WHEN LAGUARDIA WAS MAYOR— NEW YORK'S LEGENDARY YEARS

Other books by August Heckscher

The Public Happiness
Alive in the City
Open Spaces—The Life of American Cities
(with Phyllis Robinson)

When LaGuardia Was Mayor

New York's Legendary Years

August Heckscher

with *Phyllis Robinson*

W · W · Norton & Company · New York · London

Library of Congress Cataloging in Publication Data
Heckscher, August, 1913–
When LaGuardia was Mayor—New York's legendary years.

Bibliography: p.
Includes index.
1. New York (City)—Politics and government—
1898–1951. 2. La Guardia, Fiorello Henry,
1882–1947. 3. New York (City)—Mayors—
Biography. I. Robinson, Phyllis, joint author.
II. Title.
F128.5.H44 1978   974.7′1′040924 [B]   78–18203
ISBN 0-393-07534-6
1 2 3 4 5 6 7 8 9 0

Contents

List of Illustrations

Introduction

Every four years when New Yorkers go to the polls to elect a mayor someone is sure to say, "What this city needs is another LaGuardia." Thirty years after his death Fiorello H. LaGuardia is still the touchstone by which other public officials are judged. Diminutive in stature (a bare five feet two inches); stocky, even corpulent, with a high-pitched voice which under emotion could rise to what his contemporaries described as a "scream," he was a legendary figure in his lifetime and has long been acclaimed as the greatest mayor of the country's greatest city. For twelve years—from 1934 through 1945—this dynamo of mental and physical energy galvanized the New York scene and attracted national and even international attention.

Under his leadership New York set the pace for dealing with such Depression-born problems as relief and welfare, with education, health, housing, recreation and the arts. He was responsible in large measure for the physical transformation of the old city into the metropolis of today. He established an entirely new relationship between urban America and the national government in Washington. He set an example in municipal honesty, in fiscal probity, and in the never-ending fight against organized crime. When World War II overwhelmed earlier problems and priorities, within the limits of his office (and not seldom beyond those limits) he became an effective interpreter of the national will.

The man has survived largely in images—simplistic and highly colored. He is remembered with a sledgehammer in hand physically destroying the hated pinball machines; in a fireman's hat and drenched slicker attending one of a thousand fires; or coatless, his eyeglasses pushed over his head, as he read the comics to children during a newspaper strike. It was indeed a part of LaGuardia's genius that he could dramatize events and give to evanescent incidents a permanent, unforgettable form. But he was a more complex figure than these images suggest.

The story of his years as mayor is full of ups and downs, of advances and retreats, and it shows a man more variable in his fortunes, more vulnerable, and on the whole more human, than the impressions and anecdotal memoirs of his contemporaries would lead us to imagine. Beneath the showiness there was an immensely solid man, deeply committed to bettering social conditions, who came to power in New York after a career in national politics which would by itself have entitled him to the notice of history. Beneath the spunky exterior was an individual doomed to grave disappointments. His first term as mayor was an acknowledged triumph; but by the third, compromises, withdrawals, and a growing irritability had set in. Amid electoral triumphs he slipped into what might have been an inner defeat—except that it could not be defeat, for he never lost his energy, his sense of humor, or his hope.

The three terms of LaGuardia's mayoralty constitute an extraordinary period in recent history. Elected in 1933, in the depth of the Depression, his years in office brought the country through World War II and out into an uncertain postwar world. Franklin D. Roosevelt had been president nine months when LaGuardia was sworn in; he died nine months before LaGuardia retired. The new mayor stepped into the glow left by Roosevelt's first hundred days, and in New York added his own special sense of excitement to public events. Few periods in the country's history have been marked by so much action, such intensity of discussion, such conviction that political changes could affect, for better or worse, the nature of society. Men and women took part in the political process aware that they were involved in causes greater than themselves; they applauded or viewed with alarm, convinced that what they saw enacted on the public stage would restore or would ruin the nation. As happens in all high moments of political drama, men of exceptional talent were drawn into public service. When the drama faltered and the great age passed, they looked back upon those years of the 1930s as the high point of their lives.

Central to this excitement was the figure of Franklin D. Roosevelt. At the height of his popularity in 1934 he was held in intimate affection by the masses of the people. His words were fresh; his deeds were marked by boldness. The comings and goings of the president had about them the air of vast popular celebrations filled with simplicity and good humor. Not yet circumscribed by the protectiveness and secrecy of the war years, the smiling, continually surprising figure of the early New Deal days will be seen moving on great occasions through the New York scene. His presence magnified LaGuardia, whose own fate was to be crucially interlocked with the moods and policies of the national leader.

But not only Roosevelt enlivened LaGuardia's New York. Outstanding leaders crowded the narrow stage—nearly everyone who aspired to power in that time. Al Smith, Tom Dewey, Wendell Willkie, Herbert Lehman—each plays a part in the LaGuardia mayoralty. A little removed, such figures as Ickes, Hopkins, Wallace, Stimson, and the two La Follettes make their influence felt. An extraordinary cast of characters was involved in an extraordinary destiny; and New York's combustible, pugnacious mayor was an irrepressible participant in much of the action.

This book relates the principal events in the long LaGuardia administration in New York. It seeks to set in perspective the issues with which he dealt, the almost constant crises he faced. The mayor's early years and his record in Congress have already been dealt with in a definitive work, at once scholarly and graceful, by Arthur Mann; they are merely summarized here as a means of providing a background for the three terms in City Hall. It is in 1934 that our narrative begins, and with 1945 that it ends.

The LaGuardia record may seem ripe for a "revisionist" approach. It could easily lend itself to being judged differently from the way the man's contemporaries saw it. His dramatic leadership too often led to dazzling momentary results rather than to permanent reforms, and in retrospect his style could be made to look slightly ridiculous. Knowing as we do the subsequent history of New York (and of other large urban centers), we could hold his policies to blame for many of the difficulties which later accumulated. But it is important to see a man as he was seen in his own time: the perception of him by his contemporaries is in itself a major historical fact and is not to be altered by subsequent reevaluations. Yet if not revisionist, this narrative does aim to be objective, as few of the earlier appraisals could claim to be.

The following pages do not gloss over the mistakes and the frequent deviations from his own proclaimed standards. Repressive police tactics, unhappy dismissals, an obscurantist attitude in the Bertrand Russell case, and failure to meet the issue of the five-cent fare—these and other aspects of his administration are fully treated. But the LaGuardia of this book remains a striking, an important, and on the whole a highly effective leader.

These pages, in short, take seriously a serious man, one who fell just short of greatness but one who played a commanding part in his own time. He plays a part in our time, too, to the extent that we think responsibly about urban government and the men and women who run our cities.

August Heckscher

June 1978

WHEN LAGUARDIA WAS MAYOR— NEW YORK'S LEGENDARY YEARS

I

The Road to City Hall

Now We Have a Mayor!

On January 1, 1934, a new epoch began for New York City. At precisely 8:29 A.M.—a reasonable hour said the author of *Topics of the Times:* one did not want to have one's mayor getting up with the milkman—there emerged from the entrance of an old-style tenement just off Fifth Avenue at 109th Street a short, stocky figure in the wide-brimmed fedora which was to become a national trademark, wearing a blue serge suit that clung to him "with the affection of years of companionship." Fiorello LaGuardia was embarked on his first day's work as mayor.

The new administration had come in with an old-time, almost forgotten kind of celebration. Prohibition had been repealed and the great city, its merrymakers aglow with legal spirits, was prepared to make the most of the occasion. Not for fifteen years had there been such crowds in the restaurants and hotels, or so huge a gathering in the streets, as New Yorkers waited impatiently for the old year to tick out its remaining seconds. In the tide of faces along the avenues a temporary reprieve from the woes of the Depression was evident. The night was overhung with clouds; light snows were a portent of the blizzards which were shortly to fall so heavily on the town; but nothing dimmed the exuberance of the crowds. Police estimated their number in the theater district alone as 300,000, and a rough guess put Manhattan celebrants at a total of 750,000. From Harlem to Greenwich Village the citizens were out; they streamed down Flatbush Avenue in Brooklyn, through the Borough Hall district and along Fulton Street. It was a special night for the country—and special for New York City.

The gaiety seemed innocent enough, but the next day it was to strike somber thoughts in the minds of local philosophers and clergymen. The rector of St. Thomas Church, Rolif H. Brooks, said that such a new year should be ushered in not with revelry but with serious thoughts about the future. Yet the future, said Dr. Charles Jefferson of the New York Tabernacle, was unknowable. The stage on which the modern drama was being played out had become enormous in size and the actors had become too numerous to allow anyone to predict their moves. Moreover, a new note was stealing into the music of the times, he said, an undertone suggesting that Western civilization might be returning to the Dark Ages.

Undaunted by these prophets, and unheeded by the surging crowds, a simple ceremony took place at five minutes after midnight in the library of Judge Samuel Seabury's town house on East 63rd Street. The man who had played the crucial role in exposing Tammany Hall's corruption was now presiding over the swearing-in of the man who was to lead the city into a fresh chapter of honest government. Surrounded by a handful of supporters, most of whom were to play a role in the new administration, by family and a few close friends, LaGuardia took the traditional oath. In the silence which followed Seabury spoke eight words movingly appropriate to the occasion: "Now we have a mayor of New York." LaGuardia's brief response brought into that small room a consciousness of the national significance of the moment. "We are embarked on an experiment," he said, "to try to show that a nonpartisan, nonpolitical government is possible, and, if we succeed, I am sure that success in other cities is possible."

And so, early the next morning, LaGuardia was off to begin his task. From the first hour he managed to impress upon New Yorkers the particular quality of his leadership, a decisiveness of action, a strenuous impetuosity in word and deed—leading the *News* to speak of his "lion-like charge into the arena." Swearing in his police commissioner, the day's first event, his admonition to the men of the force was blunt: "Drive out the racketeers or get out yourselves." To his commissioner of taxes and assessments: "There's something wrong in the tax department. I don't know what it is. See

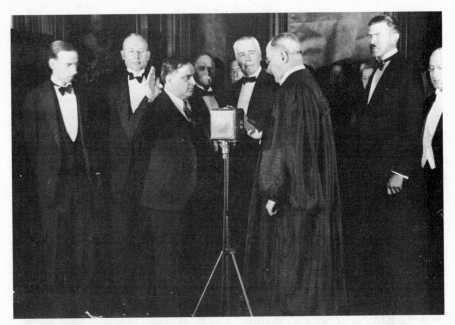

1. Seabury's moment of triumph. Watching the new mayor sworn in. January 1, 1934. UPI

2. End of an era. Tammany chieftains with Al Smith. WIDE WORLD

if you can find out"; to his health commissioner: "I know you'll not try to advertise quack medicine or practice medicine by correspondence. That would be contrary to the policy of my administration"; to the fire commissioner: "You can't fight fires from a swivel chair in a district political club." Thus there were words for each, bristling and enigmatic, a delight to the reporters who dogged the new mayor's footsteps.

The political powers were not disregarded. Breaking precedent, the mayor personally addressed the Board of Aldermen. The new president of the board, the Fusionist Bernard S. Deutsch, had already referred to the Tammany majority as "an assemblage of errand boys"; now the mayor was asked how he would deal with the majority. "It all depends," said he, "on who the majority is. I am the majority in this administration."

A visitor to LaGuardia's office later in the afternoon of his first day found him flanked at his desk by Deutsch and the comptroller, W. Arthur Cunningham—three small, compact men. The mayor was tossing letters at a "pint-sized" secretary as he shouted his commands: "Say yes, say no. Throw it away. Tell him to go to hell." Two phones and an elaborate row of pushbuttons stood on the desk. They got in the mayor's way and he ordered them removed. But he called for a big wastebasket—"the most important file in City Hall." Evidently, said the visitor, "the Fusion regime was warming up."

A gift of showmanship played a part in these first days, as it was to do throughout the new administration, but beneath it observers saw a disciplined purpose at work. "Perhaps never before," said the *New York Times,* "did a mayor of New York begin his term with such an air of getting down to business and enforcing industry and honesty on the part of every city employee." LaGuardia knew what he wanted to do. The path leading him to that office and that desk had wound across two continents and over the broad face of America; but the goal had almost always been clear.

Who was LaGuardia? And how did he get to be mayor?

Prescott and Budapest

He was born on December 11, 1882, in a tenement in the Italian section of Greenwich Village. His father and mother had settled in the United States three years before. These bare facts evoke the image of a typical immigrant family and of a childhood spent in the squalor of the slums. Al Smith and Jimmy Walker, raised only a few blocks away, grew up with an instinctive sympathy for the city and its poor; the sights and colors of the street scene, the cries, the quick movements, formed the enduring imagery of their lives. It has usually been assumed that LaGuardia, too, was a product of this native soil. But LaGuardia, if he came to understand New York as few men have done, was nurtured under a different sun. He left New York when he was three; the environment of slum and tenement was supplanted by the broad skies of an Arizona frontier town. He did not return to the city he was to make his own until after a young manhood spent in the Old World capitals of Budapest and Fiume.

LaGuardia's parents, although poor, were neither from the peasantry nor from the urban proletariat. Theirs was not the traditional immigrant background. The father, Achille, grew up in a large, middle-class family; a cornetist, composer, and bandmaster, he traveled over Europe as a young man, learning to speak several languages and making a first visit to America as a musician in 1878. Deciding then to put down roots in the New World, he returned to Europe to find a wife. In 1880 he married Irene Coen, of a cultivated Jewish family, and the couple installed themselves that same year in the Lower East Side tenement where first Gemma, and then Fiorello, were born.

The move westward occurred when Achille enlisted in 1885 as chief musician in the Eleventh Infantry Regiment of the U.S. Army. During the next years the family moved several times, to the Dakotas (where a third child, Richard, was born), back to the East, and then to Whipple Barracks at Prescott, Arizona. In Prescott, LaGuardia spent his most important and happiest years, from the age of ten to sixteen. Throughout his life he considered this his real hometown. He learned to know at firsthand the cowboys and Indians of every boy's imagination; and he lived in the midst of a cultured, harmonious family. As bandmaster and music teacher Achille had a favored position at the army post; and Irene recreated within the simple adobe home some of the amenities of her Old World upbringing. Fiorello not only learned to ride and to shoot, but regularly played the cornet at social functions, accompanied by his sister Gemma at the piano.

In 1898 war with Cuba put an end to the Prescott years. The Eleventh Infantry went into training at Mobile, Alabama, while the families were sent to St. Louis. The young Fiorello's one desire was to join the troops, and indeed he did so, though he was turned down by the army for being underage and undersized. Instead, he wangled an assignment as a reporter on the St. Louis *Post Dispatch,* and journeyed to Mobile, where his first published article assured his readers that the morale of the troops was high. "They are a nice lot of good-spirited boys," he wrote, "and the right sort of men to defend their country." But Fiorello never got to Cuba, nor did his father. In Tampa, Achille suffered an illness exacerbated by his eating "embalmed beef," the distribution of which was one of the notorious scandals of the war. He was honorably discharged for service-incurred disease, and with his family he returned to Europe, where he died six years later.

The young LaGuardia found his first job as a clerk in the American consular office in Budapest, and was promoted to the head of a one-man branch agency in Fiume. In 1906, rebuffed in efforts to have the office made a consulate with himself promoted to full consul, he bid farewell to his widowed mother, his sister and brother, and sailed to make his own way in the city which he had left as a small child.

In the record of these years can be glimpsed the LaGuardia who was to be the passionate champion of the underdog, and a peppery, almost uncontrollable public character. He said later that at Prescott he was first aroused to hatred of injustice by seeing U.S. agents deal out short measures to the Indians; in a devastating way he had witnessed the effects of graft in the selling of the "embalmed beef." His diminutive stature, moreover, had played a significant role in creating a stance of belligerence. Like many small men he compensated for lack of heft by being prepared to take on all comers, on any issue. In later life it was observed that his first reaction on meeting a man was to test his strength—intellectual, moral, and even physical—against that of the adversary.

By the time of Fiume, LaGuardia clearly saw himself as one born to protect the emigrants whose health he was charged with certifying before they embarked for America. Heretofore the medical examiners had been lax, with the result that hundreds were declared unfit when they arrived at Ellis Island and were returned to the port of embarkation. LaGuardia insisted on thorough examinations to eliminate the sick before they boarded ships for America. In this cause he was prepared to stand, as occasion arose, against Hungarian officialdom, Austrian royalty, his superiors in Budapest, and, finally, the State Department itself. For all his brilliance he began to be considered unruly and uncooperative. His chief, Consul-General Frank Chester, a man who had befriended and guided him, was soon begging Washington to inform the embassy that *he* was the principal officer, and that the Fiume consul was not to be called upon by diplomats in Austria except through his office. The LaGuardia who returned in 1906 to New York was in fact already the man who was to bedevil the Establishment throughout his career.

Making a Life

Deprived of the excitements of office and the first taste of power, immured in a city which must have seemed stifling to the senses after European airs and the wide spaces of the West, LaGuardia at twenty-four settled down to the hard task of making a living. He held poorly paid jobs as clerk and as translator at Ellis Island while he studied law at night. From the start of his practice he sought the cases of immigrants, however low their fees, and soon was known as a specialist in labor law. He joined the local Republican club, was nominated for Congress in what seemed a hopeless race, and after one defeat was elected congressman in 1916. By now life was opening up. In Greenwich Village he was part of a circle of musicians and artists; he fell in love with a young dress designer from the garment district—"porcelain-like, frail, blonde, and willowy" —who like his mother had been born in Trieste.

LaGuardia had been fascinated by aviation since its earliest days, and during the summer of 1915 he went out regularly to Long Island to take flying lessons in a plane built by Giuseppe Bellanca in a vacant Brooklyn storefront. The courage, the quick perception, and the responses necessary to make the plane hop for a half mile through the air, these LaGuardia undeniably possessed. By 1917, when the United States entered World War I, he was ready to enlist. The first aviator-legislator—he was also the first Republican congressman from the Tammany-ruled Fourteenth Congressional District, and the first Italian-American representative in the country's history—he was in Europe from October 1917 to October 1918. In Italy he survived two crashes, played a significant role in restoring Italian morale after the defeat at Caporetto, and throughout remained the American congressman, carrying his office with him into the thickets of diplomacy and into the glare of battle. He came home a major and a hero. The election of 1918 saw him in the role of patriot and he was overwhelmingly returned to his congressional seat.

Something in LaGuardia's fate never let him get too far from New York. The possibility of running for mayor was already stirring as waves of publicity rose about him and he found himself on the pinnacle of early success. In the midst of his new term as congressman he undertook a campaign for president of the Board of Aldermen—a top city post which carried with it the assurance he would be a candidate for mayor in 1921. He was elected; but the victory was followed by public and private disasters.

After a campaign based almost entirely on opposition to Woodrow Wilson's international policies, LaGuardia devoted himself to a demeaning feud with the city comptroller. He turned against Governor Nathan L. Miller who had been his sponsor and who held control over the 1921 mayoralty nomination. Meanwhile, at home a devastating personal tragedy was being enacted.

On returning from war LaGuardia had married the girl from Trieste, the blonde Thea, and entered upon a season of radiant domestic happiness. A daughter, also named Thea, was born. But all too soon the shadows gathered about the young couple. While LaGuardia was carrying out his contentious but onerous political duties, the young wife sickened with tuberculosis, and then the child began to fail. Desperate, LaGuardia moved his family to the Bronx where he hoped for healthier airs. From the new house, which had put him heavily into debt, he took his little family to Long Island and then to Saranac in the Adirondacks. In May 1921 the baby died. Thea was too weak to attend the burial, and six months later she, too, succumbed. LaGuardia descended into the pit of despair, his personal life in ruins and his hopes for a political future seemingly blighted. Public silence soon settled over his name.

From this nadir of his fortunes LaGuardia recovered—politically, at least, a changed man. When he ran for Congress again in 1922, it was from a new political base, the Twentieth Congressional District, an upper Manhattan kaleidoscope of nationalities, most conspicuous among which were the Italians and the Jews. (Here, shortly, blacks and Puerto Ricans were to predominate.) It was also upon a different political platform. The reformer had taken the place of the professional patriot. With Al Smith driving Governor

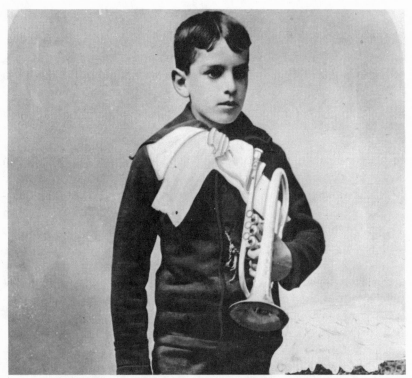

3. Cornetist at his grade school graduation. Prescott, 1898. WIDE WORLD

4. A hero in World War I. WIDE WORLD   5. First love, Thea. KEYSTONE VIEW CO.

Miller from office, the 1922 election was interpreted as a triumph of popular democracy over the forces of the old guard. Responding to this mood as well as to deeper forces within himself, LaGuardia joined with western progressives in the Congress, becoming a disciple and ally of Robert M. La Follette of Wisconsin and playing his role as a link between the eastern and western wings of the movement. The years 1923–1929 saw LaGuardia as the radical opponent of Prohibition, the supporter of social welfare legislation far in advance of its time, a critic of the conventional wisdom, and a voice howling in what seemed an endless wilderness. He was loud, abrasive, frequently alone. He was what Arthur Mann has well called "H. L. Mencken on the Potomac." He was also "America's most liberal congressman."

In 1929 New York beckoned again. James J. Walker was the city's mayor—dapper, wisecracking, outrageous in his neglect of official duties, yet none the less appealing because of his human weaknesses. The Republican enrollment citywide was less than half that of the Democrats; yet LaGuardia was convinced he could put together loosely associated groups in a coalition to defeat Tammany. He campaigned vigorously, but under restrictions of style and substance imposed by his party sponsorship and the fact that he had been picked by the Republican bosses. His charges against Walker would be backed up by the Seabury investigation, but in that year they sounded shrill and extreme. As so often, LaGuardia was ahead of his time, and in November he went down to a crushing defeat.

He had not really expected to win, yet the defeat was bitter. He knew now that he wanted to be mayor—that in the governing of the seething polyglot city, rotten with corruption yet possessed of undiminished vitality, he could find a challenge matched to his own gifts and temperament. But the chance had been denied him, and denied on terms so humiliating as to make it seem unlikely he could ever run again. He did not carry a single assembly district; he received only 26 percent of the total vote. Not since the creation of greater New York had a Republican-Fusion candidate made so poor a showing.

A week after the election, the stock market crashed. Jimmy Walker, who had danced and joked through the blithe twenties, found himself in a light which would soon make him appear an incongruous, and then a pathetic, figure. Returning to his work in Congress, LaGuardia on the other hand was in the role of a prophet whose predictions were being grimly realized. He had long preached that bankers and the leaders of big business were taking the country down the primrose path while true prosperity eluded the workers, the farmers, the poorly educated and dispossessed minorities. His calls for social reform drew a growing response in Congress and among the public at large, while to Herbert Hoover he appeared the arch demagogue. In 1932, his national prestige was higher than it had been in any previous election. Pitted against James L. Lanzetta, an unknown young Italian-American, he campaigned with the air of truculent authority and unresting energy which had become his trademark. Surprisingly, he lost.

The mayoral defeat of 1929 was understandable. It is still difficult to explain the 1932 defeat in a district where LaGuardia had appeared unassailable. Roosevelt's presidential sweep undoubtedly played a part; it was not, to put it mildly, a Republican year. Yet in his own district LaGuardia was scarcely tagged as a Republican; he had been a spokesman for the "forgotten man" long before Roosevelt. More significant, it appears, were social changes within the Upper East Side neighborhood. Puerto Ricans for the first time played a political role, a constituency which LaGuardia had not seriously courted. A new generation of Italian-Americans had come of age, upon whom the old warrior could not exert the same spell as on their parents. They looked for a kind of leadership less heated and less sharply identified with older stereotypes. It seems probable, too, that amid growing national acclaim he had neglected the endlessly renewable favors and indications of concern which maintain the loyalty of a diverse political community.

Thus, at fifty-one, LaGuardia found himself reeling from the blows of two successive defeats and soon to be out of office for the first time in fifteen years. He was fortunate, nevertheless, in his private life. In 1929 he married Marie Fischer, who had come into his office a blonde wisp of a girl just out of high school during his first term as a congressman, and had been his secretary and political confidante through the vicissitudes of private and public life. This marriage was by no means one of convenience. The congressman first fired his secretary, then courted her in a formally romantic manner. LaGuardia's private world was filled with a happiness that had long been absent and the union steadied him against the political setbacks of 1929 and 1932.

He was fortunate, too, in a second encounter. A young office aide, just out of law school in 1931, introduced LaGuardia to his

Columbia professor. Paul Kern, of whom we shall have much to say in subsequent chapters, was the aide, and the professor was Adolf A. Berle, Jr. The meeting took place at Berle's home on East 19th Street, and the two men formed a friendship which lasted throughout LaGuardia's life. The spare, tense, intellectual Berle, socially secure and independently wealthy, saw in this people's representative the qualities necessary to bring an idealist's dreams to fruition. "If he was a demagogue," said Berle long after, "he was a demagogue in the right direction." Now in this season of defeat, Berle was responsible for giving LaGuardia a political lift and making it possible for him to end his congressional career in a blaze of glory.

At the time of his first meeting with LaGuardia, Berle was among the small group of advisors to the president-elect who would later be publicized as the "brain trust." When it was decided to introduce New Deal legislation into the Congress prior to Roosevelt's inauguration, Berle scouted the field in Washington and picked on LaGuardia to lead the fight. Speaker of the House John Nance Garner approved: he was "a good little wop," he said. And so as a lame duck LaGuardia came into his own, recognized as the most important single member of the House, the authoritative spokesman for a reform movement of which in lonely battles he had long been the precursor. Under his impetus were gathered the forces necessary to enact major pieces of legislation, including amendment of the National Bankruptcy Act and creation of the Farm and Credit Home Bank. The wild jackass had become the responsible legislator. Yet the expiration of his congressional term seemed to leave him with nowhere to go politically.

Into Power

We are now nearing the crucial year of 1934, and as a floating object slows down before plunging over a waterfall, so our narrative begins to move at a more measured pace. It is first worth noting how LaGuardia appeared to contemporaries at this juncture of his career. He struck the observer above all as a noisy man. He was full of bombast and would pour into his speeches the kind of energy most men reserve for a five-mile jog. His arms waved, his lower lip jutted out, his voice ranged from a confidential whisper to a piercing falsetto. In private a variety of moods expressed itself in seemingly uncontrolled fits of rage and in moments of unexpected personal consideration. He had cultivated the habit of peremptory command, and many of his tempers were no doubt contrived for effect.

Yet years of politics, as they do with most men in this trade, had coarsened him. Little in the visible LaGuardia of this period recalled the slim, dark-eyed youth who had cut a figure with the ladies of Fiume. Albert Spalding, the violinist who became his close friend in World War I, described him as being in 1917 "stockily built" but he was impressed by the man's quick and well-coordinated movements. He was already dynamic and unpredictable, but Spalding found a kind of gentleness which was rarely seen in the public figure of fifteen years later. "It was incredible that he should like me," wrote Spalding of that earlier time. "But he did. We lived together almost as brothers."

The city that was now his natural habitat was a very different place from the Budapest of beauty and music which he was to recall in his autobiography. It was different, too, from Italy's wartime glamor. LaGuardia's intense social awareness shaded and darkened even such charms as were part of the contemporary American metropolis. He breathed the stench of decay; he lived vicariously among the violent emotions of deprived and thwarted minorities. In the world of his fervid imagination evil spirits lurked behind every conventional front, filling him with anger and suspicion. To meet a man for the first time was to suspect the worst of him, and an offer of help or support seemed to carry a concealed price. A loud and erratic manner masked the deeper wells of his personality, and to most responsible people of the city—to those civic leaders who in 1933 would be selecting a candidate for mayor—LaGuardia appeared faintly ridiculous and decidedly vulgar.

He was not worried, however, about the opinions of these respectable people. Once again, as with the young man starting out on his career, he had his way to make. He spoke of withdrawing with Marie to the country or of teaching at a small college. Then he turned to the practice of law as a means of livelihood. Yet always he watched the shifting scene of New York politics—and he never quite gave up hope.

The first year of the Depression had seen Walker's mayoralty stripped of its glitter by the Seabury investigation and then brought down in hearings before New York's governor. Franklin Roosevelt faced Walker with implacable equanimity, and after Walker's resignation went on to win the Democratic nomination for the presidency. The once-jaunty mayor sailed off to exile in Europe. An interregnum followed during which the city was led by a clean-cut young politician, Joseph V. McKee. In the election called in the autumn of 1932 John P. O'Brien was elected. A portly Tammany judge, he faced the music of the city's financial breakdown, deserving more praise than he got for his efforts to economize and to preserve the city's credit.

As the regular election of 1933 approached, a small group of civic leaders, most of them veterans of reform movements going back to the brief mayoralty of John Purroy Mitchel, saw that now, if ever, was their chance to defeat Tammany. Led by Judge Seabury, whose hatred of the Tiger was almost pathological, they resolved to pick a candidate capable of restoring nonpartisan, fusion government. Throughout the spring and early summer they gathered regularly. Seabury early declared himself out of the race, and made it clear to doubters that he meant it. Robert Moses, fresh from his triumphs in the state parks, hoped to win with Al Smith's blessing; General John F. O'Ryan, World War I hero, was the choice of ex-Governor Whitman. And then, of course, there was LaGuardia. At the end of his congressional term he had by no means withdrawn to the country, but was now being heard up and down the city.

Sometime during that spring Berle called on Seabury and urged LaGuardia's cause. The judge, after being reassured on certain points of LaGuardia's temperament and style, promised to give the matter careful consideration. It was not an easy choice for him. Measured, grave, reserved, the embodiment of tradition and descended from America's first Episcopal bishop, he was now being asked to throw the immense weight of his prestige behind a brash upstart. But LaGuardia knew his own mind. He wanted to be mayor, wanted it with a quite embarrassing candor; and he was convinced he could be a great mayor. Whatever doubts Seabury may have had, they were resolved by his slowly formed conviction that of all possible candidates, this one seemed most likely to defeat Tammany. He threatened to walk out of the Fusion group if another candidate were named. Once committed, he never wavered. And afterward he remained loyal through twelve long years. In taking LaGuardia's measure, we should give weight to his retaining through so many vicissitudes the respect of this formidable, high-minded man.

Moses had fallen back after seeing that he could not get Seabury's support (or that of his old chief Al Smith, who was too orthodox a Democrat to play the Fusion game). But O'Ryan was still an announced candidate and indeed, according to a formal statement of ex-Governor Miller, was the Fusion choice. A decisive meeting on August 3 saw unfold what Charles Culp Burlingham was to call "a frank and not too mild discussion." In fact it was explosive. Seabury stood adamant in his support of LaGuardia and, in the end, prevailed. O'Ryan, reached at the last minute, was persuaded to withdraw his name from the race. The nomination was LaGuardia's; but victory was still to him who could get it.

To defeat O'Brien, the official Democratic candidate, a genial bumbler given to naive enthusiasms and amusing malapropisms, did not seem too difficult a task. But halfway through the campaign the Democratic boss of the Bronx, Edward J. Flynn, intervened. He persuaded the honest and personable McKee to enter the race under the banner of the newly formed Recovery party. In vain Adolf Berle appealed to the White House. Roosevelt assured his friend he was neutral and maintained with a straight face that he had no control over Flynn. Whosoever wanted to believe that was free to do so. But the benefits of the McKee candidacy were evident: if McKee lost, Roosevelt would stand on his position as an outsider. If he won, the Democrats would have for mayor of New York a regular party man, an acceptable and promising figure; whereas LaGuardia would always be an alien presence, an unorthodox Republican, a liberal whose ties to the New Deal would often appear ambiguous.

McKee's entrance into the race confronted Fusion with a real crisis. Years later Mitzi Somach, who was to become one of the most trusted members of LaGuardia's staff, recalled arriving by chance at headquarters on the day of the announcement and being immediately drafted into the vast telephonic operation that was set in train. At the very least, McKee provided the Democrats with an alternative to the faltering O'Brien. More than that, he provided an alternative to the tough, brazen Fusionist candidate.

LaGuardia responded to the challenge as a man fighting for his life, with a blow which remains a blot on his record. McKee assailed Seabury, who had been so imprudent as to attack Herbert Lehman, the Democratic governor who happened to be a Jew. LaGuardia replied in effect, if McKee suspects Seabury of anti-Semitism, let him explain his own attack on the Jews in an article published some years previously in an educational journal. The article in question had been written fifteen years before, when McKee was a young schoolteacher, and only by a strained interpretation could it be said to be anti-Semitic.

The blow, nevertheless, was effective. More than any other single factor it was responsible for turning the tide in LaGuardia's favor. Toward the end of the campaign he was helped, too, by having Robert Moses come to his side in a series of witty, devastating speeches. That Moses was impelled almost as much by his desire to embarrass those—including the president—who were involved in the McKee candidacy, as he was in supporting LaGuardia, cannot be doubted. But the fact remained that he endorsed the man who had been his chief rival for the nomination, and did it when it counted and in a highly effective way. The alliance between La-Guardia and Moses was formed in that hour of need.

On Election Day LaGuardia received 40 percent of the vote to McKee's 28 and O'Brien's 27 percent. He was thus a minority mayor, though he consoled himself with the dubious notion that all the votes cast for McKee would in the normal course of things have gone to him. But LaGuardia had achieved his dream—he was mayor of New York. Victory was sweet, whatever the terms on which it had been given him. He was entitled to savor it to the full. On election night when the excitements were over, when the crowds, the congratulations, the happy acknowledgements had been dealt with, he returned to his four-room apartment and finally closed the door of privacy behind him. Donning one of his wife's household aprons, he said, "Come, Marie, we're going to cook dinner." And the mayor-elect bustled off into the kitchen.

New York Alive

The city which LaGuardia was now prepared to rule extended over 229 square miles, with a population larger than that of the country's fourteen smaller states together. Among cities it stood supreme. Taken as a whole it not only outstripped all others, but four of its separate boroughs stood at that time among the eight most populous U.S. cities. Brooklyn was larger than Philadelphia, Manhattan larger than Detroit, the Bronx larger than Los Angeles. Queens trailed the eighth, but was in itself a busy metropolis, soon to be known everywhere as the home of the World's Fair.

The megalopolis of today was only beginning to emerge from the chrysalis of nineteenth-century forms. A congeries of more or less independent boroughs, the city in 1934 lacked the physical net of bridges, parkways, and expressways which would unify its parts. It lacked the centralizing force of efficient social services. Vestiges of an earlier time were evident in crowded tenements, in localities deprived of recreational facilities and immured by lack of easy communication. One has the impression, revisiting in the imagination this New York of the early 1930s, of a mist of time separating us from that day. Not until World War II was over would the modern city in all its faults and grandeurs stand revealed.

Beneath the exterior of a pleasantly easy-going urban existence, of neighborhoods keeping an older scale and a traditional way of life, was a city grown rotten with corruption and bled white by a long period of public abuse. It was a city, as Horace said of ancient Rome, in which every man had his price. Money passed from hand to hand mysteriously at the highest levels when a contract was given or an office procured. Intimidation made its way through the affairs of the small shopkeeper, through the police force threatened with political retribution, through the largest of industries willing to pay for "protection." The finances of New York were in a desperate condition, with not enough money to pay for routine services except as a group of bankers allowed special funds to be paid out. Of its seven million inhabitants, one out of six was unemployed and in need.

Yet it was a city, too, of extraordinary brilliance. Renowned cultural institutions, the museums, the opera, the symphony orchestra, attracted large audiences—though they were (as they have almost always been) short of funds. On Broadway, in the week when the new administration began, a group of plays and musical comedies was being presented the very names of which seem legendary. *Tobacco Road* was then a new play, at the start of its fabulous run. Katharine Hepburn was appearing in her first starring role on Broadway. Eugene O'Neill had two plays, *Ah Wilderness* and *Days Without End.* Dorothy Parker, Maxwell Anderson, Sidney Kingsley, and Alexander Woolcott were among the playwrights whose works were running simultaneously. There were also, for those who preferred musical comedies, the *Ziegfeld Follies* and Earl Carrol's *Vanities, Roberta, As Thousands Cheer,* and *Let 'Em Eat Cake.*

In New York bookstores that same week *Anthony Adverse* by Hervey Allen was the reigning bestseller, sharing favor with *The Bird of Dawning* by John Masefield and *Within This Present* by Margaret Ayer Barnes. Readers of nonfiction were buying that portent of things to come *Life Begins at Forty* by Walter B. Pitkin, and also *Crowded Hours* by Alice Roosevelt Longworth and *Man of the Renaissance* by Rolph Roder.

All these contributions to the literary and dramatic scene—like the contributions of political leaders—were the subject of lively discussion and criticism in a press of competing newspapers both morning and evening. The *World* had already passed from the scene, but the *Times, Herald Tribune, World-Telegram, Post, Sun, Journal, American, Brooklyn Eagle, News,* and *Mirror* carried commentaries on cultural and political events of varying quality, but at best—as in the breezy humors of the *News* or the grave analyses of the *Tribune*—of a very high order. The *Times*'s local coverage was remarkably detailed, and occasionally its editorials struck a human and even lyrical note. LaGuardia was to deal with the press establishment as one might with a many-headed monster. Yet through it his own dramatic gifts were highlighted and his personality was made intimately familiar.

The times were good, the times were bad. New York City in 1934 was at least intensely alive, ready for the added zest provided by a political leader with a genius for eccentricity.

6. Bread line. UPI

PART ONE

2

Getting Started

First Battle

On taking office, LaGuardia's first concern was the city's financial condition. Even the light snows falling on New Year's Eve had seemed like one more dismal challenge: where would the city, in its bankrupt state, find the money to clear the streets? While he was still organizing the administration and setting the tone for events to come, LaGuardia took up the budgetary problem, boldly and with a flourish. In Berle he had a principal aide who had shared in the transition from Hoover to Roosevelt, and now he was prepared to follow the pattern of those dramatic days. As Roosevelt had done, LaGuardia moved swiftly to restore confidence with a demand for broad executive powers.

The city's plight was evident, even if it was not accompanied by the panic that had marked the last days of the Hoover administration in Washington. The city had been able to meet its current bills, but only because of an arrangement worked out with the bankers the previous September. Under its terms the bankers would approve withdrawals from a reserve fund provided the budget was balanced—but the gap between receipts and expenditures was approximately $30 million. The city was unable to sell its bonds; and grants from the federal government —the new administration's one hope for dealing with unemployment—similarly required a balanced budget.

To deal with the situation, in advance of his inauguration the new mayor prepared a sweeping measure, known as the economy bill, the terms of which permitted him to cut through existing charter provisions and to override laws relating to city governmental agencies. It drastically affected New York's dependence on the state government as well as the mayor's relationship to the municipal assembly. Under the bill, the mayor would be able to reorganize the city bureaucracy, to institute an enforced month each year of service without pay for city workers, and by executive order to fix the remuneration of any city or county employee. The bill was drafted to meet an emergency and was to expire after two years.

On January 2, the same day Roosevelt opened the Seventy-third Congress with a precedent-breaking speech delivered in person, LaGuardia appeared before the Board of Estimate to ask approval of his economy bill. Its terms had already been sent to the state legislature for consideration at its opening session. Governor Lehman, consulted the previous month, had indicated his readiness to send the "home rule" message necessary for its consideration. Every expectation was for prompt if not immediate passage. LaGuardia made what seemed to him a generous concession in granting the city lawmakers a delay sufficient to let them at least read the bill before action was taken; and with some care he explained the financial urgencies that lay behind it.

From the mayor's point of view there was no reasonable cause for delay. The emergency was clear. The powers he was requesting were essential and would place responsibility for unpopular acts plainly at his own door. Two recent federal precedents paved the way for the bill: a law enacted in the last days of the Hoover administration allowing government reorganization by the executive, and the Roosevelt Economy Act permitting the president to reduce the pay of government workers. The mayor, fresh from his electoral victory, was convinced that the voters were in no mood to tolerate obstruction from Tammany Hall and its henchmen, whether in the city or the state legislature.

But LaGuardia misjudged the degree of political opposition which the bill was to generate. In the first days of the new legislative session a setback occurred which might have warned him of the forces in play. Carefully prepared in advance by Robert Moses, a bill had been introduced aimed at altering governmental structure in regard to a particular field—that of parks. Under its terms the existing park board would be abolished; a single head appointed by the mayor would replace five commissioners responsible to their respective borough presidents. Here was the politicians' chance to try their strength within the new order of things. The bill was promptly amended so as to leave significant powers to the boroughs and the borough chieftains.

For Tammany it was a shrewd stroke. In one move the politicians had been able to set back LaGuardia and to take the rug from under his esteemed parks commissioner. Within a few weeks the bill would be restored to its original form and would set the stage for a spectacular growth in New York City's parks. But for the moment its defeat was a portent. It was a clear indication of the opposition to be expected on any reform which consolidated offices and altered existing political arrangements.

The economy bill ran into unexpected trouble from another source. Governor Lehman had maintained his doubts and reservations in silence, but after considering the full text he sent a letter to the mayor expressing profound alarm. "No man in this country had ever asked for or received the dictatorial powers which would be yours through the enactment of this bill," he wrote. "Frankly I am deeply disturbed and apprehensive of the thought of a fiscal and political dictatorship, which I regard not only as entirely unnecessary but as unAmerican."

The governor had been urged by his advisors to express his opinion in less extreme form. People were beginning to accuse Roosevelt of dictatorial tendencies, and the president and the mayor were not altogether dissimilar in their approach. A few days later when Senator Borah sent a message of warm congratulations to Lehman, there were some who saw it as an oblique way of attacking the president. But Lehman went on in his own searing words. He challenged LaGuardia's assertion that the city was on the verge of bankruptcy and in financial chaos. "If efficiently administered it should have better credit than it has had for years." He defended the authority of the existing charter. "In effect the proposed bill would permit you to modify or destroy the present charter and to rewrite it in such a way as might suit your individual point of view." Representative and democratic government, he concluded, "bestowed upon us by centuries of human struggle, should not be so hastily scuttled."

LaGuardia was incredulous that the governor should have written such a letter—"we had a frank and friendly conversation," he said, referring to a telephone call of recent days. At first he considered a radio appeal to the people, but was dissuaded. Still, he was determined to fight; he saw no need to change the bill, and two days later sent off a message to Albany offering little hope for conciliation. "Your charge of dictatorship," he said to the governor, "comes as a hollow mockery to overburdened homeowners, taxpayers, rent payers, and wage earners, who for more than a decade have suffered under as cruel and vicious a secret political dictatorship as has ever existed in an American community." He suggested that Lehman had been motivated by politics, a charge particularly offensive to the straight-laced governor. "There is no point making political capital out of the situation," LaGuardia wrote, "and I therefore overlook many of your statements." Yet through the major political and economic arguments ran a note of sober statesmanship, and the signature came after traditional expressions of esteem, and the somewhat surprising assurance that the writer remained the recipient's "humble servant." Berle had worked upon the message and his good counsel was evident in the result.

The controversy was embarrassing to the supporters of both the mayor and the governor, and a way out of the impasse had to be found. The *Times* noted with relief that LaGuardia's letter, though vigorously written, "was without a touch of violence." It went on to assert (what it had not noticed before) that the bill was "unhappily drawn" and suggested that LaGuardia realized it could not be enacted in its original form. Meanwhile, Washington maintained an eloquent silence.

LaGuardia had suggested a conference between himself and the governor and this now seemed to offer the way out. In a reply to the mayor the governor continued to assert his "unalterable opposition" but now added a pregnant phrase. He would never sanction the bill as drawn, he said, "granting you the extraordinary powers to be lodged in you alone." The words "in you alone" indicated an escape route. Might it not be possible to lodge the same powers in the Board of Estimate, where Fusion maintained a safe majority of the votes?

The mayor and his aides arrived in Albany on January 10, armed with detailed reports on the city's financial condition. It seemed that the city had been technically in default since the middle of December when revenue bills totaling $4.5 million had come due and the city had been unable to pay. The security holders were pressing for payment; the bankers were free to renege on their four-year agree-

ment, and Washington would surely withhold essential loans. La-
Guardia also arrived armed with the backing of the Citizens Union
and of the City Club headed by John Haynes Holmes and Rabbi
Stephen S. Wise.

The two principals met at noon, talked until evening, and La-
Guardia enjoyed the overnight hospitality of the governor's mansion. When their talks were done, agreement had been reached on
a bill granting all the necessary powers to the Board of Estimate,
to be exercised by at least ten of its sixteen votes. (The mayor could
count on controlling twelve.) LaGuardia announced jubilantly that
the city budget would be balanced by February 1, and that he could
confidently expect from the federal government loans of $23 mil-
lion for completion of the New York subway system. On the same
day LaGuardia was the beneficiary of a striking victory in the state
legislature. The parks bill was passed, its restoration being moved
by John J. Dunnigan, the Democratic leader who had originally led
the opposition.

Asked about the change of view, Senator Dunnigan replied with
a smile: "You know, I had a conference with the mayor last week."

The omens were favorable, with the mayor and the governor
united and the Albany politicians at least temporarily subdued. Two
days later the Board of Estimate unanimously requested the state
legislature to invest it with the powers authorized in the economy
bill. Washington, which had kept hands off during the "dictator
quarrel," now let it be known that the president was looking favorably on LaGuardia's efforts to reflect in New York his own New
Deal approach. The administration would stand behind the mayor
and the governor if difficulties arose. Presently Irwin Steingut,
minority leader of the Assembly, betook him to Washington, and
after seeing the president agreed to give all help to Lehman in
seeing that the economy bill was passed.

The mayor and the governor had come through this first fire with
credit to each. Lehman had perhaps been unnecessarily dogmatic.
A city charter was not, after all, the same thing as a state or federal
constitution; and LaGuardia had common sense on his side when
he asserted that while politicians might refer to a change in the
charter as "dictatorship," businessmen referred to it as "good management." Moreover, Lehman had retreated a little too rapidly to
the position that all was solved by giving powers to the Board of
Estimate. From legislative bodies, too, tyranny could arise. Yet the
governor had shown himself in the fray to be a solid anti-Tammany

man and to be a somewhat more colorful figure than he had previously appeared.

For LaGuardia the results of the controversy were almost all positive. He had restrained himself from the intemperate and demagogic course which must have tempted him; he had accepted a tactical retreat but had emerged with a major substantive victory. He had won, besides, the goodwill of Washington. Then at the start of what were to be twelve years of struggle, LaGuardia was not tired; habituation to power had not insensitized him. He was the statesman speaking for a great city, in accents uniquely his own.

The end of the story of the economy bill has not, however, been reached. With the governor and mayor united, the battle was transferred to another arena. The state legislature was to be the setting for a tussle in which the bill's foes were to go down to defeat only after the most protracted efforts, and after victory for the mayor had been robbed of much of its significance.

Before the Legislature

The extraordinary events which now unfolded can only be understood by remembering that in the legislature the economy bill was seen basically as a political bill. The fight was not over dollars but over votes, and in the long run over power. Assemblymen and state senators were more concerned with saving their political skins than with saving the credit of New York City.

Tammany Democrats saw in LaGuardia's determination to eliminate useless jobs a basic threat to their position—which in fact it was, and was intended to be. A machine which could survive political defeat could not survive the destruction of its essential base. Behind these Democrats were the municipal employees whose outrage knew no bounds on finding that the economy package meant salary cuts and job furloughs. The noisy, irrepressible Frank J. Prial, lobbyist for these city workers, was a close ally of the wounded and menaced Tammany stalwarts.

To keep the county offices safe from the mayor's control became a particular cause of the Tammanyites. These forty-five jobs, most of them sinecures and some of them purely honorary, had long served as a source of patronage to Tammany and as a refuge for organization leaders during political storms. By March, when it looked as if the battle might go against them, an unprecedented activity was noted in the dens of these chieftains. One sheriff, Tammany leader in the First Assembly District, was seen coming down to his office at 9:30 A.M. for the first time in years. Others failed to get the word and their staffs reported a flood of illness or a sudden surge in out-of-town business. Savings from the abolition of these posts would amount to a little over $500,000 annually, but to LaGuardia, as to his opponents, the stakes were far higher than dollars.

In the legislative struggles from New Year to Easter this first year, LaGuardia won recognition as a fighter who knew how to hold his ground when the going was against him, and yet how to appear reasonable and even conciliatory. Again and again, his back to the wall, he compromised; and in the end, considering the demands he had first made, he suffered defeat. But even defeat he bore without apparent rancor.

The picture of the mayor as a doughty warrior, a tough professional in the game of political infighting, was not new to anyone who had watched his congressional career closely. But for the average New Yorker the image was shaped during the struggles over the economy bill. To see him, morning after morning in the dawn of that bitter-cold winter setting out for Albany, a large bundle of papers and reports under his arm; to observe his persistence in argument, his shrewdness in maneuver; to see him deploy his forces as an experienced commander, was to take a new measure of the man. Awe began to be touched by affection. "Wear your rubbers, Mr. Mayor," counseled the *News* as he renewed the journey after suffering the effects of a cold. "You're turning out to be too good a mayor to lose."

The first round in the battle for the economy bill went against the mayor and the governor. In the Assembly it received only 80 votes, with 100 necessary for passage. No one, however, was greatly surprised. This was viewed as a preliminary skirmish; the bill's protagonists still had large forces to bring into play. The first of these was an aroused public opinion. Having sent Berle to Albany to negotiate behind the scenes, LaGuardia went on radio on the evening of February 10, with Mrs. LaGuardia and members of his cabinet grouped impressively around him. The speech was a persuasive mixture of logic and passion, and when it was over it seemed that at least one element of victory had been secured.

In the address LaGuardia spared no feelings in denouncing the system that placed incompetents in highly paid posts; the county jobs, he said, were "beyond decency." He lashed out at such fortresses of patronage as the Boards of Water Supply and of Education, whose members were supplied with limousines, chauffeurs, and secretarial services. Extravagances such as these, combined with deeply rooted dishonest practices, had brought the city to its present financial plight. "There isn't a well-conducted business or a well-regulated family in the country that has not reduced expenses," the mayor told the working people and housewives in his audience.

Then, step by step, LaGuardia explained the provisions of the economy bill and how they would reduce city expenses by eliminating unnecessary jobs, consolidating city departments, and making public service more efficient. He was conciliatory toward the state and had warm words for Governor Lehman, without whose help, he acknowledged, the city would have been declared insolvent. He held out hope for the provision of jobs through vast federally financed projects once the deficit was eliminated and the budget brought into balance. In keeping with a nonpolitical stance, he concluded by denouncing both parties for continuing machine politics in time of crisis.

LaGuardia was remarkably effective in rallying the public to his side. Before the speech he could count on support from Raymond V. Ingersoll, borough president of Brooklyn; Peter Grimm, of the Citizens Budget Commission; the Citizens Union; and the City Club. After hearing him every civic leader and good-government group in the city was on his side. From their pulpits, ministers appealed to their parishioners to give the mayor their backing. Civic organizations plied the legislative leaders with messages demanding passage of the bill with no weakening amendments. Popular figures like former heavyweight champion Gene Tunney commended LaGuardia and urged the public to sustain him. Bishop Manning pledged support and put his influence behind the bill.

With public backing assured, support of major political leaders was needed next. James J. Farley, national and state chairman of the Democratic party, was a key figure whose influence with the Albany politicians could be decisive. Where, precisely, did Farley stand? Where did Edward J. Flynn stand, the savvy Bronx leader who was known to play a discreet anti-Tammany game? Farley made general statements urging New Yorkers to unite behind their mayor, but was rumored to have indicated in private that these persuasions should not be taken too literally. Flynn's views were unknown, but when he paid a leisurely call on the governor he let it be surmised that he was not eager for the bill's prompt passage, even with the Lehman-inspired amendments which preserved civil service and pension rights and limited the controversial payless furloughs. Word of the visit was enough to stiffen opposition, especially among assemblymen from the Bronx.

Two upstate leaders, the O'Connell brothers, Daniel P. and Edward J., issued a statement denouncing any measure that failed to afford complete protection to teachers, firemen, and policemen, and which gave the mayor powers over the county officers. The O'Connells were close friends of Farley and their statement cast further doubt on the sincerity of his public declarations. Entrenched political interests were now quite plainly at the root of the opposition, and in this area LaGuardia, though he compromised on much else, was prepared to be adamant.

The legislative situation grew increasingly complex. Berle and Corporation Counsel Paul Windels were almost constantly in Albany as negotiators with minority leaders Steingut and Dunnigan, while the mayor and Lehman kept in close touch by telephone. In February a revised bill was defeated, though by a narrower margin than the first, with all but seven Democrats refusing to follow Lehman's lead. More than ever, Farley seemed to be at the bottom of the revolt. On March 6, the day after a third defeat, an impatient LaGuardia faced Farley across the table at a public dinner in the Bronx.

It was a dramatic encounter, with the mayor letting fly at the eminent politician and his ally Ed Flynn. If these two had lined up seven Bronx Democratic votes, he asserted, New York City would be on the way to balancing its budget. The audience was surprised by this open attack and hailed LaGuardia with a storm of cheers. Farley rose to reply, a robust physical figure towering over the diminutive mayor. But he had no defense; he was reduced to lame excuses that he did not have the powers attributed to him. As for Flynn, he had taken the precaution of not appearing at the dinner.

Still another card remained to be played: Lehman decided to appeal to President Roosevelt. Inviting Steingut and Dunnigan to accompany him to Washington, ostensibly to discuss relief funds for the state, Lehman gave Roosevelt his first opportunity to meet face to face with the chief opponents of the bill. The president had maintained a cool distance from the Albany debates; now he informed the leaders in no-nonsense terms that the city must be put on a sound basis or lose federal loans. The blame for the suffering of the unemployed would be theirs if they continued to oppose the measure. In a private conference with Steingut the president repeated his warnings, adding that federal money was ready to flow once the bill had been passed.

On their return from Washington the leaders arranged to meet with the mayor at City Hall. LaGuardia had with him his comptroller, the president of the Board of Aldermen, and Bronx Borough President Lyons, a sign that Flynn might be relenting. The Democratic leaders invited representatives of the teachers and other civil service groups. Together they hammered out a bill which all sides would live with. Even so, the fight was not over. Despite the president's instructions and LaGuardia's reasonableness, the Democratic legislators in Albany scrapped the compromise version and called a conference to discuss a new bill.

A final scene brings the legislative history of the economy bill to a stormy close. With the stage set for final passage, Steingut turned to Abbot Low Moffat, the Republican assemblyman who had sponsored the bill from the beginning, and requested a recess for members to confer. Moffat looked to Windels for his instructions. "Vote," ordered Windels.

What followed was described by the *New York Times* as "probably unprecedented in the legislative annals of the state." All the pent-up anger and frustration against LaGuardia and their own party leadership was released as the Democrats in the Assembly hurled abuse at Lehman and even jeered the president's name. When the vote was taken, the city bill had been crushed. That it could be revived in the present session seemed unlikely.

Reproaches were swift in coming. An angry Lehman placed the defeat squarely on LaGuardia's Albany representatives; Windel's action he termed "inexplicable." He had himself urged the recess and had assured Windels that passage of the bill would follow the conference. It was his leadership that had been imperiled, claimed the governor, and it was he, not LaGuardia, who had been made to bear the brunt of defeat. Windels much later recalled that the recess had been proposed at the most inappropriate time, just before the Easter holidays; he feared that many upstate Republicans, lacking real interest in a bill affecting New York City, would go home. He was sure the Democrats who called for the recess were engaging in one more maneuver to defeat a measure which they had opposed from the start.

Nevertheless, both the mayor and the governor had too much at stake to let the bill die. LaGuardia, fedora in hand, journeyed once more to Albany. It was an experience he was not likely to forget. He had been accustomed to the maneuvering of the Congress; there he had proved himself a master parliamentarian, and in his last term, steering New Deal legislation through the lame-duck session, he had been the one to call the shots. In Albany the tables were turned. His opponents dictated the terms. In a bitter six-hour session the mayor was handled roughly by his Democratic foes as, one by one, they struck down every advantage he had gained. Through it all LaGuardia maintained his composure; he even managed to smile at the criticism. If he was to salvage anything at all he had to appease.

On April 5, a weary Assembly passed the bill by a vote of 120 to 23. Four days later, after an all-night session, the Senate grudgingly concurred.

In its final form the bill imposed drastic curbs on the mayor and severely limited Fusion's power. A badly beaten LaGuardia confessed he felt like a new father who, having eagerly awaited the birth of a healthy, bouncing offspring, was presented with a "small, puny, anemic, undernourished, undersized baby." But in a good-natured capitulation, perhaps indicating that he had never expected too much, he went on to say, "I love the little brat. I will try to nourish it into something useful."

The mayor was as good as his word, and on the day following the bill's passage, he secured from the Board of Estimate provision for leaves ranging from seven days to a month for all city employees earning more than $1,200 a year. Throughout April the city announced paycuts, usually at the top levels. Commissioners who two years before had had their salaries cut assented to further sizeable reductions. Jobs were abolished in almost every city department. In all roughly half of the city's $30 million deficit was made up as a result of the economy bill. Higher taxes would make up the rest. As for the county offices, they remained immune from the mayoral axe, and LaGuardia's warfare against Tammany would have to be renewed upon other fields of battle.

The New Men

With the economy bill passed and the budget on the way to being balanced, we return to the beginning and meet the men who were to serve with the mayor in the new administration. The ideal of a nonpartisan, nonpolitical government was taken seriously in making appointments—"I have sought high and low for men who could effectively do the job," said LaGuardia. His mercurial temperament would frequently make relations with his commissioners stormy and several of them were to fall by the wayside. He could act as if they were inconsequential minions, subjecting them to a constant surveillance and to humiliating corrections. Yet withal he was proud of his commissioners, and justifiably so.

Two of his top appointments were made, admittedly, as a payment of political debts. O'Ryan, LaGuardia's top competitor for the mayoral nomination, was made police commissioner. Moses, another major contender, was made parks commissioner. (We shall presently return to these men, both strong and difficult characters.) Langdon Post, also an original Fusionist and mayoral hopeful, was an expert on housing and was appropriately put in charge of the new housing programs.

For corporation counsel LaGuardia picked a long-standing political associate, an able and ambitious figure who in one way or another was to be influential throughout the next twelve years. Paul Windels was a Brooklynite who had worked his way through law school and early found himself attracted to politics. He first met LaGuardia during the 1919 campaign for presidency of the Board of Aldermen, and in 1933 became one of the inner circle—composed of Berle, Burlingham, Seabury, the newspaper publisher Roy Howard, and civic leader William M. Chadbourne—who met regularly at breakfast to plot strategy. Windels was reluctant to enter the new administration, pleading business and family reasons. But Seabury intervened persuasively, and when LaGuardia offered him the post of corporation counsel Windels accepted on the understanding that he would have complete control over appointments in his office without interference from anyone. There was to be one corporation counsel, he insisted—and it was not to be the mayor. A little wistfully, LaGuardia asked if he would be permitted to make suggestions. The bargain made between the two men was kept

7. New appointees. Flanking the mayor-elect, O'Ryan and McElligott. Standing, Hodson, Windels, Blanshard, and his counsel, Irving Ben Cooper. WIDE WORLD

in good faith, though not without some strains and friction.

Windels made the corporation counsel's office one of the best law firms in the country. Graduates of outstanding law schools were not finding jobs in the private sector, and the new administration offered a challenge hard to reject. Three of this group, destined to have highly successful careers, we shall meet later on in our narrative: Edmund L. Palmieri, who was detached to become legal counsel in the mayor's office; William C. Chanler, who succeeded Windels as corporation counsel; and Frederick van Pelt Bryan, who would go off into World War II before he could, as planned, succeed Chanler.

Berle became city chamberlain (in charge of city finances), and Paul Blanshard, the well-known socialist and friend of Norman Thomas, was made commissioner of accounts in charge of investigations. Soon after the 1933 election LaGuardia called into his office the scion of an old New York family engaged in the freezing and storage of fish for the New York trade. "Who will make a good markets commissioner?" the caller was asked; and then, to his astonishment, the mayor-elect offered him the job. William Fellowes Morgan, Jr., his "Social Register commissioner," became one of LaGuardia's faithful lieutenants, his link with the consumer in the battle against graft and the artificially high prices plaguing the poor.

For fire commissioner the new mayor broke precedent in elevating from the ranks John J. McElligott. With Sanitation he was less immediately lucky; it took trial and error before he settled on William F. Carey, a millionaire builder who treated the post with some degree of detachment, though managing to keep the streets cleaner than, or at least as clean as, they had been at any previous time.

The most significant breakthrough came with the appointment of four experts, men outstanding in their fields whom LaGuardia searched for through the country at large and appointed without regard to political affiliation. It was at that time unimaginable to go outside New York in making such appointments, and the anguish of the politicians was great. Austin H. McCormack in the corrections department, John L. Rice in health, Sigismund S. Goldwater in hospitals, and William Hodson in welfare—these were administrators who served the mayor well and were responsible for much of the solid work accomplished by the administration.

A LaGuardia enthusiast contrasted these appointees with the

"fat-bellied, bull-necked ex-bartenders" whose presence had formerly adorned City Hall. That was unjust to many earlier public servants, but it expressed the sense of a clean break with the past which the mayor had brought into city affairs. The ideals of good government were being lived up to honorably. With some backsliding and some peculiar aberrations they were to be maintained through twelve years of power.

The new men set to work with a will, clearing out the remains of Tammany's long rule. Everywhere were signs of slipshod, outmoded administrative methods. Windels in his first annual report described the physical disarray which he had found in his offices—broken chairs and desks, files in disorder, their contents piled in every conceivable corner of the ill-lit and musty premises. Similar conditions existed in other departments, mute evidence of lack of care and concern in carrying out the public business. After the cleanup would come the introduction of new policies and standards to deal with the people's needs.

Moses and Public Enjoyments

No commissioner moved more rapidly against the old order than Robert Moses. Sworn in as the first citywide parks commissioner on January 18, immediately after passage of the enabling legislation in Albany, he replaced five borough commissioners and a board which had overseen them all. Like Windels, his first task was to clean out the smell of inefficiency and abuse. More than $100,000 in materials and labor had been misappropriated by one top official under the old regime; the man had the effrontery, besides, to explain his not having paid taxes by the fact that he practiced bootlegging on the side. Out he went, together with others whose explanations were hardly less weird. "Loafers must go" was the order of the day, and the men of the parks force, having been thoroughly lectured on the subject of petty graft, were put into uniform to uplift their morale.

Moses was not satisfied with efficiency, or even with honesty; he had far larger ideas of what should concern a parks department. Under Governor Smith he had been the initiator of a statewide park system, culminating in the creation of Jones Beach. This striking accomplishment, brought about by tough administrative skill, untiring labors, and an imaginative eye for design, was the model of a modern recreation facility for the millions. Now he looked at the scattered, rundown parks of New York City and laid his plans for what they might become.

The parks which LaGuardia and Moses inherited were largely the result of the nineteenth-century civic movement that had seen in green spaces romantically landscaped a means of improving and democratizing the new immigrant population. Tenements condemned the newcomers to dwelling without air and light; the congestion of city life bred crime and disease. In landscaped "pleasure grounds" so far as possible removed in aspect from the crowded city streets, the immigrants were to find not only delight but an escape from vice. Central Park, completed just before the Civil War, and Prospect Park in Brooklyn, completed shortly after it, set a standard imitated nationwide. Toward the end of the century, sparsely settled areas of the Bronx were carved out into large parks united by parkways into a continuous greenbelt. Smaller playgrounds, inadequate in number, had been introduced as a result of the social welfare movement of the new century.

New York parks were sensitive reflectors of the changing morals of the city. The Tweed ring had played havoc with the design of Central Park, subjecting its lawns and shady retreats to what an embittered Olmsted called "the spoils of office." Tammany under Jimmy Walker had introduced its own forms of corruption in the park services, and in the glittering, high-cost nightlife at the Central Park Casino had created the symbol of elitist decay. LaGuardia rightly saw the parks as a place where a reformation of city life could begin. Emperor Bonaparte II did not find in Haussmann a more ardent lieutenant than the new mayor found in Robert Moses. The only trouble was that it was sometimes difficult to tell which of the two was emperor.

Moses moved with incredible swiftness to start the reconstruction of a dilapidated parks system, and then toward the addition of breathtaking new facilities. Hardly a day passed by in the first months of 1934 but the press carried the announcement of a new park venture. Not one new golf course but five were announced; not one playground but a hundred. Marine Park in Brooklyn, Pelham Bay Park in the Bronx, and Wards Island in Queens were projected in quick succession. In Manhattan massive Westside improvements were begun, and so crucial a civic square as Bryant Park, left as little more than a vacant lot after subway construction, was rapidly restored—not in the form of a small-scale Versailles (as an earlier plan was described by the commissioner), but sensibly enough with plenty of benches and with large trees.

For the planning of such undertakings Moses called upon the vast resources of unemployed engineers, architects, and landscape architects within the city. At its peak the design and engineering section of the Parks Department totalled 1,800 employees, working through the night in improvised quarters behind the Central Park Arsenal. By February 1934, as many as 64,000 men on public relief, in addition to regular parks forces, worked in the field to get the various public works under way. Arguing that relief funds might end in the spring, Moses kept forces at work under floodlights. His passion for results was insatiable. Besides, he knew that only by such methods could he forestall community pressures capable of sidetracking or delaying his projects.

The man responsible for this surge of construction was then forty-five years old, and we must see him as he was in that heyday of his creative force. His cantankerousness not yet hardened into malice, his love of action not yet congealed into an appetite for power, he possessed an amazing capacity to charm and inspire men. Lean and athletic in build, quick to smile and possessed of an endless flow of allusions, stories, recollected incidents, he believed that the world's work is done by men who put loyalty above other virtues and imprint their personalities on friend and foe. "A wonderful creature who has done wonderful things," so Burlingham was to describe him at the very moment he was warning against his imperial nature.

Yet even at this season, when he was the darling of the press and of the civic groups, when salvos of applause greeted his every act, there were incidents revealing the basic arrogance of his nature. "No law, no regulation, no budget stops Bob Moses in his appointed task," LaGuardia would say. Now at an early stage he seemed anxious to affirm his style and was soon enough embroiled in controversies with the public.

One of Moses's first resolves was to displace the Columbia University Yacht Club, which by long usage occupied lands upon the shore of the Hudson River in Riverside Park. At the same time he wanted to get rid of a group of squatters who in miserable but much-cherished huts were impeding plans for the rehabilitation of Pelham Bay Park. An outcry arose from the two groups—one representing the rich and powerful, the other representing the poor of the city. In the courts Moses lost the first round.

"A burning zeal for the public interest," ruled Supreme Court Justice Aaron J. Levy, "should not dazzle an official, no matter how well intentioned. . . . Tyranny, whether it consist of oppressive measures or 'brutal severity' is never justified." The Pelham Bay case was appealed and the squatters lost; the yacht club case was settled out of court. In both incidents Moses had his way, but the reprimand of Judge Levy, as deferential as it was severe, could well have been taken to heart.

Activities within Central Park showed the amalgam of charm and insensibility so often characteristic of the man. He introduced dancing on the mall, a huge popular success in a city looking for release from care and for inexpensive entertainment. But when a group set themselves down upon a red banner spread out on the grass they received rough treatment from the commissioner, who called out the police to remove them. A crowd of 1,500 gathered to observe. Police blew their whistles with no effect. The sitters claimed there were no signs indicating they should keep off the grass, but offered to move if the spectators would also disband. The latter showed no inclination to do so. Whereupon the police called up emergency squads and the youths were routed.

Then there was the mother whose two-year-old son was caught digging a hole in Central Park. The mother was arrested and fined $2, and when she proved too poor to pay the fine she was put in jail for a day. The matter might have ended there, a pitiful example of bureaucratic bungling, if Moses had not come out with a lengthy statement defending the action. He declared the mother to be a Communist, and added darkly that she was also an actress.

The least attractive side of Moses came out a few days after his installation when the deputy comptroller raised objections to the placing of permanent improvements on lands turned over to parks by the Sinking Fund Commission. Immediately Moses let out a blast, carried by the *Times* on its front page, to the effect that members of the city administration were intent on obstructing park and playground developments. He promptly turned back to the Sinking Fund two politically sensitive areas in Brooklyn, "regretting" that he could not make neighborhood playgrounds. Others, he said, might get involved in compromises and long battles; *he* did not have the time for such things. "It is a question," he declared, "of whether there is enough cohesion in this administration and enough central purpose to get things accomplished, or whether the old hacks and red-tape boys are going to gum things up."

It is not surprising that while LaGuardia referred to others of his appointees as "my commissioners," he referred to Robert Moses as "our parks commissioner." From the beginning he seemed to feel that in dealing with Moses he was dealing with a distant and not altogether to be trusted power.

Meanwhile the public works went forward. In February 1934, just two weeks after design began, ground for a new Central Park Zoo was broken. During the next months construction was pushed on the project that was dear to the commissioner's heart. It was indeed an imaginative and, for the time, an innovative zoo. Scaled to its park site, a kind of animals' village surrounding a pool where seals played and basked, the brick structures were relieved by amusing touches, the bronze statue of a dancing bear or a frieze of primitive beasts. When it was ready for opening a short nine months after its conception, Moses decreed the occasion should be a very special one. His old friend Al Smith, who took particular delight in children and in animals, was offered the post of honorary night superintendent and seemed as pleased as if the doors of the White House had been opened to him.

That night the mayor was on hand in a sentimental mood. After the speeches a quartet of trumpeters performed; two fantastically decorated boxes burst open to reveal a gorilla and a lion. The scarlet-and-white-clad fife and drum corps of P.S. 71 escorted a pony-drawn barouche in which sat tiny Martha Jane Andrews, daughter of the park superintendent. By such occasions cities are made human and the strains of politics abated. Unfortunately, the begettor of it all, Robert Moses, was confined to his home, exhausted from the labors of an extraordinary year.

O'Ryan and Public Order

Moses's equal as a focus of controversy and of press attention in the first hundred days of the administration was the police commissioner whose appointment evened an old political score. In the choice of O'Ryan LaGuardia found, too, a means of allaying suspicions about the radical nature of his own leadership. The old soldier manifestly stood for a down-to-earth policy toward all disturbers of the public peace; he could be counted on to encourage the more militant hard-line elements within the police force. The only trouble was that LaGuardia was not at bottom—and was certainly not consistently—of such a mind. He was, moreover, inclined to intervene directly in the affairs of the police department. Except at certain critical junctures Moses was left to go his own way, with the mayor reaping his rewards upon the pleasant days when playgrounds were opened and swimming pools dedicated; but O'Ryan was held under a galling rein. Although Moses lasted throughout the administration and far beyond, O'Ryan's term was to be brief.

The opening months of 1934 seemed particularly marked by mass demonstrations and street disturbances. A first critical test of the administration's attitude occurred in the taxi strike which had flared intermittently, causing serious inconvenience to a small but significant part of the population during that first cold winter. A five-cent fare increase had been granted taxi owners prior to LaGuardia's incumbency; the drivers were now demanding a share in it. The mayor entered into the negotiations and arrived at a solution with the union leaders which in effect divided the benefit three ways, among the owners, the drivers, and the public. The settlement was turned down by the men and on the nights of March 20 and 21 serious rioting broke out. Taxis were overturned and their doors were torn off, as the police moved in full force to quell the disturbance.

It was soon revealed that the mayor and his police commissioner were in serious disagreement over the right way to handle strikes and other disturbances. Testimony given by O'Ryan in executive session to the Board of Alderman leaked out, and on April 9 the commissioner had his say publicly. The mayor, contrary to his commissioner's judgment, favored giving considerable leeway for picketers and demonstrators. "The mayor told me he felt very strongly as to the right of assemblage and the right of speech, and that technical deficiencies in permits [for parades and mass meetings] should not be a reason for breaking up the demonstrations." O'Ryan added that the next time he would follow his own judgment or else resign.

A difference of this kind between the police commissioner and the mayor has the gravest implications for a municipal government, comparable only on the national scale to such a difference between the president and his secretary of defense. The charge that a mayor is "soft" on violence and disorder is enough to damage fatally the head of most administrations, particularly when the mayor is known, as LaGuardia was, for his sympathy with the underdog, and when Communists are overtly active. Yet LaGuardia survived this revelation by his police commissioner without serious criticism, a fact that only can be attributed to the profound impression his honesty and diligence had already created in the public mind.

Worse, however, was to come. The grand jury investigating the taxi riots came out with a statement strongly adverse to the mayor, finding that he had "imposed upon the police department a special obligation of consideration for the striking drivers." What was required, the report continued, was "a clear statement from City Hall that all assemblages threatening disorder will hereafter be dispersed immediately by the police and violence will be suppressed with whatever force is necessary." The jury had overstated its case—an assemblage "threatening disorder" could hardly be dispersed without some indication that disorder was likely to occur. LaGuardia perhaps realized he could wait for public opinion to size up the issue; in any case his only comment at the time was an offhand, disarming remark. "I hope it doesn't happen again," he said of the violence, "but I can't be responsible for the activities of seven million people."

Two days later, on April 11, LaGuardia struck a different note. He rebuked the grand jury and blamed the owners of the taxicab fleets for the outbursts. They had shown themselves, he said, to be "arbitrary and cruel." He hotly rejected the grand jury's suggestion that assemblages of workers be confined to certain areas and be held under particular restrictions. As mayor of all the people, pledged to protect the rights of speech and assembly for all, he would assent to no restrictions that fell upon one group—the workers—and not upon others.

Again the mayor escaped with comparatively mild editorial criticism, and, needless to say, with eternal gratitude on the part of those local publicists and philosophers, the New York taxi drivers.

Yet LaGuardia could be moved to anger by those who exploited the rights of free speech and assemblage, especially when their actions came close to his own door. He seemed determined to tread a course between the acknowledged civil rights defender (which at heart he was) and the harsh administrator. There were moments when O'Ryan's militaristic propensities seemed useful, and then the two men would walk a short while in harness. The almost constant agitations of relief workers provided the mayor with one occasion to display his toughness. He had long had sympathy for industrial strikers but organized discontent among the unemployed evoked in him a different response, particularly because Communist influence within the leadership was indisputable. So one day in June when the relief workers had been demonstrating noisily in front of City Hall, LaGuardia agreed to receive James Gaynor, their leader, and put on for him one of those wrathful performances which observers could never believe were entirely spontaneous or unplanned.

"I don't want your help, Gaynor," the mayor shouted. "I know your kind. You don't want relief. You want to incite unfortunate people to riot. You really want people to starve to serve your own ends." Charging the leader with having run away from a previous police assault, the mayor literally screamed: "I won't stand for yellow-dog leaders inciting these people." Commissioner O'Ryan took the cue, and a few days later announced new and stringent measures against street demonstrators.

Not the least effective instrument of leadership in these first months was a series of impromptu visits to city departments. The mayor would descend unannounced, and woe to any commissioner whose men were found to be shirking! At the Transit Commission one February afternoon he found only a handful of the several hundred employees on duty, and declared forthwith that the commission ought to be abolished. He could also, on rare occasions, give praise. Inspecting the Health Department's biological laboratory, he found "everyone on the job and everyone enthusiastically working." It was, he said, the first really satisfactory inspection trip since he took office.

One such expedition was made without the mayor's presence. Though feeling ill after a mild but painful attack of pleurisy, he was on his way to Albany to plead the city's financial cause. It must have been with a good deal of regret that he left the excursion in charge of his commissioner of corrections, Austin H. McCormick, who with military precision swept down with his aides upon the penitentiary at Welfare Island. There they found narcotics, knives, and hatchets in various cells, while in the rooms of the prison hospital they came upon the group that ruled the place, living in comparative luxury and exacting tribute from the other prisoners. In their rooms were such items of booty as radio sets, rugs, canes, and even glass-topped tables. The two chief racketeers were removed on the spot and put behind bars. For the press, which had been brought along under secret orders, it was a field day. For the mayor, when he was informed of the results of the raid, it was just "a typical example" of what he had inherited from his predecessors.

Another expedition was less successful and worsened the tensions between the mayor and his police commissioner. In the company of Inspector Valentine he went on a foray described by the press as being in quest of evidence of prostitution. He returned for once reticent and evasive. He had, he said, just been driving about. In fact he had stopped at the three-story brownstone of one Christian Klosset in Brooklyn. Upon entering he was reported to have found lodgers of several months. On the top floor, Klosset informed him, was "a married couple"—did he want to inspect *them?* Annoyed, LaGuardia turned to the cellar, where he had apparently thought to find a still. But even a still was lacking.

The story would not seem to die. Klosset objected to the search and later complained that he had been framed by having undesirable elements encouraged to apply to his rooming house. He was briefly arrested and then freed. The aldermen found satisfaction in coming to Klosset's defense, and particularly to the defense of Brooklyn, whose fair name, they charged, had been shadowed by the raid. Could anyone really suppose that prostitution existed in Brooklyn? But most embarrassing was the fact that the police commissioner, General O'Ryan, felt impelled to come to the mayor's defense.

O'Ryan was not the most tactful of men, and on this occasion he outdid himself by stating that the Brooklyn rooming house raid was "justified by fusionist campaign promises." He went on to say that "all elements of the population—and they differ widely in their point of view and in the measure of their skepticism—must be made to believe that the rights of the least will be upheld and maintained." Revealing a little too explicitly for comfort the spirit and method of the LaGuardia administration, O'Ryan asserted that as commissioner he had not been as "conservative" as he would have chosen and had been "butting in" on many matters which would normally be left to subordinates. It was all undoubtedly true but it was condescending in tone and it wasn't the kind of thing one says in public. Besides, LaGuardia had not ever been deficient when it came to speaking in his own defense!

Christian Klosset now returns to the anonymity from which he was momentarily lifted, having provided an example of how good methods of leadership can sometimes go wrong. And how good men can step on each other's toes.

The Depression in New York

With New York City in the grip of the Great Depression, the cause of the jobless became a consuming preoccupation during the first months of the new administration. The hard realities of the situation would have forced action on the least social-minded of mayors; but in LaGuardia's case this had been a field of expertise throughout his legislative career. Even in the prosperity of the 1920s he had cried out in Congress on behalf of minorities left behind by economic forces; he had harped endlessly on the pockets of poverty remaining like stagnant pools amid the swirling tides of new wealth. When the Depression came he was a prophet vindicated. His voice was shrill, but now it was heeded. His actions were still impulsive, but they were in harmony with major legislative figures like Robert Wagner, the senator from New York, and John Nance Garner, the vice-president.

Unemployment had been LaGuardia's major concern as a congressman. He was Wagner's chief ally in working out bills for the establishment of federal insurance offices, for the gathering of unemployment statistics, and for public works programs. As a solitary ombudsman for the poor he spent his energies on such causes as trying to persuade Mayor Walker to put three shifts of workers on the George Washington Bridge, rebuking the Brooklyn Edison Company for laying off six hundred employees, or vindicating a Purple Heart veteran who claimed that his fellows in a veterans' hospital at Northport, Long Island, were being fined for broken dishes. The high point of constructive action was the Garner–Wagner bill, which LaGuardia shepherded through the Seventy-second Congress, providing for $3 billion in direct federal relief.

So it was that after the first priority of restoring the city's solvency, he took up the urgent task of saving individuals from demoralization and maintaining the community as a functioning organism. He turned with a kind of fierce satisfaction to a job quite different from the penny-pinching, dismissals, and salary cuts which had been his top concern on coming into office. The battle over the economy bill had tested him and had provided the relish of political combat and confrontation. But the issues of unemployment and relief were, quite literally, the bread of life, and they were to continue paramount through his first term.

Within this field he was to find occasion for the manipulations of public opinion, the sudden sallies, and the equally sudden reversals which were characteristic of his leadership. Within it he was to experience some of his most frustrating conflicts and on more than one occasion was to turn savagely on those with whose lot he had a deep-rooted sympathy. Yet, throughout, his sense of obligation and his priorities were clear. He was a mayor who would see that the poor were fed and the dignity of those who suffered was not needlessly affronted.

The problem was clear enough. Since the 1929 stock market crash unemployment had spread rapidly through the nation. Eighteen million were idle by this winter of 1934, a figure which would have to be almost doubled if put in proportion to the country's present population. New York was particularly hard hit. A sixth of the population, more than 400,000 families, were on some form of relief, a number equivalent at that time to the population of Detroit, and larger than that of Los Angeles. By May another fifteen thousand persons were being added monthly. The proportion of the city's population on relief was to rise, according to one estimate, to 23 percent, which put it highest among the cities. The equivalent figure for Philadelphia, for example, was 15 percent; for Pittsburgh, 16 percent; for Minneapolis, 10 percent. New York's plight was explained by the city's still-important industrial base and by the large number of jobs in the hard-hit construction industry. In addition, its preeminence in banking and financial services made it particularly vulnerable.

As the Depression deepened, the poor, always existing on slim economic margins, found themselves totally without resources. A new class of poor developed, families who had seen the breadwinner laid off and their savings exhausted. No group within the city's population seemed immune to the scourge. Lawyers, doctors, engineers, along with construction and factory workers, were found ready to turn to whatever aid might be derived from public sources.

LaGuardia's own attitude toward relief was unequivocal. He believed it the duty of society to provide relief, and the duty (no less) of the individual to accept it where necessary. "I'm dead against private charity," he had said while still a congressman, "whether it is through the medium of the Red Cross or the bounty of hell-fearing millionaires." Direct public relief, to farmers and city people alike, was his plea. Once in office as mayor he reiterated this philosophy, maintaining that the city had the inescapable charge of caring for its own. "It is our duty, it is our responsibility, it is economy to do so," he said. The city did not extend relief as charity, and those who applied did not ask for charity. "For its own protection the city must maintain in as good condition as possible of physical and mental health all those who cannot find work. Everyone who needs it is entitled to relief. It is an obligation of those in need to apply for it."

A small but characteristic incident gave LaGuardia a chance to dramatize this conviction. In the summer of 1934 he chose to try out the role of chief magistrate, taking his seat in the Jefferson Market Courthouse. It was a role, he announced after several cases had come before him, "hard, laborious, and nerve-wracking." Among these cases were charges against four bootblacks who had plied their trade in an area for which they were not licensed. LaGuardia, in a judgment that might have seemed quixotic, upheld the charge. Brushing aside protests that the men could not earn a living except through such illegal excursions, he told the defendants that bootblacking was *not* their only means of livelihood. Relief existed precisely so that men would be able to support themselves in legal ways and to maintain the dignity of their trade. "Apply for relief," he said. "You'll get it."

There was support for this doctrine at the time. While many other cities were failing in their treatment of the unemployed, New York was considered to have assumed its obligations through generosity combined with a sense of self-preservation. "New York has done its relief job in a way to make it a model before the country, *and hundreds drift here,*" commented the New York *Times* in a feature article.

The last phrase (italics added) was stated with no apparent censoriousness. Today it would be used to imply that New York was carelessly administered or was politically motivated in its largesse. At the time a long-standing tradition of hospitality to the newcomer muted such criticism. A city which had so recently prided itself on being able to receive and assimilate a vast flow of immigrants was not yet prepared to boggle at the arrival of a few indigent and needy. This generous attitude on the part of the public, however, was to undergo a change as the economic burdens of relief were fully felt and as politicians used the issue for their advantage.

The winter of 1934 was particularly cold and snowy. The light fall on the night of LaGuardia's inauguration presaged repeated storms, with the streets frozen and almost impassable for days. Early in February nine inches of snow fell overnight and winds of gale force roared through the city. The temperature dropped to fourteen below, an all-time record. For the unemployed the prolonged cold meant new miseries. LaGuardia opened the armories and made single men, hitherto denied relief, qualified for aid. Where jobs were available, they were often in conditions rendered even more wretched by the weather.

In the city's parks 69,000 were supposedly employed; but a third of these led a phantom existence, unable to be accounted for in any way. Many thousands huddled around fires on the marshland of Marine Park, a pathetic spectacle of uselessness and demoralization. A few others, trying to convince themselves they were doing something worthwhile, poked at the earth without tools and without protection against the cold. In Central Park 2,000 shuffled aimlessly along the snow-covered bridle paths. Yet the blizzards could be a boon of sorts, and long lines of the unemployed converged on City Hall plaza, lured by the promise that they would be paid every three days. At the height of the February storm, 50,000 men were at work cleaning up the streets. Then it was back on home relief for them, with the weekly payments that were never enough to cover even the bare necessities of life.

Inevitably these ranks of the poor were torn by conflicts and subject to manipulation by radical agitators. They had understandable cause for grievance. Though LaGuardia made the administration of relief more humane than heretofore, substituting cash for the hated relief chits, doing his best to regularize payments and to provide more adequate levels of support, available relief never seemed enough to cover the cost of coal or to provide food and shelter beyond the level of mere survival. Investigators from the Social Welfare Department were attacked on their rounds, and it was predicted that by the following autumn distribution of relief would have to be under police protection. The nearly half million on relief constituted, said one observer, "a swirling, turgid cauldron of resentments."

The assumption in Washington at this time, and generally in the public mind, was that relief was temporary. As private industry recovered, jobs were expected to eliminate the need for further programs. In the city, relief costs were calculated on a basis of 25 percent of the total, with an additional 25 percent coming from the state and 50 percent from the federal government. The mayor presented the full amount needed to the Board of Aldermen on a monthly basis, an amount which rose from about $17 million in the early months of 1934 to over $20 million a year later. Because relief was considered a short-range burden, it was not thought (until LaGuardia decreed otherwise) that borrowing for this purpose was unsound.

In Washington relief funds were on a similarly short-range basis. The Civil Works Administration, administered by Harry Hopkins, had been created in November 1933 with the idea of providing jobs for four million workers through the winter months and was due to expire at the end of March. In addition, the Public Works Administration was charged with making loans for major civic improvements such as subways, schools, and hospitals. The CWA, besides being marked for an early termination, was regularly running out of funds. The PWA, under the suspicious eye of Harold Ickes, was slow in making disbursements, as the cities were slow in formulating plans for suitable public works. It was upon these precarious and humanly fallible arrangements that the unemployed depended for survival in the first phase of the LaGuardia administration.

The situation would be alleviated as Ickes looked with momentary favor on New York's condition, and made loans which could provide immediate employment to workers on subways and bridges. The CWA received fresh appropriations when its resources were on the point of running dry, and Roosevelt let it be known that he was studying the possibility of extending it beyond the April 1 deadline. Nevertheless, as the time for its expiration drew near, tension mounted in New York and in other cities across the country. Silent demonstrators gathered in New York's Cathedral of St. John the Divine as 30,000 were dropped from the relief rolls. In Minneapolis serious rioting broke out on April 5, with fifteen persons seriously injured, eight of them police. The Minneapolis City Council yielded to the pressure and granted additional relief funds from its own budget. New York, getting the signal, similarly took up the slack from its hard-pressed resources.

May Day, 1934, approached as an ominous date. LaGuardia put the city on the alert, and Commissioner O'Ryan massed thousands of police, as Communists and Socialists held rival parades. But the day, with its rally of more than 100,000 persons, passed without serious disorder. The Communists raised a red flag to the top of a sixty-foot flagpole in Queens. The police stood around helpless while an unsung park worker, James Vanata, climbed the pole, took down the offending symbol, and restored Old Glory to its proper place. Meanwhile, in Berlin Hitler enthralled a mass estimated at two million at Tempelhof Field. The field, one reporter noted, was as large as Central Park.

The administration of relief was subject to endless controversy, and was as readily exploited by the politicians as were the unemployed by self-serving leaders. In New York the whole burden fell at the start upon the ill-equipped and understaffed Department of Social Welfare. Prior to the Depression the department had been concerned with limited programs dealing mostly with dependent children, the old, and the homeless. LaGuardia appointed for its commissioner a highly qualified professional, William Hodson, with whom at first he seemed to have a close rapport. As the political pot began to boil, however, Hodson was repeatedly made a scapegoat by the mayor, and he bore with ill-disguised anxiety the public humiliations and the private tongue-lashings which were one of the least attractive features of the LaGuardia style.

The staff of the Department of Social Welfare mushroomed to take care of the enormous new tasks. The 30,000 new workers were themselves recruited from the unemployed; most of them had been recently on relief, they were making salaries on the average of $35 weekly, and they carried into the department the grievances and often the mental habits of their clientele. Hodson's office would repeatedly be picketed by reliefers dissatisfied with their payments or conditions of work, and the sympathies of the administrative force could be equally volatile.

The problems were intensified when the Board of Aldermen discovered relief to be a politically profitable field for investigation. In the disputes between the mayor and the board, Hodson invariably found himself in the middle. When the board got wind of the fact that the staff of the Department of Social Welfare had received a small salary increase, LaGuardia called Hodson to account. The latter claimed that the mayor had been informed and had given his approval. One suspects the commissioner was right, given his professional approach and given the mayor's erratic methods of administration. In any case the commissioner was publicly rebuked and ordered forthwith to rescind the increases. The mayor threatened an investigation of his own, to counter that proposed by the Board of Aldermen. Nothing further was heard for the time being of either of these investigations, and Hodson went on to do his impossible job as best he could.

He suffered a similar rebuke in the case of the so-called potato scandal. Several million pounds of potatos destined for the poor had been allowed to spoil, apparently through inefficiency on the part of the state relief administration. This came at a time when LaGuardia needed the support of Governor Lehman, and so his commissioner once more took the rap. Hodson was denounced for having made the announcement, and LaGuardia, citing other alleged shortcomings in Hodson's department, declared he was not satisfied with the explanations. Once again, there would be an investigation.

A further cause for aldermanic sniping was the type of person found to be receiving relief. This area shows LaGuardia in a better light. A story is told of a confrontation in a meeting of the Board of Aldermen where one horrified member declared it his understanding that some relief funds were going to prostitutes. "I thought that question was settled two thousand years ago," La-Guardia shouted, "but I see I was wrong!" Then, twisting about as if in search of someone: "Mr. Sergeant-at-Arms, clear the room! Clear the room—so this big bum can throw the first stone!"

Again, there were endless disputes over whether "eurythmic dancers" were entitled to aid. Frances Bordine, "a determined young woman with bushy hair and keen eyes," was the head of the newly formed dancer's union. She explained that, like artists and writers, eurythmic dancers took any material that appealed to them and interpreted it in their own way. "We have developed this rhythm of the body," quoth she, "to such an extent that it is sensitive to anything." That gave the boys a good time. Harry Hopkins denounced the critics as being "too damn dumb to appreciate the finer things of life." LaGuardia simply added that he had "no apologies" for the programs.

We are getting ahead of our story, but it will cause no surprise to reveal that the impossible situation could not endure indefinitely. In 1935 LaGuardia reorganized the administration of relief in New York so as to put a coordinator over the long-suffering Hodson. Roosevelt recognized the fact that the problem of relief was not going to go away and under the banner of PWA launched an entirely new approach. But the problems that LaGuardia faced at the start of his term were to remain until the crisis of unemployment disappeared with the coming of World War II. They were to shadow New York's future long after the war was over.

A Breathing Space

Summer in the city brings a change of scene, and usually a change of pace. The streets become outdoor promenades where men and women stroll and pause to talk with one another. "Girls in their summer dresses" are watched by young men as they pass by. A population exceeding that of most of the cities on the globe is suddenly released from school, and kids and teenagers flood the public environs. Parks and beaches that have lain fallow much of the year come to life with a surge of nature and of humanity.

For LaGuardia the arrival of summer, his first as mayor, did not mean any slackening of the pace which he had followed since his first day in office. If anything he was busier, more visible, and more voluble. But now many of his activities were out of doors; a park would often take the place of the City Hall office or council chamber. In this relaxed mood his thoughts seemed to range more widely over the possibilities ahead and a vision of New York's future took form.

The first six months had been a time of remarkable achievement and had brought the mayor increasing signs of support and recognition. He had established himself with the people of his own city, won the confidence of Washington, and imposed upon the nation the image of his chipper, fighting style. The effects of the economy bill were beginning to be felt. Bankers were willing to reduce the interest rate on city borrowing; the sale of city bonds improved. There were even moments when Ickes seemed anxious to make PWA funds available. Troublesome problems remained unsolved as the mayor looked to the next half year—relations with his police commissioner festered, charter reform was on a rocky road, the funding of relief nagged at his mind. Ahead lay the autumn's gubernatorial campaign and (as we shall see) a contest for comptroller. Yet problems for LaGuardia, at least amid the euphoria of the first six months, only excited him to greater activity.

In a nationally broadcast radio speech, his third since taking office, LaGuardia summed up the accomplishments of the first six months. It was a curiously dry speech, a hurriedly delivered summary of a longer accounting which he submitted as a written report. The mastery of broadcasting which he was to develop later was at this time totally absent. In his six-months summary he summoned up some characteristic passion denouncing the "niggardliness" of the economy bill as passed by the state legislature, but for the most part the speech was a cold recital of facts, devoid of references to even the names of his commissioners. It told, nevertheless, an important story of reform in such areas as city hospitals, citywide purchasing and health plans, park development.

The mayor was more philosophic when he looked back over the record in an interview with Russell Owen of the *Times*. "I am the captain of a brokendown ship," he declared, "who must patch and repair and struggle continually to keep it afloat." Then he compared himself to an artist or sculptor. "I wonder if you can understand how I feel about it. I can see New York as it should be and as it will be if we all work together. But now I am like the man who has a conception of what he would like to carve or to paint, but hasn't a chisel or a brush." If only he had been elected mayor in 1929 when there was money to work with—"Then I would have rebuilt the city!" When asked what it was in his job that annoyed him most, LaGuardia snapped characteristically: "Limitation of power."

The mayor's duty, LaGuardia said, was not only to deal with present problems honestly, but to think twenty-five years ahead. In a speech at Hamilton Fish Park on the Lower East Side LaGuardia had already given a glimpse of what he saw in the future: slums cleared, city markets reorganized, traffic accidents reduced, and a vast proliferation of neighborhood playgrounds. Not in the Manhattan skyscrapers did he see proof of progress, but in the elimination of firetraps and in streets that were really clean. Now in his anniversary interview he added the goal of "the healthiest city in the world" and then—what was to become a major preoccupation —a high school of music and art.

At the beginning of June the fleet came to New York, providing one of those civic pageants which reflect a city's pride. The president came from Gettysburg, where a plea for national unity had provided the theme for one of the most eloquent of his peacetime addresses. Emerging the next morning from his house on East 65th Street a smiling, supremely confident man, he went on to review an armada of eighty-one men of war and hundreds of supporting vessels. The whole city seemed to be out on the quays or in the waterside parks. At Roosevelt's side that day was old Josephus Daniels, who as secretary of the navy had been the president's wartime chief; and Mayor LaGuardia was beside the two, as jubilant as if he had himself staged the whole great show. In the midst of an ovation Franklin Roosevelt departed from Pennsylvania Station to attend his son John's graduation at Groton.

Through the city poured 35,000 officers and men of the fleet, who would spend, it was estimated, the sum of $1 million. That night the mayor presided over a banquet at the Commodore Hotel honoring the fleet's officers.

A few evenings later there was dancing on the mall in Central Park. Five hundred couples stepped gingerly out, while ten times that number of spectators looked on. Then the sailors from the fleet joined in, and the night was alive with romance. The mayor was pleased but, never quite able to leave well enough alone, he announced that henceforth there would be no more dancing at the park-sponsored Claremont Inn, a restaurant overlooking the Hudson, or at the Tavern on the Green in Central Park. "You'll have to ask the mayor," said Robert Moses when questioned on the ban. Then he indicated slyly that LaGuardia objected not only to the minimum charge at these restaurants but also to jazz. For the next several days the mayor was hard put to it to explain his sentiments toward the offending music. He did like jazz, he explained ingenuously, if it wasn't too loud or wild.

As the summer advanced heat descended over the city, almost as extreme in its own way as had been the cold of the previous winter. In Times Square early in July an old gray horse by the name of Mallory Black (one of thirty-five thousand such horses still in the city) lay down at 2:00 P.M. in a heat of eighty-nine degrees. For three hours bus, trolley, taxi, and pedestrian traffic was held up as a crowd of spectators tried various remedies to encourage and revive him. LaGuardia quarrelled with his police commissioner over whether men on the beat should be allowed to appear without their heavy jackets. (The mayor won and the jackets came off.) The beaches were said to be polluted and two officials of the Health Department volunteered to go swimming to prove they were not. LaGuardia announced that large incinerators would take care of the litter, and then appointed a new sanitation commissioner, Thomas W. Hammond.

On the Fourth of July, amid the oratorical outbursts that were still popular, more than two thousand persons were injured by fireworks, three died by drowning, and four as a result of automobile accidents. Alderman Louis S. Isnardi declared himself shocked at seeing shirtless men in bathing. "Something ought to be done for decency," he said. LaGuardia, however, had already vetoed a bill which would have struck at this particular evil.

Meanwhile heat and drought were working their devastation across the country. By mid-July the Midwest was turning into a dust bowl, with temperatures standing at over a hundred degrees in seven states, and hundreds of deaths were reported from the heat. Franklin Roosevelt left Washington for a cruise of nearly six weeks that was to take him through the Panama Canal and out to Hawaii. While he was hailed everywhere on this triumphant tour, the West simmered, the farm crops withered. Returning, he traversed the country slowly by train, his very presence seeming to refresh the land, and with redoubled purpose promised a continuance of the New Deal.

In the city people found relief from the heat in the parks where the miracle of Moses's energy and creative imagination had begun to bear fruit. Not since the days of great park building under Frederick Law Olmsted and Calvert Vaux had New York's parks been so much the center of attention and of delight. Perhaps with some hyperbole the *Times* reported in the middle of July that dead trees had been replaced by living ones; "smooth swards of verdant grass have taken the place of bumpy and mangy lawns." More questionable was the satisfaction taken by the reporter (and by Moses) in the fact that "outmoded structures, dripping with Victorian curlicues," had been razed while modern brick buildings were being erected in their place. Moses himself was ready to deal with the diverse constituency of the LaGuardia administration, and despite the uneasiness of Mrs. Arthur Hayes Sulzberger, unofficial guardian of the pastoral tradition, was providing areas for active recreation. Vaux and Olmsted, said Moses, "did not foresee the teeming tenements which would arise a short distance from the walls of Central Park."

New or reconstructed playgrounds opened with regularity. On July 15 LaGuardia dedicated nine memorial playgrounds, while a crowd of five thousand cheered and a dozen spectators were overcome by the heat. A radio hookup relayed his address from a small playground in Brooklyn to eight simultaneous celebrations. Later in the summer Bryant Park, whose rehabilitation had been a matter of endless controversy, was formally opened. Moses dismissed the occasion as the completion of a "housekeeping job," and the mayor, declaring the park "beautiful—and so restful," arrived too late to make a formal address. But he was much in evidence later that day at the Lower East Side to dedicate the eight-acre Sara Delano Roosevelt Park. Tammany had wanted to give the area over to housing, he announced, but he had rescued it for a better use. Hundreds of children followed the mayor as he left, making a procession for blocks and holding up traffic along the way.

Through the city's outdoor spaces the sound of actors declaiming and of musicians tuning up their instruments began to be heard. The task of coordinating activities of unemployed performing artists fell to Hodson, whose Welfare Department now contained offices of drama and music. The first play to be presented was in Jefferson Park, in the mayor's old East Harlem district. LaGuardia sat watching a performance of *Uncle Tom's Cabin* from eight-thirty one evening in July until after midnight, while five thousand spectators, mostly Italians, strained the police lines and repeatedly threatened to conclude the performance by their hissing. Before the summer was over more money was being spent on the arts than has perhaps been true before or since. It was not called "funding the arts," however. It was called "relief".

The musicians who now were organized to play in the parks of the five boroughs had for the most part been living precariously, many of them actually sleeping on park benches, while they earned the $24 a week allowed for their services. But at least they had instruments in their hands and audiences who delighted in hearing them play. There never seemed enough music to go around, whether it was the long-established Goldman Band performing before five thousand on the Central Park mall, or a small group in a neighborhood square. By night Robert Moses's KEEP OFF THE GRASS signs were obscured and the people of the city, with their longings and dreams, sat at ease under the glimmering stars.

LaGuardia had indeed caught the vision of a city where public enjoyments should flourish even in the midst of human and economic woes. "Not in the Athens of Pericles, the Rome of Augustus, the Florence of the Medicis, or the Moscow of the Soviets," declared an enthusiastic reporter, had there been such a program of popular arts—or such a response. Through the summer, without a penny in his pocket, or with only a few nickels for subway fare, a New Yorker could pursue delights of the spirit. Perhaps starting the day with classes in woodworking or life drawing, he could attend amateur theatricals or puppet shows in the afternoon, and in the evening he had a choice of pleasures (to quote our reporter once more) "beyond the dreams of Haroun al Raschid." Any night one of ten professional companies was to be seen presenting a dramatic performance; three dance and five concert bands played in the warm airs.

One midsummer evening at a Goldman Band concert in Prospect Park in Brooklyn LaGuardia took over the conductor's baton and led the musicians in a stirring Sousa march. It was, according to a critic on the scene, "a workmanlike interpretation in the pianissimo patches." The mayor lifted his left hand and signaled for just the proper volume; in the more spirited bars his right arm moved vigorously. The crowd was delighted. The mayor bowed many times as the applause rose to a deafening crescendo. Then he stepped down to resume his seat, and was again called back for a series of bows.

A First Round of Politics

The rituals of summer were over. The rituals of autumn included the political campaigns for the election of a governor and of a New York City comptroller. LaGuardia, though not directly involved, found his acumen put to the test as he sailed his course between obligations to a member of his cabinet (Moses), a chief supporter (Seabury), a governor with whom he was bound to work closely, and the big boss down in Washington. His standing as a champion of Fusion was at issue, and finally, in the midst of subsidiary battles, he had to begin to work out his own position on the national political scene and lay the groundwork for his future.

The politics of the season began, tragically and unexpectedly, one afternoon in May. The city comptroller elected with LaGuardia on the Fusion ticket was horseback riding on Long Island when he died suddenly of a heart attack. W. Arthur Cunningham was only thirty-nine years old, one of the young men of promise whom LaGuardia had attracted to his banner. No less important, he controlled three votes on the Board of Estimate. His death, not the last which the Fusion movement was to experience, opened the floodgates of political opportunism. Then in the throes of reorganization, Tammany saw its chance to block LaGuardia, discredit Fusion, and show the national party leaders that its influence was once again in the mainstream of Democratic politics.

LaGuardia named as Cunningham's temporary successor the deputy comptroller, Joseph McGoldrick, a rising star at Columbia University. In July James J. Dooling, at forty-one a younger figure in the local Democratic hierarchy, assumed the leadership of Tammany Hall. He immediately pledged his full support to Franklin Roosevelt. Presently the three old stalwarts of the party—Robert F. Wagner, Alfred E. Smith, and Surrogate James A. Foley—could be seen returning in triumph to the fold. A new day seemed to have dawned for Tammany. And with the nomination of Frank J. Taylor the lines of the contest for the comptrollership were drawn.

LaGuardia had promised Marie, his wife, that the 1933 mayoralty campaign was the last city campaign he would engage in. The promise would have been forgotten in any case when 1937 came around, but now, in 1934, he declared himself ready to enter the battle on McGoldrick's behalf. "If the people of this city want us to disrupt the work we are doing, and to return to the dirty politics, the graft, and all the other things that they repudiated last year, I'm ready to go to the polls," he said, "and to meet the issue now or any other time." The courts ruled the time should be the November elections.

As autumn approached the situation at the gubernatorial level began to clear. Lehman, who had been making noises of a man reluctant to run, was now definitely in the race. Judge Seabury, lusting for Tammany blood in any and all forms—"the most vicious pirate crew that ever scuttled a ship"—let it be known that he would like the nomination. A Democrat, Seabury would have to be named on a Republican–Fusion ticket. But the old guard of the Republican party had already expressed its desire to see Robert Moses the nominee.

LaGuardia was now between the devil of his parks commissioner and the blue sea of the benign but testy Seabury. After a period of unaccustomed silence, he sent Windels to the Republican convention in Rochester to let the delegates know that he favored Seabury. The liberal wing of the Republicans, led by W. Kingsland Macy, fought Seabury's battle, but on the third ballot Moses was nominated, with Seabury receiving an ignominious 57 votes to Moses's 824.

LaGuardia had paid his debt to his loyal friend, but in doing so had shown how slight was his own influence with the dominant wing of the party to which he nominally belonged. As for Seabury, he withdrew embittered, and in the course of the campaign announced that he would vote for neither Moses nor Lehman. Whichever was elected, he announced, would be bad for the state.

Moses as the nominee of the Republican old guard was in an awkward position, and he placed the mayor in a quandary. The New York *Post* pointed out the anomoly. An editorial titled "The Mysterious Mr. Moses" asked how he could ever have accepted the nomination at the hands of the power trust barons. The platform to which he was pledged was as "garrulous as a reminiscent old gent in a club window. . . . The brilliant Mr. Moses, the courageous Mr. Moses, the student of politics Mr. Moses, runs for office on this doddering document." Moses let it be known, nevertheless, that he was confident of the mayor's support.

Besides annoyance at this remark, the mayor had reasons for wanting to weigh carefully his choice between the two candidates. Moses was in his cabinet and was doing a superb job in administering the city's parks. "I can't get along with him, and I can't get along without him," LaGuardia once confided to Windels. LaGuardia might have used the argument that, to his dismay, was to be used later against himself when he was seeking a higher post—that he was too valuable where he was to allow him to be transferred. But he didn't ; he was too understanding of men's ambitions to do that.

Toward Lehman, the mayor evidently had a mixture of feelings. As the standard-bearer of the Democratic party Lehman was close to Roosevelt and the Roosevelt forces. Yet something in LaGuardia's characteristic stance made him reluctant to ally himself wholly with the Democrats, or to alienate himself wholly from the Republican party with which he had been tied throughout his political career. His position vis-à-vis Roosevelt he sensed instinctively to be stronger for his not being one of the clan. Besides, it was his nature always to be something of an outsider, a man in balance and under tension.

LaGuardia needed Lehman almost as much as he needed Moses. Yet at the personal level the relations between them were always strained. It was one of respect, tempered by outbursts of ill-feeling and by occasional touching indications of affection. The Lehman files show a correspondence in which each was solicitous of the other's health, quick with congratulations or with condolences. As the years went by the two aging warriors were to be drawn closer together until LaGuardia found himself in the role of Lehman's successor at UNRRA. The two men seem to have been subject to missed appointments and crossed schedules. Lehman is constantly implying that he should have been asked earlier to some official event; he asserts plaintively that LaGuardia might have taken ad-

vantage of his presence in New York rather than strive for an
Albany meeting. LaGuardia, in due course setting out for Lehman's
inauguration, having gotten up "long before daybreak," is turned
back at Peekskill by bad weather. An almost inevitable coolness
colored the two men's political relationships. Lehman looked on
the mayor as volatile and unpredictable—"I simply can't understand him," he would say; and LaGuardia saw the plodding, consistent governor as one lacking in essential fire.

LaGuardia, diffidently and unenthusiastically, came out in the
end for Moses. "Are you going to support him?" a newspaperman
put the question in early October. "He's a member of my cabinet.
He'd make a good governor," the mayor replied. "Gosh, he'll
make an excellent governor." And when the questioner persisted,
"Yes, I'll vote for him," the mayor said quietly. And vote for him
was about all LaGuardia did. After this half-hearted endorsement
LaGuardia busied himself with other matters.

The gubernatorial campaign of Robert Moses lies outside the
scope of this narrative, except as it was important in the career of
one of the mayor's chief lieutenants and in the relations between
the two men. It was a campaign surprising, to say the least, in its
lack of new ideas and large political impulses. Moses left the convention backed by a genuinely enthusiastic and united Republican
party, convinced he would bring fire and light to the autumn's
political contest. He quickly dissipated the excitement by speeches
delivered with an almost aggressive disregard of his audiences,
built around the narrowest of debating points. It was extraordinary
that a man whose vision and energy were transforming so large a
part of the physical environment of the city should have had virtually nothing to say about the larger needs of New York State. It was
extraordinary that one whose wit had brought such life into the last
weeks of the 1933 LaGuardia campaign should have been so unat-
tractively plodding when speaking on his own behalf. He had rescued another; himself he could not save.

LaGuardia had known what it was to be hobbled in a campaign
by the backing of a party with which he was basically out of sympathy. "You know I was running only as a Republican," he had
remarked plaintively to Norman Thomas when reproached for the
illiberalism of his 1929 effort. But Moses was not altogether out of
sympathy with the old guard which had chosen him. Disdain them
though he might in human and personal terms, he was no less at
odds than they with the New Deal and with the novel currents

which were animating American politics. Even the conservative cause, however, he could not set forth effectively. His campaign degenerated into personal attacks and heavy-handed vituperation. It was as if the man, frustrated for so long by beings he considered less brilliant than himself, took the occasion of the campaign to pay off old grudges against the human race. The low point of the autumn came on October 22 when in a speech at Utica he charged that Lehman had "lied" in statements about the milk industry, an industry which Moses admitted he knew very little about.

The *Herald Tribune* did not waver in support of its favorite park commissioner—but then, in political campaigns that ordinarily enlightened paper never did waver, no matter how disappointing its candidate might prove. "He is bluntly honest in his speech because he is bluntly honest morally and mentally" opined that worthy journal, even after the Utica speech. The *Times* was awkwardly embarrassed, but other papers expressed their views succinctly. "Someday, it may be soon, political candidates will discover that the surest way to political defeat is the dirty way. Moses is about to discover it." And looking back, the *News* declared: "Such violent campaign talk, unless you're precise and have facts to back it up, is something of an affront to democratic government."

We return now to McGoldrick and the campaign for comptroller. For LaGuardia this seemed important, not only in that the fortunes of a young aide were at stake, but those of the Fusion movement. The latter cause was in danger of becoming obscured. LaGuardia believed in Fusion, but largely, it must be said, as a means of securing the widest possible support for himself. The consistent, painstaking building up of a nonpartisan movement dedicated to the abstract ideal of good government did not engage his basic energies. It was the essence of his politics that he personalized them and made the cause of virtue his own. At a lunch of the Citizens Budget Commission, LaGuardia had been gently rebuked for his failure to put the McGoldrick race in the context of Fusionism. "There is no use celebrating the appointment of McGoldrick," said Peter Grimm, the chairman. "We have done that. Let's get down to the business of the meeting. We are here for the purpose of developing a great nonpolitical, nonpartisan movement." LaGuardia was not so much interested in a movement as in a particular election.

He had, meanwhile, larger purposes than Fusion to serve, and these far from New York. Boarding the Broadway Limited on October 21, he journeyed to Wisconsin to make several speeches on behalf of the La Follettes—Senator Bob and Governor Phil. Having abjured Republicanism, these two were now taking a position somewhat to the left of the New Deal and were reviving the old label of Progressivism. Gotham's mayor had no difficulty in explaining his presence in Milwaukee: "Today, what concerns Wisconsin concerns New York," he declared. The Progressive party, he argued, was not a splinter party, but was destined to become a third national party, uniting the progressives in both the existing structures. LaGuardia was at home in the free atmosphere of Wisconsin and must have felt glad to escape temporarily the confinements of New York's political scene. During these days he often recalled Robert M. LaFollette, Sr., and spoke nostalgically of earlier relations with him.

On Election Day the returns showed Lehman winning an outstanding victory for the governorship and Moses going down to abject defeat. Moses's percentage of the votes cast was the smallest polled by a gubernatorial candidate of any major party in the 159-year history of New York State. His party, for the first time in twenty-one years, lost both houses of the state legislature. In the city McGoldrick lost narrowly to Frank Taylor. At twenty-eight he returned to Columbia as a full professor, leaving LaGuardia to contend with the results of Tammany's resurgence and its added votes in the Board of Estimate.

Of more importance to New York in the long run than its local contests were results in the country at large. Congressional elections had put the New Deal to its first test at the polls, and the result was a triumph. The president had achieved what was considered at the time the most overwhelming victory in the history of American politics. In state after state the pillars of the old guard went down, with Democratic strength in both the House and the Senate greatly increased. In Wisconsin the two La Follettes won over their opponents, a fact LaGuardia filed away among the matters which were to be important to him in the future.

New Taxes

On August 22, in the midst of the summer lull, LaGuardia went on the air to make a plea for new taxes to finance the city's regular and growing relief costs. The city, he said, was in a situation "more desperate than any in its entire history." Borrowing was not the answer to a fiscal burden which could no longer be looked upon as temporary. Even an increase of employment in the private sector would not take up the whole slack in manpower; unemployment insurance, which it was then hoped might be passed during 1935, would not solve the problem. LaGuardia was in advance of his time in seeing the persistence of a hard core of unemployment, and he was determined to have its costs borne by those who were most capable of bearing them. For him, that meant the business community.

The proposals of August 22, for general taxes on business, raised an immediate and fierce storm. The press, which had been ready to applaud the mayor at every turn, now joined with business and financial forces in expressing its dismay. The *Herald Tribune* called the proposed business tax "inequitable and dangerous," and claimed that LaGuardia had simply not made it clear why the whole sum of relief expenditures must be covered immediately by the budget. The *Times* said that even borrowing was better than the ill-considered tax. Grover Whalen headed a committee of businessmen to defeat the proposal, while talk of a mass exodus from the city became current and Westchester eagerly started to woo the malcontents. In the city legislature political ranks were in disarray and several Fusion members joined with the Democrats in opposition.

On August 26 a thousand businessmen and merchants marched on City Hall. They were invited to offer proposals of their own. The mayor submitted a compromise, raising the exemption from $5,000 to $15,000 and then made an emotional appeal before the Board of Aldermen. "If the tax is bad, the fault is mine, but for God's sake don't neglect and don't abandon our neighbors, our brothers and sisters who need relief at this time."

Going out a few days later to Chicago for a Labor Day speech at the World's Fair, LaGuardia made clearer than ever the dynamism at the heart of his proposed business taxes. It was a speech which had been carefully prepared, and its full text was carried in the *Times*. He called for a "new order" that would end unemployment and went on to blame the Depression on those in control of finances and industry. The country was at that time in the grip of a major textile strike: LaGuardia was at pains to state his sympathy with labor and to absolve it of blame for the nation's economic ills.

Alternate proposals for funding relief included everything that businessmen or legislators could dream up, and ranged from taxes on sales to taxes on subway fares. Action on the business tax was deferred several times; then on September 14, when the Board of Estimate turned down a compromise proposal, LaGuardia retaliated with one of the bold moves which characterized his leadership. He announced that since the taxes had been rejected, and since there was no more money in the till, all relief payments would be stopped as of nine o'clock the next morning. A sum of nearly $1 million was involved, and 400,000 families were affected.

The federal government let it be known that its 50 percent share of relief for New York City would also cease. It would provide nothing unless the city continued to meet its 25 percent share.

LaGuardia's action was immediately challenged by press and public. The comptroller explained that the government had been drawing for several weeks upon funds earmarked for other purposes and that this could not go on any longer. "Then the decision whether funds are available," queried a reporter, "is purely a matter of judgment on the part of the city's fiscal authorities?" McGoldrick replied in the affirmative. Hodson, on being questioned, said he only knew he had official word that no further funds existed. LaGuardia promised a statement on the subject, which was not offered. Alderman Lambert Fairchild, a Manhattan Republican, called the stoppage "inhuman, needless, and infamous."

The act of withholding the checks was a gesture. Four days after the stoppage, mailings were resumed. It could be said that LaGuardia had caused needless worry among those on relief, that he had been arbitrary and high-handed. Yet in fact, as was so often the case with his seemingly capricious acts, he had dramatized an important issue and raised questions which would be debated on the national as well as the local level. The exact type of tax to be levied by the city remained a question for weeks. Besides the business tax, a city income tax and a lottery were seriously considered. The latter, declared "a blow at public morals" by church and business leaders, was quickly dropped. A loan of $2 million was rejected by the bankers, while the municipal assembly voted a record relief appropriation. Finally, on November 10, the immediate crisis was relieved when a loan was successfully negotiated.

The breathing space was to be brief, and LaGuardia used it in strenuous efforts to find some sort of long-range solution. "I'm not going to the bankers with my hat in my hand to borrow money for relief," he said. The middle of November found him in Washington for day-long conferences with Harry Hopkins, while the ever-resourceful Berle was sent down to see whether some new ideas could be worked out. LaGuardia argued forcibly before the Committee on Economic Security that additional loans to municipalities would be of no avail. A $54-million loan for public works had already been approved for New York; an additional $50 million was on the way. But this did not remove the crisis. "You can't have relief on a 4 percent interest basis," he cried out. "I repeat that the municipalities cannot absorb more debt." In urging direct relief allotments LaGuardia conceded this would mean the expenditure by the federal government of "millions and millions of dollars. I say that without blushing. Don't forget that the remedy for the crisis must be drastic."

A week later he was in Chicago, putting his case before the U.S. Conference of Mayors. Though not yet president of the organization, LaGuardia was the recognized national leader. He was in advance of Washington in appreciating that improvement in business would not solve the problem of unemployment, and his prescience gave weight to a reiterated demand for large policy decisions. On other urban issues he was equally informed and militant. Taking up the terms on which PWA funds were made available to the cities, he forced renewed discussion in Washington and could take some credit for Roosevelt's ultimate policy of a 45 percent grant with the rest a loan at 3 percent interest. When the U.S. Conference of Mayors was given representation on the Advisory Committee on Allotments, the policy body for the vast public works program, LaGuardia was made the mayors' representative. He claimed that work in this field had been "the happiest time of his life." It was, he said, "the first time the conditions of the cities had been considered by the federal government in any plan for the whole country."

Back home it became increasingly evident that a sales tax, projected at 2 percent, was most likely to win the necessary public and legislative support. For LaGuardia, assent to this tax was one of the most difficult compromises of his career. He had been the arch foe of a sales tax in the Congress. His virtually single-handed opposition to the Hoover-sponsored sales tax in the Revenue Bill of 1932 brought about a stunning reversal and was an outstanding incident in his long House career. "Not within our time has an individual won such a striking legislative victory," wrote Heywood Broun:

"Attaboy, Fiorello." The congressman from East Harlem had stood up against the leadership of Speaker John Nance Garner, against a seemingly united House, and against a press almost uniformly in favor of the tax. For two weeks the debate raged with LaGuardia never leaving the floor as he made his arguments, now humorously, now eloquently, and rallied supporters slowly to his side. He pleaded the case of low-income groups on whom such a tax falls most heavily, and put his own policy in brutally simple terms: "Soak the rich! Soak the rich!"

Now, in the exercise of power, he was called on to take responsibility for a sales tax in New York City. LaGuardia did not apologize or explain himself; he simply went ahead and did the thing which he conceived to be inescapable. But Berle went into the fray on his behalf, declaring that the bankers, working hand in hand with Tammany to embarrass the mayor, had forced the sales tax on the city. Berle characterized the tax as "unjust and indefensible" and cited an unnamed banker after a recent conference: "This time we've made the mayor commit political suicide."

"Yes," Berle went on, quoting himself, "I understand you have just opened negotiations with Tammany Hall." "Well," said the banker, "the mayor is an ingenious little devil, and he may be able to get out of it."

The tale of relief and taxes may be left here for the time being, where it ends happily. The mayor did "get out of it." Early in December he secured a loan from the banks of $15 million at 1 3/4 percent interest. The sales tax came into effect without any serious complaint or opposition from the public and with no ascertainable drop in business. LaGuardia was taxed on his luncheon, which consisted of two sandwiches, a glass of milk, and a bottle of carbonated water. Mrs. LaGuardia, buying a dining room suite at W. & J. Sloanes' on Fifth Avenue, found that her tax amounted to $7.42.

Christmas was coming on, in any case, and goodwill was spreading through the city. Thousands got pay raises and bonuses. Railroad traffic was heavy; Pennsylvania Station had its busiest day since it opened in 1910. Mail was up 20 percent over the previous Christmas and turkey prices had risen (in those days a price rise was a favorable sign) to 33 cents a pound.

In the city government the Department of Sanitation, remembering the previous winter's unprecedented cold, was laying plans with military precision to meet the threats of new snowfalls. (The snow did indeed fall in 1935, the heaviest accumulation since the blizzard of 1887.) Commissioner Hammond had been instructed above all not to repeat the mistake of letting outlying districts in Queens remain impassable. Snow-fighting equipment had been newly repaired and painted, and the 14,000 regular departmental employees were to be augmented by as many emergency snow fighters as might be necessary.

Even the acerbities of politics seemed to be momentarily softened. Members of the Board of Aldermen exchanged compliments and forgave old scores. The chairman of the Board of Aldermen, Bernard Deutsch, described the past year as one of the most pleasant in his life. His fellow aldermen, whom he had dubbed "messenger boys" on first taking office, he now described as "able men who are sincerely devoted to their constituencies and to the city of New York."

At the annual lighting of the Christmas tree in front of City Hall two small children, recently adopted, were the focus of attention. Their names were Jean and Eric and they had recently become part of the family of Fiorello and Marie LaGuardia. A Parks Department band, composed of relief workers, played the traditional Christmas tunes and a mixed choir from the Department of Welfare sang. As the tree was lighted LaGuardia may well have reflected that his first year in office was one to remember.

3

In the Thick of the Fight

New York–Washington Axis

LaGuardia had come to office convinced of the need for close cooperation between Washington and New York; his first year saw the ties effectively developed. Before his inauguration he went down to pay his respects to the new secretary of the interior, the vain and testy but incurably honest Harold Ickes. In his diary entry for November 29 Ickes recorded the visit, indicating he liked what he saw. Later the journey was to be repeated regularly until Washington seemed almost as important in the mayor's life as City Hall. "It's no further than the Bronx," he would say, a remark not entirely flattering to that borough. But in fact, as an early enthusiast of the airlines, he was able to get off in the first morning hours and after accomplishing what seemed prodigious results, return for late-afternoon conferences at his City Hall office. He was the first mayor of New York to have been a Washington figure before election; and he remained one despite his new Manhattan base.

From Washington's point of view the mayor was a crucial figure in its plans for recovery and reform. To the extent that the city rid itself of corruption and balanced its budget it could be the proving ground for New Deal ideas, an important lever in lifting the whole economy. The fact that New York was the president's own state, and a bastion of Democratic politics, made the prospect more inviting. So the new mayor was watched with close interest in Washington, and as the success of his first year became apparent, was encouraged by large promises and—more important—by decisive grants.

On February 5, 1934, LaGuardia made his first visit to Washington as mayor. Roosevelt was ill with a cold and could not see him, but the mayor had a busy enough day, calling on Hopkins and Ickes, on Hugh Johnson, then head of the National Recovery Administration, and his old colleague Senator Wagner. His reward: the assurance of $68 million in loans for New York, including $20 million for the proposed New York City Housing Authority and $1.5 million for the stalled Triborough Bridge. On that same day, as if by happy prearrangement, an additional $950 million was authorized for the nationwide needs of CWA. LaGuardia would see that New York got at least its fair share of that sum.

Three months later, in May, LaGuardia again visited Hopkins and Ickes and again brought home a highly satisfactory prize. After holding up the money for months, the seemingly penurious Ickes released funds that would put three thousand men to work on subway construction, with prospects of another four thousand being employed on other PWA projects. Ickes praised the city for its "long hard fight" to set its house in order, and LaGuardia returned to New York with the clear impression that the national administration smiled upon him and his cause.

He had an additional reason for being pleased by this particular trip. Received by the president, he emerged from the interview "wreathed in smiles." Despite his services to Roosevelt in introducing New Deal legislation during his last lame-duck days in the Congress, LaGuardia had never met—or had met only in passing, as an air force captain in Italy when Roosevelt was assistant secretary of the navy—the man who was to play so decisive a part in most of his remaining career. Evidently at this first meeting the two got on well. Roosevelt was to grow genuinely fond of LaGuardia, and to find himself amused and stimulated, though easily bored, by the exuberant mayor's temperamental excesses. As for LaGuardia, he was to develop toward Roosevelt feelings of almost boyish devotion. It was an attitude which could come close to sycophancy, leading him to suffer rebuffs and slights with an embarrassing patience.

LaGuardia could persuade himself that he needed Roosevelt—needed his goodwill and support if New York was to extricate itself from its financial woes, and needed his political backing if he was himself to escape from the toils of the mayoralty. Yet beyond these explanations lay a genuine admiration for the patrician leader and an awe of the power which he seemed to wield with so light a hand. Roosevelt was, and yet never was to be wholly, a Seabury-like figure in the LaGuardia pantheon: an image of stability and of enduring values, a fixed mark in contrast to the seething forces which kept LaGuardia's own universe in constant turmoil.

Politically, when the fortunes of these two men came close it was usually to LaGuardia's disadvantage. Roosevelt's reluctance to begin an investigation of Walker's mayoralty had doomed La-Guardia's try for the office in 1929; and his sweep of New York in 1932 was a significant factor in LaGuardia's loss of his House seat. In the successful 1933 race the White House had ill concealed its involvement in the McKee candidacy.

Even after the election a certain ambiguity remained in Roosevelt's attitude. LaGuardia, he sensed, could be politically troublesome in the future. Ickes and Hopkins might discourse upon the advantage of having an honest New York administration through which New Deal funds could be channeled; still, it would have been preferable to have an administration that, in addition to being honest, was also solidly and conventionally Democratic. Besides, in Albany sat the president's personal friend Herbert Lehman, and the fight over the economy bill had shown how tenuous political relations between the mayor and the Democratic governor could be. Berle declared himself engaged in trying to "navigate" New York City into "a friendly and cooperative basis with both the state and the national administrations." Berle added, as a warning to the president, that for the first time in years a Republican, presumably LaGuardia himself, stood a chance to become governor of New York State.

Roosevelt was not a poor hand at navigating things himself, and used his personal charm as well as the flow of federal largesse to keep LaGuardia in line. At the same time he took care to see that through Ed Flynn the orthodox party machinery was oiled and maintained in good order. Thus matters stood between Washington and New York—between LaGuardia and Roosevelt —as the year 1935 began. But in the first months the relationships were suddenly to be strained. A situation putting all LaGuardia's political skills to the test developed like a summer squall and showed him confused as to whether his first obligations lay on the Hudson or on the Potomac. At issue was the role of the mayor's

parks commissioner, Robert Moses, in building the new Triborough Bridge.

Between Two Fires

In December 1934, Moses was at the lowest ebb of his prestige
and power. Physically exhausted and politically eclipsed, he seemed
a long way from the sunny heights he had walked before the ill-
fated gubernatorial campaign. Then an extraordinary reversal of
fortune took place. Franklin Roosevelt aimed what he thought to
be a decisive blow at Robert Moses; Moses not only prevailed but
caused the president of the United States to accept a rare defeat.
LaGuardia, caught in the middle of the bitter cross fire, saw his
authority as mayor directly challenged and his relations with the
Washington administration placed in jeopardy.

The crux of the famous imbroglio was Moses's position as chief
executive officer of the Triborough Bridge Authority, builder of
the giant link between the boroughs of Manhattan, the Bronx, and
Queens. The bridge had been proposed as early as 1916 and work
on the abutments had begun under Mayor Walker. On coming to
power LaGuardia made the completion of this bridge one of his
major objectives. He saw it not only as a greatly needed civic
improvement but as a source of jobs and a means of bringing larger
infusions of federal funds. One of his first tasks was the reorganization of the moribund, patronage-ridden Triborough Bridge Authority.

Under pressure from the mayor one commissioner of the authority resigned, having been found the receiver of brokerage fees for
an office rented to the authority. Another, after a hearing on
charges held at City Hall, was fired for incompetence and neglect
of duty. LaGuardia, according to Moses's account, then "sent for
me and asked me to take over direction of the authority." With
characteristic aplomb Moses replied this would be "ok if he appointed my friend George V. McLoughlin and agreed to transferring executive functions from the chairman to myself." McLoughlin
was an independent Democrat and had been a McKee supporter in
the recent campaign. His appointment, as well as Moses's, was well
received in the New York community and laid to rest charges of
partisanship in the mayor's rough handling of the two departed
Tammanyites. "Now we are ready to stop building patronage,"

said the mayor, "and to start building a bridge."

One factor, however, had been disregarded. The Moses appointment raised the hackles of the powerful man in Washington on whom LaGuardia counted for the funds to do the actual building. Why Franklin Roosevelt hated Moses with so implacable a hatred remains to this day something of a mystery. The roots of the animosity go back into the 1920s when Moses, in charge of state parks and parkways, neglected Roosevelt's interest in seeing the Taconic Parkway advanced. Roosevelt was then recovering from the worst effects of infantile paralysis, and his chairmanship of the Taconic Authority was one of his few links with New York politics. Moses was absorbed in his Long Island projects and did not take the squire on the Hudson very seriously. More personally, the seeds of hatred were sown when Moses treated high-handedly the future president's friend and alter ego, Louis Howe. In any case, Roosevelt was now out for revenge. In appointing Moses to the Triborough Bridge Authority, LaGuardia was ignorant of this background; it did not occur to him to ask Washington's approval.

Long before the public had an inkling of the storm to come, Roosevelt was determined to harass Moses by delaying or withholding Triborough funds. He was also contemplating measures to cause Moses's resignation from the authority. Pressure was unsuccessfully put upon the mayor; an offer disqualifying Moses because of his holding other posts was considered. "I think this is one of the things you cannot do," Berle wrote to the president as early as March 1934. LaGuardia, he added two weeks later, could not tolerate a personal ruling against Moses "without wrecking his administration." Besides, added Berle (who admired Moses in spite of their differences), "there might be more real devils to stop." He recalled dramatically the execution by Napoleon of the duc d'Enghien, a crime, amid many worse crimes, which started the emperor's downfall. To which the president replied blandly, "The case of your friend, the duc, is in no sense a personal one . . ."

The matter rested; but at the end of the year, following Moses's vituperative gubernatorial campaign, Roosevelt once more took up the cudgels. The president was then at the summit of his power; Moses was down and practically out. In December Ickes quietly issued an administrative order barring federal funds to an independent municipal authority when an officer of the authority also held a municipal post. It seemed innocent enough, and was not immediately noted by the press.

But there could be no doubt against whom it was directed.

Moses waited until January 4, when LaGuardia was on one of his frequent Washington trips, and then announced on his own the news of the soon-to-be-famous administrative order known as No. 129. In a long statement to the press he castigated the dispensers of public funds for being influenced by "personal and political reasons." Then he played his trump card. He was ready to resign from Triborough, he said, but if he did so he would at the same time resign as New York City's parks commissioner.

LaGuardia was in an awkward position. His first reaction, when asked whether he would call for Moses's resignation, was to stand on his prerogatives. "I am the mayor of this city, am I not?" His second was to shrug the matter off. The Triborough affair was "just a tangle . . . everything is capable of being straightened out by reasonable men." But soon he was forced to sing a different tune. He realized that the men involved were not "reasonable"; at stake were his good relations with Washington. By January 18 he was announcing that he would fire Moses if Triborough funds were seriously held up. "There will be no irritation with Washington because there are still too many important things to be done." A few weeks later he was being even more emphatic. He would, if necessary, accept the "dictatorship" of PWA. "Without the sympathetic understanding and cooperation of President Roosevelt and his administration I do not know what would happen. . . . We simply depend on him."

Public opinion, meanwhile, was mounting behind Moses in a tremendous wave. The threat to what the *Times* called "the integrity of local government" aroused one section of the public, especially those already hostile to the New Deal. The fear of losing Moses's invaluable services as parks commissioner aroused the rest. Each day brought the announcement of further support from civic and business groups, until virtually all the guardians of the public interest had placed themselves squarely against order No. 129. It was an extraordinary vindication for a man who only a short while before had been a political outcast, and Moses enjoyed the situation thoroughly. Standing by his resolve to resign from both posts if forced to resign from one, and insisting that his parks and Triborough duties were inextricably meshed, he could afford to sit and to await the outcome.

That the Ickes order was not entirely unjustified was noted, it is true, by a few observers. Apart from the issue of conflicting responsibilities, there were political factors which the watchdogs of civic virtue did not take into consideration. Moses's attacks on the Democrats during the recent campaign—and on Lehman personally—had made it seem incongruous that he should retain all his jobs, including those to which he had been named by the governor. From Suffolk County came a small voice criticizing LaGuardia for trying to force Moses "down the throat of the federal government." The mighty *News,* with refreshing iconoclasm, questioned whether in the circumstances Moses was justified in playing the role of martyr. "They that take the sword shall perish by the sword," it declared. To argue that "this high-minded and innocent lover of parks, little children, birds, and bridges" must not be stripped of any of his numerous offices was to ignore the realities of political life.

Surprised by the furor, Roosevelt admitted he knew of the controversy but refused to discuss it with newspapermen. Ickes squirmed with self-pity and anger under the widespread criticism directed against him. To his diary he confessed he thought the effort to oust Moses was a great mistake on the president's part. "I never had any interest in the enterprise. But I have to take it on the chin and act as if I liked it." Then he gave vent to his ire against the mayor. "I told LaGuardia on the phone just how accomplished a double-crosser he in fact is. This is a great disappointment to me. I had thought he was a man of real courage."

LaGuardia was frustrated whichever way he turned. He visited the president and Ickes without getting any relief from the pressure. If he was going to let Moses go (and there were certainly moments when he thought he would have to) he would at least extract in return for his submission a generous bounty from Washington. The president's $4 billion public works bill was then before the Congress; in anticipation of its passage he directed to the White House a claim for $1 billion of the total sum for New York City. Before the National Public Housing Conference in Washington on January 21 he made a demand further angering Ickes, calling for interest as low as 1.2 percent on WPA loans. In February the president made one of those gestures which could so often disarm antagonists and strengthen the wavering. Journeying by train to Harvard to participate in his son's initiation to the Fly Club, he invited LaGuardia to join him at Philadelphia. Under the spell of the president's charm the mayor agreed to shave his demand for a lion's share of the prospective relief funds.

We do not know what was said or promised on either side on the Moses affair, but it was not to be of any great moment for on the very next day the logjam broke. Al Smith, who had been forced by political exigencies to deny an endorsement of his old friend during the gubernatorial campaign, now saw the chance to come to his defense in a climactic way. A strongly worded statement denounced order No. 129 as "narrow, political, and vindictive," and demanded that the mayor act to assert the city's rights. With pathos the banished but not wholly defanged old lion affirmed Moses's indispensability as parks commissioner. "What with funerals, wakes, and consecrations to attend," he said, he got about the city as much as anyone, and the only projects he saw really going forward were those directed by Commissioner Moses.

From then on it was plain that a way out of the impasse had to be found—and that it could only be found at the price of the president's surrender. It was Ickes, of course, who would bear the brunt. In a March 12 reply to a letter from the mayor Ickes raised the white flag. He still growled and grumbled, but in the end asserted that, following the mayor's suggestion, order No. 129 would not apply where planning for a project had been completed before the order was promulgated. The exception was specifically granted to Langdon Post, who as head of the New York Housing Authority also held the municipal post of commissioner. Then came the sentence which evasively but dramatically signaled the president's humiliating withdrawal from a game in which he had supposed he held all the winning cards. "Since a like situation exists in regard to Commissioner Moses, this interpretation shall also apply to him."

It had been a famous victory, but like most such victories its results were less conclusive than might have been expected. Moses would soon enough find his position reversed, with all the civic groups ranged against him and with the president this time successfully killing the commissioner's pet project. LaGuardia emerged from the fray with his public support not noticeably diminished. His relations with Moses were no more nor less strained than was regularly the case and, most importantly, the New York–Washington axis was intact. A letter of April 15 from the mayor is addressed ceremoniously to "Dear Mr. Ickes" at his home and assures the secretary he will be well taken care of on an approaching visit to the city. "Perhaps a trip in the afternoon to Coney Island . . . would be a happy prelude to the Folies Bergere." The secretary was not

8. "Like being vaccinated twice." Moses sworn in as commissioner of Triborough Bridge Authority. July 10, 1935. INP

9. Aid from the secretary of the interior. August 19, 1937. WIDE WORLD

averse to such pleasantries from a man whom a few months before
he had been secretly characterizing as "the cheapest kind of double-
crossing politician."

The affair had an aftermath with comic overtones. Moses had
escaped decapitation but his term on the Triborough Bridge Authority ran out in the summer of 1935. The mayor, not anxious to
put salt into the still-fresh wounds in Washington with a formal
ceremony, indicated that a second swearing-in was unnecessary.
Moses, however, wanted his revenge and demanded full and public
reaffirmation. With the arrogance of which he was capable, he
announced in June he would resign as a member of Triborough—
and also as the city parks commissioner—unless the beginning of
a new term was marked officially by the mayor.

The two men were immovable. When the brand-new Prospect
Park Zoo was opened on the Fourth of July, neither would do the
other the courtesy of being present. It was left for Al Smith, his
deeply tanned face perspiring in the noon heat, to preside. The
former governor, reprieved for the day from attendance at wakes
and funerals, was a lonely figure in gray amid the park attendants,
white-gloved and dressed in military style, who passed out corsages
to the ladies in the first rows of the audience. A denunciation of the
"back-alley politics" of the LaGuardia–Moses row formed an incongruous note in a holiday event which would normally have seen the
public oratory confined to pleasant remarks about small children
and animals.

The question of a second swearing-in was referred to the corporation counsel. Windels solemnly concluded that being sworn in
twice was like being vaccinated twice: it would do no harm. It might
even reduce the temperature and was therefore recommended in
the case of Commissioner Moses. Still the games continued. The
mayor renamed Moses to the Triborough, but Moses again threatened to resign from both posts unless the signed appointment was
in his hands by noon of the following day. "I am Fiorello La-
Guardia, Mayor of New York, not Guilio Cazazza, director of the
Metropolitan Opera" was the weary comment from City Hall.
Moses continued to be vague as to whether he would appear for
the appointment at the time set by the mayor. LaGuardia managed
a grin when the ceremony was at last accomplished. From Washington there was only silence.

Beneath the coy maneuverings there was for Moses a more serious interest than that of embarrassing his adversaries. The Tribo-

rough post was important for him and he wanted his credentials signed and sealed. To an extent that even he could not foresee, Triborough would become the base of his activities—more important than all his other posts combined. Its jurisdiction enlarged by successive accretions and its projects extending over the face of the city, it would be the center of a web from which his power radiated. And when other citadels of his empire had fallen to age and politics, Robert Moses at the start of his tenth decade—still imposing, articulate, and cantankerous—would find in his post as consultant to Triborough the salary and the perquisites of a minor monarch.

Riot in Harlem

Meanwhile LaGuardia had to contend with a major crisis of a different kind. On March 19, a week after the dénouement of the Moses controversy, a serious riot broke out in Harlem. The facts as subsequently determined were on their surface rather ordinary, but the implications for LaGuardia's administration, and for the future of the city, were significant. A ten-year-old black youth stole a pocketknife from a store on West 125th Street; a girl screamed, and in the heated atmosphere a false rumor spread that the boy had been beaten to death. Roving bands of black men and women started on a rampage, breaking plate-glass windows and forcibly resisting squads of police. By early morning of the following day, when a downpour cooled the situation, more than a hundred persons, whites and blacks, had been clubbed, stabbed, or stoned, some of them injured critically.

Public officials acted with a restraint that prevented more serious consequences. Governor Lehman rejected the appeal of Harlem merchants that the National Guard be called out; the police behaved on the whole with care and good sense. LaGuardia resisted the temptation to go charging to the scene, contenting himself for the moment with distributing throughout Harlem two-foot-square handbills bearing the message over his signature that "the overwhelming majority of West Harlem leaders," were "splendid, law-abiding citizens" and that the "unfortunate events" had been stimulated by a few irresponsible persons. Then he appointed a citizens committee to look into the underlying causes of the riot. Among its members were such outstanding community leaders as the black poet Countee Cullen, Morris Ernst, Oswald Garrison Villard, and

Arthur Garfield Hays. The report would not be issued until more than a year had passed, and then would be withheld from publication for another three months by the mayor. But its recommendations, and the general discussion which it provoked, provided LaGuardia's first, probing efforts to come to grips with the problems of racial minorities in the city and of the ghettos in which they lived.

Harlem by the 1930s was a self-contained city with a population of roughly 300,000, a six-fold increase over that of 1900. The population was almost entirely black, 90 percent of the in-migration of Negroes having settled here, with another 10 percent going to Brooklyn. Blocks of fine old residences still existed along with notorious slums, but most of the better buildings had by now been taken over by groups of families. It was almost entirely a bedroom community, with 95 percent of its working population traveling to jobs in other parts of the city.

When the Depression struck, Harlem was the New York community hit hardest. Its unemployment was the heaviest; its social ills were the most prevalent. Housing was more expensive here where it could be least afforded, and goods of all kinds were sold at discriminatory prices. Within the area reports of police brutality were recurrent.

The citizens committee concentrated on specific needs for reform, and the mayor initiated corresponding action. Going over the report with members of the committee in July 1936, LaGuardia could point out that higher pay had been assured for "colored porters"; that foundations were complete for the first model housing units in Harlem; that new playgrounds, health centers, and schools had been started; and that a new Harlem hospital would be considered in the general program for the following year. The problem of admission of Negro doctors and nurses to all city hospitals was a particularly sensitive issue.

Useful as the measures and projects might be, they touched only the surface of the problem, as LaGuardia himself was well aware. The Depression ate into the fabric of Harlem's life and deepened discontents far beyond the city's capacity for remedial action. "I am as helpless in handling a large-scale economic problem," the mayor said to one Negro delegation, "as the League of Nations was in preventing the war between Italy and Ethiopia." Then, in a characteristic outburst, he proceeded to blame people "who go to Harlem at night to engage in all form of debauchery and immorality"—this in the midst of the jazz age and of Harlem's cultural flowering! The long-range problems were to emerge once again at a later critical stage in LaGuardia's administration. Meanwhile almost all agreed that the mayor had handled the situation well.

As for Margaret Mitchell, the girl whose screams were found to have precipitated the riot, she was charged with disorderly conduct and was offered the choice of a ten-dollar fine or three days in the workhouse.

Issues of Reform

While crises and diversions were making the mayor's first administration uniquely exciting, the real test of his leadership came in the shaping and execution of a reform program. He had come to office pledged to innovative measures. He had given assurance that not only would the day-to-day management of city business show a greater degree of honesty and efficiency, but that a fundamental reordering of municipal activities would take place. What he liked to call "scientific government" involved strict criteria, among which were the absence of conventional politics, the return to the taxpayer of full value for every dollar spent, the protection of the underprivileged and recognition of broad responsibility in such hitherto neglected areas as health, education, and the arts. LaGuardia looked upon city governance as highly experimental, convinced that measures must be tried and, if they didn't work, discarded.

By mid-1935 the outlines of reform were visible. Drastic improvements in health services were going forward under Commissioner Goldwater. Before coming to New York, Goldwater had supervised the construction of more than two hundred hospitals, perhaps more than any man in medical history. With LaGuardia's enthusiastic support he set about a program which was to include a new hospital for chronic diseases on Welfare Island, a new general hospital in Jamaica, a new Harlem hospital. The administration set itself the goal of achieving in the municipal hospitals the same standards of ward care that prevailed in liberally supported private institutions that had slowly been perfecting their work for generations. It was a rash goal (and today appears to have been illusory), but Goldwater pressed on undiscouraged with his program which included major laboratory extensions, a larger nursing force, and the development of scientific research.

Problems of sanitation and waste disposal proved baffling to LaGuardia. At the end of six months in office he admitted he was not satisfied with the cleanliness of the streets, and despite the availability of an immense force of relief workers for snow removal, snow always piled up disconcertingly. He was to try two commissioners before settling in for the long pull with William F. Carey, who was expected to apply engineering principles to disposing of the city's ever-increasing garbage. A builder of railroads and a former chief of excavations for the Panama Canal, he seemed just the right man for the job. But even Carey could introduce only minimal efficiency into the army of 6,000 sweepers who still made street cleaning largely a hand operation, and the purchase of heavy equipment was subjected to the inevitable financial constraints. When the U.S. Supreme Court forbade further dumping of garbage at sea and the discharge of polluted waters into the city's rivers came under attack, a construction program for large incinerators was begun. It was never to do more than cause a dent in the problem.

Three fields of reform—transit, public power, and housing—particularly preoccupied the mayor. He approached them energetically and optimistically, but in the case of the first two, at least, with disappointing results.

On his coming to office the unification of public transport facilities seemed a most urgent and also an immediately attainable goal. A long history had shaped the existing hodgepodge of a subway system. The city had built the first lines on its own at the beginning of the century, and had established a complex partnership with private interests for construction and operation of subsequent routes. To bring the three principal lines—Independent, IRT, and BMT—entirely under public ownership and management, and to combine these with the surface routes, gave promise of a new day in city transportation. Under a single authority fares would be established at a socially beneficial level, opening up new lines would be tied in with the city's rational growth, and a new level of efficiency would be established in all aspects of operations. Unfortunately such hopes were to be deceived. LaGuardia got unification, but after long delays; and then it brought, both in his time and later, few of the anticipated benefits.

The mayor's first move in this field was to put negotiations for purchase of the private lines into the hands of two of his most able advisors, Seabury and Berle. The pair got strenuously to work and in February 1935 were able to recommend a negotiated purchase price for one of the lines. It was "a good day's work," said La-Guardia. "Now we must see that there is no delay." Legislation was immediately prepared for submission to city authorities and the state legislature. But though the Board of Estimate approved, La-Guardia had not fully taken into account the power of the state-appointed Transit Commission. The mayor appealed to the governor to push the transit bill; he compromised to meet opposition in the legislature. But as in the fight for the economy bill he was up against firmly entrenched interests.

When two years later Berle and Seabury completed their proposals for takeover of the private lines, the Transit Commission again rejected the report. LaGuardia fumed and demanded that the commission come up with a proposal of its own within ninety days; he also vowed that he would get the commission abolished. In May 1938, in an abrupt change of tactics, he dealt directly with the commission for the first time in four years. After a cheerful City Hall welcome to the chairman he indicated he would go along with the demand for a constitutional amendment. (The problems and disappointments that arose when unification was finally completed must be left for a later section.)

Even more frustrating were LaGuardia's efforts to establish a municipally owned power plant. In December 1934 the city rejected all bids to supply electric current for its own use on the grounds that the proposed rates were exorbitant. The president, seeing a good opportunity to promote one of his favorite causes, asked the mayor to come to the White House where tentative promises were made by Roosevelt and Ickes to provide funds for a public power plant. LaGuardia was jubilant. "There is a nice little word in law for persons who take more than a reasonable profit," he exclaimed. "Until the utilities become decent, honest, and fair little boys, we will take the whole hog." A few days later, on his morning ride to City Hall, he selected a site for the new plant, whose construction he expected to see begin early in the new year.

The mayor had widespread public support for this enterprise. "The defiance shown by the great utility company leaves no choice," said the ordinarily conservative *World Telegram;* the power industry, said the *News,* "asked" for Roosevelt's support of the new plant. But again, as with unification, opposition expressed itself through political channels; this time, besides, the mayor was up against an adversary which could use its powers shrewdly to frustrate him. By February the utilities were offering to cut their rates for electricity supplied to the city; by May they were offering a reduction for the general consumer. "Why not accept the peace offer of the Consolidated Gas Co.?" asked the *Times*. "Why burden the city with the costs and risks of such a venture?" But though support weakened, LaGuardia held fast to his yardstick concept. When first the state legislature and then the Board of Estimate refused him the needed authority for constructing the power plant, the mayor continued to fight by going to the voters in a referendum.

There was a dramatic day in Albany when the mayor rode up to defend his yardstick bill. Against him were arrayed the representatives of the power lobby, headed by the influential Joseph N. Proskauer, former judge of the New York State Supreme Court. "That's what these gentlemen appearing in the opposition are bent upon," cried the mayor, "nipping in the bud any project for the municipalities to protect themselves against the extortion of the power companies." Then, with a sweep of his arm and a finger pointed at Judge Proskauer: "They are the great boys for legislative contraception." But though LaGuardia never weakened in the fight, though Washington declared itself waiting for an application for the loan, the power plant did not get built. The first referendum was rejected by the courts on a technicality; and in 1942 when a drastically reduced scheme was proposed for acquiring a utility plant on Staten Island, the Democrats on the city council blocked it.

"This is not final," the mayor said gamely even then. "I see the day when we will own all Consolidated Edison. It may not come in my time . . ."

Transit unification, though limited in its results, was an essential reform; the fight for a municipal power plant at least gave LaGuardia a chance to reaffirm his place within the political left. But it was efforts to create decent housing for the poor which created the most enduring fruits. From the beginning the improvement of housing conditions was a prime objective. Slums were figured to cover seventeen square miles within the five boroughs; a million children were being reared in blighted neighborhoods and under inherently antisocial conditions. A dollar cost of $15 billion was set upon the total job of eliminating slums once and for all, with $150 million required for the first stage. The latter amount did not seem beyond the range of possibility with Washington looking desperately for ways to put the unemployed to work.

LaGuardia was convinced that housing was a social need analogous to health and education; he related it closely to his health program, believing it to underlie all lasting treatment of disease. "If anyone had heard a hundred years ago that education would cost $125 million," commented his commissioner of housing, "he would have dropped dead." Yet that was what education was in fact costing New York in the 1930s, and what housing might be expected to require.

Rehabilitation and regulation were the conventional methods of amelioration pursued by the Department of Housing. The LaGuardia administration rejected these for wholesale clearance. What a generation later would seem a self-defeating approach, in that earlier period appeared the only means commensurate with the need and with the available resources of manpower.

The first requirement was to get started. A New York City Housing Authority was quickly set up, headed by Langdon Post; funds were authorized, and then witheld, by the quixotic Ickes. LaGuardia turned to private sources of funding, and with loans from Bernard Baruch and Vincent Astor, combined with relief labor, launched the pioneering project of First Houses on Avenue A and East 3rd Street. The initial phase contained 120 apartments, sunlit, with modern sanitary facilities, renting for $6.05 a room to families with an average income of $23 a week. Its dedication in December 1935 marked a milestone, however slightly it reached to the roots of the total problem.

Williamsburgh and Harlem River Houses were built directly by PWA and owned by the federal government. In a day when bigger still seemed better, the fact that Williamsburg Houses covered twenty-five acres was hailed as a triumph. At least the individual buildings were still small in scale, retaining a relationship to the ground on which they were built and to the streets of the surrounding city. Revisited today, they seem pleasantly human in comparison with later developments.

By 1937 the U.S. Housing Authority Act as well as a state authority were to pour funds directly into housing. New problems and controversies arose, and a new scale of building was achieved. Red Hook contained over nine thousand units; the famous Queensbridge Houses contained over eleven thousand, and made use of elevators for the first time. Without the New Deal in Washington none of this could have happened, but to LaGuardia went the credit for identifying the city's crucial needs and initiating the drive for action. Whatever the discrepancies between vision and reality, no other American city could show comparable achievements.

Arts in the City

Cultivation of the arts was an important aspect of LaGuardia's reform program. Though seemingly secondary to undertakings so highly visible as housing or parkways, it deserves to be singled out and remembered. The idea that the arts have a significant role to play in city life, and that the duty of city government is to promote them, was new to America. It was special to LaGuardia, deriving from his background, his natural gifts and training. If his judgments were often eccentric, and his appreciation of contemporary art definitely limited, that gave to policy in the field the same personal touch that marked his administration generally.

He was the son of an accomplished musician and was himself a practiced player upon the cornet. The traditions of the Old World were part of his makeup, with the presence of music, sculpture, and beauty in public places taken for granted. Among men of artistic temperament LaGuardia felt naturally at ease. In the midst of war he had sought out the young American violinist Albert Spalding, refusing to assign him to flying duty out of respect for his gifts. The happy period of his marriage to Thea saw the LaGuardia home in Greenwich Village a gathering place of musicians and artists.

The New York public never ceased to marvel, and to be slightly amused, when he took the conductor's baton at a public concert. Editorialists would contrast the harmony he elicited from musicians with the discord prevailing at City Hall; or wish that such repose as he demonstrated in the quieter passages might sometimes mark him in the conduct of official duties. But in fact his conducting was not a joke. Had he not been a mayor he might well have been a maestro. "His Honor has a few mannerisms as a *chef d'orchestre*," wrote the *Times* music critic Harold Taubman; "He beats time occasionally with his left foot. But we like his conducting. He knows what brasses are for—to be heard. He knows that band music should make the blood tingle."

In dance and drama, as we shall see, LaGuardia's persistent moralism often came between him and the work. And in the plastic arts he had a vision limited by a professed conservatism. "I think that a work of art should be beautiful," he said on receiving from the Fine Arts Federation a plaque in 1937, "should inspire instead of distress and please instead of annoy." On another occasion, visiting an outdoor sculpture show, he stood silent as the contemporary sculptor William Zorach explained the appeal of a certain piece because of the nature of its surfaces, its rhythm, its interplay of planes. On being told that Thomas E. Dewey had apparently responded to these nuances, the mayor replied, "I'm glad he did"—with an ever-so-faint emphasis on the "he" and the implication that this was an additional reason for the imperfect sympathy existing between himself and the young district attorney. "When it comes to art, I'm a Liberty Leaguer," he said; and, "if that's a bird, I'm Hitler."

Yet he understood the creative process. In a touching introduction to a volume on the work of his friend the well-known sculptor Attilio Piccirilli, LaGuardia gives expression to his feeling for the act of shaping inert material. "To see him mold, one sees the transmission of his love and labor and his affection for the task in the gentle handling of the clay. He always reminded me of a young mother bathing a newborn infant." LaGuardia had compared his own role to that of a sculptor, working upon the form of the great city, and he had himself felt something of the artist's "love and labor."

The time was ripe for an enlargement of the role of the public arts. The older patrons of cultural institutions were suffering from the hard times. Meanwhile, Washington's recognition that artists, too, were people and that they deserved to work at their own trade, had filled the open spaces of the city with music and given writers, actors, and painters new hope. LaGuardia was ready to build upon this base, but to go further. He wanted to get artists off the relief rolls, restoring them to full participation in the institutions of the arts, where their gifts could be developed and the public permanently benefitted. He particularly wanted to give opportunity to young people. Sensing the genius that so often goes to waste, he dreamed of a time when all the city's school children, as part of their regular curriculum, could be taught skills in their chosen artistic fields; and when the most gifted could have a high school of their own.

His administration's foray into the arts began modestly with the cleaning and regilding of city sculptures. Attention was even given to the notorious statue of Civic Virtue, showing triumphant manhood treading upon a prostrate female form. Moses, who shared the mayor's more conventional views on art, was glad to show his support of the new spirit by sponsoring murals and statues in his zoos. But LaGuardia had larger ambitions, and early in 1935 named the city's first Municipal Art Committee to advise him and to assure support for his initiatives. The committee was headed by Mrs. Henry L. Breckenridge. Its membership of more than a hundred glittered with names of the cultural leaders of the day. Among them were John Erskine, the writer; Robert Edmund Jones and Donald Oenslager, the scenic designers; Douglas Moore, the composer; Otis Skinner, the actor; and Mrs. Vincent Astor, the civic benefactor. At the first meeting, held amid the potted palms of the chamber of the Board of Estimate, the mayor set forth three major objectives: the establishment of a city art center, a high school of music, and an educational and cultural program disseminated through the city-owned radio station WNYC.

The committee had a checkered career. Formed without the blessing of the ever-jealous Art Commission, lacking funds, and with too large and disparate a membership for concentrated work, it managed to sponsor several excellent events—an exhibition of American art at Rockefeller Center, a July music festival with Albert Spalding as soloist at the opening concert—but found itself left out when the mayor's more far-reaching cultural plans were being laid. Then he would turn to other advisors. Mrs. Breckenridge felt neglected. "I admire you a great deal," she wrote plaintively to the mayor, "but you do not understand me."

In 1939, after four years of study, the committee made its mandated report. The major recommendation was admirable but in the nature of things not feasible—that a sum of 1 percent of the city budget be appropriated annually for the arts. Beyond that it called for an adequate municipal art center, a Harlem art center, a children's gallery, a municipal orchestra, and an expansion of community drama and contemporary dance programs. Many items on its agenda would still be live issues thirty years later; they would continue in some cases to be pressed by the same cultural leaders. The recommendations that theaters be included in high-rise office buildings, that curtain times be earlier, and that alcoholic beverages be served in theater lobbies have a distinctly present-day ring.

LaGuardia did not wait for the report to begin implementation of his three major objectives. In 1936 he dedicated at St. Nicholas Terrace and 135th Street the first high school where students could major in music and the plastic arts. "I believe this to be one of the best contributions that I will be able to make . . . as long as I am mayor of New York City," he declared on that proud day; and there are some today who think this was indeed his most original accomplishment. High-level cultural programs broadcast over WNYC were comparatively easy to achieve, though some would be so uncharitable as to complain that the culture they got from this source consisted largely of the mayor's airing of his political views. In fact the mayor took the programs very seriously, and in the midst of what seemed the busiest of days would put in a call to the station to say that he liked, or more often that he did not like, some classical program being broadcast.

More complex, and reaching a more distant solution, was the mayor's dream of a center for opera, symphony, and related forms of artistic expression, where the people of the city could come as to a place of their own, enjoying the best and paying the minimum price for tickets. By 1936 pledges by private donors of $14 million were reported, but they vanished amid the controversy aroused when it turned out that the proposed center would be in Central Park at 59th Street. In the same year the Museum of Modern Art acquired its present 53rd Street site, and it was hoped that this might be the focus of a wide grouping of institutions. Along with the museum a branch of the public library materialized here, but otherwise that plan, too, aborted.

Though it means getting ahead of our story, it seems well to recount one further major effort. In November 1937 the mayor is found commenting in a letter that "Mr. Berle is doing some investigation for me" in the matter of a municipal art center. But Berle went off to Washington and the following May LaGuardia declared Robert Moses was to be in charge. Moses, with characteristic disregard for the mayor, asserted it was the first time he had heard about such a thing. By September, nevertheless, he was ready with a report. It turned out to be a blockbuster. The idea he had been asked to investigate was the establishment "at Rockefeller or elsewhere" of a municipal music and performing arts center. The discussion concentrated on the feasibility of a large neoclassic building on land between 51st and 53rd streets on Sixth Avenue. Moses's position was simply stated: he was "not at all sure that we must have a center of this kind." Grand opera, as he saw it, was an obsolete art form on the way out; centralization of artistic institutions might well be "a step in the wrong direction." In any case, the "original grandiose plan" appeared in his judgment to be highly impractical.

The mayor was taken aback. To Nelson Rockefeller, who was involved in this and in most other plans for the arts, he wrote that the situation was not as "gloomy" as depicted. But a death blow had nevertheless been delivered to immediate hopes for a city art center. New initiatives would wait until after World War II and then, in City Center, would take an unexpected form.

Crime Fighter

Besides being committed to reform, the LaGuardia administration came to office committed to wage intensive warfare against crime. It was a war into which the mayor entered with a will. His combative nature, his sympathy for the poor and for the consumers who were so often victims of the rackets, and not least his love of the dramatic gesture, disposed him to energetic sallies against criminal elements. His lively imagination peopled the urban world with "racketeers," "chiselers," and "punks"—characters that loomed sinister and more than life-size upon the public stage; and he viewed himself as their foreordained enemy. His first order to the police in 1934 was to go mercilessly after the racketeers; twelve years later he would still be in hot pursuit.

The city he had been elected to govern seemed to be, and indeed was, infiltrated with crime. The signs of civic disorder, evident in bankrupt finances, rundown parks, and decrepit housing, were also to be found in squalid alliances between commerce and the underworld. Unable to get police protection all kinds of businessmen were paying tribute to racketeers rather than suffer the consequences in threats to their safety or vandalized property. In certain unexpected areas the rackets seemed to be particularly entrenched. Every truckload of grapes coming into the city paid its tribute. Kosher chickens were assessed at so much a head, and so were the crates in which they traveled. In the construction industry workers paid kickbacks to the contractors as the price of holding their jobs. Afraid to testify against their exploiters, and lacking confidence in the impartiality of the police and the courts, merchants, wage earners, and businessmen became connivers in a universe of lawlessness.

In the fight against crime the mayor had as his two chief agents the commissioner of police and the commissioner of investigation. The latter through the first term was Paul Blanshard, a former

10. Taking on the slot machines. TIMES WIDE WORLD

clergyman and associate of the respected Socialist leader Norman Thomas. Blanshard had shown his familiarity with the dark side of the city by writing with Norman Thomas *What's Wrong with New York,* an analysis of the deep-lying corruption of the Walker regime. The book, unfortunately for its sales and for its effect on the public, was published on the day Jimmy Walker resigned. As commissioner, Blanshard was subject not only to the normal frustrations of being in the mayor's cabinet—he was "a terrible man to work with," Thomas remembered being told—but also from the additional handicap of being in charge of a field with which the mayor was constantly concerned. Woe to the commissioner if investigative reports were issued directly from his office! Yet when sent to the mayor they risked being mysteriously submerged or having their publication delayed.

Toward the end of the first term Blanshard found his relations with the mayor imperceptibly but fatally cooling. He retired gracefully—he was on the whole a graceful figure. During his tenure he was spared (except in the depredations against Tammany) the use of his office to pursue the mayor's personal vendettas. His successor, by contrast, would often look into the affairs of discredited commissioners as if they were themselves heads of a racket.

The commissioner of police we are already acquainted with in the person of General O'Ryan. He might have been an effective crime fighter, but he was preoccupied during his term of office with problems of civil disturbances, demonstrations, and mass picketing. It was clear he would not last long in office. The mayor and he differed publicly on the handling of the taxi strike, on relief demonstrators, and even on how policemen should dress in summer. Forbearance on both sides began to wear thin by midsummer 1934, when the mayor charged O'Ryan with "unbecoming" statements. O'Ryan decided to go abroad for a vacation, fell ill, and in September offered his resignation. The mayor, he said, had gone over his head in ordering a concentration of police assigned to his old Harlem district. A parting blast accused the mayor of encouraging crime through constant interference in the police department: lawless persons were encouraged, he said, and the police were discouraged from the performance of their duties.

It is remarkable how well LaGuardia sailed through what might have been a serious challenge to his rule. Quarrels between a mayor and his police commissioner are the stuff of scandal-hungry journalists, and the public usually finds itself on the side of the police.

LaGuardia's image of aggressive rectitude helped him, as did the fact that everyone recognized the commissioner's appointment to have been politically necessary. He sensibly dismissed O'Ryan's final outburst, saying there would be no postmortems. A day or so later he characterized the statements as "false and malicious" but confined his personal judgment of O'Ryan to the mild remark that he was "an ill-tempered ex-police officer."

O'Ryan stayed on for a few days to make a report in connection with the sensational arrest of the alleged kidnapper of the Lindbergh baby; then the mayor called the department's chief inspector to City Hall and made him the new commissioner. Lewis J. Valentine was to serve in this post until the last days of the LaGuardia administration. A cop with an impeccable record of crime busting, he had been exiled during the Walker regime because his investigative activities brought him too close to the seat of power. Valentine, in the summer of 1934, was no stranger to the mayor. As mayor-elect LaGuardia had called him to a breakfast meeting where his opening question was "What's wrong with the police department?" Thereafter the mayor had consulted him regularly, even bringing him to City Hall over O'Ryan's head. Valentine could be erratic and emotional, but his solid reputation and his experienced vigilance were to serve the mayor in good stead.

In the end, of course, LaGuardia was his own chief racket buster and crime fighter. He alone defined the issues and dramatized the attack. An unforgettable example of his methods is provided by the battle of the slot machines. As a form of racketeering the lowly slot machine might not have recommended itself as a principal target; but it was particularly flagrant and the more insidious because the public seemed ready to let itself be mulched by the unfavorable odds of these "mechanical bandits." They existed in virtually every small retail outlet, under the threat of property damage if rejected. LaGuardia grasped the symbolic importance of the slot machine and early in his administration marched in to the West 100th Street police station, turning it into a temporary courtroom as he drew upon the authority of the committing magistrate vested in him by the city charter. Had any other mayor selected a police station for such a purpose? He replied to the question that he did not know: "Anyway," he added, *"we* create the precedents."

Thus began the process of rooting out a minor but pernicious racket, made difficult because court decisions, later to be revised, required proof that a particular machine, before being seized, had actually been used for gambling. Under these circumstances the wholesale arrests demanded by the mayor could not take place. Yet on one long-remembered occasion he had a number of the offending contraptions loaded on a barge and in his presence, along with that of the chief of police and the fire commissioner, consigned bodily to the sea. "These machines," said the mayor in his elegy, "were controlled by the most vicious of criminal elements." When much else of the LaGuardia years had been forgotten, the picture would remain vivid of a shirt-sleeved mayor personally smashing slot machines with a sledgehammer.

This, in a sense, was child's play. The more serious attacks on crime were strangely mixed up with a changing political situation and revealed some of the less pleasant aspects of the administration. Mass arrests and detentions on the flimsiest evidence, blood-curdling instructions to policemen on the beat, even book burnings, were resorted to in an attempt to drive the supposed criminals out of town and, presumably, to impress the public with the mayor's seriousness as a crime fighter. When placed on the political defensive LaGuardia was a man who knew—and who did not spurn—the tricks of his trade; and an aggressive posture against criminals being required, he could count on the support of Valentine's flamboyant tactics.

The course of the mayor's anticrime activities can be placed in the context of events in the political sphere. The LaGuardia who quarrelled with O'Ryan over harsh treatment of the drivers in the taxicab strike and who defended mass picketing was sure of his political base, confidently in control of the Board of Estimate, and secure in public favor. The LaGuardia who late in 1934 went along with overt encouragement of police brutality had suffered a damaging political blow. It will be recalled that in the summer of 1934 the young comptroller, Arthur Cunningham, died suddenly. Ignoring the politicians in his overconfidence, turning his back on the Republican state chairman whom he found waiting at his door, LaGuardia appointed the deputy comptroller as Cunningham's successor.

McGoldrick was a rotund witty Irishman, the darling of his Columbia students, but he was without political experience or Republican support as he campaigned in the court-mandated election of November.

On the night before the election LaGuardia met at the Advertising Club with Lowell Limpus, reporter and close friend. According to Limpus the mayor for the first time faced up to the possibility of the comptroller's defeat. "If you're right," said the mayor upon hearing the prediction, "we're facing a real disaster." There was a long pause as he fixed his eyes upon the ceiling. "If I lose my comptroller it means Tammany will stage a comeback. In that case you're going to see one hell of a fight."

McGoldrick's defeat at the polls narrowed Fusion's hold on the Board of Estimate. The small numerical majority was threatened, however, by the disaffection of the borough presidents of Queens and Staten Island, George Harvey and Joseph A. Palma. It seemed a time, if ever, to launch "one hell of a fight." Tammany's rejoicing proved premature as LaGuardia marshalled his forces. Blanshard was sent forth upon an investigation of Tammany; deputy commissioner Mike Fraschetti was dispatched to root out racketeers from the city's markets. Most important, Valentine was given orders to "get" the gangsters who formed the backbone of Tammany's shock troops.

It was at this time, in November 1934, that Valentine issued his famous "muss 'em up" order. The incident was provoked by circumstances personally affecting the police commissioner, but in the weeks that followed its resonance was suited to the mayor's mood. Valentine had returned from a bedside visit to a dying policeman, shot while on duty. In that day's lineup appeared a gunman whose dandified clothes were particularly offensive to the police commissioner. "When you meet men like that," he said, "don't be afraid to muss 'em up. Blood should be smeared all over that man's velvet collar." He followed this with the remark that "with killers, racketeers, and gangsters the sky is the limit," and added for the benefit of cops on the beat that there are certain people without rights—"you can club them with impunity."

Comment in the press almost uniformly expressed shock. Burlingham pleaded in private for a reproof from the mayor; he enclosed a letter from Felix Frankfurter: "Valentine has outbrutalized all the brutal utterances of his predecessors." But the mayor was silent. He believed he was fighting against criminal elements and for his own political life. Undoubtedly, too, having recently caused the resignation of one police commissioner, he realized he could not afford to quarrel with another.

By January 1935 the mayor and Valentine were in full hue and cry. "Numerous recent killings" of policemen by criminals had convinced LaGuardia that a state of war existed between the city and the underworld. "This is not time for coddling crooks," he continued. "When the war is on you cannot stand by and expect that a police officer is going to be shot by a cowardly crook." A week later Valentine was giving the same theme a more ominous twist. "Barbarians and savages," he said, were walking the streets of the city. The scales of justice were not balanced for the people but for the criminal: "It's about time we gave honest people a break."

There followed a roundup of more than three hundred persons considered to be undesirables, under an obscure section of the penal code making it unlawful for people with criminal records to assemble in public places. Those arrested were herded into cells; the next day—despite the commissioner's avowed intent "to root out crime in this city"—they were released. It then transpired that $500,000 worth of books considered obscene by "the courts and the police" would be burned in the furnaces of the police department, among them works by Mark Twain. Later that year, when the parks were in full use, another raid took place, this time landing some seven hundred drunkards, panhandlers, and beggars in crowded cells. It was reported after this incident that the mayor "conferred" with Valentine, but neither then nor following any of the other incidents referred to did LaGuardia issue a public disclaimer.

In June 1935 the war against crime took a new turn, with political consequences reaching far into the future. The New York County Grand Jury, appointed to investigate rackets, had been feuding with the district attorney, William C. Dodge, who refused to appoint a special prosecutor to continue their investigations. The jury had been dismissed at its own request. Governor Lehman now entered upon the scene. After conferring with the district attorney, he summoned both LaGuardia and Valentine to his Park Avenue apartment. He had demanded from the district attorney a report on what he had been doing to fight vice and crime; similarly he asked the mayor and his commissioner for a report on *their* activities. LaGuardia showed himself discreet and cooperative in public, but one wonders what emotions surged within. Soon afterward a letter sent directly by the governor to Valentine was answered by LaGuardia with the acid remark that his commissioner had forwarded the letter to him unanswered "in accordance with the customs and usual channels of communication." The mayor was not one who liked being bypassed, or being treated on a par with one of his commissioners.

Lehman next ordered Dodge to appoint a special prosecutor or face dismissal. He proposed the selection of one of four names: George Z. Medalie, Charles Evans Hughes, Jr., Thomas D. Thacher, and Charles H. Tuttle. It was a distinguished list but all four, after meeting with the governor, refused to head the rackets inquiry. They were too busy; besides, they regretted the omission from the list of the young lawyer whose name had been the only one recommended by the Bar Association. Lehman professed himself "greatly and deeply disappointed." As for the young lawyer, Thomas E. Dewey, the governor said he had withheld his name because he was not sufficiently known to inspire public confidence.

Despite what the *Times* called "the atrocious crime of being a young man," Dewey was named and was thus started on the career which at so many points was to lead him into conflict, or into strained and bitter accommodation, with LaGuardia. For the time being, though he found the special prosecutor's demands for funds, for furniture and office space, to be rather overly ambitious, LaGuardia promised, and gave, full cooperation. It must have been painful to have Dewey conferring directly with Valentine, as if he were part of his staff. Even to this the mayor made no apparent objection. There is a hint, however, of LaGuardia's unhappiness at these events and of his resentment of the governor's role. On the day of Dewey's appointment an important housing development in the Bronx was being dedicated. Governor Lehman was to make the principal address. LaGuardia was not present for the speeches; arriving late, he explained he had been detained by a firemen's and policemen's baseball game. The audience had waited for their mayor, but after a delay they dispersed and the ceremony was over.

The spotlight in the war against racketeers and related criminals was now shifted to Dewey. Much as LaGuardia hated to recognize it, the mayor of New York could have only a limited and largely symbolic role in rooting out crime. LaGuardia had focused public attention on the issue. Perhaps this very skill at dramatization was his most solid contribution to the cause. In the last month of this eventful year he was once more to seize the headlines with the kind of heroic play acting at which he was adept and which could be more useful than some were ready to admit. The miniature artichoke, valued as a delicacy by the Italian community, was this time cast as the damsel in distress; Ciro Terranova, who controlled the racket in artichokes, exacting a tribute from every retailer, was the villain.

The mayor kept his plans secret even from Fellowes Morgan, the commissioner of markets, until the latter was told to be at the mayor's home at 6 A.M. on December 20. "I remember it well," Morgan wrote many years later; "it was the shortest and coldest day of the year." On arriving at the Bronx Terminal Market, it was evident that the mayor had arranged for some sort of ceremony. Under his arm were large proclamations, and policemen with bugles were ready to herald the crowd to a place in front of the market restaurant.

In the extreme cold the bugles (or the bugle blowers) froze and had to be taken into the restaurant to be thawed out. Undaunted, the mayor climbed to the platform of a truck where, unrolling one of the large proclamations, he read it to the astonished crowd. Under an ancient law permitting the mayor in an emergency to ban the distribution of food, the sale of artichokes was now prohibited in the public markets, beginning upon the day following. Scrolls were passed out to the cops in the squad cars, to be posted throughout the market area.

The dawn foray received enormous publicity, though the press was not entirely favorable in its reactions. "It is impossible not to conclude that the world today is a bit mad," said the *Herald Tribune,* contemplating the spectacle of the mayor as protector of the virtue of artichokes. "Where does LaGuardia get the idea that he had the right to keep merchants from selling artichokes?" thundered the *Post.* "What induces him to believe that New York City can be ruled by proclamation?" Unnoted was the fact that amid these theatricals LaGuardia had dispatched Paul Kern to Washington to secure from the Department of Agriculture cancellation of Terranova's license to sell artichokes.

LaGuardia was not a fool and he knew well how to combine effective legal action with the politics of symbolism. In this case he not only ended the reign of one racketeer who had been draining a million dollars a year from the pockets of consumers, but he prepared the fall of others. It was twilight time, too, for the green pepper king, and for the notorious Socks Lanza who had long ruled over the fish market.

4
Toward the Zenith

Private Man

For the mayor the start of 1936 marked the halfway point of his first term. It seems as good a time as any to try to catch him standing still, seeing the private man among his family and friends.

In the domestic sphere the mayoralty had brought continuity rather than change. LaGuardia still lived in the Upper East Side apartment he had occupied as a congressman. Seeing it for the first time a visitor would invariably be impressed by its modesty; a tenement, Ickes called it. Valentine, on being invited for breakfast for a preinaugural conversation, was struck by the bare simplicity of the surroundings. Whatever his propensity for movement in the public sphere, LaGuardia treasured stability and calm at home. Besides, he and his wife had to keep a close watch on expenses during the early years of their marriage. Amid the triumph of the first election night, Marie found pleasure in the thought that now she would be able to buy a new rug.

Marie accepted her husband's constant busyness, his long hours of work and late returns, with entire equanimity. "I am perfectly happy to adjust myself and my life to Fiorello's plans whatever they may be," she once told a reporter. The statement may sound a bit removed from real life, but in fact Marie LaGuardia possessed an accepting, phlegmatic nature which in the later years one still sensed beneath her easy laugh and quick courtesies. This stolidity is said to have been what first impressed the young congressman when she came into his office as an untrained and inexperienced helper in 1915. For her part, she was "entranced by the tantrums" of a man whose temperament was so different from her own.

As wife, Marie put aside without apparent regret the role of political adviser and even partner which she had fulfilled during her fourteen years as secretary to the congressman. A rather surprising account of her in a New York newspaper of 1923 notes that "Miss Fischer has earned the reputation of being a 'practical politician.' She has a host of friends among the leaders throughout the city. She is known to be more progressive than the major himself." After Miss Fischer became Mrs. LaGuardia, however, she rarely visited the office and even at home refrained from giving advice. Yet she could still be a helpful intermediary and protector of her husband's privacy. One of the mayor's commissioners recalled an occasion when his wife called LaGuardia at home to protest on some matter. "For goodness sake, Mrs. Morgan, don't mention that matter right now," was Marie's good advice. "Give Fiorello a few days to cool off."

Fiorello was intensely proud of Marie. He wanted her to be above all dignified and "a lady"; he liked her to wear black and objected if she put on a hat which he considered conspicuous. He was reluctant to have her take too prominent a part in public events. Yet he could tease her, too, or speak of her with a frankness which in a nature less evenly balanced might have caused resentment. Addressing a group of young women being trained as secretaries, the mayor vouched for their important role. Then, with the actor's change of pace: "I had a good secretary once," he mused. "But I married her—and got a bad cook."

The biggest change in the LaGuardia home life came with the adoption of two children, a girl in 1933 and a boy the following year. LaGuardia loved children in general—one should take care in "lending" one's child to the mayor, a friend warned jokingly; he would totally monopolize it. He never seemed too busy to play with a child or to advise and instruct. This was true whether the child in question was the offspring of a constituent, or Richard, the son of LaGuardia's "colored" cook. And so the coming into his home of two children he could call his own was bound to cause a domestic revolution and to release a flood of sometimes contradictory feelings.

11. With Marie LaGuardia and the children. Breakfast in the East Harlem apartment. New York *Daily News Photo*

Jean, who was seven in 1933, was the daughter of his first wife's sister, dark-haired and of Italian extraction. Eric, a year her junior and of Scandinavian origin, satisfied LaGuardia's delight in fair-complexioned youth. Long in orphan homes—too long, said Dr. George Baehr many years later—Eric was a shy, nervous child, acutely apprehensive of doctors and with a tendency to shift his enthusiasms rapidly. He would settle down in due course, the father of a family of his own, and become professor of literature in a western university. Jean was known from the start to suffer from a serious form of diabetes, and lived too briefly, though for more years than had been deemed her allotted span. Her grave, giving her age as thirty-four, is beside her father's and close to Thea's and Thea's daughter, in Woodlawn Cemetery in the Bronx.

To accommodate the newcomers a room was taken over from the next apartment and a door cut through from Marie and Fiorello's bedroom. A visitor, commenting on what seemed the inconvenience of this arrangement, was told that LaGuardia enjoyed having the children pass through his bedroom, even when they awakened him at night. He derived pleasure from their antics, as from their sayings. In a letter to Julius Ochs Adler he told of Eric's response to the picture of an audience evidently enjoying one of his father's speeches: "Daddy, why are they all laughing at you?" questioned the son. And to John D. Rockefeller III he described how, after seeing the Rockettes at Radio City Music Hall, Eric wanted to know if they were real—"I mean are they real people, like us?" On being reassured, he referred to them afterward as "the beautiful ladies."

In speaking of Jean the father was all tenderness. His "little girl" had received an invitation to present the first bouquet at a church festival. "I will have to present the news very carefully to Jean that this honor has been offered her," he wrote in September 1935, "as this is the first invitation she has ever received to function officially." The invitation was politely turned down.

Yet LaGuardia was a strict father, insisting on standards of effort and decorum which were often unrealistic. He would complain that Jean was not concentrating sufficiently on her music or that Eric's attention was inclined to wander. To Ernest Gruening, an old friend then governor of Alaska, he wrote in 1942 announcing that "Eric is now interested in geology—please send a handful of specimens of Alaska stones." Indicating there was some requirement for haste, he added a little reprovingly that he did not know how long Eric's enthusiasm would last. The fear of spoiling his children, or having them spoiled as a result of his official position, was constant. Once, when Eric was invited to accompany him on a visit to a new Danish passenger ship, the mayor answered he would be happy to bring him along but that he must appeal as a parent "that no special recognition be made of Eric and that he be treated as any other child." Then for added emphasis the mayor instructed one of his aides to give a personal message to the Danish consul-general: "Besides being mayor I am also a parent, with all the difficulties of parenthood, and cannot have my children spoiled by having them in any way be made special guests."

Home life with the LaGuardias had its tensions, with Fiorello's impatient temperament and exacting judgments coming into conflict with his natural sympathy for children; and sometimes bringing reflections on Marie in her capacity as a mother. Yet from it all emerged an attractive and happy family atmosphere. A stranger in the New York streets told of hearing a pleasing voice amid the hubbub, and turning saw a lady standing beside him—"a rather petite lady with blonde hair." She was dressed in black and with her were two children, a boy and a girl. The boy wore an "outrageously rakish skull hat." The girl was "extremely intelligent-looking, and she wore glasses and I think had a red hat." The observer trailed along behind the little group, "being impressed the while by the lady and the utter charm of the little family's camaraderie." The letter, coming to the mayor amid the day's burden of official correspondence, was a nice tribute to what was, in part, one of his own best works.

Formal entertaining in the LaGuardia home was rare. Perhaps overscrupulous, LaGuardia had made it a rule not to have close social relationships with people he had not known before taking office. Besides, he liked old friends the best. Vito Marcantonio, a protégé and almost an adopted son, would come by; Paul Windels and Adolf Berle were frequent visitors. At Sunday lunch the sculptor Piccirilli was a fixture. In the dread days after Thea's death Piccirilli had been the disconsolate widower's sole companion when he sailed off in search of peace. Now more than any man he knew the mayor's thoughts and moods, and after the Sunday meal the two would go to his studio, sitting in silence under the high rafters or recalling old times. They were opposites in temperament and in their experience of life. Piccirilli was the victim of a notoriously unhappy marriage and was by nature unassuming and quietly reflective. Yet each had something to give the other. "He taught me to laugh twenty years ago," Piccirilli was to write of his friend, "and we have been laughing ever since."

Other friends LaGuardia saw in different ways: an evening meal at a favorite restaurant—Little Venice in the Village or Riccardi's on 116th Street—or at the Tavern on the Green in Central Park (perhaps with a concert afterward at Lewisohn Stadium). Most frequently he invited them for an early morning ride with him in his car to City Hall. It was thus that Anna Rosenberg recalled being with the mayor informally, and thus that Burlingham was able to impart much of his shrewd and affectionate advice. The official limousine would make various detours as projects were planned or works under way surveyed, and as conversation ranged freely over problems of the city and the world.

Friends from the mayor's past, voices speaking from his childhood and youth, reappear—usually fleetingly and often amid regrets for the pressure of official business. He writes his "first sweetheart," Mrs. Gussie R. Knight: "What happened when you passed through New York? . . . I have been looking for you all over the United States." He writes his "dear teacher," Lynn C. Stockton, asking her "to write a fellow once in a while" and signs it "lots of love." Then to Charles L. Kohlen: "Your mother was so kind to me during my law school days. I always will have pleasant recollections of how she would come to my room and put out the gas when she thought I was studying too long."

There were also friends from World War I days. Major J. W. Swann rode a hundred miles on horseback to meet him at a western rendezvous. A personal relationship was kept with "Ollie" (Dr. O. B. Kiel) and all his family in Wichita, and a series of letters deals with efforts to get together in New York or Texas. But LaGuardia drew the line at his friend's request to lobby in Washington for a military hospital in Wichita!

Beyond the immediate family in the East Harlem apartment, LaGuardia's close relatives consisted of his younger brother Richard and his sister Gemma. To unravel his relations with these is difficult. Nothing in the surviving correspondence or in the comments of living contemporaries gives much help. Richard lived in New Jersey, pursuing a career of social work and holding minor official positions, a figure with his older brother's basic inclinations but without his drive and passion. He died in February 1935, and though many letters of condolence came to the mayor, his responses are unrevealing. No evidence suggests they had been intimate. As so often, Burlingham speaks the kind and human word: "You may not have seen much of each other in the muck and turmoil of life, but time and space don't matter. . . ." The LaGuardias befriended Richard's son and namesake, who regularly spent his summers with the family.

Relations with his sister Gemma are more complex. Separated by only a year in age, the two had been close companions in their youth in Prescott, sharing musical gifts and a sense of adventure. When LaGuardia left Europe and returned for good to the United States in 1906, his mother and sister remained in Fiume, where Gemma gave English lessons to earn a small income. One of her students was an Austrian Jew named Herman Gluck whom she subsequently married. The couple moved to Budapest, taking Irene LaGuardia, the mother, with them. Irene died in 1915 and is buried in the Jewish cemetery in Budapest.

A surviving letter of July 1934, addressed to "dear Uncle Fiorello," contains a rather pathetic appeal from the niece Yolandez whom LaGuardia had never met. "Uncle Fiorello and Marie, auntie dear, do write a line now and then to dear mama. She always says she would be so happy if she would hear from you." Yolandez describes her mother as feeling well. "She has a great deal of grey hair, but her face is still fresh and young looking." Finally, a request is made for Jean's measurements—"I should like to make her a needlework dress. Here they are so sweet for little girls." If there was a reply it has not been preserved, though it seems unlikely that LaGuardia would have left unbroken the silence which had fallen between the two branches of the family.

When the Nazis came to power and through the early years of the war Gemma and her husband managed to exist relatively untroubled. But the two ultimately faced the horrors of the concentration camp, where Herman Gluck died. Inevitably, a result of LaGuardia's outspoken attacks was that the Nazis turned their attention to his sister in Budapest. LaGuardia would receive news of Gemma in the later years of the war through letters from fellow prisoners who had escaped or been released. His letters in reply are noncommittal and would appear to have been drafted by an aide. Meanwhile a second niece, Irene, had come to America in November 1938 on a temporary visa with her address given as City Hall, New York.

A few years later LaGuardia writes to W. P. Walters of the New York District Immigration and Nationalization Service stating he has no knowledge of Irene's whereabouts. "We are looking for her ourselves. No doubt she will eventually get into trouble, and then we shall hear from her."

It would seem that where LaGuardia's sister and her family were concerned, "time and space" did indeed matter. It is true they had been long separated; but then so had he been from his "first sweetheart" and his "dear teacher." A more subtle deterrent must have intervened. Perhaps Gemma stood for something alien in nationality and in religion at a time when identification with Protestant America was important for LaGuardia. Perhaps he had never really reconciled himself to having left his sister in Europe and been parted from her for so long. They were to be reunited in dramatic circumstances at the end of the war, but even then the private man was to leave his emotions veiled.

Under the Czars

The problem of relief for the poor and unemployed continued at the boiling point. We go back to where we left the issues unresolved in the spring of 1935. LaGuardia was on the defensive as aldermanic investigations picked at every minor abuse or extravagance, and the faithful Hodson seemed in growing trouble. Members of the board landed what they considered a star witness in the form of Robert Moses, whose department had made the most conspicuous, and therefore presumably the most fault-ridden, use of relief workers. In his lordly way Moses first announced he could not appear at the time fixed, and then on May 8 made a much-heralded appearance before the scandal-hungry politicians.

As drama, the hearing fizzled. Moses was at his most reasonable and convincing. During an effective defense of his own department's policies he issued a series of *obiter dicta* which the aldermen found unanswerable. The relief setup, he maintained, was a makeshift. Occupying a middle ground between private jobs and public works it was inevitably prone to abuse. Better, he suggested, that the funds be administered by private contractors than under public officials whose efficiency even he could not guarantee. LaGuardia commented that the testimony sounded as if it had been delivered at a convention of the Liberty League; but with the board in full cry and even Deutsch, the Fusionist chairman, showing signs of defection, he realized it was time to act.

Claiming his mind had been made up before the investigation, he appointed a "czar" in the form of a forty-seven-year-old department store executive, Oswald W. Knauth. The choice was cloaked in secrecy and was revealed at the last moment with appropriate ceremony. Liberal and socially conscious, Knauth met the aldermen's demand for a businessman to be in command of relief operations. Briskly he promised greater efficiency and a rooting out of radical elements. With Hodson's authority confined, he was for a time given a free hand. But, as had long been evident, the basic problems were intractable. He split with the mayor when he supported a policy requiring relief administrators to reside within the city. His czardom would in any case have been brief, but a new setup in Washington provided the means for a graceful exit and brought to New York czars more powerful, and a good deal more picturesque, than himself.

In April the president's relief bill was passed after prolonged controversy in the Congress. Under its terms a sum of $4.8 billion was appropriated, with authority for its dispersal lodged not in one, but in two men—Harry Hopkins and Harold Ickes. LaGuardia had been angling for some time to acquire more than a proportionate share of the money for New York and now he set out in earnest to get his due. With a dazzling list in hand of transit improvements, sewage disposal plants, hospitals, parks and playgrounds, schools, and housing, he announced that he would spend Monday through Thursday of each week in the capital until the relief funds were allocated. He was on good terms with both Ickes and Hopkins, and by mid-May had been assured of $27 million as a first installment of the $47 million allotted to the state. He announced that federal work projects would provide a total of 250,000 jobs in the city, with 100,000 shifted from the rolls of home relief.

There remained the question of how the program was to be administered locally. LaGuardia's aim was to have Washington appoint an outstanding national figure. No less important from his point of view, he aimed at getting the city set up as a separate administrative unit, independent of state patronage and control. That he should have succeeded in gaining both objectives is an indication of LaGuardia's political skill and of his high prestige in Washington at this time.

In vain the Albany bosses, the O'Connell brothers whom we have already met in the economy bill fight, maneuvered to have staff appointments within the city made through their friend, the WPA administrator for New York State. In vain the dynamic Hugh Johnson, former head of the National Recovery Act, pleaded against accepting the job in New York. LaGuardia saw in him a tough administrator capable of imposing order on the chaotic relief situation, and also, no doubt, of attracting even larger grants from Washington. Though backed by Hopkins, LaGuardia was largely responsible for getting Johnson's agreement to serve.

Johnson arrived at the Newark airport on the evening of June 19, conspicuous in a white necktie and Panama hat, scowling as he descended from the plane into a circle of newspapermen. How did it feel to be back in public life? It felt "like hell," he asserted. He dined that night with the mayor in a private dining room of the St. Regis as guest of the newspaper publisher Herbert Bayard Swope. Afterward the party, which included Joseph P. Kennedy and Raymond Moley, went off to the Louis–Carnera fight at Yankee Stadium.

Once down to work, the new czar could hardly expect all to go smoothly. LaGuardia, whatever his good intentions, found it difficult to accommodate himself to a local relief administrator not under his own authority. Johnson aroused his ire by declaring that the city's projects were not sufficiently advanced to warrant fund-

12. A czar arrives. Hugh Johnson at Newark Airport, June 1935. The *News*

ing; the mayor's response was to dispatch seventy new projects to the administrator's office. Moses, not unexpectedly, was ready to take on the newcomer. He insisted on complete control of WPA workers assigned to parks. A thousand men sent to him by WPA he characterized as "bums" and refused to accept them. "I won't use them, I won't use them," he stormed, demanding experienced foremen in their place. Johnson yielded and sent the foremen. Moses's only comment was that he'd "shoot them right back" if he was not satisfied with their performance.

Johnson had specified a limited term; actually he only served from July through September, his public flair dimmed by spells of ill health and the constraints and squabbles of the New York scene. He left with some discouraging advice for New Yorkers: "You've got to find something better [than existing relief procedures] for two reasons—you can't afford this, and it isn't any good if you could." The next czar was to be Victor F. Ridder, publisher of the *New York Journal of Commerce.* Making it a top priority to eliminate Communists, he was soon denouncing WPA workers as "rats and vermin" and distributing clubs to guards outside the WPA headquarters. His instructions were "to use 'em on anybody who gets tough." Partly as a consequence of this attitude, relief protests were staged regularly at his offices.

One of the protests was led by none other than LaGuardia's protégé Vito Marcantonio, now representing the mayor's old congressional district. He was seized and taken into custody by the police commissioner. LaGuardia did not make himself available for comment, but that night at a public dinner he denounced "protesters and demonstrators"—they were not "charity-minded" he asserted; nor were they "hungry and cold." Marcantonio was soon released, unsubdued by his mentor's chastisement. He recalled plaintively that in 1926 Congressman LaGuardia had called him up in the middle of the night, asking that he join him in a picket line. On that occasion both men had been held, at least until LaGuardia was formally recognized. But the LaGuardia of 1935 had his own way of dealing with his "children." As for Ridder, he was firmly convinced that all who had taken part in the demonstration were Communists.

Ridder quarrelled with the borough president of Queens, a local sacred cow, making it necessary for the mayor to step in as intermediary. He had his quarrel, too, with Moses. This one, known as the "Battle of the Posters," focused on park signs advising that a particular project was financed by WPA. Moses found the signs "flamboyant in color"—as well as New Dealish in inspiration—and ordered them removed. Ridder threatened to withdraw some 70,000 WPA workers, the relief czars' perennial weapon. Again the mayor had to intervene. Allowing himself to be photographed beside the offending graphics, he made it clear that relief would not be jeopardized because of the commissioner's aesthetic (or political) predelictions. A compromise was worked out, allowing a "reasonable" number of posters—presumably of a reasonable degree of flamboyance—in the parks commissioner's domain.

In the spring of 1936 an issue came to a boil after simmering for some time: whether relief workers should be forced to meet a test of residency. On the face of it the controversy seemed petty, but it was to cast a long shadow over the future. In play were forces that would determine whether New York conceived itself as a defensive and parochial citadel, or a metropolis glad to receive the stranger —any stranger—within its gates. When people complain today of non-New Yorkers receiving various benefits, they are talking in terms prevalent among the politicians of 1936. When they accept the city's larger responsibility to itself and to the nation, they are harking back to a concept strenuously upheld by LaGuardia.

James Lyons, borough president of the Bronx, had long crusaded against what he called "leeches" in the relief administration. Now he led a majority of the Board of Estimate in passing a bill that imposed three-year residency requirements on staffers and a six-months requirement on relief recipients. It was the former aspect of the bill that aroused immediate opposition. Of the 15,000 relief jobs, nearly 300 were held by nonresidents.

The board had scarcely passed the law before the mayor vetoed it. His message admitted there could be some plausible reasons for supporting a residence test, but the federal law made it mandatory that relief be administered without discrimination in this regard. Going beyond legalities, LaGuardia argued for a view of the city that measured its responsibilities in the broadest terms. "New York City," he wrote, "is the financial, commercial, and industrial center of the country. Without the rest of the country there would be no New York City." And he warned it would be "most dangerous" if other communities should be provoked into retaliation against New Yorkers.

The press entered joyously into the fray. "Them Danged Furriners" was the title of a *World Telegram* editorial. If the principle of the Bronx borough president were applied to other occupations, it suggested, many of New York's best known citizens would have to go into exile. According to the new standard, Mr. Ross, editor of the *New Yorker,* was "just a hick from Aspen, Colorado." The humorist O. O. McIntyre, another from Gallipolis, Ohio. What would happen to George M. Cohan from Rhode Island and the columnist FPA, late of the Windy City? The *Times* denounced "A Mean and Stupid Bill." "New York for New Yorkers," it asserted, was one of the most absurd slogans ever invented; facetiously it raised the spectre of a day when the principle of residency might be applied on a borough basis. "Why should a lot of carpetbaggers from Manhattan be allowed to invade Mr. Lyons's own borough of the Bronx? And supposing a clerk in his office should be so unpatriotic as to marry a lady from Washington Heights or Pelham Manor?"

Notwithstanding the ridicule, the Board of Estimate overrode the mayor's veto, the first time such an opposing coalition had been mustered. LaGuardia was watching the opening baseball game of the season when he was informed that the Board of Aldermen had followed suit with a 54–5 vote upholding the Lyons law. On the spot he ordered suspension of its operation, citing conflict with the state emergency relief administration. At stake was the sum of $6 million which the state had ordered withheld if the bill went through. It was averred that the state was bluffing. "That I do not know," said the mayor. "I do know I will not play poker with home relief."

This is not the end of the residency test; it would appear and reappear in various forms long after LaGuardia had left office. Nor in August, when Ridder withdrew, did the reign of the czars terminate. In his place was named General Brereton H. Somervell. A bluff man, he immediately ran into conflict with an important and highly articulate segment of the relief clientele, as will appear at the close of this chapter. Yet he was the best of the lot. He learned to work in reasonable harmony with the mayor, and under him the greatest of New York's public works, the airport at North Beach, was accomplished.

The problems of the unemployed continued. It was increasingly apparent that unemployment was not temporary and that, despite the slightly comical adventures of the relief czars, methods of dealing with it had to become a regular part of New York City's government. Complaints would continue right up to World War II. Armies of nomads, it was asserted, were flocking to New York to take advantage of its overgenerous system. Thousands of aliens were said to be on the rolls, with families trading children back and forth to secure maximum allowances under home relief. The relief worker became the butt of endless jokes. "Mutiny on the Bounty" was the tag applied to their recurrent agitations. A foreman was reported to have sent in requisitions for additional shovels. "No more shovels available," came the reply from headquarters: "Let the men lean on each other." To such an extent did this kind of humor become a staple of the comedian that the American Federation of Artists forbade further WPA jokes before any paying audience.

Politicians, too, continued to make capital out of their investigations. The long-suffering Hodson, his powers restored after having been clipped by the local czar, pleaded on the eve of World War II for a respite from constant inquiries. For six years he had been under scrutiny by public bodies almost invariably hostile. "Too much investigation," said the commissioner with admirable restraint, "can be as harmful as too little."

What was extraordinary, in the final accounting, was not the residue of ill humor or heartlessness, but the degree to which an overwhelming human problem was effectively grappled with. Home relief, despite all its shortcomings, met the minimum needs of a new underclass of unemployables. WPA used the workmen's often highly developed skills to achieve public structures of lasting civic worth. If relief in New York maintained a basic level of efficiency and dignity, it was in no small part due to LaGuardia's determination and to his social vision.

The New Charter

In April 1936 the charter revision committee, headed by the former U.S. solicitor-general, Thomas D. Thacher, completed a year's work, making public the plan for a new frame of government. Debate on the charter in the press and in public hearings, and in the political arena when it was submitted to the voters in the autumn elections, provided a lively contrast between Fusion ideology and the city's traditional political approach. For his own good reasons LaGuardia stood on the sidelines during much of this crucial debate. He was a politician who went for the gut issues—who dealt with real, not imaginary, powers. He sensed that charter reform would not be the path to basic political and social changes.

Yet reform of the city charter was part and parcel of the Fusion cause. It had been, indeed, since the Fusion movement under Seth Low in 1901. The charter as it stood at the time of LaGuardia's election was essentially no different from the charter shaped in 1897 when New York first became a consolidated city. Despite amendments in 1901 it remained a turgid document of 2,400 pages, representing the power struggles and the political compromises of a past generation. To trim the document, to bring the practices it prescribed more nearly into conformity with contemporary usages, was an understandable goal of the reformers.

But the Fusionists of 1934 were prepared to go much further. They wanted to reshape the basic structure of government and to reorganize its powers so as to create an efficient and largely nonpolitical system. Many of the reformers were impressed by the Cincinnati experiment with a city manager responsible to a single chamber elected by proportional representation. Wiser heads among them perceived that in New York you could not abolish the residues of borough autonomy—"Any charter which does not recognize the borough principle," wrote Burlingham, "is doomed"—

but they nevertheless hoped to find ways to restrain partisanship and to eliminate the political machines.

LaGuardia, at this time a child of Fusion, was in favor of charter reform, but only up to a point. The cause did not engage his passions, so easily aroused in the fight against racketeers, nor stir his basic sympathies as did problems of relief. He saw rightly that most of the schemes would have the effect of reducing the mayor's powers and prestige. Where he felt strongly the need for political change, as in the elimination of the county offices, he hoped to accomplish the results piecemeal, through the original economy bill and other ongoing measures.

It was perhaps characteristic of LaGuardia's basic attitude that he should have been found sleeping—one of the rare times he seems ever to have slept during a controversy—when the original charter reform bill reached its crucial stage in the 1934 session of the legislature. The bill had been introduced with a show of virtue by the Tammany Democrats who were ready to accept Alfred E. Smith as chairman of the proposed commission. Their enthusiams noticeably cooled when LaGuardia succeeded in getting Seabury named a member. They balanced him with Frank J. Prial, who had led the fight of the civil servants against the economy bill—and then they succeeded in voting down the measure. Governor Lehman was in doubt about LaGuardia's attitude toward the bill, now that the arch-foe Prial was a member of the commission. He called New York in the middle of the night, woke the mayor, and getting his assent, forced the bill to a reconsideration.

Immediately upon its passage, good-government groups began pushing their favorite scheme of a one-house legislative body, with the city's mayor as its chairman. LaGuardia waited in a silence unusual for him; and a few days later Seabury redressed the balance. Nothing, he announced, must limit mayoral powers. There must be no city manager, but the continuance of an elected officer solely responsible for the administration of the city through department heads over which he had unlimited control. (Seabury reiterated his own favorite prescription for a mayor elected without a party label.) Meanwhile the commission was running into internal difficulties. The majority, which the good judge described as "being under the domination of machine politicians," voted to maintain the Board of Estimate and the basic structure of the Board of Aldermen. This was a vote, in effect, to maintain the power of the borough presidents and the separate county bosses. Al Smith and Seabury, along with four other members, resigned.

LaGuardia said nothing through this struggle, and assented without enthusiasm to the governor's proposal to create a new commission composed of nine members named by the mayor. The legislators, not at all unwilling to put the mayor on the spot, voted for it unanimously. LaGuardia remarked noncommitally, "We must first decide from what viewpoint charter reform is to be approached, and then get persons who are in accord with that viewpoint." The earlier commission suffered, he added, from having tried to please everyone. Yet he was himself too busy with relief to think about who the new members might be. There the matter rested. The mayor said nothing more although the newspapermen grilled him daily on the identity of the new chairman and the new commission members.

Five months later, in January 1935, LaGuardia made his announcement. The wait had undoubtedly been wise. Neither lack of interest nor concern with other matters played so large a part in his delay as an instinct to let opinions cool down and to get a genuinely fresh start. With Thacher as the new chairman of the commission, none of the earlier members was retained; in their place was a group of acceptable but noncontroversial civic and political leaders. LaGuardia promised the commission a free hand and the money needed for its work. (It was noted, somewhat ruefully, that the first, abortive effort had cost the city the sum of $13,552.)

In April 1936 when the commission presented the fruits of its labors, it was found to have gone back to the same fundamental compromise that had caused Al Smith and his original fellow members to resign. The document was reduced to 200 pages and provision was made for more orderly government through the addition of a deputy mayor. Yet the mandate for a truly new charter had not been met. Apparently unaltered there remained as the keystone of city government the old Board of Estimate with the borough presidents safely entrenched. The Board of Aldermen, with a diminished membership and the new name of City Council, stood unshaken. Proportional representation, which could considerably modify the composition of this body, was recommended but would be put separately before the voters. The immediate reaction was lukewarm. Seabury expressed qualified approval. LaGuardia, in a letter consenting to be the first witness at public hearings, signed himself "sincerely but unhappily."

Nevertheless the proposed charter embodied a principle more

profound than simple preservation of existing structures. It introduced what its authors believed to be a means of tempering and rationalizing the more parochial of borough interests. Though they could not be accused, as Seabury had accused the members of the first commission, of being slaves of the machine politicians, they were convinced that the boroughs represented something important in New York life. What was necessary was not to abolish their influence, but to complete the transformation which had been begun in 1897—to create one city and at the same time to preserve the roots of diversity and of local autonomy. In words reminiscent of the *Federalist* the commission argued that selfish interests on the Board of Estimate should be controlled by publicly confronting them "with the interests of the public at large."

The means of securing this confrontation was the proposed City Planning Commission, the essential and the most strikingly new institution created by the reformed charter. With a faith that turned out to be naive, its authors believed the Planning Commission would be so influential and would command so wide a public hearing as to make the borough presidents moderate their more extreme demands. They thought of this Planning Commission as a powerful body. The eight-year terms of its members would, it was hoped, largely remove them from politics. Its control of zoning, its responsibility for the capital budget, its being in charge of the city map with authority to submit public and private changes to review and recommendation, seemed to give assurance of a steady, long-range judgment acting as a counterforce to political pressures.

Believing that the Board of Estimate would thus be curbed by the Planning Commission, and that proportional representation would make the new council responsive to the full range of civic interests, the authors of the new charter felt they had met both theoretical and practical tests. The borough presidents could fume appropriately—Lyons of the Bronx denounced the proposed Planning Commission as "one of the most dangerous weapons proposed for the destruction of home rule and local self-government." Tammany could subside into sullen opposition. But the general tendency was to accept what seemed a reasonable compromise.

A later evaluation by Wallace Sayre saw in the preservation of borough politics, with their visible parties and party leaders, a balance avoiding both extreme centralization and the kind of political atomization of a city like Chicago. Instead, under New York's borough system, there could be "struggle, bargaining, and accommodation" among power centers—a system of open politics marked by the absence of a single ruling elite, "inherently conservative but not incapable of innovation."

As for LaGuardia, he was at the same time practical and philosophically resigned. He gave limited support to the new charter and would campaign for it with moderate enthusiasm in the fall election. Much as he denounced the party leaders and resented the vetoes inevitable in the borough-dominated Board of Estimate, he recognized that under a strong mayor the system worked tolerably well. He was himself a sort of one-man machine, a Manhattan-based boss and an unorganized organization. The opposition from the machines of other boroughs did not deter him from his course. If he resented the useless jobs the local leaders needed in order to survive, he saw their power as a basic part of political life. When the time came for him to muster his forces for the 1937 mayoralty campaign, he showed himself entirely capable of bringing the separate power centers to his side and of capturing the local leaders one by one.

Exile in the Bronx

It was summer again. LaGuardia did not believe in vacations for himself or for others (some of his worst errors of judgment occurred in times of physical and mental exhaustion which would have been alleviated by a normal vacation schedule); but he did believe in making of the summer months a sort of ritual, with a changed pace and a change of scene. In June 1936 his family rented a home in Westport, Connecticut, and he moved his office from downtown Manhattan to the Bartow-Pell mansion in the outer reaches of the Bronx. Here he planned a somewhat more relaxed schedule—a ten to five working day, with two or three evenings a week in the country with Marie and the children, and an occasional morning swim before starting to town.

The Bartow-Pell mansion was a handsome stone building of the mid-nineteenth century, one of the old estates which had come into possession of the city and into the keeping of the Parks Department. At that date, before Moses had completed the sweeping land changes which created Orchard Beach, it looked out across the remains of formal gardens to the waters of Long Island Sound. However cooling the breezes, the move did not please everyone.

The mayor's staff complained about mosquitos and the lack of restaurants in the vicinity of Pelham Bay. The press found the site inaccessible, while a few of the more imaginative reporters, dispossessed from their traditional quarters in Room 9, considered the use of carrier pigeons. Relief workers, hearing the mayor had ensconced himself in a mansion somewhere in the Bronx, picketed in front of City Hall to remind him of his duties.

LaGuardia enjoyed the hubbub and set about remedying the worst of the inconveniences. A teletype machine was installed to connect him with City Hall. A police department patrol wagon carrying the legend CITY HALL BUS—OFFICIAL BUSINESS was commandeered to transport visitors between the summer headquarters and the nearest subway station.

Thus more or less settled, the mayor was ready for whatever the summer months might bring. He had hoped in that sylvan retreat to give concentrated attention to the upcoming budget, but in fact there were enough official ceremonies, enough visitors, and enough political activities to keep him otherwise occupied. The summer was hot, one of the hottest on record, and by a happy coincidence the opening of major swimming pools, the result of Moses's planning and of WPA labor, provided one of the frequent diversions.

On June 20 the first of the city's ten "million-dollar pools" was dedicated in Hamilton Fish Park in Manhattan. A week later in Harlem the mayor celebrated fulfillment of a promise, first made in 1929, to make a spectacular improvement in Thomas Jefferson Park. "Here it is," he cried, with a gesture embracing the new pool of Olympic dimensions. "Is not this a transformation?" It was indeed, as the cheers testified. Astoria pool in Queens opened just in time for July Fourth, this time with Harry Hopkins in attendance; and on July 31 dedication of McCarran Pool in Brooklyn provided the stage for Ridder's farewell appearance as WPA administrator. Rising above past disagreements, the mayor hailed the departing czar as "a great builder" and, with an evident touch of irony, "a great diplomat as well." Each of these events was marked by the kind of ceremony Moses staged so well: the flag-draped speakers' stand, the white-gloved park attendants in military array, and always plenty of eager children to test the waters of the new facility.

An event attracting national attention took place on July 11 as Roosevelt journeyed down from Hyde Park for the much-anticipated dedication of the Triborough Bridge. Not since the

13. Grand opening of the Triborough Bridge. Lehman, LaGuardia, and a relaxed Moses hear the president speak. *The News*

city's welcome to Lindbergh in 1927 had police arrangements been so elaborate. It had been a sweltering week; only the day before the temperature had risen to 102.3°, the highest to that point in the weather bureau's history, and LaGuardia had ordered the parks kept open all night for those who sought escape from airless rooms. By the afternoon of the eleventh, when barriers were to fall at approaches to the bridge in three boroughs, there was no break in the weather. But the huge crowd was not deterred; having looked forward to the day, they now stood patiently in the unrelieved glare of the midafternoon sun.

The drama of the occasion was not lost on those crowds. Everyone knew that the dedication ceremonies were bringing together the titans whose battle of the year before had been so widely reported. Roosevelt and Moses would come face to face—that alone was worth waiting for.

Behind the scenes, unknown to the public, week-long negotiations had been under way to minimize just such a confrontation as the crowd now waited to see. Almost to the last moment Roosevelt was refusing to attend at all. It took Harold Ickes's persuasive powers to convince him it would be unwise to slight New York, particularly in this year when he was a candidate as well as a presi-

dent. To LaGuardia fell the task of holding his parks commissioner
in check, a far from easy assignment as Moses was looking forward
with some relish to his part in the day's occurrences. Several noisy
sessions took place before an acceptable program was worked out.
Moses, it was agreed, would introduce LaGuardia, Ickes, and the
other dignitaries; LaGuardia would introduce the president.

The official group, when it assembled on the impressive new
bridge, was on its best behavior. If the crowd hoped for verbal
fireworks they were disappointed. It might have been a garden
party for all the smiles and gracious words that were exchanged.
The speeches appeared to be the usual rhetoric reserved for such
occasions. The president defended his policies of federal aid to local
public works; the mayor reflected on the change which had come
over the site, where feeble-minded children had once been cared
for.

Only the irrepressible Moses, the perfect host in his white linen
suit, insinuated a reference to past unhappy events. In a carefully
composed introduction of Ickes he referred to the famous eighteenth-century letter in which Samuel Johnson heaped vituperative
scorn on his patron, Lord Chesterfield, for having neglected him in
the time of need while he poured out praise on the work's being
completed. In his most impeccable style, Moses thumbed his nose
at Ickes and the president, so subtly as almost to conceal his sense
of triumph.

It was, as has been suggested, a summer of some political activity.
In Philadelphia Roosevelt won easy renomination for a second
term, signifying the occasion with the delivery of what was certainly
the most eloquent acceptance in the country's political history. In
Topeka the Republicans nominated Alfred M. Landon, governor of
Kansas.

For the moment LaGuardia was content to watch these events
from afar. A political dilemma, the beginning of which goes back
to the previous year, was confronting him in his own city. In November 1935 the Fusion president of the Board of Estimate, Bernard S. Deutsch, died suddenly at fifty-one years of age. For La-
Guardia it was a crushing blow. Coming after Fusion's loss of the
comptrollership (the result, also, of an untimely death) it deprived
the mayor of a respected friend—though one whose actions on the
Board of Estimate had frequently irked him—and at the same time
put Tammany once more in full control of the board. Arriving at
the Deutsch home on the fateful night, the mayor was too over-

come with emotion to issue a public statement. "I am lonely," he said a little later, "but I refuse to be discouraged." Now in this midsummer of 1936 a choice was to be made of the candidate to succeed Deutsch.

LaGuardia had a preferred candidate, Adolf Berle, whom he wistfully hoped to retain in his official family. He felt, too, that Berle's political support would come from a broad base of independents and good-government groups as well as Republicans, and that only such a coalition could defeat Tammany. In this political year, with a governor and a president to elect, the Republicans were hardly likely, however, to give their votes to a New Dealer, especially one known to be so close to Roosevelt. Besides, they were pursuing their own strategy.

They had let it be known they would select a ticket without help from the mayor. "Why should we consult with LaGuardia?" one of the county leaders put it. "He has never consulted with us." Nevertheless, Simpson was in touch with the mayor. When they were seen in conversation at a concert in Lewisohn Stadium, LaGuardia claimed they had only discussed "tonality, harmonics, and such things." Whatever was said on the subject of politics, the Republicans went ahead and announced their choice for the post—Newbold Morris, one of their own party, pledged to the state and national ticket, but well enough thought of by New York's civic establishment to pass muster with the Fusion leaders.

Morris was to play an important part in the LaGuardia story. He became one of the mayor's most dutiful supporters and would receive the chief's backing in a hapless race for the mayoralty when LaGuardia's time at City Hall was nearly over. For the present, even though Berle withdrew from the race, LaGuardia could not respond favorably to Morris's being named. "This is not his year. His time will come" was the mayor's prophetic comment.

That summer, ground was broken for the New York World's Fair. The scene was forlorn as hundreds of hungry men waited in line hoping for work. It was difficult to conceive how the immense garbage dump could be transformed into the glittering pavilions of 1939. Yet Moses saw even beyond the Fair, to the day when its site would become a verdant park in the keeping of his department. That was the long-range planner at his best. For the present there was an incident which involved the mayor and his commissioner in one of their most ludicrous and bitter controversies.

At 90th Street and the East River a ferry ran between Manhattan and Queens, made obsolete by the completion of the Triborough Bridge. The terminal serving passengers on the Queens side of the river had been turned over to Moses's Triborough Bridge Authority, a move undertaken with the mayor's blessing, but with the stipulation that ferry service not be discontinued until the summer months were over. An impatient Moses could not wait the sixty days and ordered his men to start immediately on the destruction of the old building at York Avenue on the Manhattan side.

On the afternoon of July 22 Assistant Corporation Counsel Frederick van Pelt Bryan received a telephone call in his office in the Municipal Building from John MacKenzie, the normally affable commissioner of docks. Now MacKenzie was shouting into the phone. "I have a ferryload of people in the middle of the river, and Bob Moses is tearing down the dock. What can I do?" "Send your people back to Queens," Bryan told him. "It's Bob Moses's terminal now." But the mayor thought differently. Furious that Moses had gone ahead in defiance of his orders, LaGuardia ordered the police to stop the destruction from going any further. When they arrived at the pier, it was a shambles of splintered wood and Moses had apparently won. LaGuardia, however, was too angry to give up, and demanded that the pier be rebuilt—and rebuilt in a hurry —so that the ferry could be in service by the next morning.

Like a film running backward, a contingent of workers labored through the night to restore the dock that had just been torn down. It was to have a short life. The transfer to the Triborough Bridge Authority was quietly effected, and, as Bryan had said, it was Moses's dock. Within a few weeks he tore it down again, this time for good. The affair, however, continued to rankle. The mayor had used the police against one of his own commissioners, and the newspapers had had a field day at Moses's expense. When the two men met at the opening of the first stage of Orchard Beach at the end of July, the tension between them was noticeable.

Concern with racketeering and other criminal activities continued through the warm summer months. One of the visitors to the Bartow-Pell mansion was Dewey; another was the former ambassador to Cuba, Harry F. Guggenheim, whom the mayor prevailed upon to head a citizens committee to assist law enforcement agencies in wiping out racketeering. It seemed an undefined, thankless job; but the grand jury investigating crime had recommended a corps of "civic vigilantes" and the mayor was ready to try any means of focusing attention on the city's fight against lawlessness.

The ambassador set out to raise $200,000 from private sources. The police commissioner at the same time busied himself with sweeping raids, abetted by extensive use of wiretapping, upon houses of prostitution.

Earlier there had been a raid on one of the most notorious of these houses. Polly Adler's principality was entered, her "little black book" was seized, and the names of many of her customers divulged. This struck the *News* as shocking. Polly Adler's was a "respectable" house, outwardly decent and causing no trouble to the neighbors. Yet the police had kept the lady under surveillance and had set spies upon her "as if they suspected her of being the Lindbergh kidnapper." Such excessive diligence, complained the *News,* was an affront "to the customs, ideals, and prejudices of the voters." It was the "puritanical" side of LaGuardia showing itself once more. This strain always annoyed some people, particularly the editors of the *News;* yet without such crusades against gambling and vice the image of "the Little Flower" would not have been the same.

In the parks crime and vandalism were problems accentuated by wide popular usage and extensive press coverage. Central Park was felt to have been overrun by thugs and was, according to the police commissioner, unsafe for strong men after dark, and even in broad daylight was perilous for women. The situation in Morningside, Mount Morris, and Riverside parks was no better. The Parks Department estimated vandalism as costing half a million dollars in Central Park alone, as thousands of benches were damaged and even the copper heads of the sprinkler system carried off.

This was a puzzling form of crime, not attributable to the depressed economic conditions. Moses was powerless. Valentine in his roundups and mass arrests was no more able than were later police commissioners to deal with the problem. The mayor was sympathetic to Moses's requests for added money in the budget to repair the depredations, but little tangible was done.

LaGuardia was always good copy, and amid the relaxations of summer his spontaneity and wit were a boon to reporters. Receiving a large group of students he lectured them under the burning heat for ninety minutes on civic problems and then presented them with $10, telling them to go off and buy themselves ice cream cones. Refusing to officiate at a rickshaw race in Central Park he declared indignantly that "God almighty gave men horses for transportation and also brains to devise locomotives, motors, and airplanes." At the dedication of a Sanitation Department facility he aired his own disappointments and then: "It is much easier to tell the other fellow how to do it than to do it yourself. I know—I used to be a congressman once."

One day he went over to Brooklyn to address a gathering of local leaders avid to hear him declare his support for a new public library. But he told them frankly, and at considerable length, why they would not get one. "I cannot let myself be constrained by your cordiality to me," he declared, "to give the library the right of way over schools, hospitals, and health centers. . . . I could easily pat you on the back and say 'I am with you,' but I am not that kind of a politician. I would rather have your respect later than your cheers now."

There was no question of cheers as the stony-faced audience filed out at the end of the speech. But LaGuardia had probably not misjudged the political realities. His audience represented at most a limited constituency. Besides, he never liked acting precisely as expected or being told by the "do-gooders" how he should set his priorities. The mayor could be obstinate as well as acute.

Summer in the mansion came to an end on Labor Day. The staff, and even the reporters, saw the Bronx headquarters close with regret. It had been a pleasant change for them. For the mayor it had been a lifesaver. When he faced his tasks once more in Manhattan's City Hall, he carried them forward, at least for a time, with what the *Times* called "a sunny summer disposition."

Labor, Progressives, and FDR

Labor Day signaled the start of political campaigning. At the local level, LaGuardia stood on the sidelines. He made a few speeches supporting the new charter, a rather perfunctory effort on behalf of the cause which had long been a mainstay of Fusion ideology. He continued in his stubborn refusal to back Newbold Morris, the Republican–Fusion nominee for aldermanic president. His eye was not on the New York, but on the national political stage; and here, in this autumn of 1936, he was prepared to play a significant part.

Tides were running in the nation, LaGuardia believed, which were bound to result in major realignments within the existing parties and could, perhaps as early as 1940, bring progressives together in a dominant coalition. Such a coalition might well pro-

vide a political base for a man prepared to break loose from his
Republican ties, whose passionate and unrelenting opposition to
the Tammany machine had barred his crossing over to the Democrats. Whether LaGuardia was right in his estimate of political
forces can never be proven; but if the Roosevelt administration had
been confined to the traditional two terms, the year 1940 would
almost certainly have seen him out in the front ranks and in the
midst of new political possibilities.

A first step toward the realignment of parties had taken place in
the summer. Working quietly behind the scenes with his old antagonist Jim Farley, LaGuardia had helped establish the American
Labor party in New York State. Led by such stalwarts of the movement as David Dubinsky and Jacob Potofsky, the new party was
devised first of all to give Roosevelt a second line on the ballot. But
it promptly backed LaGuardia's candidate, Berle, against Newbold
Morris in the aldermanic contest. Looking ahead to 1937 and beyond, the mayor saw many additional services it could render.
Might not the ALP provide him a base if the Republicans denied
their support for a second mayoralty race? Might it not be the
starting point for a wide coalition of the left if he should make a
try for the presidency in 1940? Regardless of these prospects, the
party added an element of fresh life to the politics of the state.

LaGuardia was now ready for a further step. Joining with Norris
and the La Follettes he issued a call for a conference of progressives
to be held in Chicago in mid-September. The avowed purpose of
the conference was to rally support for the president's reelection.
More than a hundred men and women gathered, representative of
a broad spectrum of opinion—eastern liberals, southern Democrats, western progressives, with a sprinkling of independent
Republicans and farmer-laborites. The first order of business was to
draw up a statement of principles; LaGuardia was chosen to head
the drafting committee. It was an absolutely crucial moment in his
political life. In accepting the assignment he was declaring himself
publicly and irrevocably for Roosevelt and the New Deal, and he
was also casting his lines upon the future's inscrutable waters.

That he knew what was at stake he made abundantly clear.
"Some of us are burning all our bridges ahead of us," he said,
"and we do so with our eyes wide open." That same curious
choice of words he would repeat in the years ahead: "I burned
all my bridges ahead of me for Franklin Roosevelt," he wrote
to Burlingham much later and in another connection, when his

spirits had been badly bruised and his fortunes were waning.

With this awareness of the drama and even the danger of his role, LaGuardia set before the convention his definition of a progressive: "One who will look facts squarely in the face, who will admit conditions as they are, who refuses to follow any fetish and seeks to bring his government abreast of the times. . . . You can't have progress in science, electricity, and business management and let the government stand still." Through the deliberations LaGuardia maintained his position of leadership. A shrewd observer, the senior A. A. Berle, wrote to the president that in his judgment no man at the conference had been as useful to his cause as the New York mayor.

From Chicago LaGuardia went on to a meeting of the American Legion in Cleveland, where he was received with a rip-roaring enthusiasm reserved for those in public life who have a widening future before them. Among these representatives of the conservative American tradition he was as much at home as he had been among the progressives. He paraded; he orated before the 70,000 delegates who greeted him with a twenty-minute ovation. When he invited the legion to hold its next annual meeting in New York, he received a paper-throwing, stamping demonstration of approval.

The personal triumph of this first western foray was not lost on New Yorkers. A few of his old intimates, Windels and Seabury in particular, felt uneasy at his taking so unequivocal a stand for Roosevelt. Republican leaders were furious. But most of the New York constituency, seeing their mayor for the first time as a national figure, were intrigued by the way midwestern America had taken him to its heart.

With his credentials thus established, he could meet the president on new terms, not so much a petitioner as a politician who might have some favors of his own to dispense. Journeying to Hyde Park late in September he met with Roosevelt in a two-hour discussion covering a wide range of topics. Questioned by reporters, the mayor talked blandly about housing and his fears of a shortage of low- and medium-rent dwellings in two years.

But housing was not what interested the press. What about the election? they asked LaGuardia. "There isn't any guess about it," he told them. "It's a foregone conclusion that Mr. Roosevelt will carry the city." And by enough to carry the state, he went on. The reporters continued to press him on the role he would play. "I'll vote," said LaGuardia, but then he noted that the president had not asked him to speak on his behalf. If he should, however, "the temptation would be irresistible."

That same day there had appeared a report in the *New York Times* that LaGuardia might be named to the permanent post of secretary of war. Was it true? The position had not been offered to him, he said, and if it were he would decline. "I've got a contract with the people of New York City that runs to December 31, 1937, with an option of renewal." The reporters scurried to report this early indication that the mayor would be a candidate for reelection next year.

A series of parades and immense popular demonstrations brought the 1936 campaign to a climax at the end of October. Like armies crossing and recrossing the city, the forces marshalled behind Roosevelt and Landon exhibited their enthusiasm for the respective candidates and sought to display their strength. Two hundred thousand lined the streets when the Republican candidate came to town; three hundred thousand—or was it half a million? (the estimates depended on political affiliations)—massed to welcome the leader of the Democrats. Such crowds were indicative of the high fervor national politics had aroused in that year. Roosevelt made several sallies into the boroughs, invariably greeted by wildly enthusiastic supporters. Introduced by LaGuardia at Brooklyn College, the president acknowledged the hard-working mayor of New York in words that gave them both credit. "Every time LaGuardia comes to Washington I tremble," Roosevelt said, "because it means he wants something, and he almost always gets it."

On October 29 at the conclusion of his eastern campaign Landon filled Madison Square Garden with 20,000 cheering partisans; Roosevelt the next evening addressed the traditional Democratic rally at the Brooklyn Academy. On November 1, after driving in an open car from his house on 65th Street, at the head of an automobile procession preceded by fifty motorcycle police, he ended his campaign before an American Labor party rally with a thundering denunciation of conservatives and stand-patters. "We have just begun to fight" was his refrain as one after another of the foes of labor were ticked off. LaGuardia was on the platform that night, along with Lehman and John L. Lewis. When it was the mayor's turn to speak he announced that rather than vote on the Republican-Fusion line, he would be enrolled henceforth under the sign of the clasped hand and gear wheel. It was his first public declaration of affiliation with the American Labor party.

LaGuardia still had chores of his own to attend to, and on the night before election he joined the good-government groups in a radio forum urging passage of the new charter. Significantly, a main attribute of the charter was in his eyes a negative one: the only element not in favor of it, he said, was Tammany—"that group of machine politicians which has for its creed the fostering of its own personal interests. I am grateful for many things but I am most grateful that, as usual, this group is against it." On Election Day he had the polls to watch. It was a task to which he attached great importance, having in the past seen the democratic process repeatedly thwarted by hired hoodlums and thugs.

By the late evening it was evident that Roosevelt had been elected by a landslide for a second term. He was to win all but two states, adding a new slogan to the American political vocabulary— "As Maine goes, so goes Vermont." At home Tammany had been weakened by passage of the charter and a victory for proportional representation. But its candidate, William Brunner, defeated Newbold Morris for the presidency of the Board of Aldermen. Morris, gentlemanly as always, attributed his defeat to the statewide Democratic sweep. Others blamed LaGuardia for his lack of support.

The ALP did well on its first time out, polling 300,000 votes, enough to qualify for a permanent place on the ballot. Speculation began almost at once as to what role it would play in the 1937 election and in the 1940 presidential race as well.

A feeling of euphoria was in the air that election night. Crowds gathered in unprecedented numbers in Times Square. They were judged by one New York police inspector to be the largest and noisiest group ever to celebrate, and his own memory went back to the false armistice of 1918. "This beats them all," said he. The mood carried on to a particularly joyous Thanksgiving. In December, when the Metropolitan Opera opened its season, the old house shone with pre-Depression brilliance. A first-night audience, out to hear the Norwegian soprano Kirsten Flagstad sing *Die Walküre,* was dressed in their most lavish furs, their showiest jewelry.

Yet there was to be a strange aftermath to the overwhelming New Deal victory. The party whose campaign promises were for a better life for all, whose triumph at the polls seemed to assure an easier portion for the poor and dispossessed, suddenly found itself with an empty till. Roosevelt was off on the cruiser *Indianapolis* on a peace mission to Latin American when on December 18 Harry

Hopkins announced at a meeting of mayors that WPA funds had run out and that retrenchment would be necessary all along the line. Among the first relief staffers to be affected were those of the WPA arts projects in New York City. Dismissal notices were received by several hundred artists, writers, and actors.

A visible and highly articulate group, they did not delay in putting their talents to use. Taking their cue from a novel practice recently invented by French workers, they staged a series of sit-down strikes, refusing to leave their offices until the dismissal notices were recalled. More than two hundred artists, a strange company in slouch hats and van Dyck beards, were carried off by police on the personal orders of General Somervell, the relief administrator then receiving his baptism of fire. In the melee a "septuagenarian Amazon" was knocked unconscious and several others were clubbed. All were later paroled in night court as charges of police brutality filled the air. LaGuardia responded quickly, ordering the police not to arrest sit-down strikers unless guilty of violence or destruction of property. Somervell was enraged and denounced what he called "the mayor's new conception of law and order that allows hoodlumism inside offices."

The next day in Washington, speaking for the U.S. Conference of Mayors, LaGuardia warned of further disorders if relief funds were cut. Roosevelt was still in South America; Hopkins was unavailable. A cable to the *Indianapolis* reminded the president of his campaign promises and urged him to countermand the cutbacks. Meanwhile, protected by the mayor's order, workers in the federal writers' project and the federal theater project continued their sit-ins. And the implacable Somervell went ahead with layoffs. In a situation growing increasingly critical, LaGuardia called in the city's business leaders, urging them to give jobs to the dismissed workers.

Then he returned to Washington for a showdown. This time Hopkins received him, though not, as he had hoped, in an open session. The presidential aide insisted on meeting him alone in his private office, and a testy LaGuardia was forced to accept the terms. The conference, which had begun badly, ended on a hopeful note. Hopkins repeated that relief funds were exhausted but assured him that WPA was not being disbanded and that all the needy would be cared for. Congress would be asked for an appropriation to sustain the relief program through June 30. Although the outcome was not altogether satisfactory, LaGuardia returned to New York in a less somber and a less combative frame of mind.

The demonstrations continued. As the holidays approached a young lady dressed as Santa Claus, waving a sheaf of the hated dismissal notices, headed a march of three thousand WPA workers to Somervell's office. The disgruntled general turned out to be not quite the Scrooge he had seemed. A few days later, a week before Christmas, he relented and announced he would rehire most of the dismissed sit-ins.

Protests slowly petered out as the year's end brought a flurry of political diversions. The Board of Aldermen adopted the mayor's budget intact—a healthy $554,998—with Alderman Newbold Morris magnanimously suggesting that bygones be bygones and praising the mayor's fiscal policies. A $12,000 appropriation was voted for a restoration of the historic City Hall, and the board approved a traffic code that would deny New York drivers for all time the right to make a right-hand turn on a red light. The mayor went along with that revolution in driving habits, but he refused to sign the bill until arrests for jaywalking were stricken from the final version. "I prefer the happiness of our unorganized imperfection to the organized perfection of other countries. Broadway is not Unter den Linden." It was a distinction that New Yorkers loved him for.

Of these events the most politically significant was a dinner at the Waldorf Astoria on December 14. At a testimonial to the Charter Revision Committee, the guests heard Thomas Thacher, the committee's chairman, join with LaGuardia in denunciation of Tammany and in hopeful anticipation of the better day which the new charter, when finally put into effect, would bring to the city. Officially and unofficially the Fusion campaign for 1937 was under way. And LaGuardia was still its standard-bearer. The events of the past year had strained old ties; yet he stood at the peak of his popularity, his prospects large and the hopes of his supporters undiminished.

5

Vindication

Government with a Soul

Whatever the immediate disappointments for New York, the New Deal victory confirmed LaGuardia in his political beliefs. He had long had a vision of a better society. As a congressman he had fought for an America "in which the 'little guys' would eat well, live in decent homes and know the dignity that comes with well-paid jobs, a voice in the government, and the knowledge that tomorrow can be better." In New York he had worked hard to make this vision real for the citizens. Now under the leadership of Franklin Roosevelt it seemed as if a time had come when efforts toward a more humane world would everywhere bear fruit. On Inauguration Day 1937, LaGuardia was kept to his bed by a bad cold, but his thoughts must have traveled to Washington where the unconquerable figure with whom his own fortunes were so frequently linked was setting forth upon a new stage of his journey.

We are now at a noon hour in LaGuardia's career as mayor. He is at the threshold of his campaign for a second term. Behind him lie the early-morning struggles to restore the credit of the city and establish the groundwork for basic reforms. Ahead lie the afternoon of achievement and the shadows that were to gather in his third term. His social values and views stand revealed in the clear light of this period.

"Government with a soul" was LaGuardia's own phrase. To provide it was a promise at least as important to him as the essential services of good housekeeping and honest accounting. It expressed the added dimension of a vital concern for the individual in all his aspects; for men and women as consumers, as citizens of a vast and bewildering city, as human beings who were often in doubt, in trouble, in need. LaGuardia spoke, too, of "scientific government," but this did not mean government run by engineers or scientists; it was meant to suggest a system free of the encumbances of political patronage. His kind of government, LaGuardia was fond of saying, might not be what the public was really looking for, and in theory he was prepared to be resigned if the old system were to be restored by the electorate.

LaGuardia had sounded this theme of government in his first radio address on assuming office. "Our city," he said, "does not belong to any individual or set of individuals. It belongs to all the people. New York City was restored to the people this morning at one minute past midnight." What happened after that was a bombardment of actions, often seeming random and sometimes bizarre, intended to free the citizens from exploitation of all kinds, by criminals, by politicians, by unfeeling bureaucrats. Then came the actions designed to be responsive to a range of needs with which municipal government did not ordinarily concern itself. To live free of fear in one's own city was important; so was it important to live with beauty around one, to live in health, without indignities or unnecessary frustrations, and above all with the feeling that one's government was listening and caring.

"We are trying to make our people happy," the mayor said, which was somewhat different from trying merely to make them safe or contented. Once, when he had come back from Washington where he presented an application for a major housing project, he stood in the wings of an auditorium before addressing a meeting. Unseen, he listened as the strains of the spiritual "I Have Heard of a City Called Heaven" filled the hall. "Yes," he said that night, promising the razing of slums on an undreamed-of scale, "We are going to make our city into a real heaven." And he actually meant it.

On another occasion he told a Harlem audience of his participation in the dedication of the first East Harlem Center in 1921. "We must not overdo these things," Governor Nathan L. Miller had said to him in an aside. "This is paternalistic. We must not coddle people. Adversity is good for them." But LaGuardia had other views: "Adversity is not good. Exploitation is not good. No country that thrives on these has a right to exist. That was my answer then. That is my philosophy today." Glorying in the name of "humanitarian," LaGuardia gave it an active political connotation such as it rarely possesses.

Health was almost the first necessity. Without health, housing and even education were vain. Next came a basic care for the disadvantaged—the stranger, the alcoholic, the persecuted, the member of a racial minority. The aim of the Department of Welfare under Commissioner Hodson was to be "a compassionate friend," opening hospitable doors to all in need. The politicians might rail at welfare extended to the poor coming from other states, but they were still the poor, and no one in his right mind would deny succor to men, women, and children who were starving simply because they had passed across a geographic border. The young were in a way the disadvantaged, too, with their needs so often unmet and misunderstood.

LaGuardia angered many civic leaders because he so persistently refused to view with conventional alarm the misdeeds of the young. He thought he understood boys, the temptations that afflicted them, and also their inherent decency. He knew that the city afforded a difficult environment for them to grow up in. A kid who took plumbing pipe from an empty house would in a country boyhood have stolen birds' eggs or filled his pockets with apples. The kid who stole a car would in the country have borrowed one for a "joyride." It was ridiculous to "indict the whole childhood of the city" when parents were so often at fault, or poor schools or unsympathetic churches. Juvenile delinquency was not a serious problem in the mayor's eyes, though there were some serious cases; and he set up in the children's court a new bureau to deal with those whose troubles could be rectified without penal measures.

The consumer, especially the deprived consumer, evoked his special concern. Fellowes Morgan, commissioner of markets, was the link between the consumer and City Hall along with Paul Blanshard, commissioner of accounts. A short measure in coal, or an artificially high price for milk or chicken, could occasion a demonstration of the mayor's unique capacity for anger. The distributors of milk he looked on with unalterable suspicion. "If the milk people come in," he said to one of his aides, "kick them out—and I mean that literally, not figuratively." Over the protests of those who wanted a professional in the post, he appointed as director of consumer services an attractive woman from Staten Island, Mrs. Frances Foley Gannon. She established close contact with consumer groups, and her daily radio talks were a great success, anticipating the colorful advice to housewives which the mayor himself would dispense in the war years.

One rather curious by-product of the mayor's personal involvement in all the affairs of the city was his mistrust of the civic groups. The earnest and well-intentioned citizens who composed them might have been expected to be his lieutenants in the fight for a more liveable New York. But they too often overstated their case, so that their advice became criticism. Besides, the mayor did not like advice, especially on matters where he considered his instincts to be a sure guide. He complained that they were always nagging and needling. Addressing a meeting of parents, he described how at a recent meeting of the Board of Estimate, when the citizens groups denounced conditions in the city's schools, he had asked himself whether he was mayor of New York "or some town in China." The situation had been grossly overstated. "When it comes to overstatement," he said, "I am an expert, but that was too much for me."

The other side of the coin was the mayor's reliance on communications coming directly from the people. He seemed ready to answer any question, to investigate any complaint, and if the letter was anonymous it often got more attention than if it came from a well-known source. "Now get on to that. Put your men on to that," the mayor would bark at a harassed commissioner who dared not suggest that the charge in question was exaggerated or palpably not true. One lady wrote in to inquire whether one had to get out of bed if the national anthem was played on the radio. She had a very patriotic husband and was in need of advice. The mayor, after searching all the legal authorities, admitted he was baffled on that one. With a touch of asperity the *Journal* suggested that since the mayor was into everything, he might do something about used razor blades, too.

His efforts to improve the city sometimes took unexpected forms as they were invariably pursued with a picturesque intensity. One of his well-known crusades was against noise—not just against a single kind of noise, like horn blowing or loud radios, but noise in

14. The lure of the hurdy-gurdy. One of the city's traditional rites. MUSEUM OF THE CITY OF NEW YORK

all its aspects and in all degrees of noisiness. A graduated series of penalties was devised to cover a range of illegal disturbances from the cacophony of animals or birds to the unnecessary blowing of stationary boiler steam whistles. Much attention was given in the press to the subtleties of this citywide endeavor, and the public joined in with its own suggestions. The people protested against clanging trolleys, rattling elevated trains; they urged the curbing of mewing cats. One indignant citizen objected to his neighbor's singing in the bathtub, and several complained about the unseemly noise of grave diggers. The number of suggestions gradually diminished, but as late as 1938, as we shall see, a frivolous response to an inquiry on noise helped bring about the downfall of a deputy mayor.

An offshoot of this campaign was the banishing of the organ-grinders. No policy of Mayor LaGuardia is better remembered or more widely misunderstood. Even today people ask how a mayor who contributed so much to the color and vivacity of the city could have taken so uncompromising a stand against this innocent form of music. Yet by 1936 the hurdy-gurdies were playing their swan song, the renewal of licenses having been specifically banned. A barrage of letters found LaGuardia patiently stating and restating his reasons. To encourage the organ-grinders, he said, was to condone public begging; also it was to endanger the lives of children who were tempted to gather about the itinerant musicians "and follow them through the streets despite the presence of automobiles and trucks." There was a time, the mayor would conclude, when organ-grinders were the only means of bringing "melodious tunes to the ears of many people"—now there were the phonograph, the radio, and public concerts.

To this type of argument the public responded with a degree of sentiment and imaginativeness rare in public controversy. Hurdy-gurdies aren't *supposed* to be music, wrote Elizabeth C. Onativia. "Hurdy-gurdies are romance, spring, one's childhood, dancing in the streets." An occasional hurdy-gurdy was all Miss Onativia had left to remind her that "life had not always been one-half politics and one-half relief." The organ-grinder must be licensed, wrote Viola Irene Cooper, "not for music but for everything it does to us, like taking us to Kew in lilac time." (Or was it possible, Miss Cooper inquired sternly, that the mayor had never been to Kew?)

"I am in complete disagreement with you," wrote the faithful

Burlingham; and Don Marquis in the *Times* capped with his eloquence all the other laments. The hurdy-gurdy was one of the last of the world's beloved vagabonds; it was a wandering troubadour, more than paying its way. "It is joy calling out in mean and sordid streets, art asserting its spontaneity and existence above the inconsequencies and trivialities of commerce." Marquis could not resist an appeal *ad hominem.* The mayor's very name made the policy incredible, he said. That name had always suggested to him "something like a flower garden"; the syllables flowed "with an appealing Latin liquidity which is almost the guarantee of a lyric soul." Even so, the mayor would not relent.

A rare letter of support came from Dean Virginia Gildersleeve, asserting that the hurdy-gurdies had made studying "extremely hard" for the girls at Barnard. But the pith of the matter was put in a letter from an Italian-American, Frederico Matati. Ninety-nine percent of the organ-grinders are of Italian origin, Matati declared; they ought to be banished, along with the Italian-American shoe-shine boys of tender age.

Years later, when LaGuardia wrote his fragment of autobiography, *The Making of an Insurgent,* he suggested the emotional roots of his own opposition to the organ-grinders. In banning them he was not thinking primarily about traffic hazards or about such comparatively new inventions as the phonograph and radio. He was reverting to a scarring incident of his youth. When he was about ten an organ-grinder with a monkey had come to Prescott, attracting a great deal of attention from the local kids. "A dago with a monkey!" they jeered. "Hey, Fiorello, you're a dago too. Where's your monkey?" To make matters worse, his father had come along and started to chatter Neopolitan with the organ-grinder. "It hurt," LaGuardia wrote; and it still hurt long afterward.

Whatever the basic cause, the battle of the hurdy-gurdies shows LaGuardia's tendency to be censorious. Between making New York a more humane place and imposing upon the city has own somewhat quixotic views there was a narrow line. LaGuardia crossed over this line on a number of occasions. No one seems to have protested when in March 1935 the police burned in the furnaces of their department a haul of "obscene" books. But when twenty women were seized in a West Side Manhattan residence, having been found playing poker allegedly for high stakes, at least a few eyebrows were raised. "Since when is it a crime to play poker?" asked Magistrate Anna M. Kross, dismissing all the women. The mayor's campaign against "indecent" magazines went on for several years, reaching a climax in 1940 when he invited the publishers and distributors to his summer city hall, lecturing them in language which "after reading your publications" he was certain they would understand. He had indeed read the publications in question; he had "discerned a trend where there is plain ugly nudity or direct sex appeal." On the basis of that judgment he asked for a boycott of stores where they were sold, and ordered a denial of licenses to newstands that displayed them.

The *Times* sensibly observed on this occasion that "we cannot very well abandon sex and we cannot prevent young people from thinking about it." When LaGuardia tried to form a committee to determine whether a particular publication—*Man to Man*—was lewd, he found that nearly everyone, including Judge Seabury, had reasons why he was unable to serve.

But these were aberrations, LaGuardian eccentricities, when an old-fashioned conscience became confused with civic compassion. More important than the ban on female poker players or indecent publications was a genuine concern for the arts; more important than the crusade against hurdy-gurdies was the sustained and effective attempt to give minorities a new sense of participation in the city's life. Jean Cocteau, coming as a visitor about this time, remarked on the wonder of New York—"it was not that it was so high," he said, "but that it was so *unnecessarily* high." The lord mayor of Liverpool, after seeing LaGuardia, commented on streets as clean as London's and expressed the wish that the air of his own city might be as pure. The excitement of the great metropolis was catching, and it was symbolized by a leader who rejoiced in the height of the skyscrapers but did not forget that the streets at their feet must be clean. He did not forget, either, that it was government's task to make sure that the people in the streets, even the poorest and most unfortunate, should find pleasure in their lives.

Serving the Mayor

The men and women who worked for LaGuardia endured a particular form of joy and grief. He was a chief of unusual severity, impatient, often unjust, and usually without gratitude for services rendered. It is difficult to reconstruct accurately the atmosphere within the administration as it existed in this early period when the mayor was still fresh at his job. Taken out of context, remembered incidents make him seem harsh and vindictive (which he often was); but they tend to leave out the overriding high humor, the excitement, and the sense of moral commitment. Among those who survived to tell their tales in the 1970s, the opinion without exception was that the work had been worthwhile—indeed, that these had been the great days of a lifetime.

If you were looking for gratitude, said Anna Rosenberg, speaking in this respect for her colleagues, you didn't serve LaGuardia; but if you wanted to see action, to share in the joy of accomplishment, you were more than compensated for all the heartaches. Mitzi Somach was the mayor's intermediary and confidential secretary for six years, serving without pay; Adolf Berle gave her the name of "Czecho" because she acted so effectively as a buffer; yet she saw the tensions accumulate, and left with only an offhand remark from the mayor that the city had gotten its return from her dollar-a-year salary. Forty years later Mrs. Somach could still say that nothing ever equalled being in LaGuardia's entourage. To be in the ranks, said Berle, was to have "a front-row seat at the best show in town."

The mayor, at least, had no illusions about himself or about the pains of working for him. "I'm an inconsiderate, arbitrary, authoritative, difficult, complicated, intolerant—and somewhat theatrical person": so he warned off Edmund Palmieri, a young assistant district attorney prepared to work at City Hall. Palmieri went to see Paul Kern. "What's so horrible about the job?" he asked. Kern seemed to be reassuring. It was hard labor, but the mayor was an interesting and dynamic person and the people around him were fun to work with. A little later Palmieri found out the full story for himself. The mayor expected the impossible to be done yesterday, he learned; the hours were seven days a week and seven nights. The penalty for making a mistake—you got fired.

Nevertheless, Palmieri threw himself into the job, as young men before and afterward had placed themselves gladly in the same lion's den. More than one found LaGuardia almost impossible with subordinates—"a temperamental and ruthless taskmaster," says Paul Blanshard, who at the same time admits that after his hero Norman Thomas, he enjoyed working with LaGuardia more than with any other man. David Rockefeller, who was an aide for almost two years in the mayor's office, saw him repeatedly reduce his stenographic staff to tears; and the sufferings of his secretaries and law aides—Kern, Howe, Stone—were, said Blanshard, "terrible to behold." The mayor's normal instinct was to find the actions of all his subordinates impossibly stodgy and slow, and he considered it his role to torment them into a higher level of efficiency.

When the day's drafts of responses to mail were brought to the mayor, he read through them with an almost incredible speed and with a sure grasp of their contents; then what he did not approve he flicked one by one to the floor, leaving the humiliated aides to pick them up. He actually seemed to enjoy finding mistakes or errors of judgment. This little ceremony, recalled by more than one of the survivors, typifies the office atmosphere, suggesting the mayor's undeviating attention to detail and his obliviousness to the feelings of those immediately around him.

On occasion, when he thought an aide was showing too much independence or was "stuck up," he would evolve more elaborate strategies of humiliation. Calculated silence and neglect or physical transfer to some outer desk or office were the more common methods. Palmieri recalls one of the more unusual. LaGuardia summoned him before a group of important transit officials in his office asking him to bring drafts of comments on upcoming legislation. The mayor read one draft after another. This time in his disdain he did not merely cast them to the floor; in full view he tore them successively into small pieces and threw them into the wastepaper basket. Palmieri was not only abased, but chagrined at the waste of so much laborious effort. Immediately after the mayor's departure for the day he went into the office to retrieve the fractured documents. To his astonishment they were not in the basket.

Several weeks later he was even more astonished when in a mayoral letter to the state legislature printed in the *Times,* he recognized precisely the arguments, in the very words and phrases, which had appeared in his drafts. In a relaxed mood some while later LaGuardia admitted his part in the incident; he had acted as he did to bring his law aide down a peg. Marie supplied the missing links. The mayor had brought home the scraps of paper personally retrieved from his basket and had charged his wife to piece them together. It had taken the better part of the day. Then he had asked Moses for a secretary of particular trustworthiness and had given her the papers to type.

Four decades later Palmieri, now a federal judge, mused upon the incident. One could sense the unforgotten hurt. Yet he had been flattered and grateful to the mayor, he said. "I thought he went to a great deal of trouble to help me eliminate a character trait I ought to correct. . . . Of course I didn't have the trait he accused me of, but if I had indeed been guilty of it, he was right to teach me a lesson."

Palmieri in this remark touched on a side of LaGuardia which was almost always evident in his dealings with younger men. Though harsh, he was genuinely concerned with their welfare and fatherly in his attitude toward them. He wanted to correct and teach them, somewhat as an old bear will teach her cubs, buffeting them painfully about the ears. Paul Kern and Vito Marcantonio were in this category of preempted children and both endured tenderness and its reverse. Paul Blanshard basked in a kind of rough-handed intimacy which he attributed to the mayor's somehow conceiving him to be a youngster. (Actually he was only five years LaGuardia's junior, but with the unworldiness of an ex-minister and the moral views of a later hippie.) When the paternalistic illusion passed, a cooling in their relations occurred imperceptibly, and then a break.

The problem of time for the mayor's staff was always acute. LaGuardia would not have believed in "coffee breaks" had they then been invented; and he certainly did not believe in vacations. A new member of the official family, exhausted by the long morning's work, asked, "When do they eat around here?" On being told that they generally didn't eat at lunchtime he seemed much disconcerted. When LaGuardia was on one of his western trips he sent back a crate of oranges for the office staff. The full humor of the acknowledgment (per his secretary, Lester Stone) can only be appreciated against the background of unremitting toil. "Your oranges arrived in good condition. Stop. Staff highly appreciative. Stop. Stopped all work to eat oranges." It was a gift the mayor undoubtedly regretted.

LaGuardia's relations with his commissioners were not essentially different from those with his more intimate staff: the same expectations of subservience to his wishes, the same quixotic and often harsh treatment. Keeping the reins of government tightly in his own hands, he second-guessed them or kept them in the dark about his plans. They were experts in their own fields, he would agree, but they were not experts in politics and public relations; only his overall surveillance could save the administration from costly misjudgments. He never hesitated to call attention to their obfuscations, as the official correspondence recalls. To Kenneth Dayton, director of the budget, he wrote: "You are supposed to be a first-class director of a first-class city. When I send something for comment I want an expressed, decided, and unequivocal report from you. As long as you are on the job I want you to do a little thinking. Do not ever again, in answer to a request for a comment on a report, refer to another document." To John Rice, health commissioner: "Please talk just plain English that us honest folk can understand." And even to Police Commissioner Valentine, who would reply meticulously to a veritable avalanche of memoranda from the mayor, covering everything from a taxicab with a blurred license to a cop on the beat who had lent his coat to a poor beggar: "In the name of all the saints that you have been told about, in addition to those you have forgotten, don't send a routine communication . . . let us have some intelligent action and less routine stuff."

A ceremony, somewhat embarrassing in retrospect, awarded during commissioners' meetings a bone to those officials who were judged to have committed a "boner." The object itself was a polished sheep's shank, contained in a mahogany box decorated with the city's colors. The commissioner of licenses, Paul Moss, got the bone for seating the mayor next to a well-known racketeer at a large public function. Fellowes Morgan of markets got it for writing an indiscreet letter used against the city in a law suit. Though veiled in a rather heavy-handed humor, and though often deserved, the rebuke stung and humiliated.

LaGuardia expected his commissioners to be available at all hours, and thought nothing of rousing them from their sleep if he thought he needed them. An assistant corporation counsel recalls being awakened at midnight and told that a police car would be at his door to bring him to LaGuardia's apartment: the mayor in a nocturnal inspection had found a movie he considered improper. Perhaps the most bizarre of summonses came to Walter Binger, the well-known engineer then serving in the Manhattan borough office. He was riding to hounds in Connecticut, dressed for the weekend hunt in high hat, boots, and pink coat, when a police car roared into the field and demanded he be identified. He was "over there, on the bay horse" one of the surprised huntsmen revealed. It seemed the mayor wanted Binger immediately in connection with what he deemed an erroneous clause in a contract he was reading. Telephoning from a nearby farmhouse Binger convinced the mayor the matter could wait until Monday (the clause, in any case, was valid). Afterward Binger regretted he had not commandeered the police car and, in full regalia and amid screeching sirens, bounded up the steps of City Hall.

Commissioners reacted in various ways to the mayor and his peculiar habits. John Rice among others was terrified of him, and welcomed on his own staff an emissary of the mayor's, Goodhue Livingstone, Jr., who could take some of the direct heat. But there were exceptions, and LaGuardia seemed to get on best with those who did not hesitate to stand up to him. Windels was too old an associate to be overly impressed by tantrums that would have floored another. Goldwater was unflappable. On one occasion when he was to represent the mayor he arrived late at the dinner and settled himself in a back row, leading the mayor to send a message the next day that he was "distressed and hurt" by the commissioner's seeming indifference. Nor was Goldwater one to be kept waiting when an appointment had been made at City Hall, a favorite ploy of the mayor's. He would simply leave if he was not received at the appointed hour.

Moses had established with the mayor his own stance of haughty independence, at once basically affectionate and slightly condescending. They almost never met without fighting. David Rockefeller, asked whether he had been witness to a stormy encounter between the two men, replied he had rarely seen one that *wasn't* stormy. Moses characterized the attitude toward La-Guardia of William Carey, sanitation commissioner, in words that were also descriptive of his own: "He regarded the mayor's vaudeville stunts with a mixture of humor, friendly admiration, and amazed incredulity." Willie Chanler, the later corporation counsel, was another whose independent wealth and whose base in a major law firm made it easy for him to keep his sense of humor. On being shown a memorandum addressed to him by the mayor, particularly abusive in tone and substance, he confessed—being then in his ninth decade—that he could not recall it. But what would have been his reaction on receiving it? "I knew the mayor well enough by then," he replied; "I would have roared with laughter."

A major difficulty in establishing effective working relations with his commissioners was the mayor's constant movement and his resulting inaccessibility. He was not an administrator who could lay

down lines of action to be carried out in his absence; he insisted on
being part of each incident as it developed. Yet even he could not
be everywhere. Meetings with his cabinet were scheduled, but
were held infrequently and irregularly. Officials were left to cool
their heels, often waiting in vain in the mayor's outer office and
often wondering whether they might be suffering one of those
unpredictable falls from grace which signaled the end of a man's
usefulness. When they did manage to meet with the mayor, the
circumstances were seldom conducive to prolonged or rational
discussion. One aide recalled how the mayor had called and "asked
if I would meet him for a quiet talk." The only place they could
meet, as it turned out, was on the grandstand while the mayor was
reviewing the Legion parade. "However," adds the aide resignedly, "such a place is as quiet as any other." Another such
conference was held while actually marching in a Memorial Day
parade. It is a wonder the city's business did get accomplished, and
that so many good men stayed on to suffer the inconveniences and
frustrations of office.

Outside the circle of commissioners, in a role halfway between
personal friends and official advisers, was a small group of men
whom LaGuardia treated with an instinctive courtesy. Berle was
one of these: though he held high posts within the administration,
these were as much a device to assure his ever-ready counsel on
matters in general as they were to get a particular job accomplished.
In the beginning Berle's friendship with Roosevelt was the invaluable asset, but as the relationship between the two men developed,
a reciprocal loyalty and solicitude for each other's interests grew up
between them; to a degree rare in public life.

After Berle had gone to Washington the tie remained unbroken. The mayor would send a car to meet his friend at the
airport, and over breakfast in the East Harlem apartment the
two would survey the world and their separate parts in it. Or
Berle would invite LaGuardia to lunch at the Century Club;
then for "an afternoon's ramble, inspecting the city with him."
As the years passed, each showed signs of singular thoughtful-
ness toward the other. Berle most often played the role of protector and promoter, almost as if he were the older man, for he
sensed LaGuardia's vulnerability and appreciated his great potential usefulness to the nation. It was a strange friendship, the
scholar-diplomat and the dusty fighter in the arena: "Who
gained the most from the interchange nobody could say," wrote

15. A young counselor, Adolf A. Berle, Jr., as city chamberlain in the first term. LENT BY DR. BEATRICE B. BERLE

16. And a counselor old and witty—Charles Culp Burlingham.

Max Ascoli. "What is certain is that it did honor to both."

Windels was another whose role in friendship and counsel transcended his official post, and who continued to be of service to LaGuardia after he left the administration. The Windels family lived next to the LaGuardias in Westport during the summer; there would be talk over the backyard fence, and spaghetti dinners cooked by the shirtless LaGuardia for the two families. Windels's son was one of the mayor's favorite youngsters, and his mother was a special friend of Marie's. In later years as a respected and conservative civic leader, Paul Windels often differed with the mayor—LaGuardia called him the "sage of Crabapple Street," a somewhat sour pun upon the famous Pineapple Street in Brooklyn Heights where Windels lived—but the two met and dealt kindly with each other. In this category, too, must be put Judge Seabury, a man not given to camaraderie, but a friend and adviser always treated with deference.

A remarkable relationship still remains to be mentioned, that between the mayor and C. C. Burlingham. The latter's comments run through this book, witty, utterly frank, nearly always wise. Burlingham had met LaGuardia in the early days of the Fusion movement. Already an old man, and soon to become almost blind, he was a veteran of civic reform movements and formed a special friendship with the candidate whose victorious campaign he helped mastermind. Burlingham held a unique place among New Yorkers, respected more for the liberal, civilized human being he was than for particular accomplishments at the bar or in public life. He was an intimate of all the leading men of his day and a word from C.C.B.—usually scrawled in an almost undecipherable hand—received attention in the White House as well as in City Hall.

The Burlingham–LaGuardia correspondence in the city archives is an anthology of affectionate and worldly wise exchanges on topics and controversies of the day. C.C.B. worries about the mayor's health, advises him on appointments, scolds him for his verbal intemperance, deplores his departures from liberal orthodoxy. "I wish I were commissioner of accounts," he writes. "I would quietly begin to investigate—The Fire Department [underlined three times]—and when His Honor the Mayor got wind of it and began to raise Hell, I would go right ahead until removed." Or this, in regard to a clerk in the corporation counsel's office: "Are you so anti-*senilic* that you won't give him another year?" One could quote endlessly, but it is even better to imagine his coming into the City Hall office late in the afternoon, setting the famous fedora upon the mayor's head, and saying, "Come on, Fiorello; it's time to quit. We will ride uptown together." Burlingham stands first among those who served the mayor by helping to keep him rational and human.

New York's Foreign Policy

Amid political events at home and the social crises of the Depression, events in Europe were moving toward their own grave climax. In 1932 Hitler came to power; in 1935 the League of Nations proved itself impotent in the face of Mussolini's determination to invade Ethiopia. New York City, with its nationality groups representative of every European country and its powerful religious minorities, reflected the turmoils loosed on foreign soil. LaGuardia, in turn, reflected the seething totality that was New York. He could no more keep silent on international questions than he could on the broader issues of national policy. He was a statesman who happened to be mayor, and within the necessarily constricted duties of his office he was prepared to play his role to the hilt.

LaGuardia saw events abroad in much the same black and white colors as those at home. His instincts were strong (and sound) where suffering and exploitation were involved; his sympathies were direct and quickly aroused. Hitler and Mussolini were international criminals in his eyes, not basically different from the racketeers and "tin-horns" who peopled his urban world. More terrible in their fanaticism, they nevertheless played on the poor and helpless much as did the gangsters in his own city. They were his enemies and he fought them with whatever weapons he found.

The political implications of events abroad did not escape LaGuardia. He had long realized the degree to which New York was a meeting place of nations, and he believed that citizens of foreign derivation should retain an interest in their homelands. From the times of his earliest campaigns he had played upon these sensitive strings. The ethnic melange of New York appeared to him one of its strengths, as well as one of the factors giving him a peculiar advantage. His knowledge of languages combined with the varied strains in his own background could make him seem a "balanced ticket" all by himself; nor was he averse in his political battles to exploit what was known as "the foreign vote."

In World War I he addressed his street-corner audiences, most of them recent immigrants from the countries then at each other's throats in Europe, in their native languages—Yiddish, Italian, Hungarian, German. He was adept at stirring old memories and instilling pride in the past glories of their countries. Quick to sense nationalist sympathies, he would seem to free them at a stroke from foreign rule. In the unfinished autobiography he wrote at the end of his life, LaGuardia notes amusingly that he "dismembered the Hapsburg Empire and liberated all the subjugated countries under that dynasty almost every night."

Now he had new enemies to exorcise, and more subtle political consequences to weigh. By 1937 the Nazi and Fascist regimes were appealing to the divided loyalties of their nationals abroad and sought to enlist their active support. In New York's Yorkville, the German-American Bund flourished and the swastika was freely displayed in shop windows. The influential Italian-language *Il Progresso* called upon Italian-Americans to help give Italian soldiers in Ethiopia the chance "to write another epic page of glory in the history of civilization." Jews of all nationalities were beginning to be aware of the scope of Hitler's anti-Semitism, while a steady stream of refugees was arriving in New York to bear witness to the new horrors of totalitarianism.

Jewish on his mother's side, with his sister married to a Jew and living in Budapest, LaGuardia did not play up this part of his background. His attacks on Hitler were perhaps the more impressive because they did not seem to be personally motivated. "My mother undoubtedly had Jewish blood in her veins," he once remarked, "but I never thought I had enough in mine to justify boasting about it." About his Italian background, however, he did boast; and this put him in an awkward position with a constituency still largely sympathetic to Italian Fascism. His attacks on Hitler could be unequivocal, but where Mussolini was concerned he hedged.

LaGuardia early staked out his position as an internationally conspicuous enemy of Hitler. In 1934, with Judge Seabury and Wilson's old secretary of state Brainbridge Colby, he addressed a large protest meeting called to adumbrate "The Case of Civilization against Hitler." Within the city he used his powers to combat the insidious poison. Goodhue Livingstone was dis-

patched from the mayor's office to keep an eye on Joe McWil-
liams, one of the leaders of the American Nazis; somewhat
quixotically a German massage operator was denied a permit to
practice in New York. This, said LaGuardia, was in retaliation
for the treatment of Americans by Hitler's Reich. Berlin
charged the mayor with breaking the trade agreement existing
between the two countries, and the American secretary of state,
Cordell Hull, admitted to some displeasure at having foreign
policy thus removed from his own hands.

Relations between the mayor and the German government were
not destined to improve over the next years; nor did those between
the mayor and the secretary of state immediately ease. A year later
LaGuardia did ameliorate the situation by defining their respective
spheres of influence. "I run the subways," he said, and he [Cordell
Hull] runs the state department—except when I abrogate a treaty
or something."

The political difficulties inherent in the Italian situation were
revealed in 1935, when a large Italian concert was scheduled to
take place in Madison Square Garden. Ostensibly for the purpose
of raising funds for the Red Cross, the event had more ominous
implications of which the mayor was fully apprised. The program,
declared *Il Progresso,* was organized "to show that every Italian who
resides in the United States is ready to help Italy fight the brutal
international coalition headed by England." The mayor was invited
and agreed to attend. The *Post* stormed: "The mayor has got to stop
posing as a great liberal and progressive in this country and backing
Mussolini in Europe." Norman Thomas paid a special visit to City
Hall to urge him not to go. LaGuardia on this occasion played the
role of the overbusy executive, burdened by many affairs and
harassed by those who ought to be his friends. He chose not to
comprehend. "Oh, Norman, you mean I can't even go to *Aida*?"
Thomas suggested drily that *Aida* had a different plot, and spelled
out for the mayor exactly who the sponsors were, who would
attend, and who would stay away.

LaGuardia was among those who went. He said later he might
not have gone but that "he wasn't going to be pushed around by
a handful of anti-Fascists and Norman Thomas," an example of the
perverse stubbornness the mayor could exhibit on occasion. At the
concert he sat prominently in a box and rose to an ovation when
he was introduced. "It was not," Thomas remarked, "one of his
most heroic efforts."

As the European situation worsened—as German troops occupied the Rhineland, the Loyalists in Spain fought their losing battle, and Japan joined up with the Rome–Berlin axis—the repercussions made New York tense and edgy. Communists held a huge anti-Fascist demonstration in Central Park; students signed the Oxford peace pledge and marched in peace parades even as they denounced the dictators. The swastika appeared menacingly in Jewish temples. The mayor, resorting to a rarely used prerogative as chief magistrate, issued a summons charging criminal libel against a man dispensing anti-Jewish literature from a printing office on Washington Street. And when, in 1939, 22,000 Nazis held a rally in Madison Square Garden, he assigned a detail of Jewish police to keep order.

The mayor's words and the story of his deeds reached beyond the shores of the United States. Many years later he was touched to receive a gift of $100 from a woman who had heard one of his anti-Nazi broadcasts during the dark winter of 1937. The words "there is no ersatz for justice" had long remained with her. The mayor divided the gift among Jewish, Protestant, and Catholic charities.

The German government heard his words, too. At a luncheon meeting of the Women's Division of the American Jewish Congress in March 1937, LaGuardia expressed the wish that at the forthcoming World's Fair there might be a "chamber of horrors" to contain "that brown-shirted fanatic who is now menacing the peace of the world." A diplomatic furor ensued and cables crackled across the Atlantic. Cordell Hull, once again discomfited by New York's mayor, expressed his "very earnest regrets." The German press continued in a vituperative mood. LaGuardia's luncheon audience, it announced, had been composed of "1,200 women of the streets"; it had gathered to be entertained by "a pimp and a procurer." When the Berlin government was asked to express some regrets of its own, it declined on the ground that the German newspapermen had been inspired by "heroic anger."

In Washington a shrewd Roosevelt watched the scuffling with amusement. At his cabinet meeting he asked Hull how he would feel if he expressed himself as agreeing completely with LaGuardia. When the secretary complained that LaGuardia would not ease off on his attacks, the president tapped his left wrist lightly with the first two fingers of his right hand. "We will chastise him, like that," he said.

A few days later LaGuardia visited the White House. Reminiscing about the occasion after Roosevelt's death, he described how the press and others thought he went there to be reprimanded. But the president smiled as he entered the office. Then he extended his right hand and said, "Heil, Fiorello."

"I snapped to attention," LaGuardia continued in his account; "I extended my right arm and said, 'Heil, Franklin.' And that's all that was ever said."

Political Cauldron

By mid-1937 nobody doubted that LaGuardia would run for a second term, nor that he had widespread popular support. But there was much uncertainty as to which ticket he would run on and how the leaders of the various political factions would line up. Nor was it at all clear that Tammany, which had been beaten in 1933, would stay beaten. The history of earlier reform administrations, all of them limited to one term, was not encouraging. The machine was still strong in the borough and county offices—in 1933 Fusion had captured only 25 of a total of 94 elective offices and in their elections since had taken just 7 out of a 109 positions. Manhattan, stronghold of Tammany, might be losing its dominant position, and New Deal Tammany figures like Flynn and Farley ruled other boroughs; nevertheless the old chiefs bided their time and organized for a primary which was to prove disastrous.

LaGuardia toyed with various ideas. He would have preferred to run as a Progressive and independent Roosevelt supporter, backed by the American Labor party and various unaffiliated groups. But he never quite persuaded himself he could dispense with the Republican endorsement. Sometimes he supposed he could manage to get a Democratic endorsement as well. Both Republicans and Democrats were in a state of inner conflict and the season which now led up to the autumn campaign saw New York a boiling cauldron of political speculation and maneuvering.

The prospect of a LaGuardia candidacy left the Republicans deeply divided. His contempt for the party bosses and his open support of Roosevelt infuriated the party's orthodox membership, while his tolerance of "radicals" in the taxicab and other strikes made him appear positively dangerous. The clubhouse leaders— Crews in Brooklyn, Ashmead in Queens, and Knewitz in the Bronx

—would never forgive him for having failed to repay their 1933 support by an appropriate dispensing of jobs. A Republican who would not give patronage was no better in their eyes than a Democrat.

Yet there were others in the Republican party who saw that they could not do without the mayor (as he could not do without them). Men like Chadbourne and Windels, strongly in his camp, wanted him in their party, too. Kenneth Simpson, the subtle New York county leader, took a realistic view of the situation and aimed to get from LaGuardia what concessions he could in return for what he knew to be a necessary endorsement. A sophisticated man, Simpson preferred to accumulate power behind the scenes rather than to spend his energies in flamboyant and ineffective rhetoric. It was sufficient for his purposes, as the political year opened, to be seen chatting with the mayor; and when the fact of a two-hour conversation was reported, it set political circles a-buzz. A month later Simpson announced he would consider it an act of treachery for the Republicans to go it alone in the mayoral contest; it would play directly into the hands of Tammany. ("Yes, he *is* an SOB," Simpson told his fellow Republicans; "all the things we have been saying are true. But he is *our* SOB and we must stick with him for the good of the party!")

By the spring of 1937 the first break in Republican opposition to LaGuardia occurred. The 9th A.D. Republican Club voted to endorse him, though only after a meeting notable for the violence of its language and for behavior rarely encountered in that dignified house of the Republican establishment. The mayor was abused vociferously; fists flew and the women in the audience were prepared to flee for cover before the vote was finally taken. Soon after, the Young Republicans listened to two and a half hours of equally bitter debate in which charges of "double-crosser," "secret ally of Tammany," and "Communist" were hurled at the mayor before they, too, voted to endorse him. The credit for carrying that evening went to Newbold Morris, who took the floor to say that nobody had been "kicked around" by LaGuardia more than he, but that he saw no alternative to endorsing him.

The Democrats began no less sharply divided than the opposition. In Manhattan, where Dooley held sway, the leadership was stubbornly anti-New Deal. For a while Grover Whalen, former police commissioner and now prominent business spokesman, seemed a likely candidate; he could not make up his mind whether he wanted the nomination and finally withdrew. The Democrats turned to the immensely influential Senator Robert F. Wagner. He knew his obligations to the party and was fully aware of his strength as a candidate. But Wagner cherished his Senate seat, where he was the first German-American to serve, and his dearest wish was to sit on the U.S. Supreme Court. City Hall seemed a less likely entree to the court than the Senate. In addition, he saw no real issue between himself and LaGuardia. The White House brought pressure to bear, but this time Roosevelt seems to have been cautious about injecting himself into the New York scene. He made a good case for Wagner's candidacy, but when Wagner said he would not run, the president only laughed and said, "Well, Bob, I bet three to one you wouldn't."

Wagner's refusal was a particular blow because of all possible Democratic candidates he alone could guarantee support of the American Labor party. It seemed inconceivable that the party, in whose establishment the year before Farley had played a prominent part, should desert the New Deal. Yet now, labor was disconcertingly independent and even seemed ready to ally itself with the Republicans behind LaGuardia. For his part the mayor was briskly stirring the pot, having placed his protégé Paul Kern in the party's central office and strengthened his own ties with the rank and file.

Meanwhile the city business went on, with every incident colored by the growing party strife. Governor Lehman, who despite his sanctified demeanor could act as a wily partisan and was rarely a political friend of the mayor's, appealed directly to the Board of Estimate to restore city salaries to their pre-1932 level. LaGuardia was caught by surprise, robbed of a popular, vote-getting initiative. He was left to insist lamely that he had himself suggested restoring the cuts the previous October, and he backed the governor with a request that he go forward with the necessary home rule message. LaGuardia countered with a surprise of his own, announcing an eight-hour day for nurses and other employees in city hospitals. The board passed the resolution unanimously, a small victory, but popular with labor, and in a tense political season every victory was important.

An encounter with the ever-mischievous Robert Moses, which occurred at this same time, took on political overtones. Dissatisfied with his own budget, Moses had been feuding over several hundred WPA playground leaders laid off by Somervell. Just after

LaGuardia left on a trip, he announced he was closing many of these playgrounds until the city provided funds to staff them with civil service workers. LaGuardia was kept informed of events by phone as his train sped west, and stopping briefly in Toledo he made his own announcement: "The playgrounds of the city were built for the use of its children. No playgrounds shall be closed while I am mayor of this city." With WPA workers assigned to the police department, he ordered Valentine to open the playgrounds and to see that they were kept open. Moses went to the Democratic-dominated Board of Aldermen where he received authorization for increased funds.

Many saw in this Moses coup an indication that he was himself preparing to make a run for mayor, combining the Al Smith wing of Tammany with the Republicans. "This is serious business," wrote Berle. "We expect Tammany against us anyway, but I do not know that we are adequately prepared to cope with treachery in our own ranks." Yet Moses's victory was in the end less to his advantage than to the mayor's. LaGuardia had lost the budget issue, but his quick and decisive action proved he was in control of the city's operations whether at City Hall or on a cross-country railroad train. His concern for the children of the city, so instinctive and direct, would be remembered fondly by New Yorkers.

In June LaGuardia made his plans for a summer which would see him somewhat removed from the daily pressure of politics. The family was settled on Asharokan Beach near Northport, and the summer city hall would be set up at the Chisholm Mansion in College Point on Long Island Sound. A last scheduled meeting of the Board of Estimate found the mayor in prickly humor. "I don't want a vacation," quipped William Brunner, Democratic president of the Board of Aldermen, in a mock show of civic virtue. Lyons of the Bronx agreed. "Very well," LaGuardia snapped in a sudden change of mood, "We'll have no adjournment at all this summer"; and forthwith determined to call regular weekly meetings in the soon-to-be-abandoned City Hall. It was an inconvenience to himself as well as to the members of the board, but LaGuardia did not care. "I'll call a bluff every time I see one," said he.

The mayor and his staff were greeted by the borough president and various local dignitaries when they moved to the Chisholm Mansion on July 1. Moses, calling himself "the janitor," saw that the summer quarters were made comfortable. At least the sea breezes would make it cool enough, he suggested, to keep down the high blood pressure of an election year. From here the mayor could sally forth for the ceremonial occasions he enjoyed and knew how to put to good use. Dedicating Marine Park Bridge on July 4, he told a cheerful audience at Riis Park of his special debt to the social reformer, Jacob Riis. "Thirty-four years ago," he said, "I had a pleasant job in the government, not much work and a home on the shores of the Adriatic. Then I read Jacob Riis's book *How the Other Half Lives*." He credited the book with being the single most important factor in his decision to leave the consular service. On a similar occasion, dedicating a health center in Chelsea, he declared Roosevelt entitled to all the praise, a rare gesture in a political season.

Other days saw him facing the Board of Estimate in obstreperous sessions. Members were in the worst of humor, having been compelled by the quixotic mayor to meet through the hot summer. They fumed at his demand to vote separately on 190 individual cases after the board had voted a blanket pay raise. They overrode decisively—52 to 1—his veto of the Lyons bill, with only Newbold Morris supporting him. At the same session, and over the mayor's objection, a five-day week was passed for all city employees except police and firemen. As a result, a record budget for 1938 was predicted.

When the mayor was in residence at his summer city hall the days were filled with a steady stream of visitors on a variety of missions. A dismissed WPA teacher pushed her way past the guards, hurled a telephone at a policeman, and shouted abuse until the mayor himself came out. He calmed her down, speaking quietly to her in French and promising assistance in finding another job. Norman Thomas came by with a delegation from the Socialist party. Asked if he would support LaGuardia, Thomas told reporters, "He hasn't even been nominated yet. No one has endorsed him except the Communists—and I have not yet decided to make common front with the Communist party." That was not very helpful.

A visit of a delegation of Republicans on one of the hottest days of summer was better. "Sure I'll receive them," said the mayor caustically. "I receive newspapermen, don't I?" But when they arrived, a thousand strong in buses, cars, motor boats, and seaplanes, the mayor's attitude toward his Republican constituency changed to one of bemused appreciation.

The event, seemingly spontaneous, took on the aspect of an old-fashioned picnic. Bands and banners were on hand; a busy

17. The wily and civilized Republican leader, Kenneth Simpson. ACME

ice cream vendor made his way through the crowd. Small boys in their overalls were lifted high to see the mayor when he began to speak. The bitterness of the last months was forgotten as the afternoon sun slanted across the green lawns running down to the sound. Yet one man, standing apart, refused to be carried away. The wily Simpson, admitting he was impressed, would only agree to take the day's events into account when the Republican choice was made.

By mid-July LaGuardia was assured of Fusion and of American Labor party endorsements. Still, as his friends told him, he needed the Republican nomination. Concealing his reluctance, he made the first move. Simpson, he knew, was fond of music, and now the mayor invited him and his wife to dine at the Claremont Inn and afterward to attend a concert at Lewisohn Stadium. Following the concert it was Simpson's turn to suggest that LaGuardia stop by at his home for a nightcap. The two men went into the library of the handsome house on East 91st Street, where Simpson, a reformed drinker, sipped White Rock while LaGuardia sat with a whiskey and soda. For what seemed a long while they discussed everything except what was uppermost in their minds.

Finally LaGuardia touched gently on the subject. He assumed, he said, that he would be the Republican nominee for mayor. Simpson affected surprise. It was hardly likely, he said, considering the mayor's courtship of the New Deal. But, if by some strange chance it should work out that way, the Republicans would naturally expect to choose the rest of the ticket. LaGuardia controlled himself with an effort. Did Simpson have anyone in mind, he asked. He did have some ideas, Simpson admitted, and mentioned Newbold Morris for council president and McGoldrick for comptroller. Neither was acceptable, LaGuardia snapped. He wanted Berle for comptroller and someone from Queens or Brooklyn for the council post.

It was late when LaGuardia rose to go. The two men had been talking for several hours. At the door he turned to Simpson and suggested it would be a good idea for him to meet with ALP leaders. Simpson said he would consider it; and indeed at a small gathering arranged by the mayor he did sit down with Alex Rose, Sidney Hillman, and David Dubinsky, forging with them a profitable alliance.

Simpson was not too much troubled by LaGuardia's opposition to the running mates he had selected, both of whom the mayor had endorsed on previous occasions. He might fuss and fume but he would come around. He was less certain about being able to sell the ticket to the other four Republican county chairmen. A much-publicized meeting of the leaders at the Yale Club on July 23 ended without a slate despite all Simpson's efforts at persuasion. He decided to take matters into his own hands. Avoiding reporters, he slipped through a backdoor of the club and telephoned Morris and McGoldrick that he was about to announce their nominations. Contrary to custom, he told them coolly, the New York Republican Committee had decided to make up its ticket from the bottom. The committee had selected candidates for council president and comptroller, but had not yet made its choice for mayor.

LaGuardia was furious. He ransacked his vocabulary for words with which to describe Simpson and to denounce his actions. The Republican leaders were hardly less offended. Jake Livingstone in Brooklyn vowed to deny the nomination to LaGuardia, and at a meeting in the Kismet Temple almost succeeded in doing so. It took all the political skills of that good Brooklynite, Paul Windels, to avoid having the raucous gathering conclude in disaster. An overagitated lady gave Windels his opportunity when she cried out that even Tammany would be preferable to LaGuardia. That was too much for the Kings County Republicans. They howled and booed, and after the uproar subsided Windels succeeded in forcing through a compromise proposal assuring LaGuardia's ultimate endorsement.

The next day, following a conference with Seabury and Simpson, LaGuardia agreed to accept the Simpson slate. The Republican ticket in Manhattan still needed to be completed by the selection of a Manhattan borough president and a district attorney. For the former, LaGuardia gladly assented to the patrician and public-spirited Stanley Isaacs, of whom we shall hear more presently. For district attorney, the obvious man seemed to be Thomas E. Dewey. But Dewey had his own style and was not ready to make the choice an easy one for his sponsors.

"Dewey's vanity, always disagreeable, was working overtime," Berle remarked of the occasion when he and LaGuardia picked him up in the mayor's car for an evening designed to get him into the race. Dewey made it a condition that both the president and the governor should ask him to run, that Seabury should guarantee him $300,000 for campaign expenses, and that he should have campaign quarters separate from the other Republican candidates. "My own thought," wrote Berle, "was that it was better to drop him overboard." But the mayor was less easily put off, and as he did so often when he wanted to apply political pressure, took Dewey to a Lewisohn Stadium concert. "I looked at the river for a while," Berle concluded in his diary, "and then went home to bed."

As for LaGuardia, his task was to make Dewey feel that he was absolutely essential to the mayor's victory, a piece of play acting he performed successfully. Dewey was persuaded and, according to one member of the ticket, made a most uncongenial running mate.

The mayor had one further chore—to enter and to win the Republican primary race. The anti-New Deal Democratic candidate, Senator Royal Copeland, was running in both party primaries. A medical practitioner who had won a wide following through his newspaper column on health problems, he might have made a good doctor (Max Lerner quipped in the *Nation*) if he had not become a quack senator. LaGuardia determined to run against him by simply continuing to run the city. There would be no headquarters, no bands or speeches, no appearances except for those in which, as mayor, LaGuardia would be expected to participate. The Republican chiefs were affronted at what seemed a belittling of their party.

When LaGuardia won—a bit too narrowly for comfort—they warned him that he could still lose in November.

Defeated by LaGuardia in the Republican primary, Copeland was defeated in the Democratic primary by the New Deal candidate, Jeremiah F. Mahoney. Mahoney had been a law partner of Senator Wagner's; his other distinction was that he had opposed participation in the German Olympics, a stand which his backers hoped would counteract LaGuardia's appeal to the Jewish vote. Backed by major New Deal figures, he would be the Democratic candidate pitted against LaGuardia in the November race.

Great Campaign

LaGuardia was ready now to fight hard for his election, with all the force and wit of which he was capable. Before he was through he would make his appeal to every minority as well as to the general citizenry with its vague longings for a better city and for richer individual lives. He would defend his record in detail, and have wonderful fun with the often vapid arguments of the opposition. It was a joy to see him in action, a man at the top of his bent with all his energies focused on one goal.

He began the final phase of the campaign well endowed with nominations. He had won the Republican endorsement; on September 30, before a wildly cheering, packed audience at Carnegie Hall, he accepted the nomination of the American Labor party. He was running, besides, as the Fusion, Progressive, and Communist party candidate. He lost the Socialist endorsement as a result of his support of George Harvey for borough president of Queens (LaGuardia, after sobering experiences, was counting his votes on the Board of Estimate); but since in his speeches Norman Thomas referred to a possible Democratic victory as a calamity, there was nowhere for Socialists to go except into the mayor's camp. This multiplicity of designations appealed to LaGuardia as much for the independence it gave him as for the combined strength it provided against the Democrats. He would be faithful to his supporters, but in his own fashion.

LaGuardia's determination to carry with him into office an ample majority on the Board of Estimate (besides Harvey, he backed the less-than-liberal borough president of Staten Island, Joseph Palma) was reinforced by bitter confrontations with the board during the election period. A reduction in the water rates was voted by the aldermen on October 5; LaGuardia counted on the full tax to balance his 1938 budget and he denounced the cuts, attractive as they were to voters, as a new low in legislative and political trickery. When the matter came before the Board of Estimate in executive session two days later, the Democratic comptroller smoothly urged him to make up for the $12 million loss in water rates by a cut in government salaries. In four years of political conflict nothing had so enraged the mayor.

Pounding on the table with sledgehammer blows heard through the doors of the committee room, he gave way to anger which this time had no touch of make-believe. "I'll be damned if I will," he exploded. *"You* cut the revenues," he screamed at the board members, "now you go ahead and cut the expenses." Then the mayor charged out of the room. "With a mighty tug the door of the chamber flew open," as a reporter described the scene. The mayor's face was a choleric red and tears of rage started from his eyes. He tore by everyone in the corridor, clattered down the stairs, and dashed into his office. The slam of that last door made the old Hall shudder.

But LaGuardia regained his composure and convinced himself that even the most patently unpopular acts could serve his cause if carried out with flair. He vetoed the bill providing city workers with a five-day week. It was a course, he asserted proudly, that few candidates would follow: "No matter what happens, my successor won't take over a bankrupt city." Then with the good humor that in these days was never far from his anger, he admitted he was acting selfishly, "because I know I'm going to succeed myself." The Democrats had the last word on the budget, however. Almost on election eve they restored sixty-five county jobs and approved various county pay rises. By then it didn't matter, for nothing could overcome LaGuardia's lead.

Mahoney opened what was to be an undistinguished campaign by charging the mayor with broken promises and conducting city government by whim. His running mate on the comptroller's ticket, Frank J. Taylor, called the mayor "a crackpot." (Nevertheless the mayor's parks commissioner saw fit to endorse Taylor.) Despite his taking time out for elocution lessons, Mahoney's tactics did not improve in the following weeks. His attacks on the mayor degenerated into red-baiting and name-calling, made the more extreme as the polls showed the Fusion ticket moving ahead. New York, said Mahoney, had been turned under LaGuardia into "a city of strife, a haven of agitators"; he charged the mayor with handcuffing the police and directing them "not to do their duty." For himself, he promised a restoration of "law and order."

LaGuardia's confidence increased and proved contagious to his followers. "I make no special promises; I make no exaggerated campaign claims," he would tell his audiences. If Seabury was on hand (as he often was) he would be introduced as "the greatest exterminator of crooks in the history of the country." Laying the cornerstone for a new hospital on Welfare Island, LaGuardia predicted that "no matter how long it takes to complete this hospital, I'll be around to dedicate it." And he told of the hospital's beginnings, at a breakfast meeting with Commissioner Goldwater. "That's where I meet with my commissioners," he said in a phrase calling to mind the excesses of the regime he had replaced, "at the breakfast table and not at the nightclubs."

The month of October saw the mayor already picking up labor support. John L. Lewis had come out for him early; then the endorsement of the CIO unions was reinforced by that of the State Federation of Labor. Republicans might think the mayor "soft" in dealing with the unions; labor thought otherwise. They had seen LaGuardia use repressive tactics in the past; they knew him to be capable of red-baiting. But they wanted results in social terms and knew Tammany was not the place to look for them. As for the ALP, Dubinsky and Rose were counting on LaGuardia to help make the party an independent national force in 1940. There were 750,000 union members, not counting dependents, who had been assumed to be in the Democratic camp. Now, while Tammany fumbled, LaGuardia was stealing them away.

Yet the opposition was far from powerless. With a Democratic president, governor, and senator, it remained to see how they would deploy their forces against the mayor. That Wagner would support his former law partner was taken for granted, as was Lehman's adherence to the straight party ticket. But what would Roosevelt do? "I hope you can keep out of this one," Berle had written him, "there is nothing in it for you." On the whole he followed this advice. After his abortive effort to persuade Wagner to run, he contented himself with encouraging or restraining the political enthusiasts around him.

Farley was known to be planning a week of active campaigning at the end of October. For a while, in view of LaGuardia's growing strength in the polls, it was thought Roosevelt would call him off. But the old warhorse could not keep entirely out of the fray. He called Farley to urge him on, saying that if La-Guardia got really tough, he would himself "pin his ears back." Watch out, replied Farley, "he might bite you." Meanwhile Ickes was preparing to come up to New York to dedicate a sewage treatment plant on Ward's Island in the East River. He had conferred with Roosevelt after receiving the mayor's invitation. The president saw it as an opportunity to keep events off balance and gave his consent to Ickes's visit. At the ceremonies, Ickes attributed initiation of the plant to the mayor's "persuasiveness," and those who snatched at any clue to the president's position noted that in his speech the secretary made four mentions of LaGuardia's name.

Behind the scenes the president played an equivocal role right up to the end. On the Saturday before the election La-Guardia called in Windels to show him a special-delivery letter he had just received. It was from Roosevelt; it was interpreted as tantamount to endorsement; it invited publication. Windels, who had never been an admirer of Roosevelt's, urged La-Guardia not to release it. He saw it as an effort on Roosevelt's part to cash in on the expected LaGuardia victory; he warned, too, that it might offend many Republicans. LaGuardia got the same advice from the newspaper publisher Roy Howard, and in the end withheld the letter. Roosevelt, it appears, was not displeased. As he summed up his own role in the campaign, "Jim Farley went to New York and told what a fine man Judge Mahoney was. Then Harold Ickes went to New York and told what a fine man Mayor LaGuardia was. Neither said anything against the other candidate." And that is the way, said the canniest politician of them all, "to be absolutely neutral."

With or without the president's blessing, the LaGuardia drive gained momentum, greatly aided by the innumerable official functions that were a normal part of the mayor's routine. There were public works to dedicate, parades to review, and inspections to make, all of which could be turned to advantage in an election campaign. On October 12 the improved Riverside Drive and park were opened. "I first heard about this in 1915," the mayor told the crowd assembled at the 79th Street rotunda, "and then in 1917

18. Groundbreaking ceremonies with the most durable of the relief czars, Brereton H. Somervell.
TIMES WIDE WORLD PHOTOS

when it was a campaign issue, and again in 1929 when it was a campaign promise. I was laughed out of the campaign of 1929 because I referred to it." It had also been an issue in 1933, he said, "and now I am glad to dedicate it in 1937." He was proud, too, to have been referred to as a "myth" by the increasingly desperate Mahoney. "The Triborough Bridge, that's a myth. Randall's Island is a myth, too, and just doesn't exist," he crooned in his richest, most sarcastic tones. "So long as we continue to have myths of that kind we needn't worry." The crowd loved it.

As Mahoney stepped up his rhetoric LaGuardia announced he would have to give him lessons in civics, explaining precisely how the city departments worked. He began issuing a series of reports which, in spite of their political overtones, showed persuasively the gains that had been made over the last four years. One day it would be the work of the commissioner of investigations whose activities would be traced out, providing themes for the mayor's increasingly numerous and exuberant speeches; the next it would be so comparatively obscure a department as that of licenses which had protected the blind and the crippled against the kind of political exploitation they had formerly been subject to. Altogether there would be eighteen such reports, and the mayor's enthusiasm as he discoursed upon them carried his large audiences with him.

On October 15, accompanied by Herbert Hoover, LaGuardia opened a tube of the Lincoln Tunnel. The next day, Mahoney, having charged the mayor with forging "an unholy alliance between minority groups," was formally endorsed by Lehman. This moved the *Times* to administer a rare rebuke to the governor whom it usually treated with almost reverential respect: he had rendered, said its editorialist, "a poor service to the community." On the same day Senator Wagner began the first of three speeches for Mahoney. LaGuardia went before the City Club to answer Mahoney on the "law and order" issue. "I'll face the music," he told the powerful group of civic leaders who formed his audience. "I'll face the music. I'll say there has been more order and that labor conditions have been better controlled than in any other large city in the United States."

October 22 was an especially busy day of campaigning for the mayor. He laid cornerstones for two public schools and a courthouse. And he delivered for Mahoney's benefit another "lesson," his sixteenth, on improvements in the Department of Plants and Structures. When Ickes met him at the Athletic Club that evening (he had come to town for his speech at Ward's Island) he found LaGuardia looking tired. He was having a hard campaign, Ickes thought, "but then he always works like a horse." LaGuardia told him indications were so favorable for his reelection he could hardly believe them; and then added with touching candor that he wasn't used to having things go his way.

The following day the Sanitation Department turned out in all its somewhat tattered glory and paraded new equipment in Manhattan and Brooklyn. Then, with the closing down of the campaign, came climactic meetings of all parties. A lack-luster Tammany rally at the Hippodrome was compensated for by the next night's Democratic meeting at the Brooklyn Academy of Music. Lehman, Wagner, and Farley shared the platform and the enthusiasm of the crowd. It was not the governor's finest hour. He had to defend Mahoney who had denounced as "red" the American Labor party which had supported both himself and Roosevelt. In a direct attack on LaGuardia he claimed for himself the credit for having saved the city from insolvency.

Fusion held its own huge rally in Madison Square Garden on October 30, and an exuberant, shouting, stamping crowd cheered LaGuardia and Dewey, and applauded in high spirits when they heard themselves addressed as "Fellow Communists" by Newbold Morris. There were a few sour notes. Robert Moses was booed for his support of Taylor, and when Kenneth Simpson tried to introduce Harvey, the Queens borough president met with such sustained booing that he walked out. Nothing could really spoil the evening, however. It was considered one of the most enthusiastic political rallies in the city's history. "Well, it's all over," declared Tom Dewey as he was to do in a later, and less successful campaign.

For LaGuardia it was not over until November 2 when he officially closed his campaign at his lucky corner on 110th Street and Lexington Avenue, in the heart of the East Harlem district which he had represented in Congress. Wearing his lucky overcoat—the dark-gray Chesterfield with the velvet collar that he had worn for his final campaign speeches for so many years—he addressed eight thousand of his friends and neighbors. All traffic halted until the mayor said goodnight and the crowd went home. The next morning he would be up early to vote.

Victory and Its Aftermath

LaGuardia's victory was overwhelming. He received the largest vote for mayor in the history of the city—1.3 million to Mahoney's 889 thousand. He was elected by a clear majority and he carried every borough. In the Board of Estimate, he could count on all the votes except that of Lyons of the Bronx. Along with McGoldrick and Morris he had committed to his support Ingersoll of Brooklyn, Palma of Staten Island, Harvey of Queens, and Isaacs of Manhattan. Tammany seemed finished. Christopher D. Sullivan, last of the Sullivan clan, chosen as leader only six months before, sat in the Hall on election night surrounded by only twenty friends.

In the mayor's personal triumph the American Labor party played a crucial part. From the Republicans he had garnered 672 thousand votes and from the ALP, 482 thousand (with an additional 168 thousand coming from the Progressive and City Fusion parties). It had not been supposed that the Labor party's success of 1936, when it had received 238 thousand votes for Roosevelt and Lehman, could possibly be repeated; but LaGuardia had not only

stolen the party away from the Democrats, he had greatly augmented its influence and numbers. Operating in virtually every
election district, with the Communists appearing a negligible factor, it seemed a power to contend with in 1940.

In politics nothing is ever quite as it looks, and in due course we
shall see how the picture altered in the next few years. The mayor
lost control of the Board of Estimate, Tammany showed startling
powers of revival, and the ALP was split into bitter factions. But
for the present the mayor was entitled to an hour of triumph as
sweet as any politician could desire.

The president, who sent LaGuardia a prompt message of congratulations, took notice of the magnitude of the victory, on a
smaller scale comparable to his own just one year before. Two days
after the election he invited the mayor to meet with him at his 65th
Street town house. The mayor's arrival, along with that of Farley
and Hopkins, was observed by a large contingent of the press, but
the door closed upon a meeting which aroused the more speculation because it was entirely private. Though word was given out
that it had been just a social visit, spontaneously arranged, observers questioned whether the politically sensitive president was not
anxious to keep LaGuardia in line and to head off any third-party
talks, at least until he had made his own plans for 1940.

In his memoirs Farley was to provide an amusing glimpse of the
occasion. The president's mother, learning what was up, had come
through the door cut in the wall that joined the two houses. She
warmly congratulated the mayor. "I knew your victory was assured
long before election," she said. Farley, evidently hurting because
of the failure of his own strategy in the campaign, adds that he had
no doubt where Mrs. Roosevelt had learned that LaGuardia would
win—it must have been from the president himself. Farley seems
to have received a good deal of rough kidding about his part in the
campaign and particularly because of the defection of his brain-
child, the Labor party. He was not one to forget such kidding, nor
to forgive.

Now was a time, if ever, for LaGuardia to relax, to take a vacation, and to think calmly about the future. He was halfway through
what by all the precedents would seem to be his time as mayor, and
he had important choices to make both in municipal and national
politics. But it was not in LaGuardia's nature to pause. He drove
himself forward against exhaustion of mind and body, without a day
off to celebrate, without a week to recover from the toils of the

campaign. He survived, and when the new year came he entered
upon what was to be the most rewarding and the happiest period
of his career. But meanwhile he engaged in a series of petulant and
erratic actions which he could well have spared himself had he been
persuaded to take a brief holiday. These actions are worth noting
not only for themselves, but because they foreshadow the later
LaGuardia, when a corrosive weariness had entered into his soul
causing his irritability to increase dangerously.

The first agency to become a target of the mayor's ire was the
Transit Commission, which had turned down the Seabury–Berle
plan for unification of the city's subways. He would, he said, demand the commission's abolition and would never deal with it in
any circumstances again. If the state wanted to keep it, that was all
right by him—"but let the state pay for it, as it pays for amusements
in the state parks." Then he took on a considerable part of the
police department. He insisted on the resignation of all officers
over sixty-five and of all in the detective force over sixty-three.
There was much to be said for opening the way to younger men
and revitalizing the uniformed and detective branches; but the
move was a strange echo of Roosevelt's attack on the Supreme
Court after his great victory of the previous year. All the men who
had been in power under Tammany would go out in the shakeup.
Veterans going back to the heyday of the Bowery, to the battles
against street gangs, the crusading of Dr. Parkhurst and the antics
of the notorious gambler Herman Rosenthal—all were now leaving
the stage.

Valentine was in an awkward position, loyal to his chief but
torn by the shock and consternation of the older men on the
force. Late in November he called a meeting at the police department headquarters. Before him were lined up veterans
grown grey in the service. With difficulty he started his address;
under the strain of visible emotion his voice broke as he announced the decree. LaGuardia, doing his best to soften the
blow, sent a letter to assure the men that there was no stigma
attached to retirement: those now asked to bow out were leaving the city "with a badge of honor."

Not surprisingly, a few days later Valentine found in an entirely different context an occasion to voice his suppressed dismay. In Central Park a sixty-year-old businessman, Charles H.
Klein, had been seen to topple over a wall; just before expiring,
he told of being seized by two blacks and stabbed when he re-

sisted being robbed. Calling a press conference to protest the brutal murder, Valentine took the opportunity to denounce the insufficiency of his police force. It was now one thousand under the quota; in all, he asked for an additional four thousand men. "We haven't an adequate force anywhere in the city," he declared. "I'm beginning to wonder whether this department isn't the stepchild of the administration." It was the kind of outcry to make any mayor wince.

The matter had an ironic ending. Two young blacks who were questioned said they saw Klein "beat himself" and then fall over the wall. More strangely, the body showed stab wounds but there were none in the man's coat or vest. Had it in fact been a murder or was it a bizarre suicide? The death was ultimately ruled a suicide, and Valentine and LaGuardia, rising above this crisis in their relations, went on to work for many years together.

A more serious mayoral incident, and one almost equally bizarre, was LaGuardia's attack upon the national housing administration and the ensuing disruption of the City Housing Authority. In November 1937 the implementation of the National Housing Act was getting under way. The first chairman of the federal housing authority was a New Yorker, Nathan Straus, whose selection by Roosevelt had been widely praised. There was every reason to believe that LaGuardia would be comfortable with the setup and anxious to cooperate. Instead, when Straus issued an invitation to the heads of local housing authorities to meet in Washington, LaGuardia exploded. Calling on Straus to "quit star-gazing and get down to work," he announced that no New York official would attend any conference except a hearing on a concrete application as required by law. "For ten years we have had nothing but conferences. The law is perfectly clear."

Four days later Charles Abrams, a well known housing expert and counsel to the New York authority, resigned in protest against LaGuardia's ban on attending the Washington conference. Langdon Post, chairman of the New York authority, agreed not to attend, but this seemed only to add fuel to the mayor's ire. He would get "damned rough" if the federal officials delayed further. Straus renewed the invitation, and this time Post protested. LaGuardia was trying to dominate the Housing Authority in a manner unauthorized by law, he asserted; and he recommended sending a representative to the second conference. At this, the mayor declared that he "accepted Mr. Post's resignation." Post made it plain he had not resigned, or at least that he would carry on until a successor was chosen. "Well, that's interesting," said LaGuardia, and turning to his secretary: "Stone, raise your right hand." After Lester Stone had taken the oath, LaGuardia concluded, "Well, that's that."

Newspapermen present at this extraordinary scene reminded the mayor he did not have the legal right to name a chairman; that power remained with members of the board. "Well," said he, "they'd better elect [Stone], or there will be a new board." Post's rejoinder, not unapt in the circumstances, was that the mayor was "being silly."

When the first allocations of housing money were made to eight cities, New York was not among them. No one from New York attended the Washington conference and the city's applications had been withdrawn to make them conform to the new law. LaGuardia now took complete charge (which had perhaps been his aim from the beginning) and in Washington presented personally to Straus two major projects, Red Hook and Queensbridge, their costs being almost equal to what the eight other cities had received. The meeting was apparently amicable, though Straus remarked pointedly that New York was beginning two weeks late. LaGuardia and Straus were to work on good terms, and in replacing Stone, who had the housing chairmanship temporarily, the mayor pulled one of those surprises that so often redeemed his worst errors. He named an able and experienced builder, Alfred Rheinstein, who turned out also to be a first-class administrator.

The mayor, as Post remarked, had acted in a silly way; he also had trenched upon the independence of the New York City Housing Authority. It is true, as we shall see later, that authorities could claim for themselves a disturbing degree of autonomy; but in the field of housing, freedom from political pressures was necessary. The selection of sites and the choice of tenants opened paths to patronage and corruption; to attract the private capital the assurance of independence was a prime requisite. In this as in other cases LaGuardia found himself not able to endure the frustrations of an authority set apart from his control. The threat to get a "new board" if he did not like the actions of the existing one was to be leveled in far graver circumstances against the Board of Education. In the break with Post, LaGuardia was playing a dangerous game.

We turn, as the year 1937 runs out, to happier matters. A reporter interviewing the mayor on the eve of his fifty-fifth birthday was amazed at the youthful appearance and restless energy of the man. To one who had followed his career in the Congress, he seemed to show less wear and tear than any of his contemporaries. For the birthday itself he was in Washington attending the annual dinner of the Gridiron Club; the president and he were the two guest speakers. LaGuardia, according to Ickes, was the star of the evening, "sparkling and witty," speaking without notes and reviewing, in an elaborate parody of a football game, the crisscrossings and conflicts, the advances and retreats, of the mayoral election. Farley came in for some more kidding. Ickes was especially pleased to hear LaGuardia take note of his own contribution to the victory. "It was decent of him," he remarked with that pleasure in being flattered which runs through the diaries. "All too often a man accepts support and then forgets all about it."

A last ritual was to be performed before the old year expired, but from this LaGuardia kept apart. The new charter, which had been accepted by the voters in the 1936 elections, would come into effect after the required year's delay—on January 1, 1937. Under its provisions the Board of Aldermen would be abolished, to be replaced by a new City Council. The last meeting of the board was held on December 22, an occasion which strongly affected some of its older members (though not so much as to preclude the usual, partisan criticism of the mayor) and evoked both sad and raucous memories of the past.

The Board of Aldermen had existed before the city got its charter in 1686. When New York became the first American city to have a municipal government, in 1784, the Board of Aldermen was a part of it. Morris, looking forward to its successor, the City Council, was optimistic as usual, but amid the enthusiastic applause of the dying body, proposed the establishment of a "Last Man's Club" to preserve "the best of old New York." Stories were told, most of them more sentimental than reverential, about the past members of the board who had slept or bickered through so many generations of New York life. There was the time, for instance, when the board was considering new gondolas for the lake in Central Park. One member, awaking from his afternoon nap, grasped imperfectly the nature of the discussion. "Buy two," said he, "and let nature take its course."

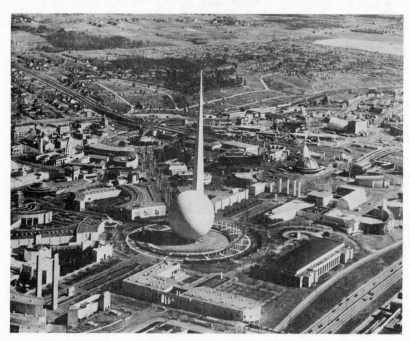

19. Between Peace and War. UPI

PART TWO

1938

6

The Feel of Power

A New Government

On January 1, 1938, just after midnight, LaGuardia was sworn in for the second time as mayor in Judge Seabury's house. Some forty persons attended—among old counselors and supporters: Windels, Berle, Burlingham; among political allies: Alex Rose and Kenneth Simpson; among comrades-in-arms: Valentine and Goldwater. Newcomers to the ceremony this year were Mr. and Mrs. Thomas Dewey. The city's first independent prosecutor in twenty years, young, brash, and ambitious, even Dewey could not have known as he watched the mayor's moment of glory that in five years he would be taking the oath as governor (and four years after that running for the presidency) while LaGuardia trudged on in the increasingly burdensome tasks of city administration.

The only Fusion government to have succeeded itself now regrouped and expanded its forces. Not only would there be the changes that occur regularly at such a watershed. The new charter had become operative and such institutions as the Planning Commission and deputy mayor's office were to be created and staffed, as well as several adjustments made in the functioning of city departments. LaGuardia took the opportunity to add some notable figures to his entourage and also to strengthen ties with his constituency. The bridge building was especially to be seen in his relations with the local Republican party, and with the Italian-American community which he had made uneasy by his repeated attacks on the European dictators.

The City Planning Commission, chief innovation under the charter, was immediately launched, to be temporarily headed by Berle and then by an outstanding recruit from the New Deal's inner circle, Rexford G. Tugwell. To the great joy of the organization, LaGuardia chose for the new post of deputy mayor a well-known Republican magistrate. Henry H. Curran had served as Manhattan borough president during LaGuardia's term as aldermanic president and in 1921 had defeated him in a bitter primary. The appointment seemed to show magnanimity as well as political prudence. LaGuardia expressed the hope that Curran and his successors would continue in office regardless of electoral changes, and indicated that he would now shed some of the detail of administration. It must be said that few took either of these pious observations very seriously.

Within his official family LaGuardia promoted to chairman of the Civil Service Commission his brilliant but erratic young protégé Paul Kern, and from Dewey's staff brought over William B. Herlands to replace the Socialist reformer Paul Blanshard as commissioner of investigation. Windels wanted to return to private practice, though as the mayor's personal lawyer he was to remain close; and to his post LaGuardia promoted William C. Chanler, the young assistant corporation counsel who had come into city government from a partnership in the powerful law firm headed by Henry L. Stimson.

Chanler had been a McKee supporter in the 1933 campaign, but to LaGuardia this seemed to make no difference. Before accepting a post in the new administration, Chanler nevertheless insisted that the mayor see and initial a particularly strong letter he had written in opposition to his candidacy. "Damn good political letter," the mayor scrawled at the bottom; "come over and write them for us." In the next four years Chanler made a highly effective record in prosecuting city cases. At forty-two, a brisk, confident figure, a graduate of St. Marks and Harvard, he carried himself with a grace which was still to distinguish him forty years later. A great favorite with the LaGuardia family, Chanler was known as a hard-bitten sailor and as a big-game hunter who hunted only with bow and arrow. He would have his battles with LaGuardia, and would yield to his imperious will, but he never doubted that work for the city carried large rewards.

Berle, his office of city chamberlain abolished by the new charter and his work of organizing the Planning Commission completed, was ready to cash in on his "ole Uncle Franklin's" promise of a good berth in Washington. "Bob," said he to his familiar adversary the parks commissioner, before leaving to become assistant secretary of state, "it's all very well for you to fuss with street openings. As for me, I'm off to settle the Chinese question." LaGuardia salted his farewell with a touch of irony, or was it simply a touch of envy? He hoped, he said, "that very soon the peace of the world would be so secure that he will be able to come back to us."

In place of Berle at the head of finances, in the newly created post of city treasurer, LaGuardia appointed Almerindo Portfolio. Retired at forty-six, Portfolio had turned over his highly successful coat manufacturing business to seven faithful employees and had set out on a journey around the world. Now president of the Bank of Sicily, a dapper bachelor living at the Plaza Hotel, he did not look his sixty years. On his first day in office workmen were called in to take down the large photograph of Franklin Roosevelt left by his predecessor. Portfolio was a Republican as well as a highly visible representative of the mayor's Italian constituency.

One further change put Kenneth Dayton into the key post of budget director, replacing McGoldrick. An original Fusionist, he had come into city government as an assistant to Deutsch, for whom he masterminded the investigations which nettled the mayor. But LaGuardia recognized his ability, not least his ability to say no in one of the city's crucial but most thankless jobs. Yet he could still be a positive force. "The important thing," Dayton said, "is to keep alert . . . so that at the right time you can still say yes." He was to serve LaGuardia with a minimum of friction until the end.

The mayor's office was now rearranged and his staff assigned to new quarters at the south side of City Hall. The room where the mayor had stormed and struggled during his first term was given over to the new deputy mayor, and the mayor moved across to the far larger and more impressive Blue Room where committee meetings and civic ceremonies had traditionally been held. It was a huge space, with the diminutive figure of the mayor crouched over a desk at the far end, "like Mussolini's office," one member of his staff was to recall. Here LaGuardia had grouped around him the team of aides headed by Stanley Howe, with Clendenin Ryan, Edmund L. Palmieri, and Mitzi Somach among its more conspicuous members.

Thus was the executive branch of city government deployed for action. In other parts of City Hall the new City Council, and the reconstituted Board of Estimate, were ready to begin their work.

Organizing the Council

Successor to the unlamented Board of Aldermen, the City Council met on January 3, launched amid high hopes that it would write a fresh chapter in New York's legislative history. The council's president, Newbold Morris, had taken the oath two days before, in the crowded aldermanic committee room where Democratic chieftains, having dominated the scene in years gone by, now formed a tattered remnant. "One of the brightest stars in the Fusion administration," Judge Seabury said of Morris on that day, and indeed the tall, youthful figure, aristocratic in bearing but modest in manner, appeared a fitting representative of the new type of civic leader.

Morris had followed a conventional route from Groton and Yale into the family law firm where he might well have spent the rest of his life working on decedent estates. In politics he saw a way out, the chance for excitement and for the breath of a new life. He was, after all, the grandson of New York's seventy-first mayor, Ambrose C. Kingsland; politics was in his blood.

Yet politics was in many ways a strange calling for Newbold Morris. Possessing all the attributes of character and background which would seem to assure success, he could never bring himself to be quite at ease in the give and take of public life. He was perhaps too diffident, too self-effacing. The qualities which should have made him most attractive, his lack of arrogance or sense of superiority, had, at times, the effect of making him seem vague and somehow inconsequential.

When Fusion came, Morris's hopes were high. In 1934 he succeeded to the seat in the Board of Alderman which had been held by Joseph Clark Baldwin, and in 1936, as we have seen, made an unsuccessful run for aldermanic president. His apprenticeship as an alderman might have tempered his optimism in regard to the City Council. But Morris was not easily disillusioned; he had been trained, besides, in an even older tradition. Despite forays into politics, he had managed to maintain a belief in the classic virtues of service and responsibility bred into him as a schoolboy. He had only to slip to be reminded of the precepts and examples of Endicott

20. A passionate voice in the new City Council, labor member B. Charney Vladeck. ACME

Peabody, headmaster of Groton. "I can feel his knee in the small of my back," Morris would say.

Other independent figures had emerged from the fires of proportional representation to take their seats in the new council. Genevieve Earle, the only woman on the council, was a forceful civic leader who had long been active in nonpartisan politics and was closely identified with social causes. The reform constituency of New York considered her one of its own, and her presence greatly enhanced the council's image. Robert K. Straus, thirty-two years old, son of the late ambassador to Turkey, had come into the arena with the mayor's strong backing. A graduate of Harvard and of Cambridge, England, he had served as secretary to the original Berle–Moley–Tugwell brain trust, and now promised qualities of initiative and commitment to service such as had never been a hallmark of the old Board of Aldermen.

An independent of a different kind and from another background was B. Charney Vladeck, a brilliant scholar and keen debater, who had been imprisoned for revolutionary activities in his native Russia. In America he earned his living as a writer and lecturer before becoming business manager of the Jewish *Daily Forward.* LaGuardia appointed him to the newly created Housing

Authority in 1935, where he served until he was elected to the
council. Vladeck was not a newcomer to the rough and tumble of
politics. In 1917 he had been the lone Socialist member of the
Board of Aldermen, and the Tammany members of that day had
learned to appreciate the talents of their unlikely colleague. He
served now as the council's minority leader.

Morris hoped that the council would conduct its business on a
high plane of reason and common sense. "We'll just debate quietly
and objectively for the good of the city," he told his fellow members at a dinner he gave for them the night before the first meeting.
He imagined them arranging themselves about him—twenty-six
good men at a round table. He learned soon enough there were few
knights among them.

It became apparent from the very first day that the council did
not conceive itself as a band of twenty-six, but as two opposed
groups of thirteen each. On one side were thirteen organization
Democrats. On the other side was a coalition composed of three
Republicans, three members of the ALP, and five independents.
With the council president prepared to vote whenever a tie occurred, the Fusion coalition appeared to have the edge. It was a
cheerful Morris who called the first meeting to order. He had
reckoned, however, without the desperation of the Democrats
who, having lost the Board of Estimate (as they had previously lost
the executive office), were determined to prevail in the only arena
left to them.

The situation was one the Democrats had never faced before.
Tammany had always dominated the Board of Aldermen, just as it
had dominated the Board of Estimate. A lone independent or a few
stray Republicans had posed no threat to the machine. But proportional representation, which Tammany had fought unsuccessfully,
spelled the end of the Democrats' monolithic rule. One old-time
Democrat plaintively recalled the days when a vote in the Board
of Aldermen would be sixty-two ayes, one nay, and two not voting.
"Now," he said, "if one man becomes sick on our side, we're
sunk."

The crucial test of strength, which was to determine the legislative history of the next several years, came to a head over the
seemingly inconsequential issue of a vice-chairman. The Democrats
named John Cashmore of Brooklyn; the Fusion bloc put up James
A. Burke. The democrats voted thirteen strong. The opposition
could muster only twelve votes because one of its members, an

ALPer from the Bronx who would one day make himself felt even more decisively by his presence in New York politics, on this day played a crucial role by his absence. Michael Quill was in Ireland, getting married. Without him, the vote stood at thirteen to twelve, and the Democrats claimed victory.

"Not at all," said Morris, citing the new charter which required a majority vote. "Thirteen is not a majority of twenty-six."

"It *is* a majority of those present and voting," the Democrats screamed, denouncing Morris as a Hitler and a thief.

The fight was on. For the next three months New Yorkers were treated to scenes of battle as the Democrats waged all-out war for control, and Morris and his motley cohorts closed ranks in opposition. The council meetings—unpredictable, rude, disorderly— were broadcast over WNYC and became one of the most popular shows in town. They were suspenseful, too, because nobody could be quite sure how the fight would turn out. Winners one day became losers the next as suits and countersuits were filed, and injunctions issued and ignored.

Tammany may have thought it was indeed "sunk" as a result of Newbold Morris's skillful maneuvering. But it had a last resort, a reservoir of power when all other channels appeared lost. The courts remained largely under justices whom Tammany patronage had put in their favored positions. It was to the courts that the dispute over organization now went, and on April 15 Cashmore was upheld as the validly elected vice-chairman. For the first time the council settled down to its real business.

To understand the passion with which the battle had been fought it is necessary to appreciate the full extent of the victory. With the Democrats in all the key positions, Tammany was now in complete control of the new council. No legislation could reach the floor, no bill could be voted out of committee, unless it served the interests of the Democratic leadership. Defeat of the county reform bill, and the 1938 budget with its protection for unnecessary jobholders, were both the work of this leadership. If emergency relief measures and essential new taxes were voted favorably in this first year, it was done grudgingly and under the heaviest public pressure. A share of the credit for these more statesmanlike results went to the minority leader Vladeck, who was a voice of conscience until he was tragically cut off. Newbold Morris never admitted to despair; La-Guardia, who raged and cajoled as his moods changed, would turn to the wider forum of public opinion to gain his ends.

Stanley Isaacs and His Strange Protégé

The Board of Estimate had survived intact under the new charter, a conclave of eight men who were supposed to act as the business managers of the city but whose roots were deep within its political structure. In the board shaped by the 1937 elections Fusion held a safe measure of control. Under the weighted voting system, La-Guardia, Morris, and McGoldrick counted together for twelve votes; borough presidents Ingersoll, Isaacs, and Palma provided more than adequate backup. The drama of the council was absent from meetings of the board; but subtle shifts in interest and alle-giance, unexpected acts of defiance or independence, would make its course fascinating to follow. Even such Fusion loyalists as Morris and McGoldrick could on occasion threaten to revolt, calling into play all the force of personal and political persuasion the mayor could exert.

One figure whose independence was never wholly crushed was the newly elected borough president of Manhattan. Stanley Isaacs held a position important in itself, made doubly so by his own personality and his outstanding, if somewhat undependable, gifts. A handsome man of great charm, the son and grandson of noted civic figures in New York, Isaacs was a Jewish counterpart to the Protestant Newbold Morris. As with Morris, it was expected of Stanley Isaacs that he would follow in the paternal way, devoting himself to philanthropic causes. But for him, too, politics acted as a magnet. He had followed with enthusiasm the career of Theodore Roosevelt, from the days when he served as police commissioner in New York; he became an active member of the same "silk stocking" Republican club from which Newbold Morris and La-Guardia himself had been launched. He had worked for LaGuardia in the 1933 campaign. Then, at fifty-six, he found himself cast into one of the major city roles, associated with the fiery mayor whose ideas were closely in harmony with his own.

Isaacs's was a vote which LaGuardia could usually count on, as his intelligence and character were of the kind LaGuardia admired. Yet relations between them were curiously prickly. To see these two men in precarious harness tells much about each of them, not least about the mayor, and gives an insight into one of the much-publicized issues of this period. At the personal level, there was something about Isaacs that irked LaGuardia. The courtly qualities

21. A humane presence on the Board of Estimate, the borough president of Manhattan, Stanley M. Isaacs. WIDE WORLD

which LaGuardia admired in Burlingham only irritated him in Isaacs. Isaacs's air of somehow being above the mob released in the mayor a deep-rooted desire to take him down a peg.

Correspondence between these two men shows the mayor prepared even on the most minor issues to pick flaws or to humiliate, and relishing the excuse to pounce upon his friend when an error of judgment or an act of questionable loyalty has been committed. Thus Isaacs, recuperating at home from a painful operation, brings to the mayor's attention a *New Yorker* cartoon suggesting the need for improved traffic signs. "Sorry you had to get the idea from the *New Yorker* in your present position," the mayor replies. "May I suggest that you read engineering periodicals instead." A passage in Isaacs's annual report occasions this rebuke: "The attempted humor . . . is neither humorous nor necessary as I see it—except to get you into another controversy, and you have had enough." "Now that you are nursing a bad leg," the mayor concludes, "you at least do not have to nurse a sore *toches.*"

These were minor examples of pique, however, compared to LaGuardia's scorn when he felt Isaacs had in some way betrayed him. On one famous occasion, arguing for higher wages for the sewer workers under his jurisdiction—a change which would entail minor increases in the mayor's budget—the overzealous Isaacs showed a film before the Board of Estimate dramatizing working conditions underground. The mayor was indignant and Isaacs attempted an apology. "It will take more than three pages of a single-spaced letter," LaGuardia replied, "to blot out the shame you have brought upon yourself by your inexcusable, unpardonable action."

Yet, as often happened with LaGuardia's outbursts, the attack seemed to clear the air, at least until the next affront. Isaacs himself didn't seem to hold such behavior against the mayor. He was a frequent speaker on behalf of the administration in places like the City Club and United Neighborhood Houses where he carried considerable weight. And LaGuardia continued to go to dinner at the Isaacs house on 96th Street.

Politically the Manhattan office under Isaacs was an asset to the mayor. LaGuardia had given his own deputy sanitation commissioner, the able engineer Walter Binger, to be Isaacs's commissioner of borough works. And Isaacs saw to it that qualified men were hired for the other engineering jobs that had formerly been filled by Tammany district leaders. That he did so and was still able to satisfy both Kenneth Simpson and Alex Rose—and the mayor, on occasion—says something for Isaacs's political skills as well as for his hiring procedures.

In one instance, however, his political skills deserted him and the lapse was to cost him dearly. Early in his term he brought into the office a young man named Simon Gerson to handle public relations. The fact that Gerson was an avowed Communist was not a disqualification in Isaacs's opinion. After all, he reasoned, if a card-carrying Communist could run for public office, he could certainly be hired for a minor post. Following his usual procedure he mentioned the appointment to Simpson and LaGuardia and there were no objections. As a matter of fact, Paul Kern told him that LaGuardia was rather pleased to be able to give something to the labor party which had been pestering him for jobs. "Good," he had said. "This'll get the boys off my neck."

Others were considerably less sanguine about the presence of an avowed Communist in a city job. The *World Telegram* and the *Journal* opened attacks that grew more heated as Gerson remained in his job and Isaacs refused to remove him. Anti-Communist sentiment increased until LaGuardia, too, came under heavy attack by the American Legion and other patriotic groups.

Ready to admit that he had made a mistake in appointing Gerson, Isaacs was not yet ready to let him go, or to force his resignation. For two years the battle raged, the legion roared and battalions of pickets marched up and down in front of the borough president's house. Finally, in September 1940, Gerson gave up and quietly resigned. But the damage had been done. By 1941 what had been an embarrassment became a millstone. The Republicans would not take the chance of running Isaacs for borough president again, LaGuardia concurred, and Isaacs was dropped from the ticket.

LaGuardia was acting as a friend when he told an anxious Edith Isaacs just after Gerson was appointed: "Cheer up, this won't last. You'll see. They'll find another victim and Gerson will be forgotten." But Gerson was not forgotten; he haunted Stanley Isaacs for the rest of his political life.

Bit Between His Teeth

Still at the start of his second term, LaGuardia turned to the issues which had formed the substance of his campaign and would preoccupy him over the next two years. Erratic and impulsive initiatives marking the postelection period gave way, first, to a concerted drive for control of the city's fate and then to a drive for the national recognition which might enable him to master even larger forces. At the end of his first year in office, when asked what he most regretted about his job, the mayor had answered without hesitation "lack of power." Now he sought power, systematically and unrelentingly. It was not power for its own sake (though LaGuardia could relish pure power and the excitements it brought) but the capacity to deal effectively with major political problems.

On February 19 the mayor left home where for several days he had been confined by illness to deliver before a luncheon of the City Affairs Committee one of the best speeches of his career. It was witty and defiant, the talk of a man completely in control of himself and of the situation he faced. He picked out the enemies one by one and issued a call to arms against them. The enemies were those agencies, boards, and institutions which resisted the cleansing force of the people's government—pockets of patronage, enclaves of bureaucracy; and, most important of all, the state government which from a privileged sanctuary treated the city like a stepchild. One of his targets, the Transit Commission, issued a statement the next day condemning the talk: the mayor, it said, had engaged in denunciation of "nearly every agency that might stop him from governing the city without restraint." The speech had been "unusual" in the variety of persons and bodies denounced: "He even denounced the pushcart peddlers."

But LaGuardia was after bigger game than the peddlers. He saw the Transit Commission standing in the way of the city's control of its own mass transportation system, its members the beneficiaries of favoritism for which they rendered scant return. He saw in the building division of the Board of Education an archaic shelter for incompetence and inefficiency, subject to a blatant and unconcealed political domination. The courts he portrayed as a bloated system, riddled with patronage, beyond the reach of a city government condemned to pay its exorbitant bills. Above all problems lay the issue of home rule for the city. New York with its vast resources was at the mercy of a state government basically unsympathetic and unresponsive.

LaGuardia was not making idle threats; he was prepared to take on the enemy in whatever form it appeared. In at least some cases he was successful. The Board of Education reorganized its building division and got on with the business of a $40 million program for new schools. The Transit Commission was eventually abolished, though LaGuardia saw that its members were moved to new jobs. County offices, the rich source of Tammany's patronage, came up before the City Council toward the end of 1938, and in a twenty-hour session tense with incipient violence ("If I come down there," cried Newbold Morris, "it will be to crack somebody's head") proposals for their abolition were turned down. The stage had been set though, and a referendum in 1941 was finally to eliminate them. Even the peddlers were abolished, as LaGuardia constructed large indoor markets where their wares could be sold without interruption for traffic.

The courts proved a far more intractable issue. A complicated system with thirty-six hundred employees, the lower courts were paid entirely by the city, the State Supreme Court and the appellate division jointly by the city and the state. The whole was immune to examination by the city's budgetary authorities, secure in a chain of patronage which led to inevitable corruption. Clerks, court attendants, and stenographers were constantly having their salaries raised; and when LaGuardia refused to accede, mandamuses for their payment were issued. Meanwhile, judges of the State Supreme Court received salaries well above those of the chief justice of the U.S. Supreme Court, and the surrogate's clerk was paid more than the city's commissioners of parks or police.

In April LaGuardia carried his attack on the court system to a meeting of the New York Bar Association. Introduced by no less a figure than Henry Stimson, with men like Seabury and Windels in his audience, LaGuardia presented a two-hour lecture with charts and graphs, showing the absurdities of a bureaucracy which cost more to maintain than the whole federal judicial establishment including the U.S. Supreme Court. The next day, as if in deliberate defiance, a local justice handed down a decision allowing additional pay for twenty-one employees of the Brooklyn supreme court and also directing the comptroller to provide salaries for three newly created positions. LaGuardia returned to the fray with an irritated gesture. A letter to justices of the court system reminded them that official stationery was paid for by the city and was subject only to official use. "You will, therefore," he continued, "keep a careful record . . . accounting for such stationery and the nature of the official business for which it is used."

Burlingham had lent the prestige of his presence to the Bar Association address; but in private he had doubts about the way LaGuardia was pursuing his war against the courts. Better than most he knew the depth of the mayor's mistrust of courts and lawyers, and he knew how easily men confuse personal predelictions with public causes. "In my opinion your attacks, so often repeated and so persistent, accomplish no good and do great harm," Burlingham wrote to the mayor. He implored him to weigh the importance of court decisions to the maintenance of civil rights and the rights of labor. "No one knows this better than you," he continued; "and yet deliberately, and not in passion, you have been playing a role I think unworthy of you, and I am truly grieved."

Incorrigible, LaGuardia noted in his reply that Burlingham still seemed to believe in "the divine right of judges." "Do not worry," he added, "for the worst is yet to come." The letter was signed "with personal regards and love."

Painful as was the maladministration of the courts to LaGuardia's sense of efficient housekeeping, the substance of judicial opinions could be even worse. Patronage had left Tammany Democrats entrenched in most judicial posts, and their bias became evident at crucial junctures. It was the courts which had given the balance of power to Democrats in the City Council; it was the courts which,

at approximately the same time, upheld the Tammany budget pro-
tecting the jobs of sixty-five county officials. LaGuardia raged and
fumed. "If all the courts in all the world" upheld the budget, it
would still be the most infamous "ever adopted in the world at any
time, anywhere." On other occasions he found himself frustrated
by the intrusion of judicial authority in matters where he felt the
executive should clearly have the last word. These went from traffic
control to the city's power to prevent dual job holding.

This authority of the courts was not all political; it was being
exercised in a continuing effort to determine the bounds of state–
city relationships. Vague in setting the original boundaries between
state and city powers, the state constitution created a no-man's land
where (in the words of one contemporary observer) "state and
local responsibilities wander almost at will, stumbling on the way
through the unexpected barbed wire and shell-holes of court decisions." The increasing complexity of government intensified the
issue. The only answer seemed to lie in a reexamination of the
divided powers and a strong campaign for home rule.

Fighting for Home Rule

In February, at roughly the same time as his City Affairs Committee speech, LaGuardia launched an attack on Governor Lehman
and the state legislature. The issues were taxes and the taxing
power, and several political strands were involved in a bitter contest. The mayor was being assailed in the council for expenditures
which had forced an increase in the property tax to the highest level
in the city's history; his administration, it was claimed, constituted
"the most expensive luxury the people have enjoyed for many
years." Simultaneously, relief costs were rising. Already tops in the
nation, New York's relief grants were considered inadequate to
meet basic needs by a mayoral committee of inquiry. The mayor at
the same time was in a controversy with Somervell over the number
of men being transferred to home relief on the grounds that they
were unemployable and therefore not subject to federal funding.
In short, LaGuardia needed more money. He accused the state
authorities of depriving the city of its due.

The city had passed a utility tax of 3 percent; the state, finding
it feasible and attractive, had imposed a utility tax of 2 percent, thus
leaving the city with the benefit of only 1 percent, or with a loss

of $12 million. On February 6 LaGuardia called the first press conference of his new term, specifically to warn that relief payments would have to be cut if the state did not restore the utility taxes which it had "carried off bodily" from the city. "The mayor cannot print money," the reporters were told; "he cannot revise the multiplication tables." Then turning back to his correspondence, he refused to answer further questions.

By March the feud between the governor and the mayor had deteriorated to name-calling, and the whole fracas would have seemed shallow politics (which in part it was) had it not been linked with LaGuardia's overall campaign to point up the necessity for home rule. In a letter to Albany LaGuardia demanded that the state, failing to restore the utility tax, assume the full burden of relief. In his reply Lehman found the mayor's arguments "inaccurate and erroneous." He chided LaGuardia for failing properly to supervise the collection of sales taxes, and added that the city possessed ample taxing power if it would use it. To which LaGuardia replied: "I wrote a letter to a statesman and I received a reply from a politician." He cancelled attendance at a dinner of the Albany legislative correspondents where he would have been expected to sit at the same table with the governor.

By the end of March he was demanding a special session of the legislature on relief and threatening to dim the streetlights and close branches of the public library. Even more drastically, he ordered a 10 percent cut in home relief allowances. When the legislature adjourned without heeding his plea, the heat was on the City Council to come up with new taxes. On March 26 the new taxes were passed—"Lehman taxes, not LaGuardia taxes," the mayor asserted. Relief cuts were restored.

That was a kind of victory; at least public moneys had been raised, and the issue of home rule had been dramatized through political infighting, as no one could do better than LaGuardia. But the larger solutions, it was evident, lay with the state constitutional convention, called for April of that year. The eighth such convention since 1776, it was intended to bring the often-amended state charter of 1894 into harmony with modern needs. It was, however, doomed to be highly political, related to the forthcoming autumn's gubernatorial campaign. Upstate Republicans were in control. Despite the omens, LaGuardia hoped to secure amendments affecting the basic balance between the state and New York City.

Court reform got nowhere; the return to the cities of control over salaries and pensions of the school systems was rejected. The mayor then tried for a general provision granting wider home rule. In a much heralded appearance before the convention he carried forward the arguments which had become his overriding theme, demanding clear and understandable safeguards against state takeover of municipal powers. The city at the very least should be able to adopt laws amending or repealing state legislative acts; the state should be forbidden to pass special acts affecting the cities, even after emergency messages of the governor. The home rule amendment adopted by the convention in August was more satisfactory than might have been anticipated. It met most of the mayor's tests, and by specifically giving the cities the right to act in fields from which the state had been excluded, confined the no-man's land hitherto open to judicial interpretation. LaGuardia would still complain, however, that the draft left "political hacks" frozen into city payrolls.

We are, however, getting ahead of our story. In April LaGuardia undertook spectacular diversions to test his own power and to lay the groundwork for further advances in the city and in national politics. A nationwide broadcast early in the month dealt with U.S. trade policy in regard to Latin America. Nazis and Fascists were subsidizing exports to gain new markets in this strategically important area; LaGuardia proposed direct federal bounties to undercut the dictators and expand American production as an aid to unemployment. Secretary Hull, an inveterate free trader, shot down the idea, and newspapers generally wondered what the mayor was doing entering upon this new field. Berle, now assistant secretary of state, had surely had a hand in the proposal. Was he gunning for Hull? Were both he and LaGuardia aiming to head off a 1940 presidential aspirant notable for his conservatism?

The mayor's next move was less ambiguous. On April 20 he left New York for a week-long foray into the West, his principal objective a speech to the Wichita Falls, Texas, Chamber of Commerce. There he rested four days with an old friend, Dr. O. B. Kiel, medical officer in the aviation unit which LaGuardia had commanded in Italy. The speech reverted to his well-developed economic and political philosophy: the nation's ills were due to lack of purchasing power; common interest linked the needs of urban and rural communities, of eastern and western regions. A political shakeup was in the making, with conservatives—many of them big businessmen and professional politicians—on one side, and on the other side, progressives, laborers, and farmers.

Wherever he passed LaGuardia left a trail of colorful stories and pungent quotes. In a brief stop at Guthrie, Oklahoma, he donned boots, spurs, and a sombrero to parade on a snorting cowpony before 100,000 cheering onlookers. The Cheyenne and Arapahoe Indians hailed him as the coming president. But he disclaimed politics: "I came out to get some western airs and some of the western virtues." Asked about Franklin Roosevelt: "I would consider him a very distinguished member of the faculty of my school of thought."

Meanwhile, in Madison, Wisconsin, important political events were taking place. The La Follette brothers, Governor Phil and Senator Bob, announced the founding of the National Progressives of America. An emotional gathering witnessed the unveiling of the new party's symbol, a circle with a cross inside it. LaGuardia, who had lingered upon his journey and punctuated it with numerous stops, now found that pressing business required him to skip Madison. He talked with the La Follettes by telephone; he had for his representative at the event none other than Berle. But he was cautious, very cautious, in his comments. The vast shakeup he foresaw would take place within the framework of existing parties. "It's all right," he added, when pressed for his opinion of the Madison rally. The general feeling was that the La Follette initiative had been premature, and also a bit scary. The mayor preferred to keep his place within the New Deal, where he had a formidable base and, it seemed, powerful friends.

LaGuardia returned with his national visibility much enhanced and with his appetite for future journeys whetted. His constituency in New York had thoroughly enjoyed the pictures of their mayor at Indian ceremonies and under the Texas sun. The *New York Times* so far departed from its usually reserved and formal language as to comment editorially upon the mayor's epic indulgences. "Mayor LaGuardia works hard, often too hard. He recuperates by playing hard. His rest is largely motion. . . . His temper and constitution are equally suited for labor and for frolic. He deserves the good times he has had." The *Times* added that "his occasional discharge of political speeches was another relief to his system." Perhaps. But perhaps, too, the mayor's excursions into national and international affairs had a more serious, and were intended to have a more influential, effect on the future than was immediately evident.

Summer in Queens

Summer of 1938 brought for LaGuardia the now-familiar change
of scene and with it a change of mood. There was, however, little
change in pace, for the mayor never really altered his work habits.
At his suggestion the police might blossom out in white gabardine
with white shorts, ties, and shoes, but the mayor would go right on
working in his dark suit, only removing his jacket as a concession
to the heat. Summer or winter he was himself, the same and yet
unpredictable; he exercised his functions, as one mayor watcher
wrote in this happy period, "with the vigor and unconventionality
of genius."

The mayor chose for his summer city hall the city building at the
unfinished World's Fair. The Fair's president, Grover Whalen, was
not altogether pleased by the incursion and was absent from the
brief welcoming ceremony. But LaGuardia enjoyed being amid the
bustle of construction, and the *Times* thought it appropriate that
"the mayor would be restoring the center to the center"; he would
be Exhibit A in the city's first exhibition building. The mayor's
quarters were dusty and hot when he arrived—the building's air
conditioning system was not working—and a picket line of striking
workers parted silently as the official black limousine came through.
Perhaps most upsetting to the mayor, a line of flagpoles stood bare
of flags.

The lack of amenities was turned, however, to an advantage. He
declared that as for himself "he liked the place fine," and then
ribbed the long-suffering boys of Room 9, who had been expecting
an agreeable change from their cramped quarters in City Hall, on
their taste for mint juleps and limousines. A little later, visiting
WPA headquarters in Manhattan where modest rooms were assigned to the press, he returned to the theme: "Why, the City Hall
reporters require a villa, tennis courts, and bathing beaches," he
told the WPA staff. It was still in the spirit of fun, very different
from the bitterly strained relations which at a later time were to
develop between LaGuardia and the press.

The summer offered its ceremonial occasions. On one memorable day LaGuardia, joined by Senator Wagner and Housing Administrator Straus, climbed into the cab of a steam shovel and turned
the earth of Red Hook in Brooklyn, the first housing project in the
country to get started under the new federal housing act. It was a

22. Dedicating Red Hook Houses. Palms courtesy of the Parks Department. July 18, 1938. NEW YORK CITY HOUSING AUTHOR-ITY

beginning which meant much to LaGuardia. Assistant Secretary of State Berle had come up from Washington for the occasion and the mayor's official family turned out in force. The Riverside, a steam-boat from the city's own fleet, took the party from Pier A at the Battery to Red Hook Park for the ceremonies. Valentine, Isaacs, Kern, McGoldrick, Vladeck, and Binger made the trip standing on the crowded deck. Landing, they were greeted by Moses and by New York City Housing Administrator Alfred Rheinstein. Quar-rels were forgotten, or at least laid aside, as Straus paid tribute to the mayor for his energetic support of the program. LaGuardia, his public charges of "star-gazing delays" lightly glossed over, had only praise for his frequent antagonist. From Red Hook, amid many expressions of good feeling, the group sailed up the East River to inspect the site of Queensbridge Houses.

Other ground breakings were less heralded, but they required the mayor's presence, and gave him a chance to expound on favor-ite topics. A new criminal courts building on Center Street was started, and a new Hunter College building on Park Avenue. Queens saw the beginning of a new hospital. On each of these occasions the mayor took the opportunity to treat city improvements against a national background, constantly returning to his theme that many governmental problems, once handled on a local basis, were really federal responsibilities.

Unanticipated diversions occurred during the hot summer. On a sunny day in mid-July New Yorkers filled the streets to cheer the young aviator Howard Hughes, even then a mythic figure, who had just circled the globe in a record-breaking three days and nineteen hours. The entire world had followed Hughes and his four-man crew in the silver monoplane, *New York World's Fair 1939*. After some confusion at the airport LaGuardia managed to meet the flyers when they landed at Floyd Bennett Field, and the next day he greeted them officially at City Hall.

Hughes insisted that the crew and their families as well as the seventeen ground technicians who had provided backup data share in the festivities. LaGuardia had invited the RFC chairman, Jesse Jones of Texas, to represent Hughes's home state. The day was stifling and the council chamber was already filled to overflowing when the group arrived. But nothing could affect the mayor's delight. It was as if his own dreams had been fulfilled by the shy, unassuming pilot. "I have a picture in my mind," he said, "of the mayor calling his wife, saying, 'Marie, I won't be home. I'm spending the weekend in Moscow.'" After an effusive round of speeches, LaGuardia donned his broad-brimmed hat and joined the flyers in a ticker-tape parade that was bigger even than Lindbergh's.

As if that were not enough excitement for one city in one summer, the celebration was unexpectedly repeated less than a month later, when thirty-one-year-old Douglas Corrigan, flying alone without benefit of passport, maps, radio, or elaborate instruments, and lacking the most elementary safety precautions, set out for California and landed in Ireland. No one, said Corrigan, was more surprised than he to find himself at Dublin's Baldonnel Airport. He had taken off from Floyd Bennett Field headed west when his compass failed and he lost his way. American officials in Dublin were disarmed. In Washington even Cordell Hull was "amused." And New York couldn't wait for "wrong-way Corrigan" to return.

For some days Brooklyn and Manhattan vied for the honor of being first to welcome the hero; he settled the matter himself when he announced by phone from shipboard that he would accept the mayor's invitation to land in Manhattan. If New Yorkers had been thrilled by Hughes, they fell head over heels for Corrigan. The young man's wit, the undaunted grin, and the sheer deviltry of his

3. Hosting the heroes. The mayor greets flyer Howard Hughes at Floyd Bennett Field, July 4, 1938. WIDE WORLD

4. And the city turns out to welcome "Wrong Way" Corrigan, August 5, 1938. WIDE WORLD

exploit were intoxicating. At City Hall he and LaGuardia exchanged mutual compliments. Corrigan proposed the mayor for
higher office; the mayor said the flyer's "deliberate impetuosity,"
his "Pickwickian impulsiveness," found a responsive chord in him
and, in fact, in the entire city. The day ended with a gala reception
and entertainment at Yankee Stadium where Corrigan was introduced by another Irishman, cut in the same devil-may-care mold,
Jimmy Walker.

Meanwhile, the routine business of the city was being conducted.
The council had gone on vacation—"I don't know what I'll do
without you," was the mayor's parting shot—and the Board of
Estimate had not been called into special session as had been threatened. But conferences with commissioners were held with unusual
regularity, and there were the now-habitual trips to Washington,
with the mayor catching the midnight train and flying back to the
city in midafternoon. The constitutional convention in Albany
dragged on through most of the summer. The mayor would be up
while the rest of the city slept, speeding to Albany to make an
appeal for a national amendment on child labor, or for the right of
municipalities to raise money without coming each year on a begging expedition to the state legislature: "Why, I have come up here
not only on my hands and knees, but literally crawling on the
floor." As the convention moved toward its close, the only subjects
which really seemed to arouse the professional politicians were
redistricting and parimutuel betting, and LaGuardia grew steadily
more disillusioned. "Don't worry too much about the convention,"
he wrote to Poletti, "it will soon be forgotten."

In the entire summer the mayor gave himself one day of un-
scheduled rest. That was at the insistence of Eric and Jean who,
although happily ensconced at Northport, Long Island, and enjoying daily trips to the beach with their mother, claimed they did not
see enough of their father. Theirs was the only summons that could
take LaGuardia from the job. Finally on September 2, declaring he
had the nicest time he'd enjoyed in a long while, he quit the city
building at the Fair and faced with relish the prospect of another
journey. As he left his summer palace, the air conditioning began
to work.

Winning the West

The mayor's second major western trip, begun on September 7, had the ostensible purpose of bringing him to Los Angeles for the national convention of the American Legion. It turned into a triumphal tour, filled with the zest, the humor, the color, which La-Guardia at his best well knew how to supply. It was played out against a shattering drama on the world stage, and against events in his own city which by themselves would have made the weeks notable.

In a holiday mood, accompanied by Marie LaGuardia and his young aide Clendenin Ryan, the mayor from the start dramatized himself in two roles: chief executive of the country's largest city, and a sort of political troubadour. He wore two watches in his vest pocket, one set on New York time, one on local; consulting them frequently and ostentatiously, he gave instructions to Ryan or rushed to the telephone when events in New York required his personal intervention. At Shreveport, Louisiana, the tone of the trip was set when the governor of the state introduced him as a guest coming from "a little town in the northeast corner of the country." He called it "a little town," he went on to explain, "because it is so much smaller than the man who guides its destiny." LaGuardia had been met at the airport by the governor and the mayor of Shreveport and driven in an open car under heavy showers, through streets lined with enthusiastic onlookers. There was only one disappointment that day: air maneuvers to have been staged in his honor were called off because of the bad weather.

The next day at Fort Worth he received an old-fashioned Texas welcome, with the governor and the mayor turning out to make him a gift of a real sombrero, though with a smaller brim than the one he ordinarily wore. Pushing on to Phoenix, Arizona, he learned that in New York Dewey's prosecution of Hines, a racketeering case on which rode the fortunes of the district attorney, had resulted in a mistrial. Justice Ferdinand Pecora had ruled that a single question of Dewey's had invalidated the proceedings, "like a drop of poison in the human system."

LaGuardia greeted the news with what a *Times* reporter called a "rueful grin." He was enjoying himself, far from the scene of Dewey's discomfiture; besides, the setback administered to his ambitious young teammate of the recent elections could not be altogether disconcerting to LaGuardia. "We spent a hundred dollars a day to air condition that courtroom," he remarked, "and now there's a mistrial . . ."

More ominously, on the same day came news of Hitler's Nuremburg speech. The dictator defied world opinion on the issue of the Sudeten Germans, and the British prime minister set off to the fateful meeting at Berchtesgaden. LaGuardia declared that the same law which applies to the underworld should apply to nations: "When an individual goes berserk, we take him in custody and put him in a place where he can do no harm."

The return to the "hometown" of Prescott was a glorious occasion for LaGuardia. The train stopped at the border of Prescott; the mayor swung effortlessly onto a cowpony, riding into town with the local mayor and a wartime comrade, with the school band bringing up the rear. He was introduced on the courthouse steps by the influential senator Henry Ashurst as one having the brightest of political futures. "He possesses youth, extraordinary vitality, and great courage. . . . He is the most constant, the most famous, and the most powerful friend Prescott will ever have—a hometown boy who has achieved worldwide renown."

LaGuardia responded with subdued emotion, recalling the "gaudy and spectacular" sight which the frontier town of his boyhood had presented. In this place he had learned the first principles of his political creed. Resentment of the exploitation of the laboring man was born when he witnessed unfairness to the railroad workers; his first experience with graft occurred when he saw an agent cheat on the food given to Indians. A little later he paid affectionate tribute to his father when a rocky Arizona outcropping was dedicated to his memory: "He was the sort of man who loved to bring cheer and happiness to those around him." Then, taking up the baton, New York's mayor led the school band of Prescott.

The arrival of the mayoral party in San Francisco was cloaked in an official secrecy satisfying to LaGuardia's romantic temperament. Only his own troops, New York City employees on their way to the Legion convention, had been informed. At the Ferry Building all present fell into line; LaGuardia gave the signal for the music to start, and the five hundred marchers moved in an "invasion" to San Francisco's City Hall. Mayor LaGuardia assured Mayor Rossi that the country was big enough for the two fairs, both at that time in the building stage, then proceeded on his way to address the

Commonwealth Club on a broad national program for U.S. cities.

In Europe, the international situation worsened. Roosevelt, who had been at the bedside of his son James in Rochester, Minnesota, told a station-side crowd that he was returning to Washington rather than to Hyde Park because of the serious events abroad. Britain and France had agreed to Hitler's demands and were exacting the surrender of Beneš, president of Czechoslovakia. In New York a trucking strike was under way. LaGuardia kept in close touch with the situation, deploying police to protect the movement of essential goods and keeping himself in readiness for an instant return.

September 19 found the mayor at Los Angeles for the climax of his tour. He was repeatedly cheered during a speech at the opening of the Legion convention as he called for loyalty to the government in its complex dealings with the European powers. The next day in the parade he led a thousand veterans then in the service of New York City. "There goes the biggest little man in the country," one legionnaire was heard to say as he passed. Interviewers that day found the mayor in a sunny disposition, ready with a quip in answer to a wide variety of questions.

As if enough trouble had not accumulated already, a severe hurricane struck the northeast region on September 21. Winds over seventy miles an hour hit New York, bringing power failures and subway tie-ups. "The visitation," said the *Herald Tribune,* "was sudden, unprecedented, and unbelievable." Boats were piled up in the city's bays and rivers; damage to parks and parkways was extensive. In the area as a whole 462 deaths were reported; in New York City, 10. That LaGuardia should not immediately have flown back to direct the cleanup, lingering instead for two days in California for an inspection of the film industry, seems surprising. That he was not condemned for his absence seems more surprising still. It suggests how far he had liberated himself at this stage from a purely local role and how widely he was recognized as a national figure.

When he did get back on September 24 he had been away for just under two weeks. He was quickly to demonstrate that he had not lost his touch in city affairs. The trucking strike had resumed after a four-day truce. LaGuardia presented a compromise settlement, winning the acceptance of the drivers but rejected by the trucking firms. He made one more direct appeal, in a stormy session where he was loudly cheered, then mobilized a thousand sanitation trucks and equipment from other departments, most of which had been condemned as obsolete by the mayor when he took office. The trucks were manned by strikers, with the permission of city drivers. At dawn the fences of City Hall Park were cut by torches and the fleet was found mobilized, ready to respond to emergency needs, when the city awoke.

Not many trucks actually left the park that day. As was often the case in the mayor's more dramatic actions, the symbol was as real as the substance. One by one the trucking firms began to sign. "With his usual air of high temper and flaming spirit," said the *Post,* "the mayor has ended the trucking strike." The manner, it added, was cleverly shaped "to conceal exceedingly careful planning."

Lehman or Dewey?

In June of 1938 LaGuardia had taken a far-reaching decision greatly affecting his personal fortunes. He declared that he would not run for the Senate in November. In purely personal terms it was the one job he most wanted. It had always been his desire to cap his long tenure in the House with a seat in the Senate and he looked back nostalgically upon his days in Congress. "As a legislator you tell people what to do," he once said; "here [in City Hall], you have to do it yourself." But it was the wrong time; perhaps he would run in 1940, but for the present he would not consider quitting New York so recently after reelection for a second term.

The question of a Senate seat had been raised in acute form by the sudden and unexpected death of Senator Royal Copeland who had been sitting as a Republican since 1922. His departure changed the political picture in New York. In the autumn two senators (in addition to a governor) would be elected; the chances were now greatly improved for a Democrat or for an independent liberal to capture a second seat and to reinforce the redoubtable Wagner. Declining to make an interim appointment to the vacancy, Lehman let it be known that in November he would himself be a senatorial candidate.

At the White House there existed little enthusiasm for Lehman, who had opposed the president's court plan. In every case such opposition had put the officeholder in the direct line of the president's fire. Lehman's foes now urged that the president's backing go to LaGuardia. It is not clear to what extent this behind-the-scenes movement developed, but there was much talk in the press, and

LaGuardia himself must have seen clearly his opportunity to gather all his strength, to ask for payment on notes due, and to make the run. He was at this time in a stronger position vis-à-vis Roosevelt than he was ever to be again. A third party in 1940 seemed a real possibility, and LaGuardia's rejection of its appeal, together with his continuing support of the New Deal, were highly desired objectives. Besides, within a short time LaGuardia was to provide, in a New York congressional district, the one success in the president's ill-fated "purge." Afterward LaGuardia would court the president's favor; now, if ever, he could lay down his own terms.

But he withstood the temptation. He did so in characteristic style, with a blow hurled in the teeth of his foes. He had run for office less than a year ago on the promise to end the spoils system, dirty politics, and inefficient municipal government. He would not now, he declared, desert the field. There were those who would gladly vote for him in order to get him out of City Hall; but "I've been trained since boyhood that it's treason to give aid and comfort to the enemy." Rhetoric aside, LaGuardia had good reasons to make a firm and quick decision. He really did believe, in that early summer of 1938, that he knew his enemies and that he had them on the run.

In the autumn he faced a more puzzling political choice. Lehman had given up his claim upon the Senate seat and had been nominated once more for the governership. The Republican gubernatorial candidate was Dewey. It was a measure of the mayor's political strength that both candidates considered his support vital to success; it was a measure of his strength, too, that he felt his interests best served by a strict neutrality. Actually, he had little feeling of warmth toward either Lehman or Dewey. Lehman's attitude in the court fight had shocked him, and the governor still persistently refused to express support for the New Deal program. Roosevelt was supporting him with some evident difficulty. When Lehman boasted of his balanced budget, the president let it be known that he, too, could balance a budget if some higher government authority paid the bills. But he was ready in the end to settle for support of an old friend and party stalwart. The ALP, supporting Lehman, was ready to settle for a show of liberalism. LaGuardia had more exacting standards.

Dewey was on LaGuardia's official team but he was always a man hard to like, and in this case he had disregarded the mayor's example, as he had resisted a personal appeal that he stay and finish the job for which he had been elected. (With the indictment of Hines in a second successful trial, Dewey had proceeded coolly to calculate his chances of success.) In addition, Dewey represented the party which had dominated the abortive constitutional convention and now supported amendments which LaGuardia found obnoxious.

LaGuardia's aim was still to drive the stolid Lehman into support of the New Deal. In October the governor had dodged following a meeting with Roosevelt; LaGuardia had insisted publicly that he declare himself. The mayor made his own visit to Hyde Park for a talk which was announced as having "politics" for its subject. On leaving, he said again he would not support Lehman unless the latter were to speak out. At the same time LaGuardia had cause for wry satisfaction in being the instrument for a considerable degree of embarrassment for the governor, in a field where he could ill afford a setback.

After an Albany hearing in 1936 Lehman had dismissed charges of "negligence and gross incompetence" made by the grand jury against Francis X. Geoghan, the Brooklyn district attorney. Geoghan was a loyal party man, well spoken and affable, a former teacher of English. The governor's exoneration had seemed, at best, to spring from a mixture of motives. Now it began to seem clearly a mistake. The mayor's commissioner of investigations, William B. Herlands, had been taking seriously his boss's injunction to explore the enforcement of criminal law in Brooklyn, including the administration of the district attorney's office. With undercover agents and with a dragnet of subpoenas he had been assembling his data and was ready to proceed publicly.

In the midst of his gubernatorial campaign Lehman announced that he would name a special prosecutor to supersede Geoghan. LaGuardia, not without a hint of malice, praised the governor's "speedy and drastic action." He also ensured that Herlands would continue his investigations into "unofficial" corruption in Brooklyn.

As for the much-coveted endorsement, LaGuardia continued to stand aloof. Prior to an ALP rally for Lehman on November 1, LaGuardia let it be known he would be unable to attend. He would be busy at that hour preparing a radio speech in support of Senator Wagner. The fact that Wagner had spoken against LaGuardia in the 1937 campaign had not been forgotten. Wagner had spoken then "as a good party man"—now the mayor was speaking "as a good-government man." Still there was silence in regard to Lehman, until aides of the mayor on November 2 leaked the information that LaGuardia had "decided" to back Lehman. The governor had finally brought himself around to praising Roosevelt's "humanitarian policies"; moreover, word had reached the mayor of Dewey's formal campaign rule never to mention LaGuardia by name.

Once again death intervened in the political process. Vladeck, minority leader of the City Council, died suddenly, and his funeral was marked by such a civic outpouring of grief and praise as occasionally unites a vast community. LaGuardia invited Lehman to ride with him to the funeral, calling for him at his Fifth Avenue apartment. The occasion was said to have been witnessed by half a million mourners and spectators, and LaGuardia's presence at Lehman's side was not overlooked.

Yet no direct word of support came from LaGuardia as the last days before the election ticked by. In the end Lehman won over Dewey by the narrow margin of 67,000 votes. Elsewhere in the country the Republicans made big gains. In the Congress the number of Republicans rose from 89 to 170; in the Senate they gained eight seats. Among many gubernatorial casualties, the defeat of Philip La Follette was widely noted. The midterm elections, as they had since 1870, brought a loss to the party in power, but this time on a scale which seemed to set back the whole liberal cause. LaGuardia, who had been largely a spectator during the campaign, now stepped forth to take an active role.

One must be realistic, he declared at a City Hall press conference; the progressive forces in several states had been decimated. Yes, the New Deal had been hurt. Now it was essential that labor transcend its differences, that there be formulated for the future "a well-defined, clear, concise progressive platform." A few days later at City Hall he received two of the defeated liberals, Governor Frank Murphy of Michigan and Senator Robert J. Buckley of Ohio. There was talk of a third party, and tentative plans were laid for a conference of progressives in Washington.

Franklin Roosevelt spiked the third-party approach; the Washington conference did not come off. But LaGuardia had his hour. He stood forth plainly at this time as the leader, under Franklin Roosevelt, of the progressive forces of the country. If Roosevelt should step down in 1940, he would be in the very forefront.

The declining year was still to have its incidents and its illuminations.

On December 20, accompanied by Comptroller McGoldrick, the mayor was returning to City Hall after having taken acetyline torch in hand and, masked and helmeted, begun the long-awaited demolition of the Sixth Avenue El. Always fascinated by the physical transformation of the city, he paused for a few moments to watch workmen tearing down the old Federal Building at the south end of City Hall Park. Then he moved to go in; an aide advanced to open the door, and a stranger tapped him from behind on the shoulder. Turning, the mayor received a violent blow which threw him to the marble steps. As he scrambled up he grabbed his attacker, a disgruntled relief recipient, by the throat. The intervention of a patrolman subdued the assailant, who was carried into City Hall while the mayor held the door open. "Why did you hit me from behind?" was LaGuardia's only comment.

"The mayor didn't get my vote," remarked a policeman on the scene. "But I'll say one thing for him. He has a lot of guts." In Germany, where the most brutal of anti-Jewish orgies had recently taken place, the Nazi press congratulated LaGuardia's assailant. "All in the day's work," said the mayor; "I've had worse blows than that below the belt."

Ten minutes later he was receiving in his office a delegation representative of various refugee organizations. Conditions in Germany, he told them, were "the shame and horror of the world." He attended police graduation ceremonies later in the day, reminding young recruits that the power of command lay in the field, not behind a desk. New policemen should get out of the force at once if they felt timid or jittery and were not prepared "to look right into the muzzle of a gun." Still the mayor's day was not quite over. It was the Christmas season, and as his daughter Jean pulled the switch lighting the traditional tree in front of City Hall, the whole country, he said, was giving heed to the greatest lesson ever given: the Sermon on the Mount.

7
Signs and Portents

The Challenge of Robert Moses

LaGuardia's drive to gain control over all agencies affecting the city's life was combined through 1938 with a growing concern for the direction and priorities of public policy. The mayor wanted to be a great builder, an artist working on the broad canvas of the city, but it began to appear that his most dramatic and vivid brushstrokes were those applied to improve the flow of automobiles. Ground breakings for a school or hospital, for a housing development or playground, occurred often enough. But they left a minor impact on the civic landscape compared to the parkways, highways, and bridges which were changing the face of New York and would soon change the living habits of millions of its citizens. By the beginning of 1938 the Triborough Bridge was completed; the Whitestone Bridge linking the Bronx and Flushing was well under way; the Queens Midtown Tunnel was going forward, and nearly fifty miles of highways and parkways linked the boroughs and made their path along the shores of bays, rivers, and oceans.

In the thinking of early civic planners roads and parkways played an important role, liberating the poorer citizens from the enclaves in which they were immured and permitting them to move freely through the city. Parks and parkways had been concepts closely allied, and indeed were usually administered, as they were in New

York, by the same agency. New York's Parks Department was weighted in favor of parkway maintenance, and its capital budget —despite the very great expansion of playground facilities—was heavily committed to parkway extensions. Grants from Washington for the development of arterial routes invariably included funds for the acquisition and development of adjacent land for recreational purposes. Not surprisingly, the parkways were considered socially beneficial, as the bridges in the eyes of all were of striking and dramatic beauty.

For LaGuardia with his love of children and his passion for engineering, the city's advances in parks, parkways, and bridges offered a specially seductive program. Yet sometime in 1938 he seems to have questioned whether such developments might not leave a lopsided city, poor in facilities ministering to other basic human needs. This line of thought was encouraged by the increasing evidence of Robert Moses's ambition and power. If Moses had built fifty miles of arterial routes, he had plans in his head for completing a hundred more. The parks and playgrounds he had constructed were in his mind only the forerunner of such massive developments as Soundview and Marine parks. For these undertakings he needed money, and he needed unchecked authority. Meanwhile the man who had collected posts and offices as other men might collect decorations acted toward the mayor's government as a potentate secure in his own realm.

Since the 1934 consolidation parks had set itself up as a quasi-sovereign department within the city organization. The commissioner regularly disregarded the pink memoranda from the mayor's office which others would acknowledge promptly with the assurance of appropriate action. He spurned the Wednesday meetings of the department heads, sending in his place a potted plant grown in his own greenhouses. The department's headquarters in the Arsenal in Central Park aroused the suspicion, or at least the envy, of commissioners confined to less sylvan surroundings. Yet Moses removed himself even from the Arsenal. He ruled from the redoubt of one of his several other offices, until he settled, invisible and aloof, at the very heart of his empire on Randall's Island under the Triborough Bridge.

Moses had his own way of dealing with such overhead agencies as budget and personnel, ordinarily the bane of department heads. The civic organizations and much of the press being constantly behind him, he could afford to dodge restraining forces, beating the drum for more money and less red tape. With Paul Kern, chairman of the Civil Service Commission, he carried on a bitter feud. When Kern issued a memorandum asking for the cooperation of departments in reporting inefficiencies, Moses responded with a broadside denunciation, inviting Kern to send the communication to the OGPU in Russia "whose representative you seem to be." In a different tactic he preempted budget personnel, and by taking them into his own department assured their compliance with his wishes.

On one occasion a young member of the corporation counsel's office had the temerity at a meeting with LaGuardia in City Hall to suggest that under the law a certain course could not be pursued. The mayor, as was not unusual with him, fired the young lawyer on the spot.

Many years later William Chanler recalled how he had received the disconsolate ex-official on his return to headquarters and was puzzling how he might set the matter straight. Just then the telephone rang. It was Moses saying he had been present at a meeting in the mayor's office where he had observed an aide with the gall to stand up and say no to the chief. He wanted that young man for his own department and promptly hired him.

The powers Moses acquired as parks commissioner were insignificant, however, beside those he was to amass as head of various independent authorities. Created as a means to develop a single major public work, the authorities were originally conceived of as going out of existence when the bondholders for that project had been paid off. Moses devised and pushed through the legislature a series of laws which ensured perpetuity for these bodies, letting them go on from one project to another. Isolated to a large degree from public scrutiny, immune to most of the rules and restraints which governed city agencies, the independent authorities were to become instruments for accomplishing great public works, and for bestowing great power on those who controlled them.

The scope to build bridges Moses possessed under the Triborough Bridge Authority; it irked him that he should be excluded from building tunnels. When LaGuardia in 1936 created a Tunnel Authority to construct an underwater link between Queens and midtown Manhattan, he deliberately refused to put Moses on the board and then skillfully fought off his attempt to undermine its operations. But the Tunnel Authority was no match for Moses's spectacular successes. The midtown tunnel languished while the superb spans of the Triborough and Whitestone Bridges cast their inverted arches against the sky. To take over the Tunnel Authority, or to merge it with Triborough, became one of Moses's long-term, steadfastly pursued goals.

Meanwhile power would be asserted from within the Triborough citadel, a degree of power which was to bring Moses and the mayor into direct confrontation. A crucial exchange between the two men, setting the stage for battles to come, occurred in April 1938. The occasion for this was significant, involving as it did not only the mayor but Paul Kern, whom Moses's hatred was to pursue until the young man's downfall four years later. The issue overtly at stake was a narrow one: the Civil Service Commission ruled that the bridge authority must select toll collectors from the lists of court attendants as well as from the prison keepers' civil service list. Going over Kern's head directly to the mayor, Moses declared, "I must absolutely refuse."

Court attendants were selected for an indoor job, whereas Mr. Moses's toll collectors would presumably be deterred by neither snow nor sleet from their appointed stands. "The difference," wrote Moses, "goes to the heart of these business enterprises which depend on the proper collection of tolls for the integrity of their bonds." Unless the matter were adjusted, Moses added, he would have to take it up with "the attorney for the bondholders and with the trustee."

LaGuardia was enraged. "I want it clearly understood that the city is not being run by attorneys for the authority bondholders," he wrote back. "The authority bondholders have absolutely nothing to say. . . . You are a city official, and will take up matters with the corporation counsel." On the day he received this letter Moses fired off in reply a decisive cannonade: "As to your statements about the powers of the bondholders, I think you had better read the arrangements and contracts." Moses topped it with one more jab at Kern, to the effect that he noted Kern often enough disregarded the corporation counsel.

There was no reply from LaGuardia. He was in an awkward position. Kern had precipitated the affair by reversing LaGuardia's original decision on the lists from which the toll collectors were to be selected; and LaGuardia knew all too well that his early protégé, the man whom he had elevated from office aide to one of the city's highest functions, was often jarringly independent. Much worse, his legal advisers confirmed that recent amendments which Moses had introduced in Albany in fact greatly extended the powers of the authorities, and specifically gave them the right to employ special counsel.

Robert Caro asserts in his book on Moses that hereafter the positions of LaGuardia and Moses were radically altered: Moses no longer saw himself as LaGuardia's subordinate but as at least his equal. It was an ascendancy he was not always to preserve. In the years ahead, particularly in the war years which Caro lightly skips over, Moses was drastically constrained by lack of men and funds to advance his building operations, and was denied a role equal to his talents. But in 1938–1939 Moses was certainly riding high, and LaGuardia was regarding him as an adversary to check, to compromise with, and occasionally to join for lack of a better alternative.

The first encounter after the above exchange came in the autumn. At issue was extension of that part of the Belt Parkway running through the Gowanus section of Brooklyn, but eventually to thread the shorelines of all the boroughs. On October 12 the mayor called on the Board of Estimate to make cuts in the capital budget, including a cut in funds for what was then called the circumferential highway. McGoldrick was insisting on a $40 million "cushion" below the debt limit; schools and health centers seemed to the mayor to have priority over the building of further automobile roads. The challenge was one Moses was fully prepared to take up. He announced that he was ready to fight.

The circumferential highway was an attractive concept, more attractive to that generation than to those who at a later time would see New York—and the many cities which followed New York's example—cut off by elevated structures and ribbons of concrete from the bays and rivers which formed its natural bounds. The report of the Municipal Art Commission for 1938 was enthusiastic over the prospect of a waterfront "ringstrasse" circling the entire island of Manhattan. LaGuardia shared the commission's vision; he was in awe of Moses's capacity to produce, and two days later he surrendered. Mass transportation extensions and other civic improvements were abandoned in favor of the new road.

The mayor, said the *Sun,* had simply been unable to halt Moses's barrage. "His recital of the fiscal conditions of the city, of its many needs, was useless against this supersalesman who dreads him not."

In his naive, persistent way, Newbold Morris refused to be convinced. One night before the budget came up for a final vote Morris sat up until 3 A.M. and decided that the circumferential highway was less important than schools. Referring to "Newbold's latest,"

Moses said he was reminded that at a prolonged session of the old Board of Aldermen, one of the brethren had sent out for "sixty sandwiches and a bale of hay." But McGoldrick also had been having some sleepless nights. "Reluctant as I am to suggest the postponement of the circumferential highway," he announced, he could not face the new construction while he saw the need for keeping the city's plant in efficient condition. "We have a stupendous investment in public bridges, buildings, and equipment which must be protected. Unless the plant is properly maintained we will undergo a repetition of the era when brokendown equipment and neglected buildings cost the taxpayers many needless millions." He argued, too, that under growing restrictions on capital expenditures, not a single school, not a single new hospital, not a new police station or firehouse, would be provided in the next two years.

Stanley Isaacs joined with Morris and McGoldrick, and the triumvirate had enough votes to defeat the proposal. But LaGuardia, though he saw the merits of their arguments, was beyond the point of compromise or retreat. On October 15, making one of his rare appearances at the Board of Estimate, he called an executive session and imposed his will on the dissenters. Outside the conference room hundreds of Moses's supporters were prepared to cheer a favorable decision; the atmosphere within was tense as the mayor made a dramatic appeal on personal grounds, and argued that millions in public funds would be lost if the highway were postponed. For four hours the fate of Fusion hung in the balance, as the minds of three men swayed between the conflicting appeals of loyalty to the cause and their own convictions. When the vote was finally taken, the highway was approved unanimously.

This was in October; the next confrontation took place a month later, and this time LaGuardia was prepared to reassert the balance. The voters in the November election had approved a constitutional amendment on housing and for the first time state money became amply available. Moses had learned well how to put state money to work in building parks; now his shrewd eyes perceived a new opportunity. On November 22, a fortnight after passage of the amendment, he took over the auditorium of the Museum of Natural History and invited the attendance of the city's leading builders and real estate men. Before his influential audience he proceeded to unfold a full-fledged housing plan, together with supplementary recreation areas. Before Moses as he spoke were the microphones of station WNYC; the broadcasting crews were at their posts. But not a word of the Moses speech went out over the air to the New York City public.

That afternoon the mayor had got wind of what was afoot; he had laid his hands on the fully illustrated brochure which was being distributed to the press but which had been carefully withheld from him. His first move was to summon Morris S. Novik, the station director, and to order him to kill the broadcast.

The Moses housing plan nevertheless filled the next day's papers. Most editors accepted the plan as coming from a master builder; but in quarters where it might have been expected to be uncritically acclaimed, there was a realization that this time Moses had over-stepped his role. "As a builder he is the ablest in the country," said the *Post,* "but his social outlook is sometimes (not always) as narrow as his technical imagination is broad." The plan came under fire for necessitating rents higher than the slum dwellers could afford and for giving private investors an unfair break, relieving them both of taxes and of costs of the new parks. "We congratulate the mayor for socking the Moses plan and for socking it hard."

The mayor had indeed made his views known and had taken further initiative from Moses's hands by inducing a powerful housing committee headed by Windels to turn down every one of the proposals. Such veterans of the housing cause as Lewis Mumford and Albert Mayer joined in opposition. In the hour of his greatest strength Moses had slipped and had opened himself to the mayor's counterthrust. But he was soon to be on the offensive once more, this time inviting a massive rebuff, and dragging the mayor with him to a defeat from forces more powerful than either one of them.

Bridge or Tunnel?

A connection between the burgeoning borough of Brooklyn and the fabled towers of lower Manhattan had been proposed as early as 1925. Under LaGuardia it seemed a likely accomplishment. But New York's Tunnel Authority was proceeding slowly with its underground link to Queens; by 1938 another two years would be required to finish it, and funding for a second tunnel seemed unavailable. Both Jesse Jones and Ickes turned down the mayor's request for loans or grants to start the Brooklyn link. Then Robert Moses came to the rescue. For a price—which included membership on the Tunnel Authority board—he agreed to finance the new tunnel by capitalizing the profits of the Triborough Bridge. With this, everything seemed in place. The War Department approved plans for the tunnel, and another LaGuardia–Moses accomplishment appeared to be in the making.

Then on January 22, 1939, Moses made a shift that completely altered the picture, churning up a civic brouhaha which was to occupy the politicians, reporters, and public-spirited citizens throughout the year. Quite simply, he abandoned the idea for a tunnel. "After considerable study," he announced, "we believe the soundness of the Brooklyn–Battery crossing lies in a bridge." The bridge would cost $41 million as opposed to the tunnel's $84 million; its maintenance costs would be halved; it would have six lanes instead of four. The public was so used to hearing grand ideas from Moses, and so long subjugated to accepting them in the form given, that it now seemed quite prepared to acquiesce in the change. Said the *Herald Tribune,* soon to be a leader in the opposition, "The scheme, unless it has flaws which do not at the moment appear, seems foolproof."

Flaws did appear soon enough. The bridge was looked on with some suspicion from the start because it so obviously seemed part of another Moses power-grab. To the startled Tunnel Authority it was plainly a case of theft, and it began to make its views known in Albany. "It is most unseemly," LaGuardia wrote to its chairman, "to have two departments in conflict with each other. . . . If a generous grant was available a tunnel would be preferable. If no grant is available a tunnel is out of the question." He called for cessation of attempts by the Tunnel Authority to thwart the enabling legislation which Moses, with his usual dispatch, had submitted to the state legislature.

When the Planning Commission held its first public hearing on February 15, Stanley Isaacs led the opposition. It was not clear to him how the new traffic could be handled in the already overburdened streets of lower Manhattan; and he was not convinced that a bridge would be asethetically acceptable. He asked for further study of the tunnel.

"An absolutely silly argument," Moses replied with an arrogance which was to become increasingly evident as the controversy proceeded. "No one is interested in studying the tunnel because it simply doesn't make sense." On March 2 the Planning Commission supported the bridge without further study or prolonged hearings. The impression deepened that Moses and the administration were out to silence legitimate doubts, even if it meant manipulating the planning body which was supposed to care for the city's long-range interests.

Leaders of the civic groups were by now thoroughly aroused. They were united as they had not been since they combined in 1935 to protect Moses from the order of banishment imposed by Harold Ickes. First the Regional Plan Association entered the fray, led by its much-respected chairman, George McAneny. The association objected to the bridge as a defacement of the skyline and of the historic Battery Park. Then the Citizens Union attacked the bridge because of its effect on real estate values. "It does not seem there is any emergency," it concluded, "which calls for hasty or inspirational action." These groups were soon augmented by the New York chapter of the American Institute of Architects, the Merchants Association, the Westside Chamber of Commerce, the Real Estate Board, the City Club, and the New York Board of Trade. Only the Park Association, long subservient to Moses and accustomed to praising his every move, refused to take a stand on the issue. It merely gave its approval to Moses's plans for relandscaping what was left of Battery Park after the bridge had been constructed.

The drama came to a public climax on March 28 when the City Council met to discuss legislation approving Triborough as the agency to construct the bridge. The day before, Moses had returned tanned and confident from a Florida vacation. He set the tone of the coming debate when he characterized opposition arguments as "the same old tripe," declaring that he would deal with them all on the morrow. The council chamber was packed at the appointed hour. Moses, having arrived with his accustomed phalanx of aides in a chain of black limousines, sat taking notes as the long arguments unfolded. Behind him were gathered the pride of New York's citizenry, fighters in civic causes, protectors of the city's fame, many with an experience going back to the days of John Purroy Mitchel. When the full case against the bridge had been exposed, Moses went to the lectern and let fly the venomous arrows of his sarcasm and his wrath.

"This is a showdown on the project," he said. "Either you want it or you don't want it, and either you want it now or you don't get it at all." Between arguments for the bridge were jibes at all who had been rash enough to stand in opposition. Picking from the audience George McAneny, darling of the reformers, he startled even those accustomed to his enormities by referring to the prematurely aged man as "an exhumed mummy . . . an extinct volcano." The expertise of civil servants having been referred to, Moses glared at the Manhattan borough president. Civil service, he said, can become a racket to the point where "nothing but a Communist state *pleasing to Mr. Isaacs and Mr. Gerson*" can deal with it.

Where was LaGuardia amid all this? Although clearly supporting the bridge and the required legislation, up to this point he had allowed Moses to bear the brunt of the controversy. During the council hearings he was holed up in his budget retreat, inaccessible to the public and the press. Without his overt pressure the bridge carried in the council; two days later Albany had rushed the enabling legislation to passage, and Moses had moved to get War Department approval. Before the end of the month he was negotiating with the Reconstruction Finance Corporation and with private bankers for the $41.2 million funding. Burlingham wrote to LaGuardia with his customary wisdom, "All I ask is that you do not exert yourself [on behalf of the bridge] in Washington or elsewhere."

Unfortunately, the mayor did not heed this advice, nor follow consistently what had been his own instincts in the matter. In Washington he went on the attack before the review board, denouncing "swivel chair admirals," an epithet at which the presiding admiral not surprisingly took umbrage. The latter recalled LaGuardia's having urged that Governor's Island, residence of the naval brass, be taken over for an airport, an idea he termed "nonsensical." The hearings were not a brilliant success. Late in April, just before the opening of the World's Fair, LaGuardia again taunted opponents of the bridge, saying Moses had promised him that before two years were out, a bridge would stand against the skies of lower Manhattan. In May the mayor appeared personally before the Board of Estimate as shepherd to a slightly revised bridge proposal.

Moses was still acting as if all the fiends were after him, replying to letters in the press and taking on his critics with savage fervor. The normally supportive *Herald Tribune* saw him as "the city's No. 1 problem child." "There is no point in arguing with a volcano," it said, "we can't understand the present heat and the present hurry. All we ask is time for more study and more light. Why, therefore, the tantrums?"

Meanwhile events were developing behind the scenes. Mrs. Roosevelt in her column "My Day" had written early in April, two days after Governor Lehman approved the bridge bill, that a "man who is greatly interested in Manhattan Island" had called her attention to the bridge; she proceeded in her rather vague way to wonder whether some consideration might not be given to preserving the skyline against this infraction. Moses afterward would be convinced that "Eleanor" was at the bottom of all that subsequently occurred. In fact another influence was at work. Burlingham, who had long been carrying on in public a campaign against the bridge (and was undoubtedly author of the letter to Mrs. Roosevelt), wrote to the president. It was a message sent in "graveyard secrecy," cryptic in style but clear enough in its implications. "The War Department can stop it . . . *Verb. suf. sap.*" This appears to have been the decisive element in Roosevelt's next move. The secretary of war, Harry H. Woodring, was brought into the picture, and on July 17, disregarding the recommendation of the army engineers, Woodring ruled against the bridge. He held that its construction in wartime would create a peril to navigation, being "seaward" of the Brooklyn Navy Yard. The fact that the Brooklyn and Manhattan bridges already existed seaward of the navy yard was brushed off by the secretary with the statement that the two bridges in question ought eventually to be demolished.

"Saved from a tragic blunder," was the *Herald Tribune*'s comment. "This administration is never daunted by anything. We will go on to the next thing," said LaGuardia. Moses was bitter. He charged that the secretary of war had perpetrated "a comic opera theory of defense," and complained about "the kicking around, discourtesy, and insulting treatment" he had personally received from Washington.

Once again, as in the case of Moses's original appointment to Triborough, LaGuardia seems to have underestimated the nature of Roosevelt's ire. Through these months he had been flirting dangerously with a buzz saw, and now—notwithstanding his resigned comments in public—he went over the head of the War Department to make a personal appeal to Roosevelt. Evidently he was not aware of the direct role Roosevelt had played in the turndown; he must have been ignorant of Burlingham's letter and the instructions to Woodring. Indeed, LaGuardia was so impolitic as to deliver personally into Roosevelt's hands a statement written by Robert Moses, denouncing as "manifestly preposterous" the secretary's arguments against the bridge.

Roosevelt received LaGuardia courteously enough. He had

come to the interview fortified by the presence of their mutual friend, Adolf Berle, and the president could afford to smile and be pleasant. For the outcome was foreordained. On November 1, just a week after the Washington meeting, Roosevelt again rejected the bridge. This time there was no appeal.

Years later, an aged man but still burning with resentment, Moses commented on the famous battle. His eyes narrowed, his jaw jutted out. "Nevertheless we did it," he muttered. "We built the Verazzano bridge *seaward of the navy yard.*"

With a loan of $57 million from Jesse Jones's Reconstruction Finance Corporation, the Brooklyn–Battery Tunnel was begun in 1940, just before the start of World War II. At least Moses had won his victory over the Tunnel Authority and was in charge of building operations. In 1946 the Tunnel Authority and the Triborough Bridge Authority were completely merged, with Moses the chairman of the new agency.

Tugwell, Gloomy Prophet

Among the casualties of the bridge fight was the City Planning Commission. That fledgling institution, the hope of the new charter, had been seriously damaged in public esteem—particularly among that part of the public whose support it most needed—by the hasty way in which it had given approval to the mayor's designs. The lesson was clear that under political pressure it would yield to the changing ideas of the administration in power. The planning commission had been conceived as a tribunal of disinterested professionals guarding the city against just such a whirlwind of passionate activity as the Moses project had generated. But it failed in its role, and failed in circumstances which confronted it with an almost insoluble dilemma.

The battle of the bridge was fought upon basically narrow grounds. No one was arguing against the idea of some sort of crossing at the mouth of the East River. Apart from personal factors, the fight turned largely upon aesthetics. Opponents of the bridge were certainly right in their feeling that a massive structure would be damaging to Manhattan's small-scale Battery Park, that the extension of a bridge from the very nose of what Melville had called "that noble mole" would destroy a world-famous image. Yet the Planning Commission was not charged with a concern for aes-

25. A philosophical planner,
Rexford G. Tugwell. UPI

thetics. It was forced, in short, to choose between enraging the mayor and alienating the civic groups on an issue peripheral to its charter responsibilities. Its political compliance did not win over the mayor, who was reluctant to see any of his prerogatives trimmed by the new institution. It fatally undermined, however, the allegiance of civic leaders whose wholehearted backing would be needed if the commission was to succeed in the long run.

This was doubly unfortunate because the commission had other obstacles, written into its very nature, which would prove insurmountable. From the first the Bureau of the Budget showed its jealousy, being unwilling to surrender traditional control over the capital budget. Even more ominously, the political establishment looked with cold hostility upon a body whose essential function was to discipline its powers and to make them conform to a vague concept of the general good.

Such difficulties were not eased by the style and character of the man whom LaGuardia had put at the head of the new agency. Then forty-seven, Tugwell was a flamboyant, opinionated figure, who had agitated Washington as one of the original brain trust and later as assistant secretary of agriculture under Henry Wallace. Markedly handsome, he had a mind "that picked you up and made your brain race along." Coming to New York as Berle's successor, he was expected to play a similar role both within the city administration and as a link between LaGuardia and the New Deal. Things never quite worked out that way. One reason was certainly the bridge controversy. "He abused commission members if they showed any independence," Tugwell wrote much later of the mayor; the memory was certainly kept green by the compulsions he had been put under in this winter of 1939.

Yet something deeper separated the two men, and ultimately separated the Planning Commission from the sympathies of New Yorkers. Tugwell was a philosophical radical, a pessimist beset by existential doubts about the future of the city and of the human race itself. He was a brooding presence ill at ease beside LaGuardia's activism. As first head, Berle's intellectualism had given the commission a quite different cast. Hardly less of a philosophical pessimist than Tugwell, he saw New York as the inheritor of the cultural tradition which in Europe was being doomed by bigotry and violence; he saw the city being enriched by the coming wave of European refugees, profiting from the follies of men in other countries. In short, Berle loved the city and loved city life. Tugwell's attitude was more ambiguous.

Taking a visitor to the thirty-sixth floor of the Municipal Building, Tugwell would lecture on the implications of the scene spread out below. Visible in the distance were the newer areas of settlement, their growing population fed by the arteries of modern transportation, insatiable in their demand for services which grew in per capita cost as the human density declined. Just below was Manhattan, brilliant, fantastically productive in change and novelty, but menaced by the increasing tax load its real estate had to bear. This fragile, beautiful agglomeration of man's making had somehow to provide tax money for a dispersed population of 7.5 million, 600,000 of whom were unemployed.

The 1939 Annual Report of the City Planning Commission was a somber document, a chilling essay on the sociology of urban change. For almost the first time, New Yorkers were confronted by the view of a city set amid intractable difficulties, one whose future might well be less than dazzling. A great cultural capital, it was almost alone in not being also a political seat of national government; a focus of great power, it was at the same time drastically affected by decisions in Washington, in Albany, and often by international forces. For decades its future had seemed one of continu-

ous population growth and limitless increase in business and industry. But in Tugwell's mind, growth no longer was the certain prem-
ise for planning. As the city's supremacy was challenged in one field
after another, it was in danger "of exchanging its place as a world
center for one on the periphery of a continent."

Given this changing position in relation to the outside world, the
city could no longer afford the indefinite expansion of its physical
plant. It was folly, Tugwell argued, to open up new areas, to build
highways to take people out of the city or to underdeveloped parts
of the newer boroughs, when the old neighborhoods, the very
heart of the city, were left to decay. The deepening financial plight
of New York might appear to be the result of a multiplication of
services, an accretion of more or less extravagant amenities. But in
fact it was not multiplication; it was rather the spreading process
which had followed real estate speculation in the other areas. In
Queens alone, New York was attempting to build a new city comparable in size to Philadelphia.

This Cassandra-like portrait of New York (refined in two later
annual reports of the commission) was somewhat lightened by a
sprinkling of hopeful recommendations, from the banishing of bill-
boards to the encouraging of museums; and the report fed the
popular fancy by picturing the long-range benefits which could
accrue from the approaching World's Fair. Indeed, the press chose
to overlook the report's deeper message in favor of these optimistic
notes. The commission was pleasantly likened by one newspaper to
a small-town physician, a specialist in a wide variety of diseases, not
all of them necessarily fatal. Tugwell, moreover, softened the rigors
of his analysis with modest reflections on what it had meant for him
to sit through a year's hearings on the capital budget, trying to meet
so many needs with such limited funds. No one could undergo such
an experience, he observed, and not be conscious of a new tolerance, a cooling of narrow enthusiasms. Without such tolerance,
which the commission itself hoped to observe, planning would
never amount to much.

But the medicine was bitter, however the pill might be coated.
The report could expect to find small favor with the business community; what Tugwell regarded as dissipation of the city's resources
—the vast housing projects with their new schools, roads, sewers
—was the stuff of life to a building industry just starting to come
out of the doldrums of the Depression. The citizens of Queens and
other newer areas would await the next election to show their

displeasure at the prospect of neglect while older neighborhoods were being sustained. Robert Moses said little at the time, but he had taken the measure of a man whose views were so diametrically opposed to his own. On one occasion Tugwell came to him, saying that the city was evidently not big enough for them both. "In that case," said Moses, "I suggest that you leave."

Reading the commission's reports today one is impressed by their prophetic character. Tugwell's vision is more in keeping with the preoccupations of the 1970s than of those who lived just prior to World War II, or who engaged in the enormous growth of the 1960s. Tugwell was right in the long run and Moses was wrong, but then Moses never claimed to be dealing with anything except immediately attainable goals. As for LaGuardia, he managed to stay aloof, taking some of the credit when good-government groups praised the commission, but neither endorsing nor condemning its reports. When Tugwell announced his departure, taking advantage of a job offered him by Ickes in Puerto Rico, the mayor played the injured party and claimed that Tugwell was abandoning him just as the third-term election was getting under way. But he knew full well that he had long since abandoned Tugwell.

A first major controversy provoked by the planning commission arose from Tugwell's conviction that the decline of older New York neighborhoods must be reversed. He saw clear signs of decay in the blatant street signs, parking garages, and gas stations which infected once-stable residential areas, all nonconforming uses under the city's zoning laws. His efforts to get retroactive conformance was roundly defeated by the pressure of business interests, and the commission narrowly escaped having its zoning powers cropped. A second controversy arose over the master plan, the formulation of which was a major charge laid on the commission.

In 1940, at a meeting in Hunter College, Tugwell presented the plan in elaborate land use maps before five hundred business and civic leaders. The objective, it was explained, was to make New York "a more convenient, a more efficient, and a better and happier place." Carefully presented with the hope of avoiding controversy, the plan at first seemed to arouse little opposition. But it was soon being picked apart by defenders of various special interests and more generally attacked by those who, as a matter of principle, disliked planning in any form. Moses, who had bided his time, now entered into the fray. Denouncing "planning reds" and ivory-tower intellectuals, he contrasted their watercolored maps with the mighty structures which had been completed under his direction by "people who labored day and night for limited objectives in the face of great difficulties." At the conclusive hearings in December 1940, Moses single-handedly doomed the plan. Tugwell, who had lacked the support of the borough presidents, of the business community, and to a large extent of the civic groups, now found himself isolated even from members of his own commission.

Two years later, when Tugwell had withdrawn and was governor of Puerto Rico, the master plan was unceremoniously discarded. Moses was now on the Planning Commission, appointed by La-Guardia at the start of the third term, an evidence of where the mayor's real sympathies had lain all along. Not until more than twenty-five years had passed would another attempt be made to present a master plan, and then one of a very different kind.

Wit and Wisdom of a Deputy Mayor

The Planning Commission was one institution created by the new charter; a second, expected to introduce into city administration a higher degree of efficiency, was the deputy mayor's office. We have noted that LaGuardia appointed a deputy mayor, installed him in the office he had himself occupied, and expressed hopes for a long and effective term. That LaGuardia's own duties had not diminished since January 1938, nor his schedule eased, has perhaps been apparent. What was Henry H. Curran doing?

Curran was one of those amiable and by no means unintelligent men found occasionally at high levels of city service, not destined to lead and not unduly disturbed when others, going for the substance of power, leave them the forms and ceremonies. If he had ambitions in earlier years (he did, after all, run for mayor in 1922) he surrendered them amid the genial duties of a magistrate, where he was known as one who took pleasure in the minutiae of the judicial function. From this haven LaGuardia at the start of the new term summoned him unexpectedly and invited him to be deputy. "Deputy mayor? What's that?" he later recalled having answered. "I never heard of that one before." Curran had voted against the new charter, thinking it gave too much power to the mayor, but he had not come across "the little ninth article" that provided for the new post. "I knew it not," said he reflectively.

The mayor looked incredulous and then became impatient. "For

26. Deputy Mayor Henry H. Curran enjoys his City Hall office. 1939. WIDE WORLD

heaven's sake go across the street and get a copy of the new charter and find out—costs fifty cents."

In his memoirs Curran continues, "I never did find out what it was all about—the deputy mayor. . . . He [LaGuardia] must have thought he wanted a deputy, for he appointed one, but when he got it he didn't know what to do with it." Curran's duties consisted of receiving those whom the mayor was too busy to see ("callers came in great numbers at first, then thinned out"); of voting as the mayor told him at the Board of Estimate ("it saved him hours of time and gave me hours of entertainment"); and engaging in small feuds with various members of the administration.

It must be said to LaGuardia's credit that after three months he began to have doubts as to whether the new arrangements were working out. Ever watchful, Burlingham urged him not to change Curran prematurely. "It takes all dignity and significance from the office," he wrote, "to treat it as a mere secretaryship, a pawn for the mayor and filled first by one and then another." For better or worse LaGuardia heeded the advice, and the deputy settled more deeply into the gentle routine of his office.

To take on Robert Moses was a natural course for one who enjoyed the exchange of words and who felt lonely in his corner of City Hall. The redesign of City Hall Park, which Curran could survey without moving from his desk, seemed a likely issue. Moses rose magnificently to the bait. It was almost as if he were ready to parody on this level the great battles which had been involving him in a major power struggle with the president of the United States.

Curran introduced into the Board of Estimate a resolution affecting City Hall Park, and apparently did it when the Parks Department representative was absent from the chamber. "This was certainly a cute trick," wrote the parks commissioner. "What a waggish, prankish lad you must have been when you were a freshman in college." There would be no change, Moses decreed, in the design of the park. Retorted Curran: "He just gets a little upset when he can't get his own way." The fight was transferred to the Art Commission where Moses's design won out over Curran's objections. The park's proposed circle, said Curran, "would be an immediate gathering place for Communists," and added as a parting shot that Moses, with his formal expanses of asphalt, was trying "to recreate the Louvre."

More effective were Curran's campaigns against the abuse of the English language in the Board of Estimate, particularly against the word "contact" when used as a verb, and what he called "the mathematical monstrosity" of the expression "and/or." Overnight he became the darling of the editorial scribes. The *Herald Tribune* discovered that Curran had once been a copy reader on its staff, "and a very good one, too." He might lose the battle for good English, it said, but he would be long remembered for his brave stand. The *Times* judged the reforms, if they were to be achieved, as "the most enduring monument set up by the LaGuardia administration." It dissented, however, from the vigor with which Curran sought to banish all traces of the verbal "contact," even when applied to objects. To "contact" other persons was surely obnoxious; but when Mr. Lyons, the borough president of the Bronx, wanted Triborough's work speeded so that "people could pass from Westchester to Long Island without *contacting* Manhattan," that, in the opinion of the *Times,* had rather a noble sound.

The deputy mayor's downfall was preceded by his own contact with a seventeen-year-old saxophone player. The youth had written LaGuardia to inquire whether practicing the saxophone in the afternoon was a violation of the antinoise ordinance. The letter went to Curran, who framed an erudite but flippant reply, urging the young man to abandon the saxophone as a "dangerous instrument," and

to try the oboe, "a sad little pipe." When the press sought out the
recipient of this letter it found an utterly serious young musician,
affronted by the tone of the deputy mayor. "I didn't want publicity," he said chillingly; "I guess he did." The deputy mayor's letter
had told him everything except what he wanted to know. And by
the way, he told reporters, Mr. Curran was wrong when he said
saxophones were never played in symphony orchestras. Several
modern composers wrote music where a saxophone could be employed; indeed Toscanini had used one in a rendition of Ravel's
Bolero.

A short while afterward LaGuardia called Curran into his office
to inform him that he had put into the next year's budget $1.00 for
the deputy mayor's salary. Curran went to the magistrate's court,
saying he was glad to be back. In a pleasant tribute to both men the
Times bid farewell after the "official decapitation." He might have
been a good deputy mayor, it said of Curran, if anything had been
deputed to him. Despite lack of something to do he had brightened
the time with his quips; he had played the role of "a sort of comic
poet laureate." As for LaGuardia, nobody but LaGuardia himself
could be his substitute. "He is present when he is absent. His genius
can't be deputed."

Writing after the LaGuardia years, Moses described in stinging
words the office which had been created with a serious purpose and
to which considerable hope had attached. In practice, he said, La-
Guardia's deputy was something "halfway between a warrant
officer loosely attached to a retired admiral and a dignified eunuch
at the door of a squirming seraglio."

Mayor on the Move

With or without a deputy LaGuardia was busy, and he was in this
time mostly at his best. Following his victories and his travels he
basked in the spotlight which he had lighted. We see him now at
his desk in the City Hall office, "like a swarthy Buddha reaching
for one of his six buzzers to call his office slaves." When he was in
good humor, which was about half the time, there was something
cherubic about him and his enthusiasms. The other half of the time
his humor would range from the disgruntled to the splenetic; but
those close to him had learned to put up with the worst of his
explosions, while his faithful Mitzi Somach (whom the mayor called

his "counsel for the defense") smoothed the injured feelings of others.

It would be a mistake, however, to overdo the picturesque aspects of LaGuardia's office routine. He could impart to the day's events an almost unfailing sense of high drama, even of sheer fun; but he was also capable of tremendously hard and concentrated work. To examine the endless flow of documents in his private files, the memos passed back and forth between himself and his aides, is to get the impression of a highly businesslike performance. He could certainly be moody or curt, but he seems to have reserved his dramatic outbursts of anger for the occasions when a live body was present to bear the brunt. On paper he was likely to be as businesslike as he was volatile in person. Rarely on the documents which once passed over his desk does today's researcher find an expletive, or even an exclamation point; indeed, one might make the mistake of supposing these to be the output of an administrator lacking in temperament.

At times he seemed to be everywhere except at his City Hall desk. He was a man on the move, through the bustling city and through the wider domain which he considered his own. The need for action possessed him. As one close observer put it, the mayor was never disturbed when something happened: "What set him popping was when something didn't happen." He took it upon himself to make sure that the latter condition occurred rarely. His instinct, now formalized into habit, was to settle an issue on the spot, and to make sure that once settled the same issue did not come back to him. His schedule was kept highly flexible, and he avoided having any set time or place for such daily chores as answering the mail. In this way he worked hard while remaining free of fixed routine. Above all, he kept himself in readiness for the unexpected.

That he would respond to the fire bell like a warhorse to the trumpet is well known; indeed, his presence at fires in a helmet and yellow slicker—a diminutive squat figure contrasted to the fire commissioner's impressive height—often while the flames still burned and water from the firemen's hoses lay congealed in winter's subzero temperature, became one of the favorite images of the time. It was told that as a boy living in the wooden army buildings crowded close together at Fort Jefferson he had been alone when a fire broke out; on his cornet he sounded the alarm which brought aid and allowed the barracks to be saved. Perhaps such an incident in his past history, or something in his psychological makeup, in-

27. Hung with icicles. Cherry Street fire, 1939. UPI

28. Maestro. MAX PETER HAAS; THIS PHOTO SUPPLIED BY EUROPEAN
PICTURE SERVICE

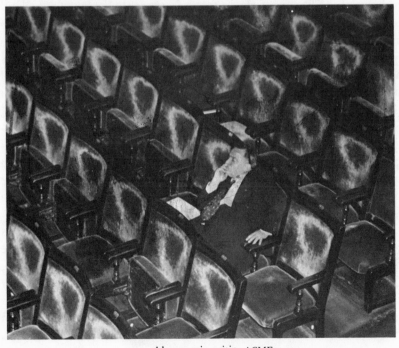

29. Also music critic. ACME

clined him to be a participant among the city's fire fighters. He grew
somewhat defensive about his role. "I hate the damn things," he
once exclaimed in answer to a question about fires. "But what
would the men think if I didn't have the guts to go where they went,
especially if there was danger?"

"The men," as a matter of fact, never had the least occasion to
doubt his disregard of personal peril. His treatment of an attacker
on the steps of City Hall became legendary in the police force.
Again, when a suitcase suspected of containing a bomb was discovered at Pennsylvania Station, LaGuardia arrived on the scene and,
despite efforts of the police to have him stand at a safe distance,
insisted on being in the front rank. When the suitcase was found
to contain only clothing and a ticking clock, "the mayor showed his
relief by twirling his big hat."

He was the most ubiquitous mayor the city had ever known. He
was equally at home in a rodeo, a tepee, a museum, or on the
conductor's podium; besides which, as John Chamberlain put it, he
could step into the pitcher's box on opening day at Yankee Stadium
"and let loose with a high, hard one in the general direction of
home plate." His dramatics, Chamberlain added, were generally
functional: "They have the intent of a parable."

The mayor's political interests covered as wide a range as his
assortment of physical roles. His capacity to deal with the problems
of the farmer as assiduously as with those of labor particularly
annoyed the conservative *Sun,* which commented after he had fired
off a telegram backing a Senate bill extending farm subsidies: "It
is good to know that the heart of that horny-handed son of the soil,
Fiorello H. LaGuardia, remains faithful to the cause of the subsi-
dized American farmer." One day it might be politically advantageous to the mayor, the editorialist continued, "to have it known
up all the forks and all the creeks, on the prairies and on the
bottomlands, that at least one New Yorker really loved the
farmer."

Most of his constituency took a more lenient view of the mayor's
wide-ranging activities, but his absences inevitably came under the
fire of the City Council. When the mayor was away in San Francisco,
Councilman Joseph E. Kinsley of the Bronx set up in the meeting
room of the finance committee, of which he was chairman, a large
map tracing LaGuardia's journeys. "Fiorello's Fanciful Flights" it
was titled. It seemed that since 1934 the mayor had traveled 38,000
miles, not counting trips to Albany and Washington. Some areas of

the map were marked as "unexplored lands, ripe for development"; Maine and Vermont were noted as being still virgin territories. The humor got ample notice in the press, but little support.
The sum of 38,000 miles was a good round figure, like the mayor's,
said the *Times;* and the council had little cause for complaint, it
argued, except that the mayor did not get enough recreation. But
then, it concluded philosophically, "His rest is motion and his play
is work." A few days later the comptroller issued figures to show
that in more than five years the mayor's travels had cost the city the
sum of $1,012.

It was difficult to deny the benefits gathered in by these journeys.
Wherever the mayor went he was an effective salesman of New
York. On one day he would fly to Burlington, Vermont (invading
a hitherto unvisited state), to sign up an airline for the airport at
North Beach then nearing completion; on another he flew upstate
to persuade the dairy farmers to forgo a strike that would be harmful to the city's interests. A single visit to Washington in February
1939 saw him engaged in the following activities: procuring $15
million for a housing development on Staten Island ("a dream
village . . . with a little cottage for every family, a little garden, with
perhaps a few chickens"); conferring with Jesse Jones on schemes
of self-financing for the Brooklyn–Battery Bridge; notifying the
Federal Communications Commission of intent to file for a full-time
allotment for WNYC; signing an agreement with the Civil Service
Commission to establish a branch at North Beach; conferring privately with Ickes and having dinner with Attorney-General Frank
Murphy. On another day in this same year he was in Wisconsin and
in Chicago; he returned home at 4:15 A.M. and was at his desk at
City Hall at 9:30 for talks on transit, for a trip to the docks to see
the president of the World's Fair off to Europe, to an inspection of
the foundations of the new criminal courts building—and so on.
"My bones ache," he admitted; "this job has aged me." Then he
used the simile of an airplane to explain his constant motion. "A
public official, you know, is very much like a plane; it needs sustained flight or it will go into a nosedive. The mayor is not going
to go into a nosedive."

His touch in the handling of city affairs was sure. When he
decided jobs would be created and the image of New York enhanced by having films made in the city, he entered into negotiations which soon had four major movies in production. When he
decided that the consumer was being deceived by the purported

difference between two grades of milk, he appealed over WNYC for a boycotting of Grade A. Grade B, he insisted, was just as good, just as wholesome, just as sanitary—and it cost less. "It took some time to convince my wife," he said; but now he was prepared to put into effect new regulations to protect the consumer. The appeal was repeated by "electrical transcription," and put the mayor in a new role as advisor extraordinary to the city's housewives.

LaGuardia's experience in labor disputes went back to service as attorney to the garment workers' trades before World War I. Now all his old skills were evoked and his fierce energies concentrated on working out settlements. The pro-labor sympathies of the early days of his administration, which had shown themselves in the taxicab strike, were muted as he proved more and more capable of reaching an understanding with both sides. LaGuardia was basically a fair man; he could talk cold facts, and capital and labor responded alike to his authority. The Industrial Relations Board which he appointed in 1937 settled hundreds of disputes without publicity, but when the issue proved intractable, the mayor himself was prepared to intervene.

"A strike which did not happen is not a spectacular thing," he wrote after the achievement of one settlement. "But to have averted the suffering in countless obscure homes, which would have otherwise ensued, is a rewarding thought." He was a confirmed believer in fact finding. "Without compulsion, and merely with the light shed by public disclosure," he believed a bridge could be built between opposing forces, and that instrumentalities of mediation and conciliation would then bring them to voluntary agreement. His achievements as mayor justified this belief, at least until the passionate irrationalities of Michael Quill introduced a new and menacing note into the processes of negotiation.

In April 1939 LaGuardia entered the national bituminous coal strike, appearing at a joint conference of miners and operators being held in New York. He discussed the situation for more than an hour, warning that vital interests were at stake and that the city might be forced to buy coal from abroad. He made a direct appeal to the president; he ordered a cut in the schedules of subways as a way of forcing attention upon the city's dwindling supplies. More directly under his control was a strike of the coal deliverers nine months later. It was winter now; the temperature was down to nine degrees, and a fifty-mph gale was howling through the city.

After a fruitless twelve-hour negotiating session the mayor observed that at that pace the strike would be settled by the Fourth of July. "That is too long to wait," he said. "I have followed the negotiations carefully and I am going to make a public offer to settle the thing." He ordered WNYC microphones placed on his desk and gave the parties until 6 P.M. to accept or reject his offer. Ten minutes before the hour LaGuardia was on the air ready to hear from both sides. The employers' committee announced it was ready to accept the offer and to take it back to its association—"They have never turned down a proposal from the mayor." The union leaders asked for a few more minutes, then they, too, assented. The mayor's role was warmly greeted. "This is not the first time," said the *Herald Tribune,* "that he has met a crisis of this kind with energy, courage, and wisdom. Yet always he seems to improve on past performances."

At approximately this time the mayor inquired at the end of one afternoon how a certain negotiation was proceeding. Progress was disconcertingly slow. A few hours later the group, deciding to break up for the night, was amazed to find the exit to City Hall firmly closed and guarded by the police. "The mayor said to keep you locked up and you'd settle the strike," explained an officer. Without food, without heat, the parties involved worked through the night and by the next morning an agreement acceptable to all had been hammered out. A strike of painters was settled in the mayor's hideaway in the Central Park Arsenal; of electrical workers when the mayor wrote a longhand decision en route to Boston; of Queens bus drivers in a conference room of the Waldorf Astoria where LaGuardia was meeting with the mayors of major cities.

Observing him at this time, Tugwell came closest to analyzing the springs of the mayor's manner and style. He possessed, said Tugwell, "an enormous capacity for business"; he had it in fantastic enlargement. "A swarming multitude of incidents, contacts, agglomerations, associations, and public posturings seethes continually in the brain of LaGuardia." From the amalgam the mayor shaped his course with sure instinct, and in this productive period of his administration put on a show which earned him the delighted approbation of a constituency far wider than New York City's alone.

World's Fair—From Peace to War

In the midst of his other activities the mayor was getting ready for the opening of the World's Fair. In March he visited the San Francisco exhibition, a courtesy call as well as a chance to beat the drums for New York's forthcoming extravaganza. To a San Francisco friend, regretting that he could not accept an invitation to dine, he had written, "I'm not coming alone. Wait until you see what I am bringing with me." What he brought was a considerable assemblage of family and of New York officials. The group which set out in holiday mood from Pennsylvania Station, in addition to Mrs. LaGuardia and Jean, included Paul Kern and the commissioner of licenses Paul Moss, their wives, and three members of the mayor's staff: Anna Clark, Byrnes MacDonald, and Clendenin Ryan. A sadly disappointed Eric was kept at home by an attack of whooping cough.

The days in San Francisco, besides giving the group a chance to act as salesmen and ambassadors, provided LaGuardia with an occasion to reinforce his image as an international statesman. A few days before his arrival, in the midst of menacing developments abroad, the German consul-general had made a defiant speech before the Commonwealth Club. Taking advantage of LaGuardia's fortuitous presence in the city, the club asked him to reply. It was a rare opportunity to speak out on a subject about which he held strong convictions. An unusually large turnout of a thousand members heard New York's mayor define the challenge to freedom and call for a united stand in the face of Hitler's aggressions.

He described himself as one who, from time to time, had given his views on Hitlerism "in more or less diplomatic language," a reference to the "chamber of horrors" speech which delighted his audience; and then fulfilled their expectations by adding that "you can only use the language of diplomacy if you are dealing with gentlemen." It was a remarkably effective speech, the more impressive because so hastily prepared, and it received wide comment around the country. Leaving San Francisco with his little expeditionary force, LaGuardia arrived home on St. Patrick's Day. He was wearing a green tie, and Eric was well again.

The New York World's Fair, for which final preparations were being made, was not only to be a great event in itself—"the mightiest exposition ever conceived and built by man," as the *Herald Tribune* described it—but was an act of city planning in the grand manner. The transformation of a garbage dump into a fair grounds and then into a park was in itself a major accomplishment. Around the fair site the scene was being reshaped by such permanent improvements as a new airport, new highways, a new bridge; and throughout the city the effects of the Fair were already being felt. New subway cars on new express lines were ready to bring visitors out to Flushing Meadows; a sanitation force enlarged by thousands of WPA workers was cleaning up the streets of the city, reaching into vacant lots where the debris of decades lay in a dismal accumulation. The Fair was looked on by LaGuardia as a vitalizing force capable of bringing immense benefits to the city. It would be dedicated to the dwindling hope for peace; but it would celebrate, no less significantly, the rebirth of a great metropolis.

Like all human undertakings, the fair was plagued by troubles and conflicts. Through the three years of preparation strikes and shortages of funds made some wonder whether it would ever actually open; right up to the eve things continued to go wrong. A bad fire broke out in one pavilion. Billie Rose's aquatic beauties refused to rehearse unless they were given more money. But on April 30, with eighty warships deployed in the East River and amid dignitaries representing every nation in the world, Franklin Roosevelt opened the Fair on schedule. His speech was a paean to democracy, a hymn of praise for a nation of many kindreds and tongues, offering a contrast to the European dictatorships scarcely needing to be underscored. Speaking briefly after the president, LaGuardia in unaccustomed cutaway and top hat declared that "the city of today greets the world of tomorrow."

The Fair itself was perhaps the last exposition which in its displays and architecture could symbolize the progress of civilization for a vast international audience. Theme structures—the unadorned white forms of the trylon and perisphere—suggested a realm of values beyond the picturesque or tawdry amusements of the hour. The introduction of television, the glimpses of tomorrow's world in a landscape of cloverleafs and overpasses, made real contributions to the popular vision. The precariousness of peace, while the crowds at Flushing Meadows dreamed of scientific progress and universal plenty, gave poignancy to even the less brilliant displays.

The mayor was not one to isolate himself from the ceremonies and excitements which the Fair generated almost daily. No longer able to possess the city building on the Fair grounds, he installed his summer city hall nearby, in the Arrowbrook Country Club,

30. The World of Tomorrow. Opening ceremonies, April, 30, 1939. ACME

31. Comfortable with the king and queen of England—on the way to the World's Fair. INP

where he worked unperturbed in an office even larger than the Blue Room, surrounded by a ragtag assortment of cretonned couches and ornate pieces in the Louis XV style. In the dining room of the former club, where a "mechanical phonograph machine" played for a dime "La Cucaracha" and "Have You Ever Been in Heaven?" the Board of Estimate held its meetings. From here the mayor sallied forth to greet celebrated visitors and to share in the opening of each newly completed pavilion.

Exhibitions sponsored by European countries gave him a splendid opportunity to make use of his many languages. At the Yugoslav pavilion he resurrected the Croatian tongue which he had learned thirty years before and had seldom used since; and on successive occasions, whatever the language, he could draw his text from the darkening scene abroad. On one memorable day in June the king and queen of England came to the Fair. LaGuardia met them as they disembarked at the Battery from the royal yacht. One observer noted approvingly that "nobody bowed too low and nobody curtsied." This democratic greeting set the tone for a day that everyone was determined to keep as simple and informal as possible. When it was over, LaGuardia, refusing to be awed, told reporters that England's royal family were "easier to entertain and live with for a day than a great many other guests we have had."

Early in July it became evident that attendance at the Fair was falling short of expectations. A financial crisis was developing and several hundred employees were dropped. LaGuardia took upon himself the responsibility of getting more people out to Flushing Meadows. He offered gentle persuasion to city employees and then gave them Saturday off so they could attend with their families. A lightning-fast, 1,700-mile selling trip was undertaken at the urging of the Fair's backers. It was just the kind of expedition the mayor liked. On August 9 he was up at dawn to inspect the site for a new market on his way to the airport; a stop in Washington allowed him to protest recent WPA cuts. He paused briefly in Cincinnati to talk with its mayor. Then at Chicago he addressed a luncheon of seven hundred businessmen, where he was introduced by Mayor Kelly as "the most dynamic personality in America," as well as the greatest mayor in the world.

He was back in New York by evening, but the day was still not over. It gave him particular pleasure, before finally retiring, to sign bonds assuring the continuance of federal programs for artists, musicians, and writers. "Don't you ever get tired?" John Haynes

Holmes wrote him around this time. "I guess you like your job—
just as millions of us like you."

Throughout the summer events in Europe steadily worsened,
climaxed in August by the signing of the Soviet-German Nonaggression Pact. In September war was formally declared. What had
been so long in the making arrived nevertheless as a shock. New
York was for a day a strange city of radio voices, as the populace
listened to tidings of doom blared forth from hot-dog stands, fruit-
drink carts, from private cars and public halls. LaGuardia moved
quickly to assure calm. The police were put on emergency duty;
bridges, tunnels, and piers were guarded. In broadcasts he appealed
for civic composure—"Battles will be fought in Europe," he said
"not in the streets of New York."

The coming of war put Fair-goers in a sober mood. Crowds
gathered in the pavilions of the chief protagonists—the French, the
English, the Italians, and the Soviets. Many came to the Polish
pavilion, a scene of anguish as bewildered men and women, holding back their tears, filed through the exhibition. It was difficult to
think of the next summer, when the Fair was scheduled to reopen.
But a new president, Harvey D. Gibson, was appointed to take over
from Whalen the management of the Fair's troubled finances, and
LaGuardia received from Roosevelt support for the idea that a
second year might provide a prop to morale.

Nearly half a million visitors, the largest crowd of the season,
turned out for the last, autumnal Sunday. "Here on 1,121.6 acres
of what once was a dismal swamp," wrote R. L. Duffus of the *Times,*
"are gardens and buildings mirroring a possible future, whose keys
have not been lost."

The Mayor Stumbles

The year 1939, for all its fanfare and its genuine accomplishments, could not quite match the *annus mirabilis,* 1938. Below the
surface, and sometimes just above it, were indications of troubles
to come. In the bridge controversy was a premonition of the kind
of turndown Franklin Roosevelt would administer far more disas-
trously a few years later; in the first report of the Planning Commission could be heard the dark undertones of the city's enduring
problems. LaGuardia in the midst of his strenuous labors and his
travels had felt twinges of the weariness which would make him

needlessly irascible as time went on. He was at the summit of his power and popularity; but he now slipped, and the abrupt dismissal of a valued aide brought down on him a kind of criticism he was not accustomed to hear.

The August issue of *Harper's* magazine carried an article by Alfred Rheinstein, successor to the ill-fated Langdon Post as commissioner of housing and chairman of the New York City Housing Authority. Entitled "Why Slum Clearance May Fail," the article angered the same Nathan Straus whom LaGuardia had bitterly attacked as a "star-gazer" in 1937. In Cincinnati for the World Series, on October 8 the mayor got word that Rheinstein was resigning. A two-word telegram, "resignation accepted," was fired back; and the next day the commissioner of investigation appeared suddenly at the office of the Housing Authority to begin an inquiry into its affairs. Scarcely any event in LaGuardia's three administrations caused so deep a disturbance in the public mind.

To understand the widespread indignation it is necessary to see Rheinstein as he appeared to contemporaries. A builder with years of experience and a strong social conscience, he seemed the ideal man to be in charge of the city's public housing programs. He was convinced construction costs could be lowered and set about proving it by the introduction of innovative methods and techniques. At Queensbridge Houses he saved a quarter of the funds allocated; at Red Hook he added within the budget 9,000 more units than had originally been planned, and reduced rents from seven dollars to five dollars a room. To a city which had long suffered from serious housing shortages, Rheinstein appeared a miracle worker, in his own field comparable to Robert Moses.

Like Moses he fought against red tape and official constraints. The *Harper's* article was a strong criticism of federal housing standards which seemed inapplicable to New York. Rigid limits upon the cost of land meant that public housing could only be constructed in the outer boroughs, where it was least needed. Income levels prescribed for the whole country were poorly suited to New York's higher wage scales. In any case, Rheinstein argued, prospective tenants should be rated by a variety of human factors and not by income alone.

In the beginning LaGuardia backed Rheinstein and the methods which so evidently produced results. On one occasion Dorothy Kenyon, first deputy in the Department of Licenses, complained that Rheinstein had disregarded civil service rules and she quoted

Paul Kern as agreeing with her. In an exchange of correspondence that would become more interesting in retrospect, LaGuardia snapped back: "You are all wrong. . . . Rheinstein was just 100 percent right and Paul 100 percent wrong. Tell him [Kern] that if he continues gossiping I will fire him without the slightest ceremony."

"I am glad to know," Kenyon replied, "that anybody in the world (except Bob Moses) is ever 100 percent right."

The day would come when Paul Kern, unceremoniously indeed, would be fired. No one could foresee that Rheinstein's hour was so close. In Washington, Nathan Straus was furious at the *Harper's* article. It was the culmination of several confrontations with New York's administrator, and Straus now threatened not to give the city another penny for housing. LaGuardia, responding swiftly to Straus's displeasure, performed a strange act of contrition. He publicly apologized for the behavior of his commissioner. Expressing regret for the article, he called it contrary to his policy of maintaining friendly relations with the Washington agencies. "I am expressing this regret without reservation," he wrote. The article itself he dismissed as "mediocre" and "amateurish," not likely to influence anyone.

On this note Rheinstein resigned and LaGuardia—without a word of praise for past services, apparently unaware of the commissioner's hold on public opinion—accepted his departure. The reaction of the press and civic groups was first one of disbelief, then of disillusionment with the mayor. Rheinstein received unqualified support. "The evidence is overwhelming," wrote the *Times,* "that Mr. Straus tried to boss local projects in a degree incompatible with local efficiency: he treated Mr. Rheinstein as if he were a subordinate employee of the federal government. He treated the great city of New York as if it were a federal pensioner." The city administration's subservience to Washington was a special cause for concern. "If Mayor LaGuardia had put himself on a doormat [and] prostrated himself on the White House steps," wrote one correspondent to the *Times,* "he could not have brought the point home more convincingly." "An irredeemable injury to the housing program" was the way the City Club and the Citizens Housing Conference described the effects of the ouster.

The mayor may not have been entirely dissatisfied with the results. Within a few days of Rheinstein's dismissal, Straus announced approval of a project in Brooklyn's Bedford–Stuyvesant area, reassuring the mayor that the federal pipeline would not run dry. Events had made it possible to remove a man who might have been another thorn in his side, another Moses, and even a threat to his own preeminence. With the dedication of Queensbridge Houses postponed, LaGuardia made his own personal inspection tour. Yet the newspapers were unrelenting. The *Times* returned to the battle with the remark that LaGuardia was looking for a new chairman "who will not mind being dropped like a hot potato whenever his opinions fail to coincide with what the mayor believes to be expedient."

The new chairman turned out to be Gerard Swope, just retired as president of General Electric. "I have not the remotest idea of policy," Swope declared in relation to his city post. Yet his appointment was generally acceptable and the press went on to other issues. Though there would be other sudden dismissals and other accommodations with Washington, no later incident stirred quite the same sense of dismay. The Rheinstein episode caused a first shadow to fall across the LaGuardia image.

His Own Airport

A happier event at the close of 1939 still waits to be noted, the opening and the successful beginnings of the airfield at North Beach. This was a triumph particularly sweet to the mayor who had conceived the project and had driven it through to completion. It was the more sweet because this was one vast building operation that was truly his own. Neither Robert Moses nor Alfred Rheinstein could claim any of the glory.

LaGuardia had always been fascinated by planes and flying. An ace in World War I and from the start of his term a constant traveler on the commercial lines, he was determined that New York should have an airport within the city limits. It was a matter of civic pride with him; it was also a realization that as the city lost its preeminence as a seaport, entrance of goods and people by air would become essential to its prosperity. And this airport he wanted to be big, fit for the age of international flight which he never doubted would come.

In 1934, returning from a trip to Chicago, his plane landed at Newark, the terminal point of commercial flights of that period. The mayor refused to disembark. His ticket read "Chicago to New

York" and he insisted on its terms being fulfilled. After he had been photographed sitting stolidly in his seat in the otherwise empty plane, a rotund and defiant figure, the airline in desperation had flown him to Floyd Bennett Field in Brooklyn. Once again La-Guardia had indulged in one of those dramatic gestures which could influence far-off events.

Next he took on the federal agencies which, being under the impression that Floyd Bennett was subject to various forms of bad weather, refused funds for its development. In a long series of letters and telegrams he set out to convince the postal service that mail could be flown into New York with a safety margin at least equal to that in New Jersey. Let a fog descend on Newark, let a flight be canceled or postponed, out would go a lengthy message from the mayor detailing the superior conditions at Floyd Bennett. In this campaign he won the support of Franklin Roosevelt, himself an aviation enthusiast, whose 1932 flight to Chicago to accept the nomination of his party had symbolized the new leader's innovative spirit.

At North Beach in Queens something far grander than Floyd Bennett was soon to be projected. Lying along the east shore of Flushing Bay, the land proposed for this use was then a nondescript marsh shelving off into muddy water. (This was before the age of ecology when a marsh was still a marsh, and was even a "dismal swamp"; it was not yet recognized as an invaluable wetland.) The bottom lands were to be dredged and piled up to form extensive runways filling part of the bay. Complemented by a new park on the site of the World's Fair grounds and served by major new highways, the airport when completed would be within a twenty-minute drive from downtown Manhattan.

One day in the early stages Roosevelt reviewed plans for the airport with LaGuardia. The president was in one of his Jeffersonian moods, playing with the image of men at work in pretechnological conditions, using shovels instead of bulldozers to spread employ-ment. Tugwell joined the conference; he was still the Washington brain truster, the advocate of centralized planning and technocratic values. Caustically he suggested that the scheme might be improved if instead of shovels the men used trowels. The project went for-ward by more orthodox construction methods, but it involved a degree of large-scale planning and administration which once and for all lifted WPA workers out of the category of leaf-rakers and gave real meaning to their toil.

32. A new day in international aviation: Opening of North Beach (LaGuardia) Airport. October 15, 1939. WIDE WORLD

As 1939 advanced LaGuardia took personal command of the drive to complete and open the airport so as to have it ready for the second summer of the World's Fair. He was backed enthusiastically by Somervell who had emerged as the most long-lived and cooperative of the federal relief czars. On a Sunday the mayor would go out to make personal inspections of the site. "It was his own baby," Marie LaGuardia later recalled. By mid-October of that year the field's advanced lighting system was turned on, bathing the runways "in golden gleams"; the beacon atop the administration building revolved slowly against a ruddy, cloud-banked sky. As the long preparations were completed, an American Airlines plane bearing six Canadian officials flew in and touched down gracefully on the runway. A new age in international aviation was beginning.

October 15 saw the field's formal dedication. The mayor arrived at noon in the perfect weather of a New York fall day. In a radio speech the previous evening he had heralded North Beach as "an airport unsurpassed and unrivalled in utility, capacity, safety, convenience, and beauty." Now amid a crowd of 325,000 he witnessed the new marvel at its birth. Coast Guard amphibians arrived, two-engined bombers and sixteen of the navy's scout bombers. Cooperating from the start in use of the field were American Airlines, United, Pan American, Transcontinental, and Western. LaGuardia was in an ebullient mood and thanked all who had stood by him in the work. He announced he was even ready to forgive those who in the early stages had opposed him.

The day's spirit of harmony carried over, and in November the Board of Estimate adjourned politics to make one of those gestures that relieve the acerbity of public life. On a motion introduced by James Lyons of the Bronx, one of the mayor's most persistent critics, the board voted to name North Beach for the mayor. And LaGuardia Airport, as the reader will no doubt have already guessed, it remains to this day. The legal implications of the board's generous gesture were left somewhat in doubt, for under the charter the commissioner of docks claimed the right to name the airport, while the City Council had the right to name streets and parks. LaGuardia, in any case, called the act of the board "very thoughtful." In August 1940 the field was christened with its new name, while a Yankee Clipper took off for one of the earliest scheduled flights to Europe. Paying tribute to the "Little Flower's" courage and pertinacity, the *Herald Tribune* added words which still seem true half a century later: "Never was there a more fitting memorial to a man than LaGuardia Field."

The mayor was not one to leave "his baby" alone and he continued his visits and inspections as if, which in some measure it did, his reputation depended on the field's success. When rental concessions in the terminal lagged, he dispatched from among his aides a young man who was himself to cause considerable alterations in the city's landscape. David Rockefeller, having just completed his graduate studies at the University of Chicago, secured an outstanding bank as a tenant and persuaded Tiffany to present a sample of its wares in one of the airport's display cases. Early in 1940, when the airport had been closed down for two days by sleet and drizzle, the mayor was on the spot to make sure that all was ship-shape. His first stop was in the men's lounge where "a Negro porter" came to attention.

"Is it clean, son?" the mayor asked. "I certainly hope so," the attendant replied. The mayor walked around, examining wash basins and corners. "It's all right, son, all right." "Thank you, sir," said the attendant with apparent relief, as the mayor went off to inspect the coffee house, the kitchen, the control tower, and the post office. Everything was in order that day. Two years later the mayor announced with satisfaction that LaGuardia was the busiest commercial airport in the world, with more than seventy-five flights taking off and landing daily.

8

The Broader Stage

At Home in the Minority

In November 1939, amid general apathy, New York citizens went to the polls in local elections. Only a million voted, roughly half those who had registered in October and the smallest proportion of those eligible since the establishment of the "Greater City" in 1897. The results were a severe setback for the Liberal-Fusion cause. Democrats elected all sixteen of their candidates for the municipal courts, and all nine supreme court justices. In the new City Council they won twelve seats out of twenty-one. A LaGuardia foe, Abner C. Surpless of Queens, was elected among the Fusionists, and the son of New York's elder statesmen, Alfred E. Smith, Jr., was launched as an independent. It was anticipated, correctly, that he would prove one of the mayor's antagonists.

Altogether it was a discouraging picture for LaGuardia, but the man who stormed at the rebuff of an individual or a hostile group was habituated to taking calmly the ups and downs of electoral politics. On election night when the lights of Tammany Hall burned brightly again for the first time since 1933, the mayor shrugged off the defeat good-naturedly. He was "not surprised" he said; he was going home to bed. Clearly he had been unable to shift his own political strength to the Fusion candidates. "A man must declare himself," he said resignedly, "even when others think differently."

In the council, as the complicated results of proportional representation became known, it was evident that a basically new situation existed. The first council, elected in 1937, had given the Democrats enough votes to bottle up, as they saw fit, almost any legislative proposals. The new council gave them a crucial two-thirds' majority, enough to override a mayoral veto. Ceasing to be a mere drag on the process of reform, they were now in a position to push forward their own programs and maneuvers.

With John Cashmore of Brooklyn the heavy-handed dictator of the Democratic majority, the first council's record had been one of stalemate or of petty accomplishments. Of the seventy-four local laws adopted since 1938, as many as forty dealt with changing street names or designating new streets. Among the important issues which had failed of action were the revision of the city's pension system, reorganization of the courts, repeal of the Lyons Law, and, above all, elimination or consolidation of Tammany-held jobs in various county posts. In the new situation, with the Democrats able to thwart the mayor's vetoes, it was hardly to be expected that a better record would be achieved.

The mayor, nevertheless, resisted any tendency to be downcast. At the opening of the new council on January 1, 1940, he made one of his best "parliamentary" speeches, indulging in nostalgia, in praise, in an expression of the modesty which he could assume on occasion, especially when any other pose would appear to be unproductive. Recalling that exactly twenty years had passed since he assumed office as president of the old Board of Aldermen, he told the council chamber: "I had all the defects then that I have today, and I haven't improved a bit. . . . I was then in the minority. I was quite at home. It has been my portion to be in the minority the greater part of my life." Among the spectators in the gallery was Alfred E. Smith, beaming upon the son and namesake who was just entering public life. Smith had preceded the mayor by just two years in the aldermanic presidency and now was the recipient of praise which carried a moral for the new council.

Smith's leadership in the state, LaGuardia declared, was proof that the legislature can never set out "to punish the executive." The Republican party had embarked upon a program opposing the governor's social and labor legislation, "and the Republican party has never been the same since in this state." They have never recovered from it, continued the mayor, because the governor was right in his proposals. "Every measure recommended by Governor Smith has since become law. The people of the city and the state are quick to realize if opposition is based on the real merits of the case, or simply following the procedure of spite and of personal opposition."

After dealing with substantive issues—a plea for economy, a warning that real estate could not indefinitely bear the costs of expanding services, observations concerning the "dislocated" school system resulting from bad subway planning ("Great were our mistakes in the laying out of the lines")—LaGuardia assumed a tone which might be termed aggressive tolerance, or belligerent accommodation. "I think a council that is alert, even a council that is unfair, is better than no council at all. I shall always think well of the legislative body of our city government. I will understand fully every blow that is struck and I will never invoke the Marquis of Queensbury rules, because you are part of the city, because it is necessary for an executive to work with a legislative body."

"I have absolute faith," he concluded, "that your interest and your love for the city are equal—just as good, just as great—as that of the mayor or anyone else in the city."

The hardest heart in the City Council may have softened (as the *Times* suggested) at these disarming words. If so, it was temporary. However much at home LaGuardia might feel in the minority, he would require all his political skills, and all his patience, to draw from the nettle of partisanship even a small flower of accomplishment.

Council v. Mayor

The council's first task, even before taking on the mayor, was to organize itself and to determine general procedures. The organizational wrangles of 1938 were not repeated. Morris, originally elected for a four-year term, continued as president; Cashmore, now in command of the large Democratic majority, was vice-president. The first regular meeting on January 22 was brief and efficient, being concluded in a bare twenty minutes with resolutions introduced by the members quickly referred to committees. One element present in the first council was now lacking, and that was thought by some to be the reason for a new air of businesslike decorum. By vote of the Democrats, microphones of the city broadcasting station were excluded from the council chamber.

During the first two years listening to the council debates, regularly broadcast over WNYC, had became a major source of popular entertainment. As many as a million people were said to be tuned in to each debate, with the broadcasts at times becoming so amusing that people left their radios and descended on City Hall to see the fun for themselves. President Lyons had even suggested that the proceedings be put on Victrola records as permanent contributions to culture. But Tammany Democrats, now in complete control, were not anxious to have their actions subjected to that kind of public scrutiny. If the old Board of Aldermen had taken 135 years to make fools of themselves, said Councilman Hart, the council had accomplished the same result in two years. He added that the broadcasts had made him blush. "And when a former alderman blushes, that's something."

This show of discretion did not escape comment. Newbold Morris suggested that next the press should be barred. Local statesmen, said the *Herald Tribune,* had reached the paradoxical point where they could only be sensible when deprived of an audience; they could only attend to business when denied "the heady intoxication of having people listen to them." As for WNYC, in place of the oratory it announced a series of all-American concerts featuring such composers as Deems Taylor, Aaron Copeland, and Oscar Levant. Who could say the public was worse off for the change?

The council had scarcely gotten itself organized before it decided to take a month's winter vacation. The vote on February 6 found Cashmore already in Florida. Don't worry, said Morris, recalling a bygone session of the Board of Aldermen when a past mayor sent a messenger to see if the current mayor would receive him. The messenger reported back: "The sergeant-at-arms is asleep, the president of the board is asleep, and most of the aldermen are asleep." "Then do not disturb them," said the mayor, "for while they sleep the city is safe." It was certainly a different atmosphere from the first council, when the tune had been set by such civic-minded idealists as Vladeck and Mrs. Earle. Indeed, Morris now urged Mrs. Earle to go to Florida herself; she would perhaps find that adjournment was "not the worst thing in the world."

Morris was right. The vacation was scarcely over before Alfred E. Smith, Jr., taking his first initiative in the council, asked for an investigation of the Civil Service Commission and of its chairman, Paul Kern. It was a blow aimed at the heart of the LaGuardia reform movement, and was bound to find joyous support among the patronage-hungry Democrats. By 1939 the number of city jobs exempt from civil service had been decisively reduced. When La-Guardia came to office more than a thousand offices were exempt; these had been cut to 600 by the end of his first term and rapid progress was being made toward the goal of 250.

The man responsible for administering civil service, and now to be subject to prolonged investigation, was by nature not averse to making enemies; he had a task which made it easy for him to do so. Paul Kern was required to take on powerful administrators like Moses and Rheinstein, or semi-independent chieftans like Grover Whalen, president of the World's Fair, and restrict their power to hire and promote. Moses had been Kern's particular foe, mistrusting him for his liberalism as much as resenting the interference of civil service regulations in his operations. It is notable that the young Smith based his resolution on the same charge Moses had first leveled against Kern, and phrased it in almost exactly the same words: namely, that Kern had attempted to establish "an alien espionage system." One must suspect that Moses, who remained close to the former governor and his family, counseled the son on this move, which turned out to be so wasteful of the council's time and energy, so painful to the mayor, and in the end so destructive of a high-minded and promising public servant.

Of all the figures who move across the public stage in these years, none is so difficult to see clearly or to judge fairly as Paul Kern. Only thirty in 1938 when LaGuardia promoted him to the chairmanship of the Civil Service Commission, and looking no older, he could certainly annoy people by an air of insouciance. "Never liked him—he was a light-weight," was the verdict of William Chanler many years later. But Edmund Palmieri, who succeeded him as LaGuardia's law secretary, found him the soul of kindness as he patiently elaborated the details of the work.

A rebel from college days, tall and slouching, with a boyish smile and a drawling voice, Kern did not take easily to expectations of deference or the demands of conformity. During the council hearings his offhand manners and his attitude of bored indifference were as much a source of indignation for the council members as his other, supposedly more heinous, offenses. Over and above everything else were the independent views of a man who sympathized with the Spanish Loyalists and did not see why Communists should be barred from schools unless they sought to indoctrinate

33. Paul Kern testifies before the City Council Investigating Committee at an open hearing.

their students. Of those around the mayor, he came nearest to the professorial type. "Engrossed in intellectual problems," a friendly observer described him at this time, "free from conventional relaxations, abstemious, usually overworked in spite of a great capacity for work, mild-mannered but at the same time vigorously outspoken, he is a reformer, but gifted with humor and a talent for friendship."

Kern had particularly close relations with LaGuardia. He was one of the young men whom the mayor looked upon as a protégé, and almost as a son. The story of their first encounter is revealing of the character of both men. Immediately after graduating from Columbia Law School, Kern dropped in unannounced at the Washington office of Congressman LaGuardia. Picking up a brief (which happened to have been written by Felix Frankfurter) he remarked casually that he could do a better one. He was abruptly thrown out. The next day he returned and the congressman relented to the extent of letting him try his hand at rewriting the brief. Kern was as good as his promise and included in the new brief court decisions subsequent to those Frankfurter had used.

For the following eight months Kern worked for LaGuardia in Washington, and then returned to teach at Columbia until LaGuardia, newly elected, brought him back into his office as law secretary. Promoted two years later to the Civil Service Commission, Kern remained within the inner circle of the mayor's friends, a regular visitor to the apartment at 109th Street and a participant in the spaghetti dinners cooked by the mayor's own hand.

Such was the person whom Al Smith, Jr., now set out to destroy. Through 1939 and 1940 the increasingly bitter inquiry unfolded, with no one showing at his best. Kern was certainly insolent in his replies, and even more so in his silences. Smith, Jr., in spite of occasional attempts at impartiality, showed himself a tool in the hands of others who had longer experience and higher stakes in the controversy than himself. The shadow of red-baiting hung over all the sessions. When a lone spectator applauded Kern at one of his first appearances, the chamber's reaction was one of astonishment close to horror. Smith, Jr., rapped his gavel; "Throw the Communist out!" he cried. Repeatedly over the following months Kern was charged with noncooperation. When he refused to testify because only Smith, Jr., was present at the hearing, he was cited for contempt; the charge was upheld in court, and the chairman of the Civil Service Commission narrowly escaped imprisonment. Along with the wholly irrelevant issues, various unproven charges— affecting the mayor as well as Kern—claimed misuses and abuses of the civil service system.

On June 1, two months after the investigation had begun, La-Guardia reappointed Kern to a full six-year term as chairman. He claimed it was "a routine matter," but in the circumstances it was far more than that. The council understandably considered it a slap, and Kern a vindication. Yet erosion of the relationship between the two men had already begun, and was to deepen as the administration suffered from the council's constant harping and as Kern's style of behavior made him seem a liability. In the state of frayed nerves resulting on both sides, a tragic dénouement would occur in 1942, with the mayor and Paul Kern in bitter opposition to each other.

In this and other forays the council was greatly strengthened by judicial decisions extending its power of investigation. The mayor had at first taken the position that under the new charter he was entitled to veto resolutions setting up investigative committees. That was perhaps no more than a political gesture. More serious was the argument that he and his commissioners had the right to withhold information deemed confidential. In July 1939, a decision was handed down to the effect that Herlands, commissioner of investigations, must heed the subpoena of a council committee and reveal the full results of one of his own inquiries. Herlands, in effect, was held accountable not to the mayor but to the council. In a later decision the mayor himself was required to appear before a council committee to present documents he considered privileged. These decisions constituted a clear enlargement of the council's powers at a time when the Democratic majority was not loath to abuse such powers as it already possessed.

Thus stimulated, the council's investigative fever mounted. Along with the hounding of the Civil Service Commission went a continuing and frustrating inquiry into the city's relief programs. In the new situation budget making became a process even more harassing than previously. The council derived political satisfaction from directing cuts in budgets which the mayor insisted had been already reduced to the bone. In 1940 the mayor sent twenty-nine separate messages vetoing such cuts, each couched in derisive language. The Democrats rejoined in kind, but despite their numerical majority could not muster sufficient votes to override the vetoes. In the end they refused to vote at all, and the LaGuardia budget was adopted by default.

Taking on Mr. Quill

The mayor's most difficult confrontation was to be not with the council but with one of its former members, now deeply embroiled in the politics of labor. Michael Quill, whom we have noted as a figure absenting himself to get married in Ireland, failed to get reelected to his council seat in 1939 when the right wing of the American Labor party refused to endorse him. Mercurial and tough, Quill could make trouble enough as head of the Transport Workers Union. With the coming of unification he saw his opportunity and grasped it eagerly.

The struggle for unification of the city's three major subway lines, which had begun in the early months of the LaGuardia administration, had dragged on inconclusively until 1939. Ceremonies marked the signing of contracts between the city and the BMT on June 30; contracts for the purchase of the IRT followed in September. Legal procedures would require several months more, running into the spring of 1940. The city stood at last on the threshold of possessing for its own use, and subjecting to its own criteria of planning, an unparalleled transportation system carrying almost two billion passengers a year, five times the number carried by all the nation's railroads.

The most complex problem posed by unification involved the status of thirty thousand employees of the combined transportation services. How were the existing contracts with the private employers to be handled? Were the workers to be integrated into the civil service of the city? If so, would their contractual rights be safeguarded? A first effort to answer these questions led to ambiguous results. A measure known as the Wicks bill went before the Albany legislature in 1939, presenting LaGuardia with an acute dilemma. Providing a place in the civil service for all subway workers, the bill was passionately opposed by the Transport Worker's Union, an influential affiliate of the CIO which had given the mayor strong support in the last campaign. Such was the practical reality; on the other side was a principle to which LaGuardia was deeply committed. Civil service status would be the only means of preventing a massive increment of exempt positions, a potentially powerful instrument of patronage.

The Wicks bill was passed by the legislature in June and lay on the governor's desk awaiting final action. The mayor's opinion was solicited. He squirmed, and the bill became known as LaGuardia's "hot potato." He indicated he considered the legislation premature; he expressed the hope that after unification the city might be able to handle the problem by local legislation. But the dilemma would not go away. As the deadline for dealing with the Wicks bill approached, Lehman sent a telegram to the mayor, asking instructions before he either signed or vetoed it. The mayor still procrastinated, and only on the last day responded to the governor. He favored signing of the bill, he wired, "provided and if you can guarantee to keep the courts off my neck and that the courts will not interfere, disturb, or otherwise prevent carrying out exactly what you and I have done in this matter."

For a man who ordinarily had no difficulty in making himself understood, this was an extraordinary piece of gobbledegook. Lehman signed the bill at the last moment. The mayor's telegram, he remarked, was "not clear"—a pardonable understatement considering the fact that the words had served conveniently to take the governor off the political hook. They had also served LaGuardia's purposes. Tens of thousands of transport workers would now augment the civil service rolls; for the time being, besides, the worst of labor's blows were averted. Quill was to see that the calm did not last.

In March 1940, while the City Council was off on its ill-deserved vacation, LaGuardia took his stand on the highly inflammatory issues surrounding the rights of transit workers under civil service. The closed shop (existing by agreements with the private employers) would not be permitted: there was no way, the mayor said, for the city to guarantee the collection of union dues. Moreover, in the future the unions would not be permitted to strike. Denouncing the mayor as the "bankers' puppet," Quill immediately defied the city. A blanket authorization to strike was voted, to be put into effect at such time as the leaders saw fit. Quill urged a march on City Hall so that workers and their families could show the mayor how large an army was "ready to fight him."

The demonstration, scheduled for March 13, passed without disorder. LaGuardia, after walking through the picket line, announced that on the following Monday he would confer with Quill. The conference was given national importance by the presence of John L. Lewis, head of the CIO, and the way was opened to a compromise settlement. It was agreed that the right to strike would

34. Adversary Michael J. Quill. WIDE WORLD

be referred to lawyers on both sides. A second meeting was set for March 26.

This second occasion saw the formidable antagonists in full eruption. During the session LaGuardia maintained that a closed shop and the right to strike were illegal and unconstitutional when applied to civil service—and then, apparently, caved in. At the end of two hours he was prepared to submit to the Transit Commission the contracts of the transit employees as they existed under private management—"every line intact," as Quill reported gleefully. But Quill continued to declare his men would walk out. "Gentlemen: what is all this I read in the papers about preparations for a general strike on subways and buses?"—so LaGuardia wrote to the Transit Workers Union on April 1. "I await your word that all this was not serious and only a little April Fool's Day fun."

The strike was in fact put off, with the understanding between LaGuardia and Lewis that the issues would be referred to the courts when and if they arose. The settlement, declared the *Times,* was "postponement and evasion." Indeed, LaGuardia's brave statements in early March which had precipitated the crisis appeared to have been considerably undermined. "The right to strike against the government is not and cannot be recognized," he had said then.

Now he was saying the courts would judge whether such a right existed. Quill was understandably pleased.

Just a year later, in March 1941, Quill called a strike of all bus lines, resulting in the most severe transportation tie-up since the subway motormen walked out in 1926. LaGuardia denounced it as "a tragic mistake." The subways were dangerously jammed; a long stoppage seemed likely. Actually the strike lasted eleven days, with both sides agreeing to have the dispute arbitrated. Once again the victory was adjudged Quill's. He vaunted his strength, threatening to follow with a subway stoppage unless the city agreed to negotiate closed-shop agreements to replace those expiring on June 30. "We hope we'll find the mayor in a better mood," said Quill. That night at a rally in Madison Square Garden LaGuardia was charged with being a strikebreaker and his name was booed.

The mayor was far from being in a better mood as April advanced and renegotiation of the contracts began. This time Philip Murray, president of the CIO, was called in, to make the argument that nothing barred the negotiation of collective bargaining contracts with employees having civil service status. He criticized the mayor's "antilabor attitude." But it was Quill, as usual, who enraged the mayor, calling him "an erstwhile friend" of labor. "I'm not going to fail in my duty for the sake of mistaken popularity," retorted LaGuardia. "I believe my contribution to American labor will long be remembered when present trends of force and violence have been eliminated from the American labor movement." Meanwhile he sent a personal appeal to the president. He asked that if the threatened strike materialized the subways be put in the business of carrying mail so as to qualify them for federal protection.

Once more the strike was averted (not until more than a quarter of a century later, at the start of John V. Lindsay's administration, would a strike of the subway workers—still under the same Michael Quill—actually take place). John L. Lewis again entered the negotiations; and again the settlement of basic issues was left to the courts and to the future. "A humiliating retreat," the *Sun* called it. "Back from Munich without even an umbrella," it added, noting that it had been Lewis, not LaGuardia, who announced the agreement. The *Herald Tribune* was a good deal more tolerant. The course the mayor had adopted was that of "a wise physician," it said; "Statesmanship is made up of that sort of thing."

However the respective gains and losses may be judged, it seems clear that in dealing with Quill LaGuardia lost the even-handed approach which had made him the certain winner in so many past confrontations. This was the same mayor who in dispute after dispute had imposed the authority of his fairness and common sense upon seemingly intractable leaders of labor and industry. Yet now he left on objective observers the impression he had given in too early, or that he had been too uncompromising. Partly this may be due to that fact that by 1941 the mayor's prestige had been diminished by national events. Partly the intransigence was due to the mayor's conviction that issues of genuine importance were at stake. But at least some of the trouble arose from the fact that Quill quite simply made him mad. And being mad he let emotion sway him instead of using emotion, as he so often did at his best, as an instrument of his own ends.

An article in the *New Republic* commented on the approach revealed by the tangles with Quill. LaGuardia, it maintained, seemed to be forgetting everything he knew about collective bargaining. He had made eleventh-hour concessions to the transport workers, intended to cut ground from under their leaders. He had pushed through a bill mandating prison sentences for vandalism against subways, a clumsy club to hold over the head of the unions. In short, "LaGuardia was provocative in more than his usually picturesque way." That Quill tempted him to this kind of provocation cannot be denied.

But there were other reasons, acting on a deeper level, interestingly hinted at in a letter from Adolf Berle to David Lilienthal, director of the Tennessee Valley Authority. Lilienthal was troubled by LaGuardia's harsh opposition to collective bargaining by civil servants. "I wonder if the mayor and his advisors are familiar with the TVA's experience," he wrote Berle. To this Berle replied that "There are other things running here beside the mere labor question. . . . Part of it, undoubtedly, the desire . . . of the Communist wing to get a heavy strategic hand on the services of the city of New York."

Berle sent a copy of the exchange to LaGuardia who did not dissent from the views expressed. Anti-Communist feeling was running strong in these years: Gerson was an admitted Communist and was anathema for that reason; Kern was unjustly charged with being a Communist; Tugwell, at least in Moses's eyes, was a "red planner"; and Quill, together with his sponsor Vito Marcantonio, was regularly branded as red in the press. LaGuardia himself was refreshingly free from anti-Communist cant; but in the struggles over transit he may well have let the deep fears of men like Berle play upon his judgment. When he denounced the "trend of force and violence" in the American labor movement he was certainly taking account of communism in his own way. The result was a hard-line approach he could not sustain in the face of the transport workers' steady and unrelenting demands.

The Case of the Noble Earl

On October 1, 1939, the Board of Higher Education of New York City named as professor at City College an erudite, disconcertingly witty Englishman who was to teach the philosophy of mathematics. Nobody took much notice of it at the time, and those who did saw nothing inappropriate in the choice. The *Sun,* bellwether of the conservatives and guardian of conventional standards, commented editorially on the new appointment. "He thinks so clearly, and writes with so much sparkle and gusto, that business should boom in the philosphy department." It did indeed, but in a quite different way from what the editorialist had anticipated.

The Englishman in question was Bertrand Russell, world-renowned mathematician, but also expounder of views upon social and political questions that often astounded and shocked his contemporaries. In particular, he held views on the relations between men and women which even today, though they are widely followed, are rarely expressed so lucidly and frankly. In a book, *Marriage and Morals,* published ten years before his New York appointment, he had written: "I am sure that university life would be better, both intellectually and morally, if most university students had temporary childless marriages that would afford a solution to the sexual urge neither restless nor surreptitious, neither mercenary nor casual, and of such nature that it need not take up time that should be given to work." All sex relations that do not involve children should be regarded as a purely private matter, he urged; adultery was permissible and even desirable, and as for Christianity: "Through its whole history it has been a force tending toward mental disorders and unwholesome views of life."

That was strong language. The book was attacked at the time but in due course was forgotten; at the start of the war Russell accepted a teaching appointment at the University of California. But there was one man, Bishop William T. Manning of New York, who did

35. The noble earl—the mayor
was not sympathetic.
WIDE WORLD

not forget and carried on in the press and elsewhere a continuing crusade against the English earl. The issue as it was posed by the bishop, and as it was seen by most others who took up the fight, was not quite the one we would expect today: not civil liberties and the right to teach, but the right to speak unpopular views. It was, in short, the old issue of toleration, and Bishop Manning was one of those who could not bear to put up with views so different from his own and so personally offensive.

In the volatile community of New York the Russell appointment was not likely to be passed over in silence. When the mathematical operation of adding one to one was performed—when the opinions of Bertrand Russell were set in conjunction with the post of City College professor—the ensuing controversy reached through all levels of public opinion, shook up the Board of Education, the courts, and the City Council, and posed a crisis for the LaGuardia administration. The mayor himself was in an acutely embarrassing position. He did not, it must be said, emerge with honors from this trial. His battles for the rights of minorities and the oppressed, his stand against the suppression of free thought in the European dicta-torships, seemed to be ignored when highly unpopular opinions were expressed in his own backyard.

LaGuardia at this time and later was much influenced by the religious hierarchies, both Catholic and Episcopalian. Bishop Manning, who referred to Russell as "an ape of genius," had enlisted the mayor's aid in various church matters and was in regular communication with City Hall. In fairness it must be added that the mayor, as a sensitive politician, was aware of the repercussions throughout his New York constituency likely to be aroused by Russell's views on sex and religion. When the chips were down, the liberals and the defenders of toleration were but a small group within the city complex, and by no means the most powerful. Finally, the mayor's own views on sexual morality, orthodox and conventional as they were, made him susceptible to being genuinely shocked by the writings of the noble earl.

"I am not a prude," the mayor stated, with the kind of innocence which made people think he very probably was. He added, to prove his point, that he had been an aviator in the war and had traveled "all over Europe." His attitude toward women was certainly old-fashioned. When his secretary, Anna Clark, visited Washington on official business, he insisted she stay at a hotel which demanded of its residents that they check in by midnight. When, at the end of a day's work, he suggested to Mitzi Somach that she ride home with him in his city car, he made sure that a third person in addition to the driver accompany them. All this might have been set down as one more of the mayor's amiable eccentricities. But when the Bertrand Russell appointment divided true believers from the bigots and the nervous nellies, it placed LaGuardia on the wrong side of the line.

Between October and March the Bertrand Russell affair boiled along below the surface of public opinion, but enough discontent was aroused to cause the council on March 14 to adopt a resolution ordering the Board of Higher Education to rescind the appointment. The St. Patrick's Day Parade that year was held under a driving snow; one can imagine that among the notables on the platform (several of whom stayed like the mayor until the end) the case was fully discussed. Here were leading representatives of the religious and political establishment, and the Russell appointment had grown as heated as the weather was cold. "Why is it we always select someone with a boil on his neck or a blister on his fanny?" LaGuardia had grumbled a few days before, and his sentiments at the grand Irish tribal rite must have been expressed in similar vein. Two days after the parade, the Board of Education was to meet to reconsider the appointment.

On the eve of the meeting the mayor received from Charles H. Tuttle, a respected member of the board, a somber letter warning that the appointment, if carried through, would do harm to City College and would be an affront to the religious people of the city. "I lay the facts before you so that you may take such action as your judgment dictates." With the letter was a memorandum setting forth lengthy quotations, most of them from Russell's controversial *Marriage and Morals* of a decade earlier. At the same time the mayor was receiving advice from Burlingham. "I hope you will keep out of the Bertrand Russell mess," wrote that wise mentor. "If Bishop Manning had kept his fourteenth-century trap shut, the noble earl would have come and gone without notice." At about the same time, in a letter addressed to "My dear and good bishop," La-Guardia was extending to Manning profuse apologies for the appointment and promising to act "within the limits of such powers as I have."

These powers included pressure on the Board of Higher Education. One member, having resisted such pressure, appealed later for LaGuardia's "forgiveness," saying that his vote could only be laid to "conscience or human fallibility." Others, though less penitent, were suffering from the same debilities. The board at its March 19 meeting voted eleven to seven against reconsideration of the appointment. A taxpayer's suit started court action, while in Albany an inquiry was voted into the activities of reds and other subversives in the New York City schools.

The decision of the court came rapidly, on March 31, in the form of an opinion delivered by Justice John E. McGeehan. McGeehan was a Catholic who had once tried to have the portrait of Martin Luther expunged from a city mural depicting the history of religions. Not surprisingly he now found Russell unfit for the post of professor. Russell's attitudes toward sex were "immoral and salacious"; besides, he was not a United States citizen. The next move was the mayor's. On April 6, when the LaGuardia budget was presented, it was noted that funds for the Bertrand Russell post had been dropped. This was in keeping, it was blandly explained, "with the policy to eliminate vacant positions." On the same day two thousand students at City College left their classes at noon in protest. At Carnegie Hall a rally urged restoration of the $8,800 budget item and called for an appeal of the McGeehan decision.

At this point LaGuardia's course becomes least comprehensi-

ble. He set himself rigidly against appeal, and Chanler, the corporation counsel, announced under evident pressure that his
office would not take the Russell case to a higher court.
Chanler's face-saving defense of this position was that it was a
poor case on which to base an appeal; there was "the gravest
danger" that it might be affirmed. He refused also to permit
other counsel to take over. The Board of Higher Education
thereupon flouted the mayor by naming special counsel of its
own, top lawyers from the conservative law firm of Root, Clark,
Bushby, and Ballantine. At the University of California, meanwhile, Russell found his post barred to him when he sought to
continue there rather than to subvert New Yorkers.

The strains resulting from the mayor's stand were intense, both
within and outside his official family. John Dewey, the noted educator, wrote LaGuardia a letter which must have hurt. After expressing shock at the mayor's refusal to allow an appeal, he stated, "I
have regarded you as a person who could be counted on to do the
straightforward thing independent of political pressure." Burlingham was deeply dismayed. His letter of April 18 is worth quoting
at length:

> I strongly urge you to direct Chanler to consent to appeal. I seriously
> doubt his right to tell the Board of Education they cannot appeal and
> I regard this refusal . . . as high-handed. . . .
>
> You know how foolish I think the Department of Philosophy and
> the Board of Higher Education were in nominating and appointing
> Russell, and how abhorrent Russell's doctrines are to me. But why
> should a man with your record in a free country do to the CCNY
> what the Nazis have done to Heidelberg and Bonn? . . .
>
> Your attempts to dispose of the case while it was in the courts was
> bad enough; but to prevent the Board appealing to higher courts is
> far worse. . . .
>
> It is not like *you.*

To this cry from the heart LaGuardia's reply was a disingenuous
brush-off. "The pressure groups are certainly bearing down on
you," the mayor wrote. "A lawyer has advised his client (the
mayor) not to appeal, and the client has accepted. . . . That is all
there is to that."

The actual relations between "the lawyer" and "the client" are
suggested by a letter of April 27 to Chanler. Referring to a "memo

re the Russell case," evidently suggesting some means to placate the liberal groups, LaGuardia thus addressed his corporation counsel:

> In reference to your memo *re* the Russell case, it might be becoming to a scrivener in the office of a barrister in the 18th century, but utterly unworthy of a law officer in the greatest city in the world. . . . The city's law department is pettifogging on technical procedural matters. The city provides third-grade clerks for that purpose. . . . I fear you are under a misapprehension as to the duties of your office and the responsibilities which go with these duties. Further correspondence will not be helpful; nor is it desirable.

Avoidance of an open break with the corporation counsel was fortunate for the LaGuardia administration. Chanler evidently was able to adjust his conscience to the mayor's interpretation of "the duties of his office." No doubt he did believe that in the hysterical atmosphere of the moment an appeal would risk confirmation. He must have understood, too, the physical strain under which the mayor was laboring. Dr. George Baehr, the mayor's personal physician, was forbidding him to make any appointments at night. Mitzi Somach found the mayor's conduct of office affairs too burdensome to endure further; she left quietly at this time, realizing only afterward that he had been an ill man. Unchanged in his affection, Burlingham wrote LaGuardia in May, "I am so worried that you are not taking proper care of yourself. Here you are, when you should be resting, in so many activities and giving so much of yourself to each of them."

The Russell affair came to its conclusion in the fall. Russell had by then accepted a teaching post with the Barnes Foundation in Merion, Pennsylvania, and the Board of Higher Education at its October meeting voted fifteen to two to drop the case. A final word in this inglorious episode may be left to Russell himself, who broke a dignified silence to answer a letter in the *Times* charging that he ought to have withdrawn voluntarily from the City College appointment:

> If I had considered only my own interests and inclinations, I should have retired at once. But it would have been cowardly and selfish. . . . I'd have tacitly assented to the proposition that substantial groups shall be allowed to drive out of public office an individual whose opinions, race, or nationality they find repugnant. . . . In a democracy it is necessary that people should learn to endure having their senti-

ments outraged. Minority groups already endure this. . . . If it is once admitted that there are opinions toward which tolerance need not extend, the whole basis of toleration is destroyed.

Toward a National Post

The year had been marked by local controversies, but these were played against a background of speculation and behind-the-scene maneuverings affecting LaGuardia's role on the national stage. From the start of his administration he had been looked on as a man with a political destiny larger than the New York scene. His long career in Congress by itself assured him a national reputation; to this was added his spectacular successes as mayor. He was the subject of much talk in White House circles in Washington as well as in the press. In the main LaGuardia treated all this with an exemplary detachment. He knew enough about politics to accept its hopes and its hazards as part of the game and he was convinced, moreover, that the best way to advance was to maintain an independent position while doing the best job he possibly could as mayor.

During the first term, prior to 1937, Roosevelt would have liked to have LaGuardia in his cabinet. LaGuardia, however, had his own work to do, and as the time for campaigning drew near he became anxious to avoid getting involved in anything that might be interpreted as "a deal." For him to take a safe berth in Washington while the stage was left clear in New York for the victory of Mr. Farley's Democrats was a course that appealed neither to his fighting spirit nor to his sense of honor. The 1937 victory gave him high visibility, enhanced by the western journeys of 1938. Yet in that year, as we have seen, he still felt it improper to make a run for the Senate. His eye was on the more distant future—on 1940 and the presidential elections. With the Roosevelt administration at the close of its second and presumably final term, the presidential and vice-presidential field would be wide open. LaGuardia with his shifting political relationships and his unconventional power base could well attract the lightning in a time of change and party realignment.

Early in 1939 Berle came up from Washington to lunch with LaGuardia. The president, Berle reported, had talked with him very frankly. He was not interested in a third term for himself, and would be satisfied with Cordell Hull as the candidate provided the convention would put a progressive in second place. He had named as acceptable possibilities Robert M. Jackson, Harry Hopkins, and LaGuardia. The mayor must have listened to all this with a good deal of interest, but his comment, according to Berle, was that he did not see the likelihood of his name getting through the convention. As late as December 1939 the indefatiguably hopeful Berle was able to note in his diary: "I still think it may be possible to have a whole LaGuardia ticket."

By 1940, where we left LaGuardia struggling with such local vexations as Quill and Russell, the question of the presidency was evidently much on his mind. In March, in an address to the City Affairs Committee, he described his ideal candidate. He would be one chosen by citizens who had put aside "fads, fancies, and hobbies," who had discarded thinking along routine lines, and who brushed aside personalities in their effort to find a leader willing and able to tackle the basic needs of the nation. Again, the leader would be one with "a brain, a heart, and a soul ready to deal with real problems." It was a description, as his audience must have noted, which nicely fitted LaGuardia himself. His own job, he remarked ruefully, was that of "a glorified janitor," without power to do anything directly about national economic and social issues: *"Yet we must think about them."*

That LaGuardia had been thinking about them was indicated by a curious and still unexplained incident a month later. In the Illinois presidential primary, where the names of the president and of Vice-President Garner were filed, the name of LaGuardia also appeared, on a petition with four thousand signatures. "Are you kidding?" was LaGuardia's comment. "I don't know anything about it." In Washington it was questioned whether John L. Lewis had been at the bottom of an anti-Roosevelt maneuver. LaGuardia withdrew his name, but only at the last moment and then in a highly visible gesture. Ceremoniously giving his letter to a police motorcycle rider, he instructed him to put it aboard the next plane for Chicago. At the same time he issued a statement to the effect that with Roosevelt in the primary, the people could express their faith in progressivism by voting for him. "They have various types of reactionaries among the other candidates. I do not believe at this time that progressives should be divided."

Speculation went on. At the end of April Berle met again with LaGuardia. They talked over "various and strange things," particularly whether LaGuardia could be a vice-presidential candidate on a ticket with Hull. "Of course it may not work out," Berle added prudently in his diary, "for the president may decide to run." Ultimately, of course, the president did decide to run. The intensification of the European war with the invasion of Belgium and Holland altered the whole political picture and made Roosevelt's candidacy for an unprecedented third term seem increasingly plausible. By June 1940 there was no longer talk of a Hull–LaGuardia ticket; but there was much talk of a cabinet post as Roosevelt considered a reorganization to meet the European crisis.

For some time it had been clear that the secretary of war, Harry Woodring, was ripe for replacement. In May Roosevelt told Ickes he had LaGuardia in mind for the post. Ickes said he thought it would be a good appointment. "Few men have the courage and intelligence to fight for ideals that LaGuardia has," he had confided to his diary a while earlier. But now he began to have second thoughts. LaGuardia might not be the best man for the job, after all: "Besides," he added, "I'd like it myself." From then on references to LaGuardia in the diary became constantly less laudatory and more critical.

Tugwell at this juncture thoroughly expected the appointment to go through. "I was confident, because the president had said so. . . . I had even been asked whether I would discuss it with LaGuardia. We did talk about it." But the post did not materialize, though LaGuardia longed for it ardently. "His hopes were so high and his eagerness so apparent," wrote Tugwell with some malice, "that his ambition became more and more apparent to others."

On June 20 Roosevelt named to his cabinet two nationally known Republicans, Henry L. Stimson and Frank Knox, the former in the post of secretary of war which LaGuardia had coveted and the second as secretary of the navy. Good Republicans were shocked by what they considered a betrayal of two of their own; the nominees were disowned by the party and attacked by Dewey. But LaGuardia showed the largeness of view he was capable of in national affairs—and also the personal magnanimity. The new men, he said, deserved and should get every possible bit of cooperation from everyone in the country. Reports of a cabinet position for himself persisted. Frances Perkins's resignation as secretary of labor was announced without qualification by the *Times*, and LaGuardia was said to be in line for the post. But Perkins did not resign, and though LaGuardia was to have several more occasions for hope, and was to be drawn into one federal office involving attendance at cabinet meetings, a place in Roosevelt's official family was not again seriously in the cards.

Several factors had provoked a change in Roosevelt's mind. He was worried about LaGuardia's capacity to work as a member of a team and disturbed by evidences of his unreliable temperament. As his own attitude toward a third term became more positive, he no longer feared LaGuardia as the leader of a third-party threat, one to be appeased or silenced by inclusion in the cabinet. But a factor perhaps as important as any other was Roosevelt's readiness to heed the pleas of noted New Yorkers, several of them LaGuardia's closest friends. Seabury and Burlingham sent messages to Roosevelt urging that LaGuardia was too important as mayor to be called to federal service. Lehman sent a letter to the president, which he followed up with a long telegram the next day, making essentially the same argument.

One may question, in view of LaGuardia's passionate eagerness to go to Washington, whether these men were acting as friends responsive to his self-interest. Berle, whose loyalty never wavered, sent a memo to the president saying that while Sumner Welles thought LaGuardia indispensable as mayor in New York, he did not himself agree. "The second-string man, Newbold Morris, though not nearly as able, could hold things together without trouble." The question inevitably arises whether Lehman was not jealous of LaGuardia's prospects, and Welles reluctant to see the mayor's avidity for international politics given undue encouragement.

In extenuation it should be remembered that New York was a highly inflammatory spot as America's involvement in the war grew more likely. In conditions of conflict it would be subject to immense tensions and dangers. LaGuardia's broad political skills over and above those needed to run New York's municipal government made him appear uniquely valuable. He could act on a national and international level, he could cope with the fierce emotions of minorities at home, and he was strong enough to keep control in the event of external threats. The irony of LaGuardia's situation was this: the qualities which led Roosevelt to consider him as a possible secretary of war were the very ones which played a crucial part in keeping him at City Hall.

The City Looks Outward

On May 10, 1940, the stalemate which had marked the first winter of the European war suddenly ended with Hitler's slashing attack on Belgium, the Netherlands, and Luxembourg. These events provided something less than a fitting atmosphere for the next day's opening of the second season of the World's Fair. The president sent a message but did not attend the ceremony; La-Guardia noted without regret the absence of the aggressor nations from among the year's exhibitors. The Fair, he said, could do without "an international rogues gallery." Increasingly the tone of events at Flushing Meadows was set by the heartbreaking news from abroad. Italy entered the war on June 11, and ten minutes after the declaration, with characteristic rapidity, LaGuardia appeared at the studios of WNYC, urging New York's vast constituency of Italian-Americans to observe a strict neutrality. The British ambassador, Lord Lothian, spoke at ceremonies marking United Kingdom Day, while England braced itself for the ultimate test of facing Hitler alone. On June 25 the tricolor sank to half-staff in front of the French pavilion, marking the day of national mourning decreed by the government of the subjugated homeland. It hung forlornly in the damp air, amid whispered expressions of sadness and sympathy from the thin line of visitors.

Elsewhere a change in the city made itself felt. A regiment composed largely of New Yorkers was in training at Plattsburgh by midsummer. Among them were two-score city employees, enough to administer a sizable town, including the president of the City Council, Newbold Morris. Morris invited the mayor to come up. He promptly responded, and in an address to the trainees urged the immediate training of 750,000 young men to guarantee the hemisphere's defense. The plea was repeated during the summer, with insistence that the appropriation of billions for war equipment was not enough. "What we want is two-fisted men," he said—and preferably young men, from eighteen to twenty-two years.

LaGuardia's summer office was established once again in the Arrowbrook Country Club. From here he could keep watch on the comings and goings of statesmen and diplomats, adding his own voice to their pleas for strength and courage in adversity, and regularly loosing his own castigations of the dictators. As he had during the earlier summer he found at the Fair the ideal international forum, and he put it to the same use, only now with the

deeper tones of urgency. "I am always told to be very, very careful
of what I say when I am speaking in diplomatic circles," he would
complain, with the air of helplessness he could assume on appropriate occasions, and then proceed to show that he did not intend to
speak carefully at all. On Ireland Day he extolled the fighting
qualities of the Irish, claiming that they had earned the right to
complete unity. Before six Latin American delegations he called for
joint defense of the hemisphere. The United States, he said, must
back its neighbors with a force sufficient to be meaningful even to
those nations that no longer understood the respect of a large
country for a small one.

As the summer advanced, LaGuardia became more and more
convinced that the war was coming close to home. He did not wait
to learn the opinion of the country or to get instructions from
Washington. In these matters he was on his own—and he was out
front. The overwhelming opinion at that time was that the United
States could, and must, keep out of the war. But LaGuardia moved
with consistent steps to put the city in shape for any emergency.

Under his driving impetus a plan to be used in case of air attack
was roughed out. A disaster control board, originally set up after
the 1938 hurricane, was refurbished, with Valentine put in control.
Lehman was asked to declare a state of emergency to enable New
York to speed its protection of the city's water supply. A local
defense board was named. In one move which was to provide an
issue of growing controversy LaGuardia asked for the deferment of
police and firemen under the newly enacted draft, claiming the
presence of these trained personnel to be essential to the city's
defense in wartime. Washington officials wobbled on the issue,
notwithstanding the mayor's appeal. The City Council, in an excess
of patriotic equalitarianism, voted against the measure, responding
to the majority leader's assertion that "every mother's son" should
take the same chances.

LaGuardia's capital budget became the vehicle of a new austerity.
Well before shortages in materials and manpower were evident, the
mayor proposed a limit of one dollar on proposals for new construction projects. Work under way could be continued, and department
heads could reassign priorities within existing funds. Exception was
made for the purchase of new subway cars and buses which, according to the mayor, were recognized by everyone "except an ignora-
mus or a willful politician" as being essential. For various reasons
of his own, the mayor was not altogether loath to impose this halt

on capital expenditures, and the outcries of his department heads, especially of Robert Moses, cannot have been too great a shock to him. Yet he was right on the big issue. He set an example which the rest of the country would soon be compelled to follow.

At the intergovernmental level LaGuardia imparted his sense of urgency to the mayors of major United States cities. Elected for the fourth time as president of the U.S. Conference of Mayors, he proposed a program under which the cities were to prepare themselves against the possibility of air raids; to restrict their capital improvements to projects capable of being finished within a year; to participate actively in federal programs for airports and highways useful to defense. He discerned new reasons for the cities to deal directly with the federal government rather than through the states. In an address at the same period to the chiefs of police of New York State he urged cooperation in devising means to prevent the panic which he saw as the chief danger under crisis conditions. The Germans, he was convinced, were developing new techniques for spreading panic among a people.

In August Roosevelt named LaGuardia to a joint U.S.–Canadian board to coordinate the defenses of the northern part of the western hemisphere. It was a fitting appointment from every point of view and LaGuardia was delighted. At home in bed with a cold when the news came, he was up the next morning to fly to Washington for briefings, and left that same night for Ottowa. He explained to the press that under the charter he could hold a second civil office if no salary were attached—it meant for him "only a little extra work and overtime." He saw an opportunity for real service. It represented, he said, "something I have been thinking and planning and dreaming about for two years." LaGuardia's membership on this joint defense board proved indeed to be one of his most rewarding experiences. It enabled him to make a contribution where his interests were deeply engaged, and remained entirely free of the bitter overtones which marked his later sallies into national defense.

So the summer passed, and the last days of the World's Fair came around. An enterprise planned in times of peace ended with the civilized world in the midst of the greatest of all wars. The hopeful prophecies of a future shaped by rational progress and technological advance turned to gloom as men saw science creating weapons of destruction on a scale hitherto unimagined. The baubles, the commercial conceits, the more or less innocent entertainments, gave forth an incongruous light beside the glare of great European cities falling under oppression. Yet it had been a grand show. Everyone felt that, and the last days were crowded with special groups of children and sightseers, anxious for a farewell glimpse of the unsubstantial pageant.

Moses had warned that everything must be cleared and empty immediately after the Fair's closing, and indeed his workmen were on hand on the morning after, converting the abandoned city of light to a new park. What remained were the highways and bridges leading to the site, which had been a prime reason for creating the Fair in the first place. In due time another World's Fair would arise on the same grounds; and a park larger than anything Olmsted, the great nineteenth-century park builder, had shaped would stand with a somewhat uncertain character at the heart of the growing borough of Queens.

All Out for FDR

Free of any illusions about presidential or vice-presidential chances for himself, and aroused by the dangers of the international situation, LaGuardia found no difficulty in making the passage to wholehearted support of a third term for Roosevelt. The Republicans in 1940 named as their candidate Wendell L. Willkie, a brilliant newcomer to national politics; Roosevelt, accepting in Chicago the "draft" of the Democratic convention, picked Henry A. Wallace for his running mate. By mid-September LaGuardia was ready to do battle for the cause of the Democrats.

A few organizational details had first to be arranged. LaGuardia considered himself a man of no party, and he was particularly anxious not to identify himself with the national Democratic chairman, who happened to be Ed Flynn, boss of the Bronx. A few days before he was to deliver a major radio speech announcing support of Roosevelt, he performed, nevertheless, an act of obeisance upon the altar of Democracy. He bestowed upon Jimmy Walker, the former mayor, a well-salaried appointment as impartial spokesman for the garment industry. This act made it all the more essential that in one way or another he affirm his position as an independent. Since returning from a three-year stay in Europe where, after his forced resignation, he had gone to escape the eye of the public and the grasp of the tax collectors, Walker had been under the benevolent eye of various Democratic bosses. It was a company LaGuardia had no desire to keep.

Attitudes of various public figures toward Walker were complex and not lacking in touches of human kindness. In 1937 Farley had arranged a Walker call at the White House, an interesting visit between men who had last met when the destinies of each were at stake. Roosevelt evidently recommended to LaGuardia the desirability of receiving his predecessor at City Hall. In due course Walker repaid the courtesy by introducing LaGuardia at a music festival in Carnegie Hall as "the greatest mayor New York ever had." An abortive effort had been made by Walker's friends to get him a minor post on the Transit Commission, in the hope of preserving his city pension. Now, as the Democratic campaign got under way, it seemed time to bring the threads of this tangled human skein into some sort of a pattern. LaGuardia paid a call on Roosevelt in September where (no doubt at the urging of Ed Flynn) the subject of Walker was brought up. A few days later LaGuardia named him arbiter of the women's suit and cloak industry at an annual salary of $20,000.

Great was the shock to LaGuardia's Fusion friends. Seabury was not a man given to charitable reconsiderations; he now found himself at the breaking point with the mayor whom he had raised up in Walker's place. "Coming from one I admire so much and am so fond of," he wrote LaGuardia, the appointment hurt him personally. Beyond that was the affront to the good judge's sense of civic righteousness. To characterize the mayor's role he used the imagery of Browning's *Lost Leader*: "Just for a handful of silver he left us." LaGuardia was surprised at the vehemence of the attack from Seabury and other friends. He denied he had discussed the appointment with Roosevelt; he claimed that he had acted only as the neutral spokesman for the garment industry. And he added—which was perhaps the truest part of his defense—that he could not forget his "Christian upbringing."

Difficult as it was for Judge Seabury to see, there was something about Walker which inclined men to be forgiving. He had done obvious wrongs, and had paid for them. He had been idle when he should have been working and had set for others a deplorable example. But he had not been self-righteous; he had never pretended to be other than he was. For New Yorkers he symbolized an epoch in the life of the city and in their own lives: they had tolerated his excesses, laughed at his wit, encouraged his escapades;

and in the end they were willing to admit that they, too, were part of the picture. Ill, subdued in spirit, almost penniless, he had returned to the city where he had glowed and shone, and gradually he had recovered a natural jauntiness. That LaGuardia should have turned to give help to this fallen angel of democracy seems in the sum of things to be to his credit. But in connecting the gesture with his support of Roosevelt's third term, he was in danger of being tarred by the brush of subservience.

The mayor's position in the forthcoming campaign was clarified by the establishment of an independent committee for Franklin Roosevelt, with LaGuardia as its chairman and Norris as honorary chairman. Thomas Corcoran, one of the early White House confidants, would be vice-president and responsible for most of the committee's organizational work. On September 24 the group called on the president. "You are a good president," LaGuardia said, "but we can't get any votes here so we are going out to the country to get them." That is precisely what LaGuardia did, embarking on a series of trips which showed him as energetic in campaigning for Roosevelt as he had ever been in expending his oratorical and political gifts on his own behalf. Afterward Robert Sherwood was to sum up the work of the independent committee as "the most spirited element" in the 1940 campaign.

From the party's point of view LaGuardia's independence was a major asset. Though he had accommodated himself to Roosevelt's wishes in the Walker appointment, though he was to bring himself perilously close to being contaminated by the Democratic bosses, he stood at the time a proud figure whose unpredictability made his allegiance the more coveted. All his political life he had been an outsider and now the stance paid off. Seeing him in the context of the New Deal, Arthur Schlesinger, Jr., wrote of him as being the New York blend of ethnic and ideological insurgency, "a broker between nationality groups and also between New York City radicalism and the progressivism of inner America: knowing Arizona as well as Ellis Island . . . a bridge between the men of the European social democratic tradition (Hillman, Dubinsky) and men of the progressive and populist tradition (Norris, LaFollette)." It was good to have praise of the president coming from such a source. LaGuardia felt this, and in the series of speeches he now embarked on, he spoke as a man knowing his own power.

Back in New York there was bound to be trouble. The mayor had made it a stern rule that city officials should not engage in political activity. "If employees were riding a subway under Carnegie Hall while a political meeting was going on, they were engaged in political activity," he said. Before the autumn's activities began Edward L. Corsi, first deputy commissioner for welfare, an important figure in the administration with wide contacts among nationality groups, resigned so as to be able to work for Willkie. But the mayor would now be absenting himself on wideranging pursuits, and in a highly partisan and controversial cause.

The third-term issue went deeply against the grain of millions of voters, adding fire to the mistrust which conservatives felt toward Roosevelt and his policies. Besides, Willkie was a leader capable of arousing large hopes and evoking a passionate dedication among those who worked for him. Big in physical and intellectual stature, with a mind capable of transcending the economic dogma which as a businessman had so recently motivated him, he was ultimately to back Roosevelt on the most significant issues of foreign policy—and one day would back LaGuardia, too. In opposing Willkie, La-Guardia broke for the time with old friends and colleagues, not only Seabury but also Thacher, Windels, Clendenin Ryan, Jr., and Chadbourne.

Following the mayor's September 12 radio address the New York Republicans let loose a blast which angered and disconcerted him. He would not be supported by the Republicans in any future election, he was assured; his speech, said Simpson, had been "a demagogic diatribe" (actually it had been a relatively restrained appeal to independents and progressives); it was a payoff for the U.S.–Canadian defense post. In his reply LaGuardia asserted that fifteen minutes before delivery of the speech, prominent Republicans begged him on their knees to support Willkie. He applied a particularly opprobrious epithet to one of his attackers, and then retracted it—saying he wanted to use it later.

With this exchange ringing in the public's ear, LaGuardia as he had promised went "out to the country." October saw him in Newark, Pittsburgh, Boston; in Detroit, Rochester, Providence, Chicago, and Cincinnati. He attacked Willkie on enslavement to the utilities, false claims as a liberal, gymnastic changes of position, reckless charges on Social Security, and hypocrisy in regard to housing. (Though foreign policy lay at the heart of the campaign it was rarely mentioned.) When John L. Lewis came out against the president, LaGuardia attacked him, too, saying he represented labor in the same way the hated Laval represented France. Besides the formal speeches, well attended and widely covered, there were motorcades, receptions, tours of industrial plants.

During a brief return to New York LaGuardia paused to address the New York *Herald Tribune* Forum, where he showed that he could still moderate his tone and recover his wits. Before a laughing audience he declared himself to be "nonpartisan," and went on to point out (which he had not heretofore been suspected of observing) that on basic issues Willkie and Roosevelt were not far apart, and that on defense they were in agreement. Turning to Helen Rogers Reid, publisher of the *Herald Tribune* and a guiding spirit in the Willkie campaign, he delighted his hearers by predicting that she would win the Nobel Prize for "diplomacy, tact, acuteness, and sweetness." It was the kind of performance with which LaGuardia in the course of his political career would repeatedly charm an audience, drawing on deep springs of sweetness and tact within his own nature.

In Detroit an incident of a different kind took place. At a City Hall reception a man inquired of the guest of honor "Are you still taking orders from Boss Flynn?" LaGuardia turned on the questioner, twisted his necktie, and tore his collar. The two men had to be physically separated. It was a reaction similar to what had occurred on the steps of his own City Hall at Christmastime two years before, but now in far less happy circumstances. The tensions of the campaign were evidently making themselves felt. LaGuardia compounded the fault when, discussing the incident on his return to New York, he characterized the questioner as "just a drunk—I turned him over to the police." The mayor was sued for assault and slander; it turned out that the questioner, whatever his sense of the proprieties, drank no liquor.

At the end of October Franklin Roosevelt came to New York for one of those grand visits that could transform the city for a day. Arriving by way of Staten Island he was met by LaGuardia, Lehman, and Wagner. The party stopped to break ground at the Brooklyn end of the famous tunnel which had aroused so much emotion two years before. LaGuardia invited Roosevelt "to come back as president" when the tunnel was opened. He couldn't promise that, Roosevelt replied; but "as president" he would come back to New York the week after election. At the Manhattan entrance to the Queens tunnel, still under construction and with the work force standing around, LaGuardia introduced Roosevelt to the crowd as "a consistent friend of labor." Valentine, who was in the entourage

36. A campaign stop with FDR at Queensbridge Houses. October 28, 1940. NYC
HOUSING AUTHORITY

all day, estimated that the president had been seen by two million
people. LaGuardia had his share of the glory, though at recurrent
intervals he would yield his place in the president's car to his
"enemies," the jealous Democratic chieftains.

The rest was in a familiar style—closing rallies in Brooklyn, in
Carnegie Hall and Madison Square Garden in Manhattan. By then
it was clear that Franklin Roosevelt would win, going on as had no
president before him into a third term. LaGuardia turned back to
the chores of city government, and to the traditional civic rites at
the year's end, with his future obscure and his mind clouded by
uncertainties.

9

Two Steps Forward...

Political Prospects

LaGuardia's all-out campaign for the New Deal had cut a deep swathe across New York politics. Fusion forces were leaderless and Republicans seemed disinclined to turn again to the man who had been a member of their party throughout most of his political life. The mayor, temporarily at least, was isolated and bitter. Whatever acclaim he had achieved on the national stage was dissipated as he faced the realities of the New York scene.

In mid-December 1940, at a Citizens Union dinner Seabury and Thacher praised the city administration and hailed progress achieved under the new charter without once mentioning La-Guardia by name. Three days later the mayor sent a letter to Fusion leaders saying he would not run again. Upon them, he said, rested the responsibility for the future of good government in New York; upon them fell the charge of having abandoned the cause through their support of Willkie. As for himself, he had a right to act according to his own judgment. The leaders of Fusion did not own or control him. Until he became mayor, he told them, the city had never been able to attain clean, decent government.

It was a sad, unnecessary communication, at once defensive and provocative, the outpouring of a mind brought to the edge of despair. LaGuardia was confused and tired; as after his own campaign of 1937, he had refused to take the vacation for which body and mind cried out. Burlingham once again had exactly the right words. "I wish you had a secretary or a friend," he wrote, "who had the courage to tell you not to send a letter which you should destroy before you signed it. If you had been well and truly served, you would have kept your letter on a higher plane, or better still would have given it to the flames." *Of course,* added the old comrade, with that reassuring common sense which was so often a boon to LaGuardia, "you had a right to vote and speak and work for FDR."

Among the Republicans anger and resentment had their day. Warren B. Ashmead, Queens leader, spoke for his party when he demanded an out-and-out Republican for the 1941 mayoral election, and banished LaGuardia in stinging words. At the same time Simpson, newly elected to Congress, planned his retirement as Manhattan chairman. A major supporter of LaGuardia's, one who had helped elect Morris, Isaacs, and other liberal candidates, his retirement as active New York leader would by itself have been a severe blow, but when he died suddenly having served but a score of days as congressman, the political loss was combined with a sense of personal bereavement. "Strange as it may seem—and public statements notwithstanding," the mayor wrote disconsolately, "we never had one exchange of harsh words in all his time in politics."

As 1941 advanced and the national election fell into the background, the political mood softened. LaGuardia turned back to the affairs of New York in a New Year's message of muted hope, praising the city as being proof of democracy's meaning, with its wide variety of races and nationalities living peaceably together. On New Year's Eve Thomas J. Curran, Simpson's successor as chairman of the Manhattan Republican committee, made a call on the mayor. It was said to be part of a traditional ceremony, but in the circumstances it was considered an omen that the door was still open and that no final stand had been taken on the 1941 mayoral elections.

LaGuardia's own plans for the future alternated between running for a third term and taking a job in Washington. In his annual address to the City Council the mayor stated frankly he might be called away before the end of his term and stressed that the city's affairs would be in good order should he leave. Later, speaking to the City Affairs Committee, he admitted he would prefer not to be a candidate for another term. "I do not want to give any comfort to politicians," he added, warning that his words should not be taken to mean he would "retire from active participation in public affairs."

John Haynes Holmes responded with a tribute which must have warmed the mayor's heart and was just the tonic he needed. "I rejoice in your joy in your job," said the noted civic leader. "I reverence your integrity, your courage, your pride in the city. . . . I love when you lock yourself in for a week on bread and water with your budget, like a saint doing devotions before the altar of his faith." This was one of the signs, and there were others, that Fusion's heart was softening toward its errant son.

The son, however, still had his reservations. The job of being mayor was losing some of its luster as possibilities of reform narrowed and old hostilities congealed. In that strange midseason when the ancient European order was being torn apart but the United States was not yet in the war, New York seemed a small stage for a man to play his part. Marie was always against a third term. Then there had been a day in 1940 when LaGuardia and Adolf Berle looked into the future, with that prescience which the young friend and counselor so often exhibited and which he encouraged in others. They met at LaGuardia Airport; it was the first time Berle had seen it in operation—"looking like a picture in an H. G. Wells novel," its runways shining in the sun, where last he had seen only a vast mud field. The two men were in a contemplative mood. LaGuardia's was the last big job that could be done in New York, Berle said. Within the limits of the existing rules of finance he had taken the city about as far as was possible. "The next mayor would merely be managing what LaGuardia had set up for him."

LaGuardia had agreed. Taxation of real estate could no longer meet the demands of the city nor, to so large a degree, the demands of the state. This was particularly true in light of the long-established policies of the federal government. Perhaps a different day would come. Would there be another mayor he wondered, who would be the interpreter of the changed financial policy of the government, which was not as yet in sight?

Washington got the message in the mayor's mood and statements; but the post which everyone assumed to be forthcoming did not materialize. It was humiliating to have Ed Flynn say, soon after the election, that at a meeting with the president a cabinet post for LaGuardia had not been discussed. In a January press conference

Roosevelt remarked that he first heard of a widely rumored defense job for LaGuardia when he read it in the morning papers. "Fine," said LaGuardia gamely, "best news I've heard in a long time." A four-man defense board was set up with William S. Knudson as director, again eliminating a possibility for LaGuardia. At the end of January Roosevelt wrote the mayor. He said he had been "really concerned about the policing of the capital for several years"— would the mayor consider lending Mr. Valentine and his principal traffic officers for several days? In the circumstances it seemed a peculiarly insensitive letter.

Though probably not himself aware of it, LaGuardia was at the center of political tides which swayed his fortunes. In Washington the old New Deal group wanted LaGuardia at their side as someone who, amid growing diversions and retrenchments, could present forcibly to the president the reformist view. Again from the New Deal point of view, he was highly important in the New York picture. Without him Ed Flynn would be in command, ambitious for national power, still representing the old wing of the party. The congressional delegation, the votes of New York's representatives at the next national convention, could only benefit from the influence of LaGuardia's abrasive liberalism. Roosevelt himself was probably divided in his feelings about LaGuardia; but above all, he had a debt to pay, and the payment would become more difficult as time went on.

In the city, when he turned to city problems, LaGuardia found particularly vexatious and frustrating conditions. The council was dominated by the opposition. In the Board of Estimate, where until recently he had had a majority, the balance of power shifted when Raymond Ingersoll, borough president of Brooklyn, a pro-LaGuardia reformer whose experience went back to the days of John Purroy Mitchel, was suddenly stricken and died. Cashmore took Ingersoll's place as borough president, assuring an additional vote for the machine politicians.

It was at this time, too, that the mayor challenged the council's right to subpoena the city's chief magistrate and call for documents he considered confidential. Through Chanler he argued in vain that only the governor and the state legislature had the power to investigate him. The raking-over of the Civil Service Commission dragged on for a second year. Early in February a preliminary report accused Kern of repeatedly violating civil service laws and showing favoritism to appointees preferred by the mayor. Councilman Robert

Straus, almost alone, carried forward the fight for a more experienced committee chairman than Alfred Smith, Jr., and a more
impartial counsel than John Ellis. By April Kern was again being
charged with communism and threatened with imprisonment because of obstructive tactics. LaGuardia stepped into the fray, ordering Kern to comply with the committee's demand for testimony,
and then counterattacked by instructing the commissioner of investigations to subpoena Ellis's bank accounts.

But more than this unseemly struggle it was the 1941 expense
budget which provided a chief issue of contention between the
mayor and his adversaries. The budget highlighted the city's condition as rapidly developing events abroad brought an approaching
end to one chapter of New York's history.

Troubled Finances

Each year the expense budget was shaped in an atmosphere of
crisis and settled amid complex political adjustments. But the year
1941 was crucial. It was to prove the last of LaGuardia's peacetime
budgets, and it brought to the fore all the latent issues which
dogged the city and clouded its future. As current revenues failed
to keep pace with the city's needs, political and civic leaders raised
questions about the adequacy of the tax base's resting so largely
upon real estate assessments; about the charges for debt service,
greatly increased as a result of recent capital improvements; about
the city's pension system; and, most of all, about the growing costs
of such social programs as relief, health, education, and recreation.
LaGuardia was determined not to leave the city in a budgetary
situation comparable to that which he had inherited. He knew,
moreover, that his own record as mayor would be judged in no
small measure by the degree to which he kept the financial house
in order.

The tax burden on real estate and the growing costs of city
pensions were two problems which particularly aroused the mayor.
We have seen the view taken by the Planning Commission, that it
was not possible for taxes based on real estate, particularly on
Manhattan real estate, to sustain the services required by the newer,
loosely populated sections of the city. It was bad enough to hear this
from within his own administration. But when the Real Estate
Board claimed the breaking point had been reached and released

37. "Like a saint doing devotions." With Budget Director Kenneth Dayton at budget retreat. AUTHENTICATED NEWS

figures to show that industry was fleeing New York to areas in New Jersey with lower taxes and labor costs, the mayor exploded. "When did they wake up? We've been working on that for several months. We've been very successful." The reasons for such moves as did occur ranged all the way, according to the mayor, from a wife's refusal to kiss her husband good morning to a desire to operate under sweatshop conditions. But the charge hurt, and a few weeks later the mayor abruptly caused the resignation of a young aide, Clendenin Ryan, Jr., who had gone out from his personal staff to head the newly established Department of Commerce.

Ryan had operated on a shoestring, from offices in Rockefeller Center loaned by Nelson Rockefeller, with a staff recruited from other agencies and with most expenses paid for out of his own pocket. The mayor's unceremonious action did not turn upon Ryan's success (or lack of it) in recruiting new business or keeping old ones in New York; but the fact that LaGuardia moved so harshly against one of his favorites suggested his nervousness on the issue. Shortly afterward he appointed a high-level business advisory committee, headed by George Sloan, to give special attention to the relation between taxes and the city's threatened industrial base.

In the field of pensions it was plain that costs were steadily mounting. Between 1929 and 1938 they had doubled, and with the addition of nearly thirty thousand transit workers the system would become the largest and most expensive in the world. An early form of social security, pensions for New York police were introduced in 1857; they were developed for other municipal workers as an expression of gratitude for public service and a compensation for the then-prevailing low wages. The system had never been placed on a sound financial basis, and by 1941 was a steady drain on New York's fiscal resources. LaGuardia made strong but only partially successful efforts to make pensions actuarially sound and to increase the contributions from city employees.

During 1940 LaGuardia was confronted by a picturesque crisis brought about by these pension reforms. It was a crisis, unlike most others, ending not in dismissals but in a refusal to allow officials to quit their jobs. In the late afternoon of February 23 the mayor was supposed to be well on his way to Des Moines, Iowa, but bad weather had caused him to make a change in his plans and instead he was motoring on official business to deal with a sanitation problem on Long Island. His car radio brought him news that his fire commissioner, John J. McElligott, had consented to the retirement of eight top aides, all fearing their pensions would be diminished under a law soon to go into effect. They had acted without taking account of LaGuardia's physical proximity or foreseeing the swiftness of his response.

Returning to City Hall where the lights were ablaze and where most of his commissioners had converged on his orders, LaGuardia dealt with the legal and practical aspects of the problem. The McElligott order sanctioning the retirements was countermanded and the "retired" firemen were called back to immediate duty. Court actions were prepared in case of a refusal and the ever-ready Herlands was instructed to start an investigation of one of the department's principal divisions. Two days later, at the bedside of his ailing commissioner, LaGuardia negotiated the final terms of the settlement. McElligot had lost his voice, but the mayor in any case would have done most of the talking. The upshot was that the commissioner escaped dismissal, continuing to be the mayor's guide and protector at the scene of many fires. The deputies remained in their jobs and a new burden on the pension fund was forestalled.

The expense budget that year was particularly hard to bring into balance. Two items in particular tell the story. Real estate assessments were down by $200 million; tax levy requirements for debt service were up by $3.9 million. In short, the basic weak spots in the city's condition were beginning to be painfully apparent. La-Guardia's emergency relief taxes, on the other hand, showed a surplus, and the mayor now proposed that from this source up to $25 million be diverted to pay for related services—old-age assistance, child welfare, hospital costs, and veterans' benefits. It appeared on the surface to be a reasonable request, and Republicans in Albany, anxious to repair their fences after the recent Democratic sweep, were prepared to look favorably on the legislation.

To the economy-minded civic groups, nevertheless, the proposed diversion seemed only slightly less heinous an offense than had been the imposition of the tax in the first place. The Merchants Association protested. The Citizens Budget Commission maintained that any surplus relief taxes should be applied to debts previously contracted and not to the financing of further social welfare activities. Massing its troops, it presented a letter signed by 420 leaders asking the mayor to meet the deficit in the expense budget by an across-the-board cut of 10 percent in the costs of city government. LaGuardia was quick to reply, calling the statement of the Citizens Budget Commission "ignorant, bombastic, malicious, and intellectually dishonest." He could not conceal, however, the fact that diversion of these taxes was a dangerous precedent and a first step away from strict financial probity.

Democrats in the City Council were not to be outdone by the private groups. The administration was assailed both for parsimoniousness and for "spending like a drunken sailor." The mayor had failed to provide sufficient funds for the most essential city needs, it was maintained, despite excessive tax rates and the largest budget in the city's history.

Beneath the rhetoric was a concern shared by all, including the mayor, for the long-range dilemma of the city. No additional help was in sight from Albany; Washington was turning away from the New Deal reforms to a total preoccupation with national defense. The country's economic condition had improved but the city, despite all its activity and brilliance, rested on an insecure base. Almost two hundred thousand unemployables languished on home relief, while whole families entered upon a second generation of dependence on governmental programs. LaGuardia had spoken of his 1940 budget as one "conceived in despair and developed in agony." The 1941 budget was in some ways worse, developed in a nagging conviction that the processes of government were no longer rational.

The real estate taxes of that year were maintained, in the end, at their previously existing level; the tax levy budget was cut by $7.3 million. In a way it was fortunate that another year would not see the same play reenacted by the same cast, for the results would surely have been disastrous. But by 1942 the nation would be at war and the scenario would be drastically altered. The next years brought their own fiscal challenges, met by LaGuardia without a complete control of the situation and with a diminishing resolve to leave a balanced budget to his successor. Much later, the 1941 budget struggle could be seen as a prototype of what New York would regularly face as it advanced into the 1950s and 1960s.

Civilian Defense

War was never far from the mayor's mind, and while he was considering his own future and the city's budget he did not take his eyes for long from international events. The first meeting of the city's Defense Council, January 18, was scrutinized by the Tammany forces with their normal degree of impartiality. They declared it to be unnecessarily alarming to the public and a first step in LaGuardia's 1941 campaign. The Defense Council, with the mayor at its head, included members of the City Council, the Board of Estimate, the police, fire, and health commissioners, members of the Tunnel Authority, the gas and electric companies, bankers, business executives, and newspaper publishers. It met behind barred doors, in an atmosphere of urgency and secrecy.

That LaGuardia was ready to put international above local politics was evidenced by his stand in the House election called after the death of Kenneth Simpson. The American Labor party, the nearest thing he had at this time to a party—he was enrolled, he said, but did not pay dues—named an able member of the bar, Dean Alfange, who was subsequently endorsed by Roosevelt. LaGuardia, however, endorsed Republican Joseph Clark Baldwin, because of the two he seemed the stronger supporter of aid to the Allies. As he took up his travels once more he played the same tune of loyalty, preparedness, and support for those fighting abroad in the good cause. In February he testified in favor of Roosevelt's Lend-Lease bill; warned in St. Louis that cities on both coasts must be aware of the possibility of attacks by bombers (a 3 percent chance, he said); and as the year progressed became more strident, declaring that those who opposed the president's policies were supplying propaganda for Hitler.

One figure, the leading spokesman for America First and a powerful opponent of Lend-Lease, LaGuardia treated with uncharacteristic gentleness. While others were assailing Charles Lindbergh in words that made him seem close to a traitor, the mayor referred to him as "a young man whom we all admire," but weak in his knowledge of European political history. Holding that Lindbergh based his opinions on false information or misunderstanding, LaGuardia refused to believe him a Nazi sympathizer. Was LaGuardia trying to offset the impression that he was an extremist, given to "hysteria" and exaggerated hostilities? It seems more likely that with his love of flying and his admiration for the daring act, he could not bring himself to see Lindbergh as anything other than a "lone eagle," misguided but still heroic.

Still, no definitive word came from Washington. On March 29 Roosevelt let it be known he had no post for LaGuardia equal in importance to the mayoralty. It was widely understood, however, that he had in fact offered him the opportunity to serve as coordinator of civil defense, but that LaGuardia had refused. We know that LaGuardia was on the mind of the president's advisors. In April James Rowe told the president that the mayor had been making "unhappy noises" since the election. By May Anna Rosenberg was acting as intermediary between the two men. On the eve of LaGuardia's May 7 visit to Washington she sent a memorandum to Roosevelt saying that yes, LaGuardia would accept the post (presumably of civil defense) if urged by the president, and that he would be willing (evidently the concern of someone in the White House) to have his utterances "supervised."

On May 17 an immense patriotic rally was held in Central Park. The crowd, estimated at 675,000 people, was the biggest in New York's history, about as big, it was noted, as the population of Munich. Ickes was the featured speaker but was overshadowed by the mayor. LaGuardia was in his best form. He seemed to be everywhere at once and to be performing in a half dozen roles. He addressed the overflow crowd in the Sheep Meadow, introduced the speakers and musicians, exchanged jokes with the celebrated comic Eddie Cantor, and twice took up the baton to conduct the 250-piece band composed of police, fire, parks, and sanitation personnel. Marian Anderson and Kate Smith sang that day. La-

Guardia's old friend, Albert Spalding, played the fiddle.

The next morning LaGuardia went to Washington, bouyed by this patriotic demonstration, and then and there accepted the post of director of civilian defense. In an address to his fellow New Yorkers he declared the new assignment would not interfere with his mayoral duties. He praised Morris and McGoldrick as members of a continuing team, and spoke modestly of his own future plans. In ordinary circumstance, he said, he would have apprised his fellow citizens before this of his intentions regarding a third-term race, but now it was difficult to plan ahead. The people themselves would make the ultimate decision as to whether he would run again, and meanwhile he promised to keep them informed.

Public reaction to the appointment was less enthusiastic than might have been anticipated, in large part because it did not seem credible that any man, even a LaGuardia, could fill the two jobs effectively. The president was judged to have paid his political debt to the restless and impatient mayor, but had it been paid in good coin? The *Herald Tribune*, less kindly inclined to Roosevelt than to the mayor, expressed toward LaGuardia an affectionate sympathy which in one way or another was widely shared. It was impossible to believe, said the *Tribune* editorial, "great as are the capacities of our mayor," that so colossal an undertaking, to be carried out by an unpaid appointee in his spare time, could be accepted with inner satisfaction or discharged with success. Elsewhere there were expressions of the deep-rooted, and to LaGuardia, extremely frustrating conviction that in his city job he was indispensable. "Every consideration of public interest," said Raymond Moley writing in *Newsweek*, "requires Mr. LaGuardia's services as mayor of New York. To the vigor, earnestness, and intelligence that Mr. LaGuardia so clearly possesses is now added a profound knowledge of the city's life and government."

The appointment was the more difficult to appraise because its scope and responsibilities were still vague. Seen in one light it involved only an extension of the efforts which normally in a period of such uncertainty and danger would be performed by the head of the U.S. Conference of Mayors. From a different perspective it called for duties comparable in the civilian field to those assigned to Knudson in the military. In England Herbert Morrison, who sent greetings and offers of any possible aid to LaGuardia, as minister of home defense was one of the major figures of the cabinet. It seemed to *Time* that the mayor's new job could be just as big as he wanted to make it; the indications were that "bustling Fiorello" was determined to make it very big.

What, precisely, *was* involved? The new agency, known as the Office of Civilian Defense, was given a three-fold charge: to organize cities and towns across America for the achievement of maximum security; to stimulate morale among the population; and to set up skeleton civilian bodies for the provision of physical defense if needed. From the beginning there was dangerous ambiguity within this broad range of duties. That a uniform air-raid precaution system should be coordinated seemed clear enough. But what was the meaning of the stress placed on maintenance of civilian morale? When the list of activities shaded off into the planning of recreation and health facilities in training camps, the new director seemed to be spread thin indeed. This was a long way from what had been understood to be the primary concern of civilian defense: to assure a maximum chance of survival in the closest proximity to a bomb explosion.

LaGuardia took up these scattered duties with his usual energy. He must have derived satisfaction from appointing Herbert Lehman, amid some genial fanfare, to be the New York State coordinator of civilian defense. For once the governor was subordinate to the mayor. In other states he hastened to make similar appointments (one of the complaints later to be made against LaGuardia's handling of the job was that he used his authority to favor political friends); again he buckled himself regularly into his seat on the day's earliest flights as he traveled over the country to confer with local officials, to make speeches or hold press conferences. By midsummer he had settled into something as close to a routine as he ever got. From Tuesday morning to Thursday night he would be in Washington; the rest of the week, installed once more (and for the last time) at the Arrowbrook Country Club, he would rule as mayor of New York. Actually he often stayed in Washington into Friday, for as an inducement to take the job he had been invited to sit in at cabinet meetings. LaGuardia was not one to neglect such an opportunity, and even Stimson was impressed by the way he conducted himself in these discussions.

The president was easily bored when it came to the details of civilian defense, but at this stage he enjoyed having LaGuardia on hand, and more than once enlisted his services in tasks beyond immediate duty. When the question came up of changes in the Social Security system, he suggested that Miss Perkins and the

38. A controversial appointment: The president and his new director of civilian defense.
KEYSTONE

39. An uneasy alliance. With Eleanor Roosevelt at Women's Trade Union dinner. TIMES
WIDE WORLD

mayor put their heads together and see what could be done. On another occasion he enrolled LaGuardia in the search for a job for his old friend, the grandfather of a future president, John Fitzgerald. (LaGuardia had nothing immediate in mind but promised to be helpful if he could.) Inevitably these flutterings so near the throne caused uneasiness among the older courtiers. Ickes's diary provides a fascinating account of jealousy at work, and also a reflection of the very real difficulties into which LaGuardia fell.

Ickes had been one of the mayor's strong supporters, but he was wary of LaGuardia (as he was of almost everyone else) lest his own relationship with the president be undercut. It was fine having LaGuardia as mayor in New York, but the civil defense appointment had ruffled him. "After all, Fiorello is not God and he has to eat and sleep like other human beings." It rankled that LaGuardia should attend cabinet meetings regularly. By July Ickes thought the post was "something he shouldn't have taken after all, either on his own account or on account of the country." With evident satisfaction he quoted Bernard Baruch and later Eugene Meyer, publisher of the *Washington Post*, to the effect that LaGuardia could not work with anybody and was "in the president's hair." An entry for November 15 noted that LaGuardia was not at the cabinet meeting of the previous day. This was the last, dry reference to a man whom Ickes had once backed for president.

The mayor's job was complicated, and his relations with Roosevelt ultimately fouled, by the singular provision that as director he should deal with civilian morale. LaGuardia desired this responsibility but saw only in the vaguest terms how he should handle it, and soon it was common knowledge in Washington that it was being neglected. At one point he considered putting the well-known journalist, Russell Davenport, in charge. But he drew back. And then he gave the task to Mrs. Roosevelt, the president's wife, as co-director with him of civilian defense. LaGuardia must have admired from a distance Eleanor's energy, the equal of his own, and no doubt thought that through association with her he would be drawn closer into the president's circle. The assumption could not have been more mistaken.

From the beginning the team did not work smoothly. Mrs. Roosevelt noted that all the matters the mayor found boring or uninteresting to deal with, he assigned to her office. She found that even she had trouble in being fitted into the director's busy schedule. As for LaGuardia, he did not find the president's wife altogether genial company. His old-fashioned ideas about the proper role of women interfered with his full appreciation of her talents: "My wife is named Marie, not Eleanor," he remarked when it was urged that Mrs. LaGuardia play a large role in public events. The first lady's abstemiousness discomfited him. Once when he had lunched with her in the little apartment she kept in Greenwich Village, he said to her on leaving: "My wife never asks me where I have been, nor whom I saw, nor what I did, but she always asks me what I have had to eat. Today I can truthfully say I did not have too much."

In more important ways the joint directorship was unfortunate. Difficult as it is to believe now when Mrs. Roosevelt is seen in the large perspective of her life and service, she was at this time a far from popular figure. Her constant engagement in social experiments, often involving younger intellectuals of advanced or radical views, had brought her into ridicule, or had made her feared as a dangerous person. Given authority within the Office of Civilian Defense, her attention to recreational activities, to crafts, to some of the more esoteric art forms, brought the agency's program under question. LaGuardia's own image, made diffuse by a well-developed tendency to engage in pep talks, was hurt by having his agency further diverted from what should have been its central purpose.

Far from bringing LaGuardia closer to the president, the association set them at an increasing distance. He could not have known that the president and his wife were often coldly apart, and in his zeal would not have appreciated that Roosevelt put civilian defense at something less than the highest priority. Anna Rosenberg became the buffer between Roosevelt and LaGuardia, with orders to keep the mayor away. "You have to keep the peace," said he cheerily, referring to problems between his wife and the mayor. The president liked LaGuardia and was entertained by him, but he didn't want to have to meet with him. "He didn't want to be bothered by Eleanor, either," Mrs. Rosenberg was later to recall. "The least you can do is to see him," she interceded. But the president was stubborn and said it would make too many problems.

Only half aware of this situation, LaGuardia plunged on through the endless labors of organizing a country which still saw war as an unlikely possibility and the dangers of aerial bombardment as utterly remote. In his own city he could at least set an example. A first obligation was to keep food prices down and assure an equable distribution in case of an emergency. For this he summoned his commissioner of markets, the able and dedicated William Fellowes Morgan. Under the fire commissioner he formed a core of local air-raid wardens and ordered the registration of all male city employees between the ages of eighteen and twenty-five who were free to assume voluntary duties. In other cities he endeavored to create the same basic machinery of defense.

The task was not easy. Early in December LaGuardia addressed the midwestern governors, the first signs of discouragement showing through his ordinarily ebullient manner. He assailed the apathy of inner America; he tried to conjure up the grim possibility of future danger. Yet he had to admit the likelihood of air raids in midwestern cities was "rather remote." He had begun to feel the tide of press comment running against him. "I confess helplessness," he said only half humorously; "I can't control the press in my own city, much less in Missouri." Then he admitted he was not satisfied with the temper of his own employees; he wanted "to chase them out of the office into the field." Two days later he was back in New York dedicating a defense housing project. "I do not know what will happen, tomorrow, next week . . ."

That was December 3. On December 7 the Japanese attacked Pearl Harbor and the whole picture of civilian defense, and of everything else, was changed.

Third-Term Campaign

The reader must now descend from these high matters of state and return to the minutiae of New York City politics. It is difficult to realize that while LaGuardia was engaged in organizing the home defense of the United States, he was at the same time deeply involved in the maneuverings of the nominating process for mayor and then conducting a strenuous campaign. Yet in fact this seemingly inexhaustible man was operating at two quite different levels, and in two spheres simultaneously—the national and the local. He moved to the rhythms of the war in Europe, and to the conventional ceremonies of parochial politicians.

Our story returns to March 1941. LaGuardia, as we have seen, was waiting hopefully for a call from Washington, was watching international developments, and was deferring any decision as to a third-term race. Undoubtedly he hoped he might work his way out of the mayoralty; or might find, if he took on responsibilities in Washington, that he could run in New York as the city's "defense mayor," with Democratic backing in addition to that of the Fusionists and ALP. Berle mentioned to Ed Flynn the possibility of a Democratic endorsement, but that particular dream got no further. "The boys wouldn't stand for it," said the boss of the Bronx. One of "the boys," James A. Roe of Queens, made it clear that what was wanted was a good old-fashioned Democrat, not a socialist, not a Fusionist, not a Communist—in short, not a LaGuardia. What's more, the Democrats thought they could win this time with one of their own.

Even the president could not alter the minds of these local chieftans. Flynn lunched at the White House and on leaving, in what was widely interpreted as a defiance of the New Deal, announced publicly that the Democrats would not pick LaGuardia. Instead, on July 16, they picked the district attorney of Brooklyn, William O'Dwyer.

That left the Fusionists, along with the Republicans, to make their choice. The patriarchs of the movement, Seabury and Thacher, gathered to revive and coordinate the forces of 1933. On July 21 it was announced that they would work through the Citizens Nonpartisan Committee for the Reelection of Fiorello H. LaGuardia. This was the signal the mayor had been waiting for; besides, it was evident by this time that the Washington job was not going to bear him aloft out of the maelstrom of city politics. That night, sitting at his desk with his daughter at his side, he delivered an address entitled "The City and the Mayor," formally announcing that he would run again.

The *Times* called the declaration "good news"; the *Post* rejoiced in "a good day for New York." The *Tribune*, *PM*, and the *World Telegram* promised full support, with only the conservative *Sun* withholding a commitment. It was the *News*, soon to turn sour on LaGuardia, that had the nicest words; its editorial paid a tribute which came near the heart of the matter. "For all his shirtsleeve vocabulary, the guy has tact. In New York City are to be found the country's widest extremes of wealth and poverty, plus the biggest assortment of racial stresses and strains. Yet it runs along on a good-natured, even keel, and LaGuardia must be credited with much of that during his first two terms." Viewed in perspective, this capacity to keep goodwill among the disparate groups of the city seemed a more notable accomplishment even than restoring fiscal credit or making a dent in the costly patronage system.

A sharp controversy now arose in Fusion ranks over the renomination of Stanley Isaacs for Manhattan borough president. Isaacs had made an excellent record, bringing to the post ability and intelligence, but his usefulness had been marred by the unhappy Gerson appointment. Admitting the appointment of a Communist had been a mistake, Isaacs nevertheless refused to remove him. On that fatal dilemma he was impaled, while his foes screamed for revenge and LaGuardia was made increasingly aware of the burden. One cannot altogether lack sympathy for the mayor, though his manner of dropping Isaacs seemed unnecessarily harsh. Mrs. Isaacs, whose account is understandably biased, tells that LaGuardia's efforts to discredit her husband culminated in a summons to City Hall where Isaacs found the mayor's office full of newspapermen. At issue was Isaacs's support of an important school project, which for reasons of economy LaGuardia wanted killed. "Stanley, I can make or break you, and if you insist on opposing me on Townsend Harris, it'll be break!" The borough president stood his ground.

Nevertheless he arrived home "white and shaken." A few weeks later LaGuardia phoned and invited him and his wife to dinner. During the evening Isaacs pleaded in vain for renomination. Afterward he wrote what he called "an immodest letter" to Seabury, and though the Fusionists on their own would have backed him, they deferred to the Republicans who were adamantly opposed. Edgar Nathan was nominated as joint candidate. Isaacs, declaring his intention to run for the City Council on an independent ticket, pledged full support to LaGuardia and his whole slate. It was a generous move, and it is pleasant to recall that this stubborn, injudicious, intensely honest man was elected, and served as minority leader of the council until his death in 1962.

When the Republican leaders met, LaGuardia was endorsed by three of them—Curran of Manhattan, Crews of Brooklyn, and Woodward of Staten Island. The three stated simply that New York under Fusion had become a better place to live, and that they were willing, therefore, to suppress their criticism of LaGuardia's offenses—his support of the New Deal and his attacks on Republican candidates for president and governor. Queens and the Bronx were not represented but put up no candidate of their own. Caught at the airport returning from Montreal, LaGuardia was told of the Republicans' action. For months he had been saying he was too busy running the city (and running civilian defense) to comment on political matters. But now he was ready with a word, and his heart was considerably softened. He praised the unselfish and patriotic spirit of the party that backed him in spite of all. He even told reporters their criticism of him had some justification, "from their point of view."

LaGuardia, nevertheless, would have to face an opponent in the Republican primary. The isolationist, anti-New Dealer John R. Davies, a highly respected old-line Republican, ran independently.

One important element that would affect the campaign remained: Who would run for Manhattan district attorney? Dewey's intentions were unknown, and neither the Republicans nor the Democrats had a candidate for the office. The Tammany Democrats had shown a readiness to nominate Dewey, on conditions that varied from his working for a straight Republican candidate for mayor to his merely remaining neutral in the negotiations. But Dewey was cool to the idea. The nice calculations by which his political choices were guided told him that to damage LaGuardia would be harmful to his own image. Besides, a canvassing of both wings of the American Labor party had resulted in an uncertain answer. On July 30, he called in the press, which for weeks had been hounding him for a decision, and announced that he would not run for district attorney. He said that he hoped one of his four assistants would succeed him in the post.

Tammany stepped into the void left by Dewey's declination, and on the very next day dropped a bombshell. They announced that their candidate for district attorney would be Frank S. Hogan, the outstanding Dewey aide who had been responsible for throwing a number of Tammany figures into jail. The Republican and Fusion leaders were left in disarray, and Hogan himself was flabbergasted. Warren Moscow writing in the *Times* summed up the situation well: "In other words, Tammany is ready to take a plea of guilty on all the political trials of the past six years if it can remove Mayor LaGuardia from City Hall."

Although the first reaction was panic, LaGuardia's supporters began to see a way out. If the Republicans also named Hogan, might it not accomplish one of the mayor's own goals of taking the district attorney out of politics? With this vote of confidence in his office, might not Dewey campaign actively for LaGuardia? So the Republicans added their endorsement to that of the Democrats. The following day Hogan dropped by at the summer city hall to pay his respects to the mayor. LaGuardia was full of curiosity and asked Hogan point blank how the Democratic nomination had come to him. Hogan told him privately who the intermediary had been, but it was never publicly divulged.

LaGuardia, in the midst of all his other concerns, now faced the primary campaign. He chose to be very largely a nonparticipant. He would not have campaign headquarters and said he would rely on all New Yorkers to be his campaign managers. He made no speeches and went about his daily business, flying regularly to Washington, presiding over the Conference of Mayors, addressing Defense Day rallies in various cities. He fought with the City Council over county reform and with Quill over the transit pay plan. He surprised reporters when he turned up suddenly for a hospital dedication and then refused to speak. It was atypical reticence, especially in an election year, but it was LaGuardia's way.

He continued to be philosophical about the opposition, saying in private he did not see why they should take any other position. Newbold Morris bore faithfully with his chief's quiescence, going around alone to face the music in the city's Republican clubs. "Did you hear what he said about us?" Morris would be asked indignantly. "Oh, he wasn't talking about *you,*" Morris would reply, and that, as he'd sum it up much later, was also LaGuardia's way. He'd attack the bankers, but Morris would assure Winthrop Aldrich that he could not have meant him personally. "He'd make some cryptic remark," Morris recalled, "and leave reporters shaking their heads."

John R. Davies, meanwhile, was a busy campaigner. He drew the issue in a way that appealed to many audiences, saying that New Dealers and left-wingers were infinitely more dangerous than the musical comedy type of bosses and ward heelers that no longer existed except in the mayor's mind. The mayor's supporters saw cause for real worry. "We cannot help recalling 1919," said the wise old *Herald Tribune,* "when likewise in the midst of exciting international issues, the defeat of another high-minded Fusion mayor, John P. Mitchel, was assured when another insignificant candidate bested him in the Republican party." But support for the mayor was coming from expected, and sometimes from unexpected, sources. Dewey came out for him (eliciting another "I'm too busy to think about it"). And on the day before the primaries Wendell Willkie announced that he would fly to New York to cast his vote for the mayor. Knowing how he had abused and vilified the Republican presidential candidate, LaGuardia could only say: "This is the most generous and sporting attitude taken in politics for a long while."

Just before the primaries the mayor even wrested an endorsement from his own parks commissioner. It was couched in the best Moses style: "I am for Mayor LaGuardia because in spite of his cussedness toward those whose support is indispensable in critical times, and in spite of excursions into the far capital where they give him nothing but husks and leavings, he has been the best mayor of New York in my lifetime." Moses has never varied from that judgment.

LaGuardia defeated Davies, but the voting was light—only 4 percent of the enrolled Republicans voted in comparison to preelection estimates of 25 to 30 percent. He did well where the county leaders supported him; his vote, ironically enough, came from the clubhouses. The Republicans had counted on a large popular turnout; now they not only felt the lash of a near defeat in the LaGuardia–Davies race, but saw unpleasant omens for the big test in November when the Democratic organization strength would be so far superior to their own. The message of the light vote was not lost on LaGuardia, who threw himself wholeheartedly into a voter registration drive and promised to end the "silent" campaign.

"I feel free now," he said, "to take up and lead the fight"—and for the sake of his opponents he added: "Don't count on laryngitis."

The Democrats, for all their traditional strength, were faced by a formidable task. A June Gallup poll showed 57 percent of the voters backing the mayor. In September Gallup measured what he called "presidential timber" and in the nationwide survey LaGuardia came in fifth—behind Willkie, Hull, Dewey, and Wallace. Nevertheless, Democrats thought LaGuardia was vulnerable on three principal issues: reds in government, specifically (and quite unjustifiably) Paul Kern; inattention to his city job because of the defense post; overspending and high assessments. They counted, besides, on having the full support of Franklin Roosevelt and the national Democratic party.

On the red issue the Democrats were shameless. O'Dwyer, his running mates, and even Jim Farley hammered away at LaGuardia, the "favorite son of Stalin." When the Communists withdrew their own candidate for the mayoralty and left their members free to vote for the mayor, LaGuardia repudiated the potential support. But that did not appease the Democrats, who accused the mayor of making a deal. In a radio broadcast directed to the city's mothers, Farley asserted the mayor consistently favored the Communist cause and that his repudiation was not to be trusted.

When he was not being called a Communist he was said to be a part-time mayor, an absentee. The attack carried a good deal of weight, though LaGuardia would answer with characteristic pugnacity that he could accomplish more for New York City in an hour's work than most politicians could accomplish in a lifetime. When O'Dwyer tried to prove mismanagement in the city's departments, he ran into real trouble. A first target was the health department. A doctor, formerly a member of the department, headed a committee responsible for a blast against Commissioner Rice. Instant support for Rice came from the medical community. The charges of the committee were demolished one by one; the good doctor was not further seen nor heard from. The Sanitation Department was said to be a sink of patronage, but new equipment and efficient operations made the charge unconvincing.

That LaGuardia was responsible for high real estate assessments was fair game for the opposition. Everyone knew, however, that he had restored the city's credit. The assessments, moreover, had been kept unchanged in the 1941 budget. Here again the mayor took the offensive, and at the airport—most of his campaign statements seem to have been made at the airport, either going to Washington or returning—characterized the majority leader of the council, Democrat Lloyd Church, as "Lulu Lloyd, the lollipop boy for Tammany Hall."

Slowly the broad public support needed by LaGuardia began to express itself. He was backed by labor, by leading Republican figures, and by the most illustrious New Yorkers of his day. There were architects committees for LaGuardia, business committees, committees for the arts and professions. The powerful civic groups supported the mayor and Bishop Manning in a sermon called for his reelection. O'Dwyer, on the other hand, seemed to be getting little independent support. But he did have the Democratic organization behind him; he had Farley, Poletti, and Governor Lehman.

LaGuardia needed the support of the president, and this time he got it in time and in full measure. Unlike 1937, when Ickes gave a cryptic signal and Roosevelt's message came so late as to be more a gesture of self-interest than of genuine help, the president gave

LaGuardia his unqualified support. In vain Flynn made a last-minute appeal for something less than complete endorsement. Berle, together with Leland Olds, chairman of the Federal Power Commission, served as the advance guard of the New Deal troops. Even Stimson, "as a private citizen," announced his support.

All seemed to be going well, and then, just two weeks before Election Day, something happened—fortuitous and unforeseen—which was to have a profound effect upon the campaign and almost to alter its outcome. It was triggered by the sudden death (how often during these years death intervened in the political process!) of the state comptroller. The attorney-general ruled that an election for the post had to take place immediately. Under any circumstances there would have been a political scramble, but in the midst of the city election the matter was greatly complicated.

The governor made a temporary appointment of Joseph V. O'Leary, a prominent ALP member, and the Democrats proceeded to back him for the election. The Republicans nominated Frank Moore, a respected upstate leader. This left LaGuardia in the highly ticklish position of choosing between a member of his own party, the ALP, and thus jeopardizing the support of the Republican organization, or backing a Republican (and a good one at that) against the ALP. It was a dilemma manufactured with exquisite skill by Lehman and his advisers.

Just a week before the election the Court of Appeals (speaking through the chief judge, the governor's brother Irving H. Lehman) overruled the attorney-general and declared that the election for comptroller must wait until the following year. The appointment of O'Leary stood, and the mayor escaped the snare which had been laid for him. That LaGuardia should make capital out of the reversal is understandable, but in the excitement of the campaign he overstepped the bounds of political prudence. Attacking Lehman for his connivance in the aborted plot, he brought down on his own head an avalanche of abuse and of shocked rebuffs.

The mayor's fatal error was in referring to Lehman as a *goniff*, a Yiddish word which can only be translated as "thief." The best account of the incident is in the *Herald Tribune* of October 28. According to this report, written before the controversy had flared into a major political storm, LaGuardia "put on a show for half a dozen audiences in Brooklyn and Manhattan" celebrating the decision of the court and reveling in the reversal of Lehman's plan. Pacing the stages of schoolhouses and public auditoriums he imitated and burlesqued Lehman's disappointment and consternation. "I think it's the funniest thing that has happened in American politics. . . . It's the first time a man has hit himself in the jaw and knocked himself out. . . . You've heard of goniffs stealing from goniffs. Well, you're now hearing of double-crossers double-crossing double-crossers." Whatever may have been the taste or the propriety of the show, LaGuardia had the crowds roaring, according to the reporter on the spot.

The next day Lehman, drawing around himself the mantle of his impregnable humorlessness, assailed LaGuardia for being "grossly abusive." The mayor, he said, had reached a new low: his "practice of abusing his opponents in both private and public life is not an eccentricity but a deliberate attempt to intimidate those who oppose him. . . . New Yorkers are sick and tired of the mayor's unbridled tongue." What is surprising is not that Lehman should have issued so self-righteous a statement (the shrewd hand of Poletti appears to have been at work in the drafting) but that others, even among the mayor's supporters, should have echoed the theme. When it was all over, the *New Republic* dated from La-Guardia's attack on Lehman the precipitous fall in his fortunes which was to occur in 1942.

Lehman held a curious place in New York political life. He was not a man whom many were moved to praise extravagantly, but attacks upon him seemed to arouse the public's latent instincts of decency and fair play. Seabury in the 1934 campaign, Moses in 1936, Dewey in 1938 had each fallen afoul of Lehman in his role as sacred cow. Now LaGuardia, who might have been judged too experienced, or perhaps too gently inclined toward the governor, stepped into precisely the same trap. It very nearly cost him the election and might well have done so had not Roosevelt intervened, declaring him "the best mayor New York ever had," and denying as having no vestige of truth the report that he had weakened in his support.

The LaGuardia of Election Day 1941 was not the frenetic frowning man of previous election days who had gone dashing about the city barking commands, "acting as if he were going to a succession of four-alarm fires." A reporter for the *Tribune,* having followed him on his day's errands, found him calm and almost indifferent. He visited Carnegie Hall and the Bronx Zoo, and the only polling place where he was seen was his own. At the end of the afternoon he entered his apartment, where his wife and mother-in-law were waiting for him, "with the manner of a man who expects to pass a pleasant interlude of leisure and rest against the morrow's work."

With O'Dwyer leading in the early returns, a close race appeared in the making. As the evening went on the result came to seem increasingly uncertain. LaGuardia won, but by only a little over 130,000 votes, the narrowest margin in any mayoral contest since 1905. At Hyde Park, Roosevelt, as he retired for the night, found the outcome too unclear to make any statement. In the lobby of LaGuardia's apartment house a small group of reporters huddled silently. But a little after midnight it was all over and the city had its first three-term mayor. A photographer from *PM* climbed the building's six flights of stairs and knocked at apartment 6C. Opening the door, Marie agreed to carry a note to the mayor. "All right," came the answer. "He says it's all right for the photographers."

On a large living-room table were a dozen ruled pads, wads of crumpled paper, several with figures, and a half dozen worn-down pencils. On one side stood a child's blackboard with rows of figures below the names of O'Dwyer and LaGuardia. The mayor's children had evidently been keeping the score, too. "You boys must be tired," Marie said, offering them a Canadian Club and soda. Soon the mayor came in, wearing a black silk dressing gown. He blinked in the sudden light. "You know I'm tired, but I don't mind getting up for photographers. But I don't like reporters." Ray Platnick, the *PM* photographer, held out his hand to the mayor and congratulated him. "Thanks," he said, "but the next four years will be hell."

In a darkened Tammany Hall a different mood prevailed. By eleven most of the stalwarts had left. "Say anything you like," said the last of these to reporters, "but be kind."

In the elections Newbold Morris and McGoldrick had been re-elected along with the mayor. The county reform bill was passed, consolidating the jobs of borough sheriffs into one citywide office, a matter of special gratification to LaGuardia. He had carried Manhattan, the Bronx, and Brooklyn. In Queens O'Dwyer won with an antiwar vote. The rest was mixed. The Irish did not give O'Dwyer the strong support expected, while some Jewish and Italian areas, which the Democrats had been ready to write off, came out strongly for O'Dwyer. All in all, as the *Times* summed it up, reform had had a close call. Had the narrow margin gone the other way, "we suspect that many who voted for O'Dwyer, including Lehman himself, would have read the news with a chilly feeling that a great humanitarian era in New York City's history was coming to an end." They would have missed, in spite of all, "an energy swift to act, an intelligence quick to understand, and a heart as big as all outdoors in the presence of human need."

War Comes to New York

War came to New York, as it came to all America, on the afternoon of Sunday, December 7. The streets were hushed as men and women in families and small groups listened to their radios, scarcely believing that so far away in Pearl Harbor events had occurred which affected their lives deeply and irrevocably. The full cost of the disaster in men and ships and in strategic implications was not immediately known; but it was plain that the United States was in a conflict of unprecedented dangers, sure to be fought with new means of terror and surprise.

For LaGuardia it was the end of a long period of waiting. Despite apathy and even ridicule he had worked with all his strength to alert the country to the likelihood of war; it had been his charge to prepare the cities against just such perils as now seemed imminent. If there was a kind of grim relief in the dénouement, there was also puzzlement and then anger. He had been criticized for trying to awaken the country to dangers which seemed unreal and remote; increasingly in the coming weeks he would be criticized for not having adequately prepared the country for the dangers when they did come. If people had said he was giving too much time to preparations for civilian defense, they now began to say that, as mayor of New York, he could not give enough time. The difficulty of juggling two jobs had been plain from the time of the president's appointment seven months before. Now it was to build up to a storm.

In his address to New Yorkers on the day of the Pearl Harbor attack LaGuardia gave painful evidence of the stress he had been under. Once again, as in 1937, he had not taken even a brief vacation after the campaign, and the accumulated weariness of mind and body expressed itself in a churlish temper. "I want to assure all persons who have been sneering and jeering at defense activities," he said, "and even those who have been objecting to them and placing obstacles in their path, that we will protect them now. But we expect their cooperation and there will be no fooling." It was an unfortunate and revealing passage in a speech (broadcast over NBC as well as WNYC) which for the rest was filled with appropriate warnings and grave advice. Worse than this would come as the crisis over the two roles developed.

For the moment, however, there were tasks to be done, and LaGuardia set about them with the breathless dispatch for which he was famous. Within a matter of hours the city was placed on a wartime footing. The emergency control board was convened and kept in continuous session. Japanese nationals were confined to their residences, while their clubs and other gathering places were put under police protection. The consul-general and his staff were carefully escorted home. A little later the police, acting on orders of the FBI, rounded up 2,500 of these Japanese and put them on Ellis Island. By midnight air-raid wardens were on duty, and precautions against sabotage of bridges, tunnels, power plants, reservoirs, and railway stations were in force.

On Monday, with Newbold Morris in place as acting mayor, LaGuardia left for a five-day trip to the West Coast. He was acting both in his capacity as director of civilian defense and president of the U.S. Conference of Mayors. Mrs. Roosevelt accompanied him and afterward made some amusing and some significant comments on the journey. The mayor had retired into his berth soon after takeoff, the plane having hit an air pocket while he was eating and spilled a glass of milk on his suit. News came that San Francisco was being bombed. Mrs. Roosevelt waited until the plane was about to land for refueling somewhere in Kansas before waking the mayor. He stuck his head out of the berth—"looking for all the world like a Kewpie doll"—and immediately instructed her to leave the plane on landing and call Washington for verification. "If it is true," he said, "we will go direct to San Francisco." The report was not true and the plane continued on its appointed route.

"It was so characteristic of him," Mrs. Roosevelt wrote in her memoirs, "that I glowed inwardly. One could be exasperated with him at times, but one had to admire his real integrity and courage."

The rest of the week was spent on the West Coast in inspections and conferences. If LaGuardia was disheartened by the lack of supplies and equipment and the general unpreparedness for war conditions, he did not show it. He had "a field day," Mrs. Roosevelt recalled, talking to everybody and meeting the sudden emergency. "His complete courage and lack of fear had a wonderful effect upon everyone." Then, with the gentle word that could conceal a dagger, "I did not know and never have known how much all our plans, both his and mine, really helped," she wrote. Before long she was to put her doubts more plainly.

On December 13 the mayor was back at this desk in New York, prepared to take personal charge of the city's defense effort— planning blackouts, promulgating air-raid rules, seeing that illegal parking did not obstruct emergency vehicles or picketing detract from morale. He announced (despite Washington's ban on giving information about troop movements) that on direct orders of President Roosevelt three thousand men of the regular army would arrive in New York to guard points considered vital. The mayor was everywhere. He reassured parents their children would be taken care of, hailed the spirit of national unity before a dinner tended in his honor by foreign born, predicted freedom for all nations then under the heel of Hitler.

City Hall, meanwhile, was undergoing a transformation, being readied to become LaGuardia's wartime headquarters. He had been back only hours from his western trip when a large force of city carpenters, painters, mechanics, and electricians took over the historic building. They installed new iron barriers outside the mayor's office, new telephone lines and light circuits, and beneath the soaring rotunda erected partitions to increase existing office space. The Art Commission, guardian of the city's antiquities, was offended because it had not been consulted; but the changes were declared temporary and in the nature of emergency action. In any case, they were completed after a weekend of overtime work, before anyone could protest very vigorously.

In the chambers of the Board of Estimate young women volunteers were quietly assembling. Behind locked doors on the mayor's orders they were fitted for blue-gray uniforms. The ladies were reticent about their duties, but a week later when they appeared for work they saluted the mayor smartly, they saluted each other, and quickly became known as "the palace guard." Scheduled to serve as receptionists, messengers, and clerical aids, the first duty assigned them by the mayor was to report on the efficacy of the air-raid sirens, then about to go off. When they did go off, no one could hear them. "An unqualified failure" was the way the mayor characterized the test. "I guess we'll have to try something else," he said, standing at the end of the Brooklyn Bridge and cocking his ear in vain.

It was difficult, in these first days of fear and uncertainty, to distinguish the activities which bordered on *opera bouffe* from those that served a real need. LaGuardia was still possessed by the fear of panic among the people. He had recently seen what happened when Orson Welles, in a famous broadcast, enacted an invasion of the earth by Martians—the contagious spread of fear, though the program was specifically described as fictional. Now he felt that a gas mask available to each civilian would reassure the public in case of unexpected enemy attack. The press made fun of the grim information that the proposed gas masks could be ordered in four sizes, from the "baby protector" to the "universal adult." At the same time the public could not but be impressed when the U.S.–Canadian Joint Defense Board, after an all-day session presided over by the mayor at City Hall, announced in a communiqué that "military, air, and naval plans heretofore made are in satisfactory operation."

This was the first wartime Christmas. Darkness was closing down on many areas of U.S. life; ahead lay years of restraints and deprivations. Yet the lights of entertainment and the arts gleamed brightly, and would continue in spite of blacked-out cities, until a postwar burst of creative energy would see New York alongside—and in certain fields superceding—the cultural capitals of Europe. Even for the moment it was doing well enough. On the Broadway stage Ethel Barrymore was playing in *The Corn Is Green*, Maurice Evans in *Macbeth*, Helen Hayes in *Candle in the Wind*. Ethel Merman, Danny Kaye, Sophie Tucker, and Gertrude Lawrence were starring in musicals. Lillian Hellman was among the playwrights represented by new works. An engaging comedy called *Life with Father* had already been running two years and had a long life before it. The films that December included Walt Disney's *Dumbo*, Alfred Hitchcock's *Suspicion*, and *Smilin' Through*, an all-new production in bright Technicolor. Edna Ferber's *Saratoga Trunk* and Fitzgerald's *Last Tycoon* were among the novels everyone was reading.

It was the Christmas when, after a secret journey, Churchill appeared as the president's guest in the White House. Despite devastating British setbacks in the Pacific, his physical presence seemed to give courage to others. On Christmas Eve he stood beside Franklin Roosevelt on the portico of the White House. The lights of the festival tree defied with their faint rays the gloom descending on Western civilization as the British leader invited all to pause in love and in hope for one night, before turning again "to the stern tasks and formidable years that lie before us."

In New York, where the mayor's staff had been on duty seven days a week since the war began, a somber greeting was extended to the city's 150,000 employees. "I hope they enjoy the holiday," said LaGuardia, "for it may be the last they will have." His own Christmas was spent at home with his family.

40. Victory. UPI

PART THREE

10

"What Has Happened to LaGuardia?"

Embattled Mayor

Despite Mrs. Roosevelt's sympathetic comments in her memoirs, on returning from the West Coast trip she was convinced that the mayor would have to be replaced as director of civilian defense. She found others in the White House sharing her opinion and she evidently spoke in the same vein to the president. Thus LaGuardia began his third term under a heavy shadow. His unprecedented electoral victory in New York, and his high visibility on the national scene, availed little against factors which were to make the next years difficult and often disappointing.

Franklin Roosevelt discussed the situation with the director of the budget, Harold Smith, who concurred in the judgment that LaGuardia could not handle the defense job under wartime conditions. There were also talks with James M. Landis of the Harvard Law School about the possibility of his taking over the administrative duties. At the end of the year Roosevelt called in LaGuardia. Entering the Oval Office, the mayor sensed something was up. He began with an aggressive argument to the effect that in his defense post he had not been treated justly by the press. Some of the journalists did not like him, others did not like Mrs. Roosevelt. The president was "fairly firm," according to Harold Smith, in insisting that a new setup was needed.

These events, which of course were not publicly known, help explain LaGuardia's conduct as the year 1941 came to an end. He was a man tormented by the sense of failure, even in the wake of his unprecedented third-term victory. He saw slipping from his grasp the role in national affairs which he had so ardently coveted and to which he had given such exhausting efforts. He was losing it, moreover, at the very moment when war, the possibility of which had been widely scoffed at, had become a reality.

One wonders whether LaGuardia contemplated the irony of his electoral victory: had the slim margin swung the other way, he would have been free to devote himself to defense. Now he had to choose—and yet there was no real choice. In politics it is not possible to run from a mandate freshly given by the voters. Besides, he was still widely believed to be indispensable as mayor. Of the many who were determined to keep him from going to Washington, some acted in good faith and some for personal reasons. So he might talk of having to choose, and in swearing in Newbold Morris as president of the council could tell him to be ready to assume the mayor's duties. But in fact he was nailed to the cross of another term; and that term, he was convinced, would be "hell."

While the machinery for a reorganization of OCD was being set in motion behind the scenes at the White House, enough was going on in public to be highly disconcerting to the mayor. On December 22 Mrs. Roosevelt stated that what the OCD required was not "reorganization" but "organization"—in other words, it had been chaos from the start. Almost all the press was in a highly excited mood, feeling after Pearl Harbor that *something* must be done, and to drop LaGuardia seemed the one simple and obvious thing. The more moderate papers could still be comparatively mild, the *Tribune* remarking that civilian defense was "mainly under the mayor's hat." Granted, it was a big hat; granted, embarrassing incidents like the failure of the air-raid sirens were not his fault—still, the work required a full-time official. Others praised his contribution to long-range planning in OCD, but called for a chief magistrate of the city undistracted by other duties.

On December 27 LaGuardia made a move which would only be interpreted as a reflection of inner tensions. Peremptorily he forced the resignation of his commissioner of markets, William Fellowes Morgan, Jr. Morgan had been with the mayor from the start, in a post crucial to the administration's consumer orientation. With the mayor's support he had built the public markets at Hunt's Point, in Brooklyn, on upper Park Avenue; it was to him, when the war came, that LaGuardia turned to make sure that food prices were not arbitrarily raised. Morgan was one of the exceptional men whom the mayor had attracted, marked by strong social commitments combined with solid business experience. He was also of a tactful and generally forgiving disposition, a factor which now contributed to the public's support.

The resignation was sparked by the mayor's insistence on making appointments without consulting the commissioner or even talking with him about them. Attempts to see the mayor had been turned aside with word that he was "out of town" or "too busy." La-Guardia did not make things easier by remarking that there was no serious dispute: "commissioners never have disputes with the mayor—you ought to know that." And two days later he dismissed the affair with the words *"E finita la comedia."* But the "comedy" was not over; it cast a shadow which was to haunt LaGuardia for the months and even the years to come.

The most obvious conclusion drawn from the resignation was that which Morgan underlined: the mayor was too preoccupied to see his own commissioners. The public's latent apprehensions were thus at a stroke given form and substance. But even worse was the suspicion that in bypassing his commissioner the mayor was making appointments directed by leaders of the national Democratic party. "We refuse to believe the mayor has suddenly become a time-serving politician," said the *Herald Tribune,* and it commented on Morgan's "courteous and temperate" description of a situation which for months had been creating alarm among the mayor's warmest and most loyal supporters. But the explosions of the Morgan incident, it concluded, "bring into sharp relief the deterioration of civic rule."

The year ended grimly. Accepting a gift of ambulances on December 30, LaGuardia gave way in public to his bitterness. "I have suffered too much during the last six months," he said, "absorbing the criticism, the abuse, the sneers and jeers of people, including some from the press, when we were seeking to train people for just this emergency." He denounced "superpatriots seeking to find flaws and to destroy the confidence of the people in their government." "I'll have more to say about that," he concluded, and turned to find New Year's Eve being celebrated by the public in a feverish and unrealistic mood, as if men and women still could not believe that the country was at war, or wished to forget it. La-

Guardia's plea to avoid sirens and bright lights was widely disregarded.

In his annual New Year's message LaGuardia had, as he had promised, more to say about his critics. He defended his Washington record, saying that the OCD was "magnificently organized"; he attacked those who disparaged him as "swivel chair scribes," "two-by-four editors," and even as "some jap or friend of a jap." That same night in the White House Harry Hopkins suggested at dinner that Wendell Willkie be made head of OCD. Mrs. Roosevelt threw up her hands in horror—it was a maneuver almost successful in winning a reprieve for LaGuardia. But the next day Roosevelt saw the mayor and told him definitely he wanted Landis appointed to the job of executive officer. This time LaGuardia agreed, and offered to talk to Landis himself.

By now Congress had become involved. Anti-New Deal forces, on the grounds that OCD was being used "to socialize America," voted to turn the organization over to the War Department. Landis took charge, with Mrs. Roosevelt remaining as his assistant, and LaGuardia announced that he welcomed being relieved of detail while he would travel even more widely about the country. This was scarcely an approach to satisfy his New York constituency. But the tension had eased, and his address to the council a few days later was agreeably different in tone from the New Year's message. "I suppose a decision will have to be made, but not yet," he said. "I don't think I've lost my grasp of the situation in New York—at least I hope I haven't."

Matters now moved rapidly to the conclusion of this chapter in LaGuardia's mayoralty. At the end of January, at a dinner of the New York University law alumni, he good-naturedly admitted he had found that "sin does not pay—I am about to give up the double life." On February 11 he formally resigned, saying his original assignment had been completed. Congress, meanwhile, had reversed its vote turning over OCD to the army. Mrs. Roosevelt quit on February 20, making it clear she was doing so under pressure of public opinion. Fellowes Morgan, now standing on the sidelines, said it was obvious that LaGuardia was a sorely overworked man whose nerves had been "shot to pieces." He urged the mayor to go away and take a much-needed rest. "When you come back, forgive and forget."

LaGuardia did not take a rest, and he never could quite bring himself to forget. The OCD experience had been a searing one and it left its mark across the third term. He had been overinsistent in reaching for it in the first place. He had been mistaken in trying to please the president by taking on Mrs. Roosevelt. But he had borne himself undauntedly when war seemed as far off as Lindbergh and Senator Nye said it was.

The fact that the country was made aware before Pearl Harbor of the rudiments of fire fighting and air-raid alerts was due to LaGuardia's efforts, and it was a tribute to him that in New York fifty-six-thousand citizens registered as air-raid wardens, while thousands of auxiliary police and firemen were enrolled. Elsewhere, it is true, local plans languished for lack of federal support or went off in directions of their own. Yet whatever the shortcomings in administration, or however irritating the impetuosities of the mayor's nature, it was war itself that in the end shattered LaGuardia's personal hopes—war which he had so prophetically foreseen but which, when it came, made his part-time efforts plainly inadequate.

Uproar over Paul Kern

The "deterioration of civic rule," which the *Tribune* had noted in the Fellowes Morgan case, was illustrated even more vividly in the extraordinary proceedings surrounding the mayor's dismissal of Paul Kern from his post as chairman of the Civil Service Commission. It will be recalled that through 1940 and 1941 Kern was under investigation by the council, a demeaning legislative spectacle in which the young Kern, at once indifferent and aggressive, stood alone against the fanaticism of the forces led by Al Smith, Jr. By 1942 Smith was in the army and the investigation was renewed under another chairman. Before this new phase of the investigation was to get very far, a wholly new situation developed, one that found LaGuardia and Kern locked in a combat far more sensational than anything the council could provide.

LaGuardia had long been indulgent toward Kern, reappointing him to a full term on the commission during the 1940 investigation. As for his being a fellow traveler, "everyone has belonged to committees at one time or another. Sometimes the purposes which have been good at one time change later." To a correspondent who had urged Kern's withdrawal during the 1941 campaign, LaGuardia defended him again. "He is indiscreet and loves to show off openly. . . . He does his work well but once in a while spoils it all by some inept or irrelevant statement. He is still young and perhaps not entirely incurable." Now, however, developments were to take place which changed this protective, almost paternal attitude.

In December, while the mayor was struggling with criticism of his role in OCD and his part in the resignation of Morgan, he found himself confronted with a gratifying piece of postelection business. The county reform bill had been passed by the voters in a referendum, eliminating the borough registrars and borough sheriffs, creating in their place two citywide offices. The reform would leave out in the cold a number of Democratic stalwarts. The Tammany machine, working through the state Civil Service Commission, moved to get these officeholders transferred without competitive examinations to the city civil service lists. Kern denied the transfers, but in the case of four particularly dear to Boss Flynn the commissioner was overruled by LaGuardia. It would be difficult to account for this if one did not see at work here the same accommodation to Democratic politicians as in the appointments to Fellowes Morgan's department. In any case, Kern set out to block the four, taking direct issue with the mayor.

When the payroll with the names of the four came up for verification, the Civil Service Commission under Kern's leadership refused to approve it. When a court order requiring payment was obtained, the Civil Service Commission voted to appeal. Chanler, the corporation counsel, refused to take the case. Admitting the mayor's support of his position, he declared in court he would not oppose the action of the state Civil Service Commission, nor would he support an "unseemly squabble" over jurisdiction. Kern retaliated by issuing a press release recalling that Chanler had supported McKee's candidacy in the 1933 election. It was not surprising, Kern argued, that Chanler should refuse to take a stand against Flynn's favorites. Thereupon the Civil Service Commission filed an action against the corporation counsel.

Up to this point the quarrel had been confined to opposing city officials. Now the mayor himself stepped in and suspended the entire Civil Service Commission. Herlands personally served the papers, performing, as he had in the cases of Rheinstein, McElligott, and Morgan, the additional service of putting his men on the premises to conduct inquiries and prevent the removal of papers.

At first the mayor was subjected to severe criticism. The *Post,* ordinarily a LaGuardia supporter, remarked on his "growing taste for assertive rule," forcing big controversies where relatively minor issues were involved. The excuse for the suspension, that he would not tolerate disputes between high officers in his administration, seemed hardly persuasive in view of the many disputes (most of them involving Moses, it is true) which he had looked on with outward equanimity—Moses *v.* Carey, Moses *v.* Curran; the Triborough *v.* the Tunnel Authority, and so on almost indefinitely. But Kern began to overstate his case, to indulge in wild exaggerations and innuendoes, which quickly lost him the sympathy of the public.

At the public hearing, where he appeared with his fellow commissioner Wallace Sayre, Kern was still comparatively self-possessed. He recalled his old relationship with the mayor. "In those days you didn't send me messengers by reporters. You called me up in the morning and at night, in all hours when you wanted me to work." He warned the mayor, in tones that made him sound like the senior partner: "Your old friends are gone with the snows of yesteryear and you have surrounded yourself with sycophants who fawn on you." Toward the end, when the mayor seemed to suggest a chance for reconsideration, both Kern and Sayre expressed regret over the whole incident.

Nevertheless, on February 16 LaGuardia formally removed the two officials. Both appealed the action (the legal results of which we shall see) and Kern let loose with a number of statements couched in the bitterest terms. He spoke of a "sinister hand" guiding the administration and denounced the mayor as a "public official who refers to the court of appeals as low-grade thieves" and "greets his own commissioners on the steps of City Hall with unprintable epithets." Kern stated that for two years the mayor had been trying to wreck the merit system in a series of behind-the-scenes moves which would have shocked the public had they known of them.

The Kern affair now took still another strange and different tack. It appeared that Commissioner Herlands had been investigating serious charges against Ed Flynn, involving the misuse of city laborers and city materials in paving with Belgian blocks the courtyard of his private residence. Kern broke the story of the paving blocks; he claimed he had himself been looking into the matter and that Herlands, far from having preceded him in the inquiry, had delib-

41. "Boss of the Bronx" Ed Flynn. WIDE WORLD

42. Democratic triumvirate. Governors Smith and Lehman with James A. Farley. WIDE WORLD

erately delayed and blocked it. LaGuardia backed Herlands and was thus placed in a position, curious for him, of having been a good deal less than aggressive in uncovering graft. He had shown his hand only when forced to do so by Kern; "and the majestic pace at which the investigation moved," said the *Tribune,* formed a strange contrast with the early days of Fusion.

The mayor now appeared on the defensive, the *Tribune* continued. "This is a melancholy change, and an ominous one. It demonstrates clearly that Mr. LaGuardia did not come back to his job as mayor too soon. It also suggests the disturbing thought that he may have remained so late as to make it an uphill task to regain the old sure touch on the reins of municipal affairs." Indeed, reading the evidence today, one asks whether the mayor's heart had ever "come back," or was not still hankering after preferment in Washington.

In May the Bronx Grand Jury, in a decision widely accepted as a whitewash, cleared Flynn of wrongdoing in the paving block charges. Kern was rebuked by the jury for hampering the investigation, and the alleged LaGuardia–Herlands–Flynn conspiracy was entirely denied. Flynn's own account, made several years later, dismisses the affair lightly. The mayor and his civil service commissioner "came to cross purposes for reasons about which I know nothing," wrote Flynn in his memoirs; Kern, in order to reinforce his case before the court "trumped up charges against me. He said anything he thought would disparage the mayor." Use or misuse of the paving blocks, he concluded, was all an innocent mistake. Mistake or not, it was to dog Flynn's career, damaging the mayor's interests as well as his own.

It remains to add that in due course the appellate court gave its decision, upholding the mayor's ouster of Kern and Sayre. The chairman, according to the majority opinion, had issued "an obviously defamatory press statement attacking William C. Chanler." That was cause enough for removal. It supported the mayor's contention at the hearing that "one agency of government cannot attack another and not impair its usefulness." But a strong dissenting opinion by Presiding Judge Francis Martin was held by the *Times* to be as "logical" as the majority verdict; it certainly raised a much deeper and more troublesome issue.

The attack on Chanler, said Justice Martin, was evidently used as a pretext to remove the commissioner "who would not perform the illegal acts directed by the mayor." Civil service commissioners, he argued, "are not under the personal supervision or control of the mayor. They should be fearless and independent and not be mere pawns."

"Fearless and independent" Kern had certainly been, but also tactless and lacking in judgment. As for the mayor, we shall observe he was not loath to tangle subsequently with the Board of Education, an agency having even stronger claims to independence. Undeterred by the Kern uproar, he was still unprepared to renounce the habit of "personal supervision and control."

Of Scraps and Scrap Iron

Shorn of power on the national scene, LaGuardia found his authority weakened when he turned back to the organization of civilian defense in New York. He received from the Board of Estimate powers he had asked for, to shift critical materials and supplies from one department to another so long as spending stayed within the overall budget. He received funds totalling $2.5 million to support blackout and dimout precautions, install sirens, provide buildings with fire-fighting equipment, and protect the all-important water system. But political opposition soon manifested itself. Air-raid wardens in Queens, emboldened by what they saw as Washington's lack of confidence in the mayor, caused a stir by asking Congress to oust him as New York's civilian defense director. Other boroughs joined in the demand that the task be placed directly under the War Department.

More cogent were arguments, in the *Times* and elsewhere, that the mayor should delegate a portion of his responsibilities to a full-time civilian defense director for the city. When LaGuardia failed to release a technical report dealing with communications, the work of a committee headed by David Sarnoff, it was widely suspected that its recommendations, if released, would lend support to the growing pressure for a full-time director. But LaGuardia stood firm. He had no intention of surrendering his prerogatives in the one area of defense still left to him. His police commissioner, he told his radio audience in February, would retain control of air-raid wardens; in case of attack from the air his Public Works Department would be in charge of salvage and clearing. And that, he said, would be his last word on the subject.

The mayor was in a less intransigent mood when, a short while later, he headed a statewide group of defense officials at civilian defense hearings in Albany. Though one of his first moves as head of OCD had been to make the city a separate administrative unit for purposes of civilian defense, he now yielded to bipartisan pressure. The city, he agreed, would be under the jurisdiction of the state in such general matters as rationing and rent control, provided a degree of local autonomy were allowed. On the issue, so crucial to him, of full mayoral control over defense he managed to keep a solid front with the other top city officials. Poletti did not endear himself to the mayor by continuing the argument for a full-time director.

LaGuardia that day was on his best behavior and his calm presentation and lack of defensiveness made a good impression in the hearing room. Queried about the Sarnoff report, his forthright answers appeared to satisfy the legislators. Its conclusions, he said, had been submitted to the relevant departments of police, fire, and public works; a general release would not have been in the interest of public safety. The report had apparently not been suppressed for his own purposes, though some were of the opinion the explanation came rather late.

The mayor's restraint in Albany had been effective, but it had not been easy for him to maintain and it masked real anger at his critics. On returning to the city he took aggressive steps to put Times Square under more stringent dimout controls, threatening to darken permanently the famous advertising signs unless they were made capable of being instantly extinguished. Then he lashed out at critics of his defense activities, charging them with an organized campaign to discredit him.

Among the critics were several of his own intimate circle led, not surprisingly, by Moses. In an effort to put the city on a wartime footing the mayor had presented a budget several millions of dollars below the current one. It meant the elimination of 5,600 jobs and shorter vacations for everyone. The cuts fell with particular severity on departments other than the uniformed services, and the usual local constituencies representing education, public health, and social services came down to City Hall in protest. But nobody was more vociferous than the parks commissioner. His original demands, he asserted, represented an irreducible minimum and the proposed cuts were arbitrary and a menace to the city. The *Herald Tribune,* taking note of the ferocious attack, remarked that in view of the compelling need for economies all along the line, it did not see how cuts in the parks budget could be avoided.

Moses's action, churlish to the point of being unpatriotic, must be viewed against the particular frustrations he was suffering. This great builder and expediter, a captain of men habituated to the largest enterprises, was left like a beached whale by the tides of war. Offered no national post commensurate with his talents, he must have found a responsibility limited to city chores almost unbearably galling. Behind the neglect of his abilities was surely the president himself. A story having the tone of authenticity records a visit to the White House by Jack Madigan, Moses's longtime associate, to whom Roosevelt offered a major construction job. Madigan had been asked by Moses "to see if there's anything down there for me," and now as he left the Oval Office he hesitated for just a moment. Franklin Roosevelt seemed to read his thoughts. "Jack," he said, "this war is going to be fought on two oceans, on several continents, and in a dozen countries. It will be fought in towns and cities across the world. And there is no place in this war for Robert Moses."

The mayor did what he could to find a place, putting Moses in charge of the city's drive for scrap metal. Scrap collection had become a thankless and controversial aspect of civilian defense, involving not only the public, which was expected to donate vital materials, but the junk dealers who were to carry it to central depots. The mayor had already had his quarrels on this subject with officials in Washington—"snipers and sneerers" as he called them —who had found his efforts in this field inadequate. In September when the mayor ordered a scrap drive of massive proportions and put none other than Robert Moses in charge, the War Production Board changed its tune. "Mighty glad to see the mayor take such an interest" became the theme. Al Smith was one of the first to respond to the mayor's call, donating his "key to the White House," a momento of his unsuccessful race for the presidency in 1928. That gesture may have helped Moses decide to accept the job.

In any case, when he took over the scrap drive on September 22 it was on his customary grand scale. Not for him the housewives' pots and pans. He wanted whole structures taken down; the zest for demolition which had always accompanied his building operations found scope as he eyed old lofts and empty plants. Only the iron fence around Gracie Mansion, recently put in place by the Parks Department, was declared untouchable—on the somewhat whimsical ground that it had been fabricated from junk in the first place. The old Aquarium at Battery Park, preserved despite Moses's wishes by the determination of civic groups, fell under the axe of his long-pent-up ire and was stripped of all its metal parts. Then, less than three weeks after he had taken over, Moses quit, blaming the federal authorities for lack of cooperation. He could not continue, he told reporters, "because I have too much to do."

The trouble, as the mayor discovered, was that Moses had been *too* successful in his drive for large-scale reserves. The junk dealers found themselves unable or unwilling to remove the debris. Not displeased to be taking things into his own hands, the mayor ordered six hundred trucks of the sanitation department to fan out through the city in a spectacular effort at collection, and then negotiated a sale to the junk men. Within a week he could announce an end to the strange episode. The results had been "magnificent," he said, and he even had kind words for the cooperation of the press.

Moses, who would no doubt have served brilliantly in the national effort had circumstances and personalities been different, was left to fight out his war in the Board of Estimate chambers and the corridors of City Hall. His confrontations with the mayor continued as he battled for the immunity of his department from cutbacks and restraints or used the emergency to vent old prejudices. The Brooklyn–Battery Tunnel, which he did not want to see built, he sought to stop by diverting—over the mayor's orders—essential structural materials. It is not a glorious chapter in the Moses saga, though it was to be forgotten as he outlived the war, and outlived LaGuardia, and went on under other mayors to more congenial peacetime tasks.

Against the war's somber background, and amid his own increasing bellicosity, LaGuardia could still strike grace notes. Over WNYC the public was treated to the unforgettable sound of the mayor warbling his own version of the alarm signal and the all-clear. They were confronted by the spectacle of the mayor's new wartime coupe, uniquely embellished and in its overall effect hitherto unimagined, except possibly in the mind of a musical comedy impresario. Four white enamel stars—"one more than a full general is permitted," noted the *Times*—gleamed on the hood. Luminous blackout paint fore and aft was supplemented by oversize lights similar to those on fire engines, and on the roof a red sign flashed MAYOR at the touch of a switch. Radio equipment completed the paraphernalia visible to the public, but the glove compartment, it was reliably reported, contained the mayor's pistol. When photographers requested the mayor to pose at the wheel of this striking vehicle he refused, saying, "I don't drive. I never faked anything in my life." But he assured them he would make use of the little car for the duration.

In June New Yorkers, who had been roundly scolded by the mayor for the levity with which they treated a major blackout test, were rewarded by what he had promised would be a great day— no carnival, but a spectacle grim and martial. More than two million citizens lined the streets for a war parade. Bombers and fighter planes roared overhead, while tanks rolled up Fifth Avenue and hundreds of thousands of men, women, and children marched in an outpouring of patriotic fervor, scarcely conscious of the day's sweltering heat. At the head of the Fifth Division, composed of the city's air-raid wardens, patrol corps, fire auxiliaries, repair batteries, welfare groups, and medical services marched the mayor, eyes straight ahead, slowing his brisk pace only now and then to acknowledge the crowds. The march was in the nature of a much-needed personal triumph and salvoes of applause greeted him on every block along the way.

Troubles with the Press

Whatever his standing with the public, LaGuardia's relations with the press seriously deteriorated through the controversies over defense. In the fall of 1942 they reached a point where the national news magazines, *Time* and *Newsweek,* both ran articles suggesting that an irreparable break had occurred between the impetuous mayor and the reporters. Perhaps more painful to La-Guardia was an article in the liberal and usually friendly *New Republic* entitled "What Has Happened to LaGuardia?" Commenting that he would undoubtedly lose the election if he were to run then, it saw LaGuardia as a tired man at a low ebb of his fortunes, his once-sure grip on city affairs disconcertingly loosened. The unseemly quarrels with Fellowes Morgan and Paul Kern had hurt him; even deeper than these, his feud with the press cut him off from what should have been a major resource. LaGuardia would have only himself to blame, the article concluded, if he did not listen to his critics and "reoccupy a position in harmony with his past."

LaGuardia and the press had rarely been on friendly terms. Each needed the other; next to the two Roosevelts LaGuardia was the greatest boon to reporters and cartoonists in the twentieth century, and the mayor's image was defined and made memorable through their skills. Yet in terms of ordinary converse, their relations were at arm's length. Early in his first term, incensed at a reporter's insistent questioning on a political matter, the mayor ceased having regular press conferences and went back to his predecessor's practice of demanding written questions. The written form, he blandly indicated, would allow the reporters to know what they wanted to ask; as for him, "I don't have to write the answers. I *know* the answers." Often enough he would forget these instructions, but in general, during his first term, verbal exchanges with the reporters were infrequent. In his second term he held a first brief press conference several months after the election, closing it peremptorily when a single topic had been covered.

Still, the mayor provided irresistible copy, and in the best period it was as if a tacit bargain had been struck. He would make news so consistently and so picturesquely as to fill, and more than fill, the local news columns; the reporters, for their part, would suffer their banishment in silence. The boys of the proverbial Room 9 were not, as a matter of fact, too unhappy under this arrangement. There would be considerable chaffing, not all of it ill-humored, and the good stories would continue to flow.

How could one be entirely at odds with a mayor whose most casual act had the force of a sledgehammer, and whose words seemed to fall naturally into quotable phrases? Caught on the steps of City Hall, or with increasing frequency at the airport as he journeyed to and from Washington, a single remark would be worth more to the attentive reporter than paragraphs extracted at the conventional press conference. "The days of the cucacano are over," he said in answer to a question on the budget as he bustled down the hall, and reporters were sent to their dictionaries for further elucidation. After a break in the long boycott of the Transit Commission, the mayor was asked whether a meeting with the chairman meant that negotiations would be resumed. "You are aware, gentlemen, of the old expression that hope springs eternal" —and with that the mayor ducked into a waiting car. It was a brief answer, but it was enough to give the City Hall reporters their story for the day.

By 1943 the spirit of these exchanges had altered. The editorial lambasting the mayor received in connection with his defense post had begun to infuse the news stories; and the mayor, his tolerance reduced by frustration and physical weariness, responded with bitterness. He would refuse to discuss an issue, he said, until the press had learned the ethics of their profession; he would denounce certain stories as "smacking strongly of sabotage." Over the radio, and in a World's Fair speech, he mounted attacks of increasing anger against "lies" in the press. In the spring of 1942 he refused for the first time to attend the reporters' annual show and "Inner Circle" dinner, sending Newbold Morris in his place.

The handling of two quite minor stories particularly infuriated the mayor. In the first months of the war he was reported as having said he would ration hot water. Strong protests were covered in news stories; then the mayor changed his mind and declared that Washington would determine the issue. Denouncing the reporters, LaGuardia charged his first statement had been inaccurately cited (it had not been) and denied he had changed his view. "You dare to want to talk to me," he growled at a reporter who wanted to discuss the matter after a Sunday broadcast. Even less consequential, but of greater importance in arousing LaGuardia's anger, was the so-called George incident.

In a broadcast in September the mayor told of having received a letter from a boy complaining that his father gambled away the household money, returning on payday without even an allowance for himself. "George," said the mayor, "you must keep me informed, and other little boys . . . please also let me know" if father should gamble, and where. The press had a field day, and no less a personage than the former president of the Board of Education, James Marshall, took the mayor to task for urging young children to inform on their fathers. "The Communists were the first to set children against their parents," he said, adding that he considered it not normal behavior for youngsters to turn their fathers over to police investigation if they were dissatisfied with their allowance. The mayor, in his next broadcast, accused the press of encouraging gambling, and in a letter to the *News* reverted to the charge of "lying."

The whole feud was unfortunate. The weekly *Time* claimed that the mayor had by then shown "unmistakable signs of being unable to distinguish between criticism of his public actions and of his oversensitive self." Yet the climax of all this ill-feeling was an episode in which LaGuardia revealed he had not lost his sense of humor.

At the end of September he laid down the rule that he would have nothing further to do with reporters. But he made a few notable exceptions: he would talk with sports writers, music critics, and women's page editors. His office was promptly besieged, and the mayor showed himself at his best. "The truth is, I've been having press trouble," he said disarmingly to Stanley Woodward, sports editor of the *Herald Tribune.* "I think I'm partly to blame. But a lot of things happen that get me mad." Then the ladies began to come in. Nancy Randolph of the *News* found him "a soft-spoken, courtly gent." Mary Draggioth of the *Post* declared him to be "a lovely mayor."

Mourned one of the disgruntled and half-repentant prisoners of Room 9, "He killed the girls with kindness, just to show what a bunch of bums we were."

New York's Waiting Season

The war brought an end to the pleasant excursions which transferred City Hall to one of the other boroughs. The mayoral staff and the press corps ploughed on that year in their regular winter quarters. For the mayor and his family, however, the season brought a major change as they moved from the cramped tenement on upper Fifth Avenue to the eighteenth-century building on the East River known as Gracie Mansion.

For some time there had been talk of providing New York's mayor with an official residence, and more particularly of prying loose LaGuardia from the inconvenient and in some ways unsafe apartment to which he had clung since his days as a congressman. Claremont Inn on the Hudson was suggested; the Charles Schwab house on 73rd Street and Riverside Drive was offered by its owner for purchase by the city. "Let my successor have it," grumbled LaGuardia. Another suggestion, that the boroughs compete to furnish a suitable house, the mayor thought particularly ridiculous. "The contest should be to furnish the tenant," he retorted.

Robert Moses had long been disturbed by lack of security at the Fifth Avenue apartment and the decline of the Upper East Side neighborhood as poor minorities moved in. (Despite his apparent reluctance, the mayor recognized that his school-age children would profit from a better environment.) Finally, in November 1941, the Board of Estimate designated Gracie Mansion as the official home of the city's mayor, allocating the sum of $20,000 to improve the building and the park area surrounding it.

Built by Alexander Gracie in 1799 on a promontory of land overlooking the river, the property had been purchased many years later by the city and had served various purposes, including a temporary home for the Museum of the City of New York. Now Moses with his customary speed set about making it liveable for the mayor and his family. In six months, with the aid of WPA labor, the work was done. Moses personally arranged to have the reception rooms furnished with antiques borrowed from the Metropolitan Museum.

The new home scarcely qualified to be known as a "mansion." From a broad porch one entered a stair hall giving on right and left to a living room and library, in those days serving as the public reception areas where meetings were held, negotiations carried on, and visitors received. Upstairs stretched a series of bedrooms such as would have been found in any home built for a growing family. Partly, perhaps, to annoy Moses, the mayor was inclined to run down the building. He affected disdain for its comparative luxury and wanted to make sure no one thought he was putting on airs. "Sixthly," he wrote to a correspondent, after giving all the reasons he could think of for belittling the move, "my family is not keen about it and it has no personal advantages for me." In particular he disliked the name of his new home. "It is not surprising," a letter of his comments, "that you cannot find anything much about Alexander Gracie. There isn't very much to record about him. I suppose he was a successful businessman, but nothing to get excited about." He wanted the building to be known, quite simply, as "The Mayor's House."

The family moving in on May 14 comprised the mayor and his wife; the two children; Richard, a son of LaGuardia's deceased brother; and the cook and her son. A custodian for the Parks Department kept an office in the basement. Much as Moses had done to make the house comfortable, wartime shortages of materials and personnel continued to justify the mayor's uneasiness about the move. The reception rooms were closed off to conserve heat and labor. It was all Mrs. LaGuardia could do without help to keep the family living quarters in shape. Still, there were compensations. The lawns provided the children with play space, the wide porch was cooled by river breezes on a summer evening, and the view was delightful as tugs, tankers, and pleasure craft plied their way through the rapid currents. Occasionally on one of the sailboats a familiar tall figure would be discovered waving toward the mansion. It was Willie Chanler, back from some cruise, sailing downtown on his yacht. Or Moses would be seen making his way across the greensward with urgent steps, coming at any hour to hold a conference with the mayor.

LaGuardia's young aides would often arrive early at the mansion for briefings on the day's activities and ride downtown afterward with the mayor. When Moses joined the group, the trip to City Hall would be made in style—in the parks commissioner's limousine and not in the mayor's Ford.

It was, nevertheless, an unhappy summer. The first wartime Fourth of July was subdued by discouraging setbacks on the fighting fronts. The Germans hacked their way into Russia and the British suffered defeats in Egypt. Churchill was under fire; Roosevelt, his economic policies unsure and undefined, warned of grim developments ahead. New Yorkers could well find the times discouraging, feeling themselves in a sort of limbo, with no one clear as to what was expected on the home front and nobody feeling altogether safe. "Wistfully we look ahead to other summers," said the *Times,* "when the length of bathing suits will again be a major issue, when pleasure seekers will again sit in their cars for weary hours on the jammed highways." For the moment the normal world seemed infinitely remote, and LaGuardia worried about the city's morale.

He attacked the problem in his own way, going directly to the people with down-to-earth advice. If they looked cheerful, he decided, it would help them to feel cheerful, and he advised women to wear gay colors. He lectured the ladies on household economy. The Germans lost World War I, he told them categorically, because of lack of fats. Save fats, but don't use the same fats for fish and meat. And don't waste bread, he advised—"Remember, there is such a thing as bread pudding."

More serious were efforts to deal with New York City's employment problem. While other cities were experiencing the beginning of wartime prosperity, New York was suffering depressed conditions, its factories bypassed when ordnance contracts were awarded and its construction and shipping industries virtually at a halt. By early summer four-hundred-thousand New Yorkers were unemployed, and the chairman of the War Powers Board, Paul McNutt, termed New York "one of the blackest spots in the nation." He suggested that workers go elsewhere to find jobs, a prescription scarcely acceptable to the mayor who saw seventy-five thousand city apartments already standing empty and many homes put up for sale in the boroughs.

The unemployment affected the entire New York metropolitan area, and the mayor made common cause with the governor in addressing an appeal to the president. Late in June he began a number of wearisome trips to the capital to seek additional war plants in the New York area and war contracts for the building of ships and the manufacture of army uniforms. By August LaGuardia reported that two hundred thousand new jobs were assured. The downward curve had been reversed and New York started on what was to be a boom in the private sector, bringing increased revenues to the city treasury.

McNutt was not the only Washington official with whom the mayor tangled. He repeatedly attacked his successor at OCD, James Landis. The army criticized his dimouts and he was quick to criticize the army. When Secretary Hull sought city tax exemption for property of the Vichy government on Fifth Avenue, LaGuardia assailed the idea that a vassal state, under a country at war with the United States, should have rights accorded to the former French government. Nor did LaGuardia neglect the officials of enemy countries.

It was disclosed at this time that he had been broadcasting regularly in Italian to the Italian people, telling them, among other things, that the Germans were stealing their food. The programs were introduced by a blare of trumpets and the by-line "Mayor LaGuardia Calling Rome." The talks were a well-kept secret at home, for which LaGuardia offered uncustomary thanks to reporters; but it was evident that in Italy they were getting through. When the Italian propaganda agency denounced "that false Italian and authenticated Jew, Fiorello H. LaGuardia," the mayor took particular pleasure, hailing the attack as proof that his provocations were effective.

A low-key political campaign that autumn provided little in the way of distraction. Dewey was now ready to try his wings on the broader political stage; Lehman at last was ready to retire as governor. With Dewey assured of the Republican nomination, the Democrats fell into intraparty squabbles. Farley was determined upon the nomination of Attorney-General John C. Bennett, an anti-New Deal spokesman, and he won out over the president's rather lukewarm support of Senator James Mead. The ALP could not accept Bennett. It put up a gubernatorial candidate of its own, Dean Alfange, who had no previous ties with labor and had made an unsuccessful run for a Democratic seat in Congress the year before.

LaGuardia supported the ALP candidate. It was not the first time he found himself in opposition to Roosevelt, but by now it cannot have been altogether unpleasing to him to needle the Democratic chief. In putting himself behind Alfange, moreover—and he was as good as his word, making several speeches over the air and at meetings on his behalf—LaGuardia helped demonstrably to ensure Dewey's large plurality for governor. On being elected (to no one's surprise and certainly not his own) Dewey himself gave credit to Alfange's effective run as a major factor in taking votes away from the Democrats. LaGuardia must have pondered quizzically on this result, but in public he said nothing. When Lehman was named director of relief for the United Nations, however, he was quick with congratulations that bespoke generosity, and perhaps also a touch of envy.

Over that wartime Labor Day LaGuardia made a point of inviting tourists to visit New York, with a special welcome reserved for servicemen. The weekend was a success from all points of view, the mayor receiving commendations on New York's warmth and hospitality, and the hotels and restaurants receiving record business. City Hall was open to all, testifying by the crowds it attracted to the fame of its chief tenant. Over Christmas the same spirit was promoted, but nothing could dispel the year-end gloom. It had been a bad year for the mayor, for the city, and for the nation. LaGuardia urged everyone to have "as cheerful a time as the conditions and the war situation would permit." But the celebrations were dim, and in Times Square, in the words of one observer, the vast crowd "tooted sluggishly."

11
Prisoner in City Hall

New Man in Albany

Republicans were once more in control of Albany. With the long administrations of Smith and Lehman ended, and a young governor of large ambitions at the helm, the mayor confronted a wholly new situation. In the circumstances he showed himself restrained and canny. He knew Dewey well; he certainly had no love for him, but he was not going to deny himself an ally if he could help it. Ahead lay inevitable conflicts with the City Council, and Albany's support could be crucial in maintaining a balance of forces.

As for Dewey, his attitude toward the mayor was as unwarmed by sentiment as were all his political kinships. He had shared in LaGuardia's 1937 victory but had kept his distance. Shrewdly calculating his own chances for advancement at the state and national levels, he watched LaGuardia's opportunities decline with what cannot have been any sense of regret. Now he would not be anxious to give to proposals of New York City's mayor an undue amount of support. Yet some sort of accommodation would be necessary if he were himself to keep the favor of downstate voters. So Dewey planned a course that would in fact leave the mayor outwitted; he projected a future in which he would soar to national heights while his rival remained mired in New York's insoluble problems.

A kind of cool contempt tempered by the respect one professional feels for another marked the LaGuardia–Dewey relationship. At Albany as at City Hall the fires were banked, ready at any instant to flame into overt antagonisms. But somehow the conflagration never occurred. Though he had often been curt or openly insulting to Lehman, in dealing with Dewey LaGuardia kept his temper. It was as if recognizing an implacable hostility based on politics as well as personality, he shunned as useless the former outbursts of indignation. Though he could so often be vituperative, LaGuardia was not prone to vent his vituperation where it could be of no advantage and where its display could bring little satisfaction. So as Dewey did on his part, LaGuardia maintained an air of correctness, while the two men jockeyed for the stakes of power.

The mayor had a habit, when the tide was against him, of showing himself magnanimous and calm. So it had been in 1940 when he first found his Fusion forces powerfully outnumbered in the City Council. Now at a meeting in City Hall he delivered a solemn New Year's message in the presence of his official family and guests. He wished them all strength to carry on during the coming hard days. "We must remember that because of the importance and size of our city we set the pace for the rest of the country," he said. "We must give the example of patience, of devotion to duty, of being able to administer government . . . in such a way as to protect the safety of our people and above all the children of our city." The mood carried over a few days later when he made his annual address to the City Council.

"Gentlemen and ladies," said he, "we have a hard time ahead of us. I hope we will be able to work together." He promised a balanced budget if the council would hold the line on salaries. Labor must recognize its responsibilities; the Sanitation Department must get along without new equipment; the hospitals must face up to the gnawing lack of personnel. As a bright spot the mayor announced steady progress at a second great city airport at Idlewild. And he indulged in a denunciation of horsemeat, a favorite anathema of his. "Whatever you do," he warned as wartime shortages of meat loomed heavily, "whether I'm here or not, don't allow horsemeat to be sold in New York City. Wherever it is sold you will find degradation."

"The mayor at his best," said the *New York Times.* The messages had been "sound and reasonable" throughout.

In Albany the governor found himself the beneficiary of unexpected accruals under the wartime economy. In a situation very different from the mayor's, Dewey's principal problem was to deal with a growing surplus. He announced a windfall of $13.5 million for the city, an act of generosity not entirely pleasing to the mayor, who was understandably touched by envy—and who had asked, besides, for a sum of more than twice that amount. Flavoring the allotment were suggestions that the mayor had perhaps not been sufficiently strict in enforcing economies. A state surplus of $148 million was declared locked up for future use, funds which were eventually to provide for the construction of the New York State Thruway, first of the postwar highway systems.

In February LaGuardia put before the governor figures showing New York's financial situation and a month later made public his formal requests to the legislature. He needed their permission to raise the city sales tax from 1 to 2 percent as well as to impose other taxes on business. He wanted the city to be relieved of mandatory budget increases, and he went back to his old plea for control of judicial salaries. The legislature was not in a welcoming mood. On March 18 it turned down the sales and business taxes, Republicans joining with Democrats in an atmosphere of personal hostility to the mayor. Assertions were made to the effect that the mayor had in the past played politics with the city's finances and had repeatedly hoodwinked the legislature and the people. The lawmakers summoned him from a sickbed to Albany to present fuller figures on the city's condition, and then found themselves too busy to read the documents.

The City Council caught the message in these actions and promptly voted deep cuts in the mayor's budget. LaGuardia vetoed the cuts, declaring they would cripple the city. He appealed to the council to pass a resolution urging the governor to grant the city additional taxing powers. Not surprisingly the appeal fell on deaf ears.

By now the legislative year was well advanced; in June, in a session wracked by bitterness, the council overrode the mayor's veto and affirmed $3.1 million in cuts. From twelve noon until the early night hours no member of the council left the chamber as name calling and fits of temper accompanied disputes over particular items, the mayor gaining some points but losing the overall battle. The faithful Morris, trying to impose order and to salvage some part of the mayor's program, was continually howled down by the opposition.

As a last resort LaGuardia turned back to Dewey, and Dewey conspicuously failed him. The governor would neither consider more state aid nor call back the legislature to review its stand on city taxes. He would entertain the possibility of a special session only if the council joined the mayor in the request and if new tax programs were made specific. LaGuardia played for time and rejected the temptation to denounce the governor. Dewey's action, he said mildly, was "politically astute," but not the course of statesmanship he had hoped for. He still counted on the governor's changing his mind. But the governor's mind did not change. A second appeal by LaGuardia was rejected in July as "an abuse of power and a futile act" in view of differences between the mayor and the council. Amid cries from the council that further economies were possible, the budget was balanced by another increase in real estate taxes.

Dewey could afford to look with satisfaction upon the outcome. He had managed to show concern for the city's financial plight, but not so much as to prove politically embarrassing to him. The Republican-dominated legislature had played the tune to which the City Council marched, and he had himself exerted just enough leadership to make sure that the unpopular sales taxes were not laid at his door. He had ended on good terms with everyone except the mayor, and the mayor did not find it politically expedient to attack him outright.

Educational China Shop

Some of the resulting vexation spilled over into LaGuardia's dealings with the Board of Education. Every mayor sooner or later discovers in the educational bureaucracy an intractable power and vows to subdue it and make it responsible to the elected government. But LaGuardia went beyond this conventional play acting. Much of his third term, as *Newsweek* commented, he spent "barging like a small bee-stung Ferdinand around New York's educational china shop." In the process he seemed determined to make the worst out of a good case.

Since 1938 LaGuardia had been attacking the board's inefficient methods of construction. Now he made its department of purchasing a prime target. Armed with a report of inefficiency and waste from the commissioner of investigation—a report released to the press before being made available to the board's chairman—the mayor resolved that the purchase of school supplies had to be transferred to the city. Early in 1943 a bill to accomplish the transfer was introduced with the mayor's urgent backing into the state legislature. There the education lobby defeated it. LaGuardia was furious and in the months ahead sought vengeance against those who had opposed the bill. Included in his ire was the chairman of the board, Ellsworth Buck, whose support the mayor considered to have been lukewarm.

A second cause of distress to the mayor was the board's rejection of Mark Starr, named to the post of adult education director of the New York City school system. Then thirty-nine, a dynamic and appealing figure, Starr's early career had been as a miner in Great Britain; subsequently he became education director of the International Ladies Garment Workers Union. His confirmation by the full board seemed assured. But on March 24 he was rejected, his labor background being held against him. Again the mayor was enraged, and this time the public agreed he had considerable justification for his wrath.

But LaGuardia overreacted. On April 11 he loosed a blistering attack on the board and its chairman, insisting on the necessity of having "complete harmony within the board, and complete confidence in every member of the board." The same people who had been supporting him in his stand on Starr now turned against him, seeing in his treatment of the board a threat to the independence of the school system. A few weeks later he was even more specific, resolving to get rid of the chairman at the earliest opportunity. The mayor put the matter in his own way, showing a kind of grim humor still at work. "I had a friendly talk with Mr. Buck," he said. "He told me he would not resign and I told him the first time I got the chance I would fire him." But the *Times* was unrelievedly solemn: "The issue appears to be very simple—shall we continue to have an independent school board, or shall the members vote upon the bidding of the mayor?"

On April 28 Starr was rejected a second time; on May 11, in defiance of City Hall, Buck was reelected chairman. Other issues became entwined with the principal ones, almost daily adding new fuel to the controversy. One board member, Albert C. Bonaschi, was held over without formal reappointment, a course interpreted as making him particularly vulnerable to mayoral pressures. Another member, Mrs. Johanna Lindloff, a labor representative, was denied reappointment because (according to her version) La-Guardia had not liked her independence of speech and action. A meeting in her honor turned into strong denunciation of the mayor, with Mark Starr joining the critics. Meanwhile the director of the budget carried on his own feud with the educational hierarchy, refusing to authorize funds for several of the board's appointments.

One of these was Trude Weil, who had been confidential secretary to Mrs. Lindloff. She was specifically rejected by the mayor and started a suit against the city for her $4,500 salary. She soon turned up at City Hall, however, as adviser on educational matters, funds for her salary having been found available. The mayor's reversal, and the young woman's good sense and professional judgment, indicated that LaGuardia might be willing at least to come to some kind of an understanding with the board. For its part the board went along with the mayor's insistence that it fire its law secretary of more than twenty years' service because he had been instrumental in the legislature's defeat of the purchasing department bill. The board's submission was ignoble, but it suggested a search for compromise in a situation growing rapidly intolerable. At this point another group moved onto center stage, and the fracas took on aspects of comedy in which the mayor played a role somewhat below his best.

The group was the National Education Association. Convening in New York to begin an investigation, the influential nationwide organization heard witnesses who had played key roles in the controversy. Most teachers were reluctant to testify, but Mrs. Lindloff claimed that LaGuardia had consistently bossed the board and interfered with its legal powers. Bonaschi, now escaped from limbo and secure on the Board of Higher Education, denied that as a member of the school board he had slavishly followed the mayor's will. LaGuardia was invited to appear, but contented himself with delivering over the air a homily on what educators ought to be doing. They ought to give, he announced, "an old-fashioned course in good manners." Kids should come to school with their hair brushed and their shoes shined—"Are you listening, Eric and Jean?"

In February of the next year the NEA made its report, charging the mayor with conduct that was "unprofessional and against public interest." The forced dismissal of the board's law clerk and the sixteen-month holdover of Dr. Bonaschi were among the actions criticized. In addition the committee attacked LaGuardia's initiation of the bill transferring school purchases to the city and claimed that the city budget did not adequately meet school needs. The mayor lightly shrugged off these conclusions. Committee members had come from smaller towns and cities; they did not fully understand New York, and many of their judgments were indeed easily refuted. But once again LaGuardia needlessly threw away support. In minimizing the report's significance, he added that he had nevertheless been impressed by its chairman, Miss Studebaker, "because she was wearing beautiful nylon stockings."

The mayor's dismissal of the report, according to the *Sun,* had been made with "a quite graceless levity." And as for Miss Studebaker, the remark in regard to her was "gratuitously offensive." Head of the NEA's department of classroom teachers, the lady was clearly "unostentatious, intelligent, well-dressed, and well-bred." Even in a day when nylon stockings were quite new, a mayor was not supposed to comment on them publicly.

Washington Says No

The scene now shifts to the national stage. That LaGuardia felt cooped up in the mayoral office while abroad the war raged on new fronts was evident. In his dealings with Dewey and with the Board of Education he showed the symptoms of his restlessness. To Burlingham he confessed he was sick of the job: "Why did I take it? I wanted it the first and second time and you asked me the third time." With some care he now prepared a way of escape.

In early March a law to make possible a leave of absence for the mayor was introduced into the legislature and passed so obscurely that almost none of the members was aware of what had been done. Without even a mention of New York City the bill gave to the governor, in the event that the mayor and the president of the City Council were called into military service, the right to name an acting mayor of the same party as the council president. This was highly acceptable to Dewey, who saw the opportunity to put a Republican of his choosing into City Hall. When the Democrats in due course learned of what they had let slip through, their cries of "treason" could be heard all the way to Times Square.

A second preliminary step was more complicated and to relate it requires a digression in this narrative. In January 1943, Roosevelt nominated Ed Flynn, boss of the Bronx, as ambassador to Australia and his personal representative in the Pacific area. A barrage of criticism was loosed in the press, where memories of the previous year's "paving block scandal" were still green. Several New York figures were called to testify in the Senate hearings. Paul Kern was given a new stage from which to issue his opinions about Flynn. Berle was hard put to explain away certain of his remarks on taking office as city chamberlain under LaGuardia. He had said the municipal accounts had been "juggled." Was not this a reflection on the previous holder of the office, none other than Boss Flynn himself? Not at all, said Berle with a straight face. And then, on January 23, it was LaGuardia's turn to testify.

The hearing room was crowded as the hour approached for the mayor's appearance. He was in a difficult spot and it was rumored he would find an excuse for not turning up. If he defended Flynn he would be betraying himself and his long record of warfare against the bosses. If he seemed in any way to give support to those who were opposing Flynn it would be a blow administered to Roosevelt in the public arena, on an issue where the president was deeply and personally involved. All LaGuardia's hopes for a post in the military service and an escape from City Hall hung upon his conduct that day.

At the appointed hour, precisely at 2:12 P.M., LaGuardia bustled into the tense hearing room. Leaning back in his chair he announced he had no general statement to make; he awaited "the pleasure of the committee." Yes, he answered to the first, inevitable question, he was aware of the charges against Flynn in the Bronx paving stone case. He had handled it in a routine manner. He had no personal knowledge of the incident and had passed on such information as he had to the Bronx Grand Jury over which he had no control. Then came the crucial question and the audience fell silent as it was asked. In the light of what he knew, did he consider Flynn suitable for the ambassadorship?

"I cannot qualify as a character witness," said the mayor, "because of the bitterness that has existed for years between us and because of my prejudice against him." The matter could not have been put more neatly and the remaining testimony was concluded after a few minutes. In a sentence he had deflated the issue. He had avoided giving aid to Flynn's foes or any cause for resentment to the president. At the same time he had cleared himself of lingering suspicions that he had been a little too close to the Bronx boss. More clearly than ever LaGuardia was in a position to receive from

Roosevelt the military appointment he coveted.

The Flynn story, however, does not end there. The furor of the press and the opposition within the committee did not abate. Early in February, under obvious pressure from the president, Flynn withdrew his name from consideration. For Roosevelt it was a stunning defeat, one of the few such rebuffs to the wartime leader. A short while later the president would again face the threat of noisy Senate hearings with the risks of a second setback. This time the figure involved would be LaGuardia himself, and the president would retreat before the issue was joined. Thus LaGuardia and Flynn, whose fates had been so curiously intertwined in the Kern episode, would find themselves linked once more. In no small measure because of the disastrous Flynn nomination as ambassador LaGuardia would see his own hopes shattered.

Landings in North Africa in the autumn of 1942 had opened the Mediterranean theater; a role in the liberation of Italy and in the establishment of civilian government seemed made for LaGuardia. It would obliterate the painful impressions left by the OCD fiasco and would give the mayor opportunity in a field ideally suited to his gifts and his past experience. Going to Italy would bring his career full circle; it was here as a young congressman that he had first found a stage wider than his Greenwich Village constituency, where he had revealed not only his physical courage but his skill as a propagandist and interpreter of the Italian national character. In Italy his name was known almost as widely as that of Roosevelt himself.

His work in New York, moreover, could be considered completed. There would still be those who argued in good faith that his leadership was necessary in case of air raids and civil disturbances. But these crises never occurred, and at least with hindsight it can be said that by the spring of 1943 LaGuardia could be spared from the New York mayoralty, as he certainly was deserving of the longed-for release.

On March 15 LaGuardia had a talk with Roosevelt during which the rank of brigadier general together with the role of civil affairs director in liberated Italy was discussed. The next day in longhand LaGuardia wrote joyfully to his White House friend Harry Hopkins: "I saw the Chief yesterday and I am so happy I can be of service to my country—besides cleaning the streets of New York City. I expect to get my medical exam next week. The Chief indicated I should be commissioned right after I finish the executive budget in early April." Talk of the appointment burgeoned in the press. "Clearly New York is about to lose a mayor and the army is about to gain an officer," said the *Herald Tribune* on March 28.

Yet there were signs that not all was going well with the mayor's cause. Word of the bill providing for a leave of absence got out. The *Times* called it a "flimsy law"; the *Post* denounced it as "a sleazy deal" with "a strong odor of fascism about it." A little too enthusiastically for comfort the *News* welcomed the mayor's rumored departure. He deserved preferment, it was admitted; but it was time he should go. He had lost interest in the job, and "with his frequent air raid alarms and assorted mock-war goings on, his quarrels with the press . . . his burlesque and bingo crusades and his other interferences with our private lives" LaGuardia had "got on the nerves of the city." Meanwhile Steve Early, the White House press secretary, announced that "all indications point to service in the army for the mayor." LaGuardia was fitted for the uniform of a brigadier general; he recruited his old friend Albert Spalding as a top aide, and started to make arrangements for a successor. Judge Thacher turned him down; Moses was approached but, as he recalled later, wasn't interested in "such shenanigans."

In the Senate Harry S Truman, then at the head of a committee on war operations, interrupted routine testimony by the assistant secretary of war to say that he was opposed to the LaGuardia appointment and to the naming of any "political generals." Stimson had strong doubts which he expressed to Roosevelt. Reluctant to face another embroglio such as that which had resulted in Flynn's withdrawal, the president the next week announced blandly at his press conference that he had no plans to name LaGuardia a brigadier general.

It was a cruel letdown for the mayor, costing him dear in self-esteem and in power to control events within his own city. Nothing afterward was to be quite the same for him. Though LaGuardia would have his successes and would continue to rouse the citizenry by his dramatic flourishes, the April rejection was a watershed in his years as mayor. Publicly he kept a game spirit. There was no overt display of emotion. "I'll carry on," he told reporters. "I've got a uniform of my own up in New York, a street cleaner's uniform. That's my little army." In private, however, he poured out his sense of resentment and despair. "I burned all my bridges ahead of me for him," he said of the man who had now abandoned him.

The anger showed itself in other ways. In June Frankfurter wrote to Burlingham saying "the Little Flower" should offer prayers of thanks to Stimson for not letting him "go soldiering." "Wouldn't it be lovely," Frankfurter asked, foreseeing the possibility of race riots in New York, "for Fiorello to be prancing around somewhere in Africa?" He added, with his customary pleasure in dropping names, that he had just lunched with Stimson and felt "inspired." Rather tactlessly Burlingham sent the letter to LaGuardia.

LaGuardia was deeply hurt. He wrote back that he would never again talk to Frankfurter as long as he lived, adding he was sorry Burlingham had forwarded the letter. What Stimson had done to him was "just plain rotten," bordering on the dishonorable. There was no justification for the "dirty deal" he got. "Do not bother to reply and please do not worry about it," LaGuardia concluded with a touching revelation of his vulnerability. "I have always been able to take care of myself. . . . I do hope you will understand. I am very unhappy."

The *Times* treatment of the matter was strangely unfeeling. La-Guardia, it seemed, had no right to leave the mayoralty: "his front line trench is right here." But the *Tribune,* as so often, could be more compassionate, in part because it understood Roosevelt better and was inclined to mistrust him. In an editorial entitled "Welcome Home" it commiserated with LaGuardia: "As with others who, supposing themselves to be on the firm ground of administration preferment, have found their heels suddenly kicking in the air, so the mayor's military ambitions seem to have been encouraged, to the point at which wolves of the Senate and the War Department could save other people the embarrassment of destroying them."

Charles Poletti, the Lehman aide for whom LaGuardia had a particular dislike, got the job of civil administrator. The uniform of a brigadier general was to be worn in Italy by William O'Dwyer.

Time Out of Joint

His enemies emboldened and his friends not averse to treating lightly his disappointed hopes, LaGuardia faced the New York scene with a sense of diminished power and for a while at least without his old zest for leadership. Everything seemed to be awry and controversies that in better days were the spice of life turned sour. The emperor had been seen not only without his uniform, but without any clothes at all. In declaring that his departure for the war fronts would be "good riddance," the *News* had breached the basic respect that must exist between a ruler and his people. Always more sensitive than his pugnacity seemed to indicate, LaGuardia suffered at this time spells of serious ill health which reflected the disorientation of his spirit.

On Good Friday 1943, a week after the Washington debacle, LaGuardia and his wife attended the Metropolitan Opera for a performance of *Parsifal.* Their old friends, the Paul Windels, were seated a few rows behind them, and with them was their son, Paul, Jr., in uniform as a private of the U.S. Army, having come home for a last weekend of leave. LaGuardia invited the young soldier to sit beside him, while Marie went back to be with his parents. It must have been a touching sight—the old warrior in mufti, the young in khaki. After one of the acts, as the music ended and the applause subsided, the mayor turned with unexpected frankness to the friend at his side, until recently one of his favorite children. "Things are not going right with me," he said. "I don't feel just right." It was Hamlet speaking to his friend Heratio

I shall win at the odds. But thou would not think how ill all's here about my heart.

Dorothy Kenyon wrote him, praising a recent speech. He thanked her for "the sweet note." "I appreciate it the more," he said, "I have had so much of the bitter given to me of late." Kenyon, like the young Windels, was struck by this open vulnerability of the mayor. "I take back all the unkind things I have ever thought and said about you—which have been plenty," she replied. As summer advanced the mood of loneliness persisted and LaGuardia's mind turned often to young soldiers fortunate enough to be at the front. "The way of prayer and sacrifice isn't the way I would personally choose," he wrote to one, "but I have told too many other fellows to make the best of a nonglamorous job to kick much about it myself—at least out loud." To his former law clerk Edmund Palmieri he confessed it a wonder that he got anything done at all, "so many of the more brilliant members of my official family are in service." But at least, he added, the WACS had not got any of his ladies!

"We city folks have our routine pretty well upset by that war of yours," he wrote in July to Joseph Lilly, formerly of the City Finance Department. How much he would like to be with Lilly in

the Pacific!—"Between us we'd chase the sons of heaven, hell for
leather, to what is waiting for them. As it seems to be, though, you
will have to do it alone." At this time the mayor began to take a
special interest in the families of his absent aides, and many years
later his kindnesses would still be recalled. Then there were the
pangs of seeing old staffers leave, or seeing them return in uniform.
Clendenin Ryan turned up one day, "sixty pounds lighter and
highly educated." David Rockefeller came by.

The corporation council, Willie Chanler, was restless, but La-
Guardia would not hear of his leaving his post—unless, he added,
"you are called into the service." For Chanler it was easy; he had
only to make a visit to his old friend and Long Island neighbor,
Secretary Stimson, and an officer's commission was arranged. The
scene on his return to the mayor's office had overtones of sadness
and irony. LaGuardia had been denied by Stimson the chance
offered so readily to his younger aide, and once again he was
presented with an occasion for regrets and farewells.

In the political field the mood expressed itself through infighting
of peculiar bitterness. Self-condemned to silence in regard to the
president and the secretary of war, LaGuardia set out to discredit
federal officials such as Chester Bowles and his Office of Price
Administration. Again and again he went into the attack, charging
Bowles with failure to protect the consumer and provoking the
counatercharge that he had sought personal control of prices beyond
the limits of the law.

He was embroiled in an ugly dispute with the firemen of his own
city. Having long maintained that firemen should be exempt from
the draft, he was now grievously disappointed when they refused
to work overtime. The department store heads, among the most
influential leaders of the community, came under the mayor's wrath
because of their opposition to the sales tax. The president of
Tiffany, Walter Hoving, exemplified the low state to which public
dialogue had sunk when he answered the mayor's assertion that the
department stores were "groggy with profits" and were under the
impression they could control the press of the city. "I say he's a
liar," said Hoving. "He should be taken to Bellevue and have some
of the competent alienists there give him a couple of treatments."

The chief manifestation of the new political atmosphere was,
however, the City Council's widely proclaimed intent to investigate
the whole LaGuardia administration. Previously there had been
investigations of individual commissioners or particular policies;

but this was something quite different and could only have taken place when the political powers were out of balance. On June 15, in the first postmidnight session on record, Republican members responded to the goading of the Democrats and voted what was in effect a fishing expedition into all aspects of the mayor's rule. In charge of the special committee was Walter Hart, Democrat from Brooklyn.

The investigation lit no fires. The local lawmakers were not capable of organizing themselves for the sustained and objective efforts which such an inquiry would entail. But they were capable, nevertheless, of making a certain amount of unpleasant noise. "It seems to be one of the rules of the game," LaGuardia wrote to one his younger wartime correspondents, "for a councilman to appear half-witted, even if he knows better." And so the remaining months of 1943 were filled with charges and countercharges, with threats of legal prosecution and removal from office, all coming to little in the end.

An early target of the investigation was Almerindo Portfolio, whom we last saw as a rich bachelor living at the Plaza when he was appointed commissioner of finance in 1938. He now emerged from obscurity, charged with using a city car for transportation to the racetrack. Considerable doubt being raised on this point, the committee chairman concluded that Portfolio was in the wrong even if he had *not* used official transportation: going to the racetrack in wartime was itself a violation of the mayor's code. A second target was the commissioner of sanitation, William Carey. He turned out to be a big fish and very difficult to land.

The charge against Carey was that he had continued to concern himself with his private business affairs, an allegation he freely admitted, having warned the mayor to this effect when he was appointed. A second charge was that he had mixed public and private funding in developing Sanita, a Long Island resort for use of Sanitation Department personnel. Again Carey was quick to confess: he had perhaps violated the city charter when it was in the public interest to do so. By avoiding red tape he had constructed a model center, widely studied by industrial leaders, for the improvement of employer–employee relations. As for city money spent on the project, it had always been the commissioner's plan to repay it from the proceeds of the department's annual baseball games. Reminded that commissioners must fit their operations to the provisions of the city charter, Carey exclaimed, "Well, let them fix up their city charter to fit the public officials." It was a bravura performance, and when it turned out that the commissioner and his wife had loaned more than $100,000 without security to permit continuation of the work at Sanita, the hearts of the councilmen seemed temporarily to melt.

Amid promises that it would come up with "more startling disclosures" the committee alternated its public hearings with long intervals of silence. Then in mid-October a dramatic reversal occurred. Herlands, who as commissioner of investigation had himself been a principal objective of the inquiry, presented evidence to show that the committee chairman had violated the charter by appearing before a city agency as attorney for a bus line. Herlands demanded that Councilman Hart be removed from office.

LaGuardia remained as aloof as possible from these proceedings. But they were rapidly reducing city government to the level of farce and taking their toll of the mayor's once-inexhaustible energies. "It is now seven o'clock and I'm not through yet," the mayor wrote a friend late in September. "I am all in. Guess I will go to bed as soon as I am through. I have a tough day tomorrow." In October he called a special session of the City Council to consider Hart's removal. Moses, not uncharacteristically, appeared as a witness supporting Hart; and Hart charged it was Herlands whose removal ought to be enforced. By December the council was charging Carey and LaGuardia with violations of the charter serious enough to constitute misdemeanors entailing forfeiture of office— the one for having engaged in private business while a commissioner, the other for having tolerated it. The year ended in something less than a charitable atmosphere, with the council on December 28 voting along party lines, fifteen to six, to adopt the adverse report of the Hart committee.

More serious in their implications than the committee's partisan rhetoric were a few words spoken this dark December by a wise man, a supporter and friend of LaGuardia's. At a luncheon of the National Lawyers Guild Stanley Isaacs served formal notice that the minority members of the recently elected council would not follow the mayor "in blind loyalty . . . because he varies in loyalty to himself and to the things he used to stand for." Beautifully understated, these were words that could not be lightly dismissed, and coming from such a source they must have hurt.

To the Barricades

But LaGuardia had proved he could still be a formidable man in a crisis. On a Sunday night in early August the city's normal routine was broken by an incident which sent shock waves throughout the community. Outside the Hotel Braddock on 126th Street and Eighth Avenue Patrolman Joe Collins made a casual arrest of a woman for disturbing the peace. The woman was noisy and obstreperous, and used abusive language as Collins prepared to take her in. A crowd gathered and a soldier, Pvt. Robert Bandy, seizing Collins's nightstick, began beating him on the head and face. Collins fell but managed to fire a shot that caught the fleeing soldier in the arm. The soldier was taken to Suydenham Hospital and the whole thing might have ended there—except that the woman and the soldier were black and the policeman was white, the weekend had been long and hot, and Harlem was in an angry mood.

The incident occurred at 9:30. Within an hour crowds had formed at three major points—the Braddock, Suydenham, and the West 123rd Street police station. What followed constituted the worst riot in Harlem's history up to that time; the outbreak of 1935 was mild in comparison. In the heart of Harlem, store windows were smashed, and bottles and stones were hurled from windows and rooftops. Thousands of people were suddenly on the streets and widespread looting ensued. A vivid footnote was provided by a young writer who happened to be on the scene that night. "In half an hour it seemed that all of Harlem was awake. Women stood on the stoops in their nightgowns and wrappers, and when the fire trucks went through with their flashing lights, you could see them framed in their tenement windows."

The mayor, arriving early with Valentine, was taken on a tour of the area to view the rioting and looting at firsthand. Three Negro leaders—Dr. Murray Yergan of the National Negro Council on African Affairs; Ferdinand Smith, secretary of the National Maritime Union; and Hope Stevens, a Harlem attorney—accompanied him. Sound trucks urged residents to get off the streets, and Walter White, riding one of the trucks all night, kept telling the crowds that, contrary to rumors, the soldier was only slightly wounded. When LaGuardia arrived back at the 123rd Street precinct he was met by an angry mob that jeered and hissed when he asked them to return to their homes.

For the next twenty-four hours the precinct, barricaded and

43. Patrolling Harlem during a tense summer night. August 3, 1943. WIDE WORLD

guarded by an army infantry detachment, became headquarters
with LaGuardia in full command of the Harlem troops. He ordered
reinforcements and deputized volunteers, most of them black, to
patrol the streets. Six thousand policemen in all were assigned, and
fifteen hundred volunteers. The rampaging reached its peak at
1:30, four hours after it began, and outbursts continued until morning. The hospitals were jammed. One newspaper described a trail
of blood from hospital steps through the corridors into the emergency room. As arrests mounted LaGuardia had the armories
opened to hold the increasing number of prisoners. Along with the
prisoners came their loot. Soon the armories looked more like giant
warehouses than jails as they filled with goods—sides of beef and
bacon, suits, women's coats, groceries, and cans of foodstuffs.
Streets, too, were cluttered with loot.

The mayor was tireless, issuing orders, rapping out commands.
He stayed at his post without rest from Sunday night until he
judged that order had been restored in the early hours of Tuesday
morning. During that time he made five broadcasts to explain what
had happened and what measures were being taken. Directing his
talks primarily to the black community, he blamed the rioting on
thoughtless hoodlums, and pleaded with the citizens of Harlem to
cooperate with the police. At 9:55 on Monday night he reported
that the situation was definitely under control. At 10:30 as a curfew
was imposed he made his last appeal to Harlem residents to go to
their homes. Then he made a final tour of the area. Harlem looked
as though it had been "blitzed." At 1 A.M. the exhausted mayor
went home.

The cost of the night's "disturbance," a word LaGuardia preferred to "race riot," had been high—five dead, four hundred
wounded, hundreds of shops wrecked and looted. Property damage had been put at $5 million. The more lasting effects were yet
to be assessed.

For the next few days Harlem remained virtually under martial
law. The curfew continued, liquor sales were banned, and wide
areas were cleared of traffic. At night the wartime dimout was lifted
and police and volunteers patroled blazing streets making Harlem
the brightest spot in the entire city. Only slowly did life return to
normal. With at least a semblance of peace restored, civic leaders
met to consider the reasons why law and order had broken down.
Opinions varied as to the causes, but the mayor's behavior throughout the crisis drew uniform praise.

The *Herald Tribune* stated that the city owed a debt to the mayor for his "just and forceful handling of the situation." The City Council paused in its investigations to speak kind words for a fine job in "the most delicate situation the city has faced in years." Black leaders in particular appreciated LaGuardia's refusal to condemn the community as a whole and his constant reminders to the rest of the city that it was the hoodlumism of a few that caused the trouble. "I approve emphatically of every word you say," Walter White told him. "The decent people of Harlem will stand by you and back you to the limit."

Why then the riot? The most widely favored theory held that basic social problems existing in Harlem for a long time had been exacerbated by the war. Shortages of materials bringing construction and repairs to a halt in all parts of the city were felt more sharply in Harlem where the physical plant was older and had been allowed to run down even before the war. Unemployment was higher there than in the rest of the city. Problems beyond the city's reach were also a factor. The treatment of Negro soldiers in the army, particularly in the South, was an especially sore point among many blacks. Walter White maintained that had it been a Negro civilian who had been shot, no matter how prominent, there would have been no riot.

The council, having risen to the occasion by praising the mayor, was soon back to business as usual, squabbling over whether a lack of recreational facilities had caused the disorders. They settled a day-long debate by requesting LaGuardia to open additional full-time playgrounds, though Moses kept insisting there were enough and Mrs. Earle argued that most of the offenders were adults.

The City-Wide Citizens Committee on Harlem, led by Algernon Black and Adam Clayton Powell, Sr., was more discerningly critical. While they had praise for the mayor's handling of the riot, they were less satisfied with his overall record in regard to Harlem. In 1941 a group of welfare and social agencies had drawn up proposals for better housing, more recreational facilities, and better personnel in Harlem schools and hospitals. LaGuardia was not insensitive to the issues raised at that time, as evidenced by his assignment of black policemen and volunteers to the area during the riot. His private correspondence over the years also gave proof of his concern for the Harlem community. Nevertheless, the citizens committee complained that recommendations had largely been ignored and that its own 1935 report had to all intents and purposes been suppressed. One of the charges, that LaGuardia's attitude toward crime and delinquency had consistently been to minimize them, was seized on by his critics and was to be heard frequently in the months ahead.

In November the charge was repeated in a Brooklyn Grand Jury report on conditions in Bedford–Stuyvesant, Brooklyn's "Little Harlem." At a meeting attended by five hundred persons, a score of them Negroes, LaGuardia defended his administration against charges of failure to curb lawlessness in Brooklyn. The mood of the audience was hostile, and there were shouts for his removal from office. An off-duty patrolman, later suspended, almost caused a riot when he attributed the rise in crime to an "influx of sun-burned citizens," and a Negro probation officer, rising in defense of his race, was booed and hissed. A week later Valentine issued a report that was, in effect, a complete denial of the grand jury charges and a vindication of LaGuardia's claim that the area had not been neglected by the city.

Nevertheless, the summer in Harlem had long-range results. The mayor and his administration were forced to take seriously the problems of the city's black population, and while they pointed to progress and achievements, they were not unaware of the narrow escape from a full-scale race riot. It had taken all the mayor's considerable skills and authority to keep the lid on, and it would take the war's end to bring any substantial improvements. But the city was beginning to plan for the postwar world, and LaGuardia, for one, knew that the needs and demands of Harlem and all the little Harlems could be ignored only at the city's peril.

Sunday Sermons

An avenue to power and a new relationship with the men and women of the city had meanwhile opened through the development of his Sunday talks over WNYC into a weekly ritual. The series had begun on January 18, 1942, a direct result of the effective broadcasts immediately following Pearl Harbor. LaGuardia had come to think of WNYC as the city's voice; and the city's voice, he came to feel increasingly, was his own. While his world was falling apart during the bitter middle months of 1943, he found he could restore his leadership by talking directly to the people of things that concerned them in their daily lives.

To the politicians LaGuardia's direct contact with the public became something close to a constitutional abuse. To the press, increasingly barred by the mayor from ordinary interviews (and not even admitted to his City Hall office while the broadcasts were in progress), they seemed a derogation of their traditional authority. But the people of New York loved them. As many as 1.8 million would tune in on a Sunday at 1:00 P.M. to the municipal station; and by letters, and sometimes by their actions, showed that they took seriously the admonitions, attacks, interpretations that poured crisply forth during the next half to three-quarters of an hour.

As a radio speaker LaGuardia's technique had developed remarkably since the first talks of his administration. Then he had approached the microphone warily, treating it like an offspring of the mistrusted telephone. He had rattled off facts and statistics, condensations of written reports, often running out of time before his material was exhausted. Now he was as comfortable on the air as in normal conversation. He usually spoke extemporaneously, spinning his remarks from notes gathered during the week, moving easily from an exposition of war news to denunciation of a neighborhood bar, reaching out to a single individual in his vast audience, or excommunicating some group from the company of good men. The garishly colored giants that peopled his imagination became alive as he excoriated gangsters, tinhorns, and plain politicians. For a little while each week the people of the mundane city could believe that they dwelt within a brightly lit and comprehensible world, under the eye of a wise parent who would reward the just and punish the wicked. In the darkest days of the war it was desperately needed reassurance.

The opening bars of the Marine hymn—the stirring "From the Halls of Montezuma," chosen because he liked the music—served each week to introduce the mayor. The setting was the executive chamber in City Hall, where two microphones were set up on the mayor's desk and a small audience of friends and family was generally gathered round. The mayor would have arrived early and by the time the broadcast was scheduled to begin would have familiarized himself with memos and reports and consulted with his staff and the director of WNYC, Morris Novick. At precisely 1:00 "with a violent gesture," he would unbutton his coat and vest, loosen his tie, and turn toward the microphone.

The usual Sunday broadcasts would begin with a roundup of world news, often with hints on strategy dropped casually as if

Franklin Roosevelt and Winston Churchill were themselves listening. The manner would be statesmanlike and cool. By 1:10 or so the delivery would grow more intense, the voice higher pitched, the language more pungent. The mayor would be dealing with city problems—the milk that was selling at too high a price (fourteen cents a quart); the meat that was being inequitably distributed, with bribery evidently playing a part ("I warn you, chicken dealers. I'm not fooling. No more monkey business"). Then the voice would become conversational and informal, almost wheedling in tone, as his honor picked up some letter written by a citizen, or recounted some personal incident of the week. Or he talked about his own household, and his listeners would hear stories about "my wife, Marie" or about the children, Eric and Jean.

On occasion (for LaGuardia knew well the secret of surprise and unpredictability) the Sunday talk would be given over to one subject—the exposition, for example, of the current budget, or the celebration of a seasonal rite. On Christmas and Easter he would leave city affairs entirely aside. Gone were the references to "cheap, dirty, low-down, low-life politicians" as the mayor discoursed upon the Bible and the Christian ethic. On such occasions he could attain true eloquence, and his repertory of roles allowed him to match the substance with a dignified and moving delivery. On Easter Sunday in 1943 his talk was preceded by selections from Wagner's *Parsifal* and followed by others from Handel's *Messiah*. His own tones were solemn as he spoke about the true meaning of the Easter parade in wartime— "the great parade of the mothers and wives, all moving toward God, all joining in the mighty chorus asking for the repose of sons or husbands, and the protection of loved ones, and constituting the great sisterhood of sorrow." As always he ended the broadcast with the words he had made so familiar, "Patience and Fortitude."

Local lawmakers were understandably disconcerted by the public's devotion to the weekly broadcasts and by an exercise of power they could neither attain nor control. They complained constantly about what they deemed the misuse of WNYC. LaGuardia had the perfect comeback when he announced that if the City Council insisted he would deliver his weekly broadcasts over a commercial station, and then proceeded to reveal an offer from a perfume manufacturer to sponsor him at $25,000 a year. LaGuardia was prepared to donate the money to the city; but the council, visibly embarrassed, declared it was undignified to have the mayor up for barter. For a while, at least, they were silent on the matter of the Sunday sermons; but the political charges came to a head following a bitter campaign in 1943 for the election of a New York Supreme Court judge.

In a postelection Sunday broadcast LaGuardia assailed the Republican organization in terms more than usually vigorous, even for him, for what he charged was their responsibility in electing Thomas Aurelio, accused of being the friend of a notorious underworld character. A top Republican figure in the state, Thomas J. Curran, demanded the right to reply on a subsequent Sunday broadcast. The mayor contended his address had been in the nature of a postmortem analysis of the election, but he faced the issue cautiously, realizing it was a test case for his right to make free use of WNYC. He asked the head of the Federal Communications Commission, James L. Fly, to rule on whether the talk in question had been of such a partisan nature as to require the granting of time for a reply.

The drama of the event was underscored by the mayor's withholding the contents of Fly's opinion, even from himself, until he opened the envelope on the air. "I thought it would be nice," he told his audience, "if you and I read the letter together." In his ruling Fly declined to say outright that the talk had been political, but held it to be accusatory and judged its charges against the Republicans to have been of a serious nature. LaGuardia accepted the verdict with good spirit and the following week Curran had a chance over WNYC, during a portion of the mayor's own hour, to make a reply. His ridicule of the mayor went unnoted as LaGuardia resumed his regular discourse.

After that LaGuardia was not noticeably more restrained, but the politicians were deprived of an issue and the public continued to enjoy their mayor in his role as preacher, news commentator, and counselor on things in general. To an increasing extent, as the last years of the administration unfolded, the Sunday broadcasts became the source of important news, and the Monday morning papers were dominated by stories which the mayor had artfully planted.

Founding of City Center

The political year ended on a sour note; but in the old Mecca Temple on West 55th Street, where LaGuardia presided over one of his outstanding successes, there were tones of a different kind. As he told the audience on the opening night of the city's new performing arts center, he was witnessing a dream come true. New York at last had a place where performances of the highest excellence could be made available at minimal prices to a large popular audience. LaGuardia had always believed that bringing the arts to the people was a responsibility of government; he had also been realistic in recognizing that funds could not come from the regular municipal budget. City Center represented a triumph of practical planning and cooperation, inspired by an ideal of civic magnificence. To the mayor went credit both for the practicality and the idealism, and the resulting institution would in years to come be regarded by many as one of his brightest achievements.

The story of the City Center goes back to the late thirties when LaGuardia turned to the WPA as the resource for a major musical undertaking. The Depression had been especially hard on musicians; ten thousand were unemployed, and when WPA offered a thousand of them a chance to work, LaGuardia saw his opportunity. He turned to Newbold Morris as a man with the will and energy to manage the WPA project for the city. Morris demurred, saying he knew little about music. But LaGuardia replied cheerfully, "You know the kind of music the average music lover wants to hear."

Why the mayor should have thought the council president would be likely to know what the people wanted to hear remains something of a mystery. Morris had cultivated tastes, but he was no connoisseur of music and could hardly claim the common touch. Nevertheless he turned out to be the best possible choice. He immersed himself in music, listening to choruses and orchestras wherever they were performing. The orchestra he finally settled on, to be known as the New York City Symphony, was an international ensemble whose members had played with the great symphonies of the world. One had even played at St. Petersburg under Tchaikovsky.

LaGuardia had been disappointed in his hopes to construct a performing arts center at Radio City, but he now learned that the Center Theater, just completed, was scheduled to remain dark for several months. Nelson Rockefeller was asked if the theater could be borrowed during the interval. Fearing an adverse reaction, Morris, who conducted the negotiations, made no mention of the fact that the orchestra would be composed of WPA musicians. He simply explained the terms: no rent, but the costs of lights, heating, and ushers to be met out of ticket sales. The young Nelson Rockefeller agreed. Next Lauritz Melchior, the popular Wagnerian tenor, was enlisted. "The people of New York City command you," Morris told him, and the effective persuasion launched the council president's career as an impresario.

The first four concerts, priced at 25¢ to a high of $1.00, were devoted to Wagner. In January Albert Spalding and Joseph Levine played an all-Tchaikovsky series. Like subsequent programs they were completely sold out and the mayor received his full credit in subway ads proclaiming, with a very small nod to Harry Hopkins's WPA, "Mayor LaGuardia presents . . ." From Radio City the symphony moved to the Metropolitan Opera House and Carnegie Hall, waiting for the day when it could have a hall of its own. In 1943 the old Mecca Temple, a whale of an auditorium, its exterior fancifully decorated in the Moorish style, came by default into the possession of the city. "You've been talking about a center for the arts," Morris told the mayor. "Here it is." The mayor had his doubts. He thought it might be better used as a garage, and only when all other possible city uses had been ruled out did he consent. Even then he questioned whether Morris could raise the $100,000 required to launch the enterprise.

Within a two-week period, creating a partnership that was the very essence of LaGuardia's New York, Morris got the money. Contributions came from public-spirited individuals—John Rockefeller, Marshall Field, Howard Cullman, Edmund Guggenheim. They came, too, from the labor unions, the Amalgamated Clothing Workers and the Jewish Labor Alliance, whose members would provide the skills, and ultimately much of the audience, for the new theater. The only cost to the city was $65,000 for capital improvements. LaGuardia was named president of the new organization; Newbold Morris, chairman of the board.

On December 11, 1943, the mayor's birthday, the building was dedicated. LaGuardia, arriving in a plain blue suit, set the tone for the occasion. A few celebrities and socialites were in evening dress, but everyone else, as the *Times* music critic described the affair, "was in ordinary clothes and a Saturday night humor and having a wonderful time." "Is it not the time," LaGuardia asked with emotion, "for us of the older generation to keep burning the flame of art . . . to hold on until the younger generation lay down their arms and come back to the peaceful, spiritual, and happy things of life?" It was as if some of his own disappointment at being left out of the war found its alleviation in that hour. Coming so transparently from the heart, the words moved the great audience; LaGuardia acknowledged their applause and was about to leave the stage when the orchestra surprised him with a thunderous rendition of "Happy Birthday to You."

If he had been skeptical in the beginning about this "adventure in the arts," LaGuardia now gave it not only his full support but invested in it the kind of all-consuming enthusiasm that could mark his leadership. He was full of plans and wanted to be in on every detail. He insisted that young American artists be given their chance, and saw to it that performances were arranged to fit the schedule of working people. "Under no circumstances," he would write in a long series of commendations or complaints to the management, "must there be any speeches before or between the acts of an opera performance at City Center. . . . You have no idea how much damage was done yesterday. The broadcast was simply rotten." On another occasion it was the playbill which drew his attention. "I enjoy reading the City Center programs. . . . However, judging by your ads, you would think New York City was nothing but perfumes and brassieres. Can't you have a few other ads?"

The vast hall was acoustically unsound, and came to be known as "LaGuardia's barn." In desperation the mayor called the governor of Connecticut, recalling that microphones stood on every desk in the state legislature which only met biannually and that this was the year when the legislators were not in session. He got the loan of four microphones, which were soon installed among the footlights.

The symphony concerts were an outstanding success, the hall bulging, as *Time* magazine remarked, "with Dubinsky's garment workers and Curran's seamen." In 1944 Leopold Stokowski agreed to serve without pay as conductor of the City Center symphony orchestra composed of eighty players of both sexes and all races— his only stipulation was that he be known as "music," not "musical" director. When plans for a Bach *Christmas Oratorio* faltered for lack of funds, Stokowski drew out his checkbook—one must assume that he drew it out with a flourish—and wrote a personal check for $10,000. "But where is opera for the people?" LaGuardia asked, and when told it was too expensive to produce, insisted there must be a way. Laszlo Halasz was persuaded to come from the St. Louis Opera Company, bringing as a loan many of the sets and costumes. *Tosca* opened triumphantly with ticket prices ranging from 85¢ to $2.20. No one seemed to mind too much when the guns of the firing squad failed to go off in the last act and the hero was forced to drop dead of apparent heart failure.

A theater company next provided the mayor with the opportunity to display his histrionic gifts. Dropping by at a rehearsal of *Susan and God* he could not restrain himself from coaching Gertrude Lawrence on the delivery of her lines. His personal intervention succeeded in getting Marc Connelly to play the stage manager in *Our Town.* When a ballet company was proposed as a natural complement to the center, LaGuardia was less enthusiastic. He did not like, he said, "to see American young men leaping around the stage in those white tights exhibiting their crotches." Nevertheless, the Ballet Russe de Monte Carlo opened in March 1944. The mayor was delighted with the "dressy" element represented by wealthy contributors, adding a special touch to the regular City Center audience.

When the League of New York Theaters expressed concern that the City Center would present unfair competition, Howard Cullman reassured the organization. "Nobody can make money out of the Center," he told them. He was almost right. At the first annual meeting in May 1944, LaGuardia announced a profit of $844.77, declaring that the center was "no longer an experiment." It was, indeed, a startling success.

12

Toward a Postwar World

A Time for Thought

LaGuardia was not a planner at heart. He was a man of the day, made for crises and indeed ready to generate them if none existed. He worked best, he believed, when he was physically overheated, and the social order seemed to him most creative when it was in ferment. Yet with the opening of 1944 a note of reflection and a concern with plans for the future manifested themselves. This period saw him engaged in activities oriented toward the world waiting to emerge at the war's end. Within the city, projects were planned to absorb the energies of returning servicemen and repair the damage and neglect of the war years. New social policies needed to be defined and new political forces to be organized. Outside the city LaGuardia saw denied to him a last chance to take part in planning for the liberated areas, but during a brief escape from city problems he participated actively in laying the ground-work for the postwar world of international aviation.

Early 1944 saw a mood of hope take possession of the country and of the city. Setbacks on the military fronts gave way to fresh advances; the fear of a protracted, indecisive struggle was replaced by the certitude of victory. The optimism proved excessive, at least in regard to hopes for a speedy end to the war, but for the moment it suited the public mind. After the nagging local preoccupations of

1943, the shortages and economic controls, men and women suddenly began thinking about an abundant future. The atmosphere of the 1944 New Year celebrations reflected the change. For the first time since Pearl Harbor there were noisy street celebrations, with laughter and cheers and the blowing of horns. In January an avalanche of available eggs seemed to portend a release from harrowing restrictions, and retail prices of food underwent a welcome decline.

On New Year's Day the mayor who had been in office for a full ten years, having seen the city move from the depths of the Great Depression through the darkness and the apprehensions of wartime, was caught in a reflective disposition. A reporter, seeing him somewhat apart from the crowd at a City Hall reception, engaged him in talk. LaGuardia was thoughtful and serious, as if glad of an opportunity to unburden his mind. His own job, he mused, had been one of "heavy labor," "a heartbreaking work" with little glamor and few of the satisfactions that had fallen to him as congressman. The time was coming when the mayor of a great city would be required to have specialized training in urban administration. Being "a good orator or a likeable fellow" would not suffice. "You just can't step into the job and learn it overnight."

Then, characteristically, the mayor looked to more immediate problems and prospects. He foresaw a vast buildup and transformation of the war about Eastertime; an Allied invasion of Germany by the summer, with Hitler killed by one of his own staff. The prophetic strain, which had not greatly misled him in regard to Europe, he then turned to events in his own country. The war's end would bring a period of trial and difficulties, especially in the larger cities which would need to establish a wholly new relationship to the federal government. "But I'm really hopeful for the country," he added. "Two years ago we were worried that no one was thinking about the future. Now everyone is, and out of it all I think we'll get something that is workable." The mayor paused. "It will be something," he said, "entirely different from what we now have."

Over the coming months LaGuardia reverted in public statements to this something "entirely different." Uniform unemployment insurance, national health insurance, a rounded program of public works combined with a shorter work week and an annual wage—these, he told a labor audience, were the minimum requisites if demobilization was not to be accompanied by severe stress. "I can't impress upon you too strongly," he added, "how serious that period is going to be." Later he proposed military training programs for boys from eighteen to twenty-one. Addressing the House Committee on Postwar Economic Policy in July he called for quick federal appropriations to make possible the implementation of city programs. Specifically he urged that immediately after the end of hostilities the cost of twenty days of the war be made available to the cities, and double that the following year.

In his own city new problems were emerging; the very nature of postwar U.S.A. would be determined by what happened in the nation's great agglomerations of skills, of talents, of services, and of unmet human needs. In fact the issues which twenty and thirty years later were to make New York a turbulent community, often held to be ungovernable as its problems were thought to be unsolvable, were then plainly in the making. The controversies of 1944 held the seeds of a troubled future. And LaGuardia's conduct in these controversies—sometimes bold and sometimes strangely hesitant—gives us a measure of his leadership.

The City's Prospects

The easy approach to postwar unemployment was to have a list of projects, long deferred and more or less obviously needed, ready to go into construction at the declaration of peace. LaGuardia was proud of having plans and specifications—complete to the last detail —for schools, hospitals, highways, recreation facilities, with a total cost figure of $700 million. He did not consider a master plan essential to the development of such projects. Moses, in 1943, was still repeating his old warning that the city must not be torn up and rebuilt "to suit an academic theory." He reflected the general view, including the mayor's, but something of the Planning Commission's earlier preoccupations remained to guide the new generation of builders. Outlying lands were to be developed more slowly, with the emphasis placed on halting the decline of established neighborhoods. Subway extensions would be limited until, in the mayor's phrase, the city had "jelled."

These good intentions and these rational precepts were not to be very strictly observed. Political pressures inevitably determined construction priorities. In certain other fields the insight was faulty from the start. Moses made light of warnings that the end of gas rationing and the postwar generation of inexpensive cars would mire the city in traffic congestion. He seemed to see the extension of highways and parkways as in itself a solution to the parking problem, as if automobiles could be kept in a state of continuous circulation; and he proposed service roads, to be used for parking, reaching from the major arteries into the hearts of the city's communities. LaGuardia urged putting cars beneath the city's parks. A major change in the zoning laws affecting the bulk of new construction was effectuated at this time, with the aim of increasing light and air around residential structures. It seemed a good idea, but by the 1950s the results would begin to appear in buildings standing isolated and surrounded by empty, unusable space.

A problem recognized by the idealists of the new city, recognized but never solved, was that of upkeep and maintenance. How were the new construction projects to be preserved from the kind of decay which LaGuardia had found prevalent throughout the city when he first took office? In 1944 the Citizens Budget Commission was warning that the city's postwar construction program was "grandiose" and would, if carried through, run the city into the blind alley of increasing maintenance costs and higher taxes. As early as 1937 a meeting of the American Society of Landscape Architects had heard a warning that the parks then being built would become "a vast system of recreational slums." "How are we to get help to groom the gift horse sent by our wealthy governmental relations? Who will pay the feed bill?" Moses replied: "Can it be your contention that the park improvements brought about by relief should not have been undertaken at all?" But in fact Moses knew better, and to his credit had constantly harped upon the need to find ways of maintaining what had been built.

His protests against inadequate park budgets centered on this necessity. New parks and parkways, he argued, had been built with the full knowledge and approval of the city: "We cannot have our cake and eat it. . . . we must be prepared to pay the bill. If there is not enough sentiment in the city in favor of maintaining such a system we should know it now." This was true of other vast enlargements of the city's plant; and it is also true that LaGuardia never got such costs incorporated within the budget. As it became clear that the federal government would not support upkeep or rehabilitation, a shadow fell over the postwar prospects. The shabby and unkempt scene of a generation later, when the whole city seemed to be falling into disrepair and no funds were available for its renewal, was in the making by the end of LaGuardia's administration.

LaGuardia warned emphatically against one danger. A startling modification saw his earlier attitude toward relief harden and grow severe. In an address before a welfare parley, denounced by the conferees as "illogical" and "antisocial," he foresaw the drift of postwar unemployed toward the larger cities: toward those that, like Los Angeles, had a pleasant climate, and especially toward New York "because it has a reputation for being big-hearted." Migration from the South he saw as a growing factor, bringing many problems of education, health, and law enforcement. "If all people have to do is to say to themselves they'll take relief, it will be impossible to meet these problems." The mayor argued cogently that the solution was bigger than any city or state and had to be met on a national level. He urged that a one-year residency be required before relief was made available.

The charge has been made that for political purposes LaGuardia encouraged in-migration, especially from Puerto Rico. In his old Harlem district his protégé Marcantonio certainly sought to organize the new minorities and to win their support with the kind of favors that politicians have traditionally bestowed upon the newcomer. But Marcantonio would complain about the obduracy of the city's Welfare Department. To the mayor he referred to the commissioner, with his strict standards and tactics of resistance, as "Mahatma Gandhi Hodson." In any case the influx of Puerto Ricans, and the problem of relief which they brought with them, did not occur until after the war and after LaGuardia's retirement.

More difficult to appraise is the charge, made by contemporaries and raised by subsequent critics, that LaGuardia left the city in a bad budgetary situation. It is true that as the war came to a close New York's finances remained impenetrable. The war had brought many fiscal advantages—added state and federal contributions, a decline in relief costs, and a diversion of thousands of civil service workers into the armed services. After the first crisis caused by the underuse of industrial plants, the city passed through a phase of war-induced prosperity bringing increases in its general tax funds. Yet by 1945 the budget would once again be several millions short.

The City Budget Commission was harsh in its judgment. "He warned but he did not act," they said of LaGuardia's record in this field. According to them he watched without effective protest as wartime spending was cloaked, windfalls poured out to meet immediate needs, and operating expenses swelled. In particular the commission was critical of the fact that LaGuardia had diverted, to pay increases for those remaining on the city's rolls, the savings from salaries of employees called into war service. Taking into account wartime inflation and the social stress of readjustment to peace, one must still conclude that the LaGuardia of these last years was not the economy-minded mayor who fought the 1934 Albany battles. By the 1940s the problems of city finances did not seem so capable of being categorically defined or of yielding as they once had to dramatic leadership.

The city's postwar finances did not lack attention from contemporary experts. A mayoral committee named in 1942, composed of city and state officials and outstanding private citizens, made a report which the mayor did not release. A committee headed by Paul Windels, then chairman of the Regional Plan Association, saw the principal means of restoring the city's financial health in a subway fare raised above the traditional nickel. It also argued persuasively for a greater degree of state support and the rebate of a larger share of the state income collected within the city. Relating borrowing for capital expenditures to the actual value of real estate, and general economies of $15 million, were also recommended as means of eliminating the "temporary patchwork expedients" by which the budget was normally balanced. LaGuardia was not pleased by the report. The five-cent fare was too touchy an issue to be embraced as a solution to the city's ills; and Windels was now a spokesman for the city's conservative interests.

Another attempt to deal with the city's future came from sources even more suspect in the mayor's eyes. Appointed by Dewey, and headed by the former undersecretary of the Treasury, John W. Hanes, the so-called Hanes Committee painted a gloomy view of New York's situation. Congestion, disproportionately high labor costs, vexatious regulations, neglect by Washington, and lack of concerted efforts to attract business were among the factors judged to be putting New York at a disadvantage in comparison to "younger" cities of the country. Most keenly felt were those criticisms which were perhaps best founded—namely, the spread of population brought about by tunnels, bridges, and highways. New York, the report asserted, already contained the country's largest areas of ghost neighborhoods, "and ghost cities are made up of ghost neighborhoods."

Windels called the report "admirable"—it confirmed, in his opinion, "what everybody had said who has been thinking about the problem." LaGuardia, needless to say, was indignant. The "alarming generalizations" of the report were attacked by city officials as being based on inconclusive evidence and inadequate statistics. The forces of George Sloan, commissioner of commerce, Herlands, commissioner of investigation, and of course the irrepressible Moses were marshalled in opposition to "the unduly dark picture." LaGuardia himself remained publicly silent, but released the successive comments of his subordinates. He must have felt in his bones the deep intractability of New York's problems; he must have sensed the shadows which lay across the future. Yet to admit them would have been to cast reflection on his three terms as mayor. His optimistic and activist nature, moreover, could not bring him to accept the thesis that a slow process of decline had set in.

A more cheerful, and as it turned out an accurately prophetic, note was struck in a series of editorials in the *Herald Tribune.* The argument made by the Regional Plan Association and others that a falling-off of industrial jobs doomed the city was summarily rejected. New York was not dependent on industry, the paper argued; its greatness among cities arose from the creative forces in its midst—from its capacity to innovate, to invent, to set styles—in short, to play the music to which the rest of the country marched. Cultural resources were as important as industrial; managerial skills —and the vast substructure of executives, junior executives, clerks, and secretaries which supported them—were as important to employment as shipping and construction. The city's "hidden industry" was in its preeminence as a center of design and the arts; the assurance of its future prosperity was in its still-unrealized capacities for the organization, communication, and distribution of ideas.

If LaGuardia has survived as the image of a successful mayor it is largely because by his very nature he encouraged these aspects of the city's life. He was in himself a metropolis, urgent, creative, busy in the shaping of new ideas and concepts; and he spoke and acted for more than seven million human beings who at their best shared something of his spirit.

Pioneering in Health Care

The mayor, complained the *Post,* had a disarming way of talking about a future "overflowing with milk and parkways." Why could

not at least a few more probation officers in the childrens court be
introduced into the shining vision? Why could not a few humble
and appropriate things be done "right now"? In one significant area
LaGuardia did act, undeterred by postwar uncertainties or shortages of funds.

A more effective way of organizing, delivering, and paying for
health services had long been one of LaGuardia's dreams. Decen-
tralized health centers, outpatient services, more city hospitals oriented toward research had been part of his basic program for New
York; and in the nation he was persuaded of the necessity for
national health insurance. In 1944 he took steps to make New York
a laboratory for nationwide reform.

LaGuardia's concern with health, not least his own health, was
constant and sometimes took bizarre forms. The assurances of his
personal physician and longtime friend, Dr. George Baehr, were
required to convince him that he had at least the average man's
chance to survive his years as mayor. His cataclysmic succession of
moods, his tendency to explosive outbursts, raised in his mind the
possibility of his being carried off like a burst balloon. To alarm the
doctors, and to befuddle them, gave him pleasure. Once he showed
Berle an x-ray which seemed to reveal a large safety pin lodged in
one of his lungs. It was the result, he confessed gleefully, of his
having placed the object—"in a fit of irritation"—beneath a shoulder blade! In fact LaGuardia was subject to illnesses, frequent and
various enough to give the doctors legitimate concern, and these,
as he himself sensed, were not unrelated to his psychic states. A man
sharply sensitive to rebuffs and setbacks, he would as often fall ill
in a period of disappointments as in periods when successful labors
brought him close to exhaustion. That he should have been aware
of others' needs for medical services, and aware of the common
man's difficulty in paying for them, was not surprising.

His concern was stimulated in 1944 by a survey of the economic
problems of city employees, showing medical costs to be the most
frequent cause of their going into debt. With characteristic direct-
ness he went about finding a means of prepaying these costs. In May
of that year he announced a plan to insure workers earning up to
$5,000 for medical services, surgery, and hospital care. In the case
of municipal employees, the city would pay half the premiums.
LaGuardia was fortunate in having as his principal adviser in these
matters the same Dr. Baehr who served as family physician, a man
of liberal views and large organizational abilities, who was to sur-

vive into the late 1970s, in his nineties still active and on the side of the angels.

Elementary as the plan for group insurance may appear at this distance, in 1944 it was a revolutionary move, and it aroused the passionate opposition of the medical establishment. LaGuardia was not displeased to have a new set of enemies who could be counted on to overstate their case and whom he could denounce with a fervor that was wearing thin when applied to "chiselers" and "punks." In important quarters, however, he found support. Such normally conservative papers as the *Herald Tribune* and the *Sun* backed the health plan—the *Tribune* seeing it as "highly significant" and the *Sun* declaring happily that with this initiative "the old LaGuardia" had come back.

When incorporation papers for the health insurance plan were filed in September, the occasion could justifiably be called "historic" by the mayor. The incorporators included such well-known names as Henry J. Kaiser, Beardsley Ruml, and Wendell Willkie. What was being achieved for New York was important, but in the mayor's view the true meaning of the day was in the example set for the rest of the country.

Incubus of the Five-Cent Fare

From this agreeable excursion we return to the persistent economic problems affecting the city, symbolized in the dilemma of the five-cent fare. The nickel subway ride had become part of New York life, a political shibboleth before which the leaders of all parties, and contestants for all offices, regularly bowed. Yet it was manifestly incapable of meeting the system's costs. A deficit of more than $40 million annually, met out of general funds, was combined with a steady deterioration of rolling stock, track, and underground stations. With the five-cent fare the hope of a balanced budget other than by windfalls and expedients was vain; yet the longer the fare remained fixed the more difficult it was to change it. To this dead end had come the large hopes evoked by municipal ownership of the city's public transportation system.

For a mayor who was into everything, and on most matters ready to declare himself unequivocally, LaGuardia proved peculiarly evasive on the subject of the five-cent fare. He might have begun his third term with a brave initiative and faced up to the problem while his political power was at its height. Burlingham was to look back regretfully upon this lost opportunity. But by 1944, with the issue ever more deeply entrenched and with his plans for a fourth term obscure, LaGuardia was as hedged in as everyone else. In his budget message of that year he asserted there was no individual in any party, and no legislative body, that would take the first step in raising the fare. He proved to be right, and he seemed to feel no embarrassment in including himself.

The budget message did at least recognize the impossibility of continuing to finance the subway deficit by ordinary means. He spoke of a "transport tax" but was mysterious in regard to its nature. "Let the critics find out what the plan is before they criticize," he said. Yet he seemed loath to reveal the facts. "All fair-minded people know that increased fares are not within the power of any one man to decide," he maintained, and "constant harping" on this point showed either "continued ignorance or continued desire to misrepresent."

Constructive leadership on this issue fell largely to Paul Windels who for some time had been advocating a raise to seven and a half or ten cents. He now proposed a new transit authority to assume ownership of the transit system and to hold power of regulating fares. In one of his March "Sunday sermons" LaGuardia took on Windels, not altogether unkindly, admitting the inevitability of a deficit under the existing fare structure but declaring the picture of the subway's deterioration to be exaggerated. Windels, he asserted, could not give the final answer on the fare, the city legislative bodies could not—only the men who controlled the two major political parties could do so. These included upstate Republican leaders and Boss Flynn of the Bronx.

The issue had thus been tossed to the politicians, and for the following week the politicians howled. Boss Flynn and Boss Frank Kelly of Brooklyn declared the mayor should have the courage and candor to state *his* views. Stanley Isaacs came to the defense of the Board of Estimate, contending the honorable members were able to think for themselves regardless of the opinions of the bosses. Reporters, citing the apparent confusion, submitted a written question to the mayor. Back came the written reply—there was no confusion and no discussion was necessary:

> Republicans have the state legislature. Democrats have the City Council.

But who has the Board of Estimate? asked Councilman Louis Cohen of the Bronx. It was not an irrelevant question.

The details of LaGuardia's transportation tax, revealed in July, provoked a new controversy. The package comprised taxes on rents and mortgages and a levy of forty cents a week on New York job holders residing out of the city. The commuters' impost, said Windels, would be enormously complicated to enforce. The evening paper *PM* was more original in its objections. The mayor, it suggested, had become the victim of "a new and super isolationism." One who understood fully the country's interrelations with England and France failed "to understand our municipal connections with New Jersey and Long Island."

In 1945 a bill creating a city transportation authority, the work of Windels and a citizens committee, was submitted to the state legislature. Still LaGuardia kept his distance. "If it passes I'll administer it and administer it well," was all he would say. The City Council opposed the bill, Isaacs maintaining that the fare should only be changed after a city referendum. Following a desultory debate and various unsuccessful efforts to smoke out LaGuardia, the state legislature dropped the matter, preferring to let New York simmer in its own indecision. LaGuardia dropped his transportation tax, and the city went forward into the postwar epoch burdened by a deficit which would nullify all rational efforts of fiscal management.

The Liberal Party

On the political front LaGuardia faced a dilemma as acute as that raised by the subway fare—and he was almost as determined to evade a choice. It will be recalled that in preparation for the 1936 campaign, Farley joined with LaGuardia in forming the American Labor party, a vehicle for support of the New Deal outside regular party labels. In 1937 LaGuardia forged his notable election victory on the basis of the ALP, stealing away its backing from the Farley-endorsed candidates. There we left the party, a major political force in New York State, with a future expected to be influential in the country at large.

After 1938, on the way to success, a strange thing happened to the ALP. As the European war approached, the Soviets performed an extraordinary about-face, signing a nonaggression pact with Hitler's Germany. Communist elements had sufficient strength in the ALP to split it wide apart. The right wing of the party, led by Alex Rose and David Dubinsky, condemned the pact and the subsequent invasion of Finland. The left wing maintained a neutral attitude and accused the right of using Fascist tactics. In a series of bitter primary battles in which the two factions put up opposing slates Rose and Dubinsky saw power slip from their grasp. In 1940 the left wing won control of the party in New York county where the rule of Rose and other garment trade leaders had never before been effectively disputed. So great was the bitterness that radio-equipped patrols were called to reinforce the police detail outside the school where the crucial meeting took place on March 1.

Then came the German invasion of Russia and the Soviets' heroic resistance. The party's left wing abandoned its neutral stand and in another spectacular reversal made common cause with the American war effort. Suddenly pro-war and pro-Roosevelt, headed by Roosevelt's longtime factotum Sidney Hillman, the leftists moved back into the mainstream. In the following elections, running on a platform with broad popular appeal, candidates of the left made considerable progress and avowed Communists in the ranks became bolder.

Now, in 1944, the issue was subtle but for LaGuardia it was excruciatingly painful. Would he continue to support—and be supported by—the ALP under its guise of being a broadly based liberal party? Or would he see it, in the words of the New York *Post,* as "a blind for the now party-less Communists"? Hillman, continuing his powerful leadership of the party's left wing, confused the issue by his connections with Roosevelt and the New Deal. LaGuardia was reluctant to choose between the two wings of the party, and refused to be drawn out despite appeals for support from both. He wanted to see Roosevelt win in the fourth-term election of 1944. And in 1945 would come the mayoralty elections when he might well need the backing of both wings of the ALP.

With less than a week to go before the primaries LaGuardia made his move, offering not a clear-cut choice but an effort at peace making. The initiative was acceptable to Hillman and the left, but was rejected by the Rose–Dubinsky forces as a cynical evasion of the issues. The *Post,* too, found the LaGuardia plan "legalistic and obscure." If he was opposed to the election of any Communist to the state committee, as he seemed to be indicating, why didn't the mayor say just that? But the mayor seemed to prefer "the state of flux" which Steingut, the minority leader in Albany, accused him of inhabiting. The *Sun,* taking a less indulgent view, charged La-Guardia with having given "the purest exhibition of fence-sitting since the heyday of 'Shipwreck Kelly.'"

Primary Day, March 28, saw the right-wing leadership routed. When the Bronx precincts, long a stronghold of right-wing support, were found giving their votes to the left, a bitter Alex Rose conceded. The next day Dubinsky, charging LaGuardia with having "made a gift of the ALP to Earl Browder," vowed to lead the International Ladies Garment Workers Union with its 132,000 members out of the party. Other leaders of the right followed suit.

What had happened to assure the victory of the left? Liberalism had not so much been defeated as rendered ambiguous. Hillman's arguments for strong prosecution of the war, for national unity, and for support of the president carried more weight than the inevitably alarmist and defensive appeal of the right. If Communist influences were at work within Hillman's ranks, they were for the time being effectively masked.

Yet the right was not ready to give up. The cause of liberalism needed more than ever a vehicle for its forthright expression. Willkie had recently been defeated in the Wisconsin primary and had withdrawn from the presidential race, dooming for the time being the espousal of liberalism by the Republican party. Within the Democratic party the liberal glow had been subdued by the long war effort, by Jim Crow elements in the South, and by machine politics in the big cities. Within a few weeks of their defeat in the ALP primaries, Dubinsky and Rose indicated their readiness to take up the banner. A new Liberal party was organized, forged from the right wing of the ALP, and at its first state convention in May prophesied for itself a long future, with a goal of 400,000 votes in the forthcoming elections.

The Liberal party in this first of its campaigns backed Roosevelt and Truman for president and vice-president, with Wagner as their candidate for senator. The ALP in its convention in August did the same. In the November elections the Liberal party received 320,000 votes; the ALP, 380,000. Thus the two parties were off to a similar start, but they were rapidly to diverge and to experience different fates. The basic line between communism and liberalism would increasingly separate them. Tactically, the ALP would be marked by support of a common front; the Liberal party by anticommunism. The ALP would have Democratic party ties, the

Liberals, ties with the Republican party going back to the original alliance forged by the wily Kenneth Simpson in 1937.

Of the two, the Liberals would have the longer life. The Communist tilt proved fatal to the ALP and the party disappeared after the fiasco of Wallace's run for the presidency in 1948. The ever-astute Alex Rose led the Liberals until his death in 1976 and the party continues to play a significant role in New York politics—now holding the balance between the major parties, now making itself felt by backing independent candidates. It was on the Liberal line in 1970 that John Lindsay ran successfully for a second term, after having suffered defeat in the Republican primaries.

We are, however, far ahead of our story. In 1944 LaGuardia was in the position of a man who had won a victory, but had won it more by stealth than by courage, and was not certain of what he had gained. He would need the endorsement of the ALP if he was to make another run; but his lack of support for its candidates in the primaries, and his coolness after their success, strained the once-unquestioned ties. Among the Liberals his position was insecure to say the least. It would soon be plain how much he had lost in sacrificing the close personal attachments of such old comrades-in-arms as Rose and Dubinsky.

To the Pacific?

Moves to send LaGuardia abroad continued in Washington, adding an undertone of uncertainty to local events. The president had been rebuffed in the spring of 1943, but he did not take the setback as final. He owed much to LaGuardia, as the approach of the fourth campaign no doubt reminded him; besides, he was not a man to give up easily. In the autumn of 1944 we find him writing to Stimson, "I do not think you and I can still say that he must remain as mayor of New York." But if not, where should he go?

A first plan, that he be sent to Italy, was turned down by the secretary of the navy, James Forrestal. The Italian situation, he wrote in a memorandum to the president, had "developed so far as to hold no substantial interest to anyone of such energy and diverse qualities as the mayor." In short, Poletti and O'Dwyer had had all the fun. Why, instead, should he not go to islands in the Pacific where there would be need of administration, "particularly the Philippines"? Roosevelt followed up the suggestion in a letter to Stimson, who soundly quashed the idea of having LaGuardia under army jurisdiction. "The light rein" envisaged for control of the civilian population, combined with plans for early withdrawal, Stimson wrote, "does not seem to be the sort of position that suits the temperament of the mayor."

Stimson then proposed that the ball be returned to Forrestal's court. "I much prefer that he be used as an advisor in the civil administration of the Pacific islands already occupied. These islands are being administered by the navy and you may wish to take this up more in detail with the navy." Stimson went on to "strongly recommend" that LaGuardia be given a rank no higher than a captain in the navy or colonel in the army; and then, in an attempt at humor, concluded in a handwritten sentence: "If Jim Forrestal wants him to have a higher rank, I should have no objection to his being made an admiral."

Roosevelt, however, was not amused. A letter in the files, dated September 29, is addressed to Stimson. It begins "Dear Harry" and reads as follows:

> I have determined that I need LaGuardia in the army with the rank of brigadier general.
>
> I have some important assignments I want him to do during the next year and their accomplishment will require his being in uniform. He should be commissioned around the middle of November.
>
> I do not plan to use him for the time being in Italy, although it may develop later that I will want him to go there for a time.

The letter is marked "not signed" and was evidently never sent. But the president discussed it with Hopkins (who had perhaps drafted it) before LaGuardia visited the White House at the end of October. The mayor was then reported to be "very unhappy" and members of the president's staff were suggesting that he be sent into areas of Connecticut and New Jersey where there were large concentrations of Italian-speaking voters.

It was another humiliating comedown, but this time LaGuardia appears to have accepted it resignedly. "I am still out of service," he wrote to a friend in mid-November, "but I haven't given up hope yet." With the reporters, who were aware that something big was going on in Washington, he reverted to his old quip about his duties as street cleaner—"I'm going to clean up the streets tonight.

I'm good at that." Letters came from across the country congratulating him on his approaching assignment and asking for positions on his staff; the St. Louis *Post Dispatch* commented favorably upon what it considered an accomplished fact. CBS asked him to appear on a national broadcast to discuss the new responsibilities. To all, in one way or another, LaGuardia replied it would be wiser to wait until something actually happened, adding that of course he would be proud to serve if the occasion arose.

Postwar Aviation

In Adolf Berle the mayor had one Washington friend who never neglected his cause, combining a desire to use his talents with a sensitive understanding of his psychological needs. Berle was now on the fringe of White House maneuvers, but in late 1944 an opportunity came to him to lead in what he called "one small part of FDR's great dream of organized peace among nations." That part was postwar international aviation, seen as an instrument of commerce and of free exchange among peoples of the world. An international conference was called, to be held in Chicago; it would run through November and into early December. The president appointed Berle head of the American delegation, and Berle asked his old friend the mayor to be one of a notable group including the assistant secretaries of war and navy. In all, fifty-seven nations were represented.

For LaGuardia the appointment was a welcome one. It provided an opportunity to get out of the confined New York scene and brought him back to aviation, one of his first loves. The excitement was not equal to what he had hoped for in Italy or the Pacific; but Berle had a way of investing even a humdrum meeting with an air of urgency and of large horizons. "We have got to get something like civil aviation ready in the event of a general German collapse in Europe," he confided to his diary in the rough-and-ready style he used. LaGuardia went to Chicago prepared to play a quiet but constructive part in the negotiations.

The conference achieved mixed results. Despite Berle's sense of immediate need the issues were prematurely posed. Russia withdrew, an ominous warning of the cold war to come. The positions of the two major wartime allies, the United States and Britain, were irreconcilably at odds on the question of whether air carriers over a long route could pick up intermittent traffic. The Americans wanted the right granted unconditionally; the British, with their more localized interests to protect, wanted it hedged and granted on a route-by-route basis. LaGuardia played his role in the dispute by pleading for unity and for the achievement of tangible results. "Let's not go back," he said, "to the old system of power politics and greed that brought us to this present situation." In the end an international civil aviation organization was established, destined to play a useful role in the postwar world.

During the month in Chicago, important events were occurring in the State Department. On November 21 Hull resigned as secretary, ending a long tenure during which his monumental integrity and patience had held together a disparate team, all of them appearing more brilliant than he. With the appointment of Edward Stettinius as secretary, Berle's position in the department was undermined. For several days he agonized over his options, and then submitted to what Max Ascoli was to term "a crude liquidation." Deprived of office but still in charge of the U.S. delegation at Chicago, he found in LaGuardia's close friendship a source of consolation and strength. The two fighters, so often an encouragement to each other in the days of strength, now comforted their common wounds.

In a letter to LaGuardia after the conference Berle bestowed praise, which others would probably have echoed, on LaGuardia's contribution. He spoke of "your own swift instinct," "your wisdom in crystallizing the discussion at the right time." Then in touching words he added his indebtedness at a deeper level: for "your tenderness to me at a time which was necessarily one of personal perplexity." "We have been working together for so many years," Berle concluded, "that I do not believe this is going to be our last venture." He took pains, as we shall see, to make sure that it was not.

Hope Deferred

The expectations of a German surrender by the year's end were not to be fulfilled. LaGuardia had almost been right in his New Year's prediction that Hitler would be assassinated by one of his own staff. The attack came in August, but it miscarried. Rome was captured on June 5 and the next day Allied landings took place on the continent as 50,000 New Yorkers, led by the mayor, prayed in Madison Square Park. DeGaulle made a first visit to the city, towering over the mayor whom he praised for having expressed faith in France "with an ardor and an energy that Frenchmen will never forget." Then in August Paris was liberated. "It is on a day such as this," said the French consul-general, Guerin de Beaumont, speaking at Rockefeller Plaza, "that fallen heroes return to the world of the living." The Allied armies continued their slashing advance through Europe—until on December 26 the Germans counterattacked and the long-drawn-out Battle of the Bulge began. The *Times* summarized the year-end mood in biblical words: "Hope deferred maketh the heart sick."

Roosevelt had been renominated almost without opposition by the Democrats, having chosen Truman over Wallace as his running mate. Dewey headed the Republican ticket. This time there was no difficulty for the mayor in coming out early and wholeheartedly for the president. "It will take a few days for Wallace's friends to reconcile themselves, but then it will be all right," he said philosophically of the choice for the vice-presidency. (He did not forget that it was Truman who in 1943 had barred his being named brigadier general.) On October 21, when the ailing Franklin Roosevelt toured New York's boroughs in the rain—more than fifty miles in an open car—LaGuardia took part in the historic odyssey. "He stood it better than I did," remarked the mayor loyally.

Roosevelt seemed to go on forever, but the world was nevertheless changing. In his official family LaGuardia saw the resignations of George Sloan, commissioner of commerce, and of his longtime commissioner of investigations, William Herlands; he felt the first blasts of McGoldrick's approaching defection. The larger world saw the passing of heroes. In October Al Smith died at the age of seventy, the elder statesman who could so often be wrong. "His monument," said the mayor discerningly, "is on the statute books of our state in the progressive social welfare laws enacted during his term as governor." Four days later, his hopes shattered by the Wisconsin defeat, Wendell Willkie passed from the scene. He had taken the brunt of LaGuardia's hostility and in a later campaign had repaid it with generosity. "His death is a great loss," the mayor said, "at a time when clear thinking and courageous leadership are much needed."

But it was another death, that of George W. Norris, which most moved the mayor. Norris had been his advisor and his model in the congressional years, and now in eulogizing him LaGuardia seemed to identify himself with the fallen hero. Tears lining his cheeks at the end of a Sunday broadcast, he recalled how Norris had been defeated in his own state because "the young voters didn't know him and the old ones had forgotten him." "I know the senator was unhappy," he continued. "You see, he was an insurgent, and the life of an insurgent in American politics is an unhappy one. He draws opposition from every side. He is always open to attack."

When Norris lost his Senate seat LaGuardia and others had advised him to remain in Washington. "Oh no, LaGuardia, you're only trying to be kind. Damn it, LaGuardia, I won't be a lame duck." LaGuardia paused in the broadcast, only this time there was in his hesitation nothing of the actor's skill. As with all independents, he said with a sigh, "I guess he will get his reward in heaven and his credit in the history books."

The last words over the air were addressed to Marie at Gracie Mansion. "I'm coming home early this afternoon. I don't think I can work much today."

13
An Epoch Passes

Fourth-Term Riddle

Would LaGuardia run for a fourth term? In New York politics that was the overarching question as 1945 opened. He had been the mayor so long it was difficult to imagine the city without him, as it would be difficult to imagine the country without Roosevelt. A generation had come of age knowing no other tenant of City Hall. The high-pitched, emphatic voice; the rotund, rapidly moving figure; the witty sallies and the innocent mystifications, had become for them as much a part of city life as Times Square or Central Park.

To tease the press had long been one of LaGuardia's pleasures. He had often played upon the emotions of the public, letting words and symbolic acts create expectations which he was free to fulfill or not. Now he had a real mystery to keep or to unravel. He had good reason, moreover, for not committing himself too early on the fourth-term issue. In his New Year broadcast he had spoken of his successor—"whenever that will be." City Hall reporters rose to the bait. Was there significance in his having used the word "whenever" instead of "whoever"? Yes, he replied solemnly, there was; he did not want to "mislead his political friends." But that was as much as he would say.

He liked to protest that he was too busy to think about politics, when politics was obviously the subject uppermost in everyone's mind, including his own. He liked to complain about the tendency to read fourth-term intentions in even his most casual remarks. If he observed he did not have much tobacco, but that it was sufficient, or if he said he would need his glasses for a long time and should have them repaired, people were exasperatingly quick to discern political significance. Yet he encouraged just such speculation, and the gnomic utterances did not cease.

No doubt he was genuinely of two minds. Could he not go on in office forever, like the indomitable man in the White House? Yet he began to be bored by the details of his job; he was often tired and would return to Marie at the day's end complaining of bad pains in his back. In the third term, and especially after the Washington turndown, he had seemed to grow increasingly irritable. It was as if the tempers that flared with a certain artistic effect in his best days had become habitual and uncontrollable. He turned easily against old friends, many of them, like Anna Rosenberg, seeing their relations with the mayor cool inexplicably.

The disillusionment he expressed at the time of George Norris's death—"the life of an insurgent in American politics is an unhappy one"—lingered to color his plans for the new year. In such moods he would toy with the prospects of a life of ease and a return to his origins in the West. He dreamed of the hills around Prescott. "When my public career ends I plan to make my home among those hills," he wrote a fellow Arizonian who wanted to return home; "You, too, must have drunk from the Hassayampa." By the hidden waters of an Indian stream he would perhaps find the peace he had so deliberately denied himself during long years in Congress and City Hall.

LaGuardia wielded the baton, orchestrating the uncertainties about his political plans; yet, in fact, others were writing the score. During the first quarter of 1945 it became increasingly questionable where, if at all, the mayor would find support for a fourth-term bid. In 1933 and 1937, though he had campaigned under independent banners, the Republican party had given him his major political backing. Hopefully in the first campaign, grudgingly in the second, the leaders had come round to him. But now they had had enough. Not only had the mayor consistently repudiated the party's state and national tickets; worse, in their eyes, was the fact that for the last eight years he had denied them patronage while dealing liberally with the ALP. Only Crews of Brooklyn had been a beneficiary of jobs, and now he alone among the local Republican leaders was sympathetic to another term for the mayor.

The ALP, or what was left of it after the defection of the right wing, could be counted on for support, but even in this quarter there were mutterings to the effect that a LaGuardia designation was not to be taken for granted. The new Liberal party was distinctly cool. Alex Rose was not a man to forget the mayor's lack of conviction in his own decisive battles of the previous year. Now he administered a sharp rebuke: nonpartisan administration, he told his followers, did not mean "a one-man rule which completely ignores public opinion or is annoyed by the instruments of our democracy which give expression to that opinion." Alfange, a Liberal after having run unsuccessfully for Congress on the ALP ticket, added that qualifications for mayor should include more than the will to resist a bribe, a cruelly narrow judgment on the LaGuardia administration.

In April Seabury entered the lists ("All I know," LaGuardia wrote his old friend Burlingham, "is that Judge Seabury was the only one who was for me in the beginning, in the middle, and up to the very end"). A letter framed by him was to go out to Republican leaders and officials urging them to rally around a fourth-term drive. "I am convinced," wrote Seabury, "that the Republicans' only hope and salvation is to support LaGuardia." There were to be fifty signatures in addition to his own, but after several weeks only forty-five had been collected. LaGuardia professed he did not know the purpose of the letter, though he was grateful to its sponsors. In the end all depended on Dewey; but Dewey, approached by Moses, remained silent and enigmatic. A *News* straw vote about this time showed 40 percent of the city's voters ready to back (of all people!) Walker for mayor, with 25 percent for O'Dwyer, and only 20 percent for LaGuardia.

LaGuardia still had the magic of his name; he had shown enormous recuperative powers before, and politically he was, as Joseph Clark Baldwin remarked, "a law unto himself." "Well, it promises to be interesting," said the *News,* after commending the mayor for being "courageous, intelligent, honest, and energetic"—a bit too energetic it added, returning to its old complaint that the mayor had crusaded "like a frustrated old woman" against such pleasures of the flesh as horse betting, Bingo, and burlesque, "Why, we cannot figure out." Meanwhile the parties juggled the names of other possible candidates. LaGuardia kept his apparent nonchalance, and the city turned to

disputes and controversies which, though often superficially unrelated to politics, constituted its very core.

Business More or Less as Usual

LaGuardia had a knack for getting into trouble with the entertainment industry almost as readily as with the politicians. In his
commissioner of licenses, Paul Moss, he had a lieutenant who was
quite prepared to lead the way. An early incident of 1944 found
the commissioner ruling that plays for which there was a large
demand must sell their tickets at the box office and not be allowed
to sell them through brokers. The cry of "harassment" went up
from the brokers, with theater owners and the press joining in. The
mayor backed the order, and then a few days later reversed himself.
For today's reader the most interesting aspect is not the mayor's
change of mind, but the titles of the plays affected. What theatrical
brilliance the Broadway of that day presented! Among the hits of
1945 were *A Bell for Adano, Harvey, I Remember Mama, Oklahoma,
Song of Norway, The Late George Apley,* and *Voice of the Turtle.*

Commissioner Moss's next invasion of Broadway caused an even
more widespread furor. A drama entitled *Trio* had opened to poor
notices; its days were numbered, but those who saw it found a
touching story, done with taste, of a girl's struggle to choose between the affections of a young man and an older woman. The
implied homosexual relationship was too much for the mayor and
his commissioner. On LaGuardia's orders Moss withdrew the license of the theater where *Trio* was playing and the offending
drama promptly shut down.

This scarcely disguised censorship united Broadway and all the
press in violent opposition. Actors Equity denounced the "outrageous action"; the Authors League demanded that Moss be fired.
City Center, which to this point had led a charmed existence, was
suddenly wracked by dissension. Moss was the mayor's assistant on
the City Center board and his resignation both as assistant and as
commissioner was demanded. The playwright Elmer Rice and the
noted actor-director Margaret Webster left the board in protest.
The mayor backed his commissioner (in the circumstances he could
hardly do otherwise), but consented to a meeting at City Hall with
representatives of the theater industry and the American Civil Liberties Union. "We had a more or less harmonious meeting," La-

Guardia declared at its close. "Everyone has retained the same views he held before the conference." But in fact LaGuardia had yielded on important points and agreed to permit the reopening of *Trio* for a test case.

Trio was beyond saving; but the damage done went beyond that single play. After such an incident the fear of censorship works a subtle poison, and John Martin of the *Times* noted that the ballet of *Frankie and Johnny,* then being presented at City Center, had undergone "laughable alterations." A brothel scene, he commented, might now be a tearoom for all evidence to the contrary.

The damage affected LaGuardia, too. He had made himself vulnerable, and indeed faintly ridiculous, by his prudery, and now the press seized on a bizarre incident to add to his discomfiture. From Pozzonti, Italy, a citizen wrote to the mayor of New York complaining that his daughter had been seduced by an American soldier, a chief pharmacist's mate. LaGuardia could not let the matter lie. "It is my understanding," he wrote to officials in Washington, "that the navy does not countenance conduct of this kind and I trust you will see to it that proper action is taken." The wheels of the naval bureaucracy began to turn, and the soldier was ordered flown back to Italy for trial.

This was too much for the *News* and for its sidekick the *Mirror.* The pharmacist's mate was not the only soldier, the *News* opined, who ever whistled at a girl in the global war: "Indeed we are informed that at least half a dozen other guys have done the same things since Pearl Harbor." Matters were made worse for the mayor when the soldier's bride, whom he had married on his return to the U.S., undertook her husband's defense, wiring the president and in general calling attention to officialdom's clumsy-footed moralism. The young woman was not only determined, she was decidedly pretty. "Bravo for her!" cried the *Mirror.* The navy recanted and cancelled the flight on which the soldier was to have been returned to the mercies of Pozzonti's irate father. The epithet "Busy-Boy Butch" was all the reward LaGuardia got for his pains.

The next scrape into which the mayor fell at this season was far broader in scope and was played out in the glare of national publicity. It was related in a subtle way both to his fourth-term political problems and to his recent attempts to enforce moral standards. In February James Byrnes, head of the Office of War Mobilization, requested a midnight curfew on restaurants, cabarets, and bars across the country. The reasons for the request were ill-defined, but it was somehow expected that by such means fuel would be saved and strains on transportation and manpower relieved. In New York the regular hours of closing were 4 A.M. on weekdays and 3 A.M. on Sunday. LaGuardia's initial reaction was one of concern for his city's special situation; but in his regular Sunday program at the end of February he declared: "We are all soldiers and you don't question orders; you just carry them out." He went so far as to secure from the City Council and Board of Estimate a change in the laws so as to make local closing hours conform to the national curfew. A week's grace was given New York by the Washington authorities and then the curfew went into effect.

Thus matters stood when on the eighteenth of March LaGuardia suddenly adopted a posture of defiance toward Washington. At the close of his Sunday radio address he announced that henceforth New York closing hours would be 1 A.M., not midnight. Why he did this can only be surmised, but it seems probable he was troubled by his growing reputation as a puritan moralist and wanted to show that he could look indulgently on New York City's nighttime activities. More significantly, he seemed to be sending a message to Roosevelt who was being urged to endorse the regular Democratic candidate in the forthcoming mayoral election. He needed a popular issue of his own, and a stand against the curfew appeared to be precisely that.

It was now LaGuardia against Byrnes and New York against the rest of the country. The results were different from what might have been expected and can only be accounted for by the highly charged political atmosphere, combined with weariness on the home front. Among the mayors of the big cities, the men he had so often led in the past, LaGuardia found himself isolated, as Cleveland, Boston, San Francisco, and Los Angeles decided to stick with the midnight curfew. In New York the City Council fell into the hyperbole of superpatriotism, denouncing the mayor and with one member calling for his resignation. "No one can reflect on the patriotism of the people of New York City, not even its chief executive," said Councilman Sharkey of the Bronx; and Councilman Phillip of Queens, not to be outdone, asserted that for anyone who interfered with the morale of the troops in wartime, "it's too little to put him against the wall and shoot him." Even Stanley Isaacs spoke of the mayor's "indefensible lawlessness."

The *Tribune,* always suspicious of Roosevelt, could once more judge LaGuardia leniently. The *Times,* however, adopted its most righteous tone. The mayor, it said, was riding "a very high horse"; all he had done was "treat with contempt a wartime request of the United States government, give the city a black eye, and declare null and void an act of the Council and Board of Estimate." The *News* missed nothing of the fun and irony in the controversy and was pleasantly objective by its own standards. Having attacked LaGuardia as a killjoy, it now heartily defended him in his role as protector of bars and cabarets. He was the only public figure of the first rank to lift a finger in opposition to the hated curfew; he was "fighting for his people and for his own city." Nor could the *News* refrain from reflecting, with sympathy for the mayor, upon the political implications of the controversy. The big boss in Washington was repaying LaGuardia for all his services "by kicking him gaily in the seat of his pants." Seeing his dearly loved powers snatched from him, LaGuardia could profit "from some long, long thoughts about it all."

Roosevelt, who was in a position to slap down LaGuardia, actually responded rather gently. He agreed with Byrnes, he said, but there was nothing the government could do about New York. In this he was proven wrong, for the armed forces, acting independently, proceeded to forbid servicemen to be in places of entertainment after midnight. For a few days LaGuardia continued his defiance—"I'm running the city" was his comment—and then, with a rueful expression, "I tried to run the army but they wouldn't let me." As a gesture to the popular mood the restaurateurs began closing when the servicemen were ordered out. That was the end. In a nationwide broadcast on the curfew LaGuardia on March 23 upheld his 1 A.M. closing hour but described it now as a way of assuring local compliance with the Byrnes's request. His tone was conciliatory. He was still game, but he had suffered a setback when he could least afford one.

The Captains and the Kings

On April 12, 1945, Franklin Roosevelt died at Warm Springs, Georgia. The news caught millions of New Yorkers on their way home from work, spreading rapidly through the streets and public places. Men and women left subways and buses to get information; still incredulous, they stopped police and passing strangers, or joined ever-growing groups standing in silence before blaring radios. Less than an hour after the news came through, shaken and desolate, LaGuardia appeared at WNYC to speak extemporaneously for ten minutes. The president's death, he said, was "the greatest loss peace-loving people have suffered in the entire war." That evening the Philharmonic concert was cancelled, as it had been only once before—the night after Lincoln's assassination.

The captain had fallen, but the armies went on to the inevitable victory. On May 7 wild crowds surged through the streets, celebrating the end of the war in Europe. The mayor's voice, more than usually emotional, pierced the other noises in Times Square at midafternoon, urging the people who had "thoughtlessly left their jobs" to go home or back to work. There were still battles to be won in the Pacific, and men were dying "at this very moment." The flag still hung at half staff, mute reminder of the president's recent death; but at night Broadway blazed again and the curfew was lifted once and for all.

A day of unshadowed rejoicing was in the making. On August 10, after the atomic explosions over Hiroshima and Nagasaki, Japan offered to surrender; for the following four days, while the war leaders negotiated in private, the Western nations held their breath. On August 13 there was a false report of surrender; the next day U.S. air forces resumed heavy attacks. Finally, after the long waiting, the rumors, and the disappointments, a light flashed on the Times Tower a few minutes past 7 P.M. on August 14. By 7:30 a crowd of three-quarters of a million people had gathered in the square; soon two million were milling about, and the celebrations went on into the dawn.

This time no restraints were imposed on the populace. The mayor declared two days of holiday, with the coming Sunday a time of prayer. For the first time in four wartorn summers, young and old wandered carefree in Central Park. They "dropped tired feet into cool waters, and felt the warm sun sink gently into flesh, making the past seem easier to forget." A patrolman noted that youthful commandos were no longer charging up the hills of the park, armed with wooden guns and flame throwers. "Why we had more casualties here than in Okinawa," he boasted. "But it's quiet today. I haven't seen a single dead Japanese."

For those in places of responsibility, however, there was to be only a brief spell of relaxation and celebration. "We must pick up now, without delay," said the mayor, "the grand task of translating into reality and action the principles of the Atlantic Charter." For

44. With the boy from Kansas—to the sound of "3,000 peals of thunder."
June 19, 1945. MUSEUM OF THE CITY OF NEW YORK

New Yorkers, he added, the work of providing jobs and economic security for all must begin "within an hour or two."

The death of Roosevelt and the return of peace marked an epoch's passing. The change of the guard was symbolized by the comings and goings of great figures through the city which had become the crossroads of the world. In August de Gaulle made a second visit, bending almost double to bestow on the mayor the Grand Cross of the Legion of Honor. "My illustrious friend," LaGuardia addressed him, and saved him from momentary embarrassment when he moved nearsightedly to bestow upon Goodhue Livingstone a decoration intended for the equally tall Newbold Morris. But the greatest welcome had been for Dwight Eisenhower, general of the victorious armies, who came to New York in June after addressing the Congress and being cheered by Washington's entire population.

City Hall plaza was packed with a quarter of a million people as LaGuardia summed up the sentiments of the occasion! "History has yet to record the achievements of a great commander of a mighty army equal in gallantry, courage, brilliance." "You can't do that to a simple country boy from Kansas," replied the general. A noise-meter operated by General Electric characterized the cheering after Eisenhower's City Hall address as the equivalent of "3,000 peals of thunder at the same time." Afterward there was a cavalcade through Manhattan and the other boroughs, a beaming mayor at the general's side. At the Waldorf Astoria that evening, moved and inspired by New York's welcome, Eisenhower spoke without notes on behalf of all American soldiers, quietly displaying the man's innate and unaffected virtue.

The End of Fusion

In his Sunday broadcast of May 5 the mayor ended uncertainties about the fourth term, announcing that he would not be a candidate "this year." To friends and city officials in the Blue Room where he spoke the timing came as a surprise. But Eric and Jean sat with Marie across the desk from him, and before he began he had turned to each of them and asked one by one, "OK?" "OK," each replied, and he embarked upon his address.

It was one of his best—"annoying, gracious, entertaining, and courageous," the *Herald Tribune* characterized it; throughout were evidences of the man's "ardent spirit," his "tireless energy." Listening to the recorded speech today one hardly wants to differ from the judgment rendered in the emotion of the hour. Despite the heartbreaks and the defeats LaGuardia never doubted but that he could run and win again. Now he recalled Al Smith: "I could run on a laundry ticket and beat those bums any time." But it was good not to stay too long in office; those who do may become bossy— "and they tell me I am sort of inclined that way at times." The characters that so long had been denizens of his imagination were paraded forth once more—"the political riffraff, the chiselers, the racketeers, the tinhorns." LaGuardia really believed he had made progress against the evil these represented, and he believed that virtue was on his side. "Not a single boss, not a single clubhouse loafer" was to be found within his administration. If the next government were to develop corruption and inefficiency, he would come back.

Meanwhile he needed a home and a job; he appealed to "all his good real estate friends" to help him find a place to live. It would be too bad if a mayor had to hold onto office just for the sake of the house which the job provided. It was all vintage LaGuardia, free of the bitterness which sometimes played below the surface; humorous, self-deprecating, generous to his foes. And it was full of love for New York: "this city of huge spaces that are too small," he said near the close, "of millions of people that are really big."

Ahead lay a campaign which never succeeded in arousing the public. Their minds were on other things, on peace and its new opportunities; and the chief actors lacked the spark to make politics come alive. The Republicans nominated General Sessions Judge Jonah J. Goldstein, a life-long Tammany Democrat, in a move approved by Dewey who saw in the choice a boost to his own forthcoming campaign. The Republican nomination for comptroller went to McGoldrick. In May the comptroller had broken irreparably with the mayor—"nothing has given me more pain and personal grief," said LaGuardia; and nothing could have ended more decisively his ability to control the Board of Estimate. Newbold Morris, up for reelection as president of the City Council, refused to accept the Republican endorsement. Seabury denounced "the sham Fusion ticket."

The Democrats, as had been expected, nominated William O'Dwyer, the Brooklyn district attorney. He had ALP backing (as Goldstein had the backing of the newly founded Liberal party) and was favorably viewed by a united Democratic party, both in Washington and New York. Then in August, prompted by LaGuardia, Newbold Morris threw in his hat as a mayoral candidate for the hastily conceived "No Deal" party.

The launching of the party and of Morris's candidacy was LaGuardia's last political caper. His motives for doing so were obscure, no doubt even to himself. We must suppose that in the end he hated to see power pass completely from his hands and hoped through Morris, as a sort of alter ego, to preserve some part of it through the next years. Yet if he wanted Morris in office he could have exerted pressure on the Republicans to nominate him; and if he was unreconciled to being out of office himself he could have run on such an independent ticket. LaGuardia's public justification, that he feared New York would be turned over "to the political bosses, to the big-shot racketeers," did not carry water in view of his acquiescence during the nominating process.

To Republicans and members of the Liberal party the motives seemed all too plain. In backing Morris, LaGuardia was splitting the Goldstein vote. He aimed to ensure O'Dwyer's victory, it was said; he wanted to gain Democratic backing for himself in a 1946 Senate race. Alex Rose, seeing the candidate of the ALP thus indirectly

45. The ever-faithful Newbold Morris with Marie LaGuardia. The *News*

served, flayed Morris who had "long been the mayor's errand boy," and who was now embarked "on the most ignominious of all his chores." Words that stung came from the nonpartisan Citizens Union, which had backed LaGuardia in three campaigns. Condemning the mayor for "an irrational and solitary caprice," it saw him deliberately betraying the Fusionists now that they could no longer serve him.

LaGuardia vigorously denied the allegations of a deal. "When I run for office," he said, "I'll come and ask the people for the nomination." He added that he would rather starve, and see his children starve, than take anything from the bosses. When on August 8 he made his first radio speech for Morris, his blunt language seemed designed to dispel the argument that he was secretly abetting the Democrats. But the mayor could never wholly dispel the impression that he had fabricated the Morris movement either in self-interest or in a last gesture of pique against the Republicans.

Why Morris lent himself to the maneuver is also unclear. He had long answered to the mayor's wishes and, as the opposition averred, perhaps found it difficult to refuse a last appeal. In the heat of the hour, moreover, it may well have seemed to him that he represented a last hope for good government. He wasn't trying to take votes from anyone, he asserted in his disarmingly vague way; he just wanted to win. He campaigned earnestly and behind the scenes the mayor exerted all his influence to get endorsements for the No Deal candidate.

"Please give a statement for Morris—for me, please," he wrote the novelist Fanny Hurst. Wendell Willkie's widow came out for Morris; so did Moses and the world-famed journalist Dorothy Thompson. But there were rankling defections among LaGuardia's New Deal affiliates. "Now Mayor LaGuardia, who has done so much for New York, backs another good man," wrote Mrs. Roosevelt in her newspaper column—but went on to give her personal endorsement to O'Dwyer. "I love Mrs. Roosevelt like a sister," Dorothy Thompson countered, "and she knows it, but once in a while I wish she would unconfuse her mind." More painful was the endorsement of O'Dwyer by the mayor's old New Deal friend Henry A. Wallace.

In the end Morris got a considerable vote, 399,000 to Goldstein's 434,000—both of them, of course, only a fraction of the vote that made O'Dwyer mayor. With no party, with no money, and with only a hastily improvised organization, Morris had undercut Dewey and the Republicans, besides being the instrument of a surprising tribute to LaGuardia. Yet nothing could disguise the fact that the Fusion cause had come to a cloudy and unworthy end.

"I feel relieved," said the mayor quietly, leaning back in his chair when it was all over. On Election Day he was the image of a man satisfied that his work was done. "You can't stay in office indefinitely," he remarked at the polling booth when reminded that this was his last ballot as mayor. And when asked what he would do next: "I'm looking through the want ads."

Last Phase

Life went on for the mayor on other fronts than the campaign. There was business to be finished up, there were battles still to be waged, and personal plans to be worked out. Over his activities as the days went by there gathered a growing sense of *fin de régime.* Power, once it is no longer actively sought, vanishes rapidly; it leaves in those who have wielded it a feeling of emptiness, and in those who have been under its sway wonderment as to how the gap will be filled. The mayor, who had played many parts since his inauguration in 1934, was not at a loss in this last role, showing just the right mixture of sentiment and pugnacity to keep the spotlight on him to the end.

In August it was announced he had bought for $40,000 a house in Riverdale, the Bronx, close to Eric's school, a pleasant Tudor-style dwelling with its four stories on the garden side disguised in the front to look like two. As the months advanced, successive writing and broadcasting assignments were made public. He would write his autobiography, contribute a column to the evening newspaper *PM,* and a signed article to be imbedded weekly in the full-page advertisement of a New York furniture store. He would broadcast regularly on programs sponsored by *Liberty* magazine and a national dairy products company. Things were so arranged, it was noted, that New Yorkers would have the opportunity every Sunday morning, noon, and night of hearing from their ex-mayor. His successor in office was wary. "We face the future without sufficient funds, with sniping and criticism already assured," commented O'Dwyer rather ungraciously on the eve of the new administration.

LaGuardia's relations with O'Dwyer were correct, and on his part mostly friendly and magnanimous. He had always liked the tall Irishman whose career in racketbusting was after his own heart; neither the acerbities of politics, nor the fact that he had usurped the rank of brigadier general, created the animosity LaGuardia felt toward Poletti and Dewey. "Give the new mayor a chance to make good," he said publicly; "be sure you have the facts before you start shooting off the ammunition." And in a private letter addressed to "Dear Bill" immediately after the elections he offered his full cooperation "if at any time between now and January I can be of help." Information and assistance from himself and his commissioners would be available for the asking. LaGuardia added some hard-earned advice. "At best the job is tough. There can be but one mayor of the city and I certainly hope you will be it. The hardest part of the job is to say no, and to say it quickly, definitively, and emphatically."

O'Dwyer, however, remained edgy. When LaGuardia posed with him at City Hall, surrounded by photographers and reporters, "They're all waiting for me to sock you," the mayor remarked. O'Dwyer laughed, a tall figure beside the diminutive mayor, but he was a little apprehensive nevertheless.

It was in this last season, when power in the city had so largely

46. "Gather 'round, children, and I will tell you about Dick Tracy." July 8, 1945. UPI

fallen from him and when his national ambitions had been quashed, that LaGuardia engaged in a performance contributing as much to his fame as anything in the twelve years of his toilsome journey. When the name of LaGuardia is mentioned today, even among a generation too young to remember him in person, "He was the man," they say, "who read the comics to the children over the radio." Indeed, he did just that. The year 1945 saw a rash of strikes, as labor unions fought to regain what they felt had been lost to them during the war years. LaGuardia intervened in strikes of longshoremen, bus drivers, office building workers, milk producers. Finally, it was the truckers delivering newspapers who walked off the job.

On July 1, in a ninety-five-degree heat, coatless and tieless before the microphones, LaGuardia undertook to make up for what the children, at least, were missing through the silence of the press. "Gather 'round, children," he declared on his regular Sunday broadcast, "and I will tell you about Dick Tracy." With appropriate gestures, his voice rising and falling according to the requirements of the plot, he enlarged upon the adventures of the comic-strip heroes. The performance was a last-minute improvization; but he loved children, and he moved in a universe inhabited by imaginary characters as simply evil or good as those created for the comics. The response was overwhelming. The mayor announced that others would carry on the readings, morning and evening over WNYC through the week, but that he would keep himself in reserve, to return to the air as virtuoso interpreter "if necessary."

"These flamboyancies," said the *Times* at the end of the regime, recalling this incident as well as others, "may be remembered long after his more solid accomplishments have been forgotten." It was an accurate prophecy, as the one-sided memories of the future would testify. But the comic-strip episode, coming as it did when so much else had been denied him, had its own pleasantly revealing character. For the busy and the quick-witted the battle is never lost. A man like LaGuardia may draw his biggest applause when others would find the audience drifting toward the doors.

One further disappointment was, nevertheless, in store for him. In July he was invited by the French municipal authorities to represent New York in the ceremonies of the first postwar Bastille Day. It seems incredible that Washington, which had so often rebuffed his more ambitious hopes, should not have looked with favor on this modest and highly appropriate request. But the old fears of LaGuardia's independence, and perhaps old resentments, persisted, and in a small but bitter reprise there was reenacted the drama that earlier had cost LaGuardia so much pain. President Truman said he could go—but in a "personal capacity." LaGuardia rejected the terms. "This private person LaGuardia that they're talking about in Washington—I don't know him," he grumbled; and the next Sunday he directed his remarks to the president himself. When Truman goes to Potsdam, the mayor said sarcastically, he hoped he would go as president of the United States, "not in a personal capacity."

It was appropriate that among the "lasts" there should be a last fire, and in this case it was spectacular. On July 29 an army bomber en route from Massachusetts to New Jersey got lost in a blinding fog and crashed into the Empire State Building. It hit 913 feet above the New York sidewalks, embedding itself between the seventy-eighth and seventy-ninth floors. The mayor was getting out of his radio-equipped limousine, arriving at City Hall for work on a Saturday, when the fourth alarm sounded. Recognizing the number of the callbox as 34th Street and Fifth Avenue, "this could be very bad," he said, and rushed off to the scene. Amid cascades of water he walked up from the sixtieth floor to where flames were still raging and remained until they were put out. Only the fact that it was a Saturday morning, with few workers in the building, saved the casualty list from rising above the actual thirteen.

It was appropriate, too, that there should be a last row with Moses. In December, with power rapidly shifting away from the mayor, the council followed O'Dwyer's lead in cutting from the capital budget $45 million for hangars at Idlewild, as well as sums for the first-stage construction of a fruit and produce market on the Lower East Side. The entire council followed the leader then waiting in the wings—with only two abstentions, those of Isaacs and Mrs. Earle. LaGuardia, hearing the news at the Lotos Club where he was guest of honor, had immediate access to the airwaves. "Don't do it, Bill, don't do it," he pleaded, saying the act of the council "smashes to smithereens" ten years of planning for the market, and five years of hard labor at the airport.

"I endorse these decisions, support them and will not be swayed by hysterics over WNYC or elsewhere," O'Dwyer responded next day, in a carefully worded statement defending the cuts.

To LaGuardia, still fuming but now virtually powerless, it seemed evident that an influence other than O'Dwyer's had been at work. Moses was to continue under the new mayor in all his posts, with the additional responsibility of general expediter of public works. He was evidently exercising his sway, asserting his priorities, and lending the edge of his carefully honed rhetoric to O'Dwyer's statements. He was angling, too, to run Idlewild through the Port of New York Authority, by then under his complete dominance. LaGuardia had expressed to O'Dwyer in November his conviction there could only be "one mayor." Now he denounced Moses as a "supermayor" whose "fine Italian hand" was behind O'Dwyer's actions.

LaGuardia had reason to know—having lived twelve years in precarious balance with Moses's undisguised ambition.

Exit

But there came an end to the flailings, as the mood of elegy and reminiscence began to take over. One day in that last autumn Truman came to City Hall, the first president in office to visit the seat of New York's government. He was in town to review the fleet on Navy Day, seven miles of battle-gray ships, veterans of such far-off battles as Midway and Guadalcanal, Saipan and Leyte Gulf and Okinawa. For Truman it was "the happiest day of his life." We can only guess at the mayor's sentiments as he received the jaunty president. His mind must have gone back to that other Navy Day, eleven years earlier, when Roosevelt had come to New York and LaGuardia had stood proudly at his side. Now he stood with Roosevelt's successor, the man who had thwarted his hopes, one from whom he could expect no favors. "It's nice to have you here," the mayor said as he shook Truman's hand. "It's nice to be here," the president replied.

The inevitable farewell occasions took place, the last meetings, the ceremonies of departure. From Florida, where he was vacationing as usual, Cashmore proposed that the city pay $2,100 for a memorial portrait of the mayor. Action on the proposal was deferred. (Morris, offered a 1946 automobile, was heard to mutter, "I'll settle for a wheelbarrow.") At a final meeting of the U.S. Conference of Mayors a crowded Madison Square Garden echoed to emotional applause as LaGuardia took the baton and led the city's combined service bands and glee clubs. "Is this your swan song," a reporter asked. "Certainly not," replied the mayor; "I'll be writing my swan song when I lose interest in the city."

47. Farewell to City Hall. ACME

Then another mood asserted itself, and LaGuardia added: "Chopin wrote my swan song long ago."

"You mean the funeral march, Mr. Mayor?"

"That's right," he said, "that's right."

At Christmas he returned to a favorite role. "Come, children; we'll celebrate Christmas together," he announced on his Sunday broadcast. "Christmas is for children, and I'll tell you what happens when you sleep." Sleigh bells sounded outside the mayor's office as he began a recitation, complete with gestures, of *'Twas the Night Before Christmas.*

There was still to be one more of his cherished Sunday programs. Eighty guests, including most of his outgoing commissioners, gathered amid the heaped-up bundles of files, the desks shoved unceremoniously into corners with chairs piled upon them—the outward signs of a dissolving order. The audience expected some climactic denunciation of the foes who were even then cutting his last budget, but the mayor, unpredictable to the last, was all courtesy and charm. He could not, however, let the occasion pass without a few remarks on gamblers and tinhorns. And he had words for a lad who, sending in eighteen cents to pay for a light he had stolen from a park, signed himself "City Ruffian." "No, son, you are not a ruffian at all. You did the right thing in sending the eighteen cents. . . . You are a good boy."

The previous day, the Saturday which was the mayor's concluding work day, City Hall had been still a bustle of activity with crowds milling through the offices and anterooms. A contract for his autobiography was signed, a delegation of Boy Scouts received, a street ceded to Mount Sinai Hospital, and two of his appointees to the bench sworn in (LaGuardia did not forget to take care of his friends). In the midst of it a certificate was presented to J. Edgar Hoover, head of the Federal Bureau of Investigation. "Edgar," said the mayor, "I have but a few hours in office, but you still have years." For better or worse, he never spoke truer words.

On January 1 O'Dwyer was sworn in at his temporary home in Queens. The next day, his special police car returned to the city garage, LaGuardia rode down with Marie in the family's Ford sedan. Stopping at the booth of the Henry Hudson Bridge, neither he nor his wife could find the dime for the toll. "I built the damn thing," LaGuardia grumbled. "Now I have to pay for it." The office was formally turned over to the new mayor and good wishes formally expressed. Then, with a wave of his familiar hat, LaGuardia was off to his new home in Riverdale and to the life of a private citizen.

14
Epilogue—The Road Away

O'Dwyer began his administration auspiciously, managing the city with vigor and efficiency and winning wide popular support. Arthur W. Wallander, the police commissioner LaGuardia had appointed when Valentine resigned during his last months in office, was kept on, and Moses—treating the new mayor with even less deference than he had the old—continued to give a forward impulse to the multifarious activities in which he was involved. Reelected in 1949, O'Dwyer seemed ready to prove that the Democrats could run the city honestly after all, notwithstanding the public's long habituation to Fusion rhetoric identifying them with bossism and club-house cronyism. O'Dwyer, however, did not have the will to stay the course. Depressed over his private affairs and mounting rumors of public scandal, at the last minute he was stayed from making public a letter of resignation prepared while in the hospital. Some months later, still at the start of his second term, he was offered a way out by Truman, who named him ambassador to Mexico.

O'Dwyer was succeeded, in accordance with the charter, by the Democratic president of the City Council, Vincent J. Impelliteri; and he by the Democrat Robert Wagner, Jr., son of the famed senator whom Roosevelt had sought in vain to persuade to make a run for the mayoralty in 1937. Wagner had three terms, alternately being perceived as a boss and as a foe of the bosses, and was

followed by the two terms of John V. Lindsay. Thus history had
come full circle. Elected—like LaGuardia—on a Fusion ticket,
Lindsay began amid expectations that he would restore the kind of
imaginative and effective government which the city had known in
the 1930s.

The city's problems did not decline and were not solved in the
years following LaGuardia's rule. The feverish growth of office
buildings in Manhattan (fulfilling the prophecy that the city's "hidden industry" was in its communication and managerial sector)
masked only superficially the decay of other areas, where the flight
of industry combined with the in-migration of the poor, especially
minorities, undermined a once-stable social and economic life. The
budget continued to be balanced by annual appeals to Albany,
growing in desperation; by gimmicks, last-minute expediencies,
and by a rise in real estate and business taxes. The glittering bridges
and parkways of the LaGuardia epoch released the city from stran-
gulating congestion, but served (as some had predicted from the
start) to hasten decentralization and to speed the flight of residents
—no longer merely to the outer boroughs but to neighboring
municipalities and states. The schools, the hospitals, the health
centers, and the new parks suffered from a lack of maintenance and,
often subjected to vandalism and neglect, survived as sad reminders
of their builders' hopes.

Of the men around LaGuardia, Moses, as has been noted, went
on practically forever. His power within the authorities consolidated, his rule over parks appearing to be by divine right, he
continued into a stalwart old age, still harboring bitter resentments
and still capable of seductive charm. Newbold Morris, named in the
last days of LaGuardia's administration to the Planning Commission, ran unsuccessfully on a Fusion ticket for mayor in 1949. He
succeeded Moses as parks commissioner in 1960, carrying out the
latter's orders (as he had once carried out LaGuardia's) until John
Lindsay replaced him in 1966. Stanley Isaacs saw his genius for
independence fulfilled. When proportional representation was
abolished under O'Dwyer, the City Council returned to being
monolithically Democratic. Its membership, in fact, was composed
of twenty-four Democrats—and Isaacs. Contented in this minority,
Isaacs became the universal do-gooder, a member of so many diverse groups and associations that in the McCarthy period he became once more a target of the red-baiters.

Others of the old circle returned to private life or subsisted in the judicial offices to which LaGuardia had appointed them as a reward for their services. Among the figures in the cast, Gerson remained faithful to his communism to the last; Kern became a lawyer as conservative in his last years as he had been ardently liberal in his youth. Berle continued as an intermittent adviser to presidents, an influential author and speaker, keeping his gift for friendship and his talent for the prophetic phrase. Burlingham lived to be over a hundred. In 1958, his hundred first year, he attended a dinner at the Century Club where he was placed between Judge Learned Hand, the guest of honor, and Justice Felix Frankfurter. Asked afterward how he had liked the party, this ancient man, deaf and almost totally blind, replied, "It was all right, but I would have preferred meeting some *new* people."

When he retired as mayor LaGuardia had only twenty months to live. At first the big house in Riverdale was busy with callers. On Sunday friends would gather in the high-ceilinged living room, as not long before they had gathered in the Blue Room of City Hall, to listen to his broadcasts. His office at Radio City, staffed with five assistants, its letterhead bearing the image of a "little flower," was a hive of activity. He still rushed for planes as if they were determined to get away before he reached them. But his driver noticed that the old energy was missing; he would not have identified this man, on the whole so considerate and so unexpectedly patient when things went wrong, with the fiery mayor who had kept a battalion of commissioners in mortal fear.

Berle, ever-faithful, knew what it was to suffer the pangs of power suddenly denied. He had himself recently experienced them when removed from the office of assistant secretary of state. Now ambassador to Brazil, a post proffered him by Roosevelt, he urged the new president to make LaGuardia the official U.S. representative at the induction of the Brazilian president. Truman was soon enough to replace Berle as ambassador; but he acceded to this request and LaGuardia had the agreeable distraction, in the first months out of office, of making a long journey, being among friends, and embodying—as he had once hoped to do on a grander scale—the influence of the United States. He still would make a fuss at attending an official luncheon—he was used to eating only a sandwich for the midday meal, and he was loath to get into formal evening clothes. But the ambassador's wife, who was equal to most tasks, did not fail in getting the famous ex-mayor to his appointments, garbed as protocol required.

Back home, the heavy schedule of writing and broadcasting did not proceed too well. As a man of action LaGuardia had been a superb stylist, precisely matching the word to the deed. It was different being forced to rely upon the word alone. His manner was shrill, and an increasingly emphatic tone took the place of what had formerly been the official exercise of authority. One of his sponsors dropped him; his schedule was eased, but the Sunday broadcasts went on to the end. The autobiography, published posthumously, runs only through the early years and shows little of the stylistic vigor which would have marked the work as his own.

An agreeable turn of fate made him Lehman's successor in charge of the United Nations organization (UNRRA) for the distribution of postwar relief. The two old warriors who had so often exchanged insults in their days of power now vied in courtesy as the succession was arranged. LaGuardia made a trip to the Midwest, reminiscent of his picturesque forays as mayor, persuading farmers to exert maximum efforts in the production of food for the war-shattered nations. Then he set out on a tour of the European capitals.

In Copenhagen his round of official meetings was interrupted by a long-deferred reunion with his sister, Gemma Gluck. She had been transferred from Ravensbruck at the war's end to a prison near Berlin where she found herself wandering, lost and helpless with a daughter and small grandchild, as the Russians completed their bloody occupation of the capital. Communication was established with her famous brother in New York, then still the mayor, and LaGuardia helped get her transferred to Scandinavia while the formalities connected with her return to the United States were proceeding with heartbreaking slowness.

Late in 1946 he arrived at the boarding house where she was living. Twenty years, adventures on both sides, and on hers incalculable suffering, had intervened since their last meeting. "Characteristically when he arrived," Gemma wrote in her memoir, "he was unsentimental, brisk, and businesslike." He told the little family he was doing all within his power to get them to the United States, but that they would have to wait their turn in the visa quotas. They would be treated no differently from thousands of other displaced persons.

The following spring LaGuardia spent some time in Mount Sinai Hospital, and when he went home to Riverdale it was with the illness which only he seemed not to recognize as mortal. Through the summer he languished uneasily, losing weight, receiving visitors who went away shaken by the change that had come over the staunch figure they remembered. Others began taking over his Sunday broadcasts—"No, no, Newbold, put *more hell* into your talk," he admonished the man he had once mistrusted for that same mildness but had come to count among the true believers. Marie headed a conspiracy of silence in regard to the nature of his disease; old friends found themselves being kept away lest some unguarded word or look betray their despair. In September LaGuardia sank into a coma and a few days later, on September 21, 1947, at the age of sixty-four, he died of cancer of the pancreas.

Long lines of New Yorkers, stricken and only half acknowledging the fact of his death, filed past the coffin lying in the huge nave of the Cathedral of St. John the Divine. How would they and others come finally to judge the small, intense figure now reduced to eternal silence? That he had been a great mayor none would deny; that he had been a man whom flaws of temperament had cost a place at the highest level of the national pantheon would be admitted by nearly all. But he was a rare enough human being just the same! Brave, mercurial, undiscourageable; the creator of a universe as rich in odd characters as a Dickens or a Trollope, he had entertained and had faithfully served a vast populace amid the ups and downs of a turbulent epoch. In the end his accomplishments would seem less important, and perhaps less durable, than the example of his tireless energy and restless zeal. What he did was often done by magic, the true magic of politics, which makes men and women believe in symbols, and through belief makes their lives the better. That was not a small thing; and the man himself, for all his human shortcomings, was never small either.

Bibliography and
Acknowledgments

The LaGuardia administration has not heretofore been covered systematically or in a narrative history. Arthur Mann's definitive works, dealing with LaGuardia as congressman and with the 1933 campaign, were not extended into the mayoral years. Early biographies by Franklin, Rodman, and Limpus are fragmentary and touch only part of the record; Manners's more recent biography is confined to a a generalized account of the administration. Other books in the form of memoirs (e.g., Cuneo, Moses) are pleasantly anecdotal or deal with LaGuardia before he became mayor. Caro's massive biography of Moses shows LaGuardia in a reflected image, and indeed invited a further volume focused on the mayor, which Caro at one time planned to undertake. The best book on the mayoralty is Garrett's *The LaGuardia Years,* but this is organized topically and is written from the point of view of the reform movement in New York. To these and to other books listed below we owe much, as we do to magazine articles from 1933 on.

Interviews, as indicated in the notes, have been useful, and we are grateful to those who submitted to questioning or answered inquiries by letter. Unfortunately many of those whose personal testimony one would have liked to receive had passed from the scene by the time work on this book began. How one envied previous writers in the field like Garrett and Caro who could call upon the memories of such men as Kern and Windels, Berle and Newbold Morris. Several of these have left their accounts in the Oral History Project at Columbia University, of variable usefulness largely depending for their value on the skill of the questioner.

The LaGuardia Papers in the New York City Archives have been a basic and invaluable resource, comprising as they do some five hundred boxes. Arranged and indexed topically, they did not lend themselves easily to the chronological form of this book, and many of the boxes contain the chaff of any mayoral administration—formal invitations, letters from cranks, correspondence with citizens drafted by aides, etc. In many areas (the correspondence with Burlingham being a notable exception) the files are disappointing. Correspondence between the mayor and Newbold Morris, to take one example, is almost nonexistent. The same is true of Windels. This being said, the Archives provide essential illumination and are significantly supplemented by the printed reports and records in the Municipal Reference Library.

Eugene J. Bockman, commissioner of the Department of Records and Information Services, and his staff, Robert Gerometta, deputy commissioner, Idilio Gracia-Pena, director of archives, and Lillian D'Aguilar, assistant director, in a period of severe municipal cutbacks continued cheerfully and effectively to guide us and to make available these essential materials.

At Hyde Park in addition to the Roosevelt Papers are those of Berle and Tugwell. William R. Emerson, director of the Franklin D. Roosevelt Library, answered our inquiries and suggested leads in a way which greatly lightened our work. The LaGuardia Papers in the New York Public Library and the Lehman Papers at Columbia University (William B. Liebman, curator) have also been examined.

At LaGuardia Community College, Queens, New York, a collection gathered by the LaGuardia Memorial Association, under the care of Colette Wagner, contains material relevant to the administration's later years. Of particular helpfulness is an indexed file of all the transcripts of LaGuardia's Sunday broadcasts. From 1942 on, the broadcasts provide a week-by-week history of the administration, and have been freely drawn on in the text.

When all was said and done, it was the newspapers of the period that provided the essential day-to-day facts of the LaGuardia administration. What newspapers they were! And how the reporters of that day could write! LaGuardia was a figure whose words and deeds were a newspaperman's delight and the press outdid itself in covering him through his twelve years in office. We have read at least one paper, usually the *Times,* daily and Sunday throughout the period. Careful perusals were supplemented by reading in the 340 scrapbooks of newspaper clippings in the New York City Archives. The New York Society Library, presided over by Sylvia Hilton, provided agreeable surroundings for the major task of going through the rag paper edition of the *Times.* In the text much is attributed to various newspapers; much other information may be assumed to have come from these sources. Only where the date of a story is not evident, or the fact of its having come from the press might be questioned, is a reference to the daily press given in the notes.

Dr. Donald Simon read the proofs with his customary good judgment. To Christine Shipman Doscher we are indebted for a prompt and perspicacious typing of the manuscript.

A.H. and P.R.

Following is a list of the books dealing with LaGuardia, his friends and associates, and with his policies, which were put to use in this study.

Books About LaGuardia

Cuneo, Ernest. *Life with Fiorello.* New York: The Macmillan Co. 1955.

LaGuardia, Fiorello H. *The Making of an Insurgent: An Autobiography, 1882–1919.* New York: J. B. Lippincott, 1948.

Limpus, Lowell M. *This Man LaGuardia.* New York: E. P. Dutton, 1938.

Mann, Arthur. *LaGuardia: A Fighter Against His Times.* New York: J. B. Lippincott, 1959.

———. *LaGuardia Comes to Power: 1933.* New York: J. B. Lippincott, 1965.

Manners, William. *Patience and Fortitude.* New York and London: Harcourt Brace Jovanovich, 1976.

Moses, Robert. *LaGuardia: A Salute and a Memoir.* New York: Simon & Schuster, 1957.

Rodman, Bella. *Fiorello LaGuardia.* New York: Hill and Wang, 1962.

Books About Politics and Other Personalities

Allen, William H. *Why Tammanies Revive: LaGuardia's Mis-Guard.* New York: New York Institute for Public Service, 1947.

Berle, Beatrice Bishop, and Jacobs, Travis Beal, eds. *Navigating the Rapids, 1918–1971.* New York: Harcourt Brace Jovanovich, 1973.

Blanshard, Paul. *Personal & Controversial.* Boston: Beacon Press, 1973.

Caro, Robert A. *The Power Broker: Robert Moses and the Fall of New York.* New York: Alfred A. Knopf, 1974.

Clark, Ronald W. *Life of Bertrand Russell.* New York: Alfred A. Knopf, 1976

Curran, Henry. *Pillar to Post.* New York: Charles Scribner's Sons, 1941.

Dalrymple, Jean. *From the Last Row.* Clifton, N.J.: Jas. T. White & Co., 1975.

Danish, Max D. *The World of David Dubinsky.* Cleveland and New York: World Publishing Company, 1957.

Dubinsky, David, and Raskin, A. H. *David Dubinsky: A Life with Labor.* New York: Simon & Schuster, 1977.

Farley, James A. *Behind the Ballots.* New York: Harcourt Brace, 1938.

————. *Jim Farley's Story: The Roosevelt Years.* New York and Toronto: Whittlesey House, McGraw-Hill Book Co., 1948.

Flynn, Edward. *You're the Boss.* New York: Viking Press, 1947.

Garrett, Charles. *The LaGuardia Years: Machine and Reform Politics in New York City.* New Brunswick, N.J.: Rutgers University Press, 1961.

Gelfand, Mark I. *A Nation of Cities: The Federal Government and Urban America, 1933–1965.* New York: Oxford University Press, 1965.

Gluck, Gemma [LaGuardia]. *My Story.* New York: David McKay, 1961.

Ickes, Harold. *The Secret Diaries of Harold Ickes:* vol. 1, *The First Thousand Days, 1933–1936;* vol. 2, *The Inside Struggle, 1936–1939;* vol. 3, *The Lowering Clouds, 1939–1944.* New York: Simon & Schuster, 1953–1954.

Ingalls, Robert P. *Herbert H. Lehman and New York's Little Deal.* New York: New York University Press, 1975.

Isaacs, Edith S. *Love Affair with a City.* New York: Random House, 1969.

Josephson, Matthew and Hannah. *Al Smith: Hero of the Cities.* Boston: Houghton Mifflin, 1969.

Lash, Joseph P. *Eleanor and Franklin.* New York: W. W. Norton & Co., 1971.

Limpus, Lowell M. *Honest Cop: Lewis J. Valentine.* New York: E. P. Dutton and Co., 1939.

Lombardo, Jos. *Vincent Piccirilli: Life of an American Sculptor.* New York and Chicago: Pitman Publishing Company, 1944.

Mitgang, Herbert. *The Man Who Rode the Tiger: The Life and Times of Judge Samuel Seabury.* Philadelphia and New York: J. B. Lippincott, 1963.

Morris, Newbold, with Dana Lee Thomas. *Let the Chips Fall: My Battle Against Corruption.* New York: Appleton-Century-Crofts, 1955.

Moses, Robert. *Public Works: A Dangerous Trade.* New York: McGraw-Hill Book Company, 1970.

Moscow, Warren. *Politics in the Empire State.* New York: Alfred A. Knopf, 1948.

Rankin, Rebecca B., ed. *New York Advancing: A Scientific Approach to Municipal Government: An Accounting of the Citizens by the Departments and Boroughs of the City of New York, 1934–1935, F. H. LaGuardia, Mayor.* New York: Municipal Reference Library, 1939.

————, ed. *New York Advancing: The Result of Five Years of Progressive Administration in the City of New York, F. H. LaGuardia, Mayor.* World's Fair Edition; New York: Municipal Reference Library, 1939.

————, ed. *New York Advancing: Seven More Years of Progressive Administration in the City of New York, 1939–1945.* Victory Edition; New York: Municipal Reference Library, 1945.

Roosevelt, Eleanor. *This I Remember.* New York: Harper & Bros., 1949.

Salter, J. T., ed. *The American Politician* (especially "Fiorello H. La-

Guardia," by Paul Kern). Chapel Hill, N.C.: University of North Carolina Press, 1936.

Sayre, Wallace S., and Kaufman, Herbert. *Governing New York City.* New York: Russell Sage Foundation, 1960.

Schlesinger, Arthur M., Jr. *The Age of Roosevelt:* vol. 2, *The Coming of the New Deal.* Boston: Houghton Mifflin, 1960.

Shaw, Frederick. *History of the New York City Legislature.* New York: Columbia University Press, 1954.

Sherwood, Robert E. *Roosevelt and Hopkins.* New York: Harper & Bros., 1950.

Spaulding, Albert. *Rise to Follow.* New York: Henry Holt & Co., 1943.

Tugwell, Rexford G. *The Art of Politics.* Garden City, N.Y.: Doubleday & Co., 1958.

———. *Roosevelt's Revolution.* New York: Macmillan Publishing Co., 1977.

Valentine, Lewis J. *Nightstick: The Autobiography of Lewis J. Valentine.* New York: Dial Press, 1947.

Walsh, George. *Gentleman Jimmy Walker.* New York: Praeger Publishers, 1974.

Weingarten, Arthur. *The Sky Is Falling.* New York: Grosset & Dunlap, 1977.

Young, Donald, ed. *Adventure in Politics—The Memoirs of Philip La Follette.* New York: Holt, Rhinehart and Winston, 1970.

Notes

In the following notes, LaGuardia Papers refers to the personal papers of Fiorello LaGuardia in the Municipal Archives and Record Center, New York City. NYT refers to the *New York Times;* HT to the New York *Herald Tribune;* WT to the *World Telegram.* The Oral History Project at Columbia University is cited as OHP. Roosevelt Papers refers to material in the Franklin D. Roosevelt Library, Hyde Park, New York. Italicized phrases refer to passages in the text. Full references to authors cited appear in the Bibliography.

Chapter 1. Road to City Hall

NOW WE HAVE A MAYOR!

p. 16 *Rector of St. Thomas; Dr. Charles Jefferson:* NYT, Jan. 2, 1934.
Seabury's town house: Mitgang, p. 337.
Seabury spoke eight words: Usually attributed to Seabury, NYT, Jan. 2, 1934; Mann, *Power,* p. 15, the words are authoritatively said to have been spoken by Maud Seabury on whom the judge "beamed." Mitgang, p. 327. The other quotations are from NYT, Jan. 2, 1934.
p. 18 *A visitor:* Moses, *A Salute,* pp. 19–20.
"I am the majority": ibid.; also Mann, *Power,* pp. 20–22.
"Perhaps never before": NYT editorial, Jan. 3, 1934.

PRESCOTT TO BUDAPEST

Chief sources for this section are Mann, *A Fighter;* LaGuardia, *The Making of an Insurgent;* and other LaGuardia biographies.
p. 20 *"good-spirited boys":* Limpus, *This Man LaGuardia,* p. 8;
p. 21 *Consul-General Frank Chester:* Mann, *A Fighter,* p. 41.

MAKING A LIFE

p. 21   *"blonde and willowy":* Fannie Hurst, cited in Mann, *A Fighter,* p. 65. Hurst, who first knew LaGuardia as early as 1910, remained a close friend throughout his career.

p. 25   *first fired his secretary:* Limpus, *This Man LaGuardia,* p. 275, describes the marriage;

p. 26   *"he was a demagogue":* Mann, *A Fighter,* p. 323. *"good little wop":* ibid., p. 324.

INTO POWER

LaGuardia's nomination and campaign are fully described in Mann's *LaGuardia Comes to Power;* also in Mitgang and Limpus. An insider's view is given in a 1943 pamphlet by Charles C. Burlingham, "Nomination of Fiorello H. LaGuardia for Mayor of New York City in 1933."

p. 27   *to meet a man:* Stanley M. Isaacs, OHP, and substantiated in interviews. For example, Mitzi Somach (March 18, 1977): "He always believed the worst of people and nothing seemed too outrageous to be believeable. . . . He had a naturally suspicious nature; he didn't trust anyone over nine years old."

         a loud and erratic manner: A contemporary view of LaGuardia is suggested in a letter of the elder Berle, A. A. Berle, Sr., to LaGuardia, Jan. 1, 1934, LaGuardia Papers. "Your enemies expect you to rave and rant." Then exercising "an old man's privilege to give advice," Berle urges: "Never write an angry letter, never let the public see you angry; speak calmly and *not* in a high voice." Clearly, the advice was not followed.

p. 29   *not too mild a discussion":* Burlingham "Nomination . . .". *in vain Adolf Berle:* Berle, *Navigating,* p. 88. *years later Mitzi Somach:* Interview.

p. 30   *on election night:* Limpus, *This Man LaGuardia,* p. 376.

Chapter 2. Getting Started—1934

FIRST BATTLE

p. 39   *"No man in this country":* The date of the Lehman letter is Jan. 8, 1934.

p. 41   *the president was looking favorably:* NYT, Jan. 19, 1934.

BEFORE THE LEGISLATURE

p. 42   *an unprecedented activity:* WT, March 1934.
p. 43   *"Wear your rubbers":* News, Jan. 26, 1934.
p. 45   *a dramatic encounter:* HT, Mar. 7, 1934.
p. 46   *Windels . . . recalled:* Windels, OHP.
p. 47   *half of $30 million deficit:* Citizens Budget Committee, *Annual Report,* 1934.

THE NEW MEN

p. 48   *"I have sought high and low":* A full account of the selection process and of the standards applied by LaGuardia is provided in "The Political and Administrative Leadership of Fiorello H. LaGuardia as Mayor of the City of New York" by William P. Brown, an unpublished thesis for New York University, 1960.

p. 48   *a long-standing political associate:* Windels, OHP.

p. 50   *the scion of an old New York family:* The incident is described in an unpublished memorandum, "LaGuardia Anecdotes," by Fellowes Morgan, dated Sept. 1, 1968, lent by William C. Chanler.

MOSES AND PUBLIC ENJOYMENTS

p. 52   *moved with incredible swiftness:* The Moses takeover of the parks is vividly described in Caro, Chapter 20.

p. 53   *the vast resources:* The figure of 1,800 in the engineering section and 64,000 on public relief may be compared with an approximate total of 10,000 at the summer peak in the entire Parks Department during the period of major park activities in the 1960s. By the end of 1977 the engineering section had been reduced to just under 100.

  loyalty above other virtues: Moses, interview, March 22, 1977. See also Moses, *A Salute,* p. 29: "My wife once charged the mayor with lack of loyalty; he replied, 'I'm loyal to principles not to men'—a very cute rejoinder . . . that still horrifies me."

  "a wonderful creature": Burlingham to LaGuardia, Nov. 9, 1937, LaGuardia Papers.

  "no law, no regulation": NYT, Dec. 28, 1944.

p. 54   *digging a hole:* NYT, April 25, 1934.

p. 55   *"our parks commissioner":* See, e.g., April 10, 1934, broadcast address on administration's first hundred days.

  a very special occasion: The description is from various newspapers of Dec. 27, 1934.

O'RYAN AND PUBLIC ORDER

p. 58   *"I don't want your help":* The Gaynor incident and the Brooklyn expedition are described in the newspapers of June 3 and March 8, 1934.

THE DEPRESSION IN NEW YORK

p. 61   *"dead against private charity":* Mann, *A Fighter,* p. 295.

  inescapable charge: NYT, Jan. 24, 1934. Note also Hodson's first communiqué on becoming commissioner: Every worker, from watchman to department head, was to receive all applicants and listen to their stories "as if they were relations, neighbors, or friends." The source is NYT, Jan. 21, 1943, Hodson's obituary. Hodson was killed in a plane accident in Dutch Guiana on temporary leave with Lehman, then director of UNRRA.

p. 62   *"hundreds drift here":* L. H. Robbins, "The City Relief Program," NYT, Sept. 23, 1934.

p. 63   *"turgid cauldron of resentments":* Ibid.

p. 64   *unsung park worker:* For a curious repetition of this incident, see August Heckscher, *Alive in the City* (New York: Charles Scribner's Sons, 1974), pp. 94–98.

p. 66   *a story is told:* Manners, p. 175.

A BREATHING SPACE

p. 69   *an old gray horse:* NYT, July 3, 1934.

p. 71   *"the Athens of Pericles":* Emma Fuller Barnard, *NYT Magazine,* Sept. 23, 1934. The Goldman Band concert is described in NYT, Aug. 15, 1934.

A First Round of Politics

p. 74 *LaGuardia once confided:* Windels, OHP.
       the Lehman files: Lehman Papers, Columbia University.
p. 75 *"running only as a Republican":* Norman Thomas, OHP.

New Taxes

p. 80 *"happiest time of his life":* Gelfand, p. 48.
       "Attaboy, Fiorello": Cited in Mann, *A Fighter,* p. 304. The whole fight
       against the sales tax is vividly described in this source.
p. 81 *"ingenious little devil":* NYT, Dec. 6, 1934.

Chapter 3. In the Thick of the Fight—1935

New York–Washington Axis

p. 83 *no further than the Bronx:* NYT, May 9, 1935.
p. 85 *trying to "navigate" New York:* Berle, p. 92.

Between Two Fires

p. 86 *"asked me to take over":* Moses, *Public Works,* p. 177.
       "stop building patronage": NYT, Feb. 6, 1934.
       something of a mystery: Ickes to Burlingham, Aug. 13, 1948: "I never
       knew the root of the high feeling that existed between FDR and
       Moses, but I do know how implacable it was"; Moses, *Public Works,* p.
       181.
p. 87 *"one of the things you cannot do"* (and the president's reply): Berle, p.
       92.
p. 88 *"I am mayor of this city"* (and following quotes): NYT, Jan. 4, 5, 18; Feb. 1.
p. 89 *the mighty "News":* Feb. 7, 1935.
       Ickes squirmed: Ickes, *Diaries,* Jan. 9, 1935.
p. 90 *a letter of April 15:* LaGuardia Papers.
       "the cheapest kind of double-crossing politician": Ickes, *Diaries,* Jan. 9,
       1935.
       an aftermath with comic overtones: This incident, including the Prospect
       Park dedication, is described in the NYT, July 4, 1935. Various direct
       quotes are from this source.

Riot in Harlem

The course of the riot is taken from the contemporary press. For conditions in
Harlem in the 1930s, see Oscar Handlin, *The Newcomers* (Cambridge, Mass.:
Harvard University Press, 1959), p. 48.
p. 94 *"I am as helpless":* NYT, July 23, 1936. LaGuardia's overall dealing
       with the problem of the blacks is favorably summarized in Garrett, pp.
       253–254.

Issues of Reform

The fullest account of the LaGuardia reforms is to be found in the three
editions, 1936, 1939, 1945 of *New York Advancing,* edited by Rebecca
Rankin, containing reports of department heads and introductions by the
mayor. Though partisan, these present a wealth of information. Garrett's *La-
Guardia Years* provides the most scholarly analysis of reform; see especially
Chapter 11, "The Welfare City."

p. 97 *a municipally owned power plant:* For background, see City Affairs Bulletin, "The Public Utilities Situation," Feb. 1935.
"a good day's work": NYT, Feb. 2, 1935.
"a nice little word": NYT, Dec. 20, 1934.
p. 98 *a dramatic day in Albany:* NYT, March 25, 1936.
"this is not final": NYT, Feb. 26, 1940.
p. 99 *"education would cost":* Langdon Post, in NYT, Nov. 22, 1936.

ARTS IN THE CITY

p. 100 *a practiced player:* He put the cornet aside and never played again after Thea's death.
Harold Taubman: NYT, Oct. 4, 1939.
p. 101 *"a work of art should be beautiful":* NYT, June 10, 1937.
an outdoor sculpture show: NYT, May 5, 1938.
Attilio Piccirilli: See Lombardo, *Piccirilli.*
to get artists off the relief roles: Russell Owen, *NYT Magazine,* March 3, 1935.
p. 102 *"I admire you a great deal":* LaGuardia Papers, Oct. 13, 1938.
the Museum of Modern Art acquired: A letter to Berle from Carleton Sprague Smith, Jan. 14, 1937, Berle Papers, Personal Correspondence, Hyde Park, sums up Berle's proposal for an art and music center "just north of Rockefeller Center" to face a square on land to be purchased by the city.
p. 103 *"Mr. Berle is doing some investigating for me":* This and other quotations to end of section are from the LaGuardia Papers, September 1938.
Moses was to be in charge: Moses's concern with cultural institutions was to continue beyond 1937. A major report to LaGuardia, Mar. 2, 1941, reviewed the situation of museums, characteristically attacking the establishment. The cultural institutions must abandon their "sacred" and "exclusive" atmosphere, must "let down the bars," and should end self-perpetuating boards. He declared the New York Historical Society to be dead. The *Times* supported much of the report, adding, "Mr. Moses hurts his argument as he has often done before, by his vehemence and unfairness." The mayor received the report in silence.

CRIME FIGHTER

p. 106 *"a terrible man to work with":* Norman Thomas, OHP.
p. 107 *"ill-tempered ex-police officer":* NYT, Sept. 26, 1934.
no stranger to the mayor: Limpus, *Honest Cop,* p. 157.
"we create the precedents": NYT, Feb. 17, 1934.
on the night before the election: Limpus, *This Man LaGuardia,* p. 397. It is plain from the context that the friendly newspaperman is Limpus himself.
p. 109 *"muss 'em up":* NYT, Nov. 27, 1934. Valentine had used the same phrase several weeks previously; Valentine, *Nightstick,* p. 177 ff. *Burlingham pleaded*—Burlingham to LaGuardia, Nov. 28, 1934, LaGuardia Papers.
p. 110 *"not the time for coddling crooks":* NYT, Jan. 27, 1935.
with the acid remark: LaGuardia to Lehman, July 3, 1935, LaGuardia Papers.
p. 112 *"I remember it well":* Fellowes Morgan to Arthur Mann, Jan. 26, 1958.

Chapter 4. Toward the Zenith—1936

PRIVATE MAN

p. 113 *seeing it for the first time:* Limpus, *Honest Cop,* p. 157.
         buy a new rug: Limpus, *This Man LaGuardia,* p. 376.
         "I am perfectly happy": News, Nov. 5, 1941.
         what first impressed the congressman: Limpus, *This Man LaGuardia,* p. 32.
         a rather surprising account: Ibid., p. 153.

p. 114 *refrained from giving advice:* Marie LaGuardia, interview.
         his wife called LaGuardia: Wm. Fellowes Morgan memorandum, "More
         Anecdotes About FHL," dated Sept. 1, 1968, lent by William C. Chanler.
         he liked her to wear black: Mitzi Somach, interview.
         "I had a good secretary once": NYT, Oct. 25, 1939.
         LaGuardia loved children in general: "If the children of this city were its
         electors the mayor would be re-elected by their votes alone," Stanley
         Howe, April 12, 1939. In his "tenement" home LaGuardia kept a wall
         covered with photographs of children in various moods and poses.
         "lending" one's child: Henry F. Pringle, "Let Fiorello Do It," *Harper's*
         Magazine, Nov. 1941.

p. 115 *long in orphan homes:* Dr. George Baehr, interview.
         inconvenience of this arrangement: Ibid.

p. 116 *enjoying one of his father's speeches:* The letters referred to in this section are
         in the LaGuardia Papers: LaGuardia to Julius Ochs Adler, Nov. 11, 1936;
         to John D. Rockefeller III, Jan. 4, 1937; to Rev. W. R. Cruickschank, Sept.
         12, 1935; to Ernest Gruening, March 20, 1942; to the Danish consul-
         general, Aug. 25, 1939. The last letter has an addition in LaGuardia's
         handwriting, emphasizing his insistence on the kind of treatment Eric was
         to receive.
         a stranger in the New York streets: Letter to LaGuardia, in the LaGuardia
         Papers, April 3, 1943.

p. 117 *Piccirilli was a fixture:* Marie LaGuardia, interview. The quotation from
         Piccirilli is from a galley proof in the LaGuardia Papers.
         friends from the mayor's past: LaGuardia to Mrs. Gussie R. Knight, Dec. 15,
         1933, May 24, 1935; to Lynn C. Stockton, July 1937, April 1944; to
         Charles L. Kohlen, Dec. 29, 1939; LaGuardia Papers.

p. 118 *letters of condolence:* Burlingham to LaGuardia, Feb. 1935, LaGuardia Pa-
         pers.
         relations with his sister: See Gluck, pass.
         a surviving letter: Yolandez Gluck to LaGuardia, July 16, 1934, LaGuardia
         Papers.

p. 119 *noncommittal:* See, e.g., E. J. Gans to LaGuardia Oct. 1, 1945; reply, Oct.
         30, 1945.
         knowledge of Irene's whereabouts: LaGuardia to W. P. Walters, April 19,
         1943.

UNDER THE CZARS

p. 121 *Johnson arrived:* HT June 20, 1936.
p. 122 *"rats and vermin":* NYT, April 3, 1936.
p. 123 *LaGuardia's protégé:* NYT, Feb. 10, 1936.
p. 125 *families trading children:* Brooklyn *Eagle,* April 28, 1938.
         the butt of endless jokes: NYT, March 12, 1939.

THE NEW CHARTER

p. 127 *found sleeping:* NYT, May 22, 1934.
p. 129 *proposed [planning] commission:* For a review of the basic principles involved, see Mark I. Gelfand, "Politics and the Public Interest: LaGuardia, Moses, Tugwell, and Planning in New York City, 1936–1941," Preliminary Draft, Boston College, Spring 1977.
a later evaluation: Sayre and Kaufman, p. 17.

EXILE IN THE BRONX

p. 131 *dedication of the Triborough:* From contemporary press; also Caro, pp. 441–443.
p. 134 *"I am lonely":* WT, Nov. 22, 1935.
a ferry ran: Bryan, interview; also contemporary news reports.
p. 136 *Polly Adler's principality:* For justifications of this raid, see Limpus, *Honest Cop,* p. 191 ff; Valentine, *Nightstick,* p. 192.
"God almighty": NYT, Aug. 17, 1936.
p. 137 *"much easier to tell the other fellow":* NYT, Aug. 13, 1936.

LABOR, PROGRESSIVES, AND FDR

p. 137 *tides were running:* LaGuardia, *Liberty Magazine,* April 15, 1936.
p. 138 *burning all our bridges: Sun,* Sept. 11, 1936; LaGuardia to Burlingham, April 25, 1942; LaGuardia Papers.
p. 139 *the senior A. A. Berle:* A. A. Berle to FDR, Sept. 16, 1936, Roosevelt Papers.
p. 142 *"septuagenarian Amazon":* NYT, Dec. 2, 1936.

Chapter 5. Vindication—1937

GOVERNMENT WITH A SOUL

p. 144 *as a congressman he had fought:* Mann, *A Fighter,* pp. 330–331.
p. 145 *"government with a soul":* See, e.g., LaGuardia's preface to Rankin, *New York Advancing,* Third Edition (1939).
"make our people happy": Speech at opening of Brooklyn market, Oct. 3, 1939.
"I Have Heard of a City Called Heaven": Burlingham, OHP.
p. 146 *"Adversity is not good":* NYT, May 7, 1936.
Fellowes Morgan was the link: See Morgan, *Confusion to Fusion,* My Eight Years as NYC's Commissioner of Markets from 1934 through 1941 under Mayor Fiorello H. LaGuardia," *Produce News,* October 1967.
p. 147 *"If the milk people come in":* Goodhue Livingston, interview, April 21, 1977.
p. 149 *hurdy-gurdies:* The LaGuardia Papers contain a file of letters from citizens on behalf of the organ-grinders. The letters quoted here, including those in support of the mayor, are from that source.
p. 150 *scarring incident of his youth:* For LaGuardia's own account of the roots of his antipathy, see LaGuardia, *Autobiography,* pp. 27–29. In *Public Works,* Moses recounts that Clara Thomas, an artist who had become annoyed at both the mayor and the parks commissioner, embodied in a mural for the Bowery Savings Bank a representation of LaGuardia as an organ-grinder with Moses as the monkey. Although Moses, thumbing his nose, is recognizable, the organ-grinder does not remotely resemble the mayor.

p. 151 *"it was so unnecessarily high"*: Cocteau's comments are from NYT, June 10, 1936; the lord mayor of Liverpool's views are from NYT, June 5, 1936.

SERVING THE MAYOR

p. 152 *"somewhat theatrical person"*: Palmieri, interview, April 11, 1977.
"ruthless taskmaster": Blanshard, *Personal and Controversial.*

p. 153 *law aide down a peg:* Undoubtedly LaGuardia had reasons for not wishing to share his memos with the transit officials at that time.

p. 154 *"when do they eat?"*: Curran, cited in Berle, pp. 147–148.
"your oranges arrived": Stone's telegram, May 19, 1937, LaGuardia Papers.
to Kenneth Dayton: Oct. 10, 1939, LaGuardia Papers.

p. 155 *a bone to those officials:* Fellowes Morgan, "Anecdotes," dated Sept. 1, 1968, lent by William C. Chanler.
the most bizarre of summonses: Walter Binger, interview, Feb. 7, 1977.

p. 156 *never met without fighting:* Captain James E. Harten, the office guard, thought Moses was particularly likely to erupt when the moon was full. He feared cranks at such times and increased the police on duty at City Hall.
Moses characterized the attitude: Moses, *A Salute,* p. 30.
"roared with laughter": Chanler, interview, March 24, 1977.

p. 157 *"quiet talk"*: Berle, p. 138.

p. 159 *Windels family lived next door:* Paul W. Windels, Jr., interview, Feb. 2, 1977.

NEW YORK'S FOEIGN POLICY

p. 161 *"dismembered the Hapsburg"*: LaGuardia, *Autobiography,* p. 124.
"Il Progresso" called upon Italians: Cited in *NY Post* editorial, Dec. 14, 1935.

p. 162 *"I run the subways"*: *NY Post,* March 25, 1936.
Italian concert: Ibid.; Norman Thomas, OHP.

p. 163 *"chamber of horrors"*: Ickes, *Diaries,* Mar. 6, 1937.
"I snapped to attention": NYT, April 14, 1945.

POLITICAL CAULDRON

p. 165 *the subtle New York County leader:* The best account of Simpson is Noel F. Busch, "Boss Without a Cigar," *The New Yorker,* October 28, 1939.
"yes he is an SOB": Garrett's interview with McGoldrick, cited in Garrett, p. 388.

p. 166 *"Well, Bob, I bet three to one"*: Ickes, *Diaries,* July 16, 1937.

p. 167 *This is serious business:* Berle, p. 127.

p. 169 *it was Simpson's turn:* Busch, "Boss Withouc a Cigar," is the source for the following paragraphs; also, Limpus, *This Man LaGuardia,* p. 406. Limpus refers to Simpson's role in choosing the ticket as "one of the most successful coups d'états New York had seen in years."

p. 171 *"Dewey's vanity"*: Berle, p. 130.
uncongenial running mate: Stanley Isaacs, OHP.

GREAT CAMPAIGN

Sources for the campaign of 1937, in addition to Noel Busch's article "Boss Without a Cigar," include "Tammany and Fusion, 1933–1937, Must History Repeat Itself?" *City Affairs Committee Bulletin,* September 1937; *New York Politics,* November 1937, Roy Fielding, ed.; Max, Lerner, "Tammany's Last Stand," *The Nation,* September 11, 1937; Ickes, *Diaries,* vol. 2; William A. Hays, *Why Tammanies Revive;* James A. Farley, *The Roosevelt Years;* and Windels, OHP. The Kismet Temple meeting is graphically covered in Limpus, *This Man LaGuardia,* p. 407.

p. 000 *with a mighty tug:* NYT, Oct. 7, 1937.

p. 175 *a special-delivery letter:* Paul Windels, OHP. Goodhue Livingston, interview, states that several years afterward LaGuardia still kept the letter in the drawer of his desk. On its face the letter seems strangely noncommittal. LaGuardia wrote Roosevelt (Oct. 18, 1937) thanking him for help in averting a subway strike through loan of a member of the National Mediation Board. Roosevelt routinely asked Secretary Perkins to draft a reply. A memorandum from her (Oct. 26) encloses the draft, which, after a simple acknowledgement, included the sentence: "all of you who participated in bringing about such a settlement are to be congratulated." Marvin McIntyre suggested to the president: "You probably will not want to sign this until after next Tuesday." Roosevelt nevertheless signed it and ordered it mailed by special delivery (Roosevelt Papers).

his own role in the campaign: Ickes, *Diaries,* Nov. 6, 1937.

p. 177 *Ickes met him:* Ibid., Oct. 23, 1937.

VICTORY AND ITS AFTERMATH

p. 179 *Farley in his memoirs:* Farley, *Roosevelt Years,* p. 102.

p. 181 *Charles Abrams . . . resigned:* LaGuardia, speaking before the U.S. Conference of Mayors, attacked Abrams for what he called the "semi-colon type of speech" and accused him of "looking for fly specks," NYT, Nov. 23, 1937.

Langdon Post . . . agreed not to attend: Langdon Post, *The Nation,* January 9, 1938, pp. 145–146.

p. 183 *"sparkling and witty":* Ickes, *Diaries,* Dec. 12, 1937.

the last meeting of the board: NYT, Dec. 22, 1937.

Chapter 6. Feel of Power—1938

THE NEW GOVERNMENT

The first days of the second term were reported extensively by the press. On January 2 the *Times* City Hall reporter, William R. Conklin, wrote a probing appraisal of the new government. And in succeeding weeks the *World Telegram* wrote a series of profiles of some of the new figures in the administration.

p. 188 *headed by Berle:* In addition the members of the first Planning Commission were: Cleveland Rodgers, Lawrence Orton, Edwin A. Salmon, and Arthur Sheridan.

"damn good political letter": Chanler, interview.

p. 189 *"ole Uncle Franklin":* Berle, p. 96.

"I'm off to settle the Chinese question": Cited in Moses, *A Salute,* p. 21.

"will be able to come back": NYT, Feb. 10, 1938.

the large photograph of Franklin Roosevelt: Brooklyn *Eagle,* Feb. 6, 1938.

"important thing is to keep alert": WT, Feb. 25, 1938.

like Mussolini's office: Anna H. Clark, interview.

ORGANIZING THE COUNCIL

p. 190 *"one of the brightest stars":* NYT, Jan. 1, 1938.

a conventional route: The sources for Morris's early life are his autobiography, *Let the Chips Fall,* and his reminiscences in OHP.

p. 192 *"We'll just debate quietly":* Morris, OHP.

p. 193 *"not a majority of twenty-six":* The council's stormy proceedings were cov-

ered in detail by the press. For Morris's account, see *Let the Chips Fall* and
OHP. We are also indebted to the manuscript of a memoir by Robert K.
Straus, in the author's possession.

p. 193 *defeat of the county reform bill:* The record of the first council is analyzed in
City Affairs Bulletin, The City Council.

STANLEY ISAACS AND HIS STRANGE PROTÉGÉ

Isaacs's reminiscenses in the Columbia Oral History Project are the source for his
personal history and for his version of the Gerson affair. See also Edith Isaacs's
memoir of her husband, *My Love Affair with New York.*

p. 195 *correspondence between these two men:* The letters are in the LaGuardia Papers.

p. 196 *"get the boys off my neck":* Cited in Edith Isaacs, p. 47.

p. 197 *"this won't last":* Ibid., p. 48.

BIT BETWEEN HIS TEETH

p. 197 *one of the best speeches:* Full text, LaGuardia Papers; Transit Commission
statement, NYT, Feb. 22, 1938.

p. 199 *New York Bar Association address:* NYT, April 20, 1938.
"keep a careful record": LaGuardia Papers; HT, May 11, 1938.
"In my opinion your attacks": Burlingham to LaGuardia July 20, 1939;
LaGuardia's reply is dated July 31, 1939; LaGuardia Papers.

p. 200 *"wander almost at will":* HT editorial, April 22, 1938.

FIGHTING FOR HOME RULE

p. 200 *"most expensive luxury":* NYT, March 1, 1938.

p. 201 *"mayor cannot print money":* NYT, Feb. 26, 1938.
a letter to Albany: Exchange of correspondence between Lehman and La-
Guardia, NYT, March 8, 11, 1938.

p. 203 *The La Follette brothers . . . announced:* In his memoirs, Philip LaFollette
writes that Berle was the only prominent liberal at the meeting. Brother
Bob was not much more enthusiastic than LaGuardia; Young, *Adventure
in Politics,* p. 255.
"Mayor LaGuardia works hard": NYT editorial, April 27, 1938.

SUMMER IN QUEENS

p. 204 The quotations are from NYT.

p. 208 *"don't worry too much about the convention":* LaGuardia to Charles Poletti,
Aug. 26, 1938, Herbert H. Lehman Papers.

WINNING THE WEST

The western trip in September was widely covered by the press around the country
as well as by reporters traveling with the mayor. Quotations, pp. 263–266 are from
NYT.

LEHMAN OR DEWEY?

p. 213 *ill-fated "purge":* Though in other primaries of that year Roosevelt's intervention on behalf of liberal candidates was self-defeating, LaGuardia's
support assured the nomination of James H. Fay in his primary race against
John O'Connor in the 16th Congressional District.
"trained since boyhood": NYT, June 26, 1938.

p. 215 *no direct word of support:* An undated memo of Poletti's in the Lehman

Papers, headed "LaGuardia's position on Re-election of Lehman," purports to show that LaGuardia had never supported Lehman in any of his elections.

p. 216 *"the mayor didn't get my vote"*: NYT, Dec. 21, 1938.

Chapter 7. Signs and Portents—1939

THE CHALLANGE OF ROBERT MOSES

p. 218 *quasi-sovereign department:* Caro, p. 268 ff. The Moses style and tactics were still much talked of by older employees of the department when the author became parks commissioner in 1967.

p. 219 *William Chanler recalled:* Chanler, interview. In any case LaGuardia would have objected to the young man: "I don't want any lawyer sitting around to decide what's in the city's interest. Keep them out of my meetings," LaGuardia could scream; ibid.

p. 220 *a crucial exchange:* Moses to LaGuardia, LaGuardia to Moses, Moses to LaGuardia, April 7, 11, 12, 1939, LaGuardia Papers.

p. 221 *at least his equal:* Caro, p. 636.
Morris refused: NYT, Dec. 2, 1938; the story of the "bale of hay," ibid.

BRIDGE OR TUNNEL?

p. 224 *"it is most unseemly":* LaGuardia to Tunnel Authority, March 1, 1939, LaGuardia Papers.

p. 226 *Burlingham wrote:* Burlingham to LaGuardia, April 10, 1939, LaGuardia Papers.
"problem child": June 6, 1939.

p. 227 *"Verb. suf. sap."* ("a word to the wise . . ."): Burlingham to FDR, April 10, 1939, Roosevelt Papers.

p. 228 *"Nevertheless we did it":* Television interview with Moses, WNET, April 5, 1977. For Moses's side of the bridge controversy, see Moses, *Public Works,* p. 197 ff.

TUGWELL, GLOOMY PROPHET

p. 228 *Casualties of the bridge fight:* See, e.g., *Sun,* July 19, 1939: "The commission bore out the old-fashioned, if cynical belief, that an appointed body is likely to be subservient to its creator."

p. 229 *Bureau of the Budget showed its jealousy; mayor too was circumspect:* These and other issues in the establishment of the Planning Commission are discussed in Mark I. Gelfand, "Politics and the Public Interest: LaGuardia, Moses, Tugwell, and Planning in New York City, 1936–1941," p. 38 ff.
markedly handsome: Maxine Block, ed., *Current Biography, Who's News and Why, 1941,* (New York:) H. W. Wilson Company, 1941.
taking a visitor: John C. Chamberlain, "Mayor LaGuardia," *Yale Review,* Autumn 1939.

p. 231 *a small-town physician:* NYT, March 27, 1940.

p. 232 *on one occasion:* Moses, interview, March 22, 1977.
played the injured party: Ickes, *Diaries,* May 17, 1941.

Wit and Wisdom of a Deputy Mayor

p. 233 *"deputy mayor? What's that?":* Curran, pp. 345–346.
p. 234 *Burlingham urged:* Burlingham to LaGuardia, April 7, 1939, LaGuardia Papers.
p. 235 *"certainly a cute trick":* NYT, Feb. 11, December 3, 1939.
        deputy mayor's downfall: NYT, Feb. 14–18, 1939.
p. 236 *LaGuardia called Curran:* Curran, p. 362.
        in stinging words: Moses, *A Salute,* p. 125.

Mayor on the Move

p. 236 *"like a swarthy Buddha":* Blanshard, p. 143.
p. 237 *"what set him popping":* Henry F. Pringle, "Let Fiorello Do It," *Harper's* magazine, Nov. 1941.
        in the wooden army buildings: Gluck, p. 7, *"I hate the damn things":* Broadcast to South Africa, Dec. 12, 1943.
        suspected of containing a bomb: NYT, Sept. 7, 1940.
p. 240 *into the pitcher's box:* Chamberlain, "Mayor LaGuardia," *Yale Review,* Autumn, 1939.
        problems of the farmer: Sun, June 23, 1939.
        LaGuardia's journeys: NYT, March 17, 1939,
p. 241 *one day he would fly:* David Rockefeller, interview.
        "a dream village": NYT, Feb. 2, 1939.
        "my bones ache": NYT, Oct. 2, 1939.
p. 242 *"A strike which did not happen":* LaGuardia to FDR, Oct. 18, 1937, Roosevelt Papers.
p. 243 *"too long to wait":* NYT, Jan. 18, 1940.
        at the end of one afternoon: Anna Rosenberg, interview.
        the mayor's manner and style: Tugwell, *Art of Politics,* p. 27.

World's Fair—From Peace to War

p. 244 *"I'm not coming alone":* LaGuardia to Florence Kahan, Feb. 14, 1938, LaGuardia Papers.
p. 246 *even larger than the Blue Room:* HT, May 12, 1938.
        "Don't you ever get tired?": John Haynes Holmes to LaGuardia, Sept. 10, 1939, LaGuardia Papers.

The Mayor Stumbles

p. 249 *on one occasion Dorothy Kenyon:* Kenyon to LaGuardia, June 3, 1939; LaGuardia to Kenyon, June 6, 1939; LaGuardia Papers.
p. 250 *"regret for the article:* LaGuardia's letter to Straus of Sept. 27 was published in NYT, Oct. 11, 1939.
p. 251 *"not the remotest idea"* NYT, Dec. 12, 1939.

His Own Airport

p. 251 *landed at Newark:* NYT, Nov. 24, 1934.
p. 252 *Roosevelt reviewed plans:* Tugwell, *Roosevelt's Revolution,* p. 45.
        "It was his own baby": Marie LaGuardia, OHP.
p. 254 *in the men's lounge:* NYT, Jan. 14, 1940.

Chapter 8. The Broader Stage—1940

COUNCIL *V.* MAYOR

p. 259 *"the sergeant-at-arms is asleep":* NYT, Feb. 7, 1940.

Alfred E. Smith, Jr.: Moses (interview, March 22, 1977) denied having set him on the Kern investigation.

p. 260 *Paul Kern:* Evaluation based on interviews with Stanley Kreutzer (Kern's lawyer in his suit against the city, June 2, 1977), Chanler, Moses, Palmieri, and others. Kern's first meeting with LaGuardia as well as other quoted phrases are from WT, Feb. 2, 1938. An article "Fiorello H. LaGuardia" by Paul Kern shows the two men at their best before the relationship became embittered: in Salter, *American Politician.*

p. 263 *Kern's style of behavior:* Straus, who was Kern's strongest defender in the council, states: "gradually over the two years the investigation lasted, I became very disenchanted" (memoir by Straus, in possession of the author).

TAKING ON MR. QUILL

p. 267 *carrying mail:* The proposal came up at a cabinet meeting where Ickes opposed it. A White House memorandum to the postmaster general approving the plan was ordered destroyed by FDR; Ickes, *Diaries,* April 1941.

p. 268 *New Republic:* May 5, 1941.

Quill . . . made him mad: Palmieri documented this hatred (interview). LaGuardia would not allow Quill in City Hall, and when Quill proposed a subway strike John L. Lewis came to town to intercede. In a conference at which Palmieri was the only other person present, LaGuardia said: "I want you to know, Lewis, that no one is going to pull a subway strike, especially not that god-damned friend of yours. . . . Tell him to take the next boat back to Ireland." Lewis: "Come, come, we're reasonably good Americans." LaGuardia (screaming): "Reasonably good Americans! . . ." and thereupon let out a stream of obscenities which, according to Palmieri, made the encounter "memorable."

Lilienthal . . . wrote to Berle: LaGuardia Papers, March 20, 1940.

THE CASE OF THE NOBLE EARL

p. 269 *In a book:* Quotations from Russell's *Marriage and Morals* and other works are cited in Tuttle memorandum, Tuttle to LaGuardia, March 18, 1940, LaGuardia Papers.

p. 270 *Bishop Manning:* For Manning's attitude, see Clark, p. 430.

p. 271 *"not a prude":* Address to news vendors, Aug. 20, 1940, LaGuardia Papers.

his attitude . . . was old-fashioned: Anna H. Clark and Mitzi Somach, interviews.

p. 272 LaGuardia Papers are the source of quotes and documents in the Russell case including the Tuttle memorandum; the Dewey and Burlingham letters; LaGuardia's letters to Bishop Manning and to Chanler. Justice McGeehan and the Luther portrait is from Clark. The repentant member of the Board was I. A. Hirschmann. Russell's letter to the *Times* is April 26, 1940. See also "The Russell Case," *Nation,* April 6, 1940.

TOWARD A NATIONAL POST

p. 275 *exemplary detachment:* Walter Binger, Memorandum, Jan. 17, 1977, to authors, quotes LaGuardia: "The son of a wop who lives in a tenement doesn't become vice-president."
Berle came up: Berle, p. 194.

p. 276 *"various and strange things":* Ibid., p. 353.
"few men have the courage": Ickes, *Diaries,* March 15, 1940.

p. 277 *"I was confident":* Tugwell, *Art of politics,* p. 95.

p. 278 *memo to the president:* Berle to FDR, May 20, 1940, Roosevelt Papers.

ALL OUT FOR FDR

p. 283 *attitudes . . . were complex:* See *Gentleman Jimmy Walker* by George Walsh, foreword by Robert Moses.

p. 284 *afterward Robert Sherwood:* Sherwood, p. 186.
"a broker between nationality groups": Schlesinger, p. 133.

Chapter 9. Two Steps Forward . . . 1941

POLITICAL PROSPECTS

p. 290 "I rejoice in your joy": NYT, April 20, 1941.
looked into the future: Berle, p. 307.

p. 291 *stricken and died:* A former parks commissioner of Brooklyn, Ingersoll is buried in Prospect Park.
he turned to city problems: Amid these vexations (February 1941) he appointed Herbert A. O'Brien to the Domestic Relations Court. The correspondence in the Archives indicates that the man (besides being a sympathizer with totalitarian regimes) was a colossal bore. The appointment raised an uproar in New York and Washington. This was the occasion for LaGuardia's immortal remark, "When I make a mistake, it's a beaut."

p. 292 *Straus, almost alone:* Memoirs by Straus, in the possession of the author.

TROUBLED FINANCES

p. 293 *newly established Department of Commerce:* The actual cause of the resignation was the mayor's firing of Ryan's deputy on the recommendation of Ethel Epstein (LaGuardia's labor advisor) while Ryan was on vacation.
in the field of pensions: For background on pensions, see speech by Harold Riegelman, counsel to Citizens Budget Commission, Dec. 20, 1939, Citizens Budget Commission report; also, 1938 *Annual Report.*

p. 295 *"ignorant, bombastic":* NYT, May 27, 1941.
"like a drunken sailor": Councilman Jos. T. Sharkey, March 25, 1941.
"conceived in despair": April 1, 1940, cited in the Citizens Budget Committee report.

CIVILIAN DEFENE

p. 297 *"unhappy noises":* James Rowe, memorandum to the president, April 21, 1941, Roosevelt Papers.
acting as intermediary: Anna Rosenberg to FDR, May 6, 1941, Roosevelt Papers.
immense patriotic rally: Description taken from *Time* Magazine, May 26, 1941.

p. 299 *as close to a routine:* Henry Pringle, "Let Fiorello Do It," *Harper's,* Nov. 1941.

Stimson was impressed: Stimson to Burlingham, April 23, 1942, LaGuardia Papers.

p. 301 *a job for his old friend:* LaGuardia's reply, Aug. 12, 1941, Roosevelt Papers.

"Fiorello is not God": This and other entries are from Ickes, *Diaries,* May 25, July 12, Nov. 15, 1941.

gave the task to Mrs. Roosevelt: See Eleanor Roosevelt, *This I Remember;* also Joseph Lash, *Eleanor and Franklin.*

p. 302 *"My wife is named Marie":* Fellowes Morgan to Arthur Mann, Jan. 6, 1958.

"My wife never asks me": Roosevelt, p. 231.

"You have to keep the peace": This and other quotations in this paragraph, from Anna Rosenberg, interview.

THIRD-TERM CAMPAIGN

p. 304 *Berle mentioned to Ed Flynn:* Berle, p. 373.

"the guy has tact": *News* editorial, May 24, 1941.

p. 305 *unnecessarily harsh:* It caused Burlingham to write, "So you did it with your little stiletto . . . so Stanley was left naked on the shores of the Council"; Burlingham to LaGuardia, August 21, 1941, LaGuardia Papers.

Mrs. Isaacs . . . tells: Isaacs, p. 49.

p. 307 *Morris bore faithfully:* Morris, OHP.

p. 308 *"I am for Mayor LaGuardia":* NYT, Sept. 16, 1941.

p. 311 *the New Republic dated:* George Britt, "What Happened to LaGuardia?" *New Republic,* March 9, 1942.

WAR COMES TO NEW YORK

p. 314 *a five-day trip:* Roosevelt, p. 236 ff.

p. 315 *"the palace guard":* Memoir by Straus (in the possession of the author). The ex-councilman had volunteered his services and was put in charge of defense preparations in City Hall.

Chapter 10. "What Has Happened to LaGuardia?"—1942

EMBATTLED MAYOR

p. 321 *the mayor would have to be replaced:* Lash, pp. 646–648.

p. 322 *he forced the resignation:* This and quotations in following paragraph, NYT, Dec. 28, 30, 1940; HT editorial, Dec. 29, 1940.

p. 324 *"swivel chair scribes":* See *Newsweek,* Jan. 12, 1942.

that same night: Lash, p. 648.

UPROAR OVER PAUL KERN

p. 325 *indulgent toward Kern:* LaGuardia to Leslie J. Tompkins, October 18, 1941, LaGuardia Papers.

p. 329 *"the old sure touch":* HT editorial, March 10, 1942.

"came to cross purposes": Flynn, p. 170 ff.

a strong dissenting opinion: Matter of Kern V. LaGuardia, App. Div., 264 (1942) 630.

OF SCRAPS AND SCRAP IRON

p. 332 *no place . . . for Robert Moses:* Anonymous Source.
fence around Gracie Mansion: NYT, June 8, 1942.
p. 333 *the old Aquarium:* NYT, Sept. 23, 1942.
he sought to stop: NYT, Oct. 7, 1942.

TROUBLES WITH THE PRESS

p. 334 *"Time" and "Newsweek":* "Hizzoner and the Press," *Newsweek,* Sept. 7, 1942; *Time,* Oct. 5, 1942.
perhaps more painful: George Britt, "What Happened to LaGuardia?" *New Republic,* March 9, 1942.
p. 335 *early in his first term:* NYT, March 11, 1934. •
p. 336 *World's Fair speech:* NYT, May 25, 1942.
climax of this ill-feeling: Newsweek, Sept. 7, 1942. The story is thoroughly reported in this source.

NEW YORK'S WAITING SEASON

p. 338 *furnished with antiques:* For an account of how Moses charged the mayor with appropriating one of these antiques, see August Heckscher, "A Slight Case of Revenge," *Christian Science Monitor,* May 20, 1977. Walter Binger quotes Robert Moses on LaGuardia's dislike of being surrounded by antiques: "They are trying to make an Early American out of LaGuardia and he is not taking it very well." Walter Binger to James Grote VanDerpool, Sept. 7, 1977.
"my family is not keen": LaGuardia to A. B. Montgomery, Jan. 17, 1942, LaGuardia Papers.
"it is not surprising": LaGuardia to Arnold E. Rattray, Nov. 15, 1945, LaGuardia Papers.
p. 339 *in the parks commissioner's limousine:* Livingston, interview.
"wistfully we look ahead": NYT editorial, July 9, 1942.
p. 341 *Dewey himself gave credit:* Alfange, interview.
"tooted sluggishly": NYT, Dec. 31, 1942.

Chapter II. Prisoner in City Hall—1943

NEW MAN IN ALBANY

The best book on Dewey is Barry Keith Beyer's *Thomas E. Dewey, 1937–1947* (University of Rochester, 1962). It says little about the LaGuardia relationship, but the evidence of the mutual dislike is clear. Goodhue Livingston (interview), cites an amusing example. In 1943 LaGuardia told Livingston to "move into the north office" where Reuben Lazarus, the mayor's Albany representative, had been handsomely installed. The reason: Lazarus had been getting "too chummy with Dewey." The dispossessed Lazarus wandered about City Hall: "I don't remember where he finally ended up." Toward Lehman LaGuardia's attitude softened in retrospect. "Thanks for all you did for the city of New York." LaGuardia to Lehman, Jan. 9, 1943, Lehman Papers.

EDUCATIONAL CHINA SHOP

p. 345 *"a bee-stung Ferdinand":* Newsweek, Sept. 27, 1943.
p. 348 *"gratuitously offensive":* HT, Feb. 8, 1943. The *Sun* quotation is from the same date.

WASHINGTON SAYS NO

p. 348 *"Why did I take it?":* LaGuardia to Burlingham, May 17, 1943, LaGuardia Papers.
p. 350 *LaGuardia wrote joyfully:* LaGuardia to Hopkins, March 17, 1943, La-Guardia Papers; Sherwood, p. 725.
p. 351 *"such shenanigans":* Moses, *A Salute,* p. 43.
his sense of resentment: LaGuardia to Burlingham, April 25, 1942, LaGuardia Papers.
p. 352 *"wouldn't it be lovely?":* Felix Frankfurter to C. C. Burlingham, June 25, 1943; LaGuardia's reply is dated July 17, 1943, LaGuardia Papers.

TIME OUT OF JOINT

p. 353 *"things are not going right":* Paul Windels, Jr., interview.
Dorothy Kenyon wrote him: This and the following letters are from the LaGuardia Papers: LaGuardia to Kenyon, Aug. 6, 1943; to Col. Lewis Landes, June 11, 1943; to E. L. Palmieri, Oct. 16, 1943; to Jos. Lilley, June 4, 1943.
p. 354 *Chanler was restless:* Chanler, interview.
"I say he's a liar": NYT, April 15, 1943.
p. 356 *"one of the rules of the game":* LaGuardia to E. L. Palmieri, Oct. 16, 1943, LaGuardia Papers.
p. 356 *"I am all in":* LaGuardia to Percy C. Magnus, Sept. 30, 1943, LaGuardia Papers.

TO THE BARRICADES

p. 357 *a vivid footnote:* The young writer on the scene was Ralph Ellison, one day to be famous as author of *The Invisible Man.* His comments are from the New York *Post,* Aug. 2, 1943.
p. 360 *his private correspondence:* See, e.g., letter to Paul Windels, July 9, 1940; to Valentine, June and August, 1937; to Dan Higgins, Aug. 29, 1941; La-Guardia Papers.

SUNDAY SEMONS

p. 362 *the opening bars:* For a description of LaGuardia's broadcasting performance, see *New Yorker,* Nov. 6, 1943; John Hutchins, NYT, July 16, 1944. The "violent gesture" is from the *New Yorker* article.

FOUNDING OF CITY CENTER

For the story of City Center we have Morris, OHP and *Let the Chips Fall;* and Dalrymple, *Last Row.*
p. 367 *letters cited:* LaGuardia Papers: LaGuardia to Harry Friedgirt, May 2, 1944; to Sigmund Gottleber, May 23, 1945.
p. 368 *"young men leaping around":* Dalrymple, p. 42 ff.

Chapter 12. Toward a Postwar World—1944

A TIME FOR THOUGHT

p. 370 *apart from the crowd:* NYT, Jan. 2, 1944.
over the coming months: E.g., address at the convention of the Hatters Union, NYT, May 2, 1944; also, seven-point program in testimony before Senate Military Affairs Committee, NYT, June 15, 1944.

The City's Prospects

p. 371 *Moses . . . was still repeating:* Moses, in *The American City,* December 1943.
subway extensions: Rankin, *New York Advancing,* Victory edition, p. xxxii:
LaGuardia foresaw that "every new extension brings with it the need for
additional public improvements—schools, water supply, sewers, etc."
mire the city in traffic congestion: LaGuardia agreed with Moses: "A lot of
traffic in Manhattan is a good thing. It means that business is prosperous."
Memoir by Straus (in possession of the author).

p. 372 *"Who will pay the feed bill?":* NYT, Oct. 4, 1936.

p. 373 *before a welfare parley:* NYT, Jan. 9, 1944.
the charge has been made: In the course of research comments were frequently heard to the effect that LaGuardia was responsible for the influx
of Puerto Ricans. Alex Rose said in September 1976 that "he would have
been a great mayor" except for the Puerto Rican issue. But, as noted in
the text, the issue did not arise until after World War II.
"but he did not act": Citizens Budget Commission, 1945 *Annual Report.*

p. 375 *a prophetic note:* HT, May 5, 1943 ff.

Pioneering in Health Care

p. 375 *a disarming way:* Post, May 26, 1934.
assurances of his personal physician: Baehr, interview.

p. 376 *a large safety pin:* Berle, p. 358.
his concern was stimulated: In LaGuardia's view debt was particularly abhor-
rent because it led employees into gambling and set them on the road to
crime.

Incubus of the Five-Cent Fare

p. 378 *Burlingham was to look back:* Burlingham to Wm. Chanler: "He should have
raised the subway fare at the beginning of his third term," April 20, 1948,
LaGuardia Papers.

The Liberal Party

p. 379 *on the political front:* For the origins of the Liberal party, see Danish, *The
World of David Dubinsky;* Dubinsky and Raskin, *A Life with Labor.* An
earlier and short-lived "liberal party" had been established in 1935 by
Nathan Straus, A. A. Berle, Jr., and Langdon Post. It endorsed Lehman
in the elections of that year.

To the Pacific?

p. 382 *writing to Stimson:* Letters cited in the following paragraphs are from the
Roosevelt Papers. FDR to Stimson, Sept. 4, 1944; Forrestal's is dated Aug.
26, 1944. Stimson's refusal to have LaGuardia under army jurisdiction and
his proposal to have him used in the navy are from a memorandum to the
president dated Sept. 7, 1944.

p. 383 *"still out of service":* The LaGuardia Papers contain a significant file of letters
commenting on the appointment, which was taken for granted.

Postwar Aviation

The description of the conference, including the quotations from Berle's diary and
his letter to LaGuardia are from Berle, p. 498 ff.

p. 385 *"Let's not go back":* NYT, Dec. 2, 1944, *"a crude liquidation":* Berle, p. xxx.

Hope Deferred

p. 386 *"on a day such as this":* NYT, Aug. 24, 1944.

Chapter 13. An Epoch Passes—1945

Fourth,-Term Riddle

p. 389 *fourth-term intentions:* NYT, June 15, 1945.
he dreamed of the hills: LaGuardia to M. D. Grunwald, June 7, 1940, LaGuardia Papers.
p. 390 *Alex Rose:* NYT, March 24, 1945.
Alfange: Ibid.
"all I know": LaGuardia to Burlingham, April 13, 1943, LaGuardia Papers.
"a law unto himself": Cited in NYT, April 22, 1945.

Business More or Less as Usual

p. 391 *scarcely disguised censorship:* Dalrymple, pp. 56, 57.
p. 392 *a bizarre incident:* This is covered in the *News* and *Mirror,* March 9, 1945. The City Council investigated the mayor's role in this episode; NYT, April 25, 1945.
p. 394 *"I'm running the city":* NYT, March 22, 1945.

The Captains and the Kings

p. 395 *"dropped tired feet":* NYT, Aug. 20, 1945.
a patrolman noted: Ibid.
p. 394 *he moved nearsightedly:* Goodhue Livingston, interview.

The End of Fusion

p. 398 *the Republicans nominated:* A young research assistant in Goldstein's campaign was Jacob Javits. The secretary to Alfange, one of Goldstein's campaign managers, was a girl named Marion. The rest is history.
p. 399 *"the mayor's errand boy":* NYT, Aug. 6, 1945.
"solitary caprice": NYT, Aug. 19, 1945.
p. 400 *"please give a statement for Morris":* LaGuardia to Fannie Hurst, Oct. 5, 1945, LaGuardia Papers.
"I love Mrs. Roosevelt": NYT, Oct. 20, 1945.

Last Phase

p. 401 *"Dear Bill":* LaGuardia to Wm. O'Dwyer, Nov. 8, 1945, LaGuardia Papers.
p. 404 *a last fire:* Thoroughly covered by the press at the time, the event is the subject of a recent book by Arthur Weingarten, *The Sky Is Falling.*

Exit

p. 405 *"nice to have you here":* NYT, Oct. 28, 1945.
p. 407 *"Chopin wrote my swan song":* NYT, Oct. 20, 1945.
his cherished Sunday programs: New Yorker, Jan. 12, 1946, p. 20.
LaGuardia rode down: Martin Liefer, interview, April 20, 1977.

Chapter 14. Epilogue—The Road Away

For a brief political history of the period following LaGuardia, see Warren Moscow, *Politics in the Empire State.*

p. 411   *in his hundred first year: Century Memorials,* The Century Association, New York 1960, p. 165.

  his driver noticed: Martin Liefer, interview.

  he still would make a fuss: Conversation with Dr. Beatrice Berle.

p. 412   *a long-deferred reunion:* Gluck, p. 114.

p. 413   *"No, no, Newbold":* Morris, p. 213.

Index

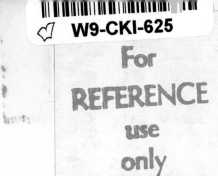

AMERICAN PLACE-NAMES

AMERICAN
PLACE-NAMES

A Concise and Selective Dictionary
for the Continental United States of America

GEORGE R. STEWART

New York
OXFORD UNIVERSITY PRESS
1970

Copyright © 1970 George R. Stewart
Library of Congress Catalogue Card Number: 72-83018
Printed in the United States of America

To
M. R. E. and S. D. S.
who have something in common,
besides intelligence and courage

Contents

Preface

As accurately as can be at present estimated, approximately 3,500,000 named places—about one to the square mile—exist currently in the United States of America. In addition, there are probably a million more such names of places that are recorded, but are no longer in use. Though this density is low by European standards, the total figure is so high that merely to print the current names alone would require volumes. From the very initiation of the dictionary, therefore, I realised that the work must be selective.[1]

First of all, the focus had to be upon the names, not upon the places —the number of names, because of repetition, being much smaller than the number of places. A single name, for instance, such as **Sand** or **Long,** may stand upon hundreds or even thousands of places. The figure for the total number of names is a matter for guess rather than for estimate. If we merely assume, however, that names are repeated, over the broad extent of the country, twenty times on the average, their total number is 175,000, and this figure may even be larger because of the many names ocurring only once or twice. But to print even 175,000 names with the necessary commentary upon each would, once more, run into volumes. Some selectivity was still necessary.

1. In the present lack of a national gazeteer including both habitation-names and names for natural features, the total number of named places may be estimated from various place-name studies, and especially from the state gazeteers, of which three are both comprehensive and recent. Of these three, unfortunately, Delaware is too small to be very useful, and Alaska is too atypical (See *Bibliography*, under Heck and Orth.) There remains Thomas P. Field's *A Guide to Kentucky Place Names,* from which the density for that state may be readily determined at just about one to the square mile. From its history, population, topography, and folk-habits, Kentucky is to be considered a fairly representative state. Naturally there is some variation of opinion as to what should be counted as a place-name, but such differences probably do not affect the total figure greatly. Some less-well-based estimates which I have made for South Dakota, Oregon, and California tend to confirm the figure derived from Kentucky.

Since a dictionary is a work of reference to be consulted rather than read, the basis of selection should be the likelihood of anyone's trying to find a certain name in it. At first thought, to proceed on such a principle might seem merely to involve the author in a gigantic guessing game with the general public. But, practically, the situation is simpler. Anyone consulting the dictionary would be likely, I concluded, to be seeking information upon names which fall into one of three categories.

1. Names of well-known places, e.g. **Philadelphia, Mississippi, Mount Rainier.**

2. Repeated names, i.e. those which appear upon several or many places, e.g. **Lost, Big, Beaver.**

3. Unusual names, i.e. those which attract attention to themselves and thus become objects of curiosity, arousing controversy. Here can be included (a) non-English names,[2] especially those of Indian origin, e.g. **Vermilion, Reliez, Kokomo, Katahdin;** (b) coined names, e.g. **Snicktaw, Ti, Birome;** (c) 'mistake names,' e.g. **Nome, Tolo, Plaski;** (d) names of unusual or provocative suggestion, e.g. **Bloody, Goodnight, Christmas.**

A standard of admission creates automatically a standard of rejection, and by a brief presentation of it the scope of the dictionary becomes better defined.

1. By far the largest number of names to be omitted are those which are derived from persons. Very few consultants of the Dictionary will be concerned with such an obvious, commonplace, and even-to-most-Joneses-uninteresting name as **Jones Creek.** Moreover, with most such names little can be said of interest in the way of elucidation. A commentator can merely present the transparent fact that the stream was named for some Jones, may then give an identification, and, if data are available, present the reason (usually commonplace) why this individual's name was thus used. But such information passes over into the field of local history, and can be omitted from a study of naming with negligible loss. Nonetheless, a large number of names of personal origin have been included because they fell within one of the positive categories.

2. As already suggested, the obsolete names have been omitted. A

---

2. Since the dictionary should be usable by people who have no knowledge of non-English languages, even the simplest terms in French and Spanish, e.g. **Rouge, Grande,** have been made entries and translated.

few may actually have been included, because the determination of complete extinction is not always possible.

3. Names of most of the very minor places have been omitted. Few people would even know about (and would much less care to investigate) the name of some small stream in the Alaskan tundra or of a desert-bound railroad siding. In general, included are counties, but not townships; lakes, but not springs; many mountains, but few hills.

4. If little or nothing can be surely stated about the name of an unimportant place, it has sometimes merely been passed over, but such cases are rare.

5. Certain names have been omitted because they are what might be called 'obviously obvious,' e.g. **Dome Mountain, Highest Lake.**

6. The names of Hawaii (as the term *Continental* in the title indicates) have not been included. The reason here, however, has not been primarily to reduce the total number, but that Hawaii has names almost wholly of the native Hawaiian (Polynesian) language. Lacking overlap, they cannot be economically treated along with the others, and demand a volume for themselves [3]. . . .

The Dictionary is the work of a single author, with only secretarial assistance. Possibly, in these times of organized research projects, it is destined to be the last dictionary to be so prepared. Being thus not limited by computers and the least common denominator of research assistants, it has not been reduced to a mechanical conformity, and may, here and there, even display a touch of personal vagary.

By the necessity of wide coverage, however, I have been forced to forgo many pleasant diversions. The study of place-names, comprising several disciplines, is all too conducive to a genial prolixity and the amiable pursuit of hobbies. The linguist, the geographer, the historian, the folk-lorist—each may write upon the subject. The linguist tends to pursue etymology to its depths; the geographer is in danger of producing a gazeteer; the historian devotes a page as to whether a certain pond was named for Joe Smith or his cousin Hank; the folk-lorist endlessly records stories about names. The toponymist, if such a chimera may exist, attempts to co-ordinate the qualities of all four. . . .

American students of place-names recognize their great debt to the

3. For a recent study of Hawaiian names, see M. W. Pukui and S. H. Elbert, *Place Names of Hawaii and Supplement to the Third Edition of the Hawaiian-English Dictionary* (1966). See also my *Names on the Land* (1960) Chap. XLV.

long and magnificent tradition of European scholarship, especially that of England, as expressed most fully in the publications of the English Place-Name Society. Nonetheless, in the study of names as in other details of civilization, there is no place for a colonial attitude. Conditions, problems, solutions—all are different. European, including English, scholarship has been concerned primarily with the etymology of those names which are of no more recent origin than 1500. In the United States, however, etymology is seldom of interest except with Indian names and a few dialectal or distorted forms.[4] European scholars rarely concern themselves with the process of name-giving or its motives—obviously because no information on such matters ordinarily exists with medieval and more ancient names. On the other hand, an American scholar scarcely considers that he has done his work fully unless he has solved—or, at least, attempted to solve—the question why. One might even put it, paradoxically, that the European onomatist argues from probability; the American, from evidence. Having collected whatever evidence (such as early forms of the name) is available, the European scholar then works out, with deep erudition, the etymological answer which seems most probable. The American scholar, on the contrary, must frequently present a highly improbable, or even fantastic, answer, because the evidence so requires, in such names, for instance, as **Primghar** and **Modesto.**

The American namer used as the tools of his trade such processes as irony, negative description, humorous distortion, coinage, literary borrowing, punning.[5] Quite possibly such processes also helped form the European name-pattern, for there is no reason to suppose that the Americans have been any more complex and nimble-witted than were the Angles, Celts or ancient Greeks. But for the older periods, the record is lacking.

In short, the chief problem of interest to the European scholar is the meaning of the name; to his American counterpart, the motivation of the namer.

The American must therefore, in at least one respect, carry his work

4. Manufactured names and names shaped by folk-etymology also raise questions of derivation, though not in the usual sense of etymology. Even the difficult problem of the translation of Indian names may in some instances be approached historically by aid of notes in early records. Thus the meanings for **Chicago, Topeka,** and **Kobeh** are recorded by early travelers who had excellent contacts with the local Indians. Their statements seem to me more authoritative than any researches of modern linguistics can possibly be.
5. Because of such naming processes even the basic tenet of European onomastics breaks down, viz. 'Every place-name has a meaning.' No 'meaning' in any ordinary sense of the word can be assigned to such names as those discussed in the *Introduction, Coined Names.*

farther than is required of the European. His task is not easier, since the discovery of the proper historical record, or the proper deduction from an imperfect record, is often highly difficult. With record lacking, the penetration of the namer's mind, as in the European situation, may become impossible, and we may quote the plaint of an early onomatist on the trail of a certain W. A. Scott, known to be the namer of Org, Wisconsin, 'No one living knows why he so named the place, where he got the name, or what it means, if it means anything.' (See *Bibliography*, Stennett, p. 84.)

An essential core of the material here presented derives from my own researches into original sources, as already presented in *Names on the Land,* my other publications, and some unpublished notes.[6] To amass the additional material, much greater in bulk, I have systematically reviewed, collated, and synthesized the still-unsuperseded scholarship on the place-names of the United States. The Sealock-Seely bibliography (see *Bibliography*) served as an indispensable check list. The more important works thus used comprise the *Bibliography*. I have, however, used a large number of smaller studies, sometimes mere notes on one name. Though they have not been included in the *Bibliography,* they are available through Sealock and Seely. . . .

As author, I myself am doubtless more cognizant of the shortcomings of this work than any critic can be. Still, it seems to me useful for the present time, and in the future offering itself as a basis for revisions, as additional local and specialized studies become available for incorporation in it.

The errors of such a work as this are those of both omission and of commission. The fundamental problem of admission is discussed earlier in this *Preface*. Undoubtedly, however, some names have been omitted which should have been discussed. More serious, presumably, are the positive errors which cannot but have crept into such a wide-sweeping work. These must be of two kinds, not even to count mere clerical and typographical lapses. 1. I must sometimes have misunderstood or inadvertently distorted my sources. 2. The most serious origin of error lies in the sources themselves, which must be considered, with

6. The connection of *Names on the Land* and the present Dictionary is close. Many names have been much more fully discussed in that earlier work than has been possible in the present concise one. That work presents both the history and the theory of place-naming in a way which the nature of a dictionary renders impossible, and some acquaintance with it will be found invaluable for enhancing the significance of the material here included.

negligible exceptions as secondary works. I have, therefore, to protect both myself and the user of the Dictionary, always considered the evidence critically. In innumerable instances, especially for the translations of Indian names, I have inserted a warning 'probably,' in the belief that uncertainty is preferable to a possible entrenchment of error. In other instances, I have merely rejected the evidence of the source, omitting the name altogether, especially if the place was not of first-rate importance. In still other instances I have even gone against the source on the basis of my own information from other sources or from general knowledge of language, literature, history, etc., in which some of the early compilers were lamentably lacking. I should not wish, however, even to seem to disparage these local toponymists. Some of them may have been comparatively unlettered and linguistically naive. But they showed the true spirit in their industrious search for knowledge and its recording. . . .

The only previous work on a national scale is that published by Henry Gannett in 1902 under the modest title *The Origin of Certain Place Names in the United States,* and reissued without revision in 1947 under the more ambitious title *American Names: a Guide to the Origin of Place-names in the United States.* Though this work contains much sound information, it is also full of errors, having been compiled before a single study at the state level was available and when research on Indian place-names had scarcely started. Although I list it in the *Bibliography,* I have consulted it only for suggestions and have based no conclusions upon it.

Traditionally, though not altogether advantageously, American study of place-names has been based upon political units—commonly, states or counties. As the result, we have a kind of patchwork. West Virginia, for instance, is excellently covered, but just over the line Virginia is, comparatively speaking, *terra incognita.*

Fortunately, a study on a national scale somewhat shades these contrasts, since many names extend across political boundaries. Moreover, many names are repeated, so that an explanation applicable in a well-studied state may be accepted in an inadequately-studied one.

In general, a three-fold classification of states may be offered, with the usual proviso that some borderline cases exist, so that the classes shade into one another.

1. A number of states have been adequately treated, usually in a

single study. In these instances I have based my work almost wholly upon this volume, the problems then being chiefly those of selection, co-ordination, and condensation. I have, however, sometimes differed even from these authorities, especially because of advantages afforded me by study on the national level. Naturally, these works differ in quality, both in their comprehensiveness of coverage, their manner of presentation, and the authoritativeness of their conclusions. Particularly, their treatment of Indian names is, in some instances, superficial. Nonetheless, this group of studies forms the firm basis upon which the Dictionary has been developed.

These well-documented states are as follows, the reference to the *Bibliography* being given in parentheses: ARIZONA (Barnes-Granger); CALIFORNIA (Gudde); FLORIDA (Bloodworth); MINNESOTA (Upham); MISSOURI (Ramsay); NEBRASKA (Fitzpatrick; Link); NEVADA (Carlson); NEW MEXICO (Pearce); OREGON (McArthur); SOUTH DAKOTA (USWP-Ehrensperger); WASHINGTON (Meany); WEST VIRGINIA (Kenny); WYOMING (Urbanek).

2. The majority of the states fall into an intermediate class. The status of research may be termed 'spotty.' No single adequate work exists, but often the amalgamation of several smaller studies produces a result about as satisfactory as is afforded for the previous group. In some cases a good study of town-names is available, or of Indian names. In other states a brief general work has been published. On the whole, for the limited objectives of a concise dictionary the treatment of these states may be considered adequate—if barely so, in some instances. They are: ALABAMA, ALASKA, COLORADO, CONNECTICUT, DELAWARE, IDAHO, ILLINOIS, IOWA, KANSAS, KENTUCKY, LOUISIANA, MAINE, MARYLAND, MASSACHUSETTS, MICHIGAN, MONTANA, NEW HAMPSHIRE, NEW JERSEY, NEW YORK, NORTH CAROLINA, NORTH DAKOTA, OHIO, OKLAHOMA, PENNSYLVANIA, RHODE ISLAND, SOUTH CAROLINA, TEXAS, UTAH, VERMONT, WISCONSIN,

3. Certain states have been inadequately studied, although the major names have usually been treated and there is no state on which material is wholly lacking: ARKANSAS, GEORGIA, INDIANA, MISSISSIPPI, TENNESSEE, VIRGINIA. Fortunately the total area of this group of states totals only about 8 per cent of that of the United States.

Acknowledgments

To express my thanks to the many persons who have generously aided in the preparation of this work is my pleasure. These individuals have, indeed, been so numerous that some may have escaped my memory and record, but I shall include them in thought, even though they may be lost in name.

My thanks are particularly due to all of those (many of them no longer living) whose work I have used, and have acknowledged formally, in the *Bibliography*. Chief among these must be mentioned Richard B. Sealock and Pauline A. Seely, whose bibliography has been my constantly-used and essential book.

As often before, Theodosia Burton Stewart has given good counsel and support. Madison S. Beeler and James D. Hart have expended time and thought in useful criticism.

Among the many others who have aided in various ways I am happy to mention William E. Ashton, Jane Burton, John Thomas Casteen, Wayne E. Corley, Kenneth E. Crouch, A. R. Dunlap, E. C. Ehrensperger, Erwin G. Gudde, Harry E. Hammer and the Missouri Pacific Lines, Louise Hanley, Kelsie Harder, Robert Hitchman, Howard Hugo, John Rydjord, Elsdon C. Smith, Wallace Stegner, Francis Lee Utley, and C. A. Weslager.

I am also endebted to several libraries and other institutions, and wish particularly to thank the Inter-library Borrowing Service of the University of California (Berkeley) Library.

Berkeley   G. R. S.
March 28, 1969

Introduction

The purpose of this introduction is to supply some aid in the use of the dictionary, not to present a general discussion of place-names. I have elsewhere delt with the history and theory of place-names (especially in the United States), and anyone wishing to make the fullest use of the present dictionary will be aided by some acquaintance with those treatises.[1] No such special knowledge, however, is required, and the present dictionary exists independently.

The Entry System

The dictionary consists of about 12,000 entries, alphabetically arranged. Each entry commonly has as its heading a single word (place-name specific), e.g. **Black, Big,** or less commonly, two or more related words which are distinguished by grammatical form, e.g. **Starve, Starvation,** or by variant spelling (see, e.g., **Lorraine**).

In some instances the full place-name (specific-generic) appears as the entry-heading, usually when the name occurs only once. Occasionally this usage is a notice that the explanation as offered applies to the specific as used with this generic only.

After the entry-heading the location, by Zip-code abbreviation of the state(s), is commonly given.[2] Omission of such a location means (1) that the name occurs in several or many states, or (2) that the place is too well known to require such statement of location.

Next in the entry the language and meaning (translation) of the

---

1. See *Names on the Land* (1945, 1960), the article *Name (in linguistics), Encyclopedia Britannica;* 'A Classification of Place Names,' *Names,* ii; 1, pp. 1–13.
2. See below, *Abbreviations.*

term are stated, unless it is a word in current American-English or a personal name.

Some detailed information may follow, e.g. the reason for the application of the term, the date of naming, the namer, and the occasion. In the numerous instances of repeated names, some specific examples may be given of typical or exceptional or of especially interesting or important occurrences.

General Background

Since the dictionary is for use by the general public, technical terms have been kept at a minimum, and almost anyone, it is hoped, can consult the text without special directions. A fuller understanding, however, will be attained by anyone giving some attention to the special topics here presented.

1. *Specific-generic.* On the analogy of biological terminology, the generic, e.g. *river, mountain, city,* indicates the class. The specific, e.g. *blue, Lincoln, battle,* modifies the generic by limitation, thus restricting the application to a single 'place,' although in practice many names are repeated.

In common usage either the specific or the generic may be omitted with resulting clipped forms, e.g. 'the river' or 'the Mississippi.'

The specific is commonly an adjective, or a noun serving as an adjective, and by regular usage in English preceding its generic, e.g. **Red Rock, Charles City, Wolf Creek.**

Double specifics are not uncommon. The secondary specific usually modifies the whole specific-generic combination. Thus **Big Black River** is distinguished from another **Black River** in the vicinity. Occasionally the secondary specific modifies the primary specific only, **Little Pete Meadows** being named for a man known as 'Little Pete.' In a case of double specific the user of the Dictionary may find it profitable to check both terms.

Because of direct or indirect influence of other languages (commonly, French or Spanish) many specifics follow the generic, e.g. **Mount Shasta, Lake Erie, Key West, Fort Wayne.** In the Dictionary these names are alphabetized under the specific, i.e. the second term.

A second type of specific consists of a prepositional (adjectival) phrase introduced by *of,* e.g. **The Gulf of Alaska, The Commonwealth of Massachusetts, The State of Maine, The City of Chicago.** Omission of the prepositional generic with names of states, cities, and towns is regular, but the full form occurs in official usage and in special cases.

By common usage, chiefly with names of towns, generics have amalgamated, even in writing, with their specifics, as has regularly occurred with compounds of *-town, -ville,* and *-burg(h).* The combined form is then treated as a specific, usually of the prepositional type, in such usages as **The City of Pittsburgh.**

Although the specific-generic combination may be considered as constituting the whole place-name, the specific is the element of interest in the ordinary name. Generics are essentially common nouns, and their meaning can be ascertained from an English dictionary. No special discussion of generics is here included. Frequently, however, the same terms occur as specifics, e.g. **City, Point, Mountain, Lake,** and in such instances they have necessarily been discussed.[3]

2. *The article.* The use or non-use of the definite article differs by localities and even by individuals, being highly complicated. It occurs with the prepositional specific, e.g. **The Gulf of Maine,** and with plurals, e.g. **The Thousand Islands.** It is commonly used with certain generics, e.g. *desert* and may or may not be used with others, e.g. *river.* See also the entry, **The.**

3. *Languages.* The great majority of the places bear names from the English language as spoken and written in the United States. Names from French, Dutch, Spanish, and various Indian languages are common. Eskimo and Aleutian names occur in their areas of occupation in Alaska, and some names survive from the Russian colonization of Alaska and California, e.g. **Tolstoi, Ross.** Small numbers of names are derived from the languages of other immigrant groups, e.g. **Shellpot, Hader.**

This direct derivation from a language should be distinguished from indirect influence through cultural or literary borrowing. For instance, *Mexico* and *coyote* are Aztecan words, but they were borrowed first by Spanish and then from that language were transferred to American-

3. For specialized treatment of generics, see *Bibliography* under headings, McJimsey, McMullan.

English. Some of the namings may be Spanish, none are Aztecan; most of them are American.[4] Similarly, Indian words taken into English, e.g. *squaw, moose, raccoon, opossum,* result in American namings. So also, literary borrowing has given rise to such names as **Paris, Odessa, Memphis,** and the acquired knowledge of classical languages has resulted in **Akron, Emporia, Eureka, Altus.**

Information as to linguistic origin with translation or explanation is offered for all names except those representing current American-English. But, to avoid excessive repetition, the different grammatical forms (such as those of French and Spanish adjectives and Spanish diminutives) are given only when such information seemed immediately pertinent.

In standardized languages (e.g. English, French, Dutch, and Spanish) modern spellings are used for entry-headings, and little problem arises. With Indian[5] languages no standardised form is commonly available, and some cross-reference is necessitated.

Since the dictionary is for general use, the system used for reference to Indian languages has been based upon practical considerations, and is not altogether consistent or likely to satisfy specialists. The name has generally been referred to the tribe, that is, to what may be in general considered the language, e.g. **Tunitcha** is labeled *Apache,* the linguistic stock, viz. *Athapascan,* not being noted. In certain areas, however, where tribal units were doubtful or where they were very small, e.g. in New England, the tribe from which the name was derived is usually uncertain, but the linguistic stock is known. Such a name as **Manatuck,** therefore, is merely labeled *Algonquian.* In some instances a double identification is given, e.g. *Muskogean (Creek),* or *Algonquian (Delaware),* especially since either of these terms may be wrongly taken if standing alone. Occasionally with obscure but separate units, such as exist particularly in the California area, a label of the type *Indian (Hupa)* has been used, since it was thought that many people would not even know that a tribe known as Hupa existed, and might suspect an error in spelling.

In a concise dictionary the detailed analysis of Indian names cannot

4. The term 'American' is used throughout as a convenient short term for 'English-speaking citizen of the United States after 1776.' In the colonial period the term 'English' is used primarily in a linguistic sense, but also to apply to the inhabitants of the thirteen colonies.
5. The term *Indian* is used always in the sense of American Indian.

be attempted, and details of phonetic shifting have likewise been passed over. Generally, however, the word order has been maintained in translation, e.g. **Bogalusa** being rendered as 'stream-black.'

The translation of many Indian names is difficult, and much research remains to be done. In some instances even the language is not surely determined, and a few names have been labeled merely 'Indian, language uncertain.' Many others, even with the language determined, have been denoted 'meaning uncertain,' or even 'meaning unknown.' The former designation generally indicates that different authorities give different translations and that, to the present lexicographer, no decision between them seems possible. Nonetheless, such names have been included in the Dictionary, since many people have an interest in knowing that a name is of Indian origin, even if they cannot learn its meaning. (See also *Tribal and national names.*)

Besides translation, Indian names offer many difficulties. 1. The forms have often been distorted in transmission through badly-informed or careless recorders, e.g. **Potomac.** 2. The names may be very old, so that they have already been transformed in the Indian context and their meaning has been obscured or shifted by folk-etymology; the significance of some names, e.g. **Tennessee,** was apparently unknown to the local Indians themselves. 3. Ambiguities exist because of homophones or near-homophones within the Indian languages, e.g. the element usually spelled in English as *talla-,* as in **Tallahassee,** may equally well represent a Muskogean term meaning 'town,' or 'stone,' or 'palmetto.' 4. Many Indian-appearing names may be more or less pseudo-Indian, i.e. they may have been coined by Americans from dictionaries or similarly produced by modern Indians, e.g. **Pasadena, Oklahoma.** In a few instances coinages have merely been made to resemble Indian names, e.g. **Wewahote, Itasca, Wewanta.** Such formations enjoyed some popularity in the mid-nineteenth century, especially under the auspices of H. R. Schoolscraft (see, e.g., **Algonac, Algoma**).

Even after the meaning of an Indian name has been determined, the reason for its application may remain difficult to fix. Most Indian names were based upon incidents (**Bear-in-the-Lodge, Boy Lake, Quilby Creek**) or were descriptive (**Mississippi, Katahdin, Kennebec**). The method of naming, however, was often different from the transplanted European methods of the colonists and later Americans. The outlet of a lake, for instance, was commonly named, though this is rarely the practice in the European tradition.

Moreover, large natural features, such as rivers, were not named as a whole but merely in sections as with **Connecticut** and **Penobscot.** The colonists, in addition, treated many Indian names as merely meaningless labels, with incongruous results, applying a name suitable to one kind of feature to another kind of feature; thus **Massachusetts,** originally descriptive of some hills, was applied to a bay and later to a colony.

4. *Linguistic transfer.* Names are transferred from one language to another by four methods, three of them in an oral situation and the fourth in a written situation.

a. An informant says the name in his own language, and the recipient then renders it by sound (perhaps later in writing) as well as he can, according to his own language habits. This process is primitive (existing even before writing and between illiterates) and is especially prevalent in situations where the recipient has little or no knowledge of the language of the informant.

b. The name is translated from the original into the receiving language. Such procedure occurs more commonly when a fair degree of mutual understanding has been established.

c. The name is reworked by folk-etymology (see *Folk-etymology*).

d. The transferral is by the written or printed form. The name is then ordinarily pronounced as the spelling suggests, and many of the 'mispronunciations' in American names thus arise, e.g. **Florida, Berlin.**

In the process of transfer many non-English generics have become specifics or parts of specifics, e.g. **Kill, Loyalhanna, Yolla Bolly.**

5. *Dual and multiple origin.* The saying that men's motives are seldom simple must be remembered in place-naming. When a colonial settlement, for instance, was given a certain name, it was not necessarily so called solely for an English town of that name or solely for a nobleman bearing that title. Instead, the one reason reinforced the other, making the name doubly appropriate. Possibly, even a family of the early settlers bore the same name, and so the appropriateness was still further enhanced. The biological analogy cannot be invoked: a man can have but one father, but a name can have two or more. An interesting case occurs with the very first European naming, i.e. **Florida.** Another important example is furnished by **New York.** (See also below, *Abbreviations.*)

6. *Abundance vs. rarity.* Since the function of a place-name is to distinguish a particular place, a name is likely to be derived from an unusual rather than a commonplace quality. Any body of water is likely to contain fish, and so their mere presence is not a distinguishing feature, except in desert areas where such a name as **Fish Spring** indicates something unusual. Ordinarily such a name as **Fish Creek** arises from a notable catch of fish made by some early visitors. So also, **Wind** is too common a phenomenon to have distinguishing value, and the name either records some heavy storm or else a place unusually exposed to wind. The common explanation, 'They called it Deer Creek; there were lots of deer there in early days,' is generally incorrect, and the name usually records the killing of a single deer or the encounter with a deer when unexpected. McArthur comments upon the rarity of the name **Fir** in Oregon, though that is a very common tree, and Gould makes the same comments about **Oak** in Oklahoma, neither of them apparently recognizing the lack of distinguishing quality of a common tree. In the same way places called **American** are rare, and the river in California was named when the region was still Mexican and Americans were rare. 'Edge-of-range' names illustrate the same principle. (See, e.g. **Alligator.**) True 'abundance-names' are comparatively uncommon, but some are noted under *Names from nature.*

7. *Habitations, natural features.* The term 'habitation-name,' borrowed from English scholars, is employed as a convenient term to include not only cities, towns, and villages, but also counties and townships—and, in fact, names in general, except for those applied to natural features (often given merely as *features*). The distinction is that the names of natural features are placed upon entities which already exist without human action, whereas a habitation-name is applied to a human creation, may even be selected before it is placed upon a site (cf. **New Orleans**), and is commonly established by official, usually legislative, act. Most habitation-names involve some commendatory quality, but such a quality is rare for names of features.

8. *Folk-names.* Based upon German usage the term 'folk' is employed by some scholars in the sense of 'tribe, people.' By American usage, as here followed, the term refers to names favored and given by people in the sense of the general anonymous public, especially such names as are often repeated, e.g. **Troublesome,** usually coupled with **Creek.**

9. *Linguistic play, humor.* Fun-making and witticism are basic human qualities, probably more pervasive among primitive and unsophisticated people than among the more educated. Many namings have at least a partially humorous motivation, expressed through the mechanism of descriptive naming or naming from incident, though such procedures are rarely recorded. (See, however, **Matrimony**) Even the application of such an important name as **California** suggests a touch of humor.

Puns are in some instances recorded or may be deduced, e.g. **Telos.**

Alliteration is common in folk-names, e.g. **Robbers Roost, Lovers Leap, Roaring Run, Horse Heaven.**

10. *Evolved names—bestowed names.* Many names develop by a kind of evolution from simple identifications which at first lack the stigmata of a name. Thus 'We shall meet at the black rock,' suggests a mere descriptive identification. Eventually, however, this may become 'We shall meet at Black Rock,' or even 'at Blackrock.' Thus, by a shift displayed both in speech and in writing, a true place-name has resulted. In contrary fashion, many names are bestowed at a particular time by a particular namer (or namers) in full consciousness that a name is thus being given, such procedure being especially common with explorers, surveyors, map makers, and town founders.

11. *'Official' names.* The names of states, counties, and incorporated cities, towns, etc. are established (in a particular spelling) by the government act creating them. Post offices are also thus established, and a certain number of vagaries of spelling arose in transmission through the Post Office Department and were then accepted by the local people, who usually did not care sufficiently how the name was spelled, provided that they got a post office. Names of unincorporated communities and of natural features are essentially a part of common language. The attempts of legislative bodies to regularize such names have sometimes been successful; sometimes, not. Since 1890 the Board on Geographic Names (and its successors) has determined governmental usage on maps and other publications, and the usage thus established may be termed 'official.' The present Dictionary considers all names to be a part of language, though in form and orthography usually accepting the 'official' decisions.

12. *Naming systems.* Anyone having to give a number of names is likely to resort to some kind of system. The most famous instance is

the naming of the 'classical belt' in New York. (See *Names on the Land,* pp. 184–86.) The numerical system (**First, Second,** etc.) has been common for street names, but has also been applied elsewhere, e.g. to chains of lakes. Alphabetical systems (sometimes the actual letters, and sometimes the letters as initials) have been common for streets, but also have been used for counties (see **Kay**) and for railroad-stations. Much of Alaska has been named on a grid-system, with **Riot, Romantic,** and **Germ** being chosen for the alphabetical requirements and uniqueness more than for any other discernable reason.

Small groups of names may spring from a kind of association which resembles a system, e.g. **Neon.** At the simplest level is 'counterpart' naming, which yields common juxtapositions (**Big-Little, Black-Red**) and unusual ones such as **Toboso-Quixote.**

13. *Literary influences.* Although the aborigines and many of the colonists and frontiersmen were illiterate, the naming of the United States, much more than that of Europe and many other areas, was accomplished by people who were familiar with the written and printed word. The occurrences of many exotic names, e.g. **Lima, Canton,** are to be explained by borrowing from books. (See also *Exotic Names.*)

The influence of the Bible was partly exercised through the spoken word, by means of sermons and established tradition, but it was primarily literary. The Bible has been the most prolific source of names of any literary work, for example, **Shiloh, Bethesda, Mount Hermon,** many of these names having been originally applied to rural churches. In second place is probably Longfellow's *Hiawatha.* Other literary influences are numerous. See, e.g., **Arden, Rob Roy, Esmond, Akela, Arklow, Nephi, Benhur, Lulbegrud.**

14. *Religious and mythological names.* French and Spanish explorers, missionaries and settlers liberally bestowed saints' names (see **Saint, San,** etc). Protestants expressed religious feeling through Biblical namings. Comparatively few place-names have been derived from Mormonism (but see **Nephi, Lemhi**). Indian religious and mythological beliefs have been preserved, sometimes in translation, e.g. **Wakan, Medicine.**

15. *Railroad stations, mines, brands.* During the rapid extension of railroads in the 19th century, thousands of stations and sidings were named, and many of these names survived, even after the abandonment of the railroad. These names were usually bestowed by railroad

officials on their own principles, so that the specific reason for naming cannot now be determined, unless a special record happens to be preserved. (See *Names on the Land,* pp. 321–25.) Many of the names were rootless, being borrowed from history or literature with no thought of their applicability to the site. The term 'railroad name' has been often employed in the Dictionary to describe a name thus arbitrarily originating.

Much the same may be said of the numerous names originating from mines, e.g. **Clan Alpine, Tombstone.** Miners characteristically gave flamboyant, colorful, and commendatory names, and were often swayed by superstition, particularly the idea of 'luck.' The motives for naming were seldom recorded.

Brand names also are arbitrary, but are commonly explicable as being merely the brand of an early ranch, e.g. **Ucross, Bar M Canyon, Teedee.**

16. *Personal names.* The majority of place-names are derived from the names of people, more commonly in the United States from family names, but also from given names, and from nicknames, e.g. **Lazbuddie.** Titles also may be considered personal names e.g. **Wilmington, Albany, Camden.** Many Indian personal names must be here included, e.g. **Osceola, Tonganoxie.** Translated, not always accurately, many of these Indian names have yielded colorful results, such as **Nettle Carrier, Kill Crazy, Almost-a-Dog, Heavy Runner.**

Because of reasons stated in the *Preface,* comparatively few of the names derived from persons have been here included. (For conditions under which personal names have been included, see *Preface.*)

The commonest source of the town-name is the personal name of the founder, of some early settler, or of the first postmaster. Many names of features spring from incidents, especially from the death of some pioneer at that point.

Family names are very numerous, 350,000 different ones being estimated for the United States.[6] They arise from different languages and sometimes have assumed bizarre and humorous forms, being, like place-names, transformed by folk-etymology and this giving rise to, e.g., **Searchlight, Birthright, Pancake, Lovelady, Moonlight.** Others, such as **Smoke Creek,** are derived from Indian personal names.

Personal names being the commonest source of place-names, anyone

6. See Elsdon C. Smith, *The Story of Our Names* (1950), p. 94.

will do well, in case of doubt, to check the local histories and directories as to whether the name may thus occur.

A few personal names are those of mythological and fictional characters, e.g. **Hobomak, Hiawatha, Ivanhoe,** and of animals, e.g. **Colo, Cuyuna.** Saints' names may be considered as forming a special class of personal names.

17. *Tribal and national names.* These may be considered personal names in a collective sense, e.g. **Shawnee, Chinese.** No attempt has been made in the Dictionary to distinguish among tribes, subtribes, clans, etc. Indian tribal names on places are common, usually having arisen because that tribe, or some individual of it, lived there.

The determination of the meaning of the tribal name itself is not properly a part of place-name study, and in a concise dictionary has to be carefully eschewed. Doubtful cases occur. Many tribes took their names from the places where they lived. If such a name first came into English as the name of a place and then was transferred to the tribe, it can properly be considered a place-name.

Tribal names away from the area of that tribe are usually late and literary, e.g. **Modoc** outside of California and Oregon. Some such names have arisen from incidents. Thus **Mohawk** in New England probably sprang from incursions of that tribe in wars against the local Indians.

18. *Names from nature.* Many names arise from the occurrence at the place of some form of animal or plant life or some mineral, e.g. **Bear, Eagle, Mosquito, Oak, Grass, Coal.** Some of these names spring from especial abundance there, e.g. **Passamaquoddy, Cobossecontee,** and may be known as 'abundance' names. (See above *Abundance-rarity.*) With animals the names most commonly arise from encounters and can be classed as 'incident names.' (See examples under **Buck, Quilby, Coyote,** etc.) Rarity also functions with minerals to produce names, e.g. **Gold, Silver.**

Extinct organisms result in names, when they are recognized as fossils, e.g. **Mammoth, Baculite.**

The origin of these nature-names is commonly so obvious that some of them have been omitted from the Dictionary. Included, however, are those which are much repeated, and those on which material of special interest has been preserved, especially when the relationship of the name to the environment may be demonstrated.

These names occur in all languages. Dialectal usage is often of interest (see, e.g. **Tiger, Painter**). Also to be noted is false identification (see, e.g. **Leopard, Crocodile, Alligator.**)

19. *Exotic names.* About the beginning of the 19th century, after the breaking of the ties with Great Britain, the habit arose of giving foreign and strange-appearing names to towns and villages, e.g. **Utica, Bogota, Memphis, Hannibal, Cairo.** Many of these names were drawn from books (see *Literary influences*), but others were from newspaper accounts of current events, e.g. **Plevna, Sebastopol, Waterloo,** and some were names brought back from foreign travel, especially by seamen. The exact reason for the use of the name has rarely become a matter of record, but such names were fashionably current. In the Dictionary the term 'exotic' has been applied to them. The use of these names was interestingly in harmony with the so-called Romanticism of the 19th century. It was also fostered by the requirement of the Post Office Department that no name should be repeated within a state. In such a situation the recourse to a very unusual name saved time and trouble, since it was unlikely to be already in use.

A Classification of Place-names
by Mechanism of Origin

Place-names originate from the need or desire to distinguish one place from others. A place will be named if people frequenting it (1) conceive it as an entity, and (2) find it to be in some way useful, and therefore worth naming. Primitive people, for instance, rarely have a name for a mountain range, since it is too large for them to see all at once and thus to conceive as an entity. Even a single mountain may not be named, because there is no advantage in its being so known, though springs and meadows on its slope will have names.

To distinguish one place from another of the same kind (generic), the users of a language employ certain devices or mechanisms, ten of which are here discussed. Nearly all (if not, indeed, all) of the place-names of the United States originate in one of these ways; sometimes (see above *Dual and multiple origin*), by more than one of them. Borderline cases also exist, but need not be our concern here.

Emphasis must be made that a particular word (specific) does not always function in the same manner. For example, *mad* may be a descriptive for a wildly-rushing stream, but in **Mad River** (California) it springs from an incident. So also, *red* is commonly a descriptive, but may also arise from an incident or a person.

These mechanisms of origin are advantageously kept distinct from the motivation of the namer, several of these having been already discussed. (See, e.g., *Linguistic play-humor, Religious and mythological names.*) Humor, for instance, is a motivation or an objective, which has to be sought by some mechanism such as descriptive or coinage (see, e.g., **Menagerie**). Religious names are generally achieved by the mechanism of commemoration.

1. *Descriptive names.* The term is here used for a specific which identifies and distinguishes a place by noting some permanent or semi-permanent characteristic which is noteworthy and thus serves to separate this particular place from others of the same generic in the vicinity. Descriptives commonly record sense impressions, e.g. **Big River, Black Rock, Stinking Spring, Roaring Run, Rushingwater Creek, Notch Mountain.** But descriptives may be more indirect and abstract, e.g. **Pliocene Ridge.**

Naming by description is common among both primitive and civilized peoples.

A special type consists of names arising by what may be called 'relative description,' e.g. **North, First.** Similarly, such terms as **Big** and **Little** may spring more from relative than from actual size. (See also *Naming Systems.*)

Negative description is rare, but occurs in such names as **Nowood Creek.** Irony, resembling negative description, is also rare, but may be seen in, for example, **Straight Creek,** a stream which is very crooked.

2. *Association names.* The phrase 'by association' is used for a type of origin related to description but profitably distinguished from it. Thus names such as **Mill River** and **Trail Creek** do not, properly speaking, describe those streams. Rather, they identify the streams by associating them with something else. The process of association is at work in numerous instances when a generic is used as a specific, e.g. **Pass, Island.**

3. *Possessive names.* These are names originating from some idea of ownership. This may be legal ownership, as when Smith's hill is so called because it is on the Smith farm, and eventually stands as **Smith Hill** on official maps. But many such names arose in the frontier

period and record merely the residence or 'squatting' of some Indian or pioneer at that place.

Since these names are generally derived from persons, see above *Personal names, Tribal and national names.*

4. *Incident names.* A name arising because something happened there is exemplified in such entries as **Cannibal, Suicide, Battle, Shivering.** A large proportion of namings for animals thus arise, as may be seen under **Wolf, Bear, Cod,** etc. This type of naming is equally as primitive as naming by description, and may be as common. Scholars, however, have tended to minimize this origin, partly because of the large number of fanciful stories which circulate. On the other hand, many authentic stories are preserved of such namings. Many times by their very nature indicate an incident, e.g. **Murder Creek, Earthquake Creek, Stray Horse Gulch.**

Exclamation-names form a rare subclass, e.g. **Helpmejack Creek, Goshelpme Creek.** Many older names, in lack of authentic information, have been thus 'explained,' but no credence can be placed in most of these stories, especially those told in connection with Indian names, e.g. that **Mooslookmeguntic** arose when a hunter cried out, 'Moose! Look! My gun, quick!' Most of these stories arose in conscious attempts at humor and were only taken seriously by humorless late-comers.

Names involving dates, e.g. **Christmas,** usually spring from incidents occurring on that date. So also many of the namings for saints arose from the fact that some explorer arrived at that place on the day of that saint, e.g. **San Diego.**

5. *Commemorative names.* Many names, especially of towns and mountains, have arisen from the desire to conserve a memory or to do honor. Noteworthy are the numerous colonial namings for places in England, e.g. **Burlington, Isle of Wight County.** Similarly, famous men (including saints) have been honored, e.g. the numerous towns, counties, and mountains called **Washington.** As a kind of commemoration may be included the namings for abstract virtues, e.g. **Union, Liberty,** though these also have commendatory value.

6. *Commendatory names.* A large proportion of towns, counties, and states have been named with a more-or-less definite idea of a 'good' name, i.e. one which would attract settlers and in various ways seem pleasant and suitable. Such names are not primarily descriptive, and

may be even misleading, as in the frequent use of **City** to designate a new settlement. Other examples are **Richland, Wheatland, Eden, Prosperity, Zenith.** Many apparent commemoratives are better classed as commendatories, as when **Birmingham** is used to suggest a future steel industry. The popular commendatories differ in different periods and places, but certain ideas are common, e.g. those of height, space, extensive view, good climate, and foreign (especially English) exclusiveness.

7. *Coined (manufactured) names.* These are names which have been consciously constructed out of fragments of other words or names, from initials, by reversals of letters or syllables, or in other ways. The practice can be observed in such names as **Saybrook, Tesnus, Romley, Carona, Somerange, Alicel, Ti, Tolono, Michillinda, Sarben, Remlap, Vadis, Primghar, Niotaze, Koldok.** Boundary-names form a subclass, e.g. **Calexico, Texarkana.**

This coinage of names is the most distinctive and creative feature of American place-naming. Nowhere else has it so flourished.

8. *Transfer and shift names, name cluster.* The term 'transfer name' is applied in a broad sense to denote names which have been moved from one location to another, e.g. **Cambridge,** from England to Massachusetts. A special case, known as a 'shift name,' occurs when a specific applied to a particular generic is shifted by association to another, near by, generic. Thus from an original **Deer Creek** may come **Deer Mountain.** A whole group of such names may develop, then being known as a 'name-cluster.' Shift names may occur even at the cost of appropriateness. Thus from an aptly named **Blue Lake** may arise **Blue Creek,** though the stream is not blue.

9. *Folk-etymology.* The term has been here used in preference to 'false etymology.' It results, theoretically, in the reshaping of an old name, but in practice it often creates a wholly new name. Some tendency toward folk-etymology occurs in nearly every transfer of a name by sound from one language to another, especially when the name is transferred merely as a name and the person receiving it is ignorant of the language of origin. In such a situation the new speaker of the name uses the sounds of his own language, and these sounds necessarily form familiar syllables, and often form words in his own language. In addition, especially for humorous ends, there may be a conscious playing with the sounds to shape them into familiar words.

Introduction

The process of folk-etymology is best grasped by observation of some examples, e.g. **Smackover, Orange, Loyalhanna, Funny Louis, Lamington.** Folk-etymology often shows in only a part of the name, e.g. **Horse Linto, Kingsessing.**

10. *Mistake names.* Undoubtedly many of our as-yet-unexplained names of apparent Indian origin remain thus obscure because they spring from a mistake made in the transmission from one language to another, either from inaccurate hearing of what was said, or because of faulty rendering of the sounds in writing. Alternate forms, e.g. **Carquinez-Tarquinez,** are thus explicable. Such early mistakes, however, can be demonstrated only in rare instances. Many actual mistakes in spelling, of later date, are authentically recorded, e.g. **Plaski, Tolo, Darrington, Bogata.** A more complicated origin may be seen in such a name as **Nome.**

Usage

1. *Qualification.* The attempt has been made to use qualifying terms consistently. 'Probably' specifies a high degree of likelihood, but indicates that (1) all the evidence may not be in, or (2) other conclusions cannot be wholly ruled out. The use of the question mark in parentheses indicates a much lower degree of likelihood, approaching a fifty-fifty situation. 'Apparently' and 'presumably' are not often used, but indicate a reasonable deduction, usually on linguistic grounds, but without direct evidence. 'Possibly' is the counterpart of 'probably,' indicating a small likelihood. It has been used but rarely, since a concise dictionary cannot ordinarily grant space to mere possibilities. The phrase 'by local story' is used when such a story cannot be confirmed and yet is not so unreasonable as to be arbitrarily rejected; it is thus about the equivalent of (?).

2. *Alphabetization.* The alphabetizing is by specific only, i.e. when a generic, such as *river* or *mountain,* occurs in the heading, it is not considered in the alphabetizing. Double specifics are alphabetized as if a single word. This usage sometimes affects the place of the entry, e.g. **A One** does not come immediately after A, but in its position as **Aone, Shake Rag** follows **Shaker.**

If alternate spellings are given, the first one determines the alphabetical position.

Introduction

If letters are put into parentheses to indicate an alternate spelling, e.g. **Ax(e)**, these letters are not considered in the alphabetizing.

Articles, including those in French and Spanish, are not considered, except (1) when the article has by usage become an integral part of a proper name, e.g. **La Pérouse,** and (2) when American usage has resulted in a firm amalgamation, e.g. **Los Angeles.** Cross references have been supplied when necessary, since differences of opinion in such matters is inevitable.

3. *Abbreviations.* The abbreviations are commonly the conventionally accepted ones, such as *e.g., i.e., viz.* The half-points of the compass are given as NE, NW, SE, SW. Other abbreviations occurring are *Co.* (County), *N.P.* (National Park), *N.M.* (National Monument), *P.O. Dept.* (Post Office Department).

The abbreviation *etc.* has usually been employed for a particular purpose. With many names the full notation should be, 'from the personal name or title or from the place in England; in later settled districts often from the original naming in America or for later places so named.' Under the necessity of conciseness, to avoid scores of such statements, the entry has sometimes been merely 'from the personal name, etc.' especially when the place involved was not one of great importance. (In any case, see *Dual and multiple origin.*)

The Zip code abbreviations have been used for the states and are listed here:

Alaska	AK	Maine	ME	Oklahoma	OK
Alabama	AL	Maryland	MD	Oregon	OR
Arizona	AZ	Massachusetts	MA	Pennsylvania	PA
Arkansas	AR	Michigan	MI	Rhode Island	RI
California	CA	Minnesota	MN	South Carolina	SC
Colorado	CO	Mississippi	MS	South Dakota	SD
Connecticut	CT	Missouri	MO	Tennessee	TN
Delaware	DE	Montana	MT	Texas	TX
Florida	FL	Nebraska	NB	Utah	UT
Georgia	GA	Nevada	NV	Vermont	VT
Idaho	ID	New Hampshire	NH	Virginia	VA
Illinois	IL	New Jersey	NJ	Washington	WA
Indiana	IN	New Mexico	NM	West Virginia	WV
Iowa	IA	New York	NY	Wisconsin	WI
Kansas	KS	North Carolina	NC	Wyoming	WY
Kentucky	KY	North Dakota	ND		
Louisiana	LA	Ohio	OH		

Bibliography

Ackerman, William K., *The Origin of Names of Stations on the Line of the Illinois-Central Railroad Company,* 1884.

Allsopp, Frederick William, *Folklore of Romantic Arkansas,* 1931.

American Guide Series. Compiled by workers of the Writers' Program of the Work Projects Administration. One volume for each state, various publishers, in the 1930's and 1940's.

Anon., 'Wyoming Place Names,' in *Annals of Wyoming,* vols. 14, 15, 1942–1943.

Arps, Louisa Ward, and Elinor Eppich Kingery, *High Country Names: Rocky Mountain National Park,* 1966.

Averett, Walter R., *Directory of Southern Nevada Place Names,* 1962.

Barge, William D., and Norman W. Caldwell, 'Illinois Place-names,' in *Journal of the Illinois State Historical Society,* vol. 29, no. 3, 1936.

Barnes, William C., *Arizona Place Names,* 1935. Revised and enlarged by Byrd H. Granger, 1960.

Beauchamp, William M., *Aboriginal Place Names of New York* in New York State Museum, *Bulletin 108,* 1907.

Becker, Donald William, *Indian Place-names in New Jersey.* 1964.

Bloodworth, Bertha Ernestine, *Florida Place-names,* 1959; (authorized facsimile, 1968, by University Microfilms, Inc.).

Board of Geographic Names (New York), *Report* in New York State Museum, *Bulletin 173,* 1914, pp. 43–58. (Names in Albany, Schenectady, and Rensselaer counties)

Bonney, Orin H., and Lorraine Bonney, *Guide to the Wyoming Mountains and Wilderness Areas,* 1960.

Branner, John Caster, 'Some old French place names in the state of Arkansas,' in *Arkansas Historical Quarterly,* vol. 19, 1960.

Bridger, Clyde A., 'The Counties of Idaho,' in *Pacific Northwest Quarterly,* vol. 31, 1940.

Brown, Virginia Pounds, and Jane Porter Nabers, 'The Origin of Certain Place Names in Jefferson County, Alabama,' in *Alabama Review,* vol. 5, 1952.

Bibliography

Carlson, Helen S., *Nevada Place Names: Origin and Meaning,* 1959, thesis, Univ. of New Mexico, typescript.

Cassidy, Frederic G., *The Place-names of Dane County, Wisconsin,* publication of the American Dialect Society, no. 7, 1947.

Chadbourne, Ava Harriet, *Maine Place Names and the Peopling of its Towns,* 1955.

Chittenden, Hiram Martin, *The Yellowstone National Park,* 1895.

Clough, Wilson Ober, *Some Wyoming Place Names,* 1943.

Corley, Wayne E., *County and community names in Kansas,* 1962.

Davis, William T., 'Staten Island Names,' in Natural Science Association of Staten Island, *Proceedings,* vol. 5, no. 5 (special no. 21), 1896.

Dawson, John F., *Place names in Colorado,* 1954.

Dexter, Franklin B., 'The History of Connecticut, as illustrated by the Names of her Towns,' in *Proceedings of the American Antiquarian Society,* n.s., vol. 2, 1885.

Donehoo, George P., *A History of the Indian Villages and Place-names in Pennsylvania,* 1928.

Dunlap, A. R., *Dutch and Swedish Place-names in Delaware,* 1956.

Dunlap, A. R., and C. A., Weslager, *Indian Place-names in Delaware,* 1950.

Dunn, Jacob Piatt, 'Glossary of Indian Names and Supposed Indian Names,' in *Indiana and Indianans,* 1919.

Dunn, Jacob Piatt, 'Indiana Geographical Nomenclature,' in *Indiana Magazine of History,* vol. 8, 1912.

Dustin, Fred, 'Isle Royale place names,' *Michigan History Magazine,* vol. 30, 1946.

Dustin, Fred, 'Some Indian place-names around Saginaw,' *Michigan History Magazine,* vol. 12, 1928.

Eels, Myron, 'Aboriginal Geographic Names in the State of Washington,' in *American Anthropologist,* vol. 5, 1892.

Eckstorm, F. H., *Indian Place-names of the Penobscot Valley and the Maine Coast, University of Maine Studies,* 2nd ser., no. 55, 1941.

Ehrensperger, Edward C., see United States Writers' Program (South Dakota).

Eno, Joel N., *A Tercentennial History of the Towns and Cities of New York: Their Origin, Dates and Names,* 1916 in New York State Historical Association, *Proceedings,* vol. 15, 1916.

Espenshade, Abraham H., *Pennsylvania Place Names,* 1925.

Farquhar, F. P., 'Naming Alaska's Mountains,' *American Alpine Journal,* vol. 11, 1959.

Farquhar, F. P., 'Naming America's Mountains,' *American Alpine Journal* ('The Cascades,' 1960; 'The Colorado Rockies,' 1961; 'The Sierra Nevada of California,' 1964).

Field, Thomas Parry, *A Guide to Kentucky Place Names,* 1961.

Field, Thomas Parry, 'The Indian Place Names of Kentucky,' in *Names,* vol. 7, 1959.

Fitzpatrick, Lillian Linder, *Nebraska Place-names,* 1925.

Bibliography

Fitzpatrick, Thomas Jefferson, Articles on the place-names of three counties in Iowa, viz. Des Moines, Lee, and Van Buren, in *Annals of Iowa,* 3rd ser., vols. 21, 17, and 18, 1937, 1929, 1931.

Fitzpatrick, Thomas Jefferson, 'The Place-names of Appanoose County, Iowa,' in *American Speech,* vol. 3, 1927.

Foscue, Virginia Oden, 'Sumter County Place-names, a Selection,' in *Alabama Review,* vol. 13, 1960.

Foster, Theodore G., 'Place-names of Ingham County,' in *Michigan History Magazine,* vol. 26, 1942.

Fox, George R., 'Place names of Berrien County,' in *Michigan Historical Magazine,* vol. 8, 1924.

Fox, George R., 'Place names of Cass County,' in *Michigan History Magazine,* vol. 27, 1943.

Fulmore, Zachary T., *The History and Geography of Texas as told in County Names,* 1915, 1926.

Gagnieur, William F., 'Indian place-names in the Upper Peninsula and their interpretation,' in *Michigan History Magazine,* vol. 2, 1918.

Gannett, Henry, Gazetteers of various states, published as bulletins of the U.S. Geological Survey, viz. Colorado, 1906; Connecticut, 1894; Delaware, 1904; Kansas, 1898; Maryland, 1904; Massachusetts, 1894; New Jersey, 1894; Oklahoma (Indian Territory), 1905; Rhode Island, 1894; Texas, 1904; Utah, 1900; Virginia, 1904; West Virginia, 1904.

Gannett, Henry, *The Origin of Certain Place Names in the United States,* 1902, reissued (without charges) in 1947 under the title, *American Names, a Guide to the Origin of Place Names in the United States.* (See *Preface.*)

Goff, John H., 'Short Studies of Georgia place names,' in *Georgia Mineral Newsletter,* vols. 7–16, 1954–1965.

Gould, Charles N., *Oklahoma Place Names,* 1933.

Granger, Byrd H. See William C. Barnes.

Gudde, Erwin G., *California Place Names,* 1949, 1960, 1969.

Halbert, Henry Sale, 'Choctaw Indian Names in Alabama and Mississippi,' in *Alabama Historical Society, Transactions,* vol. , 1898–1899.

Hamilton, Charlotte, 'Chippewa County place names,' in *Michigan History Magazine,* vol. 27, 1943.

Hanford, Franklin, 'Origin of Names of Places in Monroe County, New York,' in Rochester Historical Society, *Publication Fund Series,* vol. 5, 1926.

Hardy, Emmet Layton, *An Introduction to the Study of the Geographic Nomenclature of Kentucky's counties, cities, and towns,* thesis, Univ. on Kentucky, typescript, 1949.

Hart, John L. J., *Fourteen thousand feet,* 1925. Supplement to *Trail and Timberline,* June, 1925. (Colorado)

Heck, L. W. and others, *Delaware Place Names,* U.S. Geological Survey Bull. 1245, 1966.

Heckewelder, John G. E., *Names given by the Lenni Lenape or Delaware Indians*

Bibliography

to Rivers, Streams and Places in the Now States of New Jersey, Pennsylvania, Maryland, and Virginia. Originally in *Transactions of the American Philosophical Society,* vol. 4, 1834.

Hoffman, Frank A., 'Place Names in Brown County (Indiana),' in *Midwest Folklore,* vol. 11, 1961.

Huden, John C., *Indian Place Names of New England,* 1962.

Jenks, William L., 'History and Meaning of the County Names of Michigan,' in *Michigan History,* vol. 10, 1926.

Johnson, Amandus, *Indian Geographical Names,* Appendix to Peter Lindeström, *Geographia Americae,* 1925. (Chiefly Pennsylvania)

Johnson, William W., 'Indian Names in and about the County of Mackinac,' *Pioneer Society of the State of Michigan, Historical Collections,* vol. 12, 1887.

Johnston, Thesba N. and others, 'Vermont Town Names and their Derivations,' in *Vermont Quarterly,* n.s., vols. 20, 21, 1952–1953.

Kane, Joseph Nathan, *The American Counties,* 1962. (Valuable for its listings, but its derivations must be used with caution.)

Kenny, Hamill, *The Origin and Meaning of the Indian Place-names of Maryland,* 1961.

Kenny, Hamill, *West Virginia Place Names,* 1945.

Koch, Elers, 'Geographic Names of Western Montana and Northern Idaho,' in *Oregon Historical Quarterly,* vol. 49, 1948.

Kramer, Fritz L., *Idaho Town Names,* in Idaho State Historical Dept., *Twenty-third Biennial Report,* 1951–1952.

Krolczyk, J. C., *Gazetteer of Ohio Streams,* issued by Ohio Dept. of Natural Resources, Division of Water, 1954.

Kuhn, Herbert W., 'Indian Place-names in Wisconsin,' in *Wisconsin Archeologist,* vol. 33, 1952.

Leestma, Roger A., 'Origin of Dutch place names in Allegan and Ottawa counties, Michigan,' in *Michigan Academy of Sciences, Papers,* vol. 34, 1948.

Legler, Henry Edward, 'Origin and Meaning of Wisconsin Place-names,' in Wisconsin Academy of Sciences, Arts and Letters, *Transactions,* vol. 14, 1903.

Leigh, Rufus Wood, *Five Hundred Utah Place Names,* 1961.

Leigh, Rufus Wood, *Nevada Place Names, their Origin and Significance,* 1964.

Lindsey, David, *Ohio's Western Reserve, the Story of its Place Names,* 1955.

Link, John T., *The Origin of the Place Names of Nebraska,* 1933.

Linwood, Dee, 'Wyoming Stream Names,' in *Annals of Wyoming,* vols. 15, 16, 1944.

McArthur, Lewis A., *Oregon Geographic Names,* 1928, 1944, 1952.

McCormick, William R., 'Indian names in the Saginaw Valley,' in Pioneer Society of the State of Michigan, *Pioneer Collections,* vol. 7, 1884.

McJimsey, George Davis, *Topographic Terms in Virginia,* 1940.

McKaig, Thomas H., 'Place Names of Western New York,' in *Niagara Frontier,* vol. 1, 1954.

McMullen, Edwin Wallace, Jr., *English Topographical Terms in Florida,* 1953.

Bibliography

MacReynolds, George, *Place-names in Bucks County, Pennsylvania,* 1942.

Madison, Virginia, and Hallie Stillwell, *How come it's called that?* 1958. (The Big Bend country of Texas)

Mahr, August C., 'Indian River and Place Names in Ohio,' in *Ohio Historical Quarterly,* vol. 66, 1957.

Martin, Maria Ewing, 'Origin of Ohio Place Names,' in *Ohio Archeological and Historical Quarterly,* vol. 14, 1905.

Massengill, Fred I., *Texas Towns,* 1936.

Mathews, Mitford M., *A Dictionary of Americanisms* (2 vols.), 1951.

Meany, Edmond S., *Mount Rainier, A Record of Exploration,* 1916.

Meany, Edmond S., *Origin of Washington Geographic Names,* 1923.

Milliken, Charles F., *Ontario County (N.Y.) Place Names,* in *N.Y. State Museum Bulletin,* no. 253, 1924.

Missouri Pacific Railroad Company, *The Empire that Missouri Pacific Serves,* 1956(?). (Chiefly useful for Arkansas and Kansas)

Nevada Historical Society, studies of the place-names of various counties (Washoe, Churchill, Douglas, Lyon, Ormsby, Storey) by A. W. Ohmert, V. E. Hasch, C. M. Cleator, and F. L. Bray, in *Biennial Report,* vols. 2 and 3, 1909–1910.

Orth, Donald J., *Dictionary of Alaska Place Names,* 1967.

Overman, William Daniel, *Ohio Place Names,* 1951.

Parsons, Charles W., 'Town-names in Rhode Island,' in *Rhode Island Historical Society Proceedings,* 1886–1887.

Pearce, Ruth L., 'Welsh Place-names in Southeastern Pennsylvania,' in *Names,* vol. 11, 1963.

Pearce, T. M., *New Mexico Place Names,* 1965.

Price, Eliphalet, 'The Origin and Interpretation of the Names of the Rivers and Streams of Clayton County,' in *Annals of Iowa,* vols. 4, 5, 1866, 1867.

Queens Borough Historian, The, *The First Annual Report, Supplement,* 'The Origin of Community Names in Queens Borough (N.Y.),' 1945.

Ramsay, Robert L., *Our Storehouse of Missouri Place Names,* Missouri Handbook Number Two, The University of Missouri Bulletin, vol. 53, no. 34, Arts and Science Series, 1952, no. 7.

Ramsay, Robert L., *The Place Names of Boone County, Missouri,* 1952.

Randel, William P., 'The Place-names of Tioga County, Pennsylvania,' in *American Speech,* vol. 14, 1939.

Raup, Hallock Floy, 'Names of Ohio's Streams,' in *Names,* vol. 5, 1957.

Read, Allen Walker, *Study of Iowa Place Names selected from counties A through F,* thesis, Univ. of Iowa, typescript, 1926.

Read, William A., *Florida Place-names of Indian Origin,* 1934.

Read, William A., *Indian Place-names in Alabama,* 1937.

Read, William A., 'Indian stream-names in Georgia,' in *International Journal of American Linguistics,* vols. 15 and 16, 1949–1950.

Read, William A., *Louisiana-French,* 1931.

Bibliography

Read, William A., *Louisiana Place-names of Indian Origin,* 1927.

Reynolds, Jack Adolphe, *Louisiana Place-names of Romance Origin,* thesis, Louisiana State Univ., typescript, 1942.

Reynolds, T. W., *Born of the Mountains,* 1964 (North Carolina).

Rowe, Jesse Perry, 'The Origin of some Montana Place Names.' In his *Geography and Natural Resources of Montana,* MS, no date, Microfilm #82, Univ. of Montana Library.

Ruttenber, E. M., *Footprints of the Red Men,* in New York State Historical Association, *Proceedings,* vol. 6, 1906.

Salem County Historical Society, 'Place Names in Salem County, N.J.,' in *Publications,* vol. 2, 1964.

Sands, D. B., 'The Nature of the Generics in Island, Ledge, and Rock Names of the Maine Coast,' in *Names,* vol. 7, 1959.

Sapir, Edward, 'Southern Paiute Dictionary,' in American Academy of Arts and Sciences, *Proceedings,* vol. 65, 1931.

Scomp, H. A., 'Kentucky county names,' in *Magazine of History* vol. 7, 1908.

Sealock, Richard B., and Pauline A. Seely, *Bibliography of Place-Name Literature, United States and Canada,* 1948, 1957. Supplement in *Names,* vol. 16, 1968.

Sellers, Helen Earle, *Connecticut Town Origins* (n.d.), reprinted from *The Connecticut Register and Manual,* 1942.

Shirk, George H., *Oklahoma Place Names,* 1965.

Skinner, Alanson Buck, Some Menomini Place-names in Wisconsin,' in his *Material Culture of the Menomini,* 1921.

Smith, Huron H., 'Indian Place Names in Wisconsin,' in Milwaukee Public Museum, *Yearbook,* vol. 10, 1930.

Stennett, W. H., *A History of the Origin of the Place Names Connected with the Chicago & North Western and Chicago, St. Paul, Minneapolis & Omaha Railways,* 1908. (Chiefly used for Iowa, Michigan, and Wisconsin)

Stewart, George R., 'A Classification of Place Names,' in *Names,* vol. 2, 1954.

Stewart, George R., 'Names (in Linguistics),' in *Encyclopaedia Britannica.*

Stewart, George R., *Names on the Land,* 1945, 1960, 1967.

Toll, Roger W., *The Mountain Peaks of Colorado,* 1923. Supplement to *Trail and Timberline.*

Tooker, William Wallace, *The Indian Place-names on Long Island and Islands Adjacent,* 1911, 1962.

Trumbull, James Hammond, 'The Composition of Indian Geographical Names, illustrated from the Algonkin Languages,' in Connecticut Historical Society, *Collections,* vol. 2, 1870.

Trumbull, James Hammond, *Indian Names of Places, etc., in and on the Borders of Connecticut,* 1881.

United States Writers' Program (Colorado), 'Place Names of Colorado Towns,' in *Colorado Magazine,* January 1940 to May 1943, vols. 17–20, 1940–1943.

United States Writers' Program (Massachusetts), *The Origin of Massachusetts Place Names of the State, Counties, Cities, and Towns,* 1941.

Bibliography

United States Writers' Program (New Jersey), *The Origin of New Jersey Place Names,* 1945.

United States Writers' Program (North Carolina), *How they began—the story of North Carolina county, town and other place names,* 1941.

United States Writers' Program (South Carolina), *Palmetto Place Names,* 1941.

United States Writers' Program (South Dakota), *South Dakota Place Names,* 1941. Sponsored by the Department of English, Edward C. Ehrensperger, Head, University of South Dakota.

United States Writers' Program (Utah), *Origins of Utah Place Names,* 1940.

Upham, Warren, *Minnesota Geographic Names,* 1920.

Verwyst, Chrysostom, 'Geographical names in Wisconsin, Minnesota and Michigan having a Chippewa origin,' in State Historical Society (Wisconsin), *Collections,* vol. 12, 1892.

Verwyst, Chrysostom, 'A Glossary of Chippewa Indian Names of Rivers, Lakes and Villages,' *Acta et Dicta,* vol. 4, 1916.

Vogel, Virgil J., *Indian Place Names in Illinois,* 1963.

Walker, Norman M., 'The Geographical Nomenclature of Louisiana,' in *Magazine of American History,* vol. 10, 1883.

Webb, Walter Prescott, editor-in-chief, *The Handbook of Texas,* 1952.

Weslager, C. A., *Place names on Ocracoke Island,* 1954.

Whitmore, William Henry, *An Essay on the Origin of Names of Towns in Massachusetts, settled prior to A.D. 1775,* 1873.

Williams, Mary Ann Barnes, *Origins of North Dakota Place Names,* 1966.

WPA Guides. See *American Guide Series.*

Wright, Muriel H., 'Some Geographical Names of French Origin in Oklahoma,' in *Chronicles of Oklahoma,* vol. 7, 1929.

AMERICAN PLACE-NAMES

A

A French 'to, at, with,' but in American-French usually the equivalent of *de,* i.e. the possessive 'of.' The accented form (*à*) is used in French, but in American place-names the accent is sometimes used, sometimes omitted. In combination with the definite article occur **Au,** 'of the,' 'at the' (masculine singular) and **Aux,** 'of the,' 'at the' (plural). See **Auglaize, Ozark, Auxvasse.**

AB Mountain AK So called (1952) because the snow on the face of the mountain in the process of melting displays a rough outline of the two letters.

Abagadusset ME Algonquian, to denote a stream following a course 'parallel' to the main shore.

Abajo NM Spanish 'down, below,' in a topographical sense; 'lower' in the district name **Rio Abajo** NM: 'down-river area.'

Abalone The much-sought-after mollusk has produced some ten names along the CA coast. **Point Alones** and **Point Aulon** represent other spellings of the same Indian (probably Costanoan) word.

Abbeville From the city in France. In SC named by a Huguenot settler for his former home. In AL orginally derived from **Abbie Creek** (q.v.). In LA, for the Abbé A. D. Mégret, who established a church here, ca. 1845.

Abbie From the woman's name, e.g., **Abbie Lake** MN. **Abbie Creek** AL: a shortening from **Yattayabba** (1844), Muskogean, meaning uncertain.

Abbyville KS For Abby McLean, the first child born at the settlement.

Abdal NB A railroad name, probably from an Arabic name-element, as in such personal names as Abd-al-Kadir.

Abeles AR From a family name, not further identified.

Abenaki See **Abnaki.**

Aberdeen From the city in Scotland, usually so named because of Scottish settlers.

Aberjona River MA Algonquian 'confluence,' probably named from a place where two streams flowed together.

Abeytas NM From the family name of early Spanish landholders.

Abiathar Peak WY For Charles Abiathar White of the U. S. Geological Survey.

Abilene In KS the name was taken (ca. 1860) from Luke 3:1, where it is mentioned as a tetrarchy; it was considered appropriate because of its assumed literal meaning (from Hebrew, *abel*) 'grassy plain, meadow,' the region being at that time wholly grassland. In TX the name was transferred from KS.

Abingdon From a town in England or a personal name; possibly a spelling variant of **Abington.**

Abington In MA (1712) and PA (1714) probably from a town in England; the almost simultaneous naming is apparently coincidental. It is also a personal name. See **Abingdon.**

Abiquiu NM Recorded in a Spanish context (1776) as **Abiqui,** it is probably the name of an old Indian town, meaning uncertain, though the modern Tewa connect it with *abay,* 'chokecherry.'

Abita Springs LA Choctaw 'spring, fountain.'

Abnaki From the Indian tribal name. Also **Abenaki.**

Abo Although it is an alternate name for a city in Finland, the origin in NM is Indian (Piro) of unknown meaning. In MO the name, which occurs twice, is probably Indian.

Aboite River IN Probably French *à boitte,* 'of bait,' with possible reference to the presence of minnows.

Aboroto Creek CO Probably Spanish; if not a personal name, it may be from Mexican Spanish *abarrote,* meaning a small store, especially for groceries.

Abra Spanish 'gorge.' See also **La Habra.**

Abraham From the Biblical patriarch (also a saint), probably the bay in AK; from the personal name, especially for Abraham Lincoln, as a means of avoiding too frequent use of his family name, e.g., the islands in AK.

Abram From the personal name, e.g. **Abrams Creek** TN for an 18th-century Cherokee chief.

Abreojo Rocks AK Spanish *abre ojo,* literally 'open eye,' used as a mariner's phrase of warning.

Absaroka, Absarokee, Absaraka An Indian term of disputed origin and meaning, but applied to the tribe known in English as the Crow and also to the country inhabited by that tribe; hence, some towns and the mountains in MT and WY, because they were the land of that tribe.

Absco CA From American Beet Sugar Co.

Absecon NJ A variant of **Absegami.**

Absegami Lake NJ Probably Algonquian 'small-water' with reference to **Absecon Bay** as compared with the ocean.

Acabonack NY Algonquian 'root-place,' for some edible tuber.

Academia Latin 'academy.'

Academy From the presence of the type of school once so called, e.g. in CA and SD.

Acadia From the district in Canada so known.

Acadien The French form for Acadian, with reference to the Canadians settled in Louisiana ca. 1765, e.g. **Bayou des Acadiens.**

Acala TX From a type of cotton, originally from Acala in Mexico.

Acalanes CA From the Indian tribal name, also recorded as Sacalanes.

Acampo CA Though a Spanish word, 'common pasture,' the name was placed by Americans, probably with the idea of *campo,* 'camp,' and the article 'a.'

Acasa LA From an Indian tribal name, recorded as Nacassa.

Accakeek See **Accokeek.**

Accident MD Because, in 1774, some land was marked off 'by accident.'

Accokeek MD Algonquian (Delaware), meaning uncertain.

Accomac(k) Algonquian 'other-side-at.' In VA **Accomac County** is a part of the 'Eastern Shore,' and thus on the other side of Chesapeake Bay from the point of view of people in the chief Indian settlements.

Accord MA, NY A commendatory, probably used as a variant of the commoner **Concord.**

Accotink VA Algonquian, meaning uncertain.

Accoville WV Formed from *-ville* and from the opening letters of Amherst Coal Company.

Ace In TX from Ace Emanuel, first postmaster; in mining districts used as a commendatory, e.g. **Ace Creek** AK.

Acequia Spanish 'irrigation canal.' In ID the town was founded as part of an irrigation project.

Achi AZ Papago 'ridge.'

Achille OK Though the French form of **Achilles** and used as a personal name, it is here from a Cherokee word, 'fire.'

Achilles From the Homeric hero.

Achonee, Mount CO For an Arapaho chief whose name is more commonly spelled Ochanee; reason for application uncertain.

Achsining, Mount NY Algonquian 'standing-stones.'

Acid Factory Brook RI From an acetic acid factory which operated ca. 1865–83.

Acipco AL From American Cast Iron Pipe Company.

Acme In a dozen states as a commendatory; roughly, 'highest, best.' In OK, NM, TX, it is from a cement company which founded the towns.

Acoma NM Indian (Keres) 'white-rock people.' **Acomita** NM is the diminutive.

Acomes Falls ME Algonquian 'high.'

Acquackanonk NJ Algonquian. Of record since 1679 (first form, Haquehuenunck), this name exists in more than 80 spellings and is of uncertain meaning, but it may be another 'bush-net-fishing-at.' Cf. **Aquashicola.**

Acton In MA (1735) probably for a town in England.

Acushnet MA Algonquian, probably 'cove-at.'

Adak Island AK Aleut 'father'(?).

Adamana AZ From Adam Hanna, an early cattleman.

Adam-Ondi-Ahman MO A conscious or unconscious coinage of Joseph Smith, who records in his autobiography that he came to the place in 1838 and that it was so named 'by the mouth of the Lord,' because Adam had lived there after his exile from Paradise. The last two parts of the name have not been explained.

Adams From the personal name, most commonly for John Adams, second president, e.g. **Mount Adams** WA, **Point Adams** OR. **Adams** MA: for Samuel Adams (1722–1803), Revolutionary patriot. Namings for John Quincy Adams are rarer. See **Quincy.**

Adam's Grave MO In Mormon tradition the burial place of the Biblical Adam. See **Adam-Ondi-Ahman.**

Add KY Probably from the abbreviation of a personal name, such as Addison or Adam.

Adden Mountain VT Algonquian, apparently the fragment of a longer name, what is left being the root *-adn-,* 'mountain.'

Addielee OK From the names Addie and Lee Cole, local merchants.

Addison From the personal name especially, e.g. ME (1797), for Joseph Addison, essayist and poet. In VT (1761) the naming is for the same man, but more motivated probably by his position as Secretary of State, in which capacity he signed the commission appointing John Wentworth as lieutenant-governor of NH.

Adel Generally from a woman's name; in OR named by the landowner for a former sweetheart. In IA the earlier spelling **Adell** and the site make probable the derivation from 'a dell.'

Adelanto Spanish 'progress.'

Adelphi OH Greek 'brothers,' for Reuben and Henry Abrams who were concerned with the town-founding (1804).

Adelphia NJ, VA From the Greek for 'brother,' with an ending to indicate a place; a commendatory.

Aden NM Probably from the city in Arabia, a railroad name. But it exists as a family name.

Adena In CO it was named (1910) for Edna Adena, sweetheart of one of the settlers. In OH it was coined (ca. 1805) by Gov. Thomas Worthington for his house, from the Greek 'enough,' to indicate satisfaction, and was transferred to the town.

Adiga Creek NY Iroquoian 'to-have-fire-there.'

Adin CA For Adin McDowell, early settler.

Adios, Bayou LA Shifted by folk-etymology to the form of the Spanish 'goodbye' from earlier forms Adayes, Adois, based upon an Indian tribal name Adai, apparently with an English possessive *s.*

Adirondack NY From the Indian tribal name.

Admah NB From a Biblical town.

Admiralty In WA and AK the names were given by British explorers in honor of the British Admiralty, under whose orders their voyages were being made, e.g., the inlet in WA thus named by George Vancouver in 1792. He also named the islands in AK (1794).

Admire KS For Jacob Admire, town founder.

Adobe Spanish 'sun-dried brick.' In the U.S. it has been extended to mean soil of a kind from which such bricks might be made. As a specific, it is used to describe a place having such soil, e.g. **Adobe Hill** WY, or a place having a house or houses built of such bricks, e.g. **Adobe Walls** TX.

Adrian From the personal name, e.g. in MO for Adrian Talmage: a station-name given by his father who was general passenger agent for a railroad.

Adsul TX From the Adams-Sullivan Lumber Co.

Advance A commendatory for habitation-names, in NC for the ship *Ad-Vance,* a famous blockade-runner of the Civil War.

Advent WV From the Advent Christian Church.

Adventure To record an incident, e.g. the creek in AK where the namers went astray.

Aeneas WA For an Indian so named, a guide who died ca. 1913, reputedly more than a hundred years old.

Aetna See **Etna.**

Affonee Creek AL Muskogean, meaning uncertain.

Afognak AK A 'native' name, probably Eskimo, applied first to the island; meaning uncertain.

Africa In occasional use for a community chiefly inhabited by Negroes, e.g., in OH.

Afton From the river in Scotland, but almost wholly because of Burns's song, 'Flow gently sweet Afton.' In OK it is for Afton Ayres, daughter of a railroad surveyor.

Agamenticus ME Algonquian, meaning uncertain, but with *tic,* 'river.'

Agassiz Various features are named for Louis Agassiz (1807–1873), Swiss-American naturalist, e.g. **Agassiz Peak** AZ.

Agate Usually because of the finding of agates or stones supposed to be agates, e.g. the beach OR. **Agate Passage** WA for A. T. Agate of the Wilkes Expedition of 1841.

Agathla Needle AZ Navajo 'much wool,' probably originating from some incident, possibly of mythological origin.

Agattu Island AK Aleut, meaning uncertain.

Agawam Algonquian 'overflowed land'(?).

Agency Generally because of the presence there, at some time, of an Indian agency, e.g. **Agency Creek** OR.

Agenda KS Apparently for 'things to be done,' but actual reason for naming uncertain.

Agligadak Island AK Aleut 'albatross.'

Agoura CA Probably from a misspelling of the name of some local ranchers, Agoure.

Agra From the city in India.

Agricola In several states it is probably from Latin 'farmer' rather than for one of the Romans so named, and thus a commendatory. Cf. **Farmer.**

Agua Spanish 'water, spring,' usually a generic but serving as part of a specific in habitation-names, e.g. **Agua Sal** AZ, **Agua Dulce** CA, etc. It frequently occurs in double specifics, e.g. **Agua Fria Creek** CA.

Aguila Spanish 'eagle,' also a personal name. **Las Aguilas** CA: from a family of early settlers.

Aguilares TX From Locadis Aguilar, pioneer rancher.

Aguja Spanish 'needle,' e.g. **Aguja Peak** TX.

Ahapook Creek AZ Hualapai 'water-head.'

Ahe Vonam AZ Papago 'hat on both ends,' a descriptive of the mountain.

Ahinhan Lake WI Algonquian, meaning uncertain.

Ahlosa OK Muskogean 'there-black,' probably a place that had been burned.

Ahmeek MI Ojibway 'beaver.' Also **Ahmik.**

Ahnapee WI Algonquian, probably connected with the word for 'when,' but reference uncertain.

Ahoskie NC Indian, language and meaning uncertain.

Ahozhogun Lake WI Algonquian, meaning uncertain.

Ahwahnee CA Probably the name of an Indian village or tribe.

Air Scarcely used except in a few recent names and generally in compounds which have developed from air-travel, e.g. **Airplane Flats** AK, because planes landed there during World War II. **Airs Hill** AK: for A. R. Airs who was a member of a geological party there in 1898.

Airlie In both OR and MN, the name is from the Earl of Airlie, an investor ca. 1880 in American lands and railroads.

Airy Usually as **Mount Airy,** a repeated name in the SE where the climate makes the name especially commendatory.

Aix IN For the French or German city.

Ajo AZ The Papago called the place by their word for 'paint,' because they there obtained red ore for pigment. This term (rendered approximately as *au'auho*) sounded to the Spaniards like their word *ajo,* 'garlic,' and they adopted that spelling by the process of folk-etymology.

Akaska SD Siouan, meaning uncertain

Ak Chut Vaya AZ Papago 'well in wash.'

Akela NM Probably a literary name from the leader of the wolf pack in Kipling's *Jungle Book;* a railroad name.

Akiak AK Eskimo, probably 'crossing,' because it is a point for winter crossing of the Yukon River.

Akokala Mountain MT Indian (Kootenai) 'rotten,' reference uncertain.

Akra ND Named (1878) by Icelandic immigrants for a place in Iceland.

Akron Greek 'summit.' The town in OH is at the top of the divide between two rivers. Other towns, e.g. in IA, echoed this one; sometimes, as in CO, named with the additional reason of being on a summit.

Akutan Island AK Aleut, apparently the phrase, 'I made a mistake'; if so, probably a name applied by the Russians through misunderstanding.

Alabam AR From the colloquial contraction of **Alabama. Cf. Kentuck.**

Alabama From the name of an Indian tribe, a subdivision of the Creek, often spelled Alibamu, and known to the French as Alibamons. The modern name has been shaped under Spanish influence to the appearance of a Spanish word. It was applied from the tribe to the river, and then to the territory and state. **Alabama Hills** CA: named by Confederate sympathizers in 1863 because of the exploits of the ship *Alabama.*

Alabaster Usually, e.g. in MI, from the occurrence of gypsum, considered to be a form of alabaster.

Alachua FL From an early Seminole town; meaning uncertain.

Alacran Spanish 'scorpion.'

Aladdin In WY it was named (1898) from the character in *Arabian Nights* as a commendatory suggestive of good luck and riches.

Alafia FL From the name of an early Seminole town; meaning uncertain.

Alagnak River AK Eskimo 'raspberry.'

Alamance NC Applied first to the stream, probably Indian (Siouan) 'noisy stream' (?).

Alambique Spanish 'still.' In CA the creek takes its name from a still that was operated there ca. 1840.

Alameda Spanish 'grove of poplars' (cottonwoods), but used loosely for a grove of any kind of shade-giving trees. The county (hence, the city) in CA was named for the fine growth of oaks.

Alamicut River WA Indian, probably 'deep-river.'

Alamo Spanish 'poplar, cottonwood.' In regions of Spanish background the word regularly refers to the cottonwood. Since that tree was prominent and gave indication of places where water could be found, the name is frequent; often in the plural, e.g. **Los Alamos** CA, NM. In **Alamogordo** NM it occurs with *gordo,* 'fat, big.' In **Alamo Hueco Mountains** NM it occurs with *hueco,* 'hollow.'

Alamoosak Lake ME Algonquian 'fish-spawning-at.'

Alamosa CO, NM Spanish, a feminine adjective from *alamo,* 'cottonwood.'

Alamota KS Probably for an Osage chief of the 19th century.

Alamuchee Creek AL Muskogean 'hiding-place-little' (?).

Alanreed TX For the firm Allen & Reed, the contractors who built the local railroad.

Alanthus VA Probably a simplified spelling of *ailanthus,* for the tree.

Alapah Mountain AK Eskimo 'cold,' named ca. 1930.

Alapaha River FL From the name of an early Seminole town; meaning uncertain.

Alapahoochee River GA A diminutive of **Alapaha;** therefore, the equivalent of **Little Alapaha.**

Alapocas DE Algonquian, meaning uncertain.

Alaqua Creek FL Seminole 'sweet-gum-tree.'

Alargate Rocks AK Spanish, from a warning on the map of a Spanish expedition of 1779, 'Give this a wide berth.' Cf. **Quitasueno.**

Alarka Mountains NC Cherokee, meaning uncertain.

Alarm Creek TX Because a party of surveyors who were camped here promised to give the settlers an alarm in case of Indian incursion.

Alaska From an Aleutian word, appearing in various spellings, e.g. Alaeksu, Alachschak, Alaschka, Alaxa, and meaning 'mainland,' being thus distinguished from the islands by people who were islanders. During the Russian occupation the region was known, in English, as Russian America, but the present name was put forward by Senator Charles Sumner at the time of the purchase by the U.S. in 1867, apparently under the assumption that it meant 'great land.' The name, however, was proposed by various other people also, about the same time, sometimes with the spelling Aliaska. The form **Alaska** even appeared in the newspapers before the time of Sumner's speech, and it rapidly established itself in popular usage, and thence was taken into official usage.

Alatna River AK Athapascan, with *-na,* 'river,' and the rest uncertain.

Alazan Bay TX Spanish 'sorrel-colored,' originally the name of a land grant, but reference uncertain.

Alba Usually from a personal name, e.g. in MI for Alba Haywood, a visiting elocutionist, who apparently suggested the name with the additional idea of the Latin meaning, 'white,' as a commendatory. In TX with the Latin meaning, the town being a post-Civil War foundation where Negroes were not allowed.

Albany The Dutch settlement known as Fort Orange or Beverwyck ("Beavertown"), was thus renamed in 1664 at the time of the English occupation, after the Duke of York's Scottish title, Duke of Albany (see **New York**). The name has spread to about 20 states.

Albemarle In NC and SC the name is from George Monk (1608–1669), Duke of Albemarle, one of the Lords Proprietors. The county in VA was named (1744) for the earl.

Alberhill CA From Albers and Hill, two early landowners.

Albin From the personal name; in WY for John Albin Anderson, first postmaster.

Albino From association with an albino animal. **Albino Creek** MT because a very rare albino elk was once seen there.

Albion From the mythological name of England. Francis Drake in 1579 gave the name New Albion to the coast of California because of the white cliffs near his landfall. A memory of this naming accounts for the naming of the **Albion River** CA by an Englishman in 1844. Elsewhere the name seems to have arisen from a vaguely romantic Anglophilism. **Mount Albion** CO: originally from a mine-name given by Scots.

Albuquerque NM With slight alteration of spelling for the Duke Alburquerque, viceroy of New Spain, when the town was founded (1706). The dropping of the r appears to be the work of Americans, who may have confused the name with that of the much more famous Portuguese, Alphonso d'Albuquerque.

Alburg VT A shortening from the name of Ira Allen, Revolutionary political leader.

Alcalde NM Spanish 'magistrate, mayor,' but reason for naming unknown.

Alcan A coined name from Alaska and Canada, at the time of the building of the highway during World War II; preserved in **Alcan Harbor** AK.

Alcatraz Spanish 'pelican.' The name was given (1775) to the present **Yerba Buena Island** CA in the plural, Alcatraces, because of the number of such birds there, but was later transferred in singular form to the present island.

Alcoa TN From Aluminum Company of America.

Alcolu SC Coined by using the first two letters of Alderman, Coleman, and Lulu, all existing in the family of a local lumberman.

Alcoma VA Probably a variant of **Algoma.**

Alcona County MI Coined (1869) by the **Schoolcraft** (q.v.) system to produce a pseudo-Indian result; local tradition supplies a translation as 'the-excellent-plain,' but does not offer any plausible linguistic analysis.

Alcott From the personal name, in SC for Louisa M. Alcott, the author.

Alcova WY By local story, because it is 'all coves.'

Alcove Canyon AZ Descriptive, from the many nooks in the rocks. In CA the canyon was originally **Elk Cove,** which was transformed by folk-etymology after the memory of the elk had been lost.

Alcovy River GA Muskogean (Creek) 'pawpaws-among.'

Alder Since the tree is common along streams, it has given the name widely, and many of these have been transferred to habitations.

Aldona AZ From Al Donau, early cattleman.

Aleck Island, Alecks Creek GA From the Muskogean word for 'doctor,' from a Creek chief so known.

Aleman Spanish 'German,' the town in TX being a German settlement.

Alert In occasional use for a habitation-name, apparently as a commendatory, e.g. in NC where it was named by the first postmaster.

Aleutian An adjective formed from Aleut, the name of the people inhabiting the islands so called.

Alewife From the presence of the fish so called, e.g. the cove in CT.

Alexander From the personal name. The archipelago in AK was named (1867) by the U.S. Coast and Geodetic Survey for the czar at the time of the purchase of AK.

Alexandria The form is that of the repeated Greek name for cities, especially the one in Egypt, but the occasion of the giving of the name is regularly someone named Alexander, as with the city in VA, named in 1748 for a family of local landowners.

Alexauken Creek NJ Algonquian, meaning uncertain, but probably with *sauk,* 'outlet.'

Alfalfa Generally from the crop, but the county in OK is named for William H. Murray, governor, nicknamed 'Alfalfa Bill.'

Alfarata PA From the fictional Indian girl of the 19th-century song *The Blue Juniata.*

Alfred From the personal name. In ME (1794) it honors King Alfred, an example of new heroes being sought after the Revolution. In ND (1904) named by an English landowner for King Alfred.

Algansee MI Probably a pseudo-Indian coinage of the **Schoolcraft** (q.v.) type.

Algerita TX Locally believed to be a misspelling from *agarita,* a berry-bearing bush.

Algiers From the city of North Africa, until 1830 known chiefly for its pirates; in LA the name was probably applied derogatorily to an unsavory district, but details are uncertain.

Algoa From a bay on the coast of South Africa; in TX from a British ship, which was wrecked there.

Algodon Spanish 'cotton.' **Algodones** CA: though apparently the spelling of the Spanish plural, the origin is an Indian tribe recorded as Achedomas.

Algoma A synthetic word formed by H. R. Schoolcraft for a region in Canada bordering lakes Superior and Huron, and transferred to various towns in the U.S. The *al-* is from Algonquian, the tribal and linguistic name, and the *goma* is Algonquian for 'lake.'

Algona In IA it was coined, ca. 1860, from Algonquian. In WA the name was originally **Algoma,** but was changed by error in transmission through the Post Office Dept. (1910).

Algonac Coined (1861) from the tribal name Algonquin and *ac* (taken from *ace*) 'land, earth'; this is a name of the type popularized by H. R. Schoolcraft, and is probably by him. See **Schoolcraft.**

Algonkin See **Algonquin.**

Algonquin From the Indian tribal name, though preserved from literary sources and as a linguistic term, since the tribe itself disappeared early. In IL the name was placed by a man who had served on a ship of that name.

Alhamblar Mountain AK Coined by Robert Marshall, who was exploring the area in 1931, from **Alinement, Hammond,** and **Blarney,** because its slopes drained into those streams.

Alhambra Generally from the name of the Moorish palace in Spain, popularized by the writing of Washington Irving. The valley (Contra Costa Co., CA) was originally **Canada del Hambre,** 'valley of the hunger,' probably the equivalent of American 'starvation,' and based on some frontier incident. An American woman, in the 1880s, altered the name because of the unpleasant suggestions of *hambre.*

Ali Ak Chin AZ Papago 'little mouth of wash.'

Alicel OR From the first name and last initial of Alice Ladd.

Ali Chuk Son AZ Papago 'little blackhills foot.'

Alikchi Muskogean (Choctaw) 'doctor,' with reference to a medicinal spring.

Aliquippa PA From the personal name of a Seneca woman who was reputed to be a queen and was often so termed by the English; she died in 1754.

Aliso Spanish 'alder tree.' The Mexicans used the word to refer also to the sycamore, which is a common stream-side tree in much of CA.

Alkabo ND Coined (1913) from *alkali* and *gumbo,* because the region had both kinds of soil.

Alkali A descriptive applied to waters impregnated with the salts vaguely so known or to land showing the whiteness of alkali or known to be so charged, e.g. **Alkali Lake, Alkali Creek,** both common in arid and semi-arid regions.

Alki Chinook jargon 'by and by,' probably a fanciful naming. **Alki Point** WA: locally believed to have been named with reference to the slow growth of the community.

Allagash ME Algonquian 'bark-shelter.'

Allah AZ Originally, Garden of Allah, from a novel of that title, which the place was supposed to resemble because of its location in the desert.

Allakaket AK Indian (Athapascan) 'Alatna-(river)-mouth.'

Allamakee County IA Possibly Algonquian (Cf. **Allamuchy**), but more likely from Allen Magee, an Indian trader, as his name was pronounced by the local Indians.

Allamore TX For Alla Moore, wife of an early settler.

Allamoosook Pond ME Algonquian, meaning uncertain.

Allamuchy NJ Algonquian, probably 'inward,' with reference to a pond isolated among hills.

Allapattah FL From Seminole *halpata,* 'alligator.'

Allatoona GA Probably Cherokee, meaning uncertain.

Allegan County MI Suggested (1835) by Schoolcraft (q.v.), probably as a variant of **Allegheny** (q.v.).

Allegheny, Alleghany, Allegany Algonquian (Delaware), with *-heny* equaling the commoner *-hanna,* 'stream.' The first part of the name is probably an English adaptation of Algonquian *welhik,* 'most beautiful, best.' Thus explained the name is a translation of the Iroquoian (see **Ohio**). The Delawares moved into this region in the eighteenth century, and could have translated the Iroquoian name then. The stream is actually the upper part of the **Ohio,** and was so considered both by the Iroquois and by the French. The mountains were named from the river.

Allegre KY Probably from the Italian 'happy, joyful.'

Allemand French 'German,' e.g. **Lake des Allemands** LA, which is in an area colonized by German settlers. Cf. **Teche.**

Allen, Allan From the personal name. **Allentown** PA: for William Allen, who in the 18th century held a land grant there. **Allentown** AZ: for Allan Johnson, early cattleman; the name was absorbed into the commoner spelling. **Allendale:** usually for the district in England, with the commendatory suggestion carried by *-dale;* sometimes, e.g. NJ, SC, also suggested by the presence of a person named Allen. The river and other features in AK are for Gen. H. T. Allen, who as lieutenant conducted explorations in 1885, these names being placed later by others. His apparent naming for himself (**Allenkaket**) has reverted to **Allakaket,** (q.v.). **Allenspark** CO: for Alonzo Allen, early settler.

Alliance A commendatory name for habitations, often the equivalent of **Union** as indicating such action, e.g. in OH where the town was formed by the uniting of four communities in 1854. In SC and MN, from the Farmers' Alliance, a widespread rural organization in 1890. **Belle Alliance** LA: originally a plantation name; in French the term sometimes refers to a family relationship or marriage.

Alligator Though the alligator was common in lowland waters throughout the southeastern states, comparatively few natural features are thus distinquished, an evidence that the creature did not much impress the early American either for good or bad. An occasional river, creek, or lake is thus named. These names were rarely transferred to habitations, **Alligator** MS from nearby **Alligator Lake** being one of the few examples. **Alligator River** NC: this is an example of a 'boundary name,' being at the extreme northern range of the alligator, where its presence was noteworthy. **Alligator Hole** WV: a stream pool, apparently named because of the presence of a kind of salamander, supposed by someone (perhaps humorously) to be alligators, of which there are none in the state. **The Alligator** AZ: a low-lying ridge resembling an alligator.

Allisonia VA From the personal name Allison with a Latin ending for place.

Allonahachee Creek GA Muskogean (Creek) 'potato-(wild)-stream.'

Allouez MI, WI For Father C. J. Allouez, French Jesuit missionary of the 17th century.

Alloway MD, NJ Though the spelling has become that of an English family name, the origin in NJ is from a 17th-century Indian chief, whose name itself meant 'beautiful-tail,' i.e. 'fox'; the creek in MD may be named from that animal.

Alloy WV Chosen by vote among people associated with a local company which manufactured alloys.

Alluwe OK Algonquian (Delaware), probably 'better, superior.'

Alma Latin 'nourishing.' The name, without reference to its meaning, became popular following the battle of the Alma River in the Crimean War (1854), and girl-babies were so called. Some places were named for the battle, but most of them were named in the later 19th century after women.

Almanor, Lake CA Named from Alice, Martha, and Elinore, daughters of the president of the power company which built the dam to create the lake.

Almelo, New KS From the city of the Netherlands.

Almelund MN Swedish 'elm valley,' but partly in compliment to the first postmaster, Almquist.

Almena KS, MI, WI It is probably a pseudo-Indian coinage of the **Schoolcraft** (q.v.) type.

Almeria NB For Almeria Strohl, wife of the founder.

Almo In ID it is probably an adaptation of **Alamo,** because of cottonwoods along the stream.

Almond Probably in all instances from the personal name, e.g. in NC for Bud Almond, donor of the original site.

Almonesson NJ Algonquian, meaning uncertain.

Almont A repeated name, probably coined as a contraction of **Altamont,** and especially used by railroads as a short and euphonic name. In CO it is from the name of a race horse. See **Almonte.**

Almonte In CA it is near Muir Woods, and so may be merely Spanish 'at-the-woods,' but it is also a family name, and General J. N. Almonte was a prominent Mexican figure of the mid-19th century. **Almont** IA is locally reported to have been named for him, but one cannot see any reason why it should have been. See **Almont.**

Almora From the district and city of India.

Almota WA Indian (Nez Perce) 'torch-light-fishery.'

Almshouse From the older term for a charitable 'home,' e.g. **Almhouse Branch** DE.

Almy From the personal name, e.g. in WY, for J. L. Almy, not further identified.

Alna ME From Latin *alnus,* 'alder-tree,' given a pseudo-feminine ending when the town was named (1794) because of some fine alders.

Alockaman River WA Indian, language and meaning uncertain.

Aloha From the Hawaiian greeting. Most of the names, e.g. in LA and OR, were bestowed in the first years of the 20th century when the term had been popularized in song.

Alone Occasionally, as a variant for **Lone,** e.g. **Lake Alone** MI.

Alpena In MI it is apparently a pseudo-Indian coinage of the **Schoolcraft** (q.v.) type. In WV it was applied by Swiss immigrants as a variation of *alpine.*

Alpha From the personal name, e.g. in OR for Alpha Lundey, a young girl living there; or from the first letter of the Greek alphabet with the idea of being the first, e.g. **Alpha Lake** MN, which is the first in a series named after the first six letters of the Greek alphabet. In CA, ID, and OK the name arose as a counterpart to **Omega** (q.v.).

Alpharetta GA A variant of **Alfarata,** (q.v.).

Alphoretta KY A variant of **Alfarata,** (q.v.).

Alpine, Alps A descriptive term with commendatory suggestions, usually for a high place. **Alps** is used for a village in NM, because the region was thought to resemble Switzerland. **Alps** is sometimes a quasi-generic for high and rugged mountains, e.g. **Trinity Alps** CA. In San Mateo Co., CA, the name has developed by folk-etymology from Spanish *el pino,* 'the pine-tree.'

Alplaus NY Dutch *aal-plas,* 'eel-pond,' but possibly a personal name.

Alpowa WA Indian (Nez Perce), probably meaning a spring forming a creek.

Alridge ID Locally believed to be 'all ridge,' because of the hilly topography.

Alsea River OR From an Indian tribal name, sometimes spelled Alsi.

Alsek River AK Indian (Tlingit), meaning uncertain.

Alta See **Alto.**

Altair TX From the star, named by an amateur astronomer.

Altamaha River GA Recorded (1540) in a Spanish context as the name of a province, a Creek adaptation of a Timacua name, 'chief's lodge'(?). **Altamahaw** occurs as a variant in NC.

Altamont A synthetic name, with an Italian feminine adjective *alta,* 'high,' and a French *mont,* 'mount,' used as a descriptive and commendatory habitation-name. It may also be, e.g. probably in SD, a family name. **Altamonte Springs** FL preserves the Italian form.

Altenburg MO From a town in Germany, named by immigrants in 1839.

Alto Spanish 'high, tall,' meaning also 'height, elevation'; in habitation-names often in the feminine as **Alta.** It may be descriptive, e.g. **Alto** WA which is at the summit of a divide. It also carries the commendatory quality associated with elevation. **Los Altos** CA: 'the heights.' The meaning 'stop, halting-place' may have produced a few names, especially of railroad stations. **Alta** IA: the site is the highest on a railroad line, but the name is also for Altai Blair, daughter of a railroad official.

Altoga TX Named by an early settler with the idea of 'altogether.'

Alton Commonly from the personal name, e.g. in IL for Alton Easton, son of the town founder. In NH the name was taken (1770) from one of the places so called in England.

Altona From the city in Germany.

Altonah UT Probably coined from such names as **Altona, Alto,** and nearby **Altamont,** with the commendatory idea of height.

Altoona An adaptation of **Allatoona.** The name was bestowed (1849) in PA by J. A. Wright, one of the town founders, who had lived for some time in GA.

Other places are either from **Allatoona** or from the city in PA, though sometimes the influence of **Altona** in Germany may have been felt.

Altura(s) Spanish 'heights(s),' e.g. the town in CA, named by Americans in 1876, and not very accurately since it is not on any noteworthy elevation.

Altus Latin masculine, 'high,' in OK and AR preferred to the more common feminine. See **Alta.**

Alum Natural features, generally streams or springs, have been so called from the presence or supposed presence of one of the minerals known as alum, either as a solution in the water or as a nearby deposit, e.g. **Alum Mountain** NM. In MA and RI a lake and some ponds are probably from Algonquian 'dog.' See **Wallum.**

Alumine Peak CA From the presence of a potential alum mine.

Alvadore OR For Alvadore Welch, promoter of a local railroad.

Alverstone, Mount AK Named (1908) for Lord Alverstone, a British member of the commission which settled Alaskan boundary claims in 1903.

Alzada MT For Alzada Sheldon, early settler.

Amagansett NY Algonquian 'well-at,' because of a so-called Indian well, made from the trunk of a hollow tree sunk in a meadow.

Amakomanak Creek AK Eskimo 'wolf-dung.'

Amaladeros, Arroyo TX By a shift of spelling from Spanish *amoladeras,* 'whetstones.'

Amalden CA The quicksilver mine here was originally named **New Amalden** after the famous mine in Spain.

Amalga UT From the Amalgamated Sugar Co., which operates a factory here.

Amana IA From the Biblical mountain, but directly from the Amana Society, a German communal religious group, which made the settlement in 1855.

Amargo, Amargoso Spanish 'bitter,' often as **Amargosa,** feminine, as if in agreement with *agua,* e.g. **Amargosa River** CA.

Amarillo Spanish 'yellow.' **Tierra Amarilla** NM is 'yellow earth,' with reference to an ochre earth used as paint. **Amarillo** TX: from a nearby creek, so called probably because of banks of yellow earth.

Amatignak Island AK Aleut 'woodchip.'

Amawalk NY Algonquian, the abbreviation of a longer form, meaning uncertain.

Amawk Mountain AK Eskimo 'wolf,' named ca. 1930 by Americans because of much 'wolf-sign.'

Ambejejus Lake ME Algonquian, describing a place where there are currents on both sides of an island.

Amber In most instances probably from the personal name; in IA (1878) from the name of a character in a novel, but otherwise unidentified.

Amberon Flat AZ For Amberon Englevson, who built a corral for horses here and was killed by a stampede of the horses.

Amboy NJ Algonquian, probably meaning something hollowed out, thus a valley-like depression.

Ambridge PA From American Bridge Co.

Ambrosia Lake NM By folk-etymology from Ambrosio, it being called originally, in Spanish, 'lake of the dead Ambrosio' according to a local story of a man found floating in the lake, killed by arrows.

Ambush Water Pocket AZ In 1869 three men were ambushed here by Indians.

Amchitka Island AK Aleut, meaning uncertain.

Ameagle WV From American Eagle Colliery.

Amek Lake WI Algonquian 'beaver.'

Amelia County VA For the princess, daughter of George II.

America, American 1) From a personal name, e.g. a post office in OK named for America Stewart, a local resident. 2) A border name, indicating what is part of the U.S. as opposed to Canada, e.g. **American Creek** MT which arises south of the border and flows into Canada. 3) A name in formerly Mexican territory to indicate a feature associated with Americans, e.g. **American River** CA, **American Fork** UT. 4) A name to indicate a settlement of native Americans in a region largely settled by immigrants, e.g. **America Township** MN. 5) Given for patriotic reasons, e.g. **American Flag** AZ. **American Lake** WA: because of an American settlement in the 1840's when British influence was strong in the area. **American Falls** ID: because of association with trappers of the American Fur Co.

Americus A masculine form of **America,** but probably taken from Americus Vespucius, the Latinized form of Amerigo Vespucci, the Italian navigator for whom the continent was named.

Ames From the personal name, e.g. in IA for Oakes Ames, a chief stockholder in the railroad here.

Amesbury In MA (1668) from the town in England.

Amethyst Mountain WY For amethysts found here.

Amherst A county in VA and several towns honor Lord Jeffrey Amherst (1717–1797), British general in America during the French-and-Indian War. Later names, e.g. the glacier in AK (1899), have arisen from the college in MA.

Amicalola GA Cherokee 'water-tumbling,' probably applied first to the falls.

Amine Peak OR For Harriet Amine Saltzman, member of an early pioneer family.

Aminicon River WI Ojibway 'spawning-ground.'

Amiret MN From a shortening of Amiretta Sykes, wife of the president of the railroad which had much to do with developing the village.

Amistad NM Spanish 'friendship,' given as a commendatory in 1906.

Amite River LA Choctaw 'ant'(?).

Amity A commendatory name. In PA from the Amity Presbyterian Church. In OR from a school, so named because of the amicable settlement of a dispute. In CO, named (1894) by the Salvation Army for a colony established under its auspices.

Amma WV For Amie Geary, daughter of a prominent citizen, a change of spelling working in by error.

Ammon In ID, for a leader in the *Book of Mormon;* elsewhere, probably from from the family name.

Ammonoosuc River NH Algonquian, probably 'small-narrow-fishing-place.'

Amo In AK from Eskimo *amaguk,* 'wolf,' named by a geological party in 1950 because of some wolves seen there. Elsewhere the name may be from Latin 'I love.'

Amole Spanish 'soap-root.'

Amor MN Named by Norwegian settlers for the Roman god of love.

Amota Butte OR Chinook jargon 'strawberry.'

Amoureaux, Bayou des LA Probably for *des muriers,* 'of the mulberry trees.'

Amphitheater From a formation suggestive of an amphitheater, e.g. the peak and lake in WY.

Amsterdam From the city in the Netherlands, **New York** having been **New Amsterdam** under the Dutch regime. The present **Amsterdam** NY was named in 1804, in consciousness of the Dutch tradition and in a period of the giving of exotic names. In ID the name was selected in 1909 by Dutch settlers.

Amulet, Bayou LA From French *a(au)-mulet*, 'of-the-mule,' probably an incident name.

Amwell From the town in England, e.g. **East Amwell** NJ.

Amygdaloid From the occurrence of rock of that kind, e.g. the island in MI.

Anacacho Mountain TX A Spanish adaptation of an Indian name (?).

Anacoco Bayou LA The early spelling Yanacoco indicates origin from Spanish *llana*, 'plain,' and the rest may be from Spanish *cucu*, as denoting some American bird such as the raincrow.

Anaconda MT From the mine, which was named out of a Civil War report that Grant encircled Lee like a giant anaconda.

Anacortes WA Named by the town planner, Amos Bowman, in 1876 from his wife's maiden name, Anna Curtis, the spelling being purposefully changed to a semblance of Spanish to harmonize with the Spanish names in the area.

Anacostia MD From an Indian tribal name, spelled after a Latin model, probably by Jesuit missionaries, ca. 1640.

Anadarko OK An adaptation from Nada-ka, an Indian tribal name.

Anaheim CA From **Santa Ana**, the name of the nearby river, and the German *heim*, 'home,' the town being founded by German immigrants.

Anaho Island NV Probably Northern Paiute; meaning uncertain.

Anahuac TX In the ancient Aztec this was the name of a district, 'land by the waters'; it is here probably an adaptation of the name of a local Indian chief, Anahaw.

Anak Creek AK Eskimo 'dung,' because of game sign.

Anaktuvuk AK Eskimo 'dung-everywhere,' first applied to the pass which necessitated a concentration of migrating caribou, and hence of their dung.

Analy Valley CA Named by an Irishman for Annaly in Ireland, with the *n* dropped apparently in inadvertence.

Anamoose ND Objibway 'dog.'

Anamosa IA From the name of a little Indian girl who visited the settlement ca. 1842, interpreted as 'white fawn.'

Anaqua TX From an Indian tribal name.

Anarchist Butte SD Because a homesteader, otherwise unidentified, who lived in the area was known for anarchistic tendencies.

Anarene TX From Anna Laurene Graham, not identified.

Anasagunticook Lake ME Algonquian 'sandy-bottom-river-at.'

Anastasia Island FL Probably an early Spanish naming, for St. Anastasia.

Anatone WA Probably from the personal name of a local Indian woman.

Ancho Spanish 'broad,' **Sierra Ancha** AZ: probably so called because it gave an effect of broadness by not being cut with canyons.

Anchor With seacoast names it indicates an anchorage, e.g. **Anchor Bay** CA. It may be from an inn sign, e.g. **Cross Anchor** SC, or from a brand, as in OR. As a symbol of stability and hope the name has commendatory value, whence **Anchor Hill** SD from a mine name.

Anchorage Usually a generic. The city in AK is from **Knik Anchorage,** the post office dropping the specific when established ca. 1914. **Anchorage** KY: named by a retired riverboat captain, though it was several miles from the river, because he declared that this was his 'last anchorage.'

Anclote Spanish 'kedge-anchor,' but on the river and key in FL it is apparently the equivalent of **Anchorage.** Cf. the usage of **Anchor Bay** in English.

Ancram NY Probably a transfer-name from Scotland, a variant spelling of Ancrum.

Andale KS from Anderson and Dale, two of the town-founders, not further identified.

Andalusia From the Spanish province, one of the names reflecting the romantic early-19th-century interest in Spain, e.g. in AL the name was given in the 1830's.

Andes 1) For the mountains of South America. 2) From a personal name (in some instances, perhaps, Andy's), e.g. **Andes Lake** SD probably for Edward Andes, an early trapper.

Andesite For the rock of that name.

Andice TX By error, for Audice, son of Isaac Newton, early settler.

Andover The town in MA was named (1646) for that in England, and most of the later towns from the one in MA.

Androscoggin ME, NH Algonquian 'fish-curing-place.'

Andrusia, Lake MN A pseudo-Latinized form of Andrew, given in honor of President Jackson.

Aneroid Lake OR Named in 1897 because the altitude of the lake was taken by means of an aneroid barometer.

Angel In an English context, generally from the personal name, e.g. **Angels Camp** CA for George Angel, early settler. The Spaniards used the name with religious connections, e.g. **Angel Island** CA, which is a translation of Isla de los Angeles. **Port Angeles** WA: named by the Spanish explorer Eliza in 1791 Puerto de Nuestra Señora de los Angeles, 'Port of Our Lady of the Angels,' one of the titles of the Virgin Mary. **Mount Angel** OR: a translation of the German, Engelbert, given by the founder of a religious community. **Angel Terrace** WY: Because a white peak tinted with color suggested something angelic to the namer. See **Los Angeles.**

Angelina The river (hence, the county) in TX is from the name bestowed (ca. 1690) by the Spaniards upon a remarkable Indian girl who was Christianized and aided in the establishment of missions.

Angelus KS, SC From the religious service, reason for naming unknown.

Angle Usually from the personal name, e.g. **Angleton** TX for G. W. Angle, early developer. In MN the term has reference to the Northwest Angle of the U. S. boundary, as defined in the treaty of 1783; a township, a river, and a general area bear this name. **Angle Lake** WA Because it has a right-angled bend in it.

Anglesea NJ From the Welsh island, but also situated at an angle on the seacoast.

Angleworm Lake MI From its wormlike shape.

Angola From the former kingdom and present Portuguese colony in Africa.

Angora The spelling by which the present city of Ankara in Turkey was previously known; also associated with a breed of goats. As a habitation-name in NB, it was used by the railroad officials to replace a previous Antelope Hill; antelope were frequently known as goats.

Angostura Spanish 'narrows,' usually a generic but as a village name in NM.

Anguilla Spanish 'eel,' e.g. the bay and island in AK. In MS the name is borrowed from the West Indian island.

Anguille French 'eel.' The name of the stream (AR) apparently represents what is left of such a name as Rivière à l'Anguille.

Animas Spanish 'souls' survives usually as all that is left of a phrase. **Animas** CA: originally a land grant so called from All Souls' Day. **Las Animas** CO Spanish 'the souls,' is what remains from El Rio de Las Animas Perdidas en Purgatorio. See **Purgatoire.**

Aniwa WI Ojibway, apparently the remnant of a longer name, since this element is used to indicate a comparative, usually something bigger, probably a name applied by Americans in the 19th century.

Anjean WV From Ann and Jean, mother and daughter, of a Mr. Leckie, local mine owner.

Anmoore WV From Ann Moore Run, named from a local woman.

Ann, Anna, Annie, Anne As one of the commonest women's name, it is found commemoratively on many features, especially lakes. **Ann** is the usual form, and **Anne** the rarest. MN has **Ann** with *lake* 5 times; Anna, 3; Annie, 1. **Cape Ann** MA: for Queen Ann, wife of James I and named by her son, Prince Charles (later, Charles I), who wrote it on John Smith's map of New England (1616). **Anna River (North Anna,** etc.): these streams in VA are sometimes said to be for Queen Anne or some other Anna, but the name seems more likely to be a rendering of the Algonquian *hanne,* 'stream,' or *hanough,* 'people.' Cf. such nearby stream-names as **Rappahannock, Rapidan,** the last even explained as rapid Ann. In habitation-names **Annapolis** echoes the capital of MD, named in 1695 for Princess (later, Queen) Anne, and the Greek *polis,* 'city.' **Princess Anne Co.** VA: for the same person, named in 1695. **Ann Arbor** MI: the wives of the two first settlers (1824) were named Ann; by traditional story, they trained wild grapevines into an arbor, and their husbands called the place Anns' Arbor, later reduced to the present name. **Ann** is often, because of its brevity, joined to other personal names, e.g. **Annfred, Anmoore. Anne Arundel County** MD: for Lady Anne Arundel, who married the second Lord Baltimore, ca. 1628.

Anna See **Ann.**

Annabella UT From Ann Roberts and Isabella Dalton, the first two women residents.

Annabessacook Lake ME Algonquian, meaning uncertain.

Annada MO For Ann and Ada Jamison, daughters of Carson Jamison, an early settler.

Annahooksett Falls NH Algonquian 'beautiful-trees-at.'

Annaricken Brook NJ Algonquian, meaning uncertain.

Annarose TX For Anna Rose Scott, not identified.

Annas Bay WA Originally **Anna's Bay.**

Annasnappet Brook MA Algonquian, probably 'head-(of)-stream-at.'

Annawan IL Probably a transfer from MA. See **Annawon's Rock.**

Annawon's Rock MA A chief of this name was captured here during King Philip's War in 1675.

Anncar NB For Ann Carroll O'Neill, maiden name of the woman at whose house the first post office was established; Carroll was not used because another office of that name already existed.

Anne See **Ann.**

Anneewakee Creek GA From a Cherokee personal name.

Annelly KS Named (1885) by a railroad official for his wife Ann and his daughter Ellie.

Annemessex MD From an Indian tribal name, with the final *s*-sound being an English plural.

Annfred WV From the given names of a local railroad official and his wife.

Annis ID Coined (1896) from Ann Kearney first postmistress, and the first two letters of *island,* the area being known as **Poole's Island.**

Annisquam On several mountains in NH it is Algonquian (Abnaki) 'summit'; in MA it is probably of the same meaning, but of Natick dialect.

Annona TX Named (1884) for an Indian girl, not further identified.

Annursnack Hill MA Algonquian, probably 'summit,' or by associated meaning 'lookout-place.'

Anoka In MN the name was chosen from a Siouan dictionary without reference to its meaning ('on both sides'), because of its euphony; the town in NB is from that in MN.

Anona FL Spanish 'custard-apple,' a wild fruit growing locally, but probably chosen for euphony.

Ano Nuevo Spanish 'New Year.' The point in CA was named by the explorer Viscaíno on January 3, 1603, being the first point to be sighted in the new year.

Another River AK A name of desperation given by two geologists in 1927, 'because of the many new rivers.'

Anranta Creek TX By mistake from an earlier Arana, which is probably the Spanish term for a kind of grass.

Anse American-French 'cove, bay,' sometimes the peninsula forming the bay, rarely as a specific by association or as a habitation-name, e.g. **L'Anse** MI.

Anson From the personal name; the county in NC is for Admiral George Anson, famous voyager, who did a tour of duty along the Carolina coast in the early 18th century.

Ansonia A Latinized form from Anson, e.g. in CT for Anson G. Phelps, local magnate. In PA the name is for the same man.

Ant Rarely of sufficient note to produce a name, **Ant Canyon** ID is one of the few examples. **Ant Hill** WY: because its shape is thus suggestive.

Antelope The pronghorn, usually called antelope, was a conspicuous animal in the open country which it inhabited, and was also an important game animal. An incident, or a mere sighting, often gave rise to a name, and several hundred exist. It occurs commonly with creek (six in S.D.), and also as a habitation-name. **Antelope Co.** NB: some early settlers, on an expedition, having run out of food, managed to kill an antelope, and one of them, being a member of the legislature, later asked for this name. **Antelope House** AZ: a prehistoric ruin, so called because of pictographs of antelope on it. The valley in Douglas Co., NV, was named because in early times it was frequented by a herd of 30 to 50 antelope. **Antelope Island** UT: on Oct. 18, 1845, J. C. Frémont named the island because he had killed several antelope there.

Antepast KY The term exists in the sense of 'foretaste, something served before a meal,' but this derivation seems unlikely; it may be from Antipas, which was sometimes used as a baptismal name.

Antero CO From a Ute chief of the 19th century, friendly to the whites.

Antes Fort PA From a stockade built by Col. J. H. Antes in 1776.

Anthony's Nose See **Nose.**

Anthracite From the presence of that kind of coal, e.g. the creek in CO.

Anticline Ridge CA A geologists' term, because of the folded rocks existing there.

Antietam MD Algonquian, meaning uncertain.

Antigo WI Ojibway 'evergreen,' the shortening of a longer Indian name.

Antimony From the presence of that metal or its ore.

Antioch From the ancient city, but almost entirely religious in origin, from the association of that city with the beginnings of Christianity, as recorded in the *New Testament.* The name has been a favorite one for churches, and a number of these names have been transmitted to towns. In CA the name was chosen by the residents at a picnic on July 4, 1851.

Antipodes, Gate of the CA A narrow pass, probably so called because it leads to a place named **China.**

Antiquity OH Because the first settlers saw old markings on the rocks, apparently made by ancient inhabitants.

Antler(s) In OK, because some antlers had been nailed to a tree at a camping place. In ND from a stream whose forkings suggested antlers.

Antone Usually, e.g. **San Antone Lakes** NM with **San,** as an Americanization of **San Antonio.**

Antonino KS Named (1904) for Anthony Sauer, the oldest living inhabitant at the time; because of duplication of name within the state, a variant was used.

Antonito CO Spanish, a diminutive of Anthony, derived from **San Antonio** as a name for the nearby mountains and river; probably the diminutive was used for differentiation.

Antora Mountain CO Apparently a variant of **Antero.**

Antrim From the county in Northern Ireland, generally named by immigrants.

Antwerp From the city in Belgium.

Anvik AK Eskimo 'going-out-place'(?).

Anvil From real or supposed resemblance to an anvil, e.g. **Anvil Rock** WA, WV. **Anvil Spring** CA: from an old anvil found there.

Anxiety Point AK Named (1826) by Sir John Franklin because he had been somewhat worried about ever reaching it.

A One (A1) Mountain AZ From the brand-name of a nearby ranch.

Aowa Creek NB A variant of **Iowa.**

Apache From the Indian tribal name.

Apalachee AL, GA From the Indian tribal name.

Apalachicola FL From the tribal name (see also **Appalachian),** shaped by the early Spaniards to the appearance of a Spanish name.

Apalachin NY Recorded (1845) as Apalacon Creek, it is probably Iroquoian, of uncertain meaning, shifted by folk-etymology to resemble **Appalachian.**

Apananawapeske River ME Algonquian, describing a place where the river widens at some ledges.

Apex A repeated name, usually of habitations, used as the equivalent of summit, to indicate the high point on a road or railroad.

Apiatan Mountain CO From the name of a Kiowa chief, given to the mountain, ca. 1915, by Americans commemoratively.

Apishapa Ute 'standing (stagnant)-water,' occurring by association on several features in CO.

Apollinaris Spring WY Because its water resembles Apollinaris water.

Apollo PA So called in the period of classical naming (1827), the name of the Greek god, patron of poetry, being suggested probably by Dr. Robert McKisson, who had published two volumes of poetry.

Apookta Creek MS From the name of an ancient Choctaw village, meaning uncertain.

Apoon AK The mountain, named in 1931, is from the Eskimo 'snow.' The pass is apparently an old Eskimo name, from a similarly-sounding word, 'thumb.'

Apopka FL Seminole, 'eating-place,' in this instance a shortening of 'potato-eating-place.' The same term appears in other place-names, e.g. **Charley Apopka,** in the same literal significance, though its precise reference is doubtful.

Apostle Applied, e.g. **The Apostle Islands** WI with the idea of there being twelve, though the namers were rarely exact counters, and in the case mentioned there are actually more than 20 islands in the group.

Apostolic Ridge KY Probably by transfer from a church-name.

Apoxsee FL A 20th-century naming, a respelling of Seminole *apaksi,* 'tomorrow,' but reason for naming uncertain.

Appalachian, Appalachia Cabeza de Vaca recorded Apalachen (1528) as the Indian name of a province, and it got on maps as a vague name for the mountainous interior. In changed spelling the English applied the name to the southern part of the mountain system. In the late 19th century the name was extended to cover the whole system. Although the *n* had been a part of the original name, it was later conceived as being adjectival, after the model of Latin, and **Appalachia** was thus produced as a noun derived from a supposed adjective. Washington Irving advocated it as a name for the nation, at a time when the country was still considered as stretching along the Atlantic coast. In the 19th century it came into use as a regional term. For names derived more directly from the tribal name than from the 'province,' see **Apalachee.**

Appam ND Coined (1916) by officials of the Great Northern Railway, chiefly to be different from other names; no positive reason is known for the selection of these sounds or letters. The attempt was successful, and the name seems to remain unique.

Appanoose IL, IA, KS From the name of a Sauk chief of the early 19th century.

Appaquag, Appaquogue CT, NY Algonquian 'where flags grow,' a plant used by the Indians for making mats.

Appekunny Mountain MT Indian (Blackfoot) 'scabby-face,' the Indian name of J. W. Schultz, author, who lived many years with the Blackfoot tribe.

Appistoki Mountain MT Indian (Blackfoot), probably 'old-mountain,' a shortening of Natos Api Istuki, 'sun-old-mountain,' from a Blackfoot personal name, borne by the sun priest.

Apple Often from the personal name, as regularly in **Appleton, Applegate.** On features, e.g. **Apple Creek** NB, it is usually for the wild crab apple. Cultivated fruit has given rise to some names, e.g. **Apple Farm** WV. **Apple Springs** TX was originally **May Apple Springs** from the abundance of that wild fruit there. **Apple Valley** CA arises from an attempt to grow apples in that desert area. **Applesauce Creek** CA is from the habitual exclamation of an early settler. **Apple Tree Cove** WA was named in 1841 by the Wilkes expedition 'from the numbers of that tree which were in blossom around its shores.'

Appolacon Creek PA Algonquian (Delaware) 'messenger-returned,' apparently an incident-name.

Appomattox VA From an Indian queen, recorded in 1607 as Apumetec, so that the stream became Apumetec's River. The name was also applied to the Indians of that region, and may have been originally a tribal name.

Apponagansett Bay MA Algonquian, meaning uncertain.

Apponaug RI Algonquian, meaning uncertain.

Appoquinimink DE, PA Algonquian, meaning uncertain.

Approach Hill AK Because it is on the line of approach for planes coming in to an airfield.

Apshawa Lake NJ Algonquian, meaning uncertain.

Aptakisic IL From the name of a Potawatomi chief of the early 19th century.

Apukwa Lake WI Algonquian (Menominee) 'slippery.'

Apulia NY From the ancient district of Italy, one of the numerous classical names of this area.

Aqua Latin 'water,' probably, in most instances, from a confusion with Spanish *agua.*

Aquaquamset River ME Algonquian, meaning uncertain.

Aquarius Mountains AZ, UT Named by A. W. Whipple when exploring in 1854 because of the numerous streams flowing from the range. In Latin the term means 'water-bearer.'

Aquasco MD Algonquian (Delaware), probably 'edge-(of)-grass.'

Aquashicola Creek PA Algonguian (Delaware) 'bush-net,' with reference to an Indian method of catching fish.

Aquebogue NY Algonquian 'head- (of)-water.' Cf. **Riverhead,** in which town **Aquebogue** is located.

Aquednet MA, RI Algonquian 'island-at.'

Aquetuck NY Algonquian, from an earlier Hockatock, 'hooklike-stream'(?).

Aquia Creek VA Attracted to a pseudo-Latin form from an Algonquian term, probably 'sea-gull.'

Aquidneck RI Algonquian 'island-at.'

Aquilla AL, OH, TX The name was a given one for men, and the place-names probably thus arise, though local stories suggest Indian origin or Latin *aquila,* 'eagle.'

Aquone NC Cherokee 'by-river'(?).

Arab Probably, e.g. in AL, from a family name. See **Arabi.**

Arabi GA, LA From the family name, usually spelled Arabie.

Arabia Such names usually arise from love of the exotic, but in NB the sandy soil gave the suggestion.

Arago, Cape OR For D. F. J. Arago, French geographer, friend of Alexander von Humboldt, named ca. 1850, in counterpart to **Humboldt Bay.**

Aragon In NM from a family of Spanish immigrants of the 17th century; in GA probably from the Spanish province and former kingdom.

Aransas TX From Aranzazu, a title of the Virgin Mary, bestowed on a stream in 1746 by Spanish explorers, the full name being **Nuestra Señora de Aránzazu.** The form, being rare and of unusual spelling, was later simplified.

Arapaho From the Indian tribal name.

Ararat From the Biblical mountain, famous as the grounding place of Noah's Ark, generally as **Mount Ararat,** four of which exist in CA. In WA the name was given by a man who thought he had discovered traces of the ark there.

Arastra An alternate spelling for **Arrastre.**

Arbela MO From Alexander's victory over the Persians.

Arboga CA Named in 1911 by a Swedish immigrant for his former home in Sweden.

Arbol Spanish 'tree'; in the plural **Arboles,** e.g. in CO as a habitation-name with reference to tree growth along a stream.

Arboleda Spanish 'grove.'

Arbovale WV From the first syllable of the personal name Arbogast, plus *-vale.*

Arbre French 'tree,' e.g. **Arbre Croche** MI, 'tree-crooked (bent),' apparently for a landmark-tree.

Arbyrd MO For A. R. Byrd, landowner.

Arcadia From the district of ancient Greece, poetically envisioned as a land of rural simplicity and loveliness, as a commendatory habitation-name in many states.

Arcanum OH, VA Latin 'hidden thing, mystery' of uncertain reference, but perhaps merely the equivalent of **Hidden.**

Arcata CA Of uncertain origin; locally said to mean 'union' in some Indian language, **Union** having been the town's original name.

Arch Sometimes as a generic, but often by association for a place having a natural arch of rock, e.g. **Arch Cape** OR, **Arches N.M.** UT, **Arch** OK. From a personal name, or its shortening, e.g. **Arch** NM, though the naming may not have been for a special person but merely a short name for the post office. **The Royal Arches** CA: named by a Mason for the Seventh Degree of that order; also showing some resemblance to an arch.

Archuleta County CO For A. D. Archuleta, state political figure when the county was formed in 1885.

Arco Spanish 'arch,' but its usage is chiefly in non-Spanish areas, and is obscure. In MN it is a shortening of **Arcola** to avoid duplication of that name in the state.

Arctic Rare, except in AK, where it seems commonly to have been given from a general sense of association with the arctic region or with arctic conditions.

Arden Some are from the personal name, but the popularity undoubtedly springs in part from use in Shakespeare's *As You Like It,* even though a forest and several villages of the name exist in England. In SC the name was bestowed because fine trees suggested a romantic forest.

Ardenwald OR From Arden M. Rockwood, the *wald* being the German word for 'forest, wood,' used both because of nearby woods and for the second syllable of Rockwood.

Ardeola MO Locally believed to have been coined from the names of several now forgotten men.

Ardmore In PA, from the town in Ireland; in OK, from PA.

Aredale IA An artificial railroad name, obviously fabricated on the model of various names in **Dale.**

Arena Spanish 'sand,' e.g. **Point Arena** CA. In areas without Spanish background the English meaning of the word may apply, especially for a place situated in a hollow of the hills.

Arenac County MI Manufactured by Schoolcraft (q.v.) from Latin *arena,* 'sand,' and Algonquian *auk,* 'place.'

Arenal Spanish 'sandy place.'

Arenosa Spanish 'sandy.'

Argentine 1) From the South American country, e.g. in PA, an exotic name. 2) From the meaning, 'having to do with silver,' e.g. for a mining town in CO.

Argo It is a rare family name, and **Argo** KY probably thus originated. As a short and distinctive name, it was of the sort favored for railroad stations, and was generally known as the name of the ship of the Argonauts in Greek mythology.

Argonia KS From **Argo** (q.v.) expanded into the form of a Latin place-name.

Argonne From the forest in France, made known by the battle of 1918, e.g. in MO, named in 1918.

Argos IN From the city of Greece.

Argus From the all-seeing personage of Greek mythology, hence applied to newspapers and from a newspaper to **Argusville** NY.

Argyle A habitation-name in a dozen states, it is from the county in Scotland, sometimes given because of Scottish immigrants.

Arickaree, Aricare, Rickaree From the Indian tribal name.

Arido Creek UT Spanish 'arid,' probably because in dry country. Cf. **Seco.**

Arimo ID Probably named by railroad officials for a local Indian chief.

Arion IA From the semi-mythical early Greek poet and musician, probably applied artificially by the railroad.

Aripeka FL For a local Indian chief of the early 19th century, known in English as Sam Jones.

Aripine AZ From the first three letters of the state name, plus *pine,* because of the presence of those trees.

Arivaca AZ Probably an American alteration of a Pima name meaning 'little reeds.'

Arivaipa Canyoл AZ From the Indian tribal name.

Arizmo AZ Coined from Arizona and Missouri, by settlers from the latter state.

Arizola AZ From Arizona and Ola Thomas, daughter of an early settler.

Arizona From the Papago *ali,* 'small,' and *shonak,* 'place of the spring,' i.e. 'place of the small spring.' The name was first rendered into Spanish as *Arizonac,* and later reduced more nearly to the form of a Spanish word. The place became famous because of rich finds of silver, and so the name spread to cover the whole surrounding country, and eventually to be adopted for a territory and state. The original spring is south of the border, in Mexico.

Ark The term was applied to a type of boat used on canals and rivers in the early 19th century, and has left an occasional name, e.g. **Arkport** NY.

Arkadelphia AR From the first syllable of the state name and *-adelphia* (Greek 'brother-place') probably taken from its use in **Philadelphia.**

Arkansas A village and tribe, Arkansea, are recorded in a French context as of 1673. The French usually spelled the name Arkansa, and added the *s* as a plural, to indicate members of the tribe. The name in the plural was soon applied to the river near the original village, and then to the territory and state. After the region was Americanized in the early 19th century, an approximation of the French pronunciation was kept, and the spelling conformed as **Arkansaw,** which was used in the Act creating the territory. Later the present spelling became official, but the old pronunciation was kept among the people of the state, though many outsiders accented the second syllable, on the analogy of the spelling and of **Kansas.** The "French" pronunciation now prevails for the state, but **Arkansas City** KS keeps the second-syllable accentuation, and **Arkansaw** WI uses the older spelling.

Arkansaw See **Arkansas.**

Arkinda AR A boundary name from Arkansas and Indian Territory.

Arkoe MO A fictitious literary name from Robert Paltock's *Peter Wilkins;* an 'arkoe' meant, in the imaginary language of the story, a smooth stretch of water. The name was given by Dr. P. H. Talbot, a great reader, who apparently conceived the location to be at an 'arkoe' of the river.

Arkoma OK A boundary-name from AR and OK.

Arlee MT From the name of a local Indian chief.

Arletta WA Named ca. 1893 by combining Arla, the name of a local girl, with Valetta, the city of Malta, because of its reputed beauty.

Arlington The name of several English villages, and the title of a prominent earl, it was brought to VA (Northampton Co.) ca. 1650 as a house or plantation name by John Custis II. It was later transferred to an estate bought by the same family in 1778, the site of the present **Arlington** VA. The name was transferred to MA in 1867, and its popularity begins about this time, partly for sentimental reasons, since it was the home of R. E. Lee, and later the site of a famous national cemetery. It also came to have commendary value for habitations, following its use as a street name in the Back Bay district of Boston. It now exists as a town name in about 30 states, and is widespread also for streets, cemeteries, subdivisions, etc.

Armagh PA From the town in Northern Ireland.

Arminto WY For Manuel Armento, local rancher, spelling changed by the railroad.

Armonk NY Algonquian, probably 'beaver.'

Armuchee Creek GA Cherokee 'hominy,' but uncertain.

Army A name applied because of some association with the army or with soldiers. **Army Pass** CA: a trail here was constructed by the 4th Cavalry. **Army Point** CA: first appeared as Navy Point, but was changed after the army established a post there in 1851. **Army Hill** OR: named because it used to be frequented by soldiers from Fort Umpqua nearby.

Arnheim MI From the town in the Netherlands, usually spelled Arnhem.

Arno In CA from the Italian river; also, a personal name.

Arock OR For 'a rock,' because a large rock was nearby.

Aromas CA Spanish 'odors,' so called because of the presence of a sulphur spring.

Aromatic Creek MO A euphemism, probably for **Stinking Creek.**

Aroostook ME Algonquian 'beautiful (fine) river.'

Aroya CO A simplified spelling of **Arroyo,** after the common pronunciation.

Arpin WI From a shortening of Arpino, a town in Italy, probably applied by the railroad.

Arramopskis Falls ME Algonquian 'falls-(at)-rocks-little.'

Arraster A variant of **Arrastre** (q.v.).

Arrastre, Arrastra In American-Spanish an *arrastre* means a primitive mill used in gold mining for crushing quartz. Like **Mill** it has been used to designate natural features where such a device was once located, e.g. **Arrastre Flat** CA, **Arrastra Creek** OR.

Arrecife Spanish 'reef.'

Arriba Spanish 'above,' in a topographical sense, 'upper,' e.g. **Rio Arriba Co.** NM.

Arrow Various features are so called 1) because shaped like an arrow; 2) because of the finding of Indian arrowheads.

Arrowhead 1) From the finding of arrowheads; 2) from the shape. **Arrowhead Lake** CA: a remarkable configuration on the mountainside is shaped like an arrowhead. **Arrowhead Terrace** AZ: so called from its shape.

Arrowsic Island ME Algonquian, meaning uncertain.

Arroyo In Spanish meaning 'brook,' but in the Southwest usually transferred to mean 'canyon, gulch.' It is rarely a true specific but occurs tautologically in names like **Arroyo Seco Creek** CA, and in habitation-names, e.g. **Arroyo Grande** CA.

Arsenic From the presence, or supposed presence, of arsenic, usually applied to springs.

Arshamomaque NY Algonquian, from a recorded (1659) **Hashamomuck,** 'where-springs-flow.'

Art Usually as an abbreviation for Arthur, but in TX selected for its brevity, by local story, with "no significance whatever."

Artanna OH Coined (ca. 1934) from the names of Arthur Wolfe and his wife Anna, owners of a local store and filling station.

Artas SD A misspelling of the Greek *artos,* 'bread,' so applied because the town was in a wheat-growing area.

Artesia (n) From the presence of artesian wells, e.g. **Artesia** CA, NM, **Artesian** SD.

Arthur From the personal name. **Port Arthur** TX: for Arthur Edward Stilwell, who had the town site surveyed and named for himself (1895). **Arthurs Seat** MA: the hill echoes the name of the famous hill in Edinburgh, Scotland. **Arthur Kill** NJ, NY: by folk-etymology from Dutch *achter kill,* 'back stream,' because of its situation on the opposite side of Staten Island from New Amsterdam. **Arthur Peak** WY: one of the rare namings in honor of Chester A. Arthur, occasioned by his visit to this area (in Yellowstone N.P.) during his presidency.

Arthyde MN For the founders, Arthur and Clyde Hutchins.

Artic WA In the 1880's the name of Mrs. Arta Saunders, a local woman, was sent in to the Post Office Dept., but by error the name was approved in the present form.

Artichoke From wild artichokes, i.e. the edible tuber so known in much of the U.S., e.g. the lake in MN.

Artillero Creek TX From Spanish, the name used for a locally growing weed.

Artillery Mountains AZ In 1854 A. W. Whipple named **Artillery Peak,** a volcanic cone which may have reminded him of a cannon, but having been an officer of artillery he may have given the name commemoratively. **Artillery Creek** OK was thus named because artillery served in the area.

Artois CA A World War I name, placed in 1918 at a time of enthusiasms for things French, replacing **Germantown.**

Artray Creek CA From two Forest Service men, Arthur Barrett and Raymond Orr.

Arumsunkhungan Island ME Algonquian 'below-outlet-fishing-place.'

Arvada From the personal name, e.g. in CO for Hiram Arvada Hoskin of the family of the town founders.

Arvilla In ND it was named (1882) for Arvilla Hersey, wife of a landowner.

Asaph PA From the Biblical personal name.

Asbestos Canyon AZ From the presence of the mineral.

Asbury From the personal name especcially, e.g. in NJ for Bishop Francis Asbury, pioneer of Methodism.

Ascension The name occurs, e.g. **Ascension Parish** LA, probably as one given on or to commemorate Ascension Day.

Ascutney Mountain VT Algonquian, to denote a location at the end of a river fork.

Ash 1) From the personal name; 2) From place-names or titles in England, e.g. **Ashburnham** MA, **Ashby** MA; 3) Most commonly, from the ash tree which, being conspicuous, wide-spread, and useful, has yielded many names both of natural features and of habitations, e.g. **Ash Creek, Ash Grove. Ashland** is common as a habitation-name from having been famous as the estate of Henry Clay, but in most cases was probably applied to a site where ash trees were growing; 4) In volcanic areas it is applied because of volcanic ash, e.g. **Ash Butte** OR, **Ashpan Butte** CA, **Ash Creek** (Siskiyou Co., CA), **Volcanic Ash Valley** NB. **Ashwood** OR: a combination of Ash Butte and the

personal name, Wood. **Ashepole Swamp** SC: probably named for its production of ash timber. Some names probably arose because of the ash produced by the early industry of burning trees for potash, e.g. **Ashcamp** KY, **Ashhopper Branch** KY.

Ashawaug, Ashaway, Ashawog, Ashowat CT, RI Algonquian 'between-place,' probably the equivalent of 'middle' or 'halfway.'

Ashaway See **Ashawaug.**

Ashburnham MA From a town in England (1765).

Ashippun WI Algonquian, probably 'raccoon.'

Ashkum IL From the name of a Potawatomi chief of the early 19th century.

Ashland See **Ash.**

Ashley From the personal name. In SC the river is for Lord Anthony Ashley Cooper, one of the original Lords Proprietors.

Ashokan NY Algonquian, probably 'mouth-little,' i.e. the outlet of a small stream.

Ashtabula OH Algonquian 'there-are-always-enough-moving' (?), with possible reference to fish.

Ashuelot NH Algonquian, meaning uncertain. The same as **Ashwillet.**

Ashwaubenon Creek WI Ojibway 'lookout-place,' probably with the idea of watching for enemies.

Ashwillet River NH Algonquian, meaning uncertain, a partial adaptation by folk-etymology of **Ashuelot.**

Asilomar CA A name coined in the American period, ca. 1913, from Spanish *asilo,* 'refuge,' and *mar,* 'sea.'

Askeaton WI Ojibway *ashkidon,* 'rawmouth,' probably an Indian personal name.

Askew From the personal name, e.g. **Askewville** NC for a local family.

Asnebumsket Hill MA Algonquian 'rocks-rocks-at,' probably with the sense of rocks rising into a cliff.

Asneconick Pond MA Algonquian 'rock-field,' probably with reference to an 'Indian field' marked by a rock or having rocky soil.

Asotin WA Nez Percé 'eel creek,' originally applied to the stream.

Asp OK For H. E. Asp, attorney.

Aspatuck Creek NY Algonquian 'fish-net-stream'(?).

Aspen Though the tree is not of commercial value its conspicuous yellow foliage in the autumn makes an impression, and a number of natural features, chiefly in the western mountains, have been so named, e.g. **Aspen Hill** NM. A few towns have been named, e.g. in CO.

Aspermont TX Latin, *asper,* 'rough,' and *-mont,* because close to a mountain in rough country, but perhaps also from literary sources, since a well-known poem and several European places have similar names.

Aspero Spanish 'rough.'

Aspetong Mountain NY Algonquian 'height.'

Aspetuck CT Algonquian 'high-place-at.'

Asphalt Commonly from the occurence of natural asphalt; in NC from an asphalt plant.

Asquam NH Algonquian 'salmon-place.'

Asquango MD Algonquian (Delaware) probably 'high-bank.'

Asqueanunckton Brook NH Algonquian 'rapid-stream-reaching-as-far-as-mountain' (?).

Ass Except in **Jackass,** it is regularly from the anatomical term (British, *arse*), rating as an obscenity, circulating colloquially but not usually in print. Of such origin is probably **Skinned Ass Canyon** NM, which has doubtless been preserved in print because explained as referring to burros being skinned because of the tightness of the passage. In parts of the West **Tight-Ass Hill** is, or was, a quasigeneric for a place at which a road went over a sharp summit with resultant difficult pulling. **The Asses Ears** AK describes a rock formation, a semi-literary usage. See **Ragged, Soak.**

Assabet Brook MA Algonquian 'miry-(place)-at.'

Assabumbedock Falls ME Algonquian, probably 'sloping-sandy-(bottom).'

Assacorkin Island MD Algonquian, 'across-land-is'(?).

Assamoosic VA Algonquian, probably with *assa-,* 'across,' and the rest uncertain.

Assaria KS Named from a Swedish Lutheran church.

Assateague MD Probably first applied to the island, Algonquian 'beyond-river.'

Assawaga Algonquian 'place between,' a repeated name in southern New England, equivalent to 'middle.'

Assawanama Pond NY Algonquian 'middle-fishing-place.'

Assawoman DE, MD, VA Algonquian 'middle-fishing-stream'(?). The earliest form **Assawaman** (1677) has been partly shifted by folk-etymology.

Assawompset MA Algonquian, the latter part meaning 'rock-at;' *assaw* is uncertain, but may be 'middle.'

Assekonk CT Algonquian 'grass-place.'

Assinapink NY Algonquian 'stone-water-at.'

Assiniboine From the Indian tribal name. It is chiefly Canadian, but appears in **Assiniboine Bluff** MN.

Assinins MI Ojibway 'pebble.'

Assinipi MA Algonquian 'rock-water.'

Assiscunk Creek NJ Algonquian (Delaware) 'clay-at.'

Assonet MA Algonquian 'rock-at,' with reference to a rock bearing aboriginal markings.

Assumption A religious, usually Catholic name, given in commemoration of the assumption of the Virgin Mary, celebrated on August 15, e.g. the township in MN.

Assunpink Creek NJ Algonquian, probably 'stone-water-at.'

Assyria MI From the ancient country.

Astatula FL Indian (probably, Seminole), meaning uncertain.

Asti CA From the Italian town, named by immigrants.

Astoria OR Named in 1811 for John Jacob Astor, with the -*ia* added in simulation of a Latin place-name. Astor had organized and financed the expedition which made the first settlement at this point. The peak in WY was named commemoratively for the Astor party which traversed this region in 1811.

Asuncion Spanish 'assumption,' usually with reference to the Virgin Mary and the day August 15, traditionally associated with that event.

Aswaguscawadic ME, NH Algonquian, apparently because of a shallow place, and roughly rendered, 'where we have to drag canoe through stream.'

Asylum Though now restricted, in popular usage, to an institution for mental patients, it previously meant a place of refuge, and as such, in PA, refers to a colony established in 1794 for refugees from the French Revolution.

Atanchiluka Creek AL Muskogean 'there-corn-shelled,' probably an incident-name.

Atanum River WA By local tradition, of Indian origin, 'creek by the long mountain.'

Atarque NM Spanish 'dam,' usually meaning a small earthen dam; hence, applied to a village, creek, and lake.

Atascadero Spanish 'miry place, obstruction,' a common Mexican-Spanish geographical term, which has been used for a town in CA in spite of the unpleasant literal meaning.

Atascosa Mexican-Spanish 'miry, muddy,' placed in the feminine form on a river in TX and, by transfer, on a county and town.

Atchafalaya LA Choctaw 'river-long.'

Atchee CO Named (1904) for a local Ute chief, an advocate of peaceful relations.

Atchison From the personal name, e.g. the city in KS and the county in MO for D. R. Atchison (1807–1886), political figure.

Atchuelinguk River AK Eskimo, probably 'clear-stream.'

Atco In NJ it is from Atlantic Transport Company.

Atglen PA Adopted (1875) because the site is close to **Glen Run.**

Athalia OH From the daughter of the town founder, not further identified.

Athena OR For the Greek goddess (1889), named by a man said to have been 'of a romantic and classical turn of mind.'

Athenia NJ From **Athena**, with the *i* inserted to give the appearance of a Latin place-name.

Athens From the Greek city, through literary sources and with reference to the ancient, not the modern, city. Its popularity arose in the post-Revolutionary period of classical naming, e.g. in GA 1801. One special association has been with culture, learning, and education, and the name in GA and elsewhere has been given because of the intention to found an institution of learning.

Athlone From the town in Ireland.

Athol From the district in Scotland or the title. **Athol** MA: in honor of the Duke of Athol (1762). **Athol** ID: from the personal name of an Indian chief.

Atlanta In GA the name was coined in 1845 by J. E. Thomson, railroad-builder, for the terminus of the Western & Atlantic Railroad, from 'Atlantic' apparently under the assumption that this was the feminine form, thus conforming to the general idea that names of towns fittingly end in *a*. Most other places of the name echo this one. In ID the name commemorates the battle of 1864. In MN the name was applied fancifully, because the undulating plain was thought to resemble the Atlantic Ocean.

Atlantic From association with that ocean, usually because of location upon it, e.g. the city and county in NJ. **Atlantic Peak** and **City** in WY are so called because they are close to the Continental Divide but on the Atlantic side. **Atlantic** IA: at the time of naming it was believed to be halfway between the oceans: a coin was flipped and fell for **Pacific,** but that name had to be given up because it had been used too much elsewhere, and **Atlantic** was then chosen.

Atlas From the mythological figure; in TX from a vague association with rocks and a quarry.

Atlasta Creek AK From a woman's expression on the completion of a building, 'At last a house!'

Atlatl Rock NV The term by which anthropologists designate the ancient spear thrower; here applied, apparently, by general association, because the rock has many Indian (or pre-Indian) petroglyphs.

Atoka The county in OK is for a well-known Choctaw, Captain Atoka. Elsewhere, e.g. AL, TN, it is from the Muskogean word for 'ball-ground.'

Atolia CA From Atkins and DeGolia, two officers of a local mining company.

Atomic City ID A mid-20th century name; it is near the National Reactor Testing Station.

Atravesada Hill TX Spanish 'passed-over,' but reference uncertain.

Atsion NJ Algonquian 'stone-at.'

Attal(l)a AL, MS Cherokee 'mountain.'

Attalia WA Locally believed to have been named in 1906 for a town in Italy; it suggests an adaptation of the Italian form for the country, i.e. Italia.

Attapulgas Creek FL, GA Seminole 'dogwood-grove,' the name of a former Indian town.

Attawaugen CT Algonquian, probably 'hill, knoll.'

Attean ME The lake and mountains are for Attean (Etienne) Orson, of the late 18th century.

Attica From the district in ancient Greece, with the town in NY probably being the first; it was named in 1811 at a time and place of much interest in classical names.

Attilah Mountain NH Probably Algonquian, meaning uncertain.

Attleboro MA From Attleborough in England (1684).

Attoway VA Probably Algonquian, a shortening of **Piscataway.**

Attu Island AK Aleut, meaning uncertain.

Au French, see **A** and such names as **Auglaize.**

Aubbeenaubbee IN From the personal name of a Potawatomi chief of the 19th century.

Auberry CA From Al Yarborough, an early settler, following the common pronunciation of his last name.

Auburn This name of a Yorkshire village was used in Goldsmith's *Deserted Village* (1770), a much-read poem. In 1805 the name was adopted at a town-meeting in NY, someone quoting, "Sweet Auburn, loveliest village of the plain." Being both euphonic and of poetic suggestion, it has spread to many states. In WY some abandoned cabins gave the suggestion of a deserted village.

Auchumpkee Creek GA Muskogean (Creek) 'hickory-all-about.'

Aucilla FL From the name of an early Timucua town, meaning unknown.

Aucoot MA Algonquian 'cove.'

Audrain Lake CA Probably a misspelling of the first name of Adrian Johnson, a local farmer.

Audubon Generally for J. J. Audubon, ornithologist and artist.

Auggie From the nickname for Augustus or August, e.g. the creek (MT) for August Riggert of the Forest Service.

Aughwick Creek PA Delaware, probably 'bushy.'

Auglaize MO, OH From the American-French *au glaise,* 'at the lick'; originally applied to streams, it has been transferred to two townships in MO and to a county in OH. See **Glaise.**

Augusta The city in GA and the county in VA are for the Princess of Wales, daughter-in-law of George II. The later namings spring from these, from the personal name, and from classical references. In ME the city was named (1797) probably in honor of Pamela Augusta Dearborn, daughter of the locally prominent General Henry Dearborn. **Mount Augusta** AK: named (1891) by I. C. Russell, geologist, for his wife.

Augustine From the personal name, e.g. the creek (DE) for Augustine Herrman, early settler (See **Bohemia**). For **St. Augustine,** see **Saint.**

Auk(e) The repeated use of the term in AK is for the Indian tribe, not the bird.

Auld Lang Syne Peak NV Probably from a mine-name.

Aumentos Rock CA Probably a misspelling of the last name of J. M. Armenta, an early landowner.

Aumsville OR Amos Davis was known as Aumus; he was the son-in-law of the man on whose land the town was founded, and he died in 1863. His father-in-law then named the town for him. The reduction to one syllable is not explained, but may have been the usual pronunciation.

Aunt From the colloquial use to mean 'old woman,' e.g. **Aunt Gertie's Hill** NY.

Aura Probably Latin 'breeze' and a commendatory.

Auraria Latin 'gold-mine,' a commendatory in mining regions, e.g. in CO and GA.

Aurelius From the Roman name, in NY probably for Emperor Marcus Aurelius, a part of the classical naming of 1790.

Auries Creek NY Probably from an Indian personal name; so, **Aurieville** NY.

Aurora Latin 'dawn' and also the goddess of the dawn. Having commendatory value and also being Latin, the name enjoyed some popularity during the Classical revival of the early 19th century. In NY the suggestion may also have come from an original Iroquoian name, 'constant dawn.' In OH the derivation is probably from a woman's name.

Ausable NY American-French *au sable,* 'of-the-sand,' applied first to the river.

Austerlitz From Napoleon's victory. In NY the name was given by Martin Van Buren, an admirer of Napoleon, when he heard that another place was to be named Waterloo.

Austin From the personal name especially, e.g. in TX for Stephen F. Austin, prominent in the struggle for Texan independence. In MN, for Austin R. Nicholls, first settler. In NV, for George Austin, town founder.

Austonio TX For Stephen F. Austin (see **Austin**) and **San Antonio,** for the trail which led to that settlement.

Austrian Gulch CA Named by Austrian immigrants in the 1870's.

Austwell TX From P. R. Austin and J. C. McDowell, ranch owners.

Autauga AL From the name of an ancient Indian town; literal meaning 'border'(?).

Au Train MI French, probably 'at (of)-the-drag,' being a place where early voyagers dragged their canoes across a shallows; doubtless applied first to the bay or river.

Auvergne AR Probably from the French province.

Aux French 'at-the' (plural), e.g. **Aux-vasse,** in American usage sometimes spelled after the pronunciation as *o,* e.g. **Okaw,** or *oz,* e.g. **Ozark.** See **A.**

Aux Vasse, Auxvasse MO For American-French *aux vases,* 'at-the-swamps.'

Auxwasse Creek MO From the French *aux vases,* 'at the swamps (or muddy places).'

Ava In MO and elsewhere, probably from a woman's name.

Avalanche A common name in high mountain country because of some association, e.g. the canyon in WY and the basin in MT where avalanches are a common occurrence. **Avalanche Mountain** CO: because it is scarred with rock slides presumably caused by avalanches.

Avalo CO Probably from Spanish 'earthquake,' but reason for naming uncertain.

Avalon Known from Arthurian legend as a paradisal spot, the name has been given for commendatory reasons and sometimes with special application. **Avalon** PA: chosen in 1893, when Tennyson's *Idylls of the King* had made the name well-known; Avalon is etymologically connected with the Celtic word for *apple* and the town occupied a site where there had been an orchard. **Avalon** CA: located on a western island in the ocean, the town was situated similarly to the legendary Avalon.

Avawatz Mountains CA Southern Paiute, probably 'white sheep,' from the presence of mountain sheep.

Avena Spanish 'oats,' usually for wild oats. Hence **Avenal** CA: 'oat field.'

Avenel MD, NJ From a family name.

Avenue A common generic, sometimes standing alone as a habitation-name, usually for a railroad station, e.g. IL, MD.

Avert MO Locally believed to have arisen because the first postmaster was instructed to choose a name that would *avert* confusion.

Avoca From a place in Ireland, famous as 'the meeting of the waters,' but chiefly known because of Thomas Moore's poem of that title, which was known as a song and contains the line "Sweet vale of Avoca." In LA the name has arisen from an earlier **Avocat,** an American-French name for the marsh snipe, common in the region.

Avocat See **Avoca.**

Avon Several English rivers are so called, but Shakespearean associations ('The bard of Avon') are responsible for making this a popular name, often as **Avondale.**

Avoyelles LA From an Indian tribal name, shaped to a French form.

Avra Valley AZ Probably from Spanish *abra,* 'open.'

Awanda Creek NY Probably Iroquoian, a remnant of some such name as **Tonawanda.**

Awapa Plateau UT Paiute 'at-cedar spring.'

Awasoos Island ME Algonquian 'bear' [the animal].

Awatobi AZ Hopi 'high place of the Bow People,' indicating that the Hopi clan of that name once lived there.

Awixa NY Algonquian 'it-is-end,' i.e. a boundary.

Ax(e) As with other common frontier implements (Cf. **Hatchet, Knife**) the name, e.g. **Axe Lake** KY, MN, may be assumed to have arisen commonly from incidents which have not been recorded. **Axhandle Spring** OR: named by people who found here a broken axhandle. But the name may elsewhere record a place where such handles were made; so also, **Ax Factory Run** OH. **Axhandle Spring** NV: because a man, engaged in a fight here, wielded an axhandle.

Axemann PA A seat of the Mann family, noted makers of axes.

Axial CO Ca. 1870, the geologist J. W. Powell applied the name **Axial Basin** because the valley seemed to be the axis of the nearby geological upheaval.

Azalea Usually for the wild flowering bush, e.g. in OR where it is conspicuous. It is also a woman's name.

Azansosi Mesa AZ A slight adaptation of a Navajo term, 'slim woman,' a name given by the Navajo to Mrs. Louisa Wetherill who, with her husband, established the first trading post in this vicinity.

Azotea Spanish 'flat roof.' The mesa in NM is probably named descriptively.

Aztec The Aztec tribe did not reach the area of U.S. in historical times, but the name has been applied on the theory that they once did, and various places where ruins exist have been thus named, e.g. **Aztec Peak** AZ. **Aztec** NM is close to an ancient ruined pueblo.

Azucar Spanish 'sugar,' in FL being a town developed by a sugar company.

Azul Spanish 'blue,' e.g. **Azul Creek** NM. **Azule Mountains** CA: an American spelling, probably to indicate the pronunciation.

Azure A rare substitute for the too common **Blue,** e.g. **Azure Ridge** NV.

Azusa CA From the Gabrielino Indian dialect, probably meaning 'skunk,' from a nearby hill.

B

Baadam Point WA Altered from the name of an Indian village, Baadah; meaning unknown.

Babel The river in AK was named (1956) by D. J. Orth, 'because of the "confusion of tongues" (see *Genesis* 11:7) [among] authorities with respect to the name of this stream.' The name was so recorded by him in his *Dict. of Alaska Place Names* (1967), thus creating an entry of unusually high validity. **Babel Slough** CA: for Frederick Babel, an early German settler.

Baboosic NH Algonquian, meaning uncertain.

Baboquivari AZ Papago 'mountain narrow-in-the-middle,' a descriptive referring to a mountain with two high ends.

Baby Generally as an indication of smallness in comparison with other features of the same class, e.g. **Baby Butte** SD, **Baby Lake** WA, **Baby Glacier** AK. **Babyhead Mountain** TX was named ca. 1850 when settlers found here the head of a white baby placed on a pole by Comanches.

Babylon The name of the ancient city may be an exotic transfer, but in MA and NY it is possibly an alteration of an Algonquian name by folk-etymology, the opening *bab-* occurring in such names.

Bacchus From the personal name, e.g. in UT for T. W. Bacchus, manager of a local company.

Bachawassick Pond NY Algonquian, meaning uncertain, but with *-wassick,* probably 'stone-at.'

Bachelor Though it exists as a personal name, many examples are from the residence there of an unmarried man, or men, e.g. **Bachelor Creek** MO, **Bachelor Flat** OR. **Bachelor Butte** OR: because it stands alone, and apart from the **Three Sisters.**

Back Usually for a feature which in some way is conceived as being behind some other feature or at the back rather than the front, e.g. **Back Bay** MA, which is behind the city of Boston if the latter is conceived as facing the main bay or the ocean. **Back Point** AK: for George Back, a British explorer (1826).

Backbone Usually for a ridge so rough and rocky as to be so compared; not infrequently as **The Devil's Backbone.**

Backoo ND Named (1887) by an Australian immigrant for a river in Australia, probably the **Borcoo.**

Bacon From the personal name, e.g. **Bacon's Castle** VA because the plantation-house there was held by Bacon's followers during the rebellion of 1676. Since bacon was a common item in frontier diet, many of the names, especially in the West, have doubtless arisen from incidents involving it, e.g. **Bacon-rind Creek** MT.

Bacton PA Originally **Backtown** because of its situation, but shifted when the post office was established (1887).

Bactrian Point AK Because it has two humps, like a Bactrian camel.

Baculite From the fossil cephalopod thus known, e.g. the mesa in CO.

Bad Rare, and generally used for vague descriptive purposes, e.g. **Badway Branch** WV. **Badwater** CA: apparently from a notation on a map, to indicate that the water was undrinkable. **Bad Lands, Badlands:** generally a generic, probably translating the French *mauvaises terres,* but a specific to indicate a feature thus associated, e.g. **Bad Lands Creek** SD. **Bad River** SD: ca. 1738, Indian tradition has it that many Sioux were drowned in a nighttime flood, and it was thus named; hence, the modern term. **Bad Horse Creek** SD: for Bad Horse, a Sioux chief, who lived near it. **Bad Luck** (several on natural features in MA) obviously preserves the memory of an incident, but details are lacking. **Bad Axe** MI: because surveyors found a broken axe here. **Badfish Creek** WI:

probably a translation from Algonquian of a term which usually means 'catfish' but may be taken literally as 'bad-fish.' **Bad River** MI is a translation from Algonquian; the reason for the name is uncertain, but (as is more strongly evidenced for **Bad River** in WI) the term *maskig*, 'swamp,' may have been mistaken for *matchi*, 'bad.' In KY a kind of double derogatory is supplied by **Bad Branch of Poor Creek. Bad Medicine Butte** WY: the translation of a Shoshone name, occasioned by the mysterious death here of one of their scouts.

Baddacook Pond MA Algonquian, probably 'round-(place)-at.'

Baden, Baden Baden From the city and former kingdom in Germany.

Badger Though it is sometimes from the personal name, the animal was widespread, and gave evidence of his presence by holes that were dangerous to horsemen. **Badger Lake** SD: in 1872 two men killed a badger here by kicking it. **Badger Creek** AZ: from an animal killed here, and boiled (see **Soap**). Since WI is 'The Badger State,' and its people are 'Badgers,' some names presumably thus originated.

Badin NC Named (1913) for Adrien Badin, an industrialist who founded the town.

Badito Peak CO Probably from Spanish *vadito*, 'little-ford,' and applied first to a settlement on a stream.

Badnation SD From the personal name of an Indian chief.

Badus Lake SD Named by Swiss immigrants for a lake in Switzerland, ca. 1878.

Bagaduce ME Shortened from an earlier **Majabigwaduce**, which in its turn had apparently been shifted from a still earlier form, probably meaning 'big-tideway-river.'

Bagdad From the city celebrated in *The Arabian Nights*. In CA the location in desert country provides some appropriateness.

Bahama NC From the first letters of the names of three prominent local families, Ball, Harris, Mangum.

Bahia Spanish 'bay,' e.g. **Bahia Honda** FL.

Bainbridge In GA and several other states the name is in honor of William Bainbridge, early hero of the U.S. Navy.

Baird From the personal name, e.g. several features in AK named for S. F. Baird (1823–87), ornithologist.

Bairoil WY From the Bair Oil Company.

Bajada Spanish 'descent,' e.g. **La Bajada** NM, where an early road descended a steep slope.

Bakabi AZ Hopi, 'place of the jointed reed.'

Bakagama Lake WI Ojibway 'branch-lake,' i.e. a lake which is a branch of another one.

Baked Mountain AK A fancifully descriptive name; given because of volcanic fumaroles.

Bakeoven Meadow CA Early sheepherders built a mud and stone oven here.

Baker Usually from the personal name, e.g. **Bakersfield** CA, named for Col. Thomas Baker who fenced off a field here. **Bakerville** AZ: because a baker settled there. **Mount Baker** WA: named by George Vancouver (Apr. 20, 1792) in honor of his third lieutenant, Joseph Baker.

Bala From a town in Wales; in KS and PA arising from Welsh immigrants.

Balanced Applied to rocks which are balanced; sometimes as **Balance Rock** (e.g. SD). The term is so conventional as to be almost a generic, though the phenomenon itself is rare enough to preclude the use of a second specific.

Balaton MN From Lake Balaton in Hungary, but reason for application is unknown.

Balaxy Creek TX Named for **Biloxi** by settlers who had come from that region in MS; the shift of spelling is unexplained.

Balboa CA For V. N. de Balboa, discoverer of the Pacific Ocean.

Balcon Spanish 'balcony,' e.g. the creek in TX, probably named because of a rock formation. Also, **Balcones Creek** TX.

Bald, Baldy A common descriptive for an eminence bare of trees at the time of naming, often with 'mountain,' 'peak,' 'island.' Since the bareness may have been the result of fire or logging, the descriptive quality sometimes is lost. **Baldy** generally occurs as a kind of affectionate diminutive, especially as **Old Baldy** for a mountain, used without a generic. **Bald Head Chris Island** AK is an example of a naming for a person, and others exist, since Baldy is a common nickname. **Bald Porcupine Island**: distinguishes this island from others in the group. **Bald Eagle Peak** MT: here descriptive of the eagle. By common use, the term has become a generic, especially in the southern Appalachians, e.g. **Siler's Bald** TN.

Balize LA From French *balise*, 'beacon, lighthouse.'

Balko OK Probably from the name, or nickname, of Bob Coe, early settler.

Ball From the personal name, e.g. **Ball's Bluff** VA. **Ball Bluff** MN: originally **Bald Bluff**, for a bare hill, probably shifted under the influence of the preceding, which became well-known because of its Civil War battle. **Ball Club** MN: translated from the Ojibway, since the form of the lake suggested the shape of the club or bat used by the Indians for playing their ball game. Many Indian tribes had a ball game, e.g. lacrosse, and regular fields for playing; hence, **Ball Play** TN, **Ball Play Creek** GA, **Ball Ground** GA.

Ballarat CA A gold-mining town, it was named ca. 1890 after the gold-mining site in Australia.

Ballast A seacoast name, indicating that material suitable for ballasting early ships could be there obtained, e.g. **Ballast Point** CA.

Ballena Spanish 'whale.' **Ballena Valley** CA: from a ridge suggestive of a whale's back.

Ballona Creek CA Probably from Bayona, the home in Spain of the early landowners, *y* and *ll* being identically pronounced in Mexican Spanish.

Bally, Bolly, Bully, Bailey Wintun *buli*, 'peak'; perhaps influenced by Wintun *bola*, 'spirit,' since spirits are easily associated with high mountains. The term has been applied so widely in northern CA that it has even become a generic, e.g. **Hayfork Bally, Shasta Bally**. It appears as **Bully Choop Mountain**, meaning 'high,' as **Yolla Bolly Mountains**, 'snow-covered.' By folk-etymology it has apparently produced in that area several uses of **Baldy**, together with **Billys Peak, Ball Mountain, Bully Hill** (twice), and **Bailey Hill. Mount Bailey** OR: probably from the same. In other areas **Bally** is a personal name, e.g. **Bally Creek** MN, named for Samuel Bally, local landowner.

Balsam From a tree yielding 'balsam,' i.e. some kind of aromatic, resinous gum, most commonly indicating a fir, often called *balsam fir*, or simply *balsam*. The term was also applied to the spruce, pine, hickory, cottonwood, willow, and other trees. In place-names it is rare, and usually refers to a fir, as in **Balsam Lake** MN.

Baltic From the sea; an exotic habitation-name, usually given without much reason; in OH, by local story, chosen chiefly because it was short and easy to pronounce.

Baltimore From Lord Baltimore, founder of MD. The city was incorporated in 1729 and called **Baltimore City** to distinguish it from the already-founded county.

Baluarte Spanish 'bulwark, bastion,' e.g. **Arroyo Baluarte** TX, probably because of a rock formation.

Bamboo For a local plant thus known, e.g. **Bamboo Key** FL.

Bamedumpkok Lake ME Algonquian 'sandbar-place.'

Banana For a local plant thus known, e.g. **Banana River** FL.

Banded From a rock formation giving that appearance, e.g. the mountain in CO

Bandera TX For a Mexican general (not further identified) who, ca. 1720, fought a battle with Indians at **Bandera Pass.**

Bandon For the town in Ireland.

Bangor In ME the town is said to have been named for the hymn tune. More probably the name was transferred from Bangor in Wales or in Northern Ireland. In PA the town was named by a Welshman because of slate deposits, as at Bangor in Wales.

Banida ID A boundary-name, from **Bannock** and **Oneida** counties.

Bankersmith TX For T. D. Smith, president of the first bank in the region, who was known as 'Banker' Smith.

Bannack See **Bannock.**

Banner 1) From the personal name. 2) From the idea of winning or carrying a banner, i.e. for commendatory reasons, e.g. for the county in NB named when "banner" crops were harvested. 3) **Banner Peak** CA From cloud banners streaming from it on the day of its naming in 1883. 4) In WY, from a brand name. **Banner Elk** NC: from the Banner family, early settlers, and for the site on **Elk River.**

Bannock Generally from the Indian tribal name; also **Bannack.** In OH the town was originally **Bruce,** for the son of a land donor, but this caused confusion with other places and the new name was chosen because of the historical association of Bruce with the battle of Bannockburn.

Bano For Spanish *baño,* 'bath.' **Los Banos** CA: because pools in the stream offered a chance for early travelers to bathe.

Banquete Spanish 'banquet,' but the reason for the use of the name in TX is uncertain.

Bantam CT Algonquian 'he prays,' probably with reference to early missionary work.

Baptist A few features, e.g. **Baptist Fork** KY, are so known because of association with members of that church, streams being so named having been used for baptismal services; for similar reasons, a few habitation-names occur, e.g. **Baptist** KY, **Baptistown** NJ.

Bar 1) Regularly a generic, but used as a specific to indicate a place associated with a sand bar, e.g. **Bar View** OR, which commands a view of the bar at the entrance of a bay. 2) In brand names, e.g., **Bar M Canyon** AZ, since the bar was frequently used in brands.

Barabara A repeated name in AK; used by the Russians for a native hut, being a word borrowed by them from some Siberian language.

Baraga MI For Bishop Frederick Baraga, missionary to the Chippewas (1831–1868), and compiler of a dictionary of their language.

Baranof A repeated name in AK, it is for A. A. Baranof, first governor of the Russian American colonies.

Baranshea See **Barrenshe.**

Barateria LA Spanish 'deception.' The name was probably applied as **Deception** (q.v.) has been in English; here the bay appears to give access to the Mississippi River, but actually does not.

Barbe French 'beard.' **Point la Barbe** MI, by traditional story was the place at which returning voyagers stopped to shave and otherwise make themselves presentable before continuing the few more miles to Mackinac.

Barbenceta Butte AZ From a noted Navajo chief of the 1870's.

Barber From the personal name, e.g. in OH for O. C. Barber, town founder in 1892.

Barbershop Canyon AZ At an early sheep-shearing plant here, one of the men served as a barber.

Barbue French 'catfish,' e.g. the bayou in LA.

Barcelona From the city in Spain. On Long Island (NY) the name occurs as **Bassalona** and may be Algonquian.

Bare Though sometimes from a personal name, it is usually descriptive of a place where trees might be expected but are not to be seen, e.g. **Bare Island** OR. **Bare Island** WA: Originally named in counterpart to **Wooded Island.**

Barebone(s) Probably by folk-etymology from a family name, e.g. in LA from Barbonne.

Barefoot Probably from the family name, e.g. **Barefoot Hollow** KY.

Barela CO For Casimero Barela, state senator from 1876 to 1916.

Bargaintown NJ Probably a developer's commendatory, with the idea that property could be bought at bargain prices.

Bariboo WI A semi-phonetic spelling of the name of Jean Baribault, an early French trapper who lived on the river now bearing his name.

Barium From the occurrence of barium compounds, e.g. **Barium Springs** NC.

Bark In combination it is usually part of a personal name, e.g. **Barker** and **Barkhurst,** or else from an English place-name, e.g. **Barkhamsted. Bark River** MI: railroad surveyors named the stream because, when they first saw it, it was full of floating bark. **Bark Creek** OR: named in 1856 by some men who laid down pieces of bark to keep their horses from miring when crossing a soft spot near the stream. **Bark Road,** in KY, indicates an early road thus surfaced. The repeated **Bark Camp** (especially in the SE) indicates a place where a shelter of bark had been erected to serve the needs of hunters and travelers.

Barkaboom NY From Dutch 'birch-tree,' but possibly a family name.

Barkhamsted CT Named (1732) from the common pronunciation of Berkhamsted, a town in England.

Barley Though the grain has been widely cultivated, it has rarely been a principal crop, and so the name has not been given for commendatory reasons, in contrast to **Wheat.** On an occasional natural feature, the name may be for early cultivation but is more likely for one of the grasses known as wild barley, as in **Barley Hollow** KY, **Barley Gulch** CO. **Barley Sheaf** NJ is probably from an inn sign.

Barn By association, from the existence of a barn, e.g. **Barn Hollow** KY, **Barn Bluff** MN.

Barnard From the personal name, e.g. **Mount Barnard** CA, named in 1892 for E. E. Barnard, astronomer at the Lick Observatory (1888–1895).

Barnegat NJ From the Dutch, appearing first on a 1656 map as 'barndegat,' for *barende gat,* to indicate a break in the barrier islands where surf was breaking; literally, 'foaming passage.'

Barnes From the personal name. **Barnes Butte** In AZ is for Will C. Barnes (1859–1936), winner of the Congressional Medal of Honor and author of *Arizona Place Names.*

Barnet(t) Commonly from the personal name, but **Barnet** VT, named in 1770, is probably from the town in England.

Barneveld WI For Jan van Barneveld, hero of the Dutch wars of independence in the 17th century, known especially from J. L. Motley's *Life and Death of John Barneveld* (1874).

Barnstable MA From the town in England, ca. 1639.

Baroda MI From the city of India.

Barometer Mountain AK Because its appearance, with clouds, etc., was supposed to forecast weather.

Baron From the personal name, but in OK an adaptation of **Barren,** from a nearby creek.

Barque French for a type of medium-sized vessel used on rivers and lakes; hence **Point aux Barques** MI.

Barranca Spanish 'gorge, ravine.' A generic, but a specific by association, e.g. **Barranca Creek** NM.

Barre In MA the name is from Col. Isaac Barre, an English supporter of American liberties before the Revolution. In VT the name was transferred from MA after a fist fight between a champion who supported that name and one who fought for Holden. Both fighters were contending for the name of the town in which they had lived in MA. After decisively pummeling his opponent, the victor exclaimed, 'There, the name is Barre, by God!' See **Wilkes-Barre.**

Barrel By association with a barrel; most commonly, e.g. in SD, with 'spring,' because barrels were often set into springs to provide a collection basin.

Barren Primarily a generic used, chiefly in the Appalachian region and somewhat farther west, to indicate an area without trees, supposed to be so because of poor soil. It has specific use to denote a natural feature thus associated, e.g. **Barren River** KY, **Barren Run** PA, **Barren Springs** VA. It occurs rarely as a pure descriptive, e.g. **Barren Island** WA, AK.

Barrenshe Creek KY Probably from a personal name, e.g. Barrenche; also spelled **Barrenshee, Baranshea.**

Barrier A descriptive term; for instance, the falls in MT are so called because fish cannot surmount them.

Barrillas Mountains TX Spanish, probably with reference to the saltwort or some other desert plant.

Barrington Though an English place-name, in RI (1717) it is for Viscount Barrington (1678–1734), lawyer and theologian. **Great Barrington** MA: named in 1761, probably for the second viscount (1717–1793), political figure, the **Great** being prefixed as distinction from the original town, which had been a part of

MA until 1746. Local story in NH derives the name from that of a ship.

Barro Spanish 'clay, mud.'

Barroso Spanish 'muddy.'

Barrow Usually for the personal name, e.g. **Point Barrow** AK, named in 1826 for John Barrow, English geographer and a promoter of the Arctic expedition that discovered the point. **The Barrows** SC: from some Indian burial mounds nearby.

Barry From the personal name; in MN for Edward Barry, heroic railroad engineer, who rescued 500 people from death in a forest fire in this area (Sept. 1, 1894). In IL the name was altered from **Barre** to avoid duplication within the state.

Barstow In CA the name is for William Barstow Strong, railroad president, his middle name being used because his last name had been applied to another place.

Barter Island AK From a note reading 'place of barter,' on a map by John Simpson (1855), because of contacts there with Eskimos.

Barton From the personal name; the county in KS is for Clara Barton (1821–1912), nurse in the Civil War who was involved in the founding of the American Red Cross.

Basalt From the presence of that rock.

Basha NY On several features, e.g. **Basha's Kill,** from the name of a squaw traditionally believed to have died at this stream.

Bashan For the Biblical kingdom. It has been applied to features, e.g. in CT and MA, to some extent as a commendatory, since the original kingdom was renowned for its cattle, sheep, and oaks.

Bashaw WI From a well-known Ojibway chief, usually recorded as Wabashaw.

Bash Bish Falls MA In one of the Indian wars a chief Basha was shot here, and the name is apparently a semi-humorous adaptation of some Algonquian phrase commemorating this event, but of unknown meaning to the English.

Bashful Mountain AK Fancifully named (1958) by some mountaineers because it often seemed to hide behind clouds and other mountains.

Bashi AL Muskogean, meaning uncertain.

Basic Creek NY Probably from Algonquian *quassik,* 'stone.'

Baskahegan River ME Algonquian, probably 'branch-downstream,' i.e. a stream that branches into two parts lower down.

Basking Ridge NJ Probably from the personal name Baskin.

Bass Usually for the presence of the fish or for some incident connected with them, e.g. **Bass Lake** in many states. Sometimes from a personal name, e.g. **Bass Hill** CA, **Bassfield** MS. **Basswood** occurring with 'lake,' etc., is from an alternate name for the linden tree, and is sometimes abbreviated to **Bass.**

Bastard Peak WY Locally believed to have been so named because it stands alone.

Bastrop LA Named (1844) because the Baron de Bastrop had held a land grant here under the French regime.

Bat Because frequented notably by bats, especially if the source of bat guano, e.g. **Bat Canyon** AZ. **Bat's Creek** WY: for a French-Canadian trapper named Baptiste, and known as 'Little Bat.'

Batamore Mountains AZ. From a well, named because of the presence of a plant so called, probably of Indian origin.

Batavia From the Latin name of an ancient district, later applied to the Netherlands, used generally, e.g. in NY, for a place settled by Dutch immigrants.

Bateese Lake MI A spelling from the usual pronunciation of the French personal name Baptiste, for John Baptiste Boreau, a trader of about 1815.

Batequitos Lagoon CA A Spanish adaptation of an Indian word, *batequi,* 'water-hole.' It was apparently of the Cahita language of Sinaloa, and in that case must have been brought along by Spanish settlers, many of whom came from Sinaloa.

Bath Commonly from the city of England. The literal meaning usually appears with a more precise term, e.g. **Bathtub Spring** WY. **Bath County** KY was named because of many medicinal springs, but here too there may have been reference to England.

Baton Rouge French 'stick-red.' In LA the name translates an Indian term because of a red stick or post which had been placed to mark the boundary between the hunting grounds of two tribes; in SC, of similar origin, named by French colonists.

Batsto River NJ Dutch 'bath-house.'

Battery Commonly for a place, e.g. **The Battery** in New York City, which was once the site of coast-defence artillery; or for a place resembling a fortification, e.g. **Battery Point** AK. Another **Battery Point** in AK is a translation from a Russion name which was given because the sound of the waves suggested artillery.

Battiest OK For Byington Battiest, a Choctaw judge (1928).

Battle A common term to denote a place where fighting has occurred, usually with Indians, e.g. **Battle Bar** OR for a conflict of 1856 and **Battle Mountain** NV for one of 1861. Sometimes given humorously to commemorate some minor dispute, e.g. **Battle Creek** MI from a dispute between an Indian and a land surveyor. **Battle Creek,** Clatsop Co., OR: from a boundary dispute between two farmers. **Battle Creek,** Wallowa Co., OR: from a squabble between two old prospectors. **Battle Mountain** CA: from its proximity to San Pasqual where an engagement of the Mexican War was fought. **Battle Creek,** Grant Co., OR: from a fight between two bands of Indians. **Battle Creek,** Tulare Co., CA: where a burro fought off a mountain lion in a bloody encounter. **Battle River** MN: so named because of a fight here between Ojibways and Sioux. **Battle Brook** MN: from a fight among some loggers. **Battle Creek** MN: from a conflict of 1842 between Ojibway and Sioux. **Battleground** IN is the site of the battle of Tippecanoe in 1811. **Battle Butte** WY: because U.S. troops and Indians fought here, ca. 1876. **Battle Mountain** WY: because a posse had a skirmish here with Indians at the late date of 1895. A few occurrences are from the personal name, e.g. **Battleboro** NC for James and Joseph Battle, large stockholders in a local railroad. **Battle Mountain** CO: named by the naturalist Enos Mills, ca. 1900, because of the evidences of the battle of nature, i.e. the effects of wind, snow, and fire. **Battle Ground** WA: from an encounter of the 21st Infantry with some hostile Indians, ca. 1860.

Battleship Island WA: From its appearance.

Batupan Boque MS Muskogean 'fountainhead-creek,' for a stream arising from a spring (?).

Bauxite AR From a deposit and mine of that particular aluminum ore.

Bavaria KS From the state in Germany, named by German settlers.

Bay Occasional places are named for the color, e.g. **Bay Horse** MT, or for the bay tree, but it is commonly used, especially for habitation-names, to indicate a place associated with a bay, e.g. **Bayside, Bayview,** with commendatory purposes. **Bayocean** OR: for a summer resort on a neck of land between a bay and the ocean.

Bayonne From the city of France; in NJ (1869) perhaps with a pun 'bay-on,' because of its site.

Bayou Primarily a generic, but becoming a specific to identify a place thus associated, e.g. **Bayou Creek** KY, and in habitation-names, such as **Bayou** KY, TX, **Bayouville** MO. As a generic it commonly precedes its specific, e.g. **Bayou Bushley, Bayou Funny Louis.** For such names, see under the specific.

Bazaar KS Named in memory of a shop or bazaar that one of the early settlers had once kept.

Bazetta OH Named ca. 1804; a woman's name (?).

Bazine KS John Farnsworth, early postmaster, was an admirer of A. F. Bazaine, French commander in the war of 1870–1871, and named the postoffice for him in 1874; in some unexplained manner the 'a' was dropped.

Beach Usually from the personal name, e.g. **Beach Glen** NJ for Benjamin Beach, ironmaster, and **Beach City** OH for Henry Beach, engineer during the building of a railroad here in 1872. On features it is commonly a generic, but becomes a specific in habitation-names, e.g. **Long Beach,** and in a occasional naming by association.

Beacon Before the development of the telegraph, fires on hilltops served as alarm signals, and the name **Beacon Hill** is common, especially in New England; it moved by transfer to other features and to habitations, e.g. **Beacon Falls** CT.

Beaklance, Bayou LA From the French *bec-a-lancette,* for a bird, known in English as lancet-beak; partially shifted by folk-etymology.

Bean Often from the personal name. It may also be from beans, especially baked beans, a favorite food of gold miners **Bean Hollow** CA translates **Arroyo de los Frijoles. Bean Soup Lake** NB: some cowboys had to subsist here largely on bean soup, other supplies being low. **Bean Porridge Hill** MA: unexplained; either from an incident or from an Algonquian name by folk-etymology. **Bean Blossom Creek** IN: probably from the personal name of an Indian.

Bear It may be for a personal name, e.g. **Bear Creek** MN for Benjamin Bear, early settler. It may also be a shifted spelling from the descriptive **Bare** or such personal names as **Baer, Behr.** Ordinarily it is for the animal, and thus exists in thousands of examples (500 in CA alone), as a striking evidence of the impression which this animal made upon the early Americans. In the East the black bear was thus recorded. In the West the name is more commonly for the grizzly, and is often thus specified (see **Grizzly**). The name occurs upon all sorts of natural features, being especially common with 'mountain,' probably because bears lingered in mountain areas after being exterminated in the valleys. Though it survives on some habitations by transfer, its suggestion of uncouthness has prevented its wide use.

As with animal-names generally, it occasionally indicates mere presence, as in marginal areas of habitat, and regions where bears were especially numerous. Usually, however, the name springs from an incident. In the East these incidents are of such an early date that authentic record does not often survive. In the West many credible traditional tales still exist, some of them recorded at the time or soon afterwards. **Bear** AZ: when the railroad was being built, a bear was shot here (probably an instance of an impression made because of rarity). **Bear Creek**, Greenlee Co., AZ: a place noted for a heavy population of bears. **Bear River**, Humboldt Co., CA: in 1850 Lewis K. Wood was badly mangled by a grizzly here. **Bear Creek**, Wallowa Co., OR: a sheepherder reported seeing nine bears, frolicking by the stream. **Bear Gulch** OR: a bear here jumped on a pack-horse, with memorable confusion. **Bear Creek**, Bennett Co., SD: a translation of the Sioux name, given because a lone Indian once killed a bear here with a tomahawk. **Bear Gulch**, Custer Co., SD: an early prospecting party found a bear den here. **Bear Valley** MN: because the early settlers once pursued a bear here. **Bear Poplar** NC: probably named because an early settler once treed a bear in a poplar tree. Occasional features have been named descriptively because of resemblances to a bear or some part of one, e.g. **Bear Headland** AZ. The work of bears or traces left by them have resulted in **Bearwallow, Beartrack, Bear Tree** (for a tree marked by scratches and rubbing). Evidences of early hunting survive in **Bear Trap, Bear Pen,** and **Bearskin. Bearpaw** probably springs from a paw cut off and fastened to a tree, as a trophy or marker, e.g. **Bearpaw Meadow** CA. Indian personal names, translated, have yielded some examples; **Bear-in-the-Lodge-Creek** SD records an occasion when a bear entered one of the Indian lodges and was killed there. **Beargrass** is a term usually applied to a kind of yucca, but with various applications in different regions. **Four Bear Creek** WY: one morning in the 1880's one man killed four bears along this stream. **Bear Lake**, Rocky Mountain N.P., CO: in a region where bears are extremely rare, a rancher happened to see one here, and gave the name, thus supplying a good example of naming from rarity. Since the bear was of great importance to the Indians, both for food and as a mythological and totemistic animal (often included in personal names), translations are numerous, e.g. **Beartrap River** WI.

Bearden On natural features it may indicate a bear's den, but on habitations it is usually from a family name, e.g. in OK for J. S. Bearden, prominent resident (1896).

Beasha Creek MS Choctaw 'mulberries-are-there.'

Beasore Meadow CA An adaptation of the name of a French stockman, Beausore.

Beau The French 'beautiful' (masculine) has little currency, except as it occurs as part of a personal name. **Beaumont** TX: for Jefferson Beaumont, early settler. **Beaumont** CA: because of the literal meaning, 'beautiful mountain.' **Beaukiss** TX: a name reputed locally to be selected by an early settler, and of 'no significance,' but possibly suggested by the idea of a 'beautiful kiss.' See **Bel**.

Beaucop, Bayou LA Probably from French *beaucoup*, 'much,' with reference to the size or the amount of water. There once was, nearby, **Bayou Buckoo**.

Beaufort In NC and SC it is from the title of the Duke of Beaufort, one of the Lords Proprietors. **Beaufort Sea** AK was named (1826) by Sir John Franklin for his friend Sir Francis Beaufort, hydrographer.

Beauregard From the family name, especially (e.g. the parish in LA) for P. G. T. Beauregard, Confederate general.

Beautiful Scarcely used, but occurring in **Beautiful Mountain** NM, **Beautiful View Branch** TX.

Beaver Found all over the country in proper locations, of economic importance for its fur, conspicuous because of its dams, the beaver has given rise to, at a rough estimate, the names of 1,000 natural features. These are most commonly smaller streams (brooks, runs, creeks) such as the animal inhabited, and streams so named might occur so close to one another as to be scarcely distinguishable. Indeed, **Beaver Creek** came to be a quasi-generic requiring further delimitation, e.g. **Big Beaver Creek**. Historically, the process started with the settlement (John Winthrop named a **Beaver Brook** in MA in 1632), and continued until the near-extermination of the animal in the 19th century. By transfer the name spread to features not normally associated with the animal, such as **Beaver Lick**. Aided by the personal name, **Beaver** has spread to about 50 habitation-names. **Beaverdam:** a common name to indicate a feature thus associated, e.g. the lake in WI. **Beaver Tree Canyon** NB: from a tree gnawed by beavers.

Bebe TX Selected by the namer when he saw this name on a can of baking powder.

Becerro, Becerra Spanish 'calf,' e.g. a creek with each gender in TX.

Becket MA From **Beckett** in England (1765).

Beckwith, Beckwourth The name-cluster in CA is for James Beckwourth, early pioneer and explorer. **Beckwith**, which probably represents the actual pronunciation, is an alternate spelling.

Bedashosa Lake SD Siouan 'roily waters.'

Bedford From the county or town in England, etc. In MA (1729) it is probably for the town. In NH (1750) for the Duke of Bedford, political figure of the mid-18th century.

Bedias TX A variant plural of the Indian tribal name usually spelled Bidai.

Bedico Creek LA From a French personal name, probably for Michael Bitancourt, a settler of the 18th century.

Bedivere Point AZ From the Arthurian knight. One of the fanciful Grand Canyon names. Other such Arthurian names in the park are: **Elaine Castle, Galahad Point, Gawain Abyss, Guinevere Castle, King Arthur Castle, Lancelot Point, Merlin Abyss, Modred Abyss.** Dubious characters have abysses named after them.

Bedlam By local story **Bedlam Corner** CT was named because a quarrelsome family habitually 'raised bedlam' there. The brook in MA may be named from its noisiness or from an incident.

Bedminster NJ, PA From the town in England.

Bee 1) From the personal name or nickname, e.g. in TX for B. E. Bee, prominent early Texan. 2) From the insect, often in such compounds as **Bee Tree Creek**, e.g. in CA. 3) From the letter of the alphabet, because letters were originally given in place of names, e.g. **Bee** NB, which preserves one of the original precinct designations. **Bee** OK: for a girl named Dee, but altered in spelling by the Post Office Dept. **Bumble Bee** AZ: from the numerous bumble bees that made their nests in the cliffs. **Beegum:** originally a hollow gum-tree inhabited by bees; later, any bee-hive; in CA, from a mountain of limestone, containing many holes, some of them used by bees. **Bee House** TX: the settlers found many caves and cliffs inhabited by bees.

Beech Impressive as an individual tree but rarely the predominating growth, the beech was well suited for the identification of natural features, and many are thus distinguished in the eastern half of the U.S. where the tree is native. It also had commendatory value for habitation-names, as in **Beechwood, Beech Grove**. In the West the occasional name is from a personal name, e.g. **Beech Creek** OR.

Beecher From the personal name; for instance, the island in CO is named for Lt. F. H. Beecher killed in battle with the Cheyennes there in 1868, a conflict now known by a curious retrospect nomenclature as the Battle of Beecher Island.

Beef A rare name, since the term is commonly applied to the meat and not to the animal; in some instances it is probably from the French **Boeuf.** It is more commonly, e.g. **Beef Creek** SD, for a place associated with animals which had been selected as a 'beef-herd.' It occurs also in compounds, e.g. **Beefhide** KY.

Beegum See **Bee.**

Beehive From the shape of the conventional hive, e.g. **Beehive Rock** WA.

Beer The term is applied descriptively to springs that effervesce, e.g. the famous **Beer Springs** on the California trail, now beneath the water of an artificial lake. Other names such as **Beer Gulch** CA probably record some incident involving beer. **Beer Mug Mountain** WY: from a brand name. **Beer Kil** NY Dutch 'bear (animal)-stream.'

Beeren Island NY Dutch 'bears (animal).'

Beersheba Since the Biblical place is associated with a well, such a name as **Beersheba Springs** TN seems natural, but it was doubly so because the discoverer of the springs (1833) happened to be Beersheba Porter Cain.

Beetles Rest Spring OR The translation of a Klamath name, 'rest' being a loose translation of a word meaning 'live,' because of the number of beetles in that locality.

Begashibito AZ Navajo 'cow-water.'

Behm From the personal name; for instance, various places in AK are named for Major M. C. von Behm, commandant in Kamchatka (1779) when George Vancouver visited there.

Bejou MN An Ojibway rendering of French *bon jour,* 'Good day!' given by the Indians of a reservation to the first railroad station on their land.

Bekuennesee Falls WI Ojibway 'smoke-river,' from the resemblance of mist to smoke.

Bel, Belle French 'beautiful.' *Bel* is the older form for modern *beau; belle* is feminine. In American usage both forms have sometimes been used without reference to gender, e.g. **Belview** MN and **Belleview** in various states. The personal name Belle may be involved as with **Bellemont** AZ. The popular **Belmont** may be from the family name, e.g. in NC, but often is descriptive-commendatory, e.g. in MA. French survivals occur, e.g. **Belle Fourche River** WY, 'beautiful fork.' Both **Bellevue** and **Belleview** commonly have descriptive value. There is literary influence on **Belmont** from Shakespeare's *Merchant of Venice.* **La Belle** is 'the beautiful,' with some word meaning 'place' understood. **Belle Chasse** LA: literally, French 'fine hunting,' but probably for J. D. de Goutin Bellechasse, a local landowner. **Belle Isle** LA: for an early colonist de Belle-Isle, who was held captive here by Indians. **Belle Plaine** IA: named (1860) by Americans who were impressed by the view of the 'beautiful plain,' and translated it into French.

Belcher From the personal name. In MA (1761) **Belchertown** is for Governor Jonathan Belcher. The point in AK is for Edward Belcher, one of the explorers of the coast in 1827.

Belcoville NJ From the Bethlehem Company.

Belen NM Spanish 'Bethlehem,' a religious name from a land grant dedicated to Our Lady of Bethlehem.

Belfast From the city in Northern Ireland. In ME the name was placed by immigrants in 1770.

Belfort From the city in France, e.g. in NY and OH.

Belgium, Belgique From the country in Europe, e.g. in WI; the French form, **Belgique,** is used in MO.

Belgrade From the city in Yugoslavia; in NB originating because of a resemblance of site.

Beljica Peak WA From the initials of the first names of some tourists who visited the region in 1897.

Bell Commonly from the personal name. Sometimes a shortening of **Belle,** e.g.

Bellaire and **Bellfountain,** or an adaptation of **Bel,** e.g. **Bellmont. Bell Canyon** CA: from a rock that makes a bell-like sound when struck. **Bellflower:** from a popular variety of apples, the town in CA being named from an orchard of them. **Bellwood** WV: for J. W. Bell and J. E. Wood, the founders in 1918. **Bell Rock** AZ: from being shaped like a bell. **Bell Spring** CA: in 1860 two cow bells were found at the spring. **Bells** TX: because the place was notable for several churches having bells. **Bell Cow Creek** and **Bell Calf Creek** in OK record animals thus identified. **Bell Buckle** TN: by local tradition the creek was so named because the representations of a bell and a buckle were found carved in the bark of a beech tree near the stream's headwaters.

Bellair, Bellaire, Belleayr Cf. **Bel, Belle.** Obviously intended as a commendatory, 'beautiful air,' the name seems to be a long-used Old French form, of which the usage is American rather than based upon French immigration.

Bellamaqueen Bay VT Algonquian (apparently influenced by French spelling), probably 'good beaver.'

Belle See **Bel**

Bellefontaine, Bellefonte The first form is the French 'beautiful spring,' given descriptively to the site in OH, and used elsewhere. The second form was given, for the same reason, to a town in PA, though *fonte* is not properly used for 'spring' in French, and there is probably confusion with the English 'fount.'

Bellicose Peak AK Named (1963) by John and William Bousman, who had just made the first ascent, and thus expressed their feelings about the difficulties. Cf. **Benign.**

Bellingham From the personal name; in WA the bay was named in 1792 by George Vancouver, probably for Sir William Bellingham who had assisted in the preparations for the voyage.

Bellona NY From the Roman goddess of war; reason for naming uncertain.

Bellota Spanish 'acorn.'

Bellview See **Bellevue,** under **Bel.**

Belly Rare, being generally considered a semi-obscene term. **Belly River** MT: from the Indian tribe usually known by their French name, Gros Ventres, but often by its translation as Big Bellies. **Belly-Ache Mesa** NM: from an incident in which some cowboys ate bad food.

Belmont See **Bel.**

Beloit The original naming, in WI (1837), was on the analogy of Detroit, with the first syllable **Bel** (q.v.) apparently as a commendatory.

Belpre From older French *bel pré,* 'beautiful meadow,' named in OH, ca. 1789, in a period and area of strong French influence; used descriptively and perhaps for a place in France.

Belt Mountains MT Translating the Gros Ventre name, which arose probably because one butte has an outcrop of white rock around it, like a belt. The river is named from the mountains.

Beltrami For G. C. Beltrami, an Italian, who traveled widely in North America in the 1820's.

Beluga Various features in AK are named from the white whale; the word is Russian and some of the namings probably go back to the Russian period.

Belvedere, Belvidere Italian 'beautiful view,' or 'place having a beautiful view.' In earlier namings, e.g. in SC, the literal meaning was probably the origin. Farther west, places were named after places in the East, or the name simply came to have a vague commendatory quality for habitations. The proper Italian spelling is with the 'e,' but the other form is more common in the U.S. In **Belvedere** CA the idea of 'good view' is warranted, and is probably the cause of naming.

Bemidji MN From the personal name of an Ojibway chief.

Ben 1) Gaelic 'mountain,' as in **Ben Lomond** AR, CA, etc., though this name is actually borrowed directly from Scotland, with generally no thought of literal meaning. 2) Hebrew 'son,' as in **Ben**

Hur VA, **Benhur** TX, which is, again, scarcely to be taken literally, since it is lifted whole from the title of Lew Wallace's highly popular novel (1880). 3) It is the common shortening of Benjamin, e.g. **Benmoore Canyon** CA, named for an early settler. **Ben Franklin** TX: for Ben Franklin Simmons of a family of early landowners. **Ben Mar Hills** CA: from Ben Mark, a real estate promoter, the name being given in 1920, when the 'k' was dropped, in an attempt to make the name sound Spanish, as was popular at that time. **Bendavis** MO: for a popular variety of apple. **Benmore** UT: for the early surveyors, Israel Bennion and C. H. Skidmore who was called 'More.'

Bena MN, WI Ojibway 'partridge,' used in Longfellow's *Hiawatha* and probably taken from it.

Benali CA From the middle names of James Ben Ali Haggin, an early ranch owner.

Benarnold TX For Bennie Arnold, three-year-old girl, who was mascot of the first train to arrive in the community.

Bench Primarily a generic, chiefly Western, but appearing as a specific by association, e.g. **Bench Creek** WA, which flows across a bench.

Bend In TX the town is situated on a bend of a river. In OR the town is so called probably because of a bend in an early road, though there is also a river bend there.

Bendeleben, Mount AK Named (1866) by members of the Western Union Telegraph expedition for their leader Baron Otto von Bendeleben.

Benedicta ME From Bishop Benedict Fenwick who was involved with the founding; named commemoratively (1872), with 'a' added to simulate a Latin feminine ending as is customary with towns.

Benewah ID For a local (Coeur d'Alene) chief.

Bengal From the state in India.

Bengies Point MD From Robert Benger, who lived in the vicinity in the 17th century.

Benicia CA Founded by M. G. Vallejo and Robert Semple and given one of the names borne by the former's wife.

Benign Peak AK Named (1965) as a counterpart to **Bellicose Peak.**

Benld IL Named (1903) for a prominent local citizen, Benjamin L. Dorsey, by taking Ben and the initials, L. D.

Bennington The original naming was in VT (1749); in connection with a 'New Hampshire grant' by Gov. Benning Wentworth, it made use of his given name.

Bensalem PA The name dates from ca. 1700, before that having been **Salem.** It may have been an awkward attempt to dub a later creation as 'son of Salem.'

Bent With appropriate natural features, e.g. creek, it may be a descriptive, but is more commonly from the personal name, e.g. **Bent** NM for G. B. Bent, local miner and promoter. **Bents Fort** CO: from the trading post established in 1828 by William and Charles Bent.

Benton From the personal name, rather than from any of the English villages, especially for T. H. Benton, national political figure of the early 19th century, e.g. eight counties and several towns.

Benzie County MI Apparently a variant of **Betsie,** the chief river.

Benzonia MI Apparently a Latinized form from **Benzie County.**

Beowawe NV Probably Shoshone 'pass, gateway,' because of the situation. Persistent stories give the meaning as 'big posterior,' and it seems to have been the name of at least one Indian. Possibly this latter idea is Paiute, or else the word has two meanings, both involving the idea of passageway. Cf. the Dutch use of *gat.* See **Gate.**

Berclair TX From the given names of Bert and Clair Lucas, landowners.

Berdoo Canyon CA From the popular abbreviation or nickname of the nearby town, San Bernardino.

Berea From the Biblical city in Macedonia. In OH a committee, including two clergymen, was instructed to select a Biblical name for a new post office, and selected this one. The popularity of the name, which is unimportant in the Bible, results largely from its being short, simple, and euphonic.

Berg Usually in the sense of **Iceberg,** q.v.

Bergantin Creek TX Spanish 'barkentine,' probably because a ship of that type was wrecked here during the Spanish regime.

Bergen 1) From the city Bergen-op-zoom in the Netherlands, e.g. in NJ where it was placed by 17th century Dutch settlers. 2) From the city in Norway, e.g. in MN, named by immigrants in the 19th century.

Bergheim TX German 'mountain-home,' suggested by Andress Engel, town founder.

Bergoo WV From an obsolete term, meaning 'stew' or 'mush'; more commonly spelled 'burgoo,' applied first to the creek.

Bering On various features in AK it is commemorative of Vitus Bering who explored much of the coast for the Russians in 1741.

Berkeley, Berkley, Berkely Though it is a place-name in England, the namings are regularly from a family name. **Berkeley Co.** SC: from John and William Berkeley, two of the Lords Proprietors. Bishop George Berkeley probably is honored in **Berkley** MA and certainly in **Berkeley** CA, the latter being so named because he was the author of the line, "Westward the course of empire takes its way."

Berks, Berkshire From the county in England and its shortened form, the former adopted in PA the latter in MA for counties.

Berlin Usually from the capital of Prussia, and later of Germany, because of German immigrants. But in MD the name was originally Burleigh, and the shift may have been by a kind of folk-etymology, the accent remaining on the first syllable. In OR the place was originally Burrell's Inn from a personal name; this was shortened to **Burl Inn** when the post office was established, and then shortened again to **Berlin.** In CT the name dates from 1785, a period when foreign, non-English names were becoming popular. **Berlin,** King Co., WA: named by the Great Northern Railroad Co. on account of the large German investment in the railroad.

Bermuda From the Atlantic island. **Bermuda Hundred** VA: named ca. 1613, probably because of a fancied resemblance to the island, where some of the English had recently been shipwrecked. **Bermuda Island** SC: so named because some of the early settlers came from Bermuda. See **Hundred.**

Bern(e) Usage has been divided between **Bern** (Swiss, German) and **Berne** (French, and usual English) spellings. Thus PA has both **Berne** and **Bernville,** in both cases the name being from 18th century settlements of Swiss. Most of the other examples, e.g. **New Bern** NC, are of similar origin.

Berro Spanish 'watercress.'

Berry Though **Strawberry,** etc., occur, the unspecified 'berry' commonly arises from a personal name. **Berry Hill** SC is from the quantities of blackberries found there.

Berthoud CO For E. L. Berthoud, discoverer of the pass in 1861.

Bertie County NC Named (1722) for James and Henry Bertie, who had a share in the proprietary rights of the colony.

Berwick From one of the English towns, e.g., in ME (1713) for Berwick in Dorsetshire, in PA (1786) for Berwick-upon-Tweed.

Berwind From the personal name, e.g. in CO for E. J. Berwind, a chief stockholder in the locally operating coal company. See **Windber.**

Berwyn In PA it was named as a railroad station (see **Cynwyd**); elsewhere, e.g. in IL and OK, it has been a transfer from PA.

Besa Chitto Creek MS Choctaw 'mulberries-are-there,' with *chito*, 'big.' Cf. **Beasha.**

Besancon IN Named by French immigrants of the early 19th century for the city in France.

Besoco WV From Beckley Smokeless Coal Company.

Bessemer The names are associated with the steel industry and honor Sir. Henry Bessemer, whose discoveries transformed steel-making.

Bessie OK For the Blackwell, Enid and Southwestern (BES) Railroad on which it is located.

Bessmay TX For Bessmay Kirby, of the family which operated a large local lumber mill.

Best Regularly from the proper name, e.g. in TX for Tom Best, a railroad man. In such combinations as **Bestland** VA and **Bestfield** DE it has commendatory value.

Bet From the shortening of **Elizabeth.** But **Bet Cash Branch** KY is probably an incident-name, based on a wager.

Betatakin AZ Navajo 'side-hill house.'

Bethalto IL Originally **Bethel,** but shifted artificially to avoid duplication within the state.

Bethania The Latin form of the Biblical town more commonly rendered as **Bethany;** in NC the naming was by Moravian settlers, ca. 1759.

Bethany From the New Testament village, often used first for a church and then transferred to a settlement; in CT, dating from 1762.

Bethel From the Old Testament city, often used first for a church and then transferred to a settlement. In CT the name is from 1759. In VT, by local story, the name was bestowed by Dudley Chase, after he had, like the Biblical Jacob, slept here with a stone for his pillow. It is also an English family-name.

Bethera SC From the combination of the names of two nearby churches, Bethel and Berea, with a little simplification.

Bethesda Though mentioned only once in the Bible, this name became popular for churches, and was thus transfered to towns, as in MD and OH.

Bethlehem From the Biblical town; in CT, 1739. In PA the name was suggested by its mention in a German hymn sung at the foundation of the settlement on Christmas Eve, 1741.

Bethpage Apparently a spelling variation from Bethphage, a village mentioned in the New Testament.

Bethune In SC named (1899) by railroad officials for a prominent local citizen, not further identified. In CO probably for the town in France at the time of World War I.

Betsy, Betsey, Betsie Usually from the woman's name, e.g. **Betsey Layne** KY, not further identified. **Betsy River** MI: by folk-etymology from French *bec-scie*, a kind of duck, the French name being a translation from the Ojibway. So also **Betsie River** MI.

Betteravia CA A quasi-Latin formation from French *betterave*, 'sugar-beet,' named when a sugar factory was started, ca. 1897.

Betty From the personal name, e.g. **Betty Bowman Creek** KY. **Mount Betty** (also **Battie** and in other spellings) is probably by folk-etymology from some Algonquian term. Cf. **Madambettox.**

Between the Rivers KY A district name, with special reference to the land lying in the narrow strip between the Cumberland and Tennessee rivers, but in common usage sometimes applied more widely.

Beula See Beulah.

Beulah Although eventually from the vague but blessed land of the future (*Isaiah* 62:4), its popular usage is based more directly upon its occurrence in John Bunyan's *Pilgrim's Progress,* and namings are more common from its use as a woman's name, e.g. in ND for Beulah Stinchcombe, niece of one of the land developers. Also as **Beula,** e.g., in IA and in **Beulaville** NC.

Beverly From the town in England, e.g. in MA (1668). The name, for some reason, has attained a commendatory, snobbish suggestion, and has been borrowed widely. **Beverly Hills** CA: suggested from a newspaper account in 1907 that President Taft was spending some time at a place called **Beverly Farms;** at first, **Beverly,** in 1911, it became **Beverly Hills.**

Bexar TX An alternate spelling for **Bejar** the name of a town in Spain; applied to the site of present **San Antonio** in 1718, now the name of a county. It is also a title associated with the Spanish royal house, and the naming may have been thus influenced.

Bias WV For a local lawyer, a family name.

Bible Though some may be namings because of religious services, most of them are from the personal name, e.g. **Bible Creek** OR for A. S. Bible, early rancher.

Bibon WI Algonquian (Ojibway) 'winter,' but reference uncertain.

Bicknell From the personal name. In UT, T. C. Bicknell offered (1914) a library to any town in the state that would take his name. Two accepted, the second one becoming **Blanding,** Mrs. Bicknell's maiden name.

Bicycle Lake CA The lake is generally dry, its name probably arises from the fact that local people sometimes used its hard surface for bicycling.

Bidahochi Butte AZ Navajo, a term indicating the red streaks on the side of the butte.

Bidais Creek TX See **Bedias.**

Biddeford ME From a town in England (1718).

Bienvenu, Bayou LA For the plantation, named after Antoine Benvenue, who obtained a Spanish grant here in 1794.

Bierstadt From the personal name, especially for Albert Bierstadt (1830–1902), who painted landscapes of the region in CO where a lake bears his name.

Big The commonly-used descriptive with natural features, as a counterpart with **Little,** or merely to denote a feature which for some reason seems to the namer to be larger than is to be expected within the class of the generic, e.g. **Big River** and **Big Mountain.** Except in counterpart, it is not commonly used with generics which themselves impose a limitation of size, thus **Big Hill** is uncommon, because a big hill should really be a mountain. The name has been readily transferred to habitations, but has not been used in itself for habitation-names. It commonly and ambiguously stands as the first element of a double specific, e.g. **Big Diomede Island** AK, where the existence of a counterpart **(Little Diomede Island)** shows that the *big* refers to the island. **Big Bend,** is a habitation-name in several states and is a quasi-generic. It indicates a place at which a river makes a change of course, but it also may indicate a place where a river makes a curve approaching a circle. See **Grand, Great, Bighorn.**
   Bigfoot TX: for W. A. (Big Foot) Wallace, hunter and early Indian fighter. **Big Foot** IL: from the name of a Potawatami chief of the early 19th century. **Bigbone** KY, **Big Bone Creek** KY: because fossil bones of mastodons were found here.

Bighorn From the mountain sheep, e.g. **Bighorn Crags** ID, **Bighorn Basin** MT, **Bighorn Lake** CA. Since the sheep were comparatively rare, their sighting and successful shooting was often an event, and so led to frequent namings. **Big Horn River** WY, MT was named for the sheep, but written as two words, apparently on the analogy of its tributary the **Little Horn.** This latter stream was first called the **Little Big Horn,** but the contradiction of terms led to the dropping of *big*.

Bigwitch Gap NC From the name of a local Cherokee family.

Bijou French 'jewel.' It is sometimes a commendatory name, e.g. in CA. **Bijou Hills** SD: for a Frenchman, thus nicknamed. In LA it is a railroad name, honoring Bijou Wilson, wife of a local landowner. In CO the name probably arose from Joseph Bijeau, early frontiersman.

Bill, Billy Usually from the nicknames for William, e.g. **Billy Meadows** OR for William Smith, sheepherder and **Billy Creek** AZ for an Indian guide. **Bill Williams Mountain** AZ for the well-known mountain-man (1787–1849). **Bill Point** WA: the whole bay was named (1841) by the Wilkes expedition from a fancied resemblance to an eagle, and this point was the bill. **Billy Goat Creek** AK: because of mountain goats found here. **Bill** WY: because several of the inhabitants bore this name at the time of the establishment of the post office.

Billerica In MA (1653) an alternate spelling from Billericay in England.

Billings From the personal name, e.g. in MT for Frederick Billings, president of the Northern Pacific Railroad, which founded the town in 1882.

Biloxi MS From an Indian tribal name.

Biltmore NC Named (ca. 1893) by its founder G. W. Vanderbilt from Bildt, his estate in the Netherlands, and the English *moor*.

Bingen From the town in Germany, in WA being so named because its situation on the Columbia was like that of the other town on the Rhine.

Bingham From the personal name, e.g. in UT for Sandford and Thomas Bingham, who grazed livestock in the canyon, ca. 1850. **Binghamton** NY is for William Bingham, landowner and town developer; named commemoratively in 1855.

Binne Kill NY Dutch 'inner stream.'

Biola CA From Bible Institute of Los Angeles.

Birch Though sometimes from the personal name, the tree is widespread and conspicuous, especially for its white bark, and the name is fairly common. Since one variety grows near desert springs, the name is even found in arid areas. **Birch Creek** CA: since this is in the San Bernardino Mountains where there are no birches, it may have been named by mistake for another tree, or it may be a personal name.

Bird The personal name figures in most of the habitation-names. Many natural features are named from some bird or birds, not more definitely specified; most often it is used with *island* and *rock,* because these may be much frequented by various kinds of birds. **Bird Rock,** San Diego Co., CA: because a formation resembles a bird. **Big Bird Lake** CA: because the tracks of an unidentified large bird were seen on the shore in 1902 when the lake was named. **Bird Head Lake** SD: for an Indian so named. **Bird-in-Hand** PA: for the painting and inscription on an inn sign. **Bird Butte** OR: because George Bird, a forest guard, met with an accident there, and bled to death. **Birdseye Creek** OR: for David Birdseye, pioneer settler. **Birdsview** WA: from a shortening of the first name (Birdsey) of the first postmaster, plus the common *view*. **Birdtown** NC: probably for the Bird Clan of the Cherokees.

Birmingham From the city in England. Since this city was unimportant during the Colonial period, the namings are late, and are often with reference to iron- and steel-manufacture, as in PA (1797) and AL (1871).

Birnamwood WI From the wood in Shakespeare's *Macbeth,* but reason for naming uncertain.

Birome TX Named by R. L. Cartwright, early settler, for his sons, Bickham and Jerome.

Birthday Usually commemorating a birthday of one of the namers; for instance, the creek in AK is named because two members of a field party had birthdays at this time in 1924. **Birthday**

Cake Peak WY: because it is fancifully imagined to resemble a cake with candles.

Birthright TX For C. E. Birthright, an early settler.

Bisbee From the personal name, e.g. in AZ for DeWitt Bisbee, shareholder in a mining company.

Biscay MN From the Bay of Biscay, a railroad name, bestowed with little significance.

Biscayne Bay FL From Spanish *Biscaino;* named by early Spanish explorers for a man known as El Biscaino because he came from the province of Viscaya (Biscaya).

Biscuit The geyser basin in WY is so called because of the presence of geyseritic knobs that look like biscuits. The mountain, AZ, is named descriptively, because its top seems to be turned over on itself as are some kinds of biscuits.

Bishop Regularly from the personal name, e.g. **Bishop** CA: for S. A. Bishop, early cattleman. **Bishop Rock** CA: because the sailing ship *Bishop* struck here in 1855.

Bismarck Regularly for the German chancellor (1815–1898); e.g. in ND, named by railroad officials in 1873, in compliment to German bondholders who had given the railroad support.

Bison The name occurs rarely, never having been in popular usage, as a substitute for the too common *buffalo,* e.g. **Bison** OK, so named from nearby **Buffalo Springs.**

Bistineau LA Probably Caddoan, but made over into a French form. The meaning is uncertain, but early travelers give it as 'big broth,' apparently because foamy material was easily stirred up on the lake's surface.

Bitch Creek ID By folk-etymology from French *biche,* 'cow-elk.'

Bithlo FL Seminole 'canoe.'

Bitter One of the rare specifics arising from the sense of taste, occurring with water features, e.g. **Bitter Creek** and **Bitter Lake,** both in arid regions where the taste of the water is affected by alkali; often in combination, as in **Bitterwater Creek. Bitterroot River, Mountains** ID, MT: from the occurrence of the bitterroot plant. **Bittersweet Creek** SD: probably from growth of the herb bittersweet. So also, **Bittersweet Island** WI.

Bivalve MD, NJ Used as the equivalent of the usual **Oyster.**

Bivouac Peak WY In 1930 the first climbers were benighted on its slope, and had to 'bivouac,' cold and hungry, until morning.

Biwabik MN, WI Algonquian (Ojibway) 'iron, metal,' now applied to an iron-mining area.

Black Though it is also a frequently-occurring personal name (also as **Blackstone, Blackburn,** etc.) it is probably the commonest color descriptive, being applied to any natural feature on the dark side, even if not really black. It is widely applied to hills, mountains, buttes, canyons, etc., and also to water features. The name is not always applicable, having been sometimes applied on a dark day, when a body of water, for instance, appeared to be black. **Black Hills** SD: a translation of the Sioux name, applied because the hills are high enough to be covered with pines, and so are dark, though hardly black. **Blackhorse Creek** OR: because a black horse strayed and wintered near the stream. **Black Star Canyon** CA: for a mine name. The word also occurs in numerous compounds, which are generally obvious, e.g. **Black Bear, Blackberry, Black Oak. Blacktail** is usually for the deer; **Blackfoot,** for the Indian tribe. **Black Dog** MN, **Blackbird** NB and **Black Hawk** IA are for Indian chiefs. Habitation-names are generally by transfer. **Black River** WA: named by a British exploring party on Nov. 28, 1824, specifically 'from the color of its water,' probably because it ran over dark rocks and so appeared to be black. **Black Lake** WA was named by the same party because it was the source of the stream, not because it was black.

Blackwater is a common name on streams, especially in the SE. **Black Thunder Creek** WY: for a wild black stallion thus known.

Blackbeard's Point NC From the common nickname of Edward Teach, the pirate, who was killed when his vessel was captured near here in 1717. See **Teach.**

Blackburn From the personal name, e.g. **Mount Blackburn** AK named (1885) by H. T. Allen for J. C. S. Blackburn, senator from Kentucky, which was Allen's native state.

Blacksmith Canyon NM In the 1860's outlaws used this place for blacksmithing, and an old wooden anvil was found here.

Blaine From the personal name; especially, e.g. in MN, OH, and OK, for J. G. Blaine, presidential candidate in 1884.

Blanc, Blanche French 'white.'

Blanco, Blanca Spanish 'white,' e.g. **Cape Blanco** OR. **Blanco** CA: for Tom White, a sailor, whose name was translated into Spanish, ca. 1840. **Blanco** OK: for Ramón Blanco, governor general of Cuba, 1875–1898, named in 1901. **Blanco** CO: from **Mount Blanca,** so named from its snowiness.

Blanconia TX A pseudo-Latin formation from Spanish *blanco,* because it is situated on **Blanco Creek.**

Blanding From the personal name. See **Bicknell.**

Blank Regularly from the personal name, e.g. **Blank Lake** SD for E. E. Blank, landowner.

Blanket In TX, because an Indian blanket was found nearby at about the time of the settling. **Blanket Hill** PA: in 1756 a force of colonists on an Indian campaign abandoned some blankets here.

Blaze Occurs rarely, to distinguish a place marked by a blaze on a tree. **Blaze Mountain** MT is marked, as if by a blaze, by a strip of snow in a ravine, which does not melt in summer. **Blazed Alder Butte** OR: named in 1906 when a prominent tree became a landmark because of blazes made on it by a forest fire.

Blenheim SC From the castle in England.

Blessing TX Named by the town founder in 1902 because he thought the railroad a 'blessing.'

Bleu(e) French 'blue,' e.g. **L'Eau Bleu** LA.

Bligh Island AK Named by British explorers in 1794, probably for William Bligh, who had been associated with the famous *Bounty* mutiny in 1789.

Blind Generally for a feature which is a 'blind alley,' i.e. without exit. Thus **Blind Lake** MN ends in swamps, so that canoeists have to turn back; similarly **Blind Canyon** CA and **Blind Creek** SC. **Blind Spring** CA: apparently indicates a spring which was for some reason hard to find.

Bliss From the personal name, e.g. **Blissville** NY, laid out by Neziah Bliss in 1841.

Blitzen German 'lightning,' e.g. **Mount Blitzen** NV, doubtless named on the occasion of a storm. **Blitzen** OR is from **Donner und Blitzen River.**

Blizzard A western name, e.g. **Blizzard Mountain** ID, commemorating an incident at the time of naming. Cf. other weather phenomena, e.g. **Donner und Blitzen.**

Block Regularly from the personal name, e.g. **Block Island** RI for Adrian Block who explored it in 1614. **Blocksburg** CA: from Benjamin Blockburger, early settler. **Blockhouse** WA: from a fortification against Indians (1856); so also, **Blockhouse Mountain** TN, **Blockhouse Creek** KY.

Blood A rare variant of *bloody.* **Blood Gulch** CA: in the gold-mining period, miners noted that the water seemed bloody, and on going upstream found the body of a murdered man. **Blood and Slaughter Gap** GA is the pass between **Blood Mountain** and **Slaughter Mountain** (q.v.).

Bloody The regular term to indicate a place where bloodshed has occurred. Many of the stories are well authenticated. Others are vaguely reminiscent of Indian troubles. A few commemorate murders. CA, apparently the most sanguinary state, has 20 examples. Though bloody is not used, as in England, as an obscene term, its unpleasant associations have kept it from being a habitation-name. **Bloody Lake** MN: for the victims of the Sioux massacre in 1862. **Bloody Tanks** AZ: from a massacre of Apaches by Americans in 1864. **Bloody Run** OR: in a region noted for Indian troubles, probably for the killing of a man and wife on Oct. 1, 1855. **Bloody Island** CA: named in 1844, because of an Indian attack. **Bloody Point** CA: Modoc Indians here killed 63 people in 1852. **Bloody Pond** NY: at the battle of Lake George the bodies of some French soldiers were thrown into this pond. **Bloody Creek** NB: though a surveying party feared Indian attack, nothing happened and they applied the name in jest. Similar origins are probable for other names, or else they are from trivial incidents, such as a bloody nose from a fist fight. **Bloody Gulch** SD: traditionally believed to have been named because a disgusted Englishman referred to it as 'that bloody gulch.' **Bloody Dick Creek** MT: from an Englishman thus nicknamed, who lived there in the 1860's. Rarely the reference is to the red color of the water, e.g. **Bloody Run**, Berrien Co., MI. **Bloody Branch** GA: from an incident of 1794, when Indians killed a man and child. **Bloody Run** OH: two soldiers, ca. 1792, were killed here by Indians shooting from ambush. **Bloody Lake** WY: because some woodcutters for the railroad were killed here by Indians.

Bloom, Blooming A few names are from the personal name, e.g. **Bloom Township** PA in 1797 for Samuel Bloom, county commissioner; hence **Bloomsburg** PA. Generally the names spring from the esthetic pleasure experienced from blossoms and flowers, this being one of the few ways in which early Americans expressed admiration for nature. The common **Bloomington** thus arose, e.g. in IN and IL, the last having first been **Blooming Grove**. **Blooming Grove Township** MN: so named when the wild plums were in blossom. Though **Bloomfield** and **Bloomingdale** are family names, their popularity for habitation-names is chiefly descriptive and commendatory. A similar origin can also be ascribed to the repeated occurrences of **Blooming Prairie**, **Blooming Grove**, **Blooming Rose**, etc. In OH alone, thus originating, are **Bloomfield**, **Bloomingburg**, **Blooming Grove**, and **Bloomingville**. **Bloomfield** CA: for a German, F. G. Blume, early physician, whose name was altered to the common English spelling.

Bloomery From the term applied to an early ironworks; hence, e.g., **Bloomery** WV and **Laurel Bloomery** TN.

Blossom Usually for a place covered with wild flowers at the time of naming, e.g. the island in AK. Several features along the Pacific Coast are named for the exploring ship *Blossom*, e.g. **Cape Blossom** AK, thus named by Capt. Beechey for his vessel in 1826.

Blowing A rare term to indicate a current of air, as in **Blowing Cave** KY. **Blowing Rock** NC is from a rock formation so shaped as to cause a light object thrown off it to return to the thrower.

Blowout Creek OR Some pioneers had trouble getting a fire started here, because of a high wind which kept blowing the fire out.

Blue As a color-name it is less frequent than red, white, or black. It is applied to mountains, as in OR and **Blue Ridge** VA, which appear blue from a distance. Streams and lakes are frequently so called, sometimes with commendatory purpose. Streams may, however, be so named because of bluish clay in the water. The bluish cast of certain minerals such as glaucophane accounts for an occasional **Blue Rock**. Secondary formations are usually recognizable, e.g. **Bluejay Mountain** CA and **Bluejoint Lake** OR, the latter for a kind of grass. The family name Blue is not common, and accounts for only a few of the names.

Blue Ball PA: from a tavern and its sign. **Bluebell** SD, UT: from the name of a flower. **Bluebucket Creek** OR: by oral tradition, from an incident in which emigrants used a blue bucket to collect yellow stones which proved to be gold; such a name, doubtless, must be explained by an incident. **Blue Grove** TX: because a grove of trees there, seen from a distance, appeared blue because of haze. **Bluejacket** OK: for Charles Bluejacket, first postmaster. **Big Blue River** KS: partially the translation of an Indian (Kansa) name, 'blue earth,' because of clay found there and used as a pigment.

Bluenose Peak CA Because of blue-colored rocks.

Blueslide WA Because of a landslide, on the face of which the clay appears blue in wet weather; as an acute local commentator notes, 'It must have been named during rainy weather.'

Bluff Originating as a generic, it is often used as a specific to indicate a feature associated with a bluff, e.g. **Bluff Creek** MN. It is common with habitation-names, generally arising by transfer, e.g. **Red Bluff** CA, **Bluff** (several states), **Bluffton** SC.

Bly Though in some places the personal name is probably preserved, the town in OR is from the Klamath *p'lai,* 'high,' applied to a place on the upper reaches of a stream.

Blythe Commonly for the personal name, e.g. in CA. In compounds it is sometimes fancifully descriptive, e.g. in **Blythewood** SC originally the name of a school. **Blythedale** (several states) may be influenced by Hawthorne's *Blythedale Romance.*

Board It exists as a personal name, but is rare. **Boardman** is common as a personal name, and places so named are thus derived. Most commonly the name is from lumbering, i.e. a place where boards were sawn out. **Boardtree** occurs with some frequency in the SE, and is regularly from a native shrub so known, but may possibly be from a tree from which boards could be made or from a tree with a board nailed to it. **Boarding-**

house Hollow KY takes its name by association.

Boar's Tusk WY A light-colored volcanic neck, named descriptively.

Bob Generally for the personal nickname, but in **Bob Creek** OR a shortening for bob cat because some pioneers encountered bob cats there.

Bob Cat Occasionally used because of the animal, e.g. the creek in NM. Cf. **Cat, Lynx, Wildcat.**

Bobo From the personal name.

Boca Spanish 'mouth.'

Bocilla Island FL From Spanish *boquilla,* a diminutive of *boca,* 'mouth,' from association with an outlet. A settlement on the island has taken the form **Bokeelia.**

Bodarc See **Bois**

Bodcaw, Bodcau AR, LA Probably Indian, but language and meaning uncertain; there is possibly a connection with **Bodka.**

Bodega CA For J. F. de la Bodega, Spanish explorer, who entered the bay and named it in 1775.

Bodfish CA For Orlando Bodfish, early settler.

Bodie CA Respelled from the name of W. S. Body, early miner.

Bodka Creek AL Muskogean, probably 'wide.'

Bodoc LA From **Bois D'Arc.** See **Bois.**

Bodock AR For *bois d'arc.* See **Bois.**

Bodoway Mesa AZ From the name of a Paiute chief, transmitted through Navajo into English.

Boeuf French 'ox, steer,' sometimes for *boeuf sauvage,* i.e. buffalo.

Bog, Boggy For a feature associated with a bog or muddy place, e.g. **Bog Creek** AZ. **Boggy,** though generally rare, occurs as **Boggy Creek** five times in OK, being probably by folk-etymology from the Muskogean *bok, bog,* 'stream.' One of them, however, is probably a translation of the French **Rivière aux Vases.**

Bogalusa LA Choctaw. 'stream-black.' Cf. **Bogueloosa.**

Bogata TX For Bogota, the Colombian city, but with the spelling altered by mistake.

Boggistow Brook MA Algonquian 'turning-place.'

Boggy See **Bog.**

Boght NY Dutch, 'bend,' usually of a waterline, so that the term becomes the equivalent of 'bay.' See **Wallabout.**

Bogota From the capital of Colombia, but in NJ the suggestion was supplied by the name of a family of early settlers, viz. Bogert.

Boguechitto, Bogue Chitto AL, LA, MS Choctaw 'stream-big.' Cf. **Bokchito**

Bogue Falaya LA Choctaw 'stream-long.'

Boguegaba Creek MS Choctaw, with *bogue,* 'stream,' and the rest uncertain.

Bogue Homa Creek AL Choctaw 'stream-red.'

Bogueloosa Creek AL Choctaw 'stream-black.' Cf. **Bogalusa.**

Bogus A name applied to features, especially in the CA mining districts, to indicate some deception or humbug. **Bogus Thunder Bar** CA: a nearby waterfall suggests thunder. **Bogus Creek,** Siskiyou Co., CA: some counterfeiters once operated here. **Bogus Hollow** IA: locally reported as 'where Bill Calendine made the false money.'

Bohemia From the former European kingdom. **Bohemia River** MD: named by Augustine Hermann, who came from Bohemia, in the 17th century. **Bohemia Mountain** OR: for a prospector known as "Bohemia" Johnson, probably a Bohemian, who discovered and named the Bohemia Mines in 1863. **Bohemian Creek** NB: from early Bohemian settlers.

Bohemotash Mountain CA Wintu *bohem,* meaning 'big,' but otherwise unexplained.

Boiler Bay OR Because the remains of a boiler could once be seen there, left from a ship lost on May 18, 1910.

Boiling Generally a descriptive for thermal water, e.g. **Boiling River** WY, **Boiling Spring** AZ. **Boiling Point** OR is a punning name for a place on a grade where old-time automobiles were supposed to begin boiling.

Bois French 'wood,' in place-name usage regularly as 'forest, grove,' e.g. **Bois des Sioux River** MN, ND. **Bois d'Arc** is the French name for the Osage orange (literally, 'wood-of-bow,' since bows were made of it.) The name survives on a number of features and on a town in MO. It also occurs as **Bodarc** NB, where it is locally believed to have arisen by a mistake in the Post Office Dept. **Bois Blanc** is the French term for basswood, as in **Lac Bois Blanc** MN. See **Brule.**

Bois Connie, Bayou LA By partial folk-etymology for French *bois connu,* which is a clipped form for *bois inconnu,* 'unknown tree,' the American-French designation of the hackberry, which was unknown to Europeans.

Boise In ID applied first as French 'rivière boisée,' 'river-wooded,' and then to the city by transfer; in OK by transfer from ID.

Bokchito OK Muskogean (Choctaw) 'stream-big.' Cf. **Bogue Chitto.**

Bokeelia FL See **Bocilla.**

Bokhoma OK Muskogean (Choctaw) 'stream-red.'

Boklusa OK Muskogean (Choctaw) 'stream-black.'

Bokoshe OK Muskogean (Choctaw) 'stream-little.'

Bok Tuklo, Boktuklo OK Muskogean (Choctaw) 'stream-two,' so called because of two creeks there.

Bolada AZ From the family names of three early settlers, Bones, Lane, and Dandrea.

Boligee AL Probably Choctaw, meaning uncertain; first applied to the creek.

Bolinas CA Probably from an Indian tribal name; elsewhere spelled Baulenes.

Bolivar For Simón Bolívar, who in the years after 1820 was a hero in the U.S. because of his revolutionary wars in South America. In OH, WV, and TN towns were named for him in 1825. **Mount Bolivar** OR: for Simon Bolivar Cathcart, local surveyor.

Bolivia From the country in South America.

Bollibokka Mountain CA Wintu 'black bush,' with reference to the blackberried manzanita.

Bolly See **Bally.**

Bolsa Spanish 'purse, pocket,' in CA often to describe a place naturally enclosed, e.g. a neck of land nearly surrounded by swamp.

Bolshoi Russian 'big.'

Bolton In CT (1720) for an English town. In MA (1738) for Charles Paulet, Duke of Bolton, a member of the Colonial Council. Later occurrences are from the personal name.

Bolupusha Creek MS Choctaw 'slippery-elms-are-there.'

Boma TN From the town in Africa.

Bombahook ME Algonquian 'sandy-shoal.'

Bombay From the city of India. **Bombay Hook** DE: early forms, e.g. **Bomtiens** (1654), are Dutch, a diminutive of 'tree,' therefore, 'little-tree-point'; the name was shifted by folk-etymology in the English-speaking period. The resemblance to **Bombahook** is coincidental.

Bombazine Island ME From the name of a chief Bomazeen (killed, 1724), shifted by folk-etymology, since bombazine was once a common kind of cloth.

Bomber Mountain WY On July 28, 1943, a B-17 bomber crashed here.

Bomoseen Lake VT From the name of the last male Abnaki to live in the state (died, 1959); his English name was William Simon, which on Abnaki tongues became Obam-Saween, and thus **Bomoseen,** and by folk-etymology **Bombazine.**

Bon French 'good.' See also **Bonne. Bon Hon..ae Co.** SD is probably from a personal name, more commonly spelled **Bonhomme. Bon Homme Creek** MO: literally 'good man,' but probably from an Osage term applied to a tribal dignitary. **Bon** AZ: a shortening from H. G. Bonorden, early railroad dispatcher. In such names as **Bon Air** TN the adjective has been applied without regard to mixture of languages. See **Bon Wier. Bon Aqua** TN: coined by the landowner, ca. 1840, because of mineral springs, on the assumption that he was using the French, whereas *aqua* is Latin, for 'good-water.' **Bon Secour** AL, LA in American French 'welcome,' used as a commendatory, and in LA the name of a plantation.

Bona, Mount Named (1897) by the mountaineering Duke of Abruzzi for his yacht.

Bonanza Spanish 'prosperity,' used in the western mining regions to describe a rich strike of ore. Because of this general commendatory quality of suggesting riches, it has become a habitation-name, not only in mining areas, e.g. CO, but also in non-mining areas, e.g. AR. It also occurs on natural features where a rich strike once occurred or was hoped for. In OR a number of fine springs gave rise to the name.

Bonasila River AK Probably a much-altered Athapascan name; meaning uncertain.

Bon Carbo, Boncarbo CO From French *bon charbon,* 'good coal,' a name given (1915) by an official of a local coal company.

Bone Though bones are enduring and often conspicuous, their presence did not greatly impress the folk mind, and such names are few. **Big Bone Lick** KY was so called from the bones of mammoths and mastodons found there. **Bone Necklace Lake** SD: from the name of an Indian. **Bone** ID: from a family name of early settlers.

Boneta UT A variation of Spanish *bonita*, 'pretty.'

Bonetrail ND According to local belief, named for the 'bone-trail' used by the collectors of buffalo bones for fertilizer.

Boneyard Preserves the memory of places where bones were observed in large numbers. **The Boneyard** AZ and **Boneyard Creek** OR take their names from places where herds of cattle starved in time of deep snow.

Bonfouca LA The name of an 18th century Indian chief (also of a village, and probably of a tribe), made over into a Spanish form.

Bonito, Bonita Spanish 'pretty,' e.g. **Bonito Canyon** AZ. The feminine form is more common in place-names, occurring by itself as a habitation-name in several states, and often coupled with an English generic, e.g. **Bonita Creek** AZ. **Bonita Point** CA was originally **Bonetas,** which is Spanish for the English *bonnets* in the sense of extensions to a sail; but it may have been an error for **Bonetes,** because of the resemblance of three points to clergymen's bonnets.

Bonne French 'good,' (feminine), e.g. **Bonne Terre** MO. **Bonne Femme Creek** MO though meaning 'good woman,' is probably a translation of an Osage title of respect for a tribal dignitary.

Bonnet A configuration-name given to elevations for resemblance to the shape of a bonnet, e.g. **The Bonnet** RI. Since there have been many different kinds of bonnets, the descriptive quality is, at best, vague. So also, **Warbonnet** (see **War**).

Bonneville Some western towns and natural features, e.g. **Bonneville Salt Flats** UT have been named commemoratively for B. L. E. Bonneville (1795–

1878), the explorer. So also **Mount Bonneville** OR.

Bonnybeague See **Bonnynague.**

Bonnynague Pond ME Algonquian 'spread-out-lake.' Also, **Bonnybeague.**

Bono In TX, and probably elsewhere, it is a rough adaptation of Latin 'good.'

Bonus TX Originally **Bono** (q.v.), probably changed for differentiation from the other town in TX; so called because of fertile soil.

Bon Wier TX From the names of B. F. Bonner and D. S. Wier, early settlers.

Book Cliffs UT Because the formation suggests a row of books standing upright.

Booker From the personal name, e.g. **Mount Booker** WA for Booker T. Washington (1857–1915), author and educator. **Booker** TX: for B. F. Booker, a railroad locating engineer.

Boom By association with a boom for logging operations, e.g. **Boom Island** MN.

Boomer NC From the nickname of 'Boomer' Matheson, postmaster.

Boone, Boon From the personal name, most often for Daniel Boone (1735–1820), frontiersman; thus, several counties and various habitation-names, e.g. in MO, **Boonville, Boonsboro,** and **Boone** Co.

Boot Many features are so named because of shape, e.g. **Boot Lake** (various states), **Boot Island** MN, **Boot Peak** AZ. Incidents involving a boot are probably involved in some instances. **Boot Hill:** at Tombstone AZ and elsewhere this is derived from the belief that men 'who died with their boots on,' i.e. violently, were buried there, but this usage seems to have been invented by writers of fiction after 1900.

Boothbay ME From the town of Boothby in England, apparently shifted by folketymology because situated on a bay (1764).

Bootleg Canyon NV A name applied during the prohibition period of the 20th century because of the location here of an illicit still.

Bopquam Bay VT Algonquian, probably 'beaver.'

Boquillas Spanish 'little mouths,' because of small streams here debouching into a larger one, e.g. in AZ and TX.

Boracho Peak TX For Spanish *borracho,* 'drunk, drunken man,' but of uncertain reference.

Borah, Mount ID For W. E. Borah, senator from Idaho (1865–1940).

Borax Because of deposits of borax.

Borculo MI Named in the mid-19th century by Dutch immigrants for Borkulo, a town in Holland.

Bordeaux From the city in France, but in WA for Thomas Bordeaux, local lumber operator.

Border, Borderland These names are on borders, e.g. **Border** WY, which is at the UT line.

Bordulac ND From French *bord du lac,* 'edge of the lake,' a descriptive coined by an American woman, ca. 1900.

Borgne French 'one-eyed, one-eyed man.' The naming of the lake in LA is not of record, but such a name would normally arise from an encounter here with a one-eyed Indian.

Borodino NY For the Franco-Russian battle of 1812.

Boron From deposits of borax, in which the distinctive element is boron.

Borosolvay CA From the two firms that established the town, viz. Pacific Coast Borax Co. and Solvay Co.

Borrego Spanish 'lamb,' but the common Spanish term for 'sheep' in the SW; hence **Borrego Arroyo** NM, and an important name-cluster in CA. It is probably not used for the wild sheep, which is distinguished as **Cimarron.**

Boscawen NH For Admiral Sir Edward Boscawen, who visited the colony as the guest of the governor, the town receiving its name in 1758.

Bosco KY, LA Probably from the family name, though it is also Italian 'wood, forest.'

Boscobel WI Named (1855) from Italian *bosco,* 'wood, forest,' and *bel* with the general idea of 'beautiful,' as a descriptive-commendatory.

Bosebuc Mountain ME Algonquian, 'spread-out-stream-outlet-at.'

Bosky Rare, one of its few examples being **Bosky Dell** IL, an expression taken from a minister's sermon (ca. 1877); catching people's fancy, it was applied to the place.

Bosom In occasional 'refined' use instead of the commoner **Breast, Tit,** e.g. two peaks in WY.

Bosque Spanish 'forest, thicket, grove,' regularly a generic, but as a habitation-name in NM, and on a river and county in TX.

Bosquenoosic Island ME Algonquian 'little-broken-island.'

Boston The original naming, in MA, was from the town in England, by action of the General Court, Sept. 7, 1630. The practice was then to name MA towns for English towns, the particular name chosen probably because that town was in a strongly Puritan region, and because some of the early settlers had come from it.

Bostonia CA A Latinized form, from the Boston Ranch.

Botany Island SC Named for fanciful analogy to Botany Bay, which was used as a British penal colony; unruly bulls were sometimes 'banished' to the island.

Bote Mountain TN By local story, the Cherokee pronunciation of *vote* (their language lacking a *v*) because it was decided by a vote that a road should go in that direction. See **Defeat.**

Botna IA A shortening of **Nishnabotna**, on which river the town stands.

Bottle Though such receptacles for whiskey or other drinks were common, the name is rare. **Bottle Pinnacle** WY is named from its shape.

Bottlerock Mountain CA From a local term for obsidian, which is a dark-colored natural glass, resembling that used for bottles.

Bottom Regularly a generic for low land along a stream, but becoming a specific by association, e.g. **Bottom Fork** KY.

Bottomless Used for a lake or pool which has proved too deep to be plumbed by the usual methods available, e.g. **Bottomless Lakes** NM.

Bouff Creek AR For French *boeuf*. See **Boeuf.**

Boughcamp Branch KY To indicate a place at which an overnight shelter of boughs had been constructed.

Bouillon, Bayou From French *bouillant*, 'bubbling,' because of the discharge of gas.

Boulder, Bowlder From association with a boulder (bowlder being an archaic spelling), an extremely common name (about 100 in CA), especially for creeks. The name may indicate a single boulder which marks a stream crossing, or it may arise from a stream course in the mountains which is especially full of boulders. **Boulder Reef** WA: for 'a huge erratic granite boulder.' **Boulder** CO: named (1858) from the many boulders visible as the result of gold mining.

Boulevard From a place thus associated, e.g. in CA the place was thus called because of being on U.S. 80, locally known as the boulevard.

Bound In the sense of **Boundary** (q.v.), e.g. **Bound Brook** NJ, MA.

Boundary To indicate a feature at or near a boundary, e.g. **Boundary Creek** AK near the international border, and various features so named for the same reason in WA, MT, ND, etc. Other borders may also give rise to the name, e.g. **Boundary Ridge** AZ, near the northern edge of Grand Canyon N.P.

Bouquet Canyon CA From a French sailor, known by a nickname to the Spaniards as El Buque, 'the ship'; from this name, as pronounced, American surveyors manufactured a French form.

Bourbeux, Bourbeuse French 'muddy.'

Bourbon The county in KY (then a part of VA) was named for the royal family of France in the Revolutionary period of enthusiasm for things French. Later namings, e.g. in MO, are generally from the one in KY.

Bout In DE the creek takes its name from Dutch *bocht*, 'bend,' here as commonly for a bend in the shoreline. In LA the district **Bout de Bayou** is French 'end of bayou.'

Boutte LA From the Boutté family, early landowners.

Bovina Late Latin 'having to do with cattle,' in TX, CO, and probably elsewhere, developing from the cattle industry. In TX it is a more elegant term for the original **Bull Town.**

Bow Commonly from the personal name; in WA, from the district in London. **Bow Creek** AK: because it makes a loop resembling a bow. See **Broken.**

Bowery, The The district on Manhattan Island preserves the Dutch *De Bouwerij*, 'the farm.'

Bowie From the personal name, in TX for J. A. Bowie, famous frontiersman and designer of the Bowie knife.

Bowlegs Creeks in FL and OK are for a well-known Seminole chief of the early 19th century, known as Billy Bowlegs.

Bowling Green In KY, ca. 1800, because of the custom of playing bowls there. In OH, and generally elsewhere, from KY.

Box The word is used attributively in so many senses that the exact cause of the origin of the names often is uncertain. **Box Butte** NB: from its shape. **Box Springs** CA: because two springs were 'boxed in' to supply drinking water. The term 'box canyon' is in common use to denote one which is impassable at its head, and some names thus originated, e.g. **Box Creek** MT. **Box Elder, Boxelder:** various species of the ash-leafed maple, chiefly Western, are so called. Being a water-loving tree, it has given its name to many streams, and it has then passed by transfer to habitations, e.g. the county in UT. **Boxwood** TX: from the tree so called. **Boxborough** MA: probably because its original shape on the map was square, i.e. boxlike. **Box Creek,** Anderson Co., TX, is for R. W. Box, early landowner.

Boxford In MA (ca. 1685) for a town in England.

Boxholm IA Named (1887) by an immigrant for his birthplace in Sweden.

Boyero CO Spanish 'cowboy,' but probably in the sense of 'cattle-pen,' because of stockyards here.

Boy Lake MN Translated from the Ojibway, and commemorating the killing of three boys there by a Sioux war party, ca. 1768.

Boysag Point AZ Paiute 'bridge.'

Bozeman From the personal name, e.g. in MT for J. M. Bozeman, a leader of the party that made the first settlement (1864) in the region.

Bozoo WV Presumably from an altered spelling of the family name, Boso, recorded in the vicinity.

Bozrah CT From the place-name in the Old Testament (1786).

Bracken From the personal name, e.g. the county in KY for William Bracken, early settler killed by Indians.

Bracket Mountain OR The profile resembles the curves of a printer's brace, and the term bracket was apparently applied by mistake.

Braddock In PA, for Gen. Edward Braddock, British officer, who was killed in

the battle of 1755 near the spot. **Braddock Bay** NY: from Gen. John Prideaux, British officer, accidentally killed in this vicinity in 1759; his name was confused with that of the better-known general.

Bradford In MA the town was named (1675) for that in England, though there must also have been a side reference to Gov. Wm. Bradford. Later instances are from a personal name, e.g. in PA the county was named in 1812, for Wm. Bradford, attorney-general of the U.S.

Bradvelt NJ From Dutch 'broad-field,' but possibly a personal name.

Brae Scottish dialect, 'hillside, bank of stream.' It was one of the romantic terms popularized in the mid-19th century, e.g. **Braeburn, Braeholm, Millbrae.**

Braggadocio MO Probably from some incident involving boastfulness. The difference in spelling makes unlikely its direct derivation from Edmund Spenser's *Faerie Queen.*

Brahma Temple AZ One of the fanciful names given to fantastic formations in the Grand Canyon. In the same 'series,' are: **Buddha Temple, Cheops Pyramid, Confucius Temple, Hindu Amphitheatre, Isis Temple, Manu Temple, Osiris Temple, Tower of Ra, Tower of Set, Shiva Temple, Thor's Hammer, Venus Temple, Vesta Temple, Vishnu Temple, Zoroaster Temple.** All of these use the names of ancient gods, rulers or sages, chiefly Oriental, and they represent one of the lowest, in the opinion of the compiler, exercises of American place-naming.

Braintree In MA (1640) from a town in England.

Branch 1) From the personal name, e.g. **Branchland** WV for Col. Branch, coal mine operator. 2) Because associated with a branch in one of its senses, either of a stream or something else such as a road or railroad, e.g. **Branchville SC,** because of a railroad branch beginning here.

Brandon Commonly from the family name; in VT, named in 1761, for the

Duke of Hamilton and Brandon, British political figure.

Brandy Though brandy has never been a typical American drink, a number of such place-names appear, presumably commemorating an incident, the record of which is usually not preserved. **Brandy Bar** OR: a schooner grounded on the bar one evening in 1850; the passengers broke out some brandy, and passed the night in such a way as to insure the permanency of the name. **Brandy Brow Hill** MA: such an alliterative and non-meaningful name may be a derivation by folk-etymology from some Indian name. See **Brandywine.**

Brandywine A 17th-century term for brandy, its use in the colonies being reinforced by the Dutch *brandewijn.* The several occurrences of the name presumably spring from incidents involving the selling of spirits, or the use of a still. Cf. **Whiskey.** The creek in PA, famous for the battle, apparently arose by folk-etymology from Andrew Braindwine, an early settler.

Branford In CT (1653) the name is an alternate spelling of **Brentford,** an English town.

Brass Regularly from the personal name, e.g. **Brass Castle** NJ for Jacob Brass, early settler. **Brasstown** NC: probably from a misunderstanding in translating a Cherokee term, the real meaning of which was 'green place.'

Brassua Lake ME Probably from Indian pronunciation of the personal name Frank, borne by a chief; shifted by folk-etymology to **Brassway.**

Brassway See **Brassua.**

Brattleboro VT For Col. William Brattle, one of the land speculators who obtained the grant in 1753.

Brave Probably occurring only in combination, e.g. **Brave Bull Creek** SD named for Brave Bull, an early Sioux warrior.

Bravo Spanish 'brave,' but usually in the generalized sense, 'fine, outstanding,' and

so applied in 1598 as an alternate name to the present **Rio Grande.** See **Grande.**

Braymill OR W. M. Bray was chief owner of a sawmill here.

Brazil 1) From the country in South America; in IN, suggested by a man who had just read an article about it. 2) From the personal name, e.g. **Brazilton** KS for Thomas Brazil, one of the owners of the town site.

Brazo Spanish 'arm, branching,' also with the diminutive **Brazito;** hence, 'having branches,' e.g. **Brazos Canyon** NM. The river in TX was probably named because it originates in three forks; its full name in Spanish times was **Brazos de Dios** ('arms of God'), a name which has given rise to many fanciful stories, but has not been explained authoritatively. It may have resulted from an attempt to make a pious name out of a matter-of-fact one.

Brazoria TX A Latinized form from **Brazos River,** on which the town is situated.

Brea Spanish 'pitch, tar,' in CA referring to pools of petroleum or asphalt.

Bread and Cheese Applied to various small natural features in the older areas of settlement, e.g. islands DE, MA, small streams MD, NJ. The origin is uncertain, some proverbial expression of the 17th century is suggested. In MD the first recorded form (1654) is Dutch, but some of the others are in areas of English background. Cf. **Cheese.**

Bread Loaf Mountain VT Probably from shape. Cf. **Sugarloaf.**

Breakabeen NY Dutch (or German) dialect, literally suggesting 'break-a-leg,' but referring (?) to a kind of horsetail or rush growing along the stream so named.

Breakheart A variant from the commoner **Heartbreak** (see **Heart**), e.g. the hill in RI.

Breakneck A fanciful description for a steep or difficult canyon or gully, e.g. two canyons and a creek in CA. By association it occurs with features not in themselves deserving it, e.g. **Breakneck Pond** CT. **Break Neck Hill** WI: in Sept. 1846, an early settler, J. B. Runey, was killed here when his wagon overturned.

Breast Occasionally occurring for a breast-like eminence, e.g. **Breast Mountain** AK.

Breastworks Branch GA From the remains of some old fortifications, of unknown date.

Breathitt County KY Named (1839) for John Breathitt, state governor in 1832.

Breaux Bridge LA For Agricole Breaux, who built a toll-free bridge here.

Breckenridge, Breckinridge. From the personal name, e.g. in CO, MN, TX, for John C. Breckinridge, political figure and Confederate general. (Though his name is commonly spelled with an *i*, the other spelling has been used for post offices.) **Breckinridge** OK: for Breckinridge Jones, local railroad official.

Breda IA From the city in the Netherlands, named by immigrants.

Breech Clout, The WV This rock is said to resemble a breech clout—just how it does so is left uncertain. The term, however, was in common use during 'Indian times.'

Breedlove WV From a family name of early settlers.

Bremen From the city in Germany, generally named by German settlers, e.g. in MN.

Bremer From the personal name, e.g. in IA for Fredrika Bremer, Swedish author, who gave favorable comments upon parts of the state in her *Homes of the New World* (1853). **Bremerton** WA: for William Bremer, town founder.

Breslau From the city previously in Germany and thus known; now, Wroclaw in Poland. In NB it is in a district settled by German immigrants.

Breton Island LA Either from a personal name, or from a person so known from being a native of Brittany.

Bretton Woods NH From the English seat of the earls of Strafford; granted in 1772. See **Strafford.**

Brewery The name generally indicates that beer was once made there, e.g. **Brewery Canyon** NB.

Brewington Lake SC From Miles Brewton who held a colonial grant; by partial folk-etymology it became **Brewerton** and then **Brewington.**

Brewster From the personal name, in MA named commemoratively (1803) for William Brewster of the early Plymouth colony.

Briar, Briary Being a fairly common name, it is a good example of naming for mere nuisance-value, essentially as a derogatory or a name of warning.

Brick An occasional name for a place where bricks were made, e.g. **Brickton** MN, NB. From something built of brick, e.g. **Brickchurch** PA.

Bridal Veil Usually with *fall(s)*, but in Oregon occurring alone as a habitation-name. As a somewhat fanciful but often apt descriptive, the name seems to have originated, in the 1850's, in Yosemite Valley, CA. It has since spread widely.

Bridge As with *mill*, the existence of an early bridge often distinguished a stream, so that **Bridge Creek** is common. Since settlements clustered around bridges, it also occurs in habitation-names, e.g. **Bridgeville, Bridgeton. Bridgewater** MA: from the town in England (ca. 1656). **Bridgeport:** in CT the name dates from 1800, and celebrates, with a double-barreled commendatory, the opening of the first drawbridge across the river there. The name has been popular, and has spread to many towns which often are not ports and have not been notable for a bridge either. The personal name has not been a potent source of place-names. The bridge may be a natural formation, e.g. with **Bridge Canyon** UT.

Bridger From the personal name, especially for James Bridger, mountain-man and trapper, e.g. **Fort Bridger** WY. **Bridger Mountain** WV: in 1784 James and John Bridger were killed here by Indians.

Bridport VT Named in 1761 for Admiral Viscount Bridport, particular reason unknown.

Brielle NJ From a town in the Netherlands.

Brier, Briery See **Briar.**

Brigantine NJ By local story, for a brigantine that was wrecked in the inlet there in the 18th century.

Brigham From the personal name, e.g. in UT for Brigham Young, Mormon leader.

Bright Regularly from the personal name, e.g. **Brightsville** SC. Descriptively in some compounds, e.g. **Brightwaters** NY and **Bright Angel Creek** AZ, the latter named in counterpart to **Dirty Devil River** UT.

Brighton From the English beach resort, sometimes given with particular reference as with **Brighton** OR, originally **Brighton Beach,** though not directly on the ocean. But other towns, i.e. in CA and PA, have no association with beaches.

Brilliant In OH, because of a local company for the making of glass. In WY, for the type of coal mined there.

Brillion WI A misspelling of Brilon, a town in Germany, probably named by immigrants, but reason for misspelling uncertain.

Brimfield In MA, named soon after 1700, after a village in England.

Brimstone It is the older term for sulfur and such names as **Brimstone Hill** MA are probably for the occurrence, or supposed occurrence of sulfur. **Brimstone Mountain** WY: because the first mountaineers to climb it (1930) noted a smell of sulfur.

Bristol In the 17th century Bristol was the second city of England, and its name was used in MA, PA, and RI. In TN the name was applied (ca. 1852) as a com-

mendatory, in the hope that the town would be a manufacturing city. See **Bristow.**

Bristow From the personal name. Though this is the older form of **Bristol,** it is unlikely that the name in the U.S. was thus influenced. **Bristow** OK: for J. L. Bristow, U.S. Senator.

Britain Rare, but occurring as **New Britain** CT which was probably coined (1754) on the analogy of **New England.**

Britannia Occasionally appearing as a commemorative for Great Britain, e.g. the mountain in WY, which was named by an English settler. Spellings **Britania** and **Brittannia** may occur.

British Mountains AK Named by the British explorer, Sir John Franklin, in 1826 because they were thought to be in British territory, though one end of them lies in what is now U.S. territory.

Broad Uncommon as a descriptive term, though more used in the East than in the West, probably an indication that it was more used in colonial times than later. **Broad River** appears in GA, SC, and MD. It is applied to a variety of features, e.g. **Broad Mountain** PA, **Broad Ripple** IN. A few instances may be supplied by the personal name. Others are translations of the Dutch *breed,* or Swedish *bred,* e.g. **Broadkill** DE and **Broadway** NY, etc. This last (Dutch, *breede Wegh*) has not only become a common street name, but has also been used for towns. In habitation-names *broad* has commendatory quality, suggesting affluence and spaciousness, as in **Broad View, Broadacres, Broadmoor, Broadlands. Broad Axe** PA: from a tavern and its sign. **Broadwater** NB: from a personal name.

Broadalbin NY Named by Scottish immigrants for the district in Scotland more commonly spelled Breadalbane.

Broadus MT From a family of early settlers, Broaddus, with the shift of spelling occurring in transmission through the Post Office Dept.

Broady Creek OR From a broad-horned cow that ranged along this stream.

Brockatonorton Bay MD From an Indian tribal name, shaped by folk-etymology.

Brockton In MA the name was given (1874) after being proposed by a citizen who liked the name as used in Canada.

Broke Leg Creek KY Probably with colloquial 'broke' for 'broken,' to indicate an incident.

Broken As a descriptive it occurs, e.g. **Broken Mountain** AK, to designate a feature which has broken off, or so seems. **Broken Falls** WY: halfway down the fall is interrupted, suggesting that it has broken off. **Broken Egg Spring** WY: the shape of the spring resembles an egg with the top broken off. **Broken Top** OR: the mountain is so jagged at the summit that it appears to have been shattered. **Brokencot Creek** OR: an abandoned broken cot once stood along this stream. **Broken Bow** NB: at the time of naming in the 1880's a broken bow was found at an old Indian camp nearby; the town in OK was named from that in NB. **Broken Arrow** OK: from an Indian ceremony following the Civil War, in which an arrow was broken to symbolize the reunion of factions. **Brokenstraw Creek** PA: a translation from the Algonquian; significance, not known. **Broken Sword Creek** OH: by traditional accounts, because Col. William Crawford in 1782, defeated and about to be taken by the Indians, here broke his sword to prevent its use by his captors. **Brokenback Creek** WY: in an accident with a wagon in 1880, a man's back was thought to have been broken. Such names as **Brokenleg Branch** NC and **Broken Shin Hollow** KY probably arise from incidents.

Bromide OK Because of the presence of that mineral in the water of nearby springs.

Bronco Spanish 'wild, unruly,' but in American usage restricted to horses of that sort, and places thus associated have been named, e.g. **Bronco Lake** NB, **Bronco Gulch** CO. **Broncho,** a misspelling by Americans also occurs, e.g. as a habitation-name in NM.

Bronte TX Named in 1887 for Charlotte Bronte, the novelist.

Bronx, The NY Jonas Bronck, during the Dutch period, had a farm just north of Manhattan Island. People came to speak of going to the Broncks,' and in the English period, after the family was no longer remembered, the name worked into the present spelling. The highly unusual retension of the article is thus explained.

Brook Many names are from the personal name Brook(s). The term, meaning 'small stream,' is a generic in New England and in areas under strong New England influence, e.g. northern New Jersey. It appears as a specific in such names as **Brook Lake** MN and **Brookline** MA, the latter because of two brooks that formed part of the boundary of an estate. In other parts of the country it is a literary word of which the meaning is well known but which is not used as a generic to form place-names, except occasionally under literary or New England influence. **Fallbrook** CA: this habitation-name has been transferred from the East, and has no real significance in CA. The term often has commendatory value, suggesting pleasant surroundings, as in the often-repeated **Brookside.** **Brooklyn** NY: transferred from the Netherlands as **Breukelyn,** it was made over into a more English name, partly by respelling and partly by folk-etymology, after the English occupation in 1664, on the analogy of such names as **Brookland, Brookline,** and **Lynn. Brooklyn** CT was named in 1752, partly as a descriptive, but taking the NY form. **Brooks Range** and other features in AK are for A. H. Brooks, leading geologist in Alaska from 1903 to 1924.

Brookesmith TX For Brooke Smith, a railroad director.

Brookfield In MA a descriptive, because of a meadow with streams. In CT, for Thomas Brooks, first pastor (named, 1788).

Brooklyn See **Brook.**

Broom Rare, and sometimes from the personal name, which is usually **Broome.** **Broom Mountain** NM: a translation from the Spanish, who here, in early times, got grasses from which to make brooms. **Broomstraw Fork** KY carries the same indication. **Broom Creek** WY is for John McBroom, who built a cabin here in the 1850's.

Broomfield CO For a field of broom-corn.

Brosius WV From a family name, of local settlers.

Bross From the personal name, e.g. **Mount Bross** CO for William Bross (1813–1889), political figure and owner of mining-property in the vicinity.

Brother Generally appears in the plural, and may be the personal name. As a descriptive it indicates, as do **Sisters** and **Twin,** two or more features which are similar, so as to suggest family resemblance, e.g. **The Brothers** (rocks, CA), **The Three Brothers** (rocks or peaks, CA). A striking case occurs in CA where two rocks on one side of a channel are **The Brothers,** and two rocks on the other side are **The Sisters. The Brother of the Hole in the Mountain** (MN) is a translation from the Sioux, referring to a passageway through the hills much resembling another one. **Brothers** OR: named in counterpart to nearby **Sisters. Brothers Valley** PA: from the settlement of a German sect known as the Brethren. **Brother Jonathan Rock** CA: a steamer of that name was wrecked on this submerged rock, with heavy loss of life, in 1865. **The Brothers** WA were actually named in honor of two brothers.

Brown Though common, especially for habitation-names, it is almost exclusively from the personal name. **Brown Deer** WI is one of the few exceptions. On natural features the descriptive use is rare, since brown is a neutral color, seldom serving to set one feature off from another; some examples, however, are **Brown Cliffs** UT, **Brown Cone** CA, **Brown Mountain** OR, all named because of the color of the rock. **Brownsville** TX: for Major Jacob Brown, killed there in 1846 in a battle with the Mexicans.

Brownbacks PA From **Brumbaugh's,** for Gerhart Brumbaugh, settler of ca. 1725.

Bruin Occasionally used to escape the too-much-used **Bear,** e.g. **Bruin Bay** AK.

Bruin PA takes its name thus from nearby **Bear Creek. Bruins** AR is probably from a family name.

Bruinswick NY Probably a Dutch rendering of **Brunswick.**

Brulé, Brule French 'burnt,' properly with the accent, but more commonly written without it. It is a descriptive, indicating generally a place where the forest has been burned. Not infrequently as **Bois Brule,** (French 'wood-burnt'.) e.g. the creek in MO. **Brule** NB, SD, OK: from the Indian tribe, the name being thus translated into French. Bois Brulé was a French term for the son of a French father and an Indian mother, and certain place-names may have been thus derived.

Bruneau ID Probably for a French-Canadian trapper of that name, but exact identification uncertain; first applied to the river.

Bruno In MN from a personal name. In NB from the Moravian city Brno or Brünn, changed in spelling to make it easier for Americans.

Brunswick George I held the title of Elector of Brunswick-Lunëberg, and Brunswick was therefore used for commendatory reasons, as a name associated with the kings. e.g. for towns in ME and GA, and for counties, as well as for **New Brunswick** NJ. **Brunswick** NB: from the city in Germany, because sugar beets were raised there, as in NB.

Brush, Brushy These favorite US terms have been prolific, and are coupled with many different generics, probably most often with *creek* and *run* since small streams are likely to have banks thickly grown (to the despair of anglers). The names are numerous almost everywhere except in CA, where brush is perhaps too common to be distinctive. The family name, **Brush,** has also been used.

Brussels For the city in Belgium, e.g. in IL, WI.

Brutus Though it has been used as a personal name, most of the namings are for the Roman republican hero, from an original naming in NY, ca. 1800.

Bryant From the personal name, especially for the poet W. C. Bryant, e.g. in IA.

Bryce From the personal name, e.g. the canyon in UT for Ebenezer Bryce, first settler in the area.

Bryn Athyn PA Welsh 'hill-clinging,' but with the idea of 'hill of cohesion,' as a commendatory for a church site; given in an area where Welsh names were then (1890) prestigious, but by people who knew Welsh only from a dictionary.

Bryn Mawr PA Named as a railroad station for a nearby estate, which had taken its name from a town in Wales.

Bucareli Bay AK Named by Spanish explorers (1775) for the then viceroy of Mexico.

Bucatunna See **Buckatunna.**

Buchanan From the personal name, especially for President James Buchanan, e.g. the county in MO.

Buchon Spanish 'goiter. The point in CA was named because the Portolá expedition in 1769 encountered an Indian with a goiter near here.

Buck The frequent use of the name for the male deer (but not of the moose or elk) is evidence of how often names spring from incident, usually the killing of a fine buck. Unfortunately, the very frequency of these incidents has made them less remarkable and the stories are not preserved in tradition as **Grizzly** frequently is. The name also springs from a family name, from the common nickname, and from its use to denote a male Indian or Negro. **Buckland** MA: from a local deer park (1779). **Buck Creek** IA: in 1837 William Grant killed here a large buck that was standing at bay against a wolf which had driven him into the stream.

Buckabear Pond NJ Probably by folk-etymology from an Algonquian term, meaning unknown.

Buckada WI Algonquian (Ojibway) 'hungry,' perhaps from Longfellow's *Hiawatha* in which the name Bukadawin occurs.

Buckatabon Lake WI Algonquian, meaning uncertain.

Buckatunna Creek AL, MS Choctaw, with *buck* from *bok,* 'stream,' and the rest from 'weave,' signifying a place where baskets were woven (?).

Buckeye Some tree thus known grows in most parts of the U.S. It is generally large, often with conspicuous flowers, and with seeds that are treasured playthings for small boys. The numerous names are mostly descriptive of a place where buckeyes grow. Since Ohioans are known as Buckeyes, the name in the West often indicates a place where Ohioans first settled, as in AZ, TX. The term was at the beginning applied to any backwoodsman, and some place-names were doubtless thus derived, without reference to OH.

Buckhannon River WV Though the last two syllables suggest the Algonquian word for stream, *hanne,* the derivation is unsettled. A local Indian chief, Buck-on-gopha-non, has been somewhat uncertainly brought forward, and there is also a good possibility that the name is from an 18th-century missionary named Buchannon.

Buckhorn Many natural features are so named, usually because of the finding there of some shed antlers. Habitation-names are by transfer.

Buckingham From the county in England, etc. See **Bucks.**

Buckongahelas Creek IN, OH From the name of a Delaware chief (died 1804), partially shaped by folk-etymology, being recorded as Pak-gant-ci-hi-las.

Buckoo See **Beaucop.**

Buckroe VA From a nearby plantation which had been named for a place in England.

Bucks County PA From Buckinghamshire in England by use of the common shortened form, though at first officially Buckingham. The Penns were a family of that county, and many of the first settlers of PA came from it.

Buckshutem Swamp NJ Algonquian, meaning uncertain.

Buckskin Either for an incident involving a buckskin or as a color name, e.g. **Buckskin Peak** OR named because of boulders of a yellow-brown tint.

Buckwampum Mountain PA Algonquian (Delaware) 'round-swamp,' because of a boggy place at the top of the mountain, transformed by folk-etymology.

Buckwheat Though the crop has been widely cultivated in the NE, names are rare, e.g. **Buckwheat Island** NY.

Bucoda In MO for Buchanan, Coburn, and Davis, town founders; in WA for Buckley, Coulter, and David, local developers.

Bucyrus The original naming is that in OH (1821), probably a coined name, the most plausible story being that it was bestowed by the town planner, an admirer of the ancient Persian king Cyrus, with *Bu-* prefixed for the suggestion of *beautiful*. In ND the name was seen (1908) on a machine which had been manufactured at the town in OH.

Buda, Budapest From the city of Hungary.

Buddha Temple AZ See **Brahma.**

Bueno, Buena Spanish 'good,' e.g. **Mount Bueno** CO. The feminine form is much commoner, occurring as a habitation-name alone, in such hybrid combinations as **Buena Park** CA, and especially in **Buena Vista,** 'good view,' which may be taken from the Spanish directly or applied in the American period. The name, outside of regions of Spanish background, e.g. IA, OR, generally commemorates the battle of the Mexican War.

Buey Spanish 'ox,' but rare, since **Toro** is the usual term. **Buey Canyon** NM is enough like the original Tewa term to suggest folk-etymology.

Bueyeros Spanish 'ox-drivers.' The village in NM was so named because of the use of oxen there.

Buffalo The American bison was popularly so known, and the tremendous impact of that animal upon the people of the U.S. is shown by the hundreds of place-names. The buffalo ranged over about three-quarters of the country. It was greatly valued for its meat, skin, and even bones. Most of the names are presumably incident names, and authentic stories are preserved from some of these. In some instances the names are descriptive, since they indicate places where buffaloes were commonly present. By association, sometimes fanciful, it was applied attributively to a fish, to various plants, to Negro soldiers, etc. Many names of small streams are derived from the so-called buffalo fish. It also commonly occurred in Indian personal names, and was a nickname. The name in regions where the buffalo were not present historically, e.g. NV, may be from such secondary usages or from the findings of old skulls. Names in **Bull, Cow,** and **Calf** are frequently from the buffalo but cannot be distinguished ordinarily from names springing from domestic cattle. Note, however, such names as **Buffalo Bull Knob** WV and **Buffalo Cow Pasture** WV. The former preserves an incident story, to the effect that the last buffalo of the area was killed there by Isaac Gregory, shortly before 1812. **Buffalo** NY takes its name from **Buffalo Creek,** which was, in turn, named from an Indian who lived there. **Buffalo Leap** NB: probably because buffaloes were stampeded over this cliff by Indian hunters.

Bug Though the term is commonly used, to include most of the insects, names are rare. **Big Bug** AR: because of large flying beetles found there. Generally the name is humorously derogatory, and stands upon informally named communities without being officially recognized, though it occasionally gets upon standard maps, e.g. **Bug Hollow** KY. Repeated names of this sort are **Bug Tussle** and **Bug Scuffle,** implying places where a person would have to combat bugs, especially bedbugs.

Bula TX For Beulah Wilson, otherwise unidentified, with a misspelling.

Buldir Island AK From Stephan Buldirev, a sailor of Bering's ship, who died of scurvy on the day of the discovery of the island, Oct. 28, 1741, his name being incorrectly preserved in oral tradition.

Bull Most commonly from the domestic bull, but sometimes from the buffalo bull, and from the elk or moose. There are about fifty such **Bull** names in CA, twice the number of **Cow** names. This may be considered statistical evidence that meeting with a bull is twice as memorable as meeting with a cow. **Bull** is also a family name, and a not infrequent nickname. The common coupling **Bull Run** may owe something to the memory of the battle, but there is often a story about someone having to run from a bull, and some of these stories are doubtless true. **Bull Run River** OR is in an area where run is not generally known as a generic, but was first known merely as **Bull Run. Bull Creek** SD: the story is preserved that in early times a buffalo bull was found bogged down in the stream. Some places are so named because a ranch wintered its bulls there. **Bull Lake** MN: because a bull moose was killed there by Indians. **Bull Moose Township** MN: from the political party thus nicknamed, in 1912. **Bullhead Creek** CA for the fish. **Bull of the Woods Peak** OR: from a nearby mine. **Bull Mountain** OR: a bull, gone wild, ranged on this mountain. Because of derogatory suggestion the name has been avoided for habitations. **Bull Run** AZ: the Mormon battalion in 1847 encountered some wild bulls here, and fought with them in what was the battalion's only 'battle' of the war. **Bullhead** SD: for a lieutenant of the Indian police, killed near this spot in 1890. In early usage, 'oxen' were commonly called 'bulls' and some examples of the name thus arose, e.g. **Bull Spring** SD where such a 'bull outfit' camped. **Bull Lake** WY: from a Shoshone legend of a white buffalo bull whose spirit haunts the lake.

Bullfrog NV From a mine so named, because of its green ore.

Bullion A favorite 19th-century term for uncoined precious metal was given to mining camps, e.g. in NV, for commendatory reasons. **Bullion Bend** CA: because a gang of robbers hid their loot here.

Bully Creek OR According to a fairly well authenticated story, a man fell into the water, and one of his companions, being amused, stood on the bank and cried "Bully!"

Buncombe From the personal name, the county in NC being for Colonel Edward Buncombe, killed at the battle of Germantown in 1777.

Bungamic ME Algonquian 'boundary-at.'

Bungamug Brook ME Algonquian 'boundary,' probably with 'fishing-place.'

Bunganock, Bunganut ME Algonquian 'boundary-at.'

Bungay CT Though an English village-name, the origin is more likely the same as **Bungee**, q.v.

Bungee, Bungy CT Probably Algonquian 'boundary,' 'boundary-mark.'

Bungo MN The personal name of the family descended from Jean Bonga, who was brought to the U.S. from the West Indies as a slave in the 1780's; the name may be of African origin.

Bunion By folk-humor, descriptive of a small hill or mountain, e.g. **Charlies Bunion** NC.

Bunker Generally from the personal name, e.g. the lake in MN for Kendal Bunker, early settler. The hill in MA is presumably for George Bunker, early resident of Charleston. Though **Bunker Hill** is now a common name in England, it is thought to be of recent growth, and so the name was probably not transferred from England to MA. **Bunker Hill** is a common name across the country (4 in KY), influenced by the fame of the battle. **Bunker Hill, Coos Co., OR:** because bunkers for coal were located there.

Bunsen Peak WY For R. W. Bunsen, scientist, known especially in this Yellowstone N.P. area for his investigations of geyser action.

Bunyan From the personal name, usually with reference to the legendary Paul

Bunyan, e.g. the lake in MT, though the exact reason for naming is uncertain.

Buras LA From the Buras family, of seven brothers, which settled here ca. 1840.

Burbie, Bayou LA From French *bourbeux*, 'muddy.'

Bureau IL Named(?) for Pierre de Beuro, early French trapper; applied first to the stream.

Burg Commonly a generic and a second element. As a specific for habitation-names, e.g. in AR and KY, it is probably from the family name, as also in such compounds as **Burgdorf**. **Burghill** OH was originally named as being 'town on a hill,' and the name was retained when the settlement was moved to a lower location on the railroad.

Burgaw NC From a local Indian tribal name.

Burke From the family name, sometimes for Edmund Burke, English orator who was friendly to the American cause, e.g. in VT (named, 1782).

Burkburnett TX For Burk Burnett, ranch owner.

Burkemont OR For Judge J. C. Burke, early mine owner, with *mont* for *mountain*.

Burlington The town in NJ was settled largely by Yorkshire people in the late 17th century, and was called **Bridlington** after the town in Yorkshire. Probably from the beginning it was pronounced after the fashion of the alternate spelling, and that spelling was soon adopted. For reasons that are not clear, the name became highly popular, but always with the 'American' spelling, good evidence that the namers looked back to the older states, and not to England. That spelling was also used by the Earls of Burlington, and the town in VT thus took its name (1763), though the presence of the Burling family as local landowners may also have been an influence. Most of the western towns were named for one of those farther east, e.g. in IA and MN for the one in VT.

Burma OR A railroad name of 1941–1942, when the Burma Road was much in the news, and constituted a bottleneck for war supplies; there was also a bottleneck at this point on the railroad.

Burmah From the country in Asia, more commonly Burma.

Burn, Burns is usually from the personal name, e.g. in OR, where (as probably in other instances) it commemorates Robert Burns, the poet. In various compounds it is also a personal name, e.g. **Burnside**. **Burn** (Scottish dialect, 'brook') was one of the romantic terms popularized in the mid-19th century and **Burnside** is probably thus derived in some instances. **Braeburn** PA represents a double Scotticism.

Burning A descriptive for natural features because of actual burning or of some phenomenon that suggests burning. **Burning Springs** KY: the natural gas rising from the spring could be ignited. **Burning Mountain** NM: the area is anciently volcanic, and steam still rises after a slight rain. **Burning Hill** NM: fire has smoldered in the hill since 1891.

Burno Gulch SD Uncertain, though some local opinion takes it to be a misspelling of *burro*.

Burnt, Burned The regular form is *burnt*. It is frequent in all areas, coupled with many generics, e.g. **House, Ranch, Mountain**, and indicating a place that has been burned and where the signs of fire remained long enough to establish a name. **Burned Mountain** CA is a rare exception. **Burnt Cabins** PA: some cabins, erected illegally by squatters, were burned by government order in 1750. **Burnt Bridge Creek** OR: a bridge was burned here in forest fire in 1910. **Burnt out Lake** MN: from a burned peat bog. **Burnt Corn Creek** AL: an incident-name, probably a translation from some Indian language, since it is recorded from 1813.

Burr Commonly from the personal name, e.g. the village in MN from the family name of an early settler. **Burr Oak(s)** is from the presence of a tree of that variety.

Burro The more particularly Mexican name appears in place-names along with the thoroughly American **Jackass.** It is less characteristic of CA; more so, of AZ and NM. **Burro Canyon** AZ: because frequented by burros run wild.

Bush, Bushy 1) As a descriptive, e.g. **Bush Hollow** KY, **Bushy Run** PA. 2) From the personal name, e.g. **Bushland** TX for W. H. Bush, who donated the townsite. 3) From the Dutch *bosch,* 'wood, forest,' e.g. **Bushkill Creek** NY, PA and many names in NY. **Bushyhead Mountain** OK: from the name of an Indian chief. **Bush Point** WA: named by the Wilkes expedition in 1841, because it showed a few clumps of bushes. **Bushton** KS: because of an attractive row of hedge bushes which existed at the site.

Bushley, Bayou Transformed by folk-etymology into the semblance of an English name, from Choctaw, *bashli,* 'cut,' perhaps with the idea of the stream being cut off.

Bushong See **Latham.**

Bushwick NY Anglicized from Dutch *bosch-wik,* 'forest-place.'

Business Corners IA Some kind of 'business' is carried on at each of three corners where a split in the road occurs.

Bustleton NJ For the local Bustill family.

Butcher A few examples are from the personal name, though it seems rather to have been avoided, especially for habitation-names. **Butcher Creek,** Perkins Co., SD: named either for a man of that name or for one who was thus known from following that trade. **Butcher Creek,** Ziebach Co., SD: a rough translation of a Siouan name arising from a bloody battle between Indians in the prewhite era. **Butcherpen,** usually with stream names, indicates that animals have been slaughtered here. **Butcherknife Creek** OR: an old butcher-knife was found here in the 1890's; a hill and spring in TX were so named because a knife lost there was later found by another man. **Butchertown** is often an informal name for a district in a city where the slaughterhouses are situated, and it occasionally gains official acceptance.

Buttahatchee River AL Choctaw 'sumac-river.'

Butte Primarily a generic, the term has been applied as a specific to denote a place thus associated, e.g. **Butte County** CA, **Butte Creek** OR, **Butte City** CA, and several towns named **Butte.**

Butter An incident involving butter may be inferred, and seems to be confirmed for **Butter Creek** OR which is from an occurrence of 1852 when some volunteer soldiers 'took' some butter from the stores. The term is commoner in compounds, e.g. **Butternut, Buttercup. Buttermilk Hill** CA a dairy was located here at one time, and buttermilk was available for drinking. **Buttermilk Creek** OR: a dairy let its buttermilk, for which there was no sale, run into the creek, causing a memorable stench at times of low water. **Butterbread Canyon** CA: from Frederick Butterbredt, early German settler. **Butter Creek** PA: for its luxuriant meadows, suggestive of a rich dairying country. **Butter Hill** NY: a translation from Dutch Boter Berg, but reason for naming unknown.

Butterfly A rare name, usually recording an unusual occurrence of butterflies. See **Mariposa.**

Butternut From the presence of the tree so known.

Button Usually with references to the shape or insignificant size of a button, e.g. the knob in KY. **Button Springs** OR: for Lee Button, early settler. **Buttonwillow** CA: from a solitary tree of that species which once stood there conspicuously. **Buttonwood:** from the tree so called. **Buttonmold:** from resemblance to the wooded mold which was covered with cloth to make a button, e.g. **Buttonmold Ledges** ME.

Buxihatchee Creek AL Muskogean, with *hatchee,* 'river,' and the remainder uncertain.

Buxton In ME (1762) from a town in England.

Buzzard The English buzzard is a kind of hawk, and early examples of the name may have this reference. In America the word soon came to refer to the so-called turkey buzzard. Ranging over the southern half of the U.S., this bird is common and conspicuous, but of little general interest. The fairly common names for natural features arose from the sighting of a bird on the occasion of naming. There is also a family name. Because of derogatory suggestions it is almost nonexistent as a habitation name, but **Buzzards's Bay** MA has taken its name from the bird. **Buzzard Roost:** the nesting or roosting places of buzzards have been conspicuous enough to occasion descriptive names, e.g. **Buzzard Roost Mesa** AR, and the twice-used **Buzzard Roost Mountain** CA. **Buzzard Flopper Creek** GA: from a Cherokee personal name, translated; also translated as Buzzard Flapper, but significance uncertain.

Byhalia MS Choctaw 'white-oaks-standing,' probably in the sense of 'standing alone.'

Bylas AZ From the personal name of an Indian chief.

Bypro KY Probably a shortening of **By-Product,** q.v.

By-Product AL For a place where by-products of coal were produced.

Byron From the personal name. Its widespread use owes much to the popularity of Lord Byron's poetry, e.g. in NY the town was named for him in 1820, when his fame was at its height.

C

Caamano Point AK For Jacinto Caamano, Spanish explorer of 1792.

Cababi AZ Papago 'hidden springs.'

Caballo Spanish 'horse.'

Cabarrus County NC Named (1792) for Stephen Cabarrus, then speaker of the state's House of Commons.

Cabarton ID For C. A. Barton, official of the lumber company which built the town.

Cabbage Some features in FL are named from the so-called swamp cabbage or Sabal palm.

Cabbo Lake NH Algonquian 'sturgeon.'

Cabeza Spanish 'head.'

Cabezon Spanish 'big head'; in CA for an Indian so known in Spanish times. The peak in NM is identified as the head of a giant in Navajo legend.

Cabin Used most commonly with *creek*, the name indicates a place where an uninhabited cabin stood, or stands. If the cabin is inhabited, the place would normally take the name of the man living there. **Cabin Creek** OR: for a structure erected in 1846, the first to be built in the county by Americans.

Cabinet Mountains MT French 'compartment.' The river was first so named by French-Canadian trappers because of some rock formations along it.

Cable Usually from the personal name, e.g. in OH for P. S. Cable, town founder in 1853. In MT from the Atlantic Cable Mine, discovered in 1866 when the Atlantic telegraphic cable was of interest.

Cabool MO From the capital of Afghanistan, now usually spelled Kabul.

Cabot From the personal name, e.g. **Mt. Cabot** NH for Sebastian Cabot, English explorer of the 15th century.

Cabotian Mountains MN Named ca. 1820 in honor of John and Sebastian Cabot, voyagers to North America in the 15th century.

Cabra Spanish 'goat.'

Cabrillo Various places in CA commemorate J. R. Cabrillo, Spanish explorer of 1542.

Cacapon River WV Partial folk-etymology has made this into **Capecapon, Big Capon,** etc. The name is Algonquian of uncertain meaning, perhaps 'rising river,' since the stream emerges suddenly from the ground at its source.

Cacaway MD Algonquian, meaning uncertain.

Cache French 'hiding-place.' Taken over into English, ca. 1800, and used with the special meaning referring to a place where goods were concealed, usually by burying. It soon became a place-name specific to identify a feature, usually a stream, where a cache had been made. The term is especially connected with the fur trade, and **Cache Creek** exists in several states. **Cache la Poudre Creek** CO specifically shows that a cache of powder was made there. Habitation-names, e.g. **Cache County** UT, are by transfer, and **Cache** ID was named by settlers from **Cache Valley** UT. In early times the spelling **Cash** was common. **Cache Creek** WY, Yellowstone N. P.: a large prospecting party in 1863 had all their horses stolen by Indians here, and cached their goods.

Cachee An adapted spelling for French *caché(e)*, 'hidden,' e.g. **Butte Cachee** SD.

Cactus From the presence of this desert plant, e.g. **Cactus Pass** AZ, named in 1854 by A. W. Whipple at the request of a cactus-lover in his exploring party.

Cadams NB For C. Adams, a local banker.

Caddo From the Indian tribal name.

Caddoa CO Probably a variant of **Caddo,** from the adjective Caddoan.

Cadena Creek TX Spanish 'chain,' but from a family name (?).

Cadillac MI From Antoine de la Mothe Cadillac, French officer in the lakes region in the 17th century.

Cadiz For the city in Spain. In CA it occupies the third position in an alphabetical list of stations.

Cadmus KY, MI Probably from the family name.

Cadores Creek PA Iroquoian 'under-rocks' (?).

Cadosia NY An Indian (probably Algonquian) name, shaped to the appearance of a Latin place-name, meaning uncertain.

Cadott WI From an Americanized spelling of a French family name (?).

Cadron AR Apparently French, but uncertain whether from a personal name, from *cadran* 'sun-dial,' or from *quadrant,* 'quadrant.'

Caesar In WV the name **Caesar Mountain** probably preserves the memory of a slave who had been labeled with a classical name, as the custom then was. **Caesars Head** NC, SC: a profile in a rocky precipice is thought to resemble that of Julius Caesar.

Cahaba AL Choctaw 'water-above (upper).'

Cahelee Creek See **Cohelee.**

Cahokia From the Indian tribal name, e.g. the name-cluster in IL.

Cahola KS Indian (Kansa), probably 'living-by-the-river,' and applied first to an Indian village.

Cahone CO Named by the first postmaster from a spelling-after-the-sound of Spanish **Cajon.**

Cahoot Gulch MT Because two men went into 'cahoots' (partnership) here to split rails.

Cahoula LA Probably a shortening of **Catahoula.**

Cahto CA Pomo 'lake,' or perhaps 'swamp.'

Cahuilla CA From an Indian tribal name.

Cahulga AL Muskogean (Creek), probably with *cahu,* 'cane,' and the remainder uncertain.

Caillou French 'pebble,' e.g. **Caillou Bay** LA.

Cairo From the city in Egypt. Named in 1818, the city in IL shows the early 19th-century enthusiasm for exotic names, suggestive of grandeur; it is on the Mississippi, then called the Nile of America, and the traditional fertility of Egypt may have exercised a commendatory influence.

Cajon Spanish 'box,' but in place-names usually in the sense of 'box-canyon,' e.g. **Cajon Pass** CA.

Cakepoulin Creek NJ Algonquian, meaning uncertain but probably containing *kaak,* '(wild) goose.'

Cal-, Cali- The opening letters of CA have been widely used in border-names, e.g. **Calneva, Calzona;** in company names, e.g. **Caldor** from California Door Co. Other uses include **Calipatria** (from Latin *patria,* 'fatherland,') and **Calmesa** (from *mesa*).

Calabash NC By local story, for drinking gourds hung at wells. Cf. **Calabasa.**

Calabaza, Calabasa Spanish 'pumpkin, squash, gourd.' The Indians of the SW used gourds for drinking vessels and raised squash for eating. **Calabasas** CA from an Indian village, so called probably because of squashes raised there.

Calahonda Creek AK Italian 'cove-deep,' so named by the explorer Alessandro Malaspina in 1791.

Calais In ME and VT the name is from the French channel port, having been bestowed in the post-Revolutionary period of enthusiasm, because of French aid in the War.

Calamese Creek KY Probably for **Calamus.** See also **Calymess.**

Calamity Occasionally used for a place where some trouble occurred, e.g. the creek in TX where some people were drowned in a flood. The creek in SD is locally believed to have been named for the famous 'Calamity Jane,' because she once lived in a cabin there. **Calamity Peak** SD: also believed to be named for this heroine, though the special connection with the place (as with so much about her) is vague.

Calamus From the growth of the calamus or sweet flag, sometimes applied to water features, and thence transferred to habitations, e.g. **Calamus NB.**

Calapooya OR From an Indian tribal name.

Calavera Spanish 'skull.' **Calaveras River** CA: from the finding there, ca. 1836, of a number of skulls.

Calcasieu LA From the name of an Indian chief.

Calebee Creek AL Muskogean (Creek), a name for a kind of oak.

Caledonia The Roman name for the northern parts of Britain, used poetically for Scotland, generally by Scottish immigrants, e.g. in OH.

Calera Spanish 'lime-kiln.' In OK, a modification of the personal name Cale, for a man not otherwise identified (1910). **Calera** AL: because it was a center for the early production of lime.

Calf Incidents involving a calf have given rise to names for natural features, and some have been transferred to habitations. **Calfpen Bay** SC, **Calfpasture Island** CT are remnants of early cattle-raising. **Calf Creek** TX: the heavy brush along the stream served as a place where cows hid their calves.

Calhan CO A shortening, by the railroad, of Calahan, the name of a local railroad contractor.

Calhoun From the personal name, especially for J. C. Calhoun (1782–1850), statesman, for whom towns and counties were named, particularly in the SE.

Calico Chiefly Western, applied to hills or mountains, e.g. **Calico Mountains** NV, because of variegated colors of rock suggestive of printed calico. **Calico NJ**: probably by folk-etymology from Dutch *kalkoen,* 'turkey.'

Caliente Spanish 'hot.'

Califon NJ From an adaptation of **California** (?).

California The first known occurrence of the name is in the long romantic poem (ca. 1500), *Las Sergas de Esplandián* by Garcí Ordóñez de Montalvo. Similar names exist, e.g. Calaforno and Calafornina in Sicily and Califerne in the *Song of Roland;* the general opinion is that Montalvo coined the name for the purposes of his poem, perhaps influenced by the word *caliph* and the names of such Spanish cities as Calahorra. In the poem California is an island in the ocean, peopled by Amazon-like women and rich in gold and precious stones. A Spanish exploring expedition, probably in 1524, brought back a rumor of the actual existence of such an island in the Pacific. According to Herrera, the Spanish chronicler, Cortéz himself 'placed this name,' (**California**) upon the island, though he later and officially called it Santa Cruz. In his original naming Cortéz may have been ridiculing the idea of the discovery of Amazons. In any case, when the Spaniards reached, by sea, the tip of the present Baja California, they thought it to be an island, and used the name **California** for it. When Cabrillo explored the coast northward in 1542–1543, he kept the same name and thus brought it to the present state. Under Spanish and Mexican rule it was known as **Alta California,** but the adjective was dropped after the American occupation, thus following what had already become common practice, on account of the comparative unimportance of **Baja California. California Crossing, Hill NB**: wagons bound for CA crossed the South Fork of the Platte River at this point. In the older states the name is usually, e.g. in PA, a reflection of the gold excitement of 1849, but in MO it dates from 1846 when the people of that state were much interested in the covered-wagon migration to the Pacific coast. In newer states, especially in gold-mining regions, it is common, partly because of migration and partly as a commendatory; almost 40 places in AK bear the name.

Calion AR A boundary-name, from Calhoun and Union counties.

Calipatria See **Cal-**.

Calispell WA From the Indian tribal name.

Calista KS With adapted spelling from the Greek *kalliste,* 'most beautiful.'

Calistoga CA From California and Saratoga, the latter because of the medicinal springs there.

Callao From the seaport in Peru.

Callicoon NY From Dutch *kalkoen,* 'turkey,' but perhaps from the Indian tribe named after that bird.

Calmar IA From the city in Sweden, now more commonly spelled Kalmar.

Calmus A misspelling, after the pronunciation of **Calamus,** in IA originally applied to the creek.

Calno NJ From the Biblical town.

Caloosahatchee River FL From a tribal name, more commonly spelled Calusa, plus Seminole *hachi,* 'stream.'

Calpella CA From the Indian tribal name, or the name of the chief from which it was passed on to the tribe.

Calpet WY From California Petroleum Company.

Calpine CA A shortening of the former name **McAlpine,** though the suggestion of CA and *pine* must have been strong, since the place is the site of a lumber mill.

Calumet A French word for the ceremonial pipe used by Indians in consultations; the word came to have a vague commendatory meaning, as if mystically connected with peace; it also became known because of the famous and highly profitable Calumet Mining Company. It occurs chiefly as a habitation-name. But NB has **Calumet Hill,** and **Calumet Bluffs.**

Calvary From the place of the Crucifixion. In IL it was originally the name of a cemetery; in WI it arose from a convent.

Calvey Creek MO From the French personal name Calvé, probably for Joseph Calvé, fur trader in St. Louis in the 18th century.

Calymess Creek KY Probably for **Calamus.** See also **Calamese.**

Calypso The name of the nymph in the *Odyssey* has been applied in NC; reason unknown. **Calypso Cascades** CO: from the Latin name of the flower known as fairy slipper.

Camanche A variation of **Comanche,** originally so spelled in IA, as being more euphonic; transferred to CA.

Camano Island WA A simplified spelling from the name of Lt. Jacinto Caamano, a Spanish officer, from a naming in 1790.

Camargo IL, OK From the town in Mexico, probably a Mexican War name, since Doniphan's column reached this point in its march from the north.

Camas From the camas plant which produced edible bulbs much used by the Indians, e.g. **Camas Valley** OR. There are a number of habitation-names by transfer. The word was originally Chinook Jargon, but was taken into English soon after 1800. Sometimes **Camass, Kamas(s).**

Cambolassie Pond ME Algonquian 'chain-of-ponds,' but the initial *c* is not thus accounted for; apparently first applied to the chain, not to a single pond.

Cambria From the Latin name for Wales, sometimes indirectly. **Cambria County** PA: so named because of numerous Welsh settlers. **Cambria** CA: so named from the urgings of a single Welsh resident.

Cambridge From the town or county in England, etc. In MA (1636) the General Court applied the name with the intention of founding a college there.

Camden From the personal name, especially in honor of Charles Pratt, Lord Camden (1714–1794), a supporter of the American cause before the Revolution, e.g. towns in NJ, NC, and SC. **Camden on Gauley** WV: the name is for Johnson N. Camden, senator and railroad builder, but is more interesting for its rare coupling with a river name. This may have been to distinguish it from another Camden, but the town was founded by the Gauley Lumber Company, whose officials may have wished to advertise.

Cameahwait, Lake WY From a Shoshone chief.

Camel Applied to elevations because of a humped shape, often clearly, as in such names as **Camel's Hump** CA and **Camelback Mountain** AZ. **Camel Rock** AZ is hump-shaped, and sometimes called **The Camel.** Most of the names are Western, probably because treeless mountains are more suggestive of the shape. The camels introduced into the West, ca. 1850, may have left some traces, e.g. **Dead Camel Mountains** NV. **Pass of the Camels** was a former name in AZ because of the passage of a camel train there. **Camel Creek** SD: for Andy Camel, a pioneer settler of 1884. **Sitting Camel, The** WY: this rock formation bears a striking resemblance, with head and hump, to a sitting camel.

Cameo CO Named (1907) from a rock formation suggesting a cameo.

Camillus NY For the Roman republican general, part of the classical naming of 1790.

Caminada LA The bay and pass are for Francisco Caminada, colonist of the 18th century.

Camino Spanish 'road.'

Camp As a specific, *camp* can usually be distinguished from its use as a generic, though both regularly come first in the name. It is not common as a specific, but indicates a place where someone camped. It is also a family name. **Camp Lake** MN: government surveyors camped at this spot. As a generic the term often indicates a military post, and probably some specifics have thus arisen.

Campanula Creek WY For the flower, the wild blue bell, growing here.

Camphora CA From **Camp Four,** a construction camp on the railroad; by local story, influenced by the pronunciation of Mexican workmen.

Campo Spanish 'field,' but Mexicans in early CA used it as meaning 'mining-camp,' e.g. **Campo Seco. El Campo** TX: because harvesters were accustomed to camp there 'in early days.'

Campobello Spanish/Italian 'field-beautiful.' In SC the name was given for descriptive reasons.

Campti LA From the name of an Indian chief.

Camulos CA Chumash, the name of an Indian village, probably containing *mulus,* meaning a kind of edible fruit.

Cana From the New Testament city; in NC, with the additional influence of the name of the first postmaster, J. H. Cain.

Canaan Though portrayed in the Bible as the promised land, flowing with milk and honey, **Canaan** has not been very popular and is represented by about a dozen towns and villages. **Canaan** CT was promoted in 1738 as being a rich area, though actually it was hilly and barren, thus an example of euphemistic naming.

Canada 1) From a spelling without the tilde of Spanish *cañada,* 'valley, narrow valley,' originally a generic of somewhat shifting meaning, at times probably being applied to the stream as much as to the valley, surviving as a specific by association. **La Canada** CA retains the Spanish pronunciation, but the tilde is generally omitted. 2) From association with the dominion or country, e.g. **East Canada Creek** and **West Canada Creek** NY, along each of which ran a trail leading to and from Canada. 3) By folk-etymology from any of several Iroquoian words, e.g. those meaning 'hemlock,' 'bread,' 'village,' 'stream.' Since the Iroquoian area lies close to the Canadian border, the situation is confused, but several streams thus named are probably the result of folk-etymology rather than of proximity to Canada.

Canadarago NY Iroquoian 'on-the-lake.'

Canadawa Creek NY Iroquoian 'running-through-hemlocks.'

Canadian Generally, e.g. the creek in CA, from the presence of settlers from Canada. The river (NM, OK, TX) is probably by folk-etymology from the Caddoan name *canohatino* for the stream, i.e. 'red river.'

Canadice NY Iroquoian 'lake-long.' Cf. **Skaneateles.**

Canajoharie NY Iroquoian 'kettle-washing,' from a pothole or other formation in the bed of the creek.

Canal In spite of the era of canal construction in the early 19th century, few names have resulted. **Canal Fulton** OH: because it was on a canal, and in honor of Ben Fulton, early settler. **Canal Winchester** OH: named first by a settler from **Winchester** VA, with the other name added when a canal reached the town. In WA and AK the term has a limited use as a generic (the equivalent of *channel*) and names have developed by association, e.g. **Canal Point** AK.

Canandaigua NY Iroquoian 'town-set-off,' i.e. a place selected for settlement.

Canapitsit Channel MA Algonquian, probably 'long-weir-at.'

Canarsie NY A small local tribe was so called, but may have taken their name secondarily from that of their site, 'fenced-place,' i.e. a fortified, stockaded village.

Canary OR What may be called a name of desperation, i.e. given in order to find something that both the post office and the railroad would accept. It was probably suggested by the bird, rather than by the islands or the wine.

Canasawacta Creek NY From Iroquoian 'cabin-between-two-others' (?).

Canaseraga NY Iroquoian 'among-milkweeds.'

Canasixet River ME Algonquian 'witch-hazel-place.'

Canastota NY Iroquoian, probably 'lone-pine' or 'lone-pine-grove.'

Canaveral Spanish *canebrake*. The cape was probably named from its appearance as seen from the sea by an early Spanish voyager, as it was in established use in the earlier part of the 16th century.

Canchardee AL Muskogean (Creek) 'earth-red.'

Candelaria From the woman's name, e.g. in TX for a beautiful Mexican girl, not further identified.

Candia NH At the time of naming (1763) the Mediterranean island **Crete** was known as **Candia,** and Gov. Benning Wentworth had once been held prisoner there.

Candlewood In Colonial times the term was applied to wood such as pitch pine, splinters of which could be burned as candles; as a specific, usually with *hill* CT, MA, the name indicates where such wood could be found.

Cando ND From the phrase 'can do'; when the legal power for establishing the town was questioned (1884), a spokesman retorted, 'Just to show what we can do, we'll name this county seat Can-do.'

Candor In NC by local story the name was applied, ca. 1891, by three merchants who wished the town to be distinguished by frankness.

Cane, Canebrake Thick growths of canes are common only in SE, and the name occurs widely, e.g. **Cane Creek** NC, **Canebrake** LA. The personal name in this spelling is rare, and has little influence.

Caneadea NY Iroquoian 'where-heavens-rest-on-earth' (?), but reference uncertain.

Canelo Spanish 'cinnamon,' but often 'cinnamon-colored, brown,' e.g. the **Canelo Hills** AZ, because of their brown rock.

Canesto(w) MA Algonquian, probably a much changed form of the word for 'pickerel,' appearing elsewhere as **Kenosha.**

Caney, Cany See **Cane.** These adjectival forms are common in the SE, and seem to be used without distinction, though **Caney** is much the more frequent.

Canisteo River NY Iroquoian 'board-on-water,' but reference uncertain.

Canistota SD By error of spelling for **Canastata** NY.

Canjilon NM Uncertain, but probably a word in local Spanish 'deer antler.'

Cannelton Occurring also with other suffixes, the name refers to the presence of cannel coal.

Cannery Because of a cannery, usually a fish cannery, at the site, e.g. a dozen places in AK.

Cannibal Plateau CO From being the scene of an incident of the winter of 1873–1874, famous in both history and folklore, when Alfred Packer apparently killed his five companions, and subsisted through the winter by eating parts of their bodies. See **Man-Eater.**

Canning From the personal name, in AK commemorating George Canning, British statesman, who conducted the boundary negotiations between Russia and Great Britain.

Cannisnia Lake LA From the name of an Indian tribe.

Cannon Commonly from the personal name, but sometimes from a resemblance to a cannon or from an incident. **Cannon Butte** ND: some protruding rocks look like cannon. **Cannon Beach** OR: when a ship was wrecked there in 1846, part of the deck, with a small cannon attached, drifted ashore. **Lost Cannon Creek,** see **Lost.** The river in MN is derived by an error in transmission (probably a misunderstanding in pronunciation) from the French **Riviere aux Canots,** 'river of canoes.' In **Cannonball River** ND spheroidal rocks found here suggested cannonballs.

Canoa Spanish 'canoe,' but in place-names used in the Mexican sense to mean a trough or ditch for carrying irrigation water, and sometimes applied to a natural stream, e.g. **Canoas Creek** CA.

Canob Pond RI Probably Algonquian, a shortened form of **Canopaug,** i.e. 'long pond.'

Canobie Lake NH Algonquian 'much water' (?).

Canoe The canoe was so important both to the Indians and to early settlers in many parts of the U.S. that its occurrence in many names is not surprising, though the particular incident responsible cannot usually be determined. **Canoe Run** WV: according to a story, an Indian canoe was found moored beneath willows at the mouth of this stream.

Canoga NY Iroquoian 'oil-on-water,' first applied to a stream, probably because of a natural oil seepage.

Canon See **Canyon.**

Canonchet RI From the well-known Narragansett chief, killed 1675.

Canonicut Island RI From the well-known Narragansett chief, Canonicus, of the 17th century.

Canoochee GA From the name of an ancient Indian country or province, recorded as Canosi; meaning uncertain.

Canopaug RI Algonquian 'long-pond.'

Canopus NY Probably from the name of a local chief, with a possible linkage to **Canopaug,** q.v.

Canosia See **Kenosha.**

Canova In SD named (1883) for Antonio Canova, Italian sculptor.

Canterbury From the English city or a family name. Its rarity, in spite of its importance in England, suggests some actual counterforce. It was perhaps too long (contrast the popularity of **Kent**), and may have had too close an association with the archbishop and Episcopalianism, never a popular creed in the U.S. The town in CT dates from 1703.

Cantil Spanish 'steep rock.'

Canton The meaning of the word in French, 'district, sub-division,' probably gave rise to the name in TX (close to the LA border, where there was much French influence), when part of the county was cut off from the rest of it. Elsewhere the name seems to be taken from the seaport in China, an early example being in MA (1797). Boston ships were trading with China at this time, and foreign namings had become popular after the Revolution. Local stories, both in MA and SD, indicate that the motivation was a naming by opposites, i.e. that the city in China was considered to be the opposite spot on the other side of the world, though the geography was certainly faulty. Once established, the name was transferred from one town to another, but the popularity (ca. 25 states) is difficult to explain. The rare personal name is probably of no influence. In some instances, e.g. in OH, rival stories as to origin are told, i.e. as to whether it is French or Chinese. In CT the name is probably of Swiss derivation, being influenced by a local resident who was especially interested in Switzerland. See **Cantonment.**

Cantonment From an army encampment, e.g. in FL and OK. In a shortened form it is a possible source of **Canton.**

Canute OK Probably for the Danish king of England, a railroad name.

Canutillo TX Locally believed to be an Indian word, 'alkali flat,' but possibly from Spanish *cañutillo,* 'small pipe.'

Cany See **Cane.**

Canyon, Canon From the Spanish *cañon.* The first spelling is an adaptation aimed to render in English the original pronunciation. The second spelling merely drops the tilde. Primarily a generic, the term is used to denote a feature in a canyon; or otherwise it is associated with a generic, e.g. the frequent **Canyon Creek.** It is also frequent in habitation-names.

Cap French 'cape, headland.'

Capa SD Probably Siouan 'beaver,' but named by the state historian, not by the Indians.

Capac MI For Manco Capac, traditional founder of the Inca dynasty; reason for naming, unknown.

Capaha MO From the tribal name, more commonly occurring as **Quapaw.**

Capahosic VA Algonquian, recorded (1608) as Capa Howasicke, 'shelter-at' (?), with reference to shelter for canoes or to a sheltering forest.

Cap au Gris MO From French *cap au grès,* 'cape with the sandstone.'

Capay CA Wintu 'stream.'

Cape Regularly a generic, in most instances preceding its specific. It becomes a specific in habitation-names, e.g. **Cape Charles** VA, and rarely by association, e.g. **Cape Pond** MA. See **Cape Horn, Cape Poge,** and under the various specifics.

Cape Horn Many early Americans went to California by way of Cape Horn, and were impressed by the circuitousness and difficulty of that route. They applied the name to a number of places which seemed unusually remote or difficult of passage, e.g. the jutting precipice CA above the American River where passageway for the railroad has been dug out of the rock. Generally Western, the name occurs at least three times in WA and seven in CA.

Cape Labelle Creek WA Shifted from **Kate Labelle,** having been named for an old Indian woman who lived nearby.

Capell Creek, Humboldt Co., CA From the name of an Indian village, 'house-pit.' In Napa Co., CA, the same name is from an early settler.

Cape Poge MA Produced by folk-etymology from an Algonquian name, of which the first element was the common one meaning 'blockage, obstruction,' occurring in several forms, e.g. *cap-, kep-, kup-, kab-*. It apparently referred to something causing a stoppage of travel, such as rocks or driftwood in a stream or tidal passage. The last element is probably 'pond,' with **Capoag** MA representing the same original name. See also **Capissic, Capsuptic,** etc.

Capilla Peak NM Spanish 'hood, cap,' probably descriptive by shape.

Capinero See **El Capinero.**

Capioma See **Kapioma.**

Capissic River ME Algonquian 'obstructed-branch.'

Capitan Spanish 'captain.' **Canada del Capitan** CA probably is for Capitan J. F. Ortega, early grantee of a nearby rancho. The term may also occur in a figurative sense, e.g. **El Capitan,** the rock cliff in Yosemite Valley CA named in 1859 as being outstanding; so also **Capitan Peak** NM.

Capitol For a rock formation taken to resemble the national capitol, e.g. **Capitol Peak** CO. **Capitol Reef** UT: some white sandstone domes produce this effect. See **Reef.**

Capitola A coinage from *capitol,* with a Spanish ending; in CA it was given for commendatory purposes in 1876; in FL it is near the state capital.

Capoag See **Cape Poge.**

Capon Springs WV By folk-etymology from the **Cacapon River.**

Capouse Mountain PA From the name of an Indian chief.

Caprock NM From a nearby formation of the kind usually called rim rock.

Capshaw AL Probably from the personal name.

Capsuptic Lake ME Algonquian 'obstructed-spring-fed-stream.'

Captain Cook Point OR Applied in 1931 in honor of James Cook, the great English explorer who sailed along the Oregon coast in 1778.

Capulin Spanish '(wild)-cherry, choke-cherry.'

Caputa SD Probably from Latin *caput,* 'head,' with an *a* added to give it the appearance of a place-name, locally believed to mean 'head-camp.'

Caracol Spanish 'snail,' e.g. the creek in TX.

Caradan From the names, S. L. Caraway, and Dan T. Bush, early settlers.

Carancahua TX From the Indian tribal name, a variant of **Karankawa.**

Caratunk Lake ME Algonquian, meaning uncertain.

Carbon The name occurs as a substitute for the too-often-used **Coal.** For commendatory reasons **Carbondale** is a favorite form for habitation-names.

Carbonado WA A variation of **Carbon,** because of the presence of coal.

Carbonate On features because of the occurrence of one of the minerals so known (particularly for the ore of lead), e.g. **Carbonate Hill** (3 times) in CO.

Carbonera CO Spanish 'coal-mine.'

Carbuncle From the semi-precious stone, e.g. the hill in RI.

Carcus Creek OR An informal spelling of Carcass Creek, so named because the body of a dead horse was once found on its banks.

Cardonia IN For J. F. Card, president of a local coal company, with a Latin ending for place.

Careless Creek MT Named (1865) by William Berkin, because when traveling through he suffered from an unspecified incident caused by carelessness.

Carencro LA American-French 'turkey-buzzard, vulture.' (Apparently the word, not the name, is from the English *carrion-crow*.)

Caress WV Probably from the family name.

Caresso See **Carrizo**

Caretta WV From Etta Carter, a woman otherwise unknown to fame.

Carey From the personal name, e.g. in OH for Judge John Carey, president of a local railroad; **Careyhurst** WY for J. M. Carey, U.S. senator and local landowner.

Caribou, Cariboo, Carriboo The native American reindeer ranged widely in Alaska, but otherwise in the U.S. only along the northern border. Within this range it was an important game animal, and gave rise to numerous names, e.g. **Caribou Stream** ME, and numerous lakes and other features in northern MN. The gold rush of 1858 to the Cariboo region of British Columbia involved many American miners, and they brought the name back as one for mines. Several occurrences in CA are thus explicable, the animal itself not being native to the state; **Caribou Creek** in the Mohave Desert CA is about as unsuitable a habitat as can be imagined. The name was also given as a nickname to persons who had been in the gold rush. Thus explicable are **Caribou**, Plumas Co., CA and **Caribou** ID. **Caribou Lake, Pass** CO: from a mine, named, ca. 1870, by a miner who had been in the British Columbia gold mines.

Carillon, Mount CA Descriptive, from resemblance to a bell tower.

Carimona MN From the name of a Winnebago chief, with Latinized spelling.

Carisa See **Carrizo**.

Carlisle, Carlyle From the city in England, etc., e.g. in PA (1751) for the city. **Carlyle** arises directly from the personal name.

Carlsbad An Anglicized spelling from the European Karlsbad. *Bad* is 'bath' in German, and the name has been used for places where the springs were supposed to be medicinal, e.g. in NM.

Carlton, Carleton Generally for the personal name, though possibly for a village in England. **Carlton** OR: from the family name Carl, plus *-ton*.

Carmel, Mount Carmel A religious-commendatory name from the Biblical mountain. **Carmel** CA: the name-cluster originated with the river, named in Spanish by Viscaíno in 1603, and so called, probably because he was accompanied by three Carmelite friars.

Carmen In OK named in 1910 for Carmen Díaz, wife of president of Mexico; in ID, probably the family name of an early settler; in NM it may be a religious name for Nuestra Señora del Carmen.

Carmine TX Originally **Carmean** for John Carmean, early settler, but changed in spelling because of confusion with **Cameron**.

Carnadero American-Spanish 'butchering-place,' to indicate where cattle were slaughtered, e.g. **Carnadero Creek** CA.

Carnarvon IA For the town in Wales, named by an immigrant.

Carnation OR, WA From the name of a company manufacturing milk products.

Carnegie PA Named for Andrew Carnegie in 1894, not because he lived there or had any interest in the town, but apparently in hopes that he would become interested, which hopes were realized by the building of a public library.

Carnelian From the occurrence of the mineral, e.g. **Carnelian Bay** CA.

Carnero Spanish 'sheep, ram,' e.g. **Carnero Lake** AZ.

Caroga NY Probably Iroquoian, meaning uncertain.

Caroleen NC From the given name of the mother of the founder, S. B. Tanner.

Carolina The French colonists in 1564 used *la Caroline* for a fort on the coast of SC, but this name lapsed. In 1629 Robert Heath asked that his colony bear the name of King Charles I, the reigning monarch, who was making the grant, and it was thus designated in the form of a feminine Latin adjective as **Carolana,** with some such word as *provincia* or *terra* understood. In 1663 Charles II regranted the region to nine proprietors under the same name, with the spelling **Carolina,** the name being as applicable to him as it had been to his father. The distinction between **North** and **South** began informally in the later 17th century, and became official in 1710. Habitation-names, e.g. RI, WV, are from women bearing the name.

Caroline County VA For Queen Caroline, wife of George II.

Carona KS Named **Carbona** because of coal mines, with the common added 'a' to indicate a place-name; the 'b' was dropped by an unexplained process.

Carpe French 'carp,' in America applied to the buffalo-fish, e.g. **Bayou la Carpe** LA.

Carpet Hill Creek OR Men with an ox wagon laid a carpet on a slick, sloping rock to give their teams footing.

Carpinteria CA Spanish 'carpenter-shop.' Named by the men of the Portolá expedition in 1769 because they here saw an Indian making a canoe.

Carpio ND Probably from Bernardo del Carpio, the legendary Spanish hero, whose name was known from a popular 19th-century poem.

Carquinez CA From an Indian tribal name.

Carrabassett River ME Algonquian, meaning uncertain.

Carrabelle FL Named (1897) for Carrie Hall, who was considered the local belle.

Carrara NV From the town in Italy, because of local deposits of marble.

Carriboo See **Caribou**

Carrizo Spanish 'reed-grass,' e.g. **Carrizo Gorge** CA, **Carrizo Springs** TX. **Caresso Creek** NM and **Carisa Canyon** NM are probably variants, introduced when the names were taken into English.

Carrizozo NM Originally **Carrizo Springs;** an American added the syllable, ca. 1907, perhaps merely in high spirits, though he is said to have maintained that it indicated 'abundance.'

Carroll The family was a notable one in MD, with several eminent members. The names most commonly honor 'Charles Carroll of Carrollton' who signed the Declaration of Independence in that fashion.

Carron, Bayou LA For Joseph Carron, French settler.

Carson From the personal name, especially for Christopher (Kit) Carson, famous frontiersman, e.g. the river (hence, **Carson City**) and lake in NV. See **Kit Carson.**

Cartago CA Spanish 'Carthage,' a railroad name of 1909.

Carter From the personal name, e.g. in GA, for Farish Carter, important landowner in the vicinity. **Cartersville** IA was named in 1900, probably for the popular book *Colonel Carter of Cartersville,* published in 1891. **Carter** OK, **Carter Nine** OK: for the Carter Oil Co., and for Section 9, on which the settlement was made.

Carthage For the ancient city of North Africa, bestowed chiefly during the period of interest in exotic names, e.g. in NC (1806), MO (1842).

Carthagena OH From an alternate spelling for the city Cartagena, in Spain.

Cartridge Creek CA A young hunter became so excited when shooting at a bear that he ejected the cartridges without firing.

Carved Rare; generally indicative of a place of Indian petroglyphs, e.g. **Carved Rock** KY.

Carver From the personal name; in MA, for John Carver, first governor of the

Plymouth Colony. The county in MN and the glacier in OR are for Jonathan Carver, explorer and author.

Carwye SD A 'wye' (q.v.) where railroad cars were shunted.

Casa Spanish 'house.'

Casar By local story named by the people for Julius Caesar, but at some point altered in spelling.

Cascabel AZ The Spanish equivalent of 'rattle,' as applied to a rattlesnake, here applied because a man happened to kill a large rattlesnake at the time of the naming.

Cascade Though not common as a generic, it has been used as a specific for a number of habitation-names, and for some features identified by a cascade, especially in connection with **The Cascades** on the Columbia River. For example, the mountain through which the river there passes became known as the **Cascade Mountains,** or **Range,** ca. 1820.

Cascadia OR From being located in the Cascade Range, plus a Latin ending for place.

Cascara WV When a name was being discussed, one of the people present saw a bottle of Cascara on the shelf, and jokingly proposed that name—a common folktale, often true.

Casco ME Algonquian 'mud, muddy,' probably a shortening of an earlier form, applying particularly to the mud flats at the head of the bay.

Cash Usually from a personal name, or from a nickname for Cassius. **Cash** TX: named in honor of J. A. Money, first postmaster; but that name was not considered suitable, and a synonym was used. **Cash** SD: for Casius Timmons, early rancher. See also **Cache.**

Cashel From the town in Ireland.

Cashiers NC Originally applied to the valley; probably for an early Indian trader named Cashier.

Cashmere WA A commendatory, from the idea of the beautiful Vale of Kashmir in India.

Cashswan NB For the first postmaster, Cassius Swan, nicknamed Cash.

Casper WY For Caspar W. Collins, lieutenant of the 11th Ohio Cavalry, killed near here in gallant combat with Indians in 1865; the nearby post then became **Fort Caspar** in his honor. The shift in spelling probably occurred when the railroad station was established in the 1880's.

Caspian From the Caspian sea, the lake in VT somewhat resembling that sea in shape.

Cass From the personal name, especially for Gen. Lewis Cass, prominent Michigan political figure of the early 19th century, e.g. **Cass Lake** MN and several counties.

Cassadaga NY Iroquoian 'under-rocks.'

Cassadore Mesa AZ For an Indian chief so called.

Casscoe AR From General Cass and Colonel Coe, members of Jackson's staff at the Battle of New Orleans, obviously suggested by **Casco.**

Casse-Tete French, literally 'break-head,' but in the meaning 'hatchet, tomahawk,' e.g. the island in LA.

Cassia In FL it is probably from some local tree, such as the camphor tree, which is associated with cassia. In ID the name, first applied to the creek, is an adaptation by folk-etymology of the American-French *cajeux*, 'raft,' the lower part of the stream still being known as **Raft River.**

Cassopolis MI From **Cass County,** and the Greek 'city.'

Castac See **Castaic.**

Castaic CA From an Indian village; the name in Chumash means 'my eyes,' but this may be merely a coincidence. Also as **Castac.**

Castalia(n) From the famous spring of ancient Greece, e.g. **Castalian Springs** TN, used as a commendatory.

Castanea Latin 'chestnut, chestnut-tree.' In IA one of the early settlers gave the name **Castana**, thinking this to be the proper form, and because the oaks growing there resembled chestnut trees.

Castella Latin 'castles,' in CA from the nearby **Castle Crags.**

Castile From the province and former kingdom in Spain.

Castine ME From the Baron Vincent de St. Castine, who lived here from about 1667 to 1697, named commemoratively in 1796. **Castine Bayou** LA: probably Choctaw 'flea,' made over into a French form.

Castle Though most of the early Americans had never seen a castle, the idea seems to have been familiar to them, either from books or from association with immigrants from Europe. The term is widely used as a specific for peaks, mountains, rocks, etc., and has been transferred to other features and to habitations. It is a quasi-descriptive term to indicate a place with rock formations resembling towers and battlements. It is also, in some instances, from a personal name, but this is rare. **Castle Hayne** NC: for a place owned by Roger Hayne. **Castleford** ID: an early trail here crossed the river at a point dominated by a castlelike rock.

Castlewood In VA a plantation-name, probably transferred from the British Isles; in SD it is apparently a borrowing from Thackeray's *Henry Esmond.*

Castor Though it is a personal name, its occurrences are commonly from the French and Spanish 'beaver,' e.g. the river in MO and the bayou in LA.

Cast Steel Run VA By folk-etymology from **Castile** (?).

Cat Uncommon, it is chiefly an incident name involving a wildcat, but may occasionally be for the domestic cat or for the panther. **Catskill:** a Dutch map (1656) gives Kats Kill, 'Cat's stream.'

This is generally taken to indicate a wildcat, but the possessive form suggests a personal name or nickname. On the same map the region to the west is labeled Landt van Kats Kill, and the name was thus transferred to the mountains. **Cat Mountain** AZ, CA: these are named descriptively from a configuration resembling a cat; the one in AZ is also known as **Cat Back. Cat Spring** TX: an early settler killed a wildcat at the spring. **Catfish:** the name, usually upon small water features, is evidence of early interest in this widespread and delicious, but plebeian, fish. In American-French *chat* was sometimes applied to the raccoon; hence, in translation, **Cat Island** MS, the name arising in the Iberville expedition (1699) when some raccoons were killed here.

Catacoonamug Pond MA Algonquian, probably 'big-long-fishing-place.'

Catahoula A name for several bodies of water in LA, it begins with a clipped form of Choctaw *okhata,* 'lake.' The remainder probably is 'beloved,' perhaps as a kind of general commendatory

Cataldo ID For Father Cataldo, for many years in charge of the local Sacred Heart Mission.

Catalpa Though a fairly widespread tree, conspicuous for its flowers, the catalpa has left little imprint on nomenclature, being apparently known more as an artificially planted ornamental. It occurs as a habitation-name, e.g. in AR.

Catamint See **Catamount.**

Catamount A term chiefly in use during the Colonial period (i.e. 'cat-of-the-mountain') for the panther, but sometimes probably applied to the lynx or wildcat. It is rare as a place-name, but e.g. **Catamount Hill** MA. The creek in CO is an example of an earlier term being applied in one of the later-settled areas. **Catamint Brook** RI is apparently a modification by folk-etymology after the original meaning had been forgotten.

Cataouache, Lake LA Choctaw 'lake' (Cf. **Catahoula**), and *Ouache,* a tribal name.

Cataract Occasionally used as the equivalent of waterfall or rapids, e.g. **Cataract Canyon** AZ.

Cataraqui Lake NY Iroquoian 'fort-in-water,' to denote Fort Frontenac, built by the French in the 18th century.

Cataro LA From the family-name of early landowners.

Catarpa Creek MS Muskogean 'dammed, obstructed.' Cf. **Embarrass, Driftwood.**

Catasauqua Creek PA Algonquian (Delaware) 'dry-land.'

Catatoga GA Cherokee 'new-settlement-place,' the name of a Cherokee town.

Catatonk Creek NY Probably Algonquian 'big (principal)-stream.'

Cataula GA Muskogean (Creek) 'mulberry-dead,' apparently for a landmark tree, applied first to a natural feature.

Cataumet MA Algonquian, meaning uncertain.

Catawba From the Indian tribe, or some attributive use, e.g. the Catawba grape. The catalpa tree is sometimes called catawba, and the habitation-name in MD thus arises.

Catawissa Creek PA Algonquian (Delaware), probably from the words 'becoming fat,' and involving an incident with deer.

Catching Creek OR For E. C. Catching, early settler.

Cateeche SC An alternate name of Isaqueena, a Choctaw slave-woman of the Cherokees, who revealed a plot against the English, ca. 1750.

Cathance River ME Algonquian 'principal-fork,' i.e. 'main stream.'

Cathay In CA the name is from Andrew Cathay, an early settler; elsewhere, the name is probably the equivalent of China.

Cathedral As with castles, early Americans were not familiar with cathedrals, except in books and by contact with European immigrants. The term, however, is common to describe an up-standing rock formation, especially one having a suggestion of a tower or two towers, e.g. **Cathedral Ridge** OR, **Cathedral Rock** AZ. **Cathedral City** CA, one of the rare habitation-names, is by transfer from **Cathedral Canyon.**

Cathlamet OR, WA Indian, probably the name of a now-extinct tribe.

Catholic Peak AZ So called because a large cross is discernible on it.

Catholican Springs SD An unusual adjective, used as the equivalent of *Catholic,* because of a nearby sanitarium under Catholic auspices.

Cathro MI Probably from the family name.

Cato In most instances probably for the family name, e.g. in MT, for a family of early cattle ranchers. In NY it is for one (or more) of the Roman republican heroes, one of the classical namings of 1790. **Cato, Rito el** CO: Probably a badly rendered form of Mexican Spanish *rito del gato,* 'creek of the cat.'

Catoctin MD Algonquian, probably 'speckled-mountain,' because of the occurrence of mottled rock.

Catoma Creek AL From an Indian tribal name.

Catoosa County GA Cherokee, probably 'hill, high place.'

Catskill See **Cat.**

Cattaraugus NY Iroquoian 'banks-stinking,' applied first to the creek.

Caucomgomoc, Caucomgomock Me Algonquian 'gull-lake,' in the latter form transferred to a mountain.

Caughdenoy NY Iroquoian 'eel-lying,' for a place at which eels were fished.

Cavalier ND For C. T. Cavileer, first postmaster, with altered spelling.

Cavallo A common early spelling of **Caballo,** 'horse' in Spanish.

Cavalry Commemorative or incident names from cavalry service, e.g. the springs in NB, because a troop once camped there.

Cavanal Mountain OK Uncertain, possibly from a personal name such as Cavanaugh.

Cave Appears frequently, to describe features near or associated with a cave, e.g. **Cave Creek** AZ.

Cavendish From the family name, in VT (1761) for William Cavendish, Duke of Devonshire, a close connection of Benning Wentworth, governor of New Hampshire.

Cavour SD For Count Cavour, Italian statesman (1810–1861); named in 1880.

Cawanshannock Creek PA Algonquian (Delaware) 'briar-creek-at.'

Cawcaw River SC Locally believed to be from the imitation of the call of the crow, therefore the equivalent of Crow River.

Cayadutta Creek NY Iroquoian 'stone-standing-out-of-water.'

Cayo Spanish 'island, key,' occasionally as a specific by association, e.g. **Cayo Agua Key** FL.

Cayote A variant of **Coyote,** e.g. the creek in TX.

Cayuco Spanish 'kayak, small fishing boat.'

Cayuga From the Indian tribal name.

Cayuse In OR and WA the name is usually from the Indian tribe. Elsewhere it springs from the kind of horse bred by that tribe, which later came to be merely a general term for horse.

Cayuta NY Iroquoian, meaning uncertain.

Cazadero Spanish 'hunting place.' In CA named as a railroad station, in good deer country, in the 1880's.

Cazenovia NY A Latinized form from Theophilus Cazenove, land agent, named 1795.

Cebada Spanish 'barley.'

Cebadilla Mountain AZ Spanish, probably for the wild lily so called.

Cebolla Spanish 'onion,' usually applied to natural features because of the presence of wild onions.

Cedar As a valuable and conspicuous tree, the cedar has been prolific in producing place-names. *Cedar-swamp* has become a quasi-generic. Partly because of its Biblical usage (cedar of Lebanon), *cedar* has developed commendatory usage, and is common for habitation-names, being coupled especially with *Grove* and *-ville.* In the desert areas of the West, cedar is common with *spring* and *mountain,* here referring to the juniper. In CA and OR the name refers to the so-called incense cedar. The name has also been used for other trees, e.g. the cypress. **Cedaredge** CO: because it is at the edge of a growth of cedars (junipers).

Cedro Spanish cedar.

Cee Vee TX From the C. V. Ranch.

Ceja Spanish 'summit.' **Cejita Creek** NM uses the diminutive by association.

Celeron NY Probably for J. B. Celeron de Blainville, French officer of the 17th century.

Celeryville OH Because of being a center for the growing of celery.

Celilo OR Probably from an Indian tribe, elsewhere spelled Si-le-lah.

Celina OH A variant-spelling for **Salina,** after which town in NY it was named.

Celo NC For John Celo, a hunter.

Cement On several towns the name indicates the location of a plant for making cement. On natural features, e.g. **Cement Creek** CO, it indicates either a rock from which cement may be manufactured, or a kind of rock formation thus known. **Cement Well** AZ: because the sides were cemented.

Cemetery Among other works of man, such as *bridge* and *mill,* this term also served as a landmark. Since cemeteries were often on hills, **Cemetery Hill** is common, as on the battlefield of Gettysburg. It is shunned, however, as a habitation-name.

Cemochechobee Creek GA Hichiti 'sand-big,' i.e. the equivalent of **Big Sandy Creek.**

Cenchat GA A coined name, from being the junction of two railroads, the Central of Georgia and the Chattanooga Southern.

Centenary, Centennial Given when a place was named on some one-hundred-year occasion, e.g. **Centennial Prairie** SD which was settled in 1876. **Centenary** SC: for a Methodist church, which was founded ca. 1839, i.e. on the hundredth anniversary of the founding of Methodism in England. **Centennial** WY: From a mine that was discovered in 1876.

Center, Central Coupled with various generics, these names supply well over a hundred habitation-names. The spelling is nearly always *center,* but *centre* occurs occasionally. A comparatively small number of natural features are so called, e.g. **Central Chain of Lakes** MN, which lies between East and West chains. The **Central Valley** CA is a recent usage to supply a term covering both the Sacramento and San Joaquin valleys, being more or less central to the whole state. The term is often used as a habitation-name to differentiate two or more places of the same name in one state, e.g. **Marion** and **Marion Center** PA. In NH it commonly occurs thus as the first element, e.g. **Center Conway.** **Center Lake** in SD is at the center of a state park, and another is merely at the center of four sections of land. For towns and villages the preferred forms are **Center-ville** and **Center City.** These names are spread over the whole U.S., and every state seems to have a few of them. They indicate location with respect to a state, county, or other unit of territory, though the unit is sometimes vague. The terms are also used in the sense of mid way

between two points, which are themselves of little note.

Centinela Spanish 'sentinel.'

Centrahoma OK From 'central Oklahoma.'

Centralhatchee Creek GA By folk-etymology from Muskogean (Creek) *sanda-lakwa-hachi,* 'perch (fish)-stream,' an earlier recorded form being **Sundalhatchee.**

Centralia This neo- or pseudo-Latin form, with the same suggestions as Central, has been used to prevent duplication and also with a commendatory classical purpose. **Centralia** IL was at least partially named for being on the Illinois Central Railroad.

Centre See **Center.**

Centro Spanish, 'center,' e.g. **El Centro** CA, named in 1905 to indicate that it was central in the **Imperial Valley.**

Centropolis KS, MO A Latin-Greek hybrid for 'center-city.'

Cerbat Mountains AZ Mohave 'big-horn sheep.'

Ceredo KY, WV This name was given in WV (1857) by founders who were interested in agriculture and used Ceres, the name of the Roman goddess of the fields. The last part of the name is unexplained.

Ceres, Ceresco From the name of the Roman goddess of grain and the harvest, usually given as a commendatory name for habitations, e.g. in CA. **Ceresco** MI, NB is probably from Ceres, but the relationship is uncertain.

Cerro Spanish 'hill,' together with its diminutives **Cerrito** and **Cerrillo,** is usually a generic, but occurs as a specific in **Cerro** NM, **El Cerrito** CA. **Cerro Gordo,** Spanish 'hill-fat' (i.e. round). The name was introduced into the U.S. and used without reference to its literal meaning as a commemorative of the victory at Cerro Gordo in Mexico in 1847.

Cerulean As a substitute for **Blue,** e.g. **Cerulean Springs** KY.

Ceylon For the island, probably aided by its being described in the hymn as 'where every prospect pleases,' though the next line 'and only man is vile' would have to be ignored.

Chababakongkomuk See **Chaubunagungamaug.**

Chacahoula LA Choctaw 'home (house)-beloved.' Cf. **Catahoula.**

Chacala FL Probably from the name of a chief, recorded (1735) as Chikilli.

Chaco Canyon NM The term means 'desert,' in local Spanish, but as a name is probably an adaptation of a Navajo term of uncertain meaning.

Chacon NM The family name of early settlers.

Chactimahan, Bayou LA Muskogean (Choctaw), probably 'Choctaw-town.'

Chagrin The valley in CO was named by a paleontologist who was disappointed in his expectation of finding fossils there. The river in OH is much disputed. It is probably an Iroquoian name, heavily altered, and subjected to folk-etymology, but the possibility of an incident-naming from the common English meaning of the word cannot be ruled out.

Chagum Pond RI Algonquian, meaning uncertain.

Chaika Russian 'gull,' also as **Chaichei** and **Chiachi;** thus, several features in AK.

Chaistla Butte AZ Navajo 'beaver-pocket.'

Chakpahu AZ Hopi 'little water.'

Chaland French 'barge,' used in LA for certain flat-bottomed boats; the passes (LA) were probably so named as being large enough to accommodate such boats.

Chalcedony From the mineral, e.g. the peak in AZ.

Chalco NB Probably from the town in Mexico.

Chalk From chalk or some material resembling it, e.g. **Chalk Creek** NB.

Challis ID For A. P. Challis, town founder.

Chalmette LA From the plantation, taking its name from the owner, I. Martin de Lino de Chalmette.

Chalone CA From an Indian tribal name.

Chalybeate Usually with spring(s) because of the presence of iron salts in the water.

Chama NM Spanish adaptation of an Indian (Tewa) word of uncertain meaning, perhaps 'red.' **Chama** CO: named (ca. 1860) by settlers from **Chamita** NM, the latter name being a diminutive of the original **Chama.**

Chamberino NM Either Indian or Spanish, but shaped to a Spanish form; meaning uncertain.

Chamcook River ME Algonquian 'spawning-place.'

Chamise, Chamiso, Chemise In these and other spellings the name was taken by the Spaniards from some Indian language, and refers to various bushes, though it may mean *chaparral* in general. It occurs a number of times in CA. Forms in *-al* indicate a place where the bush grows, e.g. **Chamizal Creek** NM.

Chamois MO From the name of the Swiss goatlike antelope, locally believed to have been suggested because of the 'alpine' scenery.

Champagne Creek OR From a French family name.

Champagnolle Creek AR Probably from a French personal name.

Champaign A descriptive for open and level country; applied to the county in IL and by transfer to the city.

Champepadan Creek MN Siouan 'thorny wood,' because of thorn bushes.

Champion Usually from the personal name, e.g. in OH, NB. **Champion Creek** OR: from a mine name.

Champlain, Lake Samuel de Champlain discovered this lake in 1609. The narrative states that it 'was called Lake Champlain,' thus avoiding the direct statement that Champlain named it for himself.

Champoeg OR Probably an Indian word, but not satisfactorily explained.

Champwood WV Named ca. 1912 by an incongruous coupling of the political enemies Champ Clark and Woodrow Wilson.

Chanarambie MN Siouan 'wood-hidden,' because of a grove of trees not seen from a distance.

Chance 1) From the personal name, e.g. in OK, for T. C. Chance, first postmaster. 2) From the idea of chance or luck, e.g. **Chance** (MD), probably from an early land grant. It may be a shortening from **Last Chance**, which also appears, e.g. the creek in AK.

Chancellor SD For the German statesman, Bismarck, 'The Iron Chancellor.'

Chandalar River AK An oral development from American-French *gens de large,* 'nomadic people,' a name given to the local Indians in the early 19th century by French-Canadians of the Hudson's Bay Company.

Chandeleur French 'Candlemas,' the islands in LA having been discovered on that day in 1699.

Chaney Rush Creek SD By folk-etymology from the French *chaine de roches,* 'chain of rocks.'

Changewater NJ Probably from Changewater Furnace, but ultimate origin uncertain.

Chanhassen MN From two Siouan words, coined by R. M. Nichols, 'tree-sweet juice,' to mean maple sugar.

Chankaska Creek MN Siouan 'forest-enclosed.'

Channahatchee Creek AL Muskogean (Creek) 'cedar-stream.'

Channahon IL Indian, probably Algonquian, with *hanna,* 'stream,' and the remainder uncertain.

Channel For places associated with a channel, e.g. **Channel Islands CA.**

Chantilly VA From the town and chateau in France.

Chaos Applied, rarely, to a place suggesting great confusion, such as a jumble of boulders, e.g. **Chaos Canyon** CO.

Chapanoke NC From the Indian village, recorded as Chepanoc; literal meaning uncertain. Cf. **Chippokes.**

Chaparral A Spanish word for a place where live oak grows was taken into English, to describe the thick growth of brush which is especially common on the hills of CA. It is so ubiquitous in much of that state that it has not served to distinguish one place from another, and so has not yielded specific names there. It occurs, for example, as **Chaparral Creek** OR and **Chaparral AZ. Chaparrosa** CA: a Spanish adjective, 'having chaparral.'

Chapeau French 'hat.' The lake in MN was so named because its shape was like that of an old-fashioned three-cornered hat.

Chapel The term has been in limited use in the U.S., generally to indicate something too small to be termed a church, and only a few place-names have thus resulted, e.g. **Chapel Hill NC.** In TX the name is a shortening by the railroad of the name of James Chappell, early settler.

Chappaqua NY Algonquian, meaning uncertain.

Chappaquiddick Island MA Algonquian 'separated-island-at.'

Chappaquoit MA Algonquian, 'separated-place-at,' perhaps as indicating a boundary.

Chappaquonsett Creek MA Algonquian 'separate-long-at,' probably to indicate that the creek forms a long barrier.

Chappepeela Creek LA Choctaw, 'river-hurricane,' i.e. a stream associated with the occurrence of a hurricane.

Chaptico MD Algonquian, probably 'big-broad-river-it-is.'

Chaquaqua Creek CO Indian, language and meaning uncertain.

Charco Spanish 'pool.'

Chardon From the personal name, e.g. in OH for Peter Chardon Brooks, local landowner.

Chariot Mountain CA From the Golden Chariot Mine.

Chariton IA, MO Probably from a French family name, a Jean Chariton, being recorded as an early trader in that region.

Charity Rare, probably from religious associations and usually occurring first as a church-name, e.g. **Charity Branch** KY.

Charlemont MA Named in the mid-18th century, probably for the Earl of Charlemont, who was connected by marriage with Governor Francis Bernard.

Charleroi PA Laid out in 1890 and named for the city in Belgium, because it was a glass-manufacturing center and the new town was also.

Charles From the personal name. **Cape Charles** VA: named by the colonists, ca. 1610, 'in honor of the worthy Duke of York,' i.e. the future Charles I. **Charles River** MA: prince Charles, the same as the above, when he wrote the names on John Smith's map, ca. 1615, put his own name upon this river. **Charlestown** MA: in the earliest records, it is **Charlton,** so named after one of the many places of that name in England; it was influenced by the name of its river. **Charleston** SC: named for King Charles II, in 1670, as **Charles Town:** it was probably soon pronounced as **Charleston,** and that spelling was adopted in

1783. **Charleston** WV: established in 1794 as **Charlestown,** but soon changed; it was named by the founder, George Clendenin, for his father. **Charleston** UT: for Charles Sheldon, early surveyor. **Charlestown** NH: named in 1752 for Admiral Sir Charles Knowles, a naval commander in the French wars. **Charles City** IA: for Charles Kelly, son of the town founder, thus named by the father. **Charleston Peak** NV: named (1869) by a mapping expedition for the city in SC. **Lake Charles** LA: for one of the early settlers, ca. 1780, Carlos Salia, a Spaniard, who adopted the French form of his name.

Charlevoix MI For P. F. X. de Charlevoix, French missionary and author, who visited this region, ca. 1721.

Charley Apopka Creek FL By folk-etymology from Seminole *chalo-apapka,* 'trout-eating-place.'

Charlo MT For a Flathead chief with the French name Charlot; the 't' was dropped to coincide with the pronunciation.

Charlotte The name, previously rare in England, was popularized by the marriage of George III to Charlotte Sophia in 1761, and she was honored, in the next few years, by **Charlotte Co.** VA, **Charlottesville** VA, **Charlotte** NC, and other places.

Charlton Though a common name for English villages its use in MA is for Sir Francis Charlton, member of the Privy Council at the time of naming (1755). Elsewhere it is generally from the personal name. See **Charles.**

Charmco WV From Charleston Milling Company.

Charrette Creek MO In American-French 'cart,' but the name may be from Joseph Chorette, a trader of the 18th century.

Chartee Creek AL Muskogean (Creek), probably 'red.'

Chaska MN Siouan, a name given to the first-born child, also the name of a nearby creek and lake, and probably first given to one of these for some incident.

Chaski Bay OR Klamath 'weasel,' probably so named because the weasel had mythological associations for this tribe.

Chassahowitzka River FL Seminole 'pumpkins-hanging,' because of pumpkin vines climbing on the trees.

Chataignier French 'chestnut-tree,' but in **Bayou Chataignier** LA referring to **Chinquapin,** q.v.

Chatakhospee Creek AL Muskogean (Creek) 'rock-down-deep,' the equivalent of **Rock Bluff.**

Chataw MS Probably a variant of the tribal name **Choctaw.**

Chateaugay NY Originally Chateuaga (Iroquoian of uncertain meaning), it assumed its partially French form with the settlement in the area of French Canadians in 1796.

Chatham From the town in England; in MA, 1712. In CT the town dates from 1767, and to some degree must have reflected the popularity in the colonies of William Pitt, Earl of Chatham, for whom the county in VA was named (1767), and the strait in AK (1794) by George Vancouver.

Chatlin, Bayou LA From Nicholas Chatelin, settler of the early 19th century.

Chattahoochee AL, FL, GA Muskogean (Creek) 'rocks-marked,' first applied to the river, with reference to some pictured rocks.

Chattanooga TN Creek 'rock-rising-to-a-point,' probably referring first to **Lookout Mountain.**

Chattaroy WV From a local Indian tribe.

Chatterdowen Creek CA Wintu, probably 'digger-pine.' Also as **Chattidown.**

Chattooga River AL, GA, SC Cherokee, the name of several Indian towns, literal meaning uncertain.

Chaubunagungamaug Pond MA Algonquian 'boundary-fishing-place,' being apparently at a treaty-line, either between Indian tribes or between Indians and English.

Chauga River GA, SC Probably Muskogean (Creek) 'shoal.'

Chaughtanoonda Creek NY Iroquoian 'stone-houses.' (?)

Chautauqua NY Iroquoian, with the idea that someone was lost here, based upon an incident or legend.

Chawonk Neck ME Algonquian, the equivalent of **Great Neck,** or **Big Peninsula.**

Chazy NY The river is from Lieutenant de Chezy, a French officer, killed here by the Iroquois in 1666.

Cheaha See **Chehaw.**

Cheat River WV, PA Uncertain; from a nickname or shortening of a personal name such as **Cheatham** (?).

Chebacco Lake MA Algonquian, probably 'big-pond-at,' but much transformed on English tongues.

Chebanse IL From a Potawatomi chief of the early 19th century.

Chebeague ME, NH Algonquian 'separated place,' with reference to a peninsula or to a place which was sometimes divided by high tide.

Cheboygan MI Algonquian, probably from a word used for any perforated object such as a pipe stem. **Sheboygan** is a variant.

Cheboyganing Creek MI The same as **Cheboygan** (q.v.), with *-ing* as the locative 'at.'

Checagon Lake MI Ojibway 'skunk-place.' Cf. **Chicago,** the words for *skunk* and *onion* being similar and apparently both derived from the same base, having to do with a strong smell.

Chechesee River SC Indian (Cusabo), meaning uncertain.

Checotah OK From the name of an Indian chief, usually spelled Checote.

Cheektowaga NY Iroquoian 'crabapple-place.'

Cheese Like other ordinary commodities it is rare in names. **Cheese Creek** NB: a woman formerly made cottage cheese here and sold it. **Cheese Rock** MA: named by Gov. John Winthrop (Feb. 7, 1632) who, because of the negligence of his servant, had nothing but cheese for a meal. **Cheese Cake Creek** MA: apparently the same as **Cheesequake** NJ, and **Cheesekook** NY. These names are apparently by folk-etymology from some common Algonquian name. The first syllable suggests *che-*, 'big.' An Indian named Cheesecock is recorded in the NY area, ca. 1700. In VA the former **Cheesecake Church** arose from the tribal name Chiskiack, recorded in 1612.

Chef Menteur LA French 'chief-lying,' but reference uncertain.

Chefuncte River LA Choctaw 'chinquapin.'

Chegby, Bayou LA Probably Indian (Choctaw), of uncertain meaning.

Chehalem Mountains OR From the name of an Indian subtribe.

Chehalis WA From a local Indian language, 'sand,' the river being so called from a deposit of sand at its mouth; the name of the river was transferred to the tribe of Indians and to the city.

Chehaw, Chehawhaw AL, SC From an Indian tribal name, also appearing as **Cheaha.**

Chehockset NH Algonquian 'big-grove-at.'

Chelachie Creek WA A local Indian name, applied to the stream since 1853, meaning uncertain.

Chelan WA A local Indian name for the stream, recorded ca. 1810, 'bubbling water' (?).

Chelly, Canyon de AZ The *de Chelly* represents Navajo, *tséyi*, 'among the cliffs.' The name was transmitted through the Spanish, who spelled it in Spanish fashion, and partly changed it by folk-etymology. Americans further transformed the pronunciation, apparently assuming that it was of French origin. Current pronunciation is approximately *d'shay*. A museum-piece of a name!

Chelmsford In MA (1653) from a town in England.

Chelsea The name of a London district was applied to a town in MA in 1739, and has thence spread to other places.

Cheltenham From the town in England.

Chelyan WV For Chelyan Calvert, daughter of the first postmaster.

Chemehuevi From the Indian tribal name.

Chemin a Haut AR As a stream-name this appears to be French, with *chemin*, 'road,' and *haut*, high, but the use of an adjective following 'a' can hardly be French, and the name may represent an attempt at reconstruction by someone not familiar with that language. The earlier spellings, 'Tchemanahaut' and 'Chemanohow,' suggest Indian origin, but translations are uncertain.

Chemise See **Chamise**

Chemo Lake ME Algonquian 'big-bog,' transferred from the bog at the outlet to the lake itself *via* a popular song of 1871.

Chemquassabamticook Stream ME Algonquian 'big-lake-with-river-at.'

Chemult OR From the name of a Klamath chief.

Chemung NY, PA Algonquian 'big-horn,' from the finding in early times of what was probably an elephant tusk.

Chena River AK Athapascan, with *-na*, 'river,' and the rest uncertain.

Chenach Creek CA Indian (Karok), a term indicating the area around a stream-mouth.

Chenail See **Chenal.**

Chenal, Chenail American-French 'channel.' The proper plural would be *chenaux,* but **Les Cheneaux Islands** MI show a slightly altered form, being so named because of the many narrow channels among them. See also **Sni.**

Chenango NY Iroquoian 'bull-thistles.'

Chene French *chêne,* 'oak.'

Cheneaux See **Chenal.**

Chene-Fleur American-French, 'mistletoe,' e.g. the bayou in LA.

Chenequa WI The lake was named, ca. 1840, by I. A. Lapham, for what he believed to be the 'Indian' word for 'pine,' because of a few pines growing there; the source of his information is unknown and the language is uncertain.

Cheneyhatchee Creek AL Muskogean (Creek) 'cedar-stream,' but with the first part affected by folk-etymology and appearing in the form of an English personal name.

Chengwatana MN Ojibway 'pine village,' originally the name of an Indian village.

Cheniere French 'oak-grove,' e.g. the bayou in LA. In American-French the term has attained the meaning 'ridge,' e.g. **Cheniere Bois Connie.**

Cheningo NY Iroquoian 'bull-thistles,' a variant of **Chenango.**

Chenoa In IL it is an Indian name, probably Cherokee, given by the town founder in 1856 because of sentimental feelings for that name as used in KY; it may be the same as **Cheoah.** The present **Chenoa** in KY is from W. A. Chenoa, owner of a local coal company.

Chenowee KY, TN Probably Cherokee, meaning uncertain.

Chenunda Creek NY Iroquoian 'by-hill.'

Cheoah NC Occurring in various spellings (cf. **Chenoa**), it is the name of several Cherokee villages, probably 'otter-place.'

Cheops Pyramid AZ See **Brahma.**

Chepachague, Chepachet, Chepachewag Algonquian 'chief-turning-place.' See **Pachaug.**

Chequamegon WI Ojibway, probably with reference to the present point, and referring to a narrow strip of land reaching out into water, but exact meaning much disputed.

Cheque American-French 'wild-plum,' e.g. the bayou in LA.

Chequest Creek IA The form **Jake West** occurs on some maps, and the present name is probably the result of that name being passed down by oral tradition and misspelled, perhaps on the assumption that it was of Indian origin.

Cher Ami, Bayou LA From the French family name, Cherami (literally 'dear friend').

Cheraw From the Indian tribal name.

Chernabura Island AK From Russian *chernoburie,* 'black-brown.'

Cherokee From the Indian tribal name. In WY several names result from the Cherokee Trail, a route established by Cherokee participants in the 1849 gold rush.

Cherry The wild cherry, a conspicuous and valued tree, is responsible for most of the names, since the cultivation of cherries has rarely dominated an area. Popularly, many small trees and shrubs are called cherries, though they are not really such. In CA, where there is no true cherry growing wild, some twenty places have been so named. **Cherry Tree,** Indiana Co., PA: for a single tree that at one time helped mark the boundary between Indian and English territory. In arid areas the reference is usually to the so-called chokecherry.

Chesaning MI Algonquian 'big-rock-at,' for a large mass of rock, now blasted away and used for lime.

Chesapeake Bay First recorded (1585), in an English context, as **Chesepiooc;** in 1608 as **Chesapeak.** The English first knew it as the name of a village, and later transferred this name to the bay. General agreement exists that *che-* is Algonquian, 'big,' but the rest of the name has occasioned argument. On the evidence of the early recorded forms it seems to be *che-sipi-oc,* 'big-river-at.' The village (or tribe) would thus be reasonably named because of its location on a large river.

Cheshire From the county in England.

Chesnee SC From the personal name more commonly spelled Chesney; the family held land grants here in the 18th century.

Chester From the town and county in England. The county (hence, the city) in PA was named in 1682, many of its inhabitants having come from that county in England. There are ca. 30 later-named towns, some of them from personal names. **Chester** TX: for Chester A. Arthur, then senator; later, president.

Chesterfield The name in MA, NH, and SC is from the title, Earl of Chesterfield, in all these cases probably honoring the 4th earl (1694–1773), important in English politics. **Chesterfield** ID: for Chester Call, a local pioneer.

Chestnut The American chestnut was prized for beauty, wood, and nuts, and gave its name to many natural features over most of the NE. These names survived the disappearance of the tree itself because of blight in the early 20th century. Because the tree grew in the uplands, it is most commonly coupled with such generics as *hill* and *ridge.* Habitation-names are by transfer. It occurs rarely as a family name; hence **Chestnut** MT for Col. J. D. Chestnut, an early army officer.

Chesuncook ME Algonquian 'principal-outlet-at.'

Chetambe Creek MN Siouan 'hawk.'

Chetaslina River AK Athapascan 'marmot-river.'

Chetco River OR From the name of an Indian tribe that lived along the stream.

Chetek WI For an Ojibway chief, well-known locally.

Chetlo, Lake OR Chinook jargon 'oyster,' named because of shape.

Chetopa KS For an Osage chief, who held a commission in the U.S. Army during the Civil War.

Cheviot From the hills on the English-Scottish border; in WA a railroad name, described by an official as 'a chance selection.'

Chevreau, Bayou LA Probably a spelling-after-the-pronunciation of **Chevreuil,** 'deer.'

Chevrette French 'doe,' e.g. probably the bayou in LA, though the term also may mean 'shrimp.'

Chevreuil French 'deer,' e.g. **Bayou Chevreuil** LA.

Chevrolet KY After several names had been rejected by the P.O. Department, a mail carrier bestowed the name of his car.

Chewacia Creek AL A shortening of an earlier Muskogean name, 'raccoon-town-stream.'

Chewalla Creek MS Choctaw 'cedar.' The creek in AL is probably of the same meaning, but derived from some other Muskogean dialect.

Chewaucan Marsh OR Klamath 'potato-place.' The reference is to the edible arrowhead.

Chewelah WA Indian (Spokane?), referring to a kind of snake.

Chewiliken Creek WA For a local Indian chief of that name.

Chewonki Neck ME Algonquian 'big-ridge.'

Cheyava Falls AZ Hopi 'intermittent,' but named by Elsworth Kolb in 1903, and so not a true Indian name.

Cheyenne From the Indian tribal name.

Chiapuk AZ Papago 'spring.'

Chiavara Point AZ From the personal name of a Maricopa chief.

Chiawulitak AZ Papago 'barrel-cactus-sits.'

Chicago Recorded (1688) in a French context as Chigagou: Algonquian 'onion-place,' specifically stated at that time as being from the amount of wild onion or garlic growing in the meadow there. The name was soon transferred to the river, and became the name of the city in 1830. In spite of the importance of the city the name has not been popular, but CA has Chicago Park and Port Chicago. See Checagou.

Chicamacomico River MD Algonquian, probably 'big-water-town.'

Chicamuxen MD Algonquian, meaning uncertain.

Chicarica CO, NM From a Comanche term, probably 'spotted-bird,' because of the presence of some kind of bird, shaped by folk-etymology to the semblance of a Spanish word which might be taken as 'little-rich-girl.' See Sugarite.

Chichagof Island AK Named (1805) for Admiral V. Y. Chichagof of the Russian navy.

Chickahominy VA From an Indian tribal name, recorded in the earliest colonial documents.

Chickalah AR For an Indian of the 19th century, noted as an orator, his name being more commonly Chi-kil-leh.

Chickaloon AK From an Athapascan name, meaning uncertain.

Chickamauga GA, TN The creek took the name of a Cherokee town and sub-tribe, literal meaning uncertain.

Chickaming MI Algonquian 'big-lake-at.'

Chickaree For a common tree squirrel of the Western mountains, e.g. Chicka-ree Lake CO.

Chickasanoxie Creek AL Probably Muskogean (Creek) 'cane-ridge,' but with the first part shifted by analogy to the tribal name, Chickasaw.

Chickasaw From the Indian tribal name; also, e.g. in OK, as Chickasha.

Chickasawhatchee Creek GA Probably Hichiti 'house-is-there-stream,' with reference to a council house, attracted by American folk-etymology to the name of the well-known Chickasaw tribe.

Chickasawhay River MS Shaped to the form of the name of an important tribe from a name preserved in French context (1732) as Tchikahaé.

Chickawaukee Lake ME Not a local Indian name, but introduced in the 19th century; it appears to be Algonquian of one of the Middle-Western dialects, but is, in fact, suspiciously like a blend of Chicago and Milwaukee.

Chicken Usually from the personal name, e.g. the creek in SC. In the plains states it is for the game bird, the so-called prairie chicken. In rare instances it may indicate (e.g. possibly Chicken Creek in SD) a place where domestic fowls were kept in early times. The term occurs also in some rural derogatory names, e.g. Chicken Bristle KY, 'bristle' here being of uncertain meaning, perhaps to be connected with 'gristle.' In AK, with reference to the ptarmigan, it is a repeated name.

Chickenbone Lake MI From its shape, which is like that of the wishbone of a chicken.

Chickhansink Creek PA Algonquian (Delaware) 'robbery-(place)-at,' apparently an incident name.

Chickisalunga Creek PA Algonquian (Delaware), probably, 'holes-(of)-crayfish.'

Chickwolnepy Stream NH Algonquian 'frog-pond.'

Chico Spanish 'small,' also a personal name. Chico CA: from Rancho Chico, itself from Arroyo Chico, 'stream-little.' The meaning was ignored at the naming, though terms indicating smallness are not popular for habitations. Towns in OR and TX were named from the one in CA. **Chico Martinez Creek** CA: for a famous horseman ('Little Martinez') of the Mexican period, probably commemorating an incident.

Chicog WI Algonquian, with reference to a strong smell, e.g. from onions or skunks.

Chicone Creek MD Algonquian, meaning uncertain.

Chicopa MS Choctaw, 'plume' (?).

Chicopee MA Algonquian 'swift water' (?).

Chicora Of unknown meaning, but probably a tribal name. The name used by Spanish voyagers (1521) for a vague and uncertain region along what is now the coast of the Carolinas; it has been revived for a few habitation-names of that area.

Chicorica See **Chicarica.**

Chicosa CO Spanish 'having-chico' (a variety of mesquite).

Chicot AR French 'stump, snag'; since snags were important obstructions to navigation a stream could be reasonably so named, and the name was first thus applied.

Chicota TX Named for **Checotah** OK, with a spelling after the pronunciation.

Chidester AR From a family name, not further identified.

Chief Commonly with reference to an Indian chief, e.g. **Chief Lake** MN for the Ojibway, May-sha-ke-ge-shig. The naming is often more specific, e.g. **Chief Joseph Mountain** OR, for the famous Nez Perce leader. **Chief Mountain** MT: for John Rowand, a chief factor of the Hudson's Bay Co. **Chiefland** FL: by local story, because a Creek chief had a farm here in the mid-19th century.

Chien French 'dog.' **Prairie Du Chien** WI 'of the dog,' but from the name of the Sauk chief of a village when the French first arrived in that region.

Pointe au Chien LA: literally, 'point of the dog,' but probably originating from French *chêne,* 'oak,' and hence 'point of the oak-tree.'

Chigmit Mountains AK Athapascan, meaning uncertain.

Chihuahua Creek CA Named retrospectively by a Mexican recluse for his native state in Mexico.

Chikaskia River KS, OK Indian, probably Osage, with *skia* for 'salt, white,' and the rest uncertain.

Chilao CA Originally Chileo, a nickname for José Gonzales, who killed a grizzly bear with a hunting knife; from the episode he was given a name, apparently derived from *chile,* and thus meaning 'hot stuff.'

Chilatchee Creek AL Probably Choctaw 'fox-stream.'

Chilchinbito AZ Navajo 'sumac-water.'

Chileno Spanish for a native of Chile, usually applied because such a person lived at the place.

Chiles From the personal name, e.g. the valley in CA for J. B. Chiles, who held a Mexican land grant there.

Chilhowee, Chilhowie Originally of TN, the name of an important Cherokee town; meaning doubtful, but perhaps connected with *tsula,* 'kingfisher.'

Chili An older spelling of Chile, like many such names applied in the early 19th century for little apparent reason. **Chili Gulch** GA: because Chileans worked the gold mines here.

Chilicotal Mountain TX Spanish 'chili-cote-thicket,' from a shrub so called.

Chilili NM Indian, the name of a village, meaning unknown, an ancient name recorded by the Spaniards as early as 1581.

Chilipin Creek TX From *chiltipiquin,* the Spanish rendering of a local Indian name for a native pepper. Also **Chiltipin Creek** TX.

Chiliwist Creek WA From the personal name of an Indian who lived there.

Chilkoot, Chilkat AK From an Indian tribal name.

Chillicothe From an Indian tribal name, also applied to the villages where that tribe lived. The original application in OH (ca. 1795) was transferred to IL and MO; from MO it was transferred to TX.

Chillisquaque PA Algonquian (Delaware), probably 'snowbirds-place.'

Chillocahatchee Creek FL Seminole 'horse-creek'.

Chilly ID By local story, named on a chilly evening. So also, probably, **Chilly Buttes** ID.

Chilmark MA From a place in England (ca. 1671).

Chilocco OK Probably Muskogean, 'deer-big' (?).

Chiloquin OR From the name of a Klamath chief.

Chiltipin See **Chilipin.**

Chilton Commonly a family name, e.g. in TX for L. B. Chilton, first storekeeper. In WI a shortening of the English place-name, Chillington, by error of the county clerk.

Chimacum WA From an Indian tribal name.

Chimayo NM Spanish adaptation of an Indian (Tewa) term, roughly 'good obsidian,' that being an important material for making arrowheads.

Chiminea Spanish 'chimney,' but often in the sense of a kind of rock or outcropping, e.g. the mountain in AZ.

Chimmenticook ME Algonquian 'principal-islands-in-river-at.'

Chimney Usually a descriptive because of a pillarlike formation resembling a chimney, e.g. **Chimney Rock** NB, an early landmark. Other uses of the word may be involved, e.g. 1) an ore-body of special shape, 2) a chimney in the mountain-climber's sense. **Chimney Rock, Modoc Co., CA:** an early settler constructed a fireplace and chimney against this rock.

China, Chinese Generally from association, especially in western states, e.g. **China Creek** OR, WA where Chinese worked for gold. **Chinese Camp** CA: a Chinese settlement during the gold rush. **China Cap, China Hat,** peaks or buttes in OR descriptively named from resemblance to the headgear of early Chinese miners. **China Slide** CA: Chinese worked mines here, and a disastrous slide occurred on Chinese New Years Day in 1890. In the South, e.g. NC, TX, the name is for the china tree, or chinaberry tree, planted for shade. **China** ME: in 1818 the name was adopted, by local story, because of the hymn tune, but many places received foreign names in this period for no special reason. **Chinese Wall** WY: a rock formation taken to resemble the great wall of China.

Chinadere Mountain OR For a chief of the Wascos.

Chinati TX Probably Indian, locally believed to mean 'blackbird,' but apparently derived from the name of a local Indian chief.

Chinchalo OR From the name of a Klamath chief.

Chinchonte Arroyo NM From Spanish *sinsonte,* 'mockingbird,' altered either in Spanish or American times.

Chinchuba Creek LA Choctaw 'alligator.'

Chincopin Brook NJ Probably a variant of **Chinquapin.**

Chincoteague Bay MD, VA Algonquian probably 'big-stream.'

Chindeclamoose Run PA Algonquian (Delaware) 'cleared-fields.' See **Clearfield.**

Chinde Mesa AZ Navajo 'haunted,' because of an incident when some Indians were alarmed over an apparently dead man whom they took for a ghost; the geologists who were present then used the name.

Chinese See **China.**

Chingarora Creek NJ Algonquian, meaning uncertain.

Chiniak Aleut, probably to indicate a place of rough and dangerous sea, the name of two capes in AK.

Chinkapin See **Chinquapin.**

Chinle, Chin Lee AZ Navajo 'at canyon-mouth,' being at the opening of Canyon de Chelly.

Chino Spanish of various applications, meaning 'curly,' 'Chinese,' or 'man of mixed blood.' In AZ the name was applied to a valley because of a curly type of grass so called. In CA the name probably arises from the residence there in Spanish times of a person of mixed blood.

Chinook 1) From the tribal name, e.g. as a habitation-name in WA. 2) From the Chinook wind, a much beloved phenomenon in certain areas, thus arising some names in MT.

Chinquapin From the species of chestnut or oak thus known, mostly in the SE, e.g. as a habitation name in NC. Small and bushlike, the tree is generally unimportant, and names are not numerous.

Chipco Lake FL From Chipko, a prominent chief of the early 19th century.

Chipmunk For the small squirrel of the Western mountains, e.g. **Chipmunk Lake** CO.

Chipola River AL, FL Muskogean 'on-other-side-of-stream' (?). In LA, a transfer from FL.

Chippenaze Lake WI Algonquian (Ojibway), meaning uncertain.

Chippenhook VT Probably Algonquian 'big-run-of-water-at' (?).

Chippewa From the Indian tribal name.

Chippokes Creek (Lower, Upper) VA Probably from an Indian chief, recorded (1609) as Chopoke.

Chipuxet River RI Algonquian 'little-separated-place' (?).

Chipwanic Creek IN Algonquian, probably 'ghost-hole,' but reference uncertain.

Chiquito The diminutive of Spanish *chico;* therefore, 'very small,' e.g. **Chiquito Creek** CA. **Chiquita,** the feminine, is often a nickname of girls, the name-cluster in Rocky Mountain N.P., CO being from a novel of that title by Merrill Tileston (1902). See **Tileston.**

Chiricahua From the tribal name, but the term means 'mountain-big' in Apache, and as applied to the mountains may be considered a descriptive, from which the tribe was secondarily named.

Chirikof Island AK Eskimo, meaning uncertain.

Chirpchatta Creek CA Wintu 'cottonwood-valley.'

Chisago Lake MN A shortening from Ojibway *kichi-sago,* 'large-beautiful,' a coinage by Americans.

Chisana River AK Athapascan 'red-river.'

Chisca AL Muskogean, probably the name of an Indian town.

Chisholm From the personal name, e.g. **Chisholm Creek** KS. Jesse Chisholm, scout and trader, established the Chisholm Trail.

Chisos TX From the Indian tribal name.

Chispa Spanish 'spark, particle,' but in place-names usually 'nugget (of gold).'

Chistochina AK Athapascan 'marmot (?)-river.'

Chitanana River AK Athapascan 'red-lands-river.'

Chitina AK Athapascan 'copper-river.'

Chittamo WI Ojibway 'squirrel.'

Chittenango NY Iroquoian, meaning uncertain.

Chivato Mountains NM Spanish 'little he-goat.'

Chloride From that mineral, usually (AZ, NM) from silver-chloride, an important ore.

Choccolocco AL Muskogean (Creek) 'shoal-big.'

Choccolotta Bay AL A recent name, probably an adaptation of the older name **Chacaloochee** (Choctaw 'cypress-tree-little'), and with the analogy of **Choccolocco.**

Chochichok Falls NH Algonquian 'swift-current-at' (?).

Chockalaug River RI Algonquian 'fox-place' (?). So also, **Chockalog Pond** MA.

Chockie OK Formerly Chickiechockie, for twin daughters of Charles LeFlore, a Choctaw married to a Chickasaw wife; the twins were named from the tribal names. The name of the village, proving too long was simplified in 1904.

Chocktoot Creek OR For a Paiute or Shoshone chief.

Chocolate A rare descriptive as the equivalent of brown, e.g. the mountains in AZ. In TX it is by Spanish folk-etymology from a local Indian name for the same plant which is also known as *chiltipiquin.* See **Chilipin.**

Chocoloskee FL Seminole-Creek 'house-old.'

Choconot Creek PA, NY Iroquoian, meaning uncertain.

Chocorua NH Algonquian, from the name of a chief.

Chocowinity NC Originally applied to the stream, probably Algonquian, meaning uncertain.

Choctaw From the Indian tribal name.

Choctawhatchee River AL The second element (*hatchee*) represents the common Muskogean term for 'stream.' The remainder was probably, originally, Chatot, for a Muskogean tribe, but the name of the better-known tribe has been substituted.

Choice TX Because an early settler considered it to be a choice place.

Chokee Creek GA Shortened from a recorded **Chokeefichickee,** meaning uncertain, but probably Muskogean (Creek).

Chokeeliga Creek GA Muskogean (Creek) 'house-there,' with reference to a council house.

Chokio MN Siouan 'middle.'

Chokoloskee FL Seminole 'house-old.'

Chokup Pass NV For a local Indian chief of the mid-19th century.

Cholla, Choya Though various meanings are possible in Spanish, the name, e.g. in AZ and CA, is for the occurrence of cholla cactus.

Chopawamsic Creek VA Algonquian 'separation-(of)-outlet-at' (?), possibly for a stream-mouth with an island in its middle.

Chopmist RI Algonquian, probably 'boundary.'

Choppee From an Indian tribal name.

Choptank DE, MD, VA From an Indian tribal name; but possibly going back to a geographical term such as, roughly, 'tidal-stream.'

Choptie Prairie OR From a Klamath word, 'hidden,' a descriptive.

Chorro Spanish 'rapids' (in a stream), e.g. **Chorro Creek** CA.

Chosen FL In the 19th century a group of religious colonists (Dunkards) gave the name because it was their 'chosen' home.

Chouck's Hill NY From the name of an 18th-century Indian, recorded as **Chouckhass.**

Choukai Wash NM Navajo 'white spruce.'

Choulic AZ Papago 'corner.'

Choupique Applied to swamps and bayous in LA, it is American-French 'mudfish,' but is probably from an Indian (Muskogean ?) word 'muddy,' and in some instances to be taken in this meaning; sometimes, by folk-etymology, rendered by Americans as **Shoe-Peg.**

Chowan The river and county in NC are from a name recorded as that of 'a great town called Chawanook' by Amadas and Barlowe in 1584. It was probably also the name of a tribe, and has been doubtfully translated as Algonquian 'southern people.'

Chowchilla CA From an Indian tribal name.

Christian Regularly from the personal name, e.g. **Pass Cristian** MS, probably from a member of Iberville's exploring party (1699). **Christian County** KY: for Col. William Christian, Revolutionary soldier, killed by Indians in KY in 1786. **Christiansburg** VA is for the same man, and the town in OH is named for that in VA.

Christiana From the personal name; in DE, an adaptation in the English period from the Swedish **Christina.**

Christiann Creek MI Named by an early missionary for his wife, Christiana, and later altered in pronunciation and then in spelling.

Christina From the personal name. **Christina River** DE took its name from the fort which was built by Swedish colonists (1638), and named in honor of the Swedish queen.

Christmas Generally for an association with Dec. 25. **Christmas Creek** OR: some sheepmen took their flock here on Christmas Day, 1888. **Christmas Lake** OR: Frémont reached a lake on Dec. 24, 1843, and named it for the season; it is now Hart Lake, but another lake, probably by false association, is now known by the name. **Christmas** AZ: a miner, on Christmas Day, 1902, discovered that his claim had been confirmed. In MN the lake is named from W. Christmas, a surveyor. **Christmas Branch** GA: named on Dec. 25, 1825, by a surveyor who reached that stream on that day. **Christmas** FL: because a military post was established here on Dec. 25, 1837.

Chromo CO From the Greek word for 'color,' because of colored rocks in the vicinity.

Chual, Chualar The Costanoan *chual* means the plant commonly called pigweed. **Chualar** is apparently a Spanish adaptation, 'place where *chual* grows.'

Chuar Butte AZ The shortening of Chuaroompek, the personal name of a Kaibab Indian.

Chub From the presence of the fish, e.g. **Chub Lake** MN.

Chubbehatchee Creek AL Muskogean (Creek) 'halfway-stream,' altered from an earlier **Hatchee Chubbee,** apparently to distinguish it from the existing **Hatchechubbee.**

Chubby Creek MS Probably Creek 'halfway.'

Chucareto Creek TX Probably American-Spanish 'little plantation.'

Chuccocharts Hammock FL Seminole 'house-red.'

Chuchupate CA From an undetermined Indian language, referring to a plant, probably arrowhead or balsamroot.

Chuck 1) From the American nickname for Charles, e.g. **Chuck Lake** AK for Charles Forward, U.S. Forest Service, named in 1952. 2) From the common abbreviation of **Woodchuck,** e.g. **Chuck Pass** CA. 3) From the Americanism for 'food,' e.g. **Chuck Box Lake** AZ, because in the 1880's some cowboys abandoned a chuck box here. 4) From Chinook jargon, 'water,' hence probably in part **Chuckanut Bay** WA; so also **Chuck Creek** AK, **Salt Chuck** AK.

Chuckatuck VA Algonquian, with *tuck* probably 'tidal-stream,' and the rest uncertain.

Chuckawalla See **Chuckwalla.**

Chuckey TN Probably a shortening of an Indian (Cherokee) name, such as **Nolichocky.**

Chuckfee Bay AL Choctaw 'rabbit.'

Chuckney Mountain OR From the name of a local Indian.

Chuckwalla, Chuckawalla From the desert lizard thus known, e.g. **Chuckwalla Canyon** NV, **Chuckawalla Mountains** CA.

Chuctenunda Creek NY Iroquoian, probably 'rock-shelters,' from overhanging cliffs.

Chug In WY the term occurs in **Chug Springs** and **Chugwater River.** It is probably of Indian origin, usually supposed to be a translation, though the stories told in explanation are not acceptable. A form Chuguata for the river suggests an origin by folk-etymology, but is so late (1872) that it may be of secondary origin.

Chugach AK From an Eskimo tribal name.

Chugnut See **Choconut.**

Chugwater See **Chug.**

Chuichu AZ Pima 'caves.'

Chuili Shaik AZ Papago 'willow thicket.'

Chui Vaya AZ Papago 'cave well.'

Chukchi Sea AK From the name of the people inhabiting the most easterly portion of Siberia, and thus bordering on the western shore of this sea.

Chula In regions of Muskogean background, e.g. LA, AR, GA, it is probably from Muskogean 'fox,' also used as a tribal name. Cf. **Chulo. Chulo Homa** MS: Choctaw 'fox-red.'

Chulafinee Creek AL Muskogean (Creek) 'pine-footlog,' probably for a primitive bridge.

Chulitna AK Athapascan, with *-na* 'river'; otherwise, uncertain.

Chulo American-Spanish 'pretty,' more commonly in the feminine, e.g. **Chula Vista** CA, and probably **Chula** as a habitation-name in several states. Cf. **Chula.**

Chuluota FL Probably Seminole 'fox-den.'

Chumash Peak CA From an Indian tribal name.

Chunchula AL Probably Muskogean; 'alligator' (?).

Chunky Creek MS By folk-etymology from a Choctaw word for one of their games, probably because a place for playing the game was there.

Chunnenuggee AL Muskogean (Creek) 'long ridge.'

Chupadera American-Spanish 'sinkhole,' e.g. the creek in NM, but with possible reference to a sucking insect, such as a tick.

Chupedero Mexican-Spanish 'tippler, hard drinker,' on **Chupederos Creek** TX probably an incident-name.

Church The term may almost be considered a place-name generic, since in early times the establishment of a church also established a point of geographical reference. Many present-day towns and villages bear names which were originally those of churches. In PA there are **Brickchurch, Derry Church, Kellers Church, Spring Church, Stone Church.** The name has also been used to denote natural features associated with a church, e.g. **Church Hill,** which is a common name, since churches were often thus located. The influence of the personal names **Church** and **Churchhill,** however, is important, e.g. **Church Creek** CA for the first family to settle there. The term occurs, rarely, as a descriptive, i.e. something resembling a church, e.g. **Church Butte** MT, **Church Buttes** WY. **Mount Churchill** AK, **Churchill Peaks**

AK: named (1965) for Winston Churchill, British statesman, after his death in that year.

Churn Creek CA From a pothole in the rock suggesting a churn, an idea probably reinforced by the motion of the water.

Churubusco For the American victory in the Mexican War.

Chuska, Chusca AZ, NM Probably from the Navajo word for white spruce.

Chute French 'waterfall, cataract,' e.g. **Little Chute** WI from the French name, **Riviere des Chutes,** of the **Fox River.** See **Deschutes.**

Chutum Vaya AZ Papago 'bear (animal) well (spring).'

Cibecue Creek AZ Apache 'reddish bottom-land.'

Cibola, Cibolo From Spanish *cibola,* itself borrowed from some Indian language, meaning 'buffalo.' Perhaps from another source the early Spaniards used it to refer to the legendary Seven Cities of Cibola, and the name was applied widely and vaguely to the whole region of the southern Great Plains during the Spanish period of dominance in the region. It survives in TX as **Cibolo** on three streams and a town and, as **Cibola,** stands on some features in AZ.

Cicero From the Roman statesman, in NY being a part of the classical naming of 1790; in IL probably a transfer from NY.

Cid NC The name of the Spanish epic hero, but more immediately derived from the nickname of Sidney Muffley, local superintendent of mines.

Ciego Spanish 'blind,' e.g. **Boca Ciega** FL, probably in the sense of leading nowhere.

Cienaga Spanish 'marsh, miry place,' used also for a 'wet meadow,' occurring as a specific to denote a place marked thus, e.g. as a habitation-name in NM, and as **Cienaga Creek** CA. **Cieneguilla** is the diminutive. See **Seneca.**

Ciervo Spanish 'elk.'

Cima Spanish 'summit.'

Cimarron Spanish 'wild,' but regularly in the Mexican meaning of 'wild sheep,' i.e. bighorn, e.g. **Cimarron Mountains** AZ. So also, probably, the river in NM, OK.

Cinch Hook Butte AZ From the shape, as shown on the topographical map.

Cincinnati In OH named by General Arthur St. Clair in 1790 in honor of the recently formed Society of the Cincinnati, which had been named for the farmer-soldier hero of early Rome. In IA the name is transferred from OH. See **Losantville.**

Cincinnatus NY For the Roman hero, given as a part of the classical naming of 1790.

Cinco WV Named by a company official who was fond of Cinco cigars.

Cinderella WV From a trademark of a coal company, picturing Cinderella sitting before a blazing fire.

Cinnabar From the presence, or supposed presence, of that red ore of mercury, e.g. the mountain in MT, which is actually colored red by iron ore.

Cinnaminson NJ Algonquian, a much-altered form, 'stone-tree' (?), i.e. sugar-maple.

Cinnamon A descriptive from the color of the rock, e.g. **Cinnamon Butte** OR, **Cinnamon Mountain** CO; in some instances the name is probably from the so-called cinnamon bear.

Cinq Hommes, Cape MO French 'cape-five-men,' but arising by folk-etymology among speakers of French from the personal name of Father St. Cosme who was in the area in 1698.

Cipole OR In an onion-growing district, this represents an Americanization of the Italian *cipolla,* 'onion.'

Cipres Spanish 'cypress.'

Circle The village in AK is so called for being almost at the Arctic Circle. **Circleville** WV is an adaptation of the family name Zirkle. **Circle Bar** OR, **Circle Back** TX are brand names. **Circleville** OH: the town was laid out (1810) on the site of some ancient Indian earthworks, one of which was circular.

Cirque From association with a cirque, e.g. the mountain in CA.

Cirrus, Mount CO Four mountains were given the names of clouds (1914–1921), probably an indication of a dearth of names rather than of any appropriateness; thus, **Mt. Cumulus, Mt. Nimbus,** and **Mt. Stratus.**

Ciruela Spanish 'plum, wild plum.'

Cisco 1) From a personal name, e.g. in CA and TX, for J. J. Cisco, prominent railroad promoter of the 1860's. 2) Algonquian, from the name of a fish (probably the same as **Siskowit**), e.g. the village in IL, the lake in MI, and the river in WI.

Citico AL, TN From the name of a Cherokee town; literal meaning unknown.

Citimon, Bayou LA Muskogean (Choctaw) 'deer-village.'

Citra In FL it was selected as a commendatory (1882) by a committee, because of a developing citrus culture. In OK it is Latin 'on this side,' because of its situation in the Choctaw Nation.

Citronelle In AL, for the citronella grass which is common in the vicinity. In FL, probably another commendatory from **Citrus.**

Citrus, Citro, Citrona Interest in the raising of citrus fruits has given rise to some commendatory names.

City Occasionally as a specific to indicate association with a city, especially as **City Point** in several states. **City of Rocks:** a repeated name, e.g. ID, NM, for places where many large rocks give the impression of a city.

Clackamas River OR From the name of an Indian tribe living along the stream.

Clair(e) French 'clear,' usually with reference to water, e.g. **Eau Claire.**

Clallam WA From an Indian tribal name.

Clam Less prized than the oyster, the clam has furnished names for a few seacoast features, e.g. **Clam Island** CT, NJ, and to some of freshwater, e.g. **Clam Lake** WI, a few of which have been applied to habitations.

Clan Alpine Mountains NV From a mine-name, the name being familiar from Walter Scott's *Lady of the Lake.*

Claremont, Clermont, Clairmont Some twenty examples arise chiefly from a vaguely commendatory quality of the suggestion 'clear mountain.' Fulton's first steamboat, the *Clermont,* gave some vogue to that spelling. The personal name Clare is also involved. The name occurs in England, and the town in NH is probably named for an English estate.

Claremore OK From **Claremore Mound,** named for a Kiowa chief, Grah-mah, whose name was made over by folk-etymology into a French Clairmont, and finally into its English form.

Clarendon In SC for the first Earl of Clarendon, (1609–1674). In VT for one of the later earls. In PA for Thomas Clarendon, local businessman.

Clarion The river in PA was named by surveyors who thought that its distant sound had the 'silvery mellowness' of a clarion. The county and town were named from the stream, and the town in IA from that in PA.

Clark From the personal name. **Clark Fork** MT, **Clark Co.** MO For Capt. William Clark of the Lewis and Clark expedition. **Clark** TX: selected by the Post Office Dept. from a list of names submitted—'no significance whatever.'

Clarke From the personal name. The county in WA is named for Capt. William Clark (see **Clark**), with the name misspelled by ignorance or error.

Clarkia ID For William Clark of the Lewis and Clark expedition, with a Latin ending for differentiation from other places named **Clark.**

Clarnie OR Probably from Clara and Jennie, daughters of two railroad men, who coined the name.

Clarno OR For Andrew Clarno, one of the earliest settlers.

Classic The town in WA was named (1911) by its founder who sought a name to mean 'beautiful, well-located.' **Classic Ridge** OR: named by its founder, who hoped to have a community devoted to the arts.

Clatskanie River, Klaskanine River OR From the Indian tribe officially known as Tlats-kani.

Claudell NM From the combined names of Claude D. Wells, first postmaster.

Claverack NY From 17th-century Dutch *klaver rack*, 'clover-reach,' with reference to a straight stretch of the river, probably from a personal name Klaver.

Claxtar OR A form of **Clatskanie.**

Clay Much rarer than *sand* or *mud* with natural features. With streams it indicates the nature of the banks, and **Clay Bank** appears. With habitation-names Henry Clay is generally honored, and these are very common, including a number of counties. Clay's fame lasted well after his death, and the county in SD was named for him in 1862. **Clay County** KY: for Gen. Green Clay, prominent in the War of 1812.

Claycomo MO From Clay County, Missouri, using the common abbreviations for county and Missouri.

Clayhatchee AL A coined name, from the two streams on which the village stands, viz. **Claybank Creek** and **Choctawhatchee River.**

Claytonia A Latinized formation from Clayton; in NB probably because the town and creek were formerly in **Clay Co.**

Clear Most often a descriptive for water, often in the compound **Clearwater,** applied with creek, lake, spring, etc. Occasionally descriptive of the atmosphere, e.g. the habitation-name **Clearview. Clearmont** WY is near **Clear Creek,** and suggests the analogy of **Claremont.** It is also used in the sense of 'free of trees or brush,' especially as **Clearfield.** In PA this name is a translation from the Delaware. **Clear Grit** MN: named as a compliment to John Kaercher, a miller who showed great fortitude under the test of panics, fire, and flood.

Clearco WV From Clear Creek Coal Company.

Clearinghouse CA From the fact that a gold mine here dealt in clearinghouse certificates during the panic of 1907.

Cle Elum WA Indian, language uncertain, locally believed to mean 'swift waters.'

Cleetwood Cove OR Named for a boat used in its exploration in 1886; the boat was named for a word heard vividly in a dream and applied to golden arrow.

Clemenceau AZ For George Clemenceau, in gratitude for his services during World War I.

Clemscot OK From the names of two local residents, Clem Brooks and Scott Sparks.

Cleo OR From the initials, backward, of Oregon Export Lumber Company.

Cleora From a woman's name, e.g. in OK for Cleora Sunday, of the family of the first postmaster.

Clepsydra Geyser WY From the name of the ancient water clock, because the eruptions of the geyser mark the passage of time.

Cleveland Though a place-name in England, its use in the U.S. seems to be wholly from the personal name, most often for President Grover Cleveland, e.g. ID, UT. In OH the name is for General Moses Cleaveland, who chose the townsite in 1796, and was a shareholder in the land company owning the tract. The spelling was altered in 1832—according to local story, merely by a shift in newspaper usage. The reason behind the shift is probably the difficulty of maintaining a spelling, such as that with the 'a,' which is rare in personal names.

Clever In MO locally believed to be a commendatory, but in this and other cases probably from the personal name.

Cliff A generic, often used as a specific for a place thus associated, e.g. **Cliff Lake** MT, **Cliff Island** ME, WA. See **Clifton.**

Clift(y) The colloquial form for *cliff* occurs in **Clift Hill** KY and more commonly in the adjectival form, e.g. **Clifty Hill** OK, **Clifty Creek** KY.

Clifton Although the personal name exists, the usual origin is from the presence of a nearby cliff, e.g. in AZ, ID, NJ, TX, WV.

Clifty See **Clift.**

Clikapudi Creek CA Yana, connected with the word 'kill,' apparently since some Indians were once poisoned here.

Climax Used to suggest a settlement at the highest point topographically or figuratively, e.g. in NC for a town on a sharp hill. In MN, the name was suggested by an advertisement for Climax Tobacco. In OR the postmaster stated in 1926, 'no one living here knows anything about the name of Climax, how, when, or why.'

Clinch River Stated by Dr. Thomas Walker in 1750 to be named for 'one Clinch, a hunter,' further information lacking.

Clingman From the personal name, e.g. **Clingman's Dome** NC, TN for T. L. Clingman (1812–1897), political figure and developer of the region.

Clinton From the personal name, especially for DeWitt Clinton (1768–1828), governor of NY, and famous in connection with the Erie Canal. The extra-ordinary popularity of the name for habitations was probably aided by its brevity and by the suggestion of *-ton.* Many of the namings were late, e.g. CT, 1838; MA, 1850; IA, 1855. **Clinton County** NY: for Gov. George Clinton of NY.

Clio The name of the Greek muse of history has probably been used, not so much for classical enthusiasm, as because it is short and has been used as a personal name. **Clio** SC: according to tradition, named by the placing together of some initials. **Clio** CA: locally said to be named because of the name on a stove, which happened to catch someone's eye when he was wanting a name for the post office.

Clipper First applied to sailing craft, the term became synonymous with speed, especially as in 'clipper mill,' a fast-working sawmill, e.g. **Clipper Mills** CA. **Clipper** WA: from the Clipper Shingle Co. (1900).

Clonmel From the town in Ireland.

Clontarf MN From the town in Ireland, named by immigrants in 1876.

Cloquallum Creek WA Indian, language and meaning uncertain.

Cloud, Cloudy Not common, but sometimes used descriptively for a feature characteristically thus veiled, e.g. the mountain and cape in AK, or for one which was so at the time of naming, e.g. **Cloud Creek** CA. Fanciful names such as **Cloudcroft** NM, **Cloudveil Dome** WY, **Clouds Rest** CA occur chiefly in national parks.

Clove Commonly appearing in the former Dutch regions for *kloof,* 'cleft, ravine'; thus **Clove River** NJ.

Clover The presence of clover, valuable for pasture and a general commendatory term ('to be in clover') have led to its common use as a descriptive and commendatory name. **Cloverdale** is conventional for habitation-names.

Clovis In NM, by local story, it is for the king of the Franks in the 5th century, suggested in 1906 by the daughter of a railroad official who was interested in French history. In CA it is from Clovis Cole, local rancher.

Cly Butte AZ The personal name of a Navajo chief, who died in 1934 and was buried at the foot of the butte.

Clyde Commonly from the personal name, e.g. in TX it was the site where Robert Clyde in 1881 established a camp for construction workers on the railroad. **Clyde River** VT: for the river in Scotland, named by a Scottish surveyor. In KS the town was named for the river by a settler of Scottish ancestry.

Clyo GA A variant of **Clio.**

Coachella CA Before 1900 the valley was called **Cahuilla,** and this name probably helped to suggest **Conchilla** (Spanish, 'little-shell') which was applied in the same period, some fossil shells having been found. A mistake, however, was made when the name was transferred to an official map, and the present name resulted.

Coagie Creek AL Muskogean (Creek) 'cane-noise,' from the sound of wind in the canes (?).

Coahoma In MS it is Choctaw 'panther-red.' In TX it is locally believed to be an 'Indian' word for 'look-out,' but may be a transfer from MS.

Coahuila CA From the Indian tribal name.

Coaksett, Coassit, Coasuck, Coaxet, Coeset, Koessek (and other spellings) Algonquian 'pine-tree-at.'

Coal. Though in some early instances probably an adaptation of the family name Cole, the usage is generally descriptive or commendatory. Early explorers often noted coal seams. As a habitation name there are well on toward a hundred examples, mostly in coal-mining regions. A variety of suffixes occurs, or the word may stand alone.

Coaledo OR From a coal lead, or vein, and the analogy of such Spanish names as Toledo.

Coalinga CA First known as Coaling Station on the railroad, it was artificially transformed into a town name by the addition of a letter.

Coan VA A remnant of the Indian tribal name, recorded (1612) as Sekacawone and later as Chicacoan.

Coarsegold CA Given during the gold rush of 1849, apparently because of the finding of gold in granules or nuggets and not in dust.

Coast In American usage **The Coast** means the Pacific Coast. **The Coast Range(s)** is a term arising in the early years of American occupation in CA to distinguish the lower mountains near the coast from the higher ranges farther inland and generally separated from the coastal hills by a valley.

Coaticook River VT Algonquian 'pine-river-at.'

Coatopa AL Choctaw 'panther-there-wounded,' apparently an incident name.

Coatue Beach MA Algonquian 'pine-tree-at.'

Cobalt 1) From the metal, e.g. the town in ID, so named in 1950, because of a mine here. 2) As a synonym for *blue,* it has been occasionally applied, e.g. the lake in MT.

Cobble As a now obsolete generic, it is probably of Dutch origin and is preserved in NY with the apparent meaning 'hill'; it stands occasionally as a specific, tautologically, e.g. **Cobble Hill** NY. **Cobble Creek, Cobblestone River** AK because the natural boulders are like cobblestones.

Cobleskill NY From Jacob Kobell (Cobel) who had a mill on the stream, with Dutch *kil,* 'stream.'

Cobossecontee ME Algonquian 'sturgeon-plenty,' for a well-known place on the river where Indians speared sturgeon.

Cobre Spanish 'copper,' in NV it is a modern name applied to a railroad station which is the junction where copper from the mines farther to the south comes to the main line.

Cobscook Bay ME Algonquian 'rocks-under-water,' important because of tidal currents that they caused; the initial 'c' is left unexplained.

Coburg OR Probably named for a local stallion which was brought to a black-smith's shop here to be shod, the name being given by the blacksmith.

Cocalico Creek PA Algonquian (Delaware) 'snake-den.'

Coche Spanish 'coach,' but in place-names usually Mexican-Spanish 'hog,' e.g. **Coches Creek** CA.

Cocheco NH Algonquian 'swift-current-at.'

Cochecton NY Algonquian, meaning uncertain.

Cochessett MA Algonquian 'pine(s)-small-at.'

Cochetopa CO Ute 'buffalo-pass,' because of the numbers of buffalo that passed through it.

Cochgalechee Creek AL From an Indian tribal name.

Cochibo AZ Papago 'pig well,' the first syllable being an adaptation of Spanish *cochino*.

Coching Bayou TX An American re-working of Spanish *cochino*, 'hog.'

Cochise A county and some features in AZ commemorate the Apache chief.

Cochiti NM Indian, of uncertain origin and meaning.

Cochituate MA Algonquian 'swift-water-at.'

Cochnewagen Lake ME Algonquian 'obstructed-passage.' See **Newagen**.

Cochon French 'pig, hog,' e.g. the bayou in LA.

Cockenoe CT Algonquian 'he interprets,' with reference to an Indian who

arranged Norwalk deeds in 1652. The island (NY) is probably for the same man.

Cockermouth NH A grant of 1741 was named for Baron Cockermouth, political figure under George III; it remains as the name of a river.

Cockscomb A descriptive term for a ridge or mountain with a sawtooth pro-file like a cock's comb, e.g. **Cockscomb Crest** CA.

Coco WV The name **Poco** (probably Spanish 'little') was proposed by a little girl after the name of a rooster in a story, but in transmission through the Post Office Dept. it was changed to the present form.

Cocoa, Cocoanut From the cocoanut palm, limited to southern FL, e.g. **Cocoa Beach, Cocoanut Key**.

Cocodrie American-French 'crocodile,' used in Louisiana for the alligator, e.g. **Lake Cocodrie**.

Cocolalla ID Indian, probably Kootenai 'cold-water' (?).

Cocoosing Creek PA Algonquian (Delaware) 'owls-at.'

Cocopah CA From the Indian tribal name.

Cod, Cape MA The narrative of Bar-tholomew Gosnold records as of May 15, 1602, 'Near this cape . . . we took great store of codfish . . . and called it Cape Cod.'

Codell KS A railroad naming, from a family name, not further identified.

Coden AL From French *coq d'Inde* 'turkey-gobbler,' applied first to the bayou.

Codo Spanish 'elbow, sharp turn,' e.g. **Rio del Codo** CO.

Codornices Spanish 'quails.' The creek in CA was named in 1818 because of the finding there of a quail's nest.

Coeburn VA By local story, for an engineer Coe and a judge Burn.

Coesse IN From the name of a Miami chief of the early 19th century.

Coeur D'Alene ID From the Indian tribal name. It is, literally, French 'heart of awl,' but the ultimate derivation and meaning are uncertain.

Coeymans NY For Barent Peterse Coeymans, patentee in 1673.

Coffedelia Creek MS Choctaw 'sassafras-thicket.'

Coffee, Coffeepot The personal name Coffee is often involved, but the frequent coupling with *creek* suggests that the color of the water may have given rise to the name, or else that an incident was responsible. **Coffeepot Creek** OR: a pot fell out of a passing wagon, and was crushed by a wheel. **Coffee Creek** NB: it flows through a grove where early settlers held a picnic, drinking coffee. **Coffee Creek** AZ: by folk-etymology from the unusual personal name Coffer.

Coffee-Los Lake ME Since **Telos Lake** was sometimes said to be 'tea-less,' a 'coffee-less lake' was named by joking analogy.

Coffey From the personal name; for instance, **Coffeyville** KS is named for J. A. Coffey, the settlement having developed from a trading post which he established here in 1869.

Coffin The personal name is the source of **Coffin Creek** SC and probably of **Coffinton** GA. **Coffin Butte** OR, SD: because it looks like a coffin from one point of view. **Coffin Rock** OR: Indians used this spot to deposit their dead in canoes; so also, **Mount Coffin** WA.

Coginchaugh Brook CT Algonquian 'fish-drying-place-at.'

Cognac NC From the town of France (or, more likely, from its chief product), reason for application uncertain.

Cohabie, Cohabadiah AL Muskogean (Creek) 'cane stalks,' or 'cane covering.'

Cohansey NJ From the name of an early chief, recorded as Cohanzick.

Cohasset Algonquian, probably 'high-place-at, promontory-at.'

Cohelee Creek GA Muskogean (Creek) 'cane-good.'

Coho From a kind of salmon, e.g. **Coho Cove** AK.

Cohocksing Creek PA Algonquian (Delaware) 'pine-land-at.'

Cohocton NY A variant of **Conhocton**.

Cohoes, Cohoos, Coes (and other spellings) Algonquian 'pine-tree.'

Cohoke VA From an Indian term (language uncertain), 'marsh, swamp'.

Coila Creek MS Choctaw 'panther-comes-there.'

Coinjock NC A heavily altered Indian term, probably Algonquian 'blueberry-swamp-place' (?).

Cojo Spanish 'lame, lame man.' **Canada del Cojo** CA: the soldiers of the Portola expedition in 1769 gave this name because of encountering a lame Indian.

Cokan KS A boundary-name, from Colorado and Kansas.

Cokato MN Siouan 'at the middle,' originally the name of a lake.

Coker Usually from a personal name, but in TN from Cherokee *kuku*, 'squash.'

Colby Regularly from the personal name. **Colby** WA was originally **Coal Bay** because of coal found there.

Colchester In CT (1699), from the English town; in VT, see **Tunbridge.**

Cold A common descriptive name for springs, streams, and lakes, though seldom established scientifically. The water may merely have seemed cold to the namer at the time. When coupled with such terms as canyon and mountain the name usually records an incident, i.e. that the namer experienced a cold time. **Cold Mountain** CA is so called from nearby **Cold Canyon**. **Cold Harbor** VA: this English place-name referred to a shelter put up for travelers, and was apparently transferred without reference to its meaning. In MA it may have been more aptly applied. The compound **Coldwater** is common.

Colebrook In CT (1732) from an English town; in NH (granted, 1770) for Sir George Colebrooke, English political figure.

Coleman From the personal name. **Coleman Valley** CA: a misunderstanding for the name of Michael Kolmer, an early German settler.

Coleotchee Creek GA Muskogean (Creek) 'white-oak-stream.'

Coleraine, Colerain From the town in Northern Ireland. In MN it also in honor of T. F. Cole, local businessman.

Colestin OR From the personal name Coles with *-tin* probably substituted for *-ton.*

Coleta IL By local account, named, ca. 1870, from a character in a book.

Colewa, Bayou LA From an Indian tribal name, more commonly recorded as Koroa.

Colfax From the personal name, especially for Schuyler Colfax, Vice President of the U.S. from 1869 to 1873. He was extremely popular, and so his name was used by several counties and towns in western states. In CA the town was named on the occasion of his visit there in 1865.

Collano KS From the names of two early settlers, Collingwood and Gano, not further identified.

Collayomi Valley CA From an Indian tribal name. Also, **Locoallomi, Loconoma.**

College Indicates a place associated with a college, e.g. **College Creek** NB. Frequent in habitation-names, and used even when the association with the college is meager and after the college has disappeared, because of commendatory qualities suggestive of education and culture, e.g. **College City** and **Collegeville**

(both, CA) were named for institutions which no longer exist. Ordinarily the name indicates a still-existing institution as with **College Heights** CA and **College Corner** OH. **College Point** AK situated on **College Fiord** in the area where the glaciers have been commemoratively named for colleges.

Collet(t), Colleton Co. SC For Sir John Colleton, one of the Lords Proprietors. **Collettsville** NC: for James Collett, early settler.

Collicut Brook ME Algonquian, probably 'flames-at.'

Colma CA Uncertain. From a woman's name, which occurs MacPherson's *Songs of Selma;* or from Colma in Switzerland; or a shortening of Coleman.

Colo IA From a child's pronunciation of Carlo, the name of a favorite dog belonging to the landowner.

Coloma The name originated in CA; it was the name of a Maidu village, of unknown meaning.

Colomokee Creek GA From Kolomi, the name of a former Creek town, meaning uncertain.

Colon The Spanish form for Columbus, used in several states, apparently as a substitute for the too common Latinized form.

Colona CO Proposed as a name for the state in 1858, it was probably formed from the Spanish *Colon,* 'Columbus,' with an 'a'-ending, thus being a kind of equivalent of **Columbia.** It was adopted by the town in 1862.

Colonial Suggesting an admired style of architecture and also ancient ancestry, the term was in limited use, chiefly in the early 20th century, as a commendatory, e.g. the beach in VA and **Colonial Park** PA.

Colony In the 19th century cooperative groups of settlers often called themselves colonies, and this name has sometimes survived. **Colony Peak** CA: from the Kaweah Co-operative Colony founded in 1886. **Colony** OK: from the Seger Colony of the 1890's. **Colony** KS: named in 1872 because of the arrival of a colony of settlers.

Coloparchee Creek GA Muskogean, probably 'white-oak-stream.'

Colorado Spanish 'colored, reddish, red,' but generally indicating a less pronounced shade than does *rojo*. **Colorado River** AZ, CA, etc.: applied in 1602 by an Oñate expedition to the stream now known as the **Little Colorado**, 'because the water is almost red.' The name worked down this stream to the main **Colorado**, which is about the same color and readily took the same name. Because the upper branches were discovered and named separately, the name of the lower river, for many years, extended upward only as far as the junction of the **Green** and **Grand**. In 1921, at the instance of the legislature of CO, Congress took action to change the name **Grand** to **Colorado**, so that some part of that river should flow through the state of the same name. **Colorado** (state): when the territory was organized in 1861 the name was selected, out of many proposed, by Congress, largely on the grounds that the river arose in that territory, a conception warranted geographically but not by nomenclature. As a descriptive for features, **Colorado** is fairly common in regions of Spanish background, e.g. **Colorado River** TX.

Colores WY Spanish 'colors,' because of highly colored rocks in the vicinity.

Colorow Probably an American spelling from the colloquial Mexican pronunciation of *colorado* or *colorada*, e.g. **Colorow Mountain** CO, **Piedra Colorow Pintato** CO.

Colstrip MT From *coal strip* because coal is mined here by the process of stripping off the overlying earth and rock.

Colt From the personal name or for a young horse, but rare. **Colts Neck** NJ: originally **Caul's Neck**, for an early settler, but shifted after the area became a breeding-place for race horses. **Colt Creek** MT: originally named (1907) for a lumberman named Cott, but shifted in the written transmission. **Coltkilled**

Creek ID: the members of the Lewis and Clark expedition killed a colt here for food.

Colter From the personal name, e.g. several names in WY for John Colter who in 1808 was the first American to explore the region of Yellowstone N.P.

Columbia Coined in the Revolutionary period (first certain occurrence in Philip Freneau's poem, *American Liberty*, 1775) as a name for the emerging nation, derived from Columbus, who was played up as a hero at the time when the colonies were breaking off their English ties. The Latinized form was consistent with the classical leanings of the period. The name was used for the new capital of SC in 1786, and for the **District of Columbia** in 1791. **Columbia River:** named by the American captain, Robert Gray, in 1792. He was sailing in the ship *Columbia* and this helped suggest the name, but the patriotic motive must have been present, since Gray was at the time competing with the British captain, Vancouver, and the giving of the name served as a declaration that the region was claimed for the U.S. The name has been so popular for towns that the variants **Columbiana** and **Columbiaville** have been used. **Mount Columbia** CO: named in 1906 by a graduate of that University, in its honor; so also **Columbia Glacier** AK.

Columbiana AL, OH A Latin adjectival form from **Columbus**, with a feminine ending as is usually considered proper for place-names.

Columbine The state flower of CO has yielded a mountain, a lake, and a village in that state.

Columbus The name was not favored during the colonial period, since English propaganda stressed the Cabots' discovery of North America. Even after 1776 the interest was generally expressed through the name **Columbia**. The first important use of **Columbus** was that in OH (1812), followed in the 1820's by towns in IN, MS, and GA. The name, thus well established, spread to many states, being used without suffix, because of its length.

Colusa CA From an Indian village of unknown meaning, in early times often spelled **Colusi.**

Colville River AK Named (1837) by British explorers for Andrew Colville, who was important in the Hudson's Bay Company.

Colvos Passage WA From G. W. Colvocoressis, an officer of the Wilkes expedition (1841).

Colwich KS Coined (perhaps on the analogy of the English town) from syllables taken from the Colorado and Wichita Railroad Company.

Colyell The bayou and bay in LA are for Francisco Collel, Spanish officer of the 18th century.

Comal TX Mexican-Spanish, for a kind of flat pan; in a topographical sense, probably, 'basin,' in TX first applied to a river formed from many springs flowing together.

Comanche From the Indian tribal name. In MT from a horse (named from the tribe) which was the sole survivor of Custer's command at the battle of the Little Big Horn (1876).

Comargo KY A variant of **Camargo,** to avoid duplication within the state.

Comb A rare descriptive, e.g. **Comb Ridge** AZ. The reference is probably not to a hair comb, but to a cock's comb, as specified in other names, e.g. **Cockscomb Peak** CA. **Combs** is from the personal name.

Combahee River SC From an Indian tribal name.

Comfort On April 26, 1607, the Virginia colonists anchored safely, 'which put us in good comfort. Therefore we named that point of land Cape Comfort.' This naming has survived as **Point Comfort,** or **Old Point Comfort** VA. Half a dozen other examples result from similar motivation. In TX the founder believed, or hoped, that all settlers there would have 'everlasting comfort.' **Lake Comfort** MN: for J. W. Comfort, a local physician.

Comfrey MN Named by the first postmaster, 'from the plant, comfrey . . . that he had met with in his reading.'

Coming-in-Sight Point Translated from the Ojibway, reference uncertain.

Comite River LA, MS Choctaw 'red ant' (?).

Commack NY Algonquian, from a recorded (1689) *winne-comac,* 'pleasant-land (field, house).'

Commencement Bay WA Named by the Wilkes expedition (1841) because it was the first bay at the bottom of **Admiralty Sound.**

Commerce A commendatory name for a town, e.g. GA, OK, TX.

Como From the lake and city in Italy. **Lake Como** MN is a rare example of a natural feature being thus named by transfer, probably for commendatory reasons. **Como** CO: named by Italian settlers. The shortness and euphony of the name appealed to railroad namers, and it has been established in a dozen states. In Henry Co., MO, it is from Covey and Moberley, founders (1880).

Comobavi AZ Papago 'hackberry well.'

Companero Spanish 'friend, companion.'

Compano TX From the Indian tribal name, more commonly spelled Compane.

Compass The lake in FL resembles a compass by being round. **Compass** PA: from an inn with a sign of a mariner's compass. **Compass Creek** CO: the Powell expedition (1869) lost a compass here.

Competine Creek IA From the name of a local Sac Indian.

Competition MO Probably because founded in rivalry with some other settlement, but details unknown.

Complexion Spring CA Because the water was reputed to be good for the skin.

Compo CT Probably Algonquian 'long pond.'

Compounce Pond CT From the personal name of a local Indian, also known as John Compound.

Comstock From the personal name; **The Comstock Lode** NV is for H. P. Comstock, one of the earliest miners there, who was also known as 'Old Virginny.' See **Virginia City.**

Conanicut RI For an Indian chief, known to the colonists as Canonicus (died, 1647).

Conasauga GA, TN The name of several ancient Cherokee settlements; meaning unknown.

Conaskonk Point NJ Algonquian, meaning uncertain, but possibly *con,* 'long.'

Conata SD Siouan, meaning uncertain.

Concan TX Because Mexicans used to meet there to play the card game so called.

Conception Sometimes with the Spanish spelling **Concepcion.** A religious (Catholic) name, associated with December 8, the day of the Immaculate Conception. The point in CA was apparently named by Viscaíno in 1602 because he saw it on that day.

Concha Spanish 'shell.'

Conch Creek SC From the conch shells here found.

Concharty Mountain OK Probably the name of a Creek village in FL, brought by immigrant Indians.

Concho From the Indian tribal name, the river in TX being thus known to the Spaniards from ca. 1580. The form was sometimes, even at an early date, confused with **Concha,** 'shell,' and **Concho** OK was named by punning upon the name of C. E. Shell, local Indian agent.

Conconully WA Indian, language uncertain, but probably meaning 'cloudy,' and applied first to the creek.

Concord In MA, so ordered by the General Court in 1635. Different stories are told, such as, that the name commemorated a peaceful settlement between two factions, but the commendatory qualities of the name are obvious. This was, however, the only name of this sort given by the General Court. In addition to being a commendatory abstraction, **Concord,** incongruously, became a patriotic name with connotations of victory after the battle in 1775. It also gained connotations of culture in the mid-19th century by being the home of Emerson, etc. It has spread to ca. 20 states. **Concord** NH: named in 1763, it was probably so called under the influence of the town in MA, since it was settled by people from that state, though the commendatory qualities must have had an influence. **Concord** NC: rival factions, coming to an agreement, gave the name as a symbol.

Concordia Latin 'concord.' The form has been used as a variant of Concord, e.g. in KS and MO.

Concow CA From an Indian tribal name.

Concrete CO, ND, WA Because of a local cement industry.

Conda ID Named (1916) by a shortening of **Anaconda,** the town being founded by the Anaconda Copper Co.

Conde SD For one of the towns (properly Condé) in France, thus named because of numerous French settlers.

Condor A few features in CA record the presence of the now nearly-extinct condor.

Conecuh AL Probably Muskogean, but meaning uncertain.

Conehatta MS Choctaw 'skunk-white,' presumably because an albino animal was seen here.

Conejo Spanish 'rabbit,' e.g. **Conejos** CO, probably first applied to a natural feature.

Conemaugh River PA Algonquian (Delaware) 'otter.'

Conesus NY Iroquoian 'berry-place.'

Conewago PA Iroquoian 'rapid-stream' (?).

Conewango NY, PA Probably Iroquoian 'in-(the)-rapids'; **Conewingo** PA appears to be a variant, but may actually be Algonquian 'long-strip-(of)-land.' Cf. **Conewanta.**

Conewanta Creek PA Probably Iroquoian 'swift-water.' Cf. **Conewango.**

Conewingo See **Conewango.**

Coney, Cony Commonly from the family name, but on the island (NY) it is presumably an Anglicization of the Dutch 'rabbit.' In the Western mountains the name is usually for the animal so known, e.g. both **Coney Creek** and **Cony Creek** in CO.

Confederate Rare; generally with some Civil War connection, e.g. **Confederate Branch** KY.

Confidence A rare commendatory name, bearing a suggestion of false courage, as in **Confidence Springs,** etc. In Death Valley, CA, originally named for the unsuccessful Confidence Mill of the 1870's.

Confluence PA Because three streams here flow together.

Confucius Temple AZ See **Brahma.**

Confusion Mountains UT Because of their maze of gullies.

Congamond, Congamund, Congamuck Algonquian 'long fish-drying-place.'

Congamunck Creek NY Algonquian 'long-fish-drying-place.' This name was transferred to this inappropriate location by Americans in the 19th century.

Congaree River SC From an Indian tribal name.

Congo From the African river, though in some instances an Indian name may have given the suggestion. Since the river was not generally known until after 1850, the names are late, e.g. in WV ca. 1880. In American-French the

word means a water moccasin snake, and some names may have thus arisen.

Congress Occasionally applied as a commendatory, e.g. to a mine in AZ and thence to a town. A medicinal (purgative) spring discovered by a member of Congress in 1792 was given that name, and some springs producing similar water were afterwards thus named, e.g. in WY.

Conhocton River NY Iroquoian, probably 'log-in-water' or 'trees-in-water.'

Conifer From the trees or from a personal name, e.g. in CO for George Conifer, roadhouse-keeper.

Conimicut RI Probably from the name of the granddaughter of Canonicus (see **Conanicut**), recorded as Quenimiquet.

Conneaut OH Applied first to the creek, Iroquoian 'mud' (?), an early traveler noting that the stream had brown water.

Connecticut Algonquian 'long-(tidal)-river-at,' first applied to the river, and applicable to its lowest reach. The settlements were known first as those on **Connecticut River,** and the district, lacking any other name, became **Connecticut,** which was passed on to colony and state. The second 'c' has no relevancy to the original Indian words, is silent, and was probably inserted by some English scribe on the analogy of 'connect.'

Connedoguinet River PA Algonquian (Delaware), with *conn-*, 'long,' and the rest uncertain.

Connetquot Brook NY Algonquian 'long-(tidal)-stream-at,' the same as **Connecticut.**

Connie Commonly for the familiar form for Constance, e.g. **Connie Knob** KY. See also **Bois Connie.**

Conococheague Creek MD Algonquian, with *con-* probably 'long,' and the remainder uncertain.

Conolaways Creek PA Iroquoian 'running-through-(the)-hemlocks.'

Conoquenessing Creek PA Algonquian (Delaware), probably 'long-reach,' as descriptive of the stream.

Conowingo MD Iroquoian 'at-rapids,' probably with reference to the mouth of the stream. Cf. **Conewango.**

Conoy Creek PA Algonquian (Delaware), from the Indian tribal name.

Conquest NY Because of the victory of a faction who were successful in farming a new settlement and separating from the old one.

Conquistador Aisle AZ Spanish 'conquerer,' but named in honor of some explorers of the Grand Canyon.

Conshohocken PA Algonquian (Delaware) 'roar-land-at,' originally an incident name or a name for a stream. Also, **Conshohacking Hill.**

Consultation Lake CA Named in 1904 when some trailmakers consulted here as to how the trail should go.

Contact Commonly a geologists' descriptive for a feature associated with a 'contact' in the geological sense, e.g. a creek in AK where granite and coal-bearing rocks are visible together. **Contact** NV is at a line between limestone and granite.

Contadero NM Spanish 'counting-place,' probably because sheep were counted there.

Content Appearing rarely as a commendatory, e.g. **Content** MT, **Content Key** FL.

Continental Its use as vaguely referring to the colonies as opposed to the insular mother-country at the time of the Revolution is probably responsible for the town in OH. Otherwise, e.g. in NM it springs from **Continental Divide.**

Contorta Point OR Named for the presence of lodgepole pine, which has the scientific name *Pinus contorta.*

Contrabando Spanish 'contraband, smuggling'; the canyon in TX, being near

the border, was once much used from such trade.

Contra Costa CA Spanish, originally **Contracosta,** 'opposite coast.' It designated, in the Spanish period, from the point of view of the early settlements on the site of San Francisco, the north or east shore of the bay. The formation of the county (1850) officially applied the name to the east shore.

Contrary Creek VA Probably from flowing in a direction other than the one expected.

Contreras In NM for Matias Contreras, local rancher. Elsewhere the name is probably an echo of the Mexican War battle.

Conundrum Creek CO Probably from some question raised by its finding or exploration. Cf. **Riddle.**

Convent From the presence of a convent, e.g. in LA.

Convict Lake CA In 1871 escaped convicts from Nevada engaged in a gun battle with a posse, and one man was killed.

Conway From the personal name, about a dozen examples. In MA and NH, for General H. S. Conway, political figure and supporter of the colonies in the pre-Revolutionary period. In SC, for General Robert Conway, Revolutionary soldier. In NC, from the maiden name of the wife of a railroad president.

Cony See **Coney.**

Coochie Brake LA Choctaw 'cane, reed.'

Cook(e) Regularly from the personal name. **Cook County** IL: for D. P. Cook, Congressman. **Cook Inlet, Mount** AK: for Capt. James Cook, English explorer. He explored the inlet in 1778, and it was afterwards named for him by the British Admiralty. The mountain was named for him commemoratively in 1874.

Cool Rarely used. Applied descriptively in **Cool Springs,** and either descriptively or hopefully to **Cool** CA. **Coolville** OH:

for Simeon Cooley, father of one of the early settlers.

Cooleemee NC Indian, language and meaning uncertain.

Cooleewahee Creek GA Muskogean, probably a phrase, 'white-oak acorns are scattered.'

Coolidge From the personal name. **Mount Coolidge** SD: named by the state legislature in 1927 for the president, who was spending the summer in that vicinity.

Coon The popular shortening from **Raccoon**. Since the animal was widely distributed and since the coon hunt was a popular form of early diversion, the names are many. Nearly all embody now long-forgotten incidents involving coons. The animal was water-loving, though not aquatic, and for this reason **Coon Creek** is common. Though the personal name exists, it has probably not been an important influence. Habitation-names are few, and given by transfer. There was probably a humorous quality to the name which worked against it for habitations. **Coon Creek** MN: the village was named from **Dead Coon Lake,** where early surveyors found the body of a coon. **Coon Hollow** WY: from the colloquial term for a Negro, because one named Tunner once lived here. **Coon Creek,** Russel Co., KS: early settlers, in want of food, killed and attempted, with total failure, to cook and eat a large coon.

Coonamesset Pond MA Algonquian, probably 'long-fishing-place-at.'

Cooney Commonly from a family name. The creek (MT) is probably from an original *cony* (for the animal), modified by folk-etymology.

Cooper From the personal name. **Cooper River** SC: for Sir Anthony Ashley Cooper, one of the Lords Proprietors.

Coos In NH the county is from Algonquian (Pennicook) 'pine tree.' In OR the county is from the name of a local tribe.

Coosa(w) From the Indian tribal name, but also literally in Muskogean 'reed,

cane.' Cf. **Coochie. Coosawhatchie** SC: the Muskogean 'stream' is added.

Coosada AL From an Indian tribal name, recorded as Koasati.

Coosauk Falls NH Algonquian 'pines-at.'

Coosawattee River GA Probably Cherokee 'Creek (Indian)-old-place,' to indicate a former Creek town.

Cooter MO From the French personal name Coutre, a family prominent in the area in the 18th century.

Copake NY Algonquian, shortened from *achkook-paug,* 'snake-pond.'

Copalis WA From an Indian tribal name.

Copan OK From the town and ruined city in Honduras.

Copassaw Creek AL Choctaw 'cold.'

Copco CA From California Oregon Power Company.

Copecut MA Algonquian, probably 'obstructed (closed in)-place.'

Copenhagen From the city in Denmark, usually because of Danish settlers.

Copernicus Peak CA Named by astronomers of the Lick Observatory for the Polish astronomer.

Copiah MS Choctaw, probably from *koi,* 'panther,' and the rest uncertain.

Coplay Creek PA From the name of a local Indian, recorded as Kolapechki.

Copper Though the personal name exists, it is rare, and the place-names regularly originate from the presence or supposed presence of the metal or its ores. With habitation-names different suffixes occur, e.g. **Copperopolis** CA which used the Greek *polis,* 'city,' with an *o* for a connective.

Copperas From the mineral, e.g. **Copperas Creek** NM.

Coppereid NV From *copper* and John T. Reid, who was interested in a copper mine here.

Copperhead This not very dangerous, though poisonous, snake has given its name to few places, as compared with the rattlesnake. Its occasional use indicates a place where the snakes hibernated or where someone had an encounter with one of them. Its use as a derogatory term during the Civil War may account for an occasional use.

Copsie Point NY From Dutch *kaapsie,* 'pointlet.'

Copwax Creek NY Algonquian, probably 'obstructed place.' See **Cape Poge.**

Coquille French 'shell'; hence, **Lake Coquille** LA. The river in OR is from a tribal name of Indians living along it, recorded as Ku-kwil. French-Canadian trappers are apparently responsible for pronouncing the name as the French word, and thus leading to its present spelling.

Coral Rarely used; **Coral Gables** FL was named because the first house to be built had gables decorated with coral rock.

Coram NY Algonquian, much abbreviated but probably from a form meaning 'low country, valley.'

Coraopolis PA From Cora Watson, daughter of a town developer, and Greek *-polis,* 'city,' the 'o' apparently being considered a connective element.

Corapeake NC For the wife of a local Indian chief, elsewhere recorded as Orapeake.

Corazon Spanish 'heart.' In a Spanish context it is likely to have a religious suggestion, from the Sacred Heart of Jesus.

Cordillera The term, borrowed from the Spanish, was used by geologists to describe the western mountain ranges, but has largely gone out of use. The creek in CA may be a vestige of this usage, or may be an independent Spanish naming, from the general meaning, 'mountain-range.'

Cordova From the city in Spain, generally with little reason except the liking for a 'romantic' name. In NB the town was renamed in the late 19th century, the chief motivation being the desire to get a name unlike any other in the state. In NC the town was named at the suggestion of a woman in 1879, apparently for no special reason. In NM, from the name of a family of early Spanish settlers. **Cordova** AK: named, as a harbor, in 1790 by Spanish voyagers for the naval commander, Luis de Córdoba y Cordoba.

Corduroy From a road of that type, e.g. the creek in AZ where such a road was constructed by troops in 1880.

Corepoint NC From the ancient Indian tribe, more commonly known as Coree.

Corfu From the Greek island.

Coriacan Defile MT By local tradition for Koriaka, a Hawaiian, killed here by Indians while with a party of trappers. Cf. **Owyhee.**

Corinth Both as an important classical city and for its Biblical connections the name possessed commendatory value, and musters a dozen examples. The classical city should suggest primarily commercial activity, but in MS the name was bestowed on a railroad junction because the original city was 'the crossroads of ancient Greece.'

Corkscrew A descriptive term to indicate exceptional twistiness, e.g. the canyon in CA. **Corkscrew Peak** CA: from twisted folds in its rocks.

Cormant MN A shortening of 'cormorant.'

Cormorant From the presence of the bird. **Cormorant Passage** WA: for a British warship which served in these waters from 1844 to 1850.

Corn Meaning 'maize' in American usage, this plant does not occur wild, and is therefore almost nonexistent in the names of features. **Cornfield Island** MN: because of former cultivation by Indians. Indian cultivation, in a region where the grain could be raised only in favored spots, has resulted in **Cornfields** AZ. **Cornlea** NB: coined by use of the poetic *lea*, 'open land, field.' **Cornstalk** WV: for the famous 18th century Shawnee chief. **Cornplanter Run** PA: for the Seneca chief. **Cornville** AZ: by mistake of the Post Office Dept. for Coane, the name of a family of early settlers. **Corn** OK: though established (1896) as **Korn**, the meaning was because of a nearby cornfield, and the spelling became **Corn** in 1918. **Cornhouse Creek** AL: the translation of an Indian (Creek) name, meaning a place where there were corncribs.

Corne French 'horn, antler,' e.g. **Bayou Corne à Chevreuil** LA.

Corner(s) To designate a place at a corner especially at a junction of roads, usually a habitation-name, commonly bearing the personal name of the family living there, e.g. **Buckbee's Corners** NY. It is especially characteristic of New England and regions, such as upper NY, settled from New England, but exists elsewhere, though not so common in the West. It becomes a specific by association, e.g. **Corner Ridge** KY.

Cornie Bayou AR Probably by folk-etymology from a French proper name such as Corneille.

Corning From the personal name, e.g. in NY for Erastus Corning, who was involved with the town development, ca. 1850.

Cornucopia Latin 'horn of plenty,' often from a mine name.

Cornudas Mountains NM Spanish 'horned,' probably from the shape of rock formations.

Cornwall From the English county, etc., e.g. in CT, 1738.

Cornwallis WV This unique name was established, about 1850, when a local man gave four acres of land with the stipulation that it be called for Lord Cornwallis. One supposes that he wished to commemorate Cornwallis's surrender at Yorktown rather than the general himself.

Corona Latin, Spanish, 'crown,' used on habitation-names for commendatory purposes. In CA the name springs also from the secondary meaning, 'circle,' since there is a circular drive around the town. **Corona** MN: because it is close to the high point of the railroad between Lake Superior and the Mississippi.

Coronaca SC Apparently of Indian origin, locally said to mean 'place of big oaks.'

Coronado Spanish 'crowned,' but also a family name. **Coronado Butte** AZ and other names commemorate Francisco Vásquez de Coronado, 16th-century explorer. In CA the name is probably derived from Los Coronados, islands off the coast of Lower California, which were named in 1602 because they were sighted at the time of the day of the Four Crowned Martyrs.

Coronation The island (AK) was named by George Vancouver to commemorate his passing it on Sept. 22, 1793, the anniversary of the coronation of George III. The top of the peak in AZ suggests a crown.

Corpus Christi TX Latin 'body of Christ,' given in commemoration of Corpus Christi Day; the name was given to the bay in 1519 by the Spanish voyager, Alonso Alvarez de Pineda.

Corral Some place-names are Spanish survivals, and others are namings after the word had come into English. The name indicates a place thus associated, as in **Corral Creek**. It is rare as a habitation-name; **Corral** ID is from a railroad station. **Corralitos Lagoon** CA: uses the diminutive plural; **Corralillos Canyon** CA uses another diminutive. Since the word is Western, so are the names.

Correctionville IA Named (1856) because of being on a 'correction line,' established by land surveyors.

Correo Spanish, 'post office,' taken as the name of a post office in NM.

Corrumpa, Corrumpaw NM Locally believed to be an Indian word, 'wild, isolated.'

Corsica For the island, in SD because of the presence there of numerous Corsicans.

Corsicana TX A Latinized form from Corsica, given in 1848 by a Texan whose father had been born in that island.

Corte Madera CA An American shortening of the Spanish descriptive name, **Corte de Madera,** 'cut of wood,' i.e. a place where wood is cut.

Cortez From the personal name; in some instances probably commemorative of the conqueror of Mexico.

Cortina Creek CA Probably from the name of a local Indian chief.

Cortland NY Simplified from the name of the prominent Van Cortlandt family, probably with special reference to Pierre Van Cortlandt, (1721–1814) public figure in the Revolutionary and post-Revolutionary periods; the county was named in 1808.

Corunna From the city of Spain.

Corvallis OR Descriptively coined in the 1850's from Latin *cor,* 'heart,' and '*vallis,*' of-(the)-valley.'

Corydon A literary name, first appearing in Virgil's *Eclogues* and used in pastoral poetry, it was applied by W. H. Harrison to a town in IN, ca. 1810, being taken directly from a popular song of the time. In other states the name is probably derived from this one.

Cos Cob CT Algonquian 'high rock.'

Coshecton Creek PA Algonquian (Delaware) 'finished,' but reference uncertain.

Coshocton OH Algonquian, a badly shifted form (partly by folk-etymology), from a term meaning a 'river-crossing,' or possibly 'ferry.' Since the spot is just below a joining of two streams it is an advantageous place for a crossing.

Cosmopolis WA A commendatory name.

Cosmos See **Kosmos.**

Cosnino The tribal name applied by the Hopi to the Havasupai.

Coso CA Shoshonean, probably having some connection with 'fire,' and referring originally to a district that had been burned over.

Cossa Boone Branch NJ Probably from some Algonquian name, meaning uncertain.

Cossatot River AR From French *casse-tête,* 'tomahawk.'

Cossayuna NY Algonquian, probably 'pine-lake.'

Cost TX Selected from a list submitted to the Post Office Dept., and apparently of no significance.

Costa Spanish 'coast.' **Cayo Costa** FL is probably for Cayo de la Costa to indicate an island near the coast or mainland. **Costa Mesa** CA was named (1915) in a period when enthusiasm for Spanish names outran respect for grammar, and is to be taken as 'coast mesa.' **Port Costa** CA: from being a port in **Contra Costa Co.**

Costilla Spanish 'rib,' and in a topographical sense for a riblike formation; hence several features in NM. It is also a personal name, and the county in CO is from a family which held a large land grant in that area.

Cosumnes River CA From an Indian tribal name.

Cotaco Creek AL Probably Cherokee; meaning, 'swamp-long' (?).

Cotahaga Creek AL Choctaw, probably 'locust-tree-there-standing.'

Cotati CA From the name of a nearby Miwok village; meaning unknown.

Cote French *côte,* meaning either 'coast,' or 'hill.' In American-French it was frequently applied to a line of hills or bluffs along a stream. Translated in English as 'coast,' this last usage has raised misconceptions. **The Coast of Nebraska** was not a bold figure of speech comparing the plains to the sea, but was a reference to the line of hills along the **Nebraska (Platte) River.**

Coteau In American-French, 'ridge, height of land, divide,' e.g. **Coteau des**

Prairies or **Coteau du Missouri,** for the low elevation separating the upper Mississippi from the Missouri basin; hence, **Coteau** ND. **Coteau Persee Creek** SD, for *côteau percé,* flows through a break in the line of the **Coteau des Prairies,** which is thus literally 'pierced.'

Cotile, Bayou LA From the name of Paul Coutil, resident during the early 19th century.

Cotopaxi An exotic name, from the famous volcanic peak in Ecuador, in CO applied to a mountain probably from fancied resemblance.

Cottage The intimately rural suggestion was commendatory for habitation-names in the 19th century; hence, **Cottage Grove, Cottageville,** etc.

Cottaneva CA Probably Athabascan, but meaning unknown.

Cottaquilla AL Muskogean (Creek), probably 'locust-trees-dead.'

Cotton The personal name has given rise to habitation-names in MN and OR. In the SE the growing of cotton and its manufacture have produced such names as **Cottongin, Cotton Plant, Cottontown, Cotton Valley,** and **Cotton County** OK. Since cotton was not a wild plant, the name is rare on natural features.

Cottonwood These trees mark the lines of streams conspicuously in arid country, and were often a welcome sight to early travelers. **Cottonwood Creek** is therefore one of the most frequent of western names. Because of pleasant associations it is common as a habitation-name, generally standing without suffix because of its length. Although one species of cottonwood is eastern, the name is almost wholly western, probably because the eastern tree was generally called a poplar.

Cotuit MA Algonquian 'long-fields-at' (?).

Couchsachraga, Mount NY A name applied in the early 20th century, from an Iroquoian name for the region, meaning uncertain.

Couderay WI From French *courte oreille,* 'short-ear,' applied first to a lake, reference uncertain. See **Courteoreille.**

Cougar The common name in the NW for the big cat, known elsewhere as mountain lion, panther, etc. **Cougar Gulch** WA: so named by a man who killed a cougar there.

Coulee, Cooley Primarily a restricted generic, meaning, roughly, a stream course, it appears as a specific by association, e.g. **Coulee Creek** WA, and in the names of several towns. **Cooley** may also be from a personal name.

Council Generally commemorative of some kind of council, especially one held by or with Indians. **Council Bluffs** IA: named in 1804 because the leaders of the Lewis and Clark expedition held a meeting there with some Otoe Indians. **Council Butte** OR: a council, with the signing of a treaty, was held here on Aug. 12, 1865, with whites and Snake Indians participating. **Council** ID: nearby was a spot at which Indians traditionally held councils. **Council Crest** OR: in 1898 delegates to the National Council of Congregational Churches met at the crest of this hill, and the name was suggested and approved by the governor, who was present. **Council Hill** OK: because used by the Creeks for ceremonial purposes. **Council Grove** KS: named in 1825 by U. S. Commissioners who met in this wooded spot to negotiate a treaty with the Osage Indians for safe passage of wagons in the Santa Fe trade.

Counter Image Peak WY Because it is often well reflected in a nearby lake.

Countryman From the personal name, e.g. the peak in WY for a local family.

County A generic, appearing occasionally by association as a specific, e.g. **County Line Lake** MI.

Coupe American-French, 'cut-off,' with special reference to land cut off when a river changed channel, e.g. **Terre Coupe Prairie** MI.

Coupee From French *coupé, coupée,* 'cut off [participle],' e.g. **Pointe Coupee** LA.

Courage Point MN From a rough translation of an Indian personal name.

Courtableau, Bayou LA For Santiago Cortableau, a settler of the 18th century.

Courteoreille, Lake WI French 'short ear,' but reason for so calling is uncertain. See **Couderay.**

Courthouse, Court House In the SE the term was often used for what would have been known as the 'county seat' in other parts of the U.S., e.g. **Amelia Court House** VA, the name being regularly that of the county. This usage has gradually been declining, but it lasted well into the 20th century. Since the courthouse was likely to be the largest building known to a 19th-century American the term was applied descriptively, e.g. **Courthouse Rock** NB, a famous landmark on the covered-wagon trail, somewhat resembling a large, boxy building.

Courtland Commonly from the personal name, e.g. in CA for Courtland Sims, son of a local landowner. In KS, it was originally named for **Cortland** NY, but the spelling was changed, probably by a clerical error.

Court Martial FL Gen. Andrew Jackson, during one of his campaigns, held a trial here of two deserters.

Courtrock OR A shortening for **Courthouse Rock.**

Couse Nez Percé, the name of an edible root, e.g. the creek in OR, WA.

Coushatta LA From an Indian tribal name, but literally 'canebrake-white,' so possibly named descriptively. Also as **Koasati.**

Coutolenc CA An adaptation from Eugene Coutolanezes, early settler.

Covada WA A constructed name, from the names of six local mines, viz. Columbia, Orin, Vernie, Ada, Dora, and Alice.

Cove Originally a seacoast term, it was used as a generic, and occasionally with specific use, e.g. **Cove Point** MD. As the frontier advanced inland, the term went along, being applied to land features, such as the point of a meadow surrounded by forest. Chiefly, however, it came to mean a small isolated valley or 'pocket,' and the use as a specific sprang from this meaning, e.g. **Cove** AZ, OR, **Cove Orchard** OR.

Covelo CA Probably a transferred European name, perhaps from Spain, though by local tradition, it may be from Covolo in the Tirol.

Coventry From the English town-name, e.g. CT (1711), RI (ca. 1740).

Covert KS Originally for the creek; said locally to mean 'covered over,' but more likely from the personal name.

Covina CA A name applied ca. 1890, apparently coined. Local tradition may be right in deriving it from 'cove of vines.'

Covington From the personal name, e.g. in KY for Gen. Leonard Covington, a hero of the War of 1812.

Cow A common name, generally from the domestic animal, but sometimes from the bison, elk, or moose. The name generally springs from some incident, e.g. **Cow Creek** CA, where a herd, having been without water for a whole day, stampeded into the creek. **Cow Creek** SD: the land along this stream was favored by an early rancher as a calving ground. Compounds are numerous. **Cowbell Lake** AZ: known for a cow wearing a bell, which frequented the lake in the 1950's. **Cowhorn Mountain** OR: so called because of two projecting horn like pinnacles. **Cowskin Island** CA: some people built shelters here with cowhides.

Cowanesque Creek PA Algonquian (Delaware) 'briars-full.'

Cowasset, Cowassit, Cowate, Cowaude, Cowautacuck, Cowekesit, Cowesiseck. These names (CT, MA, RI) are of Algonquian origin, with the general meaning, 'pine(s)-at.'

Cowee From the name of a Cherokee town, probably a shortening of a name meaning 'Deer-Clan-place.'

Coweman River WA By partial folk-etymology from Indian (Cowlitz) *ko-wee-na*, 'short man,' because a small Indian lived there.

Coweta In GA from the name of a Creek town; literal meaning uncertain. In OK it is a transfer from GA.

Cowiche WA Indian, of uncertain origin.

Cowikee Creek AL Muskogean (Hichiti), probably 'water-carrying,' i.e. a place where water was carried.

Cowilliga Creek NY Iroquoian, meaning uncertain.

Cowlic Papago 'hill.'

Cowlitz A number of names in WA arise from the tribal name, but **Cowlitz Bay** is probably from a ship so named.

Cowpens SC A name derived literally from pre-Revolutionary cattle raising, probably because drovers penned their cattle here overnight.

Cowsigan ME Algonquian 'rough-narrows.'

Coxcomb From a formation resembling a cock's comb, e.g. **Mount Coxcomb AK.**

Coxsackie NY Algonquian, meaning uncertain, though *-sack-* suggests the common word for a stream outlet.

Coy From the personal name, e.g. **Coy City** TX for Alfonso Coy, local cowboy.

Coyote In the regions where the coyote originally lived, the beast was so common and unimportant as rarely to be impressive. Still, a fair number of names exist, especially in CA. Since the coyote was sometimes called *prairie wolf,* some wolf-names may be for the coyote. As is customary with animal-names, most of them spring from incidents. **Coyote Wells** CA: in 1857 a man saw a coyote scratching here for water, and thus the wells were discovered. The frequent use of the name in CA may be influenced by the fact that some of the Indians held the coyote to be a kind of god. In addi-tion, the name springs from the type of mining known as 'coyoteing,' i.e. the digging of small separate holes; hence, **Coyote Hill,** Nevada Co., CA.

Cozad From the personal name, e.g. in NB and OH.

Crab, Crab Orchard, Crabtree As a sea-coast name **Crab** springs from the crustacean. Inland, most commonly as **Crab Orchard,** it derives from the crabapple. The creek in CA is for W. W. Crabtree, early settler.

Crabapple From the wild crabapple, also often as **Crab** and **Apple.**

Crag Coming into use as a generic in the 19th century, the term is used as a descriptive, e.g. **Crag Peak** CA.

Cranberry Various plants with edible berries known by the same popular name have given rise to a considerable number of names in their regions of growth. Since the cranberry is water-loving, the names are usually formed with generics such as marsh, lake, brook. Cranberry bog, however, is usually a common noun.

Cranbury NJ Probably for the country-seat in Hampshire, England.

Crane. A few of the place-names are from the family name. Most of them are from the bird. Though it was of no special value, it was large and conspicuous, and did not occur in such numbers as to be commonplace. The association with the bird is demonstrated by the occurrence of these names in well-watered country, by their coupling with such generics as marsh and lake, and by such forms as **Crane Nest.**

Craneco WV From the partners Cole and Crane.

Crash Creek AK Named (1956) because the remains of a crashed airplane were near the stream.

Crate MN For F. L. Beasley, early homesteader, being the nickname derived from his middle name, Lucretius.

Crater In regions of volcanic activity, ancient or recent, the term is used as a specific to identify features associated with a crater, e.g. **Crater Lake** OR.

Crawl From a colloquial pronunciation of *corral,* especially a enclosure for swine, e.g. **Hog Crawl Creek** GA.

Crazy Occasionally used to record an incident. See **Mad. Crazy Horse Creek** SD: named for the well-known Sioux chief. **Crazy Creek** WY: because it seems to flow along a ridge instead of in a valley. **Crazyman Creek** OR: in the 1880's a hunter saw a man leaping about as if crazy; though the man turned out to be sane, the name was thus placed. **Crazy Peak** NM: the wife of an early settler became demented, and fell or leaped to her death from a cliff on this peak. **Crazy Woman Creek** (2 in WY): apparently translated from some Indian language, but significance uncertain. **Crazy Mountains** MT: the translation of an earlier Indian name, perhaps inspired by their rugged and unusual terrain. **Crazy Notch** AK: named (1954) by some geologists because the formations there were so unusual as to be termed 'crazy.' **Crazy Fish Lake** MT: because the first anglers found the fish ready to bite at any unusual kind of bait or lure. **Crazy Horse Creek** WY: two horses, being chased by their owners, jumped off a cliff into a lake and behaved so strangely in other ways as to gain this descriptive. **Crazy Man's Coolee** ND: because an early settler, ca. 1880, saw a wild man dressed in skins and with long hair, apparently demented.

Cream Because of association with dairying, e.g. **Cream Ridge** NJ. **Creamery** occurs as a habitation-name, e.g. PA.

Creek Primarily a generic, in New England retaining its British meaning, 'tidal inlet,' and in the rest of the country shifting to mean a flowing stream smaller than a river. In either sense it appears as a specific in habitation-names, e.g. the common **Big Creek,** and on natural features by association, e.g. **Creek Brook** MA, though this usage is rare. As the name of an important Indian tribe the name occurs, e.g. **Creek County** OK.

Cremation Creek AZ The Indians used to cremate bodies here, throwing the ashes over the cliff.

Creola In AL it probably represents an attempt to form a feminine of **Creole** on the analogy of the Spanish *criolla.*

Creole As used in names in LA it refers to the presence or ownership of a descendant of French or Spanish settlers.

Creque American-French 'wild-plum,' e.g. the bayou in LA.

Cresbard SD From the names of two early settlers, John Cressey and Fred Baird.

Crescent A common descriptive for a lake or other feature of crescent shape. Habitation-names are generally by transfer, but may have been aided by the commendatory literal meaning, 'growing.' **La Crescent** MN: by counterpart, probably with humorous intention, from the town of **La Crosse** WI, which had just been founded on the opposite side of the river; the Minnesotans thus set themselves up as rivals by this reference to the opposition of the cross and the crescent. See **Crosse.**

Crescenta, La See **La Crescenta.**

Cresco Latin *I grow.* A commendatory name in PA and IA.

Cresskill NJ Probably Dutch *kers-kil,* 'cherry-stream,' though *kers* can also be 'watercress.'

Crest, Cresta The second form is the Spanish equivalent. It is rare with natural features, but **Crested** appears, as with **Crested Butte** CO; common with habitations, usually because of a high location, especially along the line of a road or railroad. It has commendatory value because of the suggestion of height. **Creston** (for crest-on or crest-ton) is commonest, but also **Crestline, Crestview,** etc. The Spanish form occurs, as in **Cresta Blanca,** 'crest-white,' CA.

Crestone Peaks CO May be a phonetic spelling of Spanish *crestón,* 'big crest'; this is in an area of Spanish names. The word also can mean the outcropping of a vein of ore, and so may have a mining background.

Crestonio TX A Spanish-like coinage from Creston A. King, son of a local landowner.

Crete In ND from the nickname of Lucretia Steele, daughter of a local landowner; elsewhere undetermined, whether from a personal name or from the Mediterranean island.

Crevecoeur, Creve Coeur The fort IL was thus named by R. C. La Salle in 1689, apparently for the Dutch fortress, the capture of which in 1672 by the French had been a notable exploit. The literal meaning, 'break-heart,' may have furnished an additional reason.

Cricket Insects thus known were a pest in parts of the arid West, and some names result, e.g. **Cricket Mountains** UT, **Cricket Flat** OR.

Crillon, Mount AK Named (1786) by the French explorer J. F. La Perouse, but with no statement as what bearer of that name was being honored; a likely candidate would be Gen. Louis Crillon, Duc de Mahon (1718–1796).

Cripple 1) In its English sense, a rare name, springing from an incident in which a man or animal was crippled, usually as **Cripple Creek,** partly by the influence of alliteration, e.g. the stream in OR named because a surveyor once cut his foot there with an ax. 2) From the Dutch *kreupelbosch,* 'thicket, underbrush,' anglicized as *cripple;* it was used as a common noun or place-name generic, but its meaning was forgotten, and a new generic was often then supplied, with resulting names such as **Big Cripple Swamp** DE, **Long Cripple Brook** NJ. Also as **Kripplebush** NY.

Crisp From the personal name, e.g. **Crisp Point** MI, for Capt. Christopher Crisp of the U.S. Lifesaving Service. In TX for C. P. Crisp, political figure.

Cristianitos Canyon CA Spanish 'little Christians,' with reference to two children who were baptized here in 1769.

Cristo Spanish 'Christ,' used rarely, e.g. **Sierra De Cristo Rey** TX.

Croatoan Recorded in an English context (1586) as the name of an island of the northern coast of present NC and of a village on the island; probably Algonquian, meaning uncertain. The village **Croatan** NC is apparently the same, but a late transfer to a different location.

Croche American-French 'crooked,' e.g. **Marais Croche** MO.

Crockett From the personal name, especially for Davy Crockett, famous frontiersman, e.g. in TX. **Crockett** CA: for J. B. Crockett of the CA Supreme Court.

Crocodile The Bayou in LA takes its name from the alligator, probably under the influence of the French **Cocodrie.** The river in WI was named by an 18th-century traveler who heard a story (probably mythological) of a strange water beast killed here, which he supposed to be a crocodile.

Croft 1) From the personal name, e.g. **Croft** KS. 2) A vague commendatory second element (from older English 'enclosure'), e.g. **Ashcroft** CO; not widely used.

Cromesit Point MA Algonquian; uncertain, but probably with the idea of being deserted.

Cromwell From the personal name, e.g. in OK for J. I. Cromwell, oil operator (1924). **Cromwell Township** MN: for Oliver Cromwell, at the instance of English settlers. **Cromwell:** in CT (1851) probably because the activities of a local privateer during the Revolution and of a later steamboat had popularized the name locally.

Cronomer Valley NY By local tradition, from an Indian so named who lived here.

Crook From the personal name, especially in the West for Gen. George Crook of the Indian wars.

Crooked Occurs most commonly with *creek,* doubtless being favored because of the alliteration; also common with *lake;* with other features, rare. Because of derogatory suggestions it hardly occurs as a habitation name. **Crooked Finger Prairie** OR: from the name of an Indian chief.

Cross 1) From the personal name, e.g. **Cross** OK, for J. L. Cross, first postmaster. 2) As a descriptive term, i.e. something in the shape of a cross or marked with something thus shaped, e.g. **Cross Mountain** AZ, or something crossed by something else, such as a trail, a canoe route, or a river flowing across a lake, e.g. **Cross Lake** MN and **Cross Canyon** AZ. **Cross Anchor** SC: from a tavern kept by a former sailor. **Crossbar** NB: a brand name. **Cross River** MN: from a large cross erected by a missionary, ca. 1845. **Cross Timbers:** a term applied to a belt of wooded land, running north and south in the eastern part of present Texas, and thus running crosswise to the general route of travel. From another such belt the name **Cross Timbers** remains in MO. **Cross Keys:** from the name and sign of an inn, e.g. NJ, PA.

Crosse French 'crosier,' but in placenames referring to the crosierlike stick or racket used by the Indians in their game, since known as *lacrosse*. **La Crosse** WI: from an earlier **La Crosse Prairie,** so called because a favorite place for the Indians to play their game. A number of other towns are so named, probably for similar reasons.

Crosswicks NJ Algonquian, with the idea of separation, but reference uncertain.

Croton NJ, NY From the name of an early chief, recorded as Cnoten.

Crow Many of the names are from the family name or, in WY, etc., from the Crow Indians. The crow is common and conspicuous, and often called attention to himself by his cawing or other actions. **Crow** WV: as the namer was considering the problem, a crow flew overhead. **Crow Creek** SD: on the Lewis and Clark expedition, Lewis killed a magpie, a bird unknown to the explorers; they classified it as a member of the crow family, and gave that name. **Crowheart Butte** WY: according to legend, to which the existence of the name gives some authority, a Shoshone once killed a Crow here and

ate his heart to gain courage. **Crow Wing River** MN: a translation of an Ojibway name, probably to be better rendered as Raven's Feather, and so applied because of the shape of an island. **Crow Peak** SD and **Crows Nest Peak** SD by tradition indicate places where the Sioux fought battles with invading Crow. **Crow Test Peak** MT: a mountain where youths of the Crow tribe tested themselves by keeping winter vigils.

Crown Though a rare personal name (hence, probably **Crown Creek** in WA), it is commonly a commendatory for habitations, with the suggestion of being royal, i.e. superlative; it frequently occurs as a business- or corporation-name, especially on mines, and thus passes by transfer to habitations, e.g. **Crown King** AZ, a kind of double superlative, first used for a mine. **Crown Point** NY: an improper translation of the French *chevelure,* 'scalp,' probably for an incident.

Croyden From the name of a town in England.

Crucero Spanish 'crossing.'

Crum It is commonly from the family name, but **Crum Elbow** NY and **Crum Creek** PA are from Dutch *krom,* 'crooked.'

Cruso NC By local story, named, ca. 1885, by the first postmaster, who had just read *Robinson Crusoe;* change of spelling unexplained.

Crutcho Creek OK A brand name, from a crutch and the letter O.

Cruz Spanish 'cross,' e.g. in **Santa Cruz,** 'holy cross.' **Cruz** AZ: on the **Santa Cruz River,** but being a railroad location its name was shortened for ease in telegraphy. **Las Cruces** CA: 'the crosses,' but origin uncertain. **Las Cruces** NM: because men killed by Indians during an attack on an early train of ox carts were buried here and the graves marked by crosses, which remained long enough to establish the name.

Crystal Is often applied as a literal descriptive to caves and other features where crystals may be found. In the sense 'clear as crystal' it is applied to lakes and springs and, less commonly, to streams, having commendatory value. **Crystal Bay** MN: from the presence of crystalline rocks **Crystal Falls** MI: named when the vegetation near the falls was densely covered with ice crystals after a storm.

Crystallia MI A Latinized formation from nearby **Crystal Lake.**

Cub Because of some incident with a cub—usually of a bear, but sometimes of a wolf or other animal. **Cub Lake** CA: three lakes in a chain, growing successively smaller, are called **Big Bear Lake, Little Bear Lake,** and **Cub Lake. Cub Lake,** Rocky Mountain N.P., CO: merely because it is small, a mere cub.

Cuba Commonly from the island; in OH the name dates from 1813, the period of exotic names. Most of the examples, e.g. in CA and MN, date from the time of the Spanish-American War. In NM the name is from Spanish 'trough, tank.' In KS it was first Kuba for a settler of that name, not further identified. **Cuba City** WI was originally named **Yuba** from the place in CA; when this was rejected by the Post Office Dept., the present similar name was substituted. In AL it may have been suggested by **Cubahatchee.**

Cubahatchee Creek AL Muskogean, with *hatchee,* being the common word for stream, but the rest uncertain.

Cube, Mount NH As early as 1805 it was **Mt. Cuba,** so called by a former seaman; the present name was apparently developed by folk-etymology.

Cucamonga In CA, Shoshone, probably meaning 'sandy place'; in OR, a transfer from CA.

Cuchara Spanish 'spoon,' applied to a river in CO for uncertain reasons.

Cuchilla, Cuchillo Spanish 'knife,' also used in a topographical sense for a sharp ridge, e.g. **La Cuchilla** NM. **Cuchillo Negro** NM: for an Apache chief.

Cuckold Though known to early colonists, the term never flourished in the U.S., and the rare place-names have not been specifically explained, e.g. **Cuckolds Brook** NJ. **The Cuckolds,** some ledges off the coast of ME, may have been named from the occurrence of a fish so known because of their hornlike protuberances. As a habitation-name, it was a humorous derogatory, e.g. **Cuckoldstown** DE, now superseded, as with most such names.

Cucumber This rare name is probably from one of the wild plants so known—especially from the magnolia tree, called 'cucumber tree' because of the shape of its fruit.

Cudjoe Usually spelled Cudjo, this was a common name for negroes in the 18th century, and the key in FL was probably thus named.

Cuerno Verde CO Literally, Spanish 'horn-green,' but named from a Comanche chief.

Cuero Spanish 'hide, skin,' e.g. the creek in TX, which has been translated from an Indian name.

Cuervo Spanish 'crow [the bird].'

Cuesta Spanish 'hill, slope, grade.'

Cueva Spanish 'cave.'

Cuivre French 'copper.' Since there is no copper in the vicinity of the river in MO, the name arose either from false reports or by folk-etymology from an Indian name.

Culdesac ID For *cul-de-sac,* probably because a practicable route for a railroad came to a sudden end here.

Culebra Spanish 'snake, serpent,' e.g. **Rio Culebra** CO. Also used, by figure of speech for a snakelike curve, e.g. in NM.

Cullaby OR The name of a well-known local Indian.

Cullasaja River NC Cherokee 'honey-locust-place,' probably named because that tree had religious significance.

Culleoka TN Muskogean with *-oka,* 'water' and the rest uncertain.

Cullowhee NC Cherokee, probably a variant of **Chilhowee,** q.v .

Culstigh Creek AL Probably Cherokee 'locust-tree-place' (?).

Cultus A Chinook jargon word, 'filthy, very bad.' It expresses disgust with a place, probably because someone suffered something unpleasant there. It has sometimes been substituted for some obscene English word. Used on natural features, e.g. **Cultus Lake** OR.

Cumberland From the county in England, but more immediately for Prince William Augustus, Duke of Cumberland, famous from his victory at Culloden in 1746. Shortly afterwards the counties in PA, VA and NC, and the river were thus named. **Cumberland** NM: from the Cumberland Presbyterian Church, members of which founded the town.

Cumbo WV From the first letters of Cumberland Valley Railroad, and the initials of the Baltimore and Ohio Railroad.

Cumbre Spanish 'summit, top.'

Cumero Spanish 'hackberry.'

Cumorah, Hill NY According to the statement of Joseph Smith, this name was revealed to him in a vision as the hiding place of the gold plates, and it has since then been applied to the hill. Though it has a general resemblance to Hebrew, its language and meaning are uncertain.

Cumro NB From a town in Wales.

Cumulus See **Cirrus.**

Cunard From the family name, e.g. in WV for an otherwise-unidentified operator of a coal mine.

Cundiyo NM Spanish rendering of a Tewa word, meaning uncertain.

Cupertino CA A Spanish naming, in honor of St. Joseph of Cupertino.

Cupit Mary Mountain OR From an Indian woman, who was the youngest of her family; Cupit (for *ko-pet,* 'the end.'

Cupric Cauldron WY From its green coloring, resembling the cupric salts of copper.

Cuprum ID Latin 'copper,' because of a former mine.

Cupsaw NJ Algonquian, probably 'obstructed-outlet.'

Cupsuptic ME Algonquian 'obstructed-stream.'

Cureall MO Because, in self-esteem, a health resort.

Curecanti CO For a Ute chief.

Curiosity In OR the creek was named because the limb of a tree grew in an unusual shape. In CO the hill was so called because many uncommon minerals could be found here.

Curlew From the game bird; in IA it is one of three names (the others being **Mallard** and **Plover**) which were given when the railroad was built by C. E. Whitehead in memory of the birds that he had shot there.

Currant From the occurrence of wild currants, e.g. two lakes in MN, one of which has been shifted to **Current.**

Current A descriptive, usually with seacoast names, e.g. the cape in AK. **Current Lake,** Murray Co., MN was originally **Currant.**

Currituck In NC it is a tribal name. In ME it is from Algonquian 'crooked-swift-stream.'

Currumpaw See **Corrumpa.**

Curry He Mountain, Curry She Mountain TN From Cherokee *guarahi,* referring to a kind of salad plant, made over by folk-etymology into **Curry He. Curry She** then arose by analogy.

Cusaqua Creek NY Iroquoian 'spear.'

Cushetunk Mountain NJ Algonquian, probably with the idea of washed or overflowed land hence 'lowland,' originally a stream-name.

Cushtusha Creek MS Choctaw 'fleas-are-there.'

Cussabexis See **Cuxabesis.**

Cusseta AL, GA From an Indian tribal name.

Cussewago Creek PA Iroquoian 'in-basswood-country.'

Custer Counties in several states and a number of towns honor the spectacular George A. Custer, Civil War general and Indian fighter, killed in 1876.

Cut Occurring in compounds as in the common 'cutback,' as applied to a stream; hence **Cut Bank** MT. **Cut off** LA and **Cutoff Creek** AK refer to the meanderings of a river. **Cuthand** TX: from the personal name of a local Indian chief. **Cut Foot Sioux Lake** MN: translated from the Ojibway, with reference to a maimed Sioux who was killed there in a battle of 1748. **Cutshin Creek** KY: probably for 'cut shin' to indicate rough and rocky going. **Cut 'N Shoot** TX represents a bit of humor, locally believed to have arisen from a squabble about the shape of a church steeple.

Cutchogue NY Algonquian 'principal-place,' probably because of a chief tribal settlement.

Cutmaptico Creek MD Algonquian probably 'big-tree-it-is.'

Cuttalossa Creek PA Algonquian, meaning uncertain.

Cutthroat Though the presence of cutthroat trout has probably produced a few names, the explained ones are from incidents. The gulch in CA was named because a Chinese miner was found there, ca. 1860, with his throat cut. The gap in OK was the scene of a savage massacre of Kiowas by Osages in 1833.

Cuttingbone Creek GA Early forms, e.g. **Crittington's,** the name of a Cherokee-English family, indicate that the name developed by an error in transmission because of bad handwriting, *plus* the aid of folk-etymology.

Cuttyhunk MA Algonquian, but so badly transformed in English as to be uncertain in meaning.

Cuxabesis Lake ME Algonquian 'little-swift-water.'

Cuyahoga River OH Iroquoian 'river,' applied to an important stream so that it is the equivalent of 'the river, important river.'

Cuyama CA From an Indian village, probably Chumash 'clams.'

Cuyamaca CA From an Indian village, probably Diegueño 'rain above.'

Cuyuna Range MN Coined from the name of its discoverer, Cuyler Adams, and that of his accompanying dog, Una.

Cuzco IN, VA An exotic name, from the city in Peru.

Cuzzie WV From Mrs. Cuzzie Smith, first postmistress.

Cyanide CO, MT From a plant for treating ore by the cyanide method.

Cyclone Because of unpleasant association, rare for a habitation-name, but widespread for natural features to identify a place where a cyclone (tornado) occurred or where the effects of its passing, e.g. overthrown trees, could be seen.

Cygne French 'swan.'

Cygnet OH Probably from its meaning 'young swan,' but reference uncertain.

Cygnus Latin 'swan.'

Cynthiana KY Coined from Cynthia and Anna, daughters of the original landowner.

Cynwyd PA Named in the 19th century as a railroad station from a town in Wales by an official of Welsh ancestry.

Cypert AR From a family name, not otherwise identified.

Cypre French, an alternate form for *cypres,* 'cypress,' e.g. **Bayou Cipre** LA.

Cypremort, Bayou LA French 'cypress-dead,' traditionally for a fallen cypress which was used as a footbridge.

Cypress From the tree thus known, chiefly in the SE. Its association with water is shown by its frequent use with *slough, bottom, pond,* etc., *cypress swamp* being a generic term. A western tree of different type has produced, in CA, **Cypress Mountain** and **Point Cypress.** Artificial plantings have resulted in **Cypress Lawn** CA, etc. In spite of funereal associations, the name has been often used for habitations. **Cypress Island** WA: for a tree that is really a juniper.

D

Daaquam River ME Algonquian 'your-beaver.'

Dabop Bay WA Indian, of uncertain meaning.

Dacoma OK Coined from Dakota and Oklahoma in 1904.

Dacono CO Coined (1905) from the first names of three local women, Daisy Baum, Cora Van Vorhies, and Nona Brooks.

Dad The common appellation for a father or an old man appears in a few names, e.g. **Dads Lake** NB, **Dad Spring** OR.

Dade From the family name; in FL for Major F. L. Dade, killed in the outbreak of Seminole warfare in 1835.

Dagger Regularly, e.g. **Dagger Mountain** TX, from the presence of giant yucca, or so-called Spanish dagger.

Dahinda IL Ojibway 'bull-frog,' but the suggestion and spelling are from Longfellow's *Hiawatha*.

Dakota From the Indian tribe, that is, the western division of the people more commonly known as Sioux, established by Congress as the name of the territory in 1861. When the division had been made between north and south, each part, as a territory, tried to pre-empt the name, and the result was to compromise as **North Dakota** and **South Dakota**. Counties and towns in other states, e.g. IA, MN, NB are from the tribe, having been named before the organization of the territory.

Dalark AR A boundary-name, from Dallas and Clark counties.

Dalbo MN A Swedish naming to indicate 'home of people from Dalarne' (a region in Sweden).

Dale Sometimes from the personal name. More commonly it stands as the second part of a habitation-name, in its sense of 'valley,' e.g. **Springdale**. This was one of the Romantic terms popularized in the earlier 19th century. **Dale Township** MN: because lying chiefly in a valley. **Virginia Dale**, see **Virginia**.

Dalkena WA Formed from the names of Dalton and Kennedy, local lumber operators.

Dall From the personal name, various features in AK being for W. H. Dall (1845–1927) explorer and authority on AK.

Dallas The city in Texas and most other examples are for George Mifflin Dallas, mid-19th-century political figure, Vice President of the U.S., 1845–1849.

Dalles, The French 'flag-stone, slab of rock.' A quasi-generic, the term was applied by the early French to places where a stream ran over smooth rocks. The meaning 'gutter' is sometimes given, but the idea of a bottom as if of smooth pavement would seem to be the original one. Merely as **The Dalles** the name has been specialized to denote those of the Columbia River and the town there (OR).

Dalworth TX Because halfway between **Dallas** and **Fort Worth**.

Dam From association with a dam, e.g. **Dam Lake** MN, which has a low ridge of gravel forming a natural dam. The term is usually avoided because of profane suggestions.

Damariscotta ME Algonquian 'alewives (fish)-plenty.' This is a much changed form from an original Abnaki, which must have been about like the modern Abnaki form, viz. *madamas-contee*.

Damariscove Island ME Occurring in an English context (1616) as **Damerils Isles**, it is apparently from an English family name most likely from some association with Humphrey Damerell, who was very early on this coast, probably as a fisherman. It may have been influenced in form by the nearby **Damariscotta**.

Damascus From the city of Syria, often mentioned in the Bible. In OH the name was given because of the existence of two rivers, comparable to those mentioned in Kings II, 5.

Dame As **Notre Dame** (French 'Our Lady,' for the Virgin Mary) the name is common for Catholic churches and institutions, and occurs by association with a few railroad stations and post offices. **Dames Quarter** MD is probably from a family name; Dame (i.e. Dame's), and *quarter*, 'tract, district of settlement.' **Les Dames Anglaises** WY: French 'the-ladies-English,' applied (probably 1936) to some rock pinnacles of striking appearance, but reasons for thus naming in French and for the English reference are unexplained.

Damfino Creek WY A conventional spelling for the colloquial 'I'm damned if I know!' someone's reply when asked what the name was, and taken humorously by the namer.

Damnation Peak CA A derogatory name applied after a desperate conflict of troops with Indians in 1859.

Dan, Daniel(s) Danbury, e.g. CT in 1687, is from the name of a town in England. Other forms are from personal names, with **Danville** being the prevailing form, e.g. in KY for Walter Daniel, the founder, and in IL for Dan Beckwith, the founder. **Danville** VA is from its situation on **Dan River**, itself probably of Indian origin (cf. **Rapidan**); the -*an* could represent the Algonquian *hanne*, 'stream.' It is, however, doubtfully derived from an 'Indian' *dannaha*, 'muddy water' (?). In VT the name arose (1784) at a time when many French names were being given, and it probably honors J. B. B. D'Anville, famous geographer. **Danbury** LA: from Daniel Thomas, town founder, and the name of the county, **Woodbury.**

Dana From the personal name. **Dana Point** CA: from R. H. Dana, Jr., who tells in *Two Years Before the Mast* of being swung over the cliff on a rope. **Mount Dana** CA, **Dana Butte** AZ: for J. D. Dana (1813–1895), American geologist.

Dane 1) From the personal name, e.g. the county in WI for Nathan Dane, framer of the Ordinance of 1787. 2) From Danish settlers, e.g. the creek in NB.

Danevang TX Dane, coupled with a Danish word for valley or meadow; so named by immigrants.

Danger Arises because of a hazard to navigation, e.g. **Danger Point** AK, or from some other hazard or incident. **Danger Lake** MN: so called because of certain ice conditions. The name, because of unpleasant suggestions, is likely to be replaced, as has actually happened in both the above cases, but other names, e.g. **Danger Rock** WA survive.

Dango KY Uncertain; Cherokee (?).

Dania FL Named by Danes (1927), a Latinized form, the equivalent of Denmark.

Dannebrog NB The name of the Danish national flag was applied by the Danes who founded the town.

Dannemora NY From the site in Sweden, known for its iron mines.

Dante For the Italian poet, in SD locally believed to have been named because of his association with hell.

Danvers From a personal name. In MA the name may date from as early as 1745, and its origin is uncertain.

Danville See **Dan.**

Danzig For the city, formerly in Germany; now Gdansk in Poland.

D'Arbonne, Bayou LA From the name of a family of early settlers, usually spelled Derbonne or Darbonne.

Darby From an alternate spelling of the English county and city (**Derby**), or from a personal name. The stream in OH is from an Indian so called.

Dardanelle(s) The name, probably because publicized in the Crimean War, became a popular one for CA mines in the 1850's. Either by transfer or because of a fancied resemblance to the strait, the name is now used for **The Dardanelles** and associated names (CA) and for places in other states. **Dardanelle AR**: though probably originating from the French family name Dardenne, it may have been attracted to the form of the name of the straits.

Darden From the family name, in TN for Mills Darden, a local giant, reputed to have been 8 feet, 5 inches in height.

Dardenne Creek MO For the Dardenne family, early French settlers.

Dare County NC Named (1870) commemoratively for Virginia Dare, first child born of English parents in the New World.

Darfur MN From the province in the Sudan, named in 1899 when the region became known because of British campaigns in Africa.

Darien From the isthmus. In CT the name was given (1820) when exotic foreign names were popular; a narrow place on the Post Road here may have suggested an isthmus.

Dark Although existing as a personal name, it generally occurs descriptively, and is more common in the East than in the West, probably because of association with a heavy forest, e.g. **Darkharbor** ME, **Dark Swamp** LA, **Dark Hollow** (several, KY), **Dark Pond** NH. It is applied to elevations in some areas instead of the commoner **Black**, e.g. **Dark Knob** KY. **Dark Canyon** SD, a Western example, translates a Siouan name, apparently with the attempt to carry over an idea of superstitious dread.

Darling, Darlington Regularly from the personal name, e.g. in ID for Wayne Darlington, an early miner. It may in some instances be for the town in England, e.g., according to local belief, the county in SC (1785).

Darrington WA The intention was to honor a Mr. Barrington (otherwise unidentified), but a mistake was somewhere made.

Dartmouth In MA (ca. 1664) from the town in England.

Darwin From the personal name, e.g. **Mount Darwin** CA for Charles Darwin, scientist.

Darysaw Creek AR By folk-etymology from a French family of early settlers, named Des Ruisseaux. Also as **Dairysaw.**

Date A grove of date palms accounts for **Dateland** AZ. **Date Creek** AZ is from the abundance of yucca, known as *datal* in Spanish. **Date** SD is for Datus D. Peterson, local rancher.

Datha SC From the name of an Indian chief.

Datil NM Spanish 'date (the fruit).' The mountains were so called probably because of the presence of some cactus fruit resembling dates.

Daufuskie SC Probably Muskogean, meaning uncertain.

Daughter-of-the-Sun-Mountain MT Probably a translation of an Indian (Blackfoot) name, because the peak, being the highest in the vicinity, holds the sun's rays longest.

Dauphin County PA In 1785 petitioners who asked for the formation of a new county desired to honor France for aid in the Revolution, and so used the title of the heir to the throne of France.

Dauterive, Lake LA From the name of a local family.

Davenport From the personal name, e.g. in IA for Col. George Davenport, one of the founders.

David Douglas, Mount OR For the botanist, named commemoratively in 1927.

Davidson From the personal name, especially, e.g. **Davidson Rock** WA, **Mount Davidson** CA, **Davidson Seamount** (off the coast of CA), for George Davidson (1825–1911), astronomer and geographer, who himself gave many names and was much interested in nomenclature.

Daviess Counties in IL, IN, KY, and MO preserve the name of J. H. Daviess, public figure of the early 19th century, killed at Tippecanoe in 1811.

Davis From the personal names, especially for Jefferson Davis, president of the C.S.A. To avoid confusion with other holders of this common name, it appears as **Jefferson Davis County** MS, and **Jeff Davis County** TX. **Davis** CA: for J. C. Davis, early settler.

Daweepanoonis Creek CO Ute, probably with *weep,* 'canyon, watercourse,' and the rest uncertain.

Dawn Generally in a figurative or commendatory sense, e.g. **Dawn Mist Falls** MT. **Dawn** TX: a commendatory, because an early storekeeper used to refer to 'the dawn of the century.'

Dawtaw Island SC From the name of an Indian chief.

Day, Dayton From the personal name. In OH it is for Jonathan Dayton (1760–1824), one of the founders. The importance of the name in OH has led to its proliferation, and even places named for someone called Day often become **Dayton,** e.g. in TX. **Daylight Pass** CA: from a spring, which was first **Delightful** and next **Delight.**

Daylo NC Named (1924) by its founder, E. N. Vannoy, merchant, for a kind of flashlight that he sold.

Daytona Beach FL Named (1870) for its founder, Mathias Day, extended with the common suffix '-ton,' and the favorite '-a' for town-names.

De French and Spanish, 'of,' but in American-French often replaced by *à,* q.v. Other French forms are **Du,** 'of the' (masculine), and **Des,** 'of the' (plural). Spanish **Del** 'of the' (masculine) also occurs. Most of the names are entered under the significant word, but in some cases the opposite has seemed preferable, e.g. **Des Moines.** Many French and Spanish personal names begin with *de, du, des,* or *del,* either as a separate word or amalgamated.

Dead Applied descriptively to mountains, e.g. in CA, because of a dull, dreary, or deathlike appearance. More commonly a secondary specific as in **Dead Indian Creek** OR where the bodies of two Indians were found, ca.

1854. At **Dead Negro Draw** NM a Negro cowboy was frozen to death, ca. 1880. The finding of an animal's carcass has resulted in numerous names, e.g. **Dead Horse Creek** WA, **Dead Ox Creek** SD, **Dead Deer Canyon** NV. **Dead Point Creek** OR arises because of dead trees; so also, **Dead Tree Point** AK, **Dead Pine Creek** CA. **Deadwater** ME is descriptive of a place where water is without appreciable current, and **Dead River** ME probably so originates, as being applicable to certain reaches; **Dead Lake** (Otter Tail Co., MN) because of an Indian burial ground; **Dead Lake** (Hubbard Co., MN) because it has no visible outlet. See **Deadman. Dead Slough** IA is cut off from the river, and has no current. In the 1880's the body of a scalped white man was found at **Dead Man's Mountain** TX. **Dead Irishman Gulch** SD was so named because an early prospector lost his life here in a cave-in, his nationality being apparently better known than his name, a not-infrequent circumstance in Western mining-camps.

Deadening In forested areas the first step toward establishing a farm was to 'deaden' the trees by girding them with an ax. A few names have resulted, e.g. **Deadening Hollow** KY.

Deadfall By association with an early type of snare for animals, e.g. **Deadfall Branch** KY.

Deadman Common, it occurs more often in the West, perhaps because the more wide-ranging frontier with its deserts and mountains supplied more dead men. A fallen tree, useful for mooring a boat, was known as a deadman, and may have been the origin of some of the names. Stories are usually associated with the names, and many of them are authentic. In many instances, the presence of an unmarked grave (e.g. **Deadman's Island,** CA) establishes the name. Probably the finding of an unburied body is the commonest cause of the naming. The cause of death does not matter. It may have been murder, suicide, blizzard, or Indians. But after a long period of time, the name will more likely be **Skeleton,** or **Skull,** q.v. **Deadman Creek** SD. In all three examples the name results from the finding of a man or men killed and scalped. A man said that he would just as well be dead as to be in such a lonesome place, and the name **Deadman Creek** OR apparently arose from that statement. At **Deadman Gap** AZ the body of a man dead from thirst was found here, ca. 1913. **Dead Man's Curve** was used to designate a dangerous place on a highway, especially where people have been killed in automobile accidents.

Deadwood Applied descriptively to features where dead trees are conspicuous, usually because of fire, e.g. **Deadwood Gulch** SD; hence, the habitation-name.

Deaf Smith County TX For Capt. Erastus (Deaf) Smith, prominent in the Texas War of Independence.

Deal In NJ, for the town in England. **Deal Island** MD was originally **Devil Island** (for unknown reasons), and was changed, probably on the establishment of the post office.

Dearborn From the personal name, especially for Henry Dearborn, secretary of war in Jefferson's cabinet, e.g. the river in MT named by Lewis and Clark in 1805.

Dearfield CO Obviously suggested by the common **Deerfield**, but (according to differing local stories) either because the land was expensive or because the settlers were very fond of it.

Dearth From the personal name, e.g. the draw in WY, for Del Dearth, government trapper.

Deary ID For William Deary, local lumber company official (1907).

Death Rare, but occurs in several national parks, where fanciful naming often has been practiced. **Death Valley** CA is from the barren and hostile nature of the region together with the fatalities that occurred among emigrants in 1848–1850. Possibly some of the emigrants applied it at that time, as W. L. Manly declares to have been the case, but the name appears in print in 1861. **Deathball Rock** OR was a name given humorously to commemorate an unsuccessful attempt to make biscuits. At

Death Valley WY cowboys, in 1896, killed two sheepherders and 200 sheep.

Debebekid Lake AZ Navajo, 'sheep lake,' because sheep were often watered here.

De Borgia MT Probably named by early Catholic missionaries for St. Francis Borgia, with the *de* inserted later on the assumption that it should be there.

Decatur Usually for Stephen Decatur, early naval hero. In NB the name is from a town founder, himself named Stephen Decatur. In AL, after Decator's death in 1820, the town was so named at the instance of President Monroe.

Deceit, Cape AK Translated from the name given (1816) by the explorer Otto von Kotzebue both because he did not find there a bay which he had expected and because the natives there impressed him as deceitful.

Deception A record of the namer's feeling that he had been deceived in some fashion. **Deception Pass** WA was so named by George Vancouver in 1792, apparently because what he had thought to be a bay turned out to be a passageway. **Deception Creek** AK is a prospector's name, apparently because what was thought to be a good prospect for gold did not turn out to be so.

De Chelly, Canyon See **Chelly**.

Decipher Creek AR Probably from a French source, but uncertain.

Declo ID From the names of two families of early settlers, Dethles and Cloughly.

Decorah, Decorra Several Winnebago chiefs of the 18th and 19th centuries bore this name, which is preserved as **Decorah** IA, **Decorra** IL, and **Decorah's Peak** WI.

Decoria MN A Latinization of an Indian personal name. See **Decorah**.

Decypri MO A respelling, partly by sound, of the French *des cyprès,* 'of the cypresses.'

Dedham In MA (1636) from the town in England.

Deep A descriptive, either for water, e.g. **Deep Creek,** or for depression, e.g. **Deep Canyon,** or for a stream running in such a depression, e.g. **Deep Creek** OK. Though it occurs with river, e.g. CT, IA, WA, it is not common in this coupling, since under early conditions most rivers could be considered deep, i.e. over one's head. Similarly, it is rare with lake, since anything not deep would probably have been called a pond, but it occurs thus, e.g. FL. It is commonest with creek and run, and indicates the depth at the point of early crossing. It occurs also with seacoast features, e.g. **Deep Cove** AK where it is probably a name given after soundings. **Deephaven** as a habitation-name, e.g. in MN, is usually a commendatory to encourage shipping.

Deer The country over, the deer was the commonest larger mammal, and there were millions of encounters over the years. The very commonness of the animal made the name less useful, since almost any place could be so called. Whether deer were actually more numerous at one place than at another was a fact that the pioneer had little chance to determine. In addition, the pioneer was likely to use the terms **Buck, Doe,** and **Fawn,** so that these names are in many areas commoner than **Deer.** Still, encounters were so many that hundreds of names resulted, some of them originating in regions where deer were not numerous, and where the killing of one might be important for food. Incidents are rarely preserved. Isaac Wister killed a deer at **Deer Creek** CA in 1849. Because of generally pleasant associations habitation-names are numerous, e.g. **Deer Park** suggests English affluence. **Deerfield** is common, the earliest being in MA, ca. 1677. Though most MA towns were still being named for English towns, this seems to be an exception, and was probably named because deer were seen in a meadow. Descriptive because of rock formation are **Deer's Ears Buttes** SD, **Deerhorn Mountain** CA, etc. Other names are from Indian personal names, e.g. **Deer Flat** CA for a Wintu so named. At **Deer Lake** WA deer are accustomed to swim across a narrow place in the lake, and used to be killed there by men in boats.

Deeth NV Named by the railroad from the family name of an early settler.

Defeat, Defeated Fairly common in KY and TN arising from incidents, though these incidents are rarely recorded. **Defeat Mountain** TN, by local story, was named by counterpart for **Bote Mountain** (q.v.), because the decision was to take the road by the other route, and this one was thus defeated. **Defeated Creek** TN: from an incident of 1786 when a hunting party was roughly handled by attacking Indians.

Deferiet NY For Baroness Jenika de Ferriet, a French *emigrée* of the early 19th century, who lived here.

Defiance A commendatory name from the military point of view, it has been bestowed on forts, and the town in OH was thus derived, and probably that in PA. **Fort Defiance** remains in AZ and VA. **Mount Defiance** OR: so named because it held its snow for a long time in the spring, thus defying the sun.

Defiant, Mount AK Named (ca. 1957) by mountaineers because it had defied their efforts.

De Flag AZ A pseudo-Spanish name, humorously coined, for a small stream flowing through Flagstaff, and thus getting its name from the town.

De Gray Creek AR By partial folk-etymology from French *de grès,* 'of sandstone,' the banks of the stream supplying a very workable rock.

Degruy, Bayou LA For J. B. Degruy, a landowner of the 18th century.

Dehesa Spanish 'pasture-ground.'

De Kalb For Johann Kalb, known as 'Baron de Kalb,' (1721–1780), German-born, who served as major-general in the Revolutionary War and was killed at the battle of Camden, e.g. counties in MO, TN.

Dekkas Creek CA Wintu, connected with a word 'climb up.'

Del Spanish, 'of the,' masculine singular, occurring in many names, e.g. **Del Mar, Del Monte, Del Norte. Del City** OK: for Delaphene Campbell, daughter of the townsite owner.

Delacroix In LA the names are from a family of early landowners.

Delagua CO From Spanish, 'of the water,' applied first to the stream or canyon.

Delake OR From Devils Lake, said to be because the numerous Finnish immigrants used that pronunciation. It suggests, however, a. euphemism, i.e D-lake for Devils Lake.

Delanco NJ Because situated between the Delaware River and Rancocas Creek.

Delanson NY Coined from the rivers (or the railroad) Delaware and Hudson.

Delawanna NJ A coined name, because of its location on the Delaware, Lackawanna, and Western Railroad.

Delaware Thomas West, Lord de la Warr (Delaware), was the first colonial governor of Virginia, though he was in the colony for less than a year, 1610–1611. At this time Samuel Argoll discovered a cape which he called for the governor, Lawar. It later was written as Delaware, and the English transferred the name to the bay and the river. The Swedish colonists knew the stream as **New Sweden River** or **Swede's River.** The Dutch called it **South River,** in counterpart to **North River (Hudson).** The question of names became involved with sovereignty, but was settled by the English conquest (1664). At that time, the old Swedish-Dutch settlements to the west of the river were left without a name, and took that of the river, becoming the colony of **Delaware.** The Indian tribe living in that vicinity also came to be known by that name. The migration of this tribe westward in the 18th century and 19th century spread the name for towns and counties over the Middle West, and was of more influence than was the name of the state.

Delcarbon CO Spanish 'of the coal,' a comparatively recent name, given by a coal company to carry on the Spanish tradition of the area.

Delectable Mountain VT A commendatory, taken from John Bunyan's *Pilgrim's Progress.*

De Lesaire, Bayou LA Probably from the French family name De Lessart.

Delgado Spanish 'slender, narrow, acute,' often in the feminine as **Delgada,** e.g. the point and canyon in CA. **Delgado** NC: from the middle name of Dolores Delgado Stevens, wife of a local manufacturer.

Delhi From the city in India, generally applied as an exotic name without much reason, though its connection with gardens may account for its three-time use in CA.

Delight Lake AK Named (1911) by geologists because of its beauty. See **Day.**

Delightful Occasionally used to express the namers' feelings, e.g. **Delightful** (OH).

Dellmoor OR From a landowner, J. S. Dellinger, plus *moor,* since the area was moorlike.

Delmar Spanish 'of the sea'; also a personal name. As a repeated habitation-name it rarely has anything to do with the sea, and it appears to have become popular merely for its euphony and perhaps for a vaguely attractive suggestion. On the line between MD and DE it is a boundary-name. In **Delmar** IA, according to a story supported by officials of the railroad, the station was named by putting together the initials of six women who were on the excursion train making the first run on the new line; since all the letters are common ones, this story raises no great incredibility.

Delmarva Peninsula A coined name from DE, MD, and VA for the peninsula having land of all three states.

Delmita TX By local story an early settler had seven sons, and the name was established by having each son draw a letter of the alphabet; since the name seems to have no other likely origin, the story is plausible.

Deloit IA First named **Beloit** for the town in WI; when this was rejected by the Post Office Dept. because of duplication, a variant was substituted, probably on the analogy of **Detroit.**

De Loutre, Bayou TN French 'of otter,' but probably by false etymology, since earlier forms show **Saluter,** perhaps from a personal name.

Delphi From the ancient Greek town and shrine.

Delphia Probably a shortening of **Philadelphia,** e.g. in KY and MT.

Delphos In OH it is probably an artificial singular formed from **Delphi,** to avoid the duplication of a name.

Del Rio, Delrio Spanish 'of the river.' The spelling as one word is American.

Del Shay Basin AZ From the personal name of an Apache chief, absorbed to a semi-Spanish form, sometimes spelled Delche.

Delta 1) Because of triangular form, i.e. resemblance to the Greek letter *delta,* e.g. **Delta** CA where the level land at the top of a hill takes this form. **Delta County** TX: because it is triangular in shape. 2) Because of association with a delta of a river, e.g. **Delta Farms** LA. 3) Because of being fourth in a series, *delta* being the fourth letter in the Greek alphabet, e.g. the lake in MN.

Deluge Wash AZ In 1873 a prospector's camp was flooded out here.

Delusion Lake WY It was once believed to be an arm of **Yellowstone Lake,** and was named when this belief was proved to be a delusion.

De Luz CA Locally believed to be from **Corral de Luz,** the last word being the Spanish version of the name of an Englishman named Luce.

Demarcation Point AK This point of land is also, approximately, 'the point of demarcation' between Russian and British territory so named in 1826.

Demijohn Mountain CO From its fancied shape.

Deming From the personal name, in NM for Mary Deming, maiden name of Mrs. Charles Crocker, wife of the railroad magnate.

Democrat In **Democrat Gulch** OR most of the people were known as belonging to that party. In other places the name probably has a similar origin.

Demopolis Greek 'people-city,' named by a colony of French immigrants (1818), probably with the idea of democracy absorbed from the French Revolution.

Denbigh From the town and county in Wales; in ND, absorbed to this form from Densiof, a village in Russia, thus named by an immigrant.

Dendron VA Greek 'tree.'

Denio OR, NV For Aaron Denio, early settler.

Denlin CA Originally **Linden,** for John and Emma, local landowners. To avoid confusion with another **Linden,** the syllables were reversed.

Denmar WV From Dennison who came from Maryland.

Denmark In SC for a family name. Elsewhere it generally is for the country, most often, as in OR, because of the presence of Danes.

Dennehotso AZ Navajo 'upper end of meadow.'

De Noc, Big (Little) Bay MI The French *de,* 'of,' is joined with an Ojibway *noke,* 'bear totem,' to show the place of residence of Indians bearing that totem.

De Nova CO A 20th-century naming by C. B. Timberlake, congressman, probably with the idea of a fresh beginning; though precise neither in Spanish nor in Latin, the phrase is close to the Latin *de novo.*

Denver From the personal name. In CO it is for J. W. Denver, who was governor of Kansas Territory (then including eastern Colorado) at the time of the naming in 1858.

Denville NJ From Daniel Denton, landowner.

Deora CO Suggested by the first postmistress in 1920, from Spanish *de oro,* 'of gold,' probably as a commendatory.

De Pere WI Originally *rapides des pères* 'rapids of the priests,' because of an early mission at the site.

Depoe Bay OR For an Indian so called; he was probably named Depot, because associated with a supply depot.

Deposit Generally an early name to indicate a depot for goods.

De Queen AR By simplification and folk-etymology from the name of a Dutch capitalist DeGeoijen, who helped finance the local railroad.

Derby, Darby From the town and county in England, etc. **Darby** is a variant early spelling. Both spellings are used for personal names. **Mount Derby** CO: from being the shape of a derby hat.

Dermott AR For Charles McDermott, early settler.

Dernier(e) French 'last,' e.g. **Isle Derniere** LA, because it is, to anyone sailing westward, the last of a series of coastal islands.

Derry Commonly for **Londonderry**, q.v. It is also a personal name; in IA, for Col. Derry, who was interested in the local railroad line, not further identified.

Des Arc AR, MO, OK From French *des arcs,* literally 'of the bows,' but probably a shortening of Arkansa, i.e. the Indian tribe, applied first to a stream. Cf. **Ozark.**

Desatoya Mountains NV Shoshone, with *toya,* 'mountain,' and the rest probably 'big-black.'

Descanso Spanish 'rest, repose.'

Deschutes OR, WA French 'of the falls,' first applied to the river.

Desda KY Named by Hiram Irvin, probably the townfounder, for his fiancée.

Desdemona TX Originally **Desdemonia,** for a woman so named, but identification uncertain.

Deseret The term appears in the Book of Mormon as meaning 'honey-bee,' which was associated with a choice, far-off valley; the Mormon settlers used the name for the region around the Great Salt Lake, and it is still applied to a town. See **Utah.**

Desert As a generic, its early English use, 'deserted place, uninhabited place,' lasted into the Colonial period, but has left little, if any, remnant in modern place-names. By the 19th century, when the Americans entered the dry country, the sense 'arid place' had become well established, and a large number of place-names have thus developed by association. It was first applied to natural features, e.g. **Desert Well** (twice in AZ) for a spring which is the only water supply for a large arid area. After the development of the 'cult of the desert' in the 20th century the name was sometimes applied to habitations as a commendatory, e.g. **Desert Center** CA. American-French usage is with the meaning 'field, land without trees,' as in **Lake Vieu Desert** (*vieux desert*), 'old field,' for a former Indian cultivation. **Mount Desert Island** ME was named by Samuel de Champlain in 1604 as **Isle des Monts-Deserts;** since he mentions that the heights were bare of trees, he was probably using the word in the above French sense. **Desert Hound Peak** CA: from a mine-name.

Deserter Probably from an incident involving a military deserter, e.g. the creek in KY.

Desha AR For Benjamin Desha, early settler.

Desir, Bayou LA Early forms show an origin from *desert,* probably in the older French sense, 'field, land without trees' (see **Desert**), but possibly from a family name.

Des Lacs ND French 'of the lakes.'

Deslet MO Locally believed to be a derogatory descriptive from *desolate,* but possibly a French personal name.

Desmet, De Smet For Father Pierre De Smet (1801–1873), Jesuit missionary.

Des Moines In a French context as of 1673 a tribe was recorded as Moingouena. The river where they lived was later given their name, and was shortened by common French custom with Indian names to **Rivière Des Moings.** Either by similarity of sound or by folk-etymology this name was made into **Rivière Des Moines,** 'river of the monks.' In American usage it became **Des Moines River,** and the city was named from the stream.

Desolation Used, especially in CA, to designate places of 'desolated' appearance e.g., **Desolation Valley CA.**

De Soto, Desoto For Hernando de Soto, Spanish explorer of the 16th century, discoverer of the Mississippi River, e.g. several counties and towns, especially in the SE.

Despair, Gorge of CA In 1879, L. A. Winchell had some bad times here while exploring the Sierra Nevada.

Destrehan LA For *d'Estrehan,* Estrehan being the family name of former plantation owners.

Destruction The island in WA was named in 1787 because some voyagers suffered from an Indian attack. In AK the point was named because two Indian villages were destroyed there.

Deter OR From the family name of some early ranchers in the vicinity.

Detour Sometimes, e.g. in MD, of English origin, but more commonly from the French, e.g. **Detour Passage MI.** In French usage the word indicates (not, as in English, a temporary relocation) a roundabout or circuitous route, even though the main or only one. **Detour** MI changed its name to **De Tour Village** to avoid confusion in road signs.

Detroit French 'strait.' The city in MI took its name from being situated on the strait between lakes St. Clair and Erie. Elsewhere the name is generally derived from the city, but here and there is a direct French naming, e.g. **Detroit Lake MN.**

De View, Bayou AR Probably by folk-etymology from French *de veau,* 'of calf.'

Devil(s) Except when based upon Indian belief there is no evidence that any of the numerous names arise from genuine belief in a devil. In some instances the name springs from translation of Indian terms which really meant spirit rather than devil, but were so rendered because of the general belief that Indian spirits or gods were devils, e.g. **Devils Lake** ND renders the Sioux *minne,* 'water,' and *waukan,* 'spirit.' **Devil Track Lake** MN translates an Ojibway name containing *manitu,* 'spirit.' Other names are influenced by Indian belief without being actual translations, e.g. **Devil's Tooth** ND, where the rock resembles a tooth but also has an Indian story of something uncanny associated with it. The majority of the names, commoner in the West than in the East, attribute something to the devil in a humorous manner. The thing may be of superhuman size, e.g. **Devil's Postpile CA,** a formation of columnar basalt. **Devil's Kitchen** CA is a group of boiling springs. **Devil's Canyon** is a repeated name, and is quasi-descriptive, suggesting a place so difficult to pass that it must have been maliciously made by the devil. **Devils Den,** also a repeated name, is aided by alliteration, and indicates any unusually ferocious looking rock formation. **Devils Desk AK** is a peak descriptively named, with the additional benefit of alliteration. **Devils Elbow** is a repeated name, to describe an especially sharp turn in a road, and the place there. **Devils Slide** UT: this rough-topped dyke is named with the suggestion of the tortures of hell, as if the imps would set the souls to trying to slide down it. **Devils Golf Course CA:** a terrain so rough that it suggests devilish construction. In spite of a term often considered profane, a few habitation-names exist by transfer, e.g. **Devils Lake.**

Devon From the county in England, etc. One of the most rarely used of these county names.

Dewatto WA From a mythological under-earth region of the local Indians, known as *du-a-ta,* which was supposed to have an exit at this spot.

Deweese NB For J. W. Deweese, railroad attorney.

Dewey From the personal name, especially for Admiral George Dewey, hero of the Spanish-American War, e.g. the county in OK, **Deweyville** TX.

De Witt, Dewitt From the personal name, especially for De Witt **Clinton** (q.v.) whose extraordinary popularity sometimes led to the use of his first name because some town in the state had already pre-empted his last name.

Diablo Spanish 'devil,' generally used to indicate something unusually bad of its class, e.g. **Camino del Diablo** AZ 'road of the devil.' **Mount Diablo** CA The Spanish **Monte del Diablo,** 'wood of the devil,' was transferred to the mountain by Americans who took *monte* to mean *mount.* The origin is probably from some incident—by a story of 1850, one in which an Indian medicine man was taken for the devil.

Diagonal IA Because of the direction followed by the railroad with respect to the lines upon which the country was surveyed for property-holdings and roads.

Dial From the personal name, e.g. **Dialville** TX for J. J. Dial, who gave land for the townsite.

Diamond 1) From the personal name; 2) from the shape, especially as seen on a map, e.g. **Diamond Mesa** CA; 3) from the presence of crystals, supposed or imagined to be diamonds, e.g. **Diamond Ridge** WV; **Diamond Mountains** NV; 4) a commendatory name, especially for lakes, to suggest sparkling clarity, e.g. the lake in MN. **Diamond** OR; for the ranch of that name, which had a diamond-shaped brand. Many other names are from brands, e.g. **Diamond Bar Lake** NB. **Diamond:** the mesa WY and the hill CO apparently got their names from the so-called Great Diamond Hoax (1876).

Dickens From the personal name. In NB it is for Charles Dickens, novelist.

In IA it was named (1886) probably for a railroad man, otherwise unidentified.

Didallas Creek CA Probably Wintu 'daybreak.' Also as **Didallas, Dissallis.**

Difficult(y) With *creek* or *run,* e.g. AK, KY, VA, it indicates a stream hard to cross or to follow. The few habitation-names may arise by association, but local story in TN tells that the original suggestion for a post office was rejected by the department as too difficult, whereupon that term itself was chosen by the inhabitants. **Difficult** WY: from a creek, so named because some early riders became mired in it.

Digger The term was applied, usually in a derogatory sense, to many Western Indians, originally because they were not primarily hunters, but dug for roots. From the presence of such Indians or an incident involving them, the name survives on several features in CA, e.g. **Digger Creek.** The same name in AZ arose because wild horses pawed into the sand for water.

Dighton In MA (1712) probably for Deighton in England. Also a personal name.

Dike, Dyke Sometimes from the personal name. Often from the geological term, which is used as a specific to indicate the occurrence of a dike, e.g. **Dike Creek** CA.

Dilkon AZ The shortening of a Navajo term, 'smooth black rock.'

Dime Box TX Because a postman once placed a box where people could deposit dimes in return for errands done.

Dinber SC Coined from Hardin, name of a resident, and his wife's maiden name Barber.

Dinero Spanish 'money,' but the reason for the application in TX is unknown.

Ding Dong TX From its being in **Bell County.**

Dinkey Creek CA In 1863 a dog so named was injured here in a fight with a grizzly bear, and the hunters thus named the stream.

Dinnebito AZ Navajo 'people-spring.'

Dinne Mesa AZ Navajo 'without water.'

Dinner From an incident involving dinner, e.g. in WA probably from a landing-party of a British ship, ca. 1858. **Dinner Creek** MN: timber cruisers used to meet here for dinner. **Dinner Creek** OR: a party of surveyors stopped here for dinner in 1897. **Dinner Station** NV was a regular stop for meals on early stage lines.

Dinosaur Applied to features in the West because of the finding of fossils of dinosaurs. The town in CO changed its name from **Artesia** in 1965 because it is a point of entry to nearby Dinosaur N.P.

Dinpingora See **Pingora**.

Dinuba CA Probably a coined name for use by the railroad; as short, unique, and vaguely exotic, it was suitable for a station-name.

Diomede Islands AK Probably named (1728) by Vitus Bering because discovered on the day of St. Diomedes (Aug. 16).

Dione From Greek mythology, but in KY more likely from a personal name.

Dionondahowe Falls NY Iroquoian, probably 'there-it-has-interposed-mountain.'

Diorite From the kind of rock so known, e.g. the town in MI.

Dirigo Latin 'I guide, I direct'; being the motto of the state of Maine, it may be thus derived for a village in KY.

Dirty The rarity of the name testifies to the general clarity of streams under early conditions, and even **Dirty Creek** NB may have been named because of temporary pollution by buffalo. **Dirty Devil River** UT: named by J. W. Powell in his exploration of the Colorado River, because it was muddy and even had an unpleasant odor. **Dirty Glacier** AK is aptly descriptive, because of the appearance resulting from blown dust and morainal rocks. **Dirty Sock Hot Springs** CA was probably suggested by the smell of the sulphur water; **Dirty Woman Creek** SD probably from an Indian personal name; **Dirty Creek** OK by folk-etymology from the French family name Darden. The term appears as a nickname hence, **Dirty Ike Creek** MT. **Dirty Man Creek** WY: for a homesteader thus described.

Disappearing Used generally in a literal sense for a stream that at times goes underground, e.g. **Disappearing Creek** CA.

Disappointment A repeated name, springing from some incident which resulted in the disappointment of the namers, e.g. **Mount Disappointment** CA where in the 1890's a surveying party found a nearby peak to be higher after they had already climbed this one. **Cape Disappointment** WA: named in 1788 by John Meares, English explorer, who was disappointed by not finding a large river-mouth there.

Disaster A repeated name to designate a place at which the namers met with disaster, e.g. the peak in CA where a topographer was badly injured in 1877 by the dislodgment of a boulder. The peak in NV was named because a party of prospectors were attacked by Indians nearby in 1856. The Powell expedition (1869) suffered the loss of a boat at **Disaster Falls** CO.

Disco MI Latin 'I learn,' from the name of a mid-19th-century school.

Discovery Sometimes a prospectors' name for the finding of gold, e.g. the creek in AK. Also, to commemorate a discovery, e.g. the point in OR, because reputedly the place from which Crater Lake was first seen. **Port Discovery** WA: named in 1792 by George Vancouver, for his ship.

Disenchantment Bay AK Translated from the Spanish, as named (1792) by the explorer Alessandro Malaspina, because he here became 'disenchanted' of his hope of finding the Northwest Passage.

Dishmaugh Lake IN By partial folk-etymology from French *du chemin,* 'of the road,' because of an Indian trail in the vicinity; the French is a translation of the Potawatomi name.

Dismal The term was commonly a generic in the VA-NC region, meaning 'swamp,' and may be based upon some Indian word. On the other hand, it was early applied to **The Great Dismal Swamp** (VA, NC), and this in turn was reduced to **The Dismal.** The term may therefore have been taken to mean 'swamp,' and thus applied. As a specific it is used to indicate a gloomy place or one of a gloomy incident, such as camping in the rain, e.g. **Dismal River** NB, **Dismal Creek** MN, **Dismal Lake** ID.

Disney From the personal name, e.g. in OK for W. E. Disney, member of Congress (1938). **Disneyland** CA: For Walt Disney, motion-picture producer.

Dispatch KS Named (1891) because it was a point from which mail was dispatched.

Distant Island SC Probably because of its distance from Warsaw Island, from which it was reached.

Disputanta In KY it was so called, ca. 1885, because there was a dispute as to the name, when two post offices were combined; the formation is pseudo-Latin. In VA a similar story is told.

Ditch Though it is usually for a man-made excavation, the line of demarcation cannot be sharp, and in some areas, e.g. DE, the usage is vague; a few specifics arise by association, e.g. **Ditch Creek** DE.

Ditto In KY the hill is probably for J. L. Ditto, congressman and local landowner. In AK the islands resemble each other and are shaped so as to suggest a ditto mark.

Divide Primarily a generic for a height of land marking the dividing line between two important drainage systems, the term has been applied as a specific to denote a natural feature associated with a divide, e.g. **Divide Creek,** and has been transferred to habitations, e.g.

Divide CO. **The Great Divide** is the dividing line between the Atlantic and Pacific watersheds.

Dividend A commendatory name, associated with profits or expected profits from mining, e.g. in AK, UT.

Dividing, Division On features, e.g. **Dividing Creek** NJ, **Division Creek** NJ, to indicate some line of demarcation, usually the equivalent of **Boundary.**

Divot TX The intended name was Pivot (because of the situation at a crossroads), but an error arose in transmission.

Dix Commonly from the personal name, sometimes a respelling of **Dick's. Dix** NB is from **Dixon** IL, the former home of the landowner. **Dix Hills** NY is from the name of an Indian who lived there, Dick Pechegan. **Dix Creek** AZ: from Dick Boyles, ranchowner, i.e. Dick's.

Dixie The origin of the term (if it is to be called a place-name and not an abstraction) is much disputed. The most widely held theory connects it with the French *dix,* 'ten,' on ten-dollar bills issued by a bank in New Orleans. One of these was called a *dixie,* and the place where they flourished was Dixieland. Secondary uses are common, e.g. the southern part of UT is known as **Dixie** because of its warmer climate. Most habitation-names arose either because Southerners who settled there gave the name with pride, or because it was a nickname given by others. Most of these arose in the Civil War period. **Dixie Creek** OR was named in the 1860's because of many Southerners mining there. **Dixie Jett Gulch** OR was named for a man who lived there, though the exact form of his name has been lost. He may have been Jett, nicknamed Dixie for being a Southerner. **Dixie Canyon** AZ was originally Dick's Canyon, for a man so named, an early settler. **Dixie** MD: for Dixie Powell, daughter of the postmaster. **Dixie** WA: some early settlers, the three brothers Kershaw, were musicians, and their favorite tune was *Dixie.* **Dixie County** FL is a remarkably late (1921) revival of the name.

D'Lo MS Anomalous, especially in its preservation of the apostrophe; by local story from the French *de l'eau,* 'of the water'; possibly the adaptation of a French personal name.

Dobe Sometimes used for **Adobe,** e.g. **Dobe Canyon** NV.

Dobsy See **Sisladobsis.**

Doc See **Doctor.**

Docas CA From the last syllables of San Ardo and San Lucas, between which points the place is situated.

Dock Regularly from the presence of a dock (wharf), e.g. **Docton** WA. **Dock** AZ: by folk-etymology from the Pima, *dahk,* 'nose.' See **Doctor. Dock Watch Hollow** NJ: probably by folk-etymology from Algonquian, 'cold.'

Doctor, Doc, Dock Generally the equivalent of a personal name, from a doctor or someone so nicknamed, e.g. **Doc Lake** NB, **Doc Canyon** OR, **Doctor Rock** CA: a rough translation of an Indian term, the equivalent of **Medicine. Dock Creek** WV: for a Doctor Hampton, early resident.

Dodge From the personal name, e.g. **Dodge City** KS from Fort Dodge, established in 1864 and named for Col. Henry I. Dodge. **Fort Dodge** IA: named (1851) for Henry Dodge, U.S. senator.

Doe Usually for an incident involving a female deer, but much less common than **Buck,** as evidence that the doe was less often hunted and less treasured as a trophy. **Doe Creek** IA: in 1837 William Grant killed in a nearby stream a large doe that was 'mossing' there, and called it **Doe Creek**; later he called that stream **Buck Creek,** q.v., and shifted the former name to a small tributary, as more fitting to the smaller animal. A second **Doe Creek** IA was named by Benjamin Smith, because he shot a doe when it was in the act of leaping across the stream.

Dog Because of its brevity it often has a modifier, e.g. **Red, Big.** The names are not numerous, perhaps because the animal itself was so ubiquitous as to be of little distinguishing value. 1) From the canine, usually because of an incident, e.g. **Dog Lake** CA, because a sheepherder found a bitch there with her puppies; 2) from the prairie dog, e.g. **Dog Creek** SD; 3) from the translation of an Indian personal name, e.g. **Dog Ear Creek** SD; 4) from configuration, e.g. **Doghead Peak** CA, **Dog Lake** OR, which was first **Dogleg** because of its crookedness; 5) from the derogatory suggestions of the word, i.e. a place such as dogs might live in, e.g. **Dogtown** CA, a name which has tended to become extinct or to be preserved by natural features. **Dog Canyon** NM: ca. 1850 a party pursuing Indians here came upon a dog which the Indians had left behind. **Dogway Fork** WV: uncertain, but it may be for **Dugway.**

Dogie See **Dogy.**

Dogthresher Creek OK From an Indian personal name.

Dogwood Though the tree or bush is highly conspicuous and beautiful and occurs widely, it has given rise to only a few names. The plebean suggestion of *dog* may be responsible.

Dogy From the common Western term for a yearling, i.e. a motherless calf, e.g. **Dogy Creek** OK. Also as **Dogie.**

Dola, OH, WV Uncertain, a personal name (?).

Dolgoi Russian 'long.'

Dollar May be from the personal name, e.g. **Dollarville** MI for Robert Dollar, later the shipping magnate. **Dollar Lake** OR: named in humorous contempt because it was round and so small as to be like a silver dollar. **Dollar Lake** CA: the roundness and the silver color resulted in the name.

Dollymont MN From a place in Ireland, but more especially for Anthony Doll, pioneer settler.

Dolly Varden Eventually from the character in Dickens's *Barnaby Rudge,* who was noted for wearing bright colors. About 1870 the name was given to the so-called trout (actually a char), and some places have been named from the presence of the fish, e.g. the creek in

CA. A lake in MN was so called from a canoe thus named. In NV the name probably commemorates the political movement so called, which flourished in the 1870's, the settlement being named in 1872.

Dolomite From the occurrence of the rock so named.

Dolores Spanish 'sorrows,' also a name for women, but commonly used because of religious connections, viz. Nuestra Señora de los Dolores. The river in CO was thus named in 1776.

Dolphin Usually from the presence of that seas-mammal, e.g. **Dolphin Point** AK. **Dolphin** WA: from the presence of a so-called dolphin for mooring boats.

Dombey Since the personal name probably does not exist in the U.S., the literary influence of Dickens is to be supposed.

Dona Spanish *doña*, 'madam, lady.' The name **Dona Ana** in NM dates from so early (1682) that a folk-etymology from some Indian name is probable.

Donegal PA From the county in Ireland.

Dongola For the town in the Sudan, most of the names being given in the 1890's when the international situation brought **Dongola** into the news.

Doniphan From the personal name, e.g. the county in KS for A. W. Doniphan, Mexican War commander.

Donkey The name usually occurs in areas where the animal was not common (cf. **Burro, Jackass**), e.g. **Donkey Hills** ID, **Donkey Creek** WY.

Donna Schee Peak NV Probably an altered form, by partial folk-etymology, from some Northern Paiute original.

Donner From the personal name. In CA the lake and pass commemorate the disaster of the Donner Party in 1846–1847.

Donner Und Blitzen River OR German 'thunder and lightning.' Named in 1864 when some troops crossed it during a thunder storm; most regiments, at this time, included some German immigrants.

Donnybrook In ND the town is named for that in Ireland. In OR the community was so called because of a free-for-all fight, often known as a donnybrook, which occurred there in early times.

Donora PA Coined in 1900 from the maiden name of Nora Donner Mellon, wife of A. W. Mellon, whose company was chiefly responsible for the town.

Doolth Mountain AK Indian (Tlingit), indicating a place with abundant food resources.

Doom From the rare personal name, e.g. **Dooms Landing** KY.

Doon IA From 'bonnie Doon' of Robert Burns's poem.

Doonerak Mount AK Named by Robert Marshall, ca. 1930; it is the Eskimo word for one of the numerous spirits which the Eskimo believed to inhabit the earth in great numbers.

Door The personal name is rare. The county in WI is a translation from French **Porte des Morts Strait,** probably so called because of some incident when lives were lost. **Doorway** (e.g. in KY) is occasionally used in place of the commoner **Gateway.**

Dorado Spanish 'gilded,' but generally, from the legend of the 'gilded man' applied to a place supposedly of great riches, especially in gold, e.g. **El Dorado County** CA. **Eldorado** KS: named in the 1860's because of a gorgeous sunset seen by the founders on the day of their arrival, though the generally commendatory nature of the name was probably also in their minds.

Dorcheat LA Probably Caddoan. It may be the remnant of a tribal name, by itself meaning 'people' (?), which has been remade by partial folk-etymology into the semblance of an English name.

Dorchester In MA named from the town in England by the General Court, Sept. 7, 1630. The county in SC was named by settlers who came from the town in MA. Also a personal name, e.g. the town in TX, for C. B. Dorchester, early settler.

Doré Cliffs CA For P. G. Doré, chiefly known in the U.S. for his illustrations of Dante.

Dorena In OR coined in 1901 from Dora Burnette and Rena Martin, two women who are otherwise unidentified.

Dorfee WV Probably a variant spelling of the personal name D'Urfee or Durfey.

Dormin Prairie IN Potawatomi 'maize, corn.'

Dormont PA A commendatory name in extraordinary French, viz. *d'or mont,* 'mount of gold,' partially descriptive in that the site is hilly.

Dorp Dutch 'village.' With *oud,* 'old,' and *nieuw,* 'new,' it formerly occurred in NY, and **New Dorp** NY represents a partial translation into English.

Dorset From the county in England, etc. One of the most rarely used of English county names.

Dos Spanish 'two,' e.g. **Dos Cabezas Peak** AZ, 'two heads'; **Dos Narices Mountain** AZ 'two noses.'

Do Stop KY One of the few hortatory advertising names to have received recognition on an official map.

Dot Usually applied to islands (3 in AK) so small as to be merely a dot on the map. **Dot Island** King Co., WA: for Miss Dot McGilvra, daughter of the pioneer landowner. **Dot** OK: for Dot Zinn, daughter of the townsite developer.

Dota Creek AR It may be from French *d'eau tiéde,* 'of-water-lukewarm.'

Dothan A commendatory Biblical name. At the naming of the town in AL a minister quoted Genesis, 37, 17, "Let us go to Dothan."

Dotsero CO Locally believed to be from the daughter of a Ute chief, but, being a railroad station, it strongly suggests a coinage from dot-zero.

Double, Doubling, Doublet A common descriptive with a variety of natural features, e.g. spring(s), mountain, bay, run, bayou. It is approximately the equivalent of **Twin. Doublet Pool Spring** WY is a sophisticated naming in Yellowstone N.P., but also **Doublet Hill** MA. **Doublinggap** PA indicates that two gaps double back on each other.

Doughnut Lake CO It resembles a doughnut by being round and having an island in the middle to correspond to the hole.

Douglas From the personal name, especially for Stephen A. Douglas (1813–1861), e.g. **Douglas Co.** GA, SD; in AZ for Dr. J. S. Douglas, who was involved with the establishment of the town.

Dove A rare name. 1) From the personal name, e.g. **Doves Bar** OR: for Bethuel Dove, early settler; 2) from wild doves, e.g. **Dove Spring** AZ.

Dover From the English channel-port. It appears as a name of the Colonial period, e.g. in DE, and has been often repeated. Its popularity, especially in the Middle West and South springs partly from religious connections because of the Dover Association Report (1832), which caused many churches of the Baptist and Christian denominations to take that name.

Dovray See **Dovre.**

Dovre From the mountainous region in Norway, usually so named by Norwegian immigrants, e.g. **Dovre Peak** OR, **Dovre Hills** MN. Also as **Dovray** MN.

Dowagiac MI Algonquian (Potawatomi), probably indicating a place where fish can be netted, originally the river-name.

Dracut MA From a simplified, after-the-pronunciation spelling of Draycott in England (1701–1702).

Dragon From fancied resemblance to a dragon, e.g. **Dragon Head** and **The Dragon,** in Grand Canyon N.P. **Dragon's Mouth** is a thermal spring in Yellowstone N.P. **Dragon Lake** CA is named from nearby **Dragon Peak,** which is named from its shape. **Dragon Channel** CA was named as a counterpart to **St. George Point,** q.v. Habitation-names, e.g. **Dragonville** VA, more commonly arise from the family name.

Dragoon Until ca. 1860, the U.S. mounted troops were known as dragoons, and places associated with them were so named, e.g. a spring in AZ discovered by dragoons in 1856; the name was transferred to the **Dragoon Mountains** and other features.

Drake Regularly from the personal name. The bay in CA is named from its association with the landing of Sir Francis Drake in 1579. **Drakesbad** CA: from E. R. Drake, owner in the 1860's, plus *-bad* (German, 'bath') because of the hot springs.

Draw Commonly a generic in the sense of gully or streamcourse, but becoming a specific by association, e.g. **Draw** TX.

Drawyers Creek DE Dating from the 17th century and apparently of Dutch origin, but of uncertain meaning; a family name (?).

Dread One of the rare subjective descriptives that place upon the feature the feeling of the namer, e.g. **Dread Ledge** MA. **Dread and Terror Ridge** OR: named (1908) by C. V. Oden of the Forest Service because the dense thickets presented a fearful fire-hazard. **Dreadnaught Island** OR: named in 1925 because it resembled a battleship of the *Dreadnaught* type.

Dream So rare as to indicate that early Americans paid little attention to dreams. **Dreaming Creek** KY: Daniel Boone gave the name because he had a vivid dream here on one of his early expeditions. **Dreamland** has a little use as a commendatory, e.g. in TX.

Drenthe MI Named (mid-19th century) by Dutch immigrants for the province of the Netherlands.

Dresden From the city of Germany; usually, e.g. in ME (1794), and ND (1897) named because of immigrants.

Drewsey OR For Drewsey Miller, daughter of a local rancher.

Drift, Driftwood Accumulation of driftwood, especially at the mouth of a stream tributary to a navigable stream, was an important landmark in early periods, and streams were so named. In addition, the name could be used to serve as a notice that the stream was somewhere blocked to canoe travel by driftwood. On the Arctic coast driftwood is economically important to the Eskimo, and such names as **Driftwood Creek** AK thus arose. The shortened form **Drift** appears, especially in the West. Habitation-names are by transfer. See **Embarras, Zumbro.**

Drip, Dripping Descriptive of a place where water is dripping, e.g. **Drip Rock** KY, **Dripping Spring** KY. **Dripping Blood Mountain** CA is descriptive, because of red rock.

Dromedary Occasionally used, as a substitute for the commoner **Camel,** because of an outline like a hump, e.g. the hills in MN and the peak in AZ.

Drowning Probably, e.g. **Drowning Creek** OK, an incident name from a drowning in the stream.

Drum(m) 1) Commonly from the personal name, e.g. **Mount Drum** AK, named (1885) by H. T. Allen for R. C. Drum, adjutant-general of the U.S. Army. 2) Rarely, from semblance to a drum, e.g. **Drum Bridge** CA because its piers are large steel pipes filled with concrete and looking like drums from the end.

Dry The common descriptive term (hundreds of examples) to indicate a feature where water might normally be expected. A few indicate tidal features, e.g. **Dry Bay** AK. The others stand most often with streams, especially creek, and with lake. The name may indicate a feature that is dry except seasonally or occasionally, or it may indicate one that is only dry on rare occasions (but was dry at the time of naming.) The common use of the name even in the well-watered East is evidence of the tendency of the climate to occasional droughts. On the other hand, in desert areas dryness is not distinctive, and such a term as 'dry lake' tends to be a generic. **Dry** is most useful in such an area as CA

(200 examples) where the contrast of wet and dry seasons is marked. In spite of a noncommendatory suggestion there are some 20 habitation-names, arising by transfer. **Drylyn** CA: a coined name, the last syllable being the Gaelic for 'spring.' **Dryburg** TX: named because both lacking in rainfall and having inhabitants who voted anti-liquor. **Dryburg** MI: because it was 'dry' in the sense of prohibiting the sale of alcoholic liquor. Other small places, e.g. **Dry Branch** GA, apparently took their names from local prohibitionist tendencies.

Dryad WA The ancient Greek name for a tree-nymph, given to a railroad station, probably because of its location in a forest.

Dryden From the personal name. In NY apparently for the poet John Dryden, who for an unknown reason was included with the Greek and Latin figures in the classical naming of 1790.

Dublin From the city in Ireland, usually because of the presence of Irish settlers. In TX local story has it that the origin goes back to a double log house, later changed to **Dublin** at the instance of an Irishman.

Dubuque IA For Julien Dubuque, French-Canadian, first settler in the region (1785); the town was so named at its founding (1833).

Ducat From the personal name, e.g. in OH for E. and T. J. Ducat, two of the founders (1890).

Duchesne UT Probably for a French-Canadian trapper whose name is recorded as Du Chesne; he is known to have been in the area near the river ca. 1840.

Duck Though it occurs as a personal name, the place-names are regularly from the occurrence of wild ducks, and are commonly used with water-generics, e.g. **Duck Run, Duck River. Duckwater** NV: a swamp here is much frequented by migrating ducks.

Duckabush River WA A local Indian term, 'reddish-face,' because of the appearance of a mountainside.

Duco KY Latin 'I lead,' probably as a commendatory.

Ducor CA A shortening of **Dutch Corners,** for convenience, by the railroad.

Due West SC A rendering by folk-etymology of DeWitt or Duett, from the name of an early trader, first recorded as **Duett's Corner.**

Dufrene, Bayou LA For French *du frêne,* 'of the ash-tree.'

Dug A descriptive for a place formed wholly or partly by digging, e.g. **Dug Pond** MA. It may also be used for a place showing the effects of digging, e.g. **Dug Hill** KY.

Dugdemona LA Some early spellings for the bayou or river, e.g. **Ducdumani,** indicate an origin from Duc de Maine. A French prince bearing that title was a sponsor of the colony in 1717, but the stream may be named more directly for a ship of that name which made several voyages to the colony, ca. 1720.

Dugout Commonly used for a house, as constructed on the plains, where timber was lacking, and so, by association **Dugout** Creek NB.

Dugway From a term for a road dug out along the side of a hill, e.g. **Dugway Mountain** UT.

Duke From the personal name, e.g. in OK for F. B. Duke, territorial judge. **Dukes County** MA: named ca. 1683 because the Duke of York was the proprietor.

Dulac, Bayou LA From French *du lac,* 'of the lake.'

Dulce Spanish 'sweet,' usually with reference to potable water, e.g. **Agua Dulce Mountains** AZ, 'sweet water.'

Dull: Dull Knife Pass WY For Chief Dull Knife, who with his Cheyennes escaped by this route during the war of the 1870's. **Dull Center** WY: from the name of several local families.

Duluth MN Named commemoratively in 1856 for the 17th-century French officer and explorer Daniel Greysolon Du Luth.

Dulzura Spanish 'sweetness.' The creek in CA was given this name ca. 1870 because honey production was started in the area.

Dumbarton, Dunbarton Alternate spellings from the town and shire in Scotland, usually named under Scottish influence. See **Dunbar.**

Dumbbell Descriptive, from the shape, e.g. the lake in CA and OR.

Dumb Betty Branch KY The older meaning of the term, i.e. 'without speech,' is probably here preserved.

Dumbfoundling Bay FL Probably of English-American origin, but uncertain.

Dume Point CA For Father Francisco Dumetz, the name being carelessly recorded by the English explorer George Vancouver in 1792.

Dumpling A descriptive to indicate a rounded shape like that of a dumpling, e.g. the rock in MA.

Dunbar Usually from the personal name, though in some instances it may be for the town in Scotland. **Dunbarton** SC: for Robertson Dunbar, the founder. **Dunbar** MN: for W. F. Dunbar, a state official.

Dunbridge OH A coined name for a railroad station (1882) from Dunn and Trowbridge, two men concerned with its establishment.

Dundee From the city in Scotland.

Dunderberg Dutch 'thunder mountain.' The peak in CA is named from the one in NY.

Dung Rare, and probably in some instances a euphemism for *shit,* e.g. **Dung Creek** MD, **Dung Thorofare** NJ. **Dunghill:** the older term for *manure-pile* has given **Dunghill Summit** MD.

Dungeness WA In 1792 George Vancouver so named a point of land from its resemblance to Dungeness in England.

Dun Glen NV The name-cluster (settlement, creek, canyon, peak, range) first appears as **Dunn Glen,** ca. 1862, for L. F. Dunn, landowner. Its shift to the more Scottish form may have been aided by nearby **Clan Alpine.**

Dunkard, Dunker An occasional place has been named because of the settlement there of members of this sect. The personal name Dunker also occurs.

Dunraven W. T. Wyndham-Quinn, Earl of Dunraven, sportsman, who shot big game in the Rockies, ca. 1875, is commemorated by a mountain CO and a peak WY.

Dunstable In MA (1673) from the town in England.

Duo WV Named in the mid-19th century because it then consisted of only two houses.

Dupo IL A respelling, partly after the French pronunciation, of *du pont,* from the French **Prairie du Pont,** 'prairie of the bridge.'

Dupont From the personal name, e.g. in PA for the Dupont family, operators of a powder mill here. In LA the name was given by a storekeeper, the first postmaster, who saw it on a package of shotgun shells in his stock.

Dupuyer MT The creek was probably named from the American-French *dépouille,* 'buffalo tallow,' doubtless with reference to some incident, the spelling must have been the result of trying to pass the name on orally.

Duquesne PA Uses the name of Fort Duquesne, built at the site of Pittsburgh in 1754 and named for the then governor of New France, the Marquis Duquesne de Menneville.

Du Quoin IL The French name of a Kaskasia chief of the late-18th and early-19th centuries, known as a friend to the Americans.

Durango CO Named (1880) by former governor A. C. Hunt, for the city in Mexico which he had recently visited. In IA it was named (1850), apparently as a result of the Mexican War.

Durazno Spanish 'peach,' e.g. the bayou in TX.

Durham From the town and county in England, etc. **Durham** NC: for Dr. Bartlett Durham, who donated some land for public purposes.

Duro Spanish 'hard,' e.g. **Palo Duro Creek** OK, 'tree-hard,' with reference to the hackberry trees growing there.

Durwood OK Intended for **Deerwood,** but altered by mistake, probably from obscure handwriting, in transmission through the Post Office Dept.

Dushore PA A Frenchman, Capt. A. A. Dupetit-Thouars, founded the village, and its name is a spelling of a highly condensed, colloquial pronunciation of his surname.

Du Tart Creek SC From a French family name, more correctly, Dutartre, early residents.

Dutch Near the area of the Dutch colonial settlements, the name thus arises, e.g. **Dutch Neck** NJ, **Dutch Island** RI. Elsewhere the name more commonly applies to Germans, who were more numerous and commonly so

known. Scandinavians may even be included. Other names arise from individuals, of various national backgrounds, who were nicknamed Dutch. An individual might also give rise to the name, e.g. **Dutchman Flat** OR. It is also a personal name, and **Dutch Creek,** Shasta Co., CA, thus arises. See **German.**

Dutchess County NY For the Duchess of York, using an accepted 17th-century spelling.

Duwamish River WA From the name of a tribe of Indians living there.

Duwee Canyon OR From Klamath *ti-wi,* a name applied to the rushing sound of a cascade.

Duxbury In MA (ca. 1635) for Duxbury Hall in England, seat of the Standish family, in compliment to Miles Standish, who was prominent in the Plymouth colony.

Dwaar Kill NY Dutch 'cross-creek.' Also **Dwaas, Dwars.**

Dyea AK A shortening of Indian (Tlingit) *dyaytahk,* meaning uncertain.

Dyke See **Dike.**

E

Eagle The eagle is a conspicuous bird, but not commonplace; its nests also are often conspicuous. **Eagle Lake** occurs 23 times in MN. The name generally records the sighting of a bird or some other incident. **Eagle Nest** and **Eagle Rock** are recurrent names, but the latter in CA is from a rock formation which has a birdlike shape upon it. Because of commendatory suggestions, sometimes patriotic, the name is common for habitations. It may be, rarely, from the personal name. **Eagle Prairie** CA: for the nickname of a resident called 'Old Eagle Beak.' **Eagle Scout Peak** CA commemorates the first ascent, which was made on July 15, 1926, by some Boy Scouts of Eagle rating. The formation of **Eagletail Mountains** AZ resembles the tail feathers of an eagle. The name has often been used for companies, e.g. **Eagle Creek** NM from the Eagle Mining and Milling Co. The name may be given because of the same pair of eagles which may nest in the same location for many years, e.g. **Eagle Gorge** WA. **Eagle Point** WI: named commemoratively for 'Old Abe,' an eagle carried as a mascot by a Wisconsin regiment in the Civil War; he was originally captured near this spot.

Ear Although the human ear may sometimes be meant, **Ear Mountain** AK, named for two pinnacles of rock resembling an animal's ears, sets the usual pattern. The plural often occurs, e.g. **The Ears** AK. The animal is commonly specified, e.g. **The Rabbit's Ears** CO.

Early Commonly from the family name, e.g. in IA for D. C. Early, early settler. **Early Bird** FL is probably a humorous name, based on some incident.

Earth Its rare use in place-names is generally by translation, e.g. **Blue Earth River** MN from the Siouan. **Earth** TX: the first postmaster so named it because there was no tree in sight, "All you could see was earth."

East, etc. See **North.**

Eastanollee, Eastaunala GA, TN Variants, under the influence of folk-etymology, of **Oostanaula,** q.v.

Easter From some association with Easter. In AZ it is from a mine discovered on that day. **Easter Creek** AK was surveyed during Easter week. **Easter Bowl** CA: services have been held here on Easter.

Eastern Rare, but used for **Eastern Shore,** the parts of VA and MD lying to the east of Chesapeake Bay.

Eastham In MA (ca. 1651) probably for the town in England, but perhaps also for having an easterly location in the county.

Easton In PA the name is from Northamptonshire, England. Elsewhere it involves the idea of **East** or is from the personal name.

Easy Occurs as a descriptive, e.g. **Easy Pass** AK. **Easy Money Creek** is a goldminer's optimistic term. **Easy Day Peak** WY: named (1955) by a party of mountaineers because they spent a day resting before making the ascent.

Eau French 'water,' sometimes in the sense of 'spring, stream.' **Eau Claire** is the equivalent of **Clearwater. Eau Gallie** FL: named (1874) by its founder W. H. Gleason; though *eau* is French, the rest of the name makes no sense, and is possibly a private joke; a slight resemblance between Gleason and **Gallie** may be noted.

Ebano See **Ebony.**

Ebb FL From the nickname of A. W. Edwards, first postmaster (1904).

Ebeeme Mountain ME Algonquian, meaning uncertain.

Ebenecook Harbor ME Algonquian 'spreads-out-at,' descriptive of the harbor opening up after a narrow entrance.

Ebenezer Because of its Biblical use, it became a favorite name for churches, and thence was transferred to communities, e.g. KY, MS, NJ, NY. It has also occurred as a personal name, shortened to Eben, e.g. **Ebensburg** PA, for Eben Lloyd, who died in infancy, son of a local minister.

Ebony A small tree is known as 'Texan ebony,' and **Los Ebanos TX** thus takes its name, in Spanish form. **Ebony TX** is for Ebony Shaw, a local cowboy.

Ebro From the river of Spain.

Echashotee River FL Seminole 'beaver-house.'

Echo A common name for natural features, where the echo is notable or where even a small echo happened to be noted at the time of naming, e.g. **Echo Lake, Echo Mountain,** usually in mountainous country where echoes are commonest. The habitation-names are generally by transfer, but **Echo OR** is for **Echo Koontz,** daughter of one of the town-promoters.

Echota GA, NC, OK From the name of an ancient Cherokee town, meaning unknown, transferred to OK.

Eckley From the personal name, but in CO from Adams Eckles, a foreman on a cattle-ranch, perhaps by mistake in transmission.

Eckvoll MN Norwegian 'oak valley.'

Ecola Point OR Chinook jargon, 'whale.'

Econfina River Muskogean, probably Creek, 'earth (natural)-bridge,' because of such a formation.

Econlockhatchee River FL Muskogean (Creek), 'earth-mound-river.'

Economy A commendatory term in the older sense, i.e. 'thrift.'

Ecorce French 'bark (of a tree),' also in American-French a bark canoe. **Ecorse MI** is a variant spelling, a name first applied to the river, probably because Indians made canoes there.

Ecore Fabre Creek AR French 'bluff, high bank,' with the personal name Fabre.

Ecorse A variant of **Ecorce,** q.v.

E.C.P. Peak AZ From being on the East side of Cunningham Pass.

Ecru MS Named by W. C. Falkner from the color of the paint on the railroad station.

Edcouch TX For Ed Couch, local landowner.

Eddy It is commonly from the personal name or nickname, but the island and point in AK spring from strong currents observed in the water.

Eden Because of the Biblical garden, the name has been widely used for habitations, with commendatory purpose. The personal name also occurs e.g. **Edenton NC** is for Charles Eden, royal governor of the colony, 1714–1722. **Eden TX:** For Fred Eden, first storekeeper.

Edgar From the personal name, e.g. **Edgartown MA** for Prince Edgar, son of the Duke of York.

Edge Usually a descriptive, but at times from a personal name, e.g. **Edge TX** for John Edge, early settler. The influence of many English place-names such as **Edgefield, Edgeworth, Edgemond** has been important, but usually seems to have reinforced the descriptive idea rather than to have originated the name. **Edgefield Co.** SC: probably because it was at the edge of the colony when named. **Edgewood TX:** on the borderline between open and wooded country. **Edgewood CA:** at the edge of the forest in an open valley. **Edgemont SD:** at the edge of the mountains. **Edgewick WA:** by combination of the names of two prominent citizens, viz. R. W. Winnedge and W. C. Weeks, the latter name being pronounced *wicks.*

Edgecomb(e), Edgecumb(e) The spellings differ, but names are generally from the personal name, e.g. in WA for John Edgecomb, early lumberman. **Edgecombe Co.** NC: named (1735) for Richard Lord Edgecumbe (1680–1758); **Edgecomb ME** (1774), for George Lord Edgecumbe (1721–1795). James Cook on his exploring voyage in 1778 named **Mount Edgcumbe AK,** and also the cape, probably in memory of the eminence overlooking Plymouth harbor in England, and also, it seems likely, in honor of this same Lord Edgecumbe, who was then an admiral.

Edina A coinage of Scottish immigrants from Edinburgh, in MN originally the name of a flour mill.

Edinburg, Edinboro From the city Edinburgh of Scotland. In OH it was first **Eddysburg**, from three brothers who were prominent early settlers, but was attracted to the usual form by analogy, first in pronunciation and then in spelling.

Edison From the personal name, especially for T. A. Edison, inventor, e.g. the town in WA. In NB it sprang at least partly from a local man called Eddie.

Edisto Island SC From an Indian tribal name.

Edith From the personal name. The creek in WA was so called in 1907 by a guide, who needed a name, for a girl in one of his parties, so casually that he later did not even remember her full name.

Ediz Hook WA From the name of a Clallam village, probably 'good place.'

Edmond(s), Edmund(s) From the personal name; in WA the name was proposed in honor of Senator G. F. Edmunds, by an admirer, but the spelling was changed to Edmonds in transmission.

Edmore MI From Edwin Moore, town founder in 1878.

Edom From the Biblical country.

Edray WV Although the combination of two common personal names is strongly suggested, local tradition ascribes the name to the Biblical Edrei.

Eek River AK Eskimo, the shortening of a longer name, meaning uncertain.

Eel The eel has not been highly regarded in the U.S., and names are rare. The river in CA was so called in 1850 when a hungry party of explorers traded with Indians some pieces of a broken frying-pan for some eels.

Egan From the personal name; **Egan Range** NV is for Howard Egan, who explored the region in the 1850's.

Egeria CO, WV From the nymph of Roman mythology, but probably more directly from a woman so named.

Egg The finding of eggs of wild birds was at times of some interest, but most of the names record places where eggs for food were regularly gathered, usually by Indians, Aleuts, or Eskimos. These were commonly the rookeries of seacoast birds, such as gulls, and **Egg** therefore usually distinguishes seacoast features, such as *island, bay*. **Egg** is especially common in AK, with more than a dozen examples. **Egg Harbor** NJ is a translation from the Dutch; a name given by the Dutch in the early 17th century. **Egg Harbor** AK was named by A. S. Snow (1886) because he noted that the Indians visited it for eggs. **Egg Harbor** MI: from a lively incident of egg throwing at a picnic in 1825.

Eggemoggin Reach ME Algonquian 'fish-weir-place.'

Egg-Nog Branch TX In 1826 some settlers celebrated Christmas at this stream, and drank some egg-nog.

Eglon Apparently the several uses spring from the Biblical city and/or king, though it remains a mystery why anyone wanted to commemorate that obscure city or that constipated tyrant.

Egnar CO A reverse spelling of *range*, since the settlement is in range country.

Egoniaga Creek Muskogean, 'earth-hole' (?), i.e. cave.

Egremont MA For the Earl of Egremont, a political figure (1760), but also an English place-name.

Egypt The name was associated, because of the Bible, with a rich agricultural land, and this quality has led to its moderate use. In IL the southern tip of the state is so known for uncertain causes. In WV a district is so called because of fine crops. In TX it is for a place to which people came to buy corn, as Jacob went to the Biblical land. In MS the name was given (1858) for a variety of corn grown there. Because of the Biblical association of Egypt and darkness (and the colloquial expression 'dark as

Egypt') the name has apparently been put upon some rural communities derogatorily, e.g. **Egypt Hollow GA.**

Eider A repeated name in AK; for the eider duck.

Eight See also **One. Eight Dollar Mountain** OR: probably because of the discovery of a gold nugget worth eight dollars; if so, a derogatory name, since that is a very small nugget.

Eighty-eight KY By local story, the first postmaster, being scarcely literate, chose the name because it was easy to spell.

Eightyfour PA Because the post office was established in 1884.

Einahnuhto Hills AK Aleut 'three breasts.'

Einstein, Mount AK Named (1955) for Albert Einstein, scientist.

Eisenecke Creek CA German 'iron corner,' probably applied because the stream was hemmed in by cliffs.

Eitzen MN From a place in Germany from which some of the early settlers had come.

Ekal FL This is *lake* spelled backwards.

Ekalaka MT For a Sioux woman, wife of D. H. Russell, who lived at this site; the spelling is simplified from **Ijkalaka.**

Ekron KY From the Biblical city.

Ekwanok Mountain VT This is *equinox* spelled so as to appear Indian.

El Spanish 'the' masculine singular. It occurs in many names, either attached or separate, e.g. **El Dorado, Eldorado.** See entries under the significant part of the name, e.g. **El Reno,** see **Reno.**

Elaine Castle See **Bedivere.**

Elam From the personal name, e.g. **Elams** NC for James Elam, early resident (ca. 1880).

Elana WV In 1914 the post office had to be named, and having no better ideas

the namers took the trade name of a powder-puff.

Eland WI Named, ca. 1888, by a railroad official for the African antelope, but reason for naming uncertain.

Elba From the island off the coast of Italy, chiefly known as the place of Napoleon's exile it has been used as a short and attractive sounding name, without much idea of significance, in a number of states, in ID being substituted for a too-long name. **Elba** NB: named punningly by a railroad company because of an 'elbow curve.'

Elbe WA From the river of Germany, named by an immigrant from that region.

Elberon In NJ coined from L. B. Brown, one of the town founders; in other states apparently a transfer from NJ.

Elbert From the personal name, e.g. **Mount Elbert** CO for S. H. Elbert (1833–1899), who held various offices in the territory and state.

Elberta From a woman's name, but also, e.g. in UT, from a variety of peaches grown in the locality.

Elbing KS From a town in Germany.

Elbow A descriptive, for shape, e.g. **Elbow Lake** OR.

Elburn IL A manufactured name, probably formed from parts of two personal names.

El Capinero CA Not a Spanish word; it may be a Spanish adaptation of an Indian name or a mistake for *sapinero,* 'juniper (pine)-place.'

Elcho WI By tradition from a place in Scotland presumably Elcho Castle.

Eldena IL For Eldena Van Epps, wife of a local landowner.

Elder 1) From the occurrence of the tree or berry which is common in some areas, e.g. CA, where it has produced a dozen names. 2) Rarely, from the church title, e.g. **Elder Bowman's Bluff**

WI, for Joseph Bowman local landowner in the late 19th century.

Elderon WI Coined from *elder* (i.e. the bush or berry) and *on,* probably because the bushes grew 'on' the nearby stream.

Elderpom Creek CA Wintu, with *pom,* 'land,' and the rest uncertain.

Eldora A shortening of **Eldorado,** in IA named in 1853 when the gold-rush of 1849 had made the name popular. In CO the name was originally **Eldorado,** but had to be changed because of duplication.

El Dorado See **Dorado.**

Electra Generally for a woman so named, e.g. in TX, for Electra Waggoner, daughter of the owner of a large nearby ranch. **Electra Lake** CO: because it is a source for electric power.

Electric Usually for a habitation where electricity is generated or used, e.g. **Electric Mills** MS for an electrically operated sawmill; **Electric Peak** MT because of electric manifestations during a storm in 1872.

Electron WA Named in the early 20th century from an electric power plant.

Elephant Names sometimes originate from the finding of fossil remains, e.g. **Elephant Hill** AZ. More commonly the name is from a real or fancied resemblance of a formation to an elephant or part of one, usually coupled with elephantine size, and often with gray color, e.g. the mountain OR and the butte NM. Eloquent in their descriptive quality are **Elephant Legs** AZ, **Elephant Back** CA, WY, **Elephants Head** AK, **Elephants Nose** AK. **Elephants Playground** CA is a meadow strewn with boulders of elephantine size.

Eleroy IL For Leroy Jones, son of an early settler.

Elf The point in AK was named (1910) for its diminutive size.

Elgin Almost nonexistent as a feature-name, but with about 20 habitation-names, its popularity is probably due in large part to its being short and distinctive, and thus suitable for a 'railroad name.' The county and town in Scotland seem to have had little direct influence, although they furnish the ultimate source. The personal name is rare. None of the examples appear to be very old, and the city in IL (ca. 1830) may be the original one. By local tradition, it was named by J. T. Gifford, the owner of the townsite, for the hymn tune. Many of the later examples are named for this one, e.g. in NB, OK. In ND the name was given because one of the participants in the discussion saw it on his watch. In OR it sprang from a song, about the wreck of the lake steamer *Lady Elgin* in 1860.

Elgood WV Coined ca. 1910 from the name of a resident, L. Goodwin.

Eli Commonly from the personal name. 'Get there, Eli!' was a slang expression of the 19th century, and the lake in SD was thus named, humorously. In NB the name was at first the full phrase, which was the nickname of a local man; it was later shortened.

Elias The Greek form of the Hebrew Elijah, it is preserved as a saint's name. It was given, as **St. Elias,** by Bering's expedition to the present cape, and to what is now **Kayak Island,** because the ship anchored there on the saint's day in 1741. The name was later transferred to the mountain.

Elida Probably a combination of Ella and Ida, as locally reported in NM.

Elijah, Mount OR From Elijah J. Davidson, early settler.

Eliza Usually from a woman's name, but **Eliza Island** WA is for Francisco Eliza, Spanish explorer of 1791.

Elizabeth This common name has been favored for features, especially lakes, in compliment to some member of the namer's family or his sweetheart. MN has 3 such lakes; CA, about 10, besides several creeks and a mountain. **Elizabeth City** VA: named in 1619, probably for Queen Elizabeth I. **Cape Elizabeth** ME: for the Princess Elizabeth, daughter of James I, so named by her brother

Prince Charles, who wrote this name and others on John Smith's map of New England (1616). **Elizabeth NJ:** for Elizabeth Carteret, of the family of one of the proprietors (1665), and also probably in memory of Castle Elizabeth in the island of Jersey. As a habitation-name **Elizabeth** stands alone or is most commonly joined with **-town.** The use of this suffix is doubtless an echoing of its use in PA (named ca. 1750, for Elizabeth Hughes, wife of a local tavern-owner), and in NC, where the town was settled ca. 1770, and named for some unknown woman.

Elk The English colonists were not familiar with the European elk, and knew the word only as referring to a large animal of the deer kind. They transferred the term to the animal at present so known, sometimes called **Wapiti.** This was the more readily done because the American moose (the equivalent of the European elk) was found only in the extreme north of the U.S. Since *moose* came into use early in the 17th century, it may be questioned whether any places called **Elk** refer to the moose. The elk was to be found in most parts of the country, but was not so common as the smaller deer. It was therefore noteworthy, and its name was placed upon an extraordinary number of natural features (probably 1000) and upon at least 100 habitations. It has been coupled with nearly all the generics for natural features, and with numerous habitation-generics, e.g. *-ton, city.* Its transfer to habitations was facilitated by its brevity and by a slight commendatory quality. **Elk Creek IA:** in 1834 Louis Reynolds came upon a herd of elk 'mossing' in this stream. **Elkwood ND** was so named (1883) because seven elk had recently been shot in the vicinity.

Elkader IA For Abd-el-kader, leader of the Algerians in their war against the French from 1832 to 1847; the town was named in 1845, and is thus a late example of American honoring of revolutionaries.

Elkahatchee Creek AL Muskogean, with *hatchee,* 'stream,' and the rest 'potato' (?), shifted from the earlier **Alkehatchee** by folk-etymology.

Elkatawa KY Probably from the name of the early 19th-century chief known as 'the Prophet,' whose name is sometimes recorded as Ellskwatawa; a railroad name.

Elkhart The original naming was that of the river in IN, which was reported at an early date (1822) to have been so named by the Indians because of a heart-shaped island.

Elkhorn Since elk shed their antlers yearly, the finding of them, especially of fine specimens, gave rise to names for natural features, some of which have been transferred to habitations.

Elko Of uncertain origin, though occurring in several states. It probably appears first in SC as a plantation-name, given by an English owner. A relationship to **Elcho,** pronounced in the same way, is possible. In NV it is a railroad name of 1868, apparently borrowed from one of the already established places.

Elkol WY From nearby **Elk Mountain,** probably coupled with *coal,* since it is a coal-mining town.

Ellen A popular woman's name in the 19th century, it is found on many natural features, and also on habitations, often with a suffix, e.g. *-burg, -ton.* The repeated **Ellendale** may be influenced by **Allendale. Ellensburg WA:** for Mary Ellen Shoudy, wife of the town founder.

Elligo Pond VT Probably the remnant of an Algonquian name; meaning uncertain.

Ellijay GA, NC From the name of a former Cherokee village, recorded as Elatseyi.

Elloree SC A late 19th-century name, given by Mrs. W. J. Snyder, who believed it to be an 'Indian' word meaning 'Home I love.'

Elm Though native throughout the eastern half of the country and often a conspicuous individual tree, the elm has not been prolific of names for natural features, probably not having been as common in the original forest as it has since become in the second-growth woods and by cultivation as a street tree. Such names are probably more common in the Middle West, where the forest was thinning out, and single trees could be more noted, e.g. the habitation-name **Elm Tree** TN. The repeated **Elm Grove** is also indicative of trees growing in comparative isolation. As a later habitation-name **Elm** has carried commendatory suggestions of beauty and space, especially when in the form **Elmwood**, occurring in more than a dozen states.

Elma Usually from a woman's name, e.g. in WA for Elma Austin, early settler. **Elma** NY is locally believed to have been named for its elms.

Elmira In NY the name dates from 1828, being that of a child; local tradition has it that the mother called so loudly and often for her that people adopted the name for the settlement. The numerous later examples are derived from that in NY.

Elmo From the personal name, e.g. in TX, for Elmo Scott, who surveyed the railroad through this area. It may sometimes be from the popular novel *St. Elmo* (1867) by A. J. Evans. See **St. Elmo,** under **Saint.**

Elmodel GA A coinage, from Spanish 'the-model,' or from Elmo-dell.

Elmonica OR From Eleanor and Monica Stoy, daughters of a resident.

Elmore From the personal name, e.g. in MN for A. E. Elmore, 'the Sage of Mukwonago,' who had several friends among the early settlers.

Elo In ID a shortening of the Finnish name of a family of early settlers, viz. Eloheimo.

Elon From a Biblical place, or person.

Elovoi Russian 'spruce,' e.g. the island in AK.

Eloy AZ The only known source for this name is Biblical, viz. Mark 15, 34, where the word *Eloi* is the exclamation 'My God!' In AZ the name was placed by the railroad, ca. 1920, and may be a humorous covering up of someone's exclamation at the time.

El Paso TX Juan de Oñate in 1598 mentions fording the river at **El Paso del Norte.** Since **Norte** here refers to the Rio Grande, *paso* must be taken as meaning 'passage,' 'crossing,' or 'ford,' acceptable translations for the Spanish, and suitable to the context.

Elroy PA, WI Probably a variant of the personal name LeRoy.

Elrus OR For Elmer Russell, local mill-owner.

Elsinboro NJ The Swedes in the 17th century built a fort here, naming it **Fort Elfsborg** after a place in Sweden; the present name is an English adaptation, partly by folk-etymology.

Elsinore From the city and castle in Denmark, but usually to be considered a literary name, derived from *Hamlet.*

Elusive, Mount AK Named (ca. 1957) because it was difficult for its namers to locate from aerial photographs.

Elverta CA From Elverta Dike, whose husband was a local benefactor.

Elves Chasm AZ One of the many fanciful names of the Grand Canyon area.

Elwa Creek AL Choctaw, 'soft-shelled turtle' (?).

Elwha River WA Indian, 'elk' (?).

Elwin IL From the names of the town founders, Elwood and Martin.

Ely From the personal name. In MN, for Arthur Ely, railroad promoter. In NV for John Ely from whom the town promoter had borrowed $5000 to develop the site.

Elyria In OH the town was named by Herman Ely, apparently by coining it from his own, with the last three letters added from his wife's name, Maria. In other states the name is probably from that in OH. The influence of Illyria, which was known from Shakespeare's plays, is also suggested.

Elysian From the ancient idea of the Elysian Fields, and so, roughly, the equivalent of 'heavenly,' used as a commendatory. **Elysian Fields** TX preserves the full form. **Elysian Valley** CA was so named in 1856 for its beauty.

Emathla FL For Charley Emathla, a Seminole chief of the early 19th century.

Emauhee Creek AL Muskogean, of uncertain meaning, an Indian personal name (?).

Emaus See **Emmaus.**

Embar WY A brand name from a nearby ranch, i.e. *M* with a bar.

Embarcadero Spanish 'place of embarkation, landing-place.'

Embarras, Embarrass French *embarras,* 'obstacle.' The name was applied to streams by early voyagers to indicate a blockage by a jam of driftwood. It has spread by transfer to other features and some habitations. Cf. **Zumbro.**

Embden In ME it was named in 1804, and is probably the alternate spelling of **Emden,** for the German city. In ND it is by transfer from ME.

Emblem WY Uncertain; probably so called with patriotic intent, since the name was changed from **Germania** during World War I.

Embryo Lake CO Named because it was so small, a mere embryo.

Embudo Spanish 'funnel,' used in a topographical sense for a restricted passage, e.g. the creek in NM.

Emden From the city in Germany. See **Embden.**

Embelle AL Ca. 1910, named for Emma and Ella Dial, the name being specified by their father when he granted the railroad permission to cross his land.

Emerado ND A pseudo-Spanish formation from the name of Lewis Emery, local landowner.

Emerald Used as a heightened term for *green,* e.g. **Emerald Bay** CA. In NB the town was named because of an unusually verdant landscape. Also, from Ireland, 'the Emerald Isle,' e.g. the township in MN.

Emerson From the personal name. **Mount Emerson** CA: for R. W. Emerson, author.

Emhouse TX For Colonel E. M. House, political figure under President Wilson.

Emida ID From the names of three early settlers, East, Miller, and Dawson.

Emigrant The name is western, and is associated with the covered-wagon migration, such people being so called, and never 'immigrants.' The name was not given by the emigrants themselves, but arose in the following generation when tradition of the routes still lingered and places were identified as being on the old trail, e.g. **Emigrant Butte, Creek, Hill** OR. The name has been avoided for habitations, but was preserved as a railroad station for **Emigrant Gap** CA, near a place where wagons passed through a gap in a ridge.

Emily Generally from the personal name. **Mount Emily** Curry Co., OR: apparently by folk-etymology from an Indian name Emney of unknown meaning.

Eminence In MO, and probably elsewhere, used as a synonym for *hill* or *height,* and thus a commendatory. In KY the town is at the highest point on a railroad line.

Emmaus PA From the village mentioned in the New Testament, named by the Moravians who settled there, ca. 1745. Also, **Emaus.**

Emmet(t) From the personal name, especially for Robert Emmet, Irish patriot, e.g. the county in IA.

Empire A vague commendatory term, suggesting greatness and outstanding quality, applied to habitations, occasionally with reference to NY as the Empire State. It was a common name for mines, and is sometimes a transfer from a mine.

Emporia See **Emporium.**

Emporium From the Graeco-Latin term, current in English, 'market, place of business,' and so used as a commendatory in several states. **Emporia** FL, KS, VA is the plural, and is similarly used, though a borrowing from two ancient cities so named is possible, and is locally postulated for the city in KS (1857).

Empress Like **Empire** a vaguely commendatory name, sometimes used for mines, and thus by transfer to **Empress Creek** SD.

Emuckfaw Creek AL Muskogean (Hitchiti), 'shell,' or an ornament made of shell (?).

Encampment River WY Because, in the fur-trading period, Indians held a regular yearly encampment here.

Encanto Spanish 'charm.'

Enchanted Both the mesa in NM and the prairie in OR take their names from local Indian beliefs. The former is a translation of an Acoma term. **Enchanted Gorge** CA was named in 1895 by two fancifully inclined mountaineers, who named **Scylla** and **Charybdis** close by.

Encina, Encino Spanish 'live oak,' but used by Americans for any kind of oak. **Encino** is the colloquial Spanish form in the SW, and it thus occurs in CA, NM, and TX.

Encinal TX Spanish 'oak-grove.' See **Encina.**

Endeavor PA From a Christian Endeavor Society, which developed into a church and finally gave its name to the village.

Endee NM A brand name, from *N* and *D.*

Endion MN Ojibway 'my (your, his)-home,' applied by developers of a townsite in 1856, as a commendatory.

Endless Branch NJ Probably because the upper reach of the channel loses itself in a swamp.

Enebro Spanish 'juniper.'

Enemy Swim Lake SD A translation from the Siouan, which by legend goes back to a battle between Sioux and Chippewas, in which the latter were forced to swim.

Enentah, Mount CO Arapaho *enetah-notaiyah,* 'man-mountain,' shortened by the Colorado Geographic Board; reason for application unknown.

Energy A commendatory; in TX, because the people were considered to be energetic.

Enfield From a village in England, the first naming (1683) being in CT. It is also a personal name. **Enfield** NH See **Tunbridge.**

Engadine MI For the valley of Switzerland, a famous ski- and resort-area.

Engineer A repeated name in AK, usually indicating the presence there at some time of U.S. Army Engineers.

England Curiously unused, perhaps a comment on the unsentimentality of immigrants from that country, as compared with those from **Scotland.** In AR the name is for J. C. and J. E. England, brothers and prominent early financiers of the state.

Engle 1) From the personal name, e.g. in TX for J. E. Engle, who at the time of the building of the railroad here was the oldest engineer for the company; 2) an alternate form of **Ingle,** q.v. which also became a 19th-century commendatory, especially when joined with **Vale** and **Wood. Englewood,** though it exists as a name in England, in the U.S. is a commendatory for suburban developments, e.g. thus established in NJ (1859) by a real estate developer.

English Sometimes for the personal name, e.g. **Englishtown** NJ for James English, landowner. Generally with some reference to English people or an Englishman. Since the English were dominate in the colonies, the name on places is rare, since it had no distinguishing value. Even in later times the fact of someone's being English was not very striking. The name occurs about 10 times in CA, chiefly because of English miners. **English** WV: because the coal mines were owned by English investors. **English Turn** LA: from the French *Le Détour à L'Anglais,* 'the Englishman's turnabout,' from an incident in which an English ship turned back at this point. **English Mountain** OR was named during World War I in honor of the English people. **English Lookout** LA: a point from which the English made observations during the invasion of 1815.

Enid From the woman's name, popularized by Alfred Tennyson's *Geraint and Enid* (1859); in OK the city is locally believed to have been named from the poem, but two women of the name are known candidates, and a reverse spelling of *dine* has been suggested on the grounds that this was a dinner-halt on an early trail.

Enitachopco Creek AL Muskogean (Creek), 'thicket-long.'

Enka NC From the American Enka Company, being the initials *N* and *K* from the original Dutch name of the corporation.

Eno River NC From an Indian tribal name.

Enoch From the personal name, but in UT for the Mormon 'Order of Enoch,' under which the settlers were living in 1884 at the time of naming.

Enola In OR, **Enola Hill** is from *alone* spelled backwards, and is thus the equivalent of *lone.* In PA the name is from a character in a novel, whose name was probably so derived. In NB the name is from that of the founder T. J. Malone, his last name spelled backwards, with the *M* omitted. In SC the village was first called **Alone,** and was later reversed.

Enon A simplified form of Aenon, a place mentioned once in the New Testament. The popularity of the name may owe something to its brevity and euphony, but springs chiefly from its association with water, the Biblical account mentioning that "there was much water there." In WV the name first intended was **Lake Enon,** because of a pond.

Enoree SC First applied to the river; from an Indian tribal name.

Enough MO By local tradition, the first postmaster was informed by the Post Office Dept. that the number of names sent in was enough; though the story does not quite make sense, some unusual explanation seems to be demanded by an unusual name.

Ensenada NM Spanish 'bay, cove,' but here used for a small valley. Cf. **Cove.**

Entelodon Butte SD So named in 1920 by paleontologists from Princeton University because they found there the fossils of that animal.

Enterprise A common commendatory habitation-name, celebrating a typical 19th-century American virtue. In SC named ca. 1880, when things looked hopeful because of the growing of sea-island cotton.

Entiat River WA A local Indian word, 'rapid-water' (?).

Enumclaw WA First applied to a mountain; by local story so named by Indians ('home of evil spirits') because they were caught there in a lightning storm.

Eola, Eolia, Eolian These derive eventually from Aeolus, Greek god of winds. The initial *A* is not used, though the name appears on habitations in a number of states. It may, in some cases, have been used as a woman's name. **Eolia** MO is said to have been named on a very windy day. **Eola** OR: suggested by a music lover, on the idea of Aeolian music or the Aeolian harp. **Mount Eolus** CO is an example of rare usage for a natural feature, presumably named on a windy day.

Eolus See **Eola.**

Epaulet Peak CA From rock formations resembling epaulets.

Ephraim, Mount Ephraim From the Biblical mountain, tribe, or district, or from a personal name.

Ephrata From a second name or epithet of Bethlehem, occurring three times in

the Old Testament. In PA it was given
by an early German religious sect. In
WA it was given by surveyors because
the only orchard in the area was there,
these surveyors seemingly being possessed
of the curious knowledge that Biblical
dictionaries give the meaning of the
name as 'fertility.'

Epsilon MI From the fifth letter of the
Greek alphabet; reason for naming, unknown.

Epsom In NH it was incorporated in
1743, named for the town in England.

Epworth From the village in England,
but mostly for religious connections,
since the Wesleys, founders of Methodism, came from Epworth.

Equality A rare commendatory, but curiously standing in two former slave states
AL, KY. In WA it springs from an early
communal colony.

Equaloxie Creek FL Seminole, 'water-
round' (?).

Equinox, Mount VT It may be by folk-
etymology from an Algonquian name
(cf. **Equinunk**), but could also arise from
an incident associated with an equinox.

Equinunk Creek PA Algonquian (Delaware), probably 'distribution-at,' apparently because clothes were once given to
some Indians at this place.

Era In TX for Era Hargrove, daughter
of an early settler.

Ercildoun PA For Thomas of Ercildoun,
known from his association with the
ballad *Thomas the Rhymer.*

Erdahl MN From a district in Norway
from which some of the early settlers had
come.

Erie From the Indian tribal name, being
first applied, by the French, to the lake,
and later transferred to counties and
towns. By translation the Eries were
known as 'the Cats,' or 'the Cat Nation,'
and this translated name was sometimes
applied to the lake.

Erin, Erina The ancient name for Ireland occurs rarely, usually by Irish influence. **Erina** NB is a variation to avoid
duplication with a place in the state
already called **Erin.**

Ermine For the fur-bearing animal, e.g.
several features in AK.

Erratic Creek AK Because its valley is
strewn with so-called erratic rocks.

Esbon KS Named (1877) for Ezbon
Kellor, the first child born in the community; the spelling later shifted for
unknown reasons.

Escalante The town and various features
in UT are for Francisco S. V. de Escalante, Spanish priest, who explored the
area in 1776.

Escalon Spanish 'step (of a stairway).'
The town in CA was probably so called
because the founder liked the sound of
the word.

Escambia AL, FL Muskogean, with the
first part probably representing Choctaw
uski, 'cane,' and the remainder uncertain.

Escanaba MI Algonquian, meaning uncertain.

Escape An incident-name, e.g. the point
in AK, so named by George Vancouver
because of his escape here from Indians
on Aug. 12, 1793.

Escatawpa AL, MS Choctaw 'cane-there-
cut.'

Escoba Spanish 'broom,' in most instances probably because material for
brooms was collected there, e.g. **Escobas
Mountains** NM.

Escoheag RI Algonquian, meaning uncertain.

Escondido Spanish 'hidden.' The term
was applied to sources of water that were
difficult to find, the town in CA taking
its name from a creek.

Escorpion CA Spanish 'scorpion.'

Escudilla Mountain AZ Spanish 'bowl.' Descriptive, because of a large bowl-like formation at the top.

Escuela Spanish 'school.'

Escumbuit Island NH Algonquian 'watching-place-at.'

Escutassis ME Algonquian 'trout-small,' i.e. brook-trout.

Eskalapia KY Algonquian (Shawnee), to indicate a long stretch of a trail that was soft or wet.

Eskimo From the presence there of those people, e.g. several features in AK.

Esmeralda Spanish 'emerald.' It became widely known in the 19th century as the name of the heroine of Victor Hugo's *Notre Dame,* and thus being doubly commendatory was sometimes applied to mines, e.g. (1860) in NV; hence the county in NV. **Esmerelda** CA is a variant (probably a misspelling in transmission through the P.O. Depart.), derived from a nearby Esmeralda Mine. The mountain in AK was named because of being conspicuously green in summer.

Esmond In RI probably from a personal name; local stories in ND and SD connect the name with Thackeray's *Henry Esmond.*

Esopus NY Algonquian, often without the *e,* and thus referable to *sepu-es,* 'rivulet.' The initial letter appears in the first form (1614–1616), but is probably scribal, the name being shaped by classical analogy, e.g. Asopus, the name of several rivers in ancient Greece.

Espada Creek CA Spanish 'sword.' An Indian here stole a sword from a soldier of the Portolá expedition in 1769.

Espanola Spanish 'Spanish, Spanish woman.' This form of the adjective occurs on several places; it has probably been used chiefly for its euphony and vague Spanish suggestion, no specific causes being known.

Espanong NJ Algonquian, probably 'raccoon-place.'

Esparto Spanish 'feather grass.'

Espejo Spanish 'mirror,' but more likely from the personal name, e.g. **Espejo Spring** AZ for Antonio de Espejo, 16th-century explorer.

Esperanza Spanish 'hope.'

Espinoso, Espinosa Spanish 'thorny,' but originating regularly from a personal name, e.g. **Espinosa** CO for a fort built by Encarnación de Espinosa.

Espiritu Santo Spanish 'Holy Spirit.'

Esquagamah Lake MN Ojibway 'last,' being the final one of a series of three.

Essex From the county or title in England, an early use being that for the county in MA (1643), chosen as being farthest east and also as being a region from which many settlers had come.

Estaboga AL The name of a Creek village, literally, 'people-dwelling-place.'

Estabutchie MS Choctaw 'fallen-leaf-creek.'

Estacado, Estacada Spanish 'staked, palisaded.' **Llano Estacado** TX is rendered into English as **Staked Plain.** This is a misleading translation, since the name originated from the cliff or escarpment bordering many parts of the plain or plateau. Cf. **Palisade** as used in English, e.g. **Palisades of the Hudson.** **Estacada** OR: originally **Estacado** from the name in TX, probably changed to *a* because that is thought generally a more suitable ending for a town-name.

Estancia Spanish 'estate, ranch,' e.g. **Estancia** NM. The word also means 'resting-place,' and thus arose **Estancia Spring** NM which was a halting-place for travelers.

Estero Spanish 'estuary, bay.' The term is tautological in **Estero Bay** CA, FL.

Estes From the personal name, e.g. **Estes Park** CO, for Joel Estes, first permanent settler (in 1859).

Estiffanulga FL From an Indian tribal name.

Esto FL For an early settler, not further identified.

Estrella Spanish 'star.'

Estufa Canyon TX Spanish 'stove,' so called from an old stove abandoned there.

E.T. City UT For E. T. Benson, early settler.

Ethanac CA Coined from Ethan A. Chase, early landowner.

Ether NC For the anesthetic, named by a local physician.

Ethete WY Arapahoe 'good,' probably a late commendatory naming for a mission-site on the reservation.

Eticuera CA Probably a Spanish rendering of a Patwin name, but of unknown meaning.

Etigonik Mountain AK Eskimo 'smelling-of-(fox)-urine.'

Etiwanda CA Probably for the chief of an Indian tribe near Lake Michigan, whom the founders thus honored in a distant place.

Etlah MO Locally believed to be the spelling backwards of the German *halte,* 'stop,' bestowed by immigrants to denote their place of settlement.

Etna, Aetna From the volcano in Sicily. The name is sometimes given, e.g. **Aetna Springs** CA, because of a hot spring or other evidence of volcanic activity. It is also, e.g. in PA, associated with ironworks, since the Cyclopes were supposed to have their forge under the volcano. The name was also used for other mills, such as a flour mill, and **Etna** CA thus took its name. **Etna Green** IN: probably a variant or parody of Gretna Green. See **Gretna. Etna** WY was adopted because it was short and easy to pronounce.

Etoile French 'star.'

Etolin A repeated name in AK; for A. K. Etolin, governor of the Russian colonies in America, 1841–1845.

Eton From the town, seat of the celebrated school, in England.

Etoniah FL From an early Seminole town, meaning unknown.

Etowah In several states of the SE it is from the name of at least two early Cherokee towns, and may itself mean 'town.' Cf. **Hightower.**

Ettahoma MS Choctaw 'sourwood (the tree).'

Ettawa CA From Etta Waughtel, mother of the landowner.

Euchee FL From the Indian tribal name, more commonly recorded as **Yuchi.**

Euchre A rare name, but occurring in three widely separated parts of OR. In Curry Co., **Euchre Creek** is for the name of a local Indian tribe, attracted to the spelling of the card game. In Lake Co., **Euchre Butte** is probably from an incident involving the game. In Lincoln Co., **Euchre Mountain** is from some unknown Indian term under the influence of folk-etymology.

Euclid A township in OH was so named in 1796 by surveyors, thus commemorating the great geometrician, who might be called their patron. From this naming sprang the present town, and also the famous street in Cleveland. From the latter have been named the towns in PA and MN, a reversal of the usual pattern, that streets are named for towns.

Eufaula In AL it is from the name of an early Creek town, meaning uncertain; in OK, by transfer from AL.

Euphaubee Creek AL Muskogean; Hitchiti 'beechtree' (?).

Eureka Greek 'I have found (it).' The word draws its popularity from the famous story about Archimedes. It was used as the motto of CA in 1849, either with the implication of having found gold or of having found the proper country. It was used for the town in CA in 1850, and has spread to many states as a commendatory term for habitations. Just what has been found is often left vague, but the discovery of gold applies in some cases, e.g. NV. CO. In TX it was applied as a general commendatory. In KS the finding of a spring suggested the name.

Eutaw In SC the name is from a local Indian tribe. **Eutaw** AL: in commemoration of the Revolutionary battle of Eutaw Springs. This already established spelling occurs at an early date for the present UT, but the connection and the identity of pronunciation are only coincidental.

Evadale TX For Eva Dale, not identified.

Evan(s) The given name Evan is rare, and **Evan** MN was named by the first postmaster for his wife Eva. **Evanston** IL: for Dr. John Evans, who participated (1853) in buying the land on which the university was founded. **Evansville** IN: for Gen. Robert Evans, who was one of the town founders, ca. 1818. **Mount Evans** CO: for John Evans, territorial governor from 1862 to 1865.

Evangeline LA From the title-heroine of Longfellow's poem.

Evening Like similar terms it is uncommon in place-names, but occurs as **Evening Shade** AR, MO, in AR because three tall pines shaded the post office on the west; the term here is apparently used in the Southern sense, i.e. 'afternoon.'

Everest Regularly from the personal name, e.g. in ND for a local newspaper editor.

Everglades, The FL The term *glade* is here used as a quasi-generic with its common meaning in the SE, viz. a tract of low-lying marshy land. The element *ever* has not been wholly explained. It seems to be, however, an extension of the usual temporal sense of the word into a spacial sense, though comparable examples cannot be cited; *ever* should thus mean 'extensive,' or, by hyperbole, 'endless.' The plural form emphasizes this limitless idea, as can be seen in such a comparable name as **The Great Plains.** The name does not occur elsewhere,

doubtless because there is no other region like this one. The name is recorded from 1822, being apparently well-established at that time. **The Eternal Glades** (1823) is more likely derived from **The Everglades** than *vice versa.*

Evergreen Usually suggested descriptively by the presence of evergreen, usually coniferous, trees, e.g. in MN, CO; also commendatory from the pleasing idea of greenness.

Evolution Group CA The individual mountains were named in 1895 for scientists who promulgated the theory of evolution, and the general name was applied to the whole group.

Excalibur AZ From King Arthur's sword. See **Bedivere.**

Excello Latin 'I excel'; in OH, from the Excello Paper Company, established here in 1865.

Excelsior Latin 'higher,' usually from Longfellow's poem, with commendatory suggestions, e.g. in MN where the name was bestowed in 1853, only 12 years after the writing of the poem.

Exchange In PA, because stagecoaches changed horses at this point. In WV, locally believed to be because there was much changing around of ownership.

Exchequer Mountain CO From a mine name.

Exeter From the city of England. Colonial namings in RI and NH established the name, and it was thence spread westward.

Exira IA For Exira Eckman, named for her (ca. 1857) after her father had promised, on that condition, to buy a lot in the new town.

Exline IA For David Exline, pioneer local merchant.

Exmore VA Probably from a place in England, e.g. a variant of Exmoor.

Expectation Peak CO From a mine name.

Explorer Rare, except in AK, where several names commemorate the ship *Explorer* of the U.S. Coast and Geodetic Survey. **Explorer's Pass** AZ, CA is for an early steamboat which first navigated this portion of the Colorado River. **Explorers Peak** AK: named (1910) for the Explorers Club of New York. **Explorer Glacier** AK: because Explorer Scouts trained here.

Extra Dry Creek AK Named as being even drier than nearby **Dry Creek.**

Eye Opener, The AK The name of the rock is a translation from the Russian, probably with the same general idea as the Spanish **Abreojo** (q.v.).

Eyese Creek CA From the name of an Indian (Karok) village on the stream, influenced by folk-etymology, the pronunciation being *eye-ease.*

Eyota MN From a Siouan word, 'greatest, most,' a name applied in 1859 by white settlers, probably as a commendatory.

F

Fabius In NY it is a part of the classical naming of 1790, and is for one of the Roman heroes. **Fabius** WV: for a man named Bean, being an attempt to render that name in Latin. **Fabius** MO: from the river, appearing earlier as Fabiane (1809) and Ferbien (1822), apparently the name of a Frenchman, later shifted to the Latin form.

Face Rock OR Descriptive, from a rock formation like a human face.

Fact KS Named (ca. 1882) by a committee of residents because someone, when hearing that a post office had been established, replied 'Is that a fact!'

Factory Rare, as compared with **Mill,** in spite of the growing industrialism of the 19th century. **Factoryville** PA was named for a woolen mill founded ca. 1825; by association, on a few features, e.g. **Factory Brook** MA. **Factoria** WA, a pseudo-Latin form, was given in hope of the development of manufacturing. **Factory Hill** WY from fancied resemblance to a factory.

Fafnir, Mount From the dragon of Norse mythology, but reference uncertain.

Fagus MO Latin 'beech-tree.'

Fahkahhatchee River FL Seminole, probably 'clay (muddy)-stream.' **Fahkahatcheochee** is the diminutive.

Fahlun MN For a district in Sweden, named by immigrants.

Fair The common word for beautiful in earlier times, *fair* was obsolete even in the Colonial era, but lingered as a poetic or pleasantly archaic term. It has been commonly used as a commendatory term for habitation-names, but generally combined with the noun. It is commonest as **Fairview, Fairfield,** and **Fairmont (Mount),** but is found as **Fairport, Fairoaks, Fairgrove,** etc. In the more modern sense of *just* or *even* it occurs in **Fair Play,** e.g. in CA, in a commendatory sense, the local story often telling

that the origin was a fist-fight in which people called for fair play (e.g. in CA, SC). **Fairfax, Fairbanks, Fairfield,** etc. are also personal names but the commendatory quality may have been an influence in the giving of such names. The personal name **Fair** has also been so combined. **Fairfax** is from the personal name, in VA usually with reference to Lord Fairfax (1693–1781), e.g. **Fairfax Co. Fairground** VT: This and other names probably arise from the holding of a county fair. **Fairbanks** AK was named (Sept. 8, 1902) probably for C. W. Fairbanks, then a prominent political figure from Indiana; later, vice-president. **Fairlee** VT was probably from a family name. **Fair;** in such an early example as **Fairfield** CT, named in 1667, the influence of an English village of the same name is likely.

Fairborn OH On Jan. 1, 1950, the rival towns of **Fairfield** and **Osborn** merged under a merged name.

Fairweather, Cape, Mount AK Named (1778) by James Cook, presumably because of the fine weather there enjoyed. Cf. **Foulweather.**

Fairy In the 19th century some places were romantically so named, e.g. **Fairy Glen** WV; **Fairy** TX was named for Fairy Fort, daughter of an early settler.

Faith In NC, because J. T. Wyatt opened quarrying operations without previous experience, i.e. 'on faith'; in SD probably for Faith Rockefeller, daughter of a stockholder in the railroad.

Fake Creek AK Because, in 1938, some explorers were led out of their way by following this stream; this is an ungracious naming, for the stream itself was honest.

Falcon Names are rare, and may be for the personal name. Birds are seldom so called in the U.S. **Cape Falcon** OR was probably by shortening and error from the Spanish naming of 1775, which was Santa Clara de Montefalco, on whose day (Aug. 18) the name was given. In NC, by local tradition, at the time of naming a box of Falcon pens was noticed.

Falda Spanish 'skirt,' but in a topographical sense, 'slope, lower part of slope.' In CA the place so named is near a steep slope.

Falfa AZ, CO A shortening of *alfalfa,* which is locally an important crop.

Falfurrias TX Uncertain, though locally believed to be the Spanish name for a desert flower.

Falkner MS For Col. W. C. Falkner, soldier and novelist, grandfather of William Faulkner.

Fall(s) Coupled with a generic, usually *creek,* the name indicates a stream with a waterfall, or several of them. In earlier usage *fall* was used for what was later called a *rapid* or even a *riffle,* e.g. the **Falls of the Ohio,** at present Louisville. It is therefore unnecessary in the eastern states to look for any marked waterfall to explain this name. **Fall River** MA is a translation from the Algonquian, 'place of falling water.' **Fallbrook** CA is named for a private home in PA. **Fall(s)** is also a personal name. With habitation-names, e.g. **Falls City,** the name indicates a site at or near a waterfall. So also **Fall City** WA.

Fallen Occurs rarely, most often as the early term **Fallen Timber(s)** to indicate a place where trees had been blown down. **Fallen Leaf Lake** CA was apparently named by a surveying party to whom the lake, seen from a height, was like a fallen leaf. **Lake of the Fallen Moon** CA was so named by a man who wrote a poem of that title. **Fallen City** WY, a jumble of rocks, is compared to the ruins of a city.

Falling Though much less common than *fall,* the name has about the same meaning, but suggests a smaller and more delicate stream, thus occurring in the combination **Falling Spring. Falling Rock** WA is for a rock on **Falling Creek. Falling Glacier** AK appears to be falling. **Falling Mountain** AK is subject to rock avalanches.

Fallowfield Township PA For the Fallowfield family, settlers, ca. 1714.

Falmouth From the town in England; ME (1658), MA (1686), VA (1727). In KY the town **Falmouth** was named for that in VA by settlers who came from that town (1799).

Faloma OR From the names of the original landowners, viz. Force, Love, and Moore, somewhat altered.

False Used, especially by early navigators, to denote a place easily mistaken for another (or so mistaken on one occasion), e.g. **False Cape** CA, which may be confused with the more important **Cape Mendicino.** But there are also inland examples, e.g. **False Poplar River** MN to be distinguished from a nearby **Poplar River. False Bottom Creek** SD: so called because its bottom is sometimes dry. **False River** LA: from the French Fausse Rivière, being an old channel which looks like the present river.

Falsoola Mountain AK For **False Oolah,** because it resembles that mountain. See **Oolah.**

Falun From a town in Sweden, usually given by immigrants.

Fame OK A commendatory name, because the residents thought that their farmlands were, or should be, famous.

Famoso Spanish 'famous.'

Famous The hills in PA are for L. G. Famous, subdivider of 1954.

Fancy In occasional use, e.g. **Fancy Farm** KY, **Fancy Gap** VA, **Fancy Prairie** IL; the term is used in a wide variety of meanings in English, and its reason for application in naming is obscure; historical records are not extant.

Fandango The Mexican term for 'dance, ball,' became known to Americans during the Mexican War. In 1849 some emigrants held a fandango in a valley in CA, and a name-cluster has resulted.

Fang Occasionally used as a descriptive for toothlike appearance, e.g. the mountain in AK.

Fannegusha Creek MS Muskogean (Choctaw), 'squirrel-little' (?).

Far Rarely occurring, since it demands that the namer place a name, not where he is, but where he is not. **Far Hills** NJ may be a late and conscious name. **Far Rockaway** NY probably sprang from a duplication, so that **Near** and **Far** arose for differentiation. The term occurs several times in AK (cape, mountain, point), perhaps an evidence of the isolation felt by early travelers, so that even the place where they were seemed far off from home and safety.

Farallon Spanish 'cliff,' and thus applied descriptively to the islands off the coast of CA, and to the bay in AK.

Fargo From the personal name, e.g. in ND for W. G. Fargo, a director of the Northern Pacific Railway, and founder of Wells-Fargo Express. In OK the name is from that company.

Farina IL Latin 'flour,' probably as a commendatory, since the town is in a wheat-growing district.

Farisita CO Suggested by the postmaster A. S. Faris for his little daughter who was known by the Spanish diminutive of her family name.

Farm, Farmer, Farming In an agricultural community these words are commendatory, though **Farmer** is often from the personal name. **Farmington CT** was named in 1645, probably after the town in England, though the commendatory suggestion must also have been there. This name, thus off to an early start, has become highly popular, occurring in about 25 states. **Farmers Branch TX** was so named because of a farming community on a large branch (stream).

Farr From the personal name; the punning **Farr West** UT was so called from being west of **Farr's Fort.**

Farwell Regularly from a personal name. In NB it is from the Danish word for 'farewell,' supposedly because the Danish settlers thus said good-bye to a former Polish name.

Fashing TX Probably from a personal name, though by local story it is a spelling of *fashion,* that term being taken from a tobacco can, when a name was being sought.

Fastrill TX From the last names of F. F. Farrington (first postmaster), P. H. Strauss, and Will Hill (the last two, officials of a lumber company).

Fate TX From a shortening of Fayette, for LaFayette Brown, local sheriff.

Fathers, Crossing of the UT A translation of Spanish **El Vado de los Padres,** with reference to the fording of the river here in 1776 by the Escalante expedition, *father* being used in the meaning of 'priest.'

Fault Regularly in the geological sense, e.g. **Fault Creek** AK.

Fausse See **Faux.**

Faux, Fausse French 'false,' e.g. **Lake Faussepointe** LA.

Favoretta FL A name applied (1910) commendatorially to a turpentine still. Also appearing as **Favorita,** it is for Spanish 'favorite.'

Fawn The rarest of the names derived from different kinds of deer, the term indicates some incident involving a fawn. At **Fawnskin Meadows** CA hunters stretched some skins on trees in 1891, and these remained for several years, thus establishing the name.

Fayal MN From the island of the Azores; reason for application, unknown.

Fayette The Marquis de la Fayette served under Washington, but his great popularity was subsequent to his visit to the U.S., in 1824. As **Fayette, Lafayette,** and **La Fayette,** his name then became popular for towns and counties.

Faywood NM A blend of the names of two early residents, J. C. Fay and William Lockwood.

Fear, Cape NC An incident name, dating from an English voyage of 1585, because some of the seamen went into a panic at the fear of being wrecked at that point.

Feaster SC An adaptation of a German or Swiss personal name, probably the one commonly spelled Pfister.

Feather Generally from the personal name, also as **Featherston,** etc. **Feather River** CA: J. A. Sutter named the stream (perhaps first in the Spanish form **Rio de las Plumas**) before 1840, because the local Indians made use of feathers for clothing and blankets and many feathers were lying about.

Federal Usually because of property or an institution connected with the U.S. government, e.g. **Federal Dam** MN where the dam was thus built. **Federalsburg** MD was adopted in 1812 because of the Federal party.

Fedora SD Probably for a woman of that name.

Felda FL For the oldest settlers, Mr. and Mrs. F. L. Taylor, with the *F* and *L* from his initials and the other letters from her maiden name, now unremembered.

Feliciana LA Originating under the Spanish regime, it was probably named in compliment to Félicité, wife of the governor Bernardo de Gálvez.

Felicity The lake in LA is probably from French *félicité,* 'happiness,' a fisherman's term for the sheltered water. In OH the name is a commendatory suggested by the name of the founder William Fee, combined with *-city* and at one period spelled **Feelicity.**

Felida WA The assistant postmaster wanted to call the town **Thomas,** after his cat; thinking this too frivolous, others substituted a Latin form, from *Felidae,* the cat family.

Femme Osage French 'woman-Osage,' perhaps associated with a tribal dignitary. See **Bonne Femme.**

Fence A rare name, because fences are too common for distinction. **Fence Lake** NM: because of a reservoir enclosed by a fence. **Fence Lake** WI: a translation from the Ojibway, probably with reference to a device for trapping deer or fish.

Fenholloway FL From a former Creek town; literally, 'footlog (bridge)-high.'

Fer French 'iron,' e.g. **Pointe au Fer** LA; reason for naming uncertain.

Fern Sometimes from a personal name, but more commonly because of the natural growth of ferns. The term has commendatory value, suggesting luxuriant growth and a cool place, and occurs in many habitation-names, especially as **Ferndale** and **Fernwood.**

Fernandina FL An adjectival form, for Domingo Fernández, who received a large land grant in this area from Spain in 1785.

Ferrelo, Cape OR Named (1869) in honor of Bartolomé Ferrelo, pilot and later commander of the Spanish expedition of 1542–1543.

Ferrum Latin 'iron,' applied in 1948 to a station in CA on a railroad over which iron ore was hauled.

Ferry Before the building of bridges, small ferries served at many river-crossings, and this name has lingered upon both natural features and habitations, long after the vanishing of the ferry itself. **Ferry Branch** WV: at this stream a ferry across the Kanawha River was located. **Ferry Creek** Coos Co., OR was named for the Ferry family, early settlers.

Fertile A commendatory, for fertile soil.

Festus MO Probably from a personal name, but uncertain.

Feterita KA For a kind of grain sorghum grown here as a crop.

Feura Bush NY From *bush,* 'forest,' and Dutch *ver,* 'far' (?).

Fibre MI Because wood pulp, associated with the idea of fibre, was produced here.

Fickle IN Probably from the personal name.

Fiddle Early Americans knew the violin as a fiddle, and it was a widely used instrument. In the gold-rush period the settlement of **Fiddletown CA** was known for its fiddlers. At **Fiddle Creek OR** an injured man, ca. 1894, was laid up in a cabin here, and passed his time fiddling. **Fiddler** is generally from the personal name, but **Fiddlers Creek NB** is probably from the proficiency of local people on the violin.

Field Alone, and as a first element, it is commonly from the personal name, e.g. **Field NM** for Nelson Field, whose home housed the first post office. As a second element it is commonly the generic, e.g. **Bakersfield, Elysian Fields. Fieldton TX:** from **Littlefield** and **Olton,** two towns already existing in the county.

Fierro Spanish 'iron,' in NM because of a deposit of iron ore.

Fife For the county of Scotland.

Fifty Six AR From a school district so numbered.

Fig Of rare occurrence, since the fig is not native and is cultivated only in small areas. The name may be personal, though the common spelling is **Figg.**

Figarden CA: for **Fig Garden,** because of a large fig orchard there.

Files Creek SV A phonetic spelling after the 18th-century pronunciation of the name Foyle, a family of settlers, ca. 1750.

Fillmore From the personal name, especially for President Millard Fillmore, e.g. several towns and counties.

Fin In 1899 a ridge in CA was compared to a sea-serpent, and **Fin Dome** was the fin. **Fin Creek WA** was so named because some Finns lived there, ca. 1890.

Final, Cape AZ The last point reached by C. E. Dutton on an exploration of 1880.

Fingal ND From the legendary Irish hero.

Finger Usually descriptive of a feature as being long and thin like a finger, e.g. **The Finger Lakes NY,** and about 10 mountains and rocks in CA. **Finger-**

ville SC is from Joseph Finger, founder. **Fingerboard Gulch, Prairie OR:** each was distinguished by a signpost with a pointing finger.

Finikochika Creek AL Muskogean (Creek), 'foot-log-broken.'

Finis Latin 'end,' but see **Finn.**

Finland From the country in Europe, usually named by immigrants.

Finn 1) From the personal name, e.g. **Finn Rock OR,** for B. F. Finn, early settler; 2) from Finnish settlers, e.g. **Finn Lake MN.** In DE the 17th-century Swedish colony had many Finns in it, and **Finns Point DE, NJ** is presumably thus explained. **Finis Branch DE** also may be an adaptation of **Finn's.**

Finney and Egan Lake OR From two early landowners.

Fir Occurs rarely as a place-name, because the term hardly entered the early American vocabulary, the tree being known as balsam or larch, and considered to be a kind of pine. Perhaps the homophony with *fur* also tended to restrict the use. **Fir Top Mountain CA** is a late naming by foresters who knew their trees; the mountain is mostly bare except for the firs on its flat top.

Fire In view of the useful and sometimes terrifying nature of fire, names are surprisingly rare, and are almost wholly lacking on habitations. The chief usage is in AK. The name may indicate: 1) a fire seen at the time of naming; thus, probably **Fire Island NY;** 2) the mark of a forest fire; 3) volcanic action, e.g. in AK. **Valley of Fire NV** is descriptive, because of highly colored red rock formations.

Firehole River WY From *hole* 'small valley,' and *fire* because of a disastrous forest-fire before 1830; the intense thermal action of the area makes the name seem still appropriate, but was apparently not the origin.

Firescald Meaning an area of burned timber left by a forest fire, it has yielded a few names, e.g. **Firescald Branch KY.**

First, Second, etc. Ordinal numbers in general are treated under this heading. This system of relative description is applied to features occurring in a natural series, e.g. to a chain of similar lakes, e.g. **First Connecticut Lake** NH, etc. The order represents the direction of travel of the namer, e.g. in AZ, **First** to **Fourth Mesa** run from east to west. Names may survive after the series is broken or obscured, e.g. **Fourth Crossing** CA is a habitation-name at the site of the fourth stream-crossing on a stage line, though the stage has ceased to run, the road has been relocated, and the streams have been bridged. This system of naming is most highly developed with streets, with the series often running up into the hundreds. In **Firstview** CO no series is indicated, but this is the first point from which the Rocky Mts. can be seen.

Fish, Fisher, Fisherman Fisher is generally from the personal name. **Fish** also may be, but in many instances refers to a water-feature which has provided good fishing on the occasion of the naming. In arid areas **Fish Spring** or **Fish Creek** indicates a place where fish may be found, though they are not found in most waters of the vicinity. **Fisherman** arises from an incident, or else indicates a place frequented by fishermen. **Fisher Creek** Lincoln Co., OR: from the animal so called. See **Fishing.**

Fish-Eating Creek FL A translation of a Seminole name, containing *papka,* the common term for 'eating-place.' See **Apopka.**

Fishing Appears rarely, most often as **Fishing Creek,** in former Algonquian territory, e.g. PA, MD, WV. It seems to represent, not an original naming, but a partial translation of an Indian name, which consisted of an element meaning *fish* and a locative ending *-ing.* Cf. **Licking. Fishinghawk Creek** WV probably refers to the fish hawk or osprey. Various names, e.g. **Fishing Rocks** CT, are descriptive of their use for fishing.

Fishkill NY An Anglicization from a Dutch *vischers kil,* 'fishers-stream,' from *vischers rak,* 'fishers-reach,' probably because Indians were seen fishing in the creek at the time of a Dutch voyage on the Hudson in the early 17th century.

Fishtail A common word for something split into two parts, e.g. **Fishtail Canyon** AZ because it branches at the upper end.

Fishtrap Usually for Indian devices for taking fish, e.g. creeks in various states; whence, a town in WA.

Fisty KY From the nickname of a man named Combs, a local resident, not further identified.

Five See also **One. Five Points:** a name originally descriptive, for a place at which five roads or trails converged.

Fixico Creek AL Muskogean (Creek), 'heartless,' used in personal names, and so probably from an Indian so named.

Flag Generally for a place where a flag has flown; the personal name is usually **Flagg. Flag Island** OR was named in 1929 to commemorate the flying there of a British flag in 1792. **Flagstone Rock** OR got its name for the occurrence of rock suitable to be split into flagstones. **Flagtail Mountain** OR is from the occurrence of so-called flagtail deer. **Flagstaff** AZ, by transfer from **Flagstaff Spring,** was so named because a flag was once flown there from a tall pine cleared of branches. **Flagstaff** ME received its name because during Arnold's campaign against Quebec a flag was flown from a pole nearby. **Flag Creek** NB: a flag was flown here during an early patriotic celebration. **Flag Creek** SC: probably is for the Flagg family, early settlers.

Flambeau French 'torch,' e.g. **Lac du Flambeau** MI, WI, perhaps from the local Indian habit of attracting fish at night by torches.

Flaming Gorge UT The Powell expedition in 1869 named the gorge when they saw its red rocks gleaming in the sunlight. The gorge in WY is also named for red rock.

Flat Its usage is complicated. It is sometimes a simple specific, as with the repeated **Flat Rock,** or with **Flat Point** WA. Since tide-flat is a common term, such a name as **Flat Cove** AK designates a body of water having a flat showing at low tide. With streams, the exact meaning is sometimes hard to determine.

The common **Flat Creek** may indicate a stream associated with a *flat,* i.e. an area of flat ground, this usage probably being more common in the West. But the term may indicate a stream with little gradient, therefore having quiet or 'flat' water. In many instances, however, especially in the SE, *flat* means 'shallow,' or even a stream that was both quiet and shallow and therefore easy to ford. As applied to lakes, e.g. in MN, 'shallow' may also be the better rendering. In **Flatswood(s)** the reference is to a forest growing in a flat or merely a low-lying wooded area. **Flatiron** is applied to a feature resembling or imagined to resemble that common implement. In the SE the name **Flat Shoals Creek** occurs to indicate more specifically a stream having a crossing in quiet, shallow water.

Flatbush NY Dutch *vlak-bosch,* 'level forest,' an early spelling being **Flakkebos.** After the takeover of 1664 the name was shifted to an English form, probably by conscious design.

Flathead From the Indian tribal name, e.g. the lake in MT.

Flatonia TX For F. W. Flato, early settler, with a Latin ending.

Flattery, Cape WA Named by Capt. James Cook on March 22, 1778, because a small opening 'flattered us with the hopes of finding a harbour,' hopes which were proved false.

Flax Though it is a rare personal name, the examples are regularly from the plant, e.g. **Flaxton** ND, named in 1901 when flax was the almost universal crop. In the colonial and frontier period flax was widely grown for the home-making of linen, and a few names result, e.g. **Flaxpatch Branch** KY. Flax was formerly washed at **Flaxhole Pond** DE.

Flaxman Island AK Named (1826) by Sir John Franklin for 'the late eminent sculptor,' i.e. John Flaxman.

Flea Occasionally appearing to record some experience with fleas, e.g. **Flea Valley** CA.

Flechado Spanish 'pierced with arrows,' e.g. **Palo Flechado** NM from a tree found with arrows in it.

Flensburg MN From the city which has been in both Germany and Denmark, occasion for naming (1890) unknown.

Flint Sometimes for the personal name. **Flint** TX is named for R. P. Flynt, landowner, and by error of spelling; **Flintridge** CA for Senator F. P. Flint. Usually on features for the presence of flint, useful both to Indians for arrowheads and to whites for gunflints, e.g. **Flint River** MI, whence the city by transfer. The name may indicate some other stone of which arrowheads were made, such as obsidian.

Flirtation A favorite 19th-century word lingers on the peak in CO, doubtless commemorating a pleasant incident.

Flomich FL From syllables of FL and MI, the founder being a native of the latter state.

Flomot TX From **Motley,** the county in which the town is situated, and **Floyd,** the adjoining county.

Flood The personal name seems to have been avoided for habitations, probably because of unpleasant suggestion. As applied to a feature, usually a stream, the name is not common, and indicates an association with a flood, or a tendency in a stream to flood easily. **Floodwood** MN was first applied to the river; the term referred to timber brought down at flood-time, and sometimes left blocking the stream; it is here a rough translation of the French **Embarras,** q.v.

Flor Spanish 'flower,' commonly in the plural, e.g. **Las Flores** CA, from a lake so called because of its flowers. **Floresville** TX: from the abundant wild flowers. **Flores Peak** CA: for Juan Flores, bandit, who was captured here.

Flora(1) 1) From a personal name, e.g. **Flora** IL for the daughter of one of the founders; **Flora** OR: for Flora Buzzard, daughter of the first postmaster; **Floras Creek** OR for Fred Floras, miner in the 1850's. 2) Probably in some instances a vague commendatory, suggesting rich vegetation; so also **Floral.** In MN, **Flora Township** was named for the first horse brought there after a resettlement in 1865. **Florahome** FL offers a double commendatory. **Floranada** FL makes use of a vaguely Spanish ending. By suggestion of the state name, such namings are common in FL, which has also **Florinde, Floridale, Floral City, Florosa.**

Florence A repeated habitation-name, from a woman so named, except for the one in AL, which was named for the Italian city by an Italian surveyor, and for the one in OR which was either named for a state senator, A. B. Florence, or for a ship wrecked here.

Florida Spanish 'flowered, flowery.' Applied to the state, the name was given by Ponce de León, in 1513, probably on the evening of April 2. It is the first name surely given by Europeans in the territory of the U.S. Ponce gave the name, according to the chronicler Herrera, for two reasons—because he believed the land to be flowery (Spanish *florida*), and because this was the Easter season (Spanish, *Pasqua florida.*) In Spanish the accent is on the second syllable. In English the accent is on the first syllable, and probably has been so from the beginning, because the name would have been taken from a map, and thought to be Latin, in which the accent is on the first syllable. In NM the mountains are so named because of wild flowers. In MA and other states the name is one of the exotics which were favored in the post-Revolutionary period.

Florissant MO French 'flourishing, prosperous,' but perhaps for *fleurissant,* 'flowery,' which could have been applied to a site; the name dates from the 18th century.

Floriston CA Probably a coined name, from Spanish *flor,* 'flowers.'

Flounce Rock OR Named from a more-or-less fanciful resemblance to the flounces on a dress.

Flowell UT Because of a number of flowing wells in the area.

Flower, Flowery Rare, sometimes from a personal name. Usually descriptive,

because of wild flowers. **Flower Dieu Hundred** VA: from the family name Flowerday, changed to a quasi-French form after the family was forgotten. **Flowerfield** NB was so named because it was on the boundary of Flower and Field precincts, but also because wild flowers were blooming at the time of naming.

Flowk Creek NY An early spelling for *fluke,* a kind of fish such as the flounder.

Floyd From the personal name; in IA it commemorates Sgt. William Floyd of the Lewis and Clark expedition who died near the mouth of **Floyd River** IA.

Floydada TX From **Floyd County,** and Ada Price, mother of a local landowner.

Flush KS First named (1897) **Floersch** for Michael Floersch, early settler; simplified to its present form in 1899.

Flushing NY Named by the Dutch (1645) **Vlissingen,** for the town in the Netherlands, which was known to the English as **Flushing;** after the English conquest the English form was substituted.

Fluted Rock AZ Descriptive, because of a columnar structure.

Fluteville CT Because of a local industry of manufacturing flutes of apple-wood in the early 19th century.

Fluvanna County VA A coinage from Latin *fluvius,* 'river,' and the name Anna, probably with reference to Queen Anne, but probably in part suggested by the Algonquian *hanne,* 'stream,' which occurs in the region. See **Anna, Rivanna.**

Fly Rare, the insect apparently not being of sufficient note to occasion naming. In areas of early Dutch influence it is an Anglicization of *vallei* (by way of **Vly)** 'valley,' e.g. **Fly Creek** NY. **Fly** OH was chosen by the inhabitants, chiefly because it was short, and easy to pronounce and spell. **Shoo Fly Creek** KS is probably from the use of that term for a railroad track constructed around a temporary blockage. **Fly by Night Gulch** CO: probably from an incident of the mining period, the term being a common one for an absconder.

Flying Commonly from brand-names, e.g. **Flying W Mountain** NM. **Flying High** NM: originally **Flying H**, for a brand. **Flying Eagle Harbor** AK: probably from the sighting of an eagle.

Fodder In GA a Cherokee Indian personal name is preserved on **Fodder Creek**. **Fodderstack Mountain** NC was probably a variant from the too common **Haystack**.

Fodice TX From **Fordyce** AR, so named by former residents, but spelled according to pronunciation in Southern dialect.

Fog, Foggy A rare name in most areas, since fog was not a serious phenomenon before the era of automobiles and airplanes. Like other weather-words (e.g. **Fairweather**) it usually springs from conditions on a certain occasion, rather than from customary conditions; thus **Foggy Peak** WA was probably named because of fog encountered on a particular day. Still, the name is common in especially foggy regions, e.g. the coast of AK. **Foggy Island** AK: in 1826 Sir John Franklin was detained here eight days by fog.

Foley and Senter Lake NB Because of an incident involving the freighting company of that name.

Folly Commonly a generic to indicate a place notable for extravagant, foolish expenditure, or some other foolish action, e.g. **Follyfarm** OR, called **Neal's Folly** by its owner, because he had attempted to irrigate under adverse conditions; he suggested the present name when the post office was established, ca. 1909. Until ca. 1800 *folly* was in use as a topographic term, of meaning not always clearly determinable, but sometimes, as in England, for a clump of trees, especially on top of a hill; **Folly Beach** SC thus arose, and probably **Folly Hill** ME.

Fond French 'bottom, lower end.' The early French in America seem to have used the term loosely to mean 'farther end,' with reference to travel from the established settlements, so that **Fond du Lac** MN, WI is at what would be more exactly termed the 'head' of the lake.

Fondis CO The first postmaster suggested Fondi, taken from an Italian phrase in a newspaper, and it was adopted with an added *s*.

Fontana CA From the corporation that founded the town, viz. The Fontana Development Company, probably from the Spanish word meaning 'fountain,' since the town was dependent upon irrigation, and the name would have been commendatory. **Fontana** KS: from a local spring, known as 'The Old Fountain.'

Fool A rare name, commonly arising because someone did a foolish act, and the name was then placed, half-humorously, e.g. **Fools Lake** MN, where two men lost themselves and had to spend the night only a short way from their camp. **Fool Creek** WY is probably from the presence of grouse, known as 'fool hens.' **Fools Gulch** AZ was so named because some prospectors were considered fools for expecting to find gold here.

Forada MN Named by C. A. Campbell for his wife Ada, i.e. 'for Ada.'

Foraker, Mount AK Named (1899) for J. B. Foraker, Ohio politician, then senator.

Fordoche LA Louisiana-French 'brushwood,' as applied to a bayou being the equivalent of **Embarras**, q.v.

Forest Though occasionally from the personal name, e.g. **Forest Crossing** OR, the idea is usually that of thick or unbroken tree-growth. **Forest County** PA was named in 1848, when the area was almost completely forested. In early times, when the whole country was thickly grown-over, the term did not have distinguishing value for natural features, and it was a repellant rather than an attractive habitation-name. Later, forests came to have economic value and also to suggest rural exclusiveness, with a resultant use of such suburban names as **Forest Hills, Forest Park.** The term is rare with natural features, but such names as **Forest Lake** and **Forest Prairie** indicate a feature set in deep woods. **Forest Grove** appears as a habitation-name, though how a grove can be distinguished from a forest is hard to see; the usage probably represents very vague conception of terms.

Forester The pass in CA was discovered in 1929 by men of the Forest Service, and named for them. It is also a personal name.

Forge For a natural feature where a forge was located, e.g. **Forge Pond** CT, MA, an indication of early iron-working. It has survived in many habitation-names, usually as the second element, e.g. **Valley Forge** PA, **Clifton Forge** VA.

Fork Normally a generic, especially common in CA, to designate a branch of a stream. By association it becomes a specific to designate some feature involved with a fork, e.g. **Fork Ridge** KY. It occurs with habitations, e.g. **Forks of Salmon** CA, **Spanish Fork** UT, **Fork Township** MN. **Forked** also occurs, e.g. **Forked Lake** KY.

Formosa In several states it is probably an exotic borrowing from the island now known as Taiwan, but in some instances may have been used in its literal (Latin or Portuguese) sense of 'beautiful,' thus being a commendatory for habitations.

Formoso KS Apparently used as a masculine form of **Formosa**, q.v.

Forsan TX Locally believed to have been originally **Four Sands**, because of the strata in an oil field, but shortened in transmission through the Post Office Dept. Since the word means 'perhaps,' in Latin, however, it might have been fittingly applied to an oil field.

Fort Generally used as a generic and preceding its specific, but often as a specific for a feature associated with a fort, e.g. **Fort Point** OR, where two blockhouses were built in 1851. **Fort Rock** OR: the rock, with many perpendicular faces, has been taken to resemble a fort. The personal name has had little influence. For habitation-names with **Fort** as the first element, see under the second element, e.g. for **Fort Wayne**, see **Wayne.**

Fortuna Latin 'fortune.' A few habitations, e.g. in CA, have thus been named for commendatory reasons.

Forty Fort PA From a stockade built in 1770 by the first forty settlers in the area.

Forty-Nine Creek NV A commemorative naming, because numerous wagon-trains took this route in 1849.

Foshee AL Muskogean (Chickasaw), 'bird.'

Fossil Applied because of the occurrence of fossils, e.g. **Fossil Mountain** WY. **Fossil Forest** WY was so named because of petrified trees; **Fossil Creek** AZ, because objects such as twigs that drop into the stream are soon covered with a limestone deposit, thus resembling fossils.

Fostoria A Latinized derivation from the personal name Foster, apparently originating in OH (1854) for C. W. Foster, early merchant, and occurring in several states.

Foul As a seacoast name it occurs in the nautical sense, e.g. **Foul Passage** AK, and has been rarely thus used inland, e.g. **Foul Rift** NJ for a rapid.

Foulweather The cape in OR was named by James Cook on Mar. 7, 1778, because of a recent storm. The bluff in WA was named for a similar reason by George Vancouver in 1792.

Fountain Sometimes for the personal name, e.g. in NC for J. L. Fountain, local resident. Although rare as a generic and not common in colloquial use, the term has commendatory value, and has been used for a number of habitations, usually in the sense of a bountiful spring, as in **Fountain Green** UT. **Fountain Lake** MN is probably named for a spring feeding it, but the term may also indicate that the lake itself is the source of a river.

Four See also **One. Four States** WV: named by John H. Jones, who owned coal mines in four states. **Four Corners** is the only place in the U.S. where the corners of four states meet, viz. NM, AZ, UT, CO. **Four Bear Creek** WY: on a morning in the 1880's one man killed four bears along this stream. At **Fourlog Park** WY in the 1870's a prospector started to build a cabin here, but gave up after laying only four logs, which remained as a landmark. **Fourseam** KY: because a local mine has four seams of coal.

Fourche French 'fork,' usually with the topographical sense 'branch of a stream,' e.g. **Belle Fourche** SD, **Fourche Creek** MO.

Fourth See also **First**. **Fourth of July Wash** AZ: because some people had a fine party here on this day in the 1890's they gave this name.

Fox 1) For the animal. Though the fox was widespread and common, it made little impression and names are comparatively rare, though commoner in northern areas, where the fox was valuable for fur. **Fox Hole Creek** MD is descriptive, from evidences left by a fox. 2) **Fox** is also from the personal name. This is the commonest source, especially in habitation-names, e.g. **Foxborough** MA for Charles James Fox, who defended the American cause in the British Parliament. 3) Also from the Indian tribe, especially in WI, e.g. **Fox River**.

Foxen Kill NY Probably from Dutch *vos*, 'fox'; thus 'foxes' creek.'

Fracas Creek NB Because some early settlers had an altercation here.

Fragaria WA Named for the genus to which the strawberry belongs, because of early ripened berries found there on Feb. 15, 1912.

Fragua Spanish 'forge, smithy.' **Fraguita Mountain** AZ is the diminutive.

Framboise French 'raspberry,' but often from a personal name, e.g. **La Framboise Woods** IL for Claude Framboise, who held a reservation in that area.

Framingham MA From a town in England (1700).

Frances From the personal name, e.g. **Francestown** NH for Lady Frances Wentworth, wife of the governor (1772).

Franceway Creek AR By partial folk-etymology from the French personal name François.

Francitas TX Because a French family lived here, the place was known as 'Little France'; the present name is apparently an attempt to make a Spanish rendering.

Franconia The name is that of one of the medieval German duchies. Personal names have been absorbed to this form, e.g. **Franconia** NH from the given name of Sir Francis Bernard, who received a grant there in 1764; in AZ, from Frank Smith, son of a railroad official.

Frankford From the personal name plus *ford*, but aided by alliteration and by the well-known **Frankfort** in Germany.

Frankfort Usually for one of the German cities, commonly that one on the Main, e.g. in IN because the grandfather of the town founders had come from that city. In ME (1789) the name was given because of some German settlers. In KY the name was originally **Frank's Ford**, in memory of a man killed there by Indians, but passed over to the commoner form by a process analogous to folk-etymology. **Frankfort** WA was partly in honor of early citizens, Frank Bourn and Frank Scott.

Franklin The widespread use of the name is owed chiefly to Benjamin Franklin, who has been productive of namings second only to Washington, because of his fame as public figure and as author, and especially because of his early connection with post offices. Other people of the same name have also been honored, e.g. **Franklin** TX for W. G. Franklin, early settler; **Franklin Point Mountains** AK for Sir John Franklin, British explorer.

Frederick In the colonies the name was common, often representing the Anglicization of the German Friedrich. Many early namings are thus from unimportant settlers. **Frederick** MD is probably for Frederick Calvert, sixth Lord Baltimore; **Frederick County, Fredericksburg** VA for the Prince of Wales, son of George II; **Frederick** TX, named (1846) by German settlers, for Frederick the Great.

Frederika IA A partial Anglicization of Fredrika. See **Bremer**.

Fredon NJ A shortening of **Fredonia** (?).

Fredonia Coined by Dr. Samuel Latham Mitchill, shortly after 1800 from the English *freedom* with a Latin ending, with the idea of its meaning 'place of freedom.' He proposed it as a name for the nation, but it was never a serious contender. For a while it enjoyed some popularity for towns, and a dozen examples exist.

Free occurs often in personal names, e.g. **Freeland, Freeman, Freed, Freeborn.** As an adjective and abstract the term springs from a variety of motivations, less commonly than is generally supposed from a desire for personal or political freedom, though a number of places called **Freedom,** e.g. in NB, arose out of that feeling during the Civil War. **Freedman's Village** SC: from being a settlement of freed slaves after the Civil War. **Freedom** CA: from a saloon which displayed the flag and a sign *Flag of Freedom.* **Freestone** CA: from a deposit of freestone. **Freestone** TX: from "freestone" water. **Freehold** and **Freeland** involve the problems of getting and keeping land. **Freeport** expresses the commendatory idea that the port is open to all comers. **Freewater** OR was an inducement to settlers for irrigation-water. **Freetown** MA, named ca. 1683, was previously **Freemans Land,** probably an emphasis upon the land titles. **Free Hills** TN had a settlement of free Negroes in pre-Civil War times. **Free Creek** MT was named for Ira Free, homesteader of the 1890's. At **Freedmen's Grove** GA a former slaveholder, after the Civil War, deeded land here to his former slaves.

Freeo Creek AR From Spanish *frio,* 'cold.'

Freezeout In AZ the name originated because some cowboys once spent a cold night there. Other instances, e.g. several in CA, may arise from an incident involving a "freezeout" in a card game. Some early miners had to abandon their camp on **Freezeout Creek** CO because of a hard winter.

Freistadt WI German 'free city,' named by immigrants ca. 1840 to celebrate their religious freedom.

Freistatt MO Probably from a place in Germany, but see **Freistadt.**

Fremont A large number, both of features and habitations, especially in the West, are named for J. C. Frémont, explorer, presidential candidate, and Civil War general. Most of the names are in his honor, and some represent places which he discovered. **Fremont** NC: for a railroad official. **Fremont** MO: for A. J. Freeman, founder (1887), and *-mont.*

French The names total several hundred. 1) Some are from the personal name, e.g. **Frenchglen** OR for H. J. Glenn and his son-in-law Peter French, local landowners. 2) Some are from a nickname, based on nationality or French speech, e.g. **French Pete Creek** OR for an early sheepherder, his family name not preserved. **French Joe Canyon** AZ takes its name from one so-called (last name unknown) who lived here until his partner was killed by Apaches and he moved away. 3) Some names indicate where groups of French-speaking people lived: **French Camp** CA, a site frequented by Hudson Bay Company trappers, who were largely French-Canadians; **French Quarter** SC, from a settlement of French Hugenots; **French Prairie** OR, for early French-Canadian settlers. 4) A special group of names springs from the wars and border contacts of the Colonial period, e.g. **French Watering Place** MA and probably **French Hill** VT. **French Broad River** is a counterpart of **Broad River** NC, but flowed toward the west and was therefore associated with the French. 5) There are a few modern commemorative names: **French Mountain** OR was named by veterans of World War I in memory of their allies. See **Frenchman.**

Frenchman, Frenchman's These names, e.g. **Frenchmans Lake** CA, indicate a naming for a person who was more remembered for a quasi-nickname than for his real name. See **French.**

Frenchy From the common nickname for a Frenchman, e.g. the creek in MT, for a miner whose real name has been forgotten.

Frenepiquant, Bayou LA French 'ash (tree)-prickly.'

Fresh, Freshwater Chiefly as a seacoast name, to distinguish a body of water which is fresh though it might be expected to be salt, e.g. **Freshwater Lagoon** CA. As a generic in the eastern tidewater region, it means especially the upper end of a tidal creek which is fresh because of inflow; this becomes a specific in the habitation-name **Allen Fresh** MD.

Fresno Spanish 'ash-tree.' The river in CA was so called because of the presence of ash-trees. The name was passed to the county and city by transfer. **Fresnal** is Spanish for 'ash grove.'

Friday Most of the names are personal, e.g. **Friday** TX for Fred Friday, early settler. An English captain ca. 1845 named **Friday Harbor** WA for a man, apparently a Kanaka sheepherder unable to speak much English, who said that his name was Friday (perhaps a reminiscence of *Robinson Crusoe*). **Friday Mountain** TX was so named because a party of surveyors reached this spot on a Friday.

Fried ND For P. V. Fried, townsite owner.

Friede(n) German 'peace,' generally as a commendatory name. **Frieden Gemeinde** MO means 'community of peace' and **Friedheim** MO, 'home of peace.' **Friedensville** PA: from a church name. **Friedensau** NB means 'meadow of peace.'

Friend 1) From the personal name, e.g. **Friend** NB for C. E. Friend, first storekeeper. 2) The name developed with the idea of being friendly, usually as **Friendship** (habitation-name in several states), sometimes probably because of good relations with the Indians, as in **Friendly Reach** OR, WA so called by W. R. Broughton, English explorer, in 1792, because of a friendly chief. 3) Or the name appeared because of the Friends, or Quakers, who were settlers of the place, e.g. **Friendsville** OH, PA, **Friendswood** TX.

Friesland, Vriesland In MI and WI named by Dutch settlers (mid-19th century) for the province in the Netherlands.

Frijol Spanish 'bean.'

Frio Spanish 'cold.'

Friona TX First called **Frio,** from nearby **Frio Creek:** later, the *-na* was added for differentiation from another post office called **Frio.**

Frisco From the colloquial American shortening of San Francisco, e.g. **Frisco Canyon** AZ through which the San Francisco River flows. It occurs as a habitation-name in a number of states, an indication of the early fame of the California city.

Frog The widespread and numerous frog was of so little note, either for good or for bad, that the name was rarely given. Even among the numerous lakes of MN the name occurs only once or twice. **Frog Pond** and **Frog Hollow** are, however, almost generic terms, with slightly derogatory connotation. This connotation has kept the name from habitations, about the only one being **Frogmore,** which is from a town in England, and in SC was first applied to a plantation. **Frogville** OK, a now extinct post office, was reputedly so called because the district grew exceptionally large frogs.

Frohna MO Named by immigrants, probably for a place in Germany.

Froid(e) French 'cold'; in NB probably named because it is at a high, windswept site; in MT, a transfer from NB.

Frontenac For the famous French governor of Canada, e.g. in KS (1887).

Frontier The name is rare. In the times of the actual frontier, people usually preferred to imply that they were not on it. The county in NB was named because it was on the frontier at the time. The town in WY is from a mine-name.

Frost Regularly from the personal name, e.g. **Frostburg** MD for Meshach Frost who opened a tavern there in 1812; **Frost** TX for S. M. Frost, railroad attorney. References to cold weather are doubtful, though the village in WV is locally believed to have been so named because of its location on high ground.

Frosty, however, occurs, e.g. the bay in AK, and the creek in WA. **Frostproof** FL is a commendatory in a citrus area.

Frozen A rare name, arising because a stream or lake happened to be frozen at the time of naming. It may also arise because people were literally or figuratively frozen at the time. At **Frozen Run** WV a man rolled himself in a fresh buffalo skin, according to the story, was frozen in, and had to be thawed out in the morning. **Frozen Man Creek, Frozenman's Creek** SD: men were found frozen to death at these places.

Fruit A repeated commendatory name where fruit is grown or where there is hope of it; **Fruitland** and **Fruitvale** are the common forms. **Fruita** CO: a coined name, with *fruit* and the *a* added, as is common, for the name of a town, perhaps under the misapprehension that it was the Spanish form.

Fruto Spanish 'fruit,' occurring probably for commendatory reasons for a habitation-name in a fruit-growing region in CA.

Frying-Pan, Fry-Pan 1) A descriptive from shape, e.g. **Fryingpan Lake** OR. 2) A name arising from incident, such as the loss of such a common article as a frying-pan. 3) A name suggestive of heat, e.g. as used for a thermal spring WY, and as used in connection with **Hell Gate** NY for a nearby reef, conceived as an appurtenance of hell. The gulch in CO was named, according to local story, because an early miner used a frying-pan for panning gold.

Fucas Pillar WA This is for **Fuca's Pillar,** a prominent rock mentioned in his narrative. See **Juan de Fuca, Strait of.**

Fuego Spanish 'fire.'

Fulda From the river and city in Germany.

Fulgurite Peak MT Because of numerous fulgurites at its summit, i.e. rock structures caused by lightning.

Fulton The widespread use of the name for both counties and towns is in tribute to Robert Fulton, inventor of the steamboat.

Fumee Lake MI Probably French, from *fumée,* 'smoke.'

Funeral Mountains CA The chief reason for the naming is probably the analogy with **Death Valley,** in which area they are located. Certain masses of dark rock also add to the funeral suggestion.

Funny Louis, Bayou LA By folk-etymology from Choctaw *fani-lusa,* 'squirrel-black.'

Furman SC For Lizzie Furman, an aged and respected resident at the time of naming (1901), one of the few towns in SC named for a Negro.

Furnace Chiefly in the eastern states, to designate a natural feature where a furnace, generally for the working of iron, was located (cf. **Forge),** e.g. **Furnace Brook** CT. **Furnace Creek** CA was probably named because of the heat, being located in Death Valley. Another creek in CA (San Bernardino Co.) was named because of the extreme heat sometimes experienced there.

Fushachee Creek GA Muskogean (Creek), 'bird-stream.' Also as **Fusihatchi.**

Fusihatchi See **Fushachee.**

Fusillade Mountain MT Named by Dr. G. B. Grinnell (1890) because his party fired many times at a band of goats without hitting any of them. Cf. **Singleshot.**

G

Gabbro From the occurrence of that kind of rock, e.g. **Gabbro Lake** MN.

Gabilan See **Gavilan**.

Gables NB The first post office was in a building with high gables.

Gadsden From the personal name, especially for James Gadsden (1788–1858) who negotiated with Mexico **The Gadsden Purchase** (1853); for him also **Gadsden** AL, because he visited the area when the town was being planned. The town and the peak in AZ were named commemoratively on the centennial of the purchase.

Gagen WI From Algonquian (?), a term meaning 'no,' but reference uncertain.

Gahanna OH Originally a stream-name, Algonquian, probably with *hanna,* 'stream,' and the rest uncertain.

Gaines From the personal name. **Gainesville** FL, GA: for General E. P. Gaines, commander in the Seminole wars. **Gainesmore** TX: for John Gaines and D. P. Moore, founders.

Gakona AK Athapascan 'rabbit river.'

Galahad Point See **Bedivere**

Galatea CO Probably from the sea-nymph of Greek mythology, but the name also occurs as the title of a poem by Cervantes. The reason for choice was partly that a name in G was needed in an alphabetical list.

Galatia The form is that of the ancient province, known from the Biblical *Epistle to the Galatians,* but the suggestion of the name in IL was from Albert Gallatin (see **Gallatin**). In KS the name was taken from IL.

Galax VA From the decorative evergreen plant so called, the production of which is a local industry.

Galen MT For the ancient Greek physician; it is the site of a sanatorium.

Galena Used as a name for a place where that ore of lead is found, e.g. IL, KS.

Galice OR For Louis Galice, early miner.

Galien River MI Appearing (1725) first as **Galines,** it is probably from a French personal name.

Galilee From the Biblical district, e.g. in NJ, PA.

Galion OH In 1824 the settlers requested a post office under the name **Goshen:** this was rejected and the present name was suggested as a substitute by the Post Office Dept. Its origin is uncertain, but it has a general resemblance to **Goshen.**

Galisteo NM Recorded as the name of an Indian village in 1581, it is probably an Indian name of unknown meaning, made over into the form of a Spanish name.

Galiuro Mountains AZ The earliest recorded name is **Salitre** (Spanish 'saltpetre') for the presence of that mineral. Intermediate forms, **Calitre** and **Caliuro,** are extant, but such an evolution on purely phonetic grounds is highly unusual, and the name may have been confused with some other, perhaps of Indian origin.

Gallatin From the personal name, especially for Albert Gallatin, early-19th-century statesman, e.g. **Gallatin River** MT, **Gallatin** MO.

Gallienas Creek OK A more or less phonetic spelling of **Gallina(s)**, q.v.

Gallina Spanish 'hen,' sometimes for the sage hen or the wild turkey. The mesa in NM is **Gallineros,** 'chicken-houses,' from the shape of some rocks.

Gallipolis OH Settled (1790) by French immigrants, and named with a Graeco-Latin term, 'Gaul-city.'

Gallo Spanish 'cock, rooster.'

Galloo Island NY Probably from French *galet,* 'pebble, gravel.'

Gallows Though public executions occurred in the colonies, they gave rise to place-names in only a few instances, e.g. **Gallows Hill** NY, which was the scene of hangings until 1808. A name-cluster in PA probably arose from a suicide by hanging, ca. 1730; **Gallows Hill** NJ probably from an execution of the Revolutionary period. **Gallows Hill,** Salem Co., NJ, was the scene of a hanging and burning at the stake in 1717.

Galva IL An Americanization of Galfe, the seaport in Sweden from which the first settlers had come.

Galveston The bay in TX was named, ca. 1785, for Count Bernardo de Gálvez, viceroy of New Spain. The settlement took the name in its present form, under American auspices, ca. 1834.

Galvez LA For the same man who is commemorated in **Galveston,** q.v.

Gambier OH Named (1826) for Lord James Gambier, who was one of three chief donors for the establishment here of Kenyon College.

Gamerco NM From Gallup American Coal Company.

Gamoca WV From Gauley, Moley, and Campbell. The first is the local river; the others are personal names, but of unidentified people.

Ganado Spanish 'cattle.' In TX because of a large herd of cattle pastured here; in AZ, for a local Navajo chief, known in Spanish as Ganado Mucho.

Ganges From the river of India, but the reason for application, e.g. in MI and OH, is unknown.

Ganister PA From the occurrence of the kind of rock so called.

Gannett From the personal name, especially for Henry Gannett (1846–1914), geologist, chairman of the board on Geographical Names, student of place-names (see *Bibliography*), e.g. **Mount Gannett** AK, WY.

Gano From the personal name, e.g. in OH for Charles Gano, promoter of a local railroad.

Gap A common generic for a pass or opening in a ridge, especially in the eastern states, being used as a specific for places near a gap, e.g. **Gap Mills** WV, **Gapcreek** KY. **Gap** occurs as a habitation-name in several states.

Gar, Garfish From the fish so called.

Garapito Spanish 'water bug.'

Garcitas Creek TX Spanish 'little herons.'

Garden Common on habitations; less so, on natural features: 1) from the presence of Indian cultivation, e.g. **Garden Creek** AZ, **Garden Island** MN. 2) from the natural beauty and fertility of a place, e.g. **Garden Township** MN. 3) a commendatory name for habitations, e.g. the frequent **Garden City,** also **Garden Co.** NB. **Gardena** is also an attempt to produce a Latin-appearing form. **The Garden of the Gods** CO: in 1859 a facetious remark that this would be a good place for a beer garden led to a reply that it was a place fit to be the garden of the gods. This usage may have led to others, e.g. **The Garden Wall** for a precipice in Glacier N.P. MT, another example of fanciful naming in our parks. 4) The personal name has given rise to **Garden's Corner** SC from Benjamin Garden, a plantation owner. **Garden City** TX: originally **Gardner City,** for William Gardner, storekeeper; changed by error when the post office was established. **Garden Island** LA: by folk-etymology from Gordon, a river-pilot, not further identified.

Gardi GA From the expression 'Guard eye!' applied first to a stream because of thickets making it necessary for a man to be careful of his eyes (?).

Gareloi Island AK Russian 'burnt, burning.'

Garibaldi OR For Giuseppe Garibaldi (1807–1882), the Italian patriot.

Garita NM Spanish, the most likely meaning, 'privy.' It may be a derogatory obscenity placed by the cattlemen who used the place for a trading post and named it in 1885. **La Garita** CO: from the peak, which is locally thought to have been because Indians sent smoke signals from it; this meaning is barely possible from the Spanish which sometimes occurs as 'sentry box.'

Garnet From the occurrence of the semi-precious stone. The personal name is regularly **Garnett.**

Garo CO A phonetic spelling from Adolph Guiraud, town founder in 1863.

Garoga Creek NY Iroquoian 'stream-on-this-side,' because it was at the edge of an uninhabited area.

Garrapata Spanish 'tick,' used especially for those which infect sheep and cattle, e.g. **Garrapatas Creek** TX.

Garryowen MT From the regimental tune of the 7th Cavalry, Custer's command which was annihilated at the battle in 1876.

Garus CA Coined from the letters of *sugar,* since the place is in a sugar-beet area.

Gary From the personal name; in IN for E. H. Gary, lawyer, a prominent figure in the steel company which founded the city. **Gary** MN: a shortening from Garrett L. Thorpe, first merchant.

Garza Spanish 'heron,' e.g. **Garzas Creek** CA. It is also a personal name.

Gas The pioneer was not conscious of the occurrence of natural gas, and its development as an industry was so late that it produced little effect on names for features, though one may note **Gas Well Hollow** KY. It occurs on some habitations associated with the industry, e.g. **Gas** KS, **Gas City** IN, OK, **Gaswell** OK. **Gas Point** CA: from the colloquial usage of the word, as meaning 'talk,' because old prospectors gathered here to gossip. **Gasco** OR: for a local gas company.

Gasconade MO Originally for the river; of uncertain derivation, but possibly for an incident involving boastfulness (cf. **Braggadocio**). There is also **Gasconades Creek** in TX.

Gasoline TX One of the first plants in TX for the making of gasoline was here.

Gasparilla FL From the nickname of José Gaspar ('Little Gaspar'), who carried on piratical operations in this area in the mid-18th century.

Gaspee Point RI On June 9, 1772, the British revenue sloop *Gaspee* ran aground here and was later burned by American patriots.

Gassabias Lake ME Algonquian (Abnaki) 'small, clear-water lake.'

Gaston From the personal name, e.g. in OR for Joseph Gaston, settler of 1862. The county NC is for William Gaston, jurist and composer of the state song; for him also, in Latinized form, is **Gastonia** NC.

Gatagama Point AZ From an Indian family name.

Gate As a descriptive it indicates a feature having a gate, especially a toll-gate, e.g. **Gate Creek** OR. In habitation-names, it indicates a place conceived as the entrance to something, e.g. **Gateway** CO, an entrance by trail to certain mountain regions. **Gateway** OR: near a natural depression through which railroad and road pass. **Gate** OK: because it was the original entrance to the old Neutral Strip. In AK the term has been applied descriptively in **Gates of the Arctic**, a pass, and **The Gate(s)**, water passage. **Gates** is commonly from the personal name, e.g. the county in NC for Gen. Horatio Gates of the Revolution. In areas of Dutch settlement the term may be an Englishing of *gat,* which means both 'gate' and 'anal passage.' See **Hellgate**.

Gato Spanish 'cat.' Probably the namings are generally for wildcats, e.g. **Los Gatos** CA, **Rio Gata** CO.

Gauche French 'left, left-hand,' e.g. the bayou in LA.

Gauley WV Probably from the rare family name, doubtless the same that appears in early WV records as Gally.

Gavilan, Gabilan Spanish 'hawk.' A common name, probably because of the sighting of a hawk or a hawk's nest at the time of naming, e.g. **Gabilan Peak** CA, **Gavilan Creek** NM.

Gaviota CA Spanish 'sea-gull.' The men of the Portolá expedition in 1769 killed a sea gull here.

Gay Regularly from the personal name, e.g. **Gay Hill** TX, for G. H. Gay and W. C. Hill, pioneer citizens. **Gay Head** MA, as applied to the promontory, is commonly explained as a descriptive from the bright-colored rocks. Though this is a highly unlikely use of words, no better explanation is available. **Gayhart, Gayheart:** from the personal name.

Gazelle CA Probably a substitute for the too common **Antelope.**

Geanquakin Creek MD Algonquian, meaning uncertain.

Geary From the personal name, in OK an Anglicizing of the name of a French-Cheyenne scout, E. C. F. C. Guerrier.

Geauga OH Apparently a badly eroded form from the same Iroquoian original as **Cuyahoga,** first applied to a stream.

Gebo WY For Sam Gebo, promoter of local coal mines.

Geese Apparently because of its lack of *-s* in the plural, the term is applied to natural features, e.g. **Geese Channel** AK. Cf. **Goose, Mice.**

Geikie Mountain WY Named in 1877 for Sir Archibald Geikie, Scottish geologist.

Gelee French 'frozen,' e.g. **Cote Gelee** LA.

Gem In TX, from Gem Hibbard, wife of a landowner. In CA, from a lake originally named **Gem-O'-The-Mountains.** In ID, probably from the common idea that the state name meant Gem of the Mountains. In NM from the initials of George E. Merrilatt, early settler.

Gemini Latin 'twins.' In CA the name is used for a two-peaked mountain.

Gene Autry OK For the motion-picture actor, named Jan. 1, 1942.

Geneganstlet NY Iroquoian, probably 'sulphur-spring-at.'

Generals Springs AZ From Gen. George Crook, who had an encounter with Apaches near this spot ca. 1870.

Genesee NY Iroquoian 'valley-beautiful.' **Geneseo** NY is a variant form.

Geneva From the Swiss city and lake. In ID the name was applied by Swiss Mormon settlers. In OR it is for Geneva Monical, first postmistress.

Genoa From the city in Italy, usually with little reason, but in Texas because the climate was believed to resemble that of Italy. In WI, named by Italian immigrants. In NV the name was given (1855) by a man who had visited Italy and was impressed by the resemblance of nearby Lake Tahoe to the Mediterranean.

Genola The name of a village in Italy, but probably given merely as a euphonic name.

Gentile Occurs in Mormon districts, where non-Mormons are so known, e.g. **Gentile Spring** AZ.

Gentilly In MN, from a town in Canada. In LA, from the name of an early landowner.

Gentry From the personal name, e.g. in MO for Col. Richard Gentry, soldier, politician, and lover of fine horses in the early 19th century.

George From the personal name, in the Colonial period honoring one of the reigning kings, e.g. **King George Co.** VA for George I. The commonest form was **Georgetown,** the county in SC thus taking name from the town, which honored George II. Since the name was common from the 18th century onward, others than the kings are honored. **Prince George Co.** VA: for the consort of Queen Anne (1702). **Georgetown** DE: named in 1791 for George Mitchell, who was involved with the town-founding. **Georgetown** KY: named (1790) for George Washington. **Georgetown** ME: for George I (1716). **George, Cape** WA: a name dating from 1847, probably a commemorative for George Vancouver because of his explorations in the vicinity in 1792.

Georgia The state-name is from King George II (1732), taking the Latinized form for a place-name. **Georgiaville** RI: from the Georgia Cotton Manufacturing Company, ca. 1813. **Strait of Georgia** WA was named by the British explorer George Vancouver in 1792 for the reigning king, George III.

Georgica NY From the name of an Indian, recorded (1679) as Jeorgkee, probably an adaptation of George.

Gerdine, Mount AK For T. G. Gerdine, who as topographical engineer made several expeditions to AK in the late 19th century.

Gerled IA A boundary-name, from the townships **Germanic** and **Ledyard**.

German, Germania, Germany A settlement of Germans in 1683 produced **Germantown** PA, and similar settlements have echoed the name. Thus also has arisen the use of the Latin form **Germania**. Other occurrences generally indicate a German settlement. **New Germany** MN: given because of numerous German settlers, but changed to **Motordale** during World War I. It is also a family name, e.g. **Germansville** PA for Adam German, early miller.

Germano OH Named by German settlers in 1815.

Geronimo Spanish 'Jerome,' and so occurring as a saint's name, e.g. **San Geronimo** CA. **Mount Geronimo** AZ: for the Apache chief so called.

Gethsemane From the garden of the New Testament.

Gettysburg In PA from James Gettys, who laid out the town; in other states generally from the battle of 1863, e.g. in SD.

Gewhitt TX For George Whittenburg, early cattleman, by using the first letters of each name.

Geyser By association with a geyser, e.g. **Geyserville** CA, the term sometimes being applied to various manifestations that are not, strictly speaking, geysers.

Ghent From the city in Belgium, in MN because of immigrants. In OH and WV the name is locally believed to have been suggested by the Treaty of Ghent, which ended the War of 1812. In KY the name was given by Henry Clay, who had been one of the commissioners to negotiate the treaty.

Ghost Though 'ghost town' is a common term, the term is rare in names. **Ghost Creek** OR: from ghostlike white tree trunks, probably the result of a fire. **Ghost Creek** AK: because of numerous Indian burials. **Ghost Canyon** SD: because some people heard strange and unusual noises there one night. **Ghost Mound** OK: because of association with Indian beliefs. **Ghost Hole Ford** GA: locally believed to be derived from its being haunted by the ghost of a man killed there in frontier times.

Giant Occasionally used in the sense of *gigantic* with features, e.g. **Giant Geyser** WY. In **Giant Forest** CA the reference is to the size of the trees, not of the forest. **Giant** CA: so-called giant powder was manufactured here. As indicating both size and shape it occurs as **Giants Coffin** NB, **Giants Thumb** NB, **Giants Castle Mountain** WY. **Gianttrack Mountain** CO: from some potholes in the rocks, taken by the Arapahos to be the tracks of giants.

Giatto WV The first postmaster sent in the name Giotto, for the Italian painter. By mistake the Post Office Dept. took the spelling to be Giatto.

Gibbet From the presence of a gibbet for public executions, probably dating from Colonial times, e.g. **Gibbet Hill** MD.

Gibraltar From the famous rock, a descriptive, e.g. the lake in AK because of a nearby rock thus shaped. The island in OH was also named because of its resemblance to the original rock.

Gift MS, TN Probably from the family name.

Gig Harbor WA Named in 1841 by the Wilkes expedition because it had sufficient water for a small boat (gig).

Gigantes Spanish 'giants'; descriptive for **Los Gigantes Buttes** AZ. In NM used for two mesas because of Indian association of supernatural personages with the places.

Gila From the Indian tribal name, first applied to a region and then in 1697 to the river.

Gilboa For the Biblical site, where the Philistines defeated Saul.

Gilead, Mount Gilead From the Biblical mountain and district. In spite of commendatory suggestions, the name is not common.

Gilsum NH Granted to Samuel Gilbert and Thomas Sumner in 1763, and named by the first syllables of their names, an early example of such practice.

Gin Since gin was not a common drink in the U.S. until the invention of the martini, the names are probably from the presence of a cotton gin, e.g. **Gin Creek** VA, **Gin Hollow** KY. But 'gin-clear' is a common term among anglers, and some unusually clear streams may have been thus named. Cf. **Whiskey.**

Ginger Cake Mountain NC For a rock formation suggesting the form of a ginger cake.

Ginseng The wild ginseng root was much in demand as an article for export to China as a drug, and natural features were so named, especially in WV.

Gip WV From the slightly altered pronunciation of the surname of Frank Gibson, the first postmaster.

Girdletree MD Probably a spot marked by a tree that had been killed by girdling.

Girta WV For Girta Nutter, daughter of the first postmaster.

Girty Various places so named in the WV, OH, and PA area and from the famous renegade Simon Girty (1741–1818) or from other members of the family.

Given WV From the family name of early settlers.

Glacier By association with a glacier or because of evidence of the former existence of a glacier, e.g. **Glacier Divide** CA is from the actual presence, but **Glacier Point** CA was so named because of evidences of former glacial action.

Glade, Glady As a generic, it means in British usage (and in modern American) an open place in a forest. In early American usage, especially in the South, it meant a low tract of marshy ground, chiefly grass-grown. In either meaning, it has been used as a specific, both alone (for habitation-names) and in combination with various generics to indicate a place associated with a glade, e.g. **Glade Farms, Gladehill, Gladeville.** Some places are known locally as **The Glades. Glades Co.** FL: a shortening of **Everglades,** q.v.

Gladstell TX For Gladys and Stella Grogen, daughters of two owners of sawmills.

Glaise, Glaize The French *glaise,* 'clay,' was adapted in meaning in America to be the equivalent of the English **Lick.** The French used it as a generic, but this passed easily into specific usage in English, e.g. **Glaize Creek** MO, **Glaize Township** MO. There is much variation in spelling. See **Auglaize.**

Glamis CA From the castle in Scotland, probably because of its mention in *Macbeth.*

Glandorf OH Named (1834) by German settlers for a town in Germany.

Glarus From the town and canton in Switzerland, e.g. **New Glarus** WI, named by Swiss immigrant settlers.

Glasco, Glasgo Simplified spellings of **Glasgow. Glasco** KS was named (1886) by Scottish settlers, but the first postmaster misspelled the name, and the error was never corrected.

Glasgow From the city in Scotland, etc., sometimes, e.g. in VA, with the hope that the settlement would become a manufacturing town. The town in KY was named for that in VA (1799).

Glasko CT For Isaac Glasko, local businessman, ca. 1800.

Glass Often from such personal names as **Glass, Glassford, Glasscock.** It is rare for natural features, and generally denotes the presence of obsidian, e.g. **Glass Mountain** CA, **Glass Buttes** OR. **Glassport** PA: a riverport where a glass plant was established. **Glassy Mountain** SC: probably because of mica crystals, producing a shiny appearance. **Glass Mountains** OK: from a transparent form of gypsum which reflects light like glass. **Glassboro** NJ: because of an early glass factory.

Glastonbury In CT (1692) from an English town-name.

Glaucophane Ridge CA From the mineral so named.

Glazypeau AR From the French *glaise à Paul,* 'Paul's lick,' applied by transfer to a creek and mountain. It has passed through several forms, e.g. **Glazypool, Glacierpeau.**

Glen As a generic, the word, Celtic in origin, was introduced by the writings of Walter Scott. It became very popular in the 19th century. Though its meaning, 'valley,' or 'narrow valley,' was well known and the word entered the general vocabulary, it was not ordinarily used as a generic for natural features, though there is a usage of **The Glen.** It occurs commonly as a habitation-name, either as simply **Glen** or in combination with a specific. In accordance with Gaelic usage (and in Scott) the specific regularly follows the generic, but may be either a noun or an adjective, and need not itself be Gaelic. It may or may not form one word with the generic. Theoretically a name like **Glenbrook** should mean a glen-with-a-brook, but most Americans probably take it to mean a brook-in-a-glen. It occurs rarely as a personal name (more commonly **Glenn**). It is often used primarily for commendatory purposes, without much topographical aptness, as

would seem to be the case with **Glendale** CA, named ca. 1890. **Glen Aulin** CA: the term is here a true generic with a specific from the Irish, meaning, 'beautiful glen.' **Glendora** CA: the second part is a shortening of a woman's name, Ledora. Names such as **Glengarry** have been taken whole from Scotland. **Glen Pass** CA: for Glen H. Crow, forest ranger. **Glenda** OR: from *glen* and Ada Colter, the town-founder's wife. **Glenalum** WV: the water in the stream has a high alum content. **Glencoe:** from the valley in Scotland, famous because of the massacre of the MacDonalds in 1692, a habitation-name in a dozen states, in some instances, e.g. in MN, named because of Scottish settlers. In some instances the family name Coe is involved, e.g. in NM, for Mrs. Frank B. Coe in 1880, when the family settled there. **Glendorado** NM: coined from *glen,* and the Spanish *dorado,* 'golden.' **Glen Mar** CO: for Glenna Markle, daughter of early settlers. **Glendo** WY: named in 1887 for a nearby glen, the *-do* being added for euphony. **Glenmore:** from a place in Scotland, **Glenmora** occurring as a variant.

Glendive MT The creek was named in 1856 by Sir George Gore, visiting Irish sportsman, according to local tradition, for a stream in Ireland; this was probably the Glendine, since there is no Irish stream with the spelling here used, the mistake of one letter having arisen later.

Glenoma WA A commendatory. Though *-oma* is a conventional ending, the namer here chose it as an adaptation of the Hebrew *omer,* 'a measure of grain,' with the idea that the whole name would mean 'fruitful valley,' thus producing an unusual hybridization of Gaelic and Hebrew.

Glide OR In 1890, when Mrs. Carrie Laird was trying to think of a name for the new post office, she heard her small son singing something about the river gliding along.

Globe In some instances the name, chiefly occurring on habitations, was probably given for commendatory reasons, as being the equivalent of 'world, universal.' Local stories, however, tell of something spherical, e.g. a lump of silver or a large boulder for **Globe** AZ, or a circular clearing for **Globe** NC.

Glorieta, Glorietta, Gloryetta Probably chosen chiefly for commendatory reasons, because of the suggestion of *glory*. But the term is used in Spanish for a plaza from which streets radiate, and also for an arbor, and in some instances the name may be thus descriptive.

Glorious, Point AK Named (1890) because of the view attained from it.

Glory 1) A colloquial and semihumorous rustic term, usually as a second element, e.g. **Possum Glory** PA. It is applied to habitations, but not as a formal name, being used for small crossroads settlements, off the main lines of travel. Its meaning is vague and uncertain, but it probably implies that the specified first element is there 'in its glory,' e.g. that **Loafers Glory** NC is a location where loafers can be especially happy. From this usage and by shortening and association arises such a name as **Glory Branch** KY. 2) The name appears as a shortening for **Glory Hole,** a term used for the pit in open-pit mining, as with **Gloryhole Creek** AK, and probably **Glory Lake** AK. **Glory of Russia Cape** AK translates the Russian name, which was given for a ship which visited here in 1791.

Gloster See Gloucester.

Gloucester, Gloster From the town and county in England. The pronunciation in the U.S., as in England, is according to the second spelling, which in the U.S. may arise from a phonetic spelling or for a personal name. The name was placed in MA in 1642. The county in VA dates from 1652.

Gnadenhutten OH German, literally 'grace (in the theological sense)-huts,' but probably to be taken in Biblical language as 'tabernacle of grace,' a name given in 1772 by German (Moravian) missionaries for a settlement of Christianized Indians.

Gnaw Bone IN Local stories told in explanation lack authenticity. It is probably a rural derogatory (cf. **Lickskillet**),

implying that people there were so poor that they had to gnaw bones.

Gneiss For the rock so called, e.g. in NC.

Goat 1) From the domestic animal, chiefly in the SW, e.g. **Goat Spring** NM, where the goat has been commonest. An occasional name in New England, e.g. **Goat Hill** CT, MA, it is a relic of early Colonial experiments with the keeping of goats. 2) The Rocky Mountain goat, comparatively rare but much hunted, has given names to many features in the mountains of the NW, e.g. **Goat Harbor** AK, **Goat Lake** WA, **Goathaunt Mountain** MT. 3) The name appears for the pronghorn antelope, in early times often called a goat; names in the former range of the antelope usually arise thus, e.g. **Goat Creek** SD, so named by the Lewis and Clark exepdition in 1804, because at this point they saw their first antelope. **Billy Goat Hill** KY is from the common term for a domestic male goat.

Gobbler From the male wild turkey, e.g. **Gobblers Peak** AZ.

Gobernador(a) Spanish 'governor, governor's wife,' but as a place-name usually referring to the occurrence of a plant called *gobernadora*.

God Scarcely in use as a place-name element, partly because of Protestant objections to use of the name in common speech. **God's Grace Point** is in MD, where Catholic influence was dominant. See **Grace.** **God's Pocket Peak** NV is of uncertain reference.

Goethe, Mount CA For J. W. Goethe, German poet, named in 1949, the bicentennial of his birth.

Gogebic Lake MI Ojibway, with *bic*, 'body of water,' and the rest probably with the idea of 'high,' since the lake is at an elevation.

Gogogashugun River WI Algonquian (Ojibway), meaning uncertain.

Going-to-the-Sun Mountain MT Originally in the Blackfoot language **Lone High Mountain**: renamed in 1885 for a mythological figure, a semidivine chief who disappeared by ascending this mountain.

Golah NY Coined by the Rev. H. W. Howard, a local minister, by selecting a single letter from each of the names of five families of the locality.

Golconda From the ancient city of India, known proverbially for its riches, and thus a fitting name for a mine.

Gold, Golden Though there are many personal names such as **Gold, Golding, Goldman,** and **Golden,** the great majority of the numerous place-names are from the presence or supposed presence of gold. More than 100 features in CA are so distinguished, though gold was so widely distributed in some parts of that state that one has difficulty in seeing how one creek or gulch could thus be distinguished from another. Some places were notable for 'rushes,' e.g. **Gold Lake,** Plumas Co., CA, **Gold Bluffs,** Humboldt Co., CA, and **Gold Beach** OR. **Gold Ray** OR: in a gold region, but including the name of Frank Ray. **Goldville** SC: named figuratively because of the supposed fertility of the land. Various places in NC and GA were named in the 19th century because of gold-mining in those areas though most such names are in the western states. **Golden** is generally an equivalent of *gold,* used for variety, but **Golden Canyon** CA is from the yellow color of the clay. **Goldfinch** TX: for the bird. **Golden Trout Creek** CA: for the trout of that variety. **Golden Gate** CA: named by J. C. Frémont in 1848 as the Greek form Chrysopylae on the analogy of the Golden Horn at Constantinople, though just what he thought the analogy to be is by no means clear. The English translation was soon universal. The later discovery of gold in CA made the name appropriate. **Golden Lake** MN was for John Golden, landowner. **Goldsboro** TX: because deposits of gold-colored stones were found here. Almost 100 current place-names in AK (and many extinct ones) contain **Gold,** either alone or in compound. **Goldfield** IA: in honor of an early resident whose name was Brasfield; the association with a nobler metal was thought advisable for the town. **Goldtree** CA: an adaptation of Goldbaum, for Morris Goldbaum, early settler, *baum* being German 'tree.'

Goler Canyon CA For John Goler (Galler, or Goller), early prospector.

Goleta Spanish 'schooner.' In CA the name probably originated because an American schooner, some time before 1846, stranded there and remained visible for some years.

Goliad TX In 1829 the Congress of Coahuila and Texas applied the name to a presidio, coining it from the letters of **Hidalgo,** with the omission of the silent *h.*

Golondrina Creek TX Probably 'rattlesnake-weed,' though the term also means 'swallow (the bird).'

Golovnin AK The bay was named (1821) for a ship, which was named for Capt. V. M. Golovnin of the Russian navy.

Golva ND Coined (1915) from the name of the county, **Golden Valley.**

Gombo LA Probably from the local French usage which applies this term to the *patois* of French spoken by Negroes, this village being chiefly a Negro settlement.

Gomer OH From the Biblical name (?), perhaps used for a person.

Gondola Lake SD Because in 1935 the gondola from the stratospheric Explorer II landed in the vicinity.

Gonic NH Algonquian 'spear-place' (?), i.e. a place for spearing salmon.

Gonux NY From Moses Gonack, an Indian, drowned here in 1767, i.e. Gonack's.

Goochland VA Named (1727) for Gov. William Gooch.

Good Rarely used, probably because too vague. Most of the examples are from personal names, including such combinations as **Goodman** and **Goodyear.** From family names have arisen **Goodpasture Island** OR and **Goodwill** WV. **Goodnight** TX: for Charles Goodnight, ranchowner. In a few instances the usage may be called merely descriptive, e.g. **Goodwater Creek** OK, **Goodwell** OK,

Good Harbor Bay MN. The repeated **Goodland** may be either descriptive or commendatory. The repeated **Good Hope** is definitely commendatory, in MN having been chosen as an auspicious name by vote of the residents. **Goodsprings** NV: a descriptive, because of the good quality of the water there.

Goon Dip Mountain AK Named (1939) for Goon Dip who died in 1936, having been Chinese consul in Seattle for many years.

Goose The domestic goose was not important, and was not of a nature such as to give rise to names. Nearly all the names are from the wild goose, and they are numerous. Fifty are estimated for CA alone. MN has 20 such lakes. The coupling is usually with a body of water, especially lake, though **Goose Prairie** is used to denote a marshy place thus frequented. As with names derived from most wild animals and birds, these may be from special incidents, or may indicate a place where geese might be expected to be numerous. The migratory nature of the wild goose would suggest that the names were usually given by someone who was present at the proper time, and that they are thus to some extent names arising from incident. **Goose Creek**, Modoc Co., CA: from the name of a German settler which was spelled Goos. **Goose Creek** OR: a woman carrying a dressed goose, on her way to a Thanksgiving dinner, accidentally dropped the goose into the water. Though **Goose Creek** TX is an exception, the name is rarely used for habitations, doubtless because of foolishness associated with the noun *goose,* and because of the slightly obscene suggestion of the verb. **Gooseneck Harbor** AK: from the shape. **Goosepen Run** WV: the name probably derives from the presence of some kind of trap for wild geese, but the word is also used in some areas to mean a large hole burned in a standing tree. See **Geese.**

Gooseberry From the wild gooseberry, e.g. **Gooseberry Creek** OR because three men found some unusually good berries there.

Gooseneck A semigeneric, for a feature resembling the curves of a goose's neck, e.g. **Gooseneck Pinnacle** WY, because of a route which had to be followed in its ascent.

Gopher Though widespread, this rodent has usually been taken for granted, and has produced only an occasional name, e.g. **Gopher** SD, **Gopher Hill** MO. In the SE the name is applied to a tortoise, and **Gopher Ridge** FL is thus derived.

Gordo Spanish 'fat,' but in place-names usually in the sense of 'rounded,' e.g. the repeated **Cerro Gordo.**

Gore 1) From a personal name, e.g. in OK (1909) for Senator T. P. Gore. 2) From the generic term, especially in New England, referring to an elongated, usually wedge-shaped bit of land left over between two areas of surveyed land, e.g. **Gore** OH, **Gore Pond** MA.

Gormania WV A Latinization from the name of Senator A. P. Gorman.

Goshelpme Creek AK For 'Gosh-help-me!'

Goshen The land which the Israelites inhabited in Egypt is described in the Bible chiefly as a country for sheep, though other products are also implied. On this scanty evidence, early Americans began to apply the name for commendatory reasons to places which they believed to have rich soil, or so wished others to believe: **Goshen** CT being named ca. 1740, and **Goshen** MA some years later. Close religious connections are seen in **Goshen** IN, an Amish and Mennonite settlement. **Goshen Co.** WY: the name **Gosche's Hole** appears in the area, probably from an early trapper, before the founding of the county, and the later name is apparently an adaptation of that one.

Goshute, Gosiute, Goshiute From the Indian tribal name.

Gosier French 'pelican,' e.g. the island in LA.

Gosnold MA For the English explorer of 1602, Bartholomew Gosnold.

Gospel Hill NB Religious services were held here in early days.

Gotebo OK From the name of a Kiowa chief (1904).

Gothenburg NB From the city in Sweden.

Gothic From rock formations suggestive of Gothic architecture, e.g. the mesa in UT. **Gothic** CO: named from the nearby mountain.

Gouge Eye Gulch For a certain Luke, not further identified, who was thus nicknamed because he had had one eye gouged out in a fight.

Goula, Bayou LA More properly as one word, since it is from the Choctaw *bayuk-okla,* 'bayou-people.' It is, however, best conceived as a tribal name, for a people inhabiting that region in the early 18th century.

Government Generally because of some occupation by the federal government, e.g. **Government Camp** OR, because of a military camp there in 1849.

Governor From association with a governor, e.g. **Governor's Island** MA, because in the period following 1630 Governor John Winthrop had a house there. **Governors Island** NY: for Director Van Twiller of the Dutch period. **Governor Island** NB: because the governor of the state spoke there in dedication of a bridge.

Gowanda NY Adopted in the 19th century as a village-name, being a shortening of a longer Iroquoian term, 'almost-surrounded-by-hill.'

Gowanisque Creek NY Probably Algonquian 'briars-full,' i.e. the same as **Cowanesque.**

Gowanus NY Probably from the name of an Indian who lived there, recorded in 1638.

Gowrie IA From the town in Scotland.

Graafschap MI Named (mid-19th century) by Dutch immigrants for a place in the Netherlands from which some of them had come.

Grab KY Probably from the personal name.

Grace Regularly for a woman so named, e.g. **Grace Lake** CA for Grace Noble, daughter of an early pioneer. **Grace Coolidge Creek** SD: for the wife of President Coolidge, named by the state legislature in 1927, when the Coolidges were spending the summer in that vicinity; previously **Squaw Creek.** Its occurrence in MD, where Catholic influence was important, is probably for religious reasons, e.g. **Grace Point.** See **God.**

Gracemont OK From Grace and Montgomery, otherwise unidentified, except that they were friends of the first postmaster.

Gracioso Spanish 'graceful, pleasing.' In CA **Graciosa** dates from 1769, apparently arising because the Spanish soldiers saw some Indian women dancing.

Graeagle CA For **Gray Eagle,** because on a creek so named.

Graford TX Because it is halfway between **Graham** and **Weatherford.**

Grafton A place-name in England, but the town in MA (incorporated 1735) may have been named for the second duke (1683–1722), a member of the Privy Council. The towns in NH (hence, the county) and VT were named shortly before the Revolution and in honor of the third duke (1735–1811) who was prominent politically and an advocate of conciliation with the colonies. **Grafton:** names farther west echo these of New England, e.g. **Grafton** ND for the county in NH.

Grainola OK A commendatory coined name from *grain* and a common suffix from Latin or Spanish.

Gramercy NY The district on Manhattan Island took its name by folk-etymology from Dutch *krum-marisje,* 'crooked-marshlet.'

Grampian PA From the Grampian Hills in Scotland because of a resemblance in the landscape.

Gran Spanish, an alternate form of *grande,* 'big, great.' **Gran Quivira:** a 16th-century Spanish term for much of the western U.S. Its meaning is unknown, though **Gran** is usually assumed to be 'great.' It is probably an Indian term assuming a Spanish form.

Granada From the city and former kingdom in Spain, popularized by Washington Irving's *Conquest of Granada* (1829). **El Granada** CA: the article is not needed, and, if used, should be **La.**

Granby From the personal name; in MA (1768) for the Marquis of Granby, member of the British cabinet.

Grand As a place-name *grand* scarcely occurs in Great Britain. It is uncommon in the East where *great* is generally used. The usage of *grand* springs from the French, with a little aid from the Spanish. In areas occupied by the French, they applied *grand(e)* freely in its literal meaning of 'large, big.' These names the English took over, dropping the unsounded *e* where it occurred in spelling. A partial exception to the spelling rule is **Grande Ronde** ('circle,' or 'circular valley,' OR), which has been the subject of controversy and may be found in either form. After speakers of English took over, *grand* was likely to be understood in its English sense, i.e. 'magnificent, sublime.' It was then, especially in the later 19th century, used in that sense, chiefly in the West and for features such as mountains. The two usages can generally be distinguished on a commonsense basis. The French usage, moreover, is likely to display itself by a coupling with a French generic, e.g. *glaize* (lick), *coteau* (escarpment), *marais* (marsh), etc. In the English usage the most common coupling is as **Grandview**, which occurs in most states, and is common as a habitation-name, but other couplings of *grand* are also favored for this usage. *Grand* did not replace *great* in the East: **Great Lakes, Great Smoky Mountain;** and the latter even appears in the West: **Great Salt Lake, Great Basin.** *Grand* in the sense of 'sublime' has flourished in regions of national parks, with **The Grand Canyon** as a type usage. But **Grand Teton** ('breast') is a French survival. As 'sublime,' the term tends to be coupled with unusual generics or quasi-generics, e.g. **Grand Sentinal** CA. **Grand Rapids** MI: the reference is to the river, i.e. the rapids of the Grand. **Grand Reef Mountain** AZ: from

the Granite Reef Mine by folk-etymology, *reef* being used in the miners' sense of 'vein' or 'lode.' **Grand Forks** MN, ND: neither river was so called, and the original French indicated a place where the forking was into two streams of about equal size. **Grand Lake** CO: though it is the largest lake in the state, its name is from its association with the river, i.e. the stream now called **Colorado. Grand Junction** CO: because on the (former) **Grand River** at its junction with the **Gunnison. Grandmound** IA: intended for **Sand Mound,** for a nearby feature, but altered by mistake in transmission. **Grand Cane** LA: partially of French origin, and named for a large canebrake.

Granddaddy See **Grandfather.**

Grande Nearly always represents the Spanish adjective, 'big,' since the French feminine form has generally been lost (see **Grand**). **Grande** appears in postposition. Areas with Spanish background display examples, e.g. **Arroyo Grande** CA. **Rio Grande** NM, TX, by tautological colloquialism **Rio Grande River,** was called by the Spaniards in 1598 **Rio Grande del Norte** ('of the north'), either because they came to it after a long march from the south or because it flowed from the north. See **Bravo. Grande Ronde:** see **Grand.**

Grandfather The term is colloquially used for something very big and presumably old. **Granddaddy Knob** KY may have a similar origin, or may be from association with a grandfather or an old man. **Grandfather Mountain** NC: for a 'great stone face,' on the mountainside. Cf. **Old Man.**

Grandglaise AR French 'big-lick.' See **Grand, Glaise.**

Grandmother Rarely used, **Granny** being the popular term. **Grandmother Mountain** NC is named by counterpart from **Grandfather Mountain.**

Grange, Lagrange Though the personal names occur, other origins are commoner. 1) From the idea of 'farm,' or from The Grange, a farmers' organization of the late 19th century. 2) The frequent occurrence of **La Grange** or

Lagrange is attributable to its having been the name of Lafayette's country-seat in France. In GA the town was named in 1828, a few years after Lafayette's visit there during his tour of the country. In some instances, e.g. TN, TX, **Lagrange** is in **Fayette Co.**

Granite These names serve not only to mark the presence of a certain kind of rock, but also have commendatory value, since granite suggests beauty, permanence, and even steadfastness. Since early Americans were not always good petrologists, the rock is sometimes something else than true granite (see, e.g., **Marblehead**). Both **Granite** and **Graniteville** are favored for habitation-names, in some instances because they were the sites of quarries.

Granny, Grannie Denoting a grandmother or any old woman, the name occurs chiefly in the Appalachian country, usually upon small natural features, and indicating their association with some old woman. In many instances the actual name was originally used, and it sometimes remains, as with **Granny McCoy Swimming Hole** WV. **Granny Creek** OR: an old mare so named ranged here in the 1880's, until killed by mountain lions, her body being found near the stream.

Grano ND Named in 1905, common agreement locally being that it was formed by combining parts of two names of individuals, whether Grace-Lano, Grey-Reno, or Greene-Lano. Since none of these is a person of much interest, the problem may well be left unsolved, but with the comment that in a grain-growing area **Grano** is a commendatory.

Grant From the personal name, most commonly (especially with western counties) for U. S. Grant, general and president. The name, however, is so common that many places have been named for other people, e.g. **Grantsville** UT for G. D. Grant, early settler. **Grant Town** WV: for Robert Grant, a mine owner. **Grants Pass** OR: named for U. S. Grant in 1863 by men who were improving the road across the hills at this point; transferred to the town in 1865 for differentiation, because there was already a town named **Grant** in the state.

Granville From the personal name or title. In MA and PA it is for John Carteret (1690–1763), Earl of Granville.

Grape, Grapevine The Viking sagas tell of wild grapes and record the name **Vineland.** The later colonists were equally impressed. The name was often applied to small natural features, and is one of the commonest which arises from native plants. It is more frequent in the West where the native grape was less common and therefore more prized. By transfer the name has been applied to habitations, and it has also been so applied directly in the grape-growing regions, e.g. **Grape, Grapegrowers, Grapeland** CA. Grapevine is also used in figurative senses, as for a winding road. **The Grapevine,** on U.S. 99 in CA, was originally so called because of a canyon where grapes grew, but the continuing use of the term probably results from the figurative meaning.

Grapit CA The railway station took its name by shortening from a nearby gravel pit.

Grass, Grassy The name occurs as a descriptive term over the country, but is much less common in the grass-grown plains area where it could not so well serve for distinction. It there seems to denote a place which was especially well-grown with grass. In the wooded East any grass-grown opening where animals could be pastured was likely to become known as **Grassy Meadow** or **Grassy Cove,** the adjective being there favored. In the arid West grass was usually associated with streams, so that **Grass Creek** became common. In OR and northern CA the hills were likely to be tree-grown and the valleys bare, and so **Grass Valley** was applicable. **Grass Lake** is likely to occur anywhere to denote a lake with 'grass' growing in its shallows. Originally commendatory, grass has since come to have a bucolic suggestion. It seems to exist as a habitation-name only by transfer, but with increasing pressure of population *grass* is again starting to develop suburban, commendatory suggestions.

Gratis OH Because in the early 19th century a citizens' petition for the establishment of a new voting district was voted by the commissioners 'gratis,' i.e. without charge.

Grave The name denotes a place where an unidentified person is buried. Typically, if the name of the person is known, his name will be applied to the feature. But often the knowledge of who is there buried is forgotten, but the evidences of the burial still remain. As with other such names stories are often told as to the circumstances, and many of these stories may be accepted. Indian mounds, considered to be graves, have given rise to some names, e.g. in WV. There has been some tendency to replace the name. In 1854 the OR legislature changed the name of Grave Creek to **Leland Creek** because Martha Leland Crowley was the person who was buried there; but the original name has survived. **Graves** can often be attributed to the personal name. It exists as a habitation-name, but is rare, probably disliked because of its association.

Gravel, Gravelly, Gravely Occasionally from the personal name, e.g. **Gravelville** MN for Charles Gravel, early mill operator. As a descriptive for natural features it is not especially common, and seems more likely to refer to stream-bottoms than to deposits of gravel, e.g. **Gravel Bottom** WV, **Gravelly Ford** NV. The third spelling occurs as a variant, e.g. **Gravely Gap** KY. It occurs rarely as a habitation-name, either by transfer or from gravel pits. **Gravel Switch** KY: from a railroad switch for the handling of gravel.

Gravette AR For E. T. Gravett, early settler, the spelling being altered by the railroad.

Graveyard The common older term for cemetery, the name has remained as a designation for natural features, often long after burial had ceased in the area. **Graveyard Point** OR: two soldiers from an early military post were buried here. **Graveyard Canyon** AZ: two men, brutally killed in a frontier feud, were left unburied for a while, and then interred here in one grave.

Gravois American-French 'gravel.'

Gravy Springs WY The water picks up sediment from white clay and comes to resemble gravy.

Gray, Grey Rare as a descriptive term, it is usually the personal name. It has been occasionally applied to mountains, cliffs, and rocks because of color, but this seems to have been a late and sophisticated usage, commoner in AK than elsewhere. The term also occurs in double specifics, e.g. **Greybull** WY which originated from an Indian pictograph. **Gray Eagle** occurs in several states; the reference is to the immature bald eagle, which was popularly thought to be a different species. **Grays Peak** CO: for Asa Gray, the 19th-century botanist, named ca. 1860, as a companion to **Torreys Peak**, q.v. **Grayburg** TX: because, at the time application was made for a post office, most of the local buildings were painted gray. **Grayback** TX: a colloquialism for 'louse'; according to the local story a camp of cowboys here was badly infested, and the name thus arose. **Gray Coat Branch** GA: by folk-etymology from a recorded (1801) **Great Coat Branch,** from the article of clothing once known as a greatcoat.

Grayling, Greyling For the fish. One creek in AK is so named because a party (1925) caught the first grayling of the season from it.

Greasewood The term is applied loosely in the arid West to various species of low bushes which usually burn well because of resinous quality, thus resembling grease. By association the name is applied to features, e.g. **Greasewood Mountain** AZ.

Greasy In some dialectal usage, e.g. in KY, MO, it is the equivalent of *muddy,* and so appears repeatedly as **Greasy Creek.** In some instances it is probably used because of a slick from natural oil seepage appearing on the water.

Great Much less common than **Big,** with usage complicated. 1) Generally in Colonial times used as the equivalent of **Big,** the same features sometimes being known either as **Big** or **Great,** e.g. the present **Big Sandy River** WV. 2) An Anglicizing of the Dutch *groot,* 'big, great,' or its analogy, produced the concentration in NY and NJ, e.g. **Great Egg Harbor, Great Meadows, Great Notch.** 3) In the 19th century the term became differentiated from **Big,** and was used to distinguish something of a grander or higher order of magnitude, e.g. **Great Salt Lake, Great Divide** (for the Continental Divide), **Great Basin** (named by J. C. Frémont in 1843), **Great Central Valley** CA. **Greathouse** is a personal name. **Great Barrington** MA: incorporated in 1761, and thus displaying the Colonial usage; the adjective is probably to distinguish this town from one in RI. **Great Lakes:** so known in English from the late 17th century, and used as the equivalent of *big.* **Great Scott Township** MN: from the favorite exclamation of one of the namers. **Great Bend** has become a common name for a point at which a stream makes a major change of direction.

Greeley From the personal name, especially for Horace Greeley (1811–1872), editor and political figure, e.g. **Greeley** CO, and counties in KS, NB.

Green 1) A descriptive by color. It indicates a feature distingiushed by greenness, and often carries a commendatory suggestion. It is used in the arid regions for places which stand out because of grass or other verdure, e.g. **Green Valley.** The name is also common in the East where the general tone of the forest must have been dark enough to give *green* both a distinguishing and a commendatory value. **Green Mountains** VT: probably named by counterpart with the earlier named **White Mountains** NH; being lower, they would often be green while the **White Mountains** were still snow-covered. **Green Lake** and **Green River** indicate some peculiar coloring of the water. The exact reason for the naming of the river in WY is disputed, but it may be merely for color. **Green Bay** WI: a translation from the French, its origin is disputed, but it is probably from some color effect noted by the first French explorers. The descriptive sometimes carried a derogatory suggestion, e.g. **Green Lake** MN from its green scum. 2) From the personal name, especially for Nathanael Greene, whose name appears with simplified spelling in many places, e.g. both **Greensboro** NC and **Greenville** NC. So also, often from personal names, **Greenfield, Greenleaf,** and **Greenwood.** 3) From places in the British Isles, e.g. **Greenwich. Greencastle** PA was named in 1782 by an immigrant for his native place in Ireland. 4) For commendatory purposes. Such names are especially common in the arid West and in modern suburbs, where the idea of escaping from the grime of the city is strong, e.g. in such names as **Greenacres, Green Village. Greenback:** the occasional use probably springs from the monetary term. **Greenwood** MS: for Greenwood Leflore, Choctaw chief and early cotton planter.

Greene Its widespread use, especially as a county-name, is owed chiefly to General Nathanael Green (1742–1786). See also **Green.**

Greenhorn It occurs typically in the West, especially in the mining regions, where it originated from some incident involving a 'greenhorn,' i.e. an inexperienced person. **Greenhorn Creek,** Nevada Co., CA: so named by some just-arrived miners in 1849, who considered themselves to be greenhorns. In CO the name is a translation of *cuerno verde,* the name by which the Spaniards knew a Comanche chief, killed here in 1779.

Greensky Hill MI For a local Ottawa Indian.

Greenwich From the English town, first used in CT (1640). **Greenwich Village** NY still displays by its name that it was originally a separate settlement. The commendatory suggestion of *green* has aided in the establishment of the name.

Grenada Probably a variant of **Granada,** but possibly from the West Indian island. In MS two rival communities adopted it as a union name in 1836, a time when Spanish names were popular.

Grenola KS Two previous settlements combined at the coming of the railroad, and so combined the names **Greenfield** and **Canola.**

Grenora ND Coined (1916) from the Great Northern Railroad when a line was built to this point.

Gres French 'sandstone,' e.g. **Au Gres** MI.

Gretna From the town Gretna Green in Scotland, renowned as the place at which eloping English couples were married. In LA the place was famous in the early 19th century for a justice of the peace who gladly married all comers, and the name gradually established itself in popular usage, and finally became official.

Grey See **Gray.**

Greyling See **Grayling.**

Greylock Mountain MA From the name of a Waranoke chief of the early 18th century.

Grief Hill AZ Probably from the difficulties in hauling freight over it in bad weather, but possibly from Indian attacks, which were numerous here.

Grindstone The need of sharpening tools made the grindstone a frontier necessity, and places from which such stones might be obtained received this name, e.g. **Grindstone River** MN.

Grinnell From the personal name, e.g. **Lake Joseph Grinnell** CA for the zoologist; various features in MT for Dr. G. B. Grinnell, naturalist and author; the town in IA for J. B. Grinnell, town founder.

Gripe AZ A humorous name given by the attendants to the station where motorists were stopped for agricultural inspection, because the motorists were likely to 'gripe.'

Gris(e) French 'gray,' hence, probably as a descriptive, **Anse Grise** LA.

Grizzly The animal was fairly numerous and highly dangerous, so that both encounters and memorable incidents were common, and names are correspondingly so, especially in CA, where they are estimated at 200. The more precise form is occasionally used, e.g. **Grizzly Bear Creek** SD. On the other hand, **Bear** alone may sometimes refer to the grizzly. The name occurs upon features of all kinds, but is rare on habitations, because of suggestions of wildness, including association with *grisly.* **Grizzly Mountain,** Trinity Co., CA: Jim Wilburn had a fierce encounter here, was badly mauled, but killed the bear with a home-made hunting knife. **Grizzly Camp** CA: in 1880 some campers thought their mules were attacked by a grizzly; though the commotion was otherwise explained, they thus named the place. **Grizzly Mountain** OR: descriptively named because of its color. See **Bear.**

Grog Run OH Probably an incident-name from the common Colonial drink. Cf. **Rum, Whiskey.**

Groningen From the province in the Netherlands. **New Groningen** MI was named by Dutch settlers in the mid-19th century.

Gros, Grosse French 'big, broad, bulky,' e.g. **Gros Cap** MI, **Grosse Pointe** MI, **Grosse Ile** MI. **Grosse Tete** LA: French 'big head,' but probably the family name Grossetête.

Gros Ventres From the Indian tribal name, e.g. 'big-bellies,' in French form. See **Belly, Grovont.**

Groton From an English town-name; in MA, 1655, in CT, 1705.

Grottoes VA From caves nearby.

Groundhog A common name over much of the country for the animal elsewhere known as **Marmot** or **Woodchuck:** thus, **Groundhog Hollow** (4 in KY), **Ground Hog Brook** NJ.

Ground House River MN From wooden huts covered with earth, built by Hidatsa Indians, translated from an Indian language.

Grouse The widespread and valuable game bird has given its name to many natural features and to a few habitations.

Grouslous Mountain OR Probably by misspelling for John Grolouise, early resident.

Grove Primarily a generic, applicable in the regions where there was neither unbroken forest nor an extensive tree-less area, especially the Middle West. It is frequent as a specific to indicate a natural features associated with a grove, e.g. **Grove Lake, Grove Hill.** Because of deforestation and plantings, these groves are often no longer distinguishable. It occurs in habitation-names, with the commendatory value associated with trees in nonforested areas. **Grove City** PA: originally **Pine Grove,** from a distinct clump of pines on a hill. **Groveland** is a repeated habitation-name, to describe a place characterized by groves. The personal name is sometimes involved.

Grovont WY A phonetic rendering of the Indian tribal name **Gros Ventres.**

Growler Mountains AZ For John Growler, a prospector.

Grub Though of British origin, *grub,* meaning 'food,' is a highly popular American term, especially so in the 19th century, and such names as **Grub Gulch** CA are probably thus derived, although the personal name (usually spelled Grubb) may have contributed.

Grue French 'crane,' e.g. **Coulee des Grues** LA.

Gruetli TN Named, ca. 1869, for the canton in Switzerland by Swiss immigrants.

Grulla Spanish 'crane.' The town in TX took its name from a lake.

Grundy From the personal name; counties in MO and TN are for Felix Grundy (1777–1840), political figure.

Guachama CA From an Indian tribal name.

Gu Achi AZ Papago 'big ridge.'

Guadalupe From the patron of Mexico, the Virgin of Guadalupe, e.g. the river in CA, named by the Anza expedition in 1776.

Guagas Stream ME Algonquian, exact meaning uncertain, but a term associated with shallow boggy lakes.

Gu Aidak Papago 'big field.'

Guijas Mountains AZ Spanish 'rubble, small stones,' originally a mine-name.

Guajatoyan Creek CO Uncertain, but appearing to be an Indian word shaped by folk-etymology to the semblance of a Mexican-Spanish term.

Guaje American-Spanish 'gourd.'

Guajillo TX From a tree which is locally so called.

Guajolote Spanish 'turkey.'

Gualala CA From Indian (Kasaya) *hawálali,* the name of a village, 'river mouth.'

Guano A Spanish-American term which entered the English vocabulary because of sea-birds' dung used as fertilizer. **Guano Lake** OR: named for deposits of guano in the area. Some examples of the name are probably euphemistic renderings in print of the four-letter English equivalent.

Guard Rare, but e.g. **Guard Mountain** AK, reason for naming uncertain. **The Guardhouse** MT is a mountain named descriptively (cf. **Jail**). **Guard Jam Bluff** GA: probably a riverman's term, for boatmen to beware of the log jam at this point. See **Gardi.**

Guardian WV From the Guardian Coal and Oil Company.

Guatay CA Indian (Diegueño) 'large.'

Guemes The island and channel in WA, named by the Spanish explorer Eliza in 1791, are in honor of the Conde de Revillagigedo, viceroy of Mexico, who sent the expedition, using one of his many names.

Guenoc CA Probably Indian (Miwok), of uncertain meaning, but possibly a Spanish rendering of Greenock, the name of an early settler.

Guernsey In WY for C. A. Guernsey, rancher. In NH the name (formerly **Cow Island**) was changed to **Guernsey Island** by the state legislature in 1933 at the instance of the state Guernsey Breeders Association.

Guero, Mount CO From the name of a Ute Indian.

Guess From the personal name, e.g. the creek in AL for the notable Cherokee, commonly known as Sequoah, who also used his father's name, Guess.

Guijarral Spanish 'place of pebbles.'

Guild From the personal name, e.g. **Guild** NH; thus, probably **Guildhall** VT.

Guilderland NY From the province of the Netherlands.

Guilford, Guildford From an English town, first in CT (1639). In NC the name is directly from Lord North, Earl of Guilford (1770).

Guinda Spanish, for a kind of cherry, in CA so called because of the presence of an old cherry tree.

Guinea In the Colonial period the term was applied to a Negro from the Guinea Coast, but was soon used more generally, so that it is probably the equivalent of **Negro** in a few place-names, such as **Guinea Mountains** VA.

Guinevere Castle See **Bedivere**.

Gu Komelik AZ Papago 'big flats.'

Gulch Common in the West, especially in CA, as a generic, with the meaning, 'gully, small ravine.' Rare as a specific, but occurring in a few habitation-names, e.g. **Gulch** CO.

Gulf Usually a generic, and commonly with reference to the **Gulf of Mexico,** though occurring elsewhere, e.g. **Gulf of Alaska.** It is in occasional use as a specific for places thus associated, e.g. **Gulfport** MS, **Gulf Reef** WA, the latter from the now extinct name **Gulf of Georgia** (for present **Georgia Strait**). **Grand Gulf** MS: probably a translation from the French to indicate an enlargement of the Mississippi River, marked by eddies.

Gulkana AK Athapascan, with *-na,* 'river,' and the rest uncertain.

Gull The bird, being widespread and conspicuous, has given rise to many names for features, but has rarely been applied to habitations, doubtless because of its associated meaning, 'foolish person.' The form **Seagull** also appears.

Gulnare CO From the name of a blooded Holstein cow, Princess of Gulnare; by local story, selected by the Post Office Dept. in preference to other names submitted.

Gum The name occurs commonly on natural features throughout the East, and indicates one of the trees so known. By transfer it has occasionally spread to habitation-names, e.g. **Gum Neck** NC, **Gum Fork** VA.

Gumbo In the meaning 'sticky mud' it has produced **Gumbo Buttes** SD and a few other names. **The Gumbo** SD: to designate a large area characterized by such soil.

Gumboot Creek OR From a gumboot once found in the stream.

Gunbarrel Creek WY For an old gunbarrel once found here.

Gungy Wamps CT Algonquian, *wamps* being rock with the addition of an English plural, and *gungy,* probably, 'high.'

Gunlock UT From the nickname of William Hamblin, early settler and renowned hunter.

Gunnunks NY From the name of an Indian woman who lived there, probably in the 18th century.

Gunpowder Rarely occurring, under the same conditions as **Powder.** The river in MD, probably based upon an incident, is recorded from 1658.

Gunsight Although various incidents involving a gunsight probably aided in the establishment of this repeated name, it is most likely to be descriptive, e.g. in the name-cluster in AZ, which springs from an upstanding rock at the end of a level ridge, the latter forming the 'barrel'; **Gunsight Canyon** NM: a small hill suggests a gunsight. In TX the name is descriptive.

Gunstock Knob WV By tradition a pioneer found here some wood suitable for making a gunstock.

Gunter From the personal name. **Guntersville** AL: for John Gunter, early settler, named in 1848.

Gurli Put Vo AZ Papago 'old-man dead waterhole.' The equivalent of the American 'deadman,' but the incident of its origin is lost.

Gustine In TX from S. J. Gustine, first postmaster. In CA from Augustine Miller, daughter of a local landowner.

Gut Of limited occurrence, e.g. in DE, as a generic, 'channel, run, stream,' and a rare specific by association, e.g. **Gut Point** DE. **Muddygut** is a rare name for streams, e.g. in KY, and probably occurs in this topographical sense.

Guttenberg From the personal name; in IA for Johann Gutenberg, the early printer, with an accidentally introduced misspelling.

Gu Vo AZ Papago 'big pond.'

Guyandot, Guandotte WV Apparently another spelling of the tribal name, more commonly **Wyandot.** A French trader named Guyan lived on the river ca. 1750, and his name probably influenced the spelling.

Guyapipe CA Indian (probably Diegueño) 'rock-lie-on.'

Guyot From the personal name, especially for the geologist A. H. Guyot, e.g. mountains in TN and CA.

Gwynedd PA The Welsh name of North Wales; introduced by Welsh immigrants in the late 17th century.

Gyobscot Point ME Algonquian 'erect-rocks-at.'

Gypsum Descriptively identifying places where this mineral occurs, e.g. **Gypsum Creek** AZ.

Gypsy Though it may sometimes be from the presence of gypsies, these wanderers hardly appeared in the U.S. before 1850, and such names would have to be after that date. It has been used as a woman's name. **Gypsy** OK: from the name of an oil company.

H

Haakon From the personal name, the county in SD commemorating Haakon VII, king of Norway, in a region heavily settled by Norwegians.

Habra In **La Habra** CA it is apparently for Spanish *abra*, 'defile, pass,' with reference to an opening in the hills.

Hachasofkee Creek GA Muskogean (Creek) 'stream-deep.'

Hache French 'ax, hatchet,' e.g. **Pointe a La Hache** LA.

Hachemedega Creek AL Muskogean (Creek) 'stream-its-border,' with reference to its being a boundary line.

Hachita Spanish 'hatchet, little ax,' but also 'little torch,' the latter possibly producing the equivalent of **Signal Hill** in NM. See **Hatchet.**

Hacienda Spanish 'farm, estate.'

Hackberry Though growing in nearly every state, the hackberry was seldom in solid stands, was of little importance to the early settler, and was not usually conspicuous. Names occur rarely, e.g. as a habitation-name in several states; **Hackberry Lake** MN.

Hackensack NJ From the name of an Indian village and tribe.

Hadar Creek NB From German *hader*, 'strife,' mistakenly spelled; named because of a quarrel.

Haddam An alternate spelling from the English town-name Hadham; in CT, 1668.

Haden ID By misspelling, for F. V. Hayden, townsite surveyor.

Hadley In MA (1661) from a town in England. It is also a personal name.

Hadlyme CT Formed from **Haddam** and **Lyme**, and thus named.

Haggai MO The name of the Old Testament prophet has been substituted, euphemistically, for the previous **Hog-Eye.**

Hague 1) From the city of the Netherlands; usually, e.g. in ND, because of Dutch immigrants. 2) From the personal name; for instance **Hagues Peak** CO was named for the brothers James and Arnold who were members of an exploring party in the area ca. 1870.

Haha Branch MD Probably by folketymology from some Algonquian term.

Haiwee CA Probably Shoshonean 'dove.'

Haiyaha, Lake CO Presumably Indian, but language and meaning uncertain; placed by Americans, ca. 1915.

Hakihohake Creek NJ Algonquian 'field, plantation' (?).

Halagow Creek CA Yurok, probably having to do with the deerskin dance.

Halawakee Creek AL Muskogean (Creek), probably 'bad,' but reference unknown.

Halcyon Commendatory for habitations, with the suggestion of calmness and tranquility.

Half Generally occurring in combination. **Halfway** is applied typically to taverns, stage stops, etc. but occasionally to features, and by transfer to habitations. Because of changes, just what the name marked is sometimes difficult to determine, e.g. **Halfway** OR was half way between two known points, but is now moved so that it is much nearer one of the points than it was. **Half Breed Creek** NB: because of an area set apart by treaty for the use of half-breeds of certain tribes. **Half Moon:** a repeated configuration name, indicating a semicircular shape or curve, e.g. **Half Moon Bay** CA. **Halfmoon** NY is probably in memory of Hudson's exploring ship of that name. **Half Day** IL, KS: the translation of the name of a Potawatomi chief. **Half Mountain** CO: because one end has been cut off so sharply by glacial action as to suggest that only half of the mountain remains.

Halifax From the town in England or the title. In MA (1734) the naming is probably from the town; in NH (1750) and in NC (1757), for the second earl, who was much involved in Colonial affairs. In PA it is from Fort Halifax, which had been named for the second earl. The river in FL was named during the British occupation, probably for the second earl.

Hali Murk AZ Papago 'squash burned.'

Hallandale FL The early settlers were largely Dutch, and the name is a variant of Holland-dale.

Hallelujah Peak WY From the spontaneous exclamation of a mountaineer at first getting a clear view of it.

Halloca Creek GA Muskogean 'beloved,' probably with reference to some especially favored place.

Hallowing Point A place at one end of a ferry passage, e.g. MD, VA, where a person had to stand and 'hallow,' i.e. halloo or shout, to gain the attention of the ferryman on the other side.

Halo In OR the term is from Chinook jargon, 'none,' and on **Halo Creek** is the equivalent of 'dry.' In WV and KY the name is uncertain, but is possibly connected with *halloo*. See **Hallowing.**

Halpatiokee River FL Musokegan (Hitchiti) 'alligator-water.'

Halunkenburg WI German 'louts'-town,' an informal name given by German settlers because the frequenters of the locality had a reputation for drinking and fighting.

Halutu AK Tlingit 'peninsula.'

Ham Several lakes have apparently been named for their shape, resembling a ham.

Hamahama River WA Indian (Twana), badly shifted from *dub-hub-hub-bai,* the name of a rush.

Hambden OH Originally **Hamden,** from the town in CT, with spelling changed to avoid confusion with a post office already established in the state.

Hamburg From the city in Germany. In NY the town was settled by Germans, ca. 1808. Puns on **Ham** have doubtless occurred, e.g. in AR the name is locally believed to have arisen because of the killing of a deer with a remarkable pair of hams.

Hamden CT Named in 1786, probably for John Hampden (see **Hampden**); the shift of spelling is unexplained.

Hamilton From the personal name, most commonly for Alexander Hamilton (1757–1804), e.g. many towns and counties. In OH the name was first for **Fort Hamilton** (1791). In TX the name is for Gen. James Hamilton, diplomatic agent for the Republic of Texas.

Hamlet As a habitation-name, it occurs in several states. It is generally to be taken in the sense of 'small village,' but the personal name Hamlet occurs. The Prince of Denmark, moreover, is so well known that his influence cannot be ruled out.

Hammer Usually from a personal name, e.g. in SD for the Hammer family, early settlers. **Black Hammer** MN: because a hill had been blackened by fire, *hammer* being the name given by a Norwegian settler because of a similar place in Norway. **Hammertown** CT: because it was the site of an early iron-fabricating works.

Hammerhorn Mountain CA Because ca. 1867 a deer having deformed antlers was killed here.

Hammock A generic in FL, usually meaning a tract of fertile well-wooded land, occurring as a specific by association, e.g. **Hammock Island.** Elsewhere it may be a variant of *hummock,* e.g. probably **Hammock Point** MD.

Hammonassett CT Algonquian, meaning uncertain.

Hammond From the personal name, e.g. in IN for George H. Hammond, early meat-packer.

Hampden From the personal name; in MA the county was named in 1812 for John Hampden (1585–1643), English champion of the Parliament.

Hampshire From the county in England, etc. Later namings are likely to indicate places so called with reference to **New Hampshire.**

Hampton Though by itself a common English village-name, its original use in the U.S. is from a shortening of **Southampton,** as a small stream in VA was named (ca. 1610) in honor of the Earl of Southampton, who was interested in the colonization. The name was thence transferred to **Hampton Roads.** It is also a personal name, e.g. **Hampton Co.** SC for Wade Hampton, Civil War general.

Hamshire TX For L. Hamshire, early settler.

Hamtramck MI For Col. J. F. Hamtramck, who served in the Indian wars of the late 18th century and commanded the American garrison of Detroit.

Hanaupah CA Shoshonean, containing *pah,* 'water, spring.' The first part of the name may be connected with 'hemp,' which was used by local Indians for twine.

Hancock From the personal name, often for John Hancock, signer of the Declaration of Independence, e.g. in MA, MI. In the West the name may be for W. S. Hancock, Civil War general, e.g. in MN.

Handies Peak CO Probably from a personal name, i.e. Handy's, but not further identified.

Handsome Creek FL Probably from the family name Handsome or Hansom.

Handy Probably in all instances from the personal name, though local story in NC attributes the name to the desire of the inhabitants to have a post office handy.

Hanging In use with **Rock** and **Hill** to describe one in a precarious state, as if suspended. A hanging valley, as used by geologists, denotes a valley cut into the side of a glacial cliff. **Hanging Glacier**

AK and **Hanging Gardens** MT spring from this usage. **Hanging Woman Creek** WY records an Indian woman who committed suicide there. **Hanging Horn** and **Hanging Kettle** lakes MN translate Ojibway names, probably personal names.

Hangman At **Hangman's Hill** SD three horse thieves were hanged 'in early days.' **Hangman Creek** WA: in 1858 Col. George Wright executed several Indians here in reprisal for their defeat of Col. Steptoe.

Hangtown Creek CA The mining camp, now **Placerville,** was known as **Hangtown** during the gold rush because two men were hanged there; the name has survived on the stream.

Hanna Commonly from a personal name, e.g. in UT for W. P. Hanna, first postmaster. Also, it occurs as a second element in specifics, especially in PA, from the Algonquian *hanne,* 'stream,' e.g. **Tobyhanna** PA, **Loyalhanna** PA.

Hannahatchee Creek GA Muskogean (Creek) 'cedar-stream.'

Hannawa NY Probably Iroquoian, meaning uncertain.

Hannibal From the Carthaginian general. In NY it arose as part of the classical naming of 1790. In MO it dates from 1819, and arose probably as a counterpart to the nearby **Fabius,** named for the Roman general who was matched against the Carthaginians.

Hanover For the city in Germany, usually from 1714 to 1775 in compliment to the House of Hanover, the reigning monarchs of England, e.g. in MA, 1727. Later namings, e.g. in MO (1868), are generally by immigrants.

Hanska MN Siouan 'long,' originally the name of a lake.

Hanty From the colloquial pronunciation of *haunty,* i.e. 'having to do with ghosts,' e.g. **Hanty Hollow** AL.

Happy A common name, especially in the West, usually based upon an incident or being commendatory, particularly as **Happy Valley. Happy** TX; from **Happy Draw,** is so called because early travelers were happy at finding water there. **Happy Camp** AZ: though in a dreary location, water could be obtained there, so that the place may not have been named, as some early travelers suspected, by opposites. **Happy Camp** CA: probably because a man exclaimed that this was the happiest day of his life. Since the term is not uncommon as a nickname, it was probably at times given for a person, as is certainly true with the compounds, e.g. **Happy Jack Peak** NB. **Happy Isles** CA: a conscious naming, because the beauty of the place should make anyone feel happy. **Happy River** AK was named ironically (1898) when a party had great difficulty in navigating the stream. Aided by alliteration, **Happy Hollow** is common in regions. e.g. KY, where that generic is favored.

Harbor Descriptive for a place associated with a harbor, e.g. **Harbor River** SC. In the Colonial period the older meanings of the word were current, i.e. 'place of shelter,' and sometimes 'inn, tavern.' **Townsend Harbor** MA, an inland site, probably thus originated. See **Cold Harbor** (under **Cold**).

Harcuvar Mountains AZ Mohave, probably, 'water-very little.'

Hardiaken See **Hardyhickon.**

Harding From the personal name, several features in AK having been named for President W. G. Harding on the occasion of his visit there in 1923. The county in NM (1921) was also named for him.

Hardluck A miner's name, e.g. it is applied to several features in AK.

Hardmoney KY From the political slogan for 'hard money,' arising in the 1830's.

Hardscrabble 'Scrabble,' of somewhat vague meaning, is connected with 'scramble' and 'scrape.' From the first, **Hardscrabble** came to mean a place at which one would have a hard scramble to get across or out of, e.g. **Hardscrabble Point** MN, **Hardscrabble Wash** AZ. From 'scrape' the word meant 'hard place to

scrape out a living,' and this came to be the commoner meaning. As applied to poor farming country, the 19th century saw places so named in probably all states, many of them mere localities, and tending to be ephemeral. From the farming country the word was transferred to the mining country, and several places in CA were so named. Two examples of **Hardscrabble Creek** remain in that state.

Hardshell KY Probably from a settlement associated with so-called Hard-Shell Baptists, though the term was used in the 19th century in the general sense of 'determined, stubborn.'

Hardtack Island OR Originally Hardhack, from a plant growing there, changed by small-boat sailers, reputedly because it was a difficult place to tack.

Hardwick Though it is an English place-name, the town in MA (1738–1739) was probably named for Lord Hardwick, prominent political figure.

Hardwood MI, OK From the presence of hardwood trees.

Hardyhickon Creek PA By partial folk-etymology from an Algonquian term, probably the equivalent of 'bullet-mould creek,' thus being a naming after the Indians had established contact with the Europeans.

Hargill TX For W. A. Harding and Lamar Gill, town founders.

Harlem In NY named under the Dutch regime for the city of the Netherlands; it appears with various spellings, but was standardized under the English form after the English occupation.

Harmony An idealistic habitation-name (cf. **Amity, Concord**), it exists in a dozen states. In PA it originates from the Harmony Society, a communal group.

Harney From the personal name, especially for Gen. W. S. Harney of the mid-19th century, who campaigned against the western Indians, e.g. the peak in SD.

Harper From the personal name, e.g. **Harpers Ferry** WV for Robert Harper, who established a ferry here ca. 1748.

Haro Strait WA Named in 1790 for López de Haro, sailing master of a Spanish expedition.

Harpswell ME Named (1758) from a village in England.

Harquahala Mountains AZ Mohave, probably 'water-high,' because of a high-placed spring.

Harraseeket River ME Algonquian, meaning uncertain.

Harriman From the personal name, especially for E. H. Harriman, railroad magnate, e.g. **Mount Harriman** OR where he had a summer home, and the fiord and glacier in AK which were explored during an exploration organized under his auspices in 1899.

Harris From the personal name. **Harrisburg** PA: named in 1785 by John Harris, Jr., who laid out the town where his father had managed Harris' Ferry over the Susquehanna River.

Harrod From the personal name, e.g. in KY for James Harrod, the leader of the men who settled the site in March 1775.

Harrogate TN Named commendatorily for the town in England with the hope that it would become a health resort.

Hart Since this term for the bull elk never established itself in the U.S., the names are from personal ones, including such combinations as **Hartshorn** and **Hartwell.** See also **Hartford** and **Hartland. Hart Mountain** OR: a phonetic spelling from the sign of a heart used as a cattle-brand. **Hart Lake** MN: named because of its shape, but misspelled.

Hartford, Hertford From the town and county in England, etc. The first form is a variant spelling current in the 17th century and representing the pronunciation. **Hartford** CT: after the New England tradition, named for the town in England in 1637. As the spelling suggests, most of the later occurrences of the name are reminiscent of this use in CT. **Hertford** NC: from the Marquis of Hertford, an English supporter of the colonies, named in 1758.

Hartland The original (1733) naming in CT is uncertain, involving possibilities of an English town-name, of land settled from **Hartford,** and of a personal name. Later namings are from this one, or from the personal name, e.g. in WV for J. B. Hart, landowner. **Hartland** ME was first settled by Stephen Hartwell. In VT the town was originally **Hertford,** but was changed to avoid confusion with **Hartford** in the same state.

Hartoum CA Shortened from **Khartoum,** a name given by railroaders because of the desert location.

Harvard In MA (1732) for John Harvard; in later namings generally for the college (or university) bearing his name, e.g. the glacier in AK. So also in NB and ID, though the former occurs merely in an alphabetical sequence, and the latter in a string of railroad stations named for colleges. **Mount Harvard** CO: named in 1869 by an exploring party including J. D. Whitney who was then teaching at Harvard.

Harwich MA From the town in England (1684).

Harwinton CT One of the earliest (1732) composite coined names, so called because formed from parts of **Hartford, Windsor,** and **Farmington.**

Hasbidito Spring AZ Navajo 'dove.'

Hassacky See **Hassock.**

Hassan MN Siouan 'huckleberry,' but actually a shortening of **Chanhassan.**

Hassayampa River AZ Mohave 'water-big rocks-at.'

Hassel, Lake MN Norwegian 'hazel.'

Hassock Though the word may occur in its English sense (tussock), as used in NY (Long Island), it is apparently from a term appearing in Algonquian (Narragansett) as *hassucki,* 'marsh land.' An early spelling (1657) is Hassokie. Thus also, **Hassacky** CT.

Hasty From the personal name, e.g. in NC for a family of local landowners.

Hat Although not common, it is of diverse origin. The mountain in AZ and the island in WA are named because of shape, though the shape of a hat is far from being standardized. **Hat Creek,** Perkins Co., SD: from the Hat Ranch which took its name from its brand. **Hat Creek,** Fall River Co., SD: from the Siouan name, which would have more accurately been translated War Bonnet. The commonest origin is probably from an incident involving a hat. **Hat Creek** OR: a man's hat, lost when his horse bucked, hung on a bush, and was seen by others who came later. **Hat Creek** CA: probably named for an incident of a lost hat in 1852. The mountain and lake are named from the creek. Habitation-names are rare. **Hat Creek** WY: by transfer, and also by mistake, since the locators of a stage station thought that they were on that creek though they were really on another one. **Hatboro** PA: so called because an 18th-century hatter made the settlement known. **Hatfield** MA: from the town in England; otherwise, generally from the personal name.

Hatchechubbee AL Muskogean (Creek) 'creek-halfway.'

Hatchet Rare, in frontier times the terms *ax* and *tomahawk* having been commoner. **Hatchett** is a personal name. **Hatchet Creek** CA: probably because Indians stole a hatchet from some emigrants. In NM the mountains are by adaptation, or partial translation, from **Hachita.** In AL the creek is a translation of the name* of an early Creek town, aided by folk-etymology because of the common Muskogean term *hachi,* 'stream.' In AK the lake was named (1954) because a member of a surveying party happened there to cut his knee with a hatchet.

Hatchetigbee Bluff AL Choctaw 'river-knob.'

Hatchie River MS, TN Muskogean (Choctaw) 'stream.' This term appears as an element in many place-names, e.g. **Hachemedega, Atchapalaya, Elkahatchee, Kisatchie.**

Hatchineha Lake FL Seminole 'cypress tree.'

Hatteras, Cape NC Recorded by the English voyagers as of 1584 or 1585 with spellings of Hatrask or Hatoraske; probably an Indian tribal name.

Hattie From the personal name, e.g. **Hattiesburg** MS for Hattie Hardy, wife of the town founder in the 1880's.

Haulover For a place where small boats are hauled across from one water to another, e.g. the creek in FL.

Haunted Though the early American was not without his belief in spirits and apparitions, the comparative lack of such place-names seems to indicate that these beliefs did not go very deep, such names as **Haunted Cave** KY being rare. **Haunted Butte** SD: because a group of figures, of unknown origin, is carved in the rock.

Hauppauge NY Algonquian 'overflowed-land,' to describe a swampy area.

Haut French, as an adjective, 'high, elevated'; less commonly, as a noun, 'height, elevation.' **Isle au Haut** ME: Samuel de Champlain called it descriptively *'isle haute,'* in 1604; by later American French usage it became 'island of the height.' See under **Terre.**

Hauto PA For G. F. D. Hauto, local businessman.

Havana From the city of Cuba, probably chosen to some extent because of its euphony.

Havasu Lake AZ, CA Probably Mohave 'blue.'

Havelock From the personal name, especially, e.g. in IA, for Sir Henry Havelock, British general (1795–1857).

Haverford PA From the town in Wales, introduced by Welsh immigrants in the 17th century.

Haverhill In MA (ca. 1641) from a town in England.

Haverstraw NY Recorded (1640) as **Averstroo,** literally 'oat-straw,' but probably a Dutch personal name.

Havilah, Havillah From the Biblical land of gold, usually applied, as in CA, because of the finding of gold.

Havre MT From the city in France.

Havre de Grace MD Named under French auspices (1785), it is 'haven of grace,' but echoes the full name of the French seaport Le Havre.

Haw Generally from the personal name, but in NC **Haw River** is from a shortening of Sissipahaw, the name of a tribe of local Indians.

Hawk As a large and conspicuous bird the hawk has given names to many natural features, e.g. **Hawks Nest** WV. On habitations it is more commonly from the personal name. Though commoner than the eagle, the hawk has made much less impression on nomenclature, being less notable and lacking symbolic value. See **Hawkeye.**

Hawkeye In NY probably from the sobriquet for Cooper's Natty Bumppo. In IA and elsewhere, from the nickname for Iowans.

Haxtun CO From the name of a railroad contractor, not further identified; probably the original spelling was **Haxton.**

Haxy Creek WV A misspelling for Hazy, a name that occurs nearby.

Hay The origin is most often from the personal name, including such combinations as **Hayden** and **Hayward. Hayfield, Hayland,** and **Hay Creek** generally spring from the presence of meadows productive of natural hay. In CA, **The Hayfields,** Riverside Co., was applied humorously because of the thin growth of grass. **Hayfork** CA: at first the locality was **Hayfields,** because it was the chief cultivated area in a mountainous region; a branch of **Trinity River** then became known as the **Hay Fork,** and in turn the name was applied to a settlement. **Hay Creek** MN: the namers saw many haystacks made by Indians who had begun to practice agriculture. **Hayward** CA: Wm. Hayward opened a hotel here in 1852, and the place came to be known

as Hayward's or Haywards, being so spelled until 1900.

Haybro CO From Hayden Brothers, local coal operators.

Hayden From the personal name, e.g. the valley in WY for F. V. Hayden, early geologist of the West.

Haydon Peak AK Named (1888) for H. E. Haydon, then secretary of Alaska.

Hayes From the personal name, e.g. the county in NB for President Hayes. **Hayes, Mount** AK: for C. W. Hayes, geologist, named in 1898.

Haynach Lakes CO Arapaho 'snow-water,' a name applied by the Colorado Geographic Board ca. 1915.

Haysi VA For the partners in a store, Hayter and Sypher.

Haysop Creek AL An Indian name of uncertain origin and meaning, transformed to the appearance of an English name.

Haystack, Hayrick, Haycock The first is by much the commonest, and seems to be universal in the West, where this naming occurs most frequently. The name is descriptively applied to buttes, mountains, rocks, etc. resembling a haystack in outline, at least as seen from a certain angle. Sometimes it is merely **The Haystack.**

Hayti In PA, because of immigrants from Haiti in the late 19th century.

Hazel 1) From the hazel bush, sought after for its nuts, e.g. **Hazel Creek** CA. 2) From the woman's name, e.g. the mountain in OR, which was so named in 1913 by a member of the Forest Service because Hazel Taylor was camping there. **Hazelton** ND: for Hazel Roop, daughter of the townsite owner. 3) From various family names, e.g. **Hazelton, Hazelbusch, Hazelhurst.** See **Hazleton.**

Hazeline Lake CO Named, ca. 1913, by F. R. Koenig, by combining the names of his wife Hazel and his mother Emmaline.

Hazleton In PA the town derives from **Hazel Creek,** and may be a misspelling in the act of incorporation (1836); but it may be from a spelling used in England. Towns in other states use the same spelling, from this earliest one or from a personal name.

Hazy Rare, but occurring in the **Hazy Gap** WV, probably an incident-name because of atmospheric conditions.

Head Though it occurs as a personal name, most of the examples arise otherwise. It is frequently used as a generic for the source of a stream, and habitation-names thus originate, e.g. **Head of Grassy** KY. Of similar usage are **Head of Island** LA, **Head Tide** ME, **Head Waters** VA. **Heads Island** VT is a translation from the Iroquoian to indicate a place where heads of killed enemies were set up as trophies. See **Tete, Wheeling.**

Headache Spring CA Because drinking from it was popularly supposed to cause headache.

Headforemost Mountain VA Probably a descriptive for a slope so steep as to cause one to fall headforemost. Cf. **Breakneck.**

Headquarters In most instances it is a relic of army occupation, but the creek in OK is locally believed to be from the headquarters of a cattle-ranch; in NJ, because of local belief that Washington had temporary headquarters in a house here; in ID, because of the location here of the headquarters of a lumber company.

Heagan Mountain ME Algonquian, for a chief recorded as of 1698 (?).

Healing The term seems to be confined to springs and is probably influenced by the New Testament story of the pool of Siloam. It indicates waters supposed to possess special healing qualities.

Health(y) In occasional use as a commendatory. **Mount Healthy** OH was chosen because the inhabitants had escaped the ravages of a cholera epidemic in 1850.

Heart Commonly because a feature resembles the shape of a conventional heart, especially with *lake* and *island.* **Heartbreak Hill** MA: probably because of its steepness. **Heartwell** NB: for J. B. Heartwell, prominent local citizen. The term is fairly common in Indian names, e.g. **Crowheart Butte. Heart River** ND is another translation from the Indian (Mandan), the idea being that the stream flowed from the 'heart' of the country. **Heart Lake** WY was originally named for Hart Hunney, a hunter; since it is heartlike in shape, its name shifted.

Heath Regularly from the personal name. **Heath Springs** SC: after a man named Heath and another named Springs. **Heath** NB: named by a Scot who was familiar with the British usage of 'heath,' and thought that the vicinity resembled a Scottish heath.

Heathen In occasional use on features, e.g. **Heathen Meadow** MA, it probably indicates a place of Indian rites, often termed 'heathen' in the 17th century.

Heather The plant is not widespread in the U.S., but a few names occur, e.g. **Heather Island** WA, **Heather Lake** CA. It is also a personal name.

Heaven(ly) Rare, though **Heavenly Valley** is a recent commendatory name in CA. The use seems to be almost entirely semihumorous with names of animals, e.g. **Hog Heaven Branch** GA and **Turkey Heaven Mountains** AL, and the repeated **Horse Heaven.**

Heber From the personal name; in UT for Heber C. Kimball, prominent early Mormon.

Hebron The name of this important Biblical city occurs in some 15 states, being used for religious commendatory reasons. In CT the name dates from 1707.

Heceta Head OR Named in 1862 in commemoration of Bruno Heceta, Spanish voyager of 1775.

Heckletooth Mountain OR Because of tall rocks near its summit, thought to resemble the teeth of a heckle, an implement used for combing flax.

Hecla From the volcano in Iceland, well known in the 19th century because of its frequent and violent eruptions; the famous Calumet and Hecla mine in MI helped make the name known.

Hector In NY for the Trojan hero, given as part of the classical naming of 1790; it is also a personal name.

Hediondo Spanish 'stinking.'

Heebeecheeche Lake WY From the personal name of a Shoshone chief.

Hegira KY From the hegira of Mohammed from Mecca; probably it commemorates some local removal, but the circumstances are uncertain.

Hehe Butte OR Chinook jargon for 'laughter,' or 'fun,' but applied by the Indians because of a belief that the place was haunted by friendly spirits.

Height of Land Usually a generic, but a specific in the township name MN, which translates an Ojibway term.

Heimdal ND Norwegian 'home-valley,' but by local story named for the mythological figure of that name.

Heintooga Creek NC Cherokee, meaning uncertain.

Helen One of the commonest of given names, Helen has been bestowed upon numerous lakes by namers wishing to honor someone. It also occurs on other natural features, e.g. **Helen Mountain** MT. It is rare, however, as a habitation-name, doubtless because people shied off from the suggestion of hell. It is rare even with suffixes, though there is **Helenville** WI and **Helenwood** TN. **Helen Furnace** PA: no Helen seems to have been in that vicinity, and the name is taken to be Highland, and thence Hieland, for Alexander McNaughton who used to boast of being a Highland Scot.

Helena As a woman's name it has been prolific on habitations, now and then as an adaptation of Helen. **Helena** MT: named for the home town of a man from MN. **St. Helena** CA: the mountain was apparently named by the Russians who had settled at Fort Ross, Helena being a favorite Russian saint. **St. Helena** SC: named (1526) by Pedro de Quexas, pilot for the expedition of L. V. de Ayllon as **Punta de Santa Elena,** in gratitude to his own patron saint for the favorable landfall.

Heliograph Peak AZ During Indian troubles, the army maintained a heliograph signaling station here.

Helix In OR there was difficulty in finding a name not already in use, and a man with a sore ear proposed a name that he had heard his doctor mention. In CA the mountain is so named because the trail ascends it in a spiral.

Hell The term was freely applied during the frontier period. Many of the names were superseded in the interest of Victorian propriety, but many weathered that period and are now firmly established on the maps. They do not occur, at least officially, as habitation-names, and the Post Office Dept. would probably not approve such names, but a few survive for crossroads communities, such as **Helltown,** Butte Co, CA. The name was usually applied in a derogatory sense to a place that was hard to get through or otherwise disagreeable. The popular use of hell, however, is broad, and some of the names may commemorate 'where we had a hell of a good spree.' The word is used indifferently as **Hell** or **Hell's.** In the West, where thermal manifestations occurred, the name was applied almost technically, the first name for the Yellowstone Park area being **Coulter's Hell,** for the discoverer. The vocabulary, or the imagination, of the frontiersman was so small that these names were vastly repeated, and scarcely exceed a half-dozen in common use. **Hell Hole, Hell Hollow,** and **Hell's Half Acre** make use of alliteration. **Hell-for-Certain (Sartin)** and **Hell-for-Sure** vary only the wording. **Hell-Roaring,** and simple **Hell** about exhaust the list. **Hellgate** NY: this venerable and and wholly respectable name renders the Dutch **Hellegat** of the 17th century. 'Gate' is an approximate translation, since *gat* should be taken more widely, as 'passage.' It was named because of the difficult and dangerous tidal currents. **Go to Hell Gulch** SD: by local tradition so named because a stranger asked the name of the place and was rudely told 'Go to hell!' **Hell Hole Creek** SC: because in the Revolutionary War 28 men were massacred and mutilated here. **Hell Canyon** CO: in 1882 some surveyors, caught in a storm, were barely able to escape with their lives. **Hell Creek** KS: named, ca. 1860, by J. R. Mead, 'appropriately named from some experiences of myself and other hunters in buffalo days.'

Hellam PA From Hallam in England, by misspelling or use of a variant form of the 18th century.

Helmetta NJ For Etta Helme, daughter of a local factory owner.

Helotes TX From Mexican-Spanish *elote,* 'ear of green corn,' reason for application unknown.

Helper UT A railroad name, because an additional locomotive was attached at this point as a 'helper' on the upgrade.

Helpmejack Creek AK Apparently one of the rare exclamation incident-namings.

Helvetia The Latin name for Switzerland has been applied commemoratively to a few places, generally where Swiss families have settled.

Hematite From the iron ore so called.

Hemet CA Probably Shoshonean, meaning unknown.

Hemlock The tree was not known in England, and in the colonies was often considered a spruce or pine. It has thus created only a few names in the East, e.g. **Hemlock Mountain** MA. In the West one species is an important timber tree, and is distinguished under its own name, giving rise to such names as **Hemlock Gulch** MT and **Hemlock Pass** WA. A variety growing in the southern Appalachians has produced some names there, e.g. **Hemlock** SC.

Hemp In some instances, e.g. in NC, it is for what was once the principal crop. In compounds it is usually from a personal name, e.g. **Hemphill.**

Hempstead In NY from the town in the Netherlands dating from 1644 in the Dutch form Heemstede, under the English occupation shifted to the form of an English town. In TX for G. S. B. Hempstead, brother-in-law of an early settler.

Hen From the abbreviation for Henry or a female fowl, especially the so-called prairie hen, e.g. **Hen Lake** MN. **Hen and Chickens:** usually a seacoast term for something large associated with smaller things, e.g. the shoal in DE. **Hen Scratch** FL: probably a humorous rural derogatory.

Henlopen, Cape DE Of Dutch origin, recorded in 1633 as **Hinloopen:** uncertain, but most likely a family name, perhaps that of a crewman in one of the early exploring voyages.

Henrico County VA A shortening, on the establishment of the county in 1634, from the now-extinct **Henricopolis,** the latter being a Graeco-Latin form ('Henry-city') in honor of Prince Henry, son of Charles I.

Henry From the personal name. The county in VA is for Patrick Henry, Revolutionary patriot. **Cape Henry** VA: named on Apr. 29, 1607, in honor of Prince Henry, heir apparent to the English throne.

Henryetta OK For Henry G. Beard and his wife Etta Beard (1908).

Herbe French 'grass,' e.g. **Pointe aux Herbes** LA, the equivalent of **Grassy Point.**

Herculaneum MO Founded (1808) as a lead-mining center by Moses Austin, and named for the Roman town which was being excavated. Austin was a reader who would have known of the classical city; by local tradition, he selected the name because the smoke from lead-smelters was like that from Vesuvius.

Hercules In CA from Hercules Powder Company.

Hereford From the town and county in England. In the West, e.g. CO, SD, TX, the name arises from the breed of cattle.

Hereford AZ: for B. J. Hereford, a friend of the founder.

Hermagos Islands AK Named, ca. 1775, by a Spanish voyager as **Las Hormigas,** 'the ants.'

Herman(n) From the personal name; in MO, **Hermann** was named for the 1st-century German hero by German immigrants who wished to establish Germanic ideals in the U.S.

Hermano, Hermana Spanish 'brother, sister.' The usage is much the same as in English, e.g. NM has both **Tres Hermanos** and **Tres Hermanas** for three peaks close together.

Hermit Descriptively applied to a rock or mountain standing alone, e.g. **Hermit Butte** CA. **Hermit Basin** AZ: from a camp established there by a single man. **Hermit's Peak** NM: from J. M. Agustini, an Italian, who lived in solitude and piety in the traditional cave until killed in 1869.

Hermitage Generally southern, a name given to a plantation by a bachelor proprietor, especially known from association with Andrew Jackson at Nashville; from plantations the name has been transferred to some towns.

Hermon, Mount Hermon From the Biblical mountain.

Hermoso Spanish 'beautiful, pretty.' In **Hermosa Beach** CA the feminine form has been preferred, probably because of the usual association of beauty with the female. So also, **Hermosa** is a habitation-name in several states.

Hernando From the personal name, especially (e.g. FL, MS) for Hernando de Soto, Spanish explorer of the 16th century.

Hernshaw WV From the coal-mine owners Herndon and Renshaw.

Hero The two towns in VT (distinguished as **North** and **South**) were named in the post-Revolutionary period as **Two Heroes;** those thus honored are uncertain, but were probably the brothers Ethan and Ira Allen, both of whom had been involved in the Revolution and were also concerned with the founding of the town.

Heron Rare, sometimes from the personal name, which is, however, uncommon; usually from the bird, e.g. the lake in MN, which is a translation from the Siouan 'nesting place of herons.'

Herpoco CA From Hercules Powder Company.

Herring Though it is a family name, the use upon freshwater features, especially in MA, is from the presence of a fish locally known as herring.

Hertford See **Hartford.**

Hesper, Hesperia, Hesperus From the Greek-Latin name for the evening star, and thus a term taken vaguely to apply to the West. Since most regions of the U.S. at one time considered themselves to be the West, the name could be appropriately applied to habitations. **Mount Hesperus** CO is an unusual application to a feature, probably because of some association with the evening star.

Hessian Hill PA Hessian troops camped here in September, 1777.

Hetch Hetchy CA Miwok, denoting a place with edible seeds, probably a grass or acorn-producing oaks.

Hettenshaw CA Wintu 'camass valley.'

Hiaggee Creek AL From the name of an early Creek town, probably a tribal name.

Hialeah FL Probably Seminole 'beautiful-prairie.'

Hiamovi Mountain CO For a Cheyenne chief, a name placed in the early 20th century.

Hiawassee GA A variant of **Hiwassee.**

Hiawatha Occurs for about half a dozen habitation-names, more from Longfellow's poem than from the original mythical character.

Hibbing MN For Frank Hibbing, its founder.

Hibernia The Latin and poetic name for Ireland, usually, e.g. in FL, bestowed by namers of Irish background.

Hickahaly Creek MS Choctaw 'sweet-gum-trees-standing.'

Hickiwan AZ Papago 'zigzag,' but significance unknown.

Hickon Creek PA Algonquian (Delaware), a term denoting a location at the head of the tide.

Hickory A characteristic American tree, it was conspicuous and widespread over the eastern U.S., and was prized for nuts and wood. Its influence on nomenclature has been strong. A tree that appreciated well-watered, deep soil, it grew on streams and bottom-lands, and left its name on them. **Hickory Bottom** even tended to become a common descriptive term. Having attractive suggestions, the name was readily transferred to habitations. **Hickory Township** MN: a good example of a boundary-name, since it occurs at the extreme northern limit of the tree. The popular Andrew Jackson, nicknamed 'Old Hickory,' is honored in some of the habitation-names, e.g. **Hickory Co.** MO. **Hic(k)oria** AR, FL represents a Latinized form.

Hicksbaugh TX From S. B. Hicks and J. T. and J. P. Wurtsbaugh, lumber dealers.

Hico In TX tradition maintains that it was named from a local tribe of Indians; in WV it is similarly ascribed to a variety of tobacco. Both places may be transfers from **Hyco.** See **Hycootee.** In MO it is a shortening from **Hickory Co.**

Hi-Corum CA From the personal name of an Indian who discovered an ore deposit there.

Hicpochee Lake FL Seminole 'prairie-little.'

Hidalgo In TX and probably elsewhere the name commemorates Miguel Hidalgo (1753–1811), the Mexican revolutionary leader. The county in NM (1919) may be for the Treaty of Guadalupe Hidalgo, by which NM became part of the U.S., in which case the name is only removed from the revolutionary hero by one more degree, since the city was named for him.

Hidden Almost exclusively western, it denotes some feature which is or seems to be hidden from view. **Hidden Creek** MT: the stream flows through a deep and narrow canyon so that it is not easily seen. **Hidden Timber** SD: the grove is largely concealed by a high riverbank. **Hidden** WA: for L. M. Hidden, a railroad builder of the area, ca. 1905.

Hiddenite NC For a kind of mineral so named, found in the vicinity.

Hieroglyphic Hill AZ Because of Indian pictographs there.

Higganum CT Algonquian, meaningless as it stands, being the remnant of a phrase indicating a quarry for stone to make tomahawks.

High As a descriptive, either 'tall,' or 'located at high altitude.' Since height is a nondistinguishing quality of mountains and hills, **High** is rarely thus coupled, but is often used with smaller features, e.g. **Rock, Point.** In its second meaning it occurs on many features, e.g. **High Spring, High Valley. The High Desert** OR: a dry region, distinguished from **The Low Desert** to the south, though there is no sharp line of demarcation and only about 1000 feet difference in elevation. Similarly **The High Sierra** is a vague term for the highest part of the southern end of the range, which has the highest peaks. **High Shoals** NC: a paradoxical name, but apparently given because a part of the shoal is rocky and rises above the water. **Highwater** occasionally serves as a name for streams, either because of an incident or because of frequent flooding. As a habitation-name it is often by transfer or association, e.g. **High Bridge.** Since height is one of the regular commendatory qualities, **Highland** is a repeated name, and double commendatory quality is bestowed by such names as **Highland Park** and **High View. High Lonesome** is a repeated name in NM. **High** TX:

for Mack High, early settler. See **Hightower.**

Highco Mountain VA Probably a spelling variant of **Hyco,** under the influence of folk-etymology.

Hightower Usually from a personal name, e.g. in TX for L. B. Hightower, district judge. In AL and GA it has originated by folk-etymology from Cherokee *itawa,* meaning unknown.

Hiko NV Probably Shoshone 'white man,' but reason for application uncertain. **Hyko** (applied to the mountain range) is a variant.

Hill(s) Most commonly from the personal name, but also as a descriptive for a place associated with a hill, in this latter case, often in compounds, e.g. **Hillside** NJ. **Hillsboro** TX: for Dr. George Hill, political figure under the Texas Republic. **Hillyard** WA: for J. J. Hill of the Great Northern Railroad, which had a large 'yard' at that place. **Hillsboro** OH: probably because it was established (1807) in a hilly region. **Hills and Dales** OH: a commendatory descriptive of the 20th century.

Hillabee Creek AL From the name of an early Creek town.

Hillister TX For W. H. Hollister, early settler, but misspelled in transmission through the Post Office Dept.

Hillrose CO Mrs. Kate Emerson, who had deeded the land for the townsite, was permitted to choose a name, and took one by adapting the names of her sister Rose Hill.

Hillsborough In FL the name on river, county, etc., is for the second Viscount Hillsborough who held a large grant of land in the colony during the British regime.

Hiloka Creek GA Muskogean (Creek) 'gum-tree' (?).

Hilo Peak NM The word is 'thread' in Spanish, but here may be used in the miners' sense, 'seam, fault.'

Hilolo FL Seminole, a name for the long-billed curlew.

Hilton From the personal name, e.g. **Hilton Head** SC for William Hilton, named by him during his exploring voyage of 1663.

Himyar KY From the name of a famous English race horse whose owner had interests in the vicinity.

Hindu Amphitheatre AZ See **Brahma.**

Hi-Nella NJ Uncertain, probably a recent coinage.

Hingham In MA (1635) from the town in England from which most of the first settlers had come.

Hinnom VA From the valley near Jerusalem which in ancient times was considered an evil place of abomination; why such a name of unpleasant associations has been used in the U.S. is uncertain. Cf. **Sodom.**

Hiorra WV The name of the hamlet is shared with a coal mine, and is locally explained as the combination of the names of three men—unknown, except that one was probably Orr.

Hiram: Hiramsburg OH was named for Hiram Calvert, townfounder. **Hiram** OH was so called by Masons in the early 19th century, using the name of their 'master workman.' **Hiram** ME was probably thus named by Masons, though the Biblical king may also have been involved.

Hisega SD The original campground here was used by six young women who formed the name from their initials, viz. Helen, Ida, Sadie, Ethel, Grace, and Ada.

Hisle SD An adaptation from the last name of William Highshield, early settler.

Hitchita OK From an Indian tribal name.

Hiwassee NC, TN Cherokee 'meadow'; so also with **Hi Wassie** MO and probably **Hiwasse** AR.

Hiyu Mountain OR Chinook jargon for 'big.'

Hoard WV From the name of a pioneer family.

Hobbomoc, Hobbomocka See **Hobomak.**

Hobe Sound FL An Indian name of uncertain meaning, possibly tribal, recorded from the 17th century, with English forms such as Hobay and Hoe. The English later assumed it to be Spanish *Jobe* or *Jove,* the Roman god, and sometimes rendered it as **Jupiter,** thus producing this name in the same region.

Hobo The term, dating from ca. 1880, has been used to describe features in some way associated with an itinerant worker or tramp, e.g. **Hobo Lake** OR, because a 'hobo,' once camped there. **Hobo Hot Springs** CA: some workmen who camped there committed some depredations on the neighboring farms, soon after 1900, and were referred to, derogatorily, as hoboes.

Hoboken NJ The name of a village in Belgium, close to the Dutch border, was bestowed by Dutch settlers, but probably by the process of folk-etymology from an Algonquian term, 'tobacco-pipe,' because the site served as a quarry for stone from which pipes could be made.

Hobolochitto Creek MS Choctaw, with *chitto,* 'big,' and the rest (?) from *haboli,* 'abate, subside.'

Hobomak, Hobbomoc, Hobbomocka Algonquian, with reference to an evil spirit (cf. **Medicine, Wakan**) or the idea of a place being haunted; by the colonists taken to be 'the Indian devil,' e.g. several features in New England.

Hochatown OK The Muskogean 'river,' joined with English *town.*

Hochheim TX For Valentine Hoch, early settler, with German 'home.' Since *hoch means* 'high,' the whole is really 'high home.'

Hockamick NJ Algonquian, probably 'hook-shaped-place.' Cf. **Hockanum.**

Hockanum, Hockamock, Hocquan Algonquian, from the general idea of being hook-shaped.

Hockendauqua Creek PA Algonquian (Delaware). The first syllable is 'land,' and the latter part involves the idea of 'searching, coming for.' It may indicate a place where the colonists negotiated for land.

Hockessin DE Probably English *occasion,* applied to a Quaker meetinghouse, shaped to a pseudo-Indian form after the original and unusual meaning was forgotten.

Hockhockson NJ Algonquian, probably 'field, plantation.'

Hocking OH Algonquian, originally the river-name, a badly shifted form with earlier spellings **Hockhocking** and **Hocking Hocking,** the last translatable as 'above-there-is-(arable)-land,' with apparent reference to Indian fields near the headwaters.

Hocquan See **Hockanum.**

Hodchodkee Creek GA Muskogean (Creek) 'home-little.'

Hodzana River AK Athapascan 'male-beaver-river.'

Hoevet OK For C. R. Hoevet, local mill-owner.

Hog Though the common name for a common animal, its use as a place-name is infrequent. **Hog Island** occurs most often, indicating an island where swine were turned loose. The derogatory suggestions have been sufficient to keep it from being a habitation-name, and even the personal name Hogg does not so appear. **Hogback:** originating as a generic for a narrow ridge, the word has come into use as a specific in many combinations, e.g. **Hogback Ridge, Hogback Peak,** and has been transferred to yield **Hogback Creek,** etc. It also appears alone as **The Hogback. Hog Mountains** UT: a shortening from **Hogback.**

Hog-Eye An early derogatory habitation-name, probably based upon the small size of a pig's eye. See **Haggai.**

Hoggenoch NY By a mistake in spelling (1686) for **Hog Neck.**

Hoh River WA Indian, probably a tribal name.

Hohen Solms LA A settlement of Germans (ca. 1850) and apparently a German name, with *hohen,* 'high,' and the rest uncertain.

Hohenwald TN German 'high-forest,' named by Swiss immigrants.

Hohokus NJ From a tribal name (?).

Hoholitna River AK Athapascan 'sudden (unexpected)-river.'

Hokah MN Siouan 'root,' of which **Root River** is a translation; in form the word has become that of the Siouan 'crane,' and it is also the name of a Siouan chief, for whom the village was probably named directly.

Hokenduaqua PA Algonquian 'land-measuring,' probably named by the Indians because of the work of surveyors.

Hoko River WA Indian, of uncertain meaning.

Holanna Creek GA Muskogean (Creek), probably 'potatoes-yellow.'

Holden Regularly from a personal name, e.g. in MA (1740) for Samuel Holden, philanthropist.

Holderness NH Named by Gov. Benning Wentworth in 1751 for his friend, the Earl of Holderness.

Hole As a generic (now generally obsolete) the term means 1) a cove or small inlet of water, e.g. **Wood's Hole** MA, or 2) a low place surrounded by hills, and extended in the West to mean an isolated mountain valley, e.g. **Jackson Hole** WY. Though specifics have thus arisen, the commoner specific describes a place associated with a natural hole in the more limited sense, and generally in one of a few phrases, e.g. **Hole-in-the-Wall-Falls** MT, **Hole in the Rock Hill** AZ, **Hole in the Rock Spring** CA. Depressions are sometimes known simply as **The-Hole-in-the-Ground,** e.g. in OR.

Hole-in-the-Day's Bluff MN: because an Ojibway chief so named was buried at its top. **Big Hole River** MT: because it flows through a big hole, i.e. isolated valley.

Holetah Creek AL Choctaw 'fort.'

Holicong PA Algonquian, meaning uncertain.

Holiness Creek NB From the religious tendencies of early settlers.

Holitna River AK Athapascan, uncertain, but probably the same as **Honolina River,** which is a tributary.

Holland 1) From the personal name or title, e.g. in MA (1783) for Charles James Fox, Lord Holland, who defended American rights in Parliament. 2) From the province (or, more commonly, from the name used as the equivalent of Netherlands) generally applied because of a settlement of immigrants, e.g. MI (1847), NB (1867), MN (1888, 1898).

Hollow It is commonly a generic, but becomes a specific by association, e.g. **Hollow Brook** MA. In its adjectival use it is occasionally a descriptive specific, e.g. **Hollow Rock** TN, **Hollow Poplar** KY. As a rare personal name it has yielded **Hollowtown** OH for Anthony Hollow, early storekeeper.

Holly Aided by its Christmas associations, the native holly has given names to many natural features in the southeastern states, where it most typically grows, e.g. **Holly Springs, Hill, Grove.** Its pleasant suggestions have made it favored as a habitation-name. In CA true holly is not native, but the toyon was often so called. **Hollywood:** the name is an obvious one for a thicket of holly or some place near one, and soon after the time of settlement was spread across the southeastern states for villages and plantations. In 1887 Mr. and Mrs. H. H. Wilcox gave the name to a town-site that they had laid out in CA, probably borrowing it from one of the southern examples. **Holly** MN: for J. Z. Holly, early settler.

Holm Early English 'island,' e.g. in the romantic coinage **Braeholm.** It is rare, but occurs in some names derived from personal names or transferred directly from England or Scandinavia, e.g. **Stockholm.**

Holopaw FL Seminole, probably from the word, 'haul, draw,' but reference uncertain.

Holstein From the district in Germany.

Holston From the personal name, e.g. the river (VA, TN) for Stephen Holston, who built a cabin on the stream in 1746.

Holy In CA a religious community gave the name **Holy City. Holy Joe Peak** AZ: for a prospector who was so called because of being highly religious; his full name is not recorded. **Holy Jim Canyon** CA: given ironically for a local beekeeper, commonly known as 'Cussin' Jim.' **Mount of the Holy Cross** CO: from certain vantage points and at certain times a cross of snow appears on the side of the mountain; named in 1869 by a party which saw this cross.

Holyoke From the personal name; the city in MA is for either (or both) Elizur, an early settler, or Edward, president of Harvard.

Holyrood KS For the royal castle in Edinburgh, Scotland.

Home Sometimes for a personal name, e.g. **Home Lake** MN for John Homelvig, early resident. Usually a commendatory name for habitations, often as **Homeland, Homewood, Homeplace, Homestead.** The last may originate from the common sentimental use of that term, or in western states, e.g. OR, is connected with the legal use of the term in the later 19th century. In PA, **Homestead** originated from the name of a bank, which itself had doubtless been named for commendatory purposes. **Home** CO, originally **Mountain Home,** took the shorter form when a post office was established, because of duplication of the longer form. **Homes Hill** NY: from Algonquian *homes,* 'old-man,' for an old Indian, his name recorded in 1663. **Home on the Range** WY: a sentimental, commendatory naming, from the refrain line of a popular song.

Homer In NY for the ancient poet, given as a part of the classical naming of 1790. In many other states either for that poet or from the personal name. **Homers Nose** CA: for Joseph Homer, early surveyor, the projection having been laughingly compared to his nose.

Homestake Used chiefly for mines but also for habitations, e.g. in MT; the name springs from use of the word to denote a rich stake or treasure, generally explained as one rich enough to enable a man to go home.

Hominy As a common though homely article of diet, especially in the South, the name has been placed on a few features, probably because hominy was made there or because of some incident. In OK it is locally believed to be a modification of **Harmony,** from a mission. **Hominy Creek** GA: probably by a mistranslation of a Muskogean term 'deep,' the words for 'deep' and 'hominy' being much alike.

Homo A variant of Muskogean *houma, homa,* 'red,' e.g. in **Big Bogue Homo** MS.

Homochitto River MS Choctaw 'redbig.'

Homosassa River FL From the name of an Indian town, probably Seminole 'pepper-is-there,' because of the growth of wild pepper.

Hondo Spanish 'deep.' When coupled with *rio* or *arroyo* the form *hondo* would occur in Spanish, and **Hondo** CA preserves this form in **Rio Hondo.** But **La Honda** and **Honda** (both, CA) have shifted to the feminine form, apparently because of the American feeling that place-names more properly end in *a* than in *o.*

Honea Path SC Of Indian origin, probably from a word meaning 'path,' a curious example of a name both taken by sound and translated at the same time.

Honeoye NY Ironquoian 'finger-lying,' traditionally believed to spring from an incident in which an Indian, bitten by a snake, cut his finger off.

Honey Often from a personal name. **Honeyman** OR: for the family name of a local landowner. **Honeyville** OK: for Honey Salmon, daughter of the first postmaster. Usually the name indicates a place where wild honey was to be found or an incident involving wild honey occurred. **Honey Lake** CA: named not for actual honey, but for the secretions of the aphis, which were used by the Indians as a sweet and were found plentifully near the lake. **Honey Grove** TX: named in 1836 by David Crockett because he found wild honey in one of the trees. **Honey Island** TX: a place much frequented by hunters for wild honey. **Honey Hill** SC: an early settler purchased some land by payments of honey, and gave the name. **Honey Creek** OR: named in 1864 by some cavalrymen who found a sweet substance on the willow leaves near the stream. **Honey Brook** PA: a translation of the Welsh Nantmeal. **Honey Creek** NB: from the honey locust tree.

Honeymoon Island WY From being the place of the fictional honeymoon in Owen Wister's *Virginian.*

Honga River MD Probably Algonquian 'goose,' but it may also be a tribal name. Cf. **Hungars, Hungary.**

Honk Falls NY Probably Algonquian, from *hannek,* 'stream,' being what is left of some longer name.

Honnedaga NY Iroquoian 'hilly-place.'

Hood Regularly from the personal name, especially for Lord Samuel Hood, British admiral, e.g. the mountain in OR and **Hood Canal** WA, both named by George Vancouver in 1792.

Hoodoo A term not much in use before 1870, though **Hoodoo Bar** CA may date from the 1850's. Since the term is late, few names result. Generally they indicate that a place has bad luck attached to it in some way, though the association is humorous as often as serious. **Hoodoo Spring** OR was applied in 1907 by a forest ranger, because of poor trails and doubtless of some repeated bad luck that he encountered on them. As a separate usage **Hoodoo Rocks** is used to denote fantastically carved pinnacles in various parts of the West, especially in Yellowstone N. P.

Hook 1) From the personal name, e.g. **Hooks** TX for Warren Hooks, landowner. 2) In DE, NJ, and NY from Dutch *hoek,* 'angle,' but in America used topographically as 'point.' The generic was absorbed to the English spelling and also confused with the English word in meaning, so that it was generally considered a specific to which an English generic was added to produce names of the pattern **Bombay Hook Point** DE. It also is a specific in some habitation-names, e.g. **Marcus Hook** PA, and rarely by association, e.g. **Hook Brook** NJ. 3) From a hooklike shape, e.g. **Hook Arm** AK.

Hooksett NH A shortening of **Annahooksett,** q.v.

Hoonah AK From an Indian tribal name.

Hoop Lake MN Like a hoop, it surrounds a central island.

Hoopa CA Klamath, of unknown meaning.

Hoosac MA, NH, VT Algonquian, meaning uncertain. Also as **Hoosick, Hooksic.**

Hoosier From the appellation of a person from Indiana, e.g. **Hoosier Creek** NB.

Hoozaw River MO From an adaptation of the Indian tribal name, known in the commoner spelling as **Osage.**

Hop From the presence of wild hops, e.g. the mountain in AZ; from the cultivation of hops, e.g. **Hopland** CA, with commendatory suggestions.

Hopatcong, Lake NJ Algonquian, meaning uncertain.

Hope It may be either from a personal name ID, OR or a commendatory name expressing hope for the future MN, OK. The common **Hopewell** is commendatory, but may also be from a personal name, e.g. in MN for W. S. Hopewell, miner and rancher. **Hope Valley** CA:

named by a party of Mormons in 1848 who were crossing the mountains toward the east and began to have hope when they entered this valley. **Mount Hope:** though a commendatory in several states, the earliest, in RI, is a folk-etymology from the Algonquian **Montop,** q.v. **Marshyhope Creek** DE: the term is here preserved in its older English use, 'small bay.' **Point Hope** AK: named (1826) for Sir William Johnstone Hope, English merchant.

Hopi From the Indian tribal name.

Hopkinton From the personal name, in MA for Edward Hopkins, benefactor of Harvard College, who died in 1713 (named, 1715).

Hoppeny Creek PA Algonquian (Delaware) 'potatoes-at,' but probably for some native plant whose roots the Indian used for food, rather than for any of the domesticated potatoes. See **Potato.**

Hoppow Creek CA From the name of a Yurok village.

Hoquiam River WA Indian 'driftwood' (?).

Horace The popularity of Horace Greeley (See **Greeley**) was such that his first name was pressed into service for towns in KS, NB, and ND.

Horeb Usually as **Mount Horeb** (e.g. in WI), from the Biblical mountain.

Horicon Originally an Indian tribal name, but applied by J. F. Cooper in *The Last of the Mohicans* to **Lake George** NY. It has since been adopted as a habitation-name.

Horn Rare, and generally from the personal name. See **Cape Horn.**

Hornblende Mountains CA Because of the occurrence of the mineral of that name.

Hornbrook CA Named in 1886 because a small stream here ran through the property of David Horn.

Horno Spanish 'oven.' **Hornos** NM: for charcoal ovens used from ca. 1880 to 1920. **Hornitos** CA: the diminutive, but reason for naming unknown.

Horrid, Mount VT Probably a derogatory to reflect an unpleasant experience of the namers (cf. **Hungry, Terrible,** etc.), but the word may have been used in the older sense, 'bristling, rough.'

Horse The horse has given its name to an extraordinary number of natural features. These are commoner in the West than in the East, since the West was more specifically horse-country. The names indicate places where horses were kept or pastured, or else places where some incident occurred. In spite of the honor in which the horse has been held, few habitation names occur. The commonest name is **Horse Creek,** and every western state has a half-dozen or more; horses were commonly pastured along creeks, where grass and water were available. Also to be found are **Horse Mountain, Horse Lick, Horse Pond, Horse Island,** and almost every possible combination. **Horsefall Canyon** AZ: about 1900 a horse went off the trail here, and was killed. **Horsehead** CA: the skull of a horse was to be seen along the trail here for many years. **Horseheads** NY: named in 1845 to commemorate an incident in the Revolutionary War when some soldiers killed their horses for food, and left the heads piled up. **Horse Heaven (Haven):** a name given in parts of the West to a spot, considered to be attractive to horses. It occurs also as a specific, e.g. **Horse Heaven Creek** OR. **Horse Linto** CA: by folk-etymology from the name of an Indian (Hupa) village of unexplained meaning, spelled Haslintah. **Horse-thief:** the name is common in the West (20 estimated for CA), denoting a creek, canyon, etc., frequented by horse thieves or remembered for an incident, such as a hanging. **Horseshoe** has two meanings: 1) a place shaped like a horseshoe, especially a railroad line or a stream; 2) a place where an incident involving a horseshoe occurred, e.g. the finding of a cast shoe. **Horsefoot** NB: a brand name. **Horse Leg Lake** MN: from its shape. **Horsehead Crossing** TX: since this was in hard desert country, many animals died here, and the ford came to be marked by horse skulls. **Horsethief Butte** MI: from an early encounter in which several people were killed.

Hosapa Creek SD Siouan, referring to some kind of fish.

Hosesack Creek PA Algonquian, a variant of **Hoosac** (?).

Hoskinnini Mesa UT From the name of a Navajo headman.

Hospilika Creek AL Muskogean (Creek) 'yaupon-trees-place.'

Hospital The name has been avoided for habitations, as of unpleasant suggestion. **Hospital Lake** NB: because the area was used as a calving ground. **Hospital Rock**, Sequoia N. P., CA: because a man in 1863, hurt in a hunting accident, found shelter here. **Hospital Rock**, Modoc Co., CA: used as a temporary hospital by soldiers in the Modoc War of the 1870's.

Hosselkus Creek CA From the family name of the early settlers.

Hosta Butte NM From the personal name of the Jemez Indian who guided one of the early American explorers.

Hostility Branch TN By local story, because the locality was so rough as to seem hostile.

Hot A descriptive applied usually to water-features, especially **Hot Springs.** Since in most parts of the U.S. hot springs are not common, the term serves as a specific. Where hot springs are common, an additional specific has to be used, often with a personal name because of ownership, e.g. **Fales Hot Springs** CA. **Hot Creek** CA: a large hot spring turns it warm, though above this point the name is a misnomer, because the stream is cold there. **Hot Rock** CA: at the time of the Lassen volcanic eruption in 1915 this rock was part of the *ejecta* and remained hot for some time, so that the name has remained on it permanently. **Hot Lake** OR: the whole lake is warmed by a nearby hot spring. **Hot Coffee** MS: from a wayside store where exceptionally good coffee was served. **Hot Spot** KY: from the name of a coal company.

Hotason Vo AZ Papago 'rocky hill-foot pond.'

Hotevila AZ Hopi 'scraped back,' from a spring in a cave with an entrance so low as to cause the back to be scraped.

Hotouta Canyon AZ From a Havasupai personal name.

Houlka Creek MS Choctaw, probably 'sacred.'

Houma In LA it is from a tribal name; literally, Muskogean 'red.'

Housatonic Algonquian 'beyond-mountain-at,' probably for a definite place beyond the mountain, from which the river later was named by association.

House As the first element of a name it is rare, and regularly from the personal name, e.g. **House** NM, the family name of some early settlers. As **Red House**, etc. it is commoner, and usually of obvious origin. **House Creek** GA: by association with a house, as shown by the earlier name **Old House Creek.** **House Mountains** UT: named (1859) by Capt. J. H. Simpson, because the rock formations suggested buildings. **House Mountains** TX: a long ridge here suggests the outline of a house.

Houston From the personal name, e.g. in OH and NB for early settlers. Often, e.g. in TX, for Samuel Houston, first president of the Republic of Texas.

Hovenweep UT Ute, with *weep*, 'valley, canyon,' and the rest probably 'deserted.'

Howey in the Hills FL A commendatory, based on the name of the town founder, W. J. Howey.

Howling Usually, e.g. **Howling Dog Rock** AK commemorative of some incident involving sled-dogs' propensity to howl when disturbed.

Howlock Mountain OR For a Paiute chief, who lived nearby, named in 1916.

Hoypus Point WA Indian, recorded from 1841, meaning uncertain.

Huachuca AZ The name of a Pima Indian village, of unknown meaning.

Hualapai Canyon AZ From the Indian tribal name.

Huasna CA Chumash, probably the name of a village.

Hub As the equivalent of 'center, central point,' e.g. **The Hub** DE, **Hub City** SD, usually with a humorous idea of the place as 'the hub of the universe.'

Hubbard From the personal name, e.g. **Mount Hubbard** AK named (1890) by I. C. Russell for G. G. Hubbard, president of the National Geographic Society, which had helped finance Russell's expedition.

Huckleberry A common name on features to denote those where the berries may be found. It has been rejected for habitation-names, perhaps because of its inconsequential sound and suggestion.

Huddleston VA By misspelling from Henry Huttleston Rogers, financier of the Virginian Railroad; named in 1910, on his death.

Hudson From the personal name, the most notable example being **Hudson River,** named for Henry Hudson because of his exploration in 1609, and fixed upon the stream by English usage, as opposed to various names given by the Dutch. **Hudson** MA: for Charles Hudson, a local benefactor (1795–1881). **Hudson** OK: for L. G. Huddleston, local merchant, but modified—by the Post Office Dept., according to local tradition. **Hudson Bay Creek** MT: because its water flows eventually into Hudson Bay. **Hudson Bay** OR: a flat tract of land where the Hudson's Bay Company grazed stock ca. 1850.

Hueco In American-Spanish it generally has the meaning 'water hole, boggy place'; so, **Hueco** NM. In **Hueco Mountains** TX it means 'notched.'

Hueneme CA Indian (Chumash) 'place-where-one sleeps (rests),' because a halfway point between the two chief Chumash towns.

Huerfano Spanish 'orphan.' This is used for a feature standing by itself, and is thus the equivalent of 'lone,' e.g. the butte in AZ.

Huerhuero Springs CA Probably of Indian origin, but influenced in form by the Spanish *huero,* 'rotten,' perhaps with reference to sulphur water.

Hug Point OR It is necessary to 'hug' the rocks in order to get around the point without getting wet.

Hugo From the personal name, e.g. in CO for Hugo Richards, pioneer. In OK named by the wife of the town founder for Victor Hugo, French author (1901).

Huguenot NY For the French Protestants, many of whom settled in New Netherland.

Huichica CA Probably Pomo, the name of an Indian village.

Hulah OK Probably Osage 'eagle.'

Hull In MA (1644) from a town in England. Also a family name, e.g. **Hull** TX for W. F. Hull, prominent in local railroad affairs.

Humberg Valley CA In an early record it appears as **Humbug,** and was probably changed later for commendatory purposes. See **Humbug.**

Humboldt The German traveler and writer Alexander von Humboldt enjoyed great fame during the middle of the 19th century, when both the river in NV and the bay in CA were so named; so also, habitation-names in KS, MN, and SD, and the peak in CO. Also as **Humbolt.**

Humbolt A simplified spelling of **Humboldt,** e.g. in IL where it is for Alexander von Humboldt (1875).

Humbug A popular 19th-century phrase, e.g. in Dickens's *Christmas Carol,* the term was placed on features to indicate some kind of sham or imposition, especially for a mine or bar which promised to be rich and proved not to be. The application was often in humor. The exact reasons for the naming vary considerably, e.g. **Humbug Mountain OR,** named because a surveying party made a mistake. **Humbug Point** OR: named because people trying to reach the next point along the coast were deceived by this one into thinking that they were already there.

Hummock Pond MA From the Nantucket chief, Nana Humacke.

Humoro AL From Hugh Morrow, prominent in the affairs of a local coal company.

Hump A descriptive with hills and mountains, e.g. **The Hump** AK, **Hump Mountain** WV, **Hump Butte** SD. **Humpback** may be an equivalent, but **Humpback Creek** AK is so called for being a spawning ground of the humpback salmon. **Hump Creek** SD is from the translated name of the Sioux chief.

Humptulips River WA Indian, shaped by folk-etymology to the likeness of an English name, meaning uncertain.

Hunchback Mountain CO From its appearance.

Hundred In WV, by local tradition, named for Henry Church who lived here and reached the age of 109, his wife reaching 106; once called **Old Hundred,** probably under the influence of the hymn so named. **Old Hundred** NC is from being at the 100-mile post on the railroad, the **Old** being probably sentimental, from the hymn. Occasionally, e.g. **Bermuda Hundred** VA, the name is a former term for a division of a county. Commonly for distance, e.g. **Hundred and Ten Mile Creek** KS, as a measurement from the beginning of the Santa Fe Trail. See **One Hundred and One, One Hundred and Forty Mile. Hundred Thousand Creek** AK: of unknown origin, but probably setting the record for numeral names.

Hungars Creek See **Honga.**

Hungary Since contacts with the European country have not been numerous, such a name as **Hungary Creek** VA is probably a variant of the commoner **Hungry,** or may be by folk-etymology from **Honga.** In MD and VA the name

may be derived by folk-etymology from **Honga.** So also, **Hungry Mother Creek** MO is from an Osage title recorded as *Honga Monthnka* and in other forms, and the same name in NC is probably derived in similar fashion.

Hunger Hill MA Probably from a personal name, but see **Hungry.**

Hungry Generally an incident name, recording where some early Americans got hungry; it need not be taken as implying starvation. It may also indicate, derogatorily, a place where people were supposed to go chronically hungry, e.g. **Hungry Hill** OR, which was a poor mining district. It may also be from a nickname, e.g. **Hungry Jack Lake** MN and **Hungry Bills Ranch** CA. Alliteration has helped the proliferation of **Hungry Hollow,** which has itself become a specific in **Hungry Hollow Gulch** SD. **Hungry Harbor** WA: alliteration is an aid here, but the incident is uncertain.

Hunkpapa, Hunk Pa-Pa For the Indian tribe.

Hunt From the personal name, e.g. **Huntsville** AL for John Hunt, early settler. **Huntsville** TX was named by an early settler for his former home in AL.

Hunter Most of the examples are from the personal name. Some places were so called because they were frequented by hunters or were associated with a particular hunter. **Hunters Cove, Island** OR: said, on late authority, to have been frequented by sea-otter hunters, 'in early days.' **Mount Hunter** AK: named (1903) by Robert Dunn for his aunt, Miss Anna Falconer Hunter, who had helped finance his trip and to whom he was much devoted. The original naming was on another peak.

Hunterdon County NJ From Robert Hunter (1714), governor of New York and New Jersey, with the *-don* probably from analogy with the English county-name **Huntingdon.**

Hunting Sometimes a personal name, but also used to indicate a place known for good hunting or to commemorate a fortunate hunt, e.g. **Hunting Island** SC.

Huntingdon PA From the Countess of Huntingdon, a benefactress of the colony.

Huntington Regularly from the personal name, in particular for C. P. Huntington, railroad magnate (e.g. the city in WV), and from his equally rich nephew Henry E. (e.g. several towns in CA).

Hurdygurdy The term was used in the 19th century for a kind of waterwheel, sometimes used in mining. The creek in CA is probably thus derived.

Hurlwood TX For C. B. Hurlbut and W. M. Woods, early settlers.

Huron From the Indian tribe. In form the word is French, and may even be *huron,* 'rough, bristly person.' **Lake Huron** was first called by the French **Mer Douce,** 'sea-fresh' in the 17th century, but soon became **Lac des Hurons,** from which the English form is a natural development.

Hurrican A variant of **Hurricane,** q.v.

Hurricane Describes a place marked by downed trees or other evidence of high wind, or else commemorates a wind experienced there by the namers, e.g. **Hurricane Creek** KS, so named from a storm in May, 1859. A hurricane in the strict meteorological sense need not be assumed. In spite of derogatory suggestions there are several habitation-names. **Hurricane Deck** CA: a high wind-swept area, thus fancifully named.

Hurst Commonly from the personal name; sometimes in combination, e.g. **Hazelhurst.** It is also used as a second element from its Anglo-Saxon meaning 'hill, wooded hill,' being preserved in many English place-names. It was revived in the early 19th century as a commendatory for habitations, usually with little regard for its geographical accuracy, being often coupled with tree-names, e.g. **Oakhurst, Pinehurst.** As a commendatory it has the ideas of height and of English exclusiveness.

Hurst-Bush IL From W. C. Hurst and B. F. Bush, railroad officials.

Hustler WI In 1891 the citizens, unable to agree, sent to the Post Office Dept. a list of names, and this one was chosen, though it had been inserted at the end as a kind of joke. It is probably to be taken as a commendatory, to indicate an energetic person, such as the town was hoped to be; the derogatory suggestions of the term seem to have arisen later.

Hutchinson From the personal name. In KS, for C. C. Hutchinson town founder (1871). In MN, for the Hutchinson brothers, who founded the settlement in 1855.

Huxagulbee Creek Muskogean, of uncertain meaning.

Huxley From the personal name, sometimes given by scientists to natural features to honor T. H. Huxley, the English evolutionist, e.g. **Mount Huxley AK, CA.**

Huzzah Creek MO By folk-etymology from the Indian tribal name, known commonly in the spelling **Osage.**

Hyak WA Chinook jargon, 'hurry,' but reference unknown.

Hyampon CA Wintu, containing *pom,* 'land, place,' but the rest unknown.

Hyannis MA From the name of a local chief in the 17th century.

Hyco VA A shortening of **Hycotee,** which is nearby.

Hycootee Branch VA Siouan (Saponi), from *hico-oto-moni,* 'turkey-buzzard-river.' See **Hyco, Hico, Highco.**

Hydaburg AK From Haida, the tribal name of the local Indians.

Hyde From the personal name, but usually, as **Hyde Park,** a commendatory name for habitations because of the stylish and metropolitan suggestions of that park in London. **Hyde Villa** PA is apparently a double commendatory.

Hydro OK From the abundance of its well water (1901).

Hygeia The Greek goddess of health has been occasionally invoked, e.g. **Mount Hygeia** RI.

Hygiene CO From a sanatorium, built ca. 1880, called Hygiene House.

Hyko See **Hiko.**

Hylas MI, VA From the figure in Greek mythology.

Hymel LA A local French adaptation of the German family name Himmel, for an early settler.

Hymer KS Originally **Hegwer,** because on land owned by Frank and George Hegwer; the changed spelling probably resulted from a postal clerk's error because of poor handwriting.

Hymera IN By local account, named by the postmaster for his tall daughter, known as High Mary; a connection with the name of the ancient Greek city Himera is possible.

Hypocrites, The ME From an Algonquian term recorded as *epituse,* of unknown meaning, transformed by folk-etymology into **Hyppocras Island,** for *hippocras,* a spiced wine. When that kind of wine became no longer common, a further shift was made, again by folk-etymology.

Hypoluxo FL Seminole 'heap-round' (?).

Hyponeco Brook NH Algonquian 'on-both-sides-of-falls.'

I

Iago TX Locally believed to be from the character in Shakespeare's *Othello,* though why anyone should name a town for a villain is uncertain. Since Iago is a personal name in Italian, it may have another origin than the play.

Iamonia FL From the name of an ancient Seminole town; meaning uncertain.

Iaqua Buttes CA Probably from *Ay-a-qui-ya,* a salutation used by the local Indians.

Iatan MO Probably from the name of an Indian chief.

Iatt, Lake LA From the Indian tribal name, much shortened, more commonly spelled Hietan.

Iberia From an ancient name, used as a rough equivalent of **Spain. New Iberia** LA: from a settlement of Spaniards, made here during the Spanish regime.

Iberville In LA the name commemorates P. Le Moyne, Sieur d'Iberville (1661–1706), 'the first great Canadian,' founder of the French colony in Louisiana.

Ibex From the name of the European wild goat sometimes applied to the mountain sheep, e.g. **Ibex Peak** AZ. **Ibex** TX: from the Ibex Oil Company.

Ibipah UT Shoshonean 'clay (or clay-colored) spring.'

Ibis CA From a mine thus named for unknown reasons.

Icaria CA Founded as a community of the Icarians, the followers of the doctrines of Etienne Cabet.

Ice It may be from a personal name, e.g. **Ice's Ferry** WV for Frederick Ice, who settled there in 1767. **Ice Mountain** (3 in WV): in one instance the naming is for the same Frederick Ice, who was living there when his wife was killed and his children captured by Indians. Another instance may be from the presence of what is sometimes known as a natural refrigerator, where ice may be found at all times of year. From such circumstances **Ice Cave** occurs widely, as a quasi-generic. **Ice Slough** WY: pioneers found ice here, a foot or so beneath the surface, even in summer. **Ice Creek** AK: since ice is common in this area, the origin is probably a personal name or an incident. **Iceberg Lake** MT, CA: floating masses of ice, though much too small to be true icebergs, originated the name. **The Iceberg** CA: a prominent gray rock suggested an iceberg, and the name spread by transfer to a meadow and a peak. **Icehouse Canyon** AZ: ice was sold here. **Iceland** CA is a railroad name probably given 'for no particular reason.' **Iceberg Point** WA: because of glacial striations. **Ice Lake** CO: ice was once harvested here.

Ichawaynochaway Creek GA Probably by partial folk-etymology from a Muskogean (Creek) 'deer-sleep.'

Ichusa Creek MS Choctaw 'river-little.'

Ickes Slough Of record in 1940 and being near **Roosevelt Island,** it is probably for H. L. Ickes, secretary of the interior (1933–1946); this is one of a few namings for him, and his coupling with a slough may be significant in view of his notable disinclination to cultivate personal popularity.

Iconium From the city mentioned in the New Testament. In OK it is chiefly a Negro settlement, and is locally believed to have been named when a Negro preacher opened his Bible at random and came upon the name.

Ida Commonly from the woman's name; the county in IA was suggested by a local politician with an interest in naming, and is probably from Mount Ida, known from Greek mythology. **Mont Ida** KS: for a daughter of Dr. Broomhall (not further identified), the town founder, with an obvious echo of the mountain. So also **Mount Ida,** e.g. in AR.

Idabel OK For Ida and Belle Purnell, daughters of a railroad official (1904).

Idaho The Kiowa-Apache name for the Comanche is recorded as Idahi, a form from which **Idaho** may be considered to be derived since it appeared first in the region which is now **Colorado,** where both the Kiowa-Apache and the Comanche were well known. Early in 1860 **Idaho(e)** was strongly urged in Congress as the name for the new territory (what is now **Colorado**). In the same year it was applied to the settlement which is now **Idaho Springs** CO. Although its origin remained obscure, it was a name which appealed to people, who probably found it euphonic. In 1861 it was applied to a county in **Washington Territory.** When this region was organized as a territory in 1863, **Montana** was first proposed, but **Idaho** was substituted in the Senate, and the name was thus finally placed upon the region which became the state.

Idahome ID Coined from *Idaho* and *home.*

Idak AK Aleut, probably 'outlet.'

Idalia In MO, probably for the daughter of a local landowner. In CO a simplified form of the name of the wife of a town founder, Edaliah Helmick.

Idalou TX For Ida Bassett and Lou Bacon, wives of the two men who were involved with the foundation of the town.

Idamay WV For Ida May Watson, local resident.

Idana KS From the first names of Ida Howland and Anna Broughton, the wives of the men who founded the town in 1879.

Ideal A rare commendatory for habitations, e.g. GA, MN, VA.

Iditarod AK From the name of an Indian village; meaning uncertain.

Idlewild An American variant of **Idyllwild** (q.v.), a commendatory name for a resort, suggesting vacation and unspoiled nature.

Idria CA From the city, now in Yugoslavia, famous for its mercury production; the same metal was mined here. The Italian form of the name is used.

Idyllwild A commendatory name for a resort, suggesting unspoiled nature and something idyllic. See **Idlewild.**

Igloo Various places in AK take the name, either from the presence of an Eskimo snowhouse, or from a resemblance to one.

Igo Since *-ico, -igo* are common Algonquian endings, the name in VA may merely represent all that is left of some Indian name. In CA the name (especially, because of its coupling with nearby **Ono**) has caused much speculation and a proliferation of stories. Though it may have arisen because someone said 'I go!' no story has been authenticated. There is also the family name Igo.

Ikpikpuk River AK Eskimo 'big-cliff.'

Ikt Butte OR Chinook jargon, 'one.' The men of the Forest Service named several buttes in a numbered sequence.

Ilamna AK Probably Eskimo and the name of a mythical fish said to bite holes in boats, first applied to the lake.

Ilasco MO Named by a local cement company for the mineral elements iron, lead, aluminum, silicon, calcium, and oxygen.

Ile French *île,* island, isle,' in earlier periods usually appearing as *isle* even in French contexts. See Isle. In the French of the Mississippi Valley, it acquired the meaning 'grove'; hence, **Isle au Bois Creek** MO.

Ilion NY From the Greek form of the alternate name for Troy in the *Iliad,* named ca. 1800 in a period and area where classical names were popular.

Illahaw FL Based upon Seminole *valaha,* 'orange (the fruit),' a name given by Americans in the early 20th century.

Illahe Chinook jargon, 'earth, country,' applied to a post office and several features in OR. Such a general term is usually a shortening from some more specific term once in use.

Illapah Spring NV Shoshone, with *illa,* probably 'rock,' and *pah,* 'spring.'

Illilouette CA From a Miwok word, variously spelled, e.g. Tululowehack, which is reported to have been a term that would not bear translation. The present form may only indicate the difficulty of transcribing words from a foreign language, or it may be a conscious attempt at euphony.

Illinois From the name of a tribe, in a form transmitted through the French. The final consonant is the sign of the French plural. Like many tribal names, Illinois means 'men.' Its route of application has been tribe-river-district-county (Virginia)–territory-state.

Illkinask Creek AL Choctaw 'English town.'

Illmo MO A border name, from the traditional abbreviations of IL and MO.

Illumination Rock OR Named because of an illumination held on July 4, 1887.

Ilwaco WA For El-wah-ko Jim, a local Indian.

Ima NM For Ima Moncus, daughter of the first postmaster.

Image WA From **Image Canoe Island,** so named by the Lewis and Clark expedition in 1805, because of Indian evidences there.

Immaculata PA For the college founded there in 1908 by Sisters of the Order of the Immaculate Heart of Mary.

Immokalee FL, GA Cherokee 'water-tumbling.'

Imnaha River OR Probably *Imna,* the name of an Indian chief, and *ha,* indicating his country.

Imola CA From the city in Italy, because the site was to be devoted to a hospital for mental patients, and the Italian city was also so favored.

Imp Mountain NH From a rock formation appearing to be a grotesque profile, known as **Imp Face.**

Imperial A commendatory name, occasionally used for habitations or developments, often having been first a company name, e.g. **Imperial PA** from a coal company, and in WV from a glass-sand company. **Imperial Valley CA:** though the developing company used this name, it is really a commendatory term for the valley itself, in an attempt to escape the previous name, **Colorado Desert;** the name became that of the county in 1907; from CA the name spread to TX, and probably to OR.

Inabnit, Mount MT For Fred Inabnit, who worked to create public interest in the local mountains.

Inadale TX For Inadale Wooten, daughter of a railroad official.

Inavale NB A descriptive phrase, the 'vale' being the valley of the Republican River.

Inch Creek OR So named because it was about an inch long on an early map.

Inclinado Spanish 'inclined, sloping.'

Independence It is either 1) commendatory, patriotic, and idealistic, or 2) commemorative of a place named on July 4. The former is the usual one with habitation names, and about 20 exist. In TX the town was named in 1836, and commemorates independence from Mexico. Natural features are those named on or near July 4, as with **Independence Rock WY, Independence Lake CA.**

Index The butte in SD and the mountin in WA were named because rock formations suggested a pointing index finger. The peak in WY was named ca. 1870 because it resembles a closed hand with the first finger extended.

Indiahoma OK Coined from Indian and **Oklahoma** (1902).

Indian Many hundreds of these names exist. Even though the name suggests a lack of civilization, it occurs in many habitation-names, in most instances a transfer from a natural feature. Many stories are current, generally explaining the names by a hostile encounter with Indians. But the generalized and vague nature of the name suggests, rather, places where Indians were known to have lived or where they left traces. Again, the vague quality suggests that the names were given retrospectively, after the frontier period had passed. A frontiersman would have been likely to give some tribal name, whereas his grandson would merely think of Indians. The name is sometimes for individual Indians, especially those who continued to live at a spot after the region was settled by whites. This is the indication of names such as **Indian Joe Creek** CA and **Indian Jack Lake** MN. **Indian Old Fields:** used with usually generic significance for an open space in the eastern forest which was thought to be, and generally was, the result of the Indians having cleared the land for agriculture. **Indian Rock:** this widespread name may suggest, romantically, a rock used as a lookout; more commonly it is one showing Indian work, such as pictographs or holes for pounding acorns. **Indian Head:** any rock suggestive of a human head is likely to be so called. **Indian Grove** IL: some Indians continued to live here until ca. 1836.

Indiana A neo-Latin or Spanish feminine adjective meaning 'Indian' was adopted ca. 1765 by a group of land developers known as the Indiana Company, who called their tract **Indiana.** In 1800 the name was used, though in a new location, for the territory, being a natural description of a region which was at the time Indian territory. **Indiana** (county and town, PA) dates from 1805, and was suggested by the new territory as well as by the former presence of Indians.

Indianapolis Coined from the territorial name, plus the Greek *polis,* 'city.'

Indianola A repeated habitation-name, coined from Indian and a Latin or Latin-like ending, chiefly used for its euphony, and conforming to the idea that names of place should end in *a.*

Indiatlantic Beach FL A coined name, because of location on the Atlantic Ocean near Indian River.

Indio Spanish '(an) Indian.'

Indore WV Uncertain, perhaps from the Biblical Endor.

Indrio FL A coined name from nearby **Indian River,** with the substitution of Spanish **Rio.**

Indus MN From the river of India, so named by a returned missionary.

Industry A vaguely commendatory name, or from Industrial School. In TX it is locally believed to be from the industrious character of the first settlers (1831). In ME (1803) a similar story is told.

Infant Buttes CA Probably because they are small in comparison with the peaks just to the east.

Ingle Though it occurs as a personal name, it is chiefly a sentimental Scotticism, 'nook, corner.' **Ingleside,** in the sense of 'hearthside,' served as a commendatory in the 19th century. **Inglewood** may be a transfer from Great Britain *via* Canada, but it is essentially a double commendatory. See **Englewood.**

Ingomar Regularly from *Ingomar, the Barbarian* (1851), a popular play by M. A. Lovell. Col. W. C. Falkner took this name from the play, and used it in his novel *The White Rose of Memphis,* and then gave it to a town which he founded in MS.

Ingot CA A mining town where ingots of metal were cast.

Initial Point AZ The original point from which most of the surveys of the state have been based.

Ink A name probably selected largely for its brevity; in MO a local story is that someone upset a bottle of ink when a three-letter name was being sought.

Inkom ID A railroad name, probably based on the Shoshone word for 'red,' or 'red hair,' but reference uncertain.

Inkwell Lake CO Because of reflections of black rocks the water appears inklike.

Inland Occasionally given to emphasize a landlocked situation, e.g. in SD and NB. In NB it occurs in an alphabetical

sequence. **Inland Empire:** a commendatory name for the region of eastern
WA, northeastern OR, and northern ID.

Innominate, The WY A mountain, so
named by mountaineers from its resemblance to Innominate Crack in the English lake district.

Inola OK Indian (Cherokee) 'black
fox' (?).

Inspiration Chiefly as **Inspiration Point,**
a cliché, occurring in most national
parks, to suggest the effect of the view
from that location. **Inspiration** AZ: from
a mine, probably named because the
owners had a sudden idea which they
considered an inspiration.

Intake MT Because the intake of an irrigation system is located here.

Intercession City Originally **Interocean
City,** because halfway between the Atlantic and the Gulf, it was renamed by
the founders of a religious colony and
given a religious name which closely
resembles the original one.

Intercourse In PA the town was named
in 1813, before sexual implications of
the word had become current; the name
is probably a commendatory from the
then common meaning 'interchange,
commerce.' In AL the name was given
because the settlement was at a road
junction which made communication
easy.

Interior Because of location inside of
something, e.g. the town in SD which is
inside the Badlands Wall. In WA it is
from the name of a company which had
a warehouse there.

Interlachen, Interlaken, Interlochen
From the city in Switzerland. The hybrid name is generally translated 'between lakes,' and in most instances in
the U.S. has been given descriptively of
a place so located, and also with a commendatory idea, as suggesting a beautiful and cool site.

International From a situation on the
Canadian border, e.g. **International
Falls** MN.

Intervale Chiefly a term to denote flats
along streams, used in northern New
England. It exists as a specific, e.g. ME,
NH.

Intrenchment Creek GA From the presence of some old intrenchments of uncertain date.

Invasion Gulch WY From an incident of
the so-called Johnson County Cattle
War (1892) between cattlemen and
sheepmen.

Inver Grove MN Named by Irish settlers
for a place in Ireland.

Inverness From the city and county of
Scotland, generally so named by Scottish
settlers.

Inwood The personal name is rare. In
CA and WV the name is descriptive, or
commendatory, for a place located in
the woods.

Inyan Kara Mountain WY Indian, probably Siouan, 'stone-made' (?).

Inyo CA A local Indian term, probably
Shoshonean, first applied to the mountains. The meaning is given as 'dwelling
place of a great spirit,' as interpretation
which has a possible validity, since Indians sometimes conceived mountains to
be thus haunted. Cf. **Bally, Medicine.**

Inyokern CA Near the boundary of Inyo
and Kern counties.

Ioka UT From the name of a Ute chief.

Iola In some instances from a woman's
name. In CO, selected because it was
thought to have a pretty sound. In TX,
locally believed to be from an Indian
tribe. In FL, from a former Indian town
recorded as Iolee, derived from the name
of a Seminole god.

Iona, Ione Generally from a woman's
name, e.g. in OR for Ione Arthur, so
named by an admirer when she was
merely visiting in the neighborhood.
Iona MN: named by a Catholic priest
for the island off Scotland, famed as the
residence of St. Columba. In SD the
name was suggested by a Siouan word,

ionaye, probably meaning 'fire around,' and thus commemorating some fire.

Ioni Creek TX From the name of an Indian village or tribe.

Ionia From the ancient Greek district in Asia Minor, first applied (1828) to the town in NY, an area in which classical names were being freely given.

Iosco MI, MN, NJ A pseudo-Indian name, coined by H. R. Schoolcraft in a book published in 1856, possibly intended to mean 'shining-water.'

Iosepa UT For Joseph, modified by some Hawaiians who settled here (1889) as colonists, after being converted to Mormonism, for Joseph F. Smith, Mormon missionary in Hawaii.

Iowa The tribal name Ouaouiatonon is recorded on a French map, in the vicinity of the Iowa River, as of 1673. Shortened to **Ouaouia** this is apparently the origin of the later tribal name Iowa, which was applied to the river and then to the territory and state.

Iphigenia Bay AK Named (1867) for a ship of the Meares expedition, which had explored the coast in 1788.

Ipsoot, Ipsut OR, WA Chinook jargon, 'hidden.'

Ipswich MA For the town in England, but with a special note of the General Court (Aug. 4, 1634) that it was an acknowledgment of the 'honor and kindness done to our people which took shipping there.'

Iraan TX For Ira G. Yates, owner of the townsite, and his wife Ann, by combination of the two given names, a name suggested in a contest, the prize being a choice building lot.

Iredell TX For Ire Keeler, son of an early settler, coupled with the romantic *dell,* 'valley.'

Ireland The name is rare, and is generally not from the island but from the personal name, as with **Ireland Mountain** OR and **Ireland Lake** CA. **Ireland** WV: named commemoratively by a native of Ireland.

Ireteba Peaks NV For a Mohave Indian who acted as guide to an exploring expedition in 1857.

Irish In most instances from the personal name. **Irish Corner District** WV: named for the people from the northern counties of Ireland who settled it. **Irishtown:** in some cities an unofficial district name, indicating where the Irish immigrants of the 19th century once lived. The hills in MI were so called because of an appearance suggestive of Ireland.

Irmo SC From the name of an early German settler, Iremonger.

Irmulco CA Coined in 1908 for Irvine and Muir Lumber Company.

Iron A common descriptive and sometimes commendatory term indicating 1) the presence or supposed presence of iron deposits, 2) water impregnated with iron, 3) the iron industry. **Iron Mountain,** with its hyperbolic suggestions, is a repeated name. The deposits may or may not be workable, or may exist chiefly in the imagination. In MI the region has produced iron copiously. But CA has the name 30 times, and scarcely one of the places has produced commercial iron. **Iron Creek** and **Iron Spring** are typical names for waters strongly impregnated with iron or with something supposed to be iron. The iron industry is indicated by some 20 habitation-names, **Ironton** being the favorite. Long-forgotten sites of industry may be indicated by such a name as **Ironwork Brook** MA. **Iron Mountain** AZ: from R. A. Irion, early cattleman, who pronounced his name like the metal.

Irona, Ironaton Probably commendatory names to indicate ironworking.

Irondequoit NY Iroquoian 'bay,' although some more explicit meaning may also be implied.

Ironia NJ Apparently a coinage, viz. *iron* with a Latin ending *-ia* indicating place, because of iron ore.

Ironwood Various small trees, popularly so called, have given rise to a few names.

Iroquois From the Indian tribal name. The island in MI is so called because invading Iroquois once, before 1800, fought a battle here with the local Chippewas.

Irrigon OR From *irrigation* and the state name, because the site of an irrigation project.

Irville OH For John Irvine, early settler.

Irving From the personal name, especially for Washington Irving, essayist and historian, e.g. **Irvington** NJ, **Lake Irving** MN. In TX the name **Irving** was given simply because the namers liked the sound of it. **Irving's Castle** OK: named for Washington Irving by the members of his party when he visited the area in 1832.

Irvona PA A Latinized form from E. A. Irvin, the town founder.

Isa Lake WY For Isabel Jelke, named by a railroad official.

Isaban WV By combination of Isabel and Ann, unidentified; named by a coal company.

Isabella From the woman's name; in MI and perhaps elsewhere in honor of Queen Isabella of Castile, the patroness of Columbus.

Isanti MN From the Indian tribal name, more commonly spelled **Santee**. Another form appears in **Izatys** MN.

Ischua NY Uncertain, a misspelling (?) of the Italian island Ischia.

Ishawooa WY The name-cluster springs from the Shoshone 'lying warm,' probably first with reference to the mesa.

Ishi Pishi Falls CA Indian (Karok) with the general meaning of 'leveling-off,' because a trail here came down to the stream.

Ishpeming MI Ojibway 'high-place,' being on the watershed between lakes Michigan and Superior, a name coined in the 19th century by a local resident, Peter White.

Isis Temple AZ See **Brahma**.

Isla Spanish 'island.' **Isleta** NM: when first seen by the Spaniards, the pueblo was a 'little island,' because almost surrounded by the river.

Islais See **Islay**.

Islamorada FL Spanish with *isla*, 'island,' and *morada,* probably 'purple,' from the appearance as seen from a distance or as a commendatory.

Island Primarily a generic but freely used as a specific for other features identifiable by an island, e.g. **Island Cove, Island Creek, Island Lake. Island Mountain** CA is almost an island because of a looping creek. **Island County** WA is composed wholly of islands.

Islay, Islais CA Salinian, for the native bush called hollyleaf cherry, important as furnishing an edible fruit for the Indians.

Isle 1) In a French context it is the equivalent of modern French *île*, 'island'; hence **Isle au Haut, Isle la Motte,** etc. 2) In earlier English usage the term means simply 'island,' or 'small island.' **Isle of Wight County** VA: from a plantation called after the English island. **Islesborough** ME: incorporated in 1788 as 'a town located upon an island.' 3) In 19th-century American usage the term became a romantic or commendatory one for a small island, e.g. **Happy Isles,** Yosemite N.P. **Isleton** CA: situated on an island.

Isleta See **Isla**.

Islettes For modern French *îlet*, 'small island,' e.g. **Pass des Islettes** LA.

Isola MS A name given to suggest isolation and probably derived from that word, though it is Italian, 'island.'

Isolation Peak CO Because it stands by itself.

Israel From the personal name, e.g. the river in NH for Israel Glines, early settler.

Issaquah WA Indian, meaning uncertain.

Issaquena See **Cateeche**.

Istachatta FL Seminole 'man-red.'

Istokpoga Lake FL Muskogean (Creek), probably 'man-in-water-killed,' apparently from an incident.

Istopogayokee Lake FL Seminole 'people-live-at-end-of-it.'

Istrouma LA Muskogean (Choctaw) 'stick-red,' thus being the original of which **Baton Rouge** (q.v.) is the French translation.

Italian Rare, as compared with many ethnic names, since the Italian immigration was chiefly after the period of intensive naming. The mountain in CO was named because it shows the national colors—red, white, and green.

Italy In TX it is a commendatory name, because of the suggestion of 'Sunny Italy.' **Lake Italy** CA: because its shape resembles that of Italy.

Itasca, Lake MN Coined in 1832 by W. T. Boutwell and H. R. Schoolcraft, who believed it to be the 'true source' of the Mississippi. Boutwell rendered this in crude Latin as *veritas caput;* Schoolcraft joined the tail of the first word with the head of the second.

Itawamba MS Muskogean, an Indian personal name (?).

Itchepuckesassa River FL Seminole 'tobacco-blossoms-are-there,' probably with reference to a tobacco field.

Itchetucknee Springs FL Muskogean, probably with *itche-* for hichi, *'tobacco,'* and the rest uncertain.

Ithaca From the ancient Greek island, the naming in NY (1811) being at a time of classical namings and being applied to a location such as to resemble Odysseus' description of his home as being 'rugged' and not good for much except pasturing goats.

Itikmalaiyak Creek AK Eskimo 'little rectum.'

Itkillik River AK Eskimo 'Indian,' indicating a stream on which the Eskimos made contact with their enemies the Indians.

Itmann WV For I. T. Mann, a coal operator.

Itta Bena MS From Choctaw *bina,* 'camp,' and (?) *ita,* 'together.'

Iuka MS For a Chickasaw chief of the early 19th century.

Iva SC For a woman, Iva Cook, of a pioneer family.

Ivanhoe The sole source of this name, appearing in a number of states, seems to be Scott's novel.

Ivanpah, Ivanpatch Probably variants of the same Southern Paiute name, meaning 'spring-clear.'

Ivory The creek in AK was named (1950) for the finding there of some fossil mammoth ivory. **Ivorydale** OH: from the brand name of a soap manufactured there.

Ivy In spite of the dreaded poison ivy, the sylvan and poetic suggestion of the name, as well as the occurrence of the plant, has resulted in some habitation-names. **Ivy** NC: for the mountain laurel, popularly called *ivy.* **Ivy** OK: for Ivy Lewis, first postmaster.

Izaak Walton, Mount Proposed by F. P. Farquhar in 1919 to honor the author of *The Compleat Angler.*

Izatys See Isanti.

Izee OR For the **IZ** of a cattle-brand.

Izora MO Probably for Izora Irvine, wife of an early settler.

Izoro TX For Izoro Gillan, daughter of an early settler.

J

Jabalina In Mexican-Spanish usage, 'wild pig, peccary,' thus, **Jabalina Basin** NM.

Jaboncillo Spanish 'soapstone,' e.g. **Jaboncillos Creek** TX.

Jacalitos CA Mexican-Spanish 'little huts,' with special reference to Indian dwellings.

Jack Usually for the personal name or nickname. As a shortening for Jackass, e.g. **Jack Creek** OR. **Jackknife Canyon** OR: Z. Donnell lost a jackknife here, and found it the next year. **Jackass:** the common American term for a place named because of some incident involving a burro, no matter of which sex. **Jackass Flat** CA: in 1885 a burro was here hit by a locomotive. Though the large rabbit was well known in most of the West, names from it are few, probably on the principle that anything too well known is not notable enough to produce a name. **Jack Rabbit Lake** NB: because a jackrabbit seemed to be the only thing calling attention to the lake. **Jackass Pass** WY: named by early packers with the idea that it could be surmounted only by a jackass, that animal being proverbial for being able to get over and through.

Jackass See Jack.

Jackpot NV A commendatory name for a settlement chiefly devoted to gambling.

Jackson Many names of natural features and of habitations are from various holders of the common personal name. Most commonly honored is Andrew Jackson, president, generally by namings of the period 1820–1840, e.g. **Jackson** in MI and MS, and counties and towns, particularly in the southern and middle-western states, but even in OR. On account of its commonness it is sometimes used with a suffix, as in **Jacksonville** FL, named in 1822. **Jackson Hole** WY: for D. E. Jackson, early fur trader.

Jackstraw Mountain CO Named (1924) because on its side the tree trunks left by a forest fire were piled in confusion, as in the child's game called jackstraws.

Jacob's Well AZ Though someone named Jacob may have been involved, the reference is probably to the Biblical patriarch who was in one incident associated with a well.

Jacox WV From the name of a family of early settlers.

Jacumba CA Probably Indian (Diegueño), containing *aha*, 'water,' but otherwise uncertain.

Jade Lake WY For its jadelike color.

Jadito Wash AZ Navajo 'antelope-water.'

Jahuey Creek TX Probably a variant of the American-Spanish *jagüey*, meaning a place covered by temporary flooding.

Jail The rock in NB stands close to the previously named **Courthouse Rock,** and is slightly smaller. The canyon in CA is of unknown origin.

Jakehamon TX For Jake Hamon, local oil operator.

Jal NM From the JAL Ranch, itself named from the initials of its owner J. A. Lynch.

Jalapa IN From the city of Mexico, occupied by Americans during the Mexican War.

Jamacha CA Indian (Diegueño), from the word for a wild squash plant.

Jamaica Sometimes from the West Indian island, but in MA and VT from the Algonquian word for 'beaver.' In NY it is from the name of a small tribe, recorded as Jameco and Jamaco; since they were Algonquian-speaking they were thus the 'beaver people.'

James Because it is common both as a given and as a family name dozens of examples persist as both feature- and habitation-names. With the latter, *-town* is the commonest suffix, presumably because of the influence of the first English settlement. **Jamestown** VA: named by the colonists on May 14, 1607, 'in honor of the King's [James I] most excellent majesty.' **James River** VA: called originally **King's River**, and sometimes **Powhatan's River** (from the Indian tribe and chief living on it), the stream soon came to be known as the James, from the king's name, probably also influenced by the fact that **Jamestown** was the chief settlement upon it. **James River** SD: named in French (1794) **Riviere aux Jacques**, for uncertain reasons, and translated as **James**, though usually known as **Jim River**.

Jamul CA Diegueño, probably 'foaming water.'

Jane Lew WV Probably for Jane Lewis, daughter of the landowner.

Japan In MO the name is from a church dedicated to the Holy Martyrs of Japan; elsewhere it is probably an exotic of the 19th century.

Japonski Island AK Russian 'Japanese,' because in 1809 some wrecked Japanese sailors were living there.

Jara In American-Spanish, referring to a growth of reeds or willows along a stream, and thus the equivalent of 'brushy,' a common name for features in NM, e.g. **Jara Creek, Jarales, Jarita Creek, Jarosa Canyon.**

Jarbidge NV, ID Indian, probably Shoshone 'devil,' because of hot springs.

Jaroso Spanish 'having brambles'; in CO, probably applied first to a natural feature.

Jarro Spanish 'jug, pitcher.' **El Jarro Creek** CA may have been so called for a natural formation. **El Jarro Point** CA: probably preserves the name of an Indian tribe, absorbed to the form of the Spanish word.

Jasper Generally from the personal name, especially for William Jasper, sergeant and hero in the Revolutionary War, e.g. towns and numerous counties in the SE. **Jasper** MN: two villages are named for the occurrence of a red rock popularly called jasper.

Jaune French 'yellow,' e.g. **Bayou Jaune** LA from the color of its water.

Java From the island. In SD it is a railroad name, given because unusual and short.

Javon CA For Spanish *jabon*, 'soap,' so called because a mineral thought to be a natural soap was discovered there and worked for a while.

Jawbone In CA the canyon so called suggests the outline of a jawbone. Other places may have been so called for the finding of a jawbone.

Jayem In KY, from the initials of J. M. Robinson, local congressman. **Jay Em** WY: from *JM*, the brand of a ranch owned by Jim More.

Jayenne WV For the first two initials of J. N. Camden, not otherwise identified.

Jayhawker The nickname for a Kansan has established itself upon places thus associated, e.g. the spring in CA, because of the Jayhawker party of 1849.

Jay-Jay FL From the J. J. Parrish Packing House, which is at this location.

Jean de Jean, Bayou LA Probably for a French settler of the early 19th century, Jean Dejean.

Jeddo The former name of Tokyo, Japan, usually applied in the early 19th century when exotic names were in favor. Also **Yeddo**.

Jeff Davis For Jefferson Davis, president of the Confederate States, often an evidence of a naming at the time of the Civil War by settlers favoring the Confederacy, e.g. **Jeff Davis Creek** OR. Counties are so named in GA and TX, as well as **Jefferson Davis** counties in LA and MS.

Jefferson The most important namings are for Thomas Jefferson, third president, e.g. many counties, **Jefferson City** MO, **Mount Jefferson** NH, OR. See **Jeff Davis.**

Jehu From the Old Testament he is remembered for his furious driving, and in the 19th century coachmen were sometimes so designated humorously; **Jehu Mountain** NY presumably commemorates an incident of such driving.

Jellico KY, TN Probably from a family name.

Jelloway OH Originally a creek-name, for John Jelloway, a local Indian.

Jelm Mountain WY An adaptation of Gillam, from an early tie contractor for the railroad.

Jemez From the Indian tribal name.

Jena From the city in Germany, more particularly from Napoleon's victory there, e.g. in MD.

Jenera For A. B. Jener, the first physician in the area, with an *a* added as is customary with place-names.

Jenkinjones WV For Jenkin Jones, unidentified.

Jenky WV From the personal name of a friend of the founder of the post office.

Jennie, Jenny This favorite variation of Jane occurs on a few lakes and other natural features, and there are some habitation-names. **Jennie's Creek** WV: the story is that Jennie Wiley's baby was here killed by Indians, but the killed-by-Indians theory is a common one, and needs confirmation. **Jenny Lind** AR, CA: for the Swedish singer who triumphantly toured the U.S. in 1850–1852. **Jenny Lake** WY: for an Indian woman, wife of the guide of the Hayden geological expedition (1871).

Jere WV A personal name, either a shortening of Jeremiah or a name in itself.

Jericho From the Biblical city.

Jerimoth Hill RI The name of seven insignificant people in the Bible is more

likely used because of its apt Hebrew meaning, 'elevation.'

Jerked Beef Butte AZ In the 1880's some Apaches stole a number of oxen, and halted at this point to kill the animals and dry the beef.

Jersey A number of names for natural features and about a dozen habitation-names are probably all for **New Jersey,** and indicate places to which the name was carried by emigrants from that state. The shortening, **Jersey,** for **New Jersey,** has always been common. **Jersey City** NJ: the city, being on the Jersey shore, was named by counterpart from **New York City.**

Jerusalem From the Biblical rather than from the modern city. In general, it has been too holy for use, but exists as a town-name in OH and AR. **Jerusalem Mountain** AZ: apparently from a cowboys' saying about 'going to Jerusalem,' with reference to the game. **Jerusalem Creek** CA: named by Jewish settlers.

Jessamine KY Jessamine Douglas, daughter of an early settler, was surprised near the stream by an Indian, tomahawked, and killed; hence the creek and county.

Jesset, Crag of SD For Major Jesse Tucker, with the initial of the last name, given semihumorously by his friend Doane Robinson, state historian.

Jester From the personal name, e.g. in TX for G. T. Jester, political figure in the 19th century.

Jesus Scarcely used, but **Mount Jesus** (cause of naming unknown) occurs in KS. The Spaniards sometimes applied **Jesus Maria** for religious reasons, e.g. to a creek in CA which is now a part of the **Sacramento River.** Another creek of the name in CA is for an early Mexican farmer.

Jet, Jett From the personal name, e.g. **Jet** OK for W. M. Jett, first postmaster.

Jew Though Jewish pedlars and storekeepers were numerous on the frontier, the name has scarcely been used. **Jew-**

town GA is named from an original store operated by Jewish merchants.

Jewel, Jewell Occasionally **Jewel** is used as a commendatory descriptive, e.g. **Jewel Geyser,** Yellowstone N.P., WY. **Jewell** is from the personal name, e.g. the county in KS, for Lt. Col. L. R. Jewell, killed in a Civil War battle in 1862. **Jewel Lake,** Rocky Mountain N.P., CO was named (1923) to honor E. S. Jewell, president of a walking club, but the spelling was changed 'to depersonalize it.'

Jhus Canyon AZ From an Apache personal name.

Jicarilla In NM Spanish 'little basketcup,' but all the place-names are probably from the Indian tribe thus known.

Jicarita In MN Spanish 'little basketcup,' thus by description for a mountain NM shaped like an inverted cup. **Jicarita Peak** NM: on its slope is a cuplike depression.

Jiggs NV From the comic-strip character who quarrels with his wife, to commemorate such a local squabble.

Jigwallick Marsh VT Algonquian 'frogs.'

Jim Crow Although the term was commonly used with reference to a Negro, the canyon in CA was named in 1849 for a Kanaka who was thus nicknamed and who mined in that place. The creek and point in WA were named because a conspicuous tree there was much haunted by crows.

Jim Jam Ridge CA The term was commonly used for *delirium tremens* or the alcoholic jitters, and the name originated from an incident of the 1890's, when three miners had a difficult time sobering up.

Jingo From the expression 'By jingo!' popularized in 1878. In KS the name, by local story, originated when someone said, 'By jingo, we'd better decide upon a name!'

Jireh WY From the Biblical place-name Jehovahjireh, literally, 'Jehovah will pro-

vide,' an expression of hope by the early settlers.

Job Regularly for a person so named, e.g. **Jobs Peak** CA for Moses Job who kept a store at the foot of the mountain in the 1850's. In 1893 a nearby peak was named **Jobs Sister** by the U.S. Geological Survey.

Jobildunk Ravine NH By tradition, for three men named Joe, Bill, and Duncan; it has not been referred to any Indian language, and the tradition is probably correct.

Jocassee SC Locally believed to be named for an Indian woman.

Jocko River MT From the French name Jacques, probably for Jacques Findley, early fur trader.

Jo Daviess County IL See **Daviess.**

Jodie WV For the nickname of Joseph H. Gaines, a congressman.

Joes CO Among the first settlers were three men called Joe; the settlement was known as **Three Joes,** and then shortened.

Jogee Hill NY From a chief, known by the Dutch name Kokhem (Joachim), who granted land here in 1684.

Johannesburg CA Named in the 1890's after the mining center in Africa, in the hope that it too would be a center of gold production.

John From the personal name. Being traditionally the commonest of all American given names for males, it lacks distinguishing quality, and is therefore comparatively rare in habitation-names, though commoner on features. It frequently retains its possessive form, e.g. **Johns Creek. John Day River** OR: for a frontiersman who had an encounter with Indians near the mouth of this stream. **Johnstown** PA: for a Swiss immigrant, whose name was Anglicized as Joseph Johns; he owned the townsite in 1793, but it was not formally named for him until 1834. **Johntown** TX: so called because at the time of the name an especially large number of men named John were living there. See **Johnson.**

Johnson Like **John** and other extremely common personal names, it lacks distinguishing value, and has not been commonly used. President Andrew Johnson lacked popularity, and President L. B. Johnson took office after most of the naming had already occurred. **Johnson City** TX: for Jim Johnson, pioneer resident. **Johnson City** TN: originally **Hainesville,** but named in 1879 for its first mayor and prominent citizen, Henry Johnson. **Johnson City** NY: for George F. Johnson and the Endicott-Johnson Corp.; the town was built up by the corporation. **Johnsonville** TX: for John Martin, first postmaster. **Johnson Mountain** CA: for W. D. Johnson, geologist. **Johnson Peak** CA: named ca. 1890 for an otherwise unidentified teamster and guide.

Johnston From the personal name, e.g. in RI for Augustus Johnston, political figure in the 18th century. **Johnston** NY: for Sir William Johnson, prominent political figure of the 18th century, as a shortened form from **Johnsonston.**

Jo Jo WY The creek and mountain were named for two early settlers, both named Joseph and called Joe.

Joker SV For Joker Sewell, founder of the post office.

Joliet From the personal name, generally for Louis Jol(l)iet (1645–1700), French-Canadian explorer. In IL the name was first **Juliet,** for a local girl. **Joliette** ND, apparently a variant, is from the name of a town in Canada.

Jolla A Mexican spelling of the Castilian Spanish *hoya,* 'hole, pit, hollow.' It occurs several times in CA to denote places distinguished by holes, sometimes holes in rock where Indians pounded acorns, sometimes being spelled *joya* or *hoya. Joya,* however, means 'jewel' in Spanish. The name-cluster around the town **La Jolla** CA may have been suggested by the occurrence of the name nearby, or it may be a commendatory name in the sense of 'jewel,' or both influences may have worked together.

Jolly Commonly from the personal name, e.g. **Jolly** TX for W. H. Jolly, local landowner. In GA the name was suggested because someone thought that the people there were of a jolly nature. **Jolly Ann Lake** MN suggests an incident-naming.

Jolon CA Salinian, perhaps, 'valley of dead trees.'

Jones From the personal name. Like other very common personal names, it lacks distinguishing value, and is not as common as might be expected. **Jones Pass** WY: for Capt. W. A. Jones, in command of the first party to cross. **Jones Creek** WY: for the same man, who first explored it, in 1873. **Jones Valley** CA: for a woman of that name, killed there by Indians in 1864. **Jones Prairie** TX: for J. P. Jones, who obtained a grant of land here in 1833. As a habitation-name, it is too short to stand well alone, and is most commonly coupled with *-ville* and *-boro.* **Saint Jones River** DE: so known since 1671; for Robert Jones, early land-grantee; the *saint* may be from the reference to 'said Jones,' in the legal phraseology of the title; but cf. other such couplings under **Saint.**

Jonican Creek VA Apparently a variant of the commoner *jonakin,* a thin sheet of batter, toasted on a board. Cf. **Journeycake, Pone.**

J. O. Pass CA John Warren carved in a tree the first two letters of his name, and from those letters the name was given in 1889.

Joplin From the personal name, in MO for Rev. H. G. Joplin, who established (1840) the first Methodist church in the area.

Joppa A half-dozen habitation-names, repeat the name of the Biblical seaport. Since concordances connect this name with a Hebrew word meaning 'beauty,' namers may have been thus influenced.

Jordan Commonly from the personal name, but also from the Biblical river. The stream in UT was so called because the Mormons conceived their new country to be the Promised Land, thus properly having the **Jordan** as its chief river.

The **River Jordan,** an early 16th-century name on the SE coast, was from the personal name of a Spanish voyager. **Mount Jordan** CA: for David Starr Jordan, president of Stanford University. **Jordan** WV: an adaptation in honor of a local official of a coal company, whose name was actually Jorgensen. The creek in ID was named for M. M. Jordan, leader of a party which discovered gold on the stream in 1863. **Jordan** MN: for the river, as a solution of desperation after long dispute among the residents.

Jornada Spanish 'day's travel, stage of journey.' **Jornada del Muerto** NM: literally, 'of the dead man,' but usually translated as if *muerte,* 'death,' with reference to a dangerous reach of 90 miles on the Chihuahua-Santa Fe Trial.

Josina Creek IN An abbreviation and partial shifting by folk-etymology of Met-o-san-ia, the name of a Miami chief of the 18th century.

Jotank Creek VA Algonquian, for an earlier **Chotank,** probably the same as **Choptank,** q.v.

Journeycake Neck MD A variant of *johnny cake,* i.e. a bread made of cornmeal, probably from an incident.

Jovista CA From the first name of Joseph Di Giorgio, a local rancher, and the Spanish 'vista,' view.

Joy From the personal name or title. **Joy** TX: selected by settlers who were overjoyed because their first crops had been abundant. **Joy** OR: because the settlers were joyful that they were to have a post office. **Mount Joy** PA: from a personal name or title.

Joya Spanish 'jewel,' but in **La Joya** NM it may represent *hoya,* 'hole, pit,' hence, 'valley.' See **Jolla.**

Jozye TX For Willie Jo Shannon, the daughter of a local landowner; the *-zye* is apparently added for differentiation, according to local story, by the Post Office Dept.

Juab UT Goshiute 'level, valley.'

Juan de Fuca, Strait of Preserves the name, or nickname, of the Greek who told the Englishman Michael Lok of the voyage that he made in a Spanish ship in 1592, when (as he claimed) he discovered a broad strait running into the land, and, according to his belief, forming the Northwest Passage. The English explorer John Meares fixed the name in 1788 when he sailed into the strait and called it 'by the name of its original discoverer.'

Juan Miller Creek AZ From the name of an early German settler Von Muellar.

Jubilee Pass CA From a mine-name.

Jud ND For Judson LaMoure, early settler and politician, for whom the county (**LaMoure**) is also named.

Judea From the Biblical district of Palestine, e.g. **Mount Judea** AR, probably because the region was often mentioned for its mountains.

Judith From the personal name. In MT the river was named in 1804 by Capt. William Clark of the Lewis and Clark expedition for the woman who later became his wife. **Point Judith** RI: presumably for a woman, but uncertain.

Judsonia AR Named in 1869 for Adoniram Judson, American missionary in Burma, with a Latin ending added.

Judy Commonly from a personal name; **Judy Lake** MI is from J. Juday, landowner.

Jug An occasional use in **Jug Tavern** is from natural association. **The Jug** WV: apparently for Jughandle. **Jughandle:** used, like horseshoe, for a place marked by a pronounced curve, as in a stream or a road. **Jug Motte Creek** OK: from the Jug Ranch, with *motte* uncertain, though possibly from the French 'hillock.'

Juggler Lake MN The translation of an Ojibway name, with reference to a kind of medicine man.

Jugornot Hollow KY Apparently for *juggernaut,* but reference uncertain.

Julesburg CO From Jules Beni, who established a trading post in the vicinity in the 1850's; the settlement shifted among three locations, taking the name with it.

Juliaetta ID For Julia and Etta Snyder, daughters of the first postmaster.

Julian From the personal name. **Julian** PA: from the Julia Ann Furnace, itself from Julia Ann Irvin, wife of one of the owners.

Jumbo An African word, used for a person of mixed blood and in other senses, but becoming fixed in the sense of 'large' because of the elephant exhibited during the 1880's. In OK the name is directly from Jumbo Asphalt Company. In AR the name may be from the earlier usage. **Jumbo Knob** CA: from a fancied resemblance to the famous elephant.

Jumping Gully Creek SC From an incident of the Revolutionary War, in which a pursued man leaped his horse across the gully.

Jump-Off Used as a generic to indicate a place so steep that one may jump from it, often simply **The Jump-Off.** Hence, as a specific, to denote a place thus associated, e.g. **Jump-Off Creek** CA, because of the steep canyon walls. **Jumpoff Joe Creek** OR: named ca. 1838 when a man named Joe fell off a cliff and was badly injured.

Junaluska, Lake NC From the name of a Cherokee chief.

Junction A repeated name, both for features and for habitations; a descriptive, indicating a junction; e.g. of two mountain features as with **Junction Peak** CA, or most commonly of two streams, e.g. **Junction** UT, because situated at the junction of two forks of a river. The junction may be of roads or railroads, e.g. **Junction City** OH, because three railroads meet here.

Juneau From the personal name; in AK named (1881) for Joseph Juneau, one of the original discoverers of gold here. The county in WI is for Solomon Juneau, founder of the city of Milwaukee.

Juniata PA Iroquoian, meaning uncertain.

Junior WV H. G. Davis, who aided with the incorporation, named the town for his son, though the latter's name was actually John.

Juniper Americans have applied the name loosely to various kinds of conifers, but in general the trees thus known were not conspicuous in the East, and the place-names are mostly western, since in dry country the juniper (see also **Cedar**) stands out as a landmark. **Juniper Lake** CA: named because of the presence of one especially fine specimen of the tree.

Juno For the Roman goddess or a woman so named. In FL it is a counterpart name to **Jupiter.**

Junta Spanish, in place-names, 'junction,' e.g. **Juntas** CA, probably for the confluence of two streams. **La Junta** CO: from the junction of two railroads.

Juntura Spanish 'junction.'

Jupiter For the Roman diety; in WA the hills were named by the Wilkes expedition (1841) apparently because they were close to the already-named **Olympic Mountains.** See **Hobe.**

Jurupa CA A Spanish rendering of a local Indian name of unknown meaning.

Justice In WV for W. E. Justice, postmaster and landowner. **Justiceburg** TX: for J. D. Justice, landowner.

K

Kabetogama, Lake MN Ojibway 'lying-parallel lake,' i.e. from its relation to Rainy Lake.

Kabito Plateau AZ Navajo 'willow spring.'

Kable In **Kables** VA and **Kabletown** WV it is probably a variant of the locally recorded family name Cabell or Cable.

Kachemak Bay AK Eskimo 'water-cliff-big,' probably to indicate a bay with high cliffs.

Kadoka SD Siouan 'opening, hole,' because of a gap in the Badlands Wall at this point.

Kagorah Lake WY From the personal name of a Shoshone of the late 19th century.

Kahatchee AL Muskogean (Creek) 'cane-creek.'

Kahiltna River AK Athapascan with -na 'river,' and the rest uncertain.

Kahlotus WA Indian, locally believed to mean 'hole-in-the-ground.'

Kahnah Creek CO Indian, probably Ute, meaning uncertain.

Kahoka MO From an Indian tribal name.

Kahola See **Cahola**.

Kaibab Plateau AZ Paiute 'mountain lying down.'

Kaikout See **Kikeout**.

Kaiparowitz UT Paiute 'mountain-son,' probably the equivalent of a tribal name such as 'mountaineers.'

Kaiser, Keyser Probably in all instances from the personal name, e.g. in CA (San Bernardino Co.) for H. J. Kaiser, industrialist of World War II. Some places of this name suffered a change at the time of World War I, when patriotic feeling was strong against Kaiser Wilhelm.

Kaka AZ Papago 'clearing.'

Kakagon River WI Algonquian, meaning uncertain.

Kake AK From an Indian tribal name.

Kakeout Hill NY See **Kikeout**.

Kalama WA Indian 'stone' (?).

Kalamazoo MI Algonquian 'it smokes, he is troubled with smoke,' an Indian personal name (?).

Kalamut Island WA Indian, named by the Wilkes expedition (1841), meaning unknown.

Kaleetan R, WA Chinook jargon, 'arrow.' In WA it was given by a society of mountaineers in 1916.

Kalgary TX Named, with changed spelling, by settlers from Calgary, Canada.

Kalida OH Founded 1834 and, by local story, named from the Greek 'beautiful,' but this seems unlikely since that word is *kalos;* it must be considered uncertain.

Kalimink Creek MI Algonquian, meaning uncertain.

Kalispell ID, MT From the Indian tribal name.

Kalk Butte OR Chinook jargon, 'cut-off,' a descriptive.

Kalkaska MI Indian, probably Ojibway, meaning uncertain.

Kalmia MD Probably from the German family name Kalm, with a Latin ending to designate place.

Kalvesta KS From Greek *kalos,* 'beautiful,' and the Roman goddess of the hearth, Vesta, with the general idea of 'beautiful home.'

Kamankeag Pond ME Algonquian 'weir-at' (?).

Kamela OR Probably a Nez Percé word, 'tamarack.'

Kamennoi Russian 'rocky.'

Kamiah ID Indian, probably from a Nez Percé word for so-called Indian hemp, indicating a place where litter from rope-making was left on the ground.

Kamilchie WA A local Indian name, 'valley.'

Kamma Mountains NV Northern Paiute 'jackrabbit.'

Kampeska Lake SD Siouan 'shining,' with reference to the clarity of the water.

Kamrar IA For J. M. Kamrar, local judge.

Kana-A Creek AZ The Hopi name for some mythological figures believed to live in this valley.

Kanab Canyon AZ Paiute 'willows.'

Kanabec MN Ojibway 'snake,' first applied to **Snake River,** which has been translated.

Kanado KS From its location near the border of KS and CO. So also **Kanorado.**

Kanaga AK Aleut, meaning uncertain.

Kanaka From the common name for a native of the Hawaiian Islands. During the gold rush numbers of these came to CA, and places associated with them were thus named.

Kanakolus Bay ME Algonquian 'long-flame' (?).

Kanapaha FL Indian, probably Timucuan, 'palmetto-leaves-house' (?).

Kanarraville UT From Kanarra, the name of a Paiute chief.

Kanauga OH Probably an adaptation of some Indian name, e.g. **Kanawha,** since it is opposite the mouth of that river.

Kanawha River WV From the name of an Indian tribe, which occurs in various spellings.

Kancamagus Mountain NH For a Pennacook chief of the 17th century.

Kandiota, Lake ND Siouan, containing *kandi,* 'buffalo-fish.'

Kandiyohi MN Siouan 'buffalo-fish come,' originally applied to a lake where such fish were plentiful.

Kanetuck Branch AL Probably for a Choctaw whose name is recorded as Kentuck John. See **Kentuck.**

Kangaroo Often for the kangaroo rat, e.g. probably **Kangaroo Mountain** CA. **Kangaroo Headland** AZ: the outline suggests a kangaroo.

Kaniksu ID Fr. Roothaan, an early Catholic missionary, was so known by the local Indians, and this name has been perpetuated in the National Forest.

Kankakee IL, IN First applied to the river, it exists in numerous spellings, the oldest to be preserved being **Theakiki:** though much disputed, there seems little reason to doubt the explanation recorded in 1721, i.e. 'wolf-land,' because it was the residence of some Mohicans, whose name means 'wolf.'

Kannapolis NC Coined from the Cannon Mills, by J. W. Cannon, the town founder, *plus* the Greek 'city.'

Kanona NY Probably a 19th-century name coined from Ganono, the Iroquoian name for New York City.

Kanopolis KS Named (1886) from **Kansas** and the Greek *-polis,* 'city,' with a connective *-o-* for euphony, in the grandiose hope that the town, being at the center of the state, would become its chief city.

Kanorado See **Kanado.**

Kanosh UT For a well-known local Pahvant headman.

Kanouse Mountain NJ Algonqiuan, meaning uncertain.

Kanranzi Creek MN Siouan 'where the Kansas were killed,' with reference to the defeat of a Kansas war party.

Kansas From the Indian tribe, known to the Spaniards as Escansaque from 1601 and to the French as Kansa from 1673; the *s* represents the French plural. The name passed through the common progression—from tribe to river, to territory, to state. **Kansas City:** in 1838 the settlement was called **Kansas** from the river; it was officially platted as **Town of Kansas** in 1839; as **City of Kansas** in 1853; as **Kansas City** in 1889. **Kansas** OH: named for the territory in 1855 when the name was much in the news because of the slavery question.

Kantishna AK Athapascan, with *-na,* 'river,' and the rest uncertain.

Kanuti River AK Athapascan, probably 'old-man's-river.'

Kapioma KS For a Kickapoo chief of the mid-19th century. Also **Capioma.**

Kapka Butte OR Klamath 'lodgepole pine.'

Kappa IL From an Indian tribal name, probably the same as **Quapaw,** which tribe lived in southern IL for some years ca. 1700.

Karankawa From the Indian tribal name, e.g. the bayou in TX.

Karnak, Karnack From the site in Egypt, made famous in the 19th century by archaeological discoveries.

Karsaootuk Stream ME Algonquian 'pine-river.'

Karval CO An adaptation from the name of the first postmaster, G. K. Kravig.

Kashegelok AK Eskimo 'little-meeting-house.'

Kashong Creek NY Iroquoian 'the-limb-has-fallen.'

Kaskaskia IL From the Indian tribal name.

Kaskela OR The name of a local Indian chief.

Kasoag NY Probably Iroquoian, meaning uncertain.

Kasook NV Probably Northern Paiute, meaning uncertain, occurring as **Big Kasook Mountains.**

Kasota MN Siouan 'clear,' from a treeless ridge nearby.

Katahdin, Mount ME Algonquian 'big (principal)-mountain.'

Katala Mountains AL Probably Muskogean (Creek) 'mulberries-dead,' for some place where the trees had died.

Katamaug, Katama MA Algonquian, probably 'big-fishing-place,' viz. a place to smoke or dry fish.

Katemcy TX From an Indian chief, whose name is recorded as Katumse.

Kates Mountain WV For Kate Carpenter, who hid in the woods on this mountain after Indians had killed her husband in October, 1764.

Katmai AK Originally the name of an Eskimo village, meaning uncertain.

Katonah NY From the name of a local chief, recorded in 1680.

Katopskonegan ME Algonquian 'big-rocks-portage.'

Katsuk Butte OR Chinook jargon, 'middle,' because of its location.

Kattskill See **Catskill,** under **Cat.**

Katy TX From the Missouri, Kansas, & Texas Railway, universally known as 'the Katy,' on which the town is located.

Kaubeshine Lake WI Algonquian, meaning uncertain.

Kaukauna WI Ojibway 'pike-fishing-place' (?).

Kauneonga Lake NY Algonquian, probably with *kaun-,* 'long,' and the rest uncertain.

Kaw This shortening of **Kansas** is used sometimes for the river, and for the tribe, from this latter arising **Kaw** OK.

Kawa Creek KS Osage 'horse.'

Kawak Butte OR Chinook jargon, 'to fly,' arbitrarily selected by the Forest Service.

Kaweah CA From an Indian tribal name.

Kawich Range NV From the name of a local Shoshone chief of the 19th century.

Kawishiwi River MN Ojibway, probably 'full-of-beaver-lodges.'

Kawkawlin MI Algonquian, probably 'pickerel-river.'

Kawuneeche Valley Co Arapaho 'coyote,' a name placed by the Colorado Geographic Board ca. 1915.

Kay Ordinarily from the personal name or nickname, but the county in OK is for the letter *K,* thus preserving the original alphabet system for the territorial counties.

Kayaderosseras Creek NY Iroquoian, probably 'lake-outlet.'

Kayak A repeated name in AK, usually from association with, or fancied resemblance to, an Eskimo boat. **Kayak Creek** AK is from an Eskimo girl so named. **Kayak Cape** AK is probably from confusion with an Aleut word, 'hill.'

Kaycee WY From the brand, *KC,* of a local ranch.

Kayenta AZ An American rendering of **Tyende,** q.v.

Kaylor From the personal name. But the town in SD was originally **Taylor** for a local rancher, and was changed, either by mistake or to avoid duplication.

Kearn(e)y From the personal name. The county in NB, originally **Fort Kearney,** is for Gen. S. W. Kearney. The county

in KS is for Gen. Philip Kearny, of the Civil War.

Kearsarge The original name is that of the mountain in NH. It is probably Algonquian, and the most likely meaning is 'pointed mountain.' In CA the name-cluster arose at the time of the Civil War, and commemorates the sinking of the Confederate *Alabama* by the U.S.S. *Kearsarge.* Cf. **Alabama.**

Keatchie LA Caddoan, probably from the name of a tribe, though the literal meaning, 'panther,' may be involved.

Keats KS Named (1887) by some railroad men, because John Keats was their favorite poet.

Kebo Mountain ME Probably Algonquian, meaning uncertain.

Kechewaiskhe Lake WI Algonquian, meaning uncertain.

Kechi From the Indian tribal name.

Kedron In the King James Bible the name of the stream near Jerusalem is rendered **Kidron,** or (once, in the New Testament) Cedron. **Kedron** would be a proper transliteration of the Greek text, and it may appear in some versions of the Bible that continued to circulate after the King James version was authorized. Possibly **Kedron** resulted from a blend of Kidron and Cedron. See **Kidron.**

Keechelus Lake WA Indian, meaning uncertain.

Keechi TX From the Indian tribal name.

Keego Lake WI Probably Algonquian, meaning uncertain.

Keekwulee Falls WA Chinook jargon, 'falling.'

Keene From the personal name, e.g. in NH (1753) for Sir Benjamin Keene, a friend of Gov. Benning Wentworth, who was the namer.

Keesaug Brook NH Algonquian 'big (principal)-outlet.'

Keesus, Lake WI Algonquian 'sun-lake.'

Keet Seel AZ Navajo 'empty houses,' with reference to a long-abandoned cliff dwelling.

Keewatin MN Ojibway 'north,' but perhaps a name borrowed from the district in Canada.

Keewaydin PA The name of the northwest wind in Longfellow's *Hiawatha*.

Kego Lake MN Ojibway 'fish.'

Kegonsa, Lake WI Ojibway 'small-fishes,' so named (1854) by L. C. Draper, director of the Wisconsin State Historical Society.

Kekawaka Creek CA Indian, probably Lassik, locally believed to be 'creek-frog.'

Kekegama Lake WI Algonquian, with *gama*, 'lake,' and the rest uncertain.

Kekequabic Lake MN Ojibway, probably 'hawk-iron,' but reference uncertain.

Kekoskee WI From the name of a Winnebago village, literal meaning uncertain.

Kekur A repeated name in AK, from a word adopted into Russian from the language of some Siberian tribe, meaning a high isolated rock or rocky islet, e.g. **Kekur Island**. A Russian adjective formed from this word has yielded **Cape Kekurnoi**.

Keldron SD Perhaps a personal name, but locally believed to be an adaptation of *caldron*, because the town is in a kettle-shaped valley.

Kelp The seaweed, though abundant along much of the Pacific Coast, is common in names only in AK.

Kelso Commonly for the town in Scotland, e.g. in WA named by a man who had come from that place (1884).

Keluche Creek CA From the personal name of a local doctor.

Kemah TX Probably Indian, locally believed to mean 'facing the wind,' because exposed to breezes from the Gulf.

Kenabee Lake Algonquian, meaning uncertain.

Kenai AK Originally the river-name, from Athapascan, recorded as **Kakny**, with the *-ny* probably *-na*, 'river,' and the rest uncertain.

Kendaia NY Iroquoian 'open country, clearing.'

Kendalia In WV, a Latinized form from the personal name Kendall, probably also with the idea of *dale*. In TX the name is similarly derived, either from Kendall Co., or from G. W. Kendall, from whom the county was named.

Kenduskeag ME Algonquian 'eel-weir-place.'

Kenilworth From the English town, better known as the site of a famous castle and, as the title of one of Walter Scott's novels.

Kenjockety Creek NY From the name of an Indian family living there.

Kenna WV For Senator J. E. Kenna.

Kennebago ME Algonquian 'long-pond.'

Kennebec ME The river is recorded, in a French context, as **Kinibeki** as early as 1609. It is Algonquian 'long-reach,' with reference to the stretch of comparatively quiet water below Augusta.

Kennebunk ME Algonquian 'long-cut-bank.'

Kennedy From the personal name, especially for President John F. Kennedy, e.g. the cape FL and the entrance AK, both named commemoratively for him after his assassination in 1963.

Kennekuk KS Named (1858) for the so-called Kickapoo Prophet, who had died about this time.

Kennewick WA Uncertain, locally believed to be an Indian name, 'grassy place.'

Keno OR After some trouble in getting a name, the inhabitants used that of a local bird dog, which had been named after the card game.

Kenockee MI Ojibway 'he-is-long-legged,' an Indian personal name (?).

Kenoma MO Uncertain, but probably a coined name.

Kenosha, Kenoza Algonquian 'pike, pickerel.' **Canosia** MN is the same word, apparently put into a pseudo-Latin form.

Kenova In WV from the first letters of KY, OH, and VA, the town being near the point where the three states join. In WA, a 'chance selection' by a railroad official, and hence probably a borrowing from WV.

Kenoza Lake NY Algonquian 'pickerel.' Cf. **Kenosha.**

Kensee KY A border-name, from KY and TN.

Kensington From the village in England, now part of London.

Kent From the English county, e.g. the county in DE (1683); in CT (1738). The brevity of the name and its occurrence as a personal name have popularized it. In OH for the Kent family, local businessmen (1864). In WA, because the region cultivated hops, as did the county in England. In OR the name was drawn from a hat, the man who suggested it declaring his only reason to be that it was 'nice and short.'

Kentawha Creek MS Probably containing Choctaw *kinta,* 'beaver,' and the rest uncertain.

Kentenia KY A boundary-name from Kentucky, Tennessee, and Virginia.

Kentuck A common nickname for KY or for a person from that state. **Kentuck** WV: named **New Kentucky** (1875) because it reminded someone of KY, and then abbreviated. **Kentuck Slough** OR: for an early settler. It also is a personal name, e.g. **Kentuck Mountain** AZ for

Jim Kentuck, local cattleman. See **Kanetuck.**

Kentucky Probably from Iroquois *kentake,* 'meadow-land,' in which case the river would have taken its name from the region name or from some particular meadow. The name was used for the county organized by VA in 1776, and was firmly fixed by the time of the organization of the state in 1792.

Kentuctaw Creek MS Probably containing Choctaw *kinta,* 'beaver,' and the rest uncertain.

Kenvir KY A border-name from KY and VA.

Kenwood In IL named (1856) by J. A. Kennicott for his family home in Scotland, but apparently with reference also to his own name. In OK from the names William Kennedy and National Hardwood Company.

Keoka Lake ME Probably Algonquian 'where-they-get-earth-(for)-(pots)' (?).

Keokuk IA For an Indian (Fox) chief of the 19th century; applied to the city in 1834 and to the county in 1837.

Keosauqua IA Adopted ca. 1838, probably being shaped from **Keosauk,** an Algonquian (Sac, Fox) name for the Des Moines River, of uncertain meaning.

Keota The original naming was apparently in IA, where it was first **Keoton** from being on the boundary of **Keokuk** and **Washington** counties, and was later simplified by the railroad.

Keowee SC Of Indian origin, locally believed to mean 'place of mulberries.'

Kephart From the personal name, e.g. **Mount Kephart** TN for H. P. Kephart, who wrote of the southern Appalachian region.

Kerens WV For R. C. Kerens, a director of the local railroad.

Kerhonkson NY Algonquian, meaning uncertain.

Kern From the personal name. The cluster in CA is from E. M. Kern, topographer and artist, who accompanied Frémont, and in 1845 was almost drowned in the river that now bears his name.

Kesebem Lake ME Algonquian 'big (principal)-lake.'

Keshequa Creek NY Iroquoian 'spear.'

Keshina WI From the name of a Menominee chief of the mid-19th century.

Kesieway Creek NY From the name of an Indian who lived there in the late 17th century.

Ketchaponack NY Algonquian 'largest-roots-place,' for some kind of edible tubers or groundnuts.

Ketchepedrakee Creek AL Muskogean (Creek) 'mortar-spread-out,' with reference to a block of wood used in pounding corn.

Ketchikan AK Indian (Tlingit) 'wing-like' (?), because of a waterfall having such an appearance by being divided in the center by a rock.

Ketchketch Butte OR From a Klamath word, *kitchkitchli,* meaning 'rough,' or a derivative, *ketchketch,* meaning a kind of fox; it was applied by the Forest Service because of distinctive sound and a desire to establish some Indian names, rather than for a special applicability.

Kettempon Valley CA Wintu 'camass place.'

Kettle May be occasionally for the rare family name, or for an Indian personal name. Its common use, however, is as a descriptive. Certain hills and mountains are so called because they suggest having a top like an inverted kettle. Depressions, on the other hand, are named because their concavity suggests a kettle. Since kettles were common portable utensils even in frontier times, some names arose from incidents involving kettles. **Kettle River** MN is a translation from the Ojibway, but the name may have been given after the Indians obtained kettles from the traders. **Kettle Creek** OR: a pack horse bucked his pack off in this stream and ruined a kettle, which lay in the water for many years. **Kettle Falls** and **River** WA: an incorrect translation of an Indian (Salish) term, referring to a tightly woven basket, somewhat resembling a kettle, used for catching fish. **Kettle Creek** CO: the Powell expedition (1869) lost a kettle here.

Keuka In FL for W. L. Keuka, early settler. In NY probably Iroquoian 'landing-place.'

Kewadin MI For a local Indian chief of the 19th century.

Kewanee, Kewanna, Kewaunee Probably all from Potawatomi 'prairie hen,' but more specifically from the name of a chief. The names occur in IL, IN, WI, with transfers to other states.

Kewaquesaga WI Winnebago, a name given to a third daughter and thus the equivalent of a personal name.

Kewaskum WI For an Indian chief who had his camp here in 1850.

Kewaunee WI Ojibway, indicating a place where a canoe could be taken across a point of land; the town is located at the base of such a peninsula. **Kewenaw** MI and **Keweena** WI are from the same word and are similarly located.

Kewaydin Lake ME Algonquian, probably 'north.'

Keweena See **Kewaunee.**

Keweenawan Mountains WI Algonquian (Ojibway), meaning uncertain.

Kewenaw See **Kewaunee.**

Key An Anglicization of *cayo,* q.v. **Key West** FL: though an origin by folk-etymology from *cayo hueso,* 'bone key' is usually offered, a direct origin from *cayo oeste,* 'west key' seems admissable, since the key is one of the most westerly.

Keya Paha NB Siouan 'turtle-hill.' The name-cluster arises from the hills, which resemble a turtle by being low and rounded.

Keystone For natural features, the name is vaguely descriptive, viz. indicating a central or joining point. For habitation-names it may commemorate PA, 'The Keystone State,' or it may be vaguely commendatory as a place on which others may confidently rest.

Kiahsville WV From a shortening of the given name Hezekiah, a favorite name in the vicinity.

Kiamensi DE Apparently an artificial shaping, for a railroad station name, of nearby Algonquian (now extinct), **Hwis-kakimensi,** probably a tree-name.

Kiamesha NY Algonquian, meaning uncertain.

Kiamichi OK Indian (probably Caddo), the name of a village, meaning uncertain.

Kiantone NY Iroquoian, the name of an Indian village, meaning uncertain.

Kiatte Creek. OH For a local Indian chief, probably of the early 19th century, who is buried at the mouth of the stream.

Kibesillah CA Indian (Pomo), probably 'rock-flat.'

Kicco FL From Kissimmee Island Cattle Company.

Kichi Lake MN Ojibway 'big.'

Kickamuit MA, RI Algonquian 'big-spring-at' (?).

Kickapoo From the Indian tribal name.

Kickout Neck DE See **Kikeout.**

Kidney A descriptive from shape, e.g. the lake in UT.

Kidron OH From the brook mentioned in the Bible. See **Kedron.**

Kief ND Named (1906) for the Ukrainian city, by immigrants.

Kikeout From Dutch *kijkuit,* 'lookout,' occurring, usually as the name of a hill, in DE, NJ, and NY. Variants, under the influence of folk-etymology, are **Kake-out, Kickout, Kaikout, Kykout.**

Kikiktak AK Eskimo 'island.'

Kil See **Kill.**

Kilchis OR From the personal name of a local Indian chief.

Kildare From the town and county in Ireland, usually named by immigrants, e.g. in TX.

Kilkenny MN From the town in Ireland, named by immigrants.

Kill 1) The English verb occurs in a few compounds. **Killdeer Mountains** ND is a translation from the Siouan 'where they kill deer.' **Killbuck** OH was formerly **Killbuckstown,** from a Delaware chief. **Killdevil Hills** NC is probably from an incident involving *kill-devil* as the name of a strong rum. 2) From the Dutch *kil,* properly 'channel,' as in **Arthur Kill** and **Kill van Kull** (see **Kull**), but more commonly in American usage 'small stream,' e.g. **Kil Brook** NY. It is usually preserved as a second element, e.g. **Wall-kill, Catskill,** and without recognition of its meaning, so that an English generic is supplied, e.g. **Wallkill River, Catskill Mountains.**

Killawog NY Probably a much-changed form of an Algonquian name, meaning uncertain.

Killer The bay in AK was named (1928) because of a fight witnessed there by the namers between a whale and a killer whale. **Four Killer Creek** GA: from the name of a Cherokee chief, so called because he had killed four enemies.

Killingly CT Named (1708) from a manor in England.

Killingworth The name was applied in CT (1667); though it exists as an English town-name, it was applied in CT (first as **Kenelmeworth**) by a pioneer who had been born in **Kenilworth,** so that the name may be accepted as a dialectal variant of that one.

Killis Pond NY Probably from John Kelly (or Kellie), early settler.

Killpecker Creek WY Uncertain, but it may arise from the belief that certain waters contain saltpeter and thus have an adverse effect upon virility.

Kilmarnock VA From the town in Scotland.

Kilsyth WV For the town in Scotland.

Kilts OR For Jesse Kilts, first postmaster.

Kim In CO the town was named for Kipling's character. In AZ it is a railroad name, and was named for a well-liked Chinese cook on a private railroad car.

Kimama ID A railroad name, from Shoshone 'butterfly' (?). See **Kuna.**

Kimberly Regularly from the personal name, e.g. in ID for Peter Kimberly, local financier. In MO (1901) the naming was at a time when Africa was much in the news, and it may be for the city which was known from the Boer War, with the spelling changed to conform to common American practice.

Kimshew Creek CA Indian (Maidu) 'little stream.'

Kinaholi NM Navajo 'drafty house.'

Kinchafoonee Creek GA Muskogean (Creek) 'mortar-nutshells,' apparently for a device for cracking nuts.

Kinderhook NY From the Dutch, 'children's point,' dating from the early 17th century, it may record some incident involving Indian children.

Kineo ME, NH Algonquian 'sharp-peak.'

King 1) Most often for a personal name, e.g. in TX the towns **King, Kingsbury, Kingsland, Kings Mill** (for Andrew Kingsmill), and **Kingsville.** 2) In pre-Revolutionary times for the English king, e.g. the counties in VA, **King and Queen, King George** and **King William. Kingstree** SC: for a tree which was marked as being reserved for naval use. It is sometimes a counterpart name with Queen or Prince. 3) The idea of pre-eminence is probably a secondary motive in some instances. **King Bee** MD preserves a dialect word formed on the analogy of queen bee. 4) **Kings River** CA: named in Spanish for the Three Kings, because some explorers reached the stream on or about their day (Jan. 6). But **King Spur,** though in Kings Canyon N.P., is for Clarence King, as is **Mount Clarence King. King of Prussia** PA: from an inn sign representing King Frederick I, the owner in Colonial times being a native of Prussia. **King Arthur Castle** AZ, see **Bedivere. Kingston** NY: from a town in England. **King and Queen Rocks** SD: these two mounds of rocks rise close together and higher than others around them. **Kingsport** TN: probably for Col. James King who established a mill here in 1774, with *port* because it was a shipping point on the Holston River. **King Lear Peak** NV: probably from a mine-name; though the connection with Shakespeare is obvious, the name may have been suggested from miners named King and Lear.

Kingfisher Commonly for the bird, e.g. the lakes in KY. The town and county in OK are for King Fisher, early stage station keeper.

Kingsessing PA Algonquian (Delaware), by partial folk-etymology from a term meaning 'big-shells-at.'

Kinlichee AZ Navajo 'place of the red house,' thus named for the ruins of an ancient pueblo.

Kinmundy IL Named, ca. 1857, for a place in Scotland, birthplace of William Ferguson, one of the English agents for the Illinois Central Railroad.

Kinnickinnick From a substitute for tobacco, or the plant producing it, used by various Indians and by frontiersmen, the actual plants differing in various parts of the country. It was applied to features, usually places where the plant was abundantly found, and then shifted by transfer to habitation-names. Spellings differ, e.g. **Pinnickinnick, Kinniconick, Kinnikinic.** Though originally an Algonquian word, it got into English and French, and was distributed by speakers of those languages more than by Indians.

Kinnorutin Creek AK Eskimo 'you-are-crazy,' given by an explorer as a comment upon his own topographical mistake.

Kino Peak AZ For Fr. Eusebio Francisco Kino, missionary among the Papagos, 1694–1711.

Kinross IA, MI From the town in Scotland.

Kinsacks Creek AL Probably Choctaw *kushak,* 'cane,' but altered to the form of an English possessive personal name.

Kinsale VA From the town in Ireland.

Kinsman From the personal name, e.g. the notch in NH from Asa Kinsman, early pioneer, who opened a road through it.

Kinston In NC it was named (1762) as **Kingston** for King George III, but a shift in spelling was effected after the Revolution.

Kinta OK Choctaw 'beaver.'

Kinterbish Creek AL Choctaw 'beaver-lodge.'

Kin Tiel AZ Navajo 'house-broad,' being a large ruined pueblo.

Kintla Mountain MT Indian (Kootenai) 'sack,' but reference uncertain.

Kinzua Creek PA Algonquian (Delaware), literally, 'they gobble,' the equivlent of **Turkey Creek.**

Kiokee Creek GA Muskogean, probably 'falls.'

Kiomatia Originally for the river TX, probably Indian, and locally believed to mean 'clear water.'

Kiona WA Locally believed to be Indian 'brown hills.'

Kiowa From the Indian tribal name.

Kipling From the personal name; in MI, MS, and OH, for Rudyard Kipling, the names being given in the 1890's when he was at the height of his literary popularity.

Kirker Creek CA Originally **Quercus** (Latin 'oak'), presumably named because of the numerous oaks, but in Latin to avoid undue repetition of a common name. The name was not understood by most people, and was changed by folk-etymology appearing as **Kirka,** and **Kirke,** but finally becoming **Kirker,** as if from a personal name.

Kiron IA For unknown reasons two early residents were impressed by the name Kirin in Manchuria, and named the town by an adaptation.

Kisacoquilla Creek PA Algonquian (Delaware) 'already-snakes-in-dens,' but reference uncertain.

Kisatchie LA Choctaw 'reed-river.'

Kishwaukee IL Algonquian (Sauk) 'sycamore.'

Kiska AK Aleut, meaning uncertain.

Kiskatom NY Algonquian 'hickory-nut,' here the shortening of a longer name.

Kiskiminetas River PA Algonquian (Delaware), though probably analyzable as 'day-spirit,' the real meaning is uncertain.

Kisko, Mount NY Algonquian 'edge-(of)-creek-land.'

Kismet KS From the idea 'destiny, fate'; the reason for naming is uncertain, but the term had circulation in the early 20th century because of a popular play.

Kissena Pond NY A modern introduced name, from Ojibway 'it is cold.'

Kissimmee, Lake FL Probably Seminole, meaning unknown.

Kiss Me Quick Hills SD Because associated with a road full of kiss-me-quicks, i.e. bumps of the kind so called.

Kit Carson From the famous mountaineer, e.g. the pass in CA which was named by Frémont for this trusted guide when they were in its vicinity in 1844.

Kitchawan NY Algonquian 'strong (big)-running,' applied first to **Croton River.**

Kitchen Generally from the personal name. The creek in MT was originally **Catching Creek** for a local lumberman, shifted by folk-etymology.

Kitemaug CT Algonquian 'great (chief) fishing-place.'

Kitsap County WA For a local Indian chief.

Kitta Hatta Creek MS Choctaw 'mortar-white,' apparently for some special mortar for pounding corn.

Kittaning PA Algonquian (Delaware) 'big-stream-at,' from its situation on the Allegheny River.

Kittatinny Mountain NJ, PA Algonquian (Delaware) 'big-mountain-at.'

Kitten Rarely as a diminutive (cf. **Cub**), e.g. the gut NJ, which is a tributary of **Cat Gut.**

Kittery ME From Kittery Court, England, from which some of the early settlers came (1647).

Kittinelbe CA From the name of an Indian village; meaning unknown.

Kittitas WA Probably an Indian tribal name.

Kitty Hawk NC By folk-etymology from an Indian (Algonquian?) name, recorded (1729) as Chickahauk; meaning uncertain.

Kiwa Butte OR Chinook jargon, 'crooked, bent,' a descriptive.

Kiwanda, Cape OR Probably from an Indian personal name.

Klaganissecook Falls ME Algonquian 'noisy-stream-little-at.'

Klagetoh AZ Navajo 'water in the ground.'

Klamath From the Indian tribal name, in early spellings often **Tlamath.**

Klan Butte MT Because it was formerly a meeting place for the local Ku Klux Klan.

Klaskanine River OR See **Claskanine.**

Klawhop Butte OR Chinook jargon, 'hole,' a descriptive, because of a crater in the top.

Klawock AK From the name of a local Indian chief.

Kleenkoal WV Rather obviously, for clean coal, a commendatory in a mining district.

Klickitat In WA from a local Indian tribe. The mountain in OR was at a point to which this tribe sometimes made incursions.

Klim Creek AK Named (1924) by a party of geologists who found their supplies reduced to a can of Klim (powdered milk).

Klipsan Beach WA Indian, locally said to mean 'sunset.'

Kloan, Klone OR Chinook jargon, 'three,' because the place named was the third in order.

Klondike The name was popularized by the discovery of gold on the Canadian river, and in the next few years was applied to places, especially where the idea of rich gold deposits was to be suggested, e.g. **Klondike Mountain** CO.

Kloochman Creek OR Chinook jargon, 'woman.'

Klukwan AK Indian (Tlingit), probably 'old-town.'

Klutina River AK Athapascan 'glacier-river.'

Knappa OR For a man named Knapp, with the vowel added, either because his first name was Aaron, or because a habitation-name often ends in *a*.

Knife Considering the importance of the knife as an early implement, the name is rare, as compared, e.g., with **Pipe**. A name-cluster in MN probably sprang from the **Portage**, which had sharp slates, compared to knives. **Knife River** ND: because its vicinity was a source of flint from which Indians made knives.

Knik AK From an Indian village, but probably an Eskimo word, 'fire.'

Knob A generic, chiefly in the Middle West, e.g. IN, KY, for a knoblike hill; in both of these states a district is known as **The Knobs**. It becomes a specific by association, e.g. **Knob Creek** KY. **Knob Noster** MO: the second term is probably by folk-etymology from some Indian term.

Knobly Mountain WV The adjective form indicates that the mountain is not a knob itself but has knoblike protuberances on it.

Knotty Creek IA A descriptive for a very crooked stream, which might be said to tie knots in itself.

Knownothing CA The name, on two creeks, probably is a vestige of the short-lived political party, thus known in popular speech. The party was strong in CA in the 1850's, and a place where a member of the party lived might be thus called. The name was a common one for mines, perhaps for the party, but also perhaps because owners of mining claims sometimes refused to talk about the richness of the find.

Knox From the personal name, often for Henry Knox (1750–1806), Revolutionary general, e.g. **Knoxville** TN and a number of counties.

Knulthkarn Creek CA Yurok, of unknown meaning.

Koasati See **Coushatta**.

Kobeh Valley NV Indian (Shoshonean) 'face,' in the sense of 'round.'

Kobossee Island ME Algonquian 'sturgeon.'

Kobuk River AK Eskimo 'big river.'

Koch From the personal name, in MO honoring Robert Koch (1843–1910), bacteriologist, being named in 1915.

Kodak The trade name for a certain camera has been adopted as a habitation name in KY and TN. **Kodak Point** SD: a favorite point from which pictures may be taken.

Kodiak AK Eskimo (Innuit) 'island,' since this is the largest island of the area.

Kodol WV Named ca. 1900 from the name of a patent medicine, Kodol Dyspepsia Cure, one of the names submitted in a list to the Post Office Dept. Both the submitters and the department were doubtless influenced by the fact that this was an unusual name, not occurring elsewhere.

Koessek See **Coaksett**.

Kofa AZ From a brand *K of A,* derived from the King of Arizona Mine Company.

Kohanza Lakes CT Probably a garbled form of **Kenosha**, q.v.

Kohatk AZ Pima 'where a hollow has been made.' The variant **Quajota** shows Spanish influence.

Kohi Kug AZ Papago 'mulberry stands.'

Koip Peak CA Probably Northern Paiute 'mountain sheep.'

Kokadjo Mountain ME Algonquian 'kettle-mountain,' from the Indian story that the giant Glooscap, pursuing a moose calf, here threw his kettle upside down.

Kokanee For the variety of salmon so known, e.g. **Kokanee Cove** CO.

Kokechik Bay, River AK Eskimo 'has wood.'

Koko TN See **Yum Yum**.

Kokomo IN From the personal name of a local Indian.

Kokosing River OH Algonquian 'owls-at.'

Kokostick Butte OR Chinook jargon, 'woodpecker.'

Kokoweep Peak CA Southern Paiute, probably 'wind-canyon.'

Kola NB Probably from the Kola Peninsula in Russia.

Koldok ND A railroad name, a phonetic spelling from the presence there of a 'coal dock.'

Kolelemook Lake NH Algonquian 'shining-pond.'

Komelik AZ Papago 'flats.'

Kongakut River AK Eskimo 'caribou-pond.'

Kongscut CT Algonquian 'high-place-at.'

Konkapot MA, CT From the name of a chief of the early 18th century.

Konocti, Mount CA Indian (Pomo), probably 'mountain-woman.'

Konomoc Lake CT Algonquian 'long-fish (i.e. eels)-at.'

Konowa OK Muskogean (Seminole) 'string of beads,' but reference uncertain.

Koochiching County MN Cree, though adopted by the Ojibways, a name for present **Rainy River**, of uncertain meaning.

Kooi WY From Peter Kooi, owner of the site.

Koosharem UT From an edible tuber, a food staple of the local Indians.

Kooskia ID Nez Percé, a shortening of *kooskooskia*, probably 'clearwater,' originally applied to the present **Clearwater River.**

Kootenai ID From the Indian tribal name.

Korea For the country in Asia, e.g. in KY and VA.

Korona FL A commendatory from Latin *corona*, 'crown,' with spelling influenced by Polish settlers.

Kosciusko For Thaddeus Kosciusko, Polish officer who served in the American Revolution.

Kosh Creek CA For John Kosh, mine superintendent ca. 1860.

Koshkonong WI Ojibway, the name of a Winnebago village, probably 'shut-in-(with)-fog,' because of the foggy situation.

Kosmos Occurring as **Kosmos** WA and **Kosmosdale** KY, it is from the Greek 'world,' and is commendatory from its suggestion of *cosmopolitan.*

Kosoma OK Muskogean (Choctaw) 'stinking,' with reference to a sulphur spring.

Kossuth For Louis Kossuth, Hungarian patriot, whose visit to the U.S. in 1851–1852 aroused great enthusiasm, and led to the naming of towns in PA and MS.

Kosta Lake FL Seminole 'panther,' in translation, **Tiger Lake.**

Kotsina River AK Athapascan 'coal river.'

Kotzebue AK For Otto von Kotzebue, who named the sound for himself in 1816, during his exploring voyage.

Ko Vaya AZ Papago 'badger well.'

Kowanda NB From the Czech personal name of an early settler.

Koyukuk River AK From an Indian tribal name (?), probably Eskimo, since it apparently contains *kuk*, 'river.'

Krakow From the city in Poland.

Kripplebush NY From Dutch *kreupelbosch*, 'thicket, underbrush.' See **Cripple.**

Krugloi Russian 'round,' e.g. the island in AK.

Krusenstern, Cape AK Named in 1816 for Admiral A. J. van Krusenstern by Kotzebue, whose expedition was in the area at the time.

Krusof Island AK In 1805 a Russian captain named it 'Crooze Island,' reputedly for a Russian admiral; the present name has rather uncertainly developed from that one.

Krypton See **Neon.**

Kuakatch AZ Papago 'end of mountain.'

Kuamaski Butte OR Klamath 'at the cave,' but named by the Forest Service to perpetuate an Indian name, though the butte is a long way from the place originally so named.

Kuiu Island AK Indian (Tlingit), meaning uncertain.

Kuk River AK Eskimo 'river.'

Kukpuk River AK Eskimo 'river-big.'

Kula Kala Point WA Probably Chinook jargon, 'travel,' but reference not known.

Kuli, Kulli, Kully Muskogean (Choctaw) 'spring,' occurs in OK as **Kuli Inla,** 'spring-new'; **Kullituklo,** 'springs-two'; **Kully Chaha,** 'spring-high,' the last with reference to a spring on a mountainside.

Kull In **Kill van Kull** NJ, NY it is probably a family name, the ordinary formation as Kull's Kill being prevented by phonetics and *van* being used as the equivalent of English *of*.

Kulm ND Named (ca. 1893) for the city (now Chelmno in Poland) because of immigrants.

Kumiva Peak NV Northern Paiute 'sky-mountain,' because of its height.

Kumtux WA Chinook jargon, 'know,' but reference uncertain.

Kum Vo AZ Papago 'hackberry well.' Also **Comovo.**

Kuna The peak in CA is Indian, probably Shoshonean 'fire,' applied ca. 1883. In ID it is a railroad name, apparently coined ca. 1880 to avoid duplication with names elsewhere, as was done with other names in this area, e.g. **Kimama, Minidoka.** Like these, Kuna has an 'Indian' suggestion, but no meaning can be assigned. Because of the date, a transfer from CA is unlikely. The butte and caves in ID were named secondarily.

Kuncanowet Hills NH Algonquian 'long-sharp-places-at,' with reference to the range of hills.

Kuparuk River AK Eskimo, probably 'river-big.'

Kupreanof Island AK For Capt. I .A. Kupreanof, governor of the Russian American Colonies (1836–1840).

Kushaqua, Lake NY Iroquoian 'spear,' a name introduced in the 19th century.

Kuskokwim River AK Eskimo, with *-kwim,* 'stream,' and the rest uncertain.

Kussus Kook Lake ME Algonquian 'stony-falls' (?).

Kuttawa KY A variant form of **Catawba,** the Indian tribal name.

Kutztown PA For George Kutz, who founded it (1771).

Kwagunt Valley AZ For a Paiute Indian who lived there in the 1860's.

Kweo Butte OR Chinook jargon, 'circle,' a descriptive.

Kwethluk AK Eskimo 'little (bad)-river.'

Kwiguk AK Eskimo 'big-river.'

Kwinnum Butte OR Chinook jargon, 'five,' being the fifth in a series of buttes, all named at one time by the Forest Service.

Kwolh Butte OR Chinook jargon, 'aunt,' named arbitrarily by the Forest Service, an analogy to nearby 'relationship' names, e.g. **The Sisters.**

Kykout See **Kikeout.**

Kyote TX An alternate spelling for **Coyote.**

Kyrene AZ From the Greek name of the district in northern Africa in ancient times, probably given because of other classical names nearby, and to suggest the desert nature of the region.

Kyserike NY Recorded (1702) as **Keysserryck,** from Keyser, the name of the family owning the land, and the Dutch *rijk,* 'property.'

L

L Lake NB A descriptive, for shape.

La Spanish and French 'the,' feminine, singular. In proper names it has often been amalgamated with the main word, e.g. in one of the spellings of **Lafayette.** For economy of presentation, most of the names beginning in **La** (except when it is amalgamated) have been alphabetized under the main word. Sometimes e.g. **La Frank,** the **La** is not genuine, and represents a kind of pseudo-French.

Labadieville LA For J. L. Labadie, plantation owner of the 19th century.

La Batre, Bayou AL Probably from American French *batture,* a term applied to a place where the inner shore of a stream has been built up.

La Bauves, Bayou LA From the La Beauve family, early settlers, with a possessive or plural *s.*

Labette KS Probably French, a personal name (?). The local attempt to derive it from *la bête,* 'the beast,' seems unlikely.

Labish, Lake OR French 'la biche,' the female elk.

Laborcita New Mexican Spanish 'small piece of land, small farm.'

Labor in Vain Creek Occurring twice in MA, the name is probably to be taken as from an incident, such as attempting to row against the tide.

Labuco AL From Lacey-Buek Iron Company.

Lac French 'lake.' It has generally been absorbed into the English form, but exists in a number of petrified examples in areas of original French naming. **Lac du Flambeau** WI: 'lake of the torch,' perhaps so called because of torches used for attracting fish at night. **Lac Vieux Desert:** Probably a shortening of Lac au Vieux Desert, literally 'lake of the old desert.' *Desert,* however, must be taken in the common French sense of an uninhabited or deserted place. According to one account, the lake was named because of an old Indian planting ground.

Lac Court Oreilles WI: probably for Lac des Courtes Oreilles, 'Lake of the Short Ears,' of uncertain origin. **Lac Qui Parle** MN: 'lake which talks'; a translation from the Siouan, but of uncertain origin, suggested to have been for echoes or for mysterious sounds on some occasion which gave rise to the belief that the lake was haunted by spirits.

Lacassine LA From the name of an Indian (Attakapas) chief.

Lachine MI Probably from the Lachine Rapids in Canada.

Lachute, Bayou LA French 'waterfall,' named for a slight fall of water in its course. See **Chute.**

Lacjac CA From the firm of winemakers and distillers, Lachman & Jacobi.

Lack Creek CA For Dr. M. F. Lack, early settler.

Lackamissa Creek PA Algonquian (Delaware) 'sandy-soil.'

Lackawack NY Algonquian 'forks-at.'

Lackawanna, Lackawannock NY, PA Algonquian (Delaware) 'fork-stream-(at),' because at this point there was a forking in an important trail.

Lackawaxen PA Algonquian (Delaware) 'fork-trail-at.'

Lacomb OR When Tacoma was rejected by the Post Office Dept. because of duplication, a somewhat similar name was coined.

Lacombe LA From a French family name, that of a settler of the 18th century.

Lacon, Lacona Variants of **Laconia** (?).

Laconia A short-lived name for New Hampshire, given in 1629. Ferdinando Gorges, one of the grantees wrote that it was so named because of its many lakes, but it is also the name of an ancient Greek district, and its use here must be considered a punning. The present **Laconia NH** is a 19th-century revival of the old name, the town being located in a region of lakes.

La Conner WA Named in 1869 by the owner of the trading post there from the initials of his wife (Louisa Ann), and her maiden name Conner.

Lacoochee FL A shortening of **Withlacoochee.**

Lacota Probably a variant of **Lakota.**

La Crescenta CA Coined from English 'crescent,' with a Spanish article and an ending to suggest a Spanish word. The idea was suggested by crescent-shaped formations in the vicinity.

Lacrosse, La Crosse See **Crosse.**

Laddie Creek WY From Lettie Kieth, early settler, probably shifted by folketymology.

Laddonia MO For Amos Ladd, who helped lay out the town.

Ladera Spanish 'hillside.'

Ladoga From the largest European lake; used in several states, probably aided by its euphony.

Ladonia TX Manufactured from the Spanish *La Doña,* with spelling changed to approximate the Spanish pronunciation; reason for application unknown.

Ladora IA Coined by a music teacher from the notes of the scale, *la, do,* and *re.*

Ladron Spanish 'robber.' The mountains in NM doubtless harbored robbers, Indian or white, at various times, but the exact cause of the naming is unknown.

La Due MO For A. D. Ladue, a local judge.

Lady Rare, and generally of obscure origin. It may be from a personal name. **Ladies Island SC** is probably a transla-

tion of a Spanish religious naming for 'Our Lady.' **Ladies Canyon CA** is locally believed to be a euphemism for *cunt,* and elsewhere also the name may cover up an obscenity. **Lady Lake MN:** a shortening from the wild flower, lady-slipper, because of its profusion there. **My Lady's Bush Island SC:** tradition has it that a 'lady' was taken in childbirth while traveling, and bore a child in the shelter of a bush on this island. **Lady Franklin Rock CA:** for Lady Jane Franklin, widow of the Arctic explorer, who visited Yosemite Park in 1863 and admired the view from this rock. **Ladiesburg MD:** local tradition attributes the name to a preponderance of females in the early population, but it more likely is from the personal name, i.e. **Lady's Burg. My Lady Branch MD:** from **My Lady's Manor,** so called because Lord Baltimore bestowed it upon his wife in 1713.

Ladybug One of the few insects to appear in nomenclature. At certain times of year ladybugs gather into large masses, and could occasion a name, e.g. **Ladybug Peak AK** and various features in CA.

La Fave River AR From a family of early French settlers, recorded as Le Fevre.

La Favre, Fourche AR From the name of its French discoverer.

Lafitte LA From having been the establishment of Jean Lafitte, pirate and smuggler of the early 19th century.

Lafourche French 'la fourche.' See **Fourche.**

Lafox IL Originally **La Fox,** named in 1866 from its situation on the **Fox River,** apparently with a French feminine article prefixed, out of whim or ignorance.

La France SC French 'the France,' derived from a company name.

La Frank WV Named ca. 1928 by Frank Mullens, the first postmaster, who coined it from his name, with a pseudo-French article.

Lagartija Spanish 'wall lizard.'

Lagarto TX Spanish 'lizard,' but here probably with reference to the alligator.

L'Agles Creek AR From French *l'aigles,* 'the eagles.'

Lago Spanish, Italian 'lake.' In ID the name of the village may have been suggested by a similar-sounding Indian name.

La Grange See **Grange.**

Lagro IN From French *le gros,* 'the big (fat) one,' a nickname for a Miami chief.

Lagrue Creek AR From French *la grue,* 'the crane (bird).'

Laguna Spanish 'lake.' It sometimes maintains itself as a generic in American usage, e.g. **Laguna Salada** CA, but is more commonly a specific, e.g. **Laguna Beach** CA. **Lagunita** is the diminutive, as in the tautological **Lagunita Lake** CA.

Lahaska PA Algonquian (Delaware) 'writing-much,' probably because of the negotiation of a treaty there.

Lahaway Creek NJ A variant of **Rockaway,** q.v.

Lahoma OK From the last part of **Oklahoma.**

Lahontan The extinct lake and the present reservoir in NV honor the Baron de Lahontan, French explorer and author (ca. 1666–1713).

Lahore VA From the city of India.

Laingkat GA From the province in Sumatra, named (ca. 1900) by a man who was raising Sumatran tobacco.

Lajitas TX Spanish (diminutive) from *laja,* 'flagstone,' because of rock formations.

La Joy TX Probably a variant spelling of **Jolla.**

Lake A generic, but often as a specific to denote a feature associated with a lake, e.g. **Lake Creek,** from taking its rise in a lake or flowing through a lake. **Lake Mountain** may have a lake on its slope, or may stand near a lake. The name is also common for habitations, both by transfer and for high commendatory value, both for suggestion of commerce (**Lakeport, Lake City**), and for the idea of pleasant living, because of good views (**Lakeview, Lake Vista**) and other reasons. There are scores of such names as **Lake, Lakeville, Lakeland, Lakeside.** Such a name as **Lakewood** provides a double commendatory. **Lake** OR: originally it was **Christmas Lake,** because it was situated on that lake; **Christmas** was dropped, and then the post office was moved several miles from the lake, so that it is no longer descriptive. **Lake** WV: for Nicholas Lake, first postmaster.

Lakota From the Indian tribal name, a variant of **Dakota. Lakota Peak** SD is locally believed to be named for a Mrs. Lakota, a squatter, but she may have taken the tribal name.

Lama Spanish 'mud,' e.g. **Lama Canyon** NM.

Lamanda Park CA Coined in 1886 by L. J. Rose, landowner, from his wife's name Amanda, probably with the *l* added as a pseudo-Spanish article.

Lame 1) From an Indian personal name, e.g. **Lame Lake** SD for Mary Lame, a resident there. 2) As a secondary specific, e.g. **Lame Steer Lake** NB, because a lame steer was abandoned there. **Lame Johnny Creek** SD: for a notorious bandit who in 1882 robbed a stagecoach at the crossing of this creek and was later hanged by vigilantes at the same spot, and his body was then burned.

Lamelee Creek IA From the French name of a trader, Lemoliese, who lived on the stream, ca. 1820.

Lamesa See **Mesa.**

Lamine River MO For French *la mine,* 'the mine,' i.e. a stream where a mine was situated.

Lamington NJ First applied to the river; the earliest recorded form, probably 17th century, is Algonquian *allametunk,* probably 'within-hills-at.' Succeeding forms can be traced through the 18th century as Lametunk, Lamaton. This is one of the best examples of an Indian term which has shifted to the exact semblance of an English place-name, though no such English place exists.

Lamoille The river in VT appears on a French map (1744) as *la Mouelle;* this is probably for a family name, more usually spelled Lamouille. The creek in NV is for a French trapper who built a cabin there in the 1850's.

La Moine, Lamoine In ME, from an early French settler named De La Moine; in CA, a transfer from ME. In WA, by local story, when a name was being sought, this one was seen on a can of sardines.

Lamoni IA Named by members of the Reorganized Church of Latter-Day Saints for a king in the *Book of Mormon;* reason for naming, uncertain.

Lamonta OR A coined name, taken to mean 'the mountain,' from a nearby butte.

La Motte, Isle VT For the Sieur de la Motte, French commander, who built a fort here in 1666.

LaMoure See **Jud.**

Lamourie, LA Probably from French *le murier,* 'the mulberry-tree,' first applied to the bayou.

Lampasas TX First applied to the river, it is probably the same as Spanish *lampazo,* 'burdock,' in the plural.

Lampeter PA From a town in Wales, introduced by Welsh immigrants in the early 18th century.

Lampopeag Branch ME Algonquian 'like-a-rope-stream,' i.e. crooked.

Lamy NM For Archbishop J. B. Lamy, hero of Willa Cather's *Death Comes for the Archbishop.*

L'Anacoco See **Anacoco.**

Lanare CA From L. A. Nares, local promoter of the settlement.

Lanark From the town and county in Scotland.

Lancaster From the town and county in England. Counties were so named in VA (1651), and PA (1726); a town in MA (1653); a county in SC, because of settlers from PA (1798); so also, a town in OH (1800). In KY the town was named (1798) by settlers from PA.

Lance Creek WY Because ash trees growing here supplied wood to the Indians for lances.

Lancelot Point AZ See **Bedivere.**

Lancha Plana CA Spanish 'flatboat,' named because such a boat was used there for a ferry in the 1850's.

Lander From the personal name; in NV and WY in honor of Gen. F. W. Lander, who conducted explorations in the area in the 1850's.

Lando SC Called by German settlers in the 18th century after Landau, the city in Germany, simplified in spelling.

Lane Regularly from the personal name, e.g. **Lane County** OR for Joseph Lane, governor and senator. As a common noun, it appears in **Laneville** TX, so named because it stands at the junction of four lanes.

Langley From the personal name, e.g. **Mount Langley** CA for S. P. Langley, astronomer and physicist who conducted experiments in the area in 1881.

Langtry TX Probably for the well-known actress, Lily Langtry.

L'Anguille See **Anguille.**

Lannahassee Creek GA Muskogean (Creek), meaning uncertain, but from *lani,* 'yellow' (?).

Lanoka Harbor NJ An adaptation from **Lanes Oaks,** a name which was partly in honor of George Oakes, an old resident.

L'Anse MI American-French 'the bay,' but here referring rather to the peninsula forming the bay.

Lansing From the personal name, especially for John Lansing (1754–1829?), political figure and jurist, for whom the village in NY was named. Emigrants from this village carried the name to MI. In MN the name was placed partly in compliment to Alanson B. Vaughan, pioneer settler, because his first name was of similar sound.

Lantana FL From the flower, a commendatory and also euphonic.

Lanton MO For Lancaster and Sutton, founders.

Laona In WI it is by mistake in recording the legal papers, for Leona Johnson, daughter of a local businessman.

Lapatubbee Creek MS Literally 'buck-killer,' for an Indian so named.

Lapeer MI A spelling, more or less from the pronunciation, of *la pierre* (French 'the stone') with reference to the stream now known as **Flint River**, which is itself an approximate translation of the French name.

La Perouse, Mount, Glacier AK For J. F. de Galaup, comte de La Pérouse, who explored the coast in 1786, named commemoratively in 1874.

Lapile AR Probably from a French family name.

Lapine OR From the pine trees in the vicinity, apparently supposed to be French, though it should properly, then, be Le Pin.

Lapoint UT The *point* is for a projecting spur of mountain, and this has apparently been coupled with the French *la*, 'the,' to produce a coined name.

Lapomique Branch ME Algonquian 'like-a-rope,' i.e. crooked.

La Porte French 'the gate, the gateway,' the original naming being the town in IN, so called by the French in the 18th century, probably because it was the opening of a passageway into the forested country which begins at that point. **La Porte** TX: situated on a passageway into Galveston Bay; in this and other instances the suggestion of the English 'port' is strong.

Lapover Lake OR From a cabin, which was so called because part of it lapped over the other part.

La Prele See **Prele**.

La Push WA Chinook jargon, 'mouth,' probably with reference to a stream.

Lapwai ID Nez Percé, probably 'butter-fly-stream.'

Laramie The river in WY took its name from a French trapper who was killed along the stream by Indians, ca. 1825; his name was Jacques La Ramie, though the family name appears in various spellings.

Larch From either the true larch or some other species confused with it; for instance, **Larch Mountain** OR is probably named for its firs. The species made little impression, and the name is comparatively rare.

Laredo The original naming is in TX, where the town was founded in 1755 and named after the town in Spain.

L'Argent, Bayou LA French 'the silver,' but probably from a personal name.

Largo Spanish 'long.' But in CA the name is apparently an adaptation from that of L. F. Long, early resident and politician. **Lake Largo** FL is a 19th-century shift from the too common **Long Lake**: the town is named from the lake.

Lariat TX From the cowboy's rope, but reason for application unknown.

Larissa NB For Larissa Cole, daughter of the first postmaster.

Larto Lake and bayou in LA are from the French family name Lartault, recorded in the colony in the 18th century.

Las Spanish 'the,' feminine, plural. Most of the names thus beginning have been alphabetized under the main word, e.g. for **Las Aguilas**, see **Aguilas**.

La Sal UT Spanish 'the salt,' probably from 'de la sal,' 'of the salt,' used for some feature associated with a salt-deposit; now applied to mountains and a village.

La Salle Numerous namings are for Robert Cavelier, Sieur de La Salle (1643–1687), French explorer.

La Sara, Lasara TX For Laura Harding and Sara Gill, not otherwise identified.

Lasauses CO An Americanized spelling for Spanish *las sauces,* 'the willows.'

Lascar CO Probably in the meaning '(East) Indian sailor,' by local tradition a name taken from a book, and having no local significance.

Lashmeet SV From the family name, locally recorded as Lashmutt.

Lassen The name-cluster in CA is for Peter Lassen, Danish immigrant to CA in 1840, an important pioneer. His name came to be associated with the peak, probably, because of his explorations around it in the course of establishing 'Lassen's Route' of the California Trail.

Lassic CA From an Indian tribal name, which was also, apparently, the name of one of their chiefs.

Last Occasionally denotes some last feature passed before arriving at a customary destination, e.g. **Last Creek** MN. More common is **Last Chance,** often in the West used to indicate a place where water was available before the beginning of a desert, or something similar. **Last Chance Creek** OR: the last place where a camp could be made on a certain occasion in 1890. **Last Chance Spring** CA: in 1871 a party reached water here, after almost perishing in the desert. **Last Chance Canyon** NM: in 1881 a party, about to turn back for lack of water, found a running stream here. The colorful name inspires some fanciful stories, but others are authentic. **Last Dollar Mountain** CO: probably from the name of a mine on which someone staked his last dollar.

Lasuen Point CA For Father F. F. de Lasuén, prominent in the development of the missions, named by Vancouver in 1792.

Latah ID, WA Nez Percé, uncertain, but probably in part 'pine-tree.'

Latanier American-French for the dwarf palmetto, e.g. the bayou in LA.

Latex TX A boundary-name, from common abbreviations of LA and TX.

Latexo TX A company, the Louisiana-Texas Orchards, planted a large orchard here, and coined the name from the common abbreviations of the two state names, plus the first letter of 'orchard.'

Latham From the personal name, e.g. in KS for Arlie Latham, shortstop; when the Missouri Pacific built across Kansas in the 1880's, fourteen places were named for players on the champion St. Louis Brown's baseball team; of these, **Bushong** also survives, for 'Doc' Bushong, pitcher.

Latuda UT For Frank Latuda, mine owner.

Laughing Pig, The WY From the appearance of a rock.

Laundry Creek SD For Alex Laundry, early settler.

Laurel Various trees and shrubs known as laurel grow over much of the country. They are generally conspicuous and some of them bear beautiful flowers. Many natural features are named thus. The laurel also has commendatory value (cf. its classical use as a crown of victory), and either by itself or in combination occurs widely as a habitation-name. **Laurel Ridge** PA, WV, also **Hill, Mountain,** is one of the chief ridges of the Appalachians and a name dating from about 1750; as the early alternate **Laurel Thickets** indicates, the name was not commendatory, but the reverse, since the thickets impeded progress on the trail. The Spanish singular is the same as the English, but the plural, *laureles,* survives on some places in CA.

Laurens From the personal name, e.g. in SC for Henry Laurens, Revolutionary leader. In IA it is, by local tradition, for a person named in J. L. Motley's *History of the United Netherlands,* which has no such person; one Laurens is named in the same author's *Rise of the Dutch Republic;* he is, however, described as 'coarse, cruel and ignorant,' and one has difficulty in seeing how he could have been chosen for honor.

Laurium From the Latin form of the town in Greece, famous in ancient times for its mines, the town in MI being in a mining area.

Lava The occurrence of lava has produced many names in the volcanic areas of the West. The suggestions of the term seem to make it unpleasant, and it is rare as a habitation-name.

Lavaca TX Spanish 'the cow,' a translation of the earlier French name, given by La Salle in 1685 because of the presence of buffalo.

Lavalle WI Named by an early settler on the assumption that it meant 'the valley' in French.

Lavalley CO From a combination of French or Spanish *la* with English *valley,* 'the valley.'

La Verkin UT The village is named from the creek, which is a tributary of the **Virgin River:** the name is thus an American adaptation of the Spanish **La Virgen,** with an approximation of the pronunciation.

Lavernia TX Locally explained as Spanish, it is either a bad attempt at Spanish (with the idea of 'the green'), or else a personal name.

La Ward TX For Lafayette Ward, early settler.

Lawford WV A ford where a man named Law once lived, according to local accounts; but Lawford is also a personal name.

Lawn Almost never appears in names of natural features, doubtless because a lawn itself is conceived as a cultivated phenomenon. It is not very common with habitation-names, in spite of a lawn being a common American status

symbol and also existing as a personal name. It is most frequent in the commendatory **Lawndale,** e.g. in CA.

Lawrence From the personal name, especially for James Lawrence, naval hero of 1813. For him are several towns, e.g. **Lawrenceville** NJ, and a number of counties in southern and middle-western states. **Lawrence** MA: for the Lawrence family, of which Abbott and Samuel were prominent in founding the town. **Lawrence** KS: for A. A. Lawrence, prominent in connection with the founding.

Lax Lake MN An abbreviation from the family name of John Waxlax, local farmer.

Lazbuddie TX For D. L. ('Laz') Green and A. ('Buddie') Shirley, local ranchers.

Lazy As a rare specific, e.g. **Lazy Branch** KY, it apparently indicates, by figure of speech, a slow-moving stream. **Lazy Lady Islands** VT is probably by folk-etymology from the French *les îles,* but the rest of the original name is uncertain.

Le French 'the,' masculine, singular. It is often amalgamated with the main word, e.g. **Le Roy** and **Leroy** are about equally common. Unless amalgamated, the names are listed under the main word.

Lead 1) As the metal, it is used to denote a place where lead has been mined or found, e.g. **Lead Mine** WV. In the mining district of MO occur **Leadwood** and **Leadanna,** the latter apparently formed on the model of a woman's name such as Susanna. 2) In its meaning as a vein of ore there is an occasional use, e.g. **Lead** SD. **Leadville** CO: though famous for its silver mines, the town was named because this precious metal occurred in veins of lead ore.

Leaday TX Miss Doss married first W. H. Day, and, on his decease, J. C. Lea, who also died. When the double widow applied for a post office, she combined the names of the two late-departed as **Daylea,** but later shifted to **Leaday.**

Leadore ID From the occurrence of galena, i.e. 'lead-ore.'

Leaf Rare, since a leaf is commonplace and of no value; most of the few examples are probably from the surname. **Leaf Mountains** MN: from an Obijway word, fully translated as 'rustling leaf,' but reason for application unknown. **Leaves on the Hill Buttes** SD were so called because of conspicuous trees at the summits.

Leal ND Scottish dialect, 'faithful, loyal'; settled largely by immigrants of Scottish background, and named in 1883.

Leander Its occurrence in several states as a habitation-name is from men with that given name and probably not from classical mythology.

Leap, Leaping In OR the town was named in a leap year. **Leaping Rock** MN: it stands isolated and was apparently so named for being in leaping distance of the bluff. See **Lovers Leap.**

Leather Commonly from the personal name, e.g. **Leathers, Leatherberry, Leatherwood.** But **Leatherwood** is frequent in some areas, e.g. KY, because of the tree of that name. **Leatherbark** is also from a tree.

L'Eau Frais Creek AR See **Low.**

Leavenworth From the personal name, e.g. in KS the name dates from 1827 when Col. Henry H. Leavenworth built Cantonment Leavenworth; the name was later transferred to county and city.

Lebam WA The namer used a backward spelling of the name of his daughter Mabel.

Lebanon, Mount Lebanon The Biblical mountain, famed for its cedars, has been a fruitful source of habitation-names, with a vague religious-commendatory suggestion. The presence of cedar trees has sometimes helped to fix the name, as for the town in OH. In CT (ca. 1695) it is an early example of Biblical naming for habitations.

Lebec CA For an early pioneer, unknown except for an inscription cut into trees near the site, 'Peter Lebeck, killed by a bear, Oct. 17, 1837.' The spelling has been altered, apparently because of the belief that the name is French.

Lechuguilla Diminutive of Spanish 'lettuce,' but usually, in the SW meaning, the century plant.

Lechusa Canyon CA Spanish 'barn owl.'

Le Clare Probably from a phonetic spelling of Le Clerc, the family name of some early settlers.

Lecoma MO For Lenox, Comstock, and Martin, founders.

Lee From the personal name. Many places, especially counties in Southern states, have been named for the Confederate general R. E. Lee. **Lee's Ferry** AZ: for J. D. Lee, a Mormon, who was known in connection with the Mountain Meadow Massacre and who established a ferry here. **Lee** MA: for General Charles Lee of the Revolution, named in 1777, when he was still a notable figure.

Leech From the presence of leeches. The lake in MN was probably so named from the legend that the Ojibways, on first coming there, saw an enormous leech; the name in English is a translation.

Leeds From the city of England, notable for its iron industry, e.g. in AL where the name was given in 1881 when the local industry was developing.

Leelanau County MI Suggested by Schoolcraft (q.v.) in 1829, it being a name which he had used in his writings as that of an Indian girl living on the south shore of Lake Superior; he gave its meaning as 'delight of life,' but the name is apparently his own creation.

Leetonia OH For William Lee, founder of local ironworks, with a Latin ending.

Leevining CA For Lee (Leroy) Vining, who operated a sawmill in the vicinity in the 1850's.

Left The term cannot be a distinguishing one unless a fixed point of view is maintained, and this is rarely the case. In a few areas, e.g. KY, stream forks are designated **Right** and **Left** from the point of view of a person ascending the stream. **Left Cape** AK translates the Russian term and is on the left to one entering the bay. **Left Hand** is sometimes used similarly, and the village in WV takes its name from a creek. **Left Hand Spring** OK is the translation of an Arapaho personal name. **Lefthand Creek** CO: for Andrew Sublette, fur trader of the early 19th century, who was left-handed. **Lefthand Luman Creek** WY: for the left-hand branch of the stream, not because Luman was left-handed, probably aided by alliteration, there being no counterpart right-hand fork.

Legged Lump NC Two sandy reefs which once had the shape of human legs.

Legion TX The Texas division of the veterans' organization, the American Legion, established a hospital here in 1922 and later gave the name to the post office.

Lehi From the leader in the *Book of Mormon* who is described as colonizing America.

Lehigh PA Algonquian (Delaware) 'fork-stream,' but the reference is questionable—a stream with a forking, a location at a forking, or even the forking of a trail at this point.

Lehman From the personal name. The caves in NV are for Abe Lehman, who lived nearby and discovered the caves, ca. 1878.

Leicester In MA from the English town (also a county), thus named in 1712–1713. In NC for Leicester Chapman, an early settler, who himself came from Leicester in England.

Leipsic From the city of Germany, in OH named by immigrants from it.

Leisure The late, 20th-century interest in retirement homes has brought the term into use, e.g. **Leisuretown** CA, **Leisure World** CA.

Le Mars IA When the railroad was opened to this point (1869) an excursion train was run, and several names were coined from the initials of the first names of six women on the excursion; the women then voted in favor of this one.

Lemhi ID King Limhi is a character in the *Book of Mormon,* and Mormon colonists built Fort Limhi here in 1855. The shift of spelling is not explained. In the reign of Limhi the people were much oppressed by the Lamanites, and the Indians, whom the Mormons considered to be Lamanites, were very troublesome in this area; an aptness of the name may thus be established.

Lemish Butte OR Klamath 'thunder.'

Lemiti Meadow OR Chinook jargon, 'mountain.'

Lemolo Falls OR Chinook jargon, 'wild.'

Lemon Commonly for the personal name (also **Lemmon, Lemons**), e.g. **Lemon Springs** NC for a family of early settlers. In CA, where the lemon is an important crop, it has supplied a few commendatory names, e.g. **Lemoncove, Lemons, Lemongrove,** in spite of the derogatory connotation which the word developed in the early 20th century. One **Lemons** CA, however, changed name to **Walnut** in 1908. **Lemon Fair River** VT: probably by folk-etymology for the French name, Les Monts Verts, though there is no good evidence that that French term was ever current.

Lemonade Lake WY From the yellow-greenish appearance of its water.

Lemoore CA For Dr. Lovern Lee Moore, prominent local citizen in the 1870's.

Lempom CA From 'lemon' and 'pomegranate,' both of which could be grown here.

Lenann, Bayou LA Probably from Spanish *la nana,* 'the grandmother,' but reference uncertain.

Lenapah OK From the Indian tribal name, a variant of **Lenape.**

Lenape From the Indian tribal name, e.g. in KS, NJ.

Lenawee MI, WI Though it may be derived from Shawnee *lenawai,* 'man,' it is
more like to be essentially a coined,
pseudo-Indian name. Cf. **Alcona, Iosco.**

Lenexa KS From the name of a local
Shawnee woman, recorded as Len-ag-
see.

Lennep MT In honor of J. J. Lane,
congressman (?); apparently made into
a pseudo-Indian form.

Len(n)ox The name of a district in
Scotland, but in MA (1767) probably
for the Earl, which title was held by the
Duke of Richmond. The name, short
and distinctive, has been repeated across
the continent.

Lenora Usually from the woman's name;
in OK a coinage from Lee Moore and
Nora Stovall, early settlers.

Lens Creek WV From Len's, a shortening of the personal name Leonard.

Lenwood CA From Ellen Woods, whose
husband founded the town in the 1920's.

Leominster MA From a town in England (1740).

Leon Spanish 'lion,' commonly for the
mountain lion. The diminutive occurs
in **Leoncito** NM. Also a personal name,
and habitation-names in areas of non-
Spanish background are thus explicable.
In TX, in commemoration of Alonso de
León, Spanish explorer, who led five
expeditions in the area in the late 17th
century; so also **De Leon** TX. It is also
the name of a former Spanish kingdom
and of a city in Mexico, the town in IA
probably being named from the latter,
under the influence of the Mexican
War. In FL the county is for Ponce de
León, the discoverer of Florida.

Leona Regularly from the personal
name, but in TX locally believed to be
from the Spanish 'lioness,' because of
one killed there.

Leonardo NJ An adaptation from Leonard, the name of a locally prominent
family.

Leonia In NJ it is a pseudo-Latin coinage from nearby **Fort Lee.**

Leopard In PA from an 18th-century
tavern. The creek CO was so called from
the report that a leopard had been seen
there, probably a young and still-spotted
mountain lion.

Leota In MN locally recorded as being
'an Indian maiden who figured in a
story'; in other states, uncertain, but
probably a woman's name.

Leoti KS Probably for Leoti Kibbe, a
local woman.

Leoville KS Named (1885) for Pope Leo
XIII by German Catholic settlers.

Lepanto AR From the famous naval
battle of 1571.

Le Petit Pase Island LA For French
les petits pois, 'the little peas,' the name
being given by the Iberville expedition
(1699) because a bag of dried peas was
negligently left behind here.

Les French 'the,' plural. It is rare, however, in place-names, and such names
have been alphabetized under the main
words, e.g. **Les Cheneaux,** see under
Cheneaux.

Les Cheneaux See **Chenal.**

Leshara NB From a local Pawnee Indian, Pita Leshara, the latter name
itself meaning 'chief.'

Lester From the family name, a phonetic
spelling of Leicester.

Letart WV A misspelling from the name
of James LeTort, early pioneer and
trader with the Indians.

Letha ID For Letha Wilson, otherwise
not identified.

Letohatchee AL Muskogean (Creek)
'arrow-wood-stream.'

Letter A personal name probably accounts for **Letter Gap** WV. **Letter Box**
KY advertises itself as a primitive post
office. So also, **Lettered Oak** KY and
Lettered Rock KY indicate that initials
or messages were once visible on them.

Leucadia CA From the Greek island,
named by English settlers who were

enamoured of Greece; the town's streets have Greek names.

Leucite From the mineral so called, e.g. the hills in WY.

Levan UT Probably a family name, but by local belief it is from French *levant,* 'the east,' because of some association with the rising sun.

Levant ME Used as the equivalent of 'east,' since the town was located in the most eastern part of the country.

Level As a descriptive it occurs in **Level Land** SC, **Levelland** TX, **Levels** WV. In the SE it is applied to streams with little gradient, e.g. **Level Creek** GA.

Leviathan CA The peak and creek were probably named after a nearby mine of the 1860's. Mines were frequently given names suggestive of size.

Levisa Fork KY Dr. Thomas Walker in 1750 named a stream for the Princess Louisa, daughter of George II. **Levisa** is a shifting of that name, probably because of obscure writing on maps, etc., rather than for variation in pronunciation. The town on the stream, however, is **Louisa.**

Lewarae Coined, ca. 1900, from the names of three local families, Leak, Wall, and McRae.

Lewes DE As the county seat of **Sussex Co.,** it took the name of the county seat in Sussex, England (ca. 1685).

Lewis From the personal name, especially for Captain Meriwether Lewis of the Lewis and Clark expedition, e.g. **Lewiston** ID and the county in MO.

Lewis and Clark River OR In honor of the Lewis and Clark expedition, whose men camped here during the winter of 1805–1806.

Lexington From an alternate spelling of the village in England, now spelled Laxton, probably influenced by the title of Lord Lexington (1661–1723). In MA, the town was named in 1713. Because of the battle, the name spread. In KY hunters gave it to a site in 1776, where the town was founded in 1780.

Leyden From the city in the Netherlands; in MA, named because the so-called Pilgrims had lived there before coming to America. The date of naming (1784) is significant, since it shows a move for new sources of names after the Revolution had made English names somewhat unpopular.

Liard American-French 'cottonwood-tree,' e.g. **Bayou Petit Liard** LA.

Liberal In KS, because in time of drought, ca. 1886, when water was often sold, L. E. Keefer was noted for being 'liberal' in allowing people to use his well.

Liberty A frequent name, for commendatory reasons, on habitations, commonly in a vague sense, but sometimes for the cause of liberty in the Revolution, e.g. **Liberty Hill** SC. The name was chiefly popular in the first fifty years of the nation, but **Liberty** NC commemorates an incident of the Civil War. **Northern Liberties** PA: from certain areas of so-called free land. **Liberty Cap:** a name applied to mountains as descriptive of their shape, e.g. in CA. **Libertybowl Branch** WV: probably a mistake for Libertypole or Libertyboy.

Lick As a generic, a place where wild animals came to lick salt from the soil, but often applied as a specific to denote features thus distinguished, e.g. **Lick Creek** CA, **Black Lick Creek** PA. Some of the habitation-names are probably from the personal name. See, **Licking, Mahoning, Glaize.** In some areas the name occurs frequently; more than 100 streams in KY bear it.

Licking This may be merely a participle, i.e. adjectival formation, felt more suitable than 'lick' to be used as a specific, e.g. **Licking Creek.** One should note that the term occurs in Algonquian territory, where *-ing* served as a locative ending, and the name, **Mahoning** (q.v.) is common, meaning 'lick-at.' **Licking** is therefore most likely half a translation and half a taking-over of the Indian term.

Lickskillet A derogatorily humorous appellation for a place so poor or so boorish that people licked their skillets, in early times often applied as a habitation-name, usually by people who did not live there, rarely or never being official, and now largely vanished. It survives on a few feature-names, e.g. **Lickskillet Creek KY.**

Liebenthal KS German 'love-valley,' but named for a place in Russia from which German settlers had come.

Liebre Spanish 'hare,' but commonly referring to the jack rabbit.

Liege MO The defence of the Belgian city in 1914 made a deep impression in the U.S., and this name was given in 1918.

Liendre Spanish 'nit,' e.g. **La Liendre** NM, where the reference is uncertain, but may be merely derogatory.

Liesnoi Russian 'wooded.'

Light Regularly from the personal name; also in compounds, e.g. **Lightburn. Light Street** PA: transferred from the street so named in Baltimore.

Lightning A rare name, suggesting that in the folk mind lightning is a commonplace phenomenon, not much considered. The usual local explanation is that the place was so named because lightning more commonly struck there. Since this is unlikely, the real reason is probably that the place was named because of some especially remarkable lightning storm or because of one particular stroke; for instance, **Lightning Lake** MN commemorates a bolt which tore to pieces a tent of an early exploring expedition and temporarily prostrated the people.

Ligonier PA From Fort Ligonier, named for Sir John Louis Ligonier, English general.

Likely CA In 1876 the inhabitants sent three names in to the Post Office Dept. and had them all rejected because of duplication. One man then said that it was not likely they would ever get a suitable name, and someone else then picked on the word 'likely' as a name that was not likely to have been already used. Though the story is not wholly authenticated, it seems in itself to be likely as the explanation of an otherwise very unlikely name.

Lilita AL For Lilita Bizelle, daughter of the postmaster.

Lilliwaup WA Indian (Twana) 'inlet,' because of a small bay there.

Lillybrook WV Not a brook but a village, this is from the personal names Lilly and Hornbrook, of two mine operators.

Lily Commonly from the girl's name, e.g. in SD for Lily Parks, sister of the first postmaster. **Lilypons** MD: for Lily Pons, the opera singer, but also with punning reference, since the area is largely devoted to raising pond lilies.

Lima From the Peruvian city, a favorite exotic name of the early 19th century, e.g. in OH (1831). In AL it designates the place of a limestone quarry, thus being a pun for 'lime.'

Limberlost Swamp IN By local story, for a hunter, 'Limber Jim' McDowell who was once lost there.

Lime, Limestone The two are generally distinguished, but 'lime' is sometimes used loosely for 'limestone.' As always with minerals, one must remember that the namers may not have been good geologists, so that what they took for lime or limestone may have been something else. In **Limestone Mountain, Limestone Creek,** etc., the name notes the presence of native rock. **Lime** is so used also, e.g. the township in MN, but commonly denotes a place where lime was made from limestone. With water-names, e.g. creek and spring, lime may refer to extremely 'hard' water, or even to water which leaves a deposit. Limestone is associated with rich soil, and this may be one reason for its use in a good number of habitation-names; it is also a good building material. Possibly, there is commendatory value in the solid suggestion of a rock (cf. **Granite). Lime** also is fairly common for habitation-names, being suggestive of an industry, e.g. **Lime City, Limedale, Limeport. Lime** may also be from an alternate name of the linden tree (see **Linden).** Such names as **Limekiln** mark the sites of usually long-forgotten industries, e.g. **Lime Kiln Creek** MT.

Limerick From the town in Ireland; usually, e.g. in ME, so named because of the settlers who had connections with Ireland.

Limington ME Probably from the English town (1792).

Limrock CO A railroad name for the local product 'lime-rock.'

Linchester MD A coinage from the county-names, Caroline and Dorchester.

Lincoln The town and county of England gave rise to some pre-Revolutionary names, e.g. the county in ME, and town in MA. General Benjamin Lincoln of the Revolutionary War is honored with counties in GA and NC, and from the latter came counties of the name in other states; so also **Lincolnton** SC, and other towns in the South. From Abraham Lincoln have come many names, e.g. the city in NB, and towns and counties, especially in the Western states. The name became so popular that to avoid duplication of post offices it has sometimes been differentiated by the addition of City, Center, -ton, etc. **Lincoln** CA: named ca. 1859 for the middle name of its founder. **Lincoln-ville** SC: named for Abraham Lincoln by Negro settlers.

Lind An alternate name for the linden tree (see **Linden**) has produced **Lindside** WV and other names; it is also a personal name.

Linda See **Lindo**.

Linden Though the American linden, or basswood, is a well-known tree in the Eastern states, it has yielded only a few names for features, e.g. **Lake Linden** MN. As a habitation-name in as many as 20 states it is largely from the personal name, and from its literary use in Thomas Campbell's popular poem, 'Hohenlinden.' The euphonious sound has also helped to popularize it. In this last connection, note that it generally stands alone as a habitation-name. The attractive nature of the name has led to its transfer, e.g. from AL to TX. In some states, where the linden is not native, the name may be used for other trees, as for a kind of cottonwood, e.g. **Linden Wash** AZ. See **Lind, Linn, Lime.** In AL the town was named (1823) by French immigrants as **Hohenlinden** for the battle.

Lindo, Linda Spanish 'pretty, handsome.' Though CA has **Lindo Lake,** the feminine is more common, e.g. **Linda Creek, Linda Vista,** both repeated in CA. The town **Linda** CA is from a steamboat so named. The use of **Linda** as a woman's name is late and probably of little influence.

Line 1) From the personal name, e.g. **Linesville** PA, for the surveyor of the town, ca. 1825. 2) From being on or near some line, usually a state boundary, e.g. **Line Creek,** near the KS-NB boundary. **Lineville** IA lies partly in MO. **Line Lexington** PA lies on the boundary of two counties.

Linganore MD Algonquian, meaning uncertain.

Linguist Creek TX Probably a shaping by folk-etymology from some Indian original. Cf. **Terlingua.**

Link River OR Because it forms a link between two lakes.

Linlithgo A simplified spelling for Linlithgow, Scotland.

Linn An alternate name for the linden tree (see **Linden**) has produced **Linwood** in a dozen states as a habitation-name, besides some names for natural features, such as **Linn Grove** IA which has been transferred to a town. See **Lynn.**

Linneus A simplified form from the Latinized name of Carolus Linnaeus (1707–1778), the great botanist, the land in ME having been granted (1804) to establish a professorship in botany at Harvard College.

Linslaw OR Uncertain, the most likely suggestion being that it is a mistake for the nearby Siuslaw as the result of bad handwriting.

Lion Generally a shortening for mountain lion, see also **Panther, Cougar.** It is rare on natural features, except in CA, where it occurs about 50 times; in one instance, **Lion Rock** (San Luis Obispo Co.) it is for the sea lion. The animal is commonly known as *león* in Spanish; in the border states this term has been usually preserved. **Red Lion** PA: for a tavern and its sign. **Lion Gulch** WA: for Pat Lions, a prospector, named about 1900. **Lions** LA: for F. P. Lions, first postmaster.

Lipan From the Indian tribal name.

Liplip Point WA Chinook jargon, 'boiling,' probably with reference to surf.

Lisabeula WA The first postmaster combined the names of his daughters Elisa and Beulah.

Lisbon From the city in Portugal, sometimes given by Portuguese immigrants, as in SC, but often in the post-Revolutionary period, e.g. CT (1786), merely because such foreign names had become popular.

Lisburne, Cape AK Named by James Cook in 1778, probably for the first Earl of Lisburne.

Lisle NY From the city in France, an older spelling of Lille.

Litchfield From the town in England, etc. In CT the town was thus named in 1720. In ME the town was named in 1794–1795, when English connections had been broken; it may therefore have been so named for the town in CT. **Litchfield** CA: named for the Litch family, pioneer settlers, in 1912. In MN the name is in honor of the Litchfield family, local railroad builders. In NB the town is probably named from the one in CT, as is certainly true in OH.

Lithgow NY A variant for Linlithgow, Scotland.

Lithodendron Creek AZ Greek 'stone-tree,' because of a petrified forest.

Lithograph Canyon SD Because stones that were suitable for lithography were found there.

Lithopolis OH Greek 'stone-city,' for a local quarry.

Lititz PA As a settlement of Moravians, Count von Zinzendorf named the town in 1754 after Lititz in Moravia where the church had been organized.

Littcarr KY An abbreviation from **Little Carr Creek.**

Little Though the personal name must be taken into account, this is the term widely used to describe a natural feature in counterpart to one called **Big** or one which seems to the namer to be smaller than is to be expected within the class denoted by the generic. The term is not used so commonly with generics that in themselves imply small size, e.g. **Little Creek** is rare, but **Little River,** comparatively, is common. The name has been readily transferred to habitations apparently without any derogatory suggestion. On the contrary, **Little York** (for **New York**) is several times used, apparently with a pleasantly humorous suggestion. **Littleton,** however, is for the personal name Little or Littleton (or possibly for one of the towns in England) rather than for 'little town.' 'Little' is commonly, and often ambiguously, used as the first term in a double specific as in **Little Maria Mountains** CA. Here the presence of **Big Maria Mountains** makes clear that the others are not named for 'Little Maria.' But **Little Pete Meadows** CA are known to have been named for a certain 'Little Pete.' **Little Lake Valley** CA is named for a small lake. Unless a counterpart name is of record, a decision often cannot be made. A special case occurs with natural features which are so called with reference to another feature which merely bears the name, without 'Big,' e.g. **Little Mississippi River** MN exists but Big Mississippi River does not. This situation has become much commoner by the action of the U.S. Geographical Board in getting rid of 'Big' in the interests of simplification while retaining 'little' in the interests of clarity. A few features are named with reference to a well-known feature elsewhere, e.g. **Little Gibraltar** CA. The frequent use of 'little' gives our nomenclature a kind of diminutive quality, which is often fallacious. **Little Wind River** WY, and **Little Timber Creek** MT are named by counterpart, and not because the one is noted for calm weather and the other lacking in trees. Though the names themselves may be amusing and even endearing, there is nothing cute in the origins of **Little Egg Inlet** NJ, **Little Bumblebee Creek** ID, **Little Half Moon Lake** WY, and **Little Chickies Creek** PA. The last has nothing to do with chickens (see **Chickies**). One of the most striking of these names is the **Little Big Horn River** (see **Big**). **Little Rock** AR: early voyagers so named a rock which was smaller than another one farther up stream. The city took its name by transfer. **Little Belt Passage** WA: from the British ship, *Little Belt,* but so named by the Wilkes expedition (1841) as part of a plan to honor the U.S. Navy because the U.S.S. *President* had had an encounter with this British ship in 1811. **Little America** WY: Admiral R. E. Byrd gave this name to his base camp in Antarctica (1929), and the name in WY is a commendatory borrowing for a highway stop, with emphasis upon the idea of coolness in a region which is usually hot during the period of highway travel.

Litwar WV A combination of *little* and *war,* eventually from **Little War Creek.**

Live Occurs as **Live Oak,** e.g. as a habitation-name in CA and FL, in which states the evergreen oak is a common and highly conspicuous tree.

Lively VA Probably from the family name.

Livermore From the personal name, e.g. in CA for Robert Livermore, English sailor, who settled at the site, ca. 1839. In CO it is for Adophus Livernash and Stephen Moore, early settlers.

Liverpool With the growing importance of the English seaport in the 19th century, the name enjoyed some popularity in the U.S., for commendatory reasons, as suggesting a thriving city. In WV the name was given by a lumber company having connections with Liverpool, England. **East Liverpool** OH: so called to distinguish it from another Liverpool in the state; after that one disappeared, the name with the distinction still remained.

Livonia From the former Baltic province of Russia, in most instances probably given by immigrants; in MN, the name of the wife of a local judge.

Lizard The lizards of the U.S. are generally insignificant and of little interest, and names are rare. **Lizard Head** (mountain, CO) is named from a rock formation, which is fancifully taken to resemble a lizard's head.

Lizemores WV By mistake, in the Post Office Dept. for Sizemore, a local family, with the possessive *s.*

Llagas Creek CA Spanish 'wounds.' A shortening for *Las Llagas de Nuestro Padre San Francisco,* 'the wounds [stigmata] of our Father St. Francis,' a name given by a Franciscan missionary in 1769.

Llanada Spanish 'plain, level ground.'

Llano Spanish 'plain, level country,' usually as a generic, but as a habitation-name in NM, and by association for **Llano River** TX, because it in part flows through a plain.

Llao Rock OR For a Klamath diety, named by Will G. Steel in 1885.

Lo Spanish neuter article, also 'it,' but in a place-name sense, 'that which belongs . . . ,' e.g. **Lo De Mora** NM, 'Mora's property.' It existed chiefly in NM, and it is obsolete even there.

Loa UT Hawaiian 'long,' so named by a returned Mormon missionary, probably in memory of Mauna Loa, an active volcano, and the existence nearby of a mountain which seems to be volcanic.

Loachapoka AL From the name of an early Creek town, literally, 'turtle-killing-place.'

Loafer Probably in all instances, e.g. **Loafer Creek** TX from the common adaptation of the Spanish *lobo,* 'wolf.'

Loam Occasionally used as a commendatory, e.g. **Richloam** FL.

Loantaka Brook NJ Algonquian, probably with *loan* meaning 'north,' but otherwise uncertain.

Lobeco SC From the firm name, Long, Bellamy, and Company.

Lobelia WV For the flowering plant, common in the vicinity.

Loblockee AL Muskogean (Creek) 'big-cane.'

Loblolly In the SE the name of one of the common pines. The cove in MA is probably from the presence of a low, swampy place, known as a loblolly.

Lobo Spanish 'wolf,' e.g. **Lobo Peak** NM, **Lobo** TX. As a seacoast name, e.g. **Point Lobos** CA, it refers to *lobo marino,* i.e. 'seal' or 'sea lion.' **Lobitos Creek** CA may refer to coyote pups or to young seals. **Lobatos** CO: from another form of the diminutive, 'little wolves.'

Lobster From the presence of the lobster, a comparatively rare name. **Lobster Creek** OR: probably named for the crayfish, since there are no real lobsters in the area. The lake in MN has long arms, which were fancifully compared to a lobster's claws.

Lobutcha Creek MS Probably a clipped form of the name also occurring as **Yslobusha,** 'tadpoles-are-there.'

Locafoma Creek MS Choctaw 'clay-red,' from its water being colored with sediment.

Lochapopka Lake FL Seminole 'turtle-eating-place.'

Lochgelly WV For a town in Scotland. An appropriateness exists, since both the original and the namesake are coal-mining towns.

Lochloosa FL Choctaw 'turtle (terrapin)-black.'

Lochochee Creek GA Muskogean (Creek) 'turtle-little.'

Lochsa River ID Nez Percé, probably 'rough-water.'

Lock During the canal-building period of the earlier 19th century, a site at a lock was advantageous for a settlement.

Lockport is most common, but other forms are **Lock Haven** PA, **Lockbourne** OH, and **Lockington** OH. So also **Lock Seventeen** OH, **Lock Number Four** PA, etc. **Lock, Lockhart, Lockridge, Lockwood,** etc., are personal names. **Locktown** NJ: probably by folk-etymology from nearby **Lockatong Creek.**

Lockatong Creek NJ Algonquian, probably 'sand (gravel)-hills-at.'

Lockbridge WV For Lockridge Gwinn, of a family of early landowners, the *b* having been inserted by mistake or folk-etymology in the process of getting the name cleared through the Post Office Dept.

Lockchelooge Creek AL Muskogean (Creek), with *lokcha,* 'acorn,' and the rest uncertain.

Lockeford CA A ford on the Mokelumne River named for Dr. D. J. Locke, early settler.

Lockit Chinook jargon, 'four.'

Lockridge Though it exists as a personal name, the town in OK is so named because on a ridge at the meeting of four counties, their initials being used, i.e. **Logan, Oklahoma, Canadian,** and **Kingfisher.**

Locktsapopka River FL Seminole 'acorn-eating-place.'

Loco Spanish 'crazy,' but usually from the so-called loco weed which, when eaten, makes horses and cattle behave strangely, e.g. **Loco** TX. **Loco** CA: from an Indian tribal name.

Locomotive Rock AZ From its resemblance to the front end of a steam locomotive.

Loconoma See **Collayomi.**

Locust Though some places may be named because flights of locusts were seen there, the tree is the ordinary source, as in such combinations as **Locust Grove.**

Loda IL Probably from a character in one of the Ossianic poems.

Lodgepole To denote a feature, usually a creek, where Indians, or others, cut lodgepoles; sometimes from the presence of lodge-pole pines, i.e. *Pinus contorta.*

Lodi From the town in Italy and Napoleon's victory there in 1796. In OH, from the victory. In TX, named by a former resident of the town in Italy. In OK, for a woman so named. In CA, a railroad name, such names often being selected for brevity.

Lodore Canyon UT Named (1869) by the Powell expedition because of the rapids, with reference to Robert Southey's poem *The Cataract of Lodore.*

Log, Logging In habitation-names it is a frontier survival from the period of building in logs, e.g. **Log Cabin** CA, **Logtown** MS. On features it arises variously. **Log Creek** OR: named because some logs once obstructed the trail along the stream. **Log Meadow** CA: the huge trunk of a fallen sequoia lay here for many years. **Logging,** e.g. the river in FL, indicates the former existence of a lumber industry.

Logan 1) From the personal name, especially for the famous 18th-century Indian chief, e.g. **Logan** WV, and **Logansport** IN, and for Gen. J. A. Logan (1826–1886), popular with Civil War veterans, whose name appears 24 times on minor civil divisions in NB. **Logan** UT: from Logan's Fort, named for an early trapper. 2) From an Americanism meaning a small lake or a backwater of a stream, e.g. **Logan Township** MN.

Loggerhead Key FL For the loggerhead turtles found here.

Logrow WV Probably a contraction from 'locust grove.'

Lokaskal Spring AZ Navajo 'clump of reeds.'

Lokosee FL Seminole 'bear (the animal).'

Lokoya CA From an Indian tribal name.

Lola From the personal name; for instance, **Mount Lola** CA is for Lola Montez, well known as an actress and even more famous as a courtezan in the mid-19th century.

Lolah Butte OR Probably the same as **Lolo,** q.v.

Loleta, Lolita In TX the town is for Lolita Reese of a pioneer family. In CA, Loleta is locally thought to be of Indian origin, but this is doubtful.

Lolo ID, MT, OR Probably first applied to the creek, in ID and later transferred to the pass and habitations in ID and MT. It is apparently the result of Indian (Flathead) attempts to pronounce an English or French name, most likely Lawrence, an early trapper who lived on the stream, the Indians lacking an r-sound and so substituting 'l.' **Lolo Pass** OR: named by the Forest Service from Chinook jargon, 'carrying, back-packing,' because supplies had to be packed to it; this same origin is also claimed for the name in ID and MT.

Lolomai Point AZ From the name of a Hopi chief.

Loma Spanish 'hill.' It remains as a semi-generic, but in **Point Loma** CA it is what is left of Punta de la Loma, and indicates a point with a hill on it. As a specific it occurs chiefly with habitation-names where it is commendatory as being both Spanish and suggestive of elevation, e.g. **Loma Linda** CA, named ca. 1900, long after the Spanish-speaking period. The name has entered American usage, and occurs on habitations far out of the Spanish range of settlement, e.g. **Loma** MT, NB, ND. **Lomita** CA is the diminutive.

Lometa TX From Spanish *lomita.* See **Loma.**

Lon NM For Lonnie Moseley, son of the first postmaster.

Lonaconing MD Algonquian, meaning uncertain.

London From the city in England, e.g. **London** TX, named by English settlers, or from a personal name, e.g. **London Peak** OR for Jack London, the writer. **New London** CT: named by the Court in 1658 'in memory of the City of London.'

Londonderry, Derry From the city in Northern Ireland, generally mentioned in conversation by its shortened or original form; introduced by immigrants; in NH there are towns under both forms.

Lone The common English term to describe a feature standing in isolation. It occurs with features which may be generally expected to stand in groups, e.g. 'mountain,' 'lake,' 'rock,' but not with features which are ordinarily seen one at a time, e.g. 'river,' 'falls.' As the first element of a double specific it occurs especially with 'tree,' or with a particular tree, e.g. **Lone Tree Lake** (many examples) **Lone Spruce Rock** AK. The word necessarily carries a suggestion of mournfulness, and isolation in this sense was probably at times present in the namers' minds. **Lone Star:** The soubriquet of TX has undoubtedly been applied with the state in mind; the village in AZ was named from a mine, which in its turn was probably named by a Texan. **Lone Wolf** OK: from an Indian personal name. **Lake of The Lone Indian** CA: from the profile of a face (presumed, as is usual in such cases, to be that of an Indian) seen in the rocks. In combinations before a vowel there is likely to be a simplification of spelling, as in **Lonoak** CA and **Lonoke** AR both, from Lone Oak. But **Loneash** VA has resisted this tendency. See **Lonesome, Huerfano. Lone Eagle Peak** CO: Named ca. 1930 in honor of Charles Lindbergh, the aviator; the original proposal was to use his name, but a circumlocution was effected to avoid the decision of the U.S. Board on Geographic Names against naming natural features for living persons.

Lonesome A widespread but not common term, of special interest since it is not a true descriptive, but transfers to the place the feeling of the namer by a kind of pathetic fallacy, e.g. **Lonesome Valley** AZ named in 1879 when it was wholly empty. See **High.**

Long The common descriptive term for such natural features as can normally be so denoted, e.g. lakes, meadows, points, creeks. It is rare with rivers, since length is a common property of rivers. As a counterpart, 'short' is rare; 'broad,' somewhat commoner. The number of examples runs into the hundreds, of which the personal name accounts for comparatively few. Occasionally, e.g. **Long Portage** and **Long View,** the use of the word is somewhat different. **Long Island** NY: named by Adriaen Block (in Dutch form) in 1614; soon taken over into English. **Longs Peak** CO: from Stephen H. Long, who made it known through the report of his 1820 expedition. **Long Beach:** a common name for both the natural feature and a town, being commendatory as well as descriptive. The city in CA was so named, in 1887. **Long Pine** NB: this curious town name is derived from location on **Long Pine Creek,** with 'long' probably to be taken as referring to the creek. **Longtown** SC: originally **Logtown,** because built of log cabins; it became **Longtown** after the significance of the first name was lost with the disappearance of the cabins. **Longs** NM: for T. H. and R. F. Long, successive postmasters. **Long Tom River** OR: by folk-etymology from an Indian tribal name, recorded (1834) as Lung-tum-ler.

Longwood Its use is chiefly because of the Napoleonic legend, being the name of his residence in St. Helena and the place of his death.

Lonoke AR For 'lone oak,' named for a well-known individual tree.

Loogootee IN From a combination of Lowe, a railroad man, and Gootee, landowner of the town site.

Lookeba OK A coinage from Lowe, Kelly, and Baker, the town developers.

Lookingglass Usually applied to water features because of their reflecting quality. **Lookingglass Creek** OR: for an Indian, so called because he carried a small mirror with him.

Lookout A common descriptive name for a place that has been used, or might be used, as a lookout. Usually with eminences, e.g. **Lookout Mountain** TN, but may occur on other features by transfer, e.g. **Lookout River** AK. **Lookout Creek,** Wallowa Co., OR: because of a bad trail, packers had to 'look out,' that is, 'be careful,' here.

Look Shack Hill NC A colloquial designation because of a Navy lookout station of World War II, which became a permanent name.

Loom From early weaving operations, e.g. **Loomhouse Branch KY**.

Loon The well-known bird, especially notable for its cry, has given rise to the repeated **Loon Lake,** not only because the bird haunts lakes, but also because of alliteration. It is rarely found with other features. In spite of the derogatory suggestion **Loon Lake** occurs as a habitation-name. **Loon Lake** OR: in 1852 a loon's nest was found here and the eggs taken for a collection.

Looney Butte OR For Jesse Looney, a leader of the migration of 1843. In NM for the first postmaster, J. J. Looney.

Loop A rare descriptive for a stream marked by a loop or for a station at a loop on a railroad. **Loop** PA: because it is at a notable loop on Mahoning Creek. **Loop** TX: so called because the postmaster-to-be, at the time of suggesting a name, was playing with the loop of his lasso.

Loosahatchie River TN Muskogean (Chickasaw) 'black-stream.' Since the adjective follows the noun normally, the shift may have been made by Americans or the name may represent an original *luksi-hatchie,* 'terrapin-river.'

Loosa Scoona Creek MS Muskogean, meaning uncertain, though possibly with *lusa,* 'black.' See also **Scoona**.

Loosookolo Creek AL Choctaw 'turtle-water-beloved.'

Looxahoma MS Choctaw 'terrapin-red.'

Lopatcong Creek NJ Algonquian, meaning uncertain; probably a variant of **Hopatcong**.

Lorado WV Formed by syllables taken from the Lorain Coal and Dock Company.

Lorain(e) See **Lorraine**.

Loramie OH For Peter Loramie, a French trader with the Indians in the 18th century.

Lorane See **Lorraine**.

Loretto From the Italian town, famous for its shrine, generally named by Catholics or for the presence of a Catholic institution. **Loretto** NB: the original name Loran had to be replaced because of duplication; a name similar to it was chosen.

Lorne In MN for the Marquis of Lorne, for a time Governor-General of Canada.

Lorraine, Loraine, Lorain, Lorane The first spelling is correct for the French province, and the names are either thus derived or are from the woman's name. The other spellings are probably phonetic. In OH the county was named for the province in the post-Revolutionary period by a man who had traveled in France. **Loraine** TX: for Loraine Crandall, wife of a local landowner.

Los The Spanish 'the,' masculine, plural. Most of the names thus beginning have been alphabetized under the main word, e.g. for **Los Altos,** see under **Altos**. In some instances, however, the other usage has seemed preferable, e.g. **Los Angeles**.

Los Angeles Spanish 'the angels,' The Spaniards rarely named places for the angels, but see **Angel**. **Los Angeles** CA: a shortening for Nuestra Señora (Reina) de los Angeles de la Porciúncula, "Our Lady (i.e. the Virgin Mary) of the Angels (or Queen of the Angels) of the Little Portion." The Porciúncula is the Franciscan shrine near Assisi. The original naming was thus in honor of the Virgin, the name being given on Aug. 2, 1769, by the Portolá expedition to the river at which they camped, the preceding day having been the festival of the Porciúncula. The river was called **Porciúncula** for some years. The settlement was projected as early as 1779, and established in 1781, with the full name. From the beginning it was commonly used in the shortened form as **Los Angeles** as if commemorating the angels, and the Americans continued this usage.

Losantville IN An adaptation of Losantiville, the now-extinct original name of **Cincinnati,** coined with *L* for Licking, *os* (Latin 'mouth'), *anti* (Greek 'opposite') and the suffix *ville,* to mean 'town opposite the mouth of Licking Creek.'

Lospe Mountain CA From Chumash *ospe,* 'flower field,' the prefixed *l* apparently having been added on the assumption that the name was Spanish and needed an article.

Lost A widespread term, of complicated background. 1) It denotes a stream that is 'lost' by going underground, e.g. **Lost River** CA, ID. 2) It recalls an incident in which something or someone was lost, e.g. **Lost Boy Creek** MT for an incident of 1901, **Lost Horse Mountain** MT, **Lost Man Creek** CA. 3) It denotes a feature which has been reported, then 'lost,' and then rediscovered, being named by the re-discoverers, e.g. **Lost Lake** OR 4) It records an incident when the namer himself was lost, e.g. **Lost Prairie** OR. 5) In somewhat stronger manner than *lone* it indicates a place so isolated that it seems to be lost, e.g. **Lost Basin** AZ. **Lost Cannon Creek** CA: the name is connected with the howitzer abandoned near here by Frémont in 1844, but the howitzer was not really lost. Someone, however, certainly found it later, and may have given the name at that time. **Lost City** WV: from its location on Lost Creek. **Lost Hills** CA: the hills are of low elevation, and stand isolated from some higher hills, thus suggesting to someone that they were lost. **Lost Bear Lake** NM: unexplained, and tantalizingly ambiguous. **Lost Mine Peak** TX, along with other such names, arose from the common legendary tale of a rich mine, the location of which was lost. **Lost Creek** UT: so named by two men who had been lost there in a snowstorm in 1855. **Lost Temper Creek** AK: because of an incident in a camp of geologists in 1950. **Lost Nation** IA: various stories are told locally, but the name remains uncertain; some Indian connection seems likely, since the French referred to an Indian tribe by that term. The name also occurs for a local district in Peacham, VT, and the one in IA may have been borrowed from VT. **Lost Woman Canyon** CA: fancifully named because the moaning of the wind was thought to suggest the calls for help of a lost woman. **Lost Ecstasy Lake** WY: from the novel of that title written by Mary Roberts Rinehart in this region.

Lost Soldier Creek WY: in 1880 two soldiers were lost here in a snowstorm and died.

Lostant IL For the Countess of Lostant, who visited the state in 1861.

Lotus Generally, e.g. in CO (originally **Lotus Glen**) for one of the wild flowers so known. In CA, by local tradition, named (1881) by the postmaster, because the local residents were as easy going as the Lotus-eaters of the *Odyssey.*

Loudon From the personal name, especially, e.g. in NH and as **Fort Loudon** PA for the Earl of Loudoun, sometimes spelled Loudon, a general in the French and Indian War.

Louis From the personal name, especially for one of the kings of France. See **St. Louis, Louisiana. Louisville** KY: named in 1780 for Louis XVI, in recognition of the recent French alliance. **Louisburg** NC: named in 1764 in commemoration of the capture, largely by American forces, of the French fortress of that name in Nova Scotia. Because of these beginnings *Louis* has regularly been coupled with either *-burg* or *-ville.* **Bayou Louis** LA: by folk-etymology from Choctaw *lusa,* 'black.'

Louisa From the personal name, the county in VA having been named (1742) for the princess, daughter of George II. See **Levisa.**

Louisiana Named on Aug. 22, 1681, by Robert, Sieur de la Salle, in a French context, **Louisiane,** for Louis XIV, as a part of the taking possession for the French crown of the land. **Louisiane** is a normal French adjective referring to Louis. When the Spanish succeeded, they used the Spanish form **Luisiana.** The Americans mingled the two forms to produce the present one. **Louisiana Mesa** NM: by folk-etymology from the name of an early Spanish settler, probably Luciano. **Louisiana** MO: for Louisiana Bazye, so named because born in the year of the Louisiana Purchase.

Loup French 'wolf.' The river NB is from the Pawnee sub-tribe, whose name was thus translated into French and then taken into English.

L'Ours French 'the bear.' See **Ours.**

Louse, Lousy For obvious reasons. **Louse Creek** OR: so called because an early Indian camp was badly infested. **Lousy Gulch** AZ: some miners, during the winter, suffered considerably, in the 1880's. **Lousetown** at times was used as a common derogatory for a small, backward settlement; hence **Lousetown Creek** NV.

Loutre French 'otter.' See **De Loutre.**

Love Probably in all instances from the personal name, e.g. **Love's Ford** SC from a family of early settlers. So also in compounds; for instance, **Lovelady** TX is for C. Lovelady, early settler. **Loving** TX: for Oliver Loving, early cattleman. **Lovelock** NV: from the stage station kept by George Lovelock. **Loveland** CO: for W. A. H. Loveland, railroad official. See **Lover's Leap.**

Lovely Regularly from the personal name, e.g. in OK the county is for William Lovely, early Indian agent.

Lovers Lane A quasi-generic for any secluded road or path, supposedly (and usually in reality) frequented by amorous couples, especially under cover of darkness.

Lover's Leap, Lovers' Leap, Lovers Leap Aided by alliteration, the name is repeated scores of times across the country. It refers to a high point from which a person or persons might leap in suicide, and it is often a scenic viewpoint. The story is regularly told that a lover or a pair of lovers, in despair because their love was thwarted, leaped to death. The lovers are often said to have been Indians. No authentic story is recorded. The name occurs in England, and may have been brought, ready made, to this country, but the provenience is uncertain.

Low, Lower As a descriptive **Low** is rare, but occurs with *point, gap,* etc. **Lower** is a regular term to denote 1) a place downstream from, or otherwise lower than, a point of reference, e.g. **Lower Bridge** OR; 2) a place nearer the outlet of a lake, e.g. **Lower Lake** CA. In spite of derogatory suggestion **Lower** occurs in habitation-names, to indicate one at a lower level. **Low** also is a personal name, and occurs in such combinations as **Lowman. Lower Land Creek** OR: the lower stream named for T. C. Land. **Low Wassie** MO: so called in counterpart to the nearby **Hi Wassie,** probably with humorous intent, first applied to a creek. **Low Freight Creek** AR: the colloquial and historical term is by folketymology from French *l'eau froide,* 'thewater (stream)-cold,' the American-French pronunciation of *froide* being close to 'freight.' Official usage is now for **L'Eau Frais** ('fresh'), thus destroying one of the most perfect works of art among our folk-names. Moreover, the etymology is questionable and the grammar is worse, since it should be *fraiche.* Hopefully, the local inhabitants are continuing to say and to think **Low Freight. Low Moor** IA: applied to the site in 1857 when the landowners saw the name stamped on some railroad rails, presumably because they had been manufactured at a place of that name in England.

Lowake For J. Y. Lowe and C. G. Schlake, two of the oldest residents when the name was given.

Lowell From the personal name. In MA for F. C. Lowell (1775–1817), initiator of cotton manufacturing in the U.S., the town being founded in 1826 after his death. In NC the town was founded for cotton manufacturing and so echoed the name.

Lower See **Low.**

Loxahatchee River FL Seminole 'turtle-river.'

Loyal Though occurring as a personal name, the examples of place-names are regularly of a commendatory nature. **Loyal** OK: formerly Kiel; the German name was abandoned in 1918 as an indication of loyalty to the U.S. **Loyalton** CA: named in 1863 to express the strong local Union sentiment. **Loyalton** SD: because settled by a colony of Union soldiers after the Civil War. **Loyalsock** PA: Algonquian 'middle-outlet,' with a considerable tendency toward folk-etymology in both parts of the name. **Loyalhanna** PA: Algonquian 'middle stream,' with help from folk-etymology.

Luana IA Named by the town founder (1867) for his wife.

Lubbers Run NJ Probably from the Dutch family name Lubbert.

Lubbock TX For Col. T. S. Lubbock, organizer of the Texas Rangers.

Lubbub Creek AL Choctaw 'warm.'

Lubec ME Named (1811), probably for the German city, Lübeck; no special reason is known, and this may be another example of exotic naming at this period.

Lucerne, Luzerne 1) From a personal name, e.g. the county in PA, in honor of the Chevalier de la Luzerne, first French minister to the U.S. 2) From the city or lake in Switzerland, with implications of lacustrine or Alpine beauty, e.g. **Lake Lucerne** CA, NY. 3) From the alternate name for alfalfa, indicating a good place for its culture, e.g. **Lucerne** CO.

Lucin UT A railroad name, apparently by shortening of *Lucina,* the name of a genus of fossil bivalves found nearby in the dry bed of **Lake Bonneville.**

Luckiamute River OR From an Indian tribal name.

Lucknow From the city in India, made known by the famous siege of 1857; the idea of 'luck' probably aided the dissemination of the name.

Lucky A rare name, given when something fortunate was associated with a place. **Lucky Creek** OR: firefighters held a large fire along the line of this stream in 1938. **Lucky Rock** WA: from an Indian tradition of good and bad luck associated with the rock. **Lucky Mound** ND: from the creek which was originally French, *l'eau qui monte,* 'water that rises,' transformed by folk-etymology.

Ludlow The town in MA was named (ca. 1774), probably for the English town. Many instances are from a personal name, e.g. **Ludlow Creek** OH, for Israel Ludlow, early surveyor.

Lukachukai Mountains AZ Navajo, a term having to do with reeds, but exact meaning uncertain; named from a patch of reeds near the foot of the pass, the name, being first applied to the pass, extended to the mountains as a whole.

Lukanin, Lukannon AK The famous seal rookery takes its name from Ivan Lukanin, who took furs there in 1787.

Lukfata OK Muskogean (Choctaw) 'clay-white.'

Luksapalila Creek AL Choctaw 'turtle-there-crawls.'

Lulbegrud Creek KY From the fictional city, Lorbrulgrud, capital of Brobdingnag in Swift's *Gulliver's Travels,* so called by Daniel Boone and his companions because they were reading the book there when they were attacked by Indians. The name was apparently transmitted orally and the spelling was shifted to suit.

Luman From the personal name, e.g. the creek in WY, for a trapper who, ca. 1890, was fatally clawed by a bear here.

Lumbee River NC More commonly called Lumber River, the name is supposedly Indian, but is unexplained.

Lumber Not generally used for natural features (see **Timber**), the term appears in habitation-names to indicate a place associated with lumbering. **Lumber River** NC: derived from the alternate name, **Lumbee,** q.v.; **Lumberton** NC: takes its name from the river.

Lummi WA From an Indian tribal name.

Lump Gulch MT Because two miners in 1864 found gold here in lumps.

Lumpy Ridge CO Translated from an Arapaho term, descriptive of the rocks along the ridge.

Lumrum Butte OR Chinook jargon, 'whiskey, rum.'

Luna Spanish 'moon,' but more commonly from the personal name, e.g. **Los Lunas** NM for the Luna family of early settlers.

Lunada Spanish 'lunated, moon-shaped.' The bay in CA was fancifully named in the post-Spanish period.

Lund 1) From the city in Sweden, given by Swedish immigrants, e.g. **Lund Township** MN. 2) From the personal name, e.g. **Lund** UT for R. C. Lund, mine owner. **Lund** ID: with shortening, for C. J. Lundgren, first settler.

Lunenburg George I, along with other German titles, brought to the English royal family that of Elector of Brunswick-Lüneberg. The latter name was usually spelled Lunenburg by the English in the 18th century, and was bestowed on towns and counties in the colonies for commendatory reasons, as a name associated with the royal house, e.g. in MA, 1728.

Lunice Creek WV A variant spelling of **Looney's,** a common family name among the pioneer settlers of the area.

Lunksoos ME Algonquian 'lynx, panther.'

Luppatatong Creek NJ Algonquian, meaning uncertain.

Lupus MO Latin 'wolf,' probably used as a variant to replace the too common **Wolf.**

Luray VA The name apparently originated from **Lorrain Run,** recorded in 1734, which is, according to local tradition, an Indian name of unknown meaning.

Lurgan PA Probably from the town in Ireland.

Luxapallila Creek AL Choctaw 'turtle-there-crawls.'

Luxemburg From the country in Europe. In IA alternate spellings occur as **Luzembourg** and **Luxemburgh.**

Luxomni MS Muskogean (Creek) with *luxo*, 'terrapin,' and the rest uncertain.

Luxora AR For Luxora Waller, daughter of the first settler.

Luz Spanish 'light,' e.g. **La Luz** NM, from a missionary chapel dedicated to 'Our Lady of Light.'

Luzembourg See **Luxemburg.**

Luzerne See **Lucerne.**

Luzon From the Philippine island, generally, e.g. in CA, named at the time of the Spanish-American War.

Lycoming NY, PA Algonquian (Delaware) 'sand-at,' probably first applied as a descriptive to a stream.

Lyell, Mount CA For Charles Lyell (1797–1895), British geologist, named as a counterpart to **Mount Dana.**

Lykesland SC From Lykes, the family name of some early settlers.

Lyme From the name of an English town; in CT, 1667.

Lynch Regularly from the personal name, often with *-burg* from the early importance of **Lynchburg** VA, which takes its name from John Lynch, who established a ferry here in 1757.

Lynden WA Named in 1870 by Mrs. Phoebe Judson from the first line of Thomas Campbell's *Hohenlinden*, 'On Linden, when the sun was low,' with the spelling changed because she thought it prettier thus.

Lynn Often from the personal name, e.g. in NC for Lynn McAboy, son of an early settler. **Lynn** MA was named in 1637 for the town in England, and many of the later names are from it. **Lynn Grove** KY is probably another variation of **Linden** (see **Linn**). **Lynwood** CA: for Lynn Wood Sessions, wife of an early dairyman.

Lynndyl UT A railroad name; probably from **Lynn** MA, with the addition of a euphonious but meaningless final syllable, for differentiation from an already-existing **Lynn** in the state.

Lynx The term is used more generally in the north, e.g. AK, to denote a somewhat larger form of the animal widely known as wildcat or bobcat, and place-names have thus arisen. **Lynx Creek** AZ: a lynx here clawed a man in 1863; this is an instance of a southern use of the term.

Lyon(s) Commonly from the personal name, e.g. in TX for W. A. Lyon, first storekeeper (with possessive 's'). **Lyons** IA was named by French missionaries for fancied resemblance to the site of Lyon in France.

Lysander NY For the ancient Spartan general, part of the classical naming of 1790.

Lysite WY The mountain was named for Jim Lysite (or Lysaght), a miner killed in the vicinity by Indians in the 1870's.

M

Maacama See **Mayacmas.**

Maahcooatche CA Indian, probably Wintu, 'where-deer-come-to drink' (?). Also as **Maachwatchee.**

Mabana WA Named for the daughter of an old settler, Mabel Anderson, by taking the first letters from her names, and adding an *a*.

Mabank TX For Dodge Mason and Tom Eubank, early settlers.

Mabscott WV Named ca. 1906, for Mabel Scott, wife of a local coal-mine operator.

Mabton WA Probably for Mabel Baker, daughter of a pioneer railroad builder.

McAdie, Mount CA Named in 1905 in honor of A. G. McAdie, meteorologist.

Macanippuck Creek NJ Algonquian, meaning uncertain.

McCloud River CA A phonetic spelling from the name of A. R. McLeod, leader of a Hudson's Bay Company of trappers who were in the region in 1828–1829.

Macedon, Macedonia From the ancient country, known both from the fame of Alexander the Great and from the New Testament. Because of the Macedonian call (Acts 16:9) the name was a favorite one for churches, and from them was easily transferred to features and habitations.

MacFarlan Creek From the personal name, for instance, in WV the creek is for a man of that name who was wounded here by Indians in 1769.

Machado Creek NV Probably from a family name.

Machewiss Falls ME Algonquian, the same as **Machias.**

Machias Algonquian 'bad-little-falls,' applied to several places in ME; the places may have been dangerous for canoes, or otherwise troublesome.

Machipongo VA Algonquian 'bad-dust' (?).

Mach-Ki-No-Siew Lake WI Algonquian, meaning uncertain.

Macho Spanish 'mule.'

Machodoc VA Algonquian, with *mach* probably 'bad,' and the rest uncertain.

Mac-Kay-See Lake WI Algonquian, meaning uncertain.

McKees Rocks PA From the rocks in the river, associated with Alexander McKee, early settler.

Mackinac See **Mackinaw**

Mackinaw The earliest form, in a French context (1670), is **Michilimakinak** and is applied to the island MI; it is Algonquian (Ojibway), with *makina*, 'turtle,' and the whole probably 'big-turtle-at.' As applied to the island, the description is fitting and can also have mythological aptness. The name, however, may be tribal. Being long for practical use, it was soon shortened, with the French spelling it as **Mackinac**: the English, as **Mackinaw**. Both spellings survive, but there is a single pronunciation, better represented by the English spelling. In IL the name also occurs first (1773) in the longer form, as that of a river, either transferred from MI or named for literal reasons.

McKenzie From the personal name, e.g. the river in OR from Donald McKenzie of Astor's Pacific Fur Co., who explored the region in 1812.

McKinley From the personal name, especially for William McKinley, president, e.g. **McKinleyville** CA, named shortly after the assassination. **Mount McKinley** AK: named in 1896, when McKinley was a presidential candidate, by a prospector who was in the region and was of Republican leaning. Though the original naming was little more than a joke, McKinley later became president and then a 'martyred' president, so that the name was permanently established.

McKown From the personal name; for instance, in WV the creek is for Isaac and Gilbert McKown, who killed six bears here in 1850.

Maco NC From a kind of cotton grown here.

Macon From the personal name; for instance, counties and towns in AL, NC, GA, MO, and other states are for Nathaniel Macon (1758–1837), Revolutionary soldier and later political figure.

Macopin In NJ it is Algonquian 'potato,' with reference to a wild tuber (see **Potato**). **Macoupin** IL is the same.

McPherson From the personal name, especially for J. B. McPherson, Civil War general, e.g. the town in KS and counties in KS, NB, and SD.

Macungie PA Algonquian (Delaware) 'bears'-haunt.'

Macwahoc(k) ME Algonquian 'bog.'

Macy Usually from the personal name. In NB the post office was founded at the Agency for the Omaha Indians. To avoid duplication of **Omaha,** a name was coined by taking *-ma-* from 'Omaha' and *-cy* from 'Agency.' In NM the name may be from Spanish *mesa* by folk-etymology.

Mad Occurs on natural features to record an incident, usually in the sense of 'crazy' or 'frenzied,' but sometimes in the sense of 'angry.' Occasionally applied to a stream because of turbulent waters, e.g. **Mad Creek** OR. Either animals or men may be involved, for example, **Mad Mule Canyon** and **Mad Ox Canyon** (both CA), and the unlikely **Mad Sheep Mountain** WV. **Mad Tom Mountain** WV by local story, for a slave who was lost there and became demented. **Mad River** CA: named in 1849 by the first explorers, when one of them, Josiah Gregg, gave way to a violent fit of anger. **Mad River** VT: by folk-etymology from an Algonquian form, *madi tegou,* 'bad (useless)-river.' **Mad Horse Creek** NJ: because animals pastured here were once affected with a disease which made them act strangely.

Madagam Lake ME Algonquian 'near-end-of-lake.'

Madagamus Hill ME Algonquian 'snow-shoe-tracks,' but with reference to the mythological giant Glooskap, who here pursued a moose calf.

Madagascal ME Algonquian, meaning uncertain.

Madagascar VT By folk-etymology from the term seen in **Madagascal.**

Madam Bettox Mountain ME By folk-etymology from an Algonquian term elsewhere spelled **Medambettox, Medambetek,** and probably meaning 'alewife-pond,' transferred from the pond to the mountain.

Madawaska In ME it is Algonquian of uncertain meaning. In NY it is a comparatively recent name, borrowed from ME.

Madeira OH From an early settler, not otherwise identified.

Madelia MN A Latin-like coinage from Madeline Hartshorn, daughter of one of the founders.

Madeline From the personal name. In CA it commemorates a small girl killed in the vicinity by Indians when an emigrant party was attacked in the early 1850's.

Madera Spanish 'wood, timber.' In CA the name was given by a lumber company to its town in 1876 and later transferred to the county and peak. **La Madera** NM: because of sawmill operations there.

Madison The most important namings are for John Madison, fourth president, e.g. **Madison** WI, **Mount Madison** NH.

Madnaguk Island ME Algonquian 'big island.'

Madonna The Italian designation for the Virgin Mary, a rare name, but e.g. **Mount Madonna** CA.

Madras From the city of India. In OR, taken directly from the name on a bolt of cloth, that being an established term for a kind of fabric.

Madre Spanish 'mother,' as a topographical term chiefly with mountain(s), suggesting 'original' or 'basically important,' e.g. **Sierra Madre** CA, no longer officially used for the mountain range but surviving in a town. **La Madre Mountains** NV: probably a Spanish naming, but a misnomer arising from some confusion, since the range is not large or important.

Madrid From the city in Spain. **New Madrid** MO was named (1788) as **Nuevo Madrid** during the Spanish period and translated after Americans took over. **Madrid** NM probably in part commemorates the Madrid family of early settlers. Other uses of the name (e.g. in NB) spring from the 19th-century interest in foreign, especially Spanish, names.

Madrone, Madrona From the tree, a common name in the Coast Ranges of CA, and northward, e.g. **Madrona Peninsula** WA.

Magalia CA Latin 'cottages,' applied as a kind of commendatory term to a settlement previously known as **Dogtown.**

Magallo River NH Algonquian 'caribou.' The same term appears in **Magalloway** ME.

Magasewanussuck Falls ME Algonquian 'big-freshwater-falls,' as distinguished from the tidal falls farther down.

Magazine AR Originally the name of the mountain, probably from French *magasin,* 'storehouse'; reason for naming, uncertain.

Magdalena NM Probably a religious name for St. Mary Magdalene, but the local stories of its origin are conflicting.

Maggie From the woman's name; for example, **Maggie's Nipples** WY, named by cowboys for a certain Maggie Baggs, not further identified. **Mount Maggie** CA is for Maggie Kincaid, a schoolteacher of the 1870's.

Maggoty Though derivation from association with maggots is possible, the name

seems to be limited to VA and WV, thus strongly suggesting that it is a folk-etymology of **Magothy** (q.v.), also occurring in the same area.

Magic A rare commendatory, indicating some unusual qualities, e.g. **Magic Springs** AR. **Magic City** TX was named from the discovery of oil, which was sometimes said to be 'magic gold.'

Magma A geological term, in popular usage the equivalent of lava, and used to designate a place where lava is found.

Magnesia Usually with 'spring,' from the presence of magnesia in the water.

Magnet, Magnetic In the 19th century magnetism was mysterious, and various phenomena were attributed to it. Some such idea probably produced **Magnetic Springs** OH. In most instances, on natural features, the name probably arose because deposits of iron ore affected the compass needle. On habitations, e.g. NB, TX, the name is commendatory, with the idea that the place will attract people.

Magnolia Most of the southern states have a town named for the tree, which is native to that region. It is also found, by transfer or by reason of being a cultivated tree, in other regions.

Magog The Biblical name of a person and of a people. In MA probably suggested by one of the similarly-sounding Algonquian names, such as **Magonck** or **Nagog.**

Magonck CT Algonquian, probably 'grove of trees.'

Magothy, Magotha In MD and VA, probably Algonquian, 'open place in the forest, glade,' yielding **Magothy River** MD by association. **Magotha** VA: a village name, seems to represent an attempt to escape from the derogatory suggestion of **Maggoty** (q.v.), which **Magothy** closely resembles in pronunciation.

Magotsu Creek UT Paiute, probably 'long slope.'

Magpie Though the magpie is a common and conspicuous Western bird, it is of no special interest to people, and names are rare. **Magpie Peak** OR: cattle were rounded up near here, and the birds followed the cattle.

Magurrewock Lakes ME Algonquian 'caribou-(place)-at.' Also as **Megurrewock**.

Magus Hill MA For John Magus, Indian chief of the 17th century.

Mahana Peak CO The Taos Indian name for the Comanches; it was placed here about 1915 as a substitute, since **Comanche** was already the name of a peak in the area, but the namers wished to commemorate that tribe.

Mahanoy See **Mahoning**.

Mahantango Creek PA Algonquian (Delaware) 'where-we-killed-deer,' apparently an incident-name.

Maharness NY From the name of a chief, with the aid of an English possessive *s* (the same man who is remembered in **Mianus**).

Mahaska IA, KS For an Indian (Iowa) chief of the early 19th century.

Mahnomen MN Ojibway 'wild rice.'

Mahogany From one of the trees so known popularly, because the wood somewhat resembles mahogany. The name is commonest in the dry West because of the so-called 'mountain mahogany,' which is likely to be conspicuous, as the only tree growing in certain spots, e.g. **Mahogany Creek** OR, **Mahogany Flat** CA.

Mahomet IL Uncertain, whether for the prophet or from the name of an Indian chief attracted to that spelling.

Mahon River DE Probably from the common Algonquian term, 'salt-lick'; cf. **Mahoning**.

Mahoning Algonquian (Delaware) 'lick-at.' Since salt licks were frequented by game, they were of great importance both to the Indians and to the colonists, and this word became well known to speakers of English and was preserved

in many place-names, especially in PA, e.g. **Mahoning Creek** (2 in PA). It also occurs in various spellings, e.g. **Mahanoy, Mahoni, Mahony** (all in PA). It occurs in compounds, e.g. **Sinnemahoning**, and was translated as **Lick** or **Salt Lick**. See **Licking**.

Mahoosuc Range ME, NH Algonquian 'pinnacle' (?).

Mahopac NY Algonquian 'snake-lake,' probably the same as **Copake**.

Mahopenny Creek PA Algonquian (Delaware), probably 'big potato.' See **Potato**.

Mahoras Brook NJ Algonquian, meaning uncertain.

Mahto SD Siouan 'bear (the animal),' but reason for application unknown.

Mahtomedi MN Siouan 'white-bear lake.'

Mahtotopa MT Blackfoot 'four bears,' with the tradition that an Indian once killed four bears here in one morning.

Mahtowa MN A coined name from Siouan *mahto* and the last syllable of Ojibway *makwa*, each meaning 'bear.'

Mahwah NJ Algonquian, meaning uncertain.

Maiden Often from the personal name, but in the romantic period of the mid-19th century given to places associated with a young girl, particularly with an Indian legend of unrequited love, as with **Maiden Rock** WI. **The Maiden's Breast** AZ: a formation of a kind more commonly called **The Nipple**, but romanticized because in a national park, and said to be a translation from Havasupai. **Maidens Grave** CA: marks the spot of the burial of a girl who died in the migration of 1850. **Maidens Leap** NB: a variation of the commoner **Lovers Leap**.

Maidu Lake OR The name of a CA tribe, transferred to OR by means unknown.

Mailbox Gulch MT Because, where the gulch crosses a road, some mailboxes were attached to a tree.

Main Though a common descriptive in speech, it is rare in names, except in **Main Street.** Occasional uses may be noted, e.g. **Main Branch** KY, **Main Bay** AK, **Main Creek** AK. A commendatory quality still lingers, though now rather archaic, e.g. **The Main Line** PA, which refers to the suburbs built up along the chief railroad line west from Philadelphia. Cf. **Maine.**

Maine In the 17th century 'the main,' often written as 'the maine,' was used to indicate either the open sea or the continent, as in our present 'mainland.' Explorers off what is now the coast of Maine found many islands, and had constant need to refer to 'the maine.' In a charter of 1620 'the country of the Main Land' suggests a descriptive term rather than a name. In 1622 a charter declared that the grantees intended to name all that part of the mainland 'The Province of Maine.' The name fell into disuse as that of a political entity, in spite of being sharply reaffirmed by Charles I in 1629. The region continued to be popularly so known, although politically a part of MA until its organization as a state in 1820.

Maish Vaya AZ Papago 'covered well.'

Maize KS from the grain, used as an alternate for the common 'corn.'

Majenica IN For a Miami chief, whose name is recorded as Man-ji-ni-kia.

Major From the personal name, e.g. the county in OK for J. C. Major, member of the state Constitutional Convention.

Majum-Quassebem Pond ME Algonquian 'bad (useless)-pond.'

Makah WA From an Indian tribal name.

Makanda IL Uncertain; from the name of an Indian chief (?).

Maki Lake WI Algonquian, meaning uncertain.

Maklaks Klamath 'community, tribe,' or simply 'person.' The mountain in OR was named by the Forest Service.

Makoti ND Indian (Mandan) 'earth-lodge,' and thus the equivalent of 'home.'

Makushin Volcano AK Probably from Russian *makushka*, 'head, top,' because it is the highest peak of the island.

Mal Spanish 'bad.' See **Malpais,** etc.

Malabar FL On the cape it is probably from Spanish *mala barra*, 'bad bar,' Americanized partly by mere shift of pronunciation and partly by analogy with the Malabar Coast of India.

Malad ID, UT From French *malade(s)* first applied to the stream, probably as Rivière aux Malades, i.e. 'of the sick men,' because of some illness suffered there by an early party of French-Canadian trappers.

Malaga Eventually from the city in Spain, but in CA and NM for the variety of grapes so known. The islands (ME, NH) are by folk-etymology from an Algonquian word meaning 'cedar.'

Malagaie, Coulee LA Probably from French *malaguet*, 'wild-cherry.'

Malapai Hill CA An American rendering of Spanish *malpais*.

Malaspina Glacier AK Named (1874) in memory of Alessandro Malaspina, who explored the coast in 1791.

Malden In MA (1649) from a town in England; later namings are regularly transfers from MA.

Male Creek WV Probably for George Male, an early settler.

Malheur French 'misfortune.' Peter Skene Ogden, in 1826, was accompanied by French-Canadian hunters in his exploring expedition. The river in OR was so named because, on their return, they found that the Indians had plundered a cache made at that stream. The name-cluster springs from the river.

Malibu CA Probably Chumash, the name of a village; meaning unknown.

Maline In **Fourche Maline** OK it is probably French 'bad, malicious,' but the reason for naming is not known, and it may be from a personal name, such as **Malin.**

Malinta OH For Malinda Bensing, daughter of the town founder, with spelling later changed for unknown reasons.

Maljamar NM An imitation-Spanish name coined from the names (Malcolm, Janet, Margaret) of the children of William Mitchell, an oil operator in the vicinity.

Mallard From the game bird. See **Curlew.**

Mallet, Bayou LA For Pierre Mallet, landowner in the early 19th century.

Malmo From the city in Sweden.

Malone From the personal name, e.g. in NY for Edmund Malone (1741–1812), Shakespearean scholar.

Malpais Spanish 'bad country,' applied to a region difficult to travel across, especially a rough lava flow, usually a generic, but becoming a specific by association, e.g. **Malpais Mountain** AZ. Failure to sound the final consonant has produced **Mal Pai** AZ and probably **Malpie** NM.

Malpaso Spanish 'bad passage,' usually applied where a trail crossed a stream or a ravine. In CA it has been altered into **Mallo Pass Creek,** and **Mal Pass.**

Malta From the Mediterranean island. The first naming was probably that in OH (1816), where it was suggested by a former sailor who had visited the island. Being short and distinctive the name has been used by railroads in several states.

Malung MN From a town in Sweden.

Malvern From the town and hills in England, e.g. **Malvern Hill** VA.

Mamachoag, Mamaquag, Mamaquog Algonquian, a kind of small fish; the word entered English as 'mummichog.'

Mamacock CT Algonquian, probably 'great hook.'

Mamakating NY Algonquian 'bad-hill (?)' appearing by folk-etymology as **Mamacotton.** This name and **Papakating** NJ, which is not distant, have probably influenced each other by analogy.

Mamaroneck NY From the name of a local chief (recorded, 1644).

Mamasunquobscook River ME Algonquian 'rough-stones-stream.'

Mamelle French 'breast,' applied commonly to eminences shaped like a woman's breast, e.g. **Les Mamelles** MO. Cf. **Tit.**

Mammoth Regularly as a descriptive to indicate great size, e.g. **Mammoth Cave** KY, **Mammoth Hot Springs** WY, **Mammoth Peak** CA. It is sometimes a commendatory, especially for mines. A name-cluster in CA thus arose *via* the Mammoth Mining Co., and from this **Mammoth City** was the first to be named. So also, from a mine in UT. **Mammoth Creek** AK: from the finding of fossils of mammoths.

Mamou LA From the local name for the coral tree.

Man In WV from the last syllable of Ulysses Hinchman, local political figure of the 1860's. **Man Cow Rock** CA: a euphemism for bull, originating when a young lady was chased by a bull in the 1890's. **Man Trap:** see **Trap.**

Manahan Creek PA Algonquian (Delaware) 'drink-(strong)-liquor,' apparently an incident-name of an encounter with the white man's beverages.

Manahawkin NJ Algonquian 'island-small,' originally a name for the bay.

Manahowic Creek MD From an Indian tribal name.

Manakin VA From an Indian tribal name. But see **Manokin.**

Manalapan In NJ it is Algonquian, meaning uncertain. In FL it is probably a transfer from NJ.

Manan, Manhan Algonquian 'island.' In combination it occurs as *man, men, mon,* especially in New England, and is recognizable in numerous names, though some other Algonquian terms are easily confused with it. See **Manchaug, Manset, Menanhant, Monadnuck, Monanis, Monhegan,** etc.

Mananis Island ME Algonquian 'island-little.'

Manantic Creek NY Algonquian 'island-stream,' because of a small island at its mouth.

Manasquan NJ Algonquian, probably *mana,* 'island,' and the rest uncertain.

Manassa CO Named (1879) for the Biblical Manassah, or (the namers being Mormon) for the same person whose name occurs in the *Book of Mormon* as Manasseh.

Manassas VA Probably Indian, language uncertain.

Manastash Creek WA Indian, meaning unknown.

Manatawny PA Algonquian (Delaware), a repeated name, probably something like 'drinking-place-at,' being an incident name to record Indian experiences with rum.

Manatee FL The river and some habitation-names arise from the presence of the manatee or sea cow.

Manatico NJ Algonquian 'island-stream-at' (?).

Manato-Kikewe River WI Algonquian 'spirit-stooping,' probably from an Indian mythological tale.

Manatuck Algonquian, probably 'lone,' as applied to a hill and a mountain in CT, perhaps with the secondary meaning, 'lookout place.'

Manavista FL From **Manatee,** the county name, and the Spanish *vista.*

Manawa WI Ojibway, an Indian personal name (?).

Manaway Brook NJ Algonquian, probably *mana,* 'island,' and the rest uncertain.

Manchac, Bayou LA Muskogean 'strait, pass.'

Manchaug MA Algonquian, probably 'island-(of)-rushes.'

Manchester For the English city, etc. In MA the name was given in 1645, when towns were being regularly named for English ones. There may, however, be a special reference to the Duke of Manchester, who commanded the Parliamentary army. **Manchester** NH: after a visit to the thriving English city, a local citizen contrived to have his town's name changed for commendatory purposes (1810). The growing fame of the English city in the 19th century helped to popularize its name, especially where textiles were manufactured; thus **Manchester** CT in 1823. **Manchester** IA: the immediate source was William Chesterman, one of the town founders, whose name was thus inverted, though the naming may be influenced by memories of the **Manchester** in VT.

Manco Spanish 'crippled, maimed.' According to court testimony (1883), **Manco Burro Pass** NM took its name from the incident of a burro putting its knee out of place and limping. **Mancos River** CO, NM: this is probably the same word in the plural, but its origin is not known; it was previously named **San Lazaro** (St. Lazarus), and his connection with infirmities may be linked with the name.

Mandalay From the city in Burma, probably from its use in Kipling's poem.

Mandan From the Indian tribal name.

Mandaree ND Coined in 1945 from Mandan, Hidatsa, and Arickaree, as a town site for those three tribes.

Mandawessoe Island ME Algonquian 'porcupine.'

Man-Eater Canyon WY Because Alfred Packer (see **Cannibal**) was caught and arrested here in 1883.

Manetuck Neck NY Algonquian 'pine (cedar)-swamp.'

Manga Spanish 'sleeve,' 'strip of land.' Examples include **La Manga, Mangas** NM, but reasons for naming uncertain.

Manganese MN From the presence of manganiferous ores.

Mango FL For the fruit.

Mangohick VA Algonquian, meaning uncertain.

Manhan(n)ock CT, ME Algonquian 'island,' probably with the locative ending, 'at.'

Manhansuck Brook NY Algonquian 'island-outlet (brook).'

Manhasset NY From an Indian tribal name.

Manhattan NY From the tribe of Indians living there at the time of the coming of the Dutch, the word existing in various spellings. The name may be taken to mean 'island-mountain,' and thus being the Algonquian name for the island, but such a description is not well warranted. In any case, from the European point of view, the name was that of the tribe. In other states the name is from that in NY, being used as a commendatory with the suggestion of becoming a large city, and being preferred to **New York.**

Manheim From the city in Germany, generally now spelled Mannheim. In PA the town was named in 1761 by H. W. von Steigel after his native city.

Manickmung Mountain VT Algonquian 'where-mountain-bulges-up' (?).

Manikin Creek CA From the name of J. H. Mankins, early farmer in the vicinity, by folk-etymology.

Manila A half-dozen habitation-names echo the name of the Philippine city, most of them named in commemoration of the battle of Manila Bay (1898). A few use the once-current spelling **Manilla.**

Manistee MI Probably a variant of **Manistique.**

Maniste River WI See **Manistee, Manistique.**

Manistique MI Ojibway, with *tique,* 'river' and the rest, 'crooked' (?).

Manitopaymen Island MI With *manito,* 'spirit,' and the whole based upon a mythological story of the *manito* being here shot with an arrow.

Manitou A general Algonquian term, roughly to be rendered as 'spirit,' occurring in other spellings, e.g. **Manito, Manido.** It has been preserved on natural features so named by the Indians. Cf. **Spirit.** The term entered the English language, and thus has been bestowed on various towns on non-Algonquian territory.

Manitowish WI Containing the common Algonquian term 'spirit' (see **Manitou**), with a second element, 'bad' (?).

Manitowoc WI Ojibway, with *manito,* 'spirit,' and the rest, probably 'spawn' from a primitive idea that spirits propagate like fish.

Mankato MN Sioux 'earth-blue (green)' with reference to a deposit of pigmented earth used by the Indians for paint; in translation, **Blue Earth County** MN.

Manlius In NY it was given as a part of the classical naming of 1790 and certainly honors an ancient Roman hero. At least three Romans were so named and there is no way of telling which one the namers had in mind—if, indeed, they themselves knew.

Manly From the personal name. The name-cluster in CA is for W. L. Manly, author of **Death Valley in '49.**

Mannatto Hill NY Algonquian 'surpassing-hill,' i.e. the highest in the vicinity.

Mannford OK For **Mann's Ford** across the nearby river, named for Hazel and Tom Mann who lived there.

Mannington NJ Early spellings, 'Manneton' and 'Mannaton,' suggest an Algonquian origin (from *manito,* 'spirit' (?)). But the name exists as that of an English village.

Manokin River MD Algonquian (Delaware), probably, 'fortification-at,' by association either with an Indian or an English fort.

Manomet MA Algonquian 'portage.'

Manomin A variant of **Mahnomen.**

Manor 1) From the personal name, e.g. in TX, for James Manor, early settler. 2) From the term in the legal, landholding sense, the semifeudal manorial system having been established in some colonies, especially in NY; hence **Pelham Manor,** etc.

Manquin VA Algonquian, a variant of **Manakin, Manokin** (?).

Manset ME Algonquian 'island-at.'

Mansfield Although it is a town-name in England, the town in CT (1702) was named chiefly to honor Major Moses Mansfield, an important landowner. In OH the town honors Col. Jared Mansfield, Surveyor General of the U.S., named by two surveyors who were working for his department. **Mansfield** TX: for R. S. Mann and Julian Field, early settlers.

Manso Spanish 'quiet.'

Manteca CA Spanish 'lard.' The name arose in the American period, ca. 1904, and may have been taken in the less usual sense of 'butter,' being considered appropriate because of a creamery.

Manteno IL From the name of an Indian woman, recorded (1832) as Mawte-no, who held a grant of land in the vicinity.

Manteo NC, VA Named in retrospect for an Indian who was taken to England in 1584 by the Amadas and Barlow expedition.

Manti UT From one of the cities mentioned in the *Book of Mormon,* named by Brigham Young in 1849.

Mantoloking NJ Algonquian, probably *manto* represents a tribal name (see **Mantua**), and the rest, 'sand-at.'

Mantua Generally from the Italian city, in OH being an echo of Napoleon's victory in 1796. **Mantua** NJ: an adaptation by false etymology from the name of an Indian tribe, which also yields **Muncie.**

Manu Temple AZ See **Brahma.**

Manumuskin NJ Algonquian, meaning uncertain.

Manunka Chunk NJ Apparently a variant of **Mauch Chunk,** q.v.

Manwhage Swamp MA Algonquian 'refuge-at.'

Many A rare descriptive, e.g. **Many Point Lake** MN. **Many Farms** AZ is a translation from the Navajo. It occurs as a first element in many Indian personal names, and hence, e.g. **Many Skunks Creek** SD. It is a rare family name; hence, **Many** LA for Col. Many, an army officer of the early 19th century, otherwise unidentified. **Many Mind Creek** NJ: probably because it changes direction often, thus being of many minds.

Manyaska MN Siouan, with the idea of 'white,' probably 'white bluff.'

Manzana Spanish 'apple,' in some instances probably a shortening of manzanita. **Manzana Creek** CA: because in the 1870's a large apple orchard was located there.

Manzanar Spanish 'apple orchard,' but in CA applied to a fruit-growing district which did not primarily produce apples.

Manzanita, Manzanito From the bush so called, chiefly in CA, where more than 100 features bear the name. **Manzanito Creek** occurs in NM.

Manzano Spanish 'apple-tree,' the town in NM being named for some old apple orchards.

Manzanola CO From Spanish *manzana,* 'apple,' because of being in an apple-growing district, coupled with the favorite suffix, *-ola.*

Maple Although a family name, **Maples,** exists, the place-names are regularly from the widespread tree, which has been prized especially as a source of sugar and as a shade tree. See **Sugar.** Much associated with New England, it is actually commoner on natural features in the Middle West, probably because it was rarer there, and so served better for identification. Its use as a planted shade tree has given it a commendatory value beyond that of most trees and has produced many town and street names; especially liked is the name **Maplewood.**

Maquam, Maquan MA Algonquian 'beaver.'

Maquina Spanish 'machine.' In NM, **Maquina Creek** takes its name from a sawmill.

Maquoketa IA Algonquian (Iowa), probably 'bear-river.'

Maquon IL Algonquian (Illinois), from *a-ma-quon,* 'musselshell,' originally the name of **Spoon River.**

Mar Spanish 'sea.' **Mar Vista** CA is pseudo-Spanish, but suggests 'sea-view.'

Marais French 'marsh, swamp,' but in American-French commonly referring to a body of water that might be associated with a marsh, and so translatable as 'pool, slough, bayou.' Its meaning has now been largely lost, and it exists as a quasi-specific, e.g. **Marais Des Cygnes** MO and **Marais Croche** MO; used especially in habitation-names, e.g. **Grand Marais** MI.

Maramec OK Probably Indian, but uncertain in meaning; it may be a variant of **Meramec.**

Maramech Hill IL See **Meramec.**

Marana AZ From the Spanish *marana,* 'thicket,' because of thick growth of mesquite.

Maranacook Lake ME Algonquian, meaning uncertain.

Marathon From the famous Greek victory over the Persians; in TX, named by a sea captain who had visited the Greek site and was here reminded of it. **Marathon Mountain** AK: because a 'marathon' race is held here yearly.

Marble Though the personal name exists, the place-names are regularly from the occurrence of the rock or of some rock resembling marble, e.g. **Marblehill** MO and **Marble Gorge** AZ. **Marblehead** MA: named in the early 17th century, when hard rocks (here, granite) were known as marble; 'head,' in the sense of headland.

Marcellus In NY the name was given as part of the classical naming of 1790, and certainly honors an ancient Roman hero, of whom there were several so named, the most likely one being the opponent of Julius Caesar.

Marcola OR From Mary Cole, with 'a' added, as is customary with habitation-names.

Marcus Usually from the personal name, e.g. in WA for Marcus Oppenheimer, town founder. **Mount Marcus Baker** AK was named (1924) for the cartographer (1849–1903) and recorder of place-names. **Marcus Hook** PA: a form, *marikes,* recorded in a Swedish context (1660), suggests a derivation by folk-etymology from an Algonquian term, 'witchcraft,' because of some ceremonies held here.

Mardela Springs MD A boundary-name, for MD and DE.

Mardi Gras, Bayou LA French 'Shrove Tuesday,' named (1699) because an exploring expedition arrived here on that day.

Mare Uncommon, the broader term **Horse** usually serving. **Mare Island** CA: in the 1840's a mare joined a herd of elk here, and was often seen; the name is translated from Spanish. **Mare Creek** NB: by counterpart from nearby **Horse** and **Colt** creeks.

Mareep Creek CA Yurok, the name of a village, meaning unknown.

Marengo From the town in Italy and Napoleon's victory of 1800.

Marenisco MI Coined by E. H. Scott, early landowner, by taking the first two or three letters from each of his wife's names, Mary Relief Niles Scott.

Marfrance WV Named in 1919 from Margaret and Frances, as used in the names of two local coal companies.

Margaretta The township in OH was named, ca. 1812, because of several women named Margaret in the family of the developer, with the added 'a' to indicate a place-name.

Margate City NJ From Margate, England.

Maria Generally from the personal name. **Marias (Maria's) River** MT was named by Capt. Lewis of the Lewis and Clark expedition in 1804 for his cousin, Maria Wood.

Marias See **Maria**.

Maricopa From the Indian tribal name. The tribe was native to AZ, and the name in CA is apparently a transfer by Americans.

Marie Commonly from the woman's name, e.g. in TX for Marie Gentry, wife of a local landowner. **Maries River** MO is by folk-etymology from **Marias**, and the county is derived from it by transfer. **Marie Saline Landing** AR is by folk-etymology from French *marais saline*, 'marsh (pond)-salty.' **Bayou Marie Croquant** LA is probably from **Marie** as a family-name, with the other term uncertain, though possibly a derogatory, 'vagabond.'

Marienthal KS Named by German-speaking settlers from Russia, for a place from which they had emigrated.

Marietta In OH the town was named in 1788, a time of enthusiasm for things French, for Marie Antoinette, Queen of France, but with a shift to suggest an Italian or Latinized form. The name became popular and gave rise directly to others, e.g. in MN. In PA the name was coined in 1812 from Mary and Etta, wives of two founders. In NC it is from Augustus Marriel, a local promoter. In OK it is a transfer from PA.

Marin CA Probably goes back to a naming of a small bay by a Spanish explorer in 1775, Nuestra Señora de Rosario de Marinera.

Marina Spanish 'shore, seacoast.'

Marine Usually for association with the sea, e.g. **Marineland** CA, FL. In MI the city is situated on a river with heavy commerce. A settlement of some former seafaring men gave rise to **Marine IL**, and the name was thence transferred to MN.

Marinette In WI from the French name of a local Indian woman. In AZ a transfer from WI.

Maringouin LA American-French 'mosquito,' probably applied first to the bayou.

Marion From the personal name, especially for Francis Marion, Revolutionary hero, whose name was popular for towns and counties, especially in the SE, after the publication of his biography by 'Parson' Weems in 1809.

Mariposa Spanish 'butterfly.' In CA the name was applied because a Spanish expedition of 1806 encountered many butterflies.

Marissa IL By local tradition from Marisa, the Greek form of the name occurring in the Old Testament (King James version) as Mareshah; the spelling, however, suggests derivation from an Algonquian (Illinois) word for 'knife,' also the name of a chief recorded in 1818.

Markagunt UT Paiute 'highland of trees,' a name applied by A. H. Thompson, an American explorer.

Marked Tree AR From a blazed tree that once indicated the ford across a stream at this point.

Mark West Creek CA For Mark (William Marcus) West, who held a grant of land in the area about 1840.

Marlboro, Marlborough From the town in England; in MA (1660) named probably because some of the settlers had come from that town. In CT the name is probably in honor of the Duke of Marlborough, victor of Blenheim. In VT it is for Charles Spencer, Duke of Marlborough, prominent political figure of the mid-18th century.

Marmarth ND Coined (1907) from the given names of Margaret Martha Fitch, daughter of a railroad president, probably representing her childish pronunciation.

Marmaton River MO Uncertain, though apparently an Indian term made over into a French spelling.

Marmet WV Named in 1900 from the Marmet Coal Company, which was owned by William and Edwin Marmet.

Marmot The term has scarcely been colloquial in the U.S., and the names refer to various burrowing animals. In scientific parlance the term should mean the beast commonly called woodchuck, and some names have thus developed, e.g. the creek in WA. The habitation-name in OR arose from holes dug by the mountain beaver or aplodontia. In the plains area the prairie dog may be meant. **Marmot Island** AK is named from the ground squirrel (spermophilus).

Marne From the French river, which became a commendatory because of its association with American victories in World War I. **Berlin** MI became **Marne** during that war. So also **Rhine Creek** SD became **Marne Creek.**

Maroa IL From an Indian tribal name, a shortening of **Tamaroa.**

Maromas CT Algonquian 'bare.'

Maroon The peak in CO is named from the peculiar color of its rocks.

Marquette Numerous names are for Father Jacques Marquette, French missionary and explorer of the 17th century.

Marquis Creek NJ A form **Machays** indicates a development by folk-etymology from an Algonquian original of unknown meaning.

Marratooka Pond NY A variant (*via* Marritook) of **Mattituck.**

Marron, Bayou LA French 'wild' (with special reference to a feral animal or to a fugitive slave.) The bayou was probably once the haunt of an escaped slave.

Marrowbone Probably from frontier incident, for instance, in WV the name of the creek is explained by local story as being given by some half-starving men who found a bone and ate the marrow.

Marrowstone Point WA From a kind of stone so known, named by George Vancouver in 1792.

Mars From the Roman god. **Mars Bluff** SC is an adaptation from Maers, the name of an early settler. **Mars Hill** ME, NC: from the hill in Athens, thus known from the King James Bible because Paul preached there. In ME a chaplain preached with a text drawn from that passage, and the hill was thenceforth so known (1790); the town was named from the hill (1867).

Marsh Often from a personal name, e.g. **Marsh Creek** CA for John Marsh, pioneer landowner. Commonly from association with a marsh, e.g. **Marshland** OR. **Marshfield** MA was named ca. 1640, probably because of marshes in the area, though the name exists in England and may have been transferred, as was then the custom. Later towns were named for this one (e.g. in MO) without thought of marshes, especially because it was the home of Daniel Webster. An origin in some instances is to be suspected from the Algonquian *mash*, 'big,' which is common in place-names in New England, especially since *marsh* sometimes approximates *mash* in certain types of colloquial speech.

Marshall From the personal name, especially for John Marshall, Chief Justice of the U.S. Supreme Court, e.g. counties in AL, IL, IN, IA, KY, MN, MS, TN, WV, and several towns, e.g. **Marshalltown** IA, **Marshall** TX.

Marshan MN For Michael Marsh and his wife, Ann, early settlers.

Marten A few places, e.g. **Marten Buttes** OR, bear the name of the valuable fur-bearing animal. See **Martin.**

Martha From the personal name. Like other women's names it has been commonly bestowed as a sentimental commemorative. **Martha's Vineyard** MA: Gabriel Archer in 1602 noted many vines on an island, and the name undoubtedly sprang from that circumstance. Evidence is lacking for **Martha's,** though there has been much speculation. Archer was a fanciful namer, and we should probably assume here some imaginative stroke of which the record is lost.

Martin Regularly from the personal name, e.g. **Martin's Ferry** OH, where Ebenezer Martin established a town where his father had maintained a ferry, ca. 1790. **Martin** WA: because some hunters had killed a pine marten there, a shift of spelling occurring later.

Marumsco Creek MD, VA Algonquian, meaning uncertain.

Marvin From the personal name; in SD, taken from the name on the office safe, with the joke that it would be a 'safe' name.

Mary In most periods the most popular of women's names, Mary has been prolific, e.g. for lakes so named in compliment. There are about 30 towns and villages, the most common being **Marysville.** Little religious influence is indicated, but **Maryknoll** may be noted. (See also, **St. Mary, Santa Maria). Maryland:** for Henrietta Maria, queen of Charles I. Since the colony was designed for Catholics, a religious influence may be suspected, but the story is that Charles himself, a Protestant, gave the name. In early years the spelling varied (e.g. **Marieland, Mary-Land). Marysville** OH: for Mary Culbertson, daughter of the founder, in 1820. **Marysville** CA: for Mary Murphy Covillaud, wife of the principal landowner, approved at a public meeting in Jan. 1850. **Maryhill** WA: from Samuel Hill, local landowner, whose wife and mother both were named Mary. **Marylhurst** OR: coined ca. 1910 from 'Mary' (the Virgin), the ending 'hurst,' with the 'l' inserted for euphony,

the place being the seat of a Catholic order.

Marydel DE A boundary name with MD.

Maryland See **Mary.**

Marylhurst OR See **Mary.**

Masardis ME Algonquian, meaning uncertain.

Masaryktown FL For the Czechoslovakian leader, T. G. Marsaryk, founded as a Czechoslovakian agricultural colony in 1924.

Mascoma NH Algonquian, meaning uncertain.

Mascotte FL Named in the 1880's by an early settler for a ship in which he had sailed.

Mascoutah IL Algonquian 'prairie, meadow.'

Mascouten From the Indian tribal name.

Mash Although an incident involving some kind of mash may be responsible, the name could readily arise from the local pronunciation of 'marsh,' e.g. **Mash Branch** KY. In areas with a background of Algonquian speech it could arise from the word for 'big,' as in **Mashpaug,** etc.

Mashamee River NH Algonquian, meaning uncertain.

Mashapoug See **Mashpaug.**

Mashel Creek WA Probably from the French personal name Michel.

Mashentuck CT, RI Algonquian 'many-trees.'

Masheshattuck Hill NH Algonquian 'big-wooded-mountain.'

Mashipacong NJ Algonquian, probably 'big-river-at.'

Mashmoquet CT Algonquian 'chief-fishing-place-at.'

Mashoes NC From Peter Michieux (or Mashews) who was shipwrecked here in 1739, his wife and child being drowned; he then lived here in a semi-lunatic condition for many years.

Mashpaug, Mashpoag, Mashipaug, Massapaug, Massapoag, Masshapauge, Meshapock Algonquian 'big pond,' common in New England.

Mashpee MA Algonquian 'big cove (pond).'

Mashulaville MS A shortening of Mashulatubbee, a well-known Choctaw chief of the early 19th century.

Masipa Spring AZ Navajo 'gray spring.'

Maskik Run PA Algonquian (Delaware) 'swamp.'

Mason, Masonic From the personal name or the Masonic Order. **Mason and Dixon** PA: from proximity to the line marking the PA-MD boundary, named for the surveyors of 1763–1767. **Masonic Temple** AZ: one of the fanciful namings of the Grand Canyon. **Masonic Gulch** CA: because a group of Masons worked mines here in 1862. **Mason City** IA: because most of the early settlers were Masons. **Masonia** ID: probably from the name of an early settler. In AR the name is from the Marquis de Maison Rouge, an early French landowner.

Maspeth NY Algonquian, from a recorded Mespaechtes (1634), meaning uncertain.

Masquaseecook Lake ME Algonquian 'birch-stream.'

Massabesic Lake NH Algonquian 'big-brook-at.' Cf. **Mattabesec.**

Massac IL Originally as **Fort Massiac,** for the French Minister of Marine at the time of the Seven Years War.

Massachusetts Algonquian (Natick) 'big-hills-at,' originally the name of a village, recorded in 1616. The English used it as a tribal name and added the final 's' as a sign of the plural. The hills were those near the site of **Boston.** The name was transferred to the bay, then (1629) the **Massachusetts Bay Colony** was officially designated; with the Constitution of 1780 the name **Commonwealth of Massachusetts** was adopted.

Massacre A term loosely used by pioneers for a place where people had been killed, especially where whites had been killed by Indians, whether or not it might have more properly been called 'battle.' **Massacre Rocks** ID: on Aug. 10, 1862, a wagon train was attacked here, and a number of emigrants were killed. **Massacre Canyon** CA: the scene of a fight between two Indian tribes. **Massacre Lakes** NV: in a battle here in 1850, the whites were victorious, but 40 men were killed. **Massacre Bay** WA: early explorers found skulls which they took to be from Indian battles.

Massanutten VA Algonquian 'big-mountain' (?).

Massaponax VA Algonquian, meaning uncertain.

Massard AR Probably a variant, because of oral tradition and uncertain spelling, of **Mazarn.**

Massasecum Lake NH From the name of a local Indian.

Massasoit Creek KS From the 17th-century chief, who was friendly to the Plymouth colonists; the name was brought west by emigrants from New England.

Massassomineuk MA Algonquian 'big-sour(?)-berries-at,' probably for cranberries.

Massawepie Lake NY Algonquian 'big-water.'

Massena NY For André Masséna, French general, named in 1802, when he had distinguished himself in the Revolutionary wars.

Massepa River NY Algonquian, probably 'bad-river,' so called because of a difficult crossing or other hazard.

Massillon OH Named (1826) for the French author Jean Baptiste Massillon, whose works were favorites with the wife of the town founder.

Massive, Mount CO A descriptive for a broad and heavy-looking mountain.

Mastic NY Algonquian 'big-(tidal)-stream,' a variant of **Mystic.**

Mastodon From the fossils of this animal, e.g. five creeks in AK.

Mastomquoog Island ME Algonquian 'big-rocks-at.'

Mat River See **Mattaponi.**

Matacumbe See **Matecumbe.**

Matagamon ME Algonquian 'far-on-other-side.'

Matagoodus Stream ME Algonquian 'bad-landing,' i.e. for canoes.

Matagorda TX Spanish 'thicket-dense,' probably applied first to the island.

Matakehunk Brook ME Algonquian, to denote a stream that falls rapidly near its mouth.

Matamoras From the city of Mexico, captured by the Americans in the Mexican War; hence, the town in PA and **New Matamoras** in OH.

Matanawcook ME Algonquian; of special interest because the names for the three features are of different origins, though now having the same spelling. The island bears what was originally the name of the island group, viz., it means to a group of small, broken islands. The stream is 'end-island-stream-at,' viz., it has an island just off its mouth. The lake has a name taken from its outlet stream, i.e. 'end-lake-at,' with reference to the very short distance between the lake and the main river.

Matanuska AK The Russians applied the term *mednorechka*, 'copper,' to one of the rivers of the region, because of metal found there, and that name was applied to the Indians living there. It was passed on to the Americans, probably through the Indians, and ended in its present form, passing through a confusion of spellings on the way.

Matanza Spanish 'butchery, massacre,' in the plural indicating many or repeated killings, and so a slaughtering place, usually for cattle, e.g. **Matanzas Creek** CA. **Matanzas Inlet** FL: at this place, in 1565, Pedro Menéndez had 400 French prisoners beheaded.

Matapan MA Algonquian, with the element *ap*, 'sit,' the whole name probably to be taken as 'resting-place,' as on a trail or portage.

Matapeake MD From an Indian tribal name.

Matawan NJ From the tribal name recorded (1656) as Matovancons.

Matchless Mountain CO From a mine name.

Matecumbe FL Probably an Indian name shaped to a Spanish form, meaning unknown.

Mater Probably in all instances from a family name.

Mather From the personal name, e.g. **Mount Mather** AK for S. T. Mather, Director of the U.S. National Park Service (1917–1929).

Matia Islands WA By error for Spanish *mata*, 'bush, shrub,' as the name appears on Spanish charts of 1791 and 1792.

Matilija CA Chumash, the name of a village, perhaps named for the plant now known as the matilija poppy.

Matincook Mountain ME Algonquian, meaning uncertain.

Matinicus Island ME Algonquian, probably 'cut-off-island,' because of its position far at sea, a descriptive especially fitting for **Matinicus Rock.** The -*us* is unexplained.

Matinnecock NY From an Indian tribal name.

Matkatamiba Canyon AZ For an Indian family.

Matoaka This is the proper name of the Indian 'princess,' who is usually known as Pocahontas, e.g. towns in VA and WV. Sometimes as **Matoaca.**

Matrimony Creek NC, VA Named by a member of the boundary survey party of 1728, who had a poor opinion of marriage, because the stream was noisy, impetuous, and clamorous, though unsullied.

Matta See **Mattaponi.**

Mattabesec, Mattabeesick, Mattabesett Algonquian. These names, in New England, may be variants of **Massabesic** or may have developed from **Mattapoisett.**

Mattakesett Creek MA Algonquian, probably 'black-mud-at.'

Mattakeunk ME Algonquian 'end-(rapid)-stream-at.'

Mattamiscontis ME Algonquian 'alewives (fish)-plenty.'

Mattamuskeet NC From the name of a village of an Algonquian-speaking tribe; literal meaning uncertain.

Mattapan MA Algonquian, containing the element *ap*, 'sit,' the name probably meaning 'resting-place,' as at the end of a portage.

Mattapex MD See **Matapeake.**

Mattapoisett, Mattapoysett MA, RI Algonquian 'resting-place,' as on a trail or portage. Cf. **Matapan.**

Mattaponi River VA From a tribal name, recorded (1608) as Mattapanient. Dating from the mid-18th century and probably arising by conscious humor with some original stimulus from an Indian name is the present unique situation. At the chief forking the two streams are named the **Matta River** and the **Poni River:** at the forking of the former the streams are named **Mat River** and **Ta River;** at the forking of the latter the streams are named **Po River** and **Ni River.** Cf. **Poo.**

Mattaseunk Stream ME Algonquian, to denote a stream with rapids at its mouth.

Mattawamkeag ME Algonquian, to indicate a stream with a gravel bar at its mouth.

Mattawan MI Ojibway 'sand.'

Mattawoman MD From an Indian tribal name, somewhat shaped by folk-etymology, probably that recorded (1612) by John Smith as **Massawomeck.**

Matteawan NY Though apparently the same as **Matawan,** it may here be a topographical term to denote a spot at which one stream debouches into another.

Matterhorn Though the naming of mountains after mountains has not been common, the fame of this Swiss peak has led to the use of the name, e.g. in CA, CO, OR.

Mattimockamus Lake ME Algonquian 'far-off-lake-small.'

Mattituck NY Algonquian probably 'no-timber.'

Mattlacha Pass FL From the name of an Indian chief, recorded (1823) as Emathlochee.

Mattoax VA Probably a variant of **Mattox,** q.v.

Mattole CA From an Indian tribal name.

Mattox Probably shifted to the form of a family name by folk-etymology from an Algonquian name. Cf. **Matapeake, Mattapex, Appomattox, Mattoax.**

Matunuck RI Algonquian 'high place,' probably with the special meaning 'lookout.'

Maturango Peak CA From an Indian tribal name.

Mauch Chunk PA Algonquian, a badly shifted form, but meaning 'bearmountain.'

Maumee OH From the Indian tribal name, a variant of **Miami** (2).

Maumelle AR An American variant of the French *mamelle,* 'breast,' but used as a common generic for 'hill.'

Maunie IL From Maude Sheridan and Jennie Pumphrey, daughters of two early settlers.

Maurepas, Lake LA For the Comte J. F. P. de Maurepas, French political figure of the early 18th century.

Maurice From the personal name. In NJ the river and town are from a ship, *Prince Maurice,* captured and burned by the Indians in the Dutch period.

Mauvais(e) French 'bad,' e.g. **Mauvais Bois Bayou** LA.

Maverick Generally with reference to unbranded cattle, e.g. **Maverick Lake** NB. **Maverick** TX: for Samuel Maverick, early landowner, from whose name the common term is believed to be derived.

Maway River NY Probably Algonquian, meaning uncertain.

Max From the personal name, e.g. in ND for Max Freitag, son of the first postmaster. In OK it is for Mac's, from the nickname of J. P. McNaughton, local rancher. So also in combinations, e.g. **Maxville** OH for William McCormick, founder. **Maxton** NC: because it was largely settled by Scots, many of whom had names beginning with *Mac.*

Maxatawny Creek PA Algonquian (Delaware), probably 'bear-path.'

Maxinkuckee IN Potawatomi, probably 'big-stone-country.'

Maxwelton The spelling indicates that the name was borrowed, not from the town in Scotland (Maxwellton), but from the popular song, 'Annie Laurie,' in which the name has the single 'l.' The opening line, 'Maxwelton's braes are bonny,' makes the name commendatory.

May Usually for a personal name or for an English village, e.g. **Mayberry, Mayfield.** The frequency, however, suggests that the pleasant associations of the month of May have had some influence, as with **Maytown** PA, which was laid out on May 1, 1762, with dancing in the streets. **Mayflower** TX: founded and named at the time of wild flowers. But **Maywood** NB is for a girl, May Wood. **Cape May** NJ: for the Dutch captain, Cornelius Jacobsen Mey, who sailed there in the early 17th century. **May**

River SC: named by Jean Ribaut in 1563, because he landed there in May. **Mayhill** NM: for J. F. Mahill, pioneer settler, probably by mistake. **May Day** KS: a name selected by the first postmaster, because the date was on or near May 1, 1871. **Maywood** IL is for May Nichols, daughter of the town founder, with 'wood' added because of a nearby woodland. **Maybell** CO: the post office was named for May Bell, wife of a local rancher.

Mayaca, Port FL From the name of an early Indian town of uncertain meaning.

Mayacmas, Maacama CA From an Indian tribal name.

Maybe, Maybeso As applied to creeks in AK, the names (all of the 20th century) commemorate uncertainty on the part of the namers, e.g. as to where the stream led.

Mayetta In KS from Mary Henrietta Lunger, the deceased daughter of the town founder, named in 1886.

Mayodan NC Because situated at the junction of the **Mayo** and **Dan** rivers.

Maza ND For Maza Chante, a local Sioux chief.

Mazama OR, WA Spanish 'mountain-goat,' a rare word, used for a town in WA in 1899. The name was adopted by a mountaineering club, and most of the names are thus derived, e.g. the ridge in WA.

Mazarn AR An earlier **Mt. Cerne** is preserved. *Cerne* in American-French was a hunter's term, for a 'surround,' especially of buffalo, and this name apparently preserves the memory of some notable 'surround.'

Mazaska Lake WN Siouan 'white iron, silver,' but reason for application unknown.

Mazeppa MN A literary name, from Byron's poem, 'Mazeppa,' commemorating the Cossack chief (1644–1709).

Mazomanie WI Simplified from the name of a Winnebago Indian usually spelled **Manzemoneka.**

Mazon IL Algonquian (Illinois) 'nettle,' q.v.

Meacox NY Probably a shortening from Secommecock (with addition of the possessive) the personal name of an Indian recorded in 1640.

Mead The older English equivalent of 'meadow,' was introduced poetically in the early 19th century, and appears as a commendatory in habitation-names, e.g. **Rosemead.** As a detached specific, it is from the personal name; for instance, **Lake Mead** AZ, NV was named for Dr. Elwood Mead, Commissioner of the U.S. Reclamation Service, at the time of the building of the dam which resulted in the lake.

Meade From the personal name, especially for George G. Meade, Union general, e.g. several western counties.

Meadow Though basically a generic, the term is used as a specific to denote features associated with a meadow, being coupled especially with 'creek' and 'lake.' It is more numerous in regions where the tree growth is such that meadows exist or once existed. The commendatory nature of the term has led to its common use for habitation-names, esp. with such romantic endings as '-brook,' '-dale,' '-view.' **Meadowbrook** has been used as a habitation-name, ready-made, in regions (e.g. MV, MN) where 'brook' is not ordinarily used in place-names. (See **Brook.**) **Meadow Grove** NB: though seeming to state a contradiction, the town took its name from a grove standing in a meadow. The name may also be from the personal name.

Meares, Cape OR Applied in 1857 to honor John Meares, explorer and trader in the Northwest in the later 18th century.

Meat It is chiefly preserved as **Meathouse** and **Meatscaffold,** the former a place for storing meat and the latter probably an arrangement for keeping game out of the reach of prowling animals; both are, for example, names of streams in KY.

Mecan WI Algonquian (Ojibway) 'trail.'

Mecca From the city of Arabia, sometimes reinforced by the figurative sense, i.e. a center or goal for people to reach. In CA the name was additionally appropriate since the site is in the desert.

Mechanicsburg, Mechanicsville In older usage the term meant a worker in a factory and is thus used in a commendatory sense.

Mechant French 'wicked,' but as referring to the lake in LA, probably 'dirty.'

Mechescatauxin Branch NJ Algonquian, meaning uncertain.

Mecklenburg The marriage of George III to Charlotte Sophia, Duchess of Mecklenburg-Strelitz, gave rise to **Mecklenburg County** NC, VA and other places. See **Charlotte.**

Mecosta MI From the name of a Potawatomi chief of the early 19th century.

Medano Spanish 'dune,' e.g. **Point Medanos** CA.

Meddybemps ME Algonquian, probably 'plenty-of-alewives' (a fish).

Medfield MA Originally Meadfield, probably after the place of that name in Surrey, England (1650).

Medford The original naming was in MA, where the town was incorporated in 1684. In some early documents it appears as Metford, and it is probably a re-spelling, after common pronunciation, of that English hamlet-name. 'Med' is also a commoner place-name element than 'met,' and so the name might be attracted to that spelling. The influence of an actual ford is possible. Later towns are from that in MA, except that in OR the namer was also influenced by a 'middle ford' in existence.

Media PA The feminine form of the Latin adjective 'middle,' used because of the central location in the county. The choice of the name was probably also affected, in a time of classical predilections, by the name of the ancient country of the Medes.

Mediapolis IA A Latin-Greek coinage to mean 'middle-city,' because located halfway between two county seats.

Medicine, Medical The name may indicate a place with water supposed to have therapeutic value, e.g. **Medical Springs** OR. It may also record an incident, e.g. **Medicine Creek** OR. Some amateur doctors here mixed up a potion for their patient which had dire results. Most commonly the name springs from the usage of 'medicine' to mean anything that the Indians conceived to be unnatural or supernatural, e.g. **Medicine Creek** NB. Since this usage of the word did not arise until after 1800, nearly all the names are Western. Many of them are translations of Indian terms. Indian personal names are sometimes involved, e.g. **Medicine Owl Creek** MT. In many instances the names were tied up with religious belief. In other cases a merely inexplicable incident would serve, e.g. **Medicine Lake** MN where a canoe capsized in a storm and an Indian was drowned; his body could not be found, and this was mysterious enough to produce the name. **Medicine Wood** MN: a single large beech tree, growing to the north of its usual range, impressed the Indians as mysterious and so produced the name. **Medicine Bow River** WY: the name-cluster probably originated from the river. While a reference to the favorite Indian weapon may be assumed, the connection is uncertain. **Medicine Lodge** KS: from the river, to which the Indian tribes of the whole region were accustomed to resort to bathe, pray, and fast, in hope of curing their bodily ills.

Medimont ID A coinage from nearby **Medicine Mountain.**

Medina In TX the river was named on April 9, 1689, by the De León expedition, probably for Nicolás de Medina, the sergeant-major. On April 3, however, the journal makes mention of Pedro Medina, author of *Arte de Navigar,* and the coincidence of the two names may have accomplished the result. In NY probably for the city of Arabia, as part of the post-Revolutionary fervor for exotic names. In OH the town was called **Mecca,** but had to be changed because of duplication, and so took an associated name. In ND the town was formerly

Midway, but was changed under the influence of 'median'; the pronunciation was officially given a short 'i' in honor of Judge Harold Medina, who visited the town in 1956 when this honor was conferred upon him in recognition of his services in the trial of Communists in 1949.

Medio Spanish 'middle.' **Medio Dia Canyon** NM is 'mid-day.'

Medley WV From a family name of local residents.

Medo MN Siouan, for an edible root.

Medomac, Medomock ME Algonquian 'mouth-(of)-(stream)-alewives (fish)-at.'

Medora The name is from Lord Byron's poem 'The Corsair,' apparently coined by him for a woman's name, and it is probably, in some instances, e.g. IN, KS, taken directly from the poem. In ND the town was named, ca. 1883, in connection with the establishment of a large ranch, by the Marquis de Mores, for his wife.

Medumcook River ME Algonquian 'mouth-(of)-(stream)-sand-at.'

Medusa NY The name of the horrendous monster of Greek mythology was probably bestowed, without thought of its suitability, during the period of classical naming.

Meduxnekeag ME Algonquian 'mouth-(of)-(stream)-rapids-at.'

Medway In MA the town was formed from **Medfield** (1713) and retained part of the old name as a sentimental tie; the whole name is that of an English river and district. In ME the MA town must have been known, but an additional reason for naming was that the town was 'midway' between two other spots.

Meek From the personal name, e.g. in NB for Samuel Meek, local resident.

Meeme See **Mimi.**

Meeteetse Creek WY Indian, probably Shoshone, mèaning uncertain.

Meeting House In areas where this term was used commonly instead of 'church' or 'chapel' it served to identify by association, e.g. two hills, a pond, and a swamp in MA.

Megunticook ME Algonquian 'big-mountain-harbor,' first applied to the bay and then extended by transfer to other features.

Megurrewock See **Magurrewock.**

Meherrin NC, VA From an Indian tribal name.

Mekinock ND From **Mickinock,** transfered from MN.

Melakwa Lake WA Chinook jargon 'mosquito.'

Melbourne From the personal name; in FL, the name was placed by an Australian for his native city.

Meldenings Death Ridge TN In early times a man of this name was murdered here and his body concealed.

Melendreth Pass AZ Probably for an early Mexican settler named Meléndrez, though the rendering in -*th* is Castilian, not Mexican.

Melita MI, VA From the ancient name of the island of Malta.

Mellow A rare commendatory, e.g. the valley in AL. Cf. **Meloland.**

Meloland CA Named, ca. 1910, by the novelist H. B. Wright because of the mellow nature of the soil.

Melones Spanish 'melons,' but used in some figurative sense, e.g. in CA, for dry diggings that were productive of gold. A common story is that the gold was found in flakes resembling melon seeds.

Melozitna River AK Athapascan, with -*na,* 'river,' and the rest uncertain.

Melrose From the town and abbey in Scotland, popularized in the 19th century by the writings of Walter Scott. The name is euphonious, and the suggestion of 'rose' is commendatory. In MA the town was incorporated in 1850, and some later examples are from it.

Melvern KS From the Malvern Hills in England, named by a settler for his birthplace, but with spelling altered by error.

Memaloose Chinook jargon, 'death, dead,' usually applied to a place of Indian burial, e.g. the islands in OR and WA.

Memkeeswe Stream ME Algonquian 'good-landing-places' (?).

Memphis From the city of Egypt. The city in TN was incorporated in 1826; its name shows the current enthusiasm for exotic names with suggestions of grandeur, cf. **Cairo,** and the connection with Egypt suggested agricultural wealth.

Memphremagog Lake VT Algonquian, to be generally rendered as 'where there is a wide expanse of water,' i.e. approximately 'big lake.'

Mempticook Stream ME Algonquian 'overflowing-stream.'

Mena AR Originally Wilhelmina, named for the Queen of the Netherlands in 1896 by Dutch investors in a local railroad, and shortened after the fashion in railroad names.

Menagerie Island MI Humorously named, because the lightkeeper had a large family of children who were compared to a menagerie.

Menahga MN Ojibway 'blueberry.'

Menallen PA Algonquian (Delaware) 'where we drank.' See **Manahan.**

Menanhant MA Algonquian 'island-on.'

Menasha WI Algonquian, probably 'island.'

Mendenhall From the personal name, several features in AK for T. C. Mendenhall, Superintendent of the U.S. Coast and Geodetic Survey (1889–1894).

Mendocino CA Spanish, an adjective from the personal name Mendoza, recorded on a map of 1587, probably honoring L. Suárez de Mendoza, viceroy of New Spain from 1580 to 1583. A tradition, however, associated it with Antonio de Mendoza, viceroy in 1542 when the cape was believed, according to this tradition, to have been discovered. The adjectival form is highly unusual in Spanish place-naming, and the name cannot be considered as fully explained.

Mendon Apparently from Mendham, a town in England; in MA, 1667.

Mendota Siouan, apparently from either of two closely similar words, the first meaning the place where one river flows into another, and the second meaning the outlet of a lake. The first meaning gave rise to **Mendota** MN, because there the Minnesota River joins the Mississippi. This is apparently the first use of the name by Americans (ca. 1837). Probably because of its euphony it passed into general currency, and was transferred to a number of states. It was applied in IL, ca. 1854, probably because two railroads joined at this point. **Lake Mendota** WI: apparently borrowed from MN, ca. 1849, and chosen because of its euphony.

Menikoe Point ME Algonquian 'island-at,' for a small island giving shelter to canoes.

Menlo In CA, in 1854, two brothers from Menlough, Ireland, gave the name **Menlo Park** to their joint ranches. The name in other states has apparently been transferred from this early naming in CA.

Menno SD Shortened from Mennonites, because of a large settlement of that sect nearby; actually the settlement was at the place now called **Freeman,** but the railroad signs were mistakenly placed.

Meno In OK by adaptation of spelling for Menno Simons, founder of the Mennonites. In OR a shortening of **Menominee,** named by a man who had once lived in that town in MI.

Menoken ND, KS Probably Siouan, meaning uncertain.

Menominee Algonquian 'wild-rice,' and sometimes probably because of the occurrence of this valuable food plant; but ordinarily from the Indian tribal name, chiefly in MI, IL, and WI.

Mensecommook River ME Algonquian probably 'come-and-fetch,' for a place where goods were stored.

Mentasta AK Athapascan, from an earlier *mantasna,* with -*na,* 'river,' and the rest uncertain.

Mentone For the Riviera sea resort in France. In TX the naming was by a former resident of that city. In AL, applied to a resort which is in the mountains, not on the seashore.

Mentor From the personal name, e.g. in OH for Hiram Mentor, early settler.

Menunketsuck CT Algonquian 'strong-flowing stream.'

Me Own Hills NM Locally believed to be from an old man who said, 'Me own it.'

Mequon WI Algonquian *mic-wan,* 'ladle,' but with reference to a bend in a stream, thought to resemble the handle of a ladle.

Mer French 'sea,' e.g. **Mer Rouge** LA, of uncertain origin.

Meramec River MO Algonquian 'catfish,' but derived more directly from a tribal name. See **Maramech, Merrimac.**

Merced Spanish 'mercy,' usually a religious name, e.g. the river in CA was named in full Nuestra Señora de la Merced by a Spanish expedition of 1806.

Mercer Its use, especially for counties, is chiefly in tribute to General Hugh Mercer, killed at the battle of Princeton in 1777. See **Princeton.**

Merchant Generally from the family name, but **Lake Merchant** LA is by folk-etymology from the French **Lac Méchant,** 'bad.'

Mercier KS Founded by Germans and originally called **Germantown;** renamed during World War I for Cardinal Mercier, who had become well known in the U.S. for his patriotism as a Belgian and his protests against the Germans.

Mercur Peak CA For James Mercur, professor of engineering at West Point, named in 1912 by his friend, Col. W. W. Forsyth, acting superintendent of Yosemite National Park.

Mercy Hot Springs CA For J. N. Mercy, early stock raiser.

Mere The older English for 'pond, lake' was introduced poetically in the early 19th century and has been used as a second element, primarily for habitation-names, e.g. **Eagles Mere** PA.

Meredosia IL From French *marais d'osier*, 'pool-of-willow,' made over by speakers of English, by a process of folk-etymology, following the sound, into the semblance of a Greek name, such as Theodosia.

Meriden From a town in England; in CT (1664).

Meridian A surveyors' term to indicate a place at or near a meridian, usually a Principal Meridian, e.g. **Meridian** OK, **Meridian Creek** NB. **Meridian** MS: named under the mistaken idea that the term meant 'junction,' since the town was at a railroad junction.

Merino CO, MT A name used in sheep raising areas, from the variety thus known.

Merion PA Introduced by Welsh immigrants of the early eighteenth century, a shortening of Merioneth, a county of Wales.

Merit TX Originally **Merritt** was proposed as the name, but there was so much objection that a shortened, and possibly commendatory, term was substituted.

Merlin OR David Loring named the community for some birds that he saw there; they are commonly called pigeon hawks. **Merlin Abyss** AZ. See **Bedivere.**

Mermentau LA Changed under the influence of folk-etymology and of French spelling from the name of a chief, recorded as Nementou in 1784, applied to the river and transferred to the town.

Merom From the Biblical lake, probably so named from the meaning 'high place,' which fits the site.

Merrick Commonly from the personal name, e.g. in OK for J. J. Merrick, townsite owner. In NY it has arisen by folk-etymology from the name of a tribe recorded as Merickoke.

Merriconeag ME Algonquian 'lazy-portage,' i.e. one across which canoes could be taken easily.

Merrimac, Merrimack Algonquian; in MA and NH it is probably 'deep place,' but a similar word in Middle-Western Algonquian dialects is 'catfish.' See **Meramec. Merrimac** IL: so called because opposite the mouth of the **Meramec River,** but using the Eastern spelling.

Merry Commonly from the personal name, e.g. **Merry Point** VA for Thomas Merry, patentee of 1682. **Merry Oaks** NC is locally believed to be for a grove where Indians held celebrations. **Merrymeeting Bay** NH is from an incident, ca. 1770, when a meeting and festivities were held here; nearby Indian names, e.g. **Merrimack** must have helped to suggest the name.

Mesa Primarily a generic, but used as a specific to denote a feature associated with a mesa, e.g. **Mesa Peak** CA and **Mesa Creek** OR, and as a repeated habitation-name, **Mesa, Lamesa, La Mesa.**

Mesabi, Mesaba, Missabe MN Ojibway 'giant,' also the personal name of a mythological giant. The mountain was associated with him, but it was probably named because it is the chief mountain of the area.

Mescal In Spanish usage referring to various kinds of edible (or drinkable) cactus, e.g. **Mescal Island** CA, probably for the prickly pear, which bears edible fruit.

Mescalero From the Indian tribal name.

Meshodac Peak NY Algonquian 'big-mountain.'

Meshoppen Creek PA Algonquian (Delaware), probably 'big potato.' See **Potato.**

Mesic NC For S. R. Messick, second postmaster.

Mesilla NM Diminutive of Spanish *mesa,* 'table, tableland,' descriptively named because built on a small tableland.

Mesita CO The diminutive of Spanish *mesa;* thus, 'little tableland.'

Meskaskeeseehunk Brook ME Algonquian 'spruce-stream-little.'

Mesmeriser Creek TX From an early settler (not further identified) who had great faith in his powers as a mesmerist, and experimented at thus domesticating buffalo (unsuccessfully).

Mesopotamia Greek, 'between-rivers-land.' In OH and SC the name was given because of a situation between streams.

Mesqua-Ung-Gung Bay WI Algonquian, meaning unknown.

Mesquite Being the prevailing growth in many parts of the SW, the mesquite has been too common to establish many names, but is to be found occasionally, e.g. **Mesquite Spring** AZ.

Messalonskee Lake ME Algonquian 'white-clay-here.'

Messongo VA Algonquian (Delaware), probably 'bare-earth.'

Metairie LA French 'farm-house, small farm.'

Metal A rare commendatory, to suggest riches in metal ore or industry, e.g. **Metalton** WV, **Metaline** WA.

Metalia NC A Latinized form from 'metal,' so named in 1890 by a Free Silver enthusiast.

Metallak ME, NH From the personal name of an Indian who died in about 1850, last survivor of the Coosuck tribe.

Metamora From the popular play of that name by J. A. Stone (1829), an adaptation from Metacomet, the name of the 17th century chief, better known as King Philip.

Metauques Pond NY Algonquian, probably 'small-trees.'

Metawee VT Algonquian, meaning uncertain.

Metea IN For a Potawatomi chief, whose name is recorded as Mitia.

Methodist Creek AZ In about 1890 a man was attacked here by bees; as he said, the attack was so bad that it would have made a Methodist preacher swear; according to his own testimony, the name thus originated.

Methow WA From an Indian tribal name.

Metigoshe, Lake ND Algonquian, shortened from *metigoshe washegum,* 'clear-water-surrounded-by-oaks' (?).

Metinic Island ME Except for the ending, the same as **Matinicus,** q.v.

Metlakatla AK Indian (Tsimshian), a village-name transferred from British Columbia, meaning uncertain.

Meto Creek AR Also as **Meter,** and probably from French *mi-terre,* 'middle-ground,' being halfway between two larger streams.

Metolius River OR From an Indian word absorbed into a pseudo-Latin form. As first recorded it is Mpto-ly-as in the dialect of the Indians of Warm Springs, meaning 'light-colored fish.'

Metonga Lake WI Probably Algonquian, meaning uncertain.

Metongues See **Metauques.**

Metropolis, Metropolitan Commendatory names, given by town developers who expected or hoped great things for the new settlement, e.g. in IL, where the town has not as yet exceeded a few thousands in population.

Mettacahonts NY From the name of an early Indian.

Mettah Creek CA Yurok, a village name of unknown meaning.

Mettawa IL Named commemoratively (1960) for a Potawatomi chief who had a village in the vicinity ca. 1830.

Mettawee River NY Algonquian, meaning uncertain.

Metuchen NJ From the name of a 17th-century chief recorded as Metochshaning.

Metz From the city of France, e.g. in MO, or from a family name, e.g. in CA, for W. H. H. Metz, early stock raiser.

Mexhoma OK A border naming, from NM and OK.

Mexia In TX for Gen. Jorge Hammerkin y Mexia, who donated land for the town site; in AL, named for this town in TX.

Mexican By association with a Mexican or Mexicans, usually named in the Western states during the American period. **Mexican Water** AZ is a translation from the Navajo. **Mexican Creek** NM: Mexican miners worked here at a time when the area had been Americanized. **Mexican Hat** UT: from a large rock formation resembling a sombrero.

Mexico One of the exotics which were favored in the early 19th century, especially because of sympathy with the Mexican struggle for independence, e.g. in ME (1818), MO (1836).

Miakka A variant of **Myakka.** See **Mayaca.**

Miamegg Creek NY Algonquian 'together-fishing-place,' i.e. one at which people assembled.

Miami 1) In FL, applied first to the river, probably a Muskogean term, from the testimony of a 16th century Spanish explorer to be taken as 'very large'; from the river, transferred to the city. 2) In OH, a tribal name. 3) In OR, the river

is from Chinook jargon *me-mie,* 'downstream.' 4) In AZ the name is a blend from Mima Tune, fiancée of a local miner and because of some settlers from **Miami** in OH. 5) **Miami Mountain** CA: probably Yokuts, attracted to the standardized spelling. For diversity of origin this name is unique. Also of note is the tendency to attract names of varying origin to a standard spelling.

Miamogue NY A variant of **Miamegg,** q.v.

Miantanomi RI From the name of an Indian chief. See **Mianus.**

Mianus River CT Formed with the aid of an English possessive 's' from the name of a chief, Mayanno, who was killed in 1643.

Mica From the presence of that mineral, e.g. **Mica Mountain** AZ.

Micanopy FL From the name or title (literally, 'head-chief') of the chief Indian leader in the Seminole War (1835).

Micco FL Seminole 'chief,' probably with reference to a particular chief and the equivalent of a personal name.

Miccosukee FL From an Indian tribal name.

Michigamme MI Ojibway 'big-lake,' a variant of **Michigan.**

Michigan Recorded in the early 17th century as the name of a tribe, which was itself, however, named because of living near the lake (Algonquian 'big lake.'). The Territory was named (1805) from the chief natural feature near it, as was customary at the time. **Michigan Bar** and **Michigan Bluff** CA were both named in the goldmining period by miners from MI.

Michilimackinac See **Mackinaw.**

Mickinock MN From the name of an Ojibway chief, who was much respected by the Americans.

Mico TX From the Medina Irrigation Co.

Micro NC From the Greek combining-form, 'small.'

Mid Scarcely exists except in combination, e.g. **Midway, Midvale, Midland.** The meaning is generally obvious, and the term seems often to serve as a mere variant for 'middle,' e.g. **Mid West. Mid Hills** CA: these hills join two ranges of mountains. **Midwest** WY: because situated at the main camp of the Midwest Oil Company.

Midas The association with gold of the mythical Phrygian led to the placing of this name on streams in mining areas, e.g. ID, AK.

Middle A highly productive specific, both for natural features and habitations. It is joined with almost every generic to indicate a feature located between two others of more-or-less similar nature. **Middle Fork** (e.g. of the **American River**) is conventional for streams on the western slope of the **Sierra Nevada.** In some areas the 'fork' is dropped and we have, e.g. the **Middle Santiam River** OR. Family names, e.g. **Middlebrook** are to be noted. Many names were imported from England, and most of these have no significance in their U.S. locations, e.g. **Middleton** (also a family name) and **Middleborough** MA, ca. 1669. **Middletown,** an older form of **Middleton,** is to be included here. Significant uses include transfers of names of natural features, e.g. **Middle Grove** NY, and new coinages with current prefixes, e.g. **Middleville. Middletown** CT was named in 1653 as being midway between **Hartford** and **Saybrook,** but one must suspect the influence of the English name **Middleton,** in the 17th century not always distinguished from **Middletown.** This name, in general, is to be considered significant. **The Middle West** could become significant only after the development of the Far West, and is late 19th century. **Middlesboro** KY: because it lies, so to speak, in the middle, at the joining point of the states, VA, TN, and KY. **Middlebury** VT: named in 1761 as being the middle grant of three made in one area during that year.

Middlesex From the county in England. Since many colonists came from that area, the name was used for counties in CT, MA, NJ, and VA. Because of sexual suggestions, it never became popular as a town name and, ca. 1955, a CA community changed its name for this reason. The county in MA was probably named, in part, from its location in the center of the colony.

Midkiff WV From a family name common in the area.

Midlothian From the county in Scotland, in TX named by a Scottish railroad surveyor; in some instances it may be of literary origin from Scott's *The Heart of Midlothian.*

Midnight Rare, probably derived in most instances from some incident, e.g. in MS when, by local story, a man closed a poker game, remarking 'It's midnight. That's what I'm going to call my land.' The mesa in AZ was so called from its black rock. It is also a family name.

Mikado MI From the Japanese title; reason for naming, unknown.

Mikana WI Probably Algonquian, meaning uncertain.

Mikkalo OR For John Mikkalo, early settler.

Milaca MN A variation of **Mille Lacs.**

Milagro Spanish 'miracle,' but neither in CA nor in NM is the reason for naming apparent.

Milam From the personal name, especially, e.g. in TX for Ben R. Milam, hero of the Texas Revolution.

Milan From the city of Italy, after the 19th-century fashion of naming for famous foreign cities. **Milan** NM: for Salvador Milan, landowner.

Milano TX Originally **Milam,** but changed in transmission through the Post Office Dept., either by mistake or to avoid duplication of an already used name.

Milberger KS Originally, ca. 1872, named **Muhlberger** for a family of German-Russian settlers; since the German *u,* umlaut, is closer in sound to

English 'i' than to English 'u,' the change in spelling was in the direction of preserving the original sound.

Mile, Miles In the unmodified plural the name is generally a personal one, e.g. **Miles City** MT for Gen. Nelson A. Miles, prominent in the Indian wars. Unmodified in the singular, it indicates a place one mile from a point of reference, e.g. **Mile Rocks** CA, named in 1826 as being one mile south of the channel by which ships entered San Francisco Bay. The term appears most often in such combinations as **Five Mile Creek** MT, **Sevenmile Hill** CA, usage varying as to whether the form should be written as one or two words. The cause of naming is distance from a point of reference, though in some cases the distances are far from accurate and express how tired the namers felt, e.g. in CA, **Four Mile Creek** and **Five Mile Creek** are about right for the distance on this trail, but **Ten Mile Creek** is only something more than two miles farther along. Such names often occur at distances from early army posts, where the name was a memorandum to the soldier of how far he had marched or had to march on the way back. They also occur along the lines of early roads. **Three Mile Valley** CA: named because it is three miles long. **Milestone:** on natural features the name indicates association with a milestone or a rock resembling a milestone, e.g. **Milestone Mountain** CA.

Milfay OK From the names of two railroad officials, Charles Mills and Edward Fay.

Milford Chiefly from one of the English towns, but in some instances, e.g. in DE and KS, from a ford at a mill. See **Mill.**

Milk Applied to streams because of the color of the water, especially to those carrying glacial silt, e.g. **Milk Creek** OR. **Milky Wash** AZ: because a whitish clay discolors the water in time of run-off. **Milk and Mush Creek** KY: probably from an incident.

Milksick A disease of cattle known as milksickness was believed to arise from their eating a certain plant; areas fenced off to prevent them eating it were so called, e.g. **Milksick Cove** GA.

Mill Down until the later 19th century water mills were very numerous, being used chiefly for grinding flour and sawing timber. The mill often identified the stream, so that **Mill Creek** and **Mill Brook** are common. This name came to be almost synonymous with industry, and was transferred to steam mills; thus arose such frequent names as **Mill City, Millville,** and **Milltown.** The frequent occurrence of such English town-names as **Milton** and **Milford** is at least partly the result of such influence. The personal name Mill(s) is also a factor. The term may be coupled with almost any generic, e.g. **Mill Neck** NJ, **Mill Plain** CT. **Millstone** occurs with natural features to identify a place where such stones were quarried. **Millheim** PA: a hybrid coined by German settlers (*heim,* 'home'), but the German *mühl* is close enough to 'mill' in sound to create confusion. **Mill Creek,** Tehama Co., CA: named by John Bidwell in 1843, not because it had a mill, but because it looked like a good place for one. **Millbrae** CA: a name given to his country estate by D. O. Mills, *brae* being a popular term in the 1860's. **Mills Glacier, Lake, Moraine,** Rocky Mountain N.P., CO are for Enos Mills (1870–1922) closely associated with the area as naturalist and writer.

Millard From the personal name, e.g. the county in UT for President Millard Fillmore, the county seat being **Fillmore.**

Millbridge ME Named (1949) because the community had a notable bridge and an unusual tide mill.

Mille French 'thousand,' generally used as an indefinite for 'many,' e.g. **Mille Lacs** MN.

Millecoquins MI Literally, French 'thousand-rascals,' but by folk-etymology into French from Ojibway *min-nau-ko-keing,* 'hardwood-place'; note the confusion of *n* and *l,* which is common in such exchanges.

Millicoma OR An Indian (Coos) term of unknown meaning.

Millimagassett Lake ME Algonquian 'where-duckhawks-abound.'

Millinocket ME Algonquian, meaning uncertain.

Millseat Creek CA Because it once supported several water mills. Also as **Millsite.**

Millux CA From the stock-raising firm, Miller & Lux.

Milnesand NM Local tradition insists that it is from **Mill-in-the-Sand,** because of an early windmill.

Milo From the given name, e.g. in MO and WV. **Milo** OK: from the initials of the four daughters of a resident. In ME the name was given by a classical enthusiast in memory of the famous Greek athlete. Some names are probably from the name for a common kind of sorghum.

Miloma MN From the Milwaukee and Omaha railroads, being situated at their junction.

Milpa Spanish 'small field.' **Milpitas** CA is the diminutive.

Milton 1) In MA (1662) for one of the numerous places in England so named. 2) From a personal name, e.g. in WV for Milton Reece, a landowner. 3) As the equivalent of **Milltown,** because of the existence of a mill of some kind, e.g. OR, PA. 4) For the poet John Milton. There has been a latter-day tendency to ascribe namings to this literary source, but they are often doubtful, e.g. in NJ, ND. In NY the naming is certainly for the poet. In VT the naming (1763) is probably in honor of Viscount Milton, who was a family connection of Gov. John Wentworth of the colony of NH.

Milwaukee Algonquian, probably 'goodland.' It was first recorded in the 17th century, and is preserved in many spellings, a common early one being **Milwaukie,** which is used for a town in OR, presumably named by settlers from WI.

Mimbrena From the Indian tribal name.

Mimi Island WI Algonquian (Ojibway) 'dove, pigeon.' Also as **Meeme.**

Mina Commonly from a woman's name, e.g. in SD probably for Mina Earling, daughter of a railroad president. The word means 'mine (for minerals)' in Spanish, and in NV originated as a mining district.

Minatare From the Indian tribal name.

Minco GA, KS, OK Choctaw 'lord, chief.'

Mindego Creek CA A misspelling from Juan Medico, early landowner.

Mindemoya Lake MI Algonquian 'old-woman-lake,' apparently from the original name of the island, the profile of which may be taken to resemble that of a woman.

Minden From the city in Germany, usually, e.g. in LA, NB, and NV, named by immigrants for their old home. **Mindenmines** MO is for **Minden Mines.**

Mindowaskin Lake NJ From the name of one of the four Indians who sold the site in 1684.

Mine For a place associated with a mine, the name often surviving after all mining activity has long ceased and after the evidences of mining have disappeared, e.g. **Mine Creek** SC, where in Colonial times a man prospected for silver.

Minemac Lake WI Algonquian, meaning uncertain.

Mineola See **Minneola.**

Mineral A name implying mineral wealth, often applied hopefully by prospectors. **Mineral King** CA: a mining district, named as being king of them all. With **Wells, Spring,** etc., mineral is an almost generic term, indicating that the water is impregnated with some mineral, sufficiently for the taste to be affected or for deposits to be made, e.g. **Mineral Creek** AZ because of an abundance of alkali.

Minerva Generally, e.g. OR, TX, from the personal name. In OH it was the name of a daughter of one of the town founders, John Whiteacre.

Minganahone Creek NJ Algonquian, meaning uncertain.

Mingo A tribal name. It seems in origin to have been a derogatory name (cf. Cooper's novels), and so the habitation-names preserving it are chiefly traditional, established by transfer from natural features, themselves so called because Mingoes were once associated with the place.

Minidoka ID A railroad name, probably coined to resemble an Indian name, the first part being apparently from the common Siouan term for water. See **Kuna.**

Minimum MO A humorous derogatory for a small village, derived also from Mrs. Minnie Farr, wife of the first postmaster.

Minisink NJ, NY Algonquian 'Minsi-at,' from a tribal name.

Minisuing Lake WI Algonquian, meaning uncertain.

Minito Lake WI Algonquian, probably a variant of **Manitou.**

Miniwakan Lake WI Algonquian, meaning uncertain.

Minneapolis MN From a combination of **Minnehaha** and the Greek *polis,* 'city'; the 'a' is a remnant of the original name, which was coined as Minnehapolis.

Minnechadusa River SD Siouan 'water-swift.'

Minnechaug, Minnechoag Algonquian 'berry mountain.'

Minneconjou From the Indian tribal name.

Minnehaha Siouan *water-falls.* A romantic misinterpretation in 1849 gave the meaning 'laughing waters,' and on this basis Longfellow chose the name of the heroine of 'Hiawatha.' In fact, the actual coupling of the two genuine Siouan words was probably done by the Americans, beginning in 1849. The interpretation 'laughing' was apparently done under the misapprehension that *haha* was, as it might be in English, an attempt to imitate the sound of laughter. The whole jumble is a good example of the way in which romantically inaccu-

rate interpretations have confused the situation with Indian names. **Minnehaha Falls** MN: the name is still maintained on the 'original' falls, which thus is tautological, i.e. water-waterfalls-falls. The name has been transferred to the creek, and under the influence of 'Hiawatha' appears in **Minnehaha Springs** WV, though this is not in Siouan territory.

Minnehonk Lake ME Algonquian, meaning uncertain.

Minneiska MN Siouan 'water-white.'

Minnekahta SD Siouan 'water-warm.'

Minneola In MN it is Siouan 'much water.' This may be the original naming, from which the name has spread widely, aided by its euphony. In TX the surveyor of the townsite used the name of his daughter Ola, and her friend Minnie, but the use of the name elsewhere was also an influence. So also **Minneola** KS is from Minnie Davis and Ola Watson, local women. The spelling is often **Mineola.**

Minneopa MN Siouan 'water-falling-twice,' i.e. 'two waterfalls.'

Minneota MN Siouan 'water much,' because of nearby lakes.

Minnepaugs Pond NY Algonquian 'islet-pond.'

Minnesela SD Siouan 'water-red,' so called for a nearby creek, now Redwater Creek.

Minnesota From a Siouan word recorded in various forms, e.g. **Menesota, Minnay Sotor,** and meaning, 'water-cloudy,' applied to the river descriptively. After the coming of the French the Indian name was replaced, and the stream was known as the St. Peter River. In the discussion in Congress in 1847 at the organization of a new territory the old name was revived in its present form, and was applied to the territory. In 1852 an act of Congress restored the Indian name to the river.

Minnesunk Pond NY Coined by G. R. Howell, librarian in 1866, apparently from Siouan *minne,* 'water,' and Algonquian *sunk,* 'sachem's wife, queen,' probably to mean 'queen-of-the-water.' (It also suggests a variant of **Minisink**.)

Minnetonka MN Siouan 'water-big.'

Minnetrista MN *Minne* is the Siouan 'water,' but the last part of the word is apparently a semi-humorous coinage (1859) from English *twist,* the whole being 'crooked lake.'

Minnewashka, Minnewashkta MN Siouan 'water-good, originally applied to a lake.

Minnewaska NY A name introduced in the 19th century; see **Minnewashka**.

Minnewaukon ND A shortening of the Siouan name for a nearby lake *miniwaukon-chante,* 'water-spirit-bad.' See **Medicine, Devil, Wakan**.

Minnewawa River NH Algonquian 'many waters' (?).

Minniesechi Creek SD Siouan 'water-bad.'

Minnith MO A commendatory for a place devoted to farming, especially to wheat growing, because of the mention of its wheat in the Old Testament.

Minnora WV For Minnora Knotts, the daughter of a prominent local resident, given ca. 1890.

Minoa NY From one of the places so-named in ancient Greece. See **Mycenae**.

Minocqua WI Probably Algonquian (Potawatomi) 'good-land.'

Minong WI Probably the same as **Minonk**.

Minonk IL, WI Algonquian 'good-(place)-at' (?).

Minooka In PA it is Algonquian (Delaware) probably 'good-land.'

Minor Regularly for the personal name, e.g. in CA for Isaac Minor, early settler.

Minorca AR From the Mediterranean island.

Minot From the personal name; in ND for H. D. Minot, of the Great Northern Railroad.

Minotola NJ A coined name (?), with a common suffix, *-ola.*

Minqua From the Indian tribal name.

Minsi From an Indian tribal name, e.g. **Mount Minsi** PA. So also **Minisink** NJ, 'Muncies-at.' See **Muncie**.

Minster OH From Münster, the city of Germany, because of a large German settlement, with spelling changed, the better to approximate the sound.

Mint From the plant, e.g. **Mint Hill** NC, **Mint Springs** VA.

Miomi Lake FL Seminole 'bad water, whiskey' (?).

Mioxes MA In **Great Mioxes Pond**, from the name of a chief, ca. 1640, recorded as Mioxeo, with the English possessive 's' added.

Mira Spanish 'Look! Behold!' used in combination, though more by Americans than by Spanish-speakers, e.g. **Miramar, Miramonte. Miraleste** CA: here '-leste' equals *l'este,* 'the east.' **Miramontes Point** CA: from a family of early settlers.

Mirada Spanish 'look, view.' **La Mirada** CA was probably named with the idea that a view could be there attained.

Mirage Occurs rarely because of the seeing of a mirage, e.g. **Mirage Flats** NB. **El Mirage** AZ: apparently used under the assumption that 'mirage' was a Spanish word.

Miring Mule Creek SD Records an incident when a detachment of troops almost lost a mule at this stream.

Mirror A common descriptive or commendatory name for lakes, sometimes applied to other features by transfer.

Miscoe MA Algonquian, probably 'big hill.'

Misery A rare name of the type in which the feelings of the namer are transferred to the place, e.g. **Misery Gore** ME. The island in AK is a development by folk-etymology from **Lemesurier,** that name being preserved on a nearby point.

Mishaum, Mishawam Along with **Mishawamut, Mishawomut,** with suffix 'at', this name is applied to about 10 places, typically on the seacoast in MA and RI. The name contains the Algonquian *mis-,* 'big.' The latter part is uncertain, but apparently refers to a place to land canoes, and thus may be the equivalent of 'neck of land.'

Mishawaka IN Potawatomi 'dead-trees-place,' probably because of a **Deadening,** q.v.

Mishicot WI Algonquian, probably from a chief's name.

Mishnock RI Algonquian, meaning uncertain.

Miski Run MD Algonquian 'red-it-is.'

Miskimon VA Algonquian, probably with the idea of 'red.' See **Miski.**

Mispillion River DE First recorded (1664) as **Mispening,** it is Algonquian, probably 'big-tuber-at.' (See **Potato.**) The present spelling is recorded as of 1682, perhaps from Dutch folk-etymology from *mispel,* 'medlar.' **Muskmellon** (1698) shows a further but unsuccessful attempt to make sense of the name.

Misquamicut RI Algonquian 'red-salmon-at.'

Missaukee MI, WI Algonquian 'big-outlet (river-mouth)-at,' but probably from the name of an Ottawa chief of the early 19th century.

Mission, Missionary For a feature thus associated, often transferred to habitations. The frequency of **Mission** in CA (50) is a testimony to the number and activity of early Spanish missionaries, and of romantic nostalgia for 'the Mission days,' in the late 19th and early 20th centuries.

Missisquoi VT Algonquian, meaning uncertain.

Mississinewa River IN Algonquian (Miami) 'big-rock-river' (?).

Mississippi Algonquian, from one of the languages of the Great Lakes region, recorded in a French context in 1666 as **Messipi,** 'big-river.' French explorers, descending the river, carried this name along, and applied it to the stream clear to its mouth. The name thus superseded other names that had been applied to it by different tribes in their own regions and by Spanish explorers. In 1798 Congress applied this Algonquian name, from the river, to a territory which was organized in Muskogean land; from the territory the name passed to the state.

Missoula MT Part of an Indian (Flathead) name Im-i-sul-e-tiku, 'by-very-cold-water,' but with 'cold' to be taken in the sense of 'dread,' rather than of temperature; some superstition is apparently involved, and this may be apparent also in the previous name **Hellgate Canyon.**

Missouri From an Algonquian (Fox) name for a tribe living at the mouth of the river, recorded in a French context in 1673 and applied to the river. The name passed through the usual progression: river-district-territory-state.

Mistake, Mistaken From a confusion of one place with another or some similar incident, e.g. **Mistake Peak** AZ, **Mistaken Creek** KY.

Mistissin, Lake MI Algonquian, though a badly transformed name, it probably contains the roots for 'big' and 'rock,' and refers to an isolated rock nearby.

Mistletoe Its occasional use, e.g. in KY, is for the native plant.

Mistucky NY Algonquian, meaning uncertain.

Mitchell From the personal name; **Mount Mitchell** NC is for Prof. Elisha Mitchell, who first discovered it to be the highest peak in the eastern U.S.; he was killed in a fall on the mountain (1857) and is buried there.

Miter A descriptive for mountains thought to resemble a bishop's miter, e.g. **The Miter** CA, **Mitre Peak** CO.

Mitten Usually from a rock formation resembling a mitten by having one large part and a smaller part so placed as to seem a thumb, e.g. **Mitten Butte** AZ, which has two such formations thus resembling a pair of mittens. **Mitten Mountain** MT was named because of a fire scar shaped like a mitten, which has now disappeared because of new growth.

Mitteneag MA Algonquian 'abandoned fields' (?).

Mixes Food Creek SD For an Indian who lived on the stream.

Mixup Spring OR Two bands of sheep were once mixed up here.

Mizpah Hebrew 'watchtower,' the name of several places mentioned in the *Old Testament;* it owes its popularity to *Genesis* 32:49, an ambiguous passage in which the word may be taken to mean, 'The Lord watch between me and thee.'

Moab As the name of the Biblical country it has been in occasional use. In UT it is probably from Paiute *mohapa,* 'mosquito-water.' Cf. **Moapa.**

Moaning Cave CA Currents of air sometimes cause a moaning sound in the cave.

Moapa NV Paiute 'mosquito-spring,' but probably a shortening of the tribal name Moapariats, 'mosquito-spring-people.'

Moark MO From the abbreviations of Missouri and Arkansas.

Moberly MO For Col. W. E. Moberly, railroad official.

Mobile AL From the name of a tribe, known to the Spanish as Mauvila (1540), and rendered by the French (1699) in its present form, as a place-name applied first to the river.

Mobjack VA Probably Algonquian, but badly obscured by folk-etymology, 'bad-land' (?).

Mobridge SD From a bridge over the Missouri River, using the common abbreviation MO.

Moccasin 1) From some association with Indian footwear, 2) from the water moccasin or some snake supposed to be one, 3) from the moccasin flower or lady's slipper, e.g. the creek in SD. **Moccasin Lake** OR: seen from a certain height and direction, it resembles the outline of a moccasin. **Moccasin Rock** WV: the rock has a depression in it resembling the mark of a moccasin. **Moccasin Top Lake** SD: for an Indian so named. The spelling **Mocassin** also occurs.

Mocho Spanish 'cut off,' applied to a stream, e.g. **Mocho Creek** CA, which sinks into the ground; the mountain was named from the creek.

Mock From a personal name, e.g. **Mocksville** NC for a family, owners of the townsite.

Mockingbird Though thoroughly American and famed in song and story, the mockingbird has produced few names, but is represented, e.g. in **Mockingbird Gap** NM and **Mockingbird Hill** KY.

Moclips WA Indian (Quinault), indicating a place to which girls were sent at the time of the puberty rite.

Mococo CA From Mountain Copper Company.

Modale IA From the abbreviation for Missouri, the nearby river, and 'dale.'

Model Usually on habitation-names as a commendatory to suggest a community fit to form a model for others, e.g. **Modeltown** NY.

Modena From the city in Italy. **El Modena** CA: Originally **Modena;** the El was added to distinguish the place from **Madera,** but the masculine article was used. The P.O. Dept., to avoid this bad grammar, spells the name **El Modeno.** In PA the first form was **Modeville,** from a local family. Railroad officials, ca. 1870, changed it to **Modena,** either thinking it more euphonious or easier for telegraphy. It occurs elsewhere, probably as a railroad name. Americans, like Shakespeare, accent it on the second syllable.

Modesto CA Spanish 'modest, modest man.' In 1870 the namers intended to call the town for W. C. Ralston, San Francisco financier. Refusing, he was credited with modesty, and the present name was thus given.

Modoc From the name of a tribe, living in OR and CA. In the 1870's the Modoc War made the name widely known, and it was then applied in several states, in SC being suggested by a 'war' between landowners and a railroad.

Modred Abyss AZ See **Bedivere.**

Moenkopi AZ Hopi 'place of running water.'

Mogadore OH From Mogador, the African city, with an added 'e'; named ca. 1825 when, according to local story, the name was known because of its use in a popular book.

Moges Islands ME Algonquian, meaning uncertain.

Mogollon On several features in NM the name is for J. I. F. Mogollon, governor (1712–1715), whose interest in developing mines probably led to his association with particular areas.

Mogote Spanish 'hummock, hillock,' e.g. **Mogote Peak** NM, **Mogote** CO from **Los Mogotes;** Mexican usage seems to indicate shape as much as size, and the term is approximately the equivalent of **Haystack.**

Mohall ND For M. O. Hall, early settler and postmaster.

Mohantango PA Algonquian (Delaware), a repeated name, 'where we ate much meat,' apparently commemorating successful hunts.

Mohave, Mojave From the Indian tribal name. The spelling in 'h' commonly occurs in AZ; that in 'j' in CA.

Mohawk The most easterly tribe of the Iroquois gave their name to the river and valley in NY by association.

Partly for this reason and partly because the Mohawks were a well-known tribe, the name spread to many states. **Mohawk River** OR and **Mohawk Valley** CA were probably named by settlers from NY without thought of the tribe. In AZ the name was first applied to a stage station, supposedly by men from NY. The station has vanished, but a name-cluster remains by transfer, e.g. mountain, gap, valley, pass, range, peak, and post office. In New England, which was not Mohawk country, the names probably spring from incidents involving Mohawk incursions.

Mohawskin Lake WI Algonquian, a variant of **Moccasin** (?).

Mohegan An Algonquian tribe living in CT. Their name survives there for a village inhabited by some of the tribe. It has spread to a few other states by literary influence. See **Mohican.**

Mohensick, Lake NY Algonquian 'assembly-place' (?).

Mohepinoke, Mount NJ Algonquian, meaning uncertain, but -auki, 'land' (?).

Mohican Another form for **Mohegan** (q.v.). It has spread by literary influence, especially from Cooper's *The Last of the Mohicans,* and appears, for example, as **Cape Mohican** AK.

Mohonk Lake NY Algonquian, meaning uncertain, though a connection with **Mohawk** is possible.

Moiese MT For a Flathead chief.

Moingona IA Applied by the French as a tribal name; later revived for a settlement. See **Des Moines.**

Moivivi AZ Papago 'many-wells.'

Mojave See **Mohave.**

Mokane MO From the abbreviations of Missouri and Kansas, but actually thus named from the Missouri, Kansas, and Texas Railroad, with the 'e' added for euphony.

Mokelumne CA Miwok, the name of a village or small tribe. The ending *-umne* means 'people'; the rest of the name is of unknown meaning.

Mokena IL Algonquian 'turtle.' Cf. **Mackinaw.**

Mokst Butte OR Chinook jargon, 'two,' being the second in a series of buttes, as named by the Forest Service.

Molalla River OR From an Indian tribal name.

Molas Lake, Divide CO By local story it is Spanish, meaning 'moles' (the animals) of which many traces can be seen on the surface of the ground; but *molas* means 'moles' (blemishes of the skin). The name may have thus arisen by error in translation.

Molasses Creek SC Traditionally believed to be so called because it flowed as slowly as molasses in January, that being a common comparison.

Mold WA A commendatory, for rich soil.

Mole Hill WV Though Mole exists as a rare family name, the coupling with **Hill** suggests that the name was given humorously, especially since it is primarily a habitation-name. In continuing tradition of humor **Mole Hill** has now become **Mountain** by a change of name.

Molechunkemunk Lake ME Algonquian 'deep-ravine-stream' (?).

Molina From a nearby water mill (*molino* in Spanish) probably being given an 'a' ending since that is thought more suitable to towns.

Molino Spanish 'mill'; sometimes, e.g. in MO, for the battle of El Molino del Rey (1847).

Mollie, Molly The nickname for Mary has been placed on some features, particularly those of proper shape being known as **Mollie's Nipple,** e.g. in UT.

Mollywooket Brook NH Algonquian 'deep-place-at.'

Molnichwock Brook NH Algonquian 'very-deep-place, ravine.'

Molockett Mountain ME Probably from the Indian pronunciation of Mary Agatha, the last surviving member of the Pequaketts, who died in 1816.

Molunkus Stream ME Algonquian, denotes a stream flowing between high banks.

Molynuchgamog Lake ME Algonquian 'steep-banks-lake.'

Mombaccus NY First appears (1676) as 'the Mumbackers,' the 's' suggesting a plural and thus an Indian tribe or a Dutch family, but see also **Mombasha.**

Mombasha Lake NY Algonquian, probably 'lake-small,' but cf. **Basha, Mombaccus.**

Momence IL From the name of an Indian, recorded in 1832.

Momoweta Pond NY From the name of an Indian chief, recorded 1648.

Monabaugs NY Probably from an Indian so called, though without the 's' it can be taken to mean 'deep pond.'

Monache CA From an Indian tribal name.

Monadnock NH, VT Algonquian, probably 'island-mountain-at,' i.e. a mountain rising above the surrounding country as an island rises above the water.

Monango ND Uncertain; local stories suggest an Indian personal name or a pseudo-Indian coinage.

Monanis, Monasses Algonquian 'island-little.'

Monarch Applied to features in the sense of 'majestic, outstanding,' e.g. **Monarch Geyser** WY. **Monarch Divide** CA may have been applied from analogy with the existing **Kings River.**

Monasco Mountain VA Probably from the Indian tribal name or the village, a shortening of Monasukapanough.

Monaskon VA Probably a variant of **Monasko,** q.v.

Monayunk Creek NY Algonquian, meaning uncertain.

Monches WI From the name of a local Potawatomi chief.

Mondamin IA Algonquian 'corn,' probably taken from Longfellow's 'Hiawatha.'

Monday Regularly from the personal name, e.g. the creek in WY, for an early settler. The creek in OH is locally believed to be named because of the day of its discovery.

Monee IL From the name of an Indian woman who lived in the vicinity in the early 19th century.

Moneta A surname among the Romans for the goddess Juno; the suggestion of 'money' may have aided in placing the name upon several small places.

Money Regularly from the personal name, but the creek in MN springs from an incident in which a man lost his money at that stream.

Mongaup NY Algonquian 'huckleberry valley' (?).

Monhagen Pond NY Probably from Monagan, the family-name of some early settlers.

Monhegan ME Algonquian 'island-out-to-sea.'

Monia Creek NM Probably a spelling-after-the-sound of *monilla,* the Spanish name for a local shrub.

Monico WI Apparently a coined name for a railroad station, doubtless connected with the personal name Monica.

Monida MT A boundary name, being in MT and close to ID.

Monie MD Probably a tribal or village name, meaning uncertain, of Algonquian origin.

Moniteau MO Apparently a French rendering of **Manitou**, q.v.

Monitor 1) In gold-mining regions, e.g. AZ, CA, it is from the type of large nozzle used for hydraulicking. 2) In lumbering regions, e.g. OR, it is probably from a type of raft used in grappling for sunken logs. 3) It may be, in certain areas, from a primitive type of fortification against Indians.

Monkton From the personal name, e.g. in VT (1762), a simplified spelling for Gen. Robert Monckton, who served in America in the mid-18th century.

Monmouth From the town and county in England, etc.

Monnebassa Pond VT Algonquian 'deep-water.'

Mono 1) From an Indian tribal name, probably the same as **Monache,** made over into a Spanish-appearing word, probably by Americans, ca. 1850; so, the lake, county, etc., in CA. 2) The creek in Santa Barbara Co., CA, is probably Spanish for 'pretty, funny,' also, 'monkey,' but exact origin is unknown.

Monocacy, Monocasy, Monocasque MD, PA Algonquian (Delaware), a repeated name, probably 'fortified' or 'enclosed,' as a place of defence or as a cultivated field.

Monocline From the geologist's term for a formation of that kind.

Monody Creek PA Algonquian (Delaware), probably 'island.'

Monogah WV The village is on the Monongahela River, and its name is a shortening of that one.

Monomonac Lake MA Algonquian 'deep-(place)-at' (?). Also as **Monomonock** NH.

Monomoy MA Algonquian 'lookout' (?).

Monon IN Probably Potawatomi, of uncertain meaning, but to be connected (?) with **Monona.**

Monona IA, WI Algonquian (Sauk or Fox) for a mythological semidivine personage.

Monongahela River PA Algonquian (Delaware), probably 'high-banks-falling-down,' doubtless with reference to a particular place on the stream.

Monongalia County WV From the Monongahela River, which flows through the county. The name looks like an attempt to render an Indian name in a Latinized form, as was sometimes done at the time (1776) when the country was created by the VA legislature. The name may well be the coinage of Thomas Jefferson, who produced several of this kind.

Monoosmoc Brook MA Algonquian 'deep-stream' (?).

Monoskon See **Munuscong.**

Monponset Pond MA Algonquian 'deep-inlet(?)-at.'

Monroe Many counties and towns were named for President James Monroe. **Monroe** LA: the first steamboat to reach the site, in 1819, was the *James Monroe,* and the naming of the town sprang both from the steamboat and from the president for which it was named.

Monrovia CA For William N. Monroe, who helped lay the town out in 1886. The form is the Latinized one, already coined from the name of President Monroe and used for the city in Africa.

Monselaughaway Creek NJ Algonquian, but with *monse* suggesting the tribal name Minsi, and *laughaway* apparently the same as **Lahaway,** q.v.

Monserrate Mountain CA From Monserrat in Spain, probably because of a real or fancied resemblance.

Monsey NY From the name of the tribe also known as **Muncie, Minsi,** etc.

Monson In MA (1760) for Sir John Monson (1693–1748) who was a friend of Thomas Pownall, the governor, or else for the younger Monson of the same name. In ME the name arose because certain lands were granted to the academy in Monson MA, in 1807.

Mont French 'mount, mountain.' A generic, it has usually been shifted to

Mount in American usage; such names are listed under the specific. In what were already proper names, it has been preserved, e.g. **Montgomery, Montpelier.** In habitation-names it has been occasionally preserved or used where a French suggestive was thought commendary, e.g. **Mont Vernon NH, Mont Claire PA.**

Montalvo CA For the 16th century Spanish poet in whose work the name **California** first appears.

Montana In 1858 it was used as a name for a town in the Pike's Peak gold region, then a part of Kansas. Incorporation was granted, but the town died. Its name, however, was eventually passed on to Representative James M. Ashley of Ohio, a member of the House Committee on Territories. He took it to be the Spanish adjective, 'mountainous,' in feminine form. Others took the name to be Latin. It could have been either, but its attraction probably lay in its vague suggestion of mountains. Ashley proposed the name for a territory organized in 1863, but it became Idaho. Ashley, liking the name, then proposed it for a territory being organized in 1864, though most of this territory lay in the plains. After some discussion, and for want of anyone's suggestion of a better name, Mr. Ashley had his way.

Montara CA Probably a variation, perhaps by misspelling, of Spanish *montaña,* 'mountain,' or of Montero, a family name existing in the region in the Spanish period.

Montauk Algonquian 'fort-at'; originally for the point in NY.

Montaup Neck RI A variant of **Montop.**

Montazona Pass AZ From the Montana-Arizona Mining Co.

Montcalm County MI For the Marquis de Montcalm, French defender of Quebec in 1759, named in 1850 when his courage and devotion were romantically remembered.

Monte In the usage of the Spanish-Americans who settled the SW, *monte* meant 'wood, forest, thicket,' and never 'mountain.' *Monte,* however, is derived from the Latin *mons,* which archaically meant 'mountain,' and is so given in many Spanish dictionaries. Moreover, it means 'mountain' in Italian and is so much like the English 'mount' that confusion was inevitable. The general rule therefore is that in a true Spanish context the word means 'forest,' but in later American usage it ordinarily means 'mountain.' Though primarily a generic, it often is a specific for a place thus associated, and especially so in American usage. **El Monte** CA: because of a dense willow-thicket. **Del Monte** CA: 'of the grove,' because of the fine oaks. **Montecito** CA: 'little forest.' The frequent combinations, especially in CA, such as **Monte Vista** represent a kind of Anglicized Spanish, taken to mean 'mountain view,' which would be equivalent to Vista de la Sierra in Spanish, such adjectival use of a word like *monte* being un-Spanish. See **Montebello, Monte Cristo, Monterey,** etc.

Montebello Italian 'mountain-beautiful,' used as a commendatory for habitations. In MO the name may have been given (1860) because of the victory of the French over the Austrians in the preceding year.

Monte Cristo Alexandre Dumas's novel *The Count of Monte Cristo* made the name synonymous with great riches in the later 19th century, and it was bestowed on mines, thus giving rise to **Monte Cristo** in WA (1889) and to the range in NV.

Montello NV Apparently a shortening by the railroad of **Montebello.**

Monte Ne AR Coined in the 19th century from Spanish or Italian *monte* to mean 'mountain,' and a word supplied by an Indian to mean 'water'—it is probably Siouan (Cf. **Nebraska**); the whole may be taken to mean a mountain supplying water.

Monterey From a Spanish title and a town in Mexico. The approved Spanish spelling uses a doubled 'r,' but in the U.S. a spelling is used that was current at the time of the namings. The bay in CA was named thus by Sebastián de Viscaíno in 1602, honoring the Conde de Monterey, who had dispatched Viscaíno on his voyage. The name in a dozen other states is usually a Mexican War name to celebrate the victory, e.g. in MA, named in 1847.

Montesano WA A religious enthusiast proposed **Mount Zion,** but the present similar-sounding name was adopted in its stead, meaning in Italian, 'mount-healthful.'

Montevallo As a habitation-name AL, MO it is pseudo-Italian, apparently intended to mean 'mountain-valley.'

Montevideo MN From the city in Uruguay, but given with some reference to a supposed translation, 'from the mountain I see,' because of the fine view from the site.

Montezuma From the Aztec ruler of Mexico whom the Mexican War and Prescott's *Conquest of Mexico* had made a hero in the mid-19th century, from which period most of the names date. **Montezuma's Head** AZ: the formation resembles a head, and the idea of a heroic past suggested the half-legendary ruler.

Montgomery The widespread use of the personal name is largely for General Richard Montgomery, the Revolutionary hero. In AL the county was named (1816) for Major L. P. Montgomery, killed in the Creek War, but the city (at least, officially) was named (1819) for the better-known hero.

Monticello Italian 'little mountain'; a name given by Thomas Jefferson, who had some knowledge of Italian, to his hilltop residence. Because of Jefferson's fame, the name has spread to many states, aided by its euphony, and by the commendatory suggestion of height.

Montinicus Island NH Algonquian 'island-little-far-off.'

Montop Hill RI Algonquian, 'headland' (?). See **Hope.**

Montoso, Cerro AZ Local Spanish, with *montoso,* 'brushy, wooded.'

Montour PA From 'Madame Montour,' a three-quarters Indian woman of remarkable character (ca. 1682–1752). The name was first given to **Montour's Ridge** and was applied to the county in 1850, at a time of sentimental interest in Indians.

Montowese CT Algonquian, the personal name of a chief who sold land in 1638.

Montpelier In VT from the name of the French city, bestowed during the post-Revolutionary period of enthusiasm because of French aid in the War.

Montrose This favorite for habitation-names is derived eventually from a town in Scotland, but is also influenced by a literary tradition, e.g. Scott's *Legend of Montrose,* and by the commendatory suggestion of both 'mount' and 'rose.' The origin of some of the names, e.g. WV, NB, is attributed to the presence of wild roses and some kind of elevation. **Montrose** PA: the name in part commemorates Robert H. Rose, the founder. **Montrose** CA: the name was chosen in 1913 for a subdivision as the result of a contest, commendatory suggestions being chiefly in mind.

Montserrat From the mountain, or its monastery, in Spain.

Monture Creek MT For George Montour, killed by Indians near here.

Montville In CT the name was applied in 1786, a period of enthusiasm for things French, being also a commendatory from the suggestion of height.

Monument Most often for a place associated with a monument, usually one erected by surveyors. Sometimes for a natural formation suggesting a monument because of its shape, e.g. **Monument** CO, **Monument Hill** OR for rock formations. **Monument Valley** AZ: for the numerous high rocks. **Monument Peak** CA: for a granite monument erected by the CA–NV boundary survey of 1872. **Monument** NM: from an old Indian monument erected to mark the site of a spring; in keeping with the name, a modern concrete monument of an Indian has been erected. **Monument** KS: in 1888 an 85-foot monument in memory of Gen. John A. Logan was

commenced here; it was never finished and was eventually demolished, but the name remained on the town.

Moodus CT Algonquian 'noise,' a shortening from 'bad noise,' with reference to some subterranean rumblings still heard.

Moolack Mountain OR Chinook jargon, 'elk.'

Moomaw From the personal name, e.g. in NB for J. P. Moomaw, first postmaster.

Moon Often for the personal name, e.g. **Moon** SD: for Jack Moon, early settler. **Moon Lake** NB: from an Indian personal name. The name **Moon Lake** is sometimes said to be given for shape, but the explanation raises difficulties, since the moon is notoriously of many shapes. **Half Moon Bay** CA: from its fine half-circle curve. In some instances the name is probably given because of the fine showing of the moon at the time of naming, as with **Moonlight Peak** CA, although origin from the rare family name is possible. **Moonshine Lake** SD: from a ranch where 'moonshine' whisky was made. **Moonshine Lake** MN D. K. J. Clark, early settler, intended to call it for his wife, *née* Moon, but the bright moonlight of their first evening at the lake caused him to modify the name. **Moonstone Beach** CA: from the occurrence of moonstones. **Moonlight** KS for Thomas Moonlight, Secretary of State for Kansas, 1869–1871.

Moonachie NJ Algonquian, meaning uncertain.

Moonapaga, Mount WI From the name of a local Winnebago chief.

Moonax WA A local Indian word for 'woodchuck,' because Lewis and Clark in 1805 found the Indians there with a pet woodchuck.

Moordener Kill NY From Dutch *moordenaars kill,* 'murderers' stream,' (and in the past sometimes recorded as **Murderers Creek**) with reference to an incident of 1643 when seven men and two women were killed here by Indians.

Moosa CA An abbreviation of Pamoosa, an Indian village, meaning unknown.

Moosalamoo Mountain VT Algonquian; the first syllable being 'moose,' and the rest uncertain.

Moose Found only in the most northerly states, including Alaska, the largest of the deer was highly conspicuous, a prized game animal, and never so abundant as to be commonplace. Many feature-names have arisen, generally because of particular encounters or incidents. Since the animal is water-loving, **Moose Lake** is common (about 10 in MN). Perhaps because of its rather uncouth sound, **Moose** occurs rarely in habitation-names. **Moosehead, Moosehorn,** and other compounds appear. The name sometimes occurs by folk-etymology from the Algonquian *mas,* 'big,' e.g. in **Moosehausic** RI. **Moose Lake** CA: because its outline on the map resembles the head of a moose. **Moose Creek** PA: a shortening of **Chindeclamoose.** In English usage the term was not applied to the elk, but it seems to have been so used in some Algonquian dialects, so that such a name as **Moosepack Lake** NJ is translatable as 'elk-pond.' See also **Moosic. Mooseheart** IL: founded by the fraternal Loyal Order of Moose.

Moosehausic RI Narragansett 'great-marsh-at.' But see **Moose.**

Mooseleuk Mountain ME Algonquian 'moose-place.'

Mooselookmeguntic Lake ME Algonquian, probably the same as **Moosetookmeguntic.**

Moosetookmeguntic ME Algonquian 'moose-river-(with)-swampy-place.'

Moosic PA Algonquian (Delaware) 'elk-mountain.'

Moosilauke NH Algonquian, meaning uncertain.

Moosmoos Creek OR Chinook jargon, 'cattle.'

Moosup CT Algonquian, the personal name of a chief of the early 17th century.

Mopang Stream ME Algonquian, probably 'solitary-place.'

Mopeco CA Coined from Mohawk Petroleum Co.

Moquah WI Algonquian 'bear (the animal).'

Moqui From the Indian tribal name, a variant of Hopi.

Mora In NM it is from a Spanish family name, of local landowners. In AZ, **Las Moras** is Spanish, 'mulberries.' In WA, **Mora** is from a town in Sweden, so named by a man who had come from it. In ID it is one of a number of station names of uncertain origin, placed at the building of the railroad.

Moraine Common in glaciated areas for a feature thus associated, e.g. **Moraine Lake** CA.

Morapos CO First applied to the creek, probably Ute, meaning uncertain.

Moratock Coined from the names of two mine proprietors, viz., J. T. Morris and J. M. Tucker, with a change of spelling perhaps to suggest an Indian name.

Moravia Generally, e.g. PA, IA, for Moravian settlers, who were generally so called, not because of their origin in that European province, but because of their affiliation with the sect known as Moravians. **Moravian Falls** NC: because discovered by Moravian surveyors.

Moray KS Named **Morey** for the superintendent of a local railroad; he objected to the use of his name, and it was altered, to conform to the spelling of a county in Scotland.

Mordvinof, Cape AK Probably derived from Russian *morda,* 'snout,' since the point looks like the snout of an animal.

Moreau In NY for the French general J. V. Moreau, who at the time (1805) had come (or was about to come) to the United States in exile. **Moreau River** SD: for an early French trader who lived near it.

Moreland In most instances probably from the personal name. In OH it was named (1829) from George Morr, one of the founders. In IL the local story is that the site was swampy and one of the owners remarked that they needed more land and less water. In ID the name was suggested (1894) by a newcomer, John England, who had heard that in the vicinity there was 'more land' available for settlement.

Moreno Spanish 'dark, brown,' usually a descriptive. **Moreno CA**: one of the town-founders was F. E. Brown; when he did not wish his name to be used, it was translated into Spanish. **Sierra de Morena AZ**: probably from the Morena Mine. It is also a common Spanish family-name, and some place-names are probably so derived.

Morgan From the personal name. **Morgan Hill CA**: named ca. 1892 for a landowner. A sharp hill near the town is now sometimes called **Morgan Hill,** apparently on the assumption that the landowner's family name was Morgan and that the town was named from the hill. The name most commonly, e.g. the county in MO, honors Gen. Daniel Morgan of the Revolutionary War.

Morganza In PA it is from a farm, which was named for its owner, George Morgan, apparently with the help of the Spanish suffix used to form abstract nouns. In LA it is similarly coined from Col. Charles Morgan, local landowner.

Morgue On the stream in KY and a habitation-name associated, the term may be from the shortening of the common family name Morgan, with the spelling later shifted.

Moriah, Mount Moriah From the Biblical mountain.

Moriches NY From the personal name of an Indian of the 17th century.

Mormon Chiefly in the far-Western states, it denotes a place where Mormons once made a settlement or a place which was in some way associated with them. It was not ordinarily given by Mormons themselves, and is not characteristic of UT, since it would there have been non-distinctive. About 25 places in CA are thus named because of the presence of Mormons, chiefly in the period 1847–1850, e.g. **Mormon Island, Mormon Bar. Mormon Lake MN**: a Mormon missionary once lived here. As is to be expected with names denoting a special group, few of them are applied to habitations. **Mormon Hollow PA**: a number of people living here were converted to Mormonism in the 1830's.

Morning Usually from an incident which happened early in the day. **Morning Sun OH**: on the day when they had to fix a name, the namers used the first thing that they saw, i.e. the morning sun. **Morningstar Mountain MT**: for a Blackfoot mythological character.

Moro In some instances from a family name, e.g. in AR probably from the French name Moreau. **Moro Rock CA**: by local story, for a horse of a blue-roan color, known to Mexicans as a *moro,* which ranged the vicinity, but a confusion with **Morro** is possible.

Morongo CA Shoshonean, the name of an Indian village, 'largest.'

Moroni UT Named (1859) for the angel Moroni of the *Book of Mormon.*

Morphradite Creek SD The colloquial rendering of *'hermaphrodite'* records the finding of a freakish animal by a cowboy; it appears in other spellings, including the proper one.

Morrison From the personal name, e.g. in CO for George Morrison, early homesteader. **Mount Morrison CA** for Robert Morrison, who was killed here when pursuing escaped convicts in 1871. See **Convict.**

Morro Spanish 'headland, bluff, outstanding rock,' e.g. **Morro Rock CA, El Morro NM.**

Morrow From the personal name. **Morrowville KS** was originally a railroad station named **Morrow** for state senator Cal Morrow, but was changed because of confusion arising when people asked for a ticket 'to Morrow' and were thought to have said 'tomorrow.'

Mort(s) French 'dead,' and thus the equivalent of **Deadman,** e.g. **Butte des Morts WI.**

Morzhovoi AK Russian 'walrus (adjective).'

Morven GA, NC From a mountain in Scotland, in NC so named because it was the birthplace of the namer's mother.

Mosaic Canyon CA Because many flat surfaces resemble mosaic work.

Mosca Spanish 'fly,' e.g. **La Mosca Canyon** NM.

Moscow Though occurring in some 15 states as a habitation-name, it seems to have been bestowed for no important reason, except that fashion of the 19th century was to name towns after large foreign cities. **Moscow** TX: first called Greenville as a community, it could not have that name for a post office because of a nearby Greenville; a name was then selected, as being so far away that there could be no objections. **Moscow** MN: a forest fire suggested the famous burning of the Russian city in 1812.

Mosel See **Moselle.**

Moselem PA Algonquian (Delaware) 'trout,' a repeated name for water features.

Moselle From the river of Europe. **Mosel** WI is the German form.

Moshannon Creek PA Algonquian (Delaware) 'elk-creek-at.'

Moshassuck River RI Algonquian, probably 'big-meadow-stream.'

Moshawguit Lake WI Algonquian, meaning uncertain.

Moshulatubbee OK From the name of a Choctaw chief.

Mosinee WI Algonquian 'moose,' but from a tribal name (?).

Mosquero In New Mexican Spanish 'swarm of flies or mosquitoes.'

Mosquito Not used for habitation because of derogatory suggestions, but common on features, usually lakes or streams, because of the namers having been there afflicted by mosquitoes. The term seems to bear little relation to the actual prevalence of mosquitoes, and even fails to occur in many areas where they are abundant. In such areas the pests are taken for granted, and one place cannot be distinguished from another because of them. Only half a dozen such names exist in MN, though much of that state is marshy and highly infested with mosquitoes. Fifty names exist in CA, where mosquitoes are not especially common because of the dry climate in the summer. It is probably the most common insect place-name. **Mosquito Range** CO: from the Mosquito Mining Company, which was itself, by tradition, named because a mosquito lit upon the blank space where the name was to be filled in.

Mosquito Hawk CT, MA, RI By folk-etymology from Algonquian. See **Musquetohauke.**

Moss, Mossy Often from the personal name, e.g. **Moss Landing** CA for Charles Moss, who built a wharf here, ca. 1865. **Moss Beach** CA: from the presence of a mosslike plant. **Mossy** refers to a growth of moss, e.g. **Mossy Rock** WA.

Mossback Meadow VT By folk-etymology from *maasbaak,* Algonquian 'much-water, overflowed.'

Mossmain MT For P. B. Moss of nearby Billings, with 'main' probably because it is on the mainline of the railroad at the junction of a branch line.

Moswansicut RI Algonquian 'big-bend-at' (?).

Mota Spanish 'mound,' e.g. **La Mota Mountain** TX.

Mother A rare name, sometimes probably from the personal name Mothers. **Mother Lake** NB: a large lake in the midst of smaller ones, like a mother among children. **The Mother Lode** CA, **The Mother Lode Country** CA, **Mother Load Mountain** OR: based upon the belief, and a translation of the Spanish *madre,* that a gold-bearing body somewhere existed from which the placer-gold was derived. **Mother Grundy Peak** CA: because it shows the profile of a large nose and projecting chin.

Motoqua UT From an Indian tribal name.

Motordale MN Changed from **New Germany** at the time of World War I, probably as a commendatory for association with the very up-to-date automobile.

Mouchoir de l'Ourse, Bayou LA French 'handkerchief of the she-bear,' but probably arising from some error, possibly from *machoire,* 'jaw, jaw-bone,' though this does not make much sense either.

Mound The name is associated either with a small natural hill or with an artificial mound, usually called an Indian mound. The latter is especially associated with the 'Mound-builders' of the central Mississippi Valley, e.g. **Mound City** MO. Natural features account for **Mound** TX, **Mounds** OK, **Mound Prairie** MN. The term is commonest in generally flat areas, where a small elevation is notable; for instance, MN has it coupled with lake, prairie, creek, together with **The Mound, The Mounds View Hills,** and several habitation-names. **Mound Prairie** WA: because of thousands of natural low mounds.

Mount A generic, it apparently does not serve as a true specific, **Mountain** taking its place. In habitation-names, however, it is common, e.g. **Mount Pleasant, Mount Moriah. Mount Desert** ME: see **Desert.**

Mountain As a specific to indicate a place thus associated, e.g. **Mountain Brook** CT, common with habitation-names, for the commendatory suggestion of height, e.g. **Mountain Home, Mountain View.** Also in compounds, e.g. **Mountain Sheep Creek** OR, **Mountain Ash Creek** WY.

Mountsweag ME Algonquian, probably descriptive of a narrows with steep sides.

Mourne, Mount NC From the Mountains of Mourne in Ireland, so named by an immigrant.

Mouse The mouse has rarely been impressive enough to produce names, but **Mouse Island** OR was heavily infested. **Mice Meadow** CA and **Mice Lake** NM show the rare use of a plural in animal-names, probably because, not being an s-plural, it gives the effect of a different name. **Mouse Island** OH: so named (1873) because its owner said it 'was as small as a mouse.' **Mouse's Tank** NV: from the personal name of an Indian of the late 19th century.

Mousie KY Clay Martin, the first postmaster, ca. 1900, called his two daughters Kitty and Mousie, and named the office for the younger.

Moville IA From the abbreviation of Missouri, the nearby river, and 'ville.'

Moving Mountain AK So called because of landslides.

Moweaqua IL Potawatomi, 'wolf-woman' (?); if so, probably a personal name.

Mowich Chinook jargon, 'deer,' e.g. the glaciers in WA.

Moxahala Although appearing to be of Indian origin, it springs from the name of an amusement park (1906) and is probably a coined name.

Moyie River ID Recorded (1808) as French *moullier,* probably from the family name of a French-Canadian trapper, such as Mollier.

Moyock NC Algonquian 'place-of-oaks-by-trail' (?).

Mo-zo-ma-na Point MN From an Indian personal name.

Muah Mountain CA Shoshonean, meaning unknown.

Mucho Spanish 'much.' In the plural it is the equivalent of 'many,' e.g. **Muchos Canones** AZ.

Muckafoonee Creek GA A late American coinage from the two streams which unite to form it, viz. **Muckalee** and **Kinchafoonee.**

Muckalee Creek GA From the name of a Muskogean village, meaning uncertain.

Muckaloochee Creek GA The diminutive of **Muckalee;** therefore, the equivalent of **Little Muckalee.**

Muckamuck Pass Chinook jargon, 'food,' locally believed to have been named because of plentiful game there.

Muckshaw Pond NJ Probably an adaptation by folk-etymology of some Algonquian term, meaning uncertain.

Mud Common for lakes, creeks, springs, etc., usually referring to the nature of the bottom at the point of approach of the namer. More than 100 lakes in MN bear this name. It has spread by transfer to a few habitation-names. **Mud** WY takes its name from **Mud River**. **Mud Hills** CA appear to be made of mud. **Mud Volcano** WY is a geyser that spouts mud.

Muddy Less common than 'mud,' the name typically refers to the water, rather than to the bottom. It is descriptive, but some streams were so named because the namer happened to see them in flood, so that the situation approaches that of an incident naming. **Muddy Creek** WV: this is a clear stream, probably named from temporary muddiness.

Muela Spanish 'grindstone,' e.g. the creek in TX.

Muerto Spanish 'dead, dead man.' **Canyon del Muerto** AZ: many Indians were killed here in 1805 and the name was given when their bones were seen in 1886; the namer, being an American, used the singular where the plural would have been more apt. **Lomerias Muertas** CA: these 'dead hills,' were probably named because they were destitute of trees and dead-looking.

Mugaleep-Ahwangen Pond ME Algonquian 'caribou-trail.'

Mugget Hill MA Probably Algonquian, meaning uncertain.

Mugu CA Chumash, the name of an Indian village, meaning 'beach.'

Mugurrewock Lakes ME Algonquian 'caribou.'

Mugwump Lake OR From the 19th century slang term for a man who shifted parties, because the lake sometimes dried up.

Muir From the personal name, especially for John Muir, nature-lover and writer, e.g. **Muir Gorge**, etc., in CA. **Muirkirk** MD: from a place in Scotland, so named by Scottish settlers in the 18th century.

Muitzes Kill NY Probably from a Dutch personal name.

Mukewater Creek TX By folk-etymology from an Indian term recorded as Mupewarrah, language and meaning uncertain.

Mukilteo WA Indian, meaning unknown.

Muksuk Lake WI From the name of a Potawami chief, literally 'big-foot.'

Mukuntuweep UT Paiute 'straight-canyon.'

Mukwanago WI Algonquian 'bearlair' (?).

Mulat Originally on the bay, it is probably from Spanish *mulato,* perhaps in the sense of 'tawny, yellow.'

Mulatto From association with a mulatto, e.g. the mountain in NC.

Mulberry The wild mulberry made little impression, and only a few such names exist for natural features. In a few regions, e.g. CA, the mulberry was introduced in connection with abortive attempts at silk culture, and habitation-names have survived. **Mulberry Fork** WV: the name was originally that of a school, so called because of a large mulberry tree.

Mule Rare, as compared with **Horse.** Usually because of an incident, e.g. **Mule Lake,** Freeborn Co., MN so named because a team of mules was drowned there. **Mule Creek** OR: a mule named John was lost here in 1852, and the stream was known as **John Mule Creek** for a long time. There are the usual compounds, such as **Mad Mule Gulch** CA, **Dead Mule Springs** CA, and **Muleshoe Mountain** OR. **Mule Lake,** Cass Co., MN: reputed to be named because it resembles a mule's head in shape.

Mulga AL Probably from the name of a local Indian chief.

Mulhockaway Creek NJ Algonquian, meaning uncertain.

Mulino OR Because of a flour mill the name **Molino** (Spanish 'mill') was suggested in 1882 but rejected by the Post Office Dept. as too much like nearby **Molalla.** A slight variation of spelling was then adopted.

Mullica River NJ For Eric Mullica, Swedish pioneer.

Mulpus Brook MA Probably from Mulpuis, the name of a French settler.

Multnomah An Indian tribal name.

Multorpor Butte OR From **Multnomah, Oregon,** and **Portland,** a name coined for the Republican Club of Portland.

Mummy The name-cluster in CO apparently arose when someone with an active imagination thought that the profile of the **Mummy Range** resembled that of an Egyptian mummy. **Mummy Cave** WY: from the discovery here of a mummified human body.

Muncie, Muncy From the name of an Indian tribe of PA and NJ, which later migrated into IN and IL. See **Minsi.**

Munissing MI Ojibway 'island-at,' but referring to an island in a lake.

Munition WV Named during the belligerent days of World War I, traditionally as a shortening of 'ammunition.'

Munoz, Point AK For a Spanish officer who was with the Malaspina expedition of 1791. See **Muzon.**

Munster In IN for Jacob Munster, early settler.

Munsungan ME Algonquian 'humped island.'

Munt Hill NH Probably from the name of an Indian who lived there.

Munuscong MI Algonquian, probably 'reeds-at.' **Monoskon** is a variant.

Murat In FL the name is for Prince Achille Murat, Napoleon's nephew, who lived in the area for some years before his death in 1847.

Murder, Murderer These names for a place where a killing occurred were much more numerous in early times and in many areas have been wholly obliterated. The 'murder' was sometimes a killing of whites by Indians, too small to be called a 'massacre,' e.g. **Murderers Gulch** CA where three men were killed. **Murder Creek** OR: preserves the record of an early murder; attempts have been made to replace the name. **Murderkill Creek** DE: a Dutch or Swedish naming (recorded in 1654), half-translated and half-transferred (see **Kill**) into English; the particular murder is uncertain, though two early ones in the area are known.

Murieta, Murrieta From a personal name, the second form being the correct one in Spanish. The first form is used for some names in CA, thought to be named after the legendary bandit, e.g. **Joaquin Murieta Caves.**

Murky Lake WY For James Murky, early settler.

Muro Spanish 'wall.'

Muroc CA Named in 1910 from a backward spelling of Corum, the family name of two homesteaders.

Musabek NH Algonquian 'moose-head-rock.'

Muscatanupus Pond ME Algonquian 'small-red-turtle.'

Muscatatuck River IN Algonquian (probably Delaware), 'clear-river.'

Muscatine IA From the Indian tribal name, commonly spelled Mascoutin.

Muscatuapus NH Algonquian 'big-pickerel.'

Muscle See **Mussel.**

Muscoda WI Algonquian 'prairie,' but it may be a tribal name, since it is from the same word as **Mascoutin.**

Musconetcong NJ Algonquian, meaning uncertain.

Muscongus ME Algonquian, meaning uncertain.

Muscoota Algonquian 'meadow,' a repeated name, e.g. in CT, NY. Also as **Mascooten, Muscooten, Muscoot, Mosquetah,** and by folk-etymology as **Mosquito.**

Muscooten Bay (Lake) IL First recorded in a French context (ca. 1720) as **Machoutin,** 'bad-land' (?). It has apparently been absorbed to the spelling of the Indian tribal name. See **Mascouten.**

Muse Probably all instances are to be attributed to the family-name, and not to Greek mythology—even the picturesque **Muse Bottom** WV. **Muse** OK: for Joseph Muse, local minister.

Musembeah Peak WY Shoshone 'bighorn-sheep,' so named (1955) by mountaineers who found the skeleton of a bighorn near the summit.

Mush Creek SD A rendering, by shortening and folk-etymology, of the Siouan *mash-tin-cha-la,* 'cottonwood.'

Mushroom Rare, and probably from shape rather than from the presence of mushrooms, e.g. **Mushroom Rock** CA.

Music The family-name (commoner as **Musick**) probably accounts for most of the names, e.g. **Music Folk** KY. **Music Mountain** AZ is named from strata which give the appearance of a musical staff. **Music Pass** CO: named by Zebulon Pike (1805) because of sounds made by the sand when his party passed through.

Musinia Peak UT Ute 'white-mountain.'

Muskee Creek NJ Algonquian, probably 'swamp.'

Muskeget MA, RI Algonquian, probably 'big-grassy-(place)-at.'

Muskego A variant of **Muskegon,** q.v.

Muskegon MI Algonquian 'swamp-at.' A variant is **Muskego** WI.

Muskelonge For the fish, e.g. the lake in IN.

Muskesin Lake WI Algonquian, meaning uncertain.

Musketaquid MA Algonquian, probably 'grassy-island.'

Muskhog This early American term for the peccary is preserved in **Muskhog Gap** TX, where a man once was chased by a herd of the animals.

Muskingum OH Algonquian, probably the name of an Indian village, meaning uncertain. The later Indian inhabitants of the region (Delawares) apparently shifted an earlier Algonquian word by folk-etymology so that it meant 'elk-eye' to them, but there is no reason to think this the original meaning.

Muskogee FL, GA From the Indian tribal name.

Muskrat The widespread animal, valuable for its fur, has given rise to many names, especially of lakes, which are the animal's habitat. Often abbreviated to **Rat,** e.g. **Rat Lake** NB.

Musquacook River ME Algonquian, probably 'muskrat-place.'

Musquapsink Creek NJ Algonquian 'muskrat-place' (?).

Musquash Algonquian 'muskrat,' a repeated name, e.g. on natural features in ME, NH, VT.

Musquashcut Pond MA Algonquian 'muskrat-place.'

Musquetohauke Brook RI Algonquian 'grassy-land.' See **Musquito Hawk.**

Mussel, Muscle The occurrence of such molluscs, or accumulations of their shells, has produced this name, both in salt and fresh water features, e.g. **Musselshell River** MT, named by the Lewis and Clark expedition. The spelling **Muscle** was once current and has established itself for **Muscle Shoals** on the Tennessee River and for the town in AL.

Musselshell River MT The Gros Ventre name was 'moonshell,' for polished shells used in trade; the present name either is a mistranslation or arose because the shells of the local freshwater mussel were at one time used as substitute money.

Mustang From the occurrence of wild or half-wild horses thus known, common in TX with 'creek.' It occurs as a habitation-name, e.g. in OK and CO, both by transfer.

Mustard Canyon CA From the yellow rocks.

Mustinka River MN Siouan 'rabbit,' applied especially to the varying hare.

Mutual The term is vaguely commendatory, and occurs on a few small towns. In UT it is from the Mutual Coal Company. In OH the settlement had communal beginnings.

Muzon, Cape AK Probably by an accidental transposition of letters from **Munoz,** the name of a Spanish officer, q.v.

Myakka A variant of **Mayaca.**

Mycenae NY From the city of ancient Greece; along with nearby **Minoa** it was probably named after archeologists had begun to use the terms Minoan and Mycenaean.

Myrtle From the personal name, or from the plant, e.g. **Myrtle Creek** OR from the Oregon myrtle growing there.

Mystery Several streams in AK were thus named by trappers or prospectors, apparently for something uncertain about their courses or nature. The names **Problem** and **Puzzle** have similarly been applied, and there is one cluster AK of the three names in juxtaposition.

Mystic, Mistic In CT and MA it is Algonquian, 'big-(tidal)-river.' It has been transferred to other states, sometimes, e.g. in SD, with a vague idea of 'mystery.' Cf. **Medicine, Wakan.**

N

-Na The common Athapascan word, 'river,' appears as the last syllable in many river-names in AK, e.g. **Tanana, Talkeetna,** and by transfer upon many other features, e.g. **Talkeetna Mountains.** It is in many instances the only part of the name that can be translated.

Naachpunkt Brook NJ The personal name of an Indian, recorded in 1686 as Nackpunck; the spelling shows Dutch influence.

Naamans Creek DE Probably from a chief named Naaman, with the English possessive 's,' though a direct derivation from 'fish' cannot be ruled out. See e.g. **Namanock.**

Nabesna River AK Athapascan, with -na, 'river,' and the rest uncertain.

Na Bonchass, Bayou LA Probably from French *la bonne chasse,* 'the good hunting.'

Naborton LA For John Nabors, plantation-owner.

Nacedah WI Algonquian 'let-there-be-three-of-us,' but significance uncertain.

Nache Peak NV From a Paiute personal name (?). See **Natchez.**

Naches In AZ from the personal name of an Apache chief of the 19th century. In WA from an Indian name, language and meaning uncertain.

Nachusa IL Winnebago 'white-haired,' but for John Dixon, an early settler, this being the name by which the Indians knew him.

Nacimiento Spanish 'birth, Nativity.' The word also may refer to the 'birth,' i.e. the 'source' of a stream, and the name of the river in CA thus arose, by apparent confusion, a later-comer assuming the earlier explorer had thus named the stream when he had only been referring to its source. Other names are probably of religious origin, especially in connection with the festival celebrating the birth of the Virgin, September 8, e.g. several occurrences of the name in NM.

Nacogdoches TX From the Indian tribal name. See **Natchitoches.**

Nacoochee GA From the name of a Cherokee village, meaning uncertain.

Nacora NB Though said locally to be from the Spanish *nacer,* 'to be born,' the form does not make either grammar or sense, and the name may be a coined one, or a pseudo-Indian adaptation.

Nacote Creek NJ Algonquian, probably from the tribal name more commonly **Nanticoke.**

Nada Since the word means 'nothing' in Spanish, the name may have been applied in a derogatory or humorous sense. In TX it is locally said to be from Najda in Czechoslovakia, named by immigrants, but it is in a region where Spanish is widely understood, and the name could hardly have been given without knowledge of its meaning.

Naf ID For John Naf, first settler.

Nag Rare, e.g. **Nag Pond** RI, from the personal name or from the Algonquian term appearing as **Naiag,** 'point.' **Nag's Head** NC is probably a transfer from England, where the same or a similar name occurs three times.

Nagawicka WI Algonquian (Ojibway) 'sandy.'

Naghi Peak CA Indian, probably Southern Paiute 'mountain-sheep.'

Nagog MA Algonquian, meaning uncertain.

Nagrom WA A backward spelling from E. G. Morgan, local lumberman.

Nahant MA Algonquian, probably the name of a chief, elsewhere recorded as Nahantum.

Nahcotta WA Named, ca. 1880, for a local Indian chief.

Naheola AL Choctaw 'white-man.'

Nahma MI Ojibway 'sturgeon.'

Nahmakanta Lake ME Algonquian 'fish-plenty.'

Nah Supah Hot Springs ID Shoshonean, with *pah,* 'water,' and the rest uncertain.

Nahumkeag ME Algonquian, indicating a place for eel-fishing at the mouth of a stream.

Nahunta Iroquoian (Tuscarora) 'tall trees' (?), the name of an Indian town, applied to a river and swamp in NC, thence transferred to a village in GA and to a waterfall in WA, probably because of its euphony.

Naidni VT This is **Indian** spelled backwards.

Nail From the personal name, e.g. in OK from **Nail's Crossing** over a nearby river, for J. H. Nail, local merchant. **Nail Canyon** AZ: for a family of early settlers who anglicized their German name, Nagel.

Naji Point AZ From the name of a Chiracahua chief of the late 19th century.

Nakai Peak CO Navajo, a clan name, here applied, probably about 1915, in non-Navajo territory by Americans, apparently as a 'suitable' Indian name.

Naked Rare; on one island in AK it is the equivalent of 'bare'; another is so named because an Indian woman was found there, crazed and naked. As applied to a few features in the SE it is probably from the older usage, 'bare,' without reference to the body.

Nalagamoik Pond ME Algonquian 'above-lake.'

Nallahoodus Mountain ME Algonquian, meaning uncertain.

Namakan, Lake MN Ojibway 'sturgeon.'

Namanock NJ, NY, PA Algonquian 'fishing-place.'

Namareck, Namasket, Namaskik, Nameaug, Namequoit, Nameroke, Namkeag, Namkeeke, Namkook, Namquit, Namshaket, Namyak In New England these names with an initial *nam-* (Algonquian 'fish') all seem to mean 'fishing-place-at.' Their variety represents variation in Indian dialects, and also faulty transmission and uncertain spelling on the part of the English who took the names over.

Namekagon River WI Algonquian 'sturgeon-place.'

Namekeeke, Namkook See **Namareck**.

Nameless In an attempt at humor, the fact that a feature was without a name has been perpetuated, e.g. a creek and an island in AK. The name, however, tends to be replaced; thus a small settlement in TX once bore the name, and one in ND was named from it. **Nameless Cave** SD: visitors were asked to vote on a name, and at the end of a year **Nameless** had received the most votes.

Nameoki IL Uncertain; it may be an artificial coinage in imitation of an Indian name; possibly from Nahmeokee, a character in the popular play by J. A. Stone. See **Metamora**.

Namequa In IL the creek is from the name of an Indian woman who lived nearby in the early 19th century. In CO it is probably a transfer from IL.

Namequoit, Nameroke See **Namareck**.

Names Hill WY Because mountainmen and covered-wagon emigrants inscribed their names here in the soft stone, from 1822 on through the 1850's.

Namke NY Algonquian 'fish-place.'

Nammygoe Pond ME Algonquian 'lake-trout.'

Namokanok Island ME Algonquian 'turtle-shell-island,' probably from its shape.

Namorf OR For George Froman, a local resident, spelled backward.

Nampa ID For a local Shoshone chief.

Namshaket See **Namareck.**

Namyak See **Namareck.**

Nanachehaw MS Choctaw 'hill-high,' but the reference may more immediately be to the **Chehaw** or **Cheaha** tribe of Indians.

Nanafalia AL Choctaw 'hill-long.'

Nanaquaket See **Nannaquaket.**

Nanawaya Creek MS Choctaw, with *nana,* 'hill,' and (?) *waiya,* 'bend.'

Nandua VA Originally **Andua,** and by local story for an Indian 'queen.'

Nanita, Lake CO Indian, language uncertain, apparently a commemorative name applied by Americans in the 20th century, perhaps with the idea that the Comanche tribe was meant by the term.

Nanjemoy MD Algonquian, meaning uncertain.

Nankipoo TN See **Yum Yum.**

Nankoweap Butte AZ Paiute, the equivalent of 'battlefield,' commemorating a fight between Indian tribes before 1870.

Nanna Falia MS Choctaw 'hill-long.'

Nanna Hubba Bluff AL From an Indian tribal name.

Nannaquaket Pond RI Algonquian, containing *nanna,* 'dry,' and probably applied to a place that dried up at times.

Nansemond VA From an Indian tribal name, recorded (1608) as Nawsamond.

Nantahala NC Cherokee 'middle (noonday)-sun,' originally applied to a place where perpendicular cliffs kept the sun from shining until noon.

Nantasket, Nantascot CT, MA Algonquian, literally to be taken as 'narrow-ebb-at,' probably indicating a place at which only a narrow water channel was left at ebb tide.

Nanticoke From the Indian tribal name.

Nantmeal PA From Nantmel in Wales, introduced by Welsh immigrants.

Nantucket Algonquian, probably 'narrow-(tidal)-river-at,' with reference to the channel between it and **Tuckernut Island.**

Nantuxent NJ As the name of a creek and point, it is Algonquian and may be related to **Nantucket.**

Nanty Glo PA Settled by Welsh coal miners, and bearing the Welsh name, 'the coal brook.'

Nanuet NY From the name of a local Indian chief.

Naoma WV For Naoma Pettry, unidentified.

Napa CA Indian, probably Patwin, but of uncertain meaning.

Napanoch NY From the name of an Indian chief.

Napavine WA Named (1883) from a local Indian word, 'small prairie.'

Napeague NY Algonquian 'water-land,' apparently to designate an isthmus.

Naphus Peak CA For Jim Naphus, local Indian fighter and bandit.

Napias Creek ID Shoshone 'money, gold,' a name given by Americans who discovered gold here in 1866.

Naples From the city of Italy. Little reason for the naming can generally be determined, except that it was a famous name, easy to pronounce. It has been applied twice in the southern part of CA, where a Mediterranean-like climate and landscape gave some justification.

Napoleon Several places are for Napoleon Bonaparte, some of them named by French settlers, e.g. in OH. In ND the name is for Napoleon Goodsill, president of the town-site company. **Napoleonville** LA is for J. L. Napoleon, early plantation owner.

Napowan Lake WI Algonquian, meaning uncertain.

Nappanee IN Algonquian 'flour' (?), but reference uncertain.

Naquamke Falls ME Algonquian 'eel-place.'

Narada Falls WA Named by a group of Theosophists for a spiritual being of their belief, literally, 'uncontaminated,' thus a descriptive-commendatory.

Naranja Spanish 'orange,' a commendatory in a citrus-producing region.

Naranjo Spanish 'orange-tree,' but in NM from the family name of early settlers.

Nara Visa NM Apparently first applied to a creek because of a sheepherder whose name was probably Narvaez. This was first made into Narvis, and then into its present form, one would judge by someone who did not speak Spanish and merely transformed the name, as heard, into something that looked like Spanish, though neither part of the name exists as a Spanish word. An interesting case of progress toward obscurity!

Narberth PA For a town in Wales, in similar manner to **Cynwyd,** q.v.

Narcoossee FL From Seminole *nokosi,* 'bear' (the animal).

Narenta MI From the river of Yugoslavia, reason for naming not established.

Nariz Spanish 'nose.'

Narmacungawak Brook NH Algonquian 'deep-fishing-place.'

Narragansett RI From an Indian tribal name.

Narraguagus River ME Algonquian 'above-bog' (?), but much disputed. See **Guagus.**

Narraquinep Creek CO Ute, meaning uncertain.

Narraticon, Lake NJ From an Indian tribal name.

Narrow Comparatively uncommon as a descriptive, except in AK, where it is sometimes a translation of the Russian *tonkie.* As a generic, **Narrows,** used as a singular, designates a narrow place in a generally broader body of water, and sometimes becomes a specific as **The Narrows** or as a habitation, e.g. **Narrows** VA, or it is applied by association, e.g. **Narrows Point** AK.

Naschiti NM Navajo, meaning doubtful.

Nasel River WA From an Indian tribal name.

Nash From the personal name. In NC and TN for General Francis Nash, Revolutionary hero (1742–1777); because of these early uses the form is regularly **Nashville. Nashmead** CA For a postmaster named Nash, and the equivalent of 'meadow.'

Nashaquits MA Algonquian 'between-islands,' but reference uncertain.

Nashawena Island MA Algonquian, contains *nas-,* 'between,' perhaps in the phrase, 'it lies between,' which description the English took to be its name. The phrase is apt, because of the location of the island. See **Naushon.**

Nashoba OK Choctaw 'wolf.' Cf. **Neshoba.**

Nashotah WI Algonquian 'twin(s),' used in the sense of 'two, double' for natural features, in one instance Englished in **Two Rivers.**

Nashua, Nashoba, Neshobe MA, NH, VT Algonquian 'between-water,' probably the equivalent of **Middle Creek.** The name has been transferred to several states farther west.

Nasja Creek UT From Navajo 'owls.'

Naskeag Point ME Algonquian 'end,' probably because marking the eastern boundary of the bay.

Nasketucket MA Algonquian 'end-(tidal)-stream-at.'

Nassau The title Prince of Orange-Nassau was borne by Dutch rulers in the 17th century, and the name was bestowed on various places in New Netherland. The county in NY is a revival of this usage (1899). The title was also borne by King William III and used occasionally in his time. The river in FL (hence, the county) was named during the British regime (1763–1783).

Nassawadox MD, VA Algonquian 'between-streams.'

Nassawango Creek MD Algonquian 'between-land,' i.e. a place between streams.

Nasty In occasional use, usually with a stream, e.g. **Nasty Creek** SD. Though it may refer to an unpleasant color of water or to a muddy bottom, it is probably more often a euphemism to indicate a stream whose banks were more than usually defiled with human or animal excrement.

Nat WV From the nickname of the first postmaster's father.

Natalbany LA Choctaw *nita* 'bear (the animal)' probably forms the first syllable. The rest of the name has been shaped by folk-etymology to the well-known name of the city, and its meaning has been rendered uncertain.

Natanano Falls WI Algonquian (Menomini) 'smoky falls,' from the resemblance of mist to smoke.

Natanis Brook ME From the personal name of an Indian, i.e. 'Nathan-little.'

Natazhat, Mount AK Athapascan, meaning uncertain.

Natchaug CT Algonquian 'middle-country,' because lying between two streams.

Natchez In MS it is from an Indian tribal name. In NV it is probably by folk-etymology from an Indian personal name such as has yielded **Nache,** i.e. by the addition of a possessive ending to make Nache's.

Natchitoches LA From the Indian tribal name. Cf. **Nacogdoches.**

Natchka Creek CA Yurok, the name of an Indian village, meaning unknown.

Natick MA, RI From the Indian tribal name.

Nation(s) In AR, **Nations Creek** is from a family of early settlers named Nations. **Lost Nation** IA: see **Lost.**

National Habitation-names are sometimes from the existence of a Federal institution, e.g. **National Park** NJ. They may be from a company, e.g. **National** UT, WV from a coal company. **National City** CA: in Mexican times the land belonging to a presidio was called a *rancho nacional;* the town was founded on such a site.

Natividad Spanish 'birth, Nativity.' Though the reference should be to Christmas, the name in CA was given in March. It may not here be religious, but may refer to some incident or to the fact that the place was at the head of a canyon.

Natoas Peak MT For the sun priest of Blackfoot mythology.

Natoma In CA it is Indian (Maidu), the name of a village and the word for 'upstream, eastern,' the two being the same direction in this area. In KS and WI it is probably Algonquian, connected with the phrase 'on my way back' (?).

Natrona From the mineral *natron,* apparently with an added vowel to simulate a Latin form.

Natural Used, as a descriptive, with generics which usually indicate a man-made feature, especially as **Natural Bridge,** of which the one in VA is the prototype. Also occurring are e.g. **Natural Arch, Natural Tunnel. Natural Corral Creek** AZ: named from a rock enclosure used by cattlemen.

Naturita CO A diminutive of Spanish *natura,* 'nature,' applied by an early settler in an affectionate sense to indicate the beautiful tree growth along the stream in contrast to the surrounding barren country.

Naubinway MI Probably from the personal name of a local Indian.

Naufaba Creek AL Muskogean, probably Hitchiti, 'beech-tree.'

Naugatuck CT Algonquian, 'one (lone) tree,' by local tradition, applied to the river because of a special landmark tree.

Naukeag MA Algonquian 'fishing-place-at.' See **Namareck.**

Nausauket RI Algonquian, probably 'between-outlets-at.'

Nauset MA Algonquian 'between-(place)-at,' probably with reference to its situation between the bay and the ocean.

Naushon Island MA Algonquian, containing *naus-* 'between,' a descriptive suitable to the island because of its location. See **Nashawena.**

Nauvoo In 1840 the name was bestowed upon the Mormon town in IL by their leader Joseph Smith; it is probably his own coinage. After their removal from IL the Mormons abandoned the name, but it has been adopted in several states, apparently without Mormon connections in most instances, and has been retained in IL.

Navajo, Navaho From the Indian tribal name.

Navajoe An alternate spelling for **Navajo,** e.g. the mountain in OK.

Navalencia CA A coining, ca. 1919, from 'navel' and 'valencia,' the commonest varieties of orange; this is a citrus-growing area.

Navarino For the battle of that name in 1827; in WI the town was named in 1829.

Navarre The French form of the Spanish province, in OH given by a French-speaking inhabitant.

Navarro CA Probably from the family name of some early settler in CA.

Navasota TX First applied to the river, it is of Indian origin, recorded as Nabatsoto (language and meaning uncertain), later shaped to the appearance of a Spanish term.

Navesink NJ Algonquian 'point-at,' sometimes transformed by folk-etymology into **Neversink.**

Navy Generally given by naval explorers in honor of the U.S. Navy. In **Navy Archipelago** WA the individual islands were largely named for naval heroes by the Wilkes expedition (1841).

Nawadaga Creek NY Iroquoian, probably 'mud-turtle-place.'

Nawaii Lake WI Algonquian, meaning uncertain.

Nawtawaket CA Wintu 'south creek.'

Nazareth From the Biblical town, for religious-commendatory reasons. In TX the name was given by a Catholic priest, but most such names are of Protestant origin. In PA the name was given by members of the Moravian church in 1741.

Nazlini AZ Navajo 'crescent,' because the creek there flows in a curve.

Neabsco Creek VA Algonquian 'point-(of)-rock-at' (?).

Neacoxie Creek OR The name of an Indian village, probably from Chinook 'pine trees.'

Neah Bay WA From the name of a local Indian chief.

Neanscott River ME Algonquian, meaning uncertain.

Neapsco Creek VA A variant of **Neabsco.**

Near Almost nonexistent, except in AK, where it is commonly a translation from the Russian (*blizhnie*). **Near Islands** AK: so called by the Russians, because nearest to Asia; from the point of view of the U.S. they are the far islands. **Near Rockaway** NY was once used to distinguish it from **Far Rockaway.**

Neawanna Creek OR Though probably an Indian word, the source and meaning are unknown.

Nebagamon Lake WI Algonquian, to indicate a place where one watched for game at night.

Nebish Lake MN Ojibway 'tea,' with reference to the white man's beverage, but cause of application uncertain; perhaps from the color of the water. In some Algonquian dialects the more literal meaning may be preserved, 'bad water,' e.g. with **Neebish** MI.

Nebo, Mount Nebo From the Biblical mountain, famous as the place from which Moses saw the Promised Land, both as a name for features, e.g. **Mount Nebo** MN, and for several habitations, chiefly in the South.

Nebraska Siouan (Omaha or Otoe) *ni,* 'water,' and *bthaska,* 'flat,' thus meaning a river not running between high banks but spread out widely, and referring originally to the **Platte River.** J. C. Frémont, one of the first to use the present spelling, suggested the name as a suitable one for a future territory in 1844, and it was later adopted by Congress.

Necanicum River OR From the name of an Indian village, *ne* probably meaning 'place,' otherwise unknown.

Necedah WI Winnebago 'yellow.'

Necessity Occasionally used as an abstract to express something done without choice, e.g. **Fort Necessity** PA, so named by George Washington in 1754 at a critical time in his campaign against the French.

Neche ND Ojibway 'friend,' by local story named by J. J. Hill, railroad president, when he heard an Indian use it as a greeting.

Neches A Spanish plural from the Indian tribal name Neche, first applied to the river in TX, which was in the area of that tribe.

Neck Basically a generic, meaning an isthmus or peninsula, i.e. a narrow strip of land between two bodies of water. It came to be used for a narrow strip of anything, as in the colloquial 'neck of woods.' It became a specific by associa-

tion, e.g. **Neck Pond** MA, and also in habitation-names, e.g. **Dutch Neck** NJ. The cutting of forests and other changes have often destroyed the descriptive value. A certain humor may be the cause of the frequent coupling with significant specifics, especially animal names, e.g. **Bullock Neck** RI, **Horse Neck Brook** MA, **Calf Neck** RI.

Neconish WI Indian (probably Algonquian), meaning uncertain.

Neddick, Cape ME Algonquian 'lone, solitary' (?).

Nederland CO, TX Named under Dutch auspices for the Netherlands.

Neebish See **Nebish.**

Neeces SC Named (1890) by J. W. Neece who in 1889 had dreamed of a town so named.

Need In MA the name **Needham** was given, ca. 1711, for a town in England. It is also a personal name. **Needy** OR and **Needville** TX are, more or less, humorously, in reference to the impecunious condition of the settlers at the time of naming. See **Needmore.**

Needle Commonly a generic, and sometimes used absolutely, e.g. **The Needles** (sharp rocks in AZ) which have produced **Needles** (town, CA). As a descriptive it identifies something pointed or associated with such a point, e.g. **Needle Peak** CA.

Needmore A humorous derogatory, usually taken in the sense that the place needs more of everything; it is widespread and common, in KY alone being applied to eight settlements.

Neenah In WI, it is Winnebago 'water,' applied by Americans. In AL it is from a woman's name, Nina.

Neeseponsonet MA Algonquian, containing *neese-,* 'two, second,' *-pon,* 'waterfall,' *-et,* 'at.' The syllable *-son-* is uncertain.

Negani Lake WI Algonquian, meaning uncertain.

Negas ME Algonquian, meaning uncertain.

Negaunee MI From Ojibway, selected as the name in the 19th century, being considered the equivalent of 'pioneer,' in the Pioneer Iron Company, a local corporation; literally, 'he walks ahead,' coined by Peter White. See **Ishpeming.**

Negreet LA Spanish *negrito,* with reference to the growth of black haw trees.

Negro Spanish 'black,' e.g. **Negro Creek** TX; more commonly from the racial designation. Regularly now spelled **Negro,** but in most cases originally **Nigger,** and this latter is the only form preserved on many obsolete names. The term exists on many features, but not as a habitation-name, except as indicating in a generic way the section of a town chiefly inhabited by Negroes. The name usually indicates residence of a Negro at that place, and so is less common in regions where Negroes constituted a large percentage of the population, since it is there not distinctive. The name may also indicate an incident or other association. **Negro Mountain** MD: a giant Negro was killed here in a battle of the French and Indian War. **Negro Canyon** CA: from Robert Owen who lived there and became prosperous and well-known. **Negrohead, Niggerhead:** the terms are used in several ways, but in place-names usually refer to round, hard stones, and to the place where they were found. **Negrohead Mountain** CA: the reference is probably to the rounded outline. **Negro Head** AZ: a mountain of remarkably black rock. **Nigger Mesa** NM: because of a fight here involving a Negro. **Nigger Canyon,** Orange Co., CA, is by folk-etymology from **Niquel.**

Neguasseag River ME Probably the same as **Nequasset,** i.e. 'pond-at.'

Negus Mountain MA Probably Algonquian, see **Negas.**

Neguttaquid River ME Algonquian 'old-island.'

Nehalem OR An Indian tribal name.

Nehasane Lake NY Iroquoian, originally applied to a stream to indicate that it was crossed on a footlog.

Nehawka NB An adaptation of an Omaha-Otoe name for a nearby stream, meaning approximately 'murmuring water.'

Nekimi WI Algonquian, probably for a kind of berry.

Nekoma In several states, probably originating in IL. It appears to be a simplification of some Indian (Algonquian) term. In ND it is locally explained as from an Ojibway word with the general idea of 'promise,' so that it might be a commendatory.

Nekoosa WI Winnebago 'water-running.'

Nalagoney OK Probably Osage 'good water.'

Nelchina AK Athapascan, with *-na,* 'river,' and the rest uncertain.

Nellita WA Named (1900) by the postmaster, Ralph Brueger, who used a Spanish diminutive form of his wife's name, Nelli.

Nelscott OR From C. P. Nelson and W. R. Scott, the founders.

Nemadji River MN Ojibway 'left hand,' because on the left to anyone ascending the main stream out of Lake Superior.

Nemah WA Indian, of unknown meaning.

Nemaha Creek NB Omaha 'water-miry (muddy).'

Nemahbin Lakes WI Algonquian (Ojibway), for a kind of fish.

Nemo The word means 'no one' in Latin, and it is also the name of the captain in Verne's popular *Twenty Thousand Leagues under the Sea.* Its reason for use as a habitation-name, however, is uncertain. In TX it was given, in part, to harmonize in sound with nearby places ending in *-o.*

Nena Creek OR An adaptation of an Indian word, probably 'cottonwood.'

Nenana River AK Athapascan, with *-na,* 'river,' and the rest uncertain.

Neodesha KS The town founders (1869) desired something that was Indian, descriptive, and unusual. The name is therefore probably the result of coinage at that time, with Siouan *ne-*, 'water, river,' and the whole taken to mean 'meeting of the waters.'

Neoga Uncertain. It has been connected with Iroquoian 'deity-place'; if so, it must be an introduced name since it does not occur in Iroquoian country. In IL (1854) it is a railroad name, and may thus be essentially coined.

Neola From a woman's name, e.g. in OK for Neola Schooling, daughter of the first postmaster. In WV the name was coined by rearrangement of the letters in **Olean** by a man who had come from that city in NY.

Neon KY Interest in the discovery of the elements neon, krypton, and xenon. ca. 1900, apparently accounts for **Neon, Krypton,** and **Xena,** all in the same region of the state, and probably railroad names.

Neopit WI From the name of a local Menominee chief of the 19th century.

Neopolis TN Graeco-Latin 'new-city.'

Neosho In KS and MO the name was first that of a river, Siouan, with *ne-*, 'water,' and the rest probably 'main.' In WI it is also Siouan but of the Winnebago dialect, again with *ne* and the rest probably a diminutive, indicating a small source of water.

Neota CO Probably Indian, said by the Arapaho to mean 'mountain-sheep-heart,' but this may be by folk-etymology from their misunderstanding of a Ute word.

Neotuquet River ME Algonquian 'lone-river-at.'

Nepaug River CT Algonquian, with *-paug*, 'pond,' with *ne-* probably 'good,' in the sense of 'fresh, drinkable.'

Nepesta CA From **Napesta,** an early Indian (language uncertain) name for the **Arkansas River,** also used by the Spaniards, and adopted for the settlement in 1876.

Nephi From the patriarch in the *Book of Mormon,* which tells of his migration to America from Judea.

Neponset River MA Algonquian 'good (?)-waterfall-at.'

Nepp Point ME Algonquian, probably 'water,' and a shortening of some longer term.

Nequally Creek WA Probably Indian, meaning unknown.

Nequamwicke Falls ME Algonquian 'eel-place.'

Nequaseag River ME Algonquian 'clear (shallow)-water-at.'

Nequasset ME Algonquian 'pond-at.'

Nescatunga River KS Siouan (Osage) 'river-big-salt,' translated in French as **Grande Saline.**

Nesco NJ Algonquian, a shortening of **Nescochague.**

Nescochague Creek NJ Algonquian, meaning uncertain.

Nesconset NY Algonquian 'second-crossing-at,' also the name of the tribe living there.

Nescopeck PA Algonquian (Delaware) 'black-spring.'

Nesepack Ponds VT Algonquian 'two ponds.'

Neshaminy PA From the Indian tribal name.

Neshanic NJ Algonquian 'double-stream-at,' and also a tribal name.

Neshannock PA Algonquian (Delaware) 'double-stream-at.'

Neshkoro WI Winnebago, with *ne*, 'water,' and the rest uncertain.

Neshoba MS Choctaw 'wolf.' Cf. **Nashoba.**

Ne Ska River MO Siouan, probably 'river-white.'

Neskowin OR From an Indian word, probably 'place of fish.'

Nesowadnehunk Stream ME Algonquian 'between-mountains-stream.'

Nespelem WA From an Indian tribal name.

Nesquehoning Creek PA Algonquian (Delaware) 'black-lick-at.'

Ness County KS Named (1867) for Cpl. Noah V. Ness killed in 1864, one of the few examples of such a naming for a noncommissioned officer of the Civil War.

Nesselroad WV From the family name of the postmaster.

Nester A rare family name, but in **Nester Draw** NM it is probably from the western cattleman's term of reproach for a farmer, because one such had settled there.

Nestucca River OR An Indian tribal name.

Nesuntabunt Mountain ME Algonquian 'three-heads (peaks).'

Netarts OR An Indian tribal name.

Netawaka KS Probably a name applied by Americans, of doubtful Indian (Potawatomi) background, locally thought to mean 'fine-view.'

Netcong NJ Algonquian, meaning uncertain.

Netop Mountain VT Algonquian, probably 'my friend,' but reference uncertain.

Nettle The plant was useful to the Indians for the making of twine, and a few names exist, probably as translations, e.g. **Nettle Creek** IL. (See **Mazon**.) **Nettle Carrier Creek** TN: probably from an Indian personal name, translated.

Neuse From a tribal name, mentioned in 1584 by Amadas and Barlowe as 'the countrey Newsiok, situate upon a goodly river called Neus.'

Neutaconkanut Hill RI Algonquian, probably 'short-boundary-mark-at.'

Neutral In occasional informal use, e.g. **The Neutral Ground** NY, for the area lying between the two zones of occupation. **The Neutral Strip** OK was the common name for the 'panhandle,' which for 40 years was not a part of any state or territory.

Neva In some instances probably from the river of Russia or the mountain of Switzerland. In KS, probably from the name of the wife of a railroad official. In WI, from the name of an Ojibway chief. **Mount Neva** CO: from the name of an Arapaho of the mid-19th century.

Nevada Spanish 'snowed upon, snowy,' a common descriptive term in Spanish for mountains covered with snow, especially as seen from a distance. It was applied to various mountains in CA before being applied to the present range so known, ca. 1776. From the range came **Nevada Co.** and **Nevada City,** both in CA. The town in MO was named in 1855 from the county, and the town in TX from that in MO. In 1864, when the state was being organized from what had been **Washoe Territory** (q.v.), the present name was adopted by the Constitutional Convention, from the mountains.

Never-Never Lake AK So isolated that it was fancifully named (1956) as being in 'never-never-land.'

Neversink See **Navesink.**

Never Summer Mountains CO The translation of an Arapaho name, aptly descriptive for a high range.

Nevis Probably from the mountain in Scotland, though the island in the West Indies bears the same name.

New At least 100 names contain 'new,' either as a separate word (**New Castle**) or joined (**Newcastle**). On features, 'new' is comparatively rare. It may be a family name, e.g. **New Creek** WV, for Peter New, first settler at its mouth. 'New' may indicate a newly discovered feature (probably **New River** WV), and thus be a vestige of the exploratory period. It may represent an actually new feature, i.e. one formed by a landslide, earthquake, volcanic eruption, etc., e.g. **New River** CA was formed when a former dry bed was filled by overflow from another stream. On habitations 'new' is one of the commonest of all terms. It may be a family name, but as such is more common as **Newberry, Newton,** etc. It may be a transfer from England of a name already containing the element, e.g. **Newark, Newhaven, Newcastle, Newbury, Newport,** and commonly **Newton.** It may be a commemorative name from some place either in 'the old country,' or 'back east,' e.g. **Newbern** NC, **New Bedford** MA, **New London** CT. A special case of this practice exists when the commemoration is primarily for a man through his title as with **New York** (q.v.) or **New Brunswick** NJ, for George III who was also Duke of Brunswick. Most commonly the term serves merely to distinguish one place from another of the same name in the same state or vicinity. Sometimes this is because the settlement itself has moved, so that we have **Old** ——, and **New** ——. More typically one settlement remains without a distinguishing adjective, and the other adds **New.** See also the special entries that follow. **New Deal** CO, MT: named from the New Deal of the 1930's.

Newagen, Cape ME Applied first to the island, e.g. **Capemanwagan** (1623), i.e. Algonquian 'closed-route,' probably meaning a place where canoes could not pass or could pass only with difficulty. By folk-etymology the first syllable was taken to be English 'cape,' and the name was then applied to the point.

Newark From a town in England, directly in DE (1683) and probably in NJ (1666). Some advocate a religious origin, i.e. New Ark, for the latter, but it was settled from CT, where the people were given to using English names. In OH the name is from that in NJ, and other towns are also thus secondarily derived.

Newaukum WA Indian, meaning unknown.

Newaygo County MI From an Ojibway chief of the early 19th century.

New Begun Creek NC Probably by folk-etymology from the unusual family name Newbegin.

New Castle, Newcastle In DE the name dates from 1664 when Col. Richard Nicolls thus renamed the former Swedish-Dutch settlement, almost certainly in honor of the royalist earl, rather than with reference to the English city. **New Castle** PA: named for the English city, in 1802, for commendatory reasons, in the hope that it would become a manufacturing town. Later habitation-names arise chiefly from these two early ones, with the spellings varying. In WA the town was named because of coal mines.

Newcomerstown OH The second wife of Chief Eagle Feather was known as The Newcomer. Her husband was murdered; she fled, but was caught and fearfully executed. Her name clung to the place where she was captured (1750).

Newdick Point ME Algonquian 'solitary-place-at.'

New England In his voyage of 1614 John Smith applied this name, in a general way, to the region which has been so called since that time, and he entitled his book *A Description of New England* (1616). The name was an obvious one, since there were already New Spain and New France. Smith knew that Francis Drake had called the California coast Nova Albion. On one occasion Smith declares that a part of the coast was like Devonshire, but no point-by-point analogy is to be expected. James I confirmed the name in a charter of 1620. Such a name had high commendatory quality, and was also a political value in maintaining nationalistic claims, the Dutch having applied **New Netherland** in 1614.

Newent CT From the name of a village in England (or a family name).

Newfane In VT it appeared as **Fane** in 1753, for John Fane. (See **Westmoreland.**) In 1761 a new charter was granted under the name **Newfane.**

Newfound Rare; to indicate a recently discovered feature, e.g. **Newfound Lake** NH.

New Hampshire Named after the English county by John Mason, the grantee, in 1629. He was a resident of Hampshire. **Hampshire Co.** MA and WV, originally VA, were similarly named.

New Harmony IN Founded in 1815 by the Rappites, a German communal group, it was called Harmonie, with the German spelling. Robert Owen bought the land in 1825 to found his own colony, and gave it the present name to distinguish his own from the preceding settlement.

New Haven First in CT (1640), probably because it was a newly found harbor, but the English channel port was certainly known to the colonists, some of whom had come from that area. Later namings are regularly from the one in CT, 'haven' in the sense of 'harbor' having become obsolete.

Newichawannock, Newichawannuk See **Newichwanimak.**

Newichwanimak, Newichwannock ME, NH Algonquian 'between-rapids-at,' for a place at the forking of a stream, both forks having rapids. Also as **Newichawannock.**

Newington In CT (1718) from an English town-name.

New Jersey Given by the proprietors in 1664 from the island of Jersey. Sir George Carteret, one of the proprietors, was of that island.

Newllano LA Named (1918) by a colony which had come from **Llano** in CA.

New London The colonists in New England, though giving the names of many English cities, avoided that of London, perhaps as too pretentious, until **New London** CT, named in 1658. Even so, the use of **New** took away something of the pretension. The towns in OH and WI were both named by settlers from the one in CT.

New Melle MO From a place in Germany (ca. 1850).

New Mexico First applied, in Spanish, by Francisco de Ibarra, explorer, in 1562 as a commendatory, i.e. that the country lying vaguely to the north would be as rich as the original Mexico, as conquered by Cortez. The name worked north to the country along the upper Rio Grande and was well established when the Spaniards took possession in 1598. After the region became a part of the U.S. (1848), **Nuevo Mexico** was rendered as **New Mexico,** and that name persisted through the territorial period and into statehood, in spite of many propositions to change it, because it suggested a part of Mexico rather than of the U.S.

New Netherland The Dutch possessions around the Hudson River were so called in a resolution of the States General on Oct. 11, 1614. The name remained in use until replaced by New York. The use of such names was common in the period to imply that the region being settled was a natural outgrowth of the mother country.

New Orleans LA Named in 1718 by the French as Nouvelle Orléans, the latter name from the city in France and more particularly from the title of the Duc d'Orléans, regent at that time. The first word was translated into English after the city became part of the U.S. (1803).

New Paltz NY Named in 1678 by German settlers for Pfalz (Palatinate) in Germany where they had formerly lived.

Newport In RI the name dates from 1639, being probably a descriptive commendatory, though several English towns are so named and gave the example. From this beginning, and because of the attractiveness of the name, it has become a favorite, and exists in many states. **Newport News** VA: originally, ca. 1621, **New Port Newce,** the third word from the family name of the brothers who established the town, being eventually made into the common word **News** by folk-etymology. The use of **New** may here result from the fact that the brothers had already founded **Newcetown** in Ireland. **Newport** TX: in 1879 there was a squabble about what the name should be, and, to take in the largest possible number of men, the name was formed from the initials of Norman, Ezell, Welch, Pruit, Owsley,

Rieger, and Turner, otherwise unidentified.

Newry From the town in Northern Ireland.

Newskah Creek WA Indian, a village name, meaning unknown.

Newspaper Rock AZ The rock shows pictographs, and Americans gave the name on the assumption that news was thus passed about.

Newton A frequent name for habitations, because of a combination of circumstances, viz. it is a common English place-name, a common personal name, and an apt name for any new settlement. The reason for a particular name may thus be double or even triple. **Newton** MA took its name from the early name of **Cambridge**, i.e. **New Town,** of which it had been a part; it remained **New Town** until ca. 1765. **Newton Co.** IA, MO, TX: for Sgt. John Newton (1752–1780), a Revolutionary hero. **Newton** NC: for Newton Wilson, son of a man who aided in the foundation. **Newton** UT was an outgrowth of **Clarksburg,** and named as being new.

New Tripoli PA To commemorate the victory of the U.S. Navy in the war with Tripoli.

New Year's Spring AZ Named by the explorer Lt. A. W. Whipple who reached it on Jan. 1, 1854.

New York To the Dutch the city was Nieuw Amsterdam. The English took over in 1664 when the custom of prefixing 'new' was rare in the English colonies. Its existence for New York is therefore to be considered a retention of the Dutch usage. The retention suggests that the city was so named with reference to York in England. The more immediate reason, however, was the honoring of the Duke of York, to whose charge King Charles II entrusted the colony. At the same time the English also shifted the name of the colony to **New York,** on the analogy of the county in England, with its chief town of the same name.

Neyami GA From the names of three land developers, Newton, Yancy, Miller, coined ca. 1920.

Nezinscot River ME Algonquian 'descent-place,' probably for canoes.

Nez Perce From the Indian tribal name. In WY the name was given commemoratively because of a march of the tribe through that area in 1877.

Nez Piqué, Bayou LA French 'nose-tattooed.' The Indians of the region practiced tattooing, but the personal name of some Indian is here suggested.

Ni River See **Mattaponi.**

Niagara NY Iroquoian, the original application being to the situation, not to the river or fall, 'neck (of land); it is also given more specifically as 'point-of-land-cut-in-two,' to designate the place at which the river flows out into the lake.

Niangua River MO Probably Siouan, with *ni-,* 'river,' and the rest uncertain.

Niantic From the Indian tribal name.

Niatche Creek UT From a Ute personal name.

Nicasio CA Probably for a local Indian chief who had received a Spanish name in baptism.

Nicatous Lake ME Algonquian 'twin-little,' i.e. a small lake or stream of double nature, perhaps as being forked.

Nicatowis Fork ME See **Nicatous.**

Nice In CA it was named (ca. 1927) for the French city, because the topography was thought to be Mediterranean. **Niceville** FL was named as a commendatory because it was thought to be a 'nice' place.

Nichmug River NH Algonquian 'fishing-place-at-fork' (?).

Nickajack NC, GA Indian, probably Cherokee, meaning uncertain.

Nickel Though the metal has not been much produced in the U.S., it has given names, e.g. **Nickle Mines** PA and **Nickel Mountain** OR.

Nicktown PA By abbreviation from the church of St. Nicholas, around which the village grew.

Nickwacket Mountain VT Algonquian, meaning uncertain.

Nicodemus Founded in 1877 as an all-Negro community, and named for a legendary hero of the American Negroes.

Nicolaus CA For Nicholaus Allgeier, a German immigrant who held a ranch in the locality in the 1840's.

Nicollet MN The name commemorates J. N. Nicollet (1786–1843), who explored much of the region.

Nicoma OK The first syllable is from G. A. Nichols, townsite developer, and the rest from the ending of the state-name.

Nid French 'nest,' e.g. **Bayou Nid d'Aigle,** 'nest of eagle.'

Nido Spanish 'nest,' generally used in a figurative and sentimental sense for habitations, e.g. **Rionido** CA.

Nieto Spanish 'grandson, descendant,' but usually from a personal name. **Los Nietos** CA: the original grantee was Manuel Nieto (1784). In 1834 the *rancho* was regranted to his five heirs. The name thus is probably to be taken as meaning 'the Nieto family,' but it can also be taken as the *rancho* of 'the descendants.'

Nigger See **Negro.**

Night Cap CA A mountain is so named because of the resemblance to a night-cap.

Nightingale Mountains NV Probably for A. W. Nightengill, early settler and political figure, transformed by folk-etymology.

Nigu AK Eskimo 'rainbow,' but a name given to some features by geologists because of colorful rocks.

Niguel Hill CA Of Indian origin, meaning unknown.

Nihomus Run NJ Probably from the name of a chief.

Nikaagamok Lake ME Algonquian 'forked-lake.'

Nikusa Island WI A variant of **Nekoosa.**

Niland CA A contraction of Nile Land. See **Nile.**

Nil Desperandum Gulch AK Latin, roughly, 'Do not despair!' a name given by an unusual prospector who knew some Latin, on some unknown but apparently bad occasion.

Nile(s) The valley of the Egyptian river was famous for its fertility, and the name was sometimes given for commendatory reasons, e.g. **Nilegarden, Niland** CA. **Niles** is from the personal name, e.g. in OH (1834) and in MI (1835) for Hezekiah Niles, editor of the well-known *Weekly Niles Register;* **Niles** CA for A. C. Niles, who was *persona grata* to the Central Pacific Railroad.

Nimbus, Mount CO See **Cirrus.**

Nimham, Mount NY From the name of an Indian chief who aided the Americans in the Revolution.

Nimikagan River WI Algonquian (Ojibway) 'sturgeon-place.'

Nimshew CA From an Indian tribal name.

Ninaview CO From Nina Jones, wife of a local rancher, with 'view,' a common commendatory.

Nine See **One.**

Nineveh From the ancient Assyrian capital. In spite of its condemnation in the Bible as a seat of wickedness, several towns bear the name.

Ninigret Pond RI From the name of an Indian chief, ca. 1654.

Ninnekah OK Indian (Choctaw), probably connected with the word for 'night,' but reference uncertain.

Ninnescah River KS Siouan, probably 'river-salt.'

Niobe From the queen in **Greek** mythology, associated with weeping; used occasionally as a habitation-name, but reference uncertain.

Niobrara River NB From Omaha and Ponca words, 'river-spreading,' probably with reference to its flooding.

Niongwah River MO Probably Siouan, with *ni*, 'river,' and the rest uncertain.

Niota IL, TN Probably a semicoined name, with Siouan *ni-*, 'water, river,' and a convenient ending, being possibly a shortening of **Minneota.**

Niotaze KS Being named **Niota,** it was too easily confused with other places so named, and *-ze* was arbitrarily added by the postmaster for differentiation.

Nipinnawasee CA A transferred Indian name, applied ca. 1908; though locally said to mean 'plenty of deer,' *nipi* suggests the Algonquian for 'lake.'

Nipmuck From the Indian tribal name.

Nipomo CA Chumash, the name of a village, meaning unknown.

Nippenick Lake MA Algonquian, probably 'freshwater-pool.'

Nippenose Creek PA Algonquian (Delaware) 'summer-hunt,' i.e. a place where a special hunt was held in the summer.

Nippersink IL, WI Algonquian (probably Potawatomi) 'water-little-at.'

Nipple Descriptive for a formation resembling a woman's breast, or nipple, e.g. **Nipple Mountain** CO. It often approaches being a generic as in the repeated **The Nipple,** in such alliterative combinations as **Nellie's Nipple** CA, and in the highly specific **Clara Bird's Nipple,** this last having been named by the girl's father.

Nippoo Pond NH Algonquian 'freshwater-pond.'

Nisa, Mount CO An adaptation of Arapaho *nisah,* 'twins,' for a double-peaked mountain, a name placed by the Colorado Geographic Board ca. 1915.

Nishamekkackton Creek PA Algonquian (Delaware), with *nisha-*, 'double,' and the rest uncertain.

Nishayne Brook NJ Algonquian 'double-stream.'

Nishisakawick Creek NJ Algonquian 'double-outlet-house,' i.e. a habitation thus situated.

Nishnabotna River MO Probably Siouan, with *ni-* 'river,' and the rest uncertain.

Nishu ND Arikara 'arrow.'

Niskayuna NY Iroquoian, probably 'cornfields-big.'

Nisqually WA From an Indian tribal name.

Nisquitianxset RI Algonquian 'unclean (?)-(place)-at.'

Nissequogue NY From the name of a tribe, which may have taken its name from the place, which would be Algonquian but of uncertain meaning.

Nissitisset(t) MA, NH Algonquian, to indicate a place with two brooks or lying between two brooks.

Nitro WV Named during World War I, when a plant for making high explosives was located here.

Nitrolee SC W. S. Lee, ca. 1917, worked here on a scheme to fix nitrogen, and his name was thus combined to designate the village.

Nittaw FL A railroad name (1910) from Muskogean (Creek) 'day.'

Nitta Yuma MS Choctaw 'bear (the animal)-there' (?).

Nivloc NV This is the family name Colvin, spelled backward; reference uncertain.

Niwot CO For an eminent chief of the Arapahos of the late 19th century; literally 'left-hand.'

No The use of negative description is unusual, but there are some examples, e.g. **Nowood Creek** WY, **No Bottom Spring** KY, **Noluck Lake** AK, **No Name Glacier** WA, together with the Spanish **No Agua** NM, 'no water.' It occurs in Indian personal names, e.g. **No Heart Creek** SD, **No Moccasin Creek** SD. So also the curiously named **No Water Lake** SD is for Thomas No Water, the allottee. **No Man's Land** MA: the island is from a shortening of the personal name of Chief Tequenoman, known as of 1664. **Point No-Point** MN, WA: apparently in both instances a humorous description of a seeming point which at closer scrutiny turned out not to be a point. The most numerous examples are in AK, where the name may be quasi-descriptive, e.g. **No Lake Creek, No Thorofare Bay,** or may express feelings, e.g. **No Use Ledge,** or may record an incident, e.g. **No Grub Creek. Nowhere Creek** AK was named (1956) by geologists because it led to very difficult passes, i.e. 'led nowhere.' **No Business Creek:** in several southern states it is unexplained, although various local stories are circulated. **No Name Key** FL, **No Name Brook** ME, etc. are the equivalent of **Nameless,** and are retained partly for humorous ends. **No Man's Friend Pond** GA: so named apparently because in a hostile area of thickets and swamp. Followed by a numeral, **No** must be read as 'number,' e.g. **Island No 1** KY.

Noank CT Algonquian, probably 'point (of land).'

Noatak River AK Eskimo, probably 'inland river,' so named, apparently, by the coastal tribes because it flowed from far and unknown inland regions.

Nob Hill CA In San Francisco, so called because it was a fashionable place where 'nobs' lived. The name was aided by the fact that **Knob Hill** is a common descriptive term. (See **Knob.**)

Noble(s) Regularly from the personal name, e.g. the county in OK for J. W. Noble, secretary of the interior. **Noble Pass** CA: from W. H. Nobles, who discovered it in 1851; the name was often recorded as **Noble's Pass** and was eventually simplified wrongly. **Nobles Co.** MN: for the same man, who went to

MN in the mid-1850's and served in the legislature.

Nobscot, Nobska MA Algonquian 'rocky-(place)-at,' with the initial *n* unexplained.

Nobscusset, Nobsquassit MA Algonquian, probably 'rocks-little-at.' See **Nobscot.**

Noc See **De Noc.**

Nocatee FL Probably a name given by Americans, based on Seminole *nakiti,* 'What is it?' but reason for naming unknown.

Nockamixon PA Algonquian (Delaware), uncertain, but probably 'three-wigwams-at.'

Nocquebay, Lake WI Ojibway, *noc* (see **De Noc**), and the rest uncertain.

Nodaway MO Probably Siouan, meaning uncertain.

Nogal Spanish 'walnut tree,' e.g. **Nogal** NM, where a large walnut tree is a landmark. **Nogales** is commoner, being applied to features because of the presence of trees. **Nogales** AZ: named in 1855 by the Boundary Commission because of two trees, one on either side of the line.

Nohorn Creek OR From John Nachand, pioneer prospector, known as Nohorn, probably a nickname developed out of his family name.

Noir(e) French 'black,' e.g. **Terre Noir** [sic] **Creek** AR, because it flows through a region of dark soil. So also, **Bayou Lenoir** LA.

Noise Rare, but exists in **Big Noise Creek** OR, so called because a sluice gate in it was excessively noisy.

Nojogui CA Chumash, the name of a village, meaning unknown.

Nokay Lake MN From the personal name of an Ojibway chief.

Nokhu Crags CO Arapaho 'eagle's-nest,' the name having been placed by the Colorado Geographic Board ca. 1915.

Nokomis For the grandmother of Hiawatha, as made known by Longfellow's poem.

Nokoni, Lake CO Named by the Colorado Geographic Board, ca. 1915, for a well-known Comanche chief.

Noland NC For Andrew Noland, early settler.

Nolem FL This is 'melon' spelled backward, named probably from the growing of melons.

Nolia AZ Probably from Spanish *noria,* 'well,' with shift of pronunciation.

Nolichocky River TN The name of a Cherokee village, probably meaning, literally, 'spruce-tree-place.'

Nollesemic Lake ME Algonquian, meaning uncertain.

Nollidgewanticook River ME Algonquian 'above-falls-(in)-river-at.'

Noma FL From the Noma Mill Company, which operated a lumber mill here.

Nomahegan NJ From an Indian tribal name.

Nombre de Dios, Arroyo TX Spanish 'name of God,' a pious name, repeatedly used in Latin America, but reference here uncertain.

Nome On a chart prepared for a survey conducted by the British ship *Herald* the notation *? name* was placed near a certain cape in AK; this was taken by a second draughtsman to be the name itself, and he put it as **Cape Name;** the *a* being indistinct, the final copy came out as **Cape Nome.** This is a wholly authenticated instance of an origin by mistake. In TX and ND the name is derived from that in AK.

Nominick Hills NY Probably Algonquian, meaning uncertain.

Nomwaket Creek CA Wintu 'west-creek.'

Non OK From the last syllable of the name of the first postmaster, J. W. Cannon; since the Latin meaning is 'not,' a joke is to be suspected.

Nona FL For the daughter of some early settlers.

Nonames Hill NY From the name of an early Indian chief.

Nonchalanta KY Apparently from 'nonchalant,' but connection uncertain.

Nonequit, Nonquitt MA, RI Probably 'dry place.' Other names with *non,* 'dry,' are apparently **Nonacoicus** MA, **Nonnecoicus** MA. See also **Nonnewaug** and **Nunnetucket.**

None Such Occasionally as a commendatory on habitations, such as plantations, e.g. in KY. In MA its use on a pond may be by folk-etymology from such an Algonquian name as **Nonset.**

Nonnewaug CT Algonquian, apparently the equivalent of 'dry river.'

Nonoken Lake WI Algonquian (Ojibway), meaning uncertain.

Nonpareil NB Since the word means 'peerless,' this may be a commendatory name, but local story has it that it was named for nonpareil type, which is very small, and therefore was a suitable name for a very small town.

Nonsense Creek FL Probably an incident-name, but no data are available.

Nooksack WA From an Indian tribal name.

Noon, Noonday Usually from an incident involving noon. **Noonday Canyon** NM: because, on an early trail, it was a convenient place to stop for midday lunch. **Noonday Rock** CA: because the clipper *Noonday* struck here and sank on Jan. 2, 1863. **Noonday Creek** GA: by folk-etymology from the Cherokee term *nunda,* meaning 'sun' or 'moon.'

Nooning For a place at which a noonday rest was commonly taken, e.g. the creek in VA.

Nooseneck RI Algonquian, probably 'beaver-place-at.'

Nopah Range CA *Pah* is the common Shoshonean word for 'water, spring.' Probably Americans here coined a hybrid name, e.g. No-Water Range.

Noquette WI A French rendering of an Ojibway term; see **De Noc.**

Nora Usually from the woman's name, but under Norwegian influence, e.g. in MN and NB, it is for a place in Norway or a shortening and adaptation of Norway itself.

Norcatur KS Because on the boundary line of **Norton** and **Decatur** counties.

Norco CA From North Corona Land Company.

Norcross A personal name, but in MN coined from H. A. Norton and J. N. Cross, proprietors of the site.

Nord CA German 'north,' but reason for naming unknown.

Norden CA The artificial lake created in 1900 was named Lake Van Norden for Charles Van Norden of the water company; the railroad station and post office dropped Van.

Nordland MN From a district in Norway.

Norfolk From the English county, the first naming being the county in MA (1643), which was later abolished. The present county in MA dates from 1793. Also from the English county are **Norfolk** in VA (1691) and in CT (1738). In NB the town was proposed as **North Fork,** shortened to **Norfork,** but in transmission through the Post Office Dept. it was altered to the common form.

Noria Spanish 'well [of water].'

Norlina NC A coinage from **North Carolina.**

Normahiggin NJ A variant of **Nomahegan.**

Normal As in **Normalville** PA, the name indicates the location of a teachers' training center of the kind once known as a normal school.

Normandy From the French province; in IL, more remotely from the Norman family, from whom the townsite was purchased.

Normanock NJ Algonquian, probably 'fishing-place'; a variant of **Namanock.**

Normans Kill NY From Albert Andriessen, called by the Dutch 'the Norman,' because he was a Norwegian who settled here ca. 1638.

Noroton CT Probably a variant of **Roaton,** q.v.

Norridgewock ME Algonquian, probably 'torrent-descends-at,' but shaped by folk-etymology to the semblance of an English name.

North, Northern, Northeast, etc. All compass-point names, i.e. **South, East, West,** etc. are here considered; though numerous, most of them require no explanation. The adjectival form is rare, but occurs in **Southern Pines** NC, **Western Grove** AR, etc. It is also commonly used for less official descriptive purposes, and some of the usages are well on their way to being crystallized into names, being already generally capitalized, e.g. **Southern California, Western Pennsylvania.** A compass-point name ordinarily distinguishes one of five situations. 1) It distinguishes a position in a group or pair, e.g. **The Southeast Farallon** CA, and the very common distinction of stream-forks as North-South or East-West, as well as with the separation of the Carolinas and Dakotas. **North River** NY was originally so called, in Dutch, in distinction from **South River,** which was the Delaware. 2) It marks the position from the point of view of the namer. **South Mountain** PA, MD: the namer knew the ridge from PA, i.e. the northern side; it should be **North Mountain** for people living in most of MD. **East River** NY: named from the point of view of Manhattan Island; it is a western river for people living on Long Island. 3) It marks the position within the limits of a specified or assumed area. **North East** PA: the borough and township are named from lying at the northeast corner of the county, though they are actually almost at the northwest corner of the state. **Southwest City** MO lies in the extreme corner of the state. 4) The position is distinguished with respect to another place which is usually older or larger and is used without qualification, e.g. **West Virginia,** named at the time of the formation of the state (1863) from Virginia, but with the original state maintaining the unqualified name. A certain telescoping sometimes occurs, e.g. **Westborough** MA which might properly have been **Westmarlborough.** 5) Personal names occur, e.g. **Northfield** MN: for early settlers named North and Field. **Western** NB: for a landowner named West, perhaps also because it was in the western part of the U.S., though not of either the state or the county. Names containing a compass point already 'fixed' are separately considered, e.g. **Northampton.** Among compounds may be noted **South America Lake** CA from its shape. **Westfir** OR: from the Western Lumber Company, a large producer of fir lumber. **East Lynne** MO and probably **East Lynn** in other states, from the novel of that title by Mrs. Henry Wood (1861).

Northampton From the county and city in England, or the title. The county in VA (1634) probably honored the Earl of Northampton, a prominent Royalist. The city in MA (1656) must be assumed to be, after the prevailing custom, from the city in England, but it was at the time the most northerly settlement in that area, so that the name must have been considered partially descriptive. The county in NC was named for James, the third earl.

North Carolina See **Carolina.**

North Dakota See **Dakota.**

Northfield The name exists in England, but the town in MA (1713) was probably named primarily for its northern location in the colony. For **Northfield** in MN, see under **North.**

Northome MN For **North Home,** originally so called as being at the extreme north of the state and the country.

Northumberland From the county of England, etc. Counties in VA (1648) and in PA (1772) are from the English county.

Norton Often from the personal name, e.g. in TX for G. W. and W. F. Norton, landowners. In MA probably for its being the northerly part of **Taunton** from which it was set off (1711), but it also echoes a common name for English villages. **Norton Sound** AK: named (1778) by James Cook for Sir Fletcher Norton, speaker of the House of Commons.

Norumbega A ghost name, appearing on many maps of the 16th and 17th centuries, but not surviving. It covered the general area of Maine. Various forms are Arambe, Oranbego, Anorabega, and even Nuremberg, after the German city. Though an Indian original seems likely (unless the origin is pure fancy), no plausible explanation of its origin and etymology has been presented. It has been occasionally revived, but not in any important way.

Norwalk The original naming was in CT (ca. 1650) from an Indian (Siwanoy) name, probably meaning 'at the point of land,' and appearing as Norwauke or Norwaack. The pronunciation was kept, but the spelling slightly transformed by folk-etymology to suggest either a derivation from 'walk,' or a connection with some town-name in England, where the syllables *nor* and *walk* are of frequent occurrence, though not in the same name.

Norway Generally, e.g. in OR, because of the settlement there of Norwegians; so also, **Norwegian Creek** NB. **Norway** ME: in 1791 the inhabitants petitioned for the name **Norage** which is probably Algonquian (cf. **Norridgewock**), but the petition was returned from the legislature with **Norway.**

Norwich From the city in England, in CT (1659).

Norwood Though it is an English place-name, the examples are chiefly from the personal name, e.g. in NC for the family of the first postmaster. The idea of 'north wood' is sometimes involved, e.g. in NJ. In IL and KS the name is from the title of the novel by H. W. Beecher (1867). In MA the town was incorporated in 1872, and the name was suggested by a man who gave the unusually specific reasons that it 'looked well in print, had a pleasing sound, was easy to write, and had no *i* to dot or *t* to cross.'

Nosahick Lake ME Algonquian 'roiled-water-at.'

Nose Applied descriptively, e.g. **Nose Rock** CA. In **Anthony's Nose** NY it is a quasi-generic, translating the Dutch *neus,* the identity of Anthony remaining uncertain.

Nosodak ND A border name, combining abbreviations of ND and SD.

Nosoni Creek CA Wintu 'pointing south.'

Noster See **Knob.**

Notasulga AL Probably Muskogean, a tribal name (?).

Notch Used, chiefly in New England, as a generic, the equivalent of gap, and so spreading to an occasional specific use, e.g. **Notchland** NH. Elsewhere it is descriptive of a feature marked by what appears to be a notch, e.g. **Notch Peak** UT.

Notla TX A reversed spelling, from the Alton Grocery Company, which operated a store at the site ca. 1890.

Notre French 'our.' See **Dame.**

Nottaway VA From an Indian tribal name.

Nottely River GA Probably from Naduhli, the name of a Cherokee town.

Nottingham From the town, county, or title in England, etc.

Notus ID A railroad name, locally believed to be an 'Indian' phrase, 'It is all right,' but just as likely to be Latin 'well known.'

Not Vaya AZ Papago 'pampas-grass well.'

Novarupta Volcano AK A coined pseudo-Latin name, to mean 'new-eruption,' given in 1916 to denote a newly developed cone.

Novato CA From the name of a local Indian chief who had received a Spanish baptismal name.

Novelty In occasional use for villages, probably from a conscious effort to have an unusual and 'novel' name.

Novi MI Probably from the family name.

Novohrad TX Czechoslovakian 'new-town,' named by immigrants, probably for a town in Bohemia.

Nowata OK Algonquian (Delaware) 'welcome.'

Noxapater Creek MS Choctaw 'bullets-little,' but reference uncertain.

Noxubee River AL, MS Choctaw 'stinking.'

Noyack NY Algonquian 'point'; cf. **Nyack.**

Noyo CA Pomo, the name of a village, of unknown meaning.

Nub, Nubbin, Nubble A quasi-generic applied to small, conical islands or rocks off the coast of ME, sometimes merely as **The Nub,** etc.

Nubanusit NH Algonquian, meaning uncertain.

Nubble, The CA Descriptive of a small projection at the end of a hillslope. See **Nub.**

Nubieber CA A phonetic spelling for **New Bieber,** used by the railroad.

Nucla Named (1904) from 'nucleus' with the idea of its being a center of growth, the common ending *a* being substituted.

Nueces See **Nuez.**

Nuestro, Nuestra Spanish 'our,' chiefly in **Nuestra Senora,** 'Our Lady,' the ordinary appellation of the Virgin Mary, e.g. in the names of many land grants in NM.

Nuevo Spanish 'new,' frequently translated, as in **New Mexico,** but surviving, e.g. **Nuevo** CA.

Nuez Spanish 'nut'; plural, *nueces.* The river in TX was named **Nueces** by the Spanish expedition of 1689, because of the many pecan trees there.

Nugget A gold-miner's term, because of the occurrence of gold in a nugget or nuggets, e.g. the gulch in SD.

Nukacongamoc Pond ME Algonquian 'headwater-lake,' i.e. probably the point beyond which canoeing was no longer possible.

Nulhedus Mountain ME Algonquian 'waterfall-(on)-each-side.'

Nulhegan River VT Algonquian 'my-log-trap,' i.e. the site of an Indian's dead-fall.

Number Used to designate place in a series, e.g. **Island Number 1** KY; commonly abbreviated to **No.**

Numidia PA Being in the center of a county, it was to have been **Media** or **New Media** (see **Media**), but was changed by a play on words to the name of an ancient country of Africa, known from Latin writers.

Nummy NJ Algonquian, from the name of a chief.

Nunathloogagamiutbingoi Dunes AK Eskimo, meaning uncertain; probably (23 letters) the longest single word appearing in U.S. place-names.

Nunda NY Iroquoian, probably 'hilly.'

Nunivak Island AK Eskimo, probably 'big-land,' because it is a large island.

Nunnatucket River RI Algonquian 'dry creek.' Also with the element *nun,* 'dry,' are **Nunnakomac** CT, 'dry land'; **Nun-**naquahgat RI, 'dry meadow.' See **None-quit.**

Nursery TX Because a nursery for fruit trees was established here in 1882.

Nusichiya Creek Muskogean 'line, boundary,' from marking the division between Choctaws and Chickasaws.

Nutria In American-Spanish 'beaver,' e.g. several stream and lake names in NM. **Nutrioso** AZ is the adjective, 'of beavers.'

Nuyaka OK Probably a Creek rendering of New Yorker, a name transferred from AL, and there originating from a treaty which had been concluded in New York.

Nyack NY Algonquian 'point-land,' i.e. land at a point.

Nyala NV Apparently a coined name; being in **Nye Co.,** it is probably to be connected with that name, but it could just as well be from the common abbreviations for two states.

Nylon Peak WY Named (1946) by the first party to ascend the peak, because of their enthusiasm for the newly developed nylon rope that they were using.

Nymph Lake CO In 1864 the type form of a pond lily was found here, and named *Nymphaea polysepala;* the lake took its name from the Anglicized version.

Nyssa In OR a railroad station name, many such being applied merely because they were short, easy to spell, and rare. The name occurs in Greek mythology but no connection has been established. *Nyssa* is the generic name for the tupelo or gum tree, and the name in MO may be thus explainable.

O

Oacoma SD Souian 'place between,' because situated between the river and its bluff.

Oahe SD A shortening of Siouan *titankoahe,* 'place of big house,' so called because a council building once stood there.

Oak Many hundreds of places bear the name of this widely distributed and conspicuous tree, of numerous species. The names indicate the presence of trees or of a single notable example. The oak also suggests permanence, beauty, strength, etc. and has therefore been widely used for commendatory names of towns, streets, subdivisions, etc. Almost all combinations thus appear with '-grove' and '-ville' being especially numerous, along with such double commendatories as **Oak Park** and **Oakdale.** A second specific frequently occurs, generally modifying the tree rather than the generic, e.g. **Big Oak Flat, White Oak Creek. Oakland** CA: the site was known as an *encinal* (oak grove), and the descriptive name was applied at the time of incorporation in 1852, because of the fine growth of live-oaks. The personal name may be involved, as in **Oakland** NB for John Oak, early landowner. Such names as **Oakhurst** and **Oakley** are generally from personal names, but some, e.g. **Oakham** MA, were taken from English villages. **Oaks Lake** MN: the rare plural form results probably from the original name, **Lake of the Oaks. Oak Cane Branch** GA: from Daniel O'Cain, landowner, ca. 1765.

Oakalla TX Locally believed to be for **Oak Valley,** but altered somewhere in transmission.

Oakchia AL From an Indian tribal name.

Oakfuskee AL Muskogean (Creek), a term meaning a point between streams; transferred in OK as **Okfuskee.**

Oakland See **Oak.**

Oakmulgee See **Okmulgee.**

Oaknolia LA Named (1911) by combining 'oak' and 'magnolia,' for the trees here.

Oakohay Creek MS Choctaw, from *oka,* 'water,' and the rest uncertain.

Oaktark, Bayou Muskogean, from a term for an abandoned beaver pond.

Oaktibbee, Oaktibbeha See **Oktibbeha.**

Oark AR Probably a variation of Ozark, to avoid duplication.

Oasis As a place-name in its usual sense, meaning a fertile area in a desert region, so used in CA, NM, and UT.

Oat(s) Rare, but occasionally for the cultivated grain, e.g. **Oatspatch Hollow** KY. In CA the common wild oat has given rise to some 20 names, e.g. **Oat Hill.** Some names may be from the personal name **Oates.**

Obar, O Bar From a brand.

Obed From the Old Testament name; in AZ probably a Mormon naming from a character in the *Book of Mormon.*

Obelisk Occasionally, because of the suggestion of the shape of an obelisk in a formation, e.g. the mountain in CA.

Oberlin In PA and OH the name is from Jean F. Oberlin, Alsatian preacher and philanthropist; the other names are probably secondarily derived.

Oberon ND V. H. Matthews, who was appointed postmaster in 1886, selected the name from Shakespeare's *Midsummer Night's Dream.*

Obert NB Originally it was **Oberton** from a personal name. Confusion with a place named **Overton** led to the dropping of the *on.*

Obi Point AZ Paiute 'pinyon.'

Obrazo Creek MO From Brazeau, the name of a pioneer French family, probably with *au* or *aux* prefixed, thus approximately, 'at the Brazeaus' place.'

O'Brien From the personal name, the county in IA being for James O'Brien (1805–1864), Irish patriot.

Observatory, Observation Because of the presence of an astronomical observatory, e.g. **Observatory Point** CA, where actually the observatory was only projected. Sometimes merely because the peak was used as a lookout, e.g. **Observation Peak** CA for a triangulation point.

Obsidian Descriptive, for the occurrence of obsidian, i.e. natural glass.

Obumkeag River ME Algonquian 'sucker (fish)-place.'

Obwebetuck See **Ocquebituck.**

Ocala FL From the name of an ancient Timucua town and province, recorded in a Spanish context in 1539; meaning unknown.

Ocapos AZ By reversing, in reverse order, the first two letters of each of the words in the Southern Pacific Company.

Ocate NM Probably from Mexican-Spanish 'white pine.'

Occanum NY Probably Iroquoian, meaning uncertain.

Occapaspatucket Cove RI Algonquian, probably 'cove-(on)-shallow-(tidal)-river-at.'

Occidental Used as the equivalent of 'western,' e.g. the town in CA, situated not far from the Pacific Ocean and therefore about as far west as possible.

Occoneechee NC, VA From an Indian tribal name. Also as **Occaneeche, Occaneechi, Occanuchee.**

Occoquan VA Algonquian 'hooked-inlet' (?).

Occum CT For Samson Occum (1723–1792), a well-known Indian preacher.

Ocean Usually a commendatory name for seaside resorts, e.g. **Ocean Beach, Ocean Park, Oceanside,** etc.

Oceana The form results from an attempt to render 'ocean' (or the Latin *oceanus*) in a feminine form, such being considered more suitable for town-names. The town in VA is on the ocean. In WV the name is probably from Ocie Anna Cooke. The county in MI is named because it fronts on Lake Michigan, as if on the ocean.

Oceda SC Locally believed to be an adaptation of the nearby Cedar Creek. Since the name appears to be Indian, the transference may have been in the other direction, the first part representing Muskogean *oka,* 'water.'

Ocelichee Creek AL Muskogean, probably Creek, meaning uncertain.

Oceola OH From an alternate spelling of **Osceola.**

Ocheeda See **Okshida.**

Ocheesee FL Probably Seminole 'hickory-leaf.'

Ochelata OK The Indian name of Charles Thompson, Cherokee chief from 1875 to 1879.

Ocheyedan See **Okshida.**

Ochilee Creek GA Muskogean (Creek) 'sleeping' (?), i.e. for a stream that was a regular camping place on a trail.

Ochlockonee FL, GA Muskogean (Hitchiti) 'water-yellow,' first applied to the river.

Ochoco Creek OR For a local Indian chief of that name.

Ochopee FL Probably Seminole 'hickory-tree.'

Ochwalkee Creek GA Muskogean (Creek) 'water-dirty.'

Ocilla GA A variant of **Aucilla.**

Ockanicon NJ Algonquian, the name of a chief who died in 1681.

Ocklau Creek GA Muskogean (Creek), probably 'muddy.'

Ockoogangansett Hill MA Algonquian, probably 'plantation-at.'

Ocmulgee See **Okmulgee.**

Ocoee TN Cherokee 'apricot-vine-place.' **Ocoee** FL and **Okoee** OK are transfers.

Oconaluftee River NC Cherokee 'near-river' (?); if this translation is correct, the original name was probably that of a village.

Oconee Muskogean, probably with *oc-*, meaning 'water, stream.' The rest of the name is doubtful. It occurs in SC and GA, in one instance being the name of a town, which was in turn transferred to OK. In NB the name is late, and is borrowed from an older occurrence. In IL the name is doubtful.

Oconomowoc WI Algonquian 'beaver-dam.'

Oconto WI Algonquian (Menominee) 'pike-place.'

Ocoonita VA Probably Indian, meaning uncertain.

Ocosta WA Coined (ca. 1891) from Spanish *costa,* 'coast,' with *o* prefixed for euphony.

Ocotillo From the presence of the type of cactus thus known.

Ocoya IL Uncertain; probably the artificial reworking of some original Indian term.

Ocquebituck, Obwebetuck CT Algonquian, meaning uncertain.

Ocqueoc MI Algonquian 'sacred-water' (?), with possible reference to an Indian ceremony.

Ocquittunk, Lake NJ Algonquian 'swine (?)-place.'

Ocracoke NC Algonquian, first recorded (1585) as Wocokon, probably from a term meaning 'curve, bend,' from the shape of the island.

Ocran VA Probably Algonquian, meaning uncertain.

Octa OH For Miss Octa Barnes, not further identified.

Octahatchee FL Seminole 'sand-stream.'

Octave AZ The mining site was claimed by eight men, and thus named.

Octorara MD Iroquoian (Tuscarora), meaning uncertain.

Odanah WI Algonquian (Ojibway) 'town, village.'

Odart Mountain AZ A brand name, i.e. O-dart.

Odd In WV the name was established at a meeting, after a suggestion that the name should be a very odd one.

Odebolt IA From Odebeau, the name of a French trapper who lived on the stream ca. 1855.

Odense From the city of Denmark, e.g. in KS and ND.

Odessa The Russian city on the Black Sea had a large reputation in the 19th century as a wheat-shipping port, and for commendatory reasons the name was placed upon towns, e.g. in DE, MD, TX, which fancied themselves as wheat centers. The lake in CO was named by W. J. Workman, local lodgekeeper, for his daughter, ca. 1900.

Odin From the Germanic god, usually placed by Scandinavian settlers.

Odyssey Peak WY From an article, 'Wind River Odyssey' (1949), describing the region.

Oeneis, Mount WY Because a scientific group collected here a fine specimen of a butterfly of this genus.

Ofahoma MS Choctaw, with *homa,* 'red,' and the rest uncertain.

Ogallala, Ogallah, Oglala From the Indian tribal name.

Ogden From the personal name. In UT the city is from the river, which took its name from Peter Skene Ogden, of the Hudson's Bay Company, who explored the region in the 1820's.

Ogechie Lake MN Ojibway 'worm,' because of its twisted shape.

Ogeechee River GA Probably a variant of the tribal name **Uchee.**

Ogema WI Adopted as a name by Americans, ca. 1880, who heard some Indians using the word; probably Algonquian 'chief,' although the Americans took it as a personal name. Also as **Ogemaw.**

Ogemaga Lake WI Algonquian, meaning uncertain, but see **Ogema.**

Ogemaw See **Ogema.**

Ogishke Muncie Lake MN Ojibway 'kingfisher.'

Ogle From the personal name, e.g. the county in IL for Capt. Joseph Ogle, pioneer and Indian fighter.

Ogontz In MI the bay is from Algonquian for a kind of herring.

Ogunquit ME Algonquian, uncertain, but probably referring to a lagoon formed behind dunes.

Ohatchee AL Muskogean (Creek), with *hatchee,* 'stream,' and *o,* probably 'upper.'

Ohayo Mountain NY Uncertain; suspiciously like a disguised spelling of **Ohio.**

Oh-Be-Joyful Gulch CO Probably a miner's name of the rare exclamation type, the phrase generally having a bibulous suggestion.

Ohimis Lake WI Algonquian (Ojibway), meaning uncertain.

Ohio Iroquoian 'river-fine,' the *-io* (cf. **Ontario)** is a vague term of commendation, 'fine, good, beautiful.' The name appears first in a French context, and the French regularly translated it as *belle rivière,* sometimes attributing it to the Iroquois. French usage applied the name to the part of the river now known as **Allegheny,** as well as to the part now known as **Ohio.** The progression of the name is what may be called normal, viz. river-district-county-(in VA)-territory-state.

Ohiopyle PA Algonquian (Delaware) 'white-foam,' with reference to water flowing over rocks. The resemblance to **Ohio,** which is Algonquian, is chiefly coincidental, though the lesser name would naturally be attracted to the greater name in form.

Ohiowa NB Because settlers had come in about equal numbers from Ohio and from Iowa, the two names were combined.

Ohisa Creek NY Iroquoian, probably 'nettles,' another form of the word seen in **Oriskany.**

Ohomowauke Swamp ME Algonquian 'owl-place.'

Ohoopee River GA Indian, language and meaning uncertain.

Ohop WA Indian, meaning unknown.

Oie French 'goose,' e.g. **Bayou des Oies** LA.

Oil Evidences of petroleum have caused the naming of some natural features, e.g. **Oil Springs.** Most of the names spring from the oil industry. The name has been planted on natural features because of the discovery of oil there (or the hoped-for discovery), and also is common as a habitation-name, e.g. **Oil City, Oilfield, Oil Center. Oil Trough** AR: the name antedates the use of petroleum; by local tradition it is derived from an early industry of the preparation of grease or oil from the fat of bears, but the data are not well established.

Ojai CA Chumash 'moon,' but reason for application unknown; it was the name of an Indian village.

Ojalla Creek OR From a Finnish personal name, probably for an early settler.

Ojibway From the Indian tribal name.

Ojo Spanish 'eye,' but in place-names usually meaning 'spring, source of water.'

A generic in Spanish, it can be a specific in English and occurs as a habitation-name, e.g. **Ojo** CA, **Ojo Caliente** TX. The diminutive occurs, e.g. **Los Ojitos** NM.

Ojus FL Probably Seminole 'plentiful,' with possible reference to vegetation.

OK See **Okay.**

Oka MT. WV Probably for O.K.

Okahatta Creek Choctaw 'water-white.'

Okahumpka FL Muskogean 'water-bitter' (?).

Okaloacoochee Slough FL Muskogean, probably 'water-bad-little.'

Okaloosa FL, LA Muskogean 'water-black'; in LA also the name of an Indian tribe.

Okaman MN Siouan 'heron nests.'

Okanogan WA From an Indian tribal name.

Okapilco Creek GA Muskogean (Creek), probably 'water-swamp-big,' i.e. a stream associated with a big swamp.

Okarche OK Coined from the first syllables of Oklahoma, Arapaho, and Cheyenne (1890).

Okatibbee See **Oktibbeha.**

Okatoma Creek MS Choctaw, from *oka,* 'water,' and the rest uncertain.

Okaton SD Souian, meaning uncertain.

Okatuppa Creek AL Choctaw 'water-dammed.'

Okauchee WI Algonquian, with the idea of 'small' (?).

Okaw In MO, French *aux Kaws,* 'at the Kaws,' i.e. the Indians of that tribe. In IL it is from *aux Kas,* the reference here being to the Kaskaskia tribe, which was commonly abbreviated to Ka.

Okay, OK From the colloquial affirmative, but sometimes, e.g. in OR, from a brand. In OK from the OK Truck Manufacturing Company.

Okeana OH A late name (1858), it is locally believed to be for an Indian princess of the region, but may be a coined name.

Okee WI Algonquian 'land,' probably a shortening of some longer name.

Okeechobee FL Muskogean (Hitchiti) 'water-big.'

Okeeffe WV Apparently from the family name O'Keeffe.

Okeelanta FL Coined from Muskogean *oka,* 'water, lake,' and *lanta* from Atlantic, because it is near a lake and the ocean.

Okeene OK From Oklahoma, and the final letters of Cherokee and Cheyenne.

Okeetee SC An Indian term, locally taken to mean 'place of bright waters.' The first part is probably Muskogean *oka,* 'water.'

Okefenokee Swamp FL Muskogean (Hichiti) 'water-shaking,' probably because of quicksands and swamps.

Okemah OK From the personal name of an Indian who was a friend of the town founder.

Okemo Mountain VT Algonquian, meaning uncertain.

Okemos MI Algonquian 'chief-little,' a diminutive of **Ogema.**

Oketo KS Named (1870) for Arkaketah, an Oto chief, but shortened for convenience by later local usage.

Okfuskee See **Oakfuskee.**

Okhakonkonhee, Lake FL Muskogean 'water-big-crooked' (?).

Okhumpka, Lake FL Seminole 'water-one,' probably with the idea of an isolated lake.

Okisko NC From a local Indian chief, date uncertain.

Oklahoma Muskogean (Choctaw) 'people-red,' a coined name, proposed in 1866 by Allen Wright, a Choctaw chief, to designate the land held by his tribe in what was then vaguely known as the Indian Territory. It was so adopted in the Choctaw-Chickasaw treaty of 1866. In 1881 the name was used for a railroad station, which has since become Oklahoma City, and has also produced Oklahoma Co. The name thus lost its restriction to the Choctaw lands, and was passed on to the territory and thence to the state.

Oklarado CO A boundary-name between CO and OK.

Oklaunion TX From an abbreviation for OK and 'union,' given at a time when the railroad was about to bring the site into communication with the other state.

Oklawaha FL On two streams the name is Seminole 'muddy, boggy.'

Oklee MN For Ole K. Lee, on whose farm the village was founded.

Okmulgee Muskogean (Hichiti) 'water-bubbles (boils),' probably first applied to a spring; originally a name in GA, transferred to OK. In GA it is Ocmulgee.

Okobojo SD Siouan 'planting-in-spaces,' probably with reference to some kind of agriculture, the word being in the Santee dialect, i.e. in a branch of the Sioux which cultivated crops. Okoboji IA is a variant.

Okoee A variant of Ocoee.

Okoloma MS Choctaw, from oka, 'water,' and the rest uncertain.

Okolona AR, MS, OH Muskogean, probably a variant of Okoloma, but in OH partially suggested by the presence of fine oaks. In KY the name was Lone Oak, and was changed, probably on the analogy of the other towns, to avoid duplication within the state.

Okonoko WV Although looking Indian, it has not been analyzed as such, and is probably a manufactured name, made to resemble an Indian name. Note that it is a palindrome.

Okra TX Named by a local resident because okra grew well there.

Okreek SD An adaptation of Oak Creek, from a nearby stream.

Okshida, Ocheeda, Ocheyedan IA, MN The different streams thus named all represent the same Siouan word, which has to do with mourning and arose because two boys were killed in the vicinity in some war between Indian tribes.

Oktaha OK A shortening of Oktahasars, the personal name of a Creek chief in the Civil War period.

Oktibbeha MS Choctaw, with oka, 'stream,' and the rest uncertain. Tippo MS is probably a variant.

Ola From its use as a Scandinavian man's name (e.g. in SD); elsewhere (e.g. in AR) probably from a woman's name. As a suffix or quasi-generic, it appears (e.g. Indianola) apparently without much sense of meaning but merely as a euphonic element, suggestive of Latin or Spanish, offering the a-ending which is favored for habitation-names. In the SE, e.g. Ola AL, it may be from Muskogean ola, 'on this side of.'

Olalla, Olallie OR, WA Chinook jargon, 'berry.' Olele Point WA is probably the same.

Olamon ME Algonquian 'vermilion,' q.v.

Olancha CA From an Indian tribal name.

Olathe KS From Algonquian (Shawnee) 'fine, beautiful,' so named, according to local story, from a Shawnee's ejaculation when he saw the site.

Old Several hundred names contain Old, either as a separate word (Old Harbor) or joined (Oldfort), though joining is rare. In double-specific names (Old Woman Mountains CA), the first specific usually modifies the second. Old is rarely used on features, and generally in the sense of 'former,' as in Old River LA, a branch of the stream once the main one but now largely bypassed. It may carry a sentimental, commendatory value as in **Old Baldy** (peak, CA) and **Old Faithful** (geyser, WY). On habitations there is an occasional family name or English town-name, e.g. **Oldham.** Many names are from man-made features, existing either in ruins or in memory, e.g. **Old Bridge** NJ, **Old Forge** PA, **Old Diggings** CA. **Old Field** is generally a reference to an Indian old-field. When a town moves to a new location retaining the original name, the original settlement is often distinguished by the prefixing of 'old,' e.g. **Old Mystic** CT, **Old Oraibi** AZ. **Old Sun Mountain** MT: from the name of a Blackfoot Indian. **Old Man Mountain** MT: from the name of the chief of the Blackfoot gods; the name was bestowed by the tribal council, as being significant, because this was the highest mountain in Glacier N. P. So also **Oldman Mountain** CO because of a profile on its slope. **Old Maid:** the conventional 19th-century term for a middle-aged or elderly unmarried woman (slightly opprobrious) was sometimes applied, e.g. **Old Maid's Draw** WY for Miss Myrtle Dawson, who lived there ca. 1910 to 1920. **Old Glory** A patriotic name, to honor the American flag. The town in TX was originally Brandenburg, named by German settlers. It was renamed in 1917 by petition of the inhabitants.

Old Man of the Mountain NH As also with **Old Man Mountain** AZ, convention seems to demand that a natural stone face should be designated as 'old,' even though the features may not suggest old age. The idea may be that the face, being as old as the rock, is thus ancient.

Oldmans Creek NJ From the early Swedish name Aldermans Kijlen.

Olean NY For Olean Shephard, first white child born in the town, 1807.

Olele Point WA See **Olalla.**

Olema CA From an Indian tribal name, probably connected with Miwok 'coyote.'

Olena IL, OH Uncertain; a variant of **Olean** (?).

Olentangy River OH Algonquian 'paint-from-there,' because the red pigment

used for face paint was found there. Cf. **Vermillion.**

Olequa WA Indian, meaning uncertain.

Oleta From a personal name, e.g. in OK for Oleta Morris, wife of the first postmaster.

Oleum CA The site of an oil refinery, coined by dropping the first four letters of 'petroleum.'

Olex OR For Alex Smith, a local resident, but misspelled in transmission.

Oley PA Algonquian (Delaware) 'hole, valley.'

Olinda CA Originally a Portuguese name and title, transferred to Hawaii and then to CA, probably liked because of its euphony.

Olive, Olivet, Mount Olive, Mount Olivet In the New Testament the Mount of Olives is once mentioned as Olivet. Most occurrences of the name are from this source. In CA, however, several habitation-names are from the fruit. The personal name may also be involved. **Mount Olive** is the common way of rendering the Biblical Mount of Olives, e.g. in MS where it is taken from an early Presbyterian church on a hill. The spelling **Olivette** occurs in NC.

Olivo Spanish 'olive,' e.g. **Los Olivos** CA because of extensive plantings of olive trees there ca. 1890.

Ollala Creek WA Chinook jargon, 'berries.'

Olmitz KS, IA An Americanized version of Olmütz, the German name of the present city Olomouc in Czechoslovakia, so named by immigrants from that region.

Olmo Spanish 'elm.'

Olompali CA From an Indian tribal name.

Olpe KS For the city in Germany, so named by immigrants from that region.

Olsburg KS So named for Ole Thrulson, early settler, i.e. Ole's town.

Olustee In AL from Muskogean (Creek), meaning 'water-black.' In FL, from Seminole-Creek, probably with the same meaning. In OK, a transfer from AL.

Olympia, Olympus From the idea of the home of the Greek gods. In 1788 John Meares, English voyager, fancifully gave the name **Mount Olympus** WA to a tall peak. That name has spread to the **Olympic Peninsula,** and the city **Olympia.** Namings elsewhere are less specific, but seem to be from the Greek mountain, as is certainly true for **Mount Olympus** CO, named ca. 1873.

Oma MS Probably from Muskogean *homa,* 'red,' the shortening of some longer name.

Omagaar Creek CA Yurok, meaning unknown.

Omaha From the tribal name, recorded in a French context as early as 1673. The French usually rendered the name as Maha, and the modern name may have originated from the phrase *aux Mahas,* i.e. 'to or at the Maha.' But there is also justification for the actual tribal name being rendered as Omaha.

Omak WA Indian, meaning uncertain.

Omal OH A coinage, from an aluminum plant operated here by the Olin Mathieson Chemical Corporation, viz. *o* and *m* from Olin Mathieson, and *al* from aluminum.

Omega From the last letter of the Greek alphabet, used with the idea of being the last, often as a counterpart to **Alpha** as in CA, ID, OK. Also known from the Biblical book of *Revelation,* and thus named in NB, because the place was the last on the mail route.

Omemee ND Ojibway 'pigeon, dove,' but named for a town in Canada by an immigrant.

Omena MI Algonquian 'he gives to him,' but significance uncertain.

Omenoku CA Yurok, probably 'where it projects,' and therefore a suitable name for a headland.

Omjumi Mountain CA Maidu *Om-,* probably meaning 'rock,' but the rest of the word unknown.

Omlee NM From initials and name of O. M. Lee, ranchowner.

Ompompanoosuc VT Algonquian 'quaking-land.'

Omps WV From the family who owned the building where the first post office was located.

Omussee Creek AL From the tribal name, commonly occurring as Yamassee.

Onaga KS The name of a Potawatomi Indian, picked from a list of names because the namer, a railroad president, liked it. The original spelling (Onago) was shifted for euphony.

Onahu Creek CO Arapaho 'warms-himself,' the name of an Indian race horse which died near this stream.

Onaka SD Siouan, meaning uncertain.

Onalaska In 1851 T. G. Rowe, town founder and lover of poetry, gave the name in WI from the line in Thomas Campbell's *Pleasures of Hope* (with slight change in spelling), 'The wolf's long howl from Oonalaska's shore.' Rowe later became widely interested in lumbering, and bestowed the same name on places in AR, TX, and WA where his company operated.

Onamia MN Ojibway, of uncertain meaning.

Onan VA Probably a shortening from some Algonquian name, such as **Onancock.**

Onancock VA From an Algonquian tribal or village name.

Onaqui Mountains UT Gosiute 'salt-at,' probably with reference to nearby salt flats.

Onarga IL Uncertain, probably the artificial reworking of some Indian name.

Onawa See **Onaway.**

Onaway MI Algonquian (Ojibway) 'Awaken!' taken from Longfellow's Hiawatha; shortened to **Onawa** in IA and ME.

Onchiota NY Iroquoian 'rainbow,' a name given to a railroad station in the 19th century.

One, Two, etc. Numeral names in general (but see **First**) are treated under this heading, except that special entries are provided for some of the higher numbers, e.g. **Forty Fort, Ninety-Six.** Numerals may be considered descriptive. By themselves they produce a collective name, e.g. **The Three Sisters** (mountains, OR), from which the individual peaks can be separated as **The North Sister,** etc. So also, **Two Lakes, Four Gables** (mountain, CA). With **Forks** the common reference is to the meeting of roads or trails, but the term may indicate a stream junction, as in **Three Forks** CA. The common **Five Points** also springs from lines of communication. Numerals occur also as double specifics, e.g. **Twocone Point** AK, **Two Ocean Glacier** MT, the latter because it drains into both the Atlantic and the Pacific. The most frequent use is in combination with **Mile.** The omission of **Mile** for brevity may sometimes leave the numeral standing alone. The names also arise from incidents, e.g. **Three Lynx Creek** OR, because an early settler saw three wildcats. **The Three Brothers** CA: though a group of three peaks, the name springs from the capture there of three Indians who were brothers. Indian personal names may be involved, e.g. **Three Bears Lake** MT. Round numbers such as **Ten,** and lucky or commendatory numbers such as **Seven** and **Twelve** are likely to occur in habitation-names, e.g. **Seven Oaks** CA.

Oneco In CT from the name of a Mohegan chief; other uses of the name, including **Onego** WV, are probably from this one.

Onego See **Oneco.**

One Hundred and Forty Mile Creek KS From the distance as measured from the beginning of the Santa Fe Trail.

One Hundred and Two River MO A translation of French **Cent Deux,** which is probably by folk-etymology from an Indian term *çondse,* 'upland forest.'

Oneida From the Indian tribal name. In ID it is probably from the Oneida Mine (1874).

Onekama MI Algonquian 'arm,' but perhaps in a figurative sense, as a geographical term.

Oneonta NY Iroquoian 'stony-place.'

Onida SD A simplified spelling of **Oneida,** for which town in NY it was named.

Onion Though avoided in habitation-names, the wild onion has given its name to various features, especially springs.

Ono Several places bear the name of the town merely mentioned without further identification in one passage of the Bible (I Chron. 8:12). The settlers in CA adopted this name in 1883 at the suggestion of a minister, but at that time other places had already been so named. A certain sense of mystery was probably involved in this choice, and also some humor, because of the suggestion, 'Oh, no!'

Onogariske Creek NY Iroquoian 'hickory' (?).

Onondaga From the Indian tribal name.

Onoshahatchee Creek FL Seminole 'otter-stream.'

Onoto WV Probably from the pseudonym Onoto Watanna of Mrs. W. E. Babcock, who wrote popular works with a Japanese setting ca. 1900.

Ontario Iroquoian 'lake-fine.' For political reasons the French called the lake **Frontenac** for one of the governors of Canada, but the English used the present name, and it was established as the result of their victory. In CA the town was named by G. B. Chaffey in 1882 for his home province in Canada.

On the Trees Creek SD From an Indian personal name.

Ontonagon MI, WI Ojibway, probably meaning a place where game was shot by guess (i.e. without being seen), and arising from some such lucky incident.

Ontwa MI For an Indian who worked as a servant in a house where the representative of this district boarded in Detroit.

Onuck NY Algonquian 'bend,' a descriptive of the neck of land thus designated.

Onyx The name was chosen in CA, according to local story, because it was short and unique, probably meaning that it was not then in the Postal Guide. There is now another **Onyx** in AR. The name may be from the stone or from a personal name.

Oolah Mountain AK Named (1932) because it looked like an *oolah*, i.e. an Eskimo tool for scraping hides.

Oolitic IN From the kind of limestone quarried here.

Oologah OK The personal name of a Cherokee chief.

Ooltewah TN Cherokee 'resting-place' (?).

Ooskan Butte OR Chinook jargon, 'cup,' for its crater, named by the Forest Service.

Oostanaula River GA Cherokee 'place-of-rocks-across-stream,' probably indicating a ford.

Oostburg WI Named ca. 1846 by Dutch settlers, probably for a place in the Netherlands, though the literal meaning is 'east-burg.'

Ooten From the family name, e.g. **Ootens Store** KY. **Ootan Branch** KY is apparently a variant.

Oothkalooga Creek GA Cherokee 'beaver-dam.'

Opal From a personal name, or for a place where opal-like pebbles are found, e.g. **Opal Springs** OR.

Opa Locka FL Seminole 'swamp-big.'

Opcatkontycke Brook NY Algonquian, with *tycke*, probably 'stream,' and the rest uncertain.

Opechee ME, MI, NH Algonquian 'robin,' taken from Longfellow's *Hiawatha.*

Opelika AL From the name of an Indian village, literal meaning (Creek), 'swamp-big.'

Opelousas LA From an Indian tribal name, the final *s* representing a French plural.

Open In occasional use to indicate a feature, usually a water feature, which in some sense is open, generally to passage, e.g. **Open Bay** AK, **Open Fork** KY.

Opequon VA Algonquian 'white-pool-stream.'

Ophir From the land mentioned in the Bible as being rich in gold; given because of this suggestion of riches, especially of gold. Five such towns were founded in CA, and thus commendatorily named during the period of gold-mining.

Opinikaning Lake WI Algonquian 'potato (wild)-place.'

Opintlocco Creek AL Muskogean (Creek) 'swamp-big.'

Opolis KS From Greek *polis,* 'city,' the *o* apparently being conceived as a part of the word because of its occurrence in such compounds as **Kanopolis.**

Opossum Widespread over the southern U.S., the oppossum has given rise to many of features, but has been generally avoided for habitations except for a few informal neighborhood names, e.g. **Possumtown** KY. The name has thus been passed over, probably, because the animal is considered plebeian and quite unheroic. **Possum** represents the almost universal pronunciation, and it still survives in many spellings, though steamroller methods of government mapmakers have tended to replace it. Though now prevalent in CA, the animal is a recent introduction, and has not given rise to names.

Opportunity Used, rarely, as a commendatory name.

Opposition Creek CO By local story, because a boulder here opposed the digging of a ditch.

Optima, Optimo, Optimus Commendatory habitation-names, representing different forms of Latin 'best.'

Oquaga NY Iroquoian, meaning uncertain, probably the same as **Ouaguaga.**

Oquawka IL Probably Algonquian (Sauk) 'yellow-earth,' with reference to the shoreline still known as **Yellow Banks.**

Oquirrh Mountains UT Gosiute 'wooded-mountain.'

Ora Presumably for the woman's name, short and easy to spell, and so favored by railroads.

Orab, Mount OH Sometimes spelled **Oreb,** and so probably for the rock of that name mentioned in the Old Testament, but possibly, because of its coupling with **Mount,** a variant of **Horeb.**

Oracle AZ From a mine, in turn named from the ship *The Oracle* in which the mine owner had voyaged around Cape Horn.

Orafino NB A misspelling for *orofino,* Spanish 'fine gold,' because pyrite, thought to be gold, was found here.

Oral SD Probably a personal name, locally explained as having been that of a son of the first postmaster.

Oralabor IA Uncertain, but suggestive of a commendatory from the Latin 'pray-(and)-work.'

Oran 1) From the city of Algeria, in MO named by a retired sea captain who had once touched there. 2) From a personal name, e.g. in TX for Oran M. Roberts, governor of the state from 1879 to 1883.

Orange 1) From the title Prince of Orange, which King William III brought into the English royal family, e.g. the town in MA, counties in NY, NC, VA. **Orangeburg** (Co. and town in SC): for William, Prince of Orange, son-in-law of George II. The three towns known as **The Oranges** NJ may be thus derived in the Dutch period, since Prince of Orange was a Dutch title, but an Indian personal or tribal name of the region is recorded as Auronge in 1645, and these names are probably derived by folk-etymology from this. 2) From the fruit, especially in areas of commercial cultivation, e.g. CA, FL, TX, where it has commendatory value. 3) By description, from the color, e.g. **Orange Butte** AZ. 4) From the personal name, e.g. **Orangeville** UT, for Orange Seeley, early settler.

Oranoken Creek NJ Algonquian, meaning uncertain.

Oraphum Creek WA For a local Indian chief.

Orbisonia PA A Latinization from T. E. Orbison, early landowner.

Orcal OR A boundary-name from OR and CA.

Orcas Island WA From Horcasitas (shortened at both ends), one of the many names of the viceroy Revillagigedo (see **Guemes**). The shift of the name may have been aided by the fact that *orca* means 'grampus' in Spanish.

Orchard A descriptive because of the presence of an orchard, but usually with habitation-names for commendatory purposes, because of the pleasing suggestions of fruit. **Port Orchard** WA: named by George Vancouver in 1792 for H. M. Orchard, ship's clerk.

Orderville UT Because of its establishment by Mormons of the United Order.

Ordinary The common name in the 18th century for a tavern or inn, it has been preserved as an occasional habitation-name, e.g. MD, VA. It occurs sometimes as a second element, e.g. **Jennings Ordinary** VA, **Smoky Ordinary** VA.

Ore An occasional commendatory for real or supposed mineral deposits, e.g. **Ore City** TX. See **Oreana.**

Oreana It may have been suggested by the poetic Oriana and influenced by the Spanish *orejana,* 'unbranded (female) calf,' but is probably a commendatory from 'ore,' also Spanish *oro,* e.g. in the mining districts of ID and NV. See **Ore, Oro.**

Oregon The most disputed of U.S. names. Many of the theories have been highly fanciful. The serious attempt to derive it from an Algonquian (especially Ojibway or Cree) word referring to a plate or bark dish meets difficulties in view of the fact that such a name is improbable, not being in accord with known Indian habits of naming. I here abide by the theory, which I first presented in 1944, viz., that the name is from a mistake on a French map of 1715 (see the 'Ornament' issue of the Baron Lahontan's *Nouveaux Voyages*). Mistake names are a recognizable category of place-names; cf. **Bogata, Nome,** and others. This map was carelessly engraved. The name of the **Wisconsin River** was usually spelled Ouisconsink by the French, but the engraver made it Ouariconsint. Moreover, for lack of space, he put *sint* below, so that the name appears to be Ouaricon. This name was associated in later documents with an alleged great river flowing to the Pacific, and was then spelled Ouragon, Ourgan, and Ourigan. It finally appeared as **Oregon** in the work of Jonathan Carver (1778). After the discovery of the **Columbia River,** this was generally supposed to be the **Oregon,** and the name was then applied to the country in its vicinity and later to the territory and state.

Oreja Spanish 'ear,' e.g. **Tres Orejas** NM, three peaks thought to resemble coyote ears.

Orejano Spanish 'maverick.'

Orem UT For W. C. Orem, builder of a local electric railroad.

Orestimba Creek CA Costanoan *ores,* 'bear (the animal),' but the rest of the word unknown. Locally known by folk-etymology as **Orris Timbers Creek.**

Orestod CO A reversed spelling of **Dotsero,** because it is at the other end of a line of railroad.

Oretown OR A shortening from **Oregontown.**

Orford In NH (1761) for the Earl of Orford, probably the first earl (see **Walpole). Port Orford** OR is from the cape thus named by George Vancouver (1792) for the then earl.

Organ Formations resembling the pipes of an organ have given rise to **Organ Cave** WV and **Organ Mountains** NM, and by transfer have become habitation-names. The cactus has given its name to **Organ Pipe Cactus National Monument** AZ.

Orick CA From an Indian tribe or village in Yurok territory, meaning unknown.

Orient Names have been given either with the idea of 'eastern,' or as vague commendatories with the idea of 'richness.' In the latter sense, mines have been so named, and **Orient** WA thus derives. **Orient** TX is from a local railroad. **Orient** ME is located at the eastern boundary of the state, and therefore of the U.S. **Orienta** OK is from a railroad, with the addition of *a* to suggest a place-name.

Orillia WA From a town in Canada, named by an immigrant.

Orinda CA The name is apparently a poetic coinage of the 16th century, and had some currency in England in the 17th century when the poetess Katherine Fowler Philips was known as 'the matchless Orinda.' The reason for its application in CA (ca. 1880) is not known, but the euphony of the name may have been a factor, as well as the suggestion of the Spanish *oro,* names having to do with gold always having been popular in CA.

Oriska ND From the name of an Indian princess in a poem by Lydia Sigourney.

Oriskany NY Iroquoian 'nettles.'

Orland In ME of uncertain origin. In CA probably a commendatory shortening of 'orange-land' since citrus fruits were grown in the area.

Orlando From the personal name. e.g. in FL for Orlando Reeves, a soldier killed here by Indians in 1835.

Orleans From the city of France and the title, often with reference to **New Orleans**, e.g. in CA from an original **New Orleans Bar**. In IN, named in 1815, in celebration of the recent victory over the British. In MA for Louis Philippe, Duke of Orleans, named in 1797, when he visited the U.S.

Orlovista FL From nearby **Orlando** and the Spanish *vista*.

Orma WV Named in 1905 for Orma Stalnaker, unidentified.

Oro Spanish 'gold.' Because of the Spanish background this term became well known during the California gold rush, and occurs in such hybrids as **Oroville** CA, WA. Repeated names are **Oro Fino** and **Oro Grande**, i.e. 'fine-gold' and 'coarse-gold,' to indicate the type of diggings.

Orono ME For Joseph Orono, 'the blue-eyed chief,' who was a friend to the Americans in the Revolution; he was largely of French blood, and his name may not be from an Indian language.

Oronoco, Oronogo A variant spelling of the name of the South American river, usually Orinoco. In MN the name was given by settlers who lived on a large river, and were interested in developing water power. **Oronogo** MO is probably another variant. Some of the spellings suggest an origin from Thomas Southerne's often-staged tragedy *Oroonoko*.

Oronogo See **Oronoco**.

Orosi CA The first part is Spanish *oro*, with reference to fields of yellow poppies; the last part of the name may be merely the English 'See!'

Orovada NV From a mine-name, formed from Spanish *oro*, 'gold,' and a part of the state-name.

Orowac Brook NY Algonquian 'wild (uninhabited)-land.'

Orphan Butte OR Because it stands alone. Cf. **Huerfano**.

Orris Timbers Creek See **Orestimba Creek**.

Ortigalita Spanish 'nettle.'

Ortocoag River ME Algonquian 'where we mend canoes.'

Osabeg Hills ME Algonquian 'other-side-of-water.'

Osage Recorded in a French context (1673) as Ouchage, a tribal name. The name has spread to a dozen states, and is common as a name for natural features in regions, e.g. OK, where the tribe has lived. **Osage** IA: the immediate source of the name was a town benefactor named Orrin Sage, who signed himself O. Sage.

Osahatchee Creek GA Muskogean (Creek) 'pokeberry-stream.'

Osaka From the city in Japan.

Osakis Lake MN The *-sak* is for the Sauk Indians; the *o* is probably the French *aux*, and the *s* the French sign of the plural. Thus the whole is 'at the Sauks.'

Osanippa Creek AL Muskogean (Creek) 'moss-stems,' i.e. a stream marked by a growth of moss.

Osawatomie KS A name coined from the names of local Indian tribes (Osage and Potawatomi) as a compromise to end a dispute in the choosing of a name.

Osborn(e) From the personal name. **Osborne** KS was named for Pvt. V. B. Osborne, wounded in the Civil War, one of the few examples of naming for a private. But see **Rooks**.

Osca Bay LA Choctaw 'cane, canebrake.'

Oscaloosa See **Oskaloosa**.

Oscawana NY From the name of a chief of the late 17th century.

Osceola From the personal name of the Seminole chief of the early 19th century. Though he led in war against the Americans, his name later became popular, and appears on habitations in some 20 states. The later names echo the earlier ones rather than honoring the chief himself.

Oscoda MI A named coined (ca. 1881) after the **Schoolcraft** (q.v.) principles from Algonquian *ossin,* 'pebble,' and *muscoda,* 'prairie.'

Oscura Spanish 'dark, shaded.'

Osha Indian, the wild angelica root, used for medicinal purposes, and occurring on several features in NM, language uncertain.

Oshawa MN From a town in Canada.

Oshkosh WI For a well-known Menominee chief (1795–1858).

Oshoto WY Arapaho 'stormy-day,' a recent name, given on the reservation, probably because of the day on which the name was selected.

Osier From the alternate name for willow, e.g. **Osier** MI, **Osierfield** GA; also sometimes used for the dogwood.

Osiris Temple AZ See **Brahma.**

Oska Bogue Creek MS Choctaw 'cane-stream.'

Oskaloosa From the personal name of an Indian woman (one of the two wives of **Osceola**), whose name, like that of her husband, became strangely popular, though not in the area of the SE where she lived and where her Muskogean name would be natural. Instead, towns thus named are in IL, IA, KS, and MO, with **Oscaloosa** KY in addition.

Oslo From the city in Norway, though in the 19th century, at the time of the American namings, the city was called Christiania, and **Olso** was only a historical name.

Oso Spanish 'bear.' The name ocurs often in CA and other regions possessing both Spaniards and bears. **Oso Flaco Lake** CA: the men of the Portolá expedition killed a lean (*flaco*) bear here in 1769. **Canada de Los Osos** CA: the name here probably refers to hostile Indians, known as 'Bears.' **La Osa** AZ: a she-bear (*osa*) was roped and killed here, but a Spanish personal name, De La Osa, may also be involved.

Osotonac Creek ME Algonquian 'beyond-mountain-at.'

Osoyoos Lake WA Indian (Calispel), containing *sooyos,* 'narrows.'

Osprey For the bird, e.g. in FL.

Ossabaw Island GA Indian, meaning unknown.

Ossagon Creek CA Yurok, from a village name, meaning unknown.

Osseo MI, MN, WI From 'Son of the Evening Star' in Longfellow's *Hiawatha.*

Ossineke MI Ojibway 'he-gathers-stones,' but significance uncertain.

Ossining NY Algonquian 'stone(s)-little-at.' See **Sing Sing.**

Ossipee NH Algonquian 'beyond-water.'

Ostrica LA Uncertain; to be connected with the Greek 'oyster' (?).

Ostrich Bay WA Named by the Wilkes expedition (1841) from its shape.

Oswaya Creek NY, PA Iroquoian 'pine-forest.'

Oswegatchie In NY it is Iroquian, probably 'black-water.' In CT it is in Algonquian territory, but of uncertain meaning. **Oswegachie River** VT is a variant, probably of the Iroquoian name.

Oswego NY Iroquoian 'flowing-out,' a descriptive for the mouth of the river. The name has been introduced into several states.

Osyka MS Choctaw 'eagle' (?).

Otatso Lake MT Indian (Blackfoot) 'walking-stooped,' the Indian name of John Kennedy, a trader.

Otay CA Indian (Diegueno) 'brushy.'

Oteen NC A name given to a veterans' hospital by its commandant, believed to be an Indian word meaning 'chief aim,' to characterize the institution's chief object, viz. restoring health.

Otego NY Iroquoian 'to-have-fire-there,' probably the same as **Adiga**.

Oteneagen MN Ojibway, of uncertain meaning, another form of **Otonagen**.

Othello From the Shakespearean play or character; in WA, a railroad name.

Otisco Lake NY Iroquoian 'water-dried,' perhaps with the idea that the lake had shrunk.

Otocklawfa MS Choctaw, probably 'cleared-field.'

Otoe From the Indian tribal name.

Otowi NM Indian (Tewa) 'gap where water sinks.'

Otsdawa NY Iroquoian, meaning uncertain, but probably with the first syllable 'rock.'

Otsego NY Iroquoian 'rock-place,' so called from a particular rock at the outlet of the lake.

Otselic NY Iroquoian 'wild-plum' (?).

Ottauquechee River VT Algonquian, uncertain, but probably containing the idea of swift water.

Ottawa From the Indian tribal name. In MI and OH the names record the early residence of the tribe; names in KS and OK represent locations to which the tribe was later moved. In other states, e.g. WV, the name may merely echo that of the well-known capital of Canada.

Otter, Otterslide The otter, as a valuable fur-bearing animal, gave its name to a considerable number of water fea-

tures. Some of these were probably named because of the presence of an otterslide, rather than for the animal itself (Cf. **Beaverdam**). Habitation-names have arisen by transfer. **Otter Tail** MN: the name-cluster arose from the lake, which was originally so called in Ojibway, and is believed to have been named from a long and narrow sandbar, thought to resemble the tail of an otter. **Otter Rock** OR: because once the haunt of the sea otter.

Ottokee OH For a Potawatomi Indian, famous for his oratory, brother of **Wauseon**.

Ottumwa IA Probably Algonquian 'swift-water,' with reference to the Des Moines River at this location.

Otukalofa Creek MS Chickasaw 'chestnut-stump.'

Ouache, Lake LA From an Indian tribal name.

Ouachita AR, LA From the Indian tribal name. Its resemblance to **Wichita** is coincidental, and the two names are probably of different languages.

Ouaquaga NY Iroquoian, meaning uncertain, probably the same as **Oquaga**.

Ouleout NY Probably Iroquoian, with reference to the sound made by the stream.

Our Occurs on half-a-dozen creeks in AK, a prospectors' name, denoting possession.

Ouramana Lake ME Algonquian, the same as **Olamon** (vermilion),' but perhaps in the more generalized meaning of 'beautiful, shining.'

Ouray CO, UT For the well-known chief of the Utes in the 19th century.

Ours French 'bear (the animal),' e.g. **Bayou L'Ours** LA, **Bayou des Ours** LA. The form **Ourse** occurs under the influence of English-language spelling habits.

Outagamie County WI From the Indian tribal name.

Outing MN Planned as a place where people could have 'outings.'

Outlook MT, WA Probably a commendatory, either for actual view or for future prospects; sometimes applied to features because of the view.

Outside Creek CA Because on the 'outside edge' of a certain swamp area.

Ouzel From the water bird, e.g. the creek in CA, named (1899) by D. S. Jordan, because John Muir had studied the habits of the ouzel here.

Ouzinkie AK A transliteration of Russian 'very narrow,' because located on the strait, the name of which has been translated from the same Russian name, as **Narrow Strait.**

Ovalo TX Spanish 'oval' (noun), so named because in an oval-shaped valley.

Ovapa WV From abbreviations of OH, PA, and VA.

Overisel MI Named (mid-19th century) by Dutch immigrants for Overijssel, the province of the Netherlands.

Overland From association with the 19th-century overland mail and stage route, e.g. **Overland Park** KS.

Ovid In NY for the Roman poet, a part of the classical naming of 1790. In CO, for Newton Ovid, local resident.

Owaneco IL A spelling variation of **Oneco,** but how it was established in IL is uncertain.

Owanka Siouan 'camping-place.' In MN it is a name placed by 19th-century developers of a resort.

Owasco NY Iroquoian, probably 'lake-(at)-floating-bridge.'

Owascoag River ME Algonquian 'grass-at,' with the initial *o* unexplained.

Owassa AL, IA, NJ, Of Indian or pseudo-Indian origin, but uncertain.

Owasso OK Probably Osage 'end,' having been named when it was the terminus of a railroad.

Owatonna MN Siouan 'straight,' originally applied to **Straight River.**

Owego NY Iroquoian, probably 'where-valley-widens.'

Owiyukuts Plateau CO Ute, meaning uncertain.

Owl The bird was often notable because of its hooting at night, and a number of natural features bear the name, because owls thus impressed themselves upon the namers. It is rare as a habitation-name. **Owlhead** in AZ is named for a formation of that appearance; so also, probably, **Owl's Head** in ME and **Owlshead Mountain** in CA.

Owosso MI For a local Ojibway chief whose name is recorded as Wasso.

Owtanic NH Algonquian 'village-at.'

Owyhee River OR, ID This was a 19th-century spelling of Hawaii. In 1819 two Hawaiians, accompanying a trapping expedition, were killed by Indians at this stream, which was first called in memory of them Sandwich Island River. This became Owyhee as early as 1826.

Owyhigh Lakes WA From the name of a Yakima chief, elsewhere spelled Owhigh.

Ox Though a common beast of traction until the end of the 19th century, the ox has left little mark on nomenclature, partly because the word itself is so short as to be nondistinctive. In fact, the term was really avoided, except in combinations. **Ox Bow** has developed as a common term meaning something curved back upon itself, and has produced **Ox Bow** OR, etc. **Oxbow Hill** AZ: some oxbows were found here from cattle run off by Indians in 1871. **Ox Creek** ND: one of the few examples of the term by itself, is a modern shortening from **Dead Ox Creek.**

Oxford From the town and university in England; MD, 1683; MA, 1693; CT, 1741. The name has been highly popular, later namings having tended to emphasize the university, as commendatories for places of education and culture. **Oxford** OH, MS: so named because of an intended university. **Oxford** ID by local story, because tracks of oxen were found at a nearby ford.

Oxmoor In NC named by immigrants from a place in Ireland; transferred to AL ca. 1868.

Oxoboxo, Oxyboxy CT A jocular rendering of **Oxopaugsuck,** q.v.

Oxon Hill MD Probably from a place in England.

Oxopaugsaug CT Algonquian 'small-pond-outlet.' See **Oxoboxo.**

Oyster Much prized from earliest times for eating and the basis of a considerable industry, the oyster has supplied many names of coastal features, and a few habitation-names by transfer.

Ozan AR From French *aux anes,* 'of the asses.'

Ozark French *Aux Arks,* 'at the Arks,' i.e. a shortening of Arkansa, the tribal name, with an *s* added for the plural, but not sounded, and so dropped when the name came into English.

Ozaukee County WI From the Indian tribal name, literally 'river-mouth-people,' of which **Sauk** is a shortening. So also **Ozawkee** KS.

Ozette WA Probably Indian, shaped to a French form, meaning unknown.

Ozone, Ozona A repeated commendatory for habitations in the late-19th and early-20th centuries when ozone was thought to be 'good for you,' and was not known to be a poisonous component of smog. **Ozona** FL, TX substitutes a final *a,* as more suitable for a place-name.

P

Pa-A-Coon AZ Paiute 'water-boils up.'

Pabst From the personal name. The peak in WY was named in 1901 when the first two ascenders drank a bottle of Pabst beer at the summit.

Pachalka Spring CA From the personal name of a Paiute. **Pachappa** is probably a variant spelling.

Pachaug Algonquian 'turning-place.' Numerous names, especially in New England, contain the element, most commonly spelled *pach*, e.g. **Pachade, Pachassett, Pachasuck, Pachatanage, Pachest, Pachet, Pachgatgotch, Pachuach, Pachusett, Packachaug, Paskhommuck, Pauchaug, Putchaug.** The meaning is tied up with the idea of turning, dividing, or forming a boundary, but the significance is not clear, and may have varied in different names. The term may indicate a point at which a trail turned, or a boundary (necessitating a turning-back) between tribes or between the English and the Indians. See **Chepachague.**

Pachitla Creek Ga Muskogean (Creek) from *pachi*, 'pigeon,' and probably *talwa*, 'town.'

Pacific From association with the **Pacific Ocean,** especially on the western coast for habitation-names, e.g. **Pacific Beach, Grove, Palisades,** etc., also merely as **Pacific. Pacific** MO arose in the 1850's in connection with the building of a railroad which was expected to be transcontinental; the town was named in hope. A few names arose as being the destination of the covered-wagon emigrants, e.g. **Pacific Junction** IA. **Pacific Creek** WY: early travelers, having crossed the Continental Divide, bestowed this name since it was the first water flowing to the west.

Packanack Lake NJ A variant of **Pequannock.**

Packanasink NY Algonquian 'split-rocks-at.'

Packsaddle Usually for a mountain (two in TX), the profile of which resembles that of a packsaddle.

Pack-Way-Wong Lake WI Algonquian, meaning uncertain.

Packwock Stream Algonquian 'clear (shallow)-place.'

Pacoima CA Shoshonean, possibly 'running water.'

Pactola See **Pactolus.**

Pactolus From the river of Asia Minor, famous among the ancient Greeks as a source of gold, thus becoming a general commendatory with the idea of richness. **Pactola** SD was so named for being in a gold-bearing region; it was apparently formed by altering the original name to a feminine form.

Pacua Lake WI Algonquian (Ojibway) 'shallow.'

Paddy The common 19th-century adaptation of Patrick; hence, of an Irishman in general. Irish districts were commonly known as **Paddytown.** On some natural features the term is the equivalent of **Irish,** e.g. **Paddys Valley** OR.

Padilla WA The bay was named (1791) by the Spanish explorer Eliza for the viceroy Revillagigedo, using one of his many names. See **Guemes, Orcas.**

Padre Spanish 'father, priest,' generally with reference to the early Spanish missionaries. **Padre Barona Valley** CA: for a friar of that name.

Paducah In KY it is from a local (Chickasaw) chief, but is also a tribal name; in TX, because the first settlers came from the district in KY.

Paeonian Springs VA Paeonia was the ancient name for a district to the north of Greece; but the reference is uncertain. For a possible connection, see **Paonia.**

Pagan Point MD Probably Algonquian 'nut.'

Pagoda CO Originally applied to the peak ca. 1910, because of its shape, by Dean Babcock, ranger and artist.

Pagosa CO Ute 'water-healing,' for medicinal springs.

Pah 1) Eskimo 'river-mouth,' e.g. **Pah River** AK. 2) Paiute 'water, spring,' occurring in many names in the Great Basin, e.g. **Pahrump**, but commonly as a second element, e.g. **Ibipah, Tonopah.**

Paha WA Probably Indian, locally believed to mean 'big water.'

Pahaquarry NJ Algonquian, by partial folk-etymology (quarry) from **Pohaqualin**, meaning uncertain.

Pahcoon Springs NV Southern Paiute 'water (springs)-hot.'

Pahokee FL Muskogean (Hitchiti) 'grass-water,' a term applied by the Indians to the **Everglades.**

Pah Rah Mountains NV Northern Paiute, with *pah*, 'water, spring,' and the rest uncertain.

Pahranagat NV From the name of a local Indian tribe.

Pah Rock Range NV Shoshone (or Southern Paiute), with *pah-*, 'water, spring,' and the rest uncertain. The earlier spelling was **Pah Roc**, and the change is probably the result of folk-etymology.

Pah-Rum Peak NV Although it is in Northern Paiute territory, the name may be the same as **Pahrump**, q.v.

Pahrump Valley CA Southern Paiute 'water-stone,' probably for a spring in a rock.

Pahsimeroi ID Shoshone 'water-one-grove,' because of an isolated grove of trees on a stream.

Pahsupp Mountains NV Northern Paiute, with *pah-*, 'water, spring,' and the rest uncertain.

Pahute From the Indian tribal name, a variant of **Paiute.**

Pahyant On several features in UT it is from the Indian tribal name.

Paiawisit Lake WI Indian, language and meaning uncertain.

Paicines CA Costanoan, a village name, meaning unknown.

Pailles, Anse aux LA French 'straws,' but with reference to reeds and tall grass growing here.

Paimiut AK Eskimo 'rivermouth-people,' a village or tribal name.

Paincourt French 'bread-short,' a derogatory of the type common in English, e.g. **Lickskillet, Needmore.** It was an early nickname of **St. Louis** MO, and is preserved in **Paincourtville LA.**

Paint Natural features so called are from the presence there of some mineral used as a pigment by the Indians, most commonly cinnabar or some red iron compound, e.g. **Paint Creek** (two in PA). The names are often translations from some Indian language. The habitation-names are by transfer. See **Painted**

Painted The term is applied to natural features 1) because of Indian paintings or pictographs, e.g. **Painted Rock** CA, or 2) because of colorful rocks, e.g. **Painted Desert** AZ. The name occurs chiefly in the arid West, where growth does not conceal the color of the rocks, and especially in the **Colorado Plateau,** which is notable for the high colors of its formations. **Painted Woods** ND: from some trees marked with Indian paintings. **Painted Post** NY: because of a red-painted post which was erected by the Indians, apparently as a symbol.

Painter 1) From the personal name, e.g. **Paintersville** CA for Levi Painter, who laid out the town in 1879; 2) from the early variant of **Panther**, chiefly in the NE, e.g. **Painter Run** OH, PA, WV.

Paisaje Spanish 'landscape,' in CO given in compliment to the view afforded by the site.

Paisano In TX probably from the local Spanish term for the bird known in English as a road-runner.

Paisley From the town in Scotland.

Paiute From the Indian tribal name, see **Piute.**

Pajaro Spanish 'bird.' In CA the name was given to a river by the men of the Portolá Expedition in 1769, because they found there a stuffed bird left by the Indians. **Pajarito Mountains** AZ: from a rock formation that looks like a small bird.

Pakaway Lake WI Algonquian (Ojibway), probably 'shallow.'

Pakegama Lake MN Algonquian (Ojibway) 'branch-lake,' i.e. a lake having an arm branching off it.

Pakim Pond NJ Algonquian, probably 'cranberry.'

Pakouijawin Lake WI Indian, probably Algonquian, meaning uncertain.

Pala CA Indian (Luiseno), probably 'water.'

Palanush Butte Klamath 'dried up.'

Palarm AR Probably from a French personal name; an early settler Baptiste Larme is recorded.

Palatine Many 17th- and 18th-century German immigrants were so known, because coming from the Palatinate; a few names thus arose.

Palatka FL Seminole 'boat-crossing,' i.e. 'ferry.'

Palatlakaha Creek FL Seminole, probably from the name of an ancient settlement, 'swamp-big-site.'

Palco KS A coined name, probably from Palmer and Cole, two railroad officials, not further identified.

Palermo From the city in Sicily.

Palestine By religious associations this name has been considered commendatory and is used for a few habitation-names. **Palestine** TX was settled by a congregation of Baptists, who probably had in mind the idea of the promised land or the land flowing with milk and honey.

Paleta Spanish of various meanings, e.g. 'shovel, shoulder-blade, palette.' The second may be the origin of **La Paleta** CA. Cf. **Panza, Shoulderblade.**

Palisade(s) The original usage was apparently **The Palisades of the Hudson,** quotable from the early 19th century, the name probably being suggested because columnar formations of rock give the appearance of stakes set in the ground (see **Estacado**). The term became a quasi-generic for a line of cliffs. It occurs absolutely, e.g. **The Palisades** CA, CO, or as a specific by association, e.g. **Palisade Creek** CA, **Palisade Canyon** NV.

Palm Because of native palms the name occurs on some features in AZ and CA, e.g. **Palm Springs** CA. With habitation-names the palms may either be native or cultivated, and the name is usually given for its exotic and tropical suggestions, e.g. **Palm Beach** FL. It is also a personal name. See **Palmyra.**

Palma Spanish 'palm-tree.' **Palma Sola** FL, 'palm-lone,' is for a single palm marking an offshore island.

Palmetto From various small native palm trees so called, e.g. **Palmetto** FL, **Palmetto Mountain** NV.

Palmyra From the ancient city, probably known because of the story of Zenobia. It has been popular, and may have been started partly by coincidence, i.e. the personal name Palm was given to **Palmstown** PA, and this later suggested **Palmyra.**

Palo In Castilian Spanish it means 'stick, log,' but in America was often used for 'tree.' In Spanish it is a generic or a common noun, but in modern place-names it is used as a specific: **Palo Alto** 'tree-tall.' In CA one especially tall redwood was recorded in this vicinity in 1774, and the name was used to identify a *rancho*. In non-Spanish areas Palo Alto is generally an echo of the battle in the Mexican War. To form double specifics *palo* meaning 'tree,' may be found coupled with *cedro* (cedar), *verde* (green, and the name of a desert bush). The meaning 'post' is more likely with *colorado* (red), *pinto* (painted). **Palos Verdes** CA: from a slough containing some green trees. **Palo Escrito Peak** CA, 'tree-inscribed,' is probably from a tree marked with some symbols. **Palo Duro** TX refers to a kind of cedar, 'hardwood.'

Paloma Spanish 'dove,' usually for the wild dove. **Palomar:** 'dove-cot,' or more likely, 'place frequented by doves.' **Palomares Creek** CA from Francisco Palomares, early settler. **Palomas Canyon** CA: probably by folk-etymology from *pelones*, 'bald,' a name first applied to some nearby hills.

Palourde French 'mussel,' e.g. the lake in LA.

Palouse ID, WA From an Indian tribal name, appearing as Palloatpallah in the Lewis and Clark records; the name has been altered to the form of a French word, probably under the influence of French-Canadian trappers.

Pamanset River MA Algonquian 'inlet-at.'

Pamedomcook Lake ME Algonquian 'shallow-across-lake' (or 'shallow-between-two lakes').

Pamelia NY Named (1819) for Pamelia, wife of Gen. Jacob Brown, noted in the War of 1812.

Pamlico NC From the Indian tribe, more commonly recorded as Pamticough.

Pamo Valley CA Indian (Diegeño), a village name of unknown meaning.

Pampa The term is used in South America for 'plain,' especially the Pampas of Argentina, but the term is not colloquial Mexican, and its use in TX for a town is probably literary, though properly descriptive. **Pampa Peak** CA: from a railroad station, probably named from its location in the level valley.

Pamunkey VA From an Indian tribal name, recorded (1608) as Pamaunke.

Pana IL Probably from the name of a Cahokia chief ca. 1750, whose name may have been placed first upon the lake.

Panaca NV From the personal name of a local Paiute who discovered an ore ledge. But possibly the name was derived from the Paiute word for 'ore,' and the Indian was so named because he had made the discovery.

Panacea FL Because of some springs which were supposed to be all-healing.

Panama Names in several states seem to have arisen out of a general interest in the isthmus and, later, in the canal. In CA the town is probably named because situated on an isthmus between two river channels. **Panama City** FL: a commendatory name in connection with the canal, the town promoter fixing upon the idea that the town was on a straight line between Chicago and the canal.

Panamint CA From an Indian tribal name.

Panasa Lake MN Ojibway 'young bird.'

Panasoffkee FL Seminole 'valley-deep.'

Panawansot Hill ME Algonquian 'extended-fog-at.'

Pancake In PA it is for George Pancake, early settler. **Pancake Rock** AK is a descriptive, because of flat rock formations. **Pancake Summit** NV is probably of similar origin. **Pancake** TX is for J. R. Pancake, rancher of the mid-19th century.

Pando CO Probably Spanish 'slow,' to indicate a quiet place in the stream.

Pandora From ancient Greek mythology. It occurs in several states, but there seems to be no special reason for its use. **Pandora Reef** WA: for a British ship of that name, a survey vessel in that area.

Panguitch UT Paiute, a tribal name derived from the lake, 'fish-people.'

Panhandle, The A term to denote a narrow strip of land running out from a large area, and thus resembling a panhandle, when seen on the map. **The Panhandle** is pre-eminently that of Texas, but it is used with several other states. While chiefly used with states, it may be otherwise applied as in **The Panhandle** (an extension of Golden Gate Park) in San Francisco. It is essentially a generic, but **Panhandle** is a town in TX.

Panic Creek AK Named in 1950 by a geologist who was alarmed about 'overdue personnel.'

Panna Maria TX Polish 'Virgin Mary,' founded by Polish Catholic immigrants.

Pannaway Marsh NH Algonquian 'where-water-(tide)-spreads.' **Panway** is a variant.

Panoche Mexican-Spanish for a sweet substance made from reeds and wild fruit, originally by Indians. The name-cluster in CA probably arises from some incident involving panocha.

Panola In AL and OK it is Choctaw 'cotton.' In IL it is a name coined by J. B. Calhoun, land commissioner for a railroad, by the process of placing vowels and consonants in a pleasing order.

Panora IA Probably a coined name; by local story, a clipping of 'panorama,' a name suggested by the view.

Pansy, Pansey Generally from the personal name. **Pansy Mountain** OR: from the Panzy Blossom copper mine, so called because the ore had bright colors in it.

Pan Tak AZ Papago 'coyote sits.'

Pantano AZ Spanish 'swamp, hindrance.'

Panther This was the common name throughout the eastern woodland for the big cat known elsewhere as 'cougar' or 'mountain lion.' The beast was rarely seen, but, once seen, was very impressive, and many place-names result, most of them of the incident nature. MO alone has an estimated 25 such names, including the unusual **Isle of Panthers**. WV has the term coupled with creek, branch, hollow, knob, and mountain, in each case having a credible and exciting incident preserved in tradition as to the origin of the name. CA, even though the

animal is there usually called 'mountain lion,' has about 20 natural features so named. **Panther Creek** occurs nine times in OK. **Panther Peak** TX: two men were here surprised when a panther leaped between them. **Panther Creek** WA: the namer saw a panther on a log over the stream, though **Cougar** would have been the more common term in this area. **Panther Creek** IA: in 1834 Addison Sherill saw tracks in fresh snow, and set his dogs on the trail. When they brought the panther to bay at this stream, Sherill shot it and thus named the creek.

Pantigo Hill VT Algonquian 'falls-river-at.'

Panway NH See **Pannaway**.

Panza Spanish 'paunch.' **La Panza** CA, according to tradition, was so named because a paunch of beef had been left there as a bait for bears.

Paoha Island CA Mono, a word referring to imagined female spirits, sometimes called 'water babies,' applied by an American in 1882.

Paola KS An altered pronunciation from the name of Baptiste Peoria, a remarkable local Indian linguist and interpreter, an early settler in the region.

Paoli PA From a tavern named for Pasquale Paoli, known and admired during the Revolutionary period as the leader of the Corsican revolt in the mid-18th century.

Paonia CO Named (1882) by the first postmaster with the Latin name of the peony, a flower common in the region; the Latin spelling is *paeonia,* but the name was slightly simplified by the Post Office Dept.

Pap An anatomical descriptive, e.g. **The Paps** AK, **Paps Mountain** ID.

Papago From the Indian tribal name.

Papakating Creek NJ Algonquian, meaning uncertain; during the 18th century known as **Pepper-Cotton** by folk-etymology. See **Mamakating**.

Papalote TX American-Spanish 'kite.' The creek is locally believed to have been named descriptively from kite-shaped rocks along it, but the name may have arisen by folk-etymology from some Indian term.

Paper Mill Creek CA The first paper mill on the Pacific Coast was operated here in 1856.

Papillion NB Locally said to be from French *papillon*, 'butterfly,' by misspelling; probably from a French personal name.

Papoose From the term for an Indian baby, e.g. the mountain in ID.

Papscanie Island NY From the name of an early Indian who lived there.

Parada Spanish 'place of halting or stopping'; **Piedra Parada** CO is probably so named because it was a rock near a customary halting place.

Parade SD Originally Paradis, for George Paradis, early settler; changed because of duplication within the state.

Paradis French 'paradise,' but in LA named (1906) for E. L. Paradis, landowner.

Paradise The name is common, both on natural features (50 estimated for CA) and on habitations. It has usually been given in simple good faith by people who thought the place named was either very beautiful for its surroundings or wild flowers or by people who thought that it was a fine place to live. In PA an inhabitant remarked in 1804 that the place was paradise to him. In OR some cattlemen discovered a 'regular Paradise' of fine grass. In AZ a honeymoon couple thus expressed their feelings. In TX the place was said to be a paradise on earth. In CA one early spelling, **Paradice** suggests a possible derivation from 'pair of dice,' an often-told story. In SD the name was inevitable when a homesteader named Adam and one named Eve happened to settle nearby, though no marriage resulted. **Paradise Creek** WY: from the family name of an early settler. **Paradise** KS: named (1860) by J. R. Mead, who called it **Mead's Paradise**

because he found such good conditions here and such plentiful game.

Paradox In CO the valley is so called because of the unusual phenomenon that the river here cuts through its cliff walls at right angles.

Paragon Used in several states for a habitation-name, apparently as a commendatory.

Paragonah UT From an Indian tribal name.

Paragould AR Named by the railroad (1882) for the two railroad magnates J. W. Paramore and Jay Gould.

Paraiso Spanish 'paradise,' e.g. the springs in CA.

Paramount CA From the main boulevard, which in turn was named for the motion-picture company.

Paramus NJ Algonquian, uncertain, except that the *s* is all that is left of *sipus*, 'river.'

Parashont Mountain NV Southern Paiute, a variant of **Pahranagut** (?).

Parchment WV From the family name of some 18th-century settlers.

Parco WY A coined name, from the Producing and Refining Company.

Parcoal WV A town owned by the Pardee Curtin Lumber Company, which mined coal.

Parcperdue LA French 'park-lost,' from a plantation-name, but reference uncertain.

Paria River AZ, UT Paiute 'water-elk,' because of the presence of elk in the region.

Parida Creek TX Spanish 'female that has given birth.' The name may have arisen from incident; an alternate name, **Becerro,** 'calf,' suggests that a bovine birth produced the incident.

Parilla Creek TX Probably for Parrilla, a Spanish family name.

Paris Though the family name is not uncommon, the place-names generally arise from the city in France. In KY it was given as a token of gratitude for French aid in the Revolution. **Paris OR:** for G. E. Parris, the first postmaster, with spelling shortened to the French standard.

Park Primarily a generic: 1) a reserved area, usually of natural or cultivated beauty, 2) an open valley among mountains. It is also a personal name. Uses as a specific arise from all three sources, the first having especial commendatory value. Names from the second generic use are limited to the Rocky Mountains, e.g. **Park Creek, Park Co., Park Range** (all in CO). **Park River ND:** from the specialized meaning 'enclosed place where game may be driven,' in this case, such enclosures made by Indians for trapping buffalo.

Parma From the city in Italy.

Parmachenee ME Algonquian 'across-usual-path,' i.e. deviating from the most traveled trail.

Parnassus PA The name of the Greek mountain, sacred to Apollo and the Muses, was given to a tract by some surveyors in the early 19th century, a time of much giving of classical names.

Parnell From the personal name; in MN for C. S. Parnell, Irish statesman.

Paroda Junction SC From the names of the three sons of the namer, Paul, Robert, and David.

Parowan UT From an Indian tribal name, an American pronunciation of the name also spelled **Parago(o)nah.**

Parral OH A company town, named (1900) because the president had interests in silver-mining near Parral in Mexico.

Parran MD, NV From a family name.

Parsippany NJ Probably a tribal name.

Parsley WV For W. H. Parsley, first postmaster.

Parsnip For the wild parsnip, e.g. the peak in NV.

Partridge A personal name, but more often from the occurrence of the game bird or some incident involving such birds, more commonly on natural features than in habitation-names, since it apparently carries suggestions of triviality. See **Peru.**

Parunuweap UT Paiute, with *weap,* 'canyon,' and the rest probably 'roaring-water.'

Par Value Lake CA Named from a nearby mine.

Pasadena A name established by elaborate process in 1875, the idea being to find an Indian name suitable to the situation of the town. Since no local Indians were available, an appeal was made to a missionary among the Chippewas to supply a name meaning 'Crown of the Valley,' or 'Key of the Ranch,' the stories as preserved being inconclusive. The missionary sent back four long names, each ending with *Pa sa de na,* which would seem to be his idea of 'of the valley.' Dr. T. B. Elliott, who had made the appeal, quietly dropped everything but these four syllables, and presented **Pasadena** as a *fait accompli.* It was adopted by the townspeople. Other uses of the name, e.g. TX, MD, are undoubtedly borrowings from CA, although they are sometimes given other translations.

Pascack Brook NJ Algonquian, meaning uncertain.

Pascagoula MS From an Indian tribal name.

Pasco In FL it is for Samuel Pasco, political figure of the 19th century. In WA it is locally believed to be named for one of the places in Latin America, but a family name may be involved here too.

Pascoag RI Algonquian 'forking-place,' because of the forks of the river here.

Pasconuquis RI Algonquian, probably 'muddy-cove.'

Paskenta CA Indian (Wintu) 'under the bank.'

Paskuisset RI Algonquian 'muddy-(place)-at.'

Paso Spanish 'passage, crossing.' It is usually the equivalent of English 'pass (through a range of mountains or hills),' thus in CA, **Paso Robles. El Paso Peak** CA takes its name by association with a pass near it. **El Paso** TX: originally, dating from 1598, **El Paso del Norte,** to designate the spot where Juan de Oñate's expedition crossed the **Rio Grande,** then known more specifically as the **Rio Grande del Norte.** The settlement growing up at that spot retained the original name.

Pasqua AZ From Spanish *pascua,* 'Easter,' so called because it has a notable Easter celebration, as held by the Yaqui Indians.

Pasque Island MA Probably Algonquian, meaning uncertain.

Pasqueset Pond RI Algonquian 'muddy-(place)-at.'

Pasquotank NC From the tribal name of some local Indians.

Pass A generic with two basic meanings, the more widespread one being for a passageway through a mountain range (primarily western, and post-1800, 'gap' being the equivalent eastern term). Specifics arise by association, e.g. the common **Pass Creek,** for a stream flowing from a pass so that it must be followed by travelers. The other meaning is limited to tidal waters of the SE (derived from French *passe*), and by tradition of its French origin stands in the initial position, e.g. **Pass Christian** MS: in this usage **Pass** means a channel of water, usually navigable.

Passaconaway NH For a well-known Indian chief of the 17th century.

Passadumkeag ME Algonquian 'above-gravel-bar.'

Passage Commonly a generic, but becoming a specific by association, e.g. **Passage Key** FL.

Pass-a-Grille FL Probably from Spanish *paso,* 'passage,' but the rest is uncertain.

Passaic NJ Algonquian (Delaware) 'valley.'

Passamagamet Lake ME Algonquian 'many-fish-place' (?).

Passamaquoddy Bay ME Algonquian 'pollock-plenty,' because of their remarkable abundance at certain seasons.

Passapae Landing MD Probably from a tribal name.

Passapatanzy VA Algonquian, meaning uncertain.

Passatuthonsee River NH Algonquian 'muddy-shallow-place,' i.e. probably 'ford.'

Passawaukeag Lake ME Algonquian 'sturgeon-place.'

Passeonkquis Cove RI Algonquian 'muddy-place.'

Passerdyke Creek MD Shaped by folk-etymology from some Algonquian term (?).

Passissawampitts Spring AZ Paiute 'boiling water,' because of the way in which the spring bubbles up.

Passumpsic River VT Algonquian, describing a clear stream with a sandy bottom.

Passyunk PA Algonquian (Delaware) 'valley-at.'

Pastora Peak AZ Spanish 'shepherdess,' but probably an error for *pastura,* 'pasturage.'

Pasup Creek WY Arapaho 'dry-creek.'

Patagonia AZ Eventually from the region in South America, but here derived from the mountains and these in turn from a mine. The reason for the naming of the mine is not known, but many mines were fancifully named.

Pataguanset, Pattaquonset CT Algonquian 'round-shallow-at.'

Patagumkis Stream ME Algonquian 'bend-(with)-gravel-at.'

Pataha WA Indian (Nez Percé) 'brush-creek.'

Patapsco MD Algonquian (Delaware) 'jutting-(ledge)-(of)-rock-at.'

Pataskala OH Probably Algonquian, meaning uncertain.

Pataula Creek GA Muskogean, probably the Indian equivalent of 'flat.'

Patawa Creek OR From a family of Indians who lived there.

Patch As a specific (rare) it is usually from the personal name, e.g. **Sam Patch Creek** AK named (1907) by surveyors for the champion diver of that time. As a quasi-generic it has been common in colloquial speech for a small plot, either cultivated or natural, of some plant, and from this usage many place-names have resulted, especially in the Appalachian area, e.g. **Cottonpatch Knob** KY, **Laurelpatch Branch** KY, **Rye Patch** NV, **Weedpatch** CA.

Patchogue NY Probably from an Indian tribe, whose name may have been derived from the Algonquian term discussed under **Pachaug.**

Patcong Lake NJ Algonquian, probably 'round-place.'

Patera Spanish 'duck-place.' In CA the name was first applied to a stream which was known for good duck hunting.

Paterson, Patterson From the personal name. In NJ it is for William Paterson (1745–1806), who was governor at the time of the naming of the town in 1791.

Path Rare, **Trail** or **Trace** being the usual terms in place-names; but **Path Ridge** VA, **Path Fork** KY. **Pathfinder Canyon** WY: named (1812) by Robert Stuart of the Astorian party, who was exploring his way across the mountains.

Patit Creek WA Indian (Nez Percé) 'bark-creek.'

Patmos From the Greek island, known from **Revelation;** in OH, by local story, selected because a music book fell open at the tune so named.

Pato Spanish 'duck,' e.g. **Patos Lake** NM because of the wild ducks.

Patoka From a name, in different spellings, borne by more than one Indian chief. In IL the name probably springs from a Cahokia of the 18th century, and in IN from a Kickapoo of the 19th century.

Patrick From the personal name. The county in VA is for Patrick Henry, Revolutionary patriot.

Patroon Creek NY From the title of the landholder.

Patsiliga Creek AL, GA Muskogean (Creek) 'pigeon-(roosting)-place.' Also **Patsaliga.**

Pattaquattic Hill MA Algonquian 'round-hill(?)-at.' The element meaning 'round' occurs in numerous place-names in New England in various spellings, e.g. *pat, put, bet.*

Pattaquonquomis Lake ME Algonquian, meaning uncertain, seemingly joining the incongruous ideas 'round' and 'long.'

Pattawassa Lake NY Algonquian 'taken-in-trap' (?).

Pattersquash NY Probably by folk-etymology from an Indian whose name is recorded in the late 17th century as Paterquam.

Pattymocus Peak CA Wintun, meaning uncertain. Also as **Patamocas.**

Patuxent MD From an Indian tribal name.

Paug CT Algonquian 'pond.' This is the generic term in its simplest form, occurring also as *baug, pogue, poque,* etc. It is here translated as 'pond' in the New England sense of the word, i.e. a body of water which may be of a size to be called 'lake' in most parts of the U.S. It has usually been amalgamated with the specific, and thus occurs as a common second element, e.g. **Mashpaug, Quinebaug, Quonepaug.**

Paugus Algonquian 'pond-small,' e.g. in MA, but in NH from the name of an Indian of the 18th century.

Paulding From the personal name; for its use in OH, see **Van Wert.**

Paulina In LA probably from the Spanish form of Pauline. In OR from a well-known and warlike Indian chief, whose name also occurs as Paunina.

Pauma CA From the name of a Luiseño village, probably connected with the word 'water.'

Paumanok, Paumanack NY Algonquian, probably 'offering,' with reference to the shell beads made in the vicinity of Long Island and offered in exchange.

Paunsaugunt UT Paiute, probably 'beaver-place.'

Paupack Creek PA See **Wallenpaupack.**

Paupock, Paupoksuog, Poopoohquotog Algonquian 'quail(s),' the last two forms being plurals. These forms occur several times in southern New England. **Peapack** NJ may be the same. So also **Paupack Creek** PA.

Pausatuck MA Algonquian 'muddyriver.'

Pautapaug, Pautipaug Algonquian 'jutting-pond,' i.e. pond with an arm jutting out. In CT the hill has been named by transfer from the pond. **Pauto Lake** WI may be the same.

Pauto Lake WI Algonquian (Ojibway), meaning uncertain.

Pautuxet CT Algonquian 'little-falls-at.'

Pavo GA Probably Spanish 'peacock, turkey,' in an attempt to get away from the too common **Turkey.**

Pavonia A Latinized form from the name of Michael Pauw, who established a settlement NJ ca. 1630; in OH probably by transfer.

Pawcatuck CT Algonquian, probably 'open-divided-stream.'

Pawhuska OK Named in 1876 for an Osage chief.

Pawlet VT See **Shaftsbury.**

Pawn OR From the initials of four local residents who helped with the establishment of the post office, viz. Poole, Akerly, Worthington, and Nolen.

Pawnee From the Indian tribal name.

Pawpaw, Paw Paw The native tree and its fruit, being much appreciated, gave rise to names for natural features in the southeastern and middle-western states. In spite of the slightly ridiculous repetition, some of these names were transferred to habitations.

Pawticfaw Creek MS See **Tickfaw;** the rest is uncertain.

Pawtuckaway NH Algonquian, uncertain, but with *pawtuck,* probably (cf. **Pawtucket)** 'falls-(in)-river.'

Pawtucket Algonquian 'falls-(in)-river-at.'

Pawtuxent, Pawtuxet MA, RI Algonquian 'waterfall-small-at.'

Pax WV An altered spelling from **Packs Branch,** which is from the Pack family, 18th-century settlers.

Paxico KS Derived, with much shifting, from the name of a local chief whose name is recorded as Pashqua.

Paxinous PA From the name of an Indian chief, friendly to the English in the 18th century.

Paxton Creek PA Algonquian (Delaware) 'pool-at.' It is also the name of a town in England.

Payette ID Named, ca. 1820, for François Payette, Hudson's Bay Company employee.

Payment MI From the family name of early French settlers.

Paywell Mountain CO From a minename.

Pazeka Lake WY A lake containing Epsom salts was so called in the 1880's from the similarity of the effects of its water to the patent medicine laxative so named.

Pea The wild pea has occasioned a few names, e.g. **Pea Ridge** WV, AR. For **Pease,** the old plural, see **Peace. Pea Patch Island** DE is probably a development by folk-etymology; though early form are lacking. Cf. such Algonquian names as **Paupack.** So also **Peapatch Ridge** MD. **Pea Green Buttes** WY: from their peculiar color.

Peace 1) A commendatory, as probably in **Peace Dale** RI. 2) An incident name because of some treaty or of peaceful relationships, especially with Indians. **Peace River** MN marks a boundary established between Ojibways and Sioux by treaty in 1825. **Peace Township** MN: by counterpart from **Warman. Peace Creek** FL: named after the wild pea by the Seminoles, it was rendered in English as **Pease Creek,** and then shifted to its present form. **Peace Creek** FL: probably indicating a peaceful encounter with Indians, the name appears in Spanish context (ca. 1587) as Rio de Pas, apparently for *paz,* 'peace'; this name was translated into English, and then by confusion became in the 19th century **Pease** and **Peas,** which in turn was translated into Seminole.

Peach Peach-tree 'escapes' flourished greatly in the eastern region during the 17th and 18th centuries, and names of natural features are generally to be assigned to these 'wild' or 'Indian' peaches. Habitation-names are more likely from cultivated peach orchards, as in **Peachton** CA.

Peacock From the personal name, e.g. in TX for J. M. Peacock, first postmaster. The mountain in WA is from a mine, which may have borne a commendatory name.

Peak As a specific it is regularly from the personal name, e.g. **Peak** SC and **Peak** NB, the latter shortened from a personal name Peake.

Peanut CA When the original postmaster, in 1898, was asked to suggest a name, he put forward the present one, giving three reasons: 1) it would be unique, 2) he was fond of peanuts, 3) he was eating them at that time.

Peapack NJ By folk-etymology from Algonquian forms of various spellings; meaning uncertain. Cf. **Paupock.**

Peapod Rocks WA Named from their shape by the Wilkes Expedition (1841).

Pear In WV for John Pear Buckland, founder of the post office. Sometimes a commendatory name in connection with fruit-growing, e.g. **Pearblossom** CA. **Pear Lake** CA: from its shape.

Pearl Commonly on natural features from the discovery (or hoped-for discovery) of pearls, e.g. **Pearl River** MS, so named by the French. It may also be from the personal name, which is ordinarily used for women. But **Pearl** TX is for Pearl Davenport, son of the first postmaster. In some instances it is probably a general commendatory, with the sense of 'outstanding.'

Pebble A descriptive, e.g. **Pebble Creek** NB and **Pebble Beach** CA.

Peboamauk Falls NH Algonquian 'winter-place.'

Pecan The native tree has given numerous names, e.g. in TX, OK.

Pecatonica IL, WI Algonquian, applied first (1673) to the present **Missouri River** as *pekitanoui,* 'muddy'; it is recorded in various spellings, and has apparently been influenced by another Algonquian name referring to many canoes along a shore.

Pecausset CT Algonquian 'small-clearing-at.'

Pechanga CA The local Indians ascribed this name to a particular Temecula chief who at a feast remarked, 'My stomach is picha.' Such stories by Indians are rare, and this one has the misfortune of being both vague and untranslated.

Pecho Spanish 'breast,' e.g. **Pecho Rock** CA, from its shape.

Peckerwood A southern term for the woodpecker and also for a 'poor white.' The creek in AL is a translation of a Creek term for woodpecker.

Peconic NY Algonquian, a variant of **Pequonnock.**

Pecos NM, TX A Spanish adaptation of an Indian word, language and meaning uncertain. It was probably first applied to an Indian village, and later to the tribe and river.

Pecowsic MA Probably the same as **Pocasset,** q.v.

Peculiar MO By local tradition, a name selected by the first postmaster because of a letter from the department, either that he should select a name which was peculiar (unique?), or that the name that he had selected was peculiar. A similar story is told for the origin of the name in WI.

Pecumsaugan Creek IL Algonquian, meaning uncertain.

Pedee See **Pee Dee.**

Pedernal Spanish 'flint.' **Pedernales Point** CA: in 1769 the soldiers of the Portolá Expedition found flints here for their muskets.

Pedlar Down through the 19th century the itinerant pedlar with his pack was an important part of American life, and it is not peculiar that we should have **Pedlar Run** WV, **Pedlar's Run** MD, **Pedlar's Grove** PA. These probably originated from incidents involving a pedlar, but the curious fact is that in each of the three cases the incident involves death, twice by murder and once by freezing. The stories may be true, at least in some instances, since the pedlar was certainly exposed to the weather, and also was exposed to robbers, to whom he offered rich pickings.

Pedriza Spanish 'stony tract, stone wall,' e.g. the creek in TX.

Pedro Usually for a personal or a saint's name, e.g. **Pedro Valley** CA originally a *rancho* dedicated to St. Peter. **Pedro** SD: named in 1893 because the group of men who did the naming were playing the card game so called. **Pedro** WV: from the name of some Spanish settlers, the only ones of that origin in the region.

Pee Dee In NC and SC the river is from an Indian tribal name. The creek in NB is from the initials of Pennsylvania Dutch, numerous settlers in the region. **Peedee** OR: from the name in SC.

Peekamoose See **Poke-o-Moonshine.**

Peekskill NY the 'kill' was named for the Dutch trader Jan Peek, who settled there ca. 1665.

Pe Ell WA Probably from a local Indian pronunciation of Pierre, the name of an early French half-breed resident.

Pee Pee Creek OH Early settlers found the initials **PP** carved in a tree here.

Pegleg For a man thus nicknamed, e.g. the mountain in CA, for J. J. Johnson, who lived there in the 1850's.

Pejepscot ME The same as *pechipscott.* See **Sheepscott.**

Pekin From the city of China, one of the exotic names which were favored in the early 19th century.

Pekwan Creek CA From the name of an Indian village, meaning unknown.

Pelado Spanish 'bald,' and thus **Pelado Peak** NM. The term is also in common use for a worthless or poor person, especially a low-class Mexican, and some names may thus have originated.

Pelahatchie MS Choctaw 'hurricane-stream.'

Pelham Though it is an English place-name, the origin has regularly been from the personal name, e.g. in NY (ca. 1664) because of the establishment of **Pelham Manor** by John Pell. In MA for Thomas Pelham-Hollis, Duke of New Castle. In NC for Col. George Pelham, killed in the Civil War.

Pelican Both seacoast and inland names exist, since the bird flies far inland for nesting, thus giving rise, e.g., to **Pelican Creek** WY and **Pelican Lake** MN.

Pella From the ancient city of Palestine, known as a city of refuge for Christians, and thus named in IA by Dutch immigrants who were escaping intolerance at home; carried to NB by emigrants from IA.

Pellyn PA Named as a railroad station for a place in Wales, in honor of a local family claiming descent from the 12th-century Lord of Pellyn.

Pelon, Pelona Spanish 'bald,' e.g. **Sierra Pelona CA**, from having no trees.

Peloncillo Mexican-Spanish for a kind of candy made in a characteristic shape (cf. **Sugarloaf**), and hence a mountain of that form, e.g. in TX. The mountains in AZ take their name from a single peak which was named first. **Pilancillo** is a variant spelling, e.g. **Pilancillos Creek TX**.

Pelto, Lake LA From a French family name, Pelletot or Pelleteau.

Pelusha Creek MS Choctaw 'hurricane-little' (?).

Pemadumcook Lake ME Algonquian 'long-sandbar-at.'

Pemaquid ME Algonquian, a phrase to be translated 'it is far out,' with original reference to the point.

Pembina Ojibway, literally 'summer berry,' from a kind of cranberry.

Pembine WI A variant of **Pembina**, q.v.

Pembroke Eventually from the town and county in Wales. In ME (1832) because salt was produced here, as at the Welsh prototype. The pre-Revolutionary towns in MA, NC, and NH may to some extent have been named in compliment to the Earls of Pembroke, of whom one was a prominent political figure of the early 18th century.

Pemidumcook See **Pamedomcook**.

Pemigewasset NH Algonquian, probably 'long-rapids-at,' first applied to the river.

Pemiscot MO Algonquian (Fox) 'long-rock-at' (?).

Pemmaquan River ME Algonquian, probably 'slope-(with)-maples' apparently a place for making maple sugar.

Pen The term was used for an enclosure for domestic animals and also for a trap where wild animals were captured. It often occurs as a second element, e.g. **Cowpens, Wolf Pen Branch.** By association the term indicates a place thus distinguished, e.g. **Pen Creek SC**.

Pena For Spanish *peña*, 'rock.'

Penacook NH Algonquian, probably 'sloping-place, descent.'

Penalosa KS Probably for Diego de Peñalosa, who was governor of New Mexico in the late 17th century, and thus had some connection with the Kansas region.

Penantla Creek MS Choctaw 'boat-landing.'

Penasco For Spanish *peñasco*, 'rock,' e.g. **Los Penasquitos CA**, 'the little rocks.'

Penataquit Creek NY Algonquian, probably 'crooked-tree-at,' for a tree serving as a boundary mark.

Pencader DE Introduced by Welsh immigrants from a town in Wales.

Pencer MN By mistake in transmission through the Post Office Dept., for the last name of John C. Spencer, local homesteader.

Pendencia Spanish 'quarrel,' e.g. the creek in TX which probably records some incident.

Pendennis KS Named from the novel by W. M. Thackeray.

Pendleton From the personal name; in OR for G. H. Pendleton, democratic candidate for vice-president in 1864.

Pend Oreille ID, WA From an alternate name for the Indian tribe otherwise known as Kalispel.

Penecoog Ridge NH See **Penacook**.

Pengra OR For B. J. Pengra, early pioneer. The pass was named for him in 1927 to commemorate his advocacy of a railroad by that route.

Penholoway Creek GA Muskogean (Creek) 'footlog-high,' from a place where an Indian trail crossed the stream on a fallen tree. Cf. **Fenholoway.**

Peniel From the Biblical site where Jacob wrestled with the angel.

Penikese Island MA Algonquian, meaning uncertain, except that -*ese* should be a diminutive.

Peningo Point KY Probably from the name of a local chief.

Peninsula Primarily a generic, but used for a town in OH because of a large bend in a river, now no longer existing because a passage for the river has been cut across the neck.

Penitas TX From Spanish *peña*, 'stone,' a diminutive; therefore, 'small stones,' probably named from gravel beds.

Penitencia Spanish 'penitence,' the creek in CA being so called because in Spanish times a house stood there which was called La Penitencia, probably because it was associated with confession and penitence.

Penitente Peak NM Spanish 'penitent,' but probably for the religious sect known as Penitentes.

Penitentiary Rare, because such institutions were commonly established after names had been fixed on natural features, and it is not a name likely to be givn to habitations. The creek in IA was named after the penitentiary had been established at the early date of 1839.

Pen Mar MD A boundary-name for PA and MD.

Penn The repeated use of this name in the proprietory colonies of the Penns is not only from William Penn but also from the important holding of the family, e.g. **Penn Manor** PA, **Penns Grove** NJ.

Pennacook ME, NH See **Penacook.**

Pennahatchie Creek GA Muskogean (Creek) 'turkey-stream.'

Pennamaquan River ME Algonquian 'big-area-(with)-maples.'

Pennawa Creek FL Muskogean (Creek) 'turkey.'

Pennecook Falls ME See **Penacook.**

Pennichuck Brook NH Algonquian 'rapids-at.'

Pennsauken NJ Algonquian, with earlier forms such as Pemisoakin, Pimsaquim, meaning uncertain. Cf. **Pensaukee.**

Pennsuco FL From the Pennsylvania Sugar Company which operated here.

Pennsylvania William Penn, in 1681, wished his grant to be called New Wales. According to the accepted story, King Charles II gave the name, coining it from Penn and *silva* (Latin 'forest,' often spelled *sylva* in the 17th century). To escape the odium of having his own name thus used, Penn declared the naming to be in honor of his father, the admiral, and also that *pen* meant headland in Welsh.

Penn-Yan NY After a dispute over a name between two factions of settlers, Pennsylvanians and Yankees (i.e. New Englanders), the matter was settled by compromise.

Pennymottley Creek AL By folk-etymology from a Creek *pin-imala*, literally 'turkey-assistant,' probably a war name for an individual.

Pennypack Creek PA Although the present form is influenced by the name of the Pennypacker family, who were early settlers in the region, the origin is Algonquian (Delaware), with -*pack* meaning 'pond,' and the rest probably indicating a quiet or sluggish water.

Penny Pot NJ Probably derived by folk-etymology from the same Algonquian name that has produced **Pennypack,** q.v.

Peno See **Poeno.**

Penobscot ME Algonquian 'sloping-rock-at,' originally applied to about ten miles of the river above Bangor.

Penokee WI Algonquian, probably 'potato-ground,' for one of the wild tubers used by the Indians for food. In KS the town was named by people who were searching for a new name for the post office and found this one on a map.

Penon From Spanish *peñon,* 'large rock.'

Penryn From the town in Wales, in CA given by a Welsh settler.

Pensacola FL From an Indian tribal name.

Pensaukee WI Algonquian (Menominee), probably 'brant (goose)-place,' shaped by analogy with **Pensauken.**

Pensauken Creek NJ Algonquian, probably 'crooked-outlet-at.'

Pentoga MI A name coined by local mill operators, with 'no meaning'; the elements from which it was coined are uncertain.

Pentucket River MA Algonquian 'crooked-stream-at.'

Peoa UT Probably Ute, meaning uncertain.

People Commonly from the family name. **Peoples Creek** MT is a rough translation of an Indian (Gros Ventre) term to be taken in the sense of 'person, human being,' given because a deformed colt once born there was supposed to have a human head.

Peoria In IL it is recorded in a French context of 1673 as Peouarea, the name of a sub-tribe of the Illinois. In its modern form it has been spelled by Latin analogy. It has spread to about ten states.

Peosta IA For a local (Fox) chief.

Peotone IL Probably Algonquian, meaning uncertain.

Pep NM Locally said to be derived, ca. 1936, from the breakfast food, but it may merely be from the common slang shortening of 'pepper,' current from the early 20th century, from which latter meaning the town in TX probably took its name.

Pepacton NY Probably Algonquian, of uncertain meaning.

Pepin, Lake MN, WI Probably the personal name of an early French explorer or settler.

Pepper In TX the creek is for W. W. Pepper, local landowner. In NB the creek was named when the cook for a 'cow outfit' spilled too much pepper into a stew here. See also **Peppermint, Peppersauce, Pepperwood.**

Pepper-Cotton See **Papakating.**

Pepperell MA Named in 1753 for Sir William Pepperell, New England baronet.

Peppermint From the occurrence of some plant of the mint family, e.g. the creek in MN.

Peppersauce Wash AZ In the 1880's a traveler forgot and left a bottle of pepper sauce here, and was much vexed at doing so; his companions named the wash.

Pepperwood A local name for the prickly ash in the SE and for the California laurel in northern CA, in which latter region about ten names of features and a post office exist.

Pequabuck River CT Algonquian 'clear-open-pond' (?).

Pequacket Pond NH Algonquian 'broken-land.'

Pequannock NJ Algonquian 'small farm, field.' See **Pequonnock.**

Pequanwong Lake WI Probably from the name of an Ojibway village.

Pequest NJ Algonquian 'open-land' (?), probably related to **Pequannock.**

Pequod, Pequot From the Indian tribal name.

Pequonnock, Poquomock, Poquonock Algonquian 'small farm, field' **Poquetanuck** CT may be the same. **Poquonock** occurs several times in CT. The repeated examples of this name are probably an evidence of the survival of Indian agriculture, or the memory of it, into Colonial times.

Pequop Range NV From an Indian tribal name (?).

Percé(e) French 'pierced,' with application usually to a rock or cliff with a hole in it.

Per Cent An occasional commendatory for mine-names has been transferred to features, e.g. **Big Per Cent Gulch** CO.

Perche Creek MO Pronounced dissyllabically, it is probably by folk-etymology from Osage *paçi*, 'hilltop,' through an intermediate stage of French, *roche percée*.

Perdido Spanish 'lost,' e.g. the river in AL and FL.

Perdiz Spanish 'partridge,' e.g. the creek in TX.

Perdu(e) French 'lost,' e.g. **Cheniere Perdue** LA, but often from a personal name, e.g. the hill in AL, for a local family.

Pere French *père*, 'father,' in place-names generally in the meaning of 'priest,' e.g. **Des Peres River** MO because some missionaries had a post there ca. 1700.

Peridot From the mineral of that name.

Peril The peak in AK was named by mountaineers because of dangers in its ascent. **Peril Strait** AK: a translation from the Russian, so named because in 1799 a large number of Aleuts died here from eating poisonous mussels.

Perilla Spanish 'saddle-horn,' a descriptive, e.g. the mountains in AZ.

Periwinkle Creek OR From the presence of that mollusk.

Perkasie PA Algonquian (Delaware) 'hickory-nuts-cracked-at.'

Perkiomen PA Algonquian (Delaware) 'cranberries-at.'

Permanente Spanish 'permanent,' usually of a stream that flows all year, e.g. the creek in CA.

Permita Creek AL Probably Muskogean, meaning uncertain.

Perognathus Flat CA Named by the naturalist C. Hart Merriam, because of the great abundance of pocket mice of that genus which he found here.

Perote In AL probably from the fortress occupied by Americans during the Mexican War. In WI from a local judge, Sabatis Perrote.

Peroxide Well AZ Because some cowboys thought that the water tasted like hydrogen peroxide solution, at that time, ca. 1910, used as a mouthwash.

Perpetua, Cape Named for St. Perpetua by Capt. James Cook on March 7, 1778, which is the day of that saint.

Perquimans NC From the tribal name of some local Indians.

Perry Its widespread use, especially for counties and townships, is chiefly in honor of Com. Oliver Hazard Perry, victor at the Battle of Lake Erie, 1813.

Pershing Commonly for Gen. J. J. Pershing of World War I, e.g. the county in NV. The village in MO thus replaced its earlier name **Potsdam** in 1921.

Persia, Persian From a personal name, e.g. **Persian Creek** CA from John Persian, early rancher; in some instances probably from the country.

Persido Bar CA Probably a simplification of the name of a former Karok village, elsewhere recorded as Patsiluvra.

Persimmon Regularly, e.g. **Persimmon Gap** TX, from the presence of wild persimmon trees.

Persist OR Named by the first settlers, because they managed to persist, and at last had a post office after eighteen years.

Perth, Perthshire From the city and county in Scotland; **Perth Amboy** NJ for the fourth earl of Perth (1648–1716), combined with the Indian name (see **Amboy**).

Peru The name came into use in the post-Revolutionary period of interest in exotic names, e.g. in MA in 1806. The towns in IN and IL are also namings of the early 19th century. This was the period when Americans felt much interest in the South American struggle for independence from Spain, and in ME the naming in 1821 is apparently a commemoration of the independence of Peru, declared in the same year. The brevity and simplicity of the name has aided its spread. The town in MA was originally **Partridgefield,** which may have been thought too long or too insignificant in suggestion, though actually the name of a landowner. In VT the name was adopted (1804) as a commendatory, because of the riches of gold and silver associated with the South American country.

Peruque French 'wig,' a common word in the 18th century; but the reference for the creek in MO is unknown.

Pesapunck NY Algonquian 'sweat-house,' first recorded (1654) as Pissapunke.

Pescadero Spanish 'fishing-place,' e.g. the creek in CA.

Pescadito TX Spanish 'small fish,' for some fish in a nearby pool.

Pescongamoc Pond ME Algonquian 'forked-pond.'

Peshtigo WI Algonquian, meaning uncertain.

Pesotum IL From the personal name of a Potawatomi of the early 19th century.

Petaluma CA Miwok, a tribal or village name, perhaps a topographical term 'flat-back.'

Peter: Peterborough NH: probably for the Earl of Peterborough, military and political figure, named in 1737, two years after the earl's death. **Petersburg** AK: for Peter Buschmann, early resident. **St. Petersburg** FL: named (1875) by Peter Demons, president of a local railroad, for the city in Russia, his former home.

Petersham MA From the town in England.

Petit, Petite French 'small', but **Petit Lake** ID is for Tom Petit, early stage driver. See **Petty.**

Petoskey MI Algonquian, probably 'between-two-swamps.'

Petre, Bayou LA From the French family name Petre.

Petrified Descriptive, for the presence of such material, e.g. **Petrified Forest** AZ, CA.

Petroglyph Point CA Because the rock is covered with petroglyphs, i.e. figures incised by primitive people.

Petroleum, Petrolia From the presence of petroleum, the second form as a Latin word indicating a place.

Petticoat Mountain CA Locally believed to be shaped like a petticoat, whatever that may mean.

Petty From the personal name, e.g. in TX for J. M. Petty, early settler. The lake in MT is by folk-etymology from the French **Petit(e);** so also **Petty Creek** MT for David Pattee, unidentified.

Pewamo MI Algonquian 'trail-diverges,' to designate a place where a trail split or made a detour.

Pewaukee WI Algonquian 'swampy.'

Pewee Valley KY From the bird so known, also called the phoebe.

Peytona WV A Latinized formation from the personal name Peyton, probably for Madison Peyton, coal-mine operator.

Phalanx In NJ and OH the name springs from its usage by the Fourierists for one of their communities located there.

Phalla Bayou MS For Choctaw *falaia,* 'long' (?).

Phantom A fanciful descriptive to suggest something phantom-like in the feature. It is chiefly used in national parks, e.g. **Phantom Ship** OR, **Phantom Ranch** AZ, but appears elsewhere, e.g. with a lake and hill in TX. **Phantom Hill** TX: as early as 1859 the white 'ghostly' chimneys of a burned fort suggested this name. **Phantom Creek** CO: because in a 'ghost town' there, one evening at twilight, the owner of the land seemed to sense the phantoms of former inhabitants.

Pharoah OK For O. J. Pharoah, rancher.

Pharsalia NY From the battle in which Caesar defeated Pompey in 48 B.C., a classical name of the early 19th century.

Pheasant The term was applied (more commonly in the South) to the bird more generally known as a partridge, but place-names, are few, e.g. **Pheasant Branch** WI, **Pheasant Lick** KY.

Phenatchie Creek AL Choctaw 'squirrel-creek.'

Phenix A simplified spelling of **Phoenix**.

Philadelphia Greek 'brotherly love.' William Penn, when naming his new settlement in 1681/2, knew of the city mentioned in the New Testament. The name was selected, even before the settlement was made, as an expression of the ideal for which the colony was to strive. A half-dozen other places have taken the name.

Philippi WV From the ancient city, known both from the Bible and Shakespeare.

Philomath Meaning 'lover of learning,' from the Greek, it has been used, e.g. in OR, as the name of a college and then transferred to a town.

Philsmith Peak WY For Phil D. Smith, mountaineer, who climbed it in 1946.

Phoco Headland NB Pawnee 'hill-in-water-sitting,' because the river swings around the bottom of the bluff.

Phoenicia NY From the ancient Mediterranean country, a classical naming of the early 19th century.

Phoenix, Phenix The mythological bird that rose from its ashes has been widely used as a habitation-name. The other Greek meanings, 'palm tree' and 'Phoenician,' do not seem to have been of influence, though inhabitants of Phoenix AZ are known as Phoenicians. Theoretically the name should be applied to a place that had been burned and was then expected to rise from the ashes, but namers have been content to express only the idea of a hopeful future. **Phoenixville** PA: from the Phoenix Iron Works. **Phoenix** AZ because traces of an ancient Indian or pre-Indian settlement were seen at the site, and the new town was thus expected to rise again.

Phoneton OH Named (1898) because it was an important point in long-distance telephone communications, and most of the inhabitants worked for the telephone company.

Pianketank River VA Algonquian, meaning uncertain, recorded (1608) as Payankatank.

Pia Oik AZ Papago 'no fields,' but now an anomalous name since the village has fields.

Piasa IL The Illinois Indians used this name for a mythological flying creature, a large representation of which was painted on the rock of the Mississippi River shore near present Alton. The nearby creek and island took the name by association; the village, from the creek.

Pica AZ Originally **Picacho**, but shortened by the railroad officials for convenience in telegraphing.

Picabo ID A railroad name from the Shoshonean word for 'friend' (?).

Picacho Spanish 'peak.' The combination **Picacho Peak**, e.g. in CA, is tautological; so also **Picacho Mountains** NM.

Picatinny NJ Algonquian, with *-atinny*, probably 'mountain-at' (cf. **Kittatinny**), and *pic-* uncertain.

Picayune The town in MS was named ca. 1900 for the newspaper, the New Orleans *Picayune,* of which a local woman had been editor. The valley in CA was apparently named as being small.

Piccowaxen Creek MD Algonquian, probably 'pierced-moccasin.'

Piceance Creek CO Ute, meaning uncertain.

Pichet Mountain ME Algonquian 'split' (?).

Pickaway OH Another form of **Piqua**, the Indian tribal name.

Pickerel From the fish, a common name for lakes in the northern states; it may in some instances be from the family name, which occurs in numerous variations of spelling.

Picket(t) Usually from the personal name. **Picket Guard Peak** CA: because standing by itself; the equivalent of **Sentinel.**

Pickpocket Falls NH By folk-etymology from Algonquian *pakwakek*, 'arrows-at.'

Pickton TX Two men were assigned to 'pick' a name, and so they named it (1879).

Pickwick Occurring in several states, apparently always a literary name from Dickens' *Pickwick Papers,* e.g. in TX by two men who had just read the book.

Pico Spanish 'peak,' usually a generic, e.g. **Pico Blanco** CA. It is also a Spanish family name which was common in CA; hence, **Pico Creek** and **Pico Rivera**, the latter formed by amalgamation of two towns thus named.

Picoso Spanish 'pitted with smallpox.' The creek in TX may have been named for such a man, or from pittings in the rock resembling the marks left by the disease.

Pictou CO For the town in Nova Scotia, named by an immigrant.

Picture(d) Often to denote a place where Indian drawings or paintings are visible, e.g. **Picture Gorge** OR, but the name may also arise from colorful rocks, as with **Pictured Rocks** MI.

Pie In WV the name was selected by the Post Office Dept., according to local story, and that term being included because one man really liked pie 'regardless of kind.' **Pie Town** WM takes its name from the fact that a man there liked to bake pies.

Piedmont Applied in the mid-18th century, as a learned term, to denote the region still so known, i.e. the upland region just to the east of the **Appalachian Mountains.** The first spelling was **Piemont,** showing French influence, though the term is more strictly Italian (**Piemonte**). The *d* was inserted, apparently, to make more clear the connection with the French *pied,* so that the meaning foot-mountain, or foot-of-the-mountain, could be more clearly discerned. The term has become popular as a habitation-name, with high commendatory value, such as often goes with foreign-sounding words and those suggesting height. Some of the towns, e.g. in CA, are even properly located. **Piedmont** AZ: because of the variegated colors on the nearby mountains, i.e. pied.

Piedra Spanish 'stone, rock.'

Piegan From the Indian tribal name.

Pierce From the personal name, especially for President Franklin Pierce, e.g. the mountain in CA, named by surveyors in 1853.

Pierre French 'stone,' but more commonly from the personal name. In SD the town is from **Fort Pierre** (1832), which was named for Pierre Choteau, Jr., of the American Fur Company, which built the fort.

Piety Rare, but occurring occasionally as **Piety Hill,** probably for local associations of religious fervor.

Pig Although in common use for an important domestic animal, the place-names are rare. A few of them may be derived from the personal name, usually **Pigg.** Now-lost associations have produced such names as **Pig Creek** KS and **Pig Hollow** KY Obvious association has yielded **Pig Pen Branch** KY. **Pig Eye Lake** MN: from the nickname, because of a defective eye, of Pierre Par-rant, first settler in the area ca. 1842. Because of unpleasant suggestions, there are apparently no habitation-names.

Pigeon, Pigeonroost Wild pigeons gave names to many natural features. The most notable of these birds was the so-called passenger pigeon, now extinct, but in earlier times extraordinarily numerous. Places where these birds roosted in the forests covered many acres, and so highly impressed the pioneers that many names thus resulted. Most of the habitation-names arise by transfer, but the personal name also exists. **Pigeon Point** CA: from the wrecking there, May 6, 1853, of the clipper ship *Carrier Pigeon*.

Piggsgut River ME By folk-etymology from an Algonquian term recorded (1730) as **Piscot**, 'branch.'

Pike 1) a personal name, especially for for Zebulon M. Pike, explorer and hero of the War of 1812, e.g. **Pikes Peak** CO, which was made known to Americans by his report, and thus named by popular usage, since he did not place his own name upon it. **Pike Co.** occurs commemoratively in states from PA to AR. 2) From the shortening of 'turnpike,' i.e. 'toll road,' or 'main road,' e.g. **Pike** WV. 3) From the so-called Pikes, i.e. the type of backwoods frontier people who took their name from supposedly coming from **Pike Co.** MO, e.g. **Pike Co. Peak** CA. 4) From the fish, the species being generally the so-called wall-eyed pike, not the fish called 'pike' in England, which is called 'pickerel' in the U.S. Many lakes and some streams have been thus named, but **Pike Creek** OR is for Dan Pike, pioneer settler.

Pikwaming Point MI Ojibway 'tuft-(of)-trees-point.'

Pilancillo See **Peloncillo.**

Pilar Spanish 'water-basin, pillar,' also used as title for the Virgin Mary, and as a personal name, usually for a woman. **Pilares** TX: from the meaning 'water-holes.' **Pilarcitos**, the diminutive, for 'small pillar-like rocks,' occurs in two name-clusters in CA.

Pilchuck WA From a local Indian term, 'red water,' originally applied to the creek.

Pilhuena Island FL Muskogean 'swamp' (?).

Pilinterry Creek NC An altered spelling from pellitory, an herb once thought to be medicinal.

Pillager MN From the tribal name of the local Ojibways.

Pillar A common descriptive, e.g. **Pillar Rock** WA. See **Pilar.**

Pilot In seacoast usage the term indicates a place associated with a pilot, e.g. **Pilot Cove** WA. Its more characteristic use is inland, with the meaning 'landmark,' i.e. a feature easily seen, and thus serving, psychologically at least, as a guide. **Pilot Peak** NV-UT: a prominence kept in view by emigrants crossing the Salt Lake desert, named by J. C. Frémont in 1845. **Pilot Mountain** NC served as a guide to early hunters; a rare use of the name in the East, where long-range visibility is not so common. **Pilot Grove** MN: in flat country a grove thus served as a landmark. In certain areas the term is coupled especially with 'knob,' e.g. half a dozen of them in TX.

Pilpil Butte OR Chinook jargon, 'red.'

Pima From the tribal name.

Pimple A derogatory term for a small elevation, e.g. **Pimple Hills** NJ.

Pin French 'pine-tree,' e.g. **Pointe aux Pins** MI.

Pina NM For Spanish *piña*, 'pine cone.'

Pinabete NM Spanish 'fir [tree].'

Pinacate CA American-Spanish for a kind of beetle.

Pinal From the tribal name of the Pinal Apaches, the word meaning 'deer' in Apache. **Pinaleno Mountains** AZ: the Spanish term for a man of this tribe.

Pinch The personal name is rare. Names presumably arose by incident from people being in a pinch, e.g. **Pinch-Em Tight Ridge** KY, and the repeated **Pinchgut Creek,** probably referring to hunger.

Pinchona Creek AL Muskogean, meaning uncertain.

Pinchot From the personal name, especially for Gifford Pinchot, early 20th-century advocate of conservation, e.g. the mount and pass in CA.

Pinchoulee Creek AL Muskogean (Creek) with *pin,* 'turkey,' and the remainder uncertain.

Pinconning MI From an Algonquian name, *O-pin-a-kan-ning,* 'potato (wild)-place.'

Pinder Town SC Kongo 'peanut,' an African word naturalized in parts of the SE, locally thought to have been named for peanuts involved in an incident of the Revolutionary War.

Pine A rival to 'oak' in number of names, it is often used as a term to include all conifers. Though less strikingly than 'oak,' it has commendatory value for habitation-names, especially in the West, where it suggests cool mountain country of open forests, as in **Pinecrest** and **Pinehaven.** Used descriptively, it may serve to identify almost any natural feature. It is, however, not serviceable in regions that are thickly grown with pines, because it fails to make a distinction. In both East and West it is often an indicator of high altitude, so that **Pine Mountain** and **Pine Ridge** are common. A second specific is common, as in **White Pine Co.** NV, and **Lone Pine Crossing** AZ.

Pinecate Peak CA Probably a variant of **Pinacate.**

Pinellas FL From the original Spanish *pinal,* 'pine-grove,' shifted by Americans and apparently pluralized.

Pineola NC From the growth of pines and a local woman, Ola Penland.

Piney, Piny As an adjective from **Pine,** it often has a derogatory suggestion, indicating a place given over to pines, because of poor soil, most commonly as **Piney Woods** (e.g. in MS). It is typical of the SE, but is in occasional use elsewhere, e.g. **Piney Fork** OH. The spelling **Piny** is rare. **Piney** OK: for F. C. Piney, first sheriff of the county.

Pineyon AZ From an adaptation or partial Anglicizing of Spanish *piñon.*

Pingora WY Shoshone 'high, inaccessible,' named ca. 1940. Also as **Dipingora.**

Piniele MT Originally **Pinicle** (for **Pinnacle**) because of a nearby butte; the spelling was shifted in transmission.

Pink Regularly from the personal name. **Pink Creek** GA: by error or folk-etymology from an earlier recorded **Punk Creek.**

Pinnacle A common descriptive for mountains, peaks, and rocks, sometimes standing alone as with **The Pinnacles** CA.

Pinnickinnick Mountain WV Apparently a variant for **Kinnickinnick.**

Pinnochio Pinnacle WY From the resemblance of its profile to that of the fictional character.

Pinnyshook Creek MS Choctaw, the name of a village, but literally 'linden-tree.'

Pino Spanish 'pine [tree].'

Pinole CA From the Mexican-Spanish word meaning a meal ground of corn or seeds, often as made by Indians. The name apparently arose from an incident involving such meal, but details are uncertain.

Pinopolis SC From pine, and the Greek *polis,* 'city.'

Pintado Spanish 'painted.'

Pintalla Creek AL Muskogean (Creek) 'swamp-big' (?).

Pinto Though it is a Spanish family name, most examples are from the meaning 'mottled, spotted,' and arise from highly colored rock formations, e.g.

Pinto UT. **Pinto Peak** CA has been transferred to a peak that is not highly colored. The word has spread out of the Spanish-speaking area in the sense of a 'pinto' horse, and **Pinto Mountain** OR arose from a horse that ranged there. The feminine (*pinta*) occurs rarely.

Pintou, Bayou LA Spanish *pinto,* 'painted,' but reference uncertain.

Pintura Spanish 'painting,' in UT from the highly colored hills in the vicinity.

Piny See **Piney.**

Pinyon The pinyon pine is common, and often the only tree, in many parts of the arid West, and is also valued for its nuts. Names thus arising are common, e.g. **Pinyon Mountain** AZ.

Pioche NV For F. L. A. Pioche, financier, who had much to do with the development of the town (founded, 1864).

Piojo Spanish 'louse.'

Pioneer The term did not come into common use until the mid-19th century, and most of the names have been bestowed in retrospect, out of vague admiration of the pioneer settlers, e.g. in MN. **Pioneer** TX was named by W. J. Jolly for himself, since he was the first settler. **Pioneer Basin** CA: the surrounding peaks were named for four pioneer railroad builders, and the basin then given the general name. **Pioneer** OR: for the Pioneer Sandstone Company. The name may also be used in general commendatory fashion, as the equivalent of 'first,' e.g. **Pioneer** AZ from a mine-name.

Pipe Probably sometimes originating, as in the recurrent **Pipe Spring,** because a pipe had been placed to carry the water. **Pipe Lake** MN: because the shape resembles a tobacco pipe. Often an incident is involved, e.g. **Pipe Creek** AZ because a tobacco pipe was found there. **Pipe Spring** AZ: on a bet a man shot the bottom out of a pipe. **Pipe Creek** CA: two corncob pipes were found here in the 1860's. **Pipe Line Canyon** CA: from an iron pipeline laid in the 1890's. **Pipestone:** the English term for the soft stone or clay from which the Indians fashioned tobacco pipes, e.g. in MN, where the name is from a celebrated quarry for such stone. **Pipestave Hill** MA: probably where pipestaves were cut, i.e. the sections for large barrels, commonly known in Colonial times as 'pipes.' **Pipestem** WV: From a creek so called because a bush growing there produced a wood that could be used for pipe stems. **Pipe Creek** MD: probably because red clay for the making of pipes was obtained here by the Indians.

Pipit Lake CO From the water pipit, a bird found here.

Pippapasses KY Named, ca. 1915, by a schoolteacher from Browning's poem, with the idea of doing good by unconsciously influencing other people.

Piqua From an Indian tribal name, also **Pickaway.**

Piquant French 'prickly,' the bayou in LA being a shortening from *piquant amourette,* 'the thorn locust tree.'

Pirate The use of the name is chiefly as the romantic **Pirate Cove,** and seems to have no connection with genuine pirates, and to be at most 'based upon the reputation of the place.' It has been used chiefly in AK. **Pirate Lake** AK: because an excellent example of 'stream-piracy' is in the vicinity. **Pirate Peak** AK: for a steam launch so named.

Piru CA Shoshonean, probably the name of a plant.

Piscasaw Creek IL Algonquian, meaning uncertain.

Piscataqua, Piscatacook, Piscataquis, Piscataquog A repeated name in New England and NY, the Algonquian term meaning 'fork-(of)-river-at.' It is probably the origin of the tribal name **Piscataway.**

Piscataway MD, NJ See **Piscataqua.**

Piscola Creek GA Muskogean (Creek), probably 'milk-acorns,' from a place where oil was pressed from acorns.

Piseco Lake NY From the personal name of an Indian who lived there.

Pisgah From the Biblical mountain, often bestowed on a church and then transferred to a habitation. Some mountains were named directly from the Bible, e.g. in CA.

Pisgatoek River NH Algonquian 'river-branch-place,' i.e. probably a forking.

Pisinimo AZ Papago 'brown-bear head.'

Piskquoag River The same as **Pisgatoek**, q.v.

Pismire From the older word for 'ant,' e.g. **Pismire Island** MA.

Pismo CA From *pismu*, a local Indian word for 'tar,' probably Chumash.

Pispogutt MA Algonquian 'mud-pond-at.'

Pissepunk Hill CT Algonquian 'sweat-house.'

Pistakee IL Algonquian (Illinois) 'buffalo.'

Pistapaug CT Algonquian 'mud-pond.'

Pistol From an incident involving a pistol, e.g. in OR the river is named from a pistol lost in it in 1853.

Pit River CA From the pitfalls dug by the Indians in that region.

Pitahaya A name used for the saguaro cactus, e.g. **Pitahaya Canyon** AZ.

Pitas, Point CA Originally **Pitos** (Spanish 'whistle, fife') because the men of the Portolá Expedition of 1769 heard whistles blown in the Indian village there. The name was later changed to **Petes** by mistake, and this meaningless term was then changed to **Pitas**, 'century plant,' on the assumption, in American times, that this was the proper meaning.

Pitchfork Creek WY A brand name.

Pitchgussett MA Algonquian 'muddy-ledge-at.'

Pithlachascotee River FL Seminole 'canoe-cut,' apparently referring to a place where canoes were made or to an incident.

Pithlachocco Lake FL Seminole 'boat-house,' but reference uncertain.

Pitoikam AZ Papago 'sycamore place.'

Pitsua Butte OR Probably Klamath, for the kangaroo rat.

Pitt A number of towns so called in the Colonial period honor the elder William Pitt (1708–1778), e.g. **Pittsfield** MA, **Pittsboro** NC, **Pittston** PA. **Pittsburgh** PA: after the capture of Fort Duquesne, the English changed the name, but the first recorded form is still half French, as **Pitts-Bourg**. The Scottish spelling ('burgh' instead of 'boro' or 'burg') was used, probably because Gen. John Forbes, the British commander, was a Scot, and it was preserved stubbornly, even against federal pressure, in later years. The fame of the original city for coal production and steel manufacture led to the use of the name for towns thus designed, e.g. in CA and KS, but these, under pressure from the Post Office Dept., use the spelling without *h*. **Pittsburg** TX: for W. W. Pitts, early settler. See **Pittsylvania**

Pittsylvania VA Named (1769) for William Pitt, English statesman, in combination with a Latin form, 'forest-place,' on the analogy of **Pennsylvania**.

Piute From the Indian tribal name. Modern anthropologists prefer the form **Paiute**, but most of the place-names were established with the old spelling.

Piwaket Lake NY Algonquian, meaning uncertain.

Pizarro VA From the name of the 16th-century conqueror of Peru.

Pizzlewig Creek CA Formerly **Sweet Pizzlewig**, locally told to be for a woman 'deficient in virtuous ways,' who once lived there. An obscenity is to be suspected, since 'pizzle' has slang meanings of 'penis,' and 'sexual intercourse.'

Placard Swamp SC By local story, because notices were once posted there.

Placentia CA The name is that of a well-known bay in Newfoundland, but may have been used here as a kind of pseudo-Spanish to suggest 'pleasing place.'

Placer A widely used term during the gold rush in CA, either to describe the gold obtained from gravel or to designate a place where such gravel was worked, e.g. **Placer Co.**, which took its name from **Placerville**, so called because of rich workings there.

Placita Spanish, the diminutive of **Plaza,** 'little plaza.'

Plain Common for habitation-names, commendatory because of the suggestion of openness and level farming country; **Plainfield** CT dates from 1700. The commonest forms are **Plainfield, Plainview, Plainville. Plainfield** NJ: from an estate-name. **Plainview** SD is locally believed to have been named because it is on a ridge and so in 'plain view,' but from such a site the plain is also in view.

Plaine French 'plain, level country,' e.g. **Belle Plaine** in several states. In American-French the term was used for a kind of maple, and the **Des Plaines River** IL was thus descriptively named.

Plaistow NH Probably from the town in England.

Planada Spanish 'plain, level land.'

Plank Commonly from the personal name, but sometimes because of a construction in planks, especially **Plank Road** IA, for a system of road building which flourished in the mid-19th century.

Plano Spanish 'plain, level, smooth.' The name has been used for some habitations situated in flat country, e.g. TX, ID, CA. In **Rio del Plano** NM there is probably a partial Anglicization of Spanish *llano,* 'plain' (noun), but some other sense of the word may be involved.

Plant Sometimes for the family name, but also as a second element meaning 'factory, place of fabrication,' as probably in **Cotton Plant** AR, LA, MS, though the latter may in some instances be merely a shortening of **Cotton Plantation.**

Plantation Though a common term in the South, it is rare in place-names. In CA it is derived from an inn called the Plantation House.

Planter The southern term for a farmer, usually with connotations of wealth, has given rise to habitation-names, especially **Plantersville** in several states.

Plaquemine LA Louisiana French 'persimmon,' the bayou being named because of the presence there of such trees.

Plaska TX An early settler submitted **Pulaski,** the name of his former home in TN, but the name came back from the Post Office Dept. as **Plaska.**

Plaster City CA Because a cement company had its chief office there.

Plasterco VA From the product produced by the local U.S. Gypsum Company.

Plat(e) French 'flat.' In place-names the feminine appears as **Platte.** The river NB is a translation of an Omaha name, elsewhere transliterated as **Nebraska,** meaning a stream not running between high banks, but widely spread out. So also **Bayou Plat** LA. In MN the lake and river are translated from the Ojibway, the original terms apparently suggesting a man lying flat. Also on land features, e.g. **Pointe Platte** LA.

Plata Spanish 'silver,' e.g. **La Plata** NM from the occurrence or supposed occurrence of the metal. It is elsewhere, e.g. in MO (1855), a name borrowed from South America, during the period of liking for exotic names. **La Plata Peak** CO was probably named because of silver ore in the vicinity.

Plateau Commonly a generic, but occurring as a specific by association, e.g. **Plateau City** CO, **The Plateau Province** UT.

Platina CA Because the native alloy of platinum thus named was believed to exist in the area.

Platinum Because of the real or supposed occurrence of that metal, e.g. two creeks in AK.

Plato From the ancient Greek philosopher, probably given to railroad stations as being short and easy to spell. It is also a family name, and some of the place-names are probably thus derived.

Platte Commonly from the French; see **Plat.** It occasionally arises from Dutch *plat,* 'flat,' but as applied to water features 'with little current,' e.g. **Plattekill** NY.

Plausawa Mountain NH For an Abnaki warrior killed there in 1753.

Playa Spanish 'beach,' e.g. **Playa del Rey** CA, 'Beach of the King.' Over most of the SW the word refers to a dry lake, which is often beachlike in appearance, e.g. **Las Playas** AZ, **Playas Valley** NM.

Plaza Spanish 'town square, marketplace.'

Pleasant Occurs as a personal name, and some examples have so arisen, especially those with the form **Pleasants.** The great majority of the names however, are from the adjective. At least 1000 names must thus exist for quasi-descriptive and commendatory reasons. The term is coupled with many different generics to form names for natural features, e.g. **Pleasant Hill, Pleasant Valley,** both very common. It is applied, however, with the idea of habitation in mind, and so is not usually found with generics which are themselves unpleasant in suggestion and which offer no opportunity for habitation, e.g. swamp, butte, desert. Of the habitation-suffixes, '-ville' is generally used. Also noteworthy are **Pleasant Hall** PA, **Pleasant Home** OR, **Pleasant Hope** MO, **Pleasant Shade** TX, and **Pleasant Unity** PA. With 'point' and 'mount' the term stands in postposition, probably because these generics have a French origin or carry that suggestion. **Mount Pleasant** PA may be the original one, dating from the 18th century. **Pleasanton** CA, KS: for Alfred Pleasonton, Civil War general. **Pleasant Valley** CA: for James Pleasant, killed by Indians there in 1862.

Plein(e) French 'full,' but in **Eau Pleine River** WI the term is more likely a mistake in spelling for **Plaine,** q.v.

Pleito Spanish 'litigation.' The creek in CA was probably named because of some dispute in Spanish times.

Plenty Scarcely existing in place-names except as a remnant of a kind of pidgin English once used for talking with Indians and for translating their names; thus **Plenty Wolves Lake** SD for Louis Plenty Wolves, the allottee. **Plentycoos Peak** WY is for the Crow chief, whose name was more properly Plenty Coups. **Plentywood** MT: because of timber along the stream in a generally treeless country.

Plessis NY From the town in France, or a family name thus derived.

Plevna From the city in Bulgaria, the names (e.g. in MO in 1877) being given when the city became famous as the result of its siege by the Russians in 1877.

Pliny WV For Pliny Brown, local landowner.

Plomosa Mountains AZ Spanish 'leaden,' so called probably for the occurrence of lead ores.

Plotter Kill NY By folk-etymology from the Dutch; see **Plattekill.**

Plover From the game bird. See **Curlew.**

Pluck TX The namer so called it because he considered that it took pluck to settle here.

Pluckemin NJ Probably Algonquian of uncertain meaning, though the name exists in Scotland.

Plum From wild plums, e.g. **Plum Hills** OR. Habitation-names have arisen by transfer, or directly, e.g. **Plum** TX. Nine creeks in SD bear the name.

Pluma Spanish 'feather.' Generally in the plural, e.g. **Plumas Co.** CA. See **Feather.**

Plumb Creek SD Probably for **Plum,** by variation of spelling.

Plus WV For Plus Levi, town founder.

Plush OR For a well-known local Paiute Indian.

Pluto WV For the Roman god, with the local story that it was so named by the first postmaster who said that only Pluto could remain postmaster and be acceptable to the public. **Pluton** represents another form of the name, e.g. the creek in CA probably named because hot springs suggested the lower regions.

Plymouth On John Smith's map of New England (1616), Prince Charles wrote the names of many English towns, replacing the names of Indian tribes or villages. One of these was **Plymouth** at the approximate location of the present town. The 'Pilgrims' of 1620 had Smith's map with them, and kept the name when they settled there. They already had associations with the name since they were chartered under the Plymouth Company, and had sailed from Plymouth in Devonshire. Because of historical association and the resulting high commendatory value, the name has spread to some 25 states, and by transfer to a few natural features.

Plympton MA From a village in England, and also, probably, because it was close to **Plymouth** (1707).

Po River See **Mattaponi.**

P. O. Spring CA So named when a post office was established here.

Poca WV From a common local shortening of **Pocatalico.**

Pocahontas For the Indian 'princess,' daughter of Powhatan, made famous by the writings of John Smith, and married to John Rolfe, e.g. the county in IA, in which is a township **Powhatan,** and towns **Rolfe** and **Varina.** See **Matoaka.**

Pocasset Algonquian, a repeated name on water features in New England. It must be a common and useful specific for some part of a stream, and has been translated as 'where the stream widens,' but this seems doubtful, and it can just as well be rendered 'where the stream narrows.' In a sense these meanings are the same, and the term might denote any place where the stream changed in width. Related names are **Pecowsic,** and probably **Pochassic** and **Pochasuck.**

Pocatalico River SC, WV Probably from the name of an Indian tribe or village.

Pocatello ID From the name of a well-known Bannock chief of the mid-19th century.

Pochassic See **Pocasset.**

Pochasuck MA Algonquian, probably 'narrow-outlet.'

Pochuck NJ, NY Algonquian, probably 'corner, recess,' but it may also be the name of a chief.

Pochung NJ Probably a variant of **Pochuck.**

Pockwockamus Pond ME Algonquian 'little-muddy-pond.'

Pocomo Head MA Algonquian, meaning uncertain.

Pocomoke MD, VA Algonquian, probably a southern form equivalent to **Poquomock** MA; see under **Pequonnock.**

Pocono PA Algonquian (Delaware), probably 'valley-stream,' the mountain being secondarily named.

Pocopson PA Algonquian, meaning uncertain.

Pocosin, Poquoson Primarily a generic of Algonquian origin, it entered English usage in VA in the early 17th century, meaning 'swamp' or 'overflowed land.' It occurs as a specific by association, e.g. **Pocosin Fork** WV and the village **Poquoson** VA.

Pocotopaug CT Algonquian 'twin-pond.'

Pocquayahwan Lake WI Algonquian, meaning uncertain.

Pocumpcus Lake ME Algonquian 'narrow-gravelly-(place)-little-at.'

Pocumtuck MA From the Indian tribal name.

Podunk In CT it is from a tribal name. In MA and NY it is from the probable literal meaning, i.e. 'swamp (miry place)-at.' Its derogatory use to designate a rustic, out-of-the-way and insignificant village arose in the 19th century.

Poeno Creek SD An altered spelling from the name of Balboa Pynaux, an early French settler. So also **Peno Mound. Peno Creek** WY is for an early trapper who was injured here by a buffalo bull, perhaps the same man.

Poentics Kill NY From a 17th-century Dutch nickname of an early settler, with *kill,* 'stream.'

Poestenkill NY The nickname of an early Dutch settler, with *kill,* 'stream.'

Poge See **Cape Poge.**

Pogopskekok Stream ME Algonquian, probably 'shallow-gravelly-place.'

Pogromni Russian 'desolation.'

Pogue VT See **Paug.**

Pogunnock Creek PA Algonquian (Delaware) 'dark-stream.'

Pohatcong NJ Algonquian 'bare-mountain-at' (?).

Pohenagamook Lake ME Algonquian 'spread-out-lake.'

Pohick VA Algonquian 'hickory.'

Pohoco Headland NB Pawnee 'hill-in-water-sitting,' because the river swings around the bottom of the bluff.

Pohoganse Pond ME Algonquian 'shallow-sandy-pond' (?).

Pohomoosh Stream ME Algonquian 'shallow-stream.'

Poia Lake MT The Blackfoot name of Scarface, one of their mythological characters.

Point Nearly always a generic, though the fact is sometimes obscured by its standing in the first position. **Point Lake** MN: a lake identified by having a point. **Points** WV: a crossroad village, having four points of land where the roads cross. **Point** TX: a shortening from Rice's Point. **Pointblank** TX: named by a woman who is reported to have said it was because the place was 'without obstacles in the way,' probably meaning

that it was in flat country. **Eleven Points River** MO: from the American-French *pointe,* a term used along rivers for projecting points of land, the stream being at the eleventh point from some beginning. See **No,** for **Point No Point.**

Pointe French 'point,' e.g. **Pointe Coupee** LA, 'point cut-off,' named (1699) by the Iberville expedition when, on the removal of some obstructions, the water rushed through, cutting the point off. **Pointe en Pointe, Bayou** LA: French 'point in point,' perhaps with the meaning 'point upon point,' because of two points which project close together from the same side of the stream.

Poison Usually coupled with spring, less commonly with creek, because of water impregnated with alkali or some other mineral which is poisonous, particularly to cattle, e.g. **Poison Spring** WY. It is also applied to places where poisonous plants, such as the locoweed, are growing, e.g. **Poison Valley** CA. Though many unpleasant terms occur as habitation-names, this one does not seem to do so.

Pojoaque NM Indian (Tewa) 'drink water place.'

Pokagon IN, MI For Leopold Pokagon, a local Indian chief of the early 19th century.

Pokahganeh Pond ME Algonquian 'white-perch.'

Pokata Creek MD Algonquian 'cleared-it-is.' Cf. **Pequonnock.**

Pokegama MN, WI Algonquian, with *gama,* 'lake,' and the rest with the idea of jutting out, in the sense of having bays branching off.

Poke-O-Moonshine ME, NY From an Algonquian original, but so completely reworked by folk-etymology as to be obscured; 'broken-off-smooth' is the conventional translation, but cannot be considered certain. The opening *pok-* is common in Algonquian names, with various meanings, e.g. 'clear.' So also **Pok-O-Moonshine, Poky Moonshine,** and possibly **Peekamoose.**

Poker After the popularization of poker as a gambling game, ca. 1830, the name was sometimes applied by cowboys and miners to places where the game was often played or where an especially notable game had occurred. The repeated **Poker Flat** probably owes something to Bret Harte's story of 1869.

Poketo Creek PA Algonquian (Delaware), from the idea of 'abandon,' possibly because the stream could be ascended only thus far in canoes.

Pokey Lake ME Algonquian, probably 'clear, shallow, open.'

Pok-O-Moonshine See **Poke-O-Moonshine.**

Poky Moonshine See **Poke-O-Moonshine.**

Pokywaket Creek CA Wintu 'raw-creek,' probably because acorns were cured here.

Polacca AZ For Tom Polacca, Tewa Indian who established a settlement there in 1890.

Polallie Creek OR Chinook jargon, 'powdery,' with reference to glacial silt.

Poland In AR the town was named from D. R. Poland, early settler. The town in OH is probably for George Poland, early settler. In ME the town-name is probably from the hymn tune. In other instances the name may be from the European country, which was in American consciousness in the early 19th century because of its revolutions.

Polander Hollow NB From the settlement of Poles, who were often thus called.

Polar In TX, for Polar Singletary, daughter of an early settler.

Polaris The name for the North Star has been applied to a few habitations for no reason as yet discovered.

Polaski MI Probably a variant of **Pulaski,** to avoid repetition within the same state.

Pole Usually for a place where poles were cut, e.g. **Pole Knoll** AZ. **Pole Creek**

NB is a shortening for **Lodgepole Creek. Polebridge** MT, OR indicates a bridge built of undressed lumber. This usage has apparently prevented the use of the national name, but see **Polander. Twelvepole Creek** WV: the surveyor's term 'pole,' equaling 16½ feet, is here preserved, either as the width of the stream or because of its distance from a predetermined point. **Pole Bridge Creek** GA: because of a primitive bridge, in some way using poles, sometimes rendered as **Poley** or even **Polar.**

Polecat An alternate name for skunk occurs on natural features, usually in the SE. The springs in WY are named for their odor.

Polipod Brook NJ Probably Algonquian, meaning uncertain.

Polita Canyon CA An alteration of Poleta, from a nearby mine bearing a Spanish personal name.

Polk From the personal name, commonly for J. K. Polk, president, e.g. numerous towns and counties.

Polo IL Named (1856) for Marco Polo, the traveler, but reason for naming unknown.

Polonia WI Latin 'Poland,' named by Polish immigrants.

Polpis Harbor MA Algonquian 'branching-cove' (?).

Polvadera, Polvadero Dialectal variations in the SW of Spanish *polvareda,* 'dust-storm, cloud of dust,' e.g. **Polvadera Mountain** NM, **Polvadero Gap** CA.

Polychrome Pass AK Descriptive, because of multi-colored rock.

Poly Top Butte OR It has several tops (Greek *poly,* 'many').

Polywaket Creek CA Wintu 'raw-creek,' probably so named because raw acorns were brought there by the Indians for curing.

Pomaria SC From Latin *pomum,* 'fruit,' or *pomus,* 'fruit-tree,' with an ending to indicate 'place of,' named because it was a fruit-growing area.

Pomfret In CT (1713) from a spelling after the usual pronunciation of Ponte-fract, an English town; in VT (1761) probably for the Earl of Pomfret, who was prominent in the court of George II.

Pomham Rock RI Algonquian, from the name of an Indian sachem (died 1676).

Pomiches Creek NY Algonquian 'cross (athwart), crossing.'

Pomkeag ME Algonquian 'rock-place.'

Pomme French 'apple,' more commonly in place-names as **Pomme de Terre,** 'potato,' e.g. the river in MO. **Pomme d'Or Bay** LA: literally 'apple of gold,' but applied locally to a wild fruit or berry.

Pomona From the Roman goddess of fruit trees, regularly applied because of local interest in fruit-growing, e.g. CA, MO, NC.

Pomonkey Creek MD From an Indian village or tribal name.

Pompadour Bluff OR There is a peculiar rock formation suggestive of a pompadour.

Pompano FL From the fish, probably first applied to the beach.

Pompanoosuc See **Ompompanoosuc.**

Pompanuck Creek VT Algonquian, meaning a place for playing games (?).

Pompeii MI From the ancient city of Italy.

Pomperaug River CT From the name of an Indian chief who was living in 1725.

Pompeston Creek NJ Probably Algonquian; a connection with **Pompton** NJ seems likely.

Pompey From the notable Roman (106 B.C.–48 B.C.). **Pompey's Pillar** MT: named by Capt. William Clark of the Lewis and Clark Expedition, with reference to the famous monument of that name in ancient Alexandria; he may also have been thinking, humorously, of an Indian baby so called who was with the expedition.

Pomponio Creek CA For a renegade Christian Indian of that name, captured and executed in 1824.

Pompton NJ A repeated name, being some Algonquian term of uncertain meaning which has been transformed by folk-etymology into the semblance of an English town-name.

Ponaganset RI Algonquian, meaning uncertain.

Ponca From the Indian tribal name.

Ponce The discoverer of FL in 1513, Ponce de León, is commemorated in towns in FL and MO, and by numerous springs, e.g. FL, NM, his name being associated with springs because of his search for the fountain of youth.

Poncha Springs CO Probably the same as **Punche Creek** CO, both names apparently going back to some undetermined Indian original, having been attracted by folk-etymology to the semblance of Spanish words.

Ponchatalawa Creek LA Muskogean 'cattail-singing' (?), from the sound of wind in the reeds.

Ponchatoula LA Muskogean 'hair-hanging' (?), with possible reference to Spanish moss.

Poncho Rico Creek CA Probably for Francisco (Pancho) Rico, owner of a local ranch in the 1840's.

Pond Commonly a generic for a body of water too small to be called a lake, but in New England often used for what would elsewhere be a lake. It occurs as a specific by association, e.g. **Pond Gap** WV, **Pond Brook** MA. Some places are from the personal name.

Ponder From the family name, e.g. in TX for W. A. Ponder, local landowner.

Pondera County MT An American rendering of **Pend Oreille.**

Ponderay ID An alternate spelling of **Pend Oreille.**

Pondosa OR The trade name of lumber from the ponderosa pine.

Pone Its occasional use, e.g. **Pone Island** MD, is probably from the colloquial word, 'bread,' especially as 'corn pone' in the South; it would presumably have been applied because of an incident.

Ponemah Of Indian origin, from Longfellow's *Hiawatha,* 'the Land of the Hereafter.'

Poney Hollow NY Probably from Saponey, the Indian tribal name. Also as **Pony Hollow.**

Pongokwayhaymock Lake ME Algonquian 'woodpeckers-at.'

Pongonquamook Lake ME Algonquian 'muddy lake.'

Poni River See **Mattaponi.**

Poniken, Ponikin MA Algonquian, usually translated as 'put down your burden,' and apparently referring to the end of a portage.

Ponkabea Creek AL Choctaw 'grapes-are-there.' Also as **Ponkabiah.**

Ponkapog MA Algonquian 'clear (shallow)-pond,' the idea being that one can see to the bottom.

Ponkhockie NY Dutch 'point-hook-little,' i.e. a point of land with a small hook or angle in it.

Ponquogue NY Algonquian, probably a much eroded variant of the form discussed under **Pequonnock.**

Ponset Algonquian 'falls-at.'

Ponta In TX it is from Latin *pons,* 'bridge,' because of a situation near two bridges. In AL the creek is from Choctaw, meaning uncertain.

Pontchartrain, Lake LA For Louis, Comte de Pontchartrain (1643–1727), French political figure.

Ponteaux Branch SC From the French family Villeponteaux, early settlers.

Ponte Vedra FL Named (1932) for the city of Spain in an attempt to recapture Spanish atmosphere.

Pontiac From the name of the great chief of the Ottawas (ca. 1720–1765). Though he had waged bitter war against the English colonists, he made peace at the end of his life, and his character was much admired. His name was bestowed on a settlement in MI in 1818. A city in IL is named because settlers came from the one in MI, but a village **St. Clair Co.,** IL is near the site where Pontiac was killed by an Illinois Indian.

Ponton, Bayou LA French 'pontoon, floating bridge' (or from Spanish *ponton*); the reference may have been to a floating tree which served as a bridge.

Pontoocook Cove NH Algonquian 'falls-river-at.'

Pontoosuc MA Algonquian, a repeated name, analyzable as 'falls-brook-outlet,' possibly meaning a place where there was a small waterfall at the outlet of a lake.

Pontotoc Muskogean 'cattail-prairie,' a descriptive in MS, and thence transferred to other states.

Pony Widely applied in the West for a small horse or often for a horse in general, with place-names arising for the same reason. See **Horse, Poney.**

Poo Run VA Probably a shortening from some Algonquian name. Cf. **Po,** which may have been suggested by this name as well as from **Mattaponi.**

Pool Common as a generic on fishing streams, the use of the term as a specific is generally from the personal name. **Pool Knoll** AZ: in a corral here early cattlemen temporarily 'pooled' their herds.

Poonkiny Creek CA Indian (Yuki) 'wormwood.'

Poor, Poorman Both **Poor(e)** and **Poorman** are personal names, and some of the names have thus arisen, e.g. **Poor-man Creek** CA for an early miner. **Poor-house Branch** KY and similar names arise by association with an institution formerly so known; sometimes as **Poor Farm**, e.g. the branch in KY. The name may also arise as a derogatory to indicate a place where a living was supposed to be particularly hard to make, e.g. **Poor Fork** KY. **Poorman** also occurs in this sense, but tends to be replaced for habitations, **Poormans Bottom** NB becoming **Sunshine Valley**. For habitations the name is restricted to informal communities, cf. **Hardscrabble**, etc. **Poorman Creek** (several in AK) is a miners' term, either derogatory or given to cover up actual richness. **Poorman Gulch** SD: because gold was found near the surface, so that expensive sinking of shafts was not necessary, and it was a good place for a poor man.

Poosheapatope Creek LA Choctaw, probably 'sand-bottom.'

Poosumsuck River VT Algonquian 'boggy-outlet.'

Pootatuck River CT Algonquian, probably 'falls-(in)-river.'

Pophandusing Brook NJ Algonquian, meaning uncertain.

Popher Creek TX For a local Indian chief.

Poplar Though the tree was widespread and common, it apparently made little impression upon settlers, and names are comparatively rare, though it may be found coupled with spring, creek, lake, etc. **Cottonwood** and **Aspen**, which are scientifically classed as varieties of poplar, are commoner as place-names than is **Poplar**. It occurs in habitation-names, chiefly by transfer, e.g. **Poplar Bluff** MO, but is sometimes a direct naming, e.g. **Poplar** and **Poplarville**. See **Popple, Popular**.

Popo Agie River WY Siouan (Crow), probably 'head(water)-river.'

Popocatepetl, Mount OR Named in 1888 after the Mexican peak, by a party of climbers who thus complimented its difficulty, though it is only 1020 feet in elevation.

Poponoming Lake PA Algonquian (Delaware) 'looking-(place)-at,' but reference uncertain.

Poppasquash Island RI, VT Algonquian, meaning uncertain. Also as **Popasquash**.

Popple A variant form for **Poplar**, e.g. **Popple Grove** MN.

Popponesset Bay MA Algonquian, meaning uncertain.

Popular Probably from a colloquial pronunciation of 'poplar,' e.g. the point in NJ.

Poquannoc See **Pequonnock**.

Poquessing Creek PA From the name of an Indian village; literal meaning uncertain.

Poquetanuck See **Pequonnock**.

Poquoson See **Pocosin**.

Porcupine Though occurring in nearly all of the forested country of the U.S., the animal made little impression on the pioneers in the East, and names are rare. In the West names are somewhat more common, and may generally be assumed to denote a place where someone's dog 'got into' a porcupine. The butte in SD was so named because some pine trees on a level summit gave the suggestion of a crouching porcupine. Habitation-names are almost lacking, but the settlement in SD takes its name by transfer from the butte.

Porphyry From the mineral or rock.

Porpoise Rare, probably because the porpoise is not often sighted close to land. There are several seacoast names in AK. **Cape Porpoise** ME: the earliest form (1610) is **Porpas**, a regular English spelling of the time, and the name probably arose because an early voyager saw a porpoise nearby.

Port A generic, usually preceding its specific. See under the specific, e.g. for **Port Tobacco**, see **Tobacco**.

Portage As a descriptive term, applied to many natural features, especially in regions of French background and where canoe journeys were customary. In habitation-names it is by transfer, or marks the place of a portage. **Portage** UT: this is in dry country, but is named for **Portage Co., OH. Portage** PA: from the former Portage Railroad which carried canalboats by inclines across the mountains. About 60 features in AK bear the name.

Portal A repeated name for a place associated with an entrance, e.g. **El Portal** CA, the entrance to Yosemite Valley.

Porte French 'gate,' e.g. **La Porte** CO: because it is situated at an opening which leads into the back country.

Porthill ID Because a port of entry from Canada, and on a hill.

Portland From uses of the name in England. It first applied in the U.S. to **Portland Head** ME, probably for a real or imagined resemblance to the prominent Bill of Portland in England. The city ME, having previously had different names, adopted this one in 1786, using the commendatory 'port.' In OR the city was named for that in ME in 1845, in a famous incident in which two men flipped a coin to decide between the names **Portland** and **Boston.** Francis Pettygrove, who supported the **Portland** name, had come from ME. The popularity of the name is associated with its commendatory value for a harbor, e.g. in TX; with quarries and stone, e.g. in CT; with 'Portland cement,' e.g. in IN.

Portneuf The river was named for a French-Canadian trapper who was killed on its bank in 1825.

Portola CA From Gaspar de Portolá, leader of a Spanish expedition in 1769. In **Plumas Co.** the name was given retrospectively ca. 1910. The valley near **Palo Alto** is in a region which he explored, but is also retrospectively named.

Portsmouth From the English town, but with descriptive and strongly commendatory suggestions. All three of the Colonial namings NH, RI, VA were on harbors, and the double reason for naming seems to be clear. In OH the town was named for the one in RI.

Portuguese From the settlement of Portuguese immigrants, e.g. **Portuguese Flat** CA.

Porvenir TX Spanish 'future,' probably as a commendatory.

Posen From the province which was, at the time of various namings in the 19th century, a part of Germany, so named by German settlers.

Posey Regularly from the personal name, but in CA apparently by folk-etymology from Spanish **Pozo** or **Poso,** 'well.'

Posita Diminutive of Spanish *posa*, 'well, water-hole,' e.g. **Las Positas Creek** CA.

Possession The point in AK was named by James Cook on June 1, 1778 when he 'displayed the flag and took possession for Great Britain.' The sound in WA was named by George Vancouver in 1792, when he also took possession for Great Britain.

Possum See **Opossum, Possumtrot.**

Possumtrot The term 'trot' is here used in its chiefly southern sense of 'trail,' and the whole name indicates, or implies, a place so out-of-the-way that the opossums make established trails. **Possumtrot** is a common colloquial derogative for a small rural community, rarely occurring in 'official' use; but a **Possumtrot Branch** is an established name in GA.

Post Generally from the personal name. **Post Lake** NB: from association with an army post. **Post Office Bar** OR: an office was once situated on it. **Post Office Cave** CA: numerous small holes in the walls give the suggestion of post office boxes. The name was applied to a hill in AZ because the Apaches were accustomed to place stones on the grave of a man buried here, thus passing some kind of information on to the next comer. **Post Office Butte** SD: because early settlers used to leave letters under a flat rock to be picked up and carried to their destination by the first person who was going in that direction.

Posta Spanish 'post,' in the sense of 'stage station,' etc., e.g. **Posta Quemada**

AZ because the stage station was burned some time before 1875.

Postage Stamp Butte OR A rock formation looks like a letter with a stamp on it.

Postal Colony FL Because of being settled as a colony of retired postal clerks.

Potagannissing Bay MI Ojibway, probably 'gaps-at,' because of the scattered islands with gaps between them.

Potake Pond NJ, NY Algonquian 'waterfall' (?).

Potash To indicate a place where potash was manufactured, probably from wood ashes, e.g. four brooks in MA.

Potato On natural features the term often refers to some tuberous plant, such as the so-called wild artichoke, used as food by the Indians, e.g. **Potato Lake** MN. Certain features also have been named descriptively for a real or imagined resemblance to the shape of a potato, e.g. **Potato Hill** OR. Since the term is especially coupled with 'hill' the origin may, in some instances, have been a comparison to a hill of potatoes. **Potato Butte** AZ is specifically compared to a potato standing on end. Though the name may sometimes identify a place where potatoes have been grown, it is not common in the regions famous for potato culture, and seems to have flourished most in CA, where 25 such names exist. **Potato Canyon** NM: a farmer, in early times, raised potatoes here.

Potawatomi From the Indian tribal name, also as **Pottowatomie,** and in other spellings.

Potaywadjo Ridge ME Algonquian 'wind-blows-over-mountain.' Also **Potowadjo Hill** ME.

Poteau French 'post, pole.' The reference to mountain and stream (AR, OK) is uncertain, but cf. **Baton Rouge.**

Potecasi NC Indian, of uncertain language, 'parting of waters' (?).

Poteet From the personal name; in TX for F. M. Poteet, first postmaster.

Potem Creek CA Named by the local Indians for the first white settler, who befriended them, not further identified.

Pothole From association with the kind of hole thus called, e.g. **Pothole Lake** CA.

Pothtachitto Creek AL Choctaw 'broad-big.'

Potic NY Algonquian, probably 'it-is-round,' with the original reference to an Indian village or a valley.

Potlatch Chinook jargon, 'give,' and thence the Indian custom so called. The river in ID was probably named from some incident involving the term; the town was named from the Potlatch Lumber Company.

Potomac River An Indian name recorded by John Smith in 1608 as Patawomeck. He gives no meaning, and his ability to communicate with the Indians was so slight that he could not have known the meaning and may have applied to the river some phrase that meant something else. Smith undoubtedly took it to be the name of a tribe, but the Indians thus called may have been so named later. If it is a tribal name, no further meaning need be sought. If it is something else, it is probably Algonquian, and the most common explanation has been 'something brought,' with reference to trade among the Indians. But, under the circumstances, there is little chance that this is correct.

Potonapa Pond NH Algonquian 'cove-pond' (?).

Potosi From San Luis Potosí in Mexico or from the original Potosí in Bolivia, both of which had rich silver mines; towns in MO and WI were thus named for commendatory reasons, being centers of lead-mining. **Potosi Mountain** NV was an early mining center.

Potowadjo See **Potaywadjo.**

Potowomut RI Algonquian, probably 'low-meadow-at.'

Potrero Spanish 'pasture-ground,' common in CA, sometimes as a specific, e.g. with creek, hill.

Potsdam From the city in Germany.

Pottapaug Pond MA Algonquian *paug*, 'pond'; *potta* may be either 'round' or 'with a cove.'

Pottowatomie From the Indian tribal name; also as **Potawatomi,** and in other spellings.

Potuck Creek NY Algonquian 'clear-stream' (?).

Potwisha CA From an Indian tribal name.

Poughkeepsie NY Algonquian, first recorded (1683) as the name of a waterfall, 'rock-water-little-at,' probably with reference to the rock pool at the bottom of the fall.

Poughquag NY Algonquian 'cleared-land' (?). Cf. **Pequonnock.**

Poule d'Eau, Lake LA French 'hen-of-water,' but referring to the coot.

Poulsbo WA For a place in Norway, name suggested by an immigrant.

Poultney VT Named by Gov. Benning Wentworth (1761) for William Pulteney, Earl of Bath, political figure of the time.

Pound, Pounding Though **Pound** may be from the personal name, these terms (often as **Poundmill** and **Pounding Mill**) are commonly from a mill that operated by pounding, especially for the manufacture of gunpowder, being common with 'creek,' 'run,' and 'branch' in KY, VA, WV. In some instances pound may be for a pen to hold cattle or to trap wild game, especially buffalo. **Pounder** and **Pounder Mill** occur rarely, e.g. in KY.

Poverty Indicating real or supposed poverty of a place, sometimes semihumorously. The name is commonest in the former gold-mining regions, e.g. **Poverty Hill, Poverty Bar** CA, presumably named because the diggings were not rich. But **Poverty Hill** (Sierra Co., CA) suggests irony, since a rich mine was located there.

Powahkee Creek WA From the name of a Nez Percé woman who took up a claim there.

Poway CA From a local Indian village, meaning uncertain, possibly 'end of the valley.'

Powder 1) Usually because of an association with gunpowder in early times. The commonness of the name is some indication of the importance of gunpowder to the colonists. Especially places where powder was stored for safety are likely to bear the name, e.g. **Powder Island** CT, **Powder House Hill** MA. **Powder Mill Brook** MA is an evidence of early industry. The name has generally been shunned for habitations, but a few exist. **Powderhorn** CO: from the creek, probably because an old powder horn was found there by early comers. 2) From powdery soil, e.g. **Powder River** OR, WY, which latter translates an Indian (Gros Ventre) term for a natural dust, probably with reference to black dust formed from lignite beds along the stream. **Powderhorn Lake** MN: from its shape.

Powell From the personal name, especially in the western states for J. W. Powell (1834–1902), explorer, director of the Bureau of American Ethnology, e.g. **Mount Powell** CA. **Powell River** VA: for Ambrose Powell, who was an explorer of the region in 1750 and carved his name on a tree by the stream then called **Beargrass River;** those who came later saw the name and transferred it to the river.

Power A commendatory because of an electric-power project, e.g. **Power** WV and the county (ID). **Powers** is from the personal name.

Poweshiek County IA For a local (Fox) chief, named ca. 1845.

Powhatan Whatever the word may properly have meant, it has been taken as the name of an Indian chief on the authority of John Smith, and habitation-names in a dozen states are in commemoration of him.

Powwow, Pow Wow, Powaw The Algonquian term meant a 'medicine-man,' but was taken into English chiefly as meaning the kind of ceremony at which such a person might preside, and came to mean any peaceful meeting with Indians or even any kind of meeting. Place-names, though seldom established clearly, probably indicate places at which a council with Indians was held, e.g. **Pow Wow River** NH. The creek in WA was named by Americans, after the word had come into English, because of Indian councils held there.

Poxabog Pond NY Algonquian 'widening-pond,' because in wet weather it spread out to larger size.

Poygan WI Algonquian, probably 'pipe,' i.e. for tobacco, but significance uncertain.

Poy Sippi WI Algonquian, being a badly eroded form of the word for Sioux, plus 'river.'

Pozo, Poso, Poza, Posa All are apparently used for the standard Spanish *pozo,* 'well,' though *poza* more strictly means 'puddle.' In Mexican Spanish *s* and *z* are similarly pronounced, so that confusion of spelling is easy. **Poso Bueno** AZ and **El Poso** AZ are thus explainable. The term becomes a specific, e.g. **Poso Flat** CA. See **Posey.**

Praco AL From Pratt Consolidated Coal Company.

Prado Spanish 'meadow.'

Prague From the city in Czechoslovakia, usually indicating a settlement of Bohemians, e.g. in NB.

Praha From the Czech form of the city Prague.

Prairie Though a generic, the term is used to denote a place associated with a prairie, the word more commonly being thus used in its earlier sense of 'meadow.' In many instances it goes back to a French naming. It is naturally rare or absent in the heavily wooded areas and in the desert or treeless areas, but is common, e.g. **Prairie Lake,** in such regions as parts of MN, where open grasslands, i.e. prairies, occur among the trees. With its suggestion of spaciousness the term has been used in habitation-names, often in the later-developed sense of an extensive, open plain, e.g. **Prairie View** TX. **Prairie Lea** TX: the latter term is the obsolete English word, vaguely referring to meadowland, and thus having about the same meaning as prairie. **Prairie du Chien** WI is French for 'prairie of the dog,' from an Indian chief whose name was thus translated.

Prairieon, Bayou LA French, a diminutive of *prairie.*

Praise KY By local story, because a neighborhood preacher was fond of the expression 'Praise the Lord!'

Pratum OR Latin 'meadow.'

Preacher The preacher was a prominent figure on the frontier, but names are few, doubtless because the man's proper name was ordinarily known and used. **Preachers Peak** OR: probably in counterpart to **Devil's Pulpit,** a ledge on its slope. **Preachers Run** SD: a preacher was lost here from an early hunting party. **Preacher's Head** NM: from a rock formation resembling the head of a man in a serious mood.

Preakness NJ Probably from an Algonquian original, but so greatly shifted in form as to be uncertain.

Prele French *prêle,* 'rush, horsetail,' e.g. **La Prele Creek** WY, but possibly from a personal name.

Premier WV From the term in the name of a coal company.

Preparation IA Founded, ca. 1858, by a body of seceders from Mormonism, the name being given as symbolic of their belief that this life was only a preparation for the world-to-come.

Presa Spanish 'dam,' e.g. **Presita Canyon** CA, because of a small dam here.

Prescott From the personal name. In AZ it is in honor of W. H. Prescott, the historian, an instance (1864) of early enthusiasm for literature. The brook in NJ is by folk-etymology from an Indian whose name is recorded (ca. 1715) as Piscot.

President The channel WA is for the U.S. naval vessel *President,* named by the Wilkes Expedition in 1841. The point WA was named by the same expedition, which had just given names for three individual presidents.

Presidio From association with a Spanish military establishment thus known, e.g. the town and county and **Presidio Creek** in TX. The creek in CA, which is in a non-Spanish area, is the result of the transformation by folk-etymology of the name of a Karok village; meaning unknown.

Presque Isle The standardized American spelling for the French *presqu'ile,* 'peninsula,' generally an obvious descriptive for features; on habitation-names, e.g. in ME, by transfer.

Presswood Lake SC Probably because of the pressing of wood in connection with a paper mill.

Preston In CT (1687) from an English town-name; in other states, regularly from the personal name.

Presumpscot River ME Algonquian 'broken-rocks,' an apt descriptive for several places in the course of the stream.

Pretty It occurs rarely, as a descriptive, e.g. **Pretty Rock Butte** ND, **Pretty Prairie** KS.

Pribilof Islands AK Named ca. 1792 for G. G. Pribilov who had recently discovered one of the islands.

Prieto Spanish 'dark.'

Primehook DE Dutch 'plum-point,' from the occurrence of wild plum trees.

Primero Spanish 'first.' In CA the first station on a certain branch line railroad. In CO the first place at which a mining company began operations.

Primghar IA Eight commissioners laid out the townsite in 1872, but could not agree upon a name until they formed one from their own initials, their names being Pumphrey, Roberts, Inman, McCormack, Green, Hays, Albright, and Renck.

Primo, Prima Spanish 'first.'

Primrose Usually from the personal name, e.g. in NB from David Primrose, landowner.

Prince 1) From the title, e.g. **Prince Edward Co.** VA for the son of the then (1753) Prince of Wales. Such usage flourished before the Revolution and disappeared after it. **Princeton NJ:** named in 1724 in general compliment to the royal family, but also in counterpart to a nearby **Kingston.** Most of the later namings echo this one, but commemorate the battle, e.g. in WV and MO. 2) From the personal name, e.g. **Princeton** MA: for Thomas Prince (1771), a large landowner. In TX for Princeton Downing, landowner. **Princewick** WV: named ca. 1916 as a combination of two names, probably Prince and Wickham, but details are uncertain. **Prince of Wales:** the cape in AK was named by James Cook in 1778; the **Archipelago,** by George Vancouver in 1793; both voyagers were complimenting the then Prince of Wales. Some later uses of **Princeton** are for the college (or university), e.g. the mountain in CO (ca. 1873) and the glacier in AK (1909).

Princeton See **Prince.**

Principio Italian 'beginning.' The village in MD takes the name from Principio Iron Works probably so named because the first (ca. 1715) in the region.

Printer Boy Hill CO From a mine-name.

Prisoners Harbor CA Probably because certain Mexican prisoners were exiled to Santa Cruz Island in 1830, being landed at this harbor.

Proberta CA Applied by the railroad in 1889 for Edward Probert (unidentified), with an *a* added to make it seem more like a place-name.

Problem See **Mystery.**

Procious WV For Adam Proshes who later changed the spelling to that used for the post office.

Profile Because a mountain NH or a butte SD shows the profile of a face.

Progreso Spanish 'progress,' a commendatory.

Progress On a few habitations, as a commendatory.

Project City CA Adopted by a public meeting in 1939 because the town was founded in connection with the building of a dam for the Central Valley Project.

Prometheus, Mount NV From the fire-bringer of Greek mythology; reason for application unknown.

Promise In OR the founders used the name with its religious connotation, i.e. Land of Promise. **Promise City** IA was similarly named by the Mormons. **Promise** SD is the free translation (probably under religious influence) of the name of an Indian minister, whose name literally meant 'once called.'

Promised Land AR From the Biblical Canaan, a commendatory. Cf. **Promise.**

Prong Occurs as a generic, the equivalent of 'fork' (of a stream), chiefly in the SE, and is used as a specific, e.g. **Prong** WV. **Middle Prong** NB: from that branch of the Loup River.

Prophetstown IL For the Winnebago medicine man White Cloud (1794–1841), known as the 'prophet,' whose village was at this site.

Prospect 1) On many natural features, especially elevations, with the idea that an extensive view is offered, e.g. **Prospect Peak** WV, **Prospect Hill** (about 20 in MA). 2) Because of a prospect for a mine, especially for gold, e.g. **Prospect Peak** CA. 3) As a commendatory name for habitations, indicating a hopeful future, e.g. in OR, TX. The idea of a view also gives rise to habitation-names, e.g. in NC.

Prosper, Prosperity Commendatory names, generally belied by the small population of the places so called. In SC, **Prosperity** represents an attempt in 1873 to escape from the derogatory connotations of the original **Frog Level.**

Protection In NY it is from a former tavern named Protection Harbor. The island WA was named by George Vancouver in 1792 because of the protection it afforded to his vessel from northwest winds. **Protection** KS: from nearby Fort Protection, so named because of protection which it afforded against the Indians.

Protem MO By local tradition, the first postmaster was informed that he could select a name pro tem, and so he did.

Provence OK For George Provence, merchant.

Providence In RI, named by Roger Williams in 1636 from a sense of 'God's merciful providence.' In UT named by Mormon settlers who believed that their region had been divinely blessed. The name is rare, probably having been thought overly pious or even pretentiously so. A few habitation-names were taken from country churches so named.

Provident City TX From the Provident Land Company, a commendatory.

Province Rare, but to be taken with reference to the pre-Revolutionary period, when the colonies were known as provinces and public lands could be called 'province lands'; thus, **Provincetown** MA and **Province Lake** NH.

Provo, Provost From the personal name, e.g. in UT for Etienne Provot, French-Canadian trapper who explored the region in the 1820's. **Provo** SD: for Bill Provost, by spelling after the pronunciation, an early settler.

Proxy Point OR Surveyors selected this spot as a substitute station.

Prudence The island of this name RI is close to Providence and is an early name, so that it is probably named for the virtue. In WV for Prudence McGuffin, unidentified.

Prune In WY the creek was so named because its water, flowing out of a marsh, is so dark as to be compared to prune juice. **Anse a Prune Noire** LA is French for 'black plum,' with reference to the wild black sloe or hog plum.

Psazeske Stream ME Algonquian 'muddy-branch.'

Ptarmigan From the bird, e.g. the ridge WA.

Puchyan River WI Probably Algonquian, meaning uncertain.

Puckaway Lake WI From an Indian personal name.

Puckum Branch MD Probably Algonquian, from a word 'blood,' and applied to various plants yielding a red pigment.

Pudding In most instances from the existence of pudding stone, i.e. conglomerate; hence probably the hill in CT. The creek in OR takes its name from an incident of the 1820's when some hungry frontiersman killed an elk and enjoyed a blood pudding.

Pueblo Spanish 'town,' used in NM and AZ especially for an Indian settlement, and often there as a generic, e.g. **Pueblo Viejo** AZ. It becomes a specific to identify a feature thus associated, e.g. **Pueblo Canyon** AZ, for a prehistoric ruin. **Pueblo** CO: as the only settlement in the region, ca. 1842, it was known merely by the generic name, thus being simply 'The Town.'

Puente Spanish 'bridge.' In CA, the name goes back to the Portolá Expedition of 1769, whose men improvised a bridge in this vicinity. Curiously, the name stuck to the hills, but not to the stream that was bridged.

Puerco Spanish 'dirty.'

Puerto Spanish 'entrance, gate, door.'

Puffin For the bird, e.g. **Puffin Island** WA.

Pug On some lakes and ponds in ME this is probably the Abnaki equivalent of *paug*, 'pond,' in more southerly Algonquian dialects.

Puget From the personal name, especially for Peter Puget, lieutenant in George Vancouver's voyage. The sound WA was given his name after he had explored it (1792). The cape in AK was similarly named, later in the voyage.

Pukwana SD Ojibway 'peace pipe,' taken from Longfellow's *Hiawatha*.

Pulaski For Casimir Pulaski (ca. 1718–1779), Polish officer in the Revolutionary army, killed at Savannah, e.g. numerous towns and counties.

Pulga Spanish 'flea.'

Pullman From the personal name, e.g. in WA for G. M. Pullman, railroad car manufacturer, in the hope (which proved unsuccessful) of making him a benefactor.

Pulpit A repeated name, generally with 'rock,' for a formation resembling a pulpit or having been used as a pulpit. Both are true of the one in OR. During the Mormon migration of 1847 Brigham Young probably preached from **Pulpit Rock** WY.

Puma The term has been a learned one in the U.S., and names are almost nonexistent; but **Puma Hills** CO. Colloquial namings appear under **Catamount, Cougar, Lion, Painter, Panther, Tiger.**

Pumgustuck Falls ME Algonquian 'falls-goes-out-at,' i.e. falls at the mouth of the river.

Pumpkin Like most vegetables, it has given rise to few names, especially because it carries some derogatory connotation, as in 'pumpkinhead.' **Pumpkintown** SC: locally believed to have been named because of a large pumpkin once grown there. **Pumpkin Center** SD: a humorous name for a small community, with the word used in the derogatory sense to denote a place excessively rural and isolated. **Pumpkin Hook Creek** NY: by folk-etymology from an Indian name, probably the same as **Pompanuck.**

Puncha See **Poncha.**

Puncheon Before sawmills were common, the making of puncheons (semiplanks made by splitting) was an industry, and gave rise to such names as **Puncheon Creek KY, Puncheoncamp Branch WV.**

Pungo VA A shortening of some Algonquian name, such as **Pungoteague.**

Pungoteague VA Algonquian 'sand-place' (?).

Punished Woman's Lake SD Apparently a translation of the original Siouan name which was based on a legend of an Indian girl who was punished by being bound to a tree near the lake. The fork in KS previously bore the same name, but for uncertain reasons.

Punk Partially rotten wood, known as punk, was useful to Indians (and probably to early settlers) for fire material; as a name it may be a translation from some Indian language, e.g. with the creek in GA.

Punkatesset Hill MA Algonquian, probably 'shallow-brook-at.'

Punta Spanish 'point.'

Punxsutawney PA Algonquian (Delaware) 'punkie-town,' the first word having been taken into Colonial English for the sand fly. The place was notorious for its infestation, or perhaps for one special occasion in 1772.

Pup Usually for the young of the dog or of some wild animal such as the wolf or seal. It has also been used figuratively for anything small, and in AK a small ravine or gulch branching from a large one is regularly called a pup, so that a place-name generic has developed; by association a specific can thus develop and some features, e.g. **Pup Lake AK** may be thus named. **The Pup** AK: named because it is a small volcanic mountain.

Puposky MN Ojibway 'end of shaking lands,' i.e. 'of marshes.'

Purchase To designate a piece of land purchased, especially one arranged with the Indians by treaty, e.g. **Purchase Line** PA.

Purgatoire The name-cluster in CO began in Spanish as the equivalent of the

River of the Souls Lost in Purgatory in memory of some unsavory characters who, killed there by Indians about 1595, died without absolution. The Spanish was rendered into French by trappers, as in its present approved form. American pronunciation made it into **Picketwire** by folk-etymology, and this has survived to some extent in speech. See **Animas.**

Purgatory Occurs as a generic for a place difficult to get through or across 1) in New England, for a ravine; 2) in the Middle West, for a swampy prairie. In contrast to **Hell**, it is rare as a specific. **Purgatory Knob** WV may have been named from its generally rough and forbidding nature. In general, American English, partly because of its largely Protestant origins, scarcely knows this word, and the peak in WV is locally called **Pugatory.** On features in New England the names have arisen by association with the generic. **Purgatory Mountain** VA: named (1750) by Gen. Andrew Lewis with reference to an expedition which had been harassed by Indians.

Purisima Spanish 'most pure,' a religious name with reference to the Immaculate Conception of the Virgin Mary, in CA from the mission thus dedicated.

Puritan Creek SD In 1876 prospector Harry Smith was given a lecture here on the evils of drink by a stranger, and gave the name accordingly.

Purple Rare, probably because the hue is uncommon in nature. The mountain AK is named for some unusually colored rock. Other namings may be for rock or for atmospheric effects, e.g. **Purple Mountain** CO.

Purslane The U.S. Board on Geographic Names has established this as the name of a mountain WV and a run MD. The fact that the first was locally known as **Pursley** and the second as **Pusley** suggests that the origin was a personal name and not the wild purslane.

Pushaw ME For an early settler whose name is recorded as Pochard (1782).

Pushmataha In AL and OK, from the personal name of a notable Choctaw chief of the early 19th century.

Puss Cuss Creek AL By folk-etymology, from Choctaw *puskus,* 'child,' a reduction from an original meaning 'child crying,' an incident name.

Putah Creek CA Containing the Patwin *pu,* 'east,' otherwise uncertain, but originally the name of an Indian village. Many different early spellings are recorded, among them *puta,* though this is not the earliest. Since *puta* means 'whore' in Spanish, this meaning for the name has often been incorrectly assumed.

Putchaug Brook NH Algonquian 'turning-place, division-place,' i.e. probably a stream denoting a boundary.

Put-in-Bay OH In use as early as 1791, either because some particular sailing craft sheltered there, or because the bay was well suited for refuge in bad weather.

Putnam From the personal name, especially, e.g. CT (1855) for Gen. Israel Putnam, Revolutionary hero.

Puxico MO Probably from the name of an Indian chief.

Puyallup WA From an Indian tribal name.

Puye NM Indian (Tewa) 'rabbits-assemble,' probably a place for driving rabbits.

Puzzle See **Mystery.**

Pylon Peak WY Because of two pinnacles like pylons.

Pymatuning Creek PA Algonquian (Delaware) 'twisted-(one)-at,' so called because a well-known Indian with a deformed mouth lived there.

Pyote TX From the growth here of peyote weed, a spelling after the pronunciation.

Pyramid A repeated descriptive, chiefly with 'rock,' 'peak,' 'island.' The lake in NV takes its name from **The Pyramid,** a small island thus descriptively named by J. C. Frémont in 1844.

Pyrite(s) From occurrence of the mineral known as 'fool's gold,' e.g. **Pyrite Point** AK.

Pyrotechnic Hills SD Because of an early Fourth of July celebration held here.

Pysht WA Chinook jargon, 'fish.'

Q

Quabbin Mountain MA Algonquian, uncertain, from the name of a chief (?).

Quaboag Pond MA Algonquian *boag,* meaning 'pond,' and *qua* probably 'red.'

Quacken Kill NY From Dutch *kwaken,* 'herons,' and *kill,* 'stream.'

Quaco Rocks ME Algonquian, for the hooded seal.

Quaddick CT Algonquian, dialect and meaning uncertain.

Quadna Township MN Shortened from Ojibway *piquadinaw,* 'it is hilly.'

Quadrant Mountain WY Because its shape is like a quarter-circle.

Quahog, Quohog, Quogue The Algonquian word for the so-called round clam entered English in early Colonial times, and various features are so named, because of the presence of this valued shellfish. The namings may have been made by the English themselves or may have been taken over from Indian namings.

Quail As a valued game bird, it has given its name to many places, because of special concentration or because of incident. **Quail Creek** OR: for Peter Quail, prospector. **Quail Creek** AK: the idea was to name it **Ptarmigan,** but no one in the party knew how to spell that word, and so **Quail** was substituted.

Quajota See **Kohatk.**

Quakake Creek PA Algonquian (Delaware) 'pine-woods.'

Quaker Settlements of this sect have given names to **Quakertown** PA and other towns.

Quaking Asp Canyon NM From a name often applied to the aspen.

Quakish Lake ME The term is apparently dialectal for 'quaking' to indicate boggy land that shakes when trodden on; it was possibly suggested by the similar-sounding **Guagas.**

Quamphegan Falls ME Algonquian 'dip-net,' because this was an excellent place for netting fish.

Quanaduck CT Algonquian 'long-(tidal)-stream.' See **Connecticut.**

Quanah TX, OK For Quanah Parker, Comanche chief.

Quanapaug, Quinapaug, Quinebaug, Quinnipaugh, Quonepaug, Quonnipaug, Quonopaug, etc. Algonquian 'long pond.'

Quandary An expression of the feelings of the namers (cf. **Conundrum, Riddle**), e.g. the creek in AK, which was named (1950) by geologists because of its confusing way of meandering. **Mount Quandary** CO: so called by some miners in the 1860's, because they had found some ore which they did not know how to treat.

Quanicassee MI Algonquian 'lone tree' (?).

Quantabacook Lake ME Algonquian 'plenty-lake,' being a shortening of a longer term which specified what was plentiful (probably muskrats).

Quantico MD, VA Algonquian 'long-reach-at,' (?).

Quantuck NY An early (1673) form suggests that it is a contraction of **Quaquanantuck.**

Quapaw From the Indian tribal name.

Quaquanantuck NY Algonquian 'trembling-(tidal)-river,' probably because of boggy land on its margin.

Quarry Stands upon some half-dozen towns and villages because of a stone quarry, and is also used thus to identify a natural feature, e.g. **Quarry Creek** TN. The name may be given because of some natural formation resembling a quarry or for some other fancied resemblance, as probably with **Quarry Peak** CA. Like 'mill' it indicates a naming after the advent of settlement.

Quarter Though an origin from 'slave quarters' is possible, it is commonly from a measure of land. **Quartermarch Creek** VA: the latter part is a dialectal form for 'marsh.'

Quartermaster In OK the creek is an army naming, probably for J. M. Bell, who acted as quartermaster in an Indian campaign. In AZ the canyon is for an Indian so nicknamed. In WA the name was given to the harbor by the Wilkes expedition (1841), apparently as a kind of general honor for petty officers.

Quartz From the occurrence of quartz, especially in mining regions where it may be gold-bearing e.g. **Quartz Canyon** CA.

Quartzite Descriptive, from the presence of that kind of rock, e.g. **Quartzite Peak** AZ.

Quasqueton IA Indian, probably Algonquian 'swift-water, rapids' (?).

Quassaic(k) Creek NY Algonquian, meaning uncertain.

Quassapaug CT Algonquian, probably 'gravelly pond.'

Quatsap Point WA Indian, meaning unknown.

Que, Isle of PA Probably Algonquian 'pine-tree.'

Quebec From the Canadian city.

Quebeck TN From the Canadian city, but with the *k* added 'for distinction.'

Queen 1) In Colonial times, given in compliment to the queen (cf. **King**), e.g. **Queen Anne** MD, **Queens Co.** NY. 2) A commendatory with the idea of pre-eminence (cf. **King**), e.g. **Queen City** MO, TX. 3) From a personal name, e.g. **Queens** WV for A. C. Queen, early miller. **Queen Creek** AZ: from the Silver Queen mine.

Queets WA From an Indian tribal name.

Quegenump Spring NV Southern Paiute, meaning uncertain.

Quemado Spanish 'burned.'

Quemahoning PA Algonquian (Delaware) 'pine-lick-at.'

Quenemo KS For a Sac chief who lived in the region in the mid-19th century.

Queponco MD Algonquian (Delaware), probably 'pine-ashes.'

Quercus Latin 'oak,' e.g. **Quercus Grove** IN.

Quesquitcumegek Ridge ME Algonquian, meaning uncertain.

Questa NM Dating from the American period (1883), the name probably represents a misspelling of **Cuesta.**

Queue de Tortue, Bayou LA French 'tail-of-turtle,' but probably from the name of an Indian chief of the early 19th century.

Quibiquesson River ME Algonquian, probably 'long brook.'

Quick From the personal name, e.g. in NB for M. W. Quick, first postmaster.

Quicksand A descriptive, e.g. **Quicksand Creek** KY.

Quicksilver From the presence or supposed presence of ores of quicksilver (mercury), e.g. some features in CA.

Quidnet MA Algonquian 'island-at.'

Quidnic, Quidnick CT, RI Algonquian, probably 'end-(of)-hill-at.'

Quien Sabe Spanish 'Who knows?' but usually a general expression of doubt or ignorance. As a place name, e.g. the creek in CA, it may have arisen because no name was previously known, so that a speaker of Spanish, when asked, could merely have replied 'Quien sabe?' The name-cluster in AZ arose from a mine, the sort of speculative venture which might easily be characterized in terms of doubt.

Quihada Ridge NM From Spanish *quijada,* 'jaw,' because the outline resembles a jaw.

Quilby Creek AL Shifted by folk-etymology to suggest an English name, from Choctaw *koi-ai-albi,* 'panther-there-killed.'

Quilceda Creek WA Indian, meaning unknown.

Quilcene Bay WA From an Indian tribal name.

Quillayute River WA From an Indian tribal name.

Quimper Peninsula WA For Manuel Quimper, Spanish explorer of 1790.

Quinaby OR For a well-known local Indian.

Quinado Canyon CA A Spanish rendering of a Costanoan word, 'evil-smelling,' with reference to sulphur springs.

Quinapoxet, Quinnepoxet MA Algonquian, probably 'long-pond-little-at.'

Quinault WA From an Indian tribal name.

Quince River WA Indian (?), meaning unknown.

Quincy In MA the town was named (1792) for Col. John Quincy (1689–1767), prominent local resident. It occurs as a habitation-name in about 15 states, named under the influence of the MA town and more especially for John Quincy Adams, the president. His middle name was often used because Adams was already pre-empted by his father John. The town in IL passed the name along to towns farther west, e.g. OR, CA.

Quindaro KS For a Delaware-Wyandot woman whose husband founded the settlement.

Quindoxua Neck MD Algonquian, probably a variant of **Quantico.**

Quinibaak, Quinabeck The same as **Quanapaug.**

Quinn Usually from the personal name, but the river in NV was shifted by mistake or folk-etymology from **Queen,** the

stream having been so called by counterpart from nearby **King River.**

Quinnatisset CT Algonquian, probably 'long-brook-at.'

Quinnesec MI Algonquian 'smoking-river' (?).

Quinnesect Falls WI Algonquian, a word to describe the smokelike mist rising from the falls.

Quinnimont WV An attempt to coin from Latin or Romance roots a name meaning 'five mountains' to describe the location. *Quinni-* resembles Latin *quinque,* and *-mont* might be either Latin or French.

Quinnipaugh See **Quanapaug.**

Quinnipiac CT Algonquian, the equivalent of 'turning-point,' to mark a change in a direction of travel.

Quinsibis Island ME Algonquian 'long-streamlet.'

Quinsigamond Lake MA Algonquian, probably 'pickerel-fishing-place.'

Quinta Spanish 'county estate, farm (but smaller than a *rancho*).' **La Quinta** CA was originally the name of a hotel.

Quintet Mountain WY Named because of its five peaks, which were, on the occasion of the naming, all ascended by a party of five.

Quinto Creek CA Spanish 'fifth.'

Quinwood WV From the names of the founders, Quin Morton and W. C. Wood.

Quirauk Mountain MD Probably a tribal name, being the first two syllables of Quiyoucohanocks, a tribe recorded by John Smith (1612).

Quisquamego ME Algonquian 'long-high-land (ridge).' The present form (recorded, 1701) is apparently shaped under the influence of Latin.

Quitaque TX Probably Indian, locally believed to mean 'horse manure.'

Quitasueno Rock AK Spanish 'quit-sleeping, wake-up,' a navigator's name of warning, given by a Spanish expedition ca. 1775. Cf. **Alargate.**

Quitchupah Lake UT Paiute 'dung-water,' because it was a bed-ground for deer and antelope.

Quitman From the personal name, chiefly for J. A. Quitman (1798–1858), a hero of the Mexican War, commemorated in the SE.

Quito IN, TN An exotic borrowing from South America. **Quito Hill** ME is probably Algonquian 'long-flow.'

Quitobaquito AZ Apparently a fusion of Papago *ki-to-bac*, 'house ring spring,' and Spanish *-ito*, diminutive.

Quitopahilla Creek PA Algonquian (Delaware) 'pine-spring.'

Quittacus Ponds MA Algonquian, meaning uncertain.

Quiver, Mount WY In 1959 two climbers gave the name because the ascent was so difficult that it made them quiver.

Quoaug Rock RI See **Quahog.**

Quogue NY Early records indicate that it is a shortening of **Quaquanantuck.**

Quohog See **Quahog.**

Quonepaug, etc. See **Quanapaug.**

Quonoc(h)ontaug RI Algonquian, apparently a doubled form, 'long-long-pond.'

Quonset RI Algonquian 'long-place,' probably a shortening from some longer term.

Quontabacook See **Quantabacook.**

Quosatana Creek OR Probably an Indian tribal name.

R

Ra, Tower of AZ See **Brahma.**

Rabbit Though the most widespread and numerous of game animals, the rabbit was individually of so little note that names were not given as frequently as might be expected. As with most animal names, they may arise from a number of animals, but more usually from incidents, and in the case of such an unimportant animal the story of an incident is rarely preserved. In certain areas, e.g. MN, the name is sometimes a translation from an Indian language; among many tribes the rabbit was an important mythological creature, and names were given for that reason. Because of the semiderogatory nature of the term, habitation-names are rare, even by transfer. **Rabbithole Spring** NV: in 1846 the Applegate exploring party found the spring by means of the rabbit trails that converged upon it. **Rabbit Ears:** a descriptive term for mountains, e.g. CO, OR, because of a pair of upstanding rocks. **Rabbit Hash** appears as a rural derogatory, with the idea that the people there were forced to eat such lowly fare. **Rabbit Town** KY probably has a similar origin.

Raccoon The longer and more literary form for coon appears rarely, e.g. **Raccoon Mountain** GA; in speech the shortened form is probably in use for these as well. **Raccoon Straits** CA: from the British warship *Raccoon* which anchored there in 1814.

Raccourci American-French 'cut-off, short-cut,' e.g. **Bayou Raccourci** LA.

Race 1) As a coastal name, from a tide race, e.g. **Race Point** MA. 2) From horse racing, a highly popular sport from early times, e.g. **Raceland** KY, **Racetrack** TX. A few names may have arisen from an incident or from a supposed resemblance to a race track.

Racket River NY An Anglicization of **Raquette.**

Rackheap Creek OR A loggers' term for a pile of logs ready to be floated downstream. The creek is named because an eddy near its mouth piles logs up as if in a rackheap.

Racine French 'root.' The city in WI takes its name from the river on which it is situated, though this stream is now called **Root River.** The noncommendatory suggestions of 'root' probably have aided the retention of the French form. See **Root.**

Raco MI For the Richardson and Avery Company, which founded the town.

Rada WV For Rada Dany, a baby of the family who had the post office in their home.

Radisson WI Named commemoratively for P. E. Radisson, 17th-century French explorer.

Radium The discovery of radium in 1902 was widely publicized; besides, the name was short and easy; several places (most of them railroad stations) were thus named, e.g. in MN. Other places were so named because someone believed he had discovered a radium mine, e.g. in CO. **Radium Springs** NM: because the water was publicized as medicinal for the radium it contained.

Radnor In PA the name of the Welsh county was introduced by Welsh settlers in 1683.

Radom IL From the city in Poland, named by an immigrant.

Raeco WA Coined in 1908 from the names of three men (Rhodes, Appel, and Earnest) who formed a company, with *-co* added for 'company.'

Rafinesque, Mount NY For C. S. Rafinesque, botanist, who climbed it on July 30, 1833.

Raft, Rafting Occasionally used on a stream because of its being used for lumber rafts, e.g. **Rafting Creek** SC. **Raft River** ID translates the American-French *cajeux,* but the reason for the name is uncertain. See **Cassia.** Since the use of rafts is unlikely, the name may be originally Indian, and shifted by folk-etymology in passing into the French, or it may even have resulted from a confusion of sound of *cajeux* with the common **Cache.**

Rag In compounds such as **Ragland,** it is from a personal name. **Ragtown** was formerly a common term for a settlement supposed to be unusually slovenly. A well-known example was that in NV at the end of the desert stretch on the emigrant trail, where much debris was left spread around. See **Ragged.**

Ragged, Raggedy 1) A fairly common descriptive (chiefly in the West where rock profiles are not so often concealed by tree growth) given to a place where the formation suggested raggedness, e.g. **Ragged Island** AK, **Ragged Butte** SD, **Ragged Top Mountain** SD. 2) An incident name or quasi-descriptive given because someone or the people in general were in a ragged condition, e.g. **Raggedy-ass Gulch** CA. **Ragged Island** ME: by folk-etymology from **Raggertask,** itself from an Algonquian term, so badly shifted as to be uncertain. See **Rag.**

Rahway NJ Probably a variant of **Rockaway.**

Raices See **Raiz.**

Raid The lake in WY was named because of a 'raid' by cattlemen in which 1200 sheep were killed; the peak is named by transfer.

Rail Usually because of supplying rails for fences, e.g. **Rail Creek** WA.

Railroad From an association, often difficult to determine, with a railroad. **Railroad Canyon** NM: a railroad ascends to a summit through this canyon. **Railroad Lake** NB is near a railroad. **Railroad Pass** NV: no railroad has existed here, and the name apparently arose because a railroad was once projected. **Railroad Flat** CA: some hundreds of feet of wooden rails were once laid here for transporting logs. **Railroad Mountain** NM: an igneous dike of rock runs straight and smooth, and resembles a railroad.

Rain, Rainy The rarity of this word in place-names suggests that rain itself is too commonplace a phenomenon to suggest a naming. When used, it is more likely to be an incident-naming than a descriptive, i.e. it arises from a rain encountered by the namers at that place, and does not indicate a place characterized by heavy rainfall. **Rainy Lake** MN: a Cree name was taken over by the Ojibway, and then translated first into French and then into English. A form of the Cree-Ojibway name is preserved in **Koochiching Co.** MN. Though the Ojibway name could be translated as 'rainy,' there is no certainty that such was the meaning of the Cree name. An early but uncertain explanation is that the name arose from the mist produced by the waterfalls. **Rains** SC: heavy rains fell during the building of the railroad in 1941, and the station was thus named. **Rains** UT: for F. L. Rains, noted mining engineer. **Raintown** WV: for John Raine, local lumberman. **Rainy Lake** MT: a surveying party gave the name because it rained nearly all the time when the party was in the vicinity.

Rainbow 1) For a rainbow seen at the time of naming, e.g. **Rainbow** TX. 2) For variegated and highly colored vegetation or rock, e.g. **Rainbow Forest** AZ, **Rainbow Mountain** CA. 3) For the rainbows seen in spray, e.g. **Rainbow Falls** WY. 4) From the presence of rainbow trout, e.g. **Rainbow** OR. 5) From an arched shape, e.g. **Rainbow Bridge** UT; thence, by transfer, to **Rainbow Plateau** UT.

Rainelle WV From Raine, the family name of local lumber operators. When the Post Office Dept. rejected the simple name, it was resubmitted in an augmented form (1909).

Rainey Creek WA An American adaptation of René, for David René who nearly lost his life when crossing the stream with a surveying party.

Rainier, Mount WA For Peter Rainier, British admiral, named for him on May 8, 1792, by his friend the explorer Vancouver, who saw the peak from his ship.

Rainy See **Rain.**

Raiz Spanish 'root,' e.g. **Las Raices Creek** TX.

Raleigh The colonizing activities of Sir Walter Raleigh were given belated recognition by the naming for him in 1792 of the city in NC. The name has spread to other states by the usual processes or because of the personal name.

Ralston Regularly from the personal name, e.g. in OK for J. H. Ralston, town developer; in WA, from the packaged foods, a railroad name.

Ram Exists as the first element in many personal names, e.g. **Ramsay, Ramsgate,** and also **Ram** and **Ramm.** It also may be derived from English towns so named. But a few places take their names from the male sheep, either domesticated or wild, or from the resemblance in a natural feature to a ram's head or horn. **Ram's Horn** WV: from the appearance. **Ramshead Lake** WY: for the skull of a mountain sheep found there. **Rams Horn Mountain** CO: the mountain was a famous hunting ground for mountain sheep, and some accumulation of their horns probably resulted.

Ramah Though several cities in the Old Testament are so called, the name in NM was given by Mormons, probably for a hill mentioned in the Book of Mormon. In CO the community was named (1888), according to local story, from the occurrence of the name in a book about India.

Ramapo(o) NJ, NY Algonquian (Delaware) 'round-pond' (?). **Ramapoo** CT may be the same, or may be from a tribal name.

Ramirito TX From José Ramirez, early settler, the diminutive being used because the name itself was already in use for a post office in the state.

Ramo Flat OR Locally said to be for an early resident.

Ramona Though a common Spanish woman's name, the place-names are usually, e.g. in CA, literary, because of the popularity of the novel of that title (1884) by Helen Hunt Jackson.

Ramp WV From the wild leek, known as 'ramp' in local speech.

Rampart In occasional use to describe a massive rock formation like a fortification, especially **The Ramparts of the Yukon** AK.

Ranch, Rancho To designate a feature associated with a ranch, e.g. **Ranch Creek** AK. The Spanish forms occur, e.g. **Rancho Santa Fe** CA, and a diminutive, e.g. **Ranchita** CA, **Ranchito** NM. **Ranchial Creek** CA: probably from an adjective, 'pertaining to a ranch.'

Rancheria A Spanish-derived western term for an Indian village or camp, e.g. **Rancheria Island** AK.

Ranchester WY Coined in 1894 by S. H. Hardin, an Englishman, who combined 'ranch' with the common English town-ending *chester.*

Rancocas NJ From an Indian tribal name.

Randado TX Spanish, literally, 'trimmed with lace'; locally believed to have some Indian background.

Randolph From the personal name. In MA it is for Peyton Randolph (1721–1775) of VA, political figure; in NH for John Randolph (1773–1833), also of VA, political figure of the early 19th century; in NB, for Lord Randolph Churchill (1849–1895); reason for naming unknown.

Range Though used as a generic and common noun in several senses, it is infrequent as a specific. **Range** OK, OR: from being situated in range country.

Ranger It has been in use since the 17th century in a military sense, and more recently has been used in the park and forest service. It also is a personal name, though uncommon. **Ranger** TX: from some Texas Rangers who once were encamped here. **Rangerville** TX: named by people who had come from **Ranger** TX. **Ranger Lake** WY is in Yellowstone N.P., and is named for the park rangers.

Rantoul IL For Robert Rantoul, director of the Illinois Central Railroad.

Rantowles SC Probably a possessive from a personal name such as **Rantoul.**

Rapid(s) As a generic the term is an Americanism; sometimes used as a specific for a place thus associated, e.g. **Rapids City** IL. **Rapid River** MN: so named because of rapids near its mouth. It is occasionally used to describe a stream with a swift current, e.g. **Rapid Creek** NB and **Rapid City** SD, the latter named from the creek, which represents a translation of the French **L'Eau Qui Court,** itself probably translating a Pawnee name.

Rapidan River VA The stream is a tributary of the **Rappahannock,** and is probably the same name, shortened and modified by folk-etymology for the purpose of differentiation.

Rapide(s) French 'rapids,' e.g. **Rapides Parish** LA, for former rapids of the Red River, now vanished because of shifts of the riverbed.

Rappahannock River VA Algonquian 'back-and-forth-stream,' apparently because of tidal movement; an interesting question remains: 'Why apply the name to this particular stream, when all streams in this area show tidal currents?'

Raquette French 'snowshoe.'

Raritan NJ From a tribal name, which was probably first an Algonquian river name, 'stream-overflows.'

Raskohegan Island ME Algonquian 'waiting (watching)-place.' Cf. **Skohegan.**

Raso Spanish, topographically used generally in the sense of 'flat,' e.g. **Punta Rasa** FL.

Raspberry From the wild raspberry, e.g. several features in AK.

Rat Domestic rats and wild rats are widespread, but the names spring regularly from **Muskrat. Rat Root River** MN: from a kind of root eaten by muskrats. Because of derogatory suggestions the name has been avoided for habitations, except for **Rat MO,** of unexplained origin. **Rat Islands** AK: translated from the Russian, probably given

with reference to the prevalent ground squirrel, a rodent and therefore a rat-like animal. See **Marmot.**

Rathdrum ID From the town in Ireland.

Raton Spanish 'mouse.' In **Boca Raton** FL the meaning is 'hidden rock that frets cables,' like a mouse gnawing.

Rattlesnake Widespread and common, given to producing vividly remembered incidents, the rattlesnake has put its name upon hundreds of natural features. In a few instances, in spite of unpleasant suggestion, the name has been transferred to habitations. Since the meeting with a single rattlesnake is often impressive, many of the names are doubtless so given, though such incidents are rarely recorded. In other places, e.g. **Rattlesnake Tanks** AZ, the killing of several snakes is responsible, and at **Rattlesnake Basin** AZ 70 or 80 were killed. The snakes 'den up' in winter, and such places often become known, thus resulting in such names as **Rattlesnake Den** WI and **Rattlesnake Rocks** WV. About 200 features bear this name in CA, a number second only to 'grizzly' among animal names. The prairie in WA was named because some surveyors were alarmed by the rattling of some seed pods, thinking the noise to be from a snake. **Rattlesnake Draw** WY: because Frank Prager in 1895 killed a snake here, after it had frightened his wife and children.

Raunt, The NY Probably from Dutch *ruimte,* used in the nautical sense 'offing.'

Raven A large and conspicuous bird, places frequented by it have been so named, e.g. **Raven Rock** WV, **Raven Creek** WY. It is also a personal name. The use of **Ravenswood** or **Ravenwood** for a habitation-name probably springs chiefly from literary usage, e.g. from Scott's *Bride of Lammermoor.* **Ravensdale** and **Ravenscroft** also probably show literary influence. **Ravenswood Point, Slough** CA take their names from a now-vanished town.

Ravena NY Probably a variant of **Ravenna.**

Ravenna From the city in Italy. In TX the name is partly a punning one, because the location is between two ravines. **Ravenna** OH: named ca. 1808 by a landowner who had visited and admired the Italian city.

Ravinia IL, SD A pseudo-Latin form, used to indicate location near a ravine.

Rawhide Since rawhide was a common commodity in the early West, names have probably sprung from a variety of incidents involving it. **Rawhide Buttes** WY and **Rawhide Creek** NB have both given rise to legends that a white man was there flayed by Indians, but there is no authentication, and the application of the term in that sense would be unusual. **Rawhide Mountain,** Pinal Co., AZ: from a primitive Mexican goatherder who lived there, and was for some reason associated with rawhide, that being perhaps his nickname. The name may also have sprung from the use of the term to mean a Texan, or even for anything raw and rough, as seems to be the case with **Rawhide Mountain,** Mohave Co., AZ.

Rawlins WY For John A Rawlins, Union general in the Civil War, who camped at the spot in 1867.

Rayado Spanish 'streaked.' The name was applied in Spanish, descriptively, to certain tribes of Plains Indians who tattooed or otherwise marked their faces with lines, and the names in NM are probably thus derived.

Raymilton PA From the first syllable of the last name of A. W. Raymond, the founder, and *-milton,* for 'mill-town,' because he established a gristmill.

Raynham In MA from the town in England (1731); so also in NC (1884).

Raysal WV From Raymond Salvati, a local mine superintendent.

Raywick KY From the two founding families, Ray and Wickliffe.

Reading From the English city; in MA, 1644; in PA, ca. 1750. It is also a family name; see **Redding. Reading** MN: for H. H. Read, landowner.

Ready Bullion A 19th-century phrase to mean a supply of gold and silver held ready to redeem paper currency was used by prospectors for mines considered (usually with too great optimism) to be of exceptional richness; from the mines the term spread to features, e.g. several creeks in AK.

Real 1) From Spanish *reál,* 'royal,' e.g. **El Camino Real** CA, 'the road royal,' but actually about the equivalent of 'public road.' 2) From the personal name, e.g. **Real Co.** TX, named in 1912 for Julius Real (1860–1944), judge and public figure.

Rebel This term e.g. **Rebel Rock** OR, generally arises from its association with some Confederate sympathizer.

Recovery, Fort OH Named (1793) by Gen. Anthony Wayne after he had recovered the area where the Americans had been defeated in 1791.

Red Common as a descriptive because of red or reddish rock or soil, e.g. **Red Mountain, Red Bluff, Red Rock, Red Bank;** also with water similarly colored, especially if other nearby streams are clear, e.g. **Red River, Red Springs.** It sometimes exists in counterpart, especially with 'black,' e.g. the peaks **Red Kaweah** and **Black Kaweah,** to which is also added **Grey Kaweah** CA. Painted works of men add such examples as **Red Mill** NH, **Red House** (various), besides sign names, e.g. **Red Dragon** WV. Incident, resulting in a temporary redness, has produced **Red Hill** NH because of autumn coloring; **Red Hills** AK because of their appearance in a certain effect of sunlight; **Red Lake** MN a translation of the Ojibway name, but probably from sunset effects seen upon the water. Association produces **Red Glacier** AK having red boulders in its moraine.

Such names as **Redfield, Redford, Redman, Redpath,** are regularly personal. But **Redford** TX is for a ford with red clay. The common nickname for a redheaded person has produced **Red's Meadow** CA. Translated, the term is common among Indian personal names, thus producing **Red Jacket** WV, **Red Cap** CA, **Red Cloud** NV, **Red Wing** MN.

It is also common in compounds and double specifics, e.g. **Red Cedar, Red Oak,** etc. from trees; **Red Eye River** MN from a kind of fish; **Red Dog** CA probably from a card game. See **Redwood.** The repeated **Redfield** is regularly from the personal name, e.g. in SD for J. B. Redfield, railroad official; in IA for Col. J. R. Redfield, important landowner.

Redding From the personal name; in CA from B. B. Redding, land agent for the railroad, when the town was laid out in 1872. By legislative act of 1874 the town was declared to be **Reading,** so named for P. B. Reading, local pioneer, pronounced **Redding.** The railroad did not change its station-name, and the legislature changed the name to **Redding** in 1880. Because of the greater fame of Reading, the name is still often credited to him. In CT the name was originally **Reading** for John Reed, principal settler; later, because of popular dislike of him, the spelling was changed. In CT the name took the form of the town in England (1729), but was suggested by the name of the chief landowner, John Read.

Redelm SD An amalgamation of **Red Elm.**

Redess OR From 'Red Ess,' a brand.

Redondo Spanish 'round.' **Redondo Beach** CA: from the ranch **Sausal Redondo,** 'round willow-grove.'

Redoubt From a formation resembling a fortification (cf. **Castle**), e.g. **Redoubt Volcano** AK. The creek in OK was named from an actual fortification constructed there in 1870 by the 6th Infantry.

Redowl SD By amalgamation of **Red Owl,** for the nearby creek.

Redwood From the tree, except for a slight extension into OR, entirely limited in its habitat to CA, where about 50 places are so named, chiefly in the coastal counties, the tree being highly valuable and conspicuous. In modern usage the term is limited to the coastal tree (*Sequoia sempervirens*), but it was formerly used also for the *Sequoia gigantea,* now commonly called sequoia, and some names were thus given, e.g. **Redwood Meadow,** *et al.* in Tulare and Fresno Cos., CA. **Redwood City** CA was named because of fine original stands of the trees, and is one of the few habitation-names. Occasional uses outside of CA result from other trees or bushes so called, e.g. **Redwood River** MN is a translation from the Siouan for the plant usually known as **Kinnickinnick.**

Ree A shortening of the Indian tribal name **Arickaree.**

Reed, Reedy, Reid etc. In most instances the place-names arise from the common personal name. With such generics as 'creek' and 'lake' the reference may be to a growth of reeds, especially if the form is **Reedy. Red Lake** MN: named for the thick growth of reeds. **Reed-Grass River** MN, an extinct name, shows its origin clearly, and does so also in its present name **Roseau,** which merely translates 'reed' into French. **Reedy Creek** WV: from the growth of reeds.

Reedley CA T. L. Reed gave land to the town, but did not wish his name to be used for it; as a compromise it was used with a suffix, *ley* being the traditional English ending for 'open country,' suitable for the site of the town.

Reef Commonly a generic but becoming a specific by association, e.g. **Reef Point** AK. Occasionally used in the West for a cliff sticking up above level land as a reef sticks up from the sea; see **Capitol.**

Reelfoot Lake TN The translation of the name of a Chickasaw chief of the early 19th century.

Reflection A repeated name for lakes, as a descriptive.

Reform In AL an itinerant preacher, after urging people to reform, suggested that name, ca. 1820.

Refugio Spanish 'refuge,' but usually a religious name commemorating Nuestra Señora del Refugio, e.g. **Canada del Refugio** CA. In TX, from a mission thus dedicated.

Regent In ND it is a commendatory, used as the equivalent of 'royal' or **Queen City.**

Rego In NY it is from a construction company which had been named from the phrase 'Real good!' In IN the origin may be the same, but is uncertain.

Regulation Peak CA Named in 1895 because copies of Yosemite N. P. regulations were placed on trees there.

Regurgitory Spring, The WV Descriptively named because it ebbs and flows and makes gurgling noises.

Rehoboth The Biblical name means literally in Hebrew 'enlargement,' and in MA the name was given (ca. 1645) because the settlers found more room for themselves there. This meaning has aided in the establishment of the name elsewhere, e.g. in OH.

Reindeer A dozen names in AK are for the domestic reindeer, which was flourishing there around 1900. The related wild species is always **Caribou.**

Reklaw TX For Margaret L. Walker, owner of the townsite, by reverse spelling.

Relay MD Stage horses were once changed at this point.

Reliance In occasional use for habitations as a vague commendatory.

Relief A repeated name, probably commemorating some incident of the pioneer period, e.g. **Relief Valley** CA where an emigrant train in the 1850's got into difficulties and was relieved by a party sent out from the settlements.

Reliez See **Reliz.**

Reliz Mexican-Spanish 'landslide.' **Reliez Valley** CA represents a misspelling.

Reminderville OH Named (1955) for C. L. Reminder, the first mayor.

Remlap AL A reverse spelling of Palmer, a railroad station so called because at this point the line went through the farm of a family so named. It also occurs in FL.

Remlig TX A reverse spelling from Alexander Gilmer, local lumber operator.

Remote OR An apt descriptive, especially as of 1887, the date of naming.

Removal WV A name used (1888–1937) for the post office previously **Middleport** and now **Guardian.** It was given by the postmaster because the office had been moved so often.

Remove, Point AR By folk-etymology from American-French *remous,* 'whirlpool, eddy.'

Reno From the personal name; in NV for Union Gen. J. L. Reno, killed at South Mountain in 1862, the town being named a few years later on the building of the railroad. **El Reno** OK is for the same person, the Spanish article being added for distinction from an already existing **Reno City,** doubtless on the assumption that the name was Spanish, though it is French.

Renonco Creek MD Algonquian, meaning uncertain.

Renovo PA Latin 'I renew,' so called because railroad repair shops were located there.

Repaupo NJ Algonquian, meaning uncertain.

Represa Spanish 'dam.'

Republic County KS An adaptation of the tribal name, **Republican** (q.v.), but probably more directly named from the river.

Republican River NB, KS From the Pawnee subtribe, so called, who lived along it.

Requa In CA it is an Indian tribal or village name, probably 'creek-mouth.' In WI it is a name (Reque) from Norway, given by immigrants.

Resaca Local usage in southern TX applies this term as a generic to an old river channel, and thence sometimes even to a stream; by association specifics arise, e.g. **Resaca Creek.** In other states it is a Mexican War name, from the American victory at Resaca de la Palma.

Rescue In CA the name is from a mine. Other examples are probably from incidents, which have not been recorded.

Reseda CA The botanical term for a plant of the mignonette family; cause of naming unknown.

Reservation By association, most commonly from an Indian reservation, e.g. **Reservation Creek** AZ. The point in CA was so named in 1915 when the federal government reserved the land for a quarantine station.

Resting Spring CA Mormon wagon trains of the 1850's stopped here to rest and recuperate.

Reston OR When the stage station was being named, the apt **Rest** was suggested, but was eliminated because of duplication. A syllable was then added.

Restoration Point WA Named by George Vancouver (1792) in honor of Restoration Day (May 25, 1660) when the Stuart dynasty was returned to the English throne.

Retlaw OR For H. L. Walter, spelled backward, an official of the Southern Pacific Company.

Retreat Regularly with the idea of withdrawal from the world, e.g. in SC it was originally **Bachelors' Retreat.**

Retsil WA A reverse spelling, in honor of Gov. Ernest Lister.

Return The creek in CA was named, ca. 1870, by a surveying party, probably because of an incident. **Return Creek** AK: named (1911) by a prospector who intended to return there. **Return Islands** AK: named (1826) by Sir John Franklin, as **Return Reef,** because this was the farthest point reached by him and the place from which he commenced his return.

Reveille In NV the range and valley probably took their names from the newspaper *The Reese River Reveille.*

Revenue Canyon CA Probably from a mine-name.

Revere From the personal name, especially for Paul Revere (1735–1818), silversmith and rider-by-night, e.g. in MA, where the name, however, is late (1871).

Reversed Creek CA Because in a geological sense the creek now flows in a reversed direction. The peak is named from the creek.

Revillagigedo Island AK The nearby **Channel** was named (1792) by a Spanish expedition for the then viceroy of Mexico, and the **Island** by George Vancouver in 1793. The length and unusual pronunciation has worked against the name, and the island is generally known as 'the island that Ketchican's on'; it may eventually become merely **Ketchican Island.**

Revillo SD Probably for J. S. Oliver, a local railroad man, with backward spelling and slight alteration.

Revuelto Spanish 'turned-over.' The creek in NM is probably named in the sense of 'disturbed, muddied.'

Rewastico Creek MD Algonquian 'weedy-stream.'

Rex Regularly from the personal name. **Rexburg** ID: by shifted spelling for T. E. Ricks, leader in the local settlement ca. 1883. The Latin meaning of 'king' has occasionally led to its use as a commendatory, e.g. with **Rex Lake** WY.

Rey Spanish 'king.' See **Cristo, Reyes.**

Reyes, Point CA Spanish 'kings,' named by Viscaíno in 1603 because he passed the point on Jan. 6, the day of the 'three holy kings.'

Rheims From the city of France.

Rhine The Anglicized spelling of the German river-name Rhein; also a family name. **Rhinebeck** NY was introduced by immigrants in the early 18th century. The designation of the Hudson as 'The Rhine of America' led to a few names, e.g. **Rhinecliff** NY.

Rhode Island The account of Giovanni de Verrazano's voyage of 1524 mentions in this general area an island 'about the bigness of the Island of Rhodes.' By

1630 the Dutch were referring to a 'red' island, which, as generally spelled, would be 'rood' or 'rode.' In 1644 the Court of Providence Plantation ordered 'that the island commonly called Aquethneck, shall be from henceforth called the Isle of Rhodes, or Rhode Island.' The wording and spelling indicate an origin from Verrazano and thus from the Mediterranean island. The Dutch naming, however, may also have been of some influence. The government became that of **Rhode Island and Providence,** and it still remains officially **The State of Rhode Island and Providence Plantations.**

Rhododendron OR From the native rhododendron.

Rhyolite From the presence of the rock so known, e.g. **Rhyolite Gulch NV.**

Rialto From the locality in Venice. Shakespeare's *Merchant of Venice* made it known as a place frequented by businessmen, and it has been thus used for towns in a commendatory sense.

Rib River WI A translation of the Algonquian name; reason for naming unknown.

Ribaut FL The name in FL commemorates Jean Ribaut, leader of the ill-fated French colony in 1562.

Ribbon The term is applied to many waterfalls which are long and narrow, and therefore ribbon-like. So also, probably, **Ribbon Ridge OR.**

Rice In most states, from the personal name. In the restricted area where so-called wild rice was an important Indian food, chiefly MN, the name is common on lakes. **Rice Co.** MN: for H. M. Rice, U.S. senator. **Rice Hope** SC: from a plantation-name, expressing hope for successful rice-growing, one of the rare names arising from rice culture.

Rich 1) From the personal name, e.g. **Rich** OK for E. O. Rich, early merchant. 2) A descriptive or commendatory name. **Rich Bar** CA: because of its gold deposits. The idea of good soil is usually uppermost, as in the common **Richfield** and even commoner **Richland.** See **Richmond.**

Richmond From one of the towns in England, etc. **Richmond** VA: the site was named in 1733 by William Byrd, probably because of a fancied resemblance to the town in Surrey, which was on the Thames as the new site was on the James. Even in the colonies the name was several times repeated, drawing strength not only from the English towns, but also from lords of that title, from the personal name, and from the commendatory ideas of richness and height. The name has spread across the country in later times, because of the notable places already so named, and for the commendatory reasons. It has even developed into such forms as **Richmonddale. Richmond** MA: named (1765) for the Duke, who was a sympathizer with the colonies.

Richtex SC From **Richland Co.,** and the first syllable of 'texture,' the latter derived from bricks made here.

Richthofen, Mount CO For Ferdinand, Baron von Richthofen (1833–1905), geologist, probably named ca. 1870 by geologist friends with whom he had worked in CA. Curiously, **Richthofen Place** in Denver CO commemorates Walter, another and related Baron von Richthofen, who was a prominent local citizen during the last quarter of the 19th century.

Rickaree From the Indian tribal name, a variant of **Arickaree.**

Rickreall OR Probably of Indian origin, but uncertain.

Rico Spanish 'rich,' in CO a commendatory for a mining camp.

Riddle Regularly from the personal name, e.g. in ID for a numerous family of early settlers. The lake in WY was named for its enigmatic quality; there was supposed to be a lake in Yellowstone N.P. from which water flowed to both oceans; the name was finally fixed upon this lake, which is near the divide; the naming was in the late 19th century when riddles were a popular diversion.

Ridge Sometimes for the personal name, especially in compounds, e.g. **Ridgeley, Ridgeway.** Commonly for a feature or habitation associated with a ridge, e.g.

Ridgeway NC for a ridge followed by a railroad. **Ridgeville** NC: because situated on a ridge. So also **Ridge** TX. The term is rare on natural features, but e.g. **Ridge Lake** CA. It is common as the second element in habitation-names, e.g. **Chestnut Ridge** PA.

Rifle CO Originally applied to the creek; so named, ca. 1880, when a man left his rifle near the stream, but was able to find it again when returning for it.

Riflepit Canyon SD Some remains of rifle pits, dug by early pioneers as defense against Indian attack, are still discernable here.

Riga From the city of Latvia.

Right The term seems to occur only in the sense of right-handed, and is of similar usage to **Left,** q.v. to which it is often a counterpart.

Rigolet A diminutive of French *rigole,* 'ditch,' used occasionally in American-French place-names as 'little stream,' e.g. **Rigolets** LA. **Rigolet de Bon Dieu** LA is 'little stream of good God,' but the reference is uncertain. So also **Bayou Rigolettes** LA.

Riley From the personal name, e.g. **Fort Riley** KS named in 1853 for Maj. Bennett Riley who had served in the area.

Rillito Creek AZ Locally thought to be Spanish for 'little river.' If so, it must be a gross misrendering of the commoner *rito* of American Spanish. It may be connected with the personal name Rieletto.

Rimini From the city of Italy, chiefly known to the Americans of the 19th century from Francesca da Rimini, whose name was used as the title of plays and poems, e.g. the town in MT.

Rimmon Various places in the Bible bear the name. One of them was a rock, and the association **Rock Rimmon** CT is thus clear.

Rimrock The common western term for a ledge of rock forming a 'rim' has yielded names, e.g. **Rimrock Bluffs** MT.

Rincon Spanish, literarily, 'corner, nook,' but sometimes used in different senses, e.g. to indicate a place where a road is forced to make a difficult rounding of some point, as at **El Rincon** CA where the road has always been crowded between the mountains and the ocean. Its commonest use in Spanish times was to describe isolated parts of land grants, and in CA some of these names have survived on features. It is also a personal name, but there is no evidence that any place-names have thus originated.

Ring Sometimes from the personal name, as also in compounds such as **Ringrose, Ringwood. Ring Mountain** WY: because a large ring of black rock appears on its side. **Ringwood** OK: because the site was ringed with trees.

Ringgold From the personal name, chiefly for Maj. Samuel Ringgold, first American officer to be killed in the Mexican War.

Ringsted IA Named by Danish settlers for the town in Denmark.

Rio Spanish 'river.' In a Spanish context it is a generic, and stands first. Such names, e.g. **Rio Grande,** are listed under the specific (second) term. In an English context the term also stands first, e.g. **Rio Vista** CA, which must be taken to mean 'river-view.' So also with the hybrid **Rio Dell** CA, which was **Riverdale** until it had to be changed because of confusion with another post office. **Rio** stands alone on some half-dozen habitation-names.

Riparia WA Latin, feminine, 'of the bank,' an equivalent of **Riverside;** in NY the masculine **Riparius** occurs.

Ripgut Creek CA Named by an early cattleman after his clothes had been torn there by bushes.

Ripley From the personal name, e.g. the lake in MN, where F. N. Ripley was frozen to death in the winter of 1855–1856.

Ripon In WI probably from the town in England; in CA, a transfer from WI.

Rippetoe Mountain WV From a family name, but unidentified.

Rippogenus Pond ME Algonquian 'gravel' (?).

Rising Though not common, the name has various origins. **Rising Sun** MD: from an inn and its sign. **Rising Sun** IN: because of being in a good position to see the sun rise from behind the hills across the river, and for an especially noted sunrise. **Risingsun** OH: probably a commendatory name. **Rising Star** TX: **Rising Sun** was first requested as a post office name; when it was refused, the present name was substituted. **Rising Wolf Mountain** MT: for a Blackfoot chief so named. **Rising River** CA: because it rises, full-sized, from a large springlike source. **Rising City** NB: for A. W. and S. W. Rising, townsite owners.

Rito Diminutive of Spanish *rio*, 'river,' according to the usage in the SW, e.g. the tautological **El Rito River** NM and **Rito Creek** NM.

Rivanna VA As a stream-name, it is from Latin *rivus*, 'small stream' (or from English 'river') and the name Anna, probably with reference to Queen Anne, but probably in part suggested by the Algonquian *hanne*, 'stream,' which occurs in the region. The river traverses **Fluvanna Co.**, and the two names are counterparts. See **Anna, Fluvanna.**

River It is commonly a generic, and appears very rarely as a specific with natural features, e.g. **River Bay** AK. It sometimes appears as a first element, usually because it was originally the French *rivière*, e.g. **River Rouge** MI, **River Sioux** IA, **River aux Vases** MO. In habitation-names **River** may arise merely by transfer, but it is often commendatory, as suggesting a pleasant place to live.

Rivera CA A coined name, ca. 1886, because the situation was between two branches of a river.

Riviera From the French coastal district, a commendatory.

Road The name was bestowed on features because of association with a road (cf. **Trace, Trail**), e.g. **Road Canyon** NM. Since a road generally meant one that had been made, not developed by mere passage over it, these names are usually not of the earliest naming in a region. Roads often followed streams, and the name occurs most often with generics indicating smaller streams, e.g. **Run, Fork, Creek.** Compounds are common, e.g. **Horseroad Fork** WV, **Roadhouse Branch** WV. **Roads End** CA: originally at the end of the road, and existing as a name after the road has been extended.

Roan Cliffs UT From their color, resembling that of a roan horse.

Roanoke Recorded in the account of the Amadas and Barlowe Expedition of 1584, this is the first Indian name, or word, to be taken over by the English, and to survive. They understood it as being the name of the island, but their ability to communicate with the Indians was so minimal that we cannot believe this idea to have much validity, any more than we can accept the English spelling as closely representing the sounds. It is probably Algonquian, and has been analyzed in such widely variant meanings as 'white-shell place,' 'northern people,' and 'wampum.'

Roaring One of the commonest of auditory descriptives, it is applied especially to streams, e.g. brook CT, MA; creek MT, WV, fork CO, river CA, rapids AZ. **Roaring Springs** AR, OR, TX are so called because they break out noisily; **Roaring Mountain** WY, from steam vents; **Roaring Gap** NC, from the wind blowing through it. Habitation-names are by transfer.

Roatan CT Algonquian, probably from the name of a chief.

Robanna NJ Probably from a combination of personal names, e.g. Robert and Anna.

Robber(s) Typically in the plural, it indicates where robbers once haunted, or were supposed to have haunted. The name is western, especially common in CA, with about ten examples. Probably there were no more robbers in the West than in the East, but in the West the imagination pictured them more romantically. In many instances the names were fancifully given, merely because a place suggested romantic banditry. The frequent combination **Robbers Roost,** an alliterative favorite, is always to be suspected as being fanciful, though in CA two examples are associated with Tiburcio Vásquez, a bandit of the 1870's. A more trustworthy case is **Robbers Creek** CA, so called because James Doyle was robbed there by armed men in the 1860's. **Robbers Roost** NV: by local story, because two peddlers were robbed here in the 1890's.

Roberdel NC For Robert L. Steele, textile manufacturer.

Robert(s) From the personal name. **Robertsville** OH: by Anglicization, for Joseph Robard (Robart), a Frenchman, the town founder. **Robert Lee** TX: For R. E. Lee, Confederate general.

Robinhood Bay ME For an early local chief, so named by the English.

Roble Spanish 'oak,' (i.e. the deciduous oak as opposed to **Encina**). Thus **Paso Robles** CA for **Paso de Robles.** But **Robles Junction** AZ is for Bernabé Robles, an early landowner.

Rob Roy AR, IN For the Scottish hero popularized in the novel by Walter Scott.

Roche French 'rock.'

Rochelle From the city in France.

Rocher French 'rock, high rock,' e.g. **Prairie du Rocher** IL.

Rochester In MA (1686) from the town in England. **Rochester** NY: originally **Rochesterville,** named in 1817 for Col. Nathaniel Rochester, one of the owners of the land; it became **Rochester** in 1822. It has been prolific of namesakes, and most of the other places derive from this one, e.g. in PA, MN, OH, TX.

Rock, Rocky Though occurring often as a generic, 'rock' is even more common as a specific, to identify places thus distinguished. The specific is coupled with 'spring,' 'island,' 'lake,' 'mountain,' 'point,' and many others. A single conspicuous rock near a stream crossing may cause the name **Rock River** or **Rock Creek,** or the whole nature of the country may be suggestive of rock. **Rocky** refers to the general situation, and not a single rock, e.g. **Rocky Butte** OR and **Rocky Top Mountain** OR, but it is much less common than **Rock. Rocky Mountains:** it is less likely that they were named for their rocky nature (since this is not a distinguishing feature of mountains) than that they were named for the Assiniboine Indians, who were known to the English, by a translation of their name, as the Rocks or Rockies. The name for the mountains arose in the Assiniboine area.

As a habitation-name, **Rock** is very common, often as a transfer, and often with the commendatory sense of stability. Especially common are **Rockdale, Rockford, Rockland, Rockport, Rockville, Rockwood.** Even such a derogatory as **Rockfield** exists, but this is probably a personal name. So also **Rock, Rockridge,** etc. may be from personal names.

Rock as a common noun is often an element in compound nouns, so that **Rockfish** NC and **Rockoak** WV are not derived directly from 'rock.'

Rockford and **Rockyford** show the difference of the two terms. The former indicates a ford marked by a rock; the latter, a ford with a rocky bottom. **Point of Rocks** and **City of Rocks** are examples of the specific used with 'of.' Both are repeated names. The former is probably not distinguishable in meaning from **Rock Point** or **Rocky Point.** The latter refers to a place where many large rocks breaking the surface of the ground give a fanciful impression of the buildings of a city. **Rockwall Co.** TX: from a natural formation resembling a wall. The common **Rockhouse,** as a specific, may refer either to a constructed shelter or to a natural formation.

Rockabema Lake ME Algonquian 'woodpecker' (?).

Rockawalking Creek MD By folk-etymology from Algonquian (recorded in 1697 as Rockawakinmany), probably 'sandy-ground-at.' Cf. **Rockaway.**

Rockaway NJ, NY From an Indian tribal name, but originally a feature-name, 'sandy-place' (Algonquian).

Rockcastle KY The river was named for castle-like formations of rock along it.

Rockchuck Peak WY From animals living there among the rocks, probably a kind of marmot related to the common woodchuck.

Rockerville SD Once a gold-mining location, it was named for the 'rocker,' a device for working gold gravels.

Rockingham The county in NH (1769) and the town in VT (1752) are for Charles Watson Wentworth, Marquis of Rockingham, kinsman of John Wentworth, governor of NH, who was responsible for the naming.

Rockinstraw Mountain AZ An Anglicization from the name of G. R. Roggenstroh, early rancher.

Rocklin CA Extensive quarries suggested 'rock.' The second syllable may be the Celtic ending 'spring, ravine' but is just as possibly a mere ending for euphonic purposes, since the railroad gave the name.

Rockmart GA A coined name, 'rock-market,' for a place producing rock.

Rockomeko Mountains ME Algonquian, 'hoed-cornland' (?).

Rocky See **Rock.**

Rockyhock NC By folk-etymology from a form recorded as *rakiok,* probably Algonquian 'cypress-land.'

Rodeo In Spanish, 'round-up.' In English, an exhibition of riding, roping, etc. In CA the creek was named in Spanish times, and the town later by transfer. In OR and other states the name is of American application.

Roebuck From the personal name, e.g. the springs in AL for G. J. Roebuck, early settler.

Rogerene Lake NJ From an 18th-century religious sect associated with the neighborhood.

Rogue River OR French-Canadian trappers had a poor opinion of the Indians living on this stream and called them *coquins,* 'rogues.' The river became 'aux Coquins,' and by the 1840's had been translated, even appearing as **Rascally River.**

Rok AZ Probably shortened from **Rock** for convenience in telegraphing by the railroad.

Rolling Generally a descriptive, e.g. **Rolling Prairie** IN, **Rolling Green** MN. **Rolling Ground** OR: a place where cattle like to roll because of the soft ground. **Rollingstone River** MN: from a Siouan name, 'stream where the stone rolls.' **Rolling Road,** e.g. MD, SC, was so named because used for rolling hogsheads of tobacco to market. **Rolling Bay** WA: originally **Rowles Bay** for an early settler; reason for change uncertain.

Romain, Cape SC Named by one of the expeditions of L. V. de Ayllon in the years 1521–1526, presumably for one of the saints known in Spanish as San Romano; the name suffered many changes of spelling in making the transition to English, eventually dropping all designation of a saint.

Roman VA Probably from a family name, although a connection with **Romancoke** is possible.

Romance WV For Romance Parsons, in 1908, when he was a newcomer in the village and his name 'struck the villagers as a good one.' (So stated by the first postmaster.)

Romancoke MD Algonquian 'low-ground-there' (?), probably shifted by folk-etymology.

Romanzof From the personal name. The mountains in AK were named (1826) for Count Nicolas Romanzof, chancellor of Russia and also a patron of science. The cape in AK is an adaptation from the name of a Count Rumyantsov who in the early 19th century outfitted a vessel for exploration of a possible Northwest Passage.

Rome Generally for the classical rather than for the modern city. The name was used for a tract along the Potomac in 1663, doubtless with a touch of

humor. Admiration of the Roman republic was a part of early American
patriotism, and most of the important
names date from the first decades of the
19th century. A hilly site, suggestive of
Rome's seven hills, was sometimes a
factor, e.g. in GA. **Rome** NY: on the
site of **Fort Stanwix**, it was christened
in 1819, because of 'the heroic defence
of the Republic' made there. **Rome** OR:
some rock formations suggested classical
ruins.

Romeo CO Eventually from the Shakespearean character. In MI the name was
consciously chosen by an early settler
'to avoid the commonplace.' In FL a
town of **Juliette** is nearby.

Romney WV From the town in England.

Romoland CA Originally **Ramola**, a variant upon the popular **Ramona.** When
the Post Office Dept. required a change,
the present name was coined in an
effort not to break too much with the
past.

Romulus For the legendary founder of
Rome, in NY given as part of the classical naming of 1790.

Ronceverte French 'brier-green.' Named
from the Greenbriar River, on which
the town stands, this having been the
name by which the French knew the
stream. It is, however, a revival in the
late 19th century, not a survival.

Rond(e) French 'round,' e.g. **Prairie
Ronde** MI.

Ronda NC A shortening of Roundabout, originally applied to a plantation here, because of its being situated
on a river bend.

Rondowa OR The town stands at the
junction of the Grande Ronde and
Wallowa rivers, and the name is coined
out of those two.

Rondoxe NY A coined name from
Adirondack.

Rond-Pompon, Bayou LA French
'round-pumpkin (or some similar
plant).'

Ronkonkoma, Lake NY Algonquian,
with *-oma* standing for an earlier (1665)
amuck, 'fishing-place,' and the rest uncertain.

Roof Butte AZ An inexact translation
from a Navajo name referring either to
a high point or to a butte shaped like
the roof of a hut.

Rooks County KS Named in 1867 for
Pvt. John C. Rooks, fatally wounded at
the battle of Prairie Grove in 1862, one
of the few examples of a Civil War
private soldier thus honored. But see
Osborne.

Roosevelt From the personal name.
President F. D. Roosevelt became prominent after most of the names had been
placed, and was always a controversial
figure. Most of the names are for President Theodore Roosevelt, e.g. **Mount
Roosevelt** SD and habitation-names in
some ten states. The town in LA commemorates the president's bear-hunting
in that area. **Roosevelttown** NY: renamed for F. D. Roosevelt in 1934,
when he visited the town to open a
bridge.

Rooster The rock in Clackamas Co.,
OR is named from its resemblance to a
rooster's comb. The rock in Multnomah
Co., OR is a euphemistic pun with
phallic significance, i.e. it is colloquially
known as **Cock.**

Root The presence of edible roots has
given rise to the name on natural features, usually streams. These often are
translations from Indian names, sometimes through the French. See **Racine.**
The personal name has produced a few
habitation-names. **Root River** WI: a
translation from the Algonquian, which
would probably be better rendered as
'snag,' since the reference was apparently to such obstructions, which were
often roots.

Rope Creek NB Probably because a
rope had to be used to let wagons down
when crossing, because of steep banks.

Ropers Bunion OR A small hill bears
this name in honor of a local resident,
otherwise unidentified.

Rosa From the personal name. **Monte Rosa** CO, also as **Mount Rosa,** is for Rose Kingsley, the first woman (1874) to climb the mountain, who wrote articles under the pseudonym Rosa del Monte.

Rosalba Lake MS For a white rose vine growing there (Latin *rosa alba*).

Rosario WA From an original Spanish naming of 1791 in honor of the Virgin Mary, this being one of her appellations.

Rosary Lakes OR They occur in a series, like beads on a rosary.

Roscommon MI From the county in Ireland (named in 1843).

Rose Well known both as a wild and as a domesticated flower, it is a common name, both on features and for habitation-names, occurring hundreds of times. It is sometimes further qualified as **Rosebud, Wildrose, White Rose,** etc. On natural features it usually indicates the presence of the flowering wild rose. On habitations it may arise by transfer, from a personal name, or from commendatory value, especially because of its celebration in poetry and song. **Rose Creek** AZ: Al Rose was killed here in a 'war' between cattlemen in 1887. **Rose Point** AK: from the triangulation station there, probably from the compass-rose. The more common habitation-names, usually with obvious commendatory value are **Rose Hill, Rosebud, Rosedale, Roseland, Roseville, Rosewood.**

Roseau French 'reed,' e.g., in the plural, **Lake Roseaux** LA.

Roseboom NY Literally, Dutch 'rose-tree'; probably a Dutch family name.

Rosharon TX Named from the Biblical 'rose of Sharon' in 1910 because of many wild roses.

Rosier, Cape ME For James Rosier, who voyaged with George Waymouth along this coast in 1605, and wrote the existing account of the voyage.

Rosillo Spanish 'light red, roan,' and hence, by description of the rocks, the **Rosillos Mountains** TX.

Rosindale NC Because of a local manufacture of rosin.

Rosita CO The diminutive of Spanish *rosa,* so named because of wild roses at the site.

Ross Regularly from the personal name. **Fort Ross** CA: at the dedication of the Russian settlement on Sept. 11, 1812, this name was drawn by lot; it means 'Russian,' in the formal language of poetry.

Rossakatum Creek DE Algonquian, meaning uncertain.

Rothiemay MT Named by an immigrant Scot for a place near his home in Scotland.

Rotten Rare, and usually in combination, e.g. **Rotten Grass Creek** MT. **Rotten Wood Creek** GA is probably a translation of a Muskogean (Creek) name, elsewhere rendered as **Punk. Rotten Point** KY probably results from dropping some such word as 'tree.' **Rotten Thumb, The** WY: a thumb-shaped pinnacle composed of disintegrating rock.

Rotterdam From the city in the Netherlands. Since the suggestions of 'rot' and 'dam' are unpleasant, the name scarcely exists, except as a Dutch legacy in NY.

Rouge French 'red.'

Rough Its rare use is chiefly confined to the description of water, e.g. **Rough Run** WV, **Rough Channel** AK, but **Rough Mountain** NV. **Rough and Ready** CA (and in other states) is, directly or indirectly, in commemoration of Gen. and President Zachary Taylor, whose nickname it was, but the quality of being 'rough-and-ready' was also a favored one among frontiersmen, so that the name had commendatory value of its own. 'Roughs' occurs as quasi-generic for rapids, e.g. **Roughs of the Guyan** WV, **The Roughs** CA. **Rough and Tumbling Creek** CO is an unusual double-descriptive.

Roughlock Falls SD To take their wagons down a steep grade here, early teamsters were forced to rough-lock their wheels.

Roulette PA For John Roulette, local landowner.

Round One of the commonest descriptives, with hundreds of examples. It may be applied in a horizontal sense, e.g. with 'lake,' 'pond,' 'grove,' 'meadow,' 'island,' 'valley,' or in a vertical sense (rounded), e.g. with 'mountain,' 'hill,' 'mound.' MN has more than 30 lakes so designated. **Roundtop** has become a generic in its own right, so that we have such names as **Little Round Top** PA, on the battlefield of Gettysburg with which no such word as 'hill' is used. **Roundhead** OH and **Round O** SC take their names from Indian chiefs so known. Secondary formations give such names as **Round Corral Meadow** CA.

Roundout Creek NY An earlier **Rondout** is recorded; probably Dutch *rondhout,* 'logwood, timber.'

Roundup The town in MT, and various features were so named because roundups were held there. Cf. **Rodeo.**

Rowdy Occasionally used as a descriptive in place of the commoner **Rough** for a stream, e.g. creeks in CA and TN.

Rowena Generally a literary name, from the heroine of Walter Scott's *Ivanhoe,* e.g. in SD. It has also been used as a woman's name. In OR it partly honors H. S. Rowe, railroad official.

Rowley In MA (1639) from a town in England.

Roxbury In MA (1630) the first spelling was **Rocksbury.** William Wood (1634) credits the name to the rocky site. There is no English town of the name, but there is Roxborrow (various spellings) which is very close, and which is in Middlesex, a county from which some MA names were taken. If the name is purely descriptive, it is almost unique for MA of that period. From MA the name has spread, e.g. in CT, 1743.

Roxy Ann Peak OR For Roxana Baker, an early settler.

Royal Often for a personal name, e.g. **Royal** NC, NB, **Royalston** MA. Sometimes with the suggestion of being 'fit for a king,' e.g. **Royal Arch** AZ. **Royal Oak:** the coupling derives from the tree in England where Prince Charles concealed himself. In MI the name probably derives from an actual tree and the remark, 'This is indeed a royal oak!' **Port Royal** SC: given by Jean Ribaut, leader of the abortive French Huguenot colony, in 1562, as an indication of the magnificence of the harbor. **Royal Arch** CA: applied in 1851, partly to commemorate the seventh degree of Masonry, and also to describe the gigantic arch of rock.

Royale, Isle MI French 'royal island,' but the reason for application uncertain.

Royalty TX Being in an oil district, it took the idea of the amount paid on oil production.

Rozel KS Altered from Roseila, the name of the daughter of a land agent, not further identified.

Rubble Lake MT Because frequent rockslides bring much rubble down into the lake.

Rubicon River CA Bears the name of the stream in Italy made famous by Julius Caesar when he crossed it, thus taking decisive action. The name, perhaps given in jest, probably commemorates some such action on the part of the namers.

Ruby 1) From a personal name, e.g. **Ruby** AZ for Lille B. Ruby, maiden name of the wife of the first postmaster. 2) For the presence of rubies or stones thought to be, e.g. **Ruby Mountains** NV, **Ruby Creek** SD.

Rubyatt NC From an early settler, H. O. Ruby, but apparently under the influence of the immensely popular *Rubaiyat of Omar Khayyam.*

Rude ND Named (1906) for a Norwegian immigrant, the postmaster,

H. O. Studsrud, with *e* added to maintain the pronunciation, whether with humor or great lack of it.

Rudyard From the personal name, especially for Rudyard Kipling, author, e.g. **Rudyard** MI, in return for which naming Kipling sent an autographed poem which was enshrined in the cornerstone of a church.

Ruffy Lake CA For an Indian so named, who first planted trout in the lake.

Rugby From the town in England; in ND named by English stockholders (1885) in a railroad. In TN named (1877) by Thomas Hughes, author of the *Tom Brown's School Days,* a story of the Rugby school, as an experimental colony for English immigrants.

Ruidoso Spanish 'noisy.' In NM the name is from a brawling stream. **Ruidosa** TX originated from the sound of water, or (according to other belief) from the sound of wind, since it is in a windy spot.

Ruin In occasional use to designate remnants of former buildings, e.g. **Wide Ruin** AZ. **Beaver Ruin Creek** GA preserves a formerly common usage of the term to indicate the devastation to a forest which was caused by beavers.

Rulo NB With simplified spelling, for Mrs. Charles Rouleau, wife of the owner of the townsite.

Rum Before the popularization of whiskey about 1750, rum was the common spirituous liquor and was used in the Indian trade by the English. A few names, e.g. **Rum Creek** WV, thus originate, probably by incident, or else because a post for the rum trade existed there. The usual folk tale (cf. **Whiskey**) is that a keg of rum was spilled there. **Rum River** MN: its Siouan name was from *wakan,* 'spirit,' i.e. in the supernatural sense; this was turned into the present name by punning translation.

Rumney NH Named (1761) with an alternate spelling for the Earl of Romney, political figure of the mid-18th century.

Rump Generally avoided as a semi-obscene term, but existing as a descriptive, e.g. **Noahs Rump** for a hill NY.

Rumson NJ Algonquian, a shortening of Navaarumsunk (1663), meaning uncertain.

Run In the middle Atlantic states it is a common generic for a small stream. Its ambiguity has worked against its appearing as a specific. In the West it was sometimes applied as a generic by people familiar with that usage in the East. Later many of these names were assumed to be specifics, and were so incorporated, to yield names such as **Oak Run Creek** CA. The battles of **Bull Run** (1861–1862) made the name well known, but many westerners apparently did not understand the generic use. The result was a number of names like **Bull Run Peak** CA. The assumption may have been that the stream was a place where there was a 'run', i.e. a pen, for bulls. So also **Mud Run Creek** CA probably indicates a place where there was a run of mud.

Runaway Pond VT Because in 1810, when the outlet was tampered with, all the water ran away, and since then the pond has been dry.

Runbolt's Run NY From the name of an Indian preserved in an early (probably 17th-century) deed.

Runnemede See **Runnymede.**

Running A descriptive with streams, as a counterpart to **Dry,** especially in the South, e.g. **Running Water Creek** GA; so also **Running Brushy Creek** TX, **Running Springs** CA, and the habitation-name **Running Water** SD, TX.

Runningmeade See **Runnymede.**

Runnymede From the place in England, because of the association with the Magna Carta. In NJ the spelling **Runnemede** is used; the naming (1844) replaced **Marlboro,** which was thought too militantly English, and an English name more acceptable to American tastes was thus substituted. **Runnymede:** in KS the name was given (1889) by an English colony; the name was, for a while, shifted to **Runningmeade,** by folk-etymology.

Rural A 19th-century sentimental commendatory, to suggest the pleasures of country life, e.g. **Rural Hall** NC, **Rural Retreat** VA.

Rush 1) From the personal name, e.g. **Rush Township** PA for Dr. Benjamin Rush, signer of the Declaration of Independence. Also in compounds, e.g. **Rushford, Rushton.** But **Rushford** MN was so named by unanimous vote of its nine inhabitants in 1854, because of its situation on **Rush River.** 2) From the growth of rushes, common on streams and lakes (**Rush Lake,** about 20 times in MN). It is often a translation from some Indian name, since Indians were interested in rushes for weaving mats.

Rushmore From the personal name. **Mount Rushmore** SD: for C. E. Rushmore, a New York attorney who was in the region on business. When he asked the name of the mountain, someone said, jokingly, that it was Rushmore, and the name stuck.

Rushseba MN A coined hybrid from Rush River (for the bulrushes) and Ojibway 'river.'

Rushsylvania OH A coinage from Rush Creek, and the rest either taken directly from **Sylvania,** or with the literal meaning 'forest-land.'

Ruskin The mountain in CA and various habitations, e.g. in GA, NB, were named for John Ruskin, English author.

Russell From the personal name, e.g. **Mount Russell** AK named ca. 1910 by A. H. Brooks for I. C. Russell, geologist (1852–1906).

Russet Hills AZ From their brown color.

Russian From the presence of Russians, as in CA by association with the colony at **Fort Ross** in the early 19th century, e.g. **Russian River, Gulch.** In AK more than a dozen names arose from the early Russian occupation.

Russiaville IN By folk-etymology from **Richardville,** apparently under the influence of a French pronunciation; Richard was a local Miami chief.

Rustler To designate a place frequented by rustlers, e.g. **Rustler Park** AZ, or thus associated by incident, e.g. **Rustler Peak** OR. **Rustlers Roost** NB: the alliterative echo of some forgotten incident.

Ruston LA Named (1884) for R. E. Russ, local landowner.

Ruth From the woman's name; in NV it is for Ruth MacDonald, daughter of the original mining claimant.

Rutland In MA (1714) for the English county; in VT (1761) the grantee had come from **Rutland** in MA. It is possible that the Duke of Rutland was honored.

Ryde CA From the town in England, so named because of similarity of site on an island.

Rye 1) From the town in England, e.g. **Rye** NY. 2) From the tall and conspicuous wild rye grass, e.g. **Rye Patch** NV. 3) From cultivated grain, e.g. **Rye Valley** NB. 4) From the personal name, e.g. **Rye** TX for M. C. Rye, early settler. **Ryegate** VT: named (1763) for Baron Reigate, military and political figure of the mid-18th century.

Ryegate VT For Reigate, England; probably because one of the original grantees was a native of that town.

S

Sabada Pond ME Algonquian, meaning uncertain.

Sabana Spanish, the equivalent of **Savanna.**

Sabao Mountain ME Algonquian 'passage,' with reference first to a chain of lakes through which a canoe route passed.

Sabbath Used rarely as the equivalent of **Sunday,** e.g. **Sabbath Day Point** NY.

Sabbatus ME An Algonquian (Abnaki) rendering of the French personal name St. Jean Baptiste, with reference to one of two known Indians who bore that name in the 18th century. **Sabbatis Mountain** NY is of similar derivation.

Sabetha CO, KS For a Ute woman, wife of **Ouray.**

Sabina In OH for the town founder Warren Sabin, with an *a,* as is customary with place-names.

Sabine The river LA, TX was named by the Spaniards **Sabinas,** for the red cedars growing along it; speakers of French shifted it to the present form. Elsewhere the name may be from a woman's name.

Sabino In the Spanish of NM, the dwarf juniper, e.g. in the adjectival form **Sabinoso** NM; so also, probably, **Sabino Canyon** AZ. **Sabinal** TX: probably for the same tree, i.e. 'juniper-grove.'

Sable Probably all occurrences are from the French 'sand.' It occurs chiefly with features where sand is likely to be noticeable, e.g. streams, and hence arise the names **Au Sable** and **Ausable. Sable Island** MN is largely a sandbar. **Cape Sable** FL is probably of the same origin.

Sabonack See **Seponack.**

Sabougla MS Choctaw 'smoky.'

Sabraton WV For Sabra Sturgiss, wife of a local judge.

Sabrina, Lake CA For Sabrina Hobbs, wife of the local manager of a power company.

Sabula The original naming PA may be from Latin *sabulum,* 'sand, gravel,' with the *a* ending for a place-name; but a woman's name is possible.

Sac From the Indian tribal name, also as **Sauk,** and sometimes in combination representing the Algonquian word for 'stream-mouth, outlet.' See **Saco.**

Sacagawea A variant of **Sacajawea.**

Sacajawea Several western features commemorate the Shoshone woman who accompanied the Lewis and Clark Expedition.

Sacandaga NY Iroquoian, probably 'swampy.'

Sacasawaki River ME Algonquian, meaning uncertain.

Sacate, Sacaton Related terms referring to a kind of desert grass or other fodder.

Sacatone Canyon NV A variant of **Sacaton.** See **Sacate.**

Saccarappa Falls ME Algonquian, meaning uncertain.

Sachacha Pond MA Algonquian, meaning uncertain.

Sachem An Algonquian word for 'chief' came into English, in New England, being recorded in 1622. Namings are therefore English rather than Indian, e.g. **Sachem Pond** NH. **Sachem Head** CT: in 1637, during a war, two sachems were captured, and were beheaded at this 'head of land.' The name thereupon arose with a grim pun. See **Sagamore.**

Sachuest RI Algonquian 'big-hill-at.'

Sackatucket, Saquatucket, Saugatucket, etc. Algonquian 'outlet-(of)-(tidal)-river-at.' **Saugatuck** is the same name, without the locative ending.

Saco Algonquian 'river-mouth, outlet of stream.' The rivers in ME and NH are thus derived, and the city in ME is by transfer.

Sacony Creek PA See **Saucon.**

Sacramento Spanish 'sacrament,' generally referring to the Holy Sacrament, and used as a religious name. The name was applied to a river in CA in 1808, doubtless for some now-lost association with the Holy Sacrament. The county and city were named from the river.

Sacred Scarcely existing except as **Sacred Heart,** which in OK originated with a Catholic mission. In MN the origin is disputed, but probably was originally for a mission, which was abandoned, but left its name on a creek, from which it was transferred to a township and village.

Sacul TX A reverse spelling for John Lucas, early settler.

Sacut Pond NY Algonquian 'outlet-at.'

Sadawga Lake VT From the personal name of an Indian who lived there, probably 19th century.

Saddle A common descriptive for a hill or mountain, having a depression in the middle and thus more or less resembling a saddle, e.g. the recurrent **Saddle Mountain. Old Saddleback** CA: a double-peaked mountain, each peak also having its own name. **Saddle Creek** SD: a mailman abandoned a saddle here during a winter blizzard, and it was found in the spring. **Saddlebag** and **Saddlehorn** also occur as descriptives.

Sadsbury PA The township was originally **Sudbury,** from the English town. It was apparently made over when origin had been forgotten, as if it were **Sad's Bury,** from a personal name, and the town **Sadsburyville** was named.

Saenz From the personal name, e.g. **Los Saenz** TX is for the family of Miguel Saenz, granted land here in 1767.

Safety As a seacoast name it indicates a place of security, e.g. **Port Safety** AK. **Pond of Safety** NH: four paroled soldiers in the Revolutionary War lived at this secluded place to be out of the way of trouble.

Sag Algonquian 'outlet,' e.g. **Sag Pond** ME, **Sag Harbor** NY. The word has a simple meaning, which is, however, not expressed by any colloquial English word, viz. the place at which a stream flows out of a lake or pond. By association the name has been applied to a great variety of features, in a great diversity of spellings, e.g. *sauk-, saug-, suck-, saug-, sunk-, sak-, sac-*. Many names contain this element, especially in New England. The name of the important Indian tribe, usually spelled **Sauk,** is derived from the same term.

Sagadahoc ME Algonquian, taken over from the Indians in the early 17th century for the lower Kennebec River, 'river-mouth.'

Sagamore An Algonquian word for 'chief' (the same also rendered as **Sachem)** came into English, being recorded in 1613. The usage ranged from ME to VA and also spread westward, though largely replaced by **Sachem** in southern New England. Besides its use on features, e.g. a creek in NH, it acquired dignity in the Romantic period of love of Indian names and is to be found on habitations, e.g. **Sagamore** PA, **Sagamore Hills** OH.

Saganing MI From Algonquian, shortened from a name recorded as Pausaugh-e-gah-a-ning, referring to a place where cedar for canoe frames could be obtained.

Sagassett See **Sagosset.**

Sagavanirktok River AK Eskimo, probably 'strong current.'

Sagawannah Mountain NY Iroquoian, meaning uncertain.

Sage Sometimes from a personal name, e.g. the peak in AZ as a memorial to H. H. Sage who died in World War I; more often from the presence of sagebrush. This plant, however, is too ubiquitous in much of the West and so little regarded that names are comparatively rare, though a few are to be found in most of the western states on features. It is rare on habitation-names. The commonest compound is **Sagehen,** for the wild fowl, e.g. the creek in CA.

Saghibpatook Falls ME Algonquian, meaning uncertain.

Saginaw Ojibway, meaning a place where the Sauks lived; the original naming was in MI.

Sago Acording to local story in WV the name was suggested by an itinerant cattle buyer named White, who gave no reasons for his choice. The name, also in VA, is much like **Saco,** and suggests an Algonquian origin from the common word meaning 'outlet, mouth of a stream.' Possibly Mr. White was from VA, but since he is not further identified, research comes to a dead-end.

Sagola, Sagole MI, WI Probably from an Indian (Oneida) term of greeting, and applied by Americans in the 19th century.

Sagosset Island ME Algonquian 'outlet-near,' with reference to the mouth of the **Kennebec River.**

Saguache CO A shortening of Ute *sagua-gua-chi-pa,* 'blue-earth-spring,' from a blue clay found there.

Saguaro From the giant cactus so called. **Sahuarita** AZ represents a diminutive, with a different spelling, and takes its name from a ranch.

Sahale Chinook jargon, 'high,' a name applied in recent times to a waterfall OR, and a peak WA.

Sahwave Mountains NV Northern Paiute 'sagebrush.'

Sail Rock NM, WA Descriptive of a rock formation resembling a small-boat sail.

Sailor Since the navy does not function much ashore, the names generally refer to an individual sailor, either of the navy or of the merchant marine, e.g.

Sailor Creek CA, a repeated name, usually indicating that a runaway sailor worked his claim there in the gold rush.

Saint A general discussion is presented here, but for convenience of reference separate entries are reserved for **Sainte, San, Santa, Santo.** It should be always remembered that the same name may be borne by more than one saint.

1) From personal names, e.g. **St. Clairsville** OH, **St. Clair Co.** MO, etc. from Gen. Arthur St. Clair, commander in the Indian wars; **St. Johnsbury** VT for Hector St. Jean de Crevecoeur, author; **St. Vrain Mountain** CO for Ceran de St. Vrain (1802–1870), pioneer trader. **Saint Helens, Mount** WA: named (1792) by George Vancouver for Baron St. Helens (1753–1839) who conducted British negotiations with Spain regarding the northwest coast of North America.

2) By transfer from places already named in the U.S. or in other countries. Though numerous English villages bear a saint's name, early American naming was chiefly by Protestants, who did not care to use such names. **Saint Albans:** from the town in England. The town in VT was named in the late 18th century when the Puritan objection to saint's names had faded. **St. Cloud** MN: for St. Cloud, France, commemorated because the namer had been reading of the palace in a life of Napoleon. **St. Petersburg.** See **Peter.**

3) From the French usage, 'holy.' **St. Croix River** ME: French 'holy cross.' Jacques Cartier gave this name to a river because he came there on Holy Cross Day (Sept. 14, 1535). The arrangement of the river channels, suggesting a cross, may have been an additional motivation. Partly influenced by this naming, the Sieur de Monts named **St. Croix Island** in 1604.

4) From a saint. The possessive form often indicates origin from a church thus dedicated. Though such names were commonly given under Catholic auspices, many saints, especially those of the Bible, were held in honor by the Protestants. Their failure to give such names must thus be credited to the special conditions of the 17th century, under which the idea of sainthood was considered more especially Catholic. Only in the Catholic-founded col-

ony of MD do we find early namings, such as **St. George's River, St. Mary's River.** The former was an especially propitious name, for no English Protestant could make much objection to the use of the patron saint of England. With the later 18th century came a change, and some explorers began using the saint's calendar of the Church of England. James Cook named **Cape St. Augustine** AK for Augustine of Canterbury on May 26, 1778, the day of that saint. Cook indulged in similar namings without the title, probably for brevity, as with **Cape Perpetua** OR, **Cape Bede** AK. George Vancouver, also an English Protestant explorer, named **Point St. George** on April 23, 1782, the day of the saint, but probably also for patriotic reasons.

Catholic explorers bestowed saint's names freely, especially if a priest were accompanying the expedition. (See **San, Santa,** etc.) These namings were generally by the calendar, and indicate no special devotion to the particular saint, or any appropriateness, but merely the day of arrival at a certain place—commonly, a river. Later Catholic namers, especially the founders of missions and towns, were more likely to be guided by devotional reasons, and to choose a saint to whom the namer was (perhaps because of belonging to a special order) particularly attached. It thus happens that the 'great' or more popular saints are more numerous on the map, e.g. Mary, Peter, Paul, John, James, Joseph—and, because of the Franciscan Order, Francis.

In areas once French or Spanish or for other reason strongly Catholic, these names are very numerous. MO has 5 such rivers and bayous, 4 counties, and at least 50 cities, towns, and villages.

However propitious such names may be to the pious, they are highly monotonous and uninteresting to the onomatologist, and he gladly takes leave of them, by appending data on a few notable instances.

St. Joseph: in MO the settlement was named, when first platted, by Joseph Robidoux, for his name saint. It is commonly known as St. Joe, and several towns in other states are officially so spelled, e.g. **St. Joe** ID, which takes the name from the **St. Joe River,** originally called the **St. Joseph River** by the Jesuit missionary de Smet in 1844, for reasons of piety. At the same time he named another stream **St. Ignatius River. St. Augustine** FL: Pedro Menéndez de Avilés gave this name (**San Augustin**) to a fort founded in 1665 because he had sighted land on the day of St. Augustine of Hippo (Aug. 28). **St. Lawrence River:** Jacques Cartier thus named a small bay on Aug. 10, 1535, the day of St. Lawrence of Rome. The name spread to include the whole gulf and the chief river running into it. **St. Paul:** the name appears in a dozen states. The city in MN, like many towns, took its name from its church, in this instance the mission founded by the French priest Lucian Galtier in 1841. He chose the name partly in counterpart to an already established St. Peter's and partly (with a pleasant touch of humor) because St. Paul was the apostle to the Gentiles who were 'well represented in the new place in the persons of the Indians.' **St. Louis** MO: named at the founding in 1764, for Louis IX of France, partly for patriotic reasons, since it was settled by loyal Frenchmen who moved to the west of the Mississippi to remain in French territory after the treaty of 1763. The fact that the name Louis was especially associated with the French monarchy must have been an additional motivation. **St. Marys** WV: traditionally believed to have been named in 1849 by Alexander Creel, because he had seen a vision of the Virgin Mary at that spot.

5) From demi-saints, pseudo-saints, etc. Just as folk in the Middle Ages frequently called someone 'saint' on their own initiative, so Americans have often made use of the term without consulting any churchly authorities. In a surprising number of instances a place has been named for some person, and the sign of sainthood has then been prefixed. A few examples are: **St. Joe** WV: for a man (or for three men) named Joseph. **St. Joe** TX: originally called merely Joe for Joe Howell; people objected to the name (perhaps as being too short and insignificant) and it was given its present form. **St. Paul** TX: for W. H. Paul, who was nicknamed St. Paul. **St. Anna** MO: named by Bob Williams for his wife Anna, who had just died. **St. James**

MO: partly, at least, in honor of Thomas James, the founder. **St. Martha** MO: named by W. R. Wild for his wife. Two Utah towns represent attempts at a kind of canonization by the Mormons, viz. **St. George,** named in 1861 for George A. Smith, and **St. John,** named in 1867 for John Roseberry. Both of the men were prominent in the Mormon church. **St. Thomas** PA: for Thomas Campbell, first being called Campbellstown. Various places are locally said to be named **Saint** in honor of some known person, e.g. **Saint Edward** NB for a priest Edward Serrels, and **Saint Michael** NB for an Irishman named Mike Kyne. The more reasonable assumption is that such places were after the saint for whom the man himself was named. **St. Tammany** LA: from the fictitious and humorously conceived character, based upon the Delaware chief Tamanend, jocularly conceived as the patron saint of the U.S.; the name was given because the area was chiefly peopled by Indians. **St. Elmo Pass** WA: from the phenomenon of St. Elmo fire, observed there in 1887. **St. Elmo** CO: named, ca. 1879, by the local storekeeper, who had just read the novel of that title by Augusta Jane Evans. **St. Paris** OH: originally **New Paris,** but changed for differentiation, the need of a new name being probably more in mind than any honoring of the obscure 4th-century bishop. **St. Francis** KS: for Frances Emerson, wife of one of the town founders. For convenience of reference some entries are under the individual name, not under **Saint.**

Sainte French 'saint' (feminine), usually abbreviated *Ste.,* e.g. **Ste. Genevieve** MO, **Sault Ste. Marie** MI. The form is rare, since the names have generally been normalized to the English spelling.

Sakatonchee River MS Chickasaw 'hogcorn,' meaning beech mast.

Sakonnet RI Algonquian, meaning uncertain, but probably containing *sak,* 'outlet.' See **Sag.**

Salacoa Creek GA Cherokee, a kind of grass usually known as 'bear grass,' but probably derived directly from the name of a Cherokee town.

Salado Spanish 'salty,' in American usage the feminine form is regularly used in CA, even in **Arroyo Salada,** and in the hybrid **Salada Beach.** In NM and TX the masculine form is preferred, e.g. **Salado Arroyo, Salado Creek.** In AR the name, on a village and creek, is probably from some unexplained French origin, and has been attracted by folk-etymology into such forms as **Sally Doe.**

Salamanca NY Named with the building of the railroad in the late 19th century for an important stockholder; otherwise unidentified.

Salamonie River IN Algonquian (Miami), an adaptation from the word for the plant called bloodroot.

Salcha River AK Athapascan, meaning uncertain.

Salduro Spanish 'salt-hard,' so named by Americans from the nearby salt flats.

Salé French 'salty,' e.g. **Bayou Salé** LA, commonly pronounced as if **Sally.**

Salem The Indian name of the site in MA was **Naumkeag,** and this was kept by the first settlers. The Puritan divines, familiar with Hebrew, suspected this to be a name left by the Ten Lost Tribes, roughly translatable as 'comfort-haven.' This suggestion of a Hebrew original may have led to the adopting in 1629 of a Hebrew name of commendatory quality, taken to mean 'peace,' though also a shortening of Jerusalem. The fame of the original town and the commendatory qualities from a religious point of view have resulted in about 35 towns so named. Some of these originated from country churches so called, e.g. **Salem Chapel** NC. In addition, for differentiation within a state, many places bear such names as **Salemburg.** In 1951 there were listed in OH: **Salem, North Salem, West Salem, South Salem, Salem Center,** and **Lower** or **New Salem. Salem** OR: for the town in MA, named in the 1840's. **Salemsborg** KS: the combination makes use of Swedish 'castle,' probably with the literal meaning 'peace's-castle.'

Saleratus The common 19th-century term for baking soda, it was bestowed upon features in the arid West, e.g. the creek in UT, which contained or were thought to contain that mineral.

Salida Spanish 'exit, outlet.' In CO the town was named from being at the outlet of a canyon.

Salina Spanish, used broadly for something connected with salt, e.g. salt pan, salt lagoon, saltworks. **Salinas** CA: the river was named from the salt pools or marshes at its mouth. In areas lacking Spanish background the name is sometimes a mere variant of **Saline,** e.g. the city in KS is **Salina** but is on the **Saline River.** In OK the town was originally **Saline,** because of saltworks. **Saline** is apparently thought to be an unpleasant name for habitations.

Saline In arid regions for a show of salt, e.g. **Saline Valley** CA for the salt deposits there. **Saline Co.** NB: named because it was thought that salt could be produced commercially. **Salineville** OH: because salt was once produced from salt wells. In regions of French background, e.g. southern AR, it is a repeated name from American-French, 'salt-spring, salt lick, saltworks.'

Salineno TX From Ignacio Salinas, early settler.

Salisbury From the town in England; MA, 1640; in MD, 1732; in CT, 1738; in NC, 1753.

Salitpa AL Formed by transposition of consonants from **Satilpa.**

Salix Latin 'willow'; in IA and PA probably used to avoid repetition of the common English name.

Salko Hill ME Algonquian, meaning uncertain.

Sallal From the sallal bush or its edible berry, chiefly on features in OR and WA.

Sallisaw OK An Americanization from French *salaison,* 'salting,' with reference to the curing of meat, applied first to a stream where hunters cured buffalo meat.

Sally Commonly from the woman's name, e.g. the island AK. See **Sale, Salado. Sally Doe.**

Salmon From the personal name, e.g. **Salmon** TX for M. D. Salmon, first postmaster. More commonly on water features for the fish, commemorating either abundance or an incident. Such names as **Salmon Alps** CA arise by transfer, in this case from **Salmon River.** Because of the migratory habit and because rarity often causes naming, the name occurs on many small streams and in regions where salmon are uncommon. **Salmonberry:** various features are named for this wild fruit, in the NW. **Salmon Lake** AZ: so called from a case of canned salmon which was supposed to be cached there, but could not be found by the party looking for it.

Salofka FL Muskogean (Creek) 'knife,' an American naming; reference uncertain.

Salol MN So called by a former pharmacist's clerk for a drug used in treating rheumatism; the reason for naming is unknown, unless he merely considered the name to be unusual, short, and euphonious.

Salome From the personal name, e.g. in AZ for Grace Salome Pratt, wife of the town founder.

Salona PA A devout Methodist woman had been impressed by the Methodist mission at Salonika. She suggested that name, and a shortening of it was adopted.

Salquin Island ME Algonquian, meaning uncertain.

Salsipuedes A Spanish phrase, literally 'jump if you can,' used as a conventional descriptive for difficult places, e.g. several creeks in CA, so called probably because of ravines.

Salt A common descriptive for features which have salty or brackish water or are near a salt deposit, often used with creek, spring. In areas where such features are common **Salt Lick** and **Salt Lake** tend to become generics, and may attract a second descriptive, e.g. **Great Salt Lake.** In other instances such a term is used to describe another feature, e.g. **Salt Lick Creek** WV. Habitation-names arise by transfer, e.g. **Salt Lake City,** or from the salt industry, e.g. **Salt Mine** LA. **Salt River** AZ: the stream is brackish only in times of low water. **Saltblock Run** MD: probably for a block of rock salt set out for cattle. **Saltsburg** PA: though formerly sometimes spelled Salzburg and thought to be from the city in Germany, the name is from an extinct salt industry.

Saltese MT From Seltisse or Saltese, a Coeur d'Alene chief who lived near this spot.

Saltillo The city in Mexico was occupied by American troops during the war of 1846–1848, and the name was later bestowed upon several places, e.g. in TX in 1850.

Salton Sea CA One of the few bodies of water to be termed a sea in the U.S. It is apparently a coinage 'salt on,' which was applied to the dry lake bed in 1892; after the flooding the name was retained, though it could more reasonably have become 'salt in.'

Salubria ID, IA Apparently a Latin ending was used with *salubrious* to form a commendatory.

Saluda NC, SC, VA Originally a river-name, of Indian origin, probably meaning 'river of corn,' because the Indians grew corn there.

Salunga PA Algonquian (Delaware), probably 'crayfish,' cf. **Chicisalunga.**

Salvisa KY From the nearby **Salt** and **Levisa** rivers.

Samagatuma Valley CA A Spanish adaptation of the name of an Indian village; meaning unknown.

Samaniego Peak AZ For M. G. Samaniego, early settler from Mexico.

Samarcand NC Named in 1888 for the city of central Asia.

Samaria From the Biblical city.

Samfordyce TX For Samuel Fordyce, a railroad man, named ca. 1904.

Sammanonk Creek PA Algonquian (Delaware) 'horn-at,' probably an animal's horn is meant, but the reference is uncertain.

Samnorwood TX For Sam Norwood, early settler.

Samoa CA Named in 1889 for the island, at a time when it was much in the news.

Samos MO, VA From the Greek island.

Samp In Colonial English the term (originally Algonquian) meant a food prepared from maize, and is probably the origin of **Samptown** NJ.

Sampala Lake FL Probably from San Pablo, the name of a nearby Spanish mission, shifted in pronunciation either by Indians or Americans.

Sample From the personal name, e.g. in TX for A. H. and Jim Sample, early settlers.

San Spanish 'saint' (masculine). For general discussion see **Saint.** Most Spanish forms are enough like the English to be recognizable. Several of the more unusual ones are among those listed below. These names are ubiquitous in regions settled by the Spaniards, especially NM, and the southern parts of AZ, CA, TX, both for natural features and for habitation-names. Only a few need be here presented.
　　San Antonio: usually for St. Anthony of Padua, particularly common in CA, because he was a patron of the Franciscan Order. **San Antonio** TX: on May 19, 1691, the explorers Terán and Massanet came to a stream which they called by this name because the day was that of St. Anthony. The name passed to the mission and thus to the city. **San Augustine** TX: a partial Anglicizing of the Spanish San Augustín, originally for a mission. **San Bernardino** CA: the name was first placed on a subordinate settlement of the Mission San Gabriel, in the vicinity of the modern city, in 1819; it has become a

name-cluster (county, mountains, etc.). It honors St. Bernardine of Siena.

San Diego CA: though Diego is the equivalent of James, St. James is usually rendered as **Santiago** (q.v.). Viscaíno on Nov. 12, 1602, gave the name **San Diego** to a bay in honor of St. Didacus, whose day it was. The city was named by transfer. **San Dieguito** CA: the river near San Diego is known by the diminutive, the name having been first applied, probably to an Indian village subsidary to San Diego Mission. **San Fernando** CA: from the mission dedicated in 1797 to St. Ferdinand, i.e. King Ferdinand III of Spain. **San Francisco:** generally for St. Francis of Assisi. In CA the name was first applied in 1595, vaguely, to the country in general and to an uncertainly located bay. A Spanish expedition, advancing by land in 1769, looked for this bay, and applied the already existing name to the body of water now so known. The mission founded in 1770 was so dedicated. The city took that name in 1847. In AZ the peaks so called were named ca. 1629 by Franciscan missionaries in honor of their founder. **San Jacinto:** the river in TX and other names commemorate St. Hyacinth, the 13th-century Dominican, rather than one of the obscure saints of that name. **San Joaquin** CA: the name-cluster derives from St. Joachim, probably because the river was given a name on or near his day, March 20.

San Jose: though there are a dozen St. Josephs, the one usually honored was the spouse of the Virgin Mary. The popularity of this saint is reflected in a large number of place-names. The city in CA was named on its founding as a *pueblo* in 1777. **San Juan:** there are about 70 St. Johns, but those most commonly honored are the Evangelist and the Baptist (Bautista). Six different ones have been identified in the nomenclature of CA, e.g. **San Juan Capistrano** CA: the mission was dedicated to St. John Capistran, the Franciscan hero of the siege of Vienna in 1456. In certain Spanish-settled areas **San Juan** was so common that local distinctions were added, especially for land grants, e.g. **San Juan de Boquillas y Nogales** AZ. The secondary names often survived and eventually replaced the saint's name, as with both **Boquillas** and **Nogales.**

San Luis Obispo CA and **San Luis Rey** CA spring from missions dedicated to St. Louis the bishop (of Toulouse), and St. Louis the King (of France), the latter also providing the name for **St. Louis** MO. **San Pablo:** the eminence of St. Paul led to the frequent use of his name, e.g. in CA where it forms a name-cluster, originating from **Point San Pablo,** which stands as a counterpart to **Point San Pedro** on the opposite shore, the two dating from before 1811 and probably being named at the same time. **San Pedro** (see also under **San Pablo**). About 50 St. Peters exist, and the name is very common for places. Though St. Peter the Apostle is by far the most widely known, the evidence of the calendar shows that others were sometimes remembered, e.g. the name-cluster in CA springs from the naming of the bay in 1602 by Viscaíno on Nov. 26, the day of St. Peter of Alexandria. **San Saba** TX: the river was named for St. Sabbás on his day, Dec. 5, 1732, by the expedition of J. A. Bastillo y Ceballos which came to the stream on that day.

A few names present irregular development. **San Ardo** CA: it was originally called San Bernardo from the ranch of that name, but the Post Office Dept. would not approve the name because of resemblance to San Bernardino. M. J. Brandenstein, the owner of the ranch, then created what has been called a new saint by lopping off the Bern. **San Benito:** In CA a name-cluster springs from St. Benedict for calendar reasons, but in Texas the name of the town is from a ranchowner Ben Hicks, who was known to his Mexican workmen as Don Benito; one of them, a great admirer of his employer, suggested San Benito for the townsite. **San Perlita** TX: this means 'little pearl,' but there is no such saint. It is for Mrs. Pearl Johnson, but creates double confusion since it should, in that case, have been Santa Perlita. **San Quentin:** a point on San Francisco Bay was so known in Spanish by the name Quintin because of an Indian chief of that name captured there on Sept. 24, 1840. The Coast Survey in 1850 Anglicized the name to Quentin, and then prefixed San, a natural error in view of the many nearby places bearing that suffix. **San Domingo Creek** PA: an immigrant from Santo Domingo lived here in the mid-19th century. **San Pitch** See **Sanpete**.

Sancho Sank, Lake LA Probably from French *sang pour sang,* 'blood for blood,' because of revenge taken here by French settlers on Indians who had killed some of the French. The form **Sancho** probably arose by folk-etymology, the name being well known from *Don Quixote.*

Sanco TX Selected from a list submitted to the Post Office Dept., but of uncertain origin.

Sand, Sandy Very common, with many hundreds of examples. A few are from the personal name **Sands,** or from the nickname **Sandy.** Most of them are descriptives (**Sand Hill, Sandy Point, Sandy Ridge**). In connection with bodies of water, the bottom or shore is indicated (**Sand Lake, Sandy Creek**). In some instances the name is a shortening for **Quicksand** (e.g. **Sand Creek** OR). It occurs in compounds, e.g. **Sandstone Mountain** CA, but transfers from England and personal names must be distinguished, e.g. **Sandford** in the U.S. generally has nothing to do with either sand or a ford. **Sandy Bob Canyon** AZ: a man thus nicknamed, once lived here. **Sandcoulee** MT: this is in the area where *coulee* is used for a stream or stream course. **Sandy Hook:** the name occurs on a Dutch map (1656) as Sant Punt, 'Sand Point,' but *hoek* was commonly used instead of *punt,* with the same general meaning; the English form is an adaptation. **Sand Pudding Lake** NB: because, when some cowboys were camped here, sand blew into a pudding. In may areas, e.g. OK, **Sandy Creek** has become so common as to lose distinguishing capacity so that a second specific has become necessary, e.g. **Cherokee Sandy Creek, Willow Sandy Creek,** etc.

Sandia Spanish 'watermelon,' being applied in CA because watermelons were a crop of the area. The reason for the application to the mountains in NM is uncertain.

Sandisfield MA For Samuel Lord Sandys, political figure (1761).

Sandsea Kill Translated from the similar Dutch name, which was formerly in use as **Zantzee,** a fanciful description or a proper name.

Sandusky OH Iroquoian (Wyandot), applied first to the river, from a longer form recorded as Ot-san-doos-ke, referring to a source of pure water, and used on various places as a quasi-generic by the Indians.

Sandwich In MA (ca. 1637) from the town in England. In IL the name is a transfer from MA.

Sanel Mountain CA From a Pomo tribal name and also the name of one of their villages.

Sanencheck Rock AZ Navajo 'thief rock.'

Sanford From the personal name, e.g. **Mount Sanford** AK, named (1885) by H. T. Allen for the Sanford family, especially for Reuben Sanford, Allen's great-grandfather.

Sangamon IL First applied to the river, as **Saguimont** in a French context of 1721. *Sag* is probably the Algonquian 'outlet,' (see **Sag**); the rest of the name is uncertain.

Sanganois IL A combination of **Sangamon** and **Illinois.**

Sangre de Cristo Mountains Co, NM Spanish 'blood of Christ.' This unusual naming dates from the Spanish period, probably from the early 19th century; it may be connected with the growth of the Penitente sect, or may be a semireligious reaction to a red sunset.

Sanguiluela Creek NM Probably from Spanish *sanguijuela,* 'leech.'

Sanhedrin, Mount CA The name of the ancient Jewish council. By local tradition, it was named by some Missourians for a mountain in that state. An early recorded form is Sanhidrim.

Sanhickan Creek NJ From a tribal name.

Sanilac MI Named (1848) for a Wyandotte chief of earlier times, whose name was preserved in tradition.

Sanish ND Indian (Arikaran) 'real people,' originally a tribal or village name.

Sanitor SD A shortening of 'sanatorium,' because a tuberculosis hospital was located here.

Sanjon An alternative spelling for Zanjon, e.g. Sanjon de Los Alisos CA, San Jon NM. Probably for Sanjon. So also San Jon NM. See Zanja.

Sankaty Head MA Algonquian, meaning uncertain.

Sanlando FL From being between the towns Sanford and Orlando.

Sanoose Creek MS Choctaw 'deer-sleep-there.' Also as Sanusi in AL.

Sanpete UT From an Indian tribal name, recorded as Sampitch, etc., and also as the modern name San Pitch UT.

Sanpoil River WA From an Indian tribal name.

Sans French 'without.' Sans Bois Creek OK, 'without wood'; hence, the Sans Bois Mountains. Sans Souci MI, 'without care,' a commendatory name, with reference also to the palace built in Potsdam by Frederick the Great. Sans Dessein, Cote MO: American-French 'without purpose,' with côte, 'hill,' either applied to a hill which seemed cut off from the other hills, or else by folk-etymology from an Indian term, perhaps the same that appears under One Hundred and Two.

Sansarc From the Indian tribal name.

Santa For general discussion, see Saint. 1) Spanish 'holy.' Santa Cruz, 'holy cross.' A name often given, sometimes because of a place discovered on Holy Cross Day, Sept. 14. Santa Fe, 'holy faith.' A name of numerous places, a few of the habitation-names being outside of Spanish penetration, and named after one of the other places. Santa Fe NM: named La Villa Reál de la Santa

Fe de San Francisco (The Royal City of the Holy Faith of St. Francis) in 1609, but quickly shortened. Santa Fe Springs CA, Rancho Santa Fe CA: properties developed by the Santa Fe Railroad, and named for publicity, being thus secondarily derived from Santa Fe NM.

2) Spanish 'saint' (feminine). Santa Ana: probably all for St. Anne, the traditionally named mother of the Virgin Mary. Santa Ana CA: the river was named on July 28, 1769, by the soldiers of the Portolá Expedition, Saint Anne's Day being July 26. The priests called the stream by 'the most sweet name of Jesus of the Earthquakes,' because of earthquakes felt at that time. The soldiers may have considered this an unlucky name. From the river a name-cluster has developed. Santa Anita: the diminutive form of Ana is used to refer to a small or unimportant place; there is no St. Anita (cf. San Dieguito). Santa Barbara CA: the name was first applied, on the saint's day, Dec. 4, 1602, to the channel still so known between the islands and the mainland. From this has sprung a name-cluster. Santa Catalina CA: Viscaíno named the island on the day of discovery, Nov. 25, 1602, St. Catherine's Day. Santa Clara CA: the river (Los Angeles, Ventura Co.) was named on Aug. 9, 1769, by the Portolá Expedition, i.e. on the day of St. Clare of Assisi. The mission was founded in 1777 and dedicated to the same saint by previous planning; from the mission has arisen the name-cluster. Santa Maria: besides denoting the Virgin Mary, the name is repeated a dozen times in the list of saints. Since the Spanish commonly used the title Nuestra Señora for the Virgin, most of the places known as Santa Maria are for other saints. Santa Monica CA: the mountains were named on May 14, 1770, St. Monica's day, by the Portolá Expedition, and a name-cluster thus arose. Santa Rita: since Rita is the diminutive for Margarita, some places so named may be equivalents to other places named Santa Margarita. But Saint Rita is officially the name of a saint whose day falls on May 22, and most of the places so named commemorate her. Santa Rosa: both St. Rose of Lima and St. Rose of Viterbo are probably honored. The former, canonized in

1671, was popular as being the only New World saint at that time. The name is often repeated, especially in CA, where the creek in Santa Barbara Co. was named on Aug. 30, 1769, the day of St. Rose of Lima. **Santa Ynez:** the present spelling has been offically recognized, though modern Spanish uses Inés. The name-cluster in CA sprang from the mission dedicated to St. Agnes.

3) **Santa Anna** TX: the name was sent in to the Post Office Dept. as Santanta, for a friendly Indian chief, but was transformed, coming out with the English spelling of Anna.

4) **Santa Claus:** in IN the name Santa Fe having been rejected in 1846 because of duplication, Santa Claus was jocularly suggested, because it happened to be the Christmas season. The name of the 'patron saint of Christmas' has been used for other habitation-names, e.g. AK and AZ, for publicity purposes, especially because of the popularity of the postmark for Christmas mail.

5) By folk-etymology, e.g. **Santa Barb** LA, and **Santa Bogue** AL, both from Choctaw *sinti bok,* 'snake stream.'

Santanoni, Mount NY Probably from a French **St. Anthony,** but assuming a pseudo-Indian form, perhaps because of Indian transmission.

Santaquin UT For a Ute chief of the 19th century.

Santee In SC from an Indian tribal name; in NB from another such, probably unconnected with that in SC, though both tribes were of Siouan stock; in CA from the name of the first postmaster, otherwise unidentified.

Santiago Though St. James was the patron saint of Spain, his name was given to places in the U.S. less commonly than the names of certain other saints. A name-cluster in CA (Orange Co.) originated from calendar naming. **Santiago** MN: probably for the city in Spain or one of the others so named, since this is outside the direct Spanish influence and was founded too early (1856) to be named for the battle of 1898, for which a railroad station in the same state was named.

Santiam River OR An Indian tribal name.

Santo Spanish 'saint,' with certain names only, e.g. **Santo Domingo** NM for St. Dominic. **Santo** TX: for John Santo Stati, the first telegrapher there.

Santuck SC Locally said to be from Sand Tuck, with the second term meaning 'nook, cove.' But this usage is not confirmed, and the name must be considered doubtful.

Sanusi Creek See **Sanoose.**

Sapa Creek NB Sioux 'beaver.'

Sapello NM Uncertain, but going back to forms such as **Chapellote** (1821), **Shapellote** (1839), and **Chapellon** (1853). It is probably of Indian origin, and may be the personal name of a Kiowa.

Sapinero CO Named (1888) for a Ute chief who was friendly to the Americans.

Saponac Lake ME Algonquian 'big-opening,' with reference to its being the first lake encountered by anyone going upstream.

Saponi Creek VA From an Indian tribal name. Variants are **Sapona, Sappony.**

Sapowet Marsh RI Algonquian, meaning uncertain.

Sappa Creek KS Siouan, probably 'dark,' but confusion with the term for 'beaver' is possible. See **Sapa.**

Sapphire 1) As a snyonym for 'blue,' e.g. the canyon in AZ and the pool in WY. 2) From the occurrence of sapphires, e.g. the mountains in MT.

Sappony VA From the Indian tribal name.

Sapulpa OK For James Sapulpa, a Creek, early resident.

Saranac NY Probably Iroquoian, meaning uncertain.

Saranap CA From Sara Naphthaly. mother of the vice president of a railroad operating in the area in 1913.

Sarasota FL Dating from the 18th century or earlier, recorded in several different forms, the name is uncertain but is probably from an Indian original, shaped to a Spanish form.

Sarassa AR From Sarasen, the name of a famous local Quapaw chief who died in 1837.

Saratoga Probably Iroquoian, meaning uncertain. From the original NY site it has passed to several states.

Sarben NB From the first six letters of Nebraska, reversed.

Sarcillo Canyon CO Uncertain; though of proper Spanish form, it may represent the reworking of an Indian word.

Sarco, Sargo Variants of Spanish **Zarco**, 'light blue,' e.g. **Sarco Creek** CA, **Agua Sargo** NM, the latter apparently confused by Americans and appearing in masculine form.

Sarcobatus Flat NV From the Latin scientific name for the common greasewood, a name probably given to avoid duplication.

Sarcoxie KS, MO For a Delaware chief, who lived in this region in the mid-19th century.

Sardina Peak AZ Americanized from the name of an otherwise unknown Mexican, Sarvinia.

Sardine As a name of western water features it arises from the finding of an old sardine tin (as the story often goes) or some similar incident, or from reference to the size of fish caught, 'sardine' being the equivalent of 'minnow.'

Sardinia From the Mediterranean island.

Sardis Though it is a personal name, its place-name use is chiefly from the city mentioned in the Book of Revelations, e.g. in MS, OK. **Sardis Creek** GA: from **Sartain's Creek,** for James Sartain, a settler of ca. 1795.

Sarepta LA, MS From a city mentioned in the New Testament.

Sargent Commonly from a personal name, e.g. in NB a double naming, for a family of friends of the postmaster, and for G. D. Sargent, an uncle of one of the town founders. **Sargent's Bluffs** IA: for Sgt. Charles Floyd of the Lewis and Clark Expedition who was buried here, a phonetic spelling.

Sarona WI Probably from Saron, a city or district mentioned in the New Testament, with the addition of *a* to form a place-name.

Saronville NB From a local church called Saron, after a village in Sweden, named by a Swedish minister.

Sartoria NB Coined by John Swenson by making combinations of letters until he found one that was both euphonious and only to be pronounced in one way. He was apparently ignorant that the name would mean 'country of tailors' in Latin, and might be a pun for the personal name Taylor.

Sarvis See **Service.**

Sarvorum Mountain CA The name of a Karok village, meaning unknown, altered into a pseudo-Latin form.

Sasabe AZ Probably Indian, of uncertain meaning.

Sasco AZ From the Southern Arizona Smelting Company.

Saskawa OK Indian, probably Creek, 'brant goose.'

Saspamco TX From the San Antonio Sewer Pipe Manufacturing Company.

Sassafras A repeated name in the eastern U.S., because of the occurrence of the tree, which was valued by early settlers because of the 'tea' made from it.

Sassaquin Pond MA Algonquian, meaning uncertain.

Satan Occasionally used as a substitute for the too common **Devil** or as a term considered more polite, e.g. **Satan's Arbor** WY.

Satanta CO, KS From the personal name of a Kiowa chief of the 19th century.

Satartia MS Choctaw 'pumpkins-are-there.'

Saticoy CA From the name of a Chumash village, meaning unknown.

Satilpa Creek AL Probably Choctaw, meaning uncertain.

Satin TX A commendatory, i.e. that the place was as fine as silk or satin.

Satolah Mountain GA Cherokee 'six.' See **Sixes.**

Satsop River WA From an Indian tribal name.

Satsuma In several southern states, from the variety of orange.

Satucket MA Algonquian 'outlet-(tidal)-river-at.'

Satulah Mountain NC Probably a variant of **Satolah.** See also **Sixes.**

Satus Creek WA From an Indian tribal name.

Sauce Spanish 'willow,' also as **Sausal,** 'willow-grove,' whence, in the diminutive **Sausalito** CA, 'little willow-grove.' **Sauceda** also has the meaning 'willow-grove,' whence the mountains in AZ, probably a translation from the Pima. See **Sauz.**

Saucon Creek PA Algonquian (Delaware) 'outlet-at,' a name transferred from the mouth of the stream to the stream itself by the colonists. So also **Sacony.**

Sauga Point RI Algonquian 'outlet at.' See **Sag.**

Sauganash IL From the name of a Potawatomi who held land in the vicinity ca. 1830.

Saugatuck(et) In New England a variant of **Sackatucket,** q.v. In MI it is probably Algonquian for a punky material used by the Indians for tinder.

Saugerties NY Recorded (1663) as Zager's Kiletje, i.e. 'Zager's streamlet.' Zager was the first Dutch settler on the stream.

Saugus Algonquian 'outlet-small.' See **Sag.**

Sauk From the Indian tribal name. Also as **Sac,** and sometimes in combination representing the Algonquian word for 'stream-mouth, outlet.' **Sauk Center** MN: because of its central location on the **Sauk River. Mount Sauk** WA is also probably from the name of an Indian tribe, but a different one, and one local to this region.

Saule French 'willow,' e.g. **Bayou des Saules** LA.

Sault French, an archaic spelling of *saut,* 'leap,' but commonly 'waterfall,' properly a generic, but in American usage a specific as in **Long Sault Rapids** MN. Sometimes spelled phonetically, e.g. **Soo Junction** MI.

Saunemin IL From the name of a Kickapoo chief of the early 19th century.

Saunook NC From the personal name of a local Cherokee Indian.

Sauquoit NY Iroquoian, much altered from some earlier form, meaning uncertain.

Sauratown NC From an Indian tribal name.

Sauta Creek AL From Cherokee *itsati,* the name of a former Indian town; meaning unknown.

Sauvie Island OR From a personal name, either by misspelling or mispronunciation, for Laurent Sauve, early French-Canadian resident on the island.

Sauz Spanish 'willow.' See **Sauce.**

Savage Regularly from the personal name, but the lake in MN because it was a favorite haunt of Indians.

Savanna, Savannah A Carib word, taken into Spanish and thus passed to

English in the late 17th century; approximately, 'meadow,' especially one that is moist and grown with coarse grass. It soon came to be applied as a specific. **Savannah** GA, SC: the name of the river is probably an adaptation of that of the Indian tribe, but the Indians themselves may have previously been so called by the Spaniards on account of the savannas there. In any case the actual spelling of the word has been so influenced. The city takes its name from the river. Some natural features distinguished by a savanna are so named, e.g. lakes and rivers in MN. Several habitation-names, in both spellings, occur. **Savannah** MO: named for the first white child born there, her parents giving the name because of former residence in the city in GA.

Savona From the city in Italy.

Savoy Generally for the European district, but in TX for William Savoy, donor of land for the townsite. In IL named in compliment to the Princess Clotilde of Savoy, who visited the state in 1861.

Sawacklahatchee Creek AL From the name of a former Creek town, literally 'raccoon-town-stream.'

Sawadabscook River ME Algonquian 'sloping-ledges-at.'

Sawatch Creek CO A variant of **Saguache.**

Saw Buck Mountain AZ From a resemblance of the formation to a sawbuck, or a packsaddle of that type.

Sawcook NH Algonquian 'sloping land.'

Sawed Off Mountain AZ Because the flat top suggests being sawed off.

Sawhegan Falls NH Algonquian, meaning uncertain.

Sawish Lake ME Algonquian 'sluggish.'

Sawmill By association, because of the presence at some time of a sawmill, e.g. **Sawmill Hollow** KY.

Sawpit By association, from the presence at some time of one of these primitive devices for sawing timber, e.g. **Sawpit** CO.

Sawtooth Applied to mountains or ridges descriptively, e.g. **Sawtooth Range** CO, **Sawtooth Mountains** ID, **Sawteeth Mountains** MN.

Saxapahaw NC From an Indian tribal name, a variant of Sissipahaw. See **Haw.**

Saxon Generally from the personal name. **Saxonburg** PA: named in 1832 by German settlers from Saxony.

Saybrook Among the patentees in CT in 1635 were Lord Say and Sele and Lord Brooke. The name was formed by a combination of these titles. It is, as far as the record has been established, the first coined name to be used in the U.S.

Scabby Creek SD A translation of the Siouan name, arising because a herd of horses was afflicted with the scab.

Scaffold Meadow CA Because early sheepmen erected a scaffold on which to store supplies out of the reach of marauding animals. **Scaffold Camp Creek** WA: probably for such a structure made by Indians.

Scaggrock River ME Algonquian 'green (grassy)-place.'

Scajaquada Creek NY A less-transformed form of **Kenjockety,** q.v.

Scales Commonly from the personal name, e.g. in OK for Henry Scales, coal operator. **Scales** NV was the location of a railroad scales for weighing ore, ca. 1870.

Scalp The name occurs rarely, e.g. on a creek in SD, which doubtless arose from an incident involving a scalp; but divergent stories are told.

Scandia Generally placed by Scandinavian settlers for commemorative reasons; it is the Latin name of a northern island, later coming to be a vague and poetic name for Scandinavia. Also spelled **Skandia.**

Scantic, Scantuk, Squantuck Algonquian 'fork-(of)-(tidal)-river.'

Scape O'er Swamp SC Though earlier written **Scape Whore,** the name seems more likely to be derived by folk-etymology from an Indian term, recorded as *skibboo, -boo* being a term for 'stream.'

Scarboro, Scarborough, Scarbro, Scarbrough Variant forms of the same personal name, also deriving from the town in England.

Scarcity Fat Ridge IN Apparently a rural derogatory, though usually in sophisticated language, for a place lacking in food.

Scargo Mountain ME Algonquian, meaning uncertain.

Scarper Peak CA By misspelling for a local family named Scarpa.

Scarsdale NY From the Manor of Scarsdale, established in 1701 by Caleb Heathcote, who came from Scarsdale in England.

Scataway Hill ME Algonquian, meaning uncertain.

Scatchet Head WA A variant of **Skagit,** q.v.

Scenery Hill PA Named, because of the good view, by Stephen Hill, perhaps also punning on his own name.

Scenic Regularly, e.g. **Scenic Point** MT to indicate a view of good scenery.

Schaghticoke NY Algonquian 'branch-(of)-stream-at.'

Schatulga GA Muskogean (Creek) 'crayfish (plural),' probably first applied to a stream.

Schell Creek Range NV The earliest record (1859) is of **Shell Creek,** probably named for fossil shells. In the 1860's Major A. J. Schell commanded a detachment of mail guards in the area. Further delightful confusion resulted from the establishment of **Schellbourne,** a mining camp, called after a miner. At some time the creek lost the name, but it was kept for the mountains. In the end (or, anyway, at present) the 'c' has been preserved for the range, but the pass is **Shellbourne.**

Schenectady NY Iroquoian, probably 'beyond-pines.'

Schenevus NY Iroquoian, the personal name of a local Indian (?).

Schenob Brook MA Algonquian, meaning uncertain.

Schleswig IA Named (1899) for the province of Germany, from which many settlers had come.

Schley From the personal name, especially, e.g. in MN, for W. S. Schley, naval commander in the Spanish-American War.

Schochoh KY By a slight shift of spelling from Shochoh, a city mentioned in the Old Testament.

Schodac(k) Probably variants of **Schoodic.**

Schoenchen KS From a town in Russia; named by German-Russian immigrants.

Schoharie NY Iroquoian 'driftwood,' first applied to the creek.

Schohomogomoc Hill NH Algonquian 'lake-with-fire-markings-near.'

Schonchin Butte CA From a chief of the Modocs, friendly to the whites in the 1860's.

Schoodic The rendering in English represents three Algonquian terms. 1) Most commonly, 'trout,' more particularly 'brook trout,' especially on small streams in ME. 2) Literally 'fire,' and so denoting places that had been burned over, e.g. **Schoodic Lakes** on the Canadian boundary in ME. 3) **Schoodic Point** ME, 'the end.'

School As with **Church,** the term may almost be considered a generic, since in early times the establishment of a school also established a point of geographical reference. These schools, however, did not bear such distinctive names as did churches, and their influence on nomenclature is less strong. In regions where certain public lands were reserved for schools, a natural feature within that area might be so called, e.g. **School Lake,** occurring ten times in MN, **School Section Lake** MN, SD. In such names as **School House Hollow** WV the reference is more exact.

Schoolcraft From the personal name, especially e.g. in MI for H. R. Schoolcraft (1793–1864), author, ethnologist and linguist (or pseudo-linguist), who himself coined many place-names by piecing together bits and scraps of diverse languages of which he had a smattering, e.g. **Alcona, Algoma, Iosco.**

Schroeder TX Originally **Germantown,** but changed in honor of P. W. Schroeder, who was killed in France in 1918.

Schroon NY The lake and river probably go back to the first syllable of an Algonquian Sknoo-na-pus, a recorded name of uncertain meaning; the spelling indicates Dutch influence.

Schunnemunk Mountains NY Probably a variant of **Shawungunk,** q.v.

Schuyler From the personal name, especially for General Philip Schuyler of New York, Revolutionary commander, e.g. several towns and counties.

Schuylkill PA Dutch 'hiding-stream,' on the analogy of *schuilplaats,* 'hiding-place.' The reference is probably to an early incident in which a Swedish vessel lay concealed in that stream.

Schwatka Mountains AK For Frederick Schwatka, who explored in the region in 1883.

Scio From the Greek island, probably for its association with Homer, e.g. the line, 'The blind old man of Scio's rocky isle.'

Sciota IL, NY, PA A variant of **Scioto.**

Scioto OH Iroquoian, probably 'deer,' but the remnant of a longer name.

Scipio In NY from one of the Roman generals and statesmen, or for their family, as part of the classical naming of 1790.

Scitico Algonquian 'fork-(of)-(tidal)-river-at.'

Scituate MA, RI Algonquian 'cold stream' (?).

Scodoqua River Algonquian 'trout-stream.' See **Schoodic.**

Sconticut Neck MA Algonquian 'cold(?)-stream-at.'

Scooba MS Choctaw, probably 'reed-thicket.'

Scoodeag River ME Algonquian 'fireplace,' i.e. burned-over land. See **Schoodic.**

Scoodik See **Schoodic.**

Scoona Creek MS Muskogean 'leech' (?).

Scoquams NY Probably from the name of an early Indian.

Scossa NV For James and Charles Scossa, brothers, who began mining developments here, ca. 1930.

Scot, Scotch, Scotland The first two generally indicate a place where a Scot or Scots lived, e.g. **Scotch Creek** OR, **Scotch Lake** MN. Scot is rare, except in **Scotland,** which is the commonest habitation-name to indicate a place of residence of Scots, e.g. **Scotland Neck** NC, or a nostalgic naming, e.g. **Scotland** PA, **Scotland County** MO. **Scotland** TX: for Henry J. Scott, a land agent. **Scotland** CT: named ca. 1700, by its first settler, a Scot. **Scotch Plains** NJ: from a settlement of Scots in 1684. **Scotch Bonnet** NJ: probably a descriptive: cf. **Thrumcap.**

Scotia The Latin form of Scotland, being used as its equivalent for nostalgic naming, e.g. in NB, NY. **Scotia** CA: because of many settlers from Nova Scotia. **Scotia** SC: for a man named Scotia Tison, local businessman.

Scott From the personal name. **Scotts Bluff** NB: supplies one of the most famous of American naming stories. The trapper, Hiram Scott, died at this place, and his bones were later found and identified. **Fort Scott** KS: for General Winfield Scott. **Scotty:** from the common nickname, either for a Scot or for a man named Scott, e.g. **Scottys Canyon** CA.

Scrabble See **Hardscrabble.**

Scraggy Rare; an uncomplimentary descriptive with the general idea of rough and broken, e.g. **Scraggy Butte** CO.

Scranage AL For T. M. Scranage, who was an employee of the P. O. Department in Washington; it was named for him by another clerk as a compliment, neither of them having any other connection with the place.

Scranton From the personal name, in PA for the Scranton family, coal mine owners.

Scratch In occasional use as a derogatory, chiefly from the phrase 'scratch gravel,' i.e. to make a poor living by working infertile soil, but **Scratchgravel Hills** MT may be a commendatory, being locally believed to have been so named because gold could once be obtained near the surface, merely by scratching the gravel. **Scratch Hill** AL is probably a shortening of the commoner term.

Screwdriver Creek CA Because of its 'screwy' motion in flowing through a canyon, though a screwdriver itself is straight.

Scroungeout A rural derogatory, e.g. in AL, implying a place where scrounging was necessary.

Scuffle The original idea may be that suggested in **Bug Scuffle** (See **Bug**). It has been used as a rural derogatory in a somewhat vague sense and on the analogy of **Scrabble**, e.g. **Hard Scuffle.**

Scuppernong The river in NC is Southern Algonquian, 'bay-tree-at,' with reference to *Magnolia glauca* growing there. From that stream the grape was named; from the grape, the stream in MI.

Scylla From the *Odyssey,* usually as a counterpart to **Charybdis,** indicating a narrow and threatening passage, e.g. in CA, where the name was placed in 1895.

Sea In compounds it is often from a personal name, e.g. **Seaton.** Thus, in TX, **Seagraves** is for C. L. Seagraves, railroad land agent. Other compounds are obvious, e.g. **Seagull.** Though the exceptional **Billington Sea** MA is an early name (before John Billington was hanged in 1630), the term has not been a generic though it is used as a common noun. As a specific it occurs by association with 'the sea' in a general sense, most commonly as a commendatory for resorts, e.g. **Seaview, Sea Breeze, Seadrift, Sea Girt.** See also **Seabeck, Sea Warrior, Sea Lion, Salton Sea.**

Seabamuck See **Seponack.**

Seabeck WA Recorded by the Wilkes expedition (1841) as **Seabock,** an Indian name of unknown meaning; under the influence of folk-etymology the spelling was shifted to the semblance of an English name.

Seaboard Descriptive of a situation close to the sea; in NC by association with the Seaboard Railroad.

Seal From the seal or sea lion, common for seacoast features along the Pacific, including AK. It is much less used on the Atlantic coast, where the animal was less conspicuous, but e.g. **Seal Harbor** ME. Since seals are conspicuous and noisy the name is easily applied to the rocks where they congregate, e.g. **Seal Rock(s)** (seven in CA). **Seal Creek,** San Mateo Co., CA; probably for H. W. Seale. **Seal Mountain** AZ: probably because it was used as background on the first seal of the state.

Sea Lion Of rare occurrence, since the animal is commonly called **Seal,** e.g. **Sea Lion Rocks** CA. See **Lobo.**

Seama NM Indian (Keres-Laguna) 'door, gateway,' for topographical reasons.

Seaman Hills WY For Samuel Seaman, local rancher.

Searchlight NV For Floyd Searchlight, a developer of local mining claims (ca. 1897).

Seattle WA An adaptation of the name of a local Indian chief, whose name was also spelled See-yat and Sealth.

Sea Warrior Creek AL By folk-etymology from Choctaw *isi-waiya,* 'deer-crouching.'

Seawillow TX By folk-etymology from Cibolo.

Sebago Lake ME Algonquian, a shortening of **Mesibegat** (1723), 'big-lake.'

Sebasco ME A shortening from **Sebascodegan.**

Sebascodegan Island ME Algonquian 'almost-through-passage,' with reference to a place, such as an isthmus, where an easy portage for canoes was possible. The same general idea is expressed in **Sebascohegan River** ME, **Sebaskiak Neck** ME, **Sebasticook Lake** ME, **Sebesteguk River** ME.

Sebascohegan ME See **Sebascodegan.**

Sebaskiak See **Sebascodegan.**

Sebastian From the personal name, including that of the saint. **Cape Sebastian** OR: applied in 1869 to honor Sebastián Viscaíno, Spanish explorer of 1602–1603.

Sebasticook See **Sebascodegan.**

Sebastopol The city became well known because of its siege during the Crimean War, and in the 1850's the name was bestowed upon several habitations, five being recorded in CA alone, only one of which survives. That name was given, according to local story, because of a squabble among some of the residents during which one party barricaded themselves in the general store and thus stood siege.

Sebec ME Algonquian, the same as **Sebago.**

Sebeka MN Ojibway, but a late-placed name (ca. 1891), containing the word for 'river' and meaning approximately, 'river-town.'

Sebesteguk See **Sebascodegan.**

Sebethe River CT Algonquian, probably 'river-small.'

Sebewa MI Algonquian, probably 'river-little.'

Sebewaing MI Algonquian 'river-little-at.'

Seboeis ME Algonquian 'streamlet.'

Seboois See **Seboeis.**

Seboomock Lake ME Algonquian 'big-lake-at.'

Sebougla Creek Muskogean 'smoke' (?).

Seboyeta NM Probably from Spanish *cebolleta,* a diminutive of *cebolla,* 'onion,' from the nearby mountain, where wild onions could have been found.

Secarabigg Falls ME Algonquian, meaning uncertain.

Secatogue NY Algonquian 'black-land.'

Secaucus NJ Algonquian 'salt-sedge-marsh.'

Seco Spanish 'dry,' e.g. **Arroyo Seco** CA. **Seco** KY is from South East Coal Company.

Second See **First. Second Garrote** CA: when a man was hanged near here in 1850 the place was called **Garrote,** though this is not really the Spanish equivalent of 'hang.' When a similar incident occurred at this place it was distinguished as **Second Garrote.** Though of ancient origin, the story must be held suspect.

Secours French 'help,' has yielded **Bon Secour Bay** AL, sometimes occurring as **Bon Secor,** with the idea of 'good help, timely assistance,' an incident name.

Secret Usually a descriptive of a place that is isolated and hard to find. **Secret Ravine** CA: probably because a miner found it rich and tried to keep it secret. **Secret Pass** AZ: also from a mine.

Security A commendatory, in TX being from the Security Land Company, which promoted the town.

Sedalia In MO the name was given by Gen. George R. Smith, the town founder, in 1857 from Sed, the pet name of his daughter Sarah. The *-ia* represents a Latin ending, and the *-al-* was seemingly inserted for purposes of euphony. It is an interesting example of a coined name that became popular, spreading eastward, e.g. NC, SC, OH, as well as into newer states e.g. CO, ND, OK.

Sedan From the city in France, well known because of the siege of 1870; in KS the name was given late in 1870 when one of the residents noted that the landscape resembled a picture of the French site, which he had seen in a magazine.

Sedaye Mountains NV Indian, probably Shoshone 'lookout.'

Sedco CA From South Elsinore Development Company.

Sedgeunkedunk Stream ME Algonquian 'rapids-at-mouth.'

Sedona AZ For Sedona M. Schnebbly, an early settler.

Sedro-Wooley WA From the consolidation of two towns in 1898. **Cedro** was named (1884) because of the fine cedars in the vicinity, with a half-Spanish form. **Woolley** was named in 1890 for P. A. Woolley, town founder.

Seduction Point AK Named by Vancouver's expedition in 1794 because of the designing nature of the Indians encountered here.

Sedunkehunk See **Sedgeunkedunk.**

See All Mountain WV Either a highly unusual descriptive because of the view, or an equally unusual folk-etymology from the personal name **Sewell,** which occurs on a mountain elsewhere in the state.

Seeboomook ME Algonquian 'large-lake (stream)-at.'

Seekonk MA, RI Algonquian probably 'outlet-at.'

Seekseekwa Creek OR Paiute, referring to the rye grass along the stream.

Segeke Butte AZ Navajo 'square rock.'

Segetoa Spring AZ Navajo 'spring-in-forest.'

Segeunkedunk See **Sedgeunkedunk.**

Segno TX From the musical sign marking the beginning or ending of a repeat, but reason for application unknown.

Segnup Creek WY Shoshone 'muddy.'

Sego 1) For the sego lily, e.g. **Sego** UT. 2) Navajo 'canyons,' e.g. **Sego Mesas** AZ with reference to the mesas being cut by canyons.

Segovia TX Probably for the city in Spain.

Seguin 1) The island ME is Algonquian, uncertain, but possibly 'humped-up,' or 'turtle,' from its shape. 2) The town in TX was named, in gratitude for patriotic services, for J. N. Seguin (1807–1890).

Segumkendunk River ME Algonquian 'rapids-at-confluence.'

Segundo Spanish 'second.' **El Segundo** CA: because a company's second refinery was located there. **Segundo** CO: for the second coal mine opened in the area.

Seiad CA Of Indian (Shasta or Yurok) origin, meaning uncertain.

Seights Creek IA For G. Seitz, early settler.

Sejita TX Spanish, but uncertain; locally believed to be from *ceja*, 'eyebrow,' the diminutive being applied to a bank of earth thrown up as a water catch.

Selah WA From a local Indian word, 'still water,' applied first to a part of a river.

Seldovia AK Latinized form, from the Russian 'herring,' first applied to the bay.

Selkirk From the county and town in Scotland; also a personal name.

Selma In AL the name was taken (1817) from the Ossianic poems. Most of the other examples are from women so named, e.g. in CA, where two possibilities have been put forward.

Selway In MT it is from the family name of local ranchers. The river in ID is probably from the same name, though an Indian origin has been claimed.

Semiahmoo Bay WA From an Indian tribal name.

Semidi Islands AK Russian 'seven.'

Seminary From association with the type of educational institution so-called, e.g. the ridge in PA, **Seminary Hill TX**, **Seminary MS**.

Seminoe Mountains WY From the middle name of Basil Cimineau Lajeunesse, French trapper and fur trader of the mid-19th century.

Seminole This Indian tribe gave rise, from its presence there, to **Seminole County** FL, and other names in that state. Most of the tribe was later moved west, and **Seminole** and **Seminole County** OK indicate their presence. The name, probably because of its euphonious nature, has spread to several states where it is not indigenous.

Semisopochnoi Island AK Slightly shifted from the Russian name, 'seven-volcanoes.'

Sempronius NY A part of the classical naming of 1790, from the Roman family, which produced so little-notable representatives that it is hard to discover of what individual the namers were thinking; Tiberius Sempronius Longus, chiefly remembered for having been defeated by Hannibal, is probably the best-known of the family, but is hardly a heroic figure.

Senachwine IL From the name of a Potawatomi chief who lived in the vicinity in the early 19th century.

Senath For Mrs. Senath Hale Douglass, wife of the town founder.

Senatobia MS Shaped by folk-etymology to the appearance of a Latin word, containing Choctaw *sini,* 'sycamore,' and the rest uncertain.

Seneasha Creek MS Choctaw, probably 'sycamore-little.'

Seneca The Mohegan name for one of the Iroquois tribes occurs, in early documents, in a wild confusion of forms and spellings, largely depending upon whether the transcriber was French, Dutch, or English. A normal development in English might have given Sinnegar or Sennicky, the latter representing a common pronunciation. In the classically-minded 18th century the name was assimilated to the spelling of the well-known Latin writer Seneca. Before 1800, **Seneca Lake** was a fixed name, and its presence may have done much to set off the naming of the 'Classical Belt.' From NY the name has spread to a dozen states. In SC the name is from **Sinica,** an Indian town, probably derived from Esseneca, a tribal name. The Spanish **Cienaga** in colloquial speech of the SW has been made into **Seneca** by folk-etymology. In Algonquian-speaking areas, in regions where actual Seneca penetration is unlikely, the name may be from its literal meaning, 'stone.'

Senex NY Probably from the name of an early Indian, occurring (1693) as Sinnekes, attracted to a Latinized spelling.

Seng Creek WV An abbreviation of **Ginseng.**

Senita Pass AZ From a type of cactus so known.

Sennebec Pond ME Algonquian 'rock-pond.'

Senoj Lake OR Jones, spelled backward, but otherwise unidentified.

Sentinel A common name for a feature standing prominently alone, as if on guard, applied especially to mountains, rocks, buttes, etc., and in some instances transferred to habitations. The cave in CA is so called because nine pillar-like formations stand near the entrance. **Sentinel** OK: from a newspaper, the *Herald Sentinel.*

Separ NM Originally **Sepas,** which could be from Spanish *cepas,* stumps, butts of trees.' The local story that it is the beginning of **Separation** may account for the present form.

Separation The Creek in OR is so called because it flows between two mountains known as **The Husband** and **The Wife.** The rapids on the **Colorado River** in AZ were named because during the Powell expedition in 1869 three men left the main body at this point. The name-cluster in WY arises from the ridge, which is high and narrow, forming a marked dividing line. By association the name has been inaptly applied to the lake, flats, and river.

Seponack NY Algonquian 'ground-nut-place.' Also as **Sabonack** and **Seabamuck.**

Sepulcher Mountain WY Because of a rock resembling a tomb.

Sepulga River AL Probably Creek 'yaupon-tree-grove.'

Sequalitchew WA Indian, meaning unknown.

Sequatchie TN From the name of a prominent Cherokee chief of the early 18th century.

Sequim WA Indian (Clallam), probably 'quiet water,' originally applied to a harbor.

Sequoia, Sequoyah In CA several occurrences are from the tree, which was itself named from the Cherokee of the early 19th century, inventor of the Cherokee alphabet, for whom **Sequoyah County** OK and **Mount Sequoyah** TN are named.

Sergeant-Major Creek OK For Sergeant-Major W. P. Kennedy, 7th Cavalry, killed in a battle with Indians (1868).

Seroco ND From Sears Roebuck & Co., which did a large mail order business in the area.

Serrano Point OR Spanish 'mountaineer.'

Servia IN, WV From the former European nation.

Service, Serviceberry, Sarvis This widely spread berry was a favorite tidbit for the pioneers and natural features bear the name, e.g. **Service Buttes** OR, **Service Fork** WV. Early spellings (and pronunciations) were often **Sarvis,** but in the quest for 'correctness' most of the spellings are now **Service.** Actually, the derivation of the word may have nothing to do with 'service,' so that 'sarvis' might be 'correct.' The earliest spelling preserved (1784) is 'sawice.' Both **Service** and **Sarvis** are also personal names.

Servilleta NM Spanish 'napkin,' but probably a religious name from one of the commemorative titles of the Virgin Mary.

Sescawnawbekaw River WI Algonquian, meaning uncertain.

Sespe CA Chumash, the name of a village, meaning unknown.

Set, Tower of AZ See **Brahma.**

Setag TX A reversed spelling of Gates, named in about 1927 for a man (not further identified) who operated a local plant.

Setauket NY Algonquian, probably 'river-mouth-at.'

Seul Choix Point MI Literally, French 'only choice,' but by folk-etymology into French from Ojibway *shaw-sho-waig,* a term referring to the straight coast in this area.

Seven See **One.**

Seventy-Four The mountain and draw in NM derive from a brand.

Seventy-Six In KY named commemoratively for the year of the Declaration of Independence; in MO, probably for the town in KY.

Severe Spring ID Probably a phonetic spelling of the personal name Sevier.

Sevier River UT Recorded from the early years of the 19th century in Spanish context as **Rio Severo**. Though the adjective *severo*, 'severe,' exists, it makes little sense as applied to a river, and the name is more likely from San Severo, the 4th-century bishop, who as a Spaniard might well have been honored by Spanish explorers. The Americans shifted it to a name well known in the history of the U.S.

Seville From the city of Spain; in OH named because of a fancied resemblance of site.

Sewadapskak See **Souadabscook**.

Seward From the personal name, e.g. the town and county in NB and the town and several features in AK for W. H. Seward, Secretary of State (1861–1869), who negotiated the purchase of the Russian possessions in America.

Sewickley PA From an Indian tribal name.

Sexsmith Lake NY From a family name.

Seyoyah Creek AL Choctaw 'deer-crying' (?), possibly a personal name of an Indian.

S. H. Mountains AZ The rock formation is suggestive of an outhouse or outhouses. The name dates from the mid-19th century when the name was merely rendered **Shithouse**; after the arrival of white women the euphemistic initials were substituted, and the name was sometimes explained as **Shorthorn Mountains**, now often recorded as **Kofa Mountains.**

Shabakunk Creek NJ Algonquian, meaning uncertain.

Shabbona IL From a Potawatomi chief, friendly to the Americans during Indian troubles of 1827 and 1832.

Sha-Bosh-Kung Bay MN From an Ojibway chief of the 19th century.

Shackamaxon PA Algonquian (Delaware), probably 'eel- (place)-at.'

Shad From the occurrence of the valuable food-fish, e.g. **Shad Island** NJ.

Shade, Shady Though **Shade** is a personal name, most of the places are from the idea of shadow, e.g. **Shady Spring** WV, **Shady Lake** MN, **Shady Oak Lake** MN. There are some habitation names, the idea being doubtfully commendatory, since it suggests lack of sun and also dishonest or doubtfully-lawful people and actions. As might be expected, most of these names are in the South where shade is needed and enjoyed, e.g. **Shady Grove** AL, GA, KY. **Shades of Death Creek** PA, WV: used for a swampy place, 'by reason of its darkness,' in the words of an early pioneer. There is probably the suggestion not only of an unusually dark forest, but also of Indian ambush. **Shades Mountain** AL is from an earlier **Shades of Death.**

Shadow Since few phenomena of nature are more shifting and evanescent than shadows, some natural features must have been so named when seen under particular conditions, and thus be incident-names. **Shadow Point** WY is said to be so named because the shadow falls on it in the afternoon, and so it cannot have been named in the morning. But **Shadow Bay** AK is closely set among high mountains, and so is almost always shadowed. **Shadow Mountain** CA is a dark peak, standing near a lighter-colored one, and so appears to be in the shadow. **Shadow Lake** CA, MN probably indicates a naming in the evening when the lake was reflecting the shady woods. **Shadow Mountain** CO: named by the Colorado Geographic Board because it casts its shadow on **Grand Lake.**

Shaftsbury VT Named in 1761, with an alternate spelling, for the Earl of Shaftesbury, political figure; he was also Baron Pawlet, and **Pawlet** VT was likewise named in 1761.

Shagwong NY Algonquian 'side-hill-place' (?).

Shaker From a community of so-called Shakers, e.g. **Shaker Heights** OH. Names on natural features are transfers from the habitation-names.

Shake Rag In wide use as a rural derogatory. The various stories told locally in explanation lack credibility. Though the connection of 'rag' is obvious, the significance of 'shake' is uncertain.

Shakespeare Though many places bear names taken from the plays, the dramatist himself is singularly without such honor. An unsuccessful town of the name was projected in MI (1836). **Shakespeare Cliff** NV: named because the rock bears 'a striking resemblance to the features of the immortal poet,' i.e. presumably to the effigy on his tomb.

Shakopee Siouan 'six,' because the lake is six miles from some beginning point.

Shakum Pond MA Algonquian probably 'enclosed-between.'

Shale From the presence of that kind of rock, e.g. **Shale Hills** CA, **Shale Island** AK. A rare name, probably because shale is useless and undistinguished.

Shallow Though a common descriptive, it is rare as a place-name specific, but e.g. **Shallow Creek** WY. **Shallowater** TX: because water in wells occurred at a shallow depth.

Shalotte NC From **Shalot Inlet**: of uncertain origin, but possibly from *shalop,* a small sailing craft.

Shamokin PA Algonquian (Delaware), probably 'eel-(place)-at.'

Shamong NJ Algonquian 'horn-place' (?).

Shamrock Generally a sentimental naming by settlers of Irish background, as with the town in TX. **Shamrock Creek** OR: some soldiers, ca. 1885, left the shamrock painted on a tree; in the old Regular Army many of the men were Irish. **Shamrock Glacier** AK: resembles a shamrock in shape; so also, **Shamrock Lake** CA.

Shanandoa Creek NY From the name of a chief, probably of the 19th century, who lived there.

Shandaken NY Algonquian 'hemlocks-at.'

Shanghai Eventually from the city in China. In WV, from a company name. In WA, the valley was named as a joke because a man and his sons who lived there had long legs, like Shanghai chickens.

Shaniko OR For a settler, August Scherneckau, with an approximation of the spelling to American pronunciation.

Shankitunk Creek IN Algonquian 'shady-place' (?).

Shank Pooder Pond MA Probably an adaptation of an Algonquian name, but so transformed as to be uncertain of meaning.

Shannawan Creek WI Algonquian, meaning uncertain.

Shannoc Brook NJ Algonquian, probably a shortening of a longer form, with *hannoc,* 'stream-at.'

Shannock See **Shawwunk.**

Shannon Though the name may be for the Irish river, it is more commonly personal, e.g. **Shannon Co.** SD for Peter Shannon, chief justice for Dakota Territory. **Shannon** TX for Luke Shannon, early settler.

Shanty By association with a shanty, e.g. the creek in CA, because of the presence of Indian huts called shanties by the whites. The term is rare, as compared with **Cabin,** since it did not come into use until the 19th century. Its derogatory suggestions have worked against it for habitations, though 'shantytown' has become a common noun.

Shaotkam AZ Papago, for a local, edible root.

Shapnack Island NJ Algonquian, meaning uncertain.

Shappequa Hills NY Algonquian, meaning uncertain (the same as **Chappequa**).

Shark A rare name, probably because the shark does not commonly approach land so closely as to be associated with land features; an occasional visitation is commemorated in **Shark River** NJ. **Sharktooth** on various peaks is a descriptive.

Sharon Popular as a commendatory habitation-name because mentioned in the Bible as a rich region and because of its association with the rose of Sharon. In SC the town is from a church of that name.

Sharp Regularly from the personal name; for instance, **Sharpsburg** PA: for James Sharp, early landowner. It may also be a descriptive, e.g. probably **Sharp Mountain** TX.

Shasta From an Indian tribal name. **Shastina**: a coined 'feminine' form, or 'diminutive,' for the lower peak of the mountain. **Shasta Costa Creek** OR: from an Indian tribal name, elsewhere recorded as Shas-te-koos-tee.

Shato Spring AZ Navajo 'sunshine-water,' i.e. a spring exposed to the southern sun.

Shatterack MA, VT Algonquian, meaning uncertain.

Shavano CO Peak and town bear the name of a well-known Ute chief.

Shawan, Shawanee Variants of the Indian tribal name which occurs more often as **Shawnee**.

Shawangunk NY Algonquian, probably 'side-hill-at.'

Shawanni, Lake NJ Algonquian 'south.'

Shawano WI Algonquian, probably 'south-at,' and not directly connected with the tribal name **Shawnee**. The point in MI is from a 19th century Ojibway chief.

Shawkemo Creek MA Algonquian, meaning uncertain.

Shawnee From the Indian tribal name.

Shawomet MA, RI Algonquian, probably designating a place on a neck of land between two waters.

Shawsheen MA Algonquian, probably from the name of a chief.

Shawwunk Algonquian 'between-at,' i.e. a place between streams.

She Fork KY The remnant of an Indian name (?). Cf. **Curry He.**

Sheboygan WI Algonquian, probably from a word used for any perforated object such as a pipe stem. **Cheboygan** is a variant.

Shecoway River ME Algonquian, for a bird, the sheldrake or merganser.

Sheenjek River AK Athapascan, probably 'salmon.'

Sheep The name is rare in the eastern half of the U.S. where no wild sheep lived and where domestic sheep never provided an important industry, but there is an occasional one, e.g. **Sheep Run** WV. In the West the names are numerous, but the reason for naming is seldom recorded. Many places were named because flocks were pastured there. Many other places, especially mountains and rocks, were named from the presence of wild bighorn sheep, in particular, certain rocks which served as winter homes when deep snow drove the sheep out of the high mountains, e.g. **Sheep Rock** CA. Some names show more specific origin, e.g. **Sheepranch** CA, **Sheep Crossing** AZ, **Sheep Dip Creek** AZ. The mountain in WY was named because rocks on its sides looked like sheep.

Sheepeater From the Indian tribal name, e.g. the mountain in ID.

Sheepscott ME By folk-etymology from an Algonquian term recorded (1628) as *pechipscott*, 'long-rapids-rock-at,' with reference to part of the lower **Androscoggin**.

Sheetiron Springs CA Before 1880 a man built a sheet-iron hut here; it served as a landmark for many years.

Sheffield From the city in England; in MA the town was incorporated in 1733. The name has spread westward, sometimes being given with the idea of iron manufacture, e.g. in AL.

Shekomeko NY Algonquian 'big-house,' from the name of a village.

Shelburne The second earl was a prominent political figure shortly before the Revolution, and towns were named for him in VT (1761), MA (1768), and NH (1769).

Shelby From the personal name, especially, e.g. numerous counties and towns, for Isaac Shelby (1750–1826), Revolutionary commander and first governor of KY. Some names are probably for Evan Shelby (1719–1794), soldier and frontiersman (father of Isaac), or for other members of a large and active family.

Sheldahl IA An adaptation or partial Anglicizing of the family name Kjaldahl, no further identification.

Shelf Lake CO Because it is on a shelf above the nearby valley.

Shell Generally a sea coast name for places where shells are numerous, e.g. **Shell Beach** CA. Inland, it may be for freshwater shells, e.g. **Shell River** MN; for fossil shells in rock, e.g. **Shell Rock** MN; or for remains left by primitive men, e.g. **Shellmount** TN. **Shellrock:** a repeated name, literally indicates rock containing fossil shells. It is sometimes used for rock which is said to 'shell,' that is, to break up into small chunks; this may be a confusion with 'shale.'

Shellpot Creek DE By folk-etymology from the Swedish *Sköldpaddekill* (1654), 'turtle-stream.'

Shelter A common seacoast term to indicate a feature where a sailing vessel (especially, a small one) might find temporary refuge, but generally distinguished from places of greater protection denoted by **Port, Harbor,** e.g. **Shelter Island** NJ, **Shelter Cove** CA, **Shelter Bay, Point** AK.

Shenandoah VA Algonquian, probably 'spruce-stream,' but this translation leaves part of the name unexplained.

Shenango PA From an Indian village recorded as Shaningo, probably Algonquian, meaning uncertain.

Shenipsit Lake CT Algonquian 'big-pond-at.'

Shepaug Algonquian 'big-pond.'

Shepherd From association with a sheepherder, e.g. about ten features in CA, but also from the personal name, e.g. **Shepherd** TX for B. A. Shepherd, early landowner. **Shepard** and **Sheppard** are regularly from family names.

Sherborn See **Sherburn(e).**

Sherburn(e) The town in MA (now **Sherborn**) was named in 1674 and was originally spelled **Sherburne.** Later occurrences are usually from a personal name, e.g. the county in MN for Moses Sherburne, jurist.

Sheridan From the personal name, most commonly for General P. B. Sheridan of the Civil War, e.g. in WY the name was introduced by J. D. Loucks, town founder, who had served under Sheridan. In NY the town was named (1824) for R. B. Sheridan, English dramatist.

Sheriffs Springs CA Because Sheriff James Barton and his posse were murdered here by Juan Flores and his band in 1857.

Sherman From the personal name, e.g. for W. T. Sherman, Civil War general, counties in KS, NB, OR; for his brother Senator John Sherman, the town in ME; for Roger Sherman, Revolutionary statesman, the town in CT; for General Sidney Sherman, a hero of the Texan War of Independence, the town in TX.

Shesheeb Lake MI Ojibway 'duck.'

Shetek MN Ojibway 'pelican.'

Shetucket River CT Algonquian 'between-rivers-at' or 'big-river-at.'

Sheyenne A variant spelling of **Cheyenne.**

Shiawassee MI According to an unusually well-preserved traditional story, the naming of the river goes back to 1816 when Henry Bolieu, a French trapper, inquired of some Indians in their own (Algonquian) language which stream to take to reach a certain point in his canoe; they replied, *shiawasse,* 'straight-ahead-water'; he ascended this stream, built a cabin there, and used their descriptive appellation as a place-name during the years of his residence there.

Shiba, Lake MN From the initials of five members of an early exploring party, i.e. Schoolcraft, Houghton, Johnston, Boutwell, Allen.

Shick Shack Hill IL From an Indian's name, made over into English form; his identity has not been clearly established.

Shickshinny Creek PA Algonquian (Delaware), by partial folk-etymology from 'turkeys-plenty.'

Shig Lake NB From a personal nickname.

Shiloah From the Biblical spring, usually applied to a medicinal spring, e.g. in CA.

Shiloh From the Biblical name, often originating from a church.

Shin Occurs almost exclusively in compounds, e.g. **Shinbone Branch** KY, from some uncertain association. Places difficult to traverse have produced **Ripshin Creek** VA and **Cutshin Creek** KY.

Shinall Mountain AR A more-or-less phonetic spelling of Chenault, the name of a family of early French settlers.

Shingaubaosin, Point MI Algonquian (Ojibway) a term to describe the unusual quartz-veined granite found here.

Shingawassa Springs KS For a Kansa chief, his name recorded as Ching-gah-was-see, known locally as 'a good Indian.'

Shingle Regularly for a place where shingles were made, e.g. **Shingle Creek** MN, **Shingle Point** NB, **Shingle Springs** CA. As a coastal name it may arise from the term in the sense of pebbles, e.g. **Shingle Island** MA.

Shingob, Shingobee MN Ojibway, with reference to certain kinds of coniferous trees.

Shinhopple NY Probably Algonquian, meaning uncertain.

Shinnecock NY Algonquian 'level-land-at.'

Shiocton WI Algonquian, from a term meaning to float upstream, as by the force of wind.

Ship As a seacoast name, it indicates a place suitable for a ship or in some way thus associated, e.g. **Ship Harbor** ME probably from the wreck of a ship there in 1740. In the West it has been applied to mountains and rocks as a descriptive, sometimes fanciful, but usually applied to a high eminence, which might be taken to resemble a ship under sail. In some instances, the name may be derived from an original **Sheep Rock,** since such rocks would have been natural haunts of wild sheep. The rock in NM does not much resemble a ship, but efforts to explain it from Indian legends have not been successful. **Ship Bottom** NJ: though various 'legends' are related, bottom may here be the generic and have nothing to do with the bottom of a ship.

Shipetauken Creek NJ Algonquian, meaning uncertain.

Shippack Creek PA Algonquian (Delaware), literally 'urine-pond,' but probably used in the general idea of 'filthy, ill-smelling.'

Shipshewana IN Named for a local Potawatomi Indian whose name is recorded as Cup-ci-wa-no.

Shirley Though a place-name in England, it is regularly from the family name, e.g. in MA (1753) for William Shirley, governor of the colony at the time.

Shiro TX By local story, the name of a shrub, picked from a floral catalogue by the namer, who wanted a short and unusual name.

Shirtee Creek AL Muskogean (Creek) 'red' (?).

Shirttail A frontier name, usually explained by some colorful story without much authentication. **Shirttail Canyon** CA: probably named by two ex-Harvard students in 1849 because their clothes became so worn that they were working in their shirttails.

Shitike Creek OR Klamath, of unknown meaning.

Shiva Temple AZ See **Brahma.**

Shiver-de-Freeze Creek NJ By folk-etymology from *chevaux-de-frise,* arising from an obstruction placed in the Delaware River during the Revolutionary War.

Shivits UT From an Indian tribal name.

Shoal(s) A common descriptive for water features, e.g. **Shoal Lake** MN, **Shoal Creek** AK. Unless the plural is used, there is no distinction between a feature with shallow water and one with a shoal, but the distinction is not usually important. By association land features are involved, e.g. **Shoal Point** CA, and a few habitation-names have arisen by transfer. **Isles of Shoals** NH: preserves a double archaism in 'isles' and in the use of the specific with 'of.' By local belief the name originates from the local pronunciation of 'schools,' i.e. schools of fish. **Shoals** IN: because situated as a ford of the river, i.e. at the 'shoals.'

Shivering Mountain AK Named in 1931 by a climber, because he, not the mountain, was shivering.

Shoalwater A seacoast descriptive, e.g. the cape in WA, so called by the English explorer John Meares in 1788.

Shobonier IL From the name of Potawatomi chief of the early 19th century.

Shocco NC, VA From an Indian tribal name.

Shock WV From a family of that name, early landowners.

Shockaloo MS Choctaw 'cypress-tree.'

Shoe Heel Creek NC Probably by folk-etymology from an earlier Quahele, probably Indian, but language and meaning uncertain.

Shoe-Peg See **Choupique.**

Shohoken Creek PA Algonquian (Delaware) 'glue,' apparently being associated with the glue made by the Indians to fasten feathers to their arrows.

Shohola Creek PA Algonquian (Delaware) 'it faints,' being probably an incident name from someone becoming ill at this point.

Shohomagock's Hill ME From the personal name of an Indian.

Shokan NY A variant of **Ashokan.**

Shokokon IL Algonquian, probably 'flint-hill.'

Shomo AL From a personal (Choctaw) name.

Shongaloo LA Choctaw 'cypress-tree.' **Shongalo Creek** MS is a variant.

Shongo NY From the name of a local Indian of the later 18th century.

Shongum Lake NJ Algonquian, meaning uncertain, but it may be a shortening of **Shawangunk.**

Shooting Creek NC Probably an inexact translation from a Cherokee term, meaning a place of loud noise.

Shop By association with a shop, usually a blacksmith's shop, e.g. **Shop Branch** KY.

Shopiere WI A name coined (1847) by an approximately phonetic spelling of French *chaux-pierre,* literally, 'limestone,' a descriptive of the local rock.

Short 1) From the family name, e.g. **Short Springs** OK for George Short, first postmaster. 2) As a descriptive for features it is comparatively uncommon, shortness not being a quality easily seen. It occurs most commonly with 'creek' (e.g. AZ, MA, SD, NM), probably in some instances as a euphemism, but it also occurs as **Short Beach** CT, **Short Hills** NJ, etc. **Short** OK: by counterpart from a nearby post office named **Long. Short Off Mountain** NC: because a long ridge breaks off sharply in a precipice.

Shoshone From the Indian tribal name.

Shoshoni A variant of the Indian tribal name **Shoshone,** e.g. the peak in CO.

Shotgun From an incident involving a shotgun, e.g. **Shotgun Bend** CA, a place in the road believed to have been frequented by highwaymen.

Shotpouch Creek OR A shotpouch was lost here in 1856.

Shoulderblade Creek KY Probably from the finding of a bone. Cf. **Paleta.**

Shovel Creek WA From a gold hunter's wild tale that gold could be got by the shovelful.

Showanguntkil NY An Algonquian-Dutch hybrid. See **Shawwangunk** and **Kill.**

Showhacking Creek PA Probably the same as **Cohocksing,** q.v.

Showlow AZ In the 1870's two partners decided to split, and the one who could win a game of seven-up would remain at the place. The one player was ready to concede on the last hand if the other could 'show low.' He did, and the name stuck.

Shreveport LA For H. M. Shreve, who opened the Red River to navigation, ca. 1833.

Shrewsbury From the town in England; in MA, 1727, with possible reference to the Duke, who had died in 1718 after a conversion to Protestantism. In PA named (1739) by settlers from the English town.

Shubuta LA Choctaw 'smoky.'

Shumagin Islands AK Named (1741) by the Bering expedition because a sailor of this name died here of scurvy.

Shumla TX From the town in Bulgaria, because the situation was thought to be similar. The naming was in 1883 a few years after the town had figured in the Russo-Turkish War.

Shumula Creek AL Choctaw 'cottonwoods.'

Shumway From the personal name; in AZ from Charles Shumway, early Mormon settler.

Shunganunga Creek KS Siouan (Kansa) with reference to some kind of horse, but exact translation uncertain.

Shungopovi AZ Hopi 'chumoa-place,' *chumoa* being a kind of grass or reed.

Shunock Algonquian, the same as **Shawwunk** (?).

Shunpike Applied in the mid-19th century to roads by which the user could avoid paying the tolls on the turnpikes.

Shuqualak MS Choctaw, meaning uncertain.

Shushan NY From 'Shushan, the palace,' mentioned in the Old Testament.

Shushuskin Canyon WA From the name of an Indian who farmed there in the later 19th century.

Shuteye Peak CA For Old Shuteye, an Indian who was blind in one eye.

Shut-in, Shutin Usually applied to small streams (e.g. GA, KY) which are walled in by mountains.

Si, Mount WA From the shortening of the first name of Josiah Merrit, early settler.

Siah Butte OR Chinook jargon, 'far-off,' named because it is hard to get at.

Siasconset MA Algonquian 'man-bones-at,' or 'big-bones-at,' probably because of the skeletons of stranded whales.

Siberia The location in CA is very hot, and the naming, by the railroad, was apparently by opposites or anti-description. But the name-cluster in Sequoia National Park CA is from an original **Siberian Outpost,** named in 1895 because of its bleakness.

Sibiwigamick MI Ojibway 'river-(of)-house,' probably because of the presence here of a large building.

Siboco OR From Siuslaw Boom Company.

Sichomovi AZ Hopi 'mound-of-currant-bush-place.'

Sicily From the Mediterranean island, e.g. **Sicily Island** LA, by local tradition, named from a resemblance of landscape.

Sicomac NJ Algonquian, probably with *kamik,* 'enclosed-place,' with reference to an Indian burial-ground.

Sideling The descriptive seems to be limited to 'hill,' and to occur in the PA, MD, WV area. The most famous example is on the line of the National Road. Since all hills slope, the descriptive term probably arose in connection with a trail or road, meaning a hill which was ascended in a sideling fashion.

Sidewinder From the variety of rattlesnake thus known, e.g. the mountain in CA.

Sidon From the Phoenician city mentioned in the Bible. **Sidonia** TN may be formed from this name with a Latin ending, or it may be from the Spanish town Medina Sidonia.

Sierra Spanish 'mountain-range, mountain.' It is a generic in Spanish and is so used in names taken over, e.g. **Sierra Nevada, Sierra Pinta,** standing in the initial position. In many names formed under American influence the term has been equated with 'mountain' and used as an adjective in a wholly un-Spanish way, e.g. the common **Sierra Vista,** taken to mean 'mountain-view.' In Spanish it would mean 'mountain-that-has-been-seen.' It can also stand in

habitation-names, e.g. **Sierra County** CA, **Sierrita Mountains** AZ. A diminutive, for some rather low hills.

Signal A common Western name for an eminence from which signals were made, often credited to Indian signaling. The names were sometimes placed by surveyors, and this is probably the commonest origin, e.g. **Signal Hill** CA, **Mount Signal** CA. **Signal Shot Creek** CO: obviously an incident-name, but the occasion is unknown.

Sigourney IA For Mrs. L. H. Sigourney, whose poetry was popular in the mid-19th century.

Sigwanawock Stream NH Algonquian 'springtime-place,' probably a place for a spring camp.

Silaxo CA From a backward-spelling of 'oxalis,' a railroad name.

Silent Probably in most instances from the family name, e.g. in AZ for Charles Silent, early member of the Territorial Supreme Court. When applied to streams, it may be a descriptive, e.g. **Silent Run** KY.

Silesia Though it is the name of a European district, the town in MT took its name from some springs, which are locally believed to be named from the mineral contents of their water, perhaps with reference to their siliceous nature.

Siletz River OR An Indian tribal name.

Silica Generally as a synonym for sand, to avoid too frequent repetition.

Silkville KS Founded by a Frenchman in 1868 with the idea of producing silk.

Sill, Mount CA For E. R. Sill, poet and professor of English at the Univ. of CA.

Sillycook Mountain GA By folk-etymology from Cherokee *salgugi,* 'turtle.'

Sil Murk AZ Papago 'saddle-burned,' the first word being an adaptation of Spanish *silla.* Though probably an incident name, the origin is unknown.

Siloam From the pool made famous by the miracle of the blind man (*John,* 9), usually being associated with a spring or pool, which may have been supposed to have healing properties, e.g. **Siloam Springs** MO, **Pool of Siloam** NM.

Silt CO From the nature of the soil in the vicinity.

Siltcoos Lake OR Indian, probably a personal name.

Silurian Because of the presence of rock of that geological age, e.g. the hills in CA.

Silver 1) From real or supposed occurrence of the metal, very common in the West, and often for habitation names, e.g. **Silver City, Silverton.** Even states which have never produced any noticeable amount of silver have examples, e.g. **Silver Creek** WV and **Silver Run** WV, both named for a show of what was thought to be silver. So also **Silvermine** CT. 2) From the color, often with commendatory suggestion, esp. **Silver Lake, Silver Spring,** in many states. **Silver Butte** AZ: from the silvery tint of young juniper at night. **Silver Bluff** SC: from the silvery appearance of mica in the soil. **Silverstreet** SC: from silvery-looking plants that grew along the road in the days of early settlement. 3) The pleasant suggestion of silver and its euphony have led to its use with habitation-names primarily for commendatory purposes, e.g. **Silver Valley** TX, for which the word is employed for no other ascertainable reason. 4) Being next to gold in romantic suggestion of riches and buried treasure, some names spring from such tales, or else such tales are manufactured to explain the names, e.g. **Silver Lake** TX, said to be so named because the 'Spaniards' when driven out of the region dumped their silver into the lake. 5) The term occurs as a second specific in **Silver Tip Creek** MT for the grizzly bear; in **Silver Plume Mountain** CO, etc. The personal name has been of little influence. **Silvertown** GA: a town founded by the B. F. Goodrich Co., tire manufacturers, and bearing their brandname.

Silverado The name, appearing twice in CA, was coined on the analogy of Eldorado, with the commendatory idea that the mine was rich in silver (or quicksilver).

Silvies River OR From Antoine Sylvaille who explored the area in 1826.

Simi CA Chumash 'place, village.'

Similk Bay WA Indian, meaning unknown.

Similkameen River WA Indian, meaning unknown.

Simla From the town in India, which became known because of Kipling's stories.

Simnasho OR Indian 'thorn bush.'

Simoda WV From Simon Dolly, letters from each of his names, plus final 'a,' as often with habitation-names; the first post office was in his house.

Simpson From the personal name; various features in NV and UT commemorate J. H. Simpson, explorer of 1858–1859.

Simquish Lake ME Algonquian 'dip-up-a-drink' (?).

Simsbury From a colloquial pronunciation of the English town-name Symondsbury; in CT, 1670.

Sinai From the Biblical mountain. In SD the town was so called because of supposed resemblance of the region to the original Sinai.

Sinepuxent MD Algonquian, with *sine,* 'stone,' and the rest probably 'watered-place, swamp.'

Sing Peak CA For Tie Sing, a faithful Chinese cook (1888–1918) for the Geological Survey.

Singac NJ Algonquian 'boggy-ground.'

Singatze Mountains NV Probably Northern Paiute, meaning uncertain.

Singing Mountain NV A large dune on which the grains of sand, moving in the wind, make a humming noise.

Singleshot Mountain MT In 1885 Dr. G. B. Grinnell, in need of meat, here killed a mountain ram with one remarkable long-range shot. Cf. **Fusillade.**

Singletary Lake NC From a family name, not further identified.

Singrawac River NH Probably the same as **Sigwanawock,** q.v.

Sing Sing NY From Algonquian 'stone(s)-little-at,' (Cf. **Ossining),** developed by humorous folk-etymology from an original *assin-is-ing.*

Siniktaneyak A repeated name in AK, being Eskimo, to mean a place where one cannot sleep, commonly with the idea that the spot is haunted, as by the spirits of people who had died there.

Sinissippi Lake WI Algonquian 'rock-river'; the present **Rock River** is a translation.

Sink, Sinking, Sunk Sink is usually a generic, for a place at which a stream goes underground, but may occur as a descriptive as in **Sinks Grove** WV. **Sinking** is more common, e.g. **Sinking Creek** WV, **Sinking Spring** OH, PA. The personal name also occurs. **The Sinks** AZ: a number of depressions where rainwater collects. **Sinker Mountain** OR: from an incident when some hunters were forced to eat heavy biscuits, known as 'sinkers.' As a compound there is **Sinkhole Hill** KY. **Sunk,** e.g. a brook and pond in MA, probably carries the same idea.

Sinkavata Hills NV Northern Paiute, meaning uncertain.

Sinnemahoning Creek PA Algonquian (Delaware) 'stone-lick-at.'

Sinnissippi IL Algonquian (Sauk) 'rock-river.'

Sinsinawa IL, WI Algonquian 'rattle-snake,' because of a local Indian mound with the representation of a snake on it.

Sinta, Bayou MS Choctaw 'snake.'

Sioux From the Indian tribal name.

Siovi Shuatak AZ Papago 'sweet water.'

Sip Pond NH Probably shortened from Scipio, the name of a Negro man who lived there.

Sipaulovi AZ Hopi 'mosquitoes-place,' but apparently named because the people who settled there had formerly lived in a place infested with mosquitoes.

Sipe Springs TX From a local pronunciation of 'seep,' a descriptive for the springs.

Sipp Bay ME See **Sip.** But it is possibly a family name.

Sippenak Brook ME Algonquian, from the occurrence of lily roots which were eaten by the Indians.

Sippican River MA Algonquian *sippi,* 'river,' with an ending which may be merely 'at.'

Sipsey The name of several streams in AL and MS; it is from the Chickasaw-Choctaw 'poplar, cottonwood.'

Sir John's Run WV Probably for Sir John Sinclair, Quartermaster General of Forbes's army in 1758.

Sisar Canyon CA Chumash, the name of a village.

Sisi Butte OR Chinook jargon, 'blanket, cloth,' but the reason for application unknown.

Siskiyou Probably from a Chinook jargon term, in turn a shortening of a Cree word for some kind of horse, usually given as a bob-tailed horse, but more likely a pack horse, since a special term for a bob-tailed horse seems improbable. The name may have been applied in 1828 when a Hudson's Bay party lost many pack horses in a mountain snowstorm.

Siskowit, Siskiwit In MI and WI the name is Algonquian, probably Ojibway, referring to some kind of fish.

Sisladobsis Lake ME Algonquian 'shark-shaped rock,' from a rock standing out of the water like a shark's fin. Shortened to **Dobsy.**

Sisquoc CA Chumash, probably 'quail.'

Sissabogama Lake WI Algonquian (Ojibway) with *gama,* 'lake,' and the rest indicating a lake with arms running out in various directions.

Sister Usually occurring in the plural to indicate a pair (or more) of similar or balanced natural features, e.g. **The Three Sisters** (peaks in OR and CA), **Twin Sisters Peaks** WA, **The Sisters** (islands in KY). Relationship or religious status may be indicated, e.g. **Sistersville** WV for the sisters Sarah and Delilah Wells; **Sister Elsie Peak** CA for a nun. **Sisterdale** TX: from its location between two streams known as **The Sister Creeks.**

Site Six AZ Because of an emergency airfield constructed during World War II.

Sitka AK Indian (Tlingit), meaning uncertain. In other states the name is derived from this one. In KS local story has it that the naming was done on a day so cold that a man who had been in Alaska declared the place to be as cold as **Sitka.**

Sitkum OR Chinook jargon, 'half,' for a halfway house. **Sitkum Creek** OR: probably a derogatory name, since the stream is small.

Siuslaw River OR An Indian tribal name.

Siwash WA From the Indian tribal name.

Six See **One.**

Sixes 1) In GA several uses, e.g. **Sixes Creek,** probably spring from the translation of a Cherokee personal name, which would have been in full, 'six-killer,' with an English possessive 's.' See **Killer.** 2) **Sixes River** OR is from an Indian tribal name, Sik-ses-tene, shortened and respelled by folk-etymology.

Sixshooter The common western term for a revolver has produced **Sixshooter Draw** TX, probably from an incident.

Sixty-Six Mountain WY Some emigrants were once killed here by Indians, according to the story, 66 of them.

Siyeh, Mount MT For Saiyi Istuki, a noted Blackfoot warrior.

Skagit WA From the Indian tribal name.

Skagway AK Shifted by partial folk-etymology from an Indian (Tlingit) name, first recorded (1883) as *schkagué,* probably to indicate a place exposed to the north wind.

Skakane Creek WA Indian, locally thought to mean 'deep-canyon.'

Skamania WA Indian, 'swift-water' (?).

Skamokawa WA From the name of a local Indian chief.

Skanawan WI Algonquian (Ojibway) 'stream-running-through-bluffs.'

Skandia See **Scandia.**

Skaneateles NY Iroquoian 'lake-long.' Cf. **Canadice.**

Skanee MI Algonquian 'horn-river.'

Skatutakee NH Algonquian 'fire-swept-here,' doubtless first applied to the hill, which had once been burned over.

Skeag Island ME Algonquian, a shortening of **Namaskeag,** 'fishing-place,' one of the forms of **Namareck,** q.v.

Skedee OK From the Indian tribal name, often spelled **Skidi.**

Skeleton A rare Western name, generally indicating the finding of human bones. **Skeleton Canyon** AZ: a band of Mexican smugglers was slaughtered here by American bandits in 1881, and the bodies were left unburied. **Skeleton Ridge** AZ: probably a fanciful name in which the main ridge is compared to the back bone and the side ridges to ribs. **Skeleton Springs** SD: in 1876 the skeletons of a man and a bear were found; many years previous the two had apparently met in a combat which was fatal to both parties. **Skeleton Gulch**

CO: two skeletons, of men killed in a winter snow slide, were discovered here the next spring. **Skeleton Creek** OK: named (1867) by J. R. Mead, because he saw here many skeletons of Wichita Indians whose bodies had been left unburied during an epidemic of cholera.

Skell Head OR For a Klamath deity.

Ski The sport is of too new development in the U.S. to have made much impression on nomenclature, except in the names of resorts and hotels. **Ski Heil Peak** CA: chosen, ca. 1937, by winter sports enthusiasts, this being a common greeting in German among skiers.

Skiatook OK From the name of an Osage, prominent resident.

Skibo MN From the castle in Scotland, owned by Andrew Carnegie, the iron and steel magnate, this village being in an iron-ore district.

Skidi From the Indian tribal name.

Skidoo CA Named as a mining camp in 1906 when the phrase 'Twenty-three, skiddoo!' was thought to be awfully funny as a way of saying, 'Go away!' The actual reason for application is unknown.

Skilligallee MI From French *Les Iles aux Galets,* 'the islands of pebbles,' with some help from folk-etymology.

Skin A rare name-element, especially in view of the fact that the fur traders frequently used the word. **Skin Creek** WV: an early record indicates that the name resulted from a large number of deer skins collected here. **Skintown** MO: an early camp in the lead diggings, probably from one of the acquired meanings such as is still preserved in 'skin-game.'

Skinequit Pond MA Probably 'salmon-fishing-at.'

Skipanon River OR A simplification from an Indian term of unknown meaning, first appearing, in the Lewis and Clark records, as Skipanarwin.

Skipjack From the name of a fish, e.g. the island in WA.

Skitchewaug Mountain VT Algonquian 'big-mountain' (?).

Skitticook Branch ME Algonquian 'still-water.'

Skokie IL Algonquian (Potawatomi) 'marsh.'

Skokorat CT Algonquian 'snake-hill.'

Skookum Chinook jargon for a strong malign spirit, as a place-name indicating that the place is so haunted, sometimes a cemetery. It later came to be used simply as 'strong,' and **Skookumhouse Butte** OR is for a fort. **Skookum Gulch** CA apparently preserves the earlier meaning. **Skookum Butte** MT: named, ca. 1900, for a Forest Service man, Bill Woodman, nicknamed Skookum. **Skookum Chuck Brook** NH: in a region where the jargon was not used, this is either a modern introduction or an adaptation of an Algonquian name, containing the word for 'snake.'

Skowhegan ME Algonquian 'waiting (watching)-place,' because this was a spot where the Indians waited for salmon to ascend the river.

Skug River MA Algonquian 'snake.'

Skull Rare in the East, probably because quick plant growth soon concealed any bones, but fairly common in the West. Though a lake in NB was named for a buffalo skull, the term was usually restricted to places where human skulls were noticed, e.g. **Skull Creek** SD, **Skull Gulch** SD. These are generally reported as Indian skulls, probably on the assumption that a white man would be buried. **Skull Valley** AZ: skulls were left from a battle between Apaches and Maricopas, and the name was given by Americans who saw these skulls. The appearance of the place was reinforced and the name entrenched by a fight in 1866 between Americans and Indians, after which some Indians were left unburied. **Skull Valley** UT: the Indians of the region did not bury bodies but dumped them into pools of water, from which the skulls eventually came to land and were preserved. **Skull Point** CO: in 1927 an unidentified human skull was found here.

Skunk The animal was widespread, and an encounter with one was likely to be memorable; even the lingering smell itself might suggest the name. It is common on natural features, but has not been thought suitable for habitations. The name may occasionally be short for 'skunk cabbage' or one of the other animals or plants thus described. **Skunk Creek,** Charles Mix Co., SD: for an Indian so named. **Skunk Creek,** Lake Co., SD: early settlers found skunks in large numbers living in holes in the clay banks here. **Skunk's Misery,** e.g. in NY, is a repeated folk-name, usually applied to a swamp, apparently with the implication that even a skunk would be unhappy there. See **Polecat.**

Skunkscut See **Kongscut.**

Skutahzis Algonquian 'troutlet,' a diminutive of the word for 'trout' appearing in **Schoodic;** several places, chiefly in ME, are so named.

Skutarza, Skutarzy See **Skutahzis.**

Skutempah Creek UT Ute 'rabbit brush-water.'

Sky Rare, but used to suggest something very high in position, as if to be associated with the sky, usually in combination, e.g. **Sky High Butte** CA. Since height is regularly commendatory the element occurs in some habitation-names, e.g. **Skyland** NC, a mountain resort; **Sky Forest** CA on a wooded ridge, more than a mile high. **Skyline** is a repeated name for scenic roads which follow ridges, e.g. **Skyline Drive** CA.

Skyco NC For a local Indian chief whose name is also spelled Skiko.

Skykomish River WA From an Indian tribal name.

Skyrocket Hill SD Because the early settlers used it for celebrations on July 4th.

Slab Since the first cut of the log, known as slab, is chiefly bark and therefore valueless, the term in place-names is semi-derogatory, as in **Slabtown Valley** MO. Since piles of slab remained after lumbering operations had ceased, these served as points of identification and many features, especially creeks, were thus named.

Slate Often used in areas where slate or slate-like rocks occur (e.g. PA, AZ, CA) to identify a place with such rocks. **Slate Castle Creek** CA: from a formation resembling a castle. **Slate Hot Springs** CA: from the family name.

Slaughter Regularly from the personal name, e.g. the mountain in AZ for Pete Slaughter, early cattleman. **Slaughter Mountain** GA named as a counterpart to nearby **Blood Mountain,** because of a legendary Indian battle.

Slavia FL For the Slavia Colony Company, which settled Yugoslavians here (1915).

Sled Springs OR From a broken-down sled that remained there for many years.

Sleep, Sleepy, Sleeping Since 'sleepy' is a derogatory epithet for habitations, its use seems to be limited to an occasional **Sleepy Hollow,** which name owes much to Irving's story; the suggestion is that it is a place where nothing happens and people sleep a great deal. **Sleepy Eye** MN: from Sleepy Eyes, a Sioux chief. **Sleepy Hollow Draw** NB suggests the degree to which the first two words have been indissoluably coupled. **Sleeping Beauty Peak** AZ: the outline of the mountain suggests a sleeping woman, as in the fairy story; so also, **Sleeping Ute Mountain** MN. **Sleepers Bend** CA: at this river bend a reclining figure seems to be lying along the ridge. **Sleepy Creek** OR: because four campers slept late one morning there. **Sleeping Child Creek** MT: an adaptation from some Indian language, but locally believed to have been **Weeping Child,** named from some incident.

Sleeper 1) From the personal name, e.g. in OK for Gid Sleeper, local rancher. 2) From an incident, e.g. **Sleeper's**

River VT was so named because a man left as a guard by a surveying party went to sleep.

Slick A descriptive, commonly with 'rock.' The mountain in WY is of smooth rock, appearing to be polished.

Slide Generally descriptive, for a mountain or other feature marked by a landslide, e.g. **Slide Mountain** OR.

Sligo From the town in Ireland.

Slim Rare. Sometimes for the nickname, e.g. **Slim Jimmy Branch** KY. **Slim Butte** SD: because it is a slim shaft of rock and clay.

Slime Bank MA, AK Named by fishermen because of the abundance of jelly fish.

Slinger WI Simplified from the name of B. Schleisinger Weil, early storekeeper who put his name upon the settlement, ca. 1845.

Slink From the colloquial term for a young deer, e.g. **Slink Ridge** TN.

Slip Point WA Because of frequent landslides.

Slippery A rare descriptive, e.g. **Slippery Rock** PA. The ford in CA was dangerous because of smooth rocks. **Slippery Ann Mountain** MT: by folk-etymology from Cyprian Matt, early settler.

Slocum Generally from the personal name, but in TX a pun on 'slow come,' because someone thought the town would grow slowly.

Sloop From the small sailing vessel, formerly much used in river and inlet commerce, e.g. **Sloop Point** NC.

Slough Applied to a place associated with a slough, e.g. **Sloughhouse** CA originally a hotel, **Slough Creek** NB.

Slovaktown AR Because of settlers from the European province Slovakia.

Slug Canyon CA From the early miners' term for a nugget or a gold coin.

Slumgullion The term in the early West meant either the soupy mixture of gravel and clay which form the tailings of a sluice box, or else a stew of that consistency. The pass in CO was probably named because its soil, when wet, churns up into a similar mixture.

Sly Park CA For James Sly, who discovered it in June, 1848, while scouting for a Mormon wagon train.

Smackover AR By folk-etymology from French *chemin-couvert*, 'road-covered,' first applied to a creek; the reference is uncertain, but may indicate a stream arched over by branches.

Small A rare name, furnishing a good example of a common descriptive adjective which has not been taken over for topographical use, **Little** being the conventional term. Examples, however, are **Small Arm** AK, **Small Bay** AK. The name is more commonly from the personal name, but even this has been avoided for habitations because of its somewhat derogatory suggestion. **Small** ID: for a man of that name, otherwise unidentified. **Smallwood Creek** AK: for a prospector of that name. **Small Pox Bay** WA: in 1860 many Indians died here from that disease.

Smith From the personal name, but being the commonest such name it has not given much distinction and is not very common as a place-name. Being short, it occurs usually with a suffix, most often as **Smithville**. **Smith Island** VA for John Smith, its discoverer in 1608, named by Smith or his companions. **Smith River** CA: for Jedediah Smith, mountainman and explorer, though the stream which was originally so named by him (1828) is the present **Klamath**.

Smithfield Though well known as a place-name in England, the 15 or so occurrences in the U.S. are regularly associated with a person named Smith. This particular suffix, however, was probably suggested by the English name.

Smoke, Smokey, Smoky A descriptive for a place habitually smoky or for one where a smoke was seen at the time of naming. The name is applied to several mountain ranges, presumably being a naming done from a distance at which the range appeared hazy, e.g. **Great Smoky Mountains**. Though smoke from forest fires may have been present, haze or mist would have been enough to produce the name. **Smoky Butte** ND: about 1902 a column of smoke rose from the butte for some time, probably from a burning coal seam. **Smokeless** WV: from the Smokeless Coal Co. **Smoky Ordinary** VA: probably a descriptive name, 'ordinary' being used in the sense of public house. **Valley of Ten Thousand Smokes** AK: descriptive of the number of volcanic smokes rising. **Smokehouse** by association, e.g. in CA because of devices for smoking salmon. **Smoky Hill River** KS: recorded in uncertain French, ca. 1800, as La Fourche de la Côte Bucaneius (or Boucanière), the last word being an adjective from *boucane*, an American-French term for 'smoke,' and the whole being 'fork of the smoky hill'; reason for naming unknown.

Smoketree From the occurrence of trees so known, e.g. the canyon in CA.

Smolan KS Named by Swedish immigrants for a town in Sweden.

Smuggler(s) To judge from the rarity of such names, smuggling has not been a favorite American crime. The term is romantically associated with 'cove,' and there is question whether either in CA or in OR the smugglers had any more basis than someone's imagination. **Smugglers Point** ND: illicit trade from Canada is reputed to have entered here during territorial times. It has also been used as a mine-name, and in CO thus originates.

Smyrna Known both from its mention in *Revelation* and for its ancient and modern importance, the city of Asia Minor has given its name to a number of towns; specific reasons have not been preserved, but in SC it was first the name of a church.

Snag A term for an old dead tree, still standing, most commonly as **Snag Lake,** because of the trees left standing for many years after an area is flooded

as the result of a dam, or from natural reasons, such as a lava flow.

Snake The most common reason for naming is an incident involving a snake, but certain places, rightly or wrongly, get the reputation of being 'snaky' and, therefore, may get the name. With streams the name often arises because of the serpentine course, e.g. several creeks in SD are thus explained, although the actual reason for many of these namings is dubious. **Snake River** ID and other names in this area are from the Snake tribe of Indians. **Snake Knob** WV: Mr. Kyle, 'an elderly gentleman,' once killed a rattlesnake here, and the circumstantiality of the report lends it credence.

Sneffels, Mount CO Named (1874) from the mountain in Jules Verne's *Journey to the Center of the Earth,* which is itself an adaptation, for purposes of the story, from the name of the Icelandic mountain Snaefels.

Sni, Sny French *chenal,* appearing in American-French as *chenail,* as a generic for a natural, narrow passageway of water, became **Sny** in American usage, and appears as a specific in a few names, chiefly in MO. **Sniabar Creek** MO: either from *chenail-à-barre,* 'sny with a bar (blockage),' or from *chenail-à-Hubert (Hébert)* from the name of a local French family. **Snicarty** MO: probably for *chenail-ecarté,* 'lonely, narrow.'

Sniktaw CA Probably for W. F. Watkins, journalist of the 1850's, who used a reverse spelling of his name as a pseudonym.

Snipatuit MA Algonquian 'rock-river-at' (?).

Snohomish WA From an Indian tribal name.

Snokomish River WA From an Indian tribal name.

Snoqualmie WA From an Indian tribal name.

Snort Creek IA From a personal nickname (?).

Snow, Snowy For habitations, it is often from the personal name, esp. Snowville, e.g. in UT; this name is for Lorenzo Snow, fifth president of the Mormon Church. On features, and by transfer to habitations, the term often identifies mountains seen from a distance and always or usually snow-covered, e.g. Snow Peak ID, Snowcap Mountain AK, Snowcrest Range MT. Snow Hill NC: for salt giving a white appearance. Snow Hill MD: for a place in England. Snow Camp NC: in a region where heavy snow is unusual, such a name indicates an incident in which people suffered from snow when camping, but contradictory stories are told as to the incident. Snowshoe Lake MN: from its shape, but many occurrences of this name are probably from incidents of snowshoeing. Snowstake Creek AZ: because of the location of snow-stakes to indicate snow depth. Snowden is from the personal name, but Snow-doun AL preserves the spelling used in Scott's *Lady of the Lake*. Snowflake AZ: from early settlers named Snow and Flake. Many compounds exist, e.g. Snowball, Snowcrest, Snowdrift, Snow-slide, Snowshed, Snowmass.

Sny See Sni.

Soak Creek Traditionally believed, both in NB and WV to be an incident-name, resulting from some traveler falling in. That the one in WV was known first as Soakass Creek lends some reinforcement to the story.

Soap On streams, because of a soapy appearance of the water from carrying silt, e.g. Soap Creek OR. On land features, e.g. Soap Flat OR the name arises from the presence of soapweed. Soapstone Cove AK: from that rock. Soap Creek MT: probably a mistranslation of an Indian term meaning, 'warm.' Soap Creek (two in NB): from an incident involving soap. Soap Creek AZ: a badger, killed here, was put into a pot and boiled; in the morning the alkali in the water and the animal's fat were found to have combined to make soap. Soap Creek IA: a shortening from Soapstone.

Sobaba Hot Springs CA Indian (Luiseño), the name of a village.

Sobrante CA Spanish 'residue, surplus,' used as a legal term in early CA to denote what remained in a region after a land grant had been made and what therefore might be the basis of a future grant.

Socapatoy Creek AL Probably Muskogean (Creek), meaning uncertain.

Socastee SC From an Indian tribal name.

Social In occasional use, e.g. Social Circle GA, the exact reason for naming being obscure, since the term has varied applications in English, and no historical record is extant. See Society.

Society Commonly because of some particular society, e.g. Society Hill SC, because St. David's Society of Welsh Baptists founded an academy here in 1778.

Sockanosset MA, RI Algonquian, probably 'dark-earth-at.'

Sockatean Stream ME Algonquian, probably 'divided.'

Sockdolager Rapids AZ From the 19th century slang word, meaning a knock-out blow or anything very severe, given by the Powell expedition who first ran these rapids.

Sockeye Commonly for the sockeye salmon, e.g. two creeks in AK.

Sockorockets Ditch DE An Indian personal name, probably from a chief who was recorded in about 1680.

Sockrider Peak CO From a family name, not further identified.

Sock's Island ME From an Indian who lived there in the 18th century; his name represents the Indian rendering of the French name Jacques.

Sockum DE Probably a shortening of an Algonquian term occurring elsewhere as *winnasoccum*, 'fine-outlet-at,' applied by people of northern DE as a derogatory for the agricultural regions of the state in the phrase 'down Sockum,' i.e. 'in the sticks.'

Socohachee Creek GA Muskogean (Creek) 'hog-stream.'

Socorro NM Spanish 'succor, help,' from an incident of 1598, so named by the men of the Oñate expedition because the Indians of a village in this vicinity gave them corn when they were half-starved.

Soctehoma Creek MS Chickasaw 'bluff-red.'

Soctum Hill AL From Choctaw *sakti humma*, 'bank-red.'

Sod In WV the name is unexplained, but may be a nickname or an abbreviation (of **Sodom?**). The sodhouse was much used in the early settlement of the plains country, and **Sodville KS** probably thus originated.

Soda With spring the term forms a quasi-generic, sometimes calling for another specific, e.g. **Upper Soda Springs** CA arising from the presence of carbon dioxide in the water. With 'lake' the term is not so common, so that **Soda Lake** is generally sufficient. It arises from the presence in the water or crystallized around the shore of some mineral or minerals believed to be soda. On other features the name is chiefly by transfer.

Sodom From the Biblical city. In the frontier period the name was given, not infrequently, to places where the inhabitants were (or had the reputation of being) especially wicked, though usually with no particular reference to the sin of sodomy. The name was probably applied, often, in a semihumorous sense. With the increased propriety of civilization most of the names were changed. Though **Sodom** NY and a few others exist as habitation-names, the term is now more common on features, e.g. the brook in CT and the mountain in MA. **Sodom** MA: by local story the name was given for no more serious sins than spending the Sabbath gayly in drinking and singing.

Sodus NY Iroquoian, from an earlier Seodose, meaning uncertain.

Sofkahatchee Creek AL Muskogean (Creek), probably 'deep-stream.' See **Sofkee.**

Sofkee GA Muskogean (Creek) 'deep,' first applied to the creek.

Soft Shell KY From a community of so-called Soft-shell Baptists. Cf. **Hardshell.**

Solana Beach CA Spanish 'sunny place,' a commendatory name given in 1923.

Solano County CA From a mission founded in honor of St. Francis Solano, and also, specifically, for that saint and for Francisco Solano, a Christianized chief of the Suisun Indians, the county being so named in 1850.

Soldier Chiefly Western, for association with the army or with an individual soldier. **Soldier Creek** OR: because of an encampment in the Indian wars of the 1860's. **Soldier Camp Wash** AZ definitely shows its origin, probably of the early 1870's. **Soldier Creek** CA: probably for a soldier, most likely a deserter, who worked in the gold mines in 1848 or 1849. **Soldier Creek,** Corson Co., SD: from Bear Soldier, a Sioux. **Soldier River** IA: from the grave of a U.S. soldier who was buried here in early times. **Soldiers Home** as a repeated name is for a government residence for veterans. **Soldier Creek** IL: the translation of the name of a Potawatomi who lived nearby in the early 19th century.

Soledad Spanish 'solitude,' but in most instances probably a religious name from Nuestra Señora de la Soledad. In Monterey Co, CA, the name arose when an Indian said something that the Spanish soldiers of 1769 took to be that word in Spanish; the mission later founded there took the name in a religious sense.

Soleil Levante, Pointe Au LA French 'sun-rising,' but reason for naming uncertain.

Solfatara Creek WY Because of the solfataras (volcanic vents) associated with it.

Solgohachia AR Choctaw (?) 'grape-stream.'

Solitaire Lake NB Because of its isolation.

Solitario Spanish 'solitary, lone,' e.g. the range and peak in TX.

Solo MO Probably a derogatorally humorous term for a lonely place or one presumed to have only one inhabitant.

Solomon From the personal name, e.g. **Solomonville** AZ for I. E. Solomon, early settler. **Solomon River** KS: originally as **Solomon's Fork,** named (?) for Solomon Petit, trader in about 1800. Because of the reputation of the Biblical Solomon for riches and gold mines, the name was a common commendatory for mines, and thus was applied by association to features, e.g. **King Solomon Mountain** CO. In this last instance the naming was influenced by Rider Haggard's novel, *King Solomon's Mines.*

Solon Often from a personal name, e.g. in OH (1825) for Lorenzo Solon Bull, son of an early settler. **Solon Springs** WI for Thomas Solon, discoverer of the springs. In NY for the ancient Athenian lawgiver, bestowed as a part of the Classical naming of 1790.

Solromar CA Coined from Spanish *sol, oro, mar,* to suggest 'golden sunset on the sea.'

Solution Creek WY The outlet to **Riddle Lake,** q.v.

Solvang CA Danish 'sun meadow,' given by Danish settlers.

Solvay NY From a factory using the Solvay Process for making soda.

Solway From Solway Firth in Great Britain.

Somber Hill WY Probably a descriptive.

Sombrero Spanish 'hat,' e.g. **Sierra Sombrero** NM because its conical shape is like a high-peaked Mexican hat.

Somerange OR From 'summer range,' a stockman's term.

Somerset From the county in England, etc. The name in MA dates from the 17th century. In PA the county was formed in 1795, and apparently carried on the strong PA tradition of naming counties for English originals, even in the post-Revolutionary period.

Somersworth NH Probably a name coined, ca. 1754, from 'summer' and the common English suffix 'worth,' by the Rev. John Pike who spent his summers preaching here.

Somerville From the personal name, sometimes from **Somers.** In TX for Albert Somerville, local political figure. In MA, locally believed to be for Capt. Richard Somers, hero of the Tripolitan War.

Somis CA Indian, probably Chumash, the name of a village.

Somo WI Probably Algonquian and the remnant of a longer name; meaning uncertain.

Somonauk IL From a Potawatomi village-name, meaning 'pawpaw-grove.'

Songo Pond ME Algonquian 'cool-water.'

Sonoita AZ Papago, approximately 'corn-place.'

Sonny OR The owners of the Little Boy Ranch wanted that name, but the railroad thought it too long, and Sonny was substituted.

Sonoma In CA from a tribal name, recorded as Sonomi in 1816; in NV probably a transfer from CA.

Sonora In AZ and CA it is from the Mexican state, in CA having been settled by immigrants from that state. In other states the name is probably so derived, but may have been aided by its euphony.

Sonyea Of Iroquoian origin; the personal name of an Indian (?).

Soo See **Sault.**

Sookhanatcha Creek AL Choctaw 'hog-river.'

Sooner From the nickname for an Oklahoman, e.g. the river in AK.

Sooneybeag Pond ME Algonquian 'stone-pond.'

Soosap Peak OR From an Indian personal name.

Sopchoppy FL Shifted from an earlier **Lockchoppee,** from Seminole 'acorn-stem,' a term applied to the red oak.

Sopris CO In 1860 an expedition into the mountains named the peak for Richard Sopris, their leader.

Soquee River GA From the name of a former Cherokee town; literal meaning, uncertain.

Soquel CA Probably the name of an Indian village.

Soro Creek TX Probably for **Zorro,** 'fox.'

Sorrel, Bayou LA From a French family-name, probably for Joseph Sorrel, early landowner.

Sorrento From the town in Italy, with a commendatory suggestion of Mediterranean climate or of beautiful sea-coast.

Sot, Bayou de LA American-French, a term applied in LA to the rail or marsh hen.

Souadabscook River ME Algonquian 'sloping-ledge.' Also as **Sewadapskak.**

Soudan, Sudan In NB, **Soudan** was taken to mean 'land of the blacks,' and applied because the town was in the Black Hills. **Sudan** TX: because Sudan grass was grown there. **Soudan** MN supplies an example of the rare process of naming by opposites, since the naming was because the winter cold of the region was such a great contrast to the heat of the original. In FL, because of being a Negro settlement, probably with the 'land-of-the-blacks' idea.

Sougahatchee Creek AL Muskogean (Creek) 'rattle-creek.'

Souhegan River MA, NH Algonquian, meaning uncertain.

Souinlovey Creek MS Choctaw 'opossums-there-killed,' sometimes called **Possum Creek.**

Soulouque LA From a mulatto, born a slave, who took his name from the Negro leader of Hayti; Soulouque was prominent in the state legislature in the Reconstruction period.

Souneunk Stream ME Algonquian 'big-rapid-stream' (?).

Sour A rare descriptive. Occasionally used with bodies of water to indicate a sour taste produced by some chemical, e.g. **Sour Creek** WY, **Sour Lake** TX. It may also refer to the kind of soil so termed, e.g. **Sourland Mountain** NJ. **Sourdough:** from the term for a long-experienced pioneer, e.g. several streams in AK.

Sourdnahunk Lake ME See **Souneunk.**

Souris French 'mouse, mice.' The river in ND takes its name from a plague of mice suffered by a party of early trappers.

South, Southeast, etc. For general usage, see **North. South Pass** WY: after the Lewis and Clark expedition had crossed the Rockies at the head of the Missouri River, a passage farther south was sought and when finally found was given its present name. **South Bend** IN: because the site is approximately at the point where the St. Joseph River makes its 'big bend,' and reaches its farthest south point. **South America Lake** CA: from its resemblance in shape.

Southampton From the city of England, in NY dating from the 17th century. In MA the name has a special origin, being chosen in part as being the southern section of the already-named **Northampton.**

South Carolina See **Carolina.**

South Dakota See **Dakota.**

Southwick In MA (1771) it is probably for a town in England, but it is also a family name.

Souwilpa Creek AL Choctaw 'raccoons-there-killed' (?).

Sowangawas Mountain ME Algonquian 'eagle's nest.'

Sowasha Creek MS Choctaw 'coons-are-there.'

Sowbungy Mountain ME The earlier **Soubangen** (1879) indicates an original *sowangen* (Algonquian 'eagle') from which the present form has developed by folk-etymology. Also, **Sourbungy.**

Sowcook NH Algonquian, meaning uncertain.

Sowhatchee Creek GA Hichiti 'raccoon-stream.'

Spadra In AR it is of uncertain origin; in CA, a transfer in the 1850's from AR.

Spain In SD, from the European country; in MT from R. V. Spain, local landowner.

Spanaway WA Indian, meaning unknown; first recorded as Spanuch, and then shaped by folk-etymology to the semblance of an English name.

Spanish Usually indicates a place once inhabited by Spanish-speaking people, especially in the gold-mining regions, e.g. **Spanish Gulch** OR. **Spanish Fort** LA, MS, TX: from an old Spanish fortification. **Spanish Fork** UT: the town is by transfer from the stream, which was so called because an old trail known to date from Spanish times ran along it. **Spanishburg** WV: from the family name. **Spanish Hill** PA: from some archeological remains, thought to be of Spanish origin at the time of their discovery (1878).

Sparkill NY Dutch 'spruce (or fir) stream.'

Sparks From the personal name; in NV it was named (1903), by the railroad for John Sparks, state governor.

Sparta From the city of ancient Greece, usually with the symbolic idea of courage and fortitude. **Spartanburg** SC: from the Spartan Regiment, a local militia body which distinguished itself in the Revolution.

Spatterdock Usually with 'lake,' for the pond-lily so called.

Spavinaw OK Uncertain; possibly a much-altered French personal name.

Spearhead, The CO A sharp-pointed spur is thus described. Cf. **Arrowhead.**

Specimen Mountain CO Because specimens of various gemstones are found here.

Spectacle A descriptive (in the sense of eye-glasses) for a feature with two large ends connected by a narrow strip, e.g. a lake (CO, MN), and several islands and ponds in CT, MA, RI.

Specter Range NV Probably named by association with nearby **Death Valley.**

Speculator NY The land-speculator was a well-known frontier figure, though his activities were usually veiled behind commendatory names.

Spedis WA From the name of an Indian chief.

Speed From the personal name, e.g. in IN, for W. S. Speed, local manufacturer. **Speedway City** IN: because it is the site of the racetrack for automobiles.

Speelyais Columns OR From an Indian name for a local god.

Spencer From the personal name, e.g. in IA for U.S. Senator, G. E. Spencer.

Speonk NY Algonquian, the remnant of some longer name, meaning uncertain.

Spermaceti Cove NJ Probably used as the equivalent of **Whale** to avoid repetition.

Sphinx, The WY From the appearance of the mountain as seen from a certain direction.

Spice The name, fairly common for natural features in parts of the Appalachian region is from a shrub, known as spicewood or spicebush. So also, **Spicewood** TX.

Spider Rare, sometimes probably from the personal name, e.g. the village in KY. **Spider Lake** MN: probably from various branches making it suggest a spider's legs.

Spion Kop MT From the battle of the Boer War (1900), named about that time.

Spirit Used with natural features, especially lakes, and sometimes transferred to habitations. It is regularly a translation of some Indian term, which implied that there was something holy, uncanny, or haunted, and it is sometimes used for a place, e.g. **Spirit Hill** MN where the Indians held religious observances. Cf. **Manitou, Wakan, Devil.**

Splendora TX From the name of a ship in a popular song.

Splintercat Creek OR From a legendary, flying cat of the woods which was supposed to splinter branches from trees.

Split Generally for a feature with a split in it, e.g. **Split Glacier** AK, **Split Mountain** MT. **Split Lake** NB: because miscellaneous gatherings of cattle were here 'split' into their proper herds. **Split Hand Lake** MN: a translation from the Ojibway, probably an Indian personal name. **Split Tail Gulch** SD: because a duck of that variety was once shot here.

Spokane WA Indian (Siwash) from *spo-kan-ee,* 'sun,' but probably more directly from the personal name or title of a chief, who is recorded as Il-lim-spokanee (1812). A tribe of Indians was thus known, but the name may have been applied to them secondarily.

Spook(y) From the colloquial term for **Ghost,** q.v.

Spoon In the form **Spooner,** from a personal name, e.g. **Spooner** WI for J. C.

Spooner, (1843–1919), active in the region as a railroad and lumber magnate. Incidents involving a spoon, or fancied resemblance, probably account for a few names, e.g. **Spoon Glacier** AK. **Spoon Buttes** NB: a translation from the Siouan, so called because the Indians made spoons from the horns of mountain sheep which inhabited the buttes. **Spoon River** IL is a translation from the Algonquian 'mussellshell,' because the Indians used such shells as spoons. See **Maquon.**

Spoonhead, Mount AZ From an Indian personal name.

Spotsylvania VA Named in 1720 for Gov. Alexander Spotswood, from a part of his name, combined with a Latin form, 'forest-place,' on the analogy of **Pennsylvania.**

Spotted A descriptive, but generally as a secondary specific, e.g. **Spottedtail Creek** NB, **Spotted Horse** WY, both from the personal names of Indian chiefs. **Spotted Range** NV is apparently named from the variegation of its rock.

Spout Usually with **Spring(s)**. In KY a spout was laid from the spring to bring water to the roadside. Elsewhere, e.g. in VA, a spouting spring may be indicated.

Spread Eagle WI The lake was named because its outline was thought to be that of a spread eagle.

Spring Though primarily a generic, it has wide use as a specific to denote a place marked by a spring. It is also a personal name, but this has been a scarcely noticeable influence in establishing the hundreds of names. Their number, in fact, is a testimony to the interest of the pioneers in finding good drinking-water, and the names are equally as numerous in the well-watered East as they are in the arid West, where the presence of water was the more important for being rarer. It appears freely with many generics— branch, brook, creek, grove, hill, lake, valley, being especially numerous. Having high commendatory value, it passed by transfer to many habitation-names, and formed others by combination with city, dale, town, ville, etc. **Springfield** occurs in most of the states. The first was in MA, and was named after a village in England (1641). The name, both providing an apt description of many places and having commendatory quality was rapidly propagated. **Springfield** SC: for being founded in the field of a man named Spring. **Spring Hope** NC: by tradition, named because people hoped that success would spring from their settlement. But this is highly unusual. There is also the possibility that 'hope' is used in a dialectal sense, so that the name would be another Spring Valley. **Spring Garden:** originally the name of a private estate near Philadelphia, it has become the name of several towns for its commendatory value. **Spring Branch,** e.g. in TX is from the common use of that term to mean a small stream flowing from a spring.

Sprinkle TX For S. T. Sprinkle, pioneer settler.

Spruce In the East the tree is northern, except for a southward extension into the Appalachians. In this latter region 'spruce' is fairly common in place-names, probably because the tree is unusual enough to have distinctive value. In the West, though spruces are conspicuous trees in some areas, the name is not common. As with 'fir,' the nomenclature is badly confused. The 'spruce' was sometimes called 'balsam,' and on the other hand the term 'spruce' was applied to other trees, e.g. to the Douglas fir, and it even took the combination 'spruce-pine,' which itself might be applied to trees of different species. When it came to spruce, the early American knew little and cared less about taxonomy. **Spruce Pine** NC: for a single large Carolina hemlock, locally so called. **Spruce Mountain** AZ: from presence of the Douglas fir. **Spruce** WA: an unusual occurrence in a region where a tree so called predominates.

Spry UT For William Spry, governor of Utah (1909–1917).

Spuiten Duyvil NY Dutch, literally 'spout-devil,' with obvious reference to the dangerous tidal currents; the exact terms from which the present name is derived are uncertain.

Spur The lake in NM is named from its shape. Elsewhere it is generally from a brand or the name of a ranch; in TX it is a translation from the Spanish *espuela,* from the Espuela Land and Cattle Co.

Spurr, Mount AK Named, ca. 1900, by A. H. Brooks for J. E. Spurr (1870–1950), geologist and explorer in AK.

Spy Usually, e.g. **Spyrock Peak** CA with the idea of an outlook. **Spy Mountain** CA: because a man who lived there was suspected of being a spy in World War II.

Squakie Hill NY Probably from the name of a tribe recorded as Squatehega and Squawkhaw.

Squam Algonquian, a repeated name in New England. 1) Meaning 'summit,' it apparently occurs in **Squam Head** MA and other names of elevations. 2) Meaning 'salmon,' (a residual form), it probably occurs with rivers and lakes, e.g.

Squam River MA, as well in other forms, e.g. **Squamcut** RI, 'salmon-place.' See **Annisquam.**

Squamokwisseeboo Stream ME Algonquian 'salmon-in-little-stream.'

Squamscott, Squamscut NH Algonquian, either 'end-rocks-at,' or 'red-rocks-at.'

Squankum NJ Algonquian 'entrance' (?), with reference to the mouth of a stream.

Squannacook River MA Algonquian, meaning uncertain.

Squannahonk Swamps MA Algonquian, probably 'green place.'

Squantum MA Algonquian, literally 'gateway,' but perhaps preserving the name of Squantum or Squanto, who was a friend of the colonists in 1620.

Squapan ME Algonquian 'bear's den.'

Square Rare, doubtless because nature is not given to producing square forms, but existing as a descriptive, e.g. **Square Lake** MN, NB, **Square Butte** MT.

Squash Though cultivated by many Indians, the squash, like most vegetables, failed to make much impression on nomenclature. **Squash Mountains** AZ: from a peak called **Squash Blossom Butte,** which was thought to resemble the Navajo symbol of fruition, often used as a 'motif' in silver-work. **Squash Ann Creek** CA: by folk-etymology from a Yurok name for the stream, meaning unknown.

Squassucks NY From the name of a 17th-century Indian, recorded as Wesquassuck.

Squattock Lake ME Algonquian 'trout-river.'

Squaw The Algonquian term for 'woman' entered English in the early 17th century, and the namings are not to be considered Indian. They are numerous on natural features, and denote a place where an Indian woman lived or one which was in some other way thus associated. Since prostitution was not unknown among Indians, some of the names undoubtedly have that origin. The name is generally Western. Because of a derogatory suggestion, it is rare on habitation-names, and always by transfer. **Squaw Tit(s):** a common term for nipple-like formations. **Squaw Grove** IL: because one of the first settlers found some squaws camped there, the men being off hunting.

Squaxon Island WA From a local Indian word, 'lone,' originally applied to a stream which was the only one of much size in the region. The tribal name, Squakson, is probably secondary.

Squeak Creek CO For Robert Wheeler, early settler, commonly known as 'Squeaky Bob' because of his high-pitched voice.

Squealer Gulch CA For 'Squealer Bob' Gibson, an early settler, nicknamed for his high-pitched voice.

Squibnocket MA Algonquian, uncertain, except -*et*, 'at.'

Squidrayset Creek ME For an Indian chief so named.

Squirrel In the wooded areas the squirrel was so common and so insignificant as rarely to supply incidents worth a name. It occurs generally on minor features, e.g. *'swamp,' 'run.'* **Squirrel Bay** AK: because the outlines on the topographical map resemble the head and paws of a squirrel.

Squitcomegek Falls ME Algonquian 'long-ridge-at.'

Sredni Bight, Point AK From Russian *sredniy,* 'middle,' perhaps the only U.S. place-name with initial *sr-.*

Stafford The county in VA was named (1661) for Viscount Stafford; the town in CT, for the town in England (1718). Later namings are generally from the personal name, e.g. **Stafford** TX for W. M. Stafford, landowner.

Stag Sometimes probably from the personal name, usually **Stagg.** It has not been colloquially used for the male deer or elk, and a few such namings are presumably the result of reading of British books, e.g. **Stags Leap** CA.

Stage Hill NB A stage line once ran near this hill.

Staked Plain See **Estacado.**

Stalemate Bank AK When the Board on Geographic Names delayed and hesitated over the approval of a name, a name appropriate to this situation was published in the *Coast Pilot* (1954).

Stalkinghead Creek GA The Indians (and presumably some early colonists) used a so-called stalking-head, usually a buck's head with antlers, as a disguise for approaching game, and the name of the stream apparently recalls an incident thus associated. See **Stocking.**

Stalwart MI Named (1881) for the Stalwart faction of the Republican party, most of the inhabitants being so minded.

Stamford From a town in England, first used in CT (1642). Later namings, e.g. in TX, are regularly from this one.

Stampede Usually to commemorate a stampede of a cattle herd, e.g. the creek in TX. **Stampede Pass** WA: because some railroad workers quit the job in disgust, and 'stampeded' for the valley.

Stamping In the 18th century the term 'stamping ground' was used for a place frequented by game, generally because of a salt lick, and marked by trampling—hence, **Stamping Creek** WV, **Stamping Ground** KY.

Standard A popular name for corporations, on the model of the Standard Oil Company, and thence transferred to habitations, e.g. in AZ and CA, and **Standardville** UT.

Standing Descriptive of a rock or stone higher than broad, and so seeming to stand upright, e.g. **Standing Stone** PA. Certain Indian tribes noted such stones, and some of the names are translations, particularly of the Delaware *achsinnick,* 'where there is a large stone.' See **Seneca. Standing Boy Creek** GA: based upon a Muskogean term, probably a personal name.

Standish From the personal name, especially in honor e.g. CA, ME, of Miles Standish, pioneer of Plymouth Colony.

Stanislaus CA The river was called Estanislao by the Spaniards in honor of that saint, but was given a more Anglicized form by Frémont, ca. 1845.

Star 1) From the personal name, e.g. **Star Valley** AZ, for an early resident, otherwise unidentified. 2) From the shape, e.g. **Star Island** MN, **Star Lake** MN, **Star Mountain** TX. 3) From the commendatory idea of preeminence, e.g. **Star** NC, which was so called in hope of its being a 'star town.' Probably some places are named because of an especially bright star seen on the occasion.

Starr King MT Unusually honored by peaks at opposite ends of the country (CA, NH) is Starr King (1824–1864), Unitarian minister, patriot, and mountaineer.

Startup WA For G. G. Startup, manager of a local lumber company (1911).

Starve, Starvation A repeated name in the West, arises from food shortage. Though actual starvation was known among Western travelers, authenticated stories of the origin of the name for this reason are lacking, and in most instances it probably arose because people were on short rations at that point or merely had to miss a meal. The idea also occurs in **Starved to Death Creek** MT of which the story is told that some Indians thus perished after a snowstorm. **Starve Goat Island** RI: a superlative for barrenness. **Starved Rock** IL: by strong tradition, because some Illinois were besieged there (1769) by men of other tribes, and were starved out and massacred. **Starvation Flat** NV: because it offered no forage for cattle being driven across it. **Starveacre** occurs, e.g. in AL, as a degrogatory habitation-name. **Starvation Creek** TX: in the 1870's some cowboys were robbed of horses and food here and suffered from hunger before they were relieved. **Starvation Gulch** CO: kept from traveling by one of them being injured, four men remained here almost without food while a fifth went for relief.

Starwein Ridge CA An adaptation of a Yurok name; meaning unknown.

State Regularly from some association with a state, in most cases, obvious from the name itself, e.g. **State Line, State College. State Center** IA: from being thus located. **Statesburg** SC: originally intended as the capital of the state. **Statesville** NC: probably from being near the center of the state.

Staten Island NY From Dutch *staaten* 'states,' for the States General, the governing body of the Netherlands in the 17th century, a name established in the early Dutch period.

Static Peak CO Because phenomena of static electricity have frequently been observed on it.

Station Commonly a generic, but becoming a specific in habitation-names and by association. 1) In colonial times, the equivalent of residence or plantation, in the late 18th century expanding into the idea of a settlement of several families, especially a semi-fortified place for defence against Indians, particularly in KY and TN. 2) A railroad station. In habitations the term is usually a second one, e.g. **Bean Station** TN, **Adair's Station** TN but it appears first in names for natural features and in a few transfers, e.g. **Station Camp** KY, TN, **Station Run** KY.

Staunton The name of several places in England and also a family name; in VA with special reference to the wife of Gov. William Gooch, whose maiden name was Staunton.

Steamboat The ubiquitous steamboat of the 19th century impressed the American imagination, and gave rise to many names. 1) For a feature in some way looking like a steamboat, e.g. **Steamboat Mountain** NM, **Steamboat Lake** OR from a rock in the lake. 2) For a feature associated with a steamboat, e.g. **Steamboat Creek** OR where the *Norma* was once hung up on a rock; **Steamboat Slough** CA which was navigated by steamboats in preference to other channels. 3) For something making a noise like a chugging steamboat, e.g. **Steamboat Springs.** The term also had various slang usages, with the idea of swindling, and of mines with bogus claims. **Steamboat** OR probably arose from this mining usage.

Stecoah NC Cherokee, meaning uncertain.

Steel In PA, **Steelton** is from the Pennsylvania Steel Co. Most of the other namings, e.g. **Steelville** MO for James Steel, landowner, are from the personal name.

Steenykill Lake NJ From Dutch 'stony-stream.'

Steep A fairly common descriptive, applied either to elevations, e.g. **Steep Point** WA, **Steep Rock** MA, or to watercourses because of their steep gradients, e.g. **Steep Brook** MA.

Steer From some association with a steer, but uncommon, the steer being perhaps too undistinguished an animal to be thought worthy of remembrance. **Steer Creek** NB: a crippled steer wintered along this stream and survived, a

circumstance sufficiently noteworthy to produce the name. Probably because of its lack of distinction, it appears more often in a double specific, e.g. **Black Steer Lake** NB, **Lame Steer Lake** NB.

Stehekin River WA Indian (Skagit) 'way, pass.'

Steilacoom WA From the name of an Indian chief, recorded as Tail-a-koom.

Steinhatchee River FL From Seminole *isti-in-hachi,* 'man-his-river,' but significance not known.

Steller, Mount AK Named (1928) commemoratively for G. W. Steller, naturalist with Bering's expedition in 1741.

Stemlit Creek WA Indian, meaning unknown.

Step The personal name **Step(p)** is rare, and place-names are commonly from the idea of something used as a step, e.g. **Stepping Rock** KY, **Stepstone Creek** KY.

Sterling 1) From the personal name, e.g. in CT (1794) for Dr. John Sterling, who offered the town a library if it should be named for him, but never made good on his offer. 2) Occasionally for the commendatory suggestions, e.g. **Sterling** ID, for the 'sterling qualities of the soil' (1910).

Steuben Names of counties and towns are from 'Baron' von Steuben, Prussian general in the Revolutionary army.

Stewart, Mount George CA For George W. Stewart, one of the men responsible for the creation of Sequoia National Park, not for George R. Stewart, an onomatologist.

Stibnite ID From the ore of antimony so called.

Stikine River AK Indian (Tlingit) 'big-river.'

Still 1) Descriptive to indicate quiet water. **Stillwater** is used for a number of towns, and on features, e.g. **Stillwater Creek** OK and **Stillwater River** MT. **Still Creek** OR: named in contrast to the turbulent **Zigzag River,** into which it flows. 2) **Still,** or **Stillhouse,** is often used to denote a place where a whiskey still once operated, **Stillhouse** occurring as a specific more than 30 times in KY. In the SE the name often arises from a turpentine still, e.g. **Ferrel Still** FL for Clarence Ferrel. 3) From a personal name, e.g. **Still** ND for H. E. Still, railroad agent.

Stillaguamish WA From a local Indian term, 'river people,' probably the name of a tribe.

Stingray Point VA An incident name, from John Smith's being bitten there by a stingray (1608).

Stink, Stinking One of the few descriptives based on the sense of smell, usually with **Spring** or **Creek,** e.g. **Stink Creek** TX, **Stinking Spring** CO, **Stinkwater Creek** OR. The name is usually applied because of the strong smell caused by sulphur compounds in the water. Some such-named features may arise from incidents and be applied to a place that does not usually smell, e.g. **Stinking Lick** WV which is probably so called because an animal once was mired here and its decaying body raised a temporary stench. **Stinkingwater Creek** NB: the translation of an Indian name, believed to have originated because of the putrefying bodies of buffalo mired in the stream. **Stinking water** MT: because of stench caused by rotting bodies of Shoshones killed there by Gros Ventres.

Stirling From the personal name, especially, e.g. NJ, for William Alexander, so-called Lord Stirling, Revolutionary general.

Stissing NY Algonquian, probably a shortening of a longer form meaning 'great rock,' and first applied to the hill.

Stitchihatchie Creek GA From an earlier **Tickeehatchee,** Muskogean (Creek) 'border-stream.'

Stock 1) From the personal name, though more usual in compounds, e.g. **Stockdale** TX for Fletcher Stockdale, lieutenant-governor (1863–1866). **Stock-**

ton CA: for Commodore F. R. Stockton, who took possession of CA for the U.S. in the Mexican War. 2) For places in Europe. See **Stockbridge, Stockholm.** 3) From the meaning 'livestock,' e.g. **Stockton** KS and **Stockville** NV, both of which began as centers of stock-raising. **Stocktonia** FL: for a local family, with a Latin ending.

Stockbridge In MA (1739) for a town in England.

Stockholm From the city in Sweden, usually, e.g. ME, SD, named by Swedish immigrants.

Stocking Creek GA By folk-etymology from an earlier recorded (1766) **Stalking Head.**

Stockton See **Stock.**

Stoil CA Coined from Standard Oil Company, which once maintained a pumping station there.

Stone, Stoney, Stony These terms usually describe a place with many small stones, rather than a single massive rock. With streams and lakes the terms describe the nature of the bottom or the shore. Works of man supply other names. **Stonewall** TX: because stone walls were common in that area. But throughout the South the name is likely to be from General 'Stonewall' Jackson, e.g. **Stonewall County** TX. **Stonewall Canyon** CA is named for its steep, rocky slides. Other works of man are **Stone Cabin** AZ, **Stone Corral** AZ, CA, **Stone Bridge.** Towns are likely to derive from the personal name, e.g. **Stoneville** NC, for P. M. & F. J. Stone, storekeepers. **Stone Idol Creek** SD: named by Lewis and Clark in 1804 because of three prominent stones about which the Indians told a legend; there is no reason to think that these stones were properly idols, but the term was freely used by early Americans. **Stone Johnny Hill** SD: because it is marked by a so-called 'stone-johnny,' i.e. an informal monument of flat rocks piled up. **Stony Creek** WA: by folk-etymology from a recorded Stehna, an Indian name of unknown meaning. **Stone Arabia** NY: probably by folk-etymology from Dutch *steenig-raapje,* 'stony-turnip-field.' Cf.

Turnip Patch Point DE, which is also in Dutch territory. **Stones River** TN: because discovered in 1766 by a party of four men, one of whom was Uriah Stone. **Stoney Lonesome** occurs as a rural derogatory, e.g. in IN.

Stonecoal An early term applied to anthracite or other rocklike coal, descriptive in **Stonecoal Creek** WV.

Stonington In CT (1666) it is probably from an English town-name such as Stannington, though a stony site may have influenced the choice. Later namings are from this one, sometimes influenced by a quarrying indusry, as in ME.

Stono SC From an Indian tribal name.

Store Occasionally used, e.g. **Store Creek** SC to identify a feature where a store, i.e. as a place to sell goods, was located. A place where goods were stored is more commonly designated **Storehouse**, e.g. **Storehouse Branch** KY.

Storm, Stormy A few of the examples are from the personal name, but most of them are from incidents in which the namers experienced a storm, e.g. **Storm Canyon** AZ, where some cattlemen were snowed in and almost starved in 1898. **Storm Creek** AK: because a surveying party experienced severe storms here in 1925. **Storm King Mountain** NY: a romantic 19th century name, to suggest that the mountain was the haunt of the storm king. **Storm Point** WY: the point is exposed to storms.

Story From the personal name, e.g. in IA the county and city are for Judge Joseph Story of the U.S. Supreme Court.

Stove Usually from an incident, e.g. the creek in SD because some stoves issued to Indians in 1880 were stored here. **Stove Draw** WY: a stove was left here, ca. 1880, and was observed by later comers. **Stovepipe Wells** CA: the flow of water was once protected by a stove pipe.

Stow In MA from a town in England, named in 1683. Usually from the personal name, e.g. in OH for Joshua Stow, surveyor.

Straddlebug Mountain TX A brand name.

Strafford The county in NH (1769) and the town in VT (1761) are for the second Earl, so named because he was a kinsman of Benning and John Wentworth, governors of the colony of NH.

Straight A descriptive, not common, applied to creeks, canyons, etc., e.g. **Straight Creek** TX. **Straight Spring Gulch** CA. The descriptive applies to the gulch and was named in counterpart to **Crooked Spring Gulch.** Since the name may be passed by transfer, it is not always accurate, e.g. both streams known as **Straight River** in MN are crooked, but the one (Becker Co.) takes its name from a lake, and the other (Steele Co.) from the general course of its valley, both names being translated from an Indian language. **Straight Creek** KS: probably named by irony, since it is exceptionally crooked.

Strange Regularly from the personal name, e.g. the creek in WV for William Strange. Lost in the forest, he carved on a beech tree, 'Strange is my name, / and I'm on strange ground, / and strange it is / that I cannot be found.' His skeleton and inscription were later discovered.

Stranger KS Applied first to the stream, being a translation of the Siouan (Kansa) *o-keet-sha;* reason for naming unknown.

Strasburg After the Alsatian city. In PA the name was given by settlers from Alsace in 1733; in OH, by immigrants in 1828.

Stratford From one of the English towns so named, e.g. **Stratford** CT in 1643. In CA a local rancher, William Stratton, refused to allow his name to be used, and **Stratford** was then adopted. In OH the town was sometimes known, in parody, as **Stratford-on-the-Olentangy.** The popularity of the name owes much to its association with Shakespeare.

Strathmore From the Scottish district. In CA the name was given because of its literal meaning, 'valley-big.'

Stratus See **Cirrus.**

Strawberry Generally for the wild berry. In SC transferred from a plantation. **Strawberry Valley,** Eldorado Co., CA: an innkeeper here was named Berry, and nicknamed Straw. **Strawberry Peak** CA: apparently a joke name, because there were no berries there, or else from a fancied resemblance to a berry.

Stray The straying of animals was a constant problem of the early West, and such an incident is the obvious source, e.g. **Stray Horse Gulch** CO.

Stream Though current as a generic in some regions, especially northern New England, it rarely occurs as a specific. **Stream Point** AK: so called because a large stream is nearby.

Stretch Island WA For Samuel Stretch, a gunner's mate on the Wilkes expedition (1841).

Stringtown Because the settlement lacked a real center, and the houses were merely in a 'string' along the road. The explantion is locally given in MN and AR. It would thus be a humorously derogatory name. In OK it is a variation, probably humorous, from an original **Springtown.** As an informal name it occurs 12 times in MO.

Striped Mountain CA A descriptive, from the striped rock.

Strong Regularly from the personal name, e.g. in ME (1801) for Governor Caleb Strong, who is also, along with his brother John, honored in **Strongsville** OH. **Strong City** OK: for C. R. Strong, railroad developer. **Strongwater Brook** MA: probably for its strong current.

Stump, Stumpy Descriptive, suggesting cut-over and unkempt country, e.g. **Stump Creek** MT, **Stump River** MN. Some habitation-names are from the personal name, or carry a humorous derogatory touch, or are by transfer, as with **Stumpy Point** NC. **Stump Lake** NB: for a single stump, notable in generally treeless country. **Stump Creek** IA: for George Stump, early settler.

Sturbridge MA From a town in England (1738).

Sturgeon From the fish, e.g. the river in MN. It is also a personal name, and the town in MO is for I. H. Sturgeon, a railroad superintendent.

Stuttgart From the city of Germany.

Stygian Caves WY In the mythological sense 'infernal, deathly,' because poisonous fumes here have killed birds and small animals.

Styx From the mythological river of the Greek lower world. **Styx River** AL is traditionally said to have been named by a schoolmaster from VA, who found the dark water to be depressing. He may have carried the name with him from VA where there was once a stream of that name. **Styx** TX, CA: probably semi-humorously derogatory, and may be connected with 'the sticks,' i.e. an out-of-the-way place.

Suamico WI Algonquian (Menominee) 'sand-bar.'

Subiaco AR From a Catholic foundation, which took its name from the town in Italy, the site of one of the first Benedictine monasteries.

Sublette The widely scattered name in the West is from one or other of the three Sublette brothers who were prominent in the fur trade of the early 19th century. Also **Sublett.**

Subligna GA From an attempt to translate into Latin the personal name Underwood, but *ligna* is a plural form.

Sublime Sometimes used for points of lookout. **Sublimity** OR: because the namer thought the nearby scenery to be sublime.

Substitute Point OR A surveyors' name, when an alternate point of reference was selected.

Sucarnochee Creek AL Choctaw 'hog-its-stream.'

Succanesset MA Algonquian, meaning uncertain, except -*et,* 'at.'

Succasunna NJ Algonquian 'blackstone.'

Success A commendatory for habitation-names, e.g. AR, MO, VA.

Succor Flat CA Formerly **Sucker Flat,** and probably named because of settlers from Illinois, the Sucker State.

Sucio Spanish 'dirty.' In **Sucia Islands** WA the feminine form is preserved from an original **Isla Sucia;** the term here is used in its nautical sense, 'foul,' i.e. full of rocks and reefs.

Suckabone NY By folk-etymology, from an Algonquian *suc-e-bouk,* 'potato (ground-nut)-place.'

Sucker Usually on stream names for the fish. Cf. **Succor.**

Sudan See **Soudan.**

Sudbury From an English town-name; in MA, 1639.

Sudden In MT the lake was named because it is so hidden that one is not aware of it until coming upon it suddenly. In WY the lake was formed suddenly when a landslide dammed the canyon.

Suffern NY Probably from a family name.

Suffield The town in CT was originally thought to be in MA, and was named by the General Court, according to custom, after an English town; the Court also recognized the meaning 'south field,' and bestowed the name because the place was 'adjoining to the south border,' i.e. of MA, according to their belief.

Suffolk From the English county. The county in MA dates from 1643.

Sugar Commonly a place where maple sugar was made or where sugar maples (sugar trees) grew, e.g. **Sugar Grove, Sugar Creek.** Where sugar is produced from cane or beets the name also arises, e.g. **Sugar City** CO, ID. It is probably in some cases a shortening of **Sugarloaf,** e.g. **Sugar Hills** WV. **Sugar Hill** CA:

an army wagon, partly loaded with sugar, broke down and scattered the sugar. **Sugar Bush** MN, WI is originally from the Dutch, and is the equivalent of **Sugar Grove. Sugarbowl** is used for a depression or steeply sloping valley in the mountains, usually filled with snow. **Sugar Creek** NC, SC: from the Indian tribal name Sugaree. In areas where the maple is not common, the name may arise from the honey locust, especially from translations of Indian names, e.g. **Sugar Fork** NC. **Sugarcamp** is a repeated name, especially on small streams, for the site of a camp for the making of maple sugar. See **Sugarloaf.**

Sugarite NM An American rendering of **Chicarica,** by aid of folk-etymology.

Sugarloaf From early colonial times down into the 19th century sugar usually came in a so-called loaf, i.e. a rounded conical form, about five inches in diameter and standing up in a point. This was placed on the table, and bits were taken from it with spoons. This characteristic shape was transferred to topography, and many conical hills have been so-called all over the U.S. It has also become a generic.

Suicide Rare, but designating a place where a suicide occurred, e.g. the gulch in SD for one of 1877, and the pass in CA for the death of a young miner, date uncertain.

Suisun CA From an Indian tribal name.

Sukalena Creek MS Choctaw 'camps-on-bank.'

Sulfur The preferred modern spelling has not generally replaced the older **Sulphur,** q.v.

Sullivan From the personal name, especially for John Sullivan, Revolutionary general, e.g. several towns and counties.

Sulphur A descriptive to indicate the presence of sulphur, often of water smelling of sulphur (cf. **Stink**). Commonest are **Sulphur Spring(s)** and **Sulphur Creek.** Habitation-names are generally by transfer, with sometimes a commendatory suggestion, as of health-waters. A sulphur industry may be denoted, e.g. **Port Sulphur** LA, **Sulphur** NV.

Sultan WA By folk-etymology from the name of an Indian chief, recorded as Tseul-tud.

Sultana CA From a variety of grapes, commonly grown in the region when the name was given, ca. 1900.

Sumatra From the East Indian island. In FL the name is for the kind of tobacco grown here.

Sumica FL From Société Universelle, Mines, Industrie, Commerce et Agriculture which owned land here.

Summer Commonly, especially in combinations such as **Summerfield, Summerville**, from the personal name, also occurring as **Somerfield, Somerville**. There has been a tendency to change the 'o' to the 'u' spellings under the suggestion of 'summer', of the pronunciation, for instance, **Summerhill** PA was originally **Somerhill**, for two men named Somers. Though in most of the U.S. summer suggests heat and is not a commendatory term, the name has sometimes thus originated, e.g. **Summerland** CA, **Summerhaven** AZ. **Summer Lake** OR: so named by Frémont in Dec. 1843, when the area near the lake appeared green and summery in contrast to the snowy hills. **Summerton** SC: named because it was a summer resort. **Summerdale** IL: named by Robert Greer, a local businessman, who thought that it had 'pleasant sound and suggestions.'

Summit A generic, but also a common specific for both natural features associated with a summit and for habitations located at a summit. Though commonest in mountainous country, it also occurs in almost level country, sometimes indicating where a road or railroad passes over an almost imperceptable watershed, or where canoeists could expect to change from upstream to downstream paddling, e.g. **Summit Lake** (several in MN). The seemingly anomalous **Summit Hill** and **Summit Mountain** indicate one which is associated with the summit of a road or railroad, or else one which has an unusual

summit, e.g. **Summit Mountain** AZ which has a remarkable flat top.

Sumpawams Creek NY Probably from the name of an early Indian, with the possessive 's.'

Sumter From the personal name, especially (e.g. four counties in the SE) for Gen. Thomas Sumter of the Revolutionary War.

Sun, Sunny On natural features such names are not common, and indicate an incident or the weather conditions, with respect to the sun, under which the naming was done, e.g. **Sunlight Creek** MT, **Sunset Island** VT, **Sunshine Valley** AK. **Sunrise** and **Sunset** may also be equivalents of East and West. These names are common on habitations, usually with commendatory suggestion, reflecting man's seeking for the sun, even though during much of the year in the U.S. he actually seeks the shade. These names are commonest in regions which are winter-resorts FL, CA, AZ, but are by no means confined to such regions, e.g. **Sun, Sunbright, Sunburst, Sun City, Sunfield, Sunny Hills, Sunnymead, Sunnyside, Sunnyslope, Sunnyvale. Sunbury** PA: for a town in England. **Sundance** SD, WY from the mountain, where Indian ceremonies were held. **Sun Creek** NB: because the Indian sun dance was held here. **Sundown** NY, TX, MN: the equivalent of **Sunset. Sunset Peak** AZ: because it is high enough to catch the rays of the setting sun. **Sun Valley** ID: a commendatory name for a winter ski resort.

Sunapee MA, NH Algonquian 'rock-pond.'

Suncook ME, NH Algonquian 'rocks-at.'

Sunday Though the rare personal name may be involved in some instances, the common origin is from some association with the day of the week, e.g. **Sunday Creek** WA, discovered on a Sunday in 1881. The creek in TX was named by some surveyors who spent a Sunday camped here in 1887.

Sunderland MA Though it is a town in England, the naming in MA is primarily for the Earl of Sunderland, at the time (1718) prime minister.

Sunflower The native flower has resulted in an occasional name, e.g. **Sunflower Valley** AZ.

Suniland TX Probably a variant spelling for the commoner **Sunny,** used as a commendatory.

Sunk See **Sink.**

Sunkauissia Creek NY Algonquian, meaning uncertain.

Sunkhaze Stream ME Algonquian, the remnant of a longer term, roughly 'concealing-outlet,' to indicate a place where the outlet of a tributary into the main stream is such as to give concealment.

Sunspot NM Because the location there of an observatory, largely dedicated to the study of sunspots.

Suomi The Finnish name for Finland, generally given by immigrants.

Superior The lake was named by the French (Lac Superieur) in the 17th century and meant only 'upper lake,' as compared with **Lake Huron.** It assumed the English form after the ending of the French dominion, and to some extent necessarily assumed something of the English connotation, viz. 'better.' **Superior** WI: from the lake. **Superior** AZ, WV: from mining companies. **Superior** NB: a commendatory, with suggestion that the soil in this vicinity was better than elsewhere.

Superstition Mountains AZ From local Indian tales associating these mountains with supernatural happenings. The mountain in CA is similarly named.

Suponic Pond ME Algonquian 'big-opening.'

Supply Because established as a base of supply, sometimes an army term, e.g. **Fort Supply** WY. **Supply** OK was originally **Fort Supply.**

Suquamish WA From an Indian tribal name.

Sur Spanish 'south.'

Surprise A common Western name (about 20 in CA), it indicates some incident or something unexpected in a natural feature which surprised the namer. **Surprise Valley** CA: probably because the covered-wagon emigrants, having topped a range of mountains, were surprised to see a wide valley beyond, and then still higher mountains. **Surprise Creek** WY: because its course, when explored, proved to be very different from what had previously been supposed.

Surpur Creek CA Yurok, from the name of a village.

Surrey, Surry From the county in England. The VA county (1652) made use of the alternate spelling **Surry,** and later namings have generally followed this model, e.g. the county in NC (1770).

Survey, Surveyor Parties of surveyors, in the process of making maps, gave thousands of names, and the rarity of **Surveyor** is a testimony to the lack of egotism among surveyors, or to a lack of pride in their profession. Most of the names indicate a place where surveyors established a camp or where some incident occurred. **Surveyor Branch** WV: some surveyors found shelter under a cliff along the stream. **Surveyor Run** PA: a party of surveyors was once lost in the forest here. **Survey Pass** AK: A Geological Survey party crossed the range here in 1924. **Surveyor Passage** AK: for a steamer of that name.

Suscol Creek CA Patwin, the name of a village.

Susitna River AK Athapascan, shifted for euphemistic reasons from an original **Sushitna,** 'sandy-river.'

Suslota AK Athapascan, meaning uncertain.

Susquehanna River Recorded by John Smith in 1608 and 1612 as **Sasquesahanough.** Forms without a final consonant prevail after about 1675. But the final '-gh' or '-k' of the early forms indicates a tribal name with the Algonquian ending for 'men.' Also, Smith's text makes it certain that he considered the name of the river to be that of the tribe living along it. In about 1675 the

Iroquois nearly exterminated the Susquehanocks, so that they ceased to exist as a tribe, and their tribal name was no longer used. Speakers of English then, apparently, assumed the ending of the name to be *-hanna* (Algonquian 'stream'), which was common on streams in that area. It may also be argued that whatever sound Smith represented by his final '-gh,' merely became silent, as has happened in English words generally. In either case, the name should be taken as 'Susque-tribe' river.

Susquetomscut Brook CT Algonquian. The last part (*-mscut*) may be taken as 'rocks-at'; the remainder, uncertain.

Sussex From the county in England.

Sutil Island CA Named retrospectively in 1939 for a ship of a Spanish expedition of 1792.

Sutter From the personal name, especially for J. A. Sutter, prominent pioneer, e.g. the county in CA. ·

Sutton In MA (1715) probably for one of the places so named in England; in NB, for the town in MA. It is also a personal name.

Suwannee Of Indian origin, probably Muskogean. The river bears the same name as that of an early Seminole town on its bank, but which was named first is uncertain. The town in GA takes its name from Suwani, a Cherokee settlement, but thought by the Cherokees to be a Muskogean name. The meaning is unknown. The existence of the diminutive **Suwanochee Springs** FL provides additional evidence that the name is not derived from the Spanish mission San Juan de Guacara.

Svea MN From a poetic name for Sweden, named by immigrants.

Swadhums Creek WA From an Indian tribal name.

Swago Creek WV Probably the same as **Oswego.**

Swallows CO Probably from the swallows nesting in nearby cliffs.

Swamp Regularly a generic, but occurring, infrequently, as a specific by association, e.g. **Swamp Run** MD. Because of unpleasant suggestions it is rare as a habitation name, but occurs as **Swamp** VA and in a few other instances.

Swampbuggy Lake AK Named (1953) because a vehicle thus known was abandoned there.

Swampscott Algonquian 'red-rock(s)-at.'

Swan The domesticated swan is rare in the U.S., but the wild swan is a large and conspicuous bird, not too common to be commonplace. It has given rise to many names, e.g. **Swan Lake** (25 in MN). Though the personal name exists, e.g. in **Swandale** WV, nearly all the habitation-names have arisen by transfer. Even **Swanville** MN is from the nearby **Swan River. Swan Lake** NB: takes its name from its shape, having a long extension like a swan's neck.

Swango Island ME Algonquian 'eagle.'

Swannanoa NC Cherokee 'Suwali [a Tribe]-trail.'

Swansea In MA (ca. 1667) from the town in Wales.

Swanwyck DE A revival of the 17th-century Dutch **Swaenewyck,** 'swan-place.'

Swarthmore PA A Quaker settlement, taking its name from the home of George Fox, founder of the Quakers.

Swash Commonly a generic, along the Atlantic coast, for a channel, occasionally a specific by association, e.g. **Swash Hole Islands** VA, with 'hole' probably for a deep place in the channel.

Swashin(g) Creek MO By folk-etymology from the French personal name Joachim, as transmitted orally.

Swastika The symbol was native among some of the Indian tribes, and the name in NM may thus have originated (1919). After the swastika became associated with the Hitler regime, this name was changed to **Brilliant.** In NY the name, probably given merely because of the goodluck sign, has been retained.

Swatara Creek PA Iroquoian, meaning uncertain.

Swauk Creek WA Indian, meaning unknown.

Swearing Creek NC By abbreviation and folk-etymology from Swearington, a local family.

Swede, Sweden Along the lower Delaware a few names date from the 17th-century Swedish colony, e.g. **Swedesboro** NJ. The name generally has sprung for the settlement of Swedes, e.g. **Swede Prairie** MN, **Swede Hills** NB.

Sweet A personal name is often involved, e.g. **Sweetland** WV and **Sweet** MN for men so named. On natural features the common application is to water features, usually in the form **Sweetwater**, with spring or creek. In the West this name is common, and indicates potable water as opposed to salt or alkali water. The use of the term, rather than 'fresh,' may be influenced by the Spanish, i.e. it may be a translation of *dulce*, common in the combination *agua dulce*. In the East, where salt or alkali water is highly uncommon, the term may have commendatory value. The early American, in spite of a taste for rum and whiskey, considered himself a connoisseur of water, and sweet thus applied could be commendatory, indicating a source of water considered especially palatable. **Sweet Home:** a commendatory name, with reference to the song. **Sweet Briar:** from the variety of wild rose so known. **Sweet Grass** MT: a type of grass especially liked by cattle.

Swenoda Lake MN Coined from Swedish, Norwegian, and Danish, because the region was settled by people from all three nations.

Swift 1) From the personal name, e.g. **Swift Co.**, MN for Governor H. A. Swift. 2) As a descriptive for streams, e.g. **Swift River, Swiftwater, Swiftcurrent Creek.** By transfer the name is often applied, unsuitably, to other features, thus resulting in **Swift Lake** MN, **Swiftcurrent Glacier** MT, etc.

Swilling Gulch AZ For J. W. Swilling, early settler.

Swillup Creek CA By folk-etymology from the name of an Indian (Karok) village.

Swim Usually from the personal name, e.g. **Swimmer** OK for G. W. Swimmer, first postmaster. **Swimming Moose Bay** WY: because moose regularly swam across at this point to an island.

Swinomish Slough WA From an Indian tribal name.

Swiss, Switzer, Switzerland A few places have been named for Swiss immigrants, e.g. **Swisshome** OR. **Switzer** is a personal name. Both **Swiss** and **Switzerland** have been given because of the mountainous nature of the country. **Swissvale** PA: coined from the personal name Swisshelm and 'vale.'

Switchback Originally a railroad term, it has been extended to trails and roads as indicating any very twisty stretch, even though no actual switches are involved. **Switchback** WV: used in connection with a railroad. **Switchback Peak** CA: for a trail. **Switchback Falls** OR: a descriptive name for the falls.

Switzkill NY Dutch 'Swiss-stream,' from Swiss settlers.

Sword Sometimes from the personal name, but this is more commonly **Swords.** The paucity of these names is evidence of how little the sword was used by early Americans. The meadow in CA apparently was named because crossed swords were carved in a tree to commemorate a duel between two Frenchmen, one of whom was killed. See **Broken.**

Sycamore Though individually a conspicuous tree, the sycamore has given its name to only a moderate number of features. The name occurs most notably in southern California, where the tree often grows along streams where no other trees flourish, thus giving rise to **Sycamore Canyon.**

Sycan OR Klamath 'grassy plain,' first applied to the marsh.

Sylacauga AL Muskogean (Creek) 'buzzard-roost.'

Sylmar MD A boundary-name for PA and MD, the second syllable being used because the first had already been used in **Pen Mar.**

Sylvan, Silvania Commendatory, as suggesting 'forested' in a pleasant sense; usually with habitation-names. **Sylvania:** a Latinized form for 'wooded place,' was popularized by the early use of **Pennsylvania.**

Symbol Bridge CA Because the natural bridge was marked with pictures and 'writings' at the time of the naming, in 1917, probably Indian work.

Syncline Hill CA Because of the presence of a syncline, a geologist's term.

Syosset NY Probably Algonquian, meaning uncertain.

Syracuse The original naming (1825) is that in NY. It was suggested by the first postmaster, John Wilkinson, who had read of the ancient Greek city of Sicily, which he thought resembled the site in NY in being near a marsh and salt springs; he must also have been influenced by the current fashion, especially in NY, for classical names.

T

T Gulch CO From its shape, resembling a T.

Ta River See **Mattaponi.**

Taaiyalone Mountain NM Indian (Zuni) 'corn mountain.'

Tabby Mountain UT For a Ute chief of the 19th century. See **Tabiona.**

Tabequatche Creek CO From an Indian tribal name, recorded as Tabeguache.

Tabernash CO For a Ute Indian, killed here by a white man in 1879.

Tabiona UT From the name of a Ute chief (see **Tabby),** and a locative ending, i.e. 'at Tabby's place.'

Tabla Spanish 'board, plank,' e.g. **Las Tablas** NM, for a lumbering community.

Table A repeated term, most commonly with 'mountain' or 'rock,' to indicate a feature with a level top.

Tabo Creek MO The rendering of a French name of a local family, probably Tabeau.

Taboose Pass CA Probably Paiute, and meaning a groundnut.

Tabor 1) From the personal name, e.g. in TX, for John W. Tabor, early settler. 2) From the Biblical mountain, e.g. **Mount Tabor** in several states. **Tabor City** NC from the Mount Tabor Presbyterian Church.

Tabusintac Stream ME Algonquian 'they-go-paired (?), with reference to eels.

Tackawasick NY Algonquian 'stone-mortar' (?).

Taclamur CO From Tackaberry, Lamont, and Murray, local promoters.

Tacoma The lake in ME is probably of Algonquian origin, but uncertain in meaning. In WA the name appeared in Theodore Winthrop's *The Canoe and the Saddle* (1863) where it is applied to what is now **Mount Rainier,** and said to be 'a generic term also applied to all snow peaks.' Winthrop probably rendered the word more euphonic than the Indian term would have been, and thus made a more precise interpretation very difficult. It has been translated as 'the mountain,' and 'the gods,' and by various other terms. Since some Indians associated mountains and spirits, a combination of the two ideas may be considered possible. In other states, e.g. TX, the name is borrowed from WA.

Taconic A repeated name, especially for mountains, in New England and in the Algonquian area of NY, of uncertain meaning and much disputed. It is presumably Algonquian, and is most commonly connected with the root *-tugk-,* 'tree, wood, forest,' but that term fails to have distinguishing value in a heavily-forested area, and the name may therefore be merely the remnant of a longer term. An Indian deed of 1687–1688 suggests that it referred to a field; if so, the meaning might be 'field (clearing)-in-forest,' and a connection with **Poquonnock, Pequannock,** would become possible. It exists in other spellings, e.g. **Taghkanic** NY.

Taconnet River ME Algonquian 'wading-place (ford)-at.'

Tacony Creek PA Algonquian, meaning uncertain, probably the same as **Taconic.**

Tad WV From the nickname of Talmadge Dunlap, first postmaster.

Taft From the personal name, especially for President W. H. Taft, e.g. in TX, CA, OK.

Taghkanic NY See **Taconic.**

Taghum Butte OR Chinook jargon 'six.'

Tagouacha Bayou AL Probably a form of **Toucha.**

Tagus From the river of Portugal. In ND it is a shortening of the name of a local rancher Taguson.

Tahkodah Lake WI Algonquian, meaning uncertain.

Tahlequah OK Indian (Cherokee), an old town name transferred from the East, meaning unknown. See **Tellico.**

Tahneta AK Athapascan, meaning uncertain.

Tahoe, Lake CA Washo 'lake.'

Tahoka TX From the lake, locally believed to be an Indian word, meaning uncertain.

Tahoma A variant of **Tacoma,** appearing on some features in WA.

Tahosa The valley in CO was thus named, ca. 1915, by the Colorado Geographic Board. The name had been a serious contender (1859) for the name of the territory, being romantically interpreted as 'Dwellers on the Mountaintops.' It is Kiowan, being recorded as the name of a chief (1837), and probably meaning 'mountain-top.'

Tahquamenon River MI Ojibway, with reference to the dark-colored water (?).

Tahquitz CA The name of the evil spirit of the Cahuilla Indians. Since the name is not recorded until 1897, it may have been applied by whites, not by Indians.

Tahuyeh Creek WA Indian (Twana) 'that-done,' apparently an incident name.

Taiban NM Indian, but language and meaning uncertain.

Tajiguas Creek CA Chumash, the name of a village.

Tajique NM A Spanish rendering of an Indian (Tewa) name, referring to a village, but literal meaning unknown.

Tajo Spanish 'opening, gap.'

Takilma OR From an Indian tribal name.

Taku AK From an Indian tribal name.

Talahoga Creek MS Choctaw, 'rock-there-standing' (?).

Talala OK From the personal name of a Cherokee, prominent in the Civil War period.

Talamantes Creek CO From a Spanish family-name, not further identified.

Talapus, Mount OR Chinook jargon 'coyote.'

Talasha Creek MS Choctaw 'palmettos-are-there.'

Talatha SC From the name of a former Indian village (?).

Talawa, Lake CA From an Indian tribal name.

Talco TX From the Texas, Arkansas, Louisiana Candy Company.

Talega Canyon CA Spanish 'bag, sack,' perhaps because of the shape.

Taliesin AZ A fanciful name given by Frank Lloyd Wright, the architect, from the poet of the King Arthur story.

Talihina OK Choctaw 'railroad.'

Talisheek LA Choctaw 'gravel,' probably from the presence of a gravel deposit.

Talkeetna AK Athapascan, with -na, 'river,' and the rest probably 'plenty,' with reference to game and other food supplies.

Talking Rock GA From an echo, a translation of a Cherokee name.

Tall The term seems to be avoided, but occurs as a secondary (or tertiary) specific, e.g. **Tall Prairie Chicken Creek** SD for an Indian thus named, who lived at the mouth of the stream.

Talla Bena LA Choctaw 'palmetto-camp.'

Tallac, Mount CA Washo 'mountain.'

Talladega AL From the name of an early Creek town; literally, 'town-(on)-border,' i.e. the border between the Creek and Natchez tribes.

Tallahaga Creek MS Choctaw 'rock-standing.'

Tallahala Creek MS Choctaw, with *talla*, 'rock,' and the rest (?) a shortening of *halalua*, 'smooth.'

Tallahassee FL Muskogean (Creek) 'town-old.'

Tallahatchie River MS Choctaw 'rock-stream.'

Tallahatta Creek AL, MS Choctaw 'rock-white.'

Tallapoosa AL The river was named from an early Creek town; literal meaning uncertain; the first part is from *talwa*, 'town' (?).

Tallashua Creek MS Choctaw, probably 'rock-little.'

Tallassee AL From the name of an early Creek town with the first part from *talwa*, 'town,' and the remainder probably *hasi*, 'old.' Cf. **Tallahassee**. **Tallasseehatchee Creek** AL adds *hachi*, 'stream.'

Tallatchie Creek AL Choctaw, probably 'rock-stream.'

Tallatikpi AL Choctaw 'rock-knob.'

Tallawampa Creek AL Choctaw; uncertain, a personal name (?).

Tallawasse Creek AL Muskogean (Creek) 'town-old.'

Tallawyah Creek AL Choctaw 'rocks-leaning.'

Tallega KY Indian, language and meaning uncertain.

Tallula(h) In GA, from the name of a Cherokee town, meaning unknown. In MS (and probably in LA) it is a transfer from GA.

Tallyhagia Creek MS Choctaw 'rock-standing.'

Taloga OK Indian, probably Creek 'rock-water,' with possible reference to a boundary-mark.

Talpa In NM, probably from a personal name. In TX it is a shortening of **Catalpa**, from the presence of a large tree of that species.

Talucah AL Probably Muskogean, meaning uncertain.

Taluga River FL Seminole 'cowpeas.' See **Teloga**.

Tama IA From a Fox chief, whose village was in this vicinity in the early 19th century.

Tamaha OK Choctaw 'town.'

Tamalpais, Mount CA Indian (Coast Miwok), with *pais*, 'mountain,' and *tamal* probably 'western,' thus being a name given by the Indians living to the east of the peak. Since **Malpais** is a common term in Spanish, the name has apparently been somewhat shaped by folk-etymology.

Tamanos Mountain WA Chinook jargon, 'spirit,' another example of the Indian association of spirits and high places.

Tamaqua PA Algonquian (Delaware), probably 'little-beaver-stream.'

Tamarack This originally Algonquian word for the larch has supplied a large number of names. In the East it is a northern tree, generally found near water, and thus gives its name to lakes and swamps. In the West, during the frontier period, it commonly meant the tree now known as 'lodge-pole pine,' also often found near water, so that the name was still further coupled with 'lake.'

Tamaroa An Indian tribal name; see **Maroa**.

Tamassee SC Apparently of Indian origin, but uncertain.

Tamiami FL A 20th-century name, from **Tampa** and **Miami**, applied to the **Tamiami Trail** a road connecting the two cities.

Tamina TX Locally believed to be from Tammany Hall NY; if so, it was probably freely adapted, rather than misspelled.

Taminah Lake WY Shoshone 'spring (the season).'

Tam O'Shanter Peak AZ Because the top looks like a tam o'shanter.

Tampa FL Recorded in Spanish context (1565) as an Indian town, and soon transferred to the bay; the settlement was **Tampa Bay** (1831), and **Tampa** (1834). The language and meaning are uncertain.

Tan, Tanbark, Tan Yard The occurrence, e.g. in KY, is from early tanning industries and the presence of trees, usually oaks, yielding tanbark.

Tanacross AK A shortening of **Tanana Crossing,** for the point at which the original telegraph line crossed the river.

Tanadak AK Aleut 'land-little,' first applied to the island.

Tanaga AK Aleut 'land-big,' first applied to the island.

Tanana AK A shortening of Athapascan *tananatana,* 'mountain-people-river.'

Tancha Bayou TX See **Tenaha.**

Taney From the personal name, e.g. **Taneytown** MD, named for the founder in 1740, Frederick Taney. **Taney Co.** MO: for R. B. Taney (1777–1864), Chief Justice of the U.S. Supreme Court. **Taneycomo Lake** MO: from **Taney Co.,** MO. But see **Como.**

Tanforan CA For Maria and Toribio Tanforan, landowners in 1868.

Tangent OR Because of the tangent, i.e. straight stretch of track, on the railroad here.

Tangerine FL A commendatory, for the variety of oranges grown here.

Tangier Usually for the city of Africa, but **Tangier Island** VA is uncertain.

Tangipahoa LA, MS From an Indian tribal name.

Tanglewood TX Named by an early settler who had just read Hawthorne's *Tanglewood Tales.*

Tanguscoling Creek PA Algonquian (Delaware), probably 'little-valley-at.'

Tanima Peak CO Named by the Colorado Geographic Board, ca. 1915, from the name of a Comanche subtribe.

Tanipus NH A variant of **Tunipus,** q.v.

Tank In the Southwest a generic for a natural pool of water among rocks, and thence a descriptive for a place thus associated, e.g. **Tank Mountains** AZ. Sometimes from a water-tank, especially on the railroad, e.g. **Tank OK.**

Tankhanne NY Probably a variant of **Taconic.**

Tanque Spanish 'tank, waterhole.'

Tantabogue Creek TX Probably Muskogean, with *bogue,* 'stream,' and the rest uncertain.

Tantalus Creek UT From Greek mythology, used probably with the derived meaning 'tantalize,' because the stream had a habit of drying up when wanted.

Tante Phine, Bayou LA A colloquial pronunciation of Tante Josephine, 'Aunt Josephine,' not further identified.

Tantrum Glade CA Because a skittish mule once upset a camp there.

Tanwax WA By folk-etymology from an original **Tanwux** (1857), meaning unknown.

Taopi MN For a Sioux chief, who died in 1869, one of the first converts to Christianity in the area and a friend to the whites.

Taos NM Indian (Tewa), meaning uncertain.

Tapco AZ From The Arizona Power Company.

Tapiola MI Probably Finnish 'Tapio-place,' from the name of an ancient Finnish god.

Tapo Canyon CA Indian, probably Chumash, the name of a village.

Tapoco NC Coined from Tallasee Power Company.

Tappahannock VA A variant of **Rappahannock.**

Tappan NJ, NY From the Indian tribal name.

Taquahunga Falls VT Algonquian 'bittern-place.'

Tar The production of tar was an important early industry, and many places in the SE were named from that association. **Tarkiln,** e.g. 3 brooks in NJ, also springs from this industry. In other areas, e.g. OK, CA, the name has originated from seepages of asphalt, known as tar. **Tar River** NC: probably from an Indian term, meaning uncertain. **Tarboro** NC: from the river. **Tar Heel** NC: this name has become the appellation for North Carolinians, and various stories (not authenticated) have been told in explanation.

Tara From the town and hill famous as the residence of the early Irish kings.

Tarentum PA From the ancient Graeco-Roman city.

Targhee Pass ID From the name of a Bannock chief.

Tariffville CT The operators of a tariff-protected carpet factory (1827) thus showed their gratitude.

Tarkio MO Probably Indian, meaning unknown.

Tarnov NB From the eastern European city Tarnow, spelled to preserve the pronunciation.

Tarpon Several places in FL are named for the game fish.

Tarratine ME From the Indian tribal name.

Tarryall CO Probably from a family name such as Tarriel.

Tarrytown NY Probably from the family name Tarry.

Tartar Gulch OR Probably a miners' term for a place where gold was spotted in pockets.

Tartarus Lake CA Given to a lake in a volcanic region as the equivalent of **Hell.**

Tarup Creek CA Yurok, the name of a village.

Tarzan, Tarzana In CA the name **Tarzana** was given by E. R. Burroughs in 1917 for his very successful fictional character Tarzan. In TX the name probably has the same origin. In FL the name was given (1921) to a railroad station in a jungly location which seemed suitable for Tarzan's exploits.

Tasco KS From the Mexican city.

Tascosa TX The people, because the location was muddy, wished to take the name **Atascosa** (Spanish 'muddy'), but that name was already in use in the state, and so the spelling was altered.

Tassajara From American-Spanish *tasajera,* 'place where meat is dried,' e.g. several features in CA.

Tatamy PA From the name of a Delaware chief of the eighteenth century.

Tater Colloquial for 'potato,' e.g. **Tater Hill** KY.

Tatetuck CT Algonquian 'chief stream.'

Tatnic, Tatnit Algonquian 'big-hill-at.'

Tatnock Marshes ME Algonquian, probably 'shaking-place-at.'

Tatoosh Island WA From the name of an Indian chief, so named by John Meares (1788).

Tattilaba Creek AL Choctaw 'white-wood-dead-above' (?), with possible reference to a dead tree on an elevation, serving as a landmark.

Taughanick NY Probably the same as **Taghkanic.** See **Taconic.**

Taum Sauk Mountain MO Probably with Sauk, the tribal name; otherwise, uncertain.

Taunton In MA (ca. 1640) for the town in England.

Taureau French 'bull,' e.g. **Pointe a Taureau** LA, because of a well-known red bull which once pastured here.

Tauy Creek KS A shortening of Ottawa, from the nickname of J. T. Jones, a half-breed early settler, known as 'Ottawa,' because he lived with that tribe.

Tavaputs Plateau UT Ute, meaning uncertain, but possibly *tava,* 'sun.'

Tavares FL Probably from a Spanish personal name, but data are lacking.

Tawas MI From the name of a local Indian chief.

Tawawa Creek OH Algonquian, meaning uncertain.

Taycheedah WI Siouan (Winnebago) 'lake-camp.'

Tazlina AK Athapascan, a shortening of an earlier *taslintna,* 'swift-river.'

T.B. MD By local tradition because those initials were found cut into a tree or stone, presumably by Thomas Blandford, early landowner.

Tchefuncta See **Chefuncte.**

Tchula River MS Choctaw, probably 'marked,' to indicate a stream with some kind of marker to serve as a boundary.

Tea In WV, **Tea Creek** is probably from the color of its water. **Tea Bar** CA: by sound and folk-etymology from the name of a former Karok Indian village. **Tea Table Key** FL: probably from appearing to be flat and smooth as a tea table.

Teach From the personal name, e.g. **Teach's Castle** NC. See **Blackbeard.**

Teager Creek AR Probably from 'tiger,' or the French *tigre.*

Teaneck NJ From the local Dutch family-name Teneyck, shifted by folk-etymology.

Teapot The name-cluster in WY arose from the rock, which was once shaped like a teapot, but has now weathered largely away.

Tear Usually in **Tearcoat,** a name given to a place where thickets make the passage difficult, e.g. the creek in WV and the swamp in SC. **Tear Wallet Creek** VA: by local story, a hog driver while sleeping had his wallet torn by his hogs.

Teaser Creek OR For a stallion of the name which once ranged in the region.

Teaspoon Hill MI From a former nearby tavern, so known, according to local tradition, because of an incident involving some lost spoons.

Teas Toh AZ Navajo 'cottonwood-water.'

Teat(s) As a more polite form for **Tit(s),** it occurs on some maps as a substitute for the colloquial term, e.g. **Two Teats** CA. See **Tit.**

Tecalote Creek CO A variant of **Tecolote.**

Tecate CA Probably of Indian origin, the name of a village, but absorbed into a Spanish form.

Techado Spanish 'roofed,' in NM especially for the mesa, which was so called because of an old ruin with a covered well.

Teche, Bayou LA Probably a French rendering of Deutsch, the name by which the German colonists of the area would have named their stream. Cf. **Allemand.**

Tecolote Mexican-Spanish 'owl.'

Tecoma NV Shoshone, to indicate a small mountain standing by itself (?);

used as a name for two mines before being applied to a railroad station.

Tecopa CA For a Paiute chief who was friendly to the whites in the later 19th century.

Tectah Creek CA Yurok 'log.'

Tecumseh For the famous Shawnee chief, who was romanticized by the Americans after his death in 1813, though he had fought against them. The names are generally commemorative, and some of them, e.g. the mountain in NH, are in regions far-removed from the scenes of the chief's life.

Tecuya CA A Yokut name for the Chumash, some of whom occupied this area.

Teddys Teeth CO Some rocks were thus named in the early 20th century for President Theodore Roosevelt, who was portrayed by cartoonists with prominent teeth.

Teedee MT From the Tee Dee Ranch, named from its brand, i.e. T.D.

Teen Jay FL From the Tampa and Jacksonville Railroad, i.e. the 'T,' 'n' 'J.'

Teepee See **Tepee.**

Teewinot Mountain WY Shoshone 'many pinnacles.'

Tehachapi CA Southern Paiute 'frozen,' first probably applied to the creek.

Tehama CA Probably Indian, and a village or tribal name, but much disputed.

Tehipite CA Indian, probably Mono, meaning uncertain, though 'high rock' has been plausibly offered.

Tehuacana TX From a local Indian tribal name.

Tejon Spanish 'badger.' In CA it was applied because a dead badger was found here by a Spanish expedition in 1806.

Tekamah NB Uncertain. One local story is that the name is from that of a place in the far west, and it is actually enough like **Tehama** or **Tacoma** to make the story plausible.

Tekoa From the Biblical city or district.

Tekonsha MI Algonquian 'caribou-little (plural).'

Telegraph The earlier names, e.g. **Telegraph Hill** CA, dating from the 1850's record the existence of a semaphore or some other device then known as a telegraph. With the stringing up of telegraph wires, the line served to identify routes and features, e.g. **Telegraph Hill** MA and **Telegraph Canyon** AZ. **Telegraph** TX: the first telegraph poles for local use were cut here.

Telephone Since the invention was later than that of the telegraph, names are fewer, but have usually been given for the same reason, viz. that the place was distinguished by having a telephone or a line, e.g. **Telephone Flat** CA, **Telephone Canyon** NM. **Telephone** TX was suggested by the first postmaster, because he had the only telephone there at the time.

Telescope Peak CA Named because of the extensive view from it.

Tell City IN Named (1857) by Swiss settlers for their legendary hero, William Tell.

Tellico NC, TN From the name of an ancient Cherokee town, meaning uncertain. **Talequah** is a variant.

Telluride, Tellurium From deposits of the ore of tellurium.

Telocaset OR Nez Percé, 'something on the top,' a name artificially placed by the railroad.

Teloga Creek GA Muskogean (Creek) 'pea,' from the wild pea vine.

Telogia FL Probably a variant of **Taloga.**

Telos Lake ME Probably Greek 'end.' See **Coffee-Los.**

Temblor Spanish 'earthquake,' e.g. **Temblor Range** CA, usually commemorating that some early expedition suffered an earthquake here.

Temecula CA Indian, probably Luiseño, the Spanish adaptation of the name of a village, meaning unknown.

Temescal Mexican-Spanish 'bathhouse,' often with reference to Indian sweathouses or to hot springs.

Temettati Creek CA An adaptation from Mexican-Spanish 'stone mortar, metate.'

Temiscouata Lake ME Algonquian 'very-deep-everywhere.' See **Tommy Squatter.**

Tempe From the Vale of Tempe, celebrated in ancient Greece. In AZ there is no special resemblance to the ancient site, and a personal name may be involved. **Tempe Creek** TX from the name of a local Indian chief.

Temperance A common term in the 19th century because of the 'temperance movement.' The creek in OR was so named because a party there ran out of coffee and had to drink water. The river in MN was named by a pun, since it had no bar at its entrance. **Temperanceville** OH: named (1837) by Robert Gallagher, temperance advocate.

Tempiute NV A simplified variant of **Timpahute.**

Temple Usually, especially in habitation-names, from the personal name, also thus with **Templeman, Templeton.** On mountains it sometimes indicates majestic appearance or fancied resemblance to a temple, e.g. the crag in CA, and the mountain in ID. **Temple Bar** AZ: first called **The Mormon Temple;** later, absorbed to the well-known London name. **Temple** PA: from an inn called Solomon's Temple. Grand Canyon N.P. is well sprinkled with such names as **Buddha Temple** and **Confucius Temple.**

Temps Clair, Marais MO French, a translation of the name of a Kickapoo chief, i.e. 'weather-clear.'

Temvik ND Coined (1911) from Templeton and Larvik, local landowners.

Ten See **One.**

Tenabo, Mount NV Probably Shoshone, meaning uncertain.

Tenafly NJ Much disputed; containing Dutch *vly,* 'valley,' and probably Dutch *tuin,* 'garden.'

Tenaha TX Of Indian origin, language and meaning uncertain. Also as **Tancha.**

Tenaja Canyon CA An American misspelling of Spanish *tinaja,* 'waterhole, tank.'

Tenakee Indian (Tlingit) 'copper-shield,' with reference to the loss in a storm of three highly-prized copper shields.

Tenas Chinook jargon 'little.'

Tenasillahe Island OR, WA Chinook jargon, 'little-land.'

Tenaya CA Originally Ten-ie-ya, for an Indian chief so named; the lake was named on May 22, 1851, by the discoverers of Yosemite Valley.

Tencent Lake OR Because it is insignificantly small, and round like a dime.

Tendoy ID For a local Indian chief.

Tenhassan MN Siouan 'sugar-maple.'

Tenino OR, WA From an Indian tribal name.

Tennanah Lake NY Probably Algonquian, meaning uncertain except that *-anah* may represent *hanna,* 'stream.'

Tennemo TN A boundary-name from abbreviations for Tennessee and Missouri, with an inserted 'e' for euphony.

Tennessee Originally the name of a Cherokee Town, occurring in a Spanish context (1567) as **Tanasqui,** and in an English context (1707) as **Tinnase.** It was already a long-established name, and the Cherokees did not associate any literal meaning with it. The name was transferred to a small stream near the town, and as the English advanced westward, down-stream, they carried the name along, and thus called the stream until it became a large river, though it was alternately known, for many years as **Cherokee River**. The present spelling was used for the county organized as a part of NC (1788), and by a local convention (1796) for a new proposed state, and this name was accepted by Congress on the admission of the state in the same year. **Tennessee Point** CA: a streamer thus named was wrecked here in 1853.

Tennga TN A boundary-name from abbreviations of Tennessee and Georgia.

Tennyson From the personal name; in TX, for Alfred Tennyson, English poet.

Tensas See **Tensaw**.

Tensaw, Tensas AL, LA From an Indian tribal name, the 's' representing a French plural.

Tensed ID The original **Desmet** had to be changed because of duplication within the state, and the name was spelled backward as **Temsed**: a slight error in transmission through the P. O. Dept. completed the transformation.

Tensleep WY Applied first to a natural feature (creek, valley) and of Indian origin, to indicate (?) a campsite which was ten days journey from some other place; the distance is about correct for Fort Laramie. But the origin may be from an Indian personal name.

Tenstrike MN A commendatory, being used in the sense of a perfect score at bowling.

Tent Meadow CA From a large block of granite which from a distance looks like a tent.

Teoc Creek AL Choctaw 'pine-tree.'

Teocalli An Aztec word, taken into Spanish, for their temple; the mountains in AK were named (1898) from a fancied resemblance to such temples, and the mountain in CO is of similar origin.

Teoctalia Creek MS Choctaw 'pine-thicket.'

Tepee The Siouan word for their conical tent entered American usage in the later 19th century. It occurs on natural features as a descriptive, e.g. **Tepee Mountain** MT, OK, **Tepee Buttes** SD. Or it may indicate a place thus associated, e.g. **Tepee Flat** MT. Also as **Tipi, Teepee**.

Tepehemus Brook NJ Algonquian, meaning uncertain. Probably a variant of **Topanemus**.

Tequesquite Mexican-Spanish 'saltpeter, alkali,' e.g. the slough in CA and the creek in TX.

Tercio Co Spanish 'third,' for the third coal mine opened in the vicinity. See **Segundo**.

Terlingua TX Early spellings Terlingo and Tasolingo indicate an Indian origin, though language and meaning remain uncertain; the modern name represents a Spanish shaping by folk-etymology.

Terminous CA A misspelling for **Terminus**, so called because being originally at the end of a road.

Termo CA A railroad name, said to be so called because the manager liked names ending in 'o'; a connection with 'terminus' is possible.

Ternero, Ternera Spanish 'calf.'

Terra Latin or Italian 'land,' though in some instances a careless or ignorant substitution for Spanish **Tierra**. Properly a generic, but functioning as part of a double specific in habitation-names. **Terra Ceia** FL: probably for Spanish **Tierra Ceja**, which could be taken to mean 'land-summit.' **Terra Coupee** IN: for French *terre coupée*, 'land-cut-off,' presumably by the action of a river. See **Coupe. Terra Cotta** NC: from a local plant for the manufacture of terra cotta.

Terrapin For the variety of turtle so called, common on water features in the SE.

Terra Tomah Mountain CO From syllables in a chant of the Coahuila Indians of CA, which had been incorporated into an American college song. In 1914 a climber, seeing a lake, cried out this word in its usual form Terratoma as an expression of delight, and the name was later adopted by the Colorado Geographic Board in slightly changed form. Its literal meaning, if any, is unknown.

Terre French 'land, earth,' e.g. **Terrebonne,** 'good land'; **Terre Haute,** 'high land,' i.e. land out of danger of floods; **Terre aux Boeufs** LA: 'land of cattle,' because some of the first cattle in the colony were brought there. In LA the name **Terrebonne** is from a family of late 18-century landowners, whose name appears as Terrebonne or Derbonne.

Terrero NM A misspelling of Spanish *terrero,* 'mound, slag-dump,' with reference here to the dump from a mine.

Terreton ID For M. M. Terry, first storekeeper, shift of spelling not explained.

Terrible, Terror These rare names probably arose from incidents, e.g. **Terrible Creek** CO, SC. See **Dread, Fear.**

Tescott KS Coined from the name of T. E. Scott, owner of the townsite.

Teshekpak, Teshekpuk AK Eskimo 'big-lake.'

Tesla CA For Nicola Tesla, famous inventor, the town being planned as a generating point for electric power.

Tesnatee Gap GA Cherokee 'turkey' (?).

Tesnus TX **Sunset** spelled backward.

Tespusquet CA A misspelling for an earlier **Tespusque,** which itself may be for Mexican-Spanish **Tepuzque,** 'copper.'

Tesson, Bayou LA From the French family-name, for an early resident.

Testament Creek OR Because close to **Bible Creek.**

Tesuque NM Spanish rendering of Indian (Tewa) 'spotted dry place,' with reference to the partially dry bed of a stream. But the present Indians pronounce **Tesuque Pueblo** as if it were 'cottonwood tree place,' having been influenced by the Spanish rendering into a kind of folk-etymology.

Tete French 'head,' e.g. **Bayou Tete L'Ours,** literally, 'bayou-head-the-bear,' but significance uncertain. **La Tete** WA, for a peak.

Tetilla Spanish, diminutive of *teta,* 'breast, nipple.'

Tetlin AK From the name of an Indian chief (Tetling) whose village was in this vicinity in 1885.

Teton 1) French 'breast,' applied to eminences in the same way as its English equivalent, e.g. **Grand Teton** WY, **The Tetons** WY, and often transferred to habitations and to other features, e.g. **Teton River** MT, which is named for a peak near its source. 2) As a tribal name it has exercised little influence, but has produced **Teton County** WY.

Tetonia ID A Latinized formation from **Teton.**

Tetonkaha Lake SD Siouan 'the standing [site?] of the big lodging house,' originating in the 19th century when a band of Sioux were caught in a blizzard and survived by putting their tents together.

Tetracoccus Peak CA From the occurrence of a plant (spurge) known scientifically as *Tetracoccus ilicifolius.*

Teutonia Peak CA A Latinized form, the equivalent of Germany, originally the name of a mine located by a German prospector.

Tewa From the Indian tribal name. In AZ the name is from a settlement made by a group of this tribe who had migrated from NM.

Tewaukon Lake ND Algonquian, for *-waukon,* see **Wakan;** the rest is uncertain.

Tewksbury MA From the town in England (1734).

Texarkana A coined name for a town lying in TX and AR, and close to LA.

Texas Some Indians known as Teyas are recorded in Spanish records as early as 1541. This was actually a word meaning 'friends,' but was taken by the Spaniards to be a tribal name. Other Indians in 1683 told the Spaniards of what the latter thought to be 'the great kingdom of Texas.' Although this kingdom was chiefly fictional, it led to the name being established for the large area lying vaguely east of NM. It became an official designation under Spain and Mexico and was passed on to the republic and to the state.

Texhoma OK, TX Border names from the abbreviaions of the two states.

Texico In NM it is a border-name for Texas and New Mexico. In IL it is probably from Texas and Mexico, but the cause of naming is unknown.

Texline TX Because being near the boundary line with NM.

Texola OK A town on the Texas border, from Texas and a favorite suffix, somewhat sugestive of Oklahoma.

Texon TX From Texon Oil and Land Co., which operated in the area.

Thalia TX Greek 'abundance,' a commendatory. It is the name of a muse, but local tradition favors the other origin.

Thames River CT After the naming of **New London** the stream here was so called by counterpart.

Thatchtop CO In the autumn the grass on the roof-shaped mountain turns brown and resembles thatch.

The In place-name usage in the U.S. the definite article indicates pre-eminence or even uniqueness in the feature thus named, e.g. **The Jump Off** SD. The uniqueness is usually very local, e.g. two places in SD bear the above name. Such usage can exist only with rare terms. Ordinary speech is full of such expressions as **The River,** but the speaker knows that the stream has another name. When only one feature of the class exists in an area, or when one such feature is of dominating importance, its specific may be almost forgotten, e.g. the use of **The Peninsula** around San Francisco, where most people do not even know any other name. The use of **The Palisades** in New York is somewhat comparable, but most people would be able to add **of the Hudson.** With habitation-names **The** adds a slight commendatory quality by its implication of pre-eminence, e.g. **The Cedars** CA. The coupling is often with a term of commendatory quality in itself, e.g. **The Glen.** Whether or not **The** is to be used with a full (specific-generic) place-name is a matter of considerable complication, and is briefly discussed in the *Introduction*.

Thebes In all cases probably from the ancient Egyptian, rather than the Greek, city; e.g. in IL it is in the district called **Egypt.**

Thendara NY By error for **Kendaia,** thus written by a diarist of 1779.

Thermal CA From the adjective meaning 'hot,' an apt descriptive during most of the year.

Thermopolis WY Greek 'hot-city,' from the presence of hot springs.

Thermopylae From the narrow passageway in Greece, made famous by the ancient battle, e.g. the gap in MA.

Thicket In TX the town was named for being in what is known as **The Big Thicket. Thicketty** SC: from the presence of a thicket.

Thief The valley in OR got its name in 1864 when a mule-stealer was hanged there. **Thief River** MN: an Ojibway name was loosely thus translated; the original meaning was 'stolen land,' or something of that general nature.

Thimble A descriptive, because of shape, on mountains and hills, e.g. **Thimble Mountain** AZ.

Thing Valley CA For Damon Thing, rancher, ca. 1870.

Third See **First.**

Thirsty An incident-name (cf. **Hungry**) in which the feelings of the namers are transferred to the natural feature, e.g. **Thirsty Canyon** NV.

Thla-Pac-Hatchee Creek FL Muskogean 'fallen-enemy-stream.'

Thlauhatke Hills FL Probably Muskogean (Creek) 'mountain-white.'

Thompson From the personal name. The peak (Alpine Co., CA) is for John A. (Snowshoe) Thompson, famous early skier.

Thonotosassa FL Seminole 'flint-is-there.'

Thor From the ancient Germanic god, usually in a region of Scandinavian settlement.

Thoreau NM Locally believed to be named for H. D. Thoreau, author of *Walden,* though it was named in the later 19th century when his fame was not wide-spread.

Thorn, Thorny Often for the personal name, especially in such compounds as **Thornton, Thornhill,** etc. It may also be from growth of thorns or thornberries, e.g. **Thornhollow** OR. **Thorntown** IN: a translation of the name of a local Indian village, 'thorn-place.'

Thorofare, Thoroughfare A quasi-generic, by association applied as a specific because of a much-traveled route, e.g. **Thoroughfare Gap** VA. The term may have arisen because of an Indian trail or a game-trail, e.g. the gap in WV, because of game, and **Thorofare River** AK, because a heavy migration of caribou follows it. Along the Atlantic coast, especially in NJ, it is a generic for a channel offering a passageway for boats, and thus a specific by association, e.g. **Thorofare Island** NJ.

Thoroughfare See **Thorofare.**

Thor's Hammer AZ See **Brahma.**

Thousand Descriptive, indicating some number too large to be readily counted, e.g. **Thousand Cave Mountain** AZ, **Thousand Islands** NY, **Thousand Oaks** CA.

Three See **One. Threebuck Creek** OR: named by hunter who killed three bucks in 1878. **Three Fingered Jack** OR: the peak has three main rock spires.

Thrift, Thrifty Occasionally used for habitations as a commendatory; in TX, from a bank.

Through Because a feature extends through something, usually a range of hills, e.g. **Through Creek** AK, **Through Glacier** AK. Also **Thru Creek** AK.

Thru See **Through.**

Thrumcap Applied to various islands off the coast of ME; also as **The Thrumcap.** It was the knitted cap formerly worn by sailors, with a tuft at the top, to which a small conical island could be well compared, especially if it had a few trees at its top.

Thumb A descriptive for an up-standing rock or peak which can be compared to a thumb, e.g. **The Thumb** CA, **Thumb Butte** AZ.

Thunder Being an occasional phenomenon, thunder has usually been given as a name because the namer there experienced a thunderstorm, e.g. **Thunder Rock** OR, named because R. S. Shelley was caught there in a violent storm in 1906. Variants are **Thundershower Run** PA, **Thunderstruck Run** WV, **The Thunderer** (mountain, WY). **Thunderbolt** GA: the Indians, according to tradition, told that a thunderbolt struck the ground here.

Thyatira MS From the Biblical city.

Ti OK From the reversed initials of Indian Territory.

Tiadaghton PA Iroquoian, the name of a chief (?).

Tia Juana River CA An Indian name, recorded as **Tiajuan** (1833), but transformed even in Spanish times by folk-etymology to 'Aunt Jane.'

Tibbie In NV it is Northern Paiute, probably 'pinyon.' In the SE, see **Oktibbeha.**

Tibio Spanish 'tepid.'

Tiburon CA Spanish 'shark,' originally applied to the point in San Francisco Bay, apparently for the rather unusual sighting of a shark there.

Ticetonyk Mountain NY Algonquian 'ladder' (?), because of a steep slope.

Tichigan WI Algonquian, probably with *gan* 'lake,' and the rest uncertain.

Tick From the wood tick, e.g. a canyon in CA.

Tickabum AL Probably Choctaw; meaning uncertain.

Tickfaw River LA, MS Choctaw, probably 'pine-rest,' presumably for a resting place on a trail.

Ticklenaked Pond VT Uncertain, but probably by folk-etymology from some Indian name.

Ticonderoga NY Iroquoian, probably 'between-lakes.'

Tiderishi Creek OH Algonquian, meaning uncertain.

Tie 1) From association with railroad ties, e.g. **Tie Canyon** CA, **Tie Plant** AR, MS, **Tie Siding** WY. 2) **Tie Down Hill** WY: from the nickname of 'Tie Down' Brown, early cattleman and alleged rustler.

Tienda Spanish 'shop, store,' e.g. the diminutive **Tienditas** NM.

Tienekill NJ Dutch 'garden(?)-stream.'

Tierken Kill NY Probably from a Dutch dialectal nickname, and meaning 'Dirck's stream.'

Tierra Spanish 'land, earth,' a generic, but frozen in some habitation-names, e.g. **Tierra Buena** CA, **Tierra Amarilla**

NM. As a compound it occurs as a specific in **Tierra Redonda Mountain** CA.

Tifallili Creek AL Choctaw 'tree-tall.'

Tiffin Regularly from the personal name, e.g. in OH for Edward Tiffin, first governor.

Tiger, Tyger 1) From the personal name, or from one thus spelled by folk-etymology, e.g. **Tyger River** SC. Probably from an early trader, Tygert. **Tiger** OK: for Moty Tiger, Creek chief. 2) From an animal, the term often being applied to the panther, especially in the SE. It was, however, not thus limited, and **Tiger Lake** occurs twice in MN. Other cats, even the small wildcat, might be thus termed. In TX, and possibly in other states, the term may apply to the jaguar, called *tigre,* by the Mexicans. 3) From a striped appearance, e.g. probably **Tiger Glacier** AK. 4) As a vague commendatory term of pre-eminence, thus sometimes applied to mines and thus to **Tiger** AZ. **Tigerton** WI: from nearby **Tiger River.** **Tiger** GA: from an Indian chief, Tiger Tail.

Tight Eye See **Ty Ty.**

Tigiwon CO Ute 'friends'; a name applied to a campground in the early 20th century for commendatory reasons.

Tigre French, Spanish, 'tiger,' e.g. **Bayou Tigre** LA. See **Tiger.**

Tiguex Indian, probably connected with the tribal name Tewa, applied first by Coronado (1540) to a region in present NM. The name spread and on later maps was placed so as to cover a large area. It finally, however, disappeared.

Tijeras CO Spanish 'scissors,' because in some primitive adobe huts the roof poles projected in a V-shape, suggestive of scissors.

Tik Hill AK Eskimo 'rectum,' an apt name for a cinder cone.

Tilden From a personal name, especially for Samuel J. Tilden, the defeated candidate in the presidential campaign of 1876, who was honored by a township in PA, by towns in NB and TX, etc.

Tilicum Creek OR Chinook jargon, 'people, friend,' but reason for application unknown.

Tillamook OR An Indian tribal name.

Tillitoba MS Choctaw 'rock-gray' (?).

Tiltill CA Probably from an Indian village, meaning unknown.

Timbalier Island LA Probably for a soldier of the 18th century, Sylvain Filiosa, who was nicknamed Timbalier, 'kettle-drummer,' because of a notable feat of once scaring off Indians by a performance on that instrument.

Timber In OR the name refers to a heavy forest in a generally forested area, but in some regions the name springs from a grove of trees in an unforested area, thus, **Timber Lake, Jackson Co., MN. Timber Lake, Dewey Co., SD,** is in such treeless country that one theory of the origin of the name is that it arises from the presence of a single tree. **Timberlake** NC: from the name of the first postmaster. **Timber Cove** CA: because a shipping point for lumber in the 1850's.

Timbuctoo From the city in Africa, given to a mining camp in CA in the 1850's, perhaps merely because of the current liking for unusual names, but more likely for some association with a Negro miner. In early times it was occasionally used, e.g. in PA, for the Negro district of a town.

Timnath CO Named, ca. 1900, for the city mentioned in the Book of Judges.

Timothy From the personal name; more commonly, e.g. in MN, from the grass.

Timpahute Range NV From an Indian tribal name, but derived from a local spring and literally, 'rock-spring-people.'

Timpanogos, Mount UT Ute 'rock-river,' transferred to the mountain.

Timpas CO First applied to the creek, probably from Ute *timpa,* 'rock,' with an English 's' added.

Timpie UT From Goshiute 'rock.'

Timucua From the Indian tribal name.

Tin The presence of tin ore has resulted in a few names, e.g. **Tin Mountain CA, Tin Mine Canyon CA.** The omnipresent item of American life has resulted in **Tin Can Branch KY. Tin Cup Gulch CA:** from an early story that enough gold was found to fill a tin cup. **Tin Pan Canyon MN:** from a pan nailed to a post to serve as a sign post. **Tin Cup CO:** according to local story, because the first gold found in the area was in the gravel scooped up with a tin cup.

Tinaja Spanish 'large jar,' but in America commonly for a small natural or semi-artificial waterhole, and roughly the equivalent of 'tanque,' or 'tank.' By association it occurs as a specific, e.g. **Tinaja Peak AZ.**

Tinemaha, Mount CA From the name of a legendary Paiute chief.

Tinicum PA Algonquian, meaning uncertain.

Tinker From the personal name. **Tinkers Defeat Knob** CA: because J. A. Tinker, a teamster, came to grief here with an eight-horse team.

Tinmouth VT For Teignmouth, the town in England (?).

Tinnie NM For the daughter of the first postmaster, otherwise unidentified.

Tintah MN Siouan 'prairie,' also a tribal name, related to the tribal name **Teton.**

Tintic UT For a Goshiute of the 19th century, described as 'a renegade chief.'

Tinto Spanish 'dyed, dark-colored,' but **Rio Tinto** NV is from the famous mining district in Spain, applied as a commendatory.

Tioga Iroquoian 'at-(the)-forks,' applied especially to a site in northern PA. The name was used for counties in NY and PA. Being an Indian name that was both short and euphonious, it spread to many states, usually without thought of its meaning, though the erroneous translation 'gateway' may have lead to some namings. The pass in CA took its name from a mine (ca. 1878).

Tioughnioga River NY Iroquoian 'forks-(of)-river,' with reference to the dividing of the stream at **Chenango Forks.**

Tiogue Lake RI Algonquian, probably 'low-land.'

Tip In OK from the nickname of W. H. H. Mayes, prominent resident. Usually in combination to indicate height, e.g. **Tip Top Mountain CA. Tip Over Creek** NB: probably because a wagon tipped over.

Tipi See **Tepee.**

Tippah MS Muskogean, from the personal name of an Indian woman, wife of a chief (?).

Tippecanoe In IN it is by partial folk-etymology from the Potawatomi name for the river, recorded as *ki-tap-i-kon,* 'buffalo-fish.' In OH the town was named in 1840 at the time of the 'Tippecanoe and Tyler too' campaign.

Tippecansett Pond RI Algonquian 'big-clearing (field)-at.' See **Pequonnock.**

Tipperary From the town in Ireland, usually named because of Irish immigrants.

Tippipah NV Shoshone, with -*pah,* 'water, spring,' and *tippi,* 'pinyon.'

Tippo MS See **Oktibbeha.**

Tipsoo Peak OR Chinook jargon, 'grass.'

Tipton From the personal name, e.g. in OK for J. T. Tipton, a local railroad conductor; in MO for W. Tipton Seely, who laid the town out.

Tirbircio CO Probably from the Spanish personal name, Tiburcio; not further identified.

Tire Creek OR In early times a wagon wheel broke here, and its iron tire was left in the creek bed.

Tiro See **Tyro.**

Tirzah SC From a church that had been named after the Biblical city.

Tisbury MA From a place in England (ca. 1671).

Tishabee AL From a local Indian chief of the early 19th century.

Tishamingo MS, OK For a well-known Chickasaw chief of the early 19th century.

Tiskilwa IL Probably Algonquian, meaning uncertain.

Tisquaquin Pond MA From the name of a chief (also recorded as Watuspaquin) killed in King Philip's War, 1676.

Tit, Teat A common colloquial term for a formation resembling a woman's breast, e.g. **Tit Butte.** It often approaches being a generic as in **The Tit.** In the interests of decorum it sometimes takes the spelling **Teat,** but it is more commonly banished entirely from official usage by the substitution of another name. An exception is **Two Teats** CA, which is, however, a misnomer, the name now being applied to only one of the two features which gave rise to the original name. **Wildhorse Tit** CO is probably to distinguish one eminence from another, and not to indicate the anatomy of a wild horse. The term has also arisen from a colloquial shortening of French *petite,* e.g. **Tit Chateau LA, Tit Blis LA.** See **Nipple.**

Titanic OK Named (1916) for the liner Titanic which had sunk in 1912.

Titanothere Canyon CA Because fossil bones of that animal were found there.

Tite Isle LA From the colloquial pronunciation of **Petite,** 'little.'

Titi See **Ty Ty.**

Titicus CT, NY Algonquian (Mahican) 'without-trees-at.'

Titicut, Titticut MA, RI Algonquian (Narragansett, Wampanoag) 'main-river-at.'

Titie Creek FL Probably a variant of **Ty Ty.**

Titonka IA Probably Siouan, meaning uncertain.

Tittabawassee River MI Algonquian, probably 'following-shore-river,' because of its course.

Tiverton RI From a village in England (1694).

Tivoli From the town in Italy.

Tiz Nat Zin NM Navajo 'rock-black.'

Tlingit AK From the Indian tribal name.

TNT Creek OR A pack mule once bucked off a box of explosive at this point; further details unrecorded.

Toad Since the toad is not a much-regarded creature, names are rare, **Toad Lake** MN is a translation from the Ojibway. **Toad-a-Loop:** See **Tour-de-Loup.**

Toadlena NM From Navajo 'water bubbling up,' because of springs, apparently changed by folk-etymology in the American period.

Toana The spring in UT, from Goshiute, is probably 'pipe-camping-place,' from some association with a tobacco pipe.

Toandos Peninsula WA From the tribal name, commonly spelled Twana (?).

Toano VA Named ca. 1885, by a railroad; probably transferred from NV. See **Toana.**

Tobacco Like other important field crops it has not yielded numerous names, but occurs as a commendatory to indicate a place for tobacco growing, e.g. **Tobacco Run** MD, **Tobaccoport** TN, **Tobaccoville** NC, VA. **Port Tobacco** MD: by folk-etymology from Algonquian, recorded (1608) as Potapaco, the name of an Indian village or tribe. **Tobacco Root Range** MT: from a wild plant, used by frontiersmen in a pinch for tobacco.

Tobannee Creek GA Muskogean 'trees-crossed,' probably with reference to a place where trees had been laid prostrate by a hurricane.

Tobar NV For Capt. Tobar, a miner, not further identified.

Tobe Canyon CO For Tobe Benevides, early settler.

Tobegewock Pond ME Algonquian 'rapid-current-at-outlet.'

Tobenanee Creek GA Muskogean (Creek), probably 'tree-crooked,' for a landmark tree.

Tobesofkee Creek GA With Muskogean (Creek) *sofkee,* 'deep,' and the rest uncertain.

Toboso OH From *Don Quixote,* the knight's lady-love being Dulcinea del Toboso.

Tobucksy OK From the Choctaw *to-baksi,* 'coal.'

Toby Normally this would be for the colloquial abbreviation of the personal name Tobias, but in PA it has arisen by folk-etymology from the Algonquian *tobi,* 'alder-tree,' e.g. **Toby's Creek, Tobyhanna,** 'alder-stream.' In other areas of Algonquian background similar origin is to be expected, expecially with unusual spellings, e.g. **Tobey Pond** CT.

Tobytubbee Creek MS From the personal name of an Indian.

Tocaluma CA A Spanish rendering of a Miwok name for a village, with -*luma* probably an adaptation of the Miwok for 'place.'

Toccoa GA Cherokee 'Tagwa-place,' for the tribe generally known as Catawba.

Toccopola MS Choctaw, meaning uncertain.

Tocito NM A Spanish adaptation of Navajo 'hot water.'

Tocoi FL From a Timucuan village, meaning uncertain.

Tocosos River WA Indian, meaning unknown.

Todo Spanish 'all,' usually as **Todos Santos,** 'all-saints,' for a place named by association with All Saints' Day, e.g. the creek in TX.

Todokozh Navajo 'bitter water,' a repeated name for springs in AZ.

Toe River NC Indian, probably Cherkee, a shortening of *estatoe,* meaning uncertain; this term may also have yielded **Tar River.**

Togue ME Algonquian 'trout,' with reference to the large lake trout, in contrast to the brook trout. See **Schoodic, Tuladi.**

Togus ME Algonquian 'streamlet.'

Togwotee Pass WY Named (1873) by Capt. William A. Jones for his Indian guide.

Tohadistoa Spring AZ Navajo 'water-bubbling is heard.'

Tohakum Peak NV Northern Paiute, probably 'lookout-mountain.'

Tohatchi NM Navajo, with *to-* 'water,' and the rest uncertain.

Tohickon Creek PA Algonquian (Delaware), with *-on,* 'stream,' and the rest disputed, but probably 'driftwood.'

Tohopeka AL Muskogean (Creek) 'fort.'

Tohopekaliga Lake FL Seminole 'fort-site.'

Tohopkee FL Seminole 'fort.'

Toivola MI, MN Finnish, the equivalent of 'hopeville,' named by Finnish immigrants.

Toiyabe Mountains NV Shoshone, a general word for mountain, recorded (1859) as *toy-ap.*

Tok AK Athapascan, shortening of an earlier **Tokai,** which with *-na* yields **Tokaina,** q.v.

Tokaina Creek AK Athapascan, with *-na,* 'river,' and the rest, 'trees' (?). See **Tokositna.**

Toke Point WA From the name of an Indian chief of the mid-19th century.

Token Creek WI By folk-etymology from Tokaunee, the name of a local chief of the early 19th century.

Toketee Falls OR Chinook jargon, 'pretty.'

Tokewanna Peak UT Ute, meaning uncertain.

Tokio From the city in Japan, in most cases, apparently given for 'no particular reason,' but the name was most popular in the period of pro-Japanese feeling after the Russo-Japanese War. In spite of some adverse feeling against the name in the Second World War, it has generally survived. In OK from the Kiowa *towkyowy,* 'long building,' a descriptive of the building which housed the post office. In ND the name was probably suggested by a local Indian (Siouan?) word, 'gift,' of similar sound.

Tokopah Valley CA Probably Shoshonean, with *-pah,* 'water, spring,' and the whole, perhaps, 'high spring'.

Tokositna River AK Athapascan 'tree-less-river.'

Tolani Lakes AZ Navajo 'water-many bodies,' i.e. the equivalent of 'many lakes.'

Tolawanda Creek OH Algonquian, meaning uncertain.

Tolay Creek CA Recorded in 1823 as the name of a local Indian chief.

Toledo From the city of Spain. The name was given to the city OH in 1833 at a time when Spanish names were popular; probably also, the euphony of the name had its appeal; the specific reason is unknown. In OR the name was given by a settler who was homesick for OH. **Toledo Creek** NM: from the family name of local Spanish settlers.

Tolenas Creek CA From the name of an Indian tribe or village.

Tolicha Peak NV Shoshone, with *to-* probably 'black' and the rest uncertain.

Toll 1) From the personal name, e.g. **Mount Toll** CO for R. W. Toll, superintendent of Rocky Mountain N.P. from 1921 to 1929. 2) From the taking of toll on a road or bridge, e.g. **Toll Gate** WV, **Tollhouse** CA, **Tollgate Canyon** CO.

Tolland In CT (1715) from a town in England. In CO, for this same town but also for Mrs. C. H. Toll, local landowner.

Toller Bogue Creek AL Choctaw 'palmetto-stream,' shaped by partial folk-etymology to the appearance of an English name.

Tolo OR For **Yolo** CA, but the T was substituted by mistake.

Tolona MO Probably a coined name. See **Tolono.**

Tolono IL A land commissioner, J. B. Calhoun, coined the name by making a euphonious combination of vowels and consonants.

Tolstoi Russian 'broad.' The name has been preserved in AK, apparently on the assumption that it was the personal name, as in some instances it may be, since one man of that name was prominent in Russian affairs in America.

Tolstoy SD For Count Leo Tolstoi, the Russian novelist, named 1907.

Tolt River WA Indian, meaning unknown.

Toltec Like the Aztecs, the Toltecs were never historical residents of the

United States, and the name was applied from literary sources. In CO it was first a mine name.

Tolu KY From a trade name of some bitters which were sold in the local store.

Toluca From the city in Mexico, aided by its euphonic quality.

Tom Usually from a personal name, e.g. **Toms River** NJ for William Tom who explored it in 1673. Often from the common abbreviation of **Thomas,** e.g. **Tom's Run** WV for Thomas Smith, landowner. The name being highly common, the family name is often included, e.g. **Tom Dye Rock** CA for a fugitive who hid here in 1878. **Mount Tom** CA is for Thomas Clark, who first ascended it. In New England **Mount Tom** is so repetitive (4 in CT) that it is to be considered a name by folk-etymology from some Indian term meaning 'hill, mountain,' perhaps **Montop.**

Tomah In WI, from the name of a famous Menominee chief of the early 19th century. In ME the island is probably for a chief so named, and the stream may also be so derived, but is uncertain.

Tomahawk The Algonquian word for war hatchet was taken into English. Though the name may occasionally be descriptive for shape, the usual cause was an incident involving a tomahawk, though the stories have usually been forgotten. **Tomahawk Island** OR: on Nov. 4, 1805 Capt. William Clark's tomahawk pipe was stolen here by Indians, and the name was given in consequence.

Tomakokin Creek MD Algonquian, probably 'beaver-place.'

Tomales CA A Spanish-formed plural from the name of the Tamal tribe.

Tomaquag Brook RI Algonquian, containing *maquag*, 'beaver.'

Tomball TX For Tom Ball, a local lawyer.

Tombicon Creek PA Algonquian (Delaware) 'apple-creek,' because of wild fruit growing there.

Tombigbee River AL Choctaw 'coffinmakers,' so named from a class of tribesmen who cleaned the bones of the dead and placed them in boxes; for some unknown reason the river came to be associated with these persons; the name itself has been shaped by folk-etymology to the semblance of an English name, the original form having been *itombi-ikbi.*

Tombstone 1) From a rock formation resembling a tombstone, e.g. the lakes in OR and the rocks in AK. 2) From the presence of an actual tombstone from early times, e.g. the prairie in OR. 3) **Tombstone** AZ: from a mine, which was so named because the prediction was made that because of the threat from Apaches the mine would only serve as the miner's tombstone.

Tomhannock Creek ME, NY Algonquian, probably 'overflowed.'

Tomhegan Pond ME Algonquian 'ax.'

Tomichi CO Ute, originally a name for the stream, with *to-* probably 'black,' and the rest uncertain.

Tomka Valley CA Shoshonean, meaning uncertain, but having to do with eating.

Tomlike Mountain OR From an Indian personal name.

Tom Mix Wash AZ In 1940 the actor Tom Mix was killed here in an automobile accident.

Tommy Squatter VT By folk-etymology from Algonquian, *temi-isquattan,* 'deepwater-here,' a name for fishing spots in deep water. See **Temiscouata.**

Tomoka Creek FL From the Indian tribal name, commonly spelled **Timucua.**

Tomotley SC Of Yemassee origin, locally said to mean 'Hewed Timber Town.' **Tomotla** NC is apparently the same word.

Tonahutu Creek CO Arapaho 'bigmeadows,' adopted by the Colorado Geographic Board, ca. 1915.

Tonasket Creek WA From the name of an Indian chief.

Tonawanda NY Iroquoian 'swift-water.'

Tone For Wolfe Tone, Irish patriot, named by immigrants from Ireland.

Tonemy Hill ME A shortening of Algonquian *wannametoname,* 'vermilion (red earth)-it-produces.'

Tonganoxie KS For a Delaware chief who lived at the site in the mid-19th century.

Tongass AK Most of the names are from the tribe, but the tribe itself was named from the island, which is probably of Tlingit origin, but of uncertain meaning.

Tongue The point in OR was so named in 1792 because it was a projecting tongue of land. The river in WY is recorded by Lewis and Clark (1806) as the translation of an Indian name, without reason given for the naming.

Tonica IL Probably a shortening from the **Pecatonica River,** which is in the same area.

Tonk An abbreviation of the Indian tribal name **Tonkawa,** e.g. three creeks in TX.

Tonka Bay MN Shortened from **Minnetonka.**

Tonkawa From the Indian tribal name.

Tono WA A coined railroad name, locally believed to be an abbreviation of 'ton of coal.'

Tonoloway MD Algonquian 'long-tail,' i.e. 'panther' (?).

Tonopah NV Shoshone (or Northern Paiute), probably 'greasewood-spring.'

Tonti For Henri de Tonti who was La Salle's lieutenant in the exploration during the 17th century, e.g. **Tontitown** AR.

Tonto Spanish 'fool,' but the name-cluster in AZ arises from the tribal name of the so-called Tonto Apaches.

Tontogany OH For a local Indian chief, whose name was first applied to the creek.

Tony Cany Creek MS Choctaw, probably 'post-standing,' for some kind of marker.

Tony Creek OR For a pony so called.

Tonytank Creek MD Shifted by folk-etymology from an Indian tribal name, recorded in the 17th century as Tanxsnitania, Tundotenake.

Tooele Valley UT Probably Gosiute, for a species of flag growing in the vicinity of the springs.

Toolik River AK Eskimo 'loon.'

Toomsuba Creek AL, MS Choctaw, for a bird called pigeon hawk or blue darter.

Toonerville CO For the fictional town, a type of a small out-of-the-way place, popularized in a series of cartoons by Fontaine Fox in the 20th century.

Tooth Scarcely occurring, but an example is **The Tooth** WA, a descriptive. **Tooth of Time Mountain** NM: a fanciful naming based descriptively, because of a rock formation resembling a tooth. **Bears Tooth Peak** WY: because of a rock formation.

Top A generic, occasionally as a specific, more commonly as a compound, e.g. **Fir Top Mountain.**

Topanemus, Lake NJ Algonquian, meaning uncertain. Probably a variant of **Tepehemus.**

Topanga CA Shoshonean, with the locative ending -nga, otherwise uncertain.

Topatopa CA Chumash, the name of a village.

Topawa AZ Papago 'it is a bean,' named from a game.

Topaz From the occurrence of the semi-precious stone, e.g. the lake CA, NV.

Topeka Siouan (Kansa) 'potato-good-place,' with reference, in KS (the original naming) to a place where Indians could dig some wild tuber, which was usually rendered in English as **Potato.**

Tophet The Biblical place, vaguely associated in later thought with hell, has occasionally been used euphemistically to replace that name, e.g. **Tophet Brook** MA. **Tophet Springs** CA are hot springs in the volcanic region of Mt. Lassen. **Tophet** WV: the name was **Hill Top,** but this was apparently mistaken for **Hell Top** by the Post Office Dept., which made the substitution.

Topinabee MI For a Potawatomi chief of the early 19th century.

Topisaw MS Choctaw, meaning uncertain.

Topo Spanish 'mole, gopher.'

Topock CA Mohave 'bridge,' with reference to the railroad bridge across the Colorado River.

Toponas CO Ute, meaning uncertain.

Toppenish WA An Indian tribal name.

Topsail NC Originally applied to the inlet, a maritime name, but reference uncertain.

Topsfield In MA (1650) an alternate spelling, after the pronunciation, from Toppesfield in England. In ME the first settlers were from the town in MA (1838).

Topsham From the town in England; in ME (1764) because many of the original settlers had come from there.

Toquerville UT From a Paiute chief, whose name is recorded (1854) as Toker.

Toquima Range NV From an Indian tribal name.

Toquop Wash NV Southern Paiute, with reference to a plant used by the Indians for tobacco.

Toreva AZ Hopi 'crooked,' from the course of some water draining from a spring.

Torn, The NJ From Dutch *toren,* 'tower,' a descriptive of the rock formation.

Tornado Not a colloquial term, and rare in place-names, but, for instance, **Tornado Peak** AZ indicates a place where a tornado was once experienced.

Tornillo TX From the presence of the screw-pod mesquite, commonly so called.

Toro Spanish 'bull.'

Toronto From the city in Canada; commonly, e.g. OH, SD, named by an immigrant.

Toroweap Valley AZ Paiute 'gully, wash.'

Torquemada, Mount CA Probably for Juan de Torquemada, whose work contains an account of the Viscaíno expedition which named Santa Catalina Island, on which the mountain stands.

Torrey From the personal name, especially for John Torrey, 19th-century botanist, e.g. **Torrey Pines Park** CA, **Torreys Peak** CO. Cf. **Greys Peak.**

Torrington In CT from an English town-name (1732).

Tortilla The name of the characteristic Mexican corn cake has been given, informally, as **Tortilla Flat** to indicate a Mexican district. In AZ the term was suggested by some flattened rocks.

Tortu(e) French 'crooked,' e.g. **Bayou Tortu** LA, but possibly from **Tortue,** q.v.

Tortue French 'turtle, tortoise.' See **Tortu.**

Tortuga Spanish 'turtle,' e.g. **The Tortugas Islands** FL, often known as **The Dry Tortugas,** which were named by Ponce (1513) because his men took many turtles there; this is the oldest European place-name in the country, except for **Florida.**   *

Tosi Peak WY From the name of a Shoshone medicine-man of the late 19th century.

Tot Mountain OR Chinook jargon, 'uncle.' So named to harmonize with such other names of the vicinity as **Three Sisters** and **The Husband.**

Totagaticonce The same as **Totagatic** (q.v.), with an ending of uncertain significance.

Total Wreck AZ Named in 1877 when a prospector described the place as being a 'total wreck,' because of the way the rocks were piled there in confusion.

Totaro VA From the Indian tribal name, commonly recorded as Tutelo.

Tote Road Lake MT By association with such a road, i.e. an improvised rather than made road.

Toto Creek GA From *toter,* i.e. 'carrier,' this being from Child Toter, the translation of the name of a Cherokee Indian.

Totogatic River WI Algonquian (Ojibway) 'boggy-river.'

Totoket Mountain CT Algonquian 'great-(tidal)-stream-on.'

Totopitk AZ Papago 'crooked.'

Totopotomoy Creek VA For an Indian chief who was an ally of the English in the mid-17th century.

Totosahatchee Creek FL Seminole 'chicken-stream.'

Totowa NJ Algonquian, meaning uncertain.

Toucha AL From an Indian tribal name, in commoner form appearing as Tawasa.

Touchet WA From an original **Toosha** (1843), it has been reshaped as if a French word. It is of Indian origin; meaning, unknown.

Touchmenot Mountain NY Probably an incident name; one of the very rare examples of a phrasal specific in English.

Tougaloo MS Apparently a variant of **Tugaloo** transferred into Choctaw territory by Americans.

Toughkenamon PA Probably Algonquian, by local story, 'firebrand,' because of a hill used for signaling.

Touharna Creek NY Iroquoian, meaning uncertain.

Toulbah Mountains ME Algonquian 'turtle.'

Toulon IL, KS From the city of France.

Tour-de-Loup MO French 'track-of-wolf,' probably in the sense of an established track or circuit followed by a wolf or wolves. **Toad-a-Loop** MO represents a re-working by folk-etymology of a form using *à* instead of *de*.

Toutle WA From an Indian tribal name.

Towaco NJ Probably a tribal name.

Towaliga River GA Muskogean (Creek) probably 'scalp-place,' being a spot where war parties halted to dry scalps.

Towanda PA Algonquian (Delaware) 'burial-ground,' from a site used by the Nanticoke tribe.

Towantic CT Algonquian 'ford-(across)-river.'

Towaoc CO Ute 'all-right,' given as a commendatory when the Utes settled here on their reservation.

Tower Often from the personal name, e.g. **Tower City** PA for Charlemagne Tower, the founder. **Tower** MN, ND honor this same man, and also his son of the same name, both of whom were involved with the iron-ore industry in MN. Natural features are descriptively named for a formation resembling a tower, e.g. **Tower Mountain** CO. In Grand Canyon N.P. **Tower** has become a quasi-generic, e.g. **Tower of Ra. Tower Mountain** OR: because it has a triangulation tower on it.

Toweset Neck RI Algonquian, meaning uncertain.

Towhead According to Mark Twain, 'A towhead is a sand-bar that has cottonwoods on it as thick as harrow-teeth'; hence, e.g. **Towhead Island** KY.

Town Usually from the personal name, often **Towne** or **Town(e)s**, e.g. **Townville** PA for Noah Town, the founder in 1824. So also in compounds, especially **Towns(h)end, Towner**, e.g. **Townsend** MA for Charles Townshend (1674–1738), English politician. **Port Townsend** WA: named by George Vancouver (1792) for the then Marquis of Townshend, later simplified in spelling.

Townsend, Townshend See **Town.**

Towsissimock Creek PA Algonquian (Delaware) 'cattle-pasture,' a term developed after contact had been established with Europeans.

Toxaway NC, SC From the name of an ancient Cherokee town, meaning unknown.

Toyah TX Locally believed to be an Indian word, 'much water.'

Toyon From the occurrence of the bush sometimes known as California holly.

Trabuco Spanish 'blunderbuss, musket.' The creek in CA was named because in the Portolá expedition of 1769 one of the soldiers lost his weapon here.

Trace The term was used as the equivalent of 'trail,' especially in the SE, and to name a natural feature distinguished by having a trace near it. WV has **Trace Branch** (4), **Trace Creek** (3), **Trace Fork** (12), **Trace Run** (2), **Trace Fork Branch,** and the village **Trace. Trace Lake** MN: from a personal name.

Tractor Creek AK Named, ca. 1960, because 'Sam Snyder got his caterpillar tractor stuck.'

Trade Though 'trade,' 'trader,' and 'trading post' were common frontier terms, only a few permanent names have resulted, e.g. **Trading Post** KS. **Tradesville** SC was an early trading post.

Trafalgar IN For the British sea victory over the French.

Tragedy Springs CA In 1848 three men were killed by Indians here.

Trail The earlier term was 'path' or 'trace,' and 'trail' did not come into use until about 1800. The names are therefore mostly Western, or late and conscious namings in the East. On features the name indicates a place distinguished by having a trail, either of Indian origin or more recent, e.g. **Trail Creek** OR, for an Indian trail. **Trail City** SD: a watering place on a cattle trail.

Train See **Au Train.**

Traitors Cove AK Named (1793) by George Vancouver, because he considered that the local Indians had acted treacherously.

Tralee WV From the town in Ireland.

Trammel KY Probably from the personal name.

Trampa Spanish 'trap.' **Las Trampas** CA: so called because traps for elk were set in this vicinity. Various names in NM are probably mementoes of the beaver-trapping period.

Tranca Spanish 'bar, barrier.'

Tranquil(l)ity A rare commendatory for habitation-names.

Tranquillon Mountain CA Indian, of unknown meaning.

Transquaking River ME Shifted by folk-etymology from Algonquian 'cedar-swamp-there-is' (?).

Transylvania Latin 'beyond-forest,' probably given for literal meaning and not as an echo of the European region so named. The county in NC (created 1861) echoes the land-development company formed in 1775, which name must have been commendatory, since the region in TN thus denoted was still in the forest region, not beyond it.

Trap, Trapper The names are chiefly memorials of the fur-trading era, indicating a place associated by incident or otherwise with a trapper or trap, e.g. the finding of a trap. Trap may also have a reverse meaning, e.g. **The Trap** PA, a blind channel in the Ohio River, where a boat could be trapped. **Man Trap Lake** MN: it offered many hazards to the canoe-voyager attempting to pass through it because of peninsulas and swamps. **Trap Corral Canyon** NM: wild horses were captured here, because the canyon could be closed off after they had been driven in.

Trappe From a French family name, in PA from one who was an early hunter, otherwise unidentified.

Travelair Creek AK Named in about 1950 by geologists because a Travelair plane crashed and burned here.

Travellers Rest KY, SC From an inn name.

Traverse 1) A French term, 'crossing, shortcut,' used for a river crossing, e.g. **Traverse Township** MN, especially for a place at which men in canoes could cut across the mouth of a bay, as in **Grand Traverse Bay** MI. Thus also **Little Traverse Bay,** and **Traverse City** MI. 2) A technical surveyors' term; thus, **Traverse Ridge** OR. **Traverse Lake** SD; MN; hence, the county, MN: because the direction of its axis is at right angle to the trend of other lakes nearby; the French here translated an earlier Siouan term, meaning 'lake-lying-crosswise.'

Travertine From incrustation with the mineral so called, e.g. the rock and spring in CA.

Treasure Stories of buried treasure are legion, and a few have resulted in names, e.g. **Treasure Cove** OR. The popularity of R. L. Stevenson's novel has made the coupling **Treasure Island** likely; in CA, it was bestowed upon an artificial island which was made in 1939. **Treasure Lake** CA: so named because the lake was stocked with golden trout. **Treasureton** ID: for William Treasure, first postmaster. **Treasure Peak** NV: rich mines were discovered in this area in 1868.

Treaty Hill NV Because of an agreement once made here between rival Indian tribes.

Trechado NM A misspelling for **Techado,** the name of the nearby mesa.

Tred Avon River MD Probably from a family name, the early spellings (1672) being Tredaven and Tredhaven; since other streams in the area bore the names of English rivers (**Wye, Severn**), this name was apparently supposed to be another such, and the meaningless first element was separated in the spelling.

Tredyffrin PA From Welsh *tre yr dyffrin,* 'town in the valley,' named by immigrants, ca. 1700.

Trego Probably in most instances from a family name; in WI, coined by E. E. Woodman, a railroad man, from Latin *tres,* 'three,' and English 'go,' with the *s* dropped for euphony, to indicate a junction where the railroad went off in three directions.

Trelipe MN A variation of tullibee, a common fish of the region. So also. **Tulaby Lake** MN.

Trembleau Point NY See **Trempealeau.**

Trementina Spanish 'turpentine,' the creek in NM probably being named because turpentine was once made from the pines there.

Tremont The adaptation of an Italian 'three mounts,' probably originating with **Tremont Street** in **Boston,** which was itself sometimes in the early years called **Tri-Mountain,** descriptively. In ME, named (1848) because of three notable peaks.

Trempealeau From the French *trempe a l'eau,* in American-French used as a quasi-generic applied to high islands with the sense 'stands-in-the-water,' often with **Montagne Qui** ('mountain-which'); it has survived for an island WI in the Mississippi River, and thence has spread by transfer to a town, county, and river. **Trembleau Point** NY is a

variant, in a region of French background.

Trench Generally from a personal name. But the canyon in CA is so called from being deep and narrow.

Trent River NC Probably from the river of that name in England.

Trenton The original name, in NJ, dates from the early 18th century, having been at first Trent's Town, and being named by the founder (William Trent) for himself. It is one of the earliest examples of a developer naming a place after himself. Later foundations are generally echoings of this one, often with the further association of the Revolutionary battle. In TX the name was given just because a man liked the sound of it.

Tres Spanish 'three.' **Tres Palacios Bay** TX is from the family name, probably for J. F. Trespalacios, prominently associated with Texas, ca. 1820.

Trevlac IN This is Calvert spelled backwards, for an early landowner; differentiation was necessary because the name had already been used in the state.

Triadelphia WV Formed on the model of Philadelphia, from the Greek *tri*- (three), and *adelphos* (brother), though the men thus honored are uncertain. They were either three brothers or three men whose friendship was likened to that of brothers.

Triangle The hill in Oregon is descriptively named, because of the appearance from the east. The town ID is from a brand name.

Tribes Hill NY By association with Indian tribes, the hill having been used by the Iroquois for ceremonial purposes.

Tribune KS From the *New York Tribune,* whose editor, Horace Greeley, was a supporter of westward expansion, nearby towns being **Horace** and **Greeley.**

Trickham TX According to local story, it originated, ca. 1870, because the storekeeper here liked to play tricks on people.

Tridell UT Because of its situation at the joining of three small mountain valleys (dells).

Trident Peak NV From its three-cusped summit.

Trigger Mountain TX A rock formation resembles an inverted trigger.

Trigo Spanish 'wheat,' also used for various wild grasses, from one of which **Trigo Mountains** AZ take their name.

Trigo Canyon NM: because wheat was once cultivated near its mouth.

Trilby From the novel by George Du Maurier, e.g. in FL, where the town took the name shortly after the publication of the book in 1894.

Trimmed Tree Summit CO An obvious landmark-name, for a tree partially stripped of branches either artificially or by natural process.

Trimountain MI From three nearby peaks.

Trinchera Spanish 'trench,' the creek in NM being so called because of the trench-like canyon.

Trinidad Spanish 'trinity,' usually with reference to the Holy Trinity, as in CO. The bay in CA was named by the explorer Bruno de Hezeta because he took possession on Trinity Sunday, 1775. In TX the name is a translation from Trinity (for the river) which was itself earlier translated from the Spanish.

Trinity Usually of religious significance, i.e. for the Holy Trinity or by association with Trinity Sunday. The river in TX was named, in Spanish, by the De Leon-Massanet expedition on Friday, May 19, 1690, close to Trinity Sunday. The river in CA was so called in 1845 because it was supposed to flow into **Trinidad Bay.**

Triple Divide Peak MT From its summit the waters flow to the Pacific, the

Arctic, and the Atlantic. So also in WY, where the waters flow to the Missouri, Snake, and Green rivers.

Triplet Indicating a combination of three, e.g. **The Triplets, Mount Triplet** AZ.

Tripod Mountain NM Three low peaks are compared to the points on which a tripod might be placed.

Tripoli The name of several ancient cities, but in the U.S. usually with reference to the North African city, known because of the Tripolitan War (1801–1805), e.g. **New Tripoli** PA, named in 1816.

Triumph In IL, because the community had 'triumphed' in getting a post office established. In ID, from a mine. In MN from the Triumph Creamery Company.

Triunfo Spanish 'triumph.' In CA the valley was named by Father Crespi in 1770, in Spanish, for 'The triumph of the sweet name of Jesus,' but it soon suffered abbreviation.

Trojan Like **Troy** the name has a commendatory value. In SD it was a mine name, passed on to a town. **Trojan Peak** CA: from the nickname of the athletic teams of the University of Southern California, who were thus honored in 1954.

Tromperas Creek NM Probably a misspelling for Spanish *tramperas,* 'trappers.'

Trop Clair, Bayou LA French 'too clear,' but probably from a personal name such as Trosclair.

Tropic UT Because the first settlers found the climate very warm as compared with that to which they were accustomed.

Trotwood OH Named by the postmaster, a Dickensian, for Betsey Trotwood of *David Copperfield,* ca. 1854.

Trouble, Troublesome In NB, the name arose because someone had trouble getting a name for the new post office, and so suggested **Trouble. Troublesome** on natural features is widespread geographically, but not common, and is limited almost entirely to creeks, except as it has spread by transfer. Apparently the name was established in an early period as being a suitable one for a creek, and so went west with the settlers. It is an obvious incident name. In MO the name was given in 1874 because a particular creek was likely to give trouble by quickly flooding after a shower.

Trough Either from a natural formation resembling a trough or from a feature marked by a watering trough constructed for stock. **Trough Shoals** SC: the place is known from a rock formation like a trough.

Trout Rarely from the personal name, e.g. **Trout's Hill** WV, named for Abraham Trout, early settler. Common with water features to indicate the presence of trout which for some reason are to be considered remarkable for this particular stream or lake. Because of commendatory suggestions, the name has been easily transferred to habitations. **Troutdale** OR: from a small valley where a pond had been stocked with trout.

Troy Usually from the Iliad. **Troy** NY: the name was approved at a meeting of residents on Jan. 5, 1789, an important date, since it may be said to have inaugurated the fashion for classical names. The previous name had been **Vanderheyden's Ferry**, but this probably seemed too long and too specifically Dutch. The positive reasons for the choice of **Troy** are not known, but there seems to be no doubt that it was selected because of the Homeric city. It is also short, easy to pronounce and spell, and vaguely commendatory. It now stands on about 30 habitations. **Troy** WV: one of the few named for a person, in this case, the first postmaster. **Troy** NC: for J. B. Troy, state legislator.

Trucha Spanish 'trout.'

Truckee The Stevens Party in 1844 was aided by an Indian whose name they took to be Truckee; they gave this name to the river that he showed to them.

Truckland SC From fine 'truck' crops grown here.

True Blue Creek SC So called from a plantation which was itself named for the production of indigo, the blue dye stuff.

True Love Creek SC Named because of being crooked, on the analogy that the course of true love never runs straight. The name was similarly given by the VA-NC surveyors in 1728.

Truro In MA from the town in England (1707). In OH some of the early settlers had come from Truro in Nova Scotia.

Truth A rare commendatory, e.g. **Truthville** N.Y. **Truth or Consequences** NM: a name adopted by vote of the citizens of the town (formerly **Hot Springs**) on Mar. 31, 1950, the action being an acceptance of the offer of the master of ceremonies of a well-known radio show, viz. that, if the name of the program was adopted by the town, he would hold a yearly fiesta, with the program presented in the town. The town thus attained much publicity. The distinctiveness of the new name, in comparison with the triteness of the old one, was a factor in the selection. Because of length, however, the name in speech has been shortened to **T. or C.,** and on road signs is commonly **Truth or C.** In a second election (Jan. 13, 1964) the town voted to retain the new name. **Truth** NC: by local story, suggested in jest by a member of the selecting committee, and then adopted seriously.

Tryon From the personal name, especially for William Tryon, Colonial governor of NC and later of NY; he became unpopular during the Revolution and his name was removed from counties in those colonies, but it remained on **Tryon Peak** NC from which it was transferred later to the town of **Tryon.**

Tsala Apopka Lake FL Seminole 'trout-eating-place.' See **Charley Apopka.**

Tsegi Canyon AZ Navajo 'canyon.'

Tsina River AK Athapascan 'crooked-river.'

Tualatin OR Indian, meaning uncertain.

Tuana See **Toana.**

Tuba In AZ it is from the American pronunciation of the name of a local Indian chief. **Tuba Canyon** CA is from Indian (probably Southern Paiute) for pinyon nut.

Tubac AZ From a local Indian language but meaning unknown, except that -*bac* may be 'house, ruin.'

Tubby Creek AL Choctaw 'killer,' probably part of a personal name, since this was a common element in such names.

Tucannon Creek WA Indian (Nez Percé) 'bread-root-creek.'

Tucapau SC From the Tucapau Mill; probably of Indian origin.

Tuck Mountain ME Although it is an English family name, it may here be an adaptation from an Algonquian form, e.g. **Tug.**

Tuckabatchie AL From the name of an early Creek town, literal meaning uncertain, but probably containing *hachi*, 'stream.'

Tuckahoe A repeated name in the Middle Atlantic region, apparently of Algonquian origin (in the VA area (?), meaning 'round,' and applied to a root or tuber used for food. The word passed into English, probably in the 17th century, and most of the namings would seem to be English rather than Indian, and to be from the acquired meaning, i.e. a backwoods or folksy person, such as might live on wild tubers, but with a humorous more than a derogatory suggestion.

Tuckaseeking Lake GA Transformed by folk-etymology from some Indian name; connected (?) with Muskogean (Creek) *tukashina*, 'peppergrass.'

Tuckaseigee, Tuckasegee NC, TN The name of two ancient Cherokee towns, meaning uncertain. **Tuckaseeking Lake** GA is probably the same, though a con-

nection is possible with Muskogean (Creek) *tukshina*, 'peppergrass.'

Tuckernut Island MA Shaped by folk-etymology from an Algonquian term, meaning uncertain.

Tucki Mountain CA Shoshonean 'sheep,' presumably for wild sheep.

Tuckkipping Lake WI Probably Algonquian 'spring, well.'

Tucquan Creek PA Algonquian (Delaware) 'crooked-stream.'

Tucson AZ Papago 'black base,' with reference to a nearby mountain. The name was used in connection with a mission settlement at some distance from the original location, and eventually replaced the saint's name entirely.

Tucumcari NM The original naming was probably for the mountain. The name is Indian (Comanche), apparently from a word 'to lie in wait,' and thus the equivalent of 'ambush,' or 'lookout,' as a place frequented by war parties.

Tufit Mountain OR From an Indian personal name.

Tug Several mountains in New England are so called, probably from some Algonquian term; 'tree' has been suggested, but such a term is not distinctive in a region where forest was almost universal. **Tug Fork** WV: probably a shortening from the Cherokee term, 'fork of a stream.' See **Tugaloo.** See also **Taconic,** with which the term in NE may be connected.

Tugaloo River GA, SC From Cherokee *tugulu*, 'fork of a stream.' See **Tug.**

Tujunga CA Southern Paiute, probably 'mountain range.'

Tukuhnikivatz, Mount UT Ute, 'where-the-sun-shines-longest' (?), perhaps because of being the highest point in the region.

Tukwila WA When the post office was being named in 1905, a suggestion was *tuck-will-la*, 'land of hazelnuts,' supposedly Indian, but language not stated.

Tula MS Choctaw, probably 'peak.'

Tulaby See **Trelipe.**

Tuladi Brook ME Algonquian 'lake-trout,' appearing in another form as **Togue.**

Tulainyo Lake CA Coined in 1917 to indicate a location near the boundary between Tulare and Inyo counties.

Tulalip Bay WA Indian (language uncertain), locally taken to be 'bay-with-small-mouth.'

Tulamdie River ME Algonquian 'canoe-sandbar.'

Tulvanic Stream ME Algonquian, for a place where canoes were made.

Tule American-Spanish 'reed, bullrush,' e.g. **Tule Lake** CA, OR, **Tule Tank** AZ. It is especially common as a place-name in CA. A place where reeds grow should be **Tular,** but a new American term was derived from the plural **Tulares,** apparently by merely dropping the final letter; hence, **Tulare Lake,** as well as town, county, etc. CA. The diminutive appears in **Tularcitos Creek** CA.

Tuledad CA For Tuledad Matney, early settler.

Tuleta TX For Tuleta Chittum, daughter of an early settler.

Tulia TX An adaptation from **Tule Canyon,** probably an attempt to make it seem more suitable for a habitation by means of a Latin form.

Tulip From the tulip tree (yellow poplar), chiefly growing in the SE; hence habitation-names, e.g. in AR, GA.

Tullahassee OK A variant of **Tallahassee.**

Tullahoma TN Muskogean, with *-homa,* 'red,' and *tulla-* probably 'town.'

Tullifinney River SC An adaptation of an Indian word more commonly spelled Tulufina, the name of a town or tribe of unexplained meaning.

Tully In NY it is the Anglicized form for Tullius, for the Roman orator, Marcus Tullius Cicero, a part of the classical naming of 1790. The name-cluster in MA presumably springs from the family name, well-known in New England.

Tulpehauken Brook NJ Algonquian 'turtle-land,' but possibly with reference to a tribe that bore the turtle as its totem. Also, the creek in PA.

Tulsa The name of an ancient town of the Creeks (meaning, 'town-old') together with ashes from it were taken in the forced migration of the tribe, and the name was then bestowed upon the place of settlement in OK. In AL the name was given to a railroad station as **Tulse.** In TX, for differentiation, a pseudo-Spanish diminutive was formed, thus yielding **Tulsita.**

Tulsita See **Tulsa.**

Tulucay Creek CA Pomo 'red,' but probably a tribal name.

Tuluga River AK Eskimo 'raven.'

Tumacacori AZ Pima 'curved peak.'

Tumalo Creek OR Indian, of uncertain meaning.

Tumalt Creek OR From an Indian personal name.

Tumanoc Hill AZ Papago 'horned-toad hill.'

Tumble, Tumbling Occasionally applied to stream-features because of rapidly-descending water, e.g. **Tumble Creek** AK, **Tumbling Shoals** AR. **Tumbling** is associated with man-made dams which are said to tumble when they overflow, e.g. **Tumbling Shoals** SC.

Tumco CA Coined in 1910 from The United Mines Company.

Tumkeehatchee Creek AL Muskogean (Creek) 'sounding-stream,' apparently named for its noise.

Tumtum Chinook jargon, 'heart,' and also applied because of the sound of falling water; thus, **Tumtum Creek** OR, and probably **Tumtum** WA. See **Tumwater.**

Tumwater WA A shortening of **Tumtum,** with an American suffix, thus referring to falling water, especially to its sound.

Tuna From the fruit of the prickly pear, e.g. **Tuna** TX and **Tunitas Creek** CA, the latter a Spanish diminutive plural.

Tunbridge NH Viscount Tunbridge and Baron Enfield and Colchester, political figure under George II, loomed so large in the mind of Gov. Benning Wentworth that he was honored with **Tunbridge** (VT, 1761), **Enfield** (NH, 1761), and **Colchester** (VT, 1763).

Tune Creek CA Wintu 'the end.'

Tungsten Because of the occurrence of ores of the metal, e.g. the hills in CA.

Tunica LA, MS From the name of an Indian tribe.

Tunipus RI Algonquian probably 'turtle.'

Tunitas Creek CA Diminutive plural of Spanish *tuna,* for the fruit of a kind of cactus.

Tunitcha Mountains AZ Navajo 'big water.'

Tunk ME On various features, it is originally a stream-name, probably a shortening from Algonquian *k't-hunk,* 'big (principal)-stream.'

Tunkahoosen Brook CT Algonquian, meaning uncertain.

Tunkhanne Creek PA Algonquian (Delaware) 'little-stream.' **Tunkhannock Creek** PA, 'little-stream-at.'

Tunnel Usually for a railroad tunnel, and in this case commonly a habitation-name, e.g. **Tunnelton, Tunnel City.** But **Tunnel Hill** exists in several states, both for hill and town. A natural tunnel may also produce the name, e.g. **Tunnel Point** OR.

Tunxis CT Algonquian, probably, 'little river.'

Tuolumne CA From an Indian tribal name, *umne* meaning 'people,' in the Yokuts and Miwok languages.

Tupelo An occasional name in the SE from the black gum tree, so called.

Tuquas Creek KS For a Sac chief, signer of a treaty in 1842.

Turd A derogatory, not preserved in official use; a hill thus named is recorded in VA (1777).

Turin From the city of Italy.

Turkey The native wild turkey ranged over most of the U.S. A valuable source of food for the pioneers, but not so common as to be commonplace, it has given rise to the names of many natural features, e.g. creek, ridge, run. Some of these have become habitation-names by transfer, but because of a humorous suggestion the name has not had commendatory value. **Turkey Isle** VA: given in 1607, because there 'were many turkeys,' this is the first English place-name for a native animal or bird. **Turkey Springs** AZ W. C. Barnes and another man camped here in May, 1886, when the springs were nameless. Having found some turkey eggs, they gave the name. Barnes later became the author of *Arizona Place-Names* and recorded the story.

Turlock CA An adaptation of Turlough, from a place in Ireland.

Turn In NM the name was given because of a sharp turn in the highway; in CA, because of a sharp turn in a railroad. **Turnback Creek** CA: because the stream seems to turn back upon itself. **Turntable Creek** CA: because on an old road there was a place at this point where wagons could turn. **Turnpike** indicates the former existence of a road so known. **Turnout** indicates a place on a narrow road where one wagon could pull out to let another one pass. **Turner** and **Turnbull** are personal names.

Turn Island WA: it marks a turn in the channel. **Turnagain Arm** AK:

named (1778) by James Cook because from it he could penetrate no further inland. **Turnaround Creek** AK: named (1965) by D. J. Orth because on two occasions his airplane had to turn back at this point because of bad weather (and so recorded in his *Dict. of Alaska Place Names*). **Turnback River** MO: locally believed to be because some early travelers turned back at this point. Derivation by folk-etymology from a personal name, e.g. Dornback, is possible **Turnabout**, e.g. in AL, probably indicates a place where a vehicle could be turned around on a primitive road. **Turnover Creek** TX: A wagon was once upset at this stream.

Turnip The cultivation of turnips has yielded a few names, e.g. **Turnippatch Hollow** KY, **Turnip Patch Point** DE.

Turnwall Creek AR By folk-etymology from French *terre noire*, 'earth-black,' because the stream flows through an area of black soil. On many modern maps it appears as **Terre Noire.**

Turon KS Previously **Turin**, it was changed to avoid duplication within the same state.

Turquoise After the semi-precious stone, common in the SW, e.g. **Turquoise Canyon** AZ.

Turret A name given to various mountains which display turret-like formations.

Turtle Though widespread, the lowly turtle was of minimal interest and unlikely to cause exciting incidents. Still a fair number of such names occur on features, usually with creek, lake, etc. A number of these are translations from various Indian languages, since among some tribes the turtle was a totem-animal. Turtles are likely to be especially abundant in certain streams, and some names have thus originated, e.g. **Turtle River** SD. The shape of the shell has produced some names, even in regions not noted for turtles, e.g. **Turtle Back Mountain** AZ. **Turtle Lake** MI: because the shape of the lake is taken to resemble the outline of a turtle.

Turube Pond ME Algonquian 'turtle.'

Turup Creek CA Yurok, the name of an Indian village, meaning unknown.

Tusa Spanish 'prairie dog,' e.g. **Las Tusas** NM.

Tuscahoma AL Choctaw 'warrior-red.'

Tuscalameta Creek MS Choctaw 'warrior-young.'

Tuscaloosa AL Choctaw 'warrior-black,' but probably from the name of a chief recorded in an account of De Soto's expedition (1540) as Tascaluça. In translation we have the **Black Warrior River.**

Tuscan Springs CA The water contains borax, and the name was given with reference to Tuscany in Italy, where borax has been produced.

Tuscarawas OH A variant (plural) of the tribal name more commonly spelled **Tuscarora.**

Tuscarora From the Indian tribal name.

Tuscola Probably a coinage by **Schoolcraft** (q.v.) who gave its meaning once as 'warrior prairie,' and once as 'level lands,' for the county in MI (1845). The first part suggests Muskogean *tushka*, 'warrior.' The last part is probably a mere favorite euphonic ending which appears elsewhere (see **Ola**). The name has spread to several states. In MS there is the possibility that it is based upon a genuine Muskogean name.

Tuscumbia AL Named (1822) for a famous Cherokee chief.

Tushka OK Muskogean 'warrior.'

Tushkahoma OK Choctaw 'warrior-red.'

Tuskatucket River RI Algonquian, 'ford-(in)-(tidal)-river-at.'

Tuskegee AL, OK From an Indian tribal name.

Tuskoona AL Probably from an Indian personal name.

Tusquitee NC Cherokee, meaning uncertain.

Tussahaw Creek GA Probably Muskogean with *tussa-,* 'warrior,' and the rest uncertain.

Tussocky A rare descriptive for association with tussocky land, e.g. the creek in VA.

Tustenugee FL For a leading Seminole chief of the early 19th century.

Tutuilla Creek OR Probably an Indian word, 'thornbush.'

Tututni Pass OR An Indian tribal name.

Tuxedo NY Algonquian, with first syllable 'round' and the whole probably 'round-foot-he-has' i.e. 'wolf.'

Tuzigoot AZ The name for the National Monument is of recent selection, being Apache 'crooked water,' from a nearby lake.

Tuye Navajo 'scant water,' a repeated name for springs in AZ.

TV Mountain MT Because, in 1954, a television transmitting tower was built on its summit.

Twain-Harte CA Named in 1924 after Mark Twain and Bret Harte, both associated with the region in which the town is situated. Since Twain bitterly hated Harte, the coupling is ironic.

Twenty Mule Team Canyon CA To commemorate the wagons hauled by twenty mules which transported borax in this region before the building of the railroad.

Twilight Rare; usually for some incident occurring at twilight (cf. **Midnight**). But **Twilight Creek** OR is for W. H. Twilight, early landowner.

Twin The commonest term (see also **Brother, Sister**) to describe a pair of similar features. It is uncommon with features such as streams, which fail to present a precise entity, and is commonest with lakes, buttes, springs, and islands. **Twin Lake** appears about 35 times in MN. It occurs in habitation-names, most often by transfer, but also in such a case as **Twin City** GA; But **Twinsburg** OH was named for twin brothers. GA has about 200 such names, both for natural features and for habitations, including **Twin Bridges,** which presents the rather unusual case of such a name arising from a work of man. **Twin Sisters** occurs, e.g. CO, NB, WA. The two features collectively known as **Twin** are regularly distinguished by a second specific, e.g. **Upper Twin Lake. Twin Springs,** Coconino Co., AZ: the springs are not at all alike, but take the name because they are the only two springs near together in a generally dry country. **Twin Falls** ID is by transfer from the nearby falls of **Snake River.**

Twisp River WA Indian (originally **Twitsp**); meaning unknown.

Two See **One. Twodot** MT: a brand name.

Tyaskin Creek MD Algonquian 'bridge,' probably with reference to a stream-obstruction for catching fish; it was also a tribal name.

Tybo NV Probably Shoshone, meaning uncertain.

Tyee Chinook jargon, 'chief,' e.g. **Tyee Peak** WA.

Tyende Creek AZ Navajo 'where they fell into a pit,' i.e. referring to a bog where animals were mired.

Tyewhoppety See **Tywappity.**

Tygh Valley OR From an Indian tribal name.

Tyhee ID For a local Bannock chief.

Tyler From the personal name, especially for John Tyler, president. His lack of popularity, however, is reflected in a general paucity of places named for him. A county was named for him in VA (now, in WV) in regard for his service as governor (1825–1827). A town and county in TX are a token of his signing the bill that admitted TX as a state.

Tymochtee OH Algonquian 'around-plains (?), first applied to the stream.

Tyndall From the personal name. Both the mountain in CA and the glacier in AK are for John Tyndall (1820–1893), English scientist, student of glaciers.

Tyre From the ancient Mediterranean city.

Tyringham An English village-name, but in MA (1762) probably in honor of a family with which Governor Francis Bernard was connected.

Tyro, Tiro Latin 'recruit, beginner,' the name probably being given as suitable for a new settlement.

Tyrone From the county in Ireland.

Ty Ty GA Also, on various natural features in the SE as **Tye Tye, Titi, Tyty,** and **Tight Eye:** from the name of a bush, also called 'ironwood,' 'leatherwood,' etc., which forms dense thickets and is therefore likely to be memorable enough to produce a name.

Tywappity, Tywhapita, Tyewhoppety KY, MO An apparent variant, **Zewapeta,** appears in MO. Probably Algonquian (Shawnee), 'place of no return.' The examples in MO may be transfers from KY by Americans in the early 19th century. The name was probably first applied to natural features, e.g. streams, but has since been transferred to two habitations in KY. The complete significance of the term is doubtful, but it may be somewhat like the English **Halfway,** marking a place from which it is as easy to go forward as to return.

Tywhapita See **Tywappity.**

U

Ubehebe CA Probably Shoshonean, meaning unknown.

Ubet An alternate spelling for **You Bet,** e.g. in MT.

Uceta FL Named, ca. 1926, for a Timucuan chief whose name is recorded in a Spanish context of 1539.

Uchee AL, GA From the Indian tribal name, often appearing as Yuchi.

Ucon ID Chosen (ca. 1912) when a post office was to be esablished, possibly from **Yukon,** which was well known at the time because of the gold rush.

Ucross WY A brand name.

U Fish Creek CA By folk-etymology from an Indian (Karok) term, probably meaning 'salt.'

Ugly Very rare, but apparently as a descriptive in **Ugly Creek** KY.

Uharie NC Cherokee, meaning uncertain.

Uhupat Oidak AZ Papago 'cat's-claw field.'

Uinkarets Mountains AZ Paiute 'pineland,' but more directly from an Indian tribal name.

Uinta From an Indian tribal name.

Ukolnoi Island AK Russian 'stone-coal.'

Ukonom CA Various features are from an Indian (Karok) term, meaning 'fine sand' (?).

Ulatis CA An Indian (Patwin) tribal name.

Ulcohachee Creek GA Muskogean (Creek) 'pawpaw-stream.'

Uleta FL Originally **Snake Creek,** it took a new name from one used in a motion picture of the South Seas which was filmed in the vicinity.

Ullin In ND the name as **Glen Ullin** is drawn from Thomas Campbell's poem *Lord Ullin's Daughter,* the coupling with 'glen' doubtless being suggested by the occurrence of that word in the poem. In IL it is from one of the heroes in the Ossianic poems.

Ulm From the city in Germany, usually bestowed by German immigrants, as with **New Ulm** MN.

Ulmsaket Ponds ME Algonquian 'where-points-meet,' descriptive of a chain of ponds. **Umsaskis Lake** ME is a variant.

Ulster From the district in Ireland, usually named by immigrants. The county in NY took its name after the English occupation from the Irish title of the Duke of York, the proprietor.

Ulysses In NY for the hero of the *Odyssey,* given as part of the classical naming of 1790. It may be from a personal name, e.g. in KS and NB, and where it is from the first name of President Grant.

Umak AK Aleut, meaning uncertain.

Umapine OR For an Indian so named.

Umatilla OR, WA Of Indian origin, meaning unknown, the tribe taking its name late and from the river.

Umbagog Lake ME, NH Algonquian 'clear-lake.'

Umbazookskus Stream ME Algonquian 'clear-gravelly-outlet.'

Umnak Island AK Aleut, by the present Aleuts believed to be from the word for 'fish-line,' such lines having been made from a single miraculous tree that once grew on the now treeless island.

Umpewage CT Algonquian 'beyond the bend.'

Umpog Creek CT Algonquian, meaning uncertain.

Umpqua OR An Indian name for a locality, of unknown meaning, later applied to the river and the tribe.

Umsaskis See **Ulmsaket.**

Umtanum WA Indian, meaning unknown, recorded in 1853 as *em-te-num.*

Umunhum, Mount CA Indian (Costanoan), probably 'resting-place of the hummingbird,' that bird being important in local mythology.

Unadilla NY Iroquoian 'place-of-meeting.'

Unagua Spring CO Mexican-Spanish *un agua,* 'a (one)-spring.'

Unaka Mountains TN Cherokee 'white,' because of formations of white rock.

Unalakleet AK Eskimo, meaning uncertain.

Unalaska AK Aleut, the name for the island having developed similarly to that of **Alaska** itself, i.e. meaning 'mainland,' because it is a large island; *un-* is probably a demonstrative, 'this,' to distinguish the island from the farther-away mainland.

Unami From the Indian tribal name.

Unawatti Creek GA Cherokee 'shallow.'

Unaweep CO Ute 'red-canyon.'

Uncanoomuc Mountain NH Algonquian, probably 'end-fishing-place-at.'

Uncanoonucks Mountain NH Algonquian 'breast, nipple.'

Uncas In CT the name (**Uncasville**) is for the famous Mohegan chief of the 17th century. In OK the name is probably for the character in J. F. Cooper's *Last of the Mohicans.*

Uncatena Island MA Algonquian 'end-hill,' but reference uncertain.

Unchechewhaton MA Algonquian 'end-(of)-wooded-hill.'

Uncle Sam Frequently given for patriotic reasons, especially to mines; hence, the mountain in CA.

Uncompahgre CO Ute 'red-water-canyon.'

Undine The area in MN was so named in 1841, because its river and lakes seemed a fitting habitat for the heroine of Friedrich Fouqué's tale. The name, as that of a water sprite, has similarly been applied elsewhere to lakes, and by transfer to other feaures, e.g. in MA.

Uneeda WV Named ca. 1898 for Uneeda Biscuit, but doubtless with a pun such as 'You need a post office.'

Ungalooroosh Creek CO Ute, with *unga-,* 'red,' and the rest uncertain.

Ungatoowis Creek CO Ute, with *unga-,* 'red,' and the rest uncertain.

Unicoi TN Cherokee 'white,' cf. **Unaka.**

Unicorn Peak CA A formation resembles, in a somewhat fanciful way, the horn of a unicorn.

Unimak Island AK Aleut, meaning uncertain, but *un-* may be 'this,' as in nearby **Unalaska.**

Union The most popular of the abstract terms in U.S. place-naming. As applied to natural features it indicates some kind of physical union. **Union Lake,** Polk Co., MN consists of three wide parts united by straits. **Union** is more commonly a habitation-name. It is sometimes physical, as when **Unionville** OH symbolizes a settlement on a county line. **Uniontown** OR: from the name of a now-defunct packing company. The name sometimes arises from a union church, i.e. a church arising from the uniting of two congregations, e.g. **Union Ridge** NC, **Union Co.** SC, **Union Grove** MN. Typically, however, the name has arisen from political and patriotic motives, e.g. the union of England and Scotland in 1707 probably produced **Union Street** in Boston. The union of the colonies in the Revolutionary period was commemorated in names such as **Uniontown** PA. From 1830 the political atmosphere was such as to make citizens highly conscious of the idea of union, and many names resulted. The culmination was in the Civil War period, though only in the northern and western states, where such names became so numerous as to call for many differentiations, e.g. **Union Center, Uniontown, Unionville. Union Center** SD: so named because it was one of the first (1927) enterprises of the Farmers' Union.

Unita(h) CO, UT From an Indian tribal name.

United States of America The term **United Colonies** or **United Colonies of America** was used when the colonies first began to unite against England. With independence the term **States** was naturally substituted for **Colonies.** Though **United States of America** was probably used in speech at an earlier date, its first recorded usage is in connection with the discussions leading to the Declaration of Independence in 1776. The term is such a matter-of-fact one that it partakes of the nature of a description rather than of a name. **United States of North America** was used in the first treaty with France, but this more accurate term did not establish itself. If any individual is to be credited with the name, it would have to be the author of the Declaration of Independence, Thomas Jefferson. The theory that Thomas Paine invented the name is unwarranted. Paine did not use it in his writings until 1777, and seems actually to have preferred **America.**

Unity A commendatory, in ME arising from 'unison in political sentiment.'

University A commendatory name for habitations, because of suggestions of culture and education, usually near a university. **University Hills** NB: so named because the University of NB once conducted paleontological studies there.

Unkpapa For the Indian tribal name, more commonly occurring as **Hunkpapa.**

Unnamed Wash CA Probably a notation on the sketch map was inadvertently, or even purposefully, transformed into a name.

Unquamonk Hill MA Algonquian 'end-place,' possibly in the sense of 'boundary.'

Upalco UT Coined from the Uintah Power and Light Company.

Upatoi Creek GA Muskogean (Creek) 'last, farthest off' (?).

Upham ND Named (1908) for Dr. Warren Upham, eminent geologist and author of *Minnesota Geographic Names.* The peak in MT also is named for him.

Upland Usually, e.g. in CA, from being at a high location. In PA the name probably arose from the Swedish Upland (a province from which some of the Swedes had come), and may even go back to a Dutch fortification Opt-landt ('on the land') of 1631.

Upper The usual relative descriptive to indicate a place as being higher than (upstream from) another place. It is used with many names both for natural features and for habitations, being common as a second specific, i.e. to distinguish **Upper Bear Lake** from **Lower Bear Lake,** or **Bear Lake.** It may even occur as a triple specific as in **Upper Little Swatara Creek** PA.

Upquedopscook River ME Algonquian 'top-(of)-rocks-at.'

Upsala MN From an older spelling of Uppsala, the city in Sweden.

Upset Rapids AZ From an overturned boat suffered by an expedition mapping the Grand Canyon in 1923.

Upsilon, Lake ND From its Y-shape, named from the Greek letter more commonly spelled Ypsilon.

Upton In MA (1735) probably from one of the numerous villages of the name in England. Though it is a personal name, many instances, e.g. in NC, UT, arise as descriptives for a site higher up than some other site.

Urania LA From one of the muses of Greek mythology, but reason for application uncertain.

Uravan CO Named (1936) from the metals uranium and vanadium, which were being mined here.

Urbana The Latin adjective 'urban,' used in the feminine to give the preferred ending -a, a commendatory.

Urbanna VA A variant of **Urbana,** probably influenced by nearby names such as **Fluvanna, Rivanna.**

Urbita Springs CA Coined ca. 1895 from Latin *urbs,* 'city,' and Spanish *-ita,* the diminutive ending; hence, 'little city,' the habitation-name being transferred to the springs, and then dying out.

Ursina PA The form represents the Latin adjective 'bearlike,' and its use may be an attempt to escape from the too common **Bear** or it may be from a given name.

Ursine NV From the adjective 'having to do with bears,' probably to avoid repetition of a too common name.

Ursus Latin 'bear (the animal, masculine),' occasionally substituted for the too common **Bear,** e.g. **Ursus Cove** AK.

Usal CA Pomo, containing in its first syllable the word for 'south,' but otherwise of unknown meaning.

Useless Bay WA Named by the Wilkes Expedition (1841) because it offered no shelter from storms.

Useppa Island FL From Josefa, one of the several wives of Gasparilla, q.v., who was exiled to this island.

Usgah River ME Algonquian 'bitter-water' (?).

Ushkabwahka River MN Ojibway 'place of wild artichokes.'

Usk WA From the Usk River in Great Britain.

Usona Coined from the initials of United States of North America, and proposed as a name for the nation. Though never seriously considered, it had a little advocacy in the early 20th century, and was adopted as a habitation-name in CA (1913).

Usquepaug RI Algonquian 'end-(of)-pond.'

Utah From the Indian tribe, more commonly spelled Ute, but in early times Uta and **Utah.** Frémont used the last, not only for the tribe, but also for the present **Utah Lake** and for the river flowing out of it, now the **Jordan.** When the region was being organized as a territory in 1850, the Mormons preferred their own name **Deseret,** but this met opposition in Congress, and the name of the river was adopted, in the spelling which had recently been popularized in Frémont's much-read report.

Ute From the Indian tribal name.

Utica In 1798, a period when classical names were popular, the name of this ancient city of Africa, at the suggestion of a lawyer, Erastus Clark, was bestowed upon a site in NY. Since the ancient city itself was not widely known, the naming may have been inspired by the heroic Cato Uticensis, who committed suicide after the battle of Utica and thus was enshrined as a republican hero. The name has been popular, in newer states, being transferred from NY.

Utility In KY and LA it is probably a vague commendatory, suggesting that the land and its products will be useful.

Utopia Though the term has been in common usage, it has produced only a few names, e.g. **Utopia TX,** as a commendatory.

Utowanne Lake NY Iroquoian 'waves-big.'

Utoy Creek GA Probably a variant of **Upatoi.**

Utsayantha NY Iroquoian 'beautiful-spring.'

Utukok AK Eskimo 'old,' but reference uncertain.

Uva 1) Spanish 'grape,' e.g. **Uvas Creek** CA. 2) In WY, from a brand, probably UV.

Uvada NV A boundary-name, from UT and NV.

Uvalde TX Named retrospectively, but with a spelling after local pronunciation, for José de Ugalde, governor of Coahuila in the late 18th century and victor over the Comanches in this area.

Uwchland PA Originally **Uchlan,** a Welsh word meaning 'upland,' and still preserved in the township name.

Uxbridge MA Though it is a place-name in England, the naming (1727) was apparently for the Earl of Uxbridge of the King's Privy Council.

Uz Though it is a Biblical personal name, its use as a place-name is probably from the country mentioned in the Book of Job.

V

Vaca Spanish 'cow.' **Vaca Canyon** CA is probably thus derived, but **Vacaville** CA is from J. M. Vaca who was granted a ranch there in 1845. The name was often applied to the buffalo. **Lavaca River,** etc. TX: named in French by La Salle in 1685 as **Les Vaches,** for the buffalo, either translated or renamed in Spanish times.

Vache French 'cow,' e.g. **Isle aux Vaches** LA.

Vacherie LA French 'dairy-farm.'

Vade CA From a local resident Nevada Phillips, nicknamed 'Vade.'

Vade Mecum NC Latin 'go (walk) with me,' used probably as a commendatory for some medicinal springs.

Vader WA For an 'old German' resident, otherwise unidentified.

Vadis WV From a scrambling of the personal name Davis.

Vado Spanish 'ford.'

Val Spanish 'valley,' a form used chiefly in compounds, e.g. **Valrico** FL, 'valley-rich.'

Valatie NY Probably Dutch 'little valley.'

Valdasta TX According to local story, the name was imposed by the Post Office Dept.; probably the same as **Valdosta.**

Valdese NC Italian 'Waldensian,' so named (1893) by a colony of Waldensian immigrants from Italy.

Valdez From the personal name, e.g. in AK the port was named (1790) by a Spanish expedition for Antonio Valdés y Basan, famous Spanish naval officer.

Valdosta GA So called (1860) in honor of the state governor, G. M. Troup, who had given this romantic Italian name to his estate.

Vale A poetic equivalent for 'valley,' popularized by the early-19th century writers, used as a habitation-name, sometimes standing alone, more commonly as a second element, e.g. **Ballard Vale, Oakvale.**

Valeda KS Local story derives the name from Latin *valida,* 'strong, healthy,' but a woman's name is more likely.

Valencia The town in PA is probably from the city of Spain. In NM, it is from Juan de Valencia, an early settler, or his family. In CA, the name is probably from the variety of orange so known.

Valentine Usually from the personal name, e.g. in NB for E. K. Valentine, local congressman. In TX, because the first train to arrive, did so on St. Valentine's Day.

Valhalla See **Walhalla.**

Valkaria FL Named by a Swedish settler, ca. 1895, for the Valkyries of Scandinavian mythology, with a Latin ending.

Valle, Vallecito Spanish 'valley, little valley.' Though primarily generics, they become specifics by association, e.g. **Valle Grande Creek** NM, **Vallecito Mountain** CA. The word is also Italian, and **Valle Crucis** NC is probably a hybrid coinage of Italian with Latin 'of cross,' the name suggested because the view shows streams joining in the valley below in the shape of a cross.

Vallejo CA From M. G. Vallejo, prominent citizen and owner of the land on which the town was laid out in 1850.

Valles Mines MO From the Vallés family, the developers of mines here ca. 1790.

Valley As a specific, indicates a feature thus associated, e.g. **Valley Falls.** Though a stream necessarily flows in a valley, the term is sometimes used, e.g. **Valley Creek,** to denote a stream having an especially well-marked or well-known valley. The term is commoner on habitations, where it has the commendatory value of suggesting a pleasant openness and agricultural possibilities, e.g. **Valley, Valley City, Valley Park, Valley View. Valley Home** CA: during anti-German feeling at the time of World War I, **Thalheim** was thus literally translated.

Vallorso CO From the Italian words *valle,* 'valley,' and *orso,* 'bear (the animal),' coined from the already established **Bear Canyon,** when the Post Office Dept. refused to have another post office in the state beginning with **Bear.**

Valmy NV A railroad name, from the village in France, famous for the battle of 1792.

Valparaiso Though the city of Chile may have been an influence, the literal meaning 'valley of paradise' generally suggested the name for descriptive or commendatory reasons.

Valpe Ridge CA For Calvin Valpey, pioneer of 1851, or one of his sons.

Valsetz OR Coined by officials from the name Valley & Siletz Railroad.

Valverda LA From a plantation-name, probably for Spanish *val verde,* 'valley-green.'

Valverde NM From Antonio Valverde y Cosio, acting governor from 1717 to 1722.

Valyermo CA Coined in 1909 from Spanish *val,* 'valley,' and *yermo,* 'desert, desolate.'

Vamori AZ Papago 'swamp.'

Van Regularly from a personal name or its shortening, e.g. **Van** WV for Van Linville, first postmaster. **Van** NB: for T. A. Van Pelt, first postmaster. Other instances also are indicative of the desire for short names for post offices. **Van** TX: from the opening letters in the names of Vannie and Henry Vance Tunnell, not otherwise identified. **Vanport** PA: named for Martin Van Buren

(known as 'little Van') during his presidential campaign of 1836. **Van Norden, Lake** CA: see **Norden.**

Vanadium Usually, e.g. in NM, because of deposits of vanadium ore.

Vanar AZ Shortened from the personal name Vanarman, not further identified.

Van Buren From the personal name, especially for President Martin Van Buren, e.g. some towns and counties. The county in MO took the name **Cass** when Van Buren lost his popularity and was defeated in 1840.

Vancouver Several places on the Pacific Coast, e.g. **Mount Vancouver** AK, are commemoratively named for Capt. George Vancouver who conducted (1791–1795) extensive explorations by sea, and himself gave numerous names.

Vandalia A curiously popular name of uncertain origin. The first naming was probably in NY, and a derivation from a Latinization of a Dutch family name in Van (or perhaps Vondel) seems likely. The knowledge of the existence of a Germanic tribe, the Vandals, would have aided the formation, though this tribe has a bad literary reputation, being known chiefly as destroyers. No special reason is apparent for the popularity of the name and its spread to, e.g., IL and MO.

Vanderbilt From the personal name, especially from the NY family, whose name became proverbial for riches. Thus arose the name in CA (for a mining district) and in TX (for a farming district), both in the hope of suggesting wealth.

Van Wert From the personal name, in OH for Isaac Van Wert who (along with John Paulding and David Williams) captured Maj. John André, the spy, in the Revolutionary War; the county was named in 1837.

Vaquero Spanish 'cowboy,' but itself often used as an English word; thus **Vaqueros Canyon** NM.

Varina Of uncertain origin, but may be merely a variation of **Virginia:** it was the name of the plantation VA where John Rolfe lived with Pocohontas after their marriage in 1614. It later was used as a woman's name. **Varina** NC: from the name as fancifully used by the postmaster's wife in her courtship correspondence. See **Virginia.**

Varna From the city of Bulgaria, known in the 19th century because of its importance in the Crimean and Russo-Turkish wars.

Vasa MN For Gustavus Vasa, king of Sweden in the 16th century, named by Swedish immigrants.

Vashti From the personal name, e.g. in ND for Mollie Vashti Jarvis (1916), wife of an early settler.

Vassar In MI the town was named for Matthew Vassar, founder of the college, later namings are usually from the college, e.g. **Vassar Glacier** AK.

Vaucluse From the town in France, probably because of its romantic association with the poet Petrarch.

Veda Lake OR Coined in 1917 from the names of Vern Rogers and Dave Donaldson, by the local forest ranger, because the two men had stocked the lake with trout.

Vedauwoo Glen WY Named (1924) by Mabelle Land DeKay for her play of that title which was produced here, meaning 'earthborn' in Arapaho.

Vega Spanish 'meadow.' The towns of **Las Vegas** in NM and NV take their names from the natural meadows that served as camping places on early trails. **Vega** TX is also from a meadow, but **Vega** SD and other instances are probably from the star.

Velva ND Locally believed to be from 'velvet,' a descriptive for the soft- and smooth-appearing landscape of the river valley.

Venado Spanish 'deer.'

Venango PA Iroquoian, probably from a term recorded as *in-nun-gah,* absorbed to a partially French form under early French influence; the literal translation is uncertain, but by early testimony the name refers to an indecent figure carved upon a tree by Indians.

Vendovi Island WA For a South Sea islander who was with the Wilkes Expedition (1841).

Veneta OR For Veneta Hunter, daughter of the community founder.

Veniaminof, Mount AK For I. P. Veniaminof (1797–1879), bishop of Russion America, and student of the Aleut language.

Venice From the city in Italy, often because of some association with water, e.g. in CA the town was originally laid out with numerous canals. In IL the site was subject to floods, and the streets were sometimes well watered. In OH (Butler Co.) the name was originally **Venus;** reason for change unknown. In OH (Erie Co.) the situation was watery.

Venoah Lake MN Coined from the pet names of Winona and Marie Watkins, local residents.

Ventana Spanish 'window,' e.g. **La Ventana** NM, which provides a view like that from a window.

Ventero, Rio CO Spanish in form, but of undetermined connection and meaning.

Ventucopa CA Coined in 1926 from **Ventura** and **Maricopa,** being about halfway between the two.

Ventura Spanish 'happiness, luck,' but in CA a shortening of **San Buenaventura,** the saint to whom the mission was dedicated in 1782.

Venturia ND A spelling variation of **Ventura,** a name suggested because it had been seen on a wrecked boxcar nearby.

Venus The name of the Latin goddess has chiefly been applied because of her connection with beauty, e.g. both in TX and NB because of beautiful natural surroundings. In FL the name is one

in a series of names of Roman deities.
Venus Temple AZ: see **Brahma.**

Vera Regularly from the woman's name,
e.g. in TX for Vera Kellogg, daughter
of an early settler. **Vera Cruz:** from the
city in Mexico, a name commemorating
the Mexican campaign, e.g. in MO ca.
1850.

Verano Spanish 'summer.' **El Verano**
CA: so named because the summer
climate was considered excellent.

Verbena AL From the wild verbena in
the vicinity.

Verde Spanish 'green.'

Verdel NB Coined from Spanish *verde,*
'green,' with the suggestion of the commendatory 'dell.'

Verdi For Giuseppe Verdi, composer of
operas, e.g. in KS and NV.

Verdigris The term is loosely used, and
seems to indicate any greenish substance
which is or suggests a copper ore, e.g.
Verdigris OK from the river, **Verdigris
Creek** NB. The name seems to be used
under French influence, and **Verdigre**
NB represents a spelling to conform
with the usual pronunciation, which is
after the French model.

Verdon In SD it was named (1886) from
the river in France. In NB it is locally
believed to have been constructed from
'verdure.'

Verdunville WV For the city in France,
named by a veteran of World War I
who had fought near Verdun.

Verendrye For the brothers, French explorers of the mid-18th century, e.g.
Verendrye ND, named commemoratively
in the 20th century. **Verendrye Hill** SD:
in 1913 children discovered here a lead
plate buried as a record by the French
explorers in 1743.

Verfkil NY Dutch 'paint-stream.'

Vergennes In VT the name was bestowed in the post-Revolutionary period
of enthusiasm for France, in honor of
the Count de Vergennes, French minister of foreign affairs.

Veribest TX A commendatory, i.e. 'very
best,' taken from the trade name of a
packing company.

Verkerde Kill NY From Dutch *verkeerd,*
'bad, mistaken,' with *kill,* 'stream'; reference uncertain.

Vermejo For Spanish *bermejo,* 'red,
vermilion,' e.g. several names in NM,
probably for red soil, perhaps for cinnabar.

Vermilion From the French *vermillon,*
with reference to red pigment which
was dug by Indians to be used as war
paint. It is questionable whether the
French ever used the word primarily
to indicate color, but later usage has
so occurred, e.g. the valley in CA, which
was named because of its orange-red
appearance. **Vermillion Township** IA:
for W. F. Vermillion, local attorney.

Vermont Whether the French applied
the term **Le(s) Mont(s) Vert(s),** 'The
Green Mountain(s),' in this region is
uncertain, though possible, since in doing so they would merely have been
translating the term already current in
English. The actual name, however, has
not been traced farther back than a
broadside by Dr. Thomas Young (Apr.
11, 1777), where it appears in the address 'To the Inhabitants of Vermont.'
Young was self-educated and knew some
French. Obviously he intended his
name to suggest Green Mountain(s).
His failure to offer correct French, however, may not be the result of ignorance.
For euphony or other reasons, he may
have preferred his own coinage, which
may be said to be suggested by the
French rather than to be French. Critics
pointed out that the name might be
taken better to mean 'worm-mountain.'
But the coinage was successful. The
region and governmental unit had previously been called **New Connecticut,**
but such a derivative name was unsatis-
factory. The new name was adopted
officially in June 1777, soon became
identified with the territorial and
governmental integrity of the region,
and was perpetuated as the name of the
state.

Vern(e) From the personal name, e.g.
Verndale MN for Vernie Smith, grand-

daughter of one of the first settlers. **La Verne** CA: the given name of a real estate developer, with the Spanish article prefixed for color.

Vernal The falls in CA suggested to the namer a springlike shower. In UT the town was named (1893) because it was a green spot in surrounding arid country.

Vernalis CA Latin 'springlike,' probably a commendatory name.

Vernon, Mount Vernon The popular name is often derived from an early settler, e.g. in AZ, CA, UT. Its bestowal is probably influenced in most cases by **Mount Vernon,** and in some instances may be merely a shortening of it, as in TX, where a **Mount Vernon** already existed. **Mount Vernon** is from the Washington estate in VA, which was named by Lawrence Washington (older half-brother of George) for Adm. Edward Vernon, under whom Lawrence Washington had served in the campaign against Cartagena, the **Mount** being suggested by the eminence over the Potomac River on which the house stands. The suggestion of 'verdant' has probably helped popularize the name. On the sites there is normally some kind of hill, which justifies the name. In OR the name was applied to a butte, for unknown reasons, before the town was named.

Vernonia OR So named in 1876, with slight alteration from Vernona Cherrington, daughter of one of the founders; she herself was never in Oregon.

Verona From the city in Italy. **Verona** CA: originally Vernon; when a new name was necessary, one somewhat similar was chosen. **Verona** NB: the name was suggested because of a prominent local family named Veronica.

Verruga Spanish 'wart.' **Canada Verruga** CA was so called because an Indian living there had a large wart.

Versailles From the town and palace in France. The older names, e.g. KY, PA and OH, go back to the time when France was still popular because of its

aid in the Revolution and when many foreign names were being given.

Vershire VT A boundary-name, near the line between VT and NH.

Veseli MN From Weseli, a village in Bohemia from which some of the settlers had come.

Vesper From the Latin name of the evening star, but in WI also because the place was heavily frequented by Vesper sparrows.

Vesta The name of the Latin goddess of the hearth, but also used as a personal name for women, and hence some of the names, e.g. in NB where a schoolmaster gave the name for one of his pupils. **Vesta Temple** AZ: see **Brahma.**

Vestal Generally a personal name, but in CA probably with reference to the worship of Vesta, the Roman goddess of the hearth.

Vesuvius, Mount CA From the Italian volcano, and especially because in 1893 fireworks were shot off from its summit, thus giving the suggestion of a volcano.

Veta Spanish 'vein, lode,' e.g. **La Veta** CO, probably for mineral veins in the vicinity.

Veteran The names are generally self-explanatory, e.g. **Veterans Home** CA. **Veteran** WY was settled by veterans of World War I.

Vevay IN From the town in Switzerland, named by Swiss immigrants.

Veyo UT Coined, ca. 1911, by a group of Mormon girls from 'verdure' and 'youth,' or by another story from the initials of 'virtue,' 'enterprise,' 'youth,' and 'order.'

Vian OK Probably from the French *viande,* 'meat', to indicate a place where meat was cured.

Vibora Spanish 'viper, rattlesnake.'

Vichy From the spa in France, e.g. **Vichy Springs** CA, so called because the waters were supposed to be similar to those in France.

Vici OK Latin 'I conquered,' named in jest by a local resident in 1900.

Vick From the personal name, commonly as **Vicksburg,** e.g. in MS for Newitt Vick, Methodist minister and early settler.

Victim Island WA Because of the finding there of bones from Indian battles.

Victor Commonly from the personal name, e.g. **Victorville** CA for J. N. Victor, named in 1885 when he was construction superintendent here for the railroad. **Victor View** OR: for Frances Fuller Victor, poet and historian. **Victor** CO: from the mine of that name; hence, a commendatory.

Victoria From the personal name, in some instances, e.g. the lake in MN, in honor of Queen Victoria. In TX, for Guadelupe Victoria, first president of the Mexican republic. In KS the town was named (1871) by a colony of English settlers.

Victory A commendatory, usually arising from some obscure and inconsequential reason, e.g. in OK because the citizens considered themselves to have won a victory by obtaining the post office. In VT the name dates from 1780 when the Revolutionary War was still uncertain, but when a hope might be expressed.

Vida From a woman's name, e.g. in OR for Vida Pepiot, daughter of the postmaster.

Vidal, Bayou LA For Jose Vidal, Spanish officer of the 18th century. So also **Vidalia** LA.

Vidette CA With the distinction **East** and **West** these names were given to two peaks standing isolated, being thus the equivalents of **Sentinel.**

Viejo Spanish 'old, old man.' **Los Viejos** CA: probably applied by geologists, because these hills are of an old formation as compared with other hills nearby. **Viejas Valley** CA: according to tradi-

tion, on the approach of a Spanish exploring expedition all the Indians fled except some old women, for whom the name was given.

Vienna About a dozen habitation-names echo that of the capital of Austria. The town in SD is known to have been named to please some settlers from Austria in 1888.

Viento From the first two letters of the names Villard, Endicott, and Tolman, all of whom were men of importance in railroading. Also Spanish 'wind.'

Viking MN Named by a Norwegian pastor for the vikings of Norway.

Villa In Mexican-Spanish the term is roughly equivalent to 'town,' and it is so used as a quasi-generic in, e.g., **Villanueva** NM. American usage more commonly follows the Italian meaning in a vague way, i.e. 'residence, mansion,' especially in a somewhat rural setting, and place-names are generally commendatory, e.g. **Villa Park** CA, IL, NJ.

Villanow GA From the fictional palace in the popular 19th-century novel *Thaddeus of Warsaw* by Jane Porter, probably proposed also with the idea that the place, at the time of naming, was a 'village-now.'

Villar, Lake LA From the family name, probably for Numa Villar, colonist of the 18th century.

Villa Rica GA Spanish, literally 'town-rich,' but generally used in the vaguely commendatory sense of 'fine'; the name was probably taken directly from one of the places so called in Latin America.

Villisca IA Uncertain; by local belief, of Indian origin.

Vina For Spanish *viña,* 'vineyard.'

Vinal Haven ME For John Vinal who had worked to secure titles to the local land, with further emphasis upon the harbor (1789).

Vincen WV Spelled according to the local pronunciation, for Vincent Merritt, local farmer, ca. 1901.

Vincennes In IN it was named, ca. 1736, for F. M. de Vincennes (burned at the stake by Chickasaws that year), who had founded a fort and trading post at the site.

Vinco Latin 'I conquer,' e.g. **Vinco** OK and **Mount Vinco** VA, reference uncertain.

Vine, Viney, Vineyard The presence of vines, especially of wild grapes, has led to the naming of natural features, and these names have spread to habitations by transfer. In addition, the cultivation of grapes has led to such habitation-names as **Vinemont, Vineyard.** The often used **Vineland** was doubtless aided by the memory of that name given to the first European settlement by Lief Ericson. (See **Vinland.**) **Viney Mountain** WV: though this might spring from an adjective having to do with vines, tradition has it to be named for a former slave who was given land here, and whose name, Vina, became Viney in common pronunciation. **Vineyard Haven** MA: named as being the harbor on **Martha's Vineyard. Vineyard** may be from the personal name, e.g. in TX for G. N. Vineyard, early settler. See **Martha's Vineyard.**

Vinegar Rare, usually as **Vinegar Hill** CT, PA, SD, probably as a transfer name from Ireland where the name was well known because of the battle (1798).

Vinegaron A Spanish term for a large kind of scorpion, usually Americanized as 'vinegaroon,' e.g. **Vinegaron Well** AZ.

Vinita OK A coinage, in Spanish form, from the first name of Vinnie Ream, sculptor; thus named by the town founder.

Vinland The original name was given by Lief Ericson (ca. 1000), presumably to an area not in the U.S., because of the vines found there; it has been re-applied in modern times as a habitation-name, usually under Scandinavian influence. See **Vine.**

Violet Usually for a woman so named, e.g. in NB for Violet Butler, daughter of the first governor.

Viopuli AZ Papago, referring to a plant grown there to serve as tobacco.

Virgen See **Virgin.**

Virgil From a personal name, e.g. in OK for Virgil Lewis, son of the first postmaster. In NY and SD it honors the Roman poet.

Virgin, Virgen 1) From the family name, e.g. the creek in MO, from an otherwise unidentified landowner. The river AZ, NV, UT, was known, as **Virgen,** to the Spaniards, and was probably a religious naming, but the present spelling is apparently from Robert Virgin, who was with an American expedition through that area in 1826. 2) For religious reasons, i.e. for the Virgin Mary. See above. 3) With the idea of unspoiled, clean nature, e.g. a dozen creeks and springs in CA, partly with the idea of pure water. **Virginville** PA: a translation of an Indian name. **Las Virgenes Creek** CA: either an incident name of the Spanish period or a religious name from St. Ursula and the eleven thousand virgins.

Virginia According to the Amadas and Barlowe narrative, the country is described as 'now called Virginia Anno 1584,' and the name is declared to have been given 'by her Majestie,' i.e. Elizabeth I. Virginia was a designation, poetically given to the queen, in reference to her unmarried state. In the same sentence with the mention of Virginia, there is also mention of the king of the country, named Wingina. This name is so similar that it may have had something to do with suggesting the other. The name was also appropriate to describe a 'virgin land,' and this also may have given a suggestion. Otherwise Elizabeth might have used one of her other epithets such as Gloriana. Later uses of the name are with reference to the colony-state, or are from women named Virginia. **Virginia Dale** CO: named by Jack Slade, of the overland stage company, for his wife, who had been Virginia Dale before her marriage. **Virginia City** NV: named (1859) from 'Old Virginny,' the nickname of James Fennimore, one of the first prospectors of what became the Comstock Lode; why he should have been thus honored has never been made clear, and the state itself may have been in mind also. **Virginia City** MT: in 1864 sympathizers with the South named it **Varina** in honor of the wife of President Davis of the Confederate States, but a Union-minded official rejected this name, and diplomatically wrote **Virginia** on a document, a name to which Southerners could not object; since the city in NV was already famous as a mining center, the name was also commendatory. **West Virginia:** at the time of the organization of the new state (1862) various names were proposed (**New Virginia, Kanawha, Western Virginia, Augusta**), but the simple geographical distinction received a large majority in the vote of the convention, with resultant emphasis upon the fact that part of the state had not joined the Confederacy.

Viroqua WI Probably Algonquian, meaning uncertain.

Virtue Flat OR For J. W. Virtue, early settler.

Visalia In KY for a settler named Vise, with a pseudo-Latin ending supplied. In CA probably a transfer-name, though the town was founded by another member of the Vise family.

Viscaino Names in CA commemorate the explorer of 1602 Sebastian Viscaíno.

Vishnu Temple AZ See **Brahma.**

Visitation In CA the name is from the Spanish **Visitacion,** and is sometimes so spelled. The name is of religious origin commemorating the Visitation of the Virgin Mary.

Vista As a glorified term for 'view' the word is used occasionally to indicate a natural feature from which a view may be obtained, e.g. **Vista Ridge** OR. It is commoner with habitation-names, commendatory for a view, but most often, under Spanish influence, it occurs as a quasi-generic in such names as **Sierra Vista** CA, **Valle Vista** CA. It is also used in more correct Spanish as **Vista del Mar** CA, **Vista del Valle** CA, **Vista Grande** CA, **Chula Vista** CA, etc.

Vistillas OR Spanish 'viewpoint, outlook.' The post office was originally **Fairview;** when it had to be replaced because of duplication, an equivalent was substituted.

Viti Rocks From one of the Fiji islands, named by the Wilkes Expedition (1841) which had previously visited Fiji. See **Vendovi.**

Viuda Spanish 'widow,' e.g. **La Vidua Mountain** TX, probably because standing alone.

Vivo Spanish 'living,' e.g. **Agua Viva** NM, probably 'pure.'

Vliet 1) Dutch 'small stream,' e.g. **Vliettown** NJ. 2) From a personal name, e.g. **Vliets** KS for a local landowner, not further identified.

Vly From a localized pronunciation of *vallei,* 'valley' among the Dutch in the early settlements, used as a generic, apparently to mean low or marshy land, appearing as a specific by association, e.g. **Vly Lake** NY; often as **Fly,** q.v.

Voca TX When **Avoca** was impossible because of duplication, a change of name was accomplished.

Voda KS Bohemian 'water,' so called by immigrants because they dug a well and obtained a good supply of water.

Volcano, Volcanic Active volcanoes occur in CA and AK, and natural features there have been so named. Evidence, or supposed evidence, of extinct volcanoes has led to the use of the name on many features where no historical activity is known. Even in the states mentioned above many of the features are named for extinct volcanoes, and the town **Volcano** CA is apparently named for natural features that were mistakenly supposed to be volcanic. **Volcano** WV: named either because of the Volcanic Oil and Coal Company, or because many oil or gas flares made the place, at night, look like a volcano.

Volga Several towns are named for the Russian river, but for uncertain reasons.

Volga River IA was named (1836) by a surveyor, probably because of some fancied resemblance.

Volinia MI A simplified spelling for the Polish province Volhynia.

Volta CA For the Italian scientist, Alessandro Volta (1890).

Voltage OR A commendatory name (1908) given in the hope that much power could be generated here.

Voltaire ND Probably for the French author.

Voluntown CT Founded in 1708 on land granted to volunteers in King Philip's War, and thus coined, being one of the earliest coined names.

Volusia FL The county was named (1854) from **Volusia Landing:** the origin is uncertain, but local tradition derives it from the name of an early settler, and this assumption seems likely.

Vona CO Named (1888) by P. S. King, the town founder, for his niece.

Voss In TX for Mabel Lee-Voss, early settler. In ND a shortening from Vossongen in Norway, home of the town founder.

Vriesland See **Friesland.**

Vulcan The Roman god of fire and artificers has been used for a few towns, in WV, MO, because of association with ironworks. **Vulcan's Throne** AK: a fancifully named volcanic cone. **Vulcan's Castle** CA: a volcanic formation whose red color may have led to the naming, as being suggestive of fire.

Vulture Occasionally occurring, apparently as a substitute for the commoner 'buzzard.' **Vulture** AZ: from a mine-name.

W

Waadah Island WA Indian, meaning unknown.

Wabacosoos Lake ME Algonquian 'white, shining.'

Waban MA Algonquian, a name for the east wind.

Wabano Lake MN Ojibway, probably 'east.'

Wabash Algonquian, probably Miami, 'white-shining,' with reference to the white limestone bed of the upper course of the river.

Wabasha MN The personal name of the hereditary chiefs of a certain tribal group of Sioux.

Wabasso In MN the name is literary, from Longfellow's *Hiawatha,* though it is an Ojibway word, 'rabbit.' In FL it is locally believed to be **Ossabaw** spelled backward, and this may be the origin, though the influence of Longfellow is to be suspected too.

Wabassus Lake ME Algonquian, probably 'white, shining.'

Wabaunsee KS For a noted chief of the Potawatomi.

Wabbaseka AR For an Indian 'princess,' whose name was more properly Wattaseka; a railroad naming.

Wabek ND Siouan (?), meaning uncertain.

Wabeno WI The word for one of the degrees of the medicine lodge among Ojibway and Potawatomi; as a name it may have been given by Americans.

Wabikon Lake WI Algonquian 'arbutus' (?).

Wabuska NV Probably Northern Paiute, meaning uncertain.

Wacahoota FL Muskogean 'cow-home,' i.e. 'cow-barn.'

Wacasassa River FL Seminole 'cattle-are-there,' i.e. 'cattle-range.'

Waccabuc NY Algonquian 'end-(of)-lake.'

Waccamaw NC, SC From the Indian tribal name.

Wachapreague VA Algonquian, meaning uncertain.

Wachipauke Pond NH Algonquian 'mountain-pond.'

Wachocastinook CT Algonquian, the beginning and end equal 'hill . . . at.' The middle is uncertain.

Wachu CT Algonquian 'hill, mountain.' This name approaches closely the basic form of one Algonquian word for 'mountain' or 'hill,' which appears in numerous variations, e.g. *-adchu-, -achu-, wadjo, watchu,* yielding many names, especially in New England, e.g. **Massachusetts, Watchaug, Watching,** q.v.

Wachusett Mountain MA Algonquian 'mountain-at.'

Wacissa FL Indian (Timucuan), meaning unknown.

Waco In TX it is from the Indian tribal name, often spelled Hueco. In the SE it arises from the Muskogean 'heron.'

Waconda A variant of **Wakan.**

Waconia MN A Latinized form of a Siouan name, 'fountain, spring.'

Wacooche Creek AL Muskogean (Creek) 'cow-little,' i.e. the equivalent of **Calf Creek.**

Wacouta MN From a local Sioux chief.

Wadboo Swamp SC Of Indian origin, unexplained.

Wadena Ojibway 'little round hill.'

Wading Rare; applied to a stream which could be crossed by wading, e.g. **Wading River** NJ.

Wagejo, Lake MI Coined, in a region of many Indian names, to resemble another Indian name, but from the first names of three men, Walter Koelz, George Stanley, and John Brumm.

Waggy WV For Henry Waggy, local lumberman.

Wagon Though wagons, covered and otherwise, were much in use, the name is rare. **Wagon Creek** WV, CO, is probably based upon an incident. **Wagontire Mountain** OR: because an iron tire lay beside the road for many years. **Wagon Tongue Creek** NB: from the breaking of a tongue. **Wagon Mound** NM: a descriptive, for a rock formation resembling a covered wagon. **Wagonhound Creek** SD: because the stream crossing was known for some old wagonhounds abandoned there. **Wagon Wheel Gap** CO: because early comers found there a wagon wheel, supposed to have been left by a prospecting party of 1861. **Wagon Mountain** MT: from a wagon abandoned here by an early settler who was trapped by thick underbrush. **Wagontown** PA: because of a tavern using the picture of a wagon as its sign.

Wagram NC From Napoleon's victory of 1809.

Waha ID Probably Indian, meaning uncertain.

Wahachee Creek GA Probably from the Cherokee title of a chief; literally, Mighty Wolf.

Wahalak Creek AL, MS Choctaw, probably with reference to the ground lying between the forks of a stream.

Wahanna Lake OR A variant of **Neawanna,** but transferred in recent years from another location.

Wahatoya CO Indian, language and meaning uncertain.

Wahattus Mountain WA Indian 'lookout-place' (?).

Wahb Springs WY For the grizzly bear thus named, the chief character in the story *Wahb* by E. T. Seton.

Wahclella Falls OR Named in 1915 by a committee representing some outdoor groups, the name being taken from an Indian-named locality in WA, of unknown meaning, selected for pleasant sound.

Wahguyhe Peak CA, NV Indian, probably Southern Paiute, 'summit.'

Wahjamega MI Ojibway 'fish-pool,' for a deep spot where fishing is good.

Wahkeena Falls OR Selected in 1915 by a committee representing some outdoor groups, said to be a Yakima word, 'beautiful,' but probably chosen chiefly for sound and for a suggestion of Indian background.

Wahkiacus WA For Sally Wahkiacus, a well-known local Indian woman.

Wahkiakum WA From an Indian tribal name.

Wahkon See **Wakan.**

Wahluke WA Indian 'watering-place,' i.e. a place where there is a break in the high bank, so that animals can get down to drink.

Wahoo In FL and GA from the Muskogean (Creek) *uhawhu,* designating either the winged elm or the white basswood. In NB from the name applied locally to the so-called burning bush, based upon a Siouan term. In FL the name was first applied to a swamp; in NB, to a creek.

Wahpeton ND From an Indian tribal name.

Wahtoke CA From an Indian tribal name.

Wahtum Lake OR Applied by surveyors in 1901; probably an Indian word, but source and meaning uncertain.

Wah Wah Mountains, Valley UT Paiute, badly shifted, but probably containing the word for 'juniper.'

Wainscott NY Originally for a pond which was used in the process of preparing timber for 'wainscot.'

Waiska River MI For a Chippewa chief of the 19th century. **Waiski** is a variant, and sometimes **Whiskey** by folk-etymology.

Wait(s) From the personal name, e.g. **Waits River** VT because in the retreat of Roger's Rangers (1759), Joseph Waite here killed a deer when his party was threatened with starvation.

Waka TX Originally **Wakaka**, but simplified in 1927; locally believed to be of Indian origin, but meaning unknown.

Wakafudsky Creek GA Muskogean (Creek) 'heron-point' (?).

Wakan, Wakon, Wahkon, Wakanda, Wakonda All are variations of the general Siouan term for something uncanny, sacred, etc. Cf. **Spirit.**

Wakarusa KS Applied first to the stream, denoting the growth of some kind of large weed.

Wakatomika Creek OH Algonquian (Shawnee), probably 'it-is-river-bend-land,' applied first to the land thus located and later transferred to the stream.

Wakefield In RI, probably for the town in England. In MA from Cyrus Wakefield, local businessman and benefactor, named 1868. In KS for the town in England from which many of the settlers had emigrated, but also honoring Richard Wake, one of the townsite owners.

Wakenda, Wakon, Wakonda See **Wakan.**

Wakpala SD Siouan 'creek.'

Wakulla In FL it is Seminole 'loon' (?). The same name occurs in NC, but is probably not of the same origin and is of doubtful language and meaning, though by local belief 'clear-water,' because of numerous springs.

Walden Commonly from a personal name, e.g. in CO for M. A. Walden, early settler. As the name of several places in England, it may have been thus borrowed in some instances. Since transfer of such names to natural features in the colonies was rare, **Walden Pond** MA is probably from a family name.

Waldport OR Named in the 1880's by combining German *wald*, 'forest,' and English 'port.' The town is a seaport in forested country.

Wales From the British principality, e.g. in UT, or from the personal name, e.g. in MA for J. L. Wales, in 1828, on his leaving the town $2000. In ME the name was given to honor John Welch, a pioneer, whose ancestors came from Wales. **Wales Lake** CA: for F. H. Wales, early settler.

Waleska GA Named ca. 1836 for a Cherokee girl whose name is recorded as Warluskee.

Walgrove WV Shortened from Walnut Grove.

Walhalla, Valhalla From Germanic mythology, the home of the gods, used in a commendatory sense as roughly the equivalent of 'heaven.' In SC the name was placed by German immigrants in 1850. See **Gualala.**

Walhonding OH Algonquian (Delaware) 'ditch, ravine,' first applied to the river, which flows for part of its course through a ravine.

Walkaround Creek AK Because some explorers in 1931 could not ford the swollen stream and decided to walk around it.

Walker From the personal name, especially for J. R. Walker, frontiersman and guide, e.g. the pass in CA, which he discovered in 1833, and which was named for him by Frémont in 1844; also the river CA, NV and the lake NV.

Wall 1) As a habitation-name it is regularly from the personal name, e.g. **Wall** TX for J. M. Wall, early settler. But see **Adobe.** 2) On natural features it may be from a formation resembling a wall, e.g. **Wall Creek** OR. 3) In the area of early Dutch settlement it is generally from association with one or more of the people known in English as Walloons (q.v.), e.g. **Wallabout Bay** NY from Dutch **Waalen Boght,** 'Walloons' Bay,' to which the English generic has been added. So also probably **Wallkill River** NJ, NY, 'Walloons' stream.'

Wallacut River WA Indian 'stone-place,' because of smooth-worn boulders at the stream mouth.

Wallagrass ME Algonquian, meaning uncertain.

Wallahatchee Creek AL From the name of an early Creek village, a shortening of 'war-divider-creek,' indicating that this village announced the opening of a war.

Wallalute Falls OR Wasco 'strong water,' a name applied artificially in 1893.

Wallamatogus, Mount ME Algonquian 'cove-brook,' applied to the mountain by transfer.

Walla Walla OR, WA From an Indian tribal name, recorded in the Lewis and Clark journals in many spellings, e.g. Wollah Wollah, Wallow Wallow. The tribe may have been named from the river, which is from Nez Percé or Cayuse 'running water,' which is made into a diminutive by repetition, so that the whole could be translated as 'little swift river.'

Wallback WV For a 'Mr. Wallback,' early landowner.

Wallingford From an English town-name; in CT, 1670.

Wallkill See **Wall.**

Walloomsac NY, VT Algonquian 'paint-rocks-at,' for a place at which the Indians obtained paint.

Walloon From association with one or more of the French-speaking people so known, now chiefly Belgian, e.g. **Walloon Lake** MI. They were an important

element of the early NY settlement; see **Wall.**

Wallowa OR Nez Percé, with reference to a kind of fish trap, first applied to the river.

Wallula In WA it is a variant of **Walla Walla.** In KS it is from the name of a local Delaware Indian.

Wallum MA, RI Algonquian 'dog.'

Walnut Regularly from the occurrence of some species of wild walnut tree, which was valuable for timber, and was also treasured for its nuts. Even **Walnut Creek** CA, though English walnuts have been extensively cultivated here, takes its name by translation from the Spanish **Arroyo de Los Nogales.** But other CA habitation-names, e.g. **Walnut Grove** and **Walnut,** are probably from the cultivated walnut, given for commendatory reasons.

Walpack NJ Algonquian (Delaware), probably 'hole-pond,' i.e. a pond or spring with a deep hole.

Walpi AZ Hopi 'gap-place,' because of a gap in the mesa there.

Walpole From the personal name; in MA (1724) it is for Sir Robert Walpole (1676–1745), prime minister; in NH (1752) it is probably in his memory.

Walrus A few places in AK have been named for the animal.

Walsburg KS A shortening from **Walnut Creek** on which the community is located.

Walteria CA A Latinization, from the name of a certain Capt. Walters, early hotel keeper.

Waltham In MA (1738) for a town in England.

Walum ND With shortened spelling, for M. O. Wallum, early landowner.

Waluski River OR An Indian tribal name.

Wamego KS From the name of a local Potawatomi chief of the early 19th century.

Wamic OR From Womack, spelled after the ordinary pronunciation, the family name of three brothers, early settlers.

Wampecack Creek NY, VT Algonquian 'chestnut-place' (?).

Wampee SC An Indian name applied to a plant, commonly for the jack-in-the-pulpit or the pickerelweed; the creek was named from the presence of this plant.

Wamphassuck CT Algonquian, meaning uncertain.

Wampmissic NY Algonquian 'chestnut-trees-at.'

Wamponamon NY Algonquian 'east-at,' as fitting the eastern tip of Long Island.

Wampum The Algonquian term for bead-money came into English in the 17th century, and the few namings are probably by association, and English rather than Indian, e.g. **Wampum** PA. See **Buckwampum**.

Wampus In NY the pond is from the name of a local chief. In OR the butte is from a legendary monster of the forest.

Wanakah NY Probably a coined name of the 19th century, perhaps based vaguely upon Algonquian 'good-land.'

Wanakena NY Iroquoian, but a commendatory applied by Americans in the 19th century, 'pleasant-place.'

Wanamassa NJ From the name of a chief of the late 17th century.

Wanaque NJ Algonquian, probably 'sassafras-place.'

Wanatah IN From the personal name of a local Indian chief.

Wanblee SD Siouan, literal meaning uncertain, but referring to Eagle Nest Butte.

Wanchese NC Named commemoratively for one of the two Indians taken from this region to England by Amadas and Barlow in 1584.

Wanda MN Named ca. 1900, it may have been coined from an Ojibway word, 'forgetfulness'; it is, however, occasionally used as a woman's name, and this may have caused its use here.

Wandawega Lake WI Algonquian, meaning uncertain.

Wanderers Peak OR Because some hunters were lost here and wandered about for several days.

Wando River SC From an Indian tribal name.

Wanette OK An adaptation, partly by sound, of the commoner **Juanita**.

Wangan River ME Algonquian 'bend.'

Wango In MD it is a shortening of **Nassawango**; in NY it is from **Conewango**.

Wankinco River MA Algonquian, meaning uncertain.

Wannametoname. See **Tonemy**.

Wannaska MN Ojibway 'pool, deep place in river.'

Wannee FL A shortening of **Suwannee**.

Wanoga Butte OR Klamath 'son.' Named when other features of the vicinity were being given names of relationship.

Wanship UT For a local friendly Indian chief.

Wanskuck Pond RI Algonquian 'end-at.'

Wantage NJ Though assimilated to the spelling of an English town, it is probably of Algonquian origin, of uncertain meaning.

Wantagh NY Thus named at the request of the inhabitants in 1891, from the name of an early local chief, a variant of **Wyandance**.

Wantastiquet Mountain NH Algonquian 'end-(of)-river-at.'

Wapakoneta OH The name of a Shawnee village, itself named for a prominent chief.

Wapalanne, Lake NJ Algonquian 'white (bald)-eagle.'

Wapanaki Lake VT Algonquian 'from-the-east' (?).

Wapato In WI, probably Algonquian, meaning uncertain. **Wapato Lake** OR: a local Indian word for the arrowhead or wild potato.

Wapella, Wapello IL, IA From the name of a Fox chief of the early 19th century.

Wapinitia OR A Warm-Spring Indian word, 'something on the edge,' on the edge of just what, being here uncertain, perhaps on the edge of the desert.

Wapiti The learned name for 'elk' is in occasional use, e.g. the lake in WY.

Wapogasset Lake WI Algonquian (Ojibway) 'white pelican.'

Wapose Lake WI Algonquian, probably 'rabbit.'

Wappapello MO Probably the same as **Wapello.**

Wappasuning Creek PA Algonquian (Delaware) 'white-stones-at.'

Wapping CT Algonquian 'east land.' But it is an English village-name, and might also be from **Wappinger.**

Wappinger From the Indian tribal name.

Wapsipinicon River IA Algonquian 'white-potato,' for a wild tuber, an Indian food.

Waptook Lake ME Algonquian 'wild-goose.'

Wapwallopen Creek PA Algonquian (Delaware) 'white-hemp-at,' i.e. a place where that plant grew.

Waquoit MA Algonquian 'end-at,' but reference uncertain.

War, The term is generally referrable to Indian hostilities, as in **War Creek** KY, WV, hence the habitation-name **War** WV. **War Branch** KY, WV also occurs, and **Warroad** MN, the latter to mark a route followed by war parties. **War Club Lake** MN is named for its shape. **Warbonnet Peak** ID resembles a conventional Indian bonnet. **War Woman Creek** GA: the translation of a Cherokee title which was bestowed on a woman who was allowed to decide upon the fate of prisoners. **War Eagle** WV: from the name of a coal company. **Warman** MN: for S. M. Warman, quarry owner.

Waramaug CT Algonquian 'good-fish-drying-place.'

Ware Though it is an English place-name, the river in MA was probably named by translation (and spelled according to pronunciation) of the Indian name, which had to do with weirs for fish; the town took its name (1761) from the river.

Wareham In MA (1739) for a town in England.

Warm A descriptive on natural features, generally with 'spring,' though **Warm Lake** and **Warm Creek** occur. Sometimes as a double specific, e.g. **Warm Springs Creek** ID. On habitations by transfer.

Warminster From the town in England.

Warne NC From **Warren,** the name of a local family, with spelling conforming to common speech.

Warren The popularity of the name has been so great that it has been often differentiated as **Warrenton, Warrenville,** etc. From the personal name, especially, e.g. MA, PA, for Gen. Joseph Warren, hero of Bunker Hill. **Warren** OH: for Moses Warren, surveyor of the vicinity. **Warren** AR: for Warren Bradley, a slave, named by a grateful master to whom he had been body servant. In RI and NH for Adm. Sir Peter Warren, who served in America in the mid-18th century.

Warrior Usually with reference to Indians. **Warriors Mark** PA: from some strange marks on trees which were supposed to have been carved by Indians. **Warriors Ridge, Run** PA: because situated on the Indian route known as the Warriors Trail. **Black Warrior River** AL: a translation of **Tuscaloosa**. **Warrior Point** OR: because the explorer Broughton, of Vancouver's Expedition (1792), was here surrounded by some canoes full of Indian warriors.

Warsaw 1) From the city in Poland. In IN it is the countyseat of Koskiusko Co., and thus springs from the early 19th-century love of revolutionaries. In VA it was given in 1845 from sympathy for the Polish revolution. 2) In GA and SC it is by mistaken etymology or spelling from **Wassau**, q.v.

Wartburg TN From the city of Germany.

Wartrace TN Because on the trail (trace) followed by Indian war parties.

Warwick The town and county of England exercised its influence chiefly by way of its earls, for one of whom **Warwick Co.** VA was named (1634), and for another of whom **Warwick** MA was named (1763).

Wasatch UT Probably from a prominent Ute chief, ca. 1800, whose name is recorded in Spanish context as Guasache.

Wasco OR An Indian tribal name.

Waseca MN Siouan 'fertile,' especially with reference to production of food, a name given ca. 1855 by Indians in reply to settlers who were seeking a name and wished something to indicate the fertility of the soil.

Wash 1) In the SW a generic for a watercourse generally dry but subject to flooding; hence, a specific by association. 2) From a shortening of the personal name Washington, e.g. **Washes Bottom** KY.

Washabaugh The county in SD is for F. J. Washabaugh, early judge and legislator.

Washakie UT, WY For the famous Snake chief, noted for his friendship to the Americans.

Washapie Mountains CA From an Indian language, meaning unknown.

Washboard The creek in AZ was so called because the old stage road was 'rough as a washboard.' **The Washboard** CA: because the contours make the hillside look like a washboard.

Washinee Lake CT Along with its twin **Washining Lake,** the two names are probably pseudo-Indian coinages of the mid-19th century, without meaning.

Washington The family was established in VA from the 17th century, and some local names are thus derived. Most of them, however, honor George Washington, beginning with **Fort Washington** NY in 1776. Numerous names followed rapidly. **Washington** DC: named in honor of the President (1791) by the commissioners who were entrusted with establishing a national capital. **Washington** (State): the territory was so named by act of Congress in 1853, in honor of George Washington, though strenuous objection was raised against further use of a name already occurring so widely. In addition to hundreds of habitation-names (counties, townships, and towns), the name has been bestowed honorifically on high mountains, especially in NH and OR, and has also spread by transfer from habitation-names. **Washington Crossing** PA: for the crossing of the Delaware River by Washington and his army in 1776. **Washington Pass** AZ: for J. M. Washington, commander of a military expedition in the area (1849). **Washington Pass** NM: for the same man, who was governor of NM, 1848–1849. In honor of the first First Lady, and also to honor the distaff side and to avoid duplication, arose such names as **Mount Lady Washington** CO, also known as **Martha Washington Mountain.**

Washita AR, OK An alternate spelling of **Wichita.**

Washkish MN Ojibway 'deer.'

Washley LA Probably shaped by folk-etymology to the appearance of an English name from Choctaw *wushulli,* 'foam,' applied first to a creek, as having foam.

Washoe From the Indian tribe.

Washougal WA Indian 'rushing-water' (?).

Washta IA Named (1868) by A. J. Chisman, first postmaster, from an expression that he had heard Sioux Indians using when they examined his rifle; Siouan 'good, fine.' See **Wasta.**

Washtenaw MI Originally applied to a stream, Ojibway 'far-off,' perhaps with the idea of coming from far-off, and therefore 'long.'

Washtucna WA From the name of a Palouse Indian chief.

Washucke River NH Algonquian 'hills-at.'

Wasilla Creek AK From the name of a local Indian chief, probably from the Russian name Vasiliev.

Wasioja MN Siouan 'pine, pine-clad.'

Wasioto KY A Cherokee personal name (?).

Wasola MO Probably a pseudo-Indian coined name.

Wasp Since early Americans were not expert entomologists, wasps may generally have been called bees, and place-names are rare. **Wasp Islands** WA: for the U.S.S. *Wasp,* named by the Wilkes Expedition (1841). **Wasp Creek** TX: an early surveyor became involved with a wasps' nest.

Wass Island ME Algonquian 'white,' because of a beach.

Wassaic NY Algonquian, probably 'rock-place.'

Wassamassaw Swamp SC From an Indian tribal name.

Wassamma Creek CA Miwok, the name of an Indian village, meaning unknown.

Wassaquoick ME Algonquian 'clear, shining.'

Wassassabskek Rapids ME Algonquian 'slippery-rocks-at.'

Wassaticook Stream ME Algonquian 'shining (clear)-stream-at.'

Wassokeag Lake ME Algonquian, probably 'clear (shining)-fishing-place.'

Wassontha Creek NY Iroquoian 'water-fall.'

Wassuk Range NV Northern Paiute, meaning uncertain.

Wasta SD Siouan 'good,' a name selected by the state historian.

Watab River MN Ojibway, for the roots of tamarack and pine, used by the Indians for sewing canoes.

Wataga IL Probably a variant of **Watauga,** and a transfer from TN.

Watanga CO Named by the Colorado Geographic Board, ca. 1915, for an Arapaho chief.

Watannanuck Hill NH Algonquian 'we-climb-at.'

Watasa Lake WI Algonquian, meaning uncertain.

Watatick MA Algonquian, meaning uncertain.

Watauga In TN, from the name of two or more Cherokee towns; literal meaning unknown; elsewhere, by transfer.

Watch Hill See **Watchaug.**

Watcha Pond MA Algonquian 'hill.'

Watchaug, Watchic, Watchoog Algonquian 'mountain-country, mountain-at.' **Watch Hill** RI is probably thus derived by partial folk-etymology. Even though an old watchtower exists there, we should expect **Lookout Hill** because of that.

Watchemoket Cove RI Algonquian, prbably 'end-(of)-fishing-place-at.'

Watchic Pond ME Algonquian 'mountain-at.'

Watchogue NY See **Watchaug.**

Watchung See **Watchaug.**

Water Frequent as an element in habitation-names, descriptive with commendatory overtones, to indicate a place associated with water, as in being on navigable water or having an attractive view, e.g. **Water View** VA. Curiously, the element occurs chiefly in the well-watered East, and not in the arid West where the presence of water is more striking. The commonest suffixes are '-town' and '-ville.' **Watertown** MA: so ordered by the General Court on Sept. 7, 1630. It was associated with water by being designated as 'the town upon Charles River.' The first spelling was **Waterton,** and the name was probably taken (as were the other towns named at this time) from a place in England, such as the one in Yorkshire. **Watertown** NY: named in 1800, apparently because of the possibility of water power. **Watervliet** NY: Dutch *water-vliet,* 'water-brook.' **Waterbury:** first (1686) used in CT, probably as a descriptive commendatory because of the site. **Water Street** PA: from the **Water Street** branch of the **Juniata River,** where the ravine was so narrow that early travelers had to walk in the stream. The term however, would have been already known since some streets bore that name because of being on the waterfront. **Water Canyon** AZ: because irrigation water was taken from it. **Water Proof** LA: having been subjected to floods, the town was moved to a knoll and given its present commendatory name.

Wateree River SC From an Indian tribal name.

Waterford From the town in Ireland, e.g. in PA. The popularity of the name, however, indicates that it is often a descriptive for a settlement at a ford, e.g. in ME.

Watergap, Water Gap From the generic, as opposed to **Windgap,** for a gap in a ridge through which a stream flows, e.g. habitation-names in KY, PA.

Waterloo From the village in Belgium and the battle (1815). The publicity accorded the name was so great that many places received it, though without much political feeling. In NY the name was apparently given by an anti-Napoleonist. More often it was given in its acquired sense of 'defeat,' as in the phrase 'to meet one's Waterloo.' In OK the town was near a steep grade where a railroad engineer almost was defeated. In OR it was given after a severe court decision had been handed down. In IA the name was left blank in a petition until one of the signers, looking through the post office directory, picked the name as having the 'right ring to it.' In NJ it is from the Waterloo Foundry.

Waternomee Mountain NH Algonquian, probably containing the word for 'mountain,' but so badly altered by folk-etymology as to be uncertain.

Waterquechee, Waterqueechy NH, VT A form of **Ottauquechee,** shifted by folk-etymology.

Watersmeet MI Anomalously named (1884) since it is really a place where waters do not meet but where they separate, i.e. it is at a triple divide where streams head that flow to lakes Superior and Michigan and to the Mississippi River.

Waterspout In the NW some streams and gulches are thus named because of heavy flood-discharge after cloudbursts.

Watervliet NY Dutch 'water-stream.'

Waterwheel Falls CA The water is thrown into the air in arcs, resembling wheels.

Watha NC Of uncertain origin, locally believed by some to be from **Washington.**

Wathena KS Named (1856) for a Kickapoo chief who had lived on the site.

Watnong Mountain NJ Algonquian 'hill-at.'

Watonga OK For an Arapaho chief, named in 1892.

Watonwan County MN Probably Siouan, but altered in transmission, meaning uncertain.

Watova OK For an Osage chief, named in 1892.

Watsak Point WA Indian, meaning unknown.

Watseewinse Mountain WI Algonquian, meaning uncertain.

Watseka IL From the name of a Potawatomi woman (also that of a legendary character) of the 19th century; so named in her honor in 1863.

Wattanumon Brook NH From the name of an Indian chief, recorded in 1632.

Wattis UT Probably from the family name.

Watula Creek AL Muskogean (Creek) 'crane.'

Watuppa Pond MA Algonquian 'roots,' probably with reference to those gathered for use in sewing.

Waubansee Creek IL From the name of a Potawatomi chief of the early 19th century, whose village was nearby.

Waubee Lake WI Algonquian, meaning uncertain.

Waubeek IA, WI Algonquian (Ojibway) 'rock, metal.'

Waubeesee, Lake WI Algonquian 'swan.'

Waubeka WI From the name of a Potawatomi chief whose village was at this spot ca. 1850.

Waubesa, Lake WI Algonquian (Ojibway) 'swan,' so named (1854) by Draper (see **Kegonsa**) because an unusually large swan had once been killed there.

Waubun MN Ojibway 'east, morning.'

Waucedah MI Algonquian 'it-reflects-light' (?).

Wauchula FL Muskogean 'crane' (?). Cf. **Watula.**

Waucoba CA Paiute 'pine.'

Waucoma IA, WI Algonquian, meaning uncertain.

Waugoshance See **Wongooshance.**

Waukau WI Algonquian 'sweet flag (the plant)' (?).

Waukeag Neck ME Algonquian, a shortening of *adowaukeag,* what is locally known as a 'horseback,' i.e. a glacial kame or hillock.

Waukee In IA probably a variant of **Wakan.** In WA it may be a transfer, but is locally thought to be the last six letters of **Milwaukee.**

Waukeenah In FL it is for a woman bearing the Spanish name Joachina, a phonetic spelling. **Waukena** CA is probably developed in the same manner from its being in the **San Joaquin Valley.**

Waukegan IL Algonquian 'house, trading-post, fort,' adopted by vote of the citizens in 1849, but probably going back to the Indian name of a stream, recorded in 1778, and meaning 'old fort.'

Waukena See **Waukeenah.**

Waukesha WI In 1849 Joshua Hathaway recorded that the name was first used when he inscribed it on an oak tree in the area in 1846, the name being his own coinage, with the consent of other residents, an adaptation from the Potawatomi word for 'fox' which he had learned from some Indian boys ca. 1836. He believed it to be a common Indian term for crooked rivers (like the trail of a fox) and thus applicable to the local stream.

Waukewan Lake NH Algonquian 'crooked-route-at' (?).

Waukhomis OK Probably a pseudo-Indian coinage, in local belief originating when a man had to 'walk home.'

Waukon In IA from Waukon-Decorah, the name of a prominent Winnebago chief of the 19th century, who also gave rise to **Decorah** IA. In WA the name is probably borrowed from IA.

Waukonda A variant of **Wakan.**

Wauksha, Bayou LA Indian, uncertain in language and meaning.

Waullenpaupack Creek PA Algonquian (Delaware), probably 'hole-pond-at,' with possible reference to a deep pool.

Waumandee WI Algonquian, meaning uncertain.

Waumbek Mountain NH Algonquian 'white-rock-at.'

Wauna OR, WA Indian, probably Klickitat, for a particular spirit-creature, supposed to represent the Columbia River.

Waunakee WI A name coined by Americans in the 19th century, from Algonquian, and taken to mean 'he-has-peace.'

Wauneta, Waunita Phonetic spellings of Juanita, the name being popular because of the 19th-century song.

Waupaca WI Probably a pseudo-Indian name coined by Americans after the **Schoolcraft** (q.v.) system.

Waupecan Creek IL Probably from the name of a Potawatomi chief, but not clearly identified.

Wauponsee IL A variant of **Waubansee**, q.v.

Waupun WI Algonquian 'east.' Cf. **Waban.**

Wauregan Algonquian, a general word for 'good, fine.'

Waurika OK Probably a coinage or an adaptation of some Indian term; locally believed to be Indian for 'pure water.'

Wausa NB Named by Swedish settlers for Gustavus Vasa, king of Sweden, with the spelling adapted to the pronunciation of the name.

Wausau In WI probably from Algonquian 'far-away'; in FL a transfer from WI.

Wausaukee WI Algonquian 'far-away-(land).' Cf. **Wausau.**

Wauseon OH For a well-known Potawatomi Indian, brother of **Ottokee.**

Waushara WI Probably from the name of a Winnebago chief of the early 19th century, from the Winnebago word for 'fox.'

Wautoma WI Coined by Americans in the 19th century from the Algonquian *waugh*, 'good,' and the name of a chief Tomah.

Wauwatosa WI Algonquian 'firefly.'

Wauwinet MA For a chief, recorded in 1660.

Wauxamaka Creek AL From a Creek personal name or title, with *maka*, 'chief,' and the rest uncertain.

Wauzeka WI From the name of an Indian chief, probably a Potawatomi.

Waver Light AR By folk-etymology from 'wavellite,' a locally found mineral.

Waverly From Scott's *Waverley Novels,* though usually with shortened spelling. In NB the streets of the town also bear names from Scott.

Wawa In OR, from Chinook jargon, 'talk,' probably from the sound of the stream. In PA probably an abbreviation of an Algonquian name, but uncertain. **Wawaset** PA may be the same.

Wawarsing NY Algonquian, meaning uncertain.

Wawasee IN For a Potawatomi chief, whose name is recorded as Wa-wi-as-si.

Wawawai WA Indian 'council-ground' (?). It may contain Chinook jargon *waga*, 'talk.'

Wawayanda NJ, NY Algonquian, a descriptive to denote an extremely winding stream.

Wawbeek NY Algonquian (Ojibway) 'rock,' a 19th-century naming.

Wawecus Hill CT For an Indian chief of the 17th century, brother of **Uncas.**

Wawina MN Ojibway, literally, 'I name him often,' but significance unknown.

Wawona Indian (probably Miwok) 'big tree,' with reference to the sequoia.

Wawpecong IN Algonquian, for the shellbark hickories growing here.

Waxahatchee, Waxahachie In TX it is a transfer from AL, where it is Muskogean, probably Creek, with *hachi,* 'stream.' The first part is (?) by folk-etymology from *waka,* 'cow.'

Waxell Ridge AK Named (1913) commemoratively for Lt. Sven Waxall, sailing master in Bering's Expedition of 1741.

Waxhaw NC, SC From an Indian tribal name.

Waxia LA From **Wauksha,** artificially formed when the post office was named.

Wayah Gap NC Cherokee, probably 'wolf.'

Wayan ID From the first names of Wayne Nevils, first postmaster, and his wife Ann.

Waycake Creek NJ By folk-etymology from an Algonquian form recorded as Waakaack, etc., meaning uncertain.

Wayne The widespread use is due chiefly to Gen. Anthony Wayne (1745–1797). **Fort Wayne** IN: the name given to the stockade built on the site by Gen. Wayne after his victory over the Indians at the Fallen Timbers in 1794.

Waynoka OK Cheyenne 'sweet water' (?).

Wayside KS Chosen (1887) as a descriptive for a settlement 'by the side of the road.'

Wayzata MN Originating from a Siouan term, but freely adapted by white settlers, probably referring to the location on the 'north' side of a lake.

Wazeecha Lake WI Algonquian, meaning uncertain.

Wea IN, KS From an Indian tribal name.

Wealthia VA Apaprently a commendatory with 'wealth' and the Latin ending *-ia* for a place.

Weary The river in AK was named (1952) by geologists because its sluggishness and windings made it very tiresome to follow.

Weasel The animal is seldom noteworthy, and has occasioned few names. The cove AK was named in 1929 for many weasels seen there. The creek AK was named from the type of vehicle used to traverse the tundra.

Weatic, Weatogue CT Algonquian 'wigwams-at.'

Weaubleau Creek MO Either a French spelling of an Indian term or an American rendering of French *eau bleue,* 'water-blue.'

Web OR From the initials of W. E. Burke, local landowner.

Webatuck NY Algonquian, probably 'goose.'

Webhannet ME Algonquian 'clear-stream-at' (?).

Webster From the personal name, most often for Daniel Webster, 19th-century orator and statesman, e.g. in MA, PA. So also, **Webster Groves** MO, and a number of counties. **Webster** SD: from J. B. Webster, the first settler.

Wechech Basin NV Southern Paiute, meaning uncertain.

Weches TX The namers wanted it to be **Neches,** after the river, but to avoid duplication, they made a change of spelling.

Wecoma OR Chinook jargon, 'sea.' The community is near the sea.

Wedding Cake CA Named in 1870 by James King and his bride on their honeymoon, because it reminded them of a wedding cake.

Wedge Though the personal name exists, the place-names have regularly arisen from description, e.g. **Wedge Cape** AK, **Wedge Islands** AK. The term is rare, except in AK. **Wedgefield** SC: probably from a body of land so shaped. **The Wedge** DE is the body of land thus laid out by surveyors and long in dispute with PA, confirmed to DE in 1893. **Wedges Creek** WI: Originally **Wages' Creek,** for J. D. Wage, a local lumberman, shifted by carelessness in transmission.

Wedonia KY From an early settler Weedon, not further identified, shaped to the form of a Latin place-name.

Wedowee AL Named ca. 1835 with the personal name of a local Indian.

Weed Regularly for the personal name, e.g. in CA for Abner Weed, early lumberman. **Weed Patch** CA: because a luxuriant growth of weeds was once caused there by a flow of water, the rest of the area being rather barren.

Weehawken NJ Shifted by folk-etymology to a pseudo-Dutch form from some Algonquian original, meaning uncertain.

Wee-Hun-Ga, Mount WI From the name of an Indian woman, wife of the chief Moo-na-pa-ga.

Weekapaug RI Algonquian 'end-(of)-pond.'

Weekasoak Brook NH Algonquian 'small-house-at' (?).

Weekiwachee River FL Muskogean (Creek) 'spring-little.'

Weepah NV Shoshone 'watercourse-spring,' i.e. a spring with a stream running from it.

Weepecket MA Algonquian, for a bird, probably the eagle or osprey.

Weeping Usually to indicate a place where water drips, e.g. **Weeping Cliffs** AZ. **Weeping Water** NB: from an Omaha-Otoe term meaning, approximately, 'murmuring water,' taken into French as **L'Eau Qui Pleure,** and then translated literally into English.

Weepose Brook NY Algonquian, from *seapoose* (?), 'rivulet.'

Weesatche TX From the presence of a bush so called.

Weesaw MI For a local Potawatomi chief of the 19th century.

Weetamoo Mountain NH Algonquian, from the 'female chief' of a local tribe.

Wehadkee AL, GA Muskogean (Creek) 'water-white.'

Wehamba Creek FL Seminole 'water-bad.'

Weimar In TX, so named by German settlers for their city in Germany. In CA, for an Indian chief whose name appears as Weima(h); spelling changed to conform to that of the city.

Weimer MN Named by a German settler for Weimar in Germany, but misspelled in the county records.

Weippe ID Probably Indian, language and meaning uncertain.

Weiser From the personal name; in ID the river was probably named for Peter Wiser of the Lewis and Clark Expedition.

Weitchpec CA From an Indian tribal name.

Wekiwa FL Seminole 'spring (of water).'

Welaka FL Probably Seminole 'water-big.'

Welaunee Creek AL Muskogean (Creek) 'water-yellow.'

Welch, Welsh Commonly from the personal name, e.g. **Welsh** LA for Miles Welsh, early settler.

Welcome 1) From the personal name, e.g. in MN for A. M. Welcome, early landowner. 2) From the idea of hospitality, e.g. in TX. In NC, because a store displayed the sign, 'Welcome— Come in!

Welda KS Named (1870) as a railroad station, probably for a town in Germany.

Weldona CO For Gen. Weldon, not further identified, further differentiated from the already existing **Walden** by the addition of a letter.

Weleetka OK Creek 'running water' (?).

Welfare TX A commendatory, adopted at a meeting of citizens.

Well(s) 1) Most commonly from the personal name, e.g. **Wellston** OH for Harvey Wells, townfounder in 1873; **Wellsville** OH, for William Wells, town founder in 1824. 2) From the town in England, e.g. **Wells** ME in 1653. 3) From a natural feature so called, viz. a spring which in its formation resembles a man-made well, e.g. **Wells** NV, **Well Spring** OR. 4) From a man-made well, e.g. **Well Canyon** NB.

Wellesley MA From the name of the estate of H. H. Hunnewell, which he had named from his wife's family (Welles) by adding the common English suffix *-ley.*

Wellfleet MA Uncertain; for a place in England (?).

Wellington From the personal name. The dozen examples are variously derived, e.g. in UT for J. Wellington Seeley, local jurist. Though the Americans were never inclined to make a hero of the Iron Duke, some of the names, e.g. in ME, honor him. In TX the name is in honor of the Duke, having been given by British cattlemen.

Welokinbacook Lake ME Algonquian, probably to describe a lake with a much-indented shore.

Welona Creek AL Probably Muskogean (Creek) 'water-yellow.'

Welton IA Named, ca. 1850, from a resemblance of landscape to Welton Dale in England.

Welview TX A coined name, suggestive of an attractive view from the site.

Weminuche Creek CO From an Indian tribal name.

Wemrock Pond NJ Algonquian, meaning uncertain.

Wenachus Lake MA Algonquian, probably 'good hill.'

Wenaha River OR An Indian tribal name.

Wenaka OR To have been **Wenaha**, but altered by mistake.

Wenatchee WA From an Indian tribal name, but itself meaning 'river-issuing-from-canyon.'

Wenatuxet Stream MA Algonquian 'good-brook-at.'

Wenaumet Bluffs MA Algonquian 'good-fishing-place-at' (?).

Wendover UT Though it exists as a family name, it was here applied by the railroad officials, apparently from the older English *wend,* 'go' (here perhaps partly confused with 'wind'), because at this point the railroad begins a sinuous course over the hills to the west.

Wenham In MA (1643) from a town in England.

Wenona(h) A variant of **Winona**. Longfellow in his *Hiawatha* used **Wenonah**.

Wenonda VA Probably pseudo-Indian. Cf. **Wenona(h).**

Weogufka Creek AL Muskogean (Creek) 'water-muddy.'

Weohyakapka Lake FL Seminole 'water-on-walking,' but reference uncertain.

Weoka Creek AL Creek, with *oka,* 'water,' and the first syllable uncertain.

Weolustee Creek AL Muskogean (Creek) 'water-black.'

Weott CA From an Indian tribal name.

Wepawaug River CT Algonquian, probably 'crossing-place.'

Wepo Springs AZ Hopi 'onion.'

Wepuc Creek NY Algonquian, probably 'ginseng.'

Wequahic NJ Algonquian, probably 'end (boundary)-land.'

Wequetequock CT Algonquian, probably, 'end-(tidal)-stream-at.'

Wequetonsing WI Algonquian 'bay-little-at.'

Wequiock WI Algonquian (Ojibway), probably 'bladder,' but reference unknown.

Wesaw IN From the personal name of a Miami chief recorded as Wisa.

Wescosville PA From Philip Wesco, an innkeeper.

Wesickaman Creek NJ Algonquian, probably 'grapes-path.'

Weskan KS A coined name, from the location in western Kansas.

Weskeag Creek ME Algonquian 'peninsula-tidal-stream.'

Weslaco TX From the initial and opening letters of W. E. Stewart Land Company, a promoting agency in the area.

Wesley From the personal name, especially for John Wesley, founder of Methodism, e.g. **Wesley** ME and **Wesleyan** ID.

Wesobulga Creek AL Muskogean (Creek) 'sassafras-tree-grove.'

Wesserunsett Stream ME Algonquian 'bitter-water-at' (?).

West, etc. See **North. West Point** NB: at the time of naming it was the most westerly point reached by the railroad.

Westconnaug RI Algonquian, meaning uncertain.

Westecunk Creek NJ Algonquian, meaning uncertain.

Westerheim Norwegian 'western home,' given by immigrants, e.g. in MN.

Westerlo NY For Rev. Eilardus Westerlo, otherwise unidentified.

Westerly RI From its situation at the western extremity of the colony.

Westfield MA From the western part of Springfield.

Westminster Eventually from the English abbey and district in London, but in the U.S. usually by religious association with the Presbyterian Church because of the Westminster Catechism. In SC the town took its name from a church; in TX from a theological seminary.

Westmoreland, Westmorland From the county in England, now spelled Westmorland. In 1773, when the county in PA was formed, spellings were uncertain, and the other spelling was used. The fact that the examples in the U.S. are nearly all spelled with *e* indicates that they go back to the PA county, and not to England. An exception is **Westmorland** CA, which, however, was probably named to indicate that there was more land in the western part of a district. In NH (1752) the naming is primarily for the Earl of Westmoreland, soldier and political figure, who reported to the government on Gov. Benning Wentworth's plans for the organization of NH.

Weston Occasionally from the personal name, e.g. in CO for Bert Weston, first postmaster (ca. 1892). It may also be for the personal name West, with *-ton*, as probably in WV. Commonly some idea of 'west' is present, e.g. in ID where the town was named for being 'on' the 'west' side of the river. In MA the naming (1712–1713) was probably suggested by the location in the western part of **Watertown,** from which it was formed, but **Weston** is a very common name in England and the suggestion may thus have arisen.

Westphalia From the district in Germany; usually, e.g. in MI, given by immigrants.

West Virginia See **Virginia.**

Westwego LA Probably a coined name, perhaps on the analogy of **Oswego;** by local story, from the phrase 'West we go!' because the site was on the road to the West.

Wesuck Brook NY Algonquian, a shortening from Achabachawesuck, 'separation-turns-aside-brook,' probably for a stream indicating a boundary.

Wet Rare. In **Wet Mountains** CO it is a translation of Spanish *sierra mojada,* descriptive of a well-watered range. **Wet-Bottom Creek** AZ describes a stream named when it showed dampness without running water. **Wet Creek** ID is apparently by counterpart from nearby **Dry Creek.**

Westappo Creek FL Muskogean (Creek), probably 'water-broad.'

Wetaug IL A transfer from New England; see **Weatic, Weatogue.**

Wetauwanchu Mountain CT Algonquian 'wigwam-mountain.'

Wethersfield The name of an English town, used in CT (1637).

Wetipquin MD Algonquian (probably Powhatan) 'skull-at.'

Wetonka SD Chosen (1906) from a list submitted by State Historian Dane Robinson, believed to be Indian (Siouan?), and to be associated with the idea 'big,' thus being a commendatory for a habitation.

Wetterhorn Peak CO From the mountain in Switzerland.

Wetumpka In AL it is Muskogean (Creek) 'water-sounding.' In NJ it is applied to a waterfall, being descriptive; it is probably not from a local language, but a name borrowed from the South by someone who knew its literal meaning.

Wevaco WV From the West Virginia Colliery Company.

Wewahitchka FL Muskogean (Creek), probably 'water-obtain,' i.e. a place which was used for a water supply.

Wewahotee FL Muskogean (Creek) 'water-house,' for a railroad water tank, obviously a name given when the railroad was built, by Americans rather than by Indians.

Wewanta WV A coined name from 'We want a post office.'

Wewaset PA Applied by the railroad, ca. 1875, probably pseudo-Indian, reputedly for a 'brave,' who was the hero of a romantic love affair.

Wewela SD Siouan 'small spring.'

Wewoka OK Transferred into OK by the Creeks, being the name of one of their towns, probably the same as **Weoka,** q.v.

Wexford From the county (or town) in Ireland.

Weyanoke VA From an Indian tribal name. Also as **Wyanoke.**

Weyauwega WI Ojibway, literally 'he embodies it,' probably from an Indian mythological story of shape-shifting.

Weymouth In MA (1635) from the town in England, which was a port of departure for many emigrants.

Whale, Whaler As seacoast names these reflect some incident involving a whale or a place frequented by whalers, e.g. **Whale Island** AK, **Whalers Rock** CA, **Whaleboat Rock** CA, **Whaleman Harbor** CA: probably from a personal name, as also, various places named **Whalen** and **Whaley.** Inland, the name is usually descriptive, especially for a feature of curved outline resembling a whale, e.g. **Whaleback Mountain** CA. **Whale Tail Lake** MN: because of a shape suggesting that part of the whale. **Whale Branch** SC: probably because a whale entered this stream at a time of high water.

What Cheer When Roger Williams arrived (1636) at the site of Providence, he was met by some Indians knowing a little English, who greeted him with 'What cheer!' The words were used for various places in RI, but the name is now almost extinct. In IA it was applied, apparently as a commendatory, by a Scottish miner who discovered coal here.

Whatcom WA From the name of a local Indian chief.

Wheat Occurs very rarely on natural features, probably as a late name, established after wheat-farming had started. Being a valuable crop, it occurs as a habitation-name for descriptive commendatory purposes, chiefly as **Wheatland.** It is also a personal name, and **Wheaton** derives chiefly from this source. Various wild plants known as wheat account for a few names, e.g. **Wheat Flats** NB.

Wheeler From the personal name. The peak in NV is for Capt. G. M. Wheeler who led a surveying expedition in the area in 1869–1870, and first described the mountain.

Wheeling Originally for the creek in WV, thence transferred to the city, and from it to other towns. The source is much disputed, but an Indian (Delaware) *wih-link,* 'head-at,' or 'place of the head,' seems likely. Heckewelder, who gives this meaning, explains that a prisoner was decapitated here and his head placed on a pole.

Whetstone In pioneer times stone for the purpose of sharpening tools was valued highly, and places where it could be found were often so named.

Whidbey From the personal name, especially for Master Joseph Whidbey of the Vancouver Expedition, e.g. **Whidbey Island** WA, which he circumnavigated in 1792, and several places in AK.

Whippany River NJ Algonquian (Delaware), probably 'arrow-stream,' because wood for arrows was found here.

Whipperwill A variant of **Whippoorwill.**

Whippoorwill From the bird so known, e.g. several creeks in KY.

Whiskeag Creek ME Algonquian, uncertain literally, but apparently descriptive of a channel which goes nearly dry at ebb tide.

Whiskey, Whisky Common on natural features, but resisted for habitations. The name is largely western, and with 50 examples is especially common in CA, as a heritage of the boisterous mining period. There is usually a story to explain the name. Though these can rarely be checked, many of them are doubtless true. **Whiskey Creek** is commonest, and in most instances indicates that whisky was sold there, e.g. in MN where illegal liquor was once sold to soldiers. **Whisky Creek,** Jackson Co., OR: a whisky dealer ca. 1865 was caught here in the snow, and buried his whisky, which was found and dug out by others. **Whisky Creek,** Wallowa Co., OR: in a fight by local citizens, ca. 1872, illegal whisky selling to Indians was broken up, and the whisky ran in the stream. **Whiskey Creek** AZ, NB: the water is dark from vegetation, and so is compared to whisky. The manufacture of whisky may also account for the name. Cf. **Still. Whiskey Chitto Creek** LA: by partial folk-etymology from Choctaw *uski-chito,* 'cane (canebrake)-big.' **Whiskey Creek** WA: ca. 1860 three traders were engaged here in trading whisky for Indian ponies.

Whiskinboo Creek SC Indian (Cusabo), uncertain, but probably *-boo,* 'stream.'

Whistle Creek NB A translation from the Dakota, based upon an incident in which a party of Indians, caught in a storm, heard mysterious whistling, which turned out to be from one of their own people, also caught in the storm and half-crazed.

White Often from a personal name, especially in habitation-names, and in numerous compounds such as **Whitefield, Whitehead, Whiteman, Whiteside.** With features it is common, a descriptive for white rock, soil, water, or guano. **White River** OR carries glacial silt (cf. **Milk**). **White Mountains** CA:

for extremely white dolomite at the crest. **White Mountains** NH: the name goes back to 1642 as a descriptive, 'white hill,' and probably arose from the snow, which is mentioned in the first account. **White Plains** NY: an early name, probably a descriptive, but origin uncertain. Compounds are numerous, especially **Whitewater,** which usually refers to a stream with rapids, but **Whitewater River** AZ is so named because alkali makes its banks white. Also repeated are **Whitehorse, White Tail** (from the deer), and **Whitefish.** Indian personal names supply **White Bear Lake** MN and many others. Unusual, possibly albino, animals supply **White Wolf** CA, **White Deer** TX. **White Horse Pass** AZ: a white rock formation resembles a horse's head. **White Horse** NJ, PA: from an inn and its sign. **Whitewater Bay** FL: a literal translation of the Seminole term for 'ocean.' **White Post** VA: from a post, painted white, which was originally erected by Lord Fairfax in the 18th century to mark the way to his estate. **Whitecrow** MT: from a mythical being of the Blackfoot Indians.

Whiteface TX: from the 'whiteface' cattle, i.e. Herefords, which were pastured here. **Whitehall** MT: for a white ranch house, in its turn probably named in reminiscence of the district in London.

Whitney From the personal name, e.g. the mountain in CA for J. D. Whitney, geologist and chief of the State Geological Survey; so named in 1864 by four of his assistants, who sighted it from a nearby peak and recognized it as being the highest in the range.

Whittier From the personal name, especially, e.g. in CA, for J. G. Whittier, poet.

Whollochet Bay WA Indian, meaning unknown.

Whon TX A phonetic spelling of the Spanish personal name Juan, but reason for application unknown.

Whooping Island SC Of the same origin as **Hallowing,** q.v.

Whore Frontier uses of the term have vanished, almost without trace. **Whore-** kill DE: a partial translation of the Dutch **Hoeren-Kil,** 'whores'-stream,' probably going back to an incident in which Dutch sailors consorted with Indian women; now officially extinct, it is remembered as the earlier name of **Lewes.**

Whosau Trace MO From an adaptation of the tribal name, commonly known in the spelling **Osage.**

Whynot See **Wynot.**

Wichita From the Indian tribal name. See **Ouachita, Washita.**

Wickabaug Pond MA Algonquian 'end-(of)-pond.'

Wickaboxet CT, RI Algonquian 'end-(of)-pond-small-at.'

Wickapogue NY A variant of **Wickabaug.**

Wickatunk NJ Algonquian 'end-stream' (?).

Wickecheoke Creek NJ Algonquian, meaning uncertain.

Wicked Creek GA From Ned Wicked, a Cherokee Indian, probably a translation of his Cherokee name.

Wickford RI The name of a village in England, its choice may have been aided by the name of the developer (1709), Lodowick Updike.

Wickiup, Wikiup From the term for an Indian brush house, e.g. in AZ where such a structure was standing in 1922 at the time of naming.

Wickus Sippus Creek PA Algonquian (Delaware), badly altered, with *sippus* probably the word for 'stream.'

Wickyville Swamp NB A cowboy camp, i.e. a *ville* of wickiups.

Wicomico MD Algonquian (Delaware), probably 'pleasant-village.'

Wiconisco Creek PA Algonquian (Delaware) 'camp-wet' or 'camp-dirty.'

Wicopee NY, VT Algonquian 'tying-bark,' i.e. a place where the Indians obtained bark for making cords.

Wide Though a common descriptive adjective, it is rare as a place-name specific, but may be found as **Wide Lick** KY, **Widemouth Creek** WV, etc. **Wide Ruins** AZ is the translation of a Navajo form.

Widow Applied because a widow owned the place or lived there, e.g. **Widows Creek** OR, more often specifically, e.g. **Widow Preston Lake** NB, **Widow Reed Creek** CA, **Widow Reynolds Bar** KY.

Wight See **Isle.**

Wigudi River ME Algonquian 'canoe' (?).

Wigwam To indicate a place associated with an Indian house, e.g. **Wigwam Bay** MN.

Wikiup See **Wickiup.**

Wilark OR From Wilson and Clark, names occurring in the Clark & Wilson Lumber Company.

Wilawana PA Algonquian (Delaware) 'head, headgear, horns.' Reference uncertain, but perhaps in the sense 'head village,' 'chief settlement.' See **Chemung.**

Wilbraham MA From a place in England (1763).

Wild Seldom occurs alone, perhaps since all places were equally wild at the time of first settlement. The rare personal name is one source. It is occasionally applied to streams for their rough water, and may be applied to a place which has a particularly rough appearance, but such namings seem to be sophisticated and late. In combination (written either as one word or two) **Wild** is common, being used with the noun for any plant or animal that has a wild counterpart, or can 'go wild.' **Wildcat** represents an ancient coupling. We have, however, **Wild Horse** or **Wildhorse,** and similarly with combinations of **Cherry, Dog, Goose, Rice, Rose, Rye,** etc. As usual these represent places associated with the plant or animal, by incident, or otherwise. **Wild** occurs as a habitation-name, and there is even a commendatory value to it, with its rural suggestions, as in **Wildrose.** This is most striking in **Wildwood** which occurs widely, being probably aided by the sentimental 19th-century song, 'There's a church in the valley by the wildwood.' **Wildcat Canyon** AZ: named by a sheepman after a wildcat had killed several sheep. **Wildman Meadow** CA: an owl's shrieks at night led some sheepherders to think that a wildman must be loose in the vicinity, and they gave that name before learning the cause of the shrieks.

Wilderness Largely used because of Biblical associations, the term was employed as a generic to describe wild and difficult areas, and occurs occasionally as a specific, e.g. **Wilderness Road, The Wilderness** VA, MO. Its use as a quasi-generic in **Wilderness Area** is recent.

Wilkes-Barre PA Named in 1769 to honor John Wilkes and Isaac Barré, English political figures who favored the American cause, or, more directly, for two children who had recently been named for the two men.

Willachoochee Creek GA A variant of **Willochochee,** q.v.

Willamette OR Of Indian origin, meaning unknown. The earliest spelling recorded was **Wilarmet,** and the present spelling suggests French influence, though French accentual tendencies have not prevailed, and the accent remains on the second syllable.

Willapa WA From the tribal name of the Indians living on that river.

Willbridge OR Named as being near the bridge over the Willamette River.

Willdo ND Named (1890) on the analogy of the countyseat **Cando.**

William(s) Being extremely common both as a given and a family name, it has given rise to a large number of names both for natural features and for habitations, most states having a dozen or more, chiefly from early settlers or landowners. Many of these can be identified, but in some instances, e.g. **Williamsport** PA, there are several claimants, because numerous men of that name are always available in a given area. **Prince William Co.** VA: for the son of George II, the Duke of Cumberland. **Williamstown** MA: for Col. Ephraim Williams, founder of Williams College. **Williamsburg** VA: for King William III. **Williamsburg** MA: for the Williams family of Hatfield, who helped to organize the town in 1771. **Williams** AZ: a transfer from **Bill Williams Mountain,** the latter being named for the eccentric mountaineer of that name. **William:** for its use in **William Co.** OH, see **Van Wert.**

Williamson From the personal name, e.g. the mountain in CA, named in 1864 for R. S. Williamson of the Pacific Railroad Survey. **Williamson** WV: for W. J. Williamson, early owner of the townsite.

Willimantic CT, ME Algonquian 'good-cedar-swamp.'

Willington CT This is the name of a town in England, and is the spelling of the act of creation (1727), but a previous spelling (1725) is **Wellington,** and the origin may be from that town in England.

Willis From the personal name; **Williston** ND, from S. Willis James, railroad stockholder.

Williwaw Several places in AK are named from this word for a violent windstorm.

Willmont MN One local group wanted **Willumet** and the other, **Lamont:** a compromise was effected.

Willochochee Creek FL Muskogean (Creek) 'water-big-little'; since 'water-big' is the equivalent of river, the name really is another **Little River.**

Willow Because willows commonly grow by streams and springs and are conspicuous and widely spread trees, such names as **Willow Brook, Willow Creek,** and **Willow Spring** are common over most of the country including AK.

Willowemoc NY Algonquian, probably 'bottom-land.'

Willowick OH A coined name (1951) from the personal names Willoughby and Wickliffe; not further identified.

Wilmette IL Archange Ouilmette, the Potawatomi wife of a French trader, was granted lands in this vicinity in 1829, and the present name is an Anglicized spelling of hers.

Wilmington Towns in DE, MA, and NC, in the early 18th century, took their names from the title of Spencer Compton, Earl of Wilmington (1673–1743), who was prominent in English politics and had Colonial interests. In DE the name was first **Willington** for a local town developer, but was changed by the proprietor Thomas Penn, whose friend Compton was. Later towns were named from these early ones, e.g. that in OH from NC, and that in CA from DE.

Wilpen PA An abbreviation from William Penn Snyder, a local coal operator.

Wilson From the personal name. Probably because the name is very common, President Woodrow Wilson has more often been honored by the use of his first name, q.v. **Mount Wilson** CA is for B. D. Wilson, early American settler, who built a trail up the peak in 1864. **Mount Wilson** CO and also **Wilson Peak** CO are for A. D. Wilson who was a map maker and mountain climber in the area in the 1870's.

Wilton In CT (1726) from an English town. The personal name is not common, and **Wilton** has spread to many states by transfer, e.g. from NH to ME, to ND.

Wiltshire, Wilshire The English county has made almost no impression, but in the Los Angeles area CA, names have been from H. G. Wilshire (1861–1927), local developer.

Wimauma FL Coined in 1903 from the names of three women, Willie, Maud, and Mary.

Wimbee Creek SC From an Indian tribal name.

Wimico FL Seminole 'water-chief,' i.e. 'principal lake.'

Winamac IN From the personal name of a Potawatomi chief, recorded as Wi-na-mak.

Winbeam Mountain NJ Algonquian 'lone tree' (?).

Winchendon MA From a town in England (1764).

Winchester The earliest namings were for the English town, viz. CT, 1733; VA, 1744; NH, 1753. Later namings are by transfer, or from the personal name, e.g. in MA (1850) for W. P. Winchester, local philanthropist. The town in ID was named for the make of rifle. **Winchester Lake** OR: by local tradition, named because an old Winchester rifle was once found there. In KY the town was named for that in VA (1793).

Wincittico River ME Algonquian 'crooked-stream.'

Wind, Windy Descriptives for natural features, often denoting a place subject to wind, e.g. **Windy Point.** Other places were named because a heavy wind happened to be blowing at the time of discovery or naming. Since winds are not usually pleasant, habitation-names have arisen chiefly by transfer, but in the warmer parts of the country the suggestion of moving air may be pleasant and can result in such suburban names as **Windy Bush** DE, **Windy Hills** DE. **Wind River** WY: an early (ca. 1810) account mentions that the wind blew so hard here as to keep the ground free of snow, but such an observation would apply only to certain places or to a particular time.

Windber PA From the name of E. J. Berwind, chief stockholder in a coal company operating in the vicinity.

Windgap, Wind Gap From the generic term, as opposed to **Watergap,** for a gap through which no stream flows, usually caused by stream-beheading, e.g. in PA.

Windham In CT (1691) it is from the colloquial pronunciation of the English town-name Wymondham. So, probably, in ME (1762). In NH (1741) it is probably for Charles Wyndham, prominent English political figure of the time.

Windigo Lake WI From the mythical man-eating creature of Algonquian folklore.

Winding Rare, but in occasional use with natural features as a descriptive, e.g. **Winding Gap** KY. It occurs also with works of man, e.g. **Winding Way** KY, **Winding Stair,** the latter for a mountain range in OK, so called because the first road across it gave that appearance.

Windmill An occasional name testifies to the early use of such mills in the Colonies, e.g. two hills in RI. Though windmills have been a common feature of the plains states, names are few, perhaps because the ubiquity of the mills made them useless for distinguishing purposes, **Windmill Valley** NB being one of the rare examples.

Windom From the personal name, e.g. **Mount Windom** CO, named by a map maker, ca. 1902, for William Windom, then a recently deceased political figure.

Window Used descriptively when a window-like aperture appears, e.g. **Window Rock** AZ.

Windsor From the town and castle in England; in CT (1637), PA, and NC, the name is directly from England. Most of the other numerous namings are secondary. **Windsor** MA: the name **Gageborough** in honor of the last royal governor was changed for patriotic reasons in 1778, but the thoroughly English name was adopted, probably transferred from the town in CT. In VT the name (1761) is probably for the Earl of Windsor, a prominent political figure. Because of association with the castle which is the residence of royalty, the name has commendatory suggestions, and has been popular for towns.

Windy See **Wind.**

Winegegwok NH Algonquian 'otter-place' (?).

Winemas Chimneys CA From the personal name of a local Indian woman.

Winesburg OH With shifted spelling from an original **Weinsburg,** a town in Germany, suggested by German settlers.

Wing Sometimes for the personal name, e.g. **Wing Mountain** AZ for the owner of the Wing Cattle Company. **Wing Ridge** OR: from its shape. **Wingville** OR: chiefly settled after the Civil War by Southerners who were known, after the well-worked joke, as 'the left wing of Price's army,' that having been the most westerly of the Confederate armies. **Crow Wing River** MN: from the Ojibway name, which should have been translated as 'raven wing,' possibly named from the shape of an island in the river. **Red Wing** MN: from the name of several Sioux chiefs.

Winganhauppauge Brook NY Algonquian, probably 'pleasant-springs,' indicating especially good water.

Wingina VA The name of an Indian 'king,' as reported in the Amadas and Barlow narrative of the 1584 voyage. See **Virginia.**

Wingohocking Creek PA Algonquian (Delaware) 'good (rich)-land-at.'

Wingra, Lake MI Winnebago 'duck.'

Wink TX Shortened from **Winkler,** the name of the county.

Winkledoodle Creek MD Probably by folk-etymology from some Algonquian term, but no earlier form has been preserved.

Winkompaugh ME Algonquian 'good-enclosed-pond.'

Winnabow NC Probably an Indian personal name.

Winnebago From the Indian tribal name.

Winnebagoshish, Lake MN Ojibway 'filthy water,' probably with reference to its being muddy.

Winneconne WI Algonquian 'skull,' according to a Menominee story, because

of bones remaining after a French-Sauk battle. An alternate translation, 'dirty-place,' might be similarly derived, though it has been taken to refer to the mud flats. **Winneconna** IL is apparently a variant.

Winnecook ME Algonquian 'portage-at.'

Winnecott River NH Algonquian, probably 'portage-at.' Also **Winnecowet.**

Winnecunnet MA Algonquian 'good-pines-at' (?).

Winnedumah CA From the personal name of a Paiute medicine man, a legendary figure believed to have been turned into stone, thus producing the present formation.

Winnegance ME Algonquian 'little-portage.'

Winnemoiset MA Algonquian 'good-resting-place-at' (?).

Winnemucca NV Named (1868) for a local Indian chief; there were several of this name, and the one here commemorated is probably 'old Winnemucca,' who maintained friendly relations with the Americans.

Winnepaug, Winnepuck Algonquian 'fine pond.'

Winnepesaukee, Lake NH Algonquian, extant in more than 100 spellings, its meaning has been much disputed. The most-obvious-appearing roots are *winne,* 'good, fine,' and *sauk,* 'outlet,' the *ee* being the remnant of a locative ending, but many other renderings are possible.

Winnepocket Lake NH Algonquian, probably 'portage-pond-at.'

Winnequah Point WI A name manufactured by Frank Barnes when he opened a resort here in 1870, from the earlier name **Squaw Point,** and the tribal name **Winnebago,** because some of those Indians still lived in the vicinity.

Winner SD Commemorative of the victory in that the townsite won the railroad over a rival site.

Winneshiek IA, MN, WI For either of two 19th-century Winnebago chiefs, father and son.

Winnetka IL Dating from the 1850's, the name was apparently manufactured from Indian materials, e.g. the Algonquian *winne,* 'beautiful,' the latter part being shaped chiefly for euphony; it is not an Indian name originating with Indians.

Winnibuli Mountain CA Wintun 'middle peak.' See **Bally.**

Winnisquam Lake NH Algonquian, uncertain, but with *squam,* 'salmon.'

Winona First used (1853) as a placename in MN, where it was placed on the townsite by one of the owners, a Siouan personal name, given usually to the first-born daughter, in particular that of a prominent Sioux woman, known in connection with the removal of the Winnebagos (1848). The name was further popularized by its use in H. L. Gordon's poem *Winona* (1881), and was adopted as a woman's name. Later uses in several states are chiefly from women, e.g. in TX for Winona Douglass, daughter of a local railroad owner.

Winopee Lake OR Chinook jargon, 'by-and-by-wait,' apparently an incident-name.

Winston From the personal name. **Winston-Salem** NC is from Joseph Winston, Revolutionary general; a joint incorporation with nearby **Salem** in 1913 resulted in the hyphenated name.

Winter Generally from the personal name, e.g. **Winters** TX for J. N. Winters, pioneer settler. **Winter Ridge** OR: named by Frémont in 1843 because of cold weather encountered here, in contrast to **Summer Lake. Winterhaven:** a commendatory name in regions offering warm winters, e.g. FL, CA. **Winterset** IA: when **Somerset** was suggested as a name, the weather was so cold that **Winterset** was thought more appropriate. **Winterquarters** UT: a party of miners was trapped here by heavy snow and spent the winter. **Winter Road River** MN: a trail so called,

i.e. one that could be used only when the ground was frozen, ran along this stream through the swamps. **Winter Harbor** ME: because the harbor can be used all winter, being never clogged with ice. So also **Winterport** ME.

Winterthur DE Named (1819) by its founder, J. A. Binderman, who had come from that town in Switzerland.

Winthrop From the personal name; in MA for Gov. John Winthrop (1588–1649).

Wintun, Wintoon CA From an Indian tribal name.

Winyah Bay SC From an Indian tribal name.

Wiota IA, WI Probably Algonquian, meaning uncertain.

Wire As a commodity it came into common use so late in the 19th century as to produce few names. **Wire Road** SC: because of a telephone line. **Wire Bridge** WV: because of a suspension bridge thus constructed.

Wisacky SC From an Indian tribal name.

Wiscasset ME Algonquian, probably 'hidden-outlet-at.'

Wiscoal KY From Wisconsin and coal, because a mine operator from that state started a mine here.

Wisconemuck Pond NH Algonquian, meaning uncertain.

Wisconsin As of 1673 **Mescousing** and **Mesconsing** are recorded in a French context for a river that is apparently the present **Wisconsin.** The name appeared soon, also in French context, as **Ouisconsin(g)** from which the English form was derived. There is no proof that **Mesconsing** and **Ouisconsing** are the same name, but the resemblance is marked and the reference seems to be to the same stream. If they are the same, there is nothing to indicate which is the proper form from which the other is an aberration, presumably by mistake. The name has been universally taken to be a French version of an Indian (Algonquian) name, and the *-ing* ending of both forms would naturally be taken as the locative ending, 'at.' The element *mes* can be taken as 'big,' and *con* as 'long,' both being good descriptive terms for some part of a river, but Algonquinists have yet to settle the matter. Having been first applied to the river, the name passed on naturally to the territory and to the state.

Wiscoy Creek NY Iroquoian 'under-banks.' **East Coy Creek** NY is derived from this by counterpart and folk-etymology.

Wisdom In MT from the river, so named by Lewis and Clark in their honoring of the virtues, though the stream has lost the name. In KY and MO it occurs as a habitation-name, probably a commendatory.

Wishkah River WA Indian (Chealis) 'stinking-water.'

Wissahickon Creek PA Algonquian (Delaware), probably 'yellow-stream.'

Wissota Lake WI Probably Algonquian, meaning uncertain.

Wister, Mount WY For Owen Wister, novelist, who was closely associated with the region.

Wita Lake MN Siouan 'island.'

Witch Although belief in witches was widespread in the 17th century, the evidences in nomenclature are few and are chiefly from Indian beliefs, e.g. **Witch Water Pocket** AZ which is a translation from the Mohave, the place being so called because believed to be the haunt of witches. **Witch Creek** CA: the Indian name sounded like *hechicera*, 'witch,' to the Spanish settlers, and was so rendered; later translated into English.

Withla FL Shortened from **Withlacoochee**; see **Willochochee**.

Withlacoochee FL A variant of **Willochochee**, q.v.

Witoka MN Named in 1855 for a Sioux woman known in local annals.

Wittawaket Creek CA Wintun 'turn-around-creek,' probably because of a pronounced bend.

Wittenberg From the city in Germany; in WI named by Lutherans because of the association of Luther with that city.

Wizard Wells TX Because the water was supposed to have healing powers.

Woburn In MA (1642) from a town in England.

Wocus Bay OR Klamath, for the seed of the pond lily, which was used for food.

Wolf Often from the personal name, also spelled **Wolfe, Wolff,** or from a nickname. **Wolfeborough** NH: for Gen. James Wolfe, victor at Quebec. Such habitation-names as **Wolfs Store** and **Wolfton** suggest the personal name. The great majority of the names on natural features are from the ubiquitous predator, found in nearly all parts of the country, and a nuisance in pioneer times for inroads on stock. Unlike the bear, which was associated chiefly with mountains, the wolf was associated with almost any natural feature, perhaps most commonly with streams and bottomlands, which offered the shelter of thickets, e.g. **Wolf Creek, Wolf Island.** Memorials to the early counteroffensive are such names as **Wolftrap** VA, **Wolf Pen Branch** WV, and **Wolfpit Fork** WV. Incidents, rather than mere prevalence, must account for most of the names, but the stories are generally forgotten. **Wolf Run** WV: a wounded wolf, pursued by the hunter, died in the stream. **Wolf Creek** IA: on the first evening of Dennis Quigley's residence here, some wolves killed the sheep that he had brought with him. **Wolf Butte** ND: wolf dens were once visible in the sides of the butte. **Wolf Stake Knob** GA is for a type of trap making use of a stake to hold the bait in the pit.

Wolfforth TX From George Wolffarth, pioneer settler, but with a misspelling.

Wolverine It is not a commonly seen animal, and names are rare, except in AK, where more than 20 names suggest that the wolverine is more commonly encountered under arctic conditions.

Womac(k) From the personal name, e.g. in IL for J. J. Womac, early merchant.

Wombemando Island ME Algonquian 'white-devil,' but probably the name of an Indian who lived there ca. 1750.

Womenshenick Brook CT Algonquian 'steep-rocks-at.'

Wonalancet NH From the name of a local chief of the 17th century.

Wonder OR From a store, so called, according to local story, because people wondered how the store could survive in that place.

Wonderland A commendatory for something offering a spectacle, e.g. **Wonderland Cavern** KY.

Wonewoc WI Algonquian 'they-howl,' probably the equivalent of 'wolves.'

Wongooshance, Point MI Algonquian (Ojibway) 'fox-little.' So also **Waugoshance Island** MI.

Wononpacook Lake CT Algonquian 'bend-(of)-pond-at.'

Wononskopomuc Lake CT Algonquian, probably 'bend-(with)-rocks-lake-at.'

Wonsits Plateau AZ Indian (Uinkarets) 'antelope.'

Wood, Woody Many places are from the common personal name, often itself a compound name as in **Woodrow, Woodward.** Towns of England have also contributed, e.g. **Woodbury, Woodstock.** As a descriptive, the term more commonly refers to tree growth, not to wood as a material, though some names spring from the lumber industry, e.g. **Woodyard** WV, **Woodchute Mountain** AZ. In a forest-covered region the term is not distinctive, and it is therefore rare on natural features in the East. In the largely treeless areas, **Wood Creek** and **Woody Creek** attain descriptive value. Though colloquial American has used 'woods' instead of 'wood,' the place-name usage has preferred 'wood,' possibly an indication that in the West the places so named were considered sources of wood supply, and some places,

e.g. **Wood River** OR, were definitely named because of lumbering. As a habitation-name, the term is usually late, and springs from the commendatory value attached to trees, e.g. **Woodland,** and the oxymoronic **Woodlawn,** which seems, at once, to promise both trees and their absence. **Lake of the Woods** MN: a translation of the French *Lac du Bois,* i.e. 'Lake of the Forest,' which is in turn the translation of an Indian name. This lake is near the treeless country, but is itself surrounded by forest.

Woodbine The term is almost non-existent for natural features, and there is even some doubt as to what a woodbine really is, whether an ivy or a honeysuckle. The word carries, however, poetic suggestions, e.g. Milton's 'well-attired woodbine,' and a dozen habitation-names have resulted, for commendatory reasons. Some names, e.g. in KS, were suggested by the popular mid-19th-century song, 'Gone where the woodbine twineth.'

Woodbury Commonly from a personal name, e.g. in NJ for John Wood, early settler. In CT (1765) it may be from the town in England, with the additional suggestion of wooded country.

Woodchuck A common name over much of the country for the animal also known as **Marmot** or **Groundhog;** thus, **Woodchuck Hill** MA.

Wooden Valley CA For John Wooden, who purchased the land in 1850.

Woodmen CO From the fraternal order Modern Woodmen of America, on whose property it was founded.

Woodrow From the personal name, especially from the first name of President Wilson, e.g. MN, UT.

Woodstock In MA (1689–1690) from a town in England. Most of the later namings are directly or indirectly from this one, aided by Walter Scott's novel and the commendatory idea in 'wood.'

Woolaroc A coined name for a park-like game preserve in OK, from 'woods,' 'lakes,' rocks'; transferred to an airplane, and thence to AZ.

Woolstock IA Coined (1881) for this particular village, but obviously to some extent suggested by such names as **Woodstock.**

Woolwich ME From a town in England (1759).

Woonasquatucket RI Algonquian 'end-(tidal)-river-at.'

Woonsocket RI Algonquian, probably 'steep-descent-at.'

Wooster From a personal name, e.g. in OH for Gen. David Wooster of the Revolutionary War.

Woosung IL A railroad station name, given by the station agent, who had once sailed to China.

Wootenaux Creek MD From the personal name of an early 18th-century Indian, with the English possessive *s* added. By folk-etymology pronounced **Wooden Hawk,** and sometimes so spelled.

Worcester From the county or town in England, etc. The city in MA dates from 1684, and may have been named with some thought of the battle of 1651.

Worm(s) Rare, the lake in MN being so called because of its irregular, 'worm-like' shape. **Worms** NB: from the city in Germany.

Worry NC After several names for the new post office had been rejected, the local people were worried, and Virginia Eliza Caldwell proposed the name, which was accepted.

Worse In GA the name is applied to a creek (near **Bad Creek),** being a good example of relative description, probably because it was difficult for travelers to cross.

Worth For counties and towns the name is commonly from Gen. William J. Worth of the Mexican War, thus **Fort Worth** TX.

Worthla Creek CA Yurok, meaning unknown.

Worthless Creek SD Because it flows through some very poor country.

Wouldbe In occasional use to indicate aspiration, e.g. two now-extinct post offices in OK.

Wounded Occasionally occurring to record some incident, e.g. **Wounded Man Creek** MT. **Wounded Knee** SD: a translation of a Siouan name, which was given because a Sioux was once wounded there in the knee.

Wrangell A repeated name in AK, all the examples going back eventually to Baron von Wrangell (1794–1870), director of Russian-American Colonies.

Wrentham MA From a town in England (1673).

Wrong Mountain AZ Surveyors in 1910 took this to be another peak, and on discovering their mistake gave this name.

Wuh, Mount CO Arapaho 'grizzly bear,' but an American naming of 1923, after the grizzly was extinct in this area.

Wyaconda MO See **Wakan.**

Wyalusing Creek PA Algonquian (Delaware) 'old-man-at,' in commemoration of an old warrior who lived there.

Wyandance NY From a friendly local chief of the 17th century.

Wyandotte From the Indian tribal name.

Wyanet IL Originating in 1869, it is apparently (cf. **Winnetka**) a name manufactured from vaguely Indian materials, probably containing a reminiscence of Algonquian *winne,* 'beautiful,' but otherwise influenced chiefly by euphony.

Wyanoke Creek VA From an Indian tribal name, more commonly **Weyanoke.**

Wyarno WY Originally **Arno,** a railroad name; the first letters of the state name were apparently added for differentiation.

Wyasup Lake CT Algonquian, referring to some growth of plants, such as flags or rushes.

Wyco WV From Wyoming Co., suggested by the abbreviation on a map.

Wye 1) From the River Wye in England, e.g. the river in MD. 2) A term, to indicate a place where railroad tracks (or a road) had a Y-shape, generally for the purpose of reversing the direction of a train, e.g. **Napa Wye** CA, **Wye City** MO. **Wyeville** WI may be similarly named, being a railroad junction, but locally the name is believed to be from the personal name Wythe and the county in VA.

Wyeth 1) From the personal name, e.g. in OR for N. J. Wyeth, early explorer. 2) In CA the name is derived from a railroad 'Wye,' but the ending is unexplained. See **Wye.**

Wylam AL For the town in England, a coal-producing center, as its namesake was intended to be.

Wynoochee River WA Indian 'shifting' (?), with reference to a changing course.

Wynot NB From the phrase 'Why not?' The local story is that at the time of naming many suggestions were prefaced, 'Why not name it—' until someone finally suggested 'Why not name it Whynot?' So also **Whynot** MS, NC.

Wyocena WI Algonquian, connected (?) with Potawatomi 'someone-else,' but reference uncertain.

Wyoming Algonquian, a shortening of *meche-weami-ing*, 'big-flats-at,' applied originally to a valley in PA. Partly from this source, and partly from its use in Thomas Campbell's poem *Gertrude of Wyoming* (1809), the name spread to counties in NY, PA, and WV, and to habitations in several states. When a new territory was organized in 1868, James M. Ashley of Ohio, a member of the House Committee on Territories, argued the name through for it, in spite of much opposition based on the inappropriateness of thus applying an eastern Indian name to a western territory. But opponents could agree upon no suitable local name, and there was a general interest in Indian names in that period. Moreover, the proponents argued that the name was appropriate in its literal meaning, for a territory largely in plains country.

Wyreka MO For **Yreka** CA with changed spelling.

Wysaukin See **Wysox.**

Wysox PA Algonquian (Delaware) 'grapes-at,' from the occurrence of wild grapes.

Wytopitlock ME Algonquian 'alder-place.'

Wywamic PA Probably Algonquian, meaning uncertain.

X

X In the 19th century it was used commonly as the abbreviation for 'cross,' usually with 'roads.' **Owens X-Roads** AL preserves the usage locally, though the post office is officially **Owens Cross Roads.**

Xavier KS A religious community named (ca. 1942) for its founder Sister Xavier Ross, at the same time honoring St. Francis Xavier.

Xena See **Neon.**

Xenia IL, OH Greek 'hospitality'; in OH the town was named (1803) at the suggestion of a minister who thought that the idea characterized the local people.

Xerxes KY From the ancient king of Persia.

Ximeno CA An archaic spelling of the Spanish Jimeno, perhaps for Manuel Jimeno Casarin, prominent citizen of the 1840's.

X-Ray TX Though originally the X indicated a crossroads, the association with X-ray must have been considered in the naming of the post office in 1900.

Y

Yaak MT Kootenai, probably 'stream.' Also **Yakt.**

Yachats OR From an Indian tribal name.

Yacolt WA From a prairie called 'haunted place' in the local Indian language, because on one occasion some children were lost in such a mysterious way as to be blamed on spirits.

Yadkin NC Partially shifted by folk-etymology from an Indian name; language and meaning uncertain.

Yahala FL Seminole 'orange (the fruit).'

Yahara River WI Apparently a pseudo-Indian coinage (first recorded, 1954) distantly derived from Winnebago 'catfish.'

Yahoo Creek KY The term, from Swift's *Gulliver's Travels,* had some general usage to mean a rough unpleasant person, but the immediate influence of the book is possible (cf. **Lulbegrud),** and the reference may be to the Indians.

Yahoola Creek GA Probably Cherokee, meaning uncertain.

Yainax OR Klamath 'little hill,' with reference to present Council Butte.

Yaki Point AZ For the Yaqui Indians of Mexico, named ca, 1910, when the Yaquis were struggling against the Mexican government and had some sympathy in the U.S.

Yakima WA From an Indian tribal name.

Yakina Bay OR An Indian tribal name.

Yakt See **Yaak.**

Yakutat AK From an Indian tribal name.

Yale May be from the personal name, but is often commemorative of Yale University, e.g. **Mount Yale** CO, **Yale** SD. **Yale** OK: named from the make of lock on the door of the building where the post office was established. **Lake Yale** FL: originally **Lake Yulee,** for Sen. D. L. Yulee, prominent local citizen.

Yalobusha MS Choctaw 'tadpole-little.'

Yamacraw KY From a tribal name among the Creeks; the name was chosen from a book for a railroad station.

Yamhill OR From an Indian tribal name first spelled Yamhela, altered by folk-etymology.

Yampa CO, UT From the root thus known, which served as a staple food for the Indians, aided by the fact that a subtribe of Ute was also so designated.

Yamsay Mountain OR Klamath 'north wind,' probably with mythological suggestion.

Yankee In the South the term traditionally means a northerner; in the rest of the country, a New Englander. Most of the place-names spring from the latter application, in many instances being from individuals thus nicknamed, e.g. **Yankee Hill** CA. **Yank's Canyon** AZ: for 'Yank' Bartlett, an early teamster. **Yankeetown** FL: a settlement largely of Northerners, and so named by them in 1925, after it had been already informally so called by the local people.

Yankton From the Indian tribal name.

Yantacaw NJ Algonquian, uncertain, but cf. **Yantic.**

Yantic River CT Algonquian *tic* is 'tidal stream'; the rest, uncertain.

Yantley AL Made by folk-etymology into the semblance of an English name from Choctaw *yanalli,* 'running,' probably a shortening of 'running water.'

Yaphank NY Algonquian, probably 'riverbank.'

Yard TX By local story, because someone asked for a yard of cloth when the storekeeper was trying to think of a name to send to the Post Office Dept.

Yarmony CO For a Ute chief so named.

Yarmouth In MA (ca. 1638) from the town in England. In ME the town was originally (1680) called **North Yarmouth** to distinguish it from the one in MA.

Yarnaby OK Choctaw 'go and kill,' but reference uncertain.

Yauhannah SC From Algonquian *hannah,* 'river,' with *yau* locally explained as 'long.'

Yawgoo, Yawgoog RI Algonquian, meaning uncertain.

Ya Whee Plateau OR From a Klamath word meaning 'eastern.'

Yazoo MS From an Indian tribal name.

Ybor FL From a settlement founded by Vicente Martinez y Bor, cigar manufacturer.

Ycatapom Peak CA Wintun, locally said to mean 'where the big chief lives.'

Ycotti Creek CA From the personal name of a local Indian medicine man.

Ydalpom CA Wintu, a village name, probably 'north-lying-place.' (Not Moplady reversed.)

Yeddo See **Jeddo.**

Yegua Spanish 'mare,' e.g. the creek in TX.

Yei Bichei Mesa AZ Because a rock formation suggested dancers lined up in the ceremony called Yei Bichei.

Yell From the personal name, e.g. the county and **Yellville** in AR for Gov. and Col. Archibald Yell, killed at Buena Vista in 1847.

Yellepit WA For a chief of the Walla Wallas of the early 19th century.

Yellow Rare as a place-name, as compared with some other colors, but occurring as a descriptive with creek, mountain, etc. With a stream it may refer either to the color of the water or to the color of the rocks or clay banks, e.g. **Yellow Bank River** MN. **Yellowstone:** the park takes its name from the river, which is a translation of the French **Roche Jaune** (and probably of a still earlier Indian name), so called from a yellow rock near the mouth of the river. Yellow is more common as a second specific, as in **Yellowjacket, Yellow Pine. Yellow House** PA: from a tavern which was kept painted yellow. **Yellow Medicine Co.** MN: a translation of the Indian name referring to a yellow root used for medicinal purposes. **Yellow Jacket Creek** CA: for an Indian family so named, local landowners. **Yellowhawk Creek** WA: by translation, from the name of a Cayuse chief.

Yelm WA Indian, meaning unknown.

Yeocomico VA Algonquian 'four-houses.'

Yeon Mountain OR For J. B. Yeon, early settler who became a state highway commissioner.

Yeopim NC An Indian tribal name, first applied to a stream.

Yerba Spanish 'herb,' e.g. **Yerba Buena Island** CA for the sweet-scented creeper growing there.

Yermo Spanish 'desert.'

Yes Bay AK From the Indian (Tlingit) *yas,* 'mussel.'

Yesmar AL An approximate reverse spelling from the family name of Erskine Ramsay, coal operator ca. 1890.

Yettem CA Armenian 'paradise,' applied by Armenian settlers in 1902.

Yew The tree is not important in the U.S., and its name has scarcely entered the vocabulary. It is correspondingly rare in place-names. Sometimes considered a variety of pine, it yielded **Yew Pine Mountains** WV, now **Yew Mountains.**

Yewed OK Named in 1901 for Adm. George Dewey, hero of the Spanish-American War; since a post office named **Dewey** already existed, the spelling was reversed.

Yockey Creek KS For Levi Yockey, early homesteader.

Yocona River MS Choctaw 'the reach' (?).

Yokahockany River MS Choctaw 'beautiful-land' (?).

Yoker Creek OH From a kind of bush so called which grows here.

Yokohl CA From an Indian tribal name.

Yokum, Yokun MA A pond and mountain are from Chief Yokum, a Stockbridge Indian of the late 18th century.

Yolano CA Coined from **Yolo** and **Solano.**

Yolla Bolly See **Bally.**

Yolo CA Of Indian origin, probably Patwin, of uncertain meaning, but perhaps a village name, 'place where rushes grow.'

Yo-Lo-Digo Creek TX Spanish 'I say it,' probably an incident-name.

Yonaba Creek MS Muskogean 'ironwood (the tree).'

Yonaguska, Mount TN For a Cherokee chief of the early 19th century.

Yonah Mountain GA Cherokee 'bear (the animal),' from its shape (?).

Yoncalla OR From a mountain so named in the local Indian dialect as 'haunt of eagles.'

Yonkers In New Netherland, Adriaen van der Donck had a farm at this site and was known as 'Jonkheer,' a courtesy title about the equivalent of 'Squire.' People spoke of going to 'the Jonkheer's,' meaning his home, and in the English period the name was changed to a phonetic spelling, and the article was dropped.

Yorba Linda CA For Antonio Yorba, early settler, combined with **Olinda** (ca. 1913), the name of a nearby community. But see also **Linda.**

York, Yorkshire From the city or county in England, etc. The populous county supplied many emigrants, and Duke of York was a royal title. The county in VA (1634) is named from the English county, as is the one in ME, itself a remnant of the original **Yorkshire Co.** MA which included all of ME. **York Co.** PA was in the PA tradition of English county names (1741). **York Co.** SC was named in 1798 because of settlers from that county in PA. **New York** (q.v.) was named for the Duke of York. Many later namings echo these early ones, especially New York. There is also the personal name. Because of the brevity of the name, it has often been coupled with a suffix, especially **Yorkville. Yorktown** VA was so called as the town of **York Co.** Because of the Revolutionary victory there, **Yorktown** has been echoed in several towns.

Yosemite Named in 1851 by the first white men to enter the valley, for the local tribe of Indians, meaning literally 'grizzly bear.'

You Bet CA Locally said to be derived from the favorite expression of a bartender in 1857; some such origin seems called for.

Youghiogheny River PA Algonquian (Delaware) 'contrary-stream,' doubtless so named because, to a person going west from the headwaters of the Potomac, this was the first stream which did not run to the Atlantic.

Young From the personal name, almost exclusively, e.g. in OH, where it was named in 1797 for John Young, an early settler. As a descriptive, the duty is performed by **New;** in any case 'young' is not colloquially applicable to natural features. **Young America,** a village name in MN, dates from 1856; the phrase was then a political catchword of expansionists. It occurs elsewhere, e.g. as a lake in CA, which was named from a mine. **Young Hopeful** WY is the whimsical name bestowed on a geyser in Yellowstone N.P.

Youtlkut Butte OR Chinook jargon, 'long,' named by the Forest Service.

Ypsilanti MI For Demetrios Ypsilanti, Greek patriot in the struggle for independence, widely known as a hero in the U.S. in the earlier 19th century.

Ypsilon Mountain CO From the Greek letter, which is approximately the shape of a Y; named because the snow in converging gullies often appears in that shape.

Yreka CA Shasta, the name for Mount Shasta, the first syllable meaning 'north.'

Yscloskey LA From a family name (?).

Ysleta TX An alternate spelling for Spanish *isleta,* 'island' (diminutive), because the site was once surrounded by water.

Yuba CA Maidu, a village and tribal name.

Yucaipa CA Shoshonean, *-pa* meaning water, and the whole probably 'wet land.'

Yucatan MN Originally **Utica;** when that name was ruled out by the Post Office Dept. because of repetition, the citizens took a similar-sounding but rare name.

Yucca, Yuca The term is applied loosely to various kinds of conspicu-

ously flowering dry-country plants, and has given rise to a few names, e.g. **Yuca Valley** NB, **Yucca** AZ, **Yucca Mountain** CA.

Yuha CA Since the name-cluster is in Yuma territory, the name may be a variant of **Yuma,** the tribal name.

Yuhwamai CA Shoshonean 'muddy place.'

Yukon AK Athapascan, recorded (1846) as *yukon-na,* 'big-river.'

Yulee FL For Sen. D. L. Yulee, prominent sugar planter. See **Yale.**

Yulupa Uncertain, but probably from the name of an Indian village.

Yuma In AZ it is from a local Indian tribe. In CO the name is a transfer from AZ, probably having originated as a railroad station.

Yumtheska Point AZ For an Indian family.

Yum Yum TN Along with **Nankipoo** and *Koko,* this name is from the Gilbert and Sullivan opera *The Mikado,* apparently placed by an enthusiast for that work, but details unknown.

Yunosi Point AZ For an Indian woman, so called because of her frequently saying in English, 'You no see?'

Yutan NB From the name of an Otoe chief.

Z

Zaca CA The name of an Indian village (or chief), probably Chumash; meaning uncertain.

Zacatosa Spanish 'having *zacate* grass,' or approximately 'grassy,' e.g. two creeks in TX.

Zalma MO For Zalma Block, a friend of one of the railroad builders.

Zama MS From the African town, famous for the victory of Scipio over Hannibal.

Zane From the personal name, e.g. **Zanesville** OH for Ebenezer Zane, who laid out Zane's Trace to this point and founded a settlement here, which he called **Westbourne**; it came to be known, however, as **Zane's Town**, and the post office was established as **Zanesville** (1800).

Zanita Point CA In the novel of this name by M. T. Yelverton (1872), the heroine Zanita hurled herself to death from this point into the river.

Zanja, Zanjon Spanish 'ditch, irrigation-ditch.' **Zanja Cota Creek** CA: a ditch associated with the Cota family.

Zanoni Its use, e.g. MO, VA, is from the title of the romance by Edward Bulwer-Lytton (1842).

Zapad, Zapadni AK Russian 'west.'

Zapato Spanish 'shoe,' but as applied to streams in CA more likely to be from the sapote tree.

Zarah KS Established (1857) as a railroad station, using a name drawn from the Bible, with a literal meaning of 'sprout,' which may have been thought significant for a place that might grow.

Zarco Spanish 'light blue,' e.g. **Agua Zarca** NM.

Zavalla TX From Lorenzo de Zavala (with misspelling), first provisional vice president of the Republic of Texas.

Zayante Creek CA Indian, probably a personal name.

Zeandale KS Coined (1857) from Greek (chiefly Homeric) *zeia,* 'grain, spelt,' and English 'dale,' apparently with a euphonic *n*, by J. H. Pillsbury, because of the corn-producing potential of the area.

Zebulon From the personal name; in GA, for Zebulon Pike (see **Pike**); in NC, for Zebulon B. Vance, governor 1862–1865 and 1877–1879.

Zeeland From the province of the Netherlands, from which (MI, ND) the early settlers had come.

Zekiah Swamp MD From an Indian tribal name, recorded (1668) as Sacayo, apparently changed by folk-etymology to the colloquial form of the personal name Hezekiah.

Zelienople PA From Zelie Basse, daughter of the founder, and a shortening of the Greek *polis,* 'city,' on the model of such names as Constantinople. The *n* was probably inserted on that analogy.

Zell SD From a family of early settlers.

Zena From a woman's name, e.g. in OR for Arvezena Cooper, wife of an early settler. In OK for Asenith Wood, called Zeen, wife of the first postmaster.

Zenda From *The Prisoner of Zenda* by Anthony Hope, a highly popular romance of 1894.

Zenia CA So named in 1900 for an unidentified girl.

Zenith The name occurs on several small communities either because of situation at a summit or, more commonly, as a vague commendatory.

Zenobia VA From the famous queen of Palmyra, of the 3rd century, A.D.

Zeona SD Chosen by the settlers (1910) who hoped to have something unusual and different; it is probably a manufactured name.

Zephyr Generally, as meaning a pleasant breeze, a commendatory, e.g. **Zephyr Cove** NV. In TX the name was given ironically when some surveyors were struck by a severe 'norther.'

Zeta MO From the sixth letter of the Greek alphabet, named in 1910 by a railroad builder who was interested in studying Greek.

Zewapeta MO Indian, of uncertain meaning, probably the same as **Tywappity.**

Zia NM Indian (Keresan), the name of a village, meaning unknown.

Zigzag Descriptive because of the course, usually of a stream, e.g. **Zigzag River** OR, **Zigzag Branch** SC.

Zildigloi Mountain NM Navajo 'stubby mountain.'

Zile au Boy Creek MO By folk-etymology from French *aux îles au bois.*

Zillesa Mesa AZ Navajo 'mountain with bare soil around.'

Zilnez Mesa AZ Navajo 'mountain-long.'

Ziltahjini Mesa AZ Navajo, *zil* is 'mountain,' and the rest has been explained vaguely as 'standing cranes.'

Zilwaukee MI Probably a variant of **Milwaukee** (q.v.).

Zim MN A shortening from Zimmerman, the name of a local lumberman.

Zimmerdale KS For Martin Zimmermann and W. J. Truesdale, landowners.

Zinc As compared with other metals, zinc has inspired few names, but **Zinc** AR and **Zincville** OK may be noted.

Zingara VA Italian 'gipsy-girl,' probably from the title of a mid-19th century opera.

Zion The Biblical name for a hill in Jerusalem, but generally used for the city itself or by figure of speech for the New Jerusalem or for the Chosen People. It was used for churches, and was thence transferred to towns, even taking the form **Zion(s)ville.** It was used by the Mormons to apply to themselves as a chosen people and also to the region where they settled. **Zion Canyon** UT: so called by a small group of Mormons who settled there, finding it a place of refuge because Indians did not like to live in the dark canyon.

Zirconia NC A Latinized form, because of zircon mines nearby.

Zitziana River AK Athapascan, with *-na,* 'river,' and the rest uncertain.

Zoar From the Biblical city. Its literal meaning, 'little,' upon which the Biblical text makes a play of words, may have influenced its selection, e.g. in CT. In OH it was named by a German religious sect which considered it a name for a city of refuge since Lot fled for refuge from Sodom to Zoar.

Zoie, Bayou LA From the colloquial pronunciation of French *aux* (or *des*) *oies,* 'of the geese,' which later assumed singular form.

Zolotoi Russian 'golden,' e.g. **Zolotoi Sands** AK.

Zoroaster Temple AZ See **Brahma.**

Zorro Spanish 'fox.'

Zourie, Bayou LA Probably from the colloquial pronunciation of French *souris,* 'mouse,' but in this trapping area used of small fur-bearing animals generally.

Zulu IN For the African tribe, much in the news in the late 19th century, probably chosen with the idea of being at the end of most alphabetical lists.

Zumbro River MN From the French *aux embarras,* 'at (of) the obstacles,' and being known as Embarras River as late as 1836. The obstacles were jams or 'rafts' of driftwood. The present form represents an oral rendition by speakers of English from the clipped pronunciation of French frontiersmen. See **Embarras.**

Zumbrota MN From the **Zumbro River,** on which it is situated, plus the Siouan ending -*ta*, 'on, at.'

Zuni From the Indian tribal name.

Zurich From the city in Switzerland, in CA suggested by mountainous scenery.

Zwingle IA From a personal name, not further identified.

Zybra OK From a colloquial word meaning a man who moved from one settlement to another; though extinct, it deserves remembrance as the last American place-name in the alphabetical list.